Key to map pages

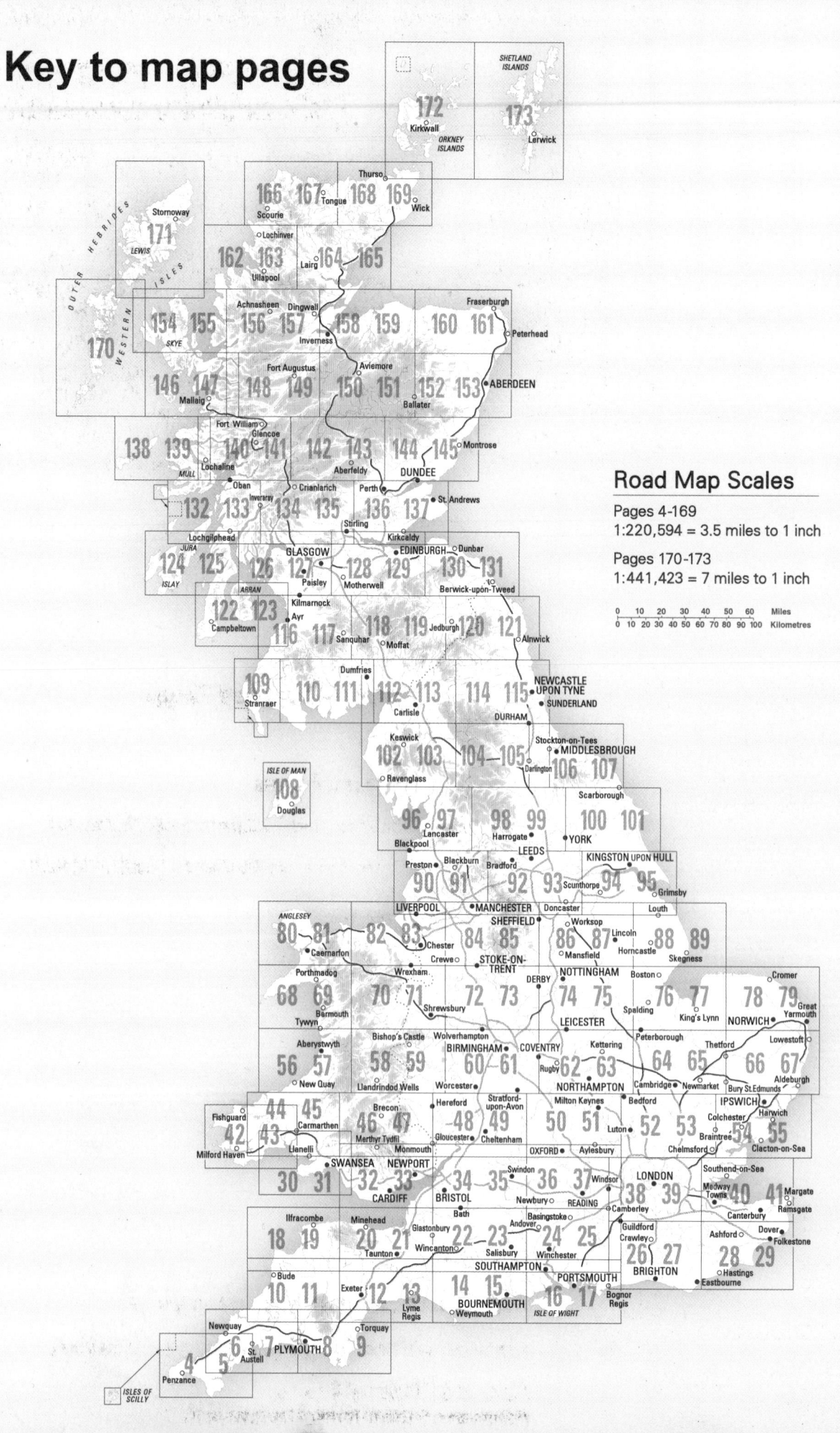

Road Map Scales

Pages 4-169
1:220,594 = 3.5 miles to 1 inch

Pages 170-173
1:441,423 = 7 miles to 1 inch

0	10	20	30	40	50	60		Miles
0	10 20	30 40	50 60	70 80	90 100			Kilometres

BRITAIN 2013

CONTENTS

Edition 2013 by Michelin Travel Partner
© 2012 Michelin, Propriétaires-éditeurs
Société par actions simplifiée
au capital de 11 629 590 EUR
27 Cours de l'Île Seguin
92100 Boulogne-Billancourt (France)
R.C.S. Nanterre 433 677 721

Cartography supplied by Geographers' A-Z Map
Company Limited.
Copyright © 2012 Geographers' A-Z Map Company Ltd.

Ordnance Survey® This product includes mapping
data licensed from Ordnance Survey® with the
permission of the Controller of Her Majesty's
Stationery Office. © Crown Copyright 2012. All
rights reserved. Licence Number 100017302.
The Grid in this atlas is the National Grid taken
from Ordnance Survey ® mapping with the
permission of the Controller of Her Majesty's
Stationery Office.
Safety Camera & Fuel Station Databases Copyright
2012 © PocketGPSWorld.com

PocketGPSWorld.com's CamerAlert is a
self-contained speed and red light camera
warning system for SatNavs and Android or Apple
iOS smartphones/tablets.
Visit www.cameralert.co.uk to download.
The Shopmobility logo is a registered symbol of
The National Federation of Shopmobility.
Relief Data within the A-Z Cartography is sourced
from Geo-Innovations.
The representation on the maps of a road, track
or footpath is no evidence of the existence of a
right of way.
All rights reserved.
No part of this publication may be reproduced
or recorded in any form or by any means of
electronic, mechanical, reprographic or other
duplication without the permission of the
Publishers and copyright holders.

While every effort is made to ensure that all
information printed in this publication is correct
and up-to-date, Michelin Maps & Guides accepts
no liability for any direct, indirect or consequential
losses howsoever caused so far as such can be
excluded by law.

In spite of the care taken in the production of this
book, it is possible that a defective copy may have
escaped our attention. If this is so, please return it
to your bookseller, who will exchange it for you,
or contact:
Michelin Maps & Guides
Hannay House - 39 Clarendon Road
WATFORD Herts WD17 1JA
www.ViaMichelin.com
Printed in Italy by Rotolito Lombarda
Cover and title photo:
Chad Ehlers/Tips/Photononstop

II - V — **Route Planning**

2 — **Mileage Chart and Journey Times**

3 — **Reference Page**

4 - 173 — **Britain Road Map Pages**

4 - 169 — Main map : 3.5 miles to 1 inch / 2.2 km to 1 cm (1 : 220,594)

170 - 173 — Northern Isles : 7 miles to 1 inch / 4.4 km to 1 cm (1 : 441,423)

174 - 184 — **Main Route Maps**

174 - 181 — London

182 - 183 — Birmingham

184 — Manchester

185 - 214 — **City & Town Centre Maps**

185 - 186 — Reference

187 - 214 — City & Town Plans

215 - 216 — **Port & Airport Plans**

217 - 275 — **Index Pages**

275 — Safety Camera Information

276 - 279 — **Index to Selected Places of Interest**

280 - 281 — **Limited Interchange Motorway Junctions**

282 — **Channel Tunnel Plans**
Folkestone & Calais Terminal access maps

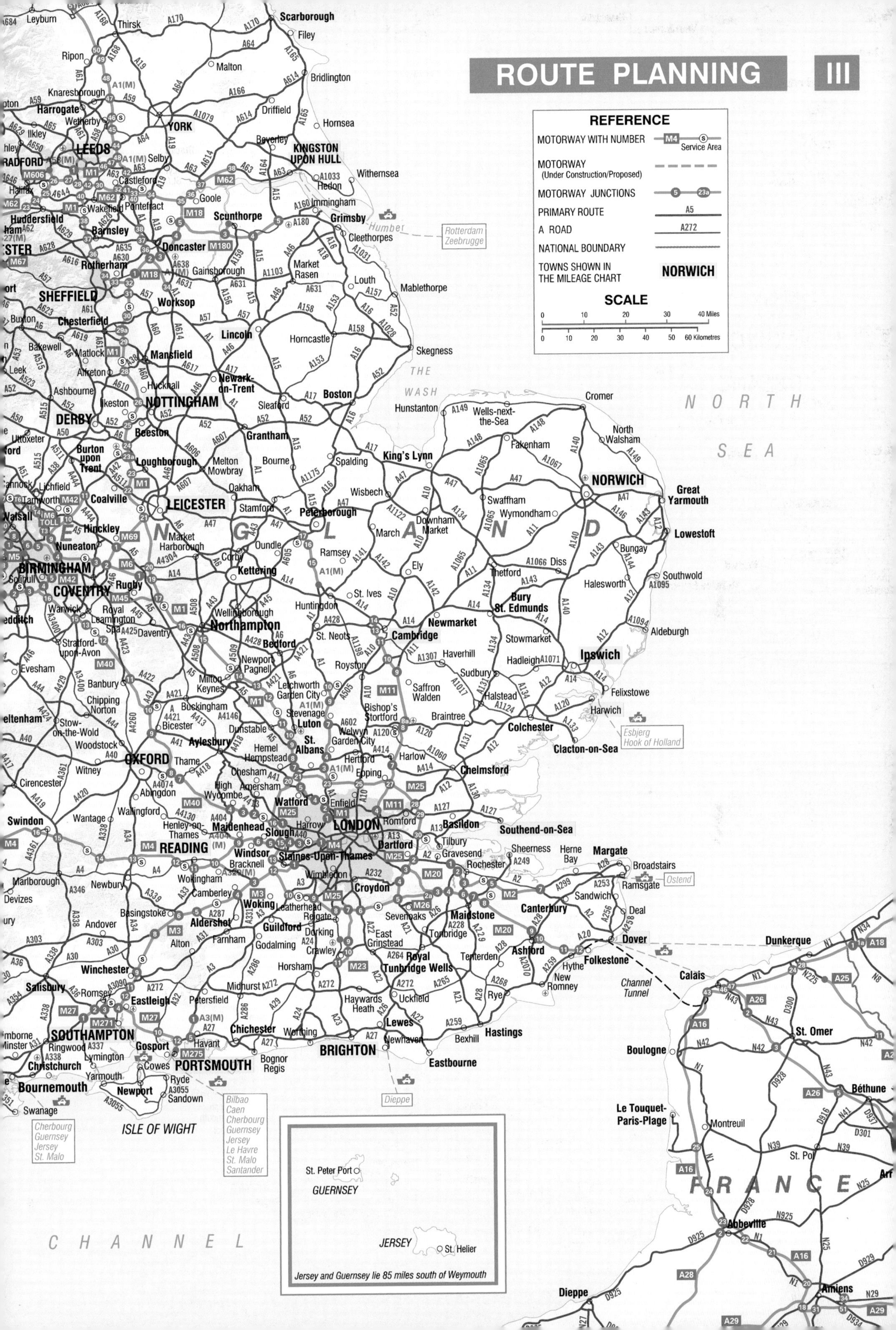

REFERENCE

MOTORWAY WITH NUMBER	M4 — S Service Area
MOTORWAY (Under Construction/Proposed)	– – –
MOTORWAY JUNCTIONS	5 — 23a
PRIMARY ROUTE	A5
A ROAD	A272
NATIONAL BOUNDARY	
TOWNS SHOWN IN THE MILEAGE CHART	**NORWICH**

SCALE

0   10   20   30   40 Miles

0   10   20   30   40   50   60 Kilometres

NORTH SEA

THE WASH

E N G L A N D

CHANNEL

F R A N C E

ISLE OF WIGHT

GUERNSEY — St. Peter Port

JERSEY — St. Helier

Jersey and Guernsey lie 85 miles south of Weymouth

Rotterdam Zeebrugge

Esbjerg Hook of Holland

Ostend

Dieppe

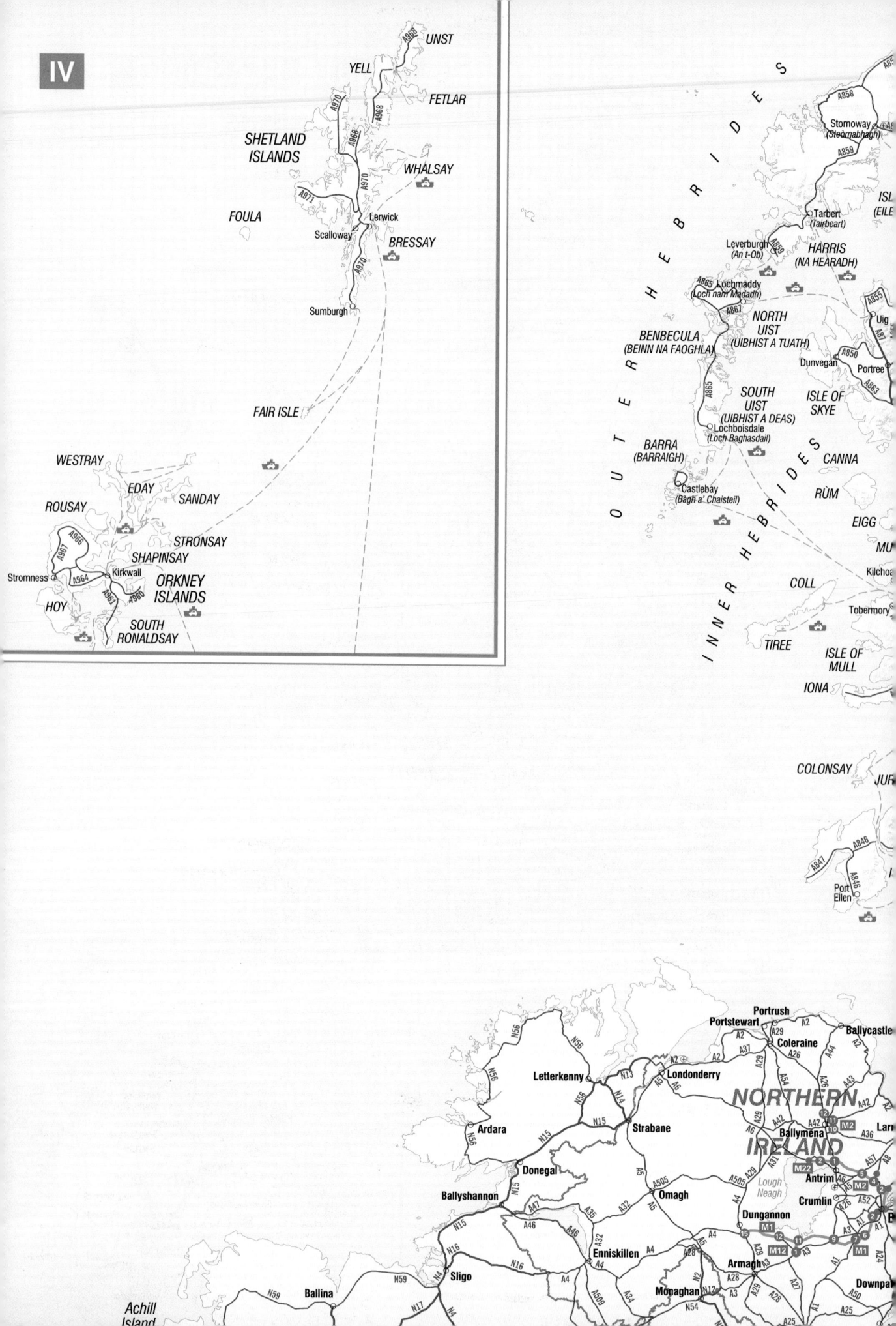

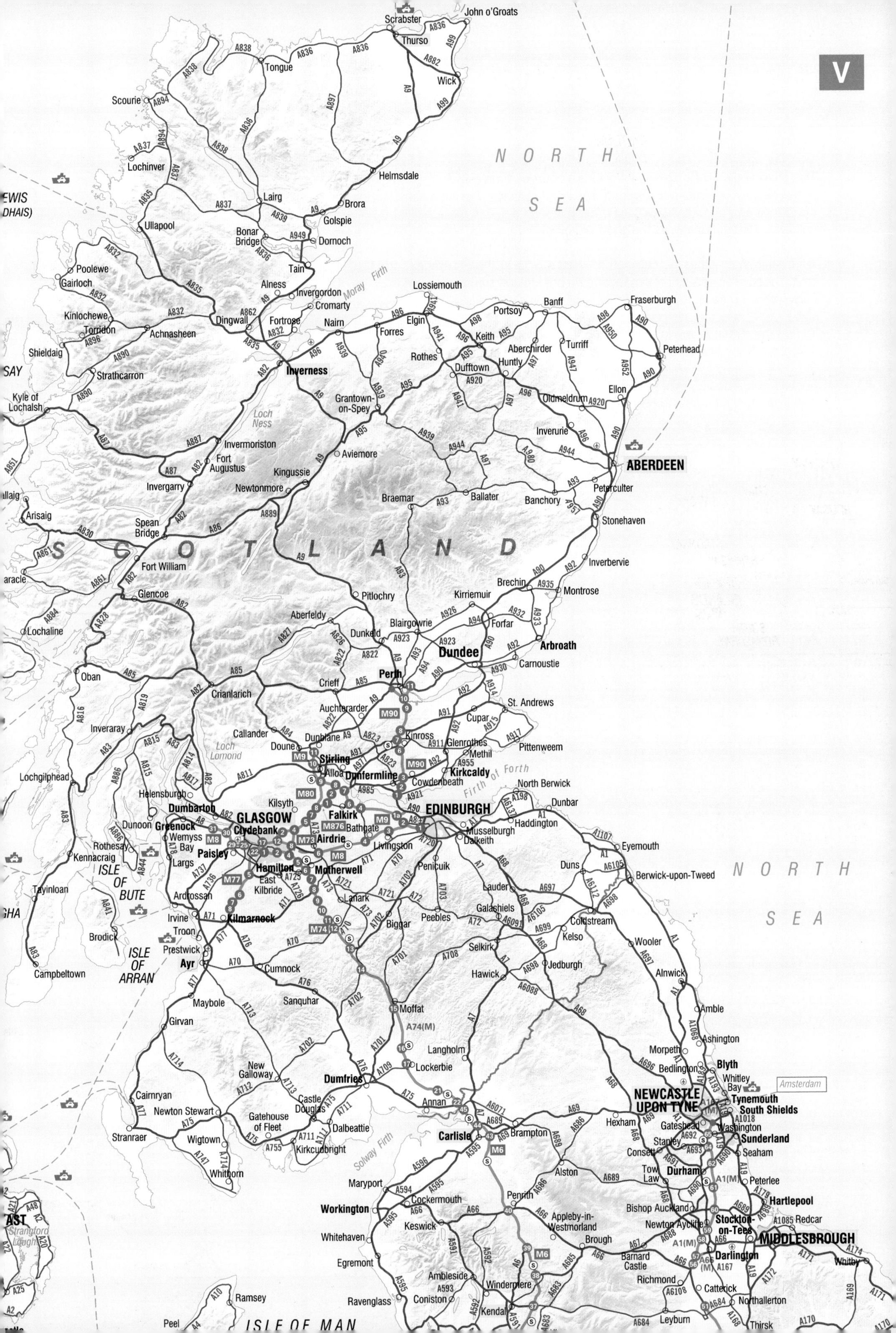

NORTH SEA

SCOTLAND

John o'Groats
Scrabster • Thurso
Tongue
Scourie
Lochinver
Helmsdale
Wick
Lairg • Brora
Golspie
Bonar Bridge • Dornoch
Ullapool
Poolewe
Gairloch
Tain
Alness • Invergordon
Cromarty
Kinlochewe
Torridon
Shieldaig
Strathcarron
Achnasheen
Dingwall • Fortrose
Nairn
Kyle of Lochalsh
Inverness
Lossiemouth
Portsoy • Banff • Fraserburgh
Elgin
Forres • Keith
Rothes • Aberchirder • Turriff
Peterhead
Dufftown • Huntly
Grantown-on-Spey
Oldmeldrum • Ellon
Invermoriston
Fort Augustus
Aviemore
Inverurie
ABERDEEN
Invergarry
Kingussie
Newtonmore
Peterculter
Arisaig
Spean Bridge
Braemar • Ballater • Banchory
Stonehaven
Fort William
Inverbervie
Glencoe
Pitlochry
Brechin • Montrose
Lochaline
Aberfeldy
Kirriemuir
Forfar
Oban
Dunkeld
Blairgowrie
Dundee • **Arbroath**
Crianlarich
Crieff
Carnoustie
Auchterarder
Perth
Inveraray
Callander
Doune
Kinross • St. Andrews
Stirling
Dunblane
Cupar
Glenrothes • Pittenweem
Helensburgh
Alloa
Dunfermline
Methil
Kirkcaldy
Lochgilphead
Dumbarton
Kilsyth
Cowdenbeath
North Berwick
Dunoon
GLASGOW
Clydebank
Falkirk
EDINBURGH
Dunbar
Greenock
Bathgate
Haddington
Wemyss Bay
Airdrie
Livingston
Musselburgh
Eyemouth
Paisley
Dalkeith
Largs
Hamilton
Motherwell
Penicuik
Duns
Berwick-upon-Tweed
Ardrossan
East Kilbride
Lanark
Lauder
Galashiels
ISLE OF BUTE
Rothesay
Irvine
Kilmarnock
Biggar
Peebles
Coldstream
Kennacraig
Troon
Prestwick
Selkirk
Kelso
Wooler
Tayinloan
Ayr
Hawick
Jedburgh
Alnwick
Brodick
Cumnock
ISLE OF ARRAN
Maybole
Sanquhar
Moffat
Amble
Campbeltown
Girvan
Ashington
Langholm
Morpeth
New Galloway
Lockerbie
Bedlington
Blyth
Whitley Bay
Cairnryan
Castle Douglas
Annan
NEWCASTLE UPON TYNE • **Tynemouth**
South Shields
Stranraer
Newton Stewart
Dumfries
Hexham
Gateshead
Washington
Sunderland
Wigtown
Dalbeattie
Brampton
Stanley
Seaham
Kirkcudbright
Carlisle
Consett
Whithorn
Alston
Tow Law
Durham
Peterlee
Maryport
Penrith
Bishop Auckland
Hartlepool
Workington
Cockermouth
Newton Aycliffe
Redcar
Whitehaven
Keswick
Appleby-in-Westmorland
Brough
Stockton-on-Tees
MIDDLESBROUGH
Egremont
Barnard Castle
Darlington
Whitby
Ambleside
Richmond
Ravenglass
Coniston
Windermere
Kendal
Catterick
Northallerton
Ramsey
Peel
ISLE OF MAN
Leyburn
Thirsk

NORTH SEA

Amsterdam

Loch Ness
Loch Lomond
Moray Firth
Firth of Forth
Solway Firth
Strangford Lough

LEWIS (LEODHAIS)

This chart shows the distance in miles and journey time between two cities or towns in Great Britain. Each route has been calculated using a combination of motorways, primary routes and other major roads. This is normally the quickest, though not always the shortest route.

Average journey times are calculated whilst driving at the maximum speed limit. These times are approximate and do not include traffic congestion or convenience breaks.

To find the distance and journey time between two cities or towns, follow a horizontal line and vertical column until they meet each other.

For example, the 285 mile journey from London to Penzance is approximately 4 hours and 59 minutes.

Great Britain

Journey times

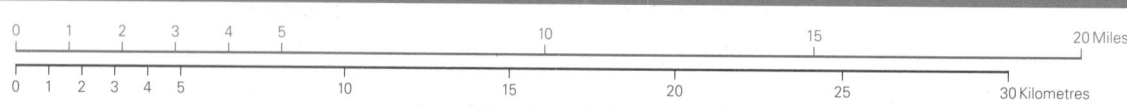

Distance in miles

0 1 2 3 4 5 10 15 20 Miles

0 1 2 3 4 5 10 15 20 25 30 Kilometres

Motorway
Autoroute
Autobahn
`M1`

Motorway Under Construction
Autoroute en construction
Autobahn im Bau

Motorway Proposed
Autoroute prévue
Geplante Autobahn

Motorway Junctions with Numbers
Unlimited Interchange **4**
Limited Interchange **5**

Autoroute échangeur numéroté
Echangeur complet
Echangeur partiel

Autobahnanschlußstelle mit Nummer
Unbeschränkter Fahrtrichtungswechsel
Beschränkter Fahrtrichtungswechsel

Motorway Service Area (with fuel station)
with access from one carriageway only

Aire de services d'autoroute (avec station service)
accessible d'un seul côté

Rastplatz oder Raststätte (mit tankstelle)
Einbahn

Major Road Service Areas
(with fuel station) with 24 hour facilities
`LEEMING`
`OLDBURY`

Aire de services sur route prioritaire
(avec station service) Ouverte 24h sur 24

Raststätte
(mit tankstelle) Durchgehend geöffnet

Truckstop (selection of)
Sélection d'aire pour poids lourds
Auswahl von Fernfahrerrastplatz

Primary Route
Route à grande circulation
Hauptverkehrsstraße
`A41`

Primary Route Junction with Number
Echangeur numéroté
Hauptverkehrsstraßenkreuzung mit Nummer

Primary Route Destination
Route prioritaire, direction
Hauptverkehrsstraße Richtung
`DOVER`

Dual Carriageways (A & B roads)
Route à double chaussées séparées (route A & B)
Zweispurige Schnellstraße (A- und B- Straßen)

Class A Road
Route de type A
A-Straße
`A129`

Class B Road
Route de type B
B-Straße
`B177`

Narrow Major Road (passing places)
Route prioritaire étroite (possibilité de dépassement)
Schmale Hauptverkehrsstaße (mit Überholmöglichkeit)

Major Roads Under Construction
Route prioritaire en construction
Hauptverkehrsstaße im Bau

Major Roads Proposed
Route prioritaire prévue
Geplante Hauptverkehrsstaße

Safety Cameras with Speed Limits
Single Camera **30**
Multiple Cameras located along road **50**
Single & Multiple Variable Speed Cameras **V V**

Radars de contrôle de vitesse
Radar simple
Radars multiples situés le long de la route
Radars simples et multiples de contrôle de vitesse variable

Sicherheitskameras mit Tempolimit
Einzelne Kamera
Mehrere Kameras entlang der Straße
Einzelne und mehrere Kameras für variables Tempolimit

Fuel Station
Station service
Tankstelle

Gradient 1:5 (20%) **& steeper**
(ascent in direction of arrow)
Pente égale ou supérieure à 20% (dans le sens de la montée)
20% Steigung und steiler (in Pfeilrichtung)

Toll
Barrière de péage
Gebührenpflichtig
`TOLL`

Mileage between markers
Distence en miles entre les flèches
Strecke zwischen Markierungen in Meilen
8

Railway and Station
Voie ferrée et gare
Eisenbahnlinie und Bahnhof

Level Crossing and Tunnel
Passage à niveau et tunnel
Bahnübergang und Tunnel

River or Canal
Rivière ou canal
Fluß oder Kanal

County or Unitary Authority Boundary
Limite de comté ou de division administrative
Grafschafts- oder Verwaltungsbezirksgrenze

National Boundary
Frontière nationale
Landesgrenze

Built-up Area
Agglomération
Geschlossene Ortschaft

Village or Hamlet
Village ou hameau
Dorf oder Weiler

Wooded Area
Zone boisée
Waldgebiet

Spot Height in Feet
Altitude (en pieds)
Höhe in Fuß
• 813

Relief above 400' (122m)
Relief par estompage au-dessus de 400' (122m)
Reliefschattierung über 400' (122m)

National Grid Reference (kilometres)
Coordonnées géographiques nationales (Kilomètres)
Nationale geographische Koordinaten (Kilometer)
100

Page Continuation
Suite à la page indiquée
Seitenfortsetzung
48

Area covered by Main Route map
Répartition des cartes des principaux axes routiers
Von Karten mit Hauptverkehrsstrecken
`MAIN ROUTE 180`

Area covered by Town Plan
Ville ayant un plan à la page indiquée
Von Karten mit Stadtplänen erfaßter Bereich
`SEE PAGE 194`

Airport
Aéroport
Flughafen

Airfield
Terrain d'aviation
Flugplatz

Heliport
Héliport
Hubschrauberlandeplatz

Battle Site and Date
Champ de bataille et date
Schlachtfeld und Datum
1066

Castle (open to public)
Château (ouvert au public)
Schloß / Burg (für die Öffentlichkeit zugänglich)

Castle with Garden (open to public)
Château avec parc (ouvert au public)
Schloß mit Garten (für die Öffentlichkeit zugänglich)

Cathedral, Abbey, Church, Friary, Priory
Cathédrale, abbaye, église, monastère, prieuré
Kathedrale, Abtei, Kirche, Mönchskloster, Kloster

Country Park
Parc régional
Landschaftspark

Ferry (vehicular, sea)
(vehicular, river)
(foot only)

Bac (véhicules, mer)
(véhicules, rivière)
(piétons)

Fähre (auto, meer)
(auto, fluß)
(nur für Personen)

Garden (open to public)
Jardin (ouvert au public)
Garten (für die Öffentlichkeit zugänglich)

Golf Course (9 hole) (18 hole)
Terrain de golf (9 trous) (18 trous)
Golfplatz (9 Löcher) (18 Löcher)

Historic Building (open to public)
Monument historique (ouvert au public)
Historisches Gebäude (für die Öffentlichkeit zugänglich)

Historic Building with Garden (open to public)
Monument historique avec jardin (ouvert au public)
Historisches Gebäude mit Garten (für die Öffentlichkeit zugänglich)

Horse Racecourse
Hippodrome
Pferderennbahn

Information Centre
Syndicat d'initiative
Information

Lighthouse
Phare
Leuchtturm

Motor Racing Circuit
Circuit Automobile
Automobilrennbahn

Museum, Art Gallery
Musée
Museum, Galerie

National Trust Property
(National Trust for Scotland)
`NT`
`NTS`

National Trust Property
(National Trust for Scotland)

National Trust- Eigentum
(National Trust for Scotland)

National Park
Parc national
Nationalpark

Nature Reserve or Bird Sanctuary
Réserve naturelle botanique ou ornithologique
Natur- oder Vogelschutzgebiet

Nature Trail or Forest Walk
Chemin forestier, piste verte
Naturpfad oder Waldweg

Place of Interest
Site, curiosité
Sehenswürdigkeit
Monument •

Picnic Site
Lieu pour pique-nique
Picknickplatz

Railway, Steam or Narrow Gauge
Chemin de fer, à vapeur ou à voie étroite
Eisenbahn, Dampf- oder Schmalspurbahn

Theme Park
Centre de loisirs
Vergnügungspark

Viewpoint (360 degrees) (180 degrees)
Vue panoramique (360 degrés) (180 degrés)
Aussichtspunkt (360 Grade) (180 Grade)

Wildlife Park
Réserve de faune
Wildpark

Windmill
Moulin à vent
Windmühle

Zoo or Safari Park
Parc ou réserve zoologique
Zoo oder Safari-Park

Please note: symbols have been enlarged for clarity

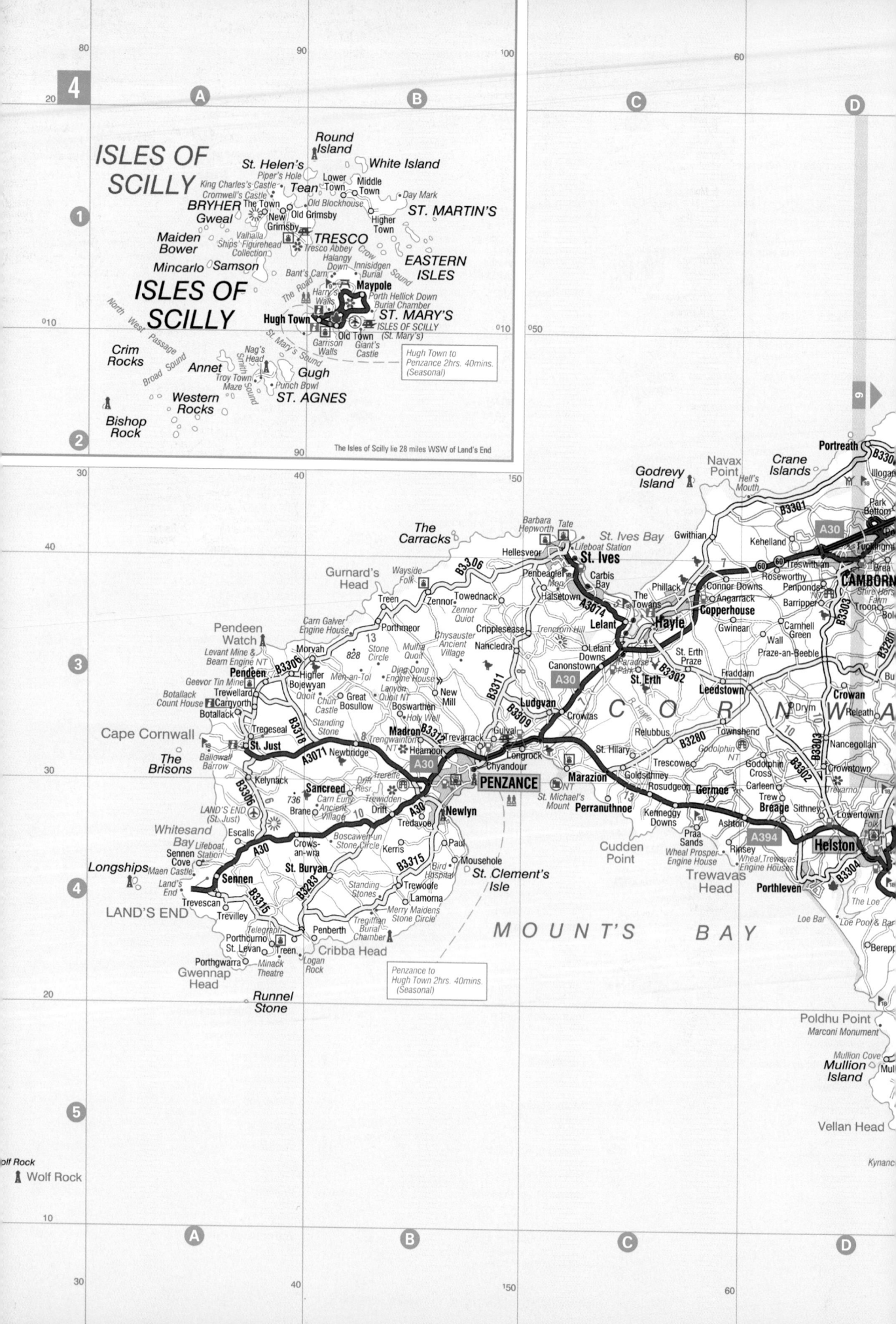

ISLES OF SCILLY

Round Island

St. Helen's   White Island
Piper's Hole   Lower   Middle
King Charles's Castle   Town   Town   Day Mark
Cromwell's Castle   Tean
BRYHER   The Town   Old Blockhouse
Gweal   New   Old Grimsby   ST. MARTIN'S
Grimsby   Higher
Valhalla   Town
Maiden   Ships' Figurehead   TRESCO   EASTERN
Bower   Collection   Tresco Abbey   Crow   ISLES
Halangy   Sound
Mincarlo   Samson   Down   Innisidgen
Bant's Carn   Burial
ISLES OF   Maypole
SCILLY   Harry's   Porth Hellick Down
Walls   Burial Chamber
Hugh Town   ISLES OF SCILLY
Old Town   ST. MARY'S
Crim   Garrison   (St. Mary's)
Rocks   Walls   Giant's
Nag's   Castle   Hugh Town to
Head   Penzance 2hrs. 40mins.
Annet   Gugh   (Seasonal)
Troy Town   Punch Bowl
Maze   ST. AGNES

Bishop
Rock

The Isles of Scilly lie 28 miles WSW of Land's End

30   40   150

The Carracks   Barbara   Tate
Hepworth   St. Ives Bay   Gwithian
Hellesveor   Lifeboat Station   Godrevy
Gurnard's   Wayside   St. Ives   Island   Navax   Crane
Head   Folk   Penbeagler   Carbis   Point   Islands   Portreath
Treen   Zennor   Towednack   Bay   Gwithian   Hell's
Pendeen   Porthmeor   Halsetown   The Towans   Mouth   Kehelland
Watch   Zennor   Chysauster   Hayle   Connor Downs   Roseworthy   Treswithian
Levant Mine &   Carn Galver   Quoit   Ancient   Cripplesease   Phillack   Angarrack   Penponds   CAMBORNE
Beam Engine NT   Engine House   13   Village   Nancledra   Lelant   Copperhouse   Barripper   Shire
Morvah   Higher   Stone   Lelant   Gwinear   Praze-an-Beeble
Pendeen   Bojewyan   828   Circle   Mulfra   New   Downs   St. Erth   Carnhell
Geevor Tin Mine   Men-an-Tol   Quoit   Mill   Canonstown   St. Erth   Green   Crowan
Trewellard   Higher   Great   Ding Dong   B3311   Praze   Fraddam
Botallack   Chûn   Bosullow   Engine House   Relubbus   Townshend   Nancegollan
Count House   Carnyorth   Quoit   Lanyon   Boswarthen   Ludgvan   St. Hilary   Crowan   Releath
Botallack   Chûn   Quoit NT   Holy Well   Crowlas   Trescowe   Reawla
Castle   Trevarrack   Godolphin   Godolphin   Crowarno
Tregeseal   Standing   Gulval   St. Hilary   NT   Cross   Trevarno
Cape Cornwall   St. Just   Stone   Madron   Longrock   Rosudgeon   Carleen
Newbridge   8   Trengwainton   Chyandour   Germoe   Trew   Breage
The   Kelynack   NT   Heamoor   A30   PENZANCE   Marazion   Goldsithney   Ashton   Sithney
Brisons   Ballowall   Sancreed   Drift   Trereife   St. Michael's   Perranuthnoe   Kenneggy   Rinsey   Lowertown   Helston
Barrow   Carn Euny   Resr   Trewidden   Newlyn   Mount   Downs   Praa   Wheal Trewavas
LAND'S END   Ancient   NT   Tredavoe   Sands   Engine Houses   Porthleven
(St. Just)   736   Village   10   Drift   Cudden   Wheal Prosper   The Loe
Whitesand   Brane   Point   Engine House   Loe Bar
Bay   Escalls   Crows-   Kerris   Paul   Trewavas   Loe Pool & Bar
Sennen   an-wra   B3315   Mousehole   Head
Cove   St. Buryan   Bird   St. Clement's   Berep
Longships   Sennen   Hospital   Isle
Maen Castle   St. Buryan   Trewoofe   MOUNT'S   BAY
Land's   Lamorna
End   Standing
LAND'S END   Trevescan   Stones
Trevilley   Penberth   Merry Maidens   Poldhu Point
Telegraph   Tregiffian   Stone Circle   Marconi Monument
Porthcurno   Burial
St. Levan   Treen   Chamber   Mullion Cove
Porthgwarra   Minack   Logan   Penzance to   Mullion   Mul
Gwennap   Theatre   Rock   Hugh Town 2hrs. 40mins.   Island
Head   Cribba Head   (Seasonal)
Runnel
Stone   Vellan Head

Wolf Rock   Kynanc

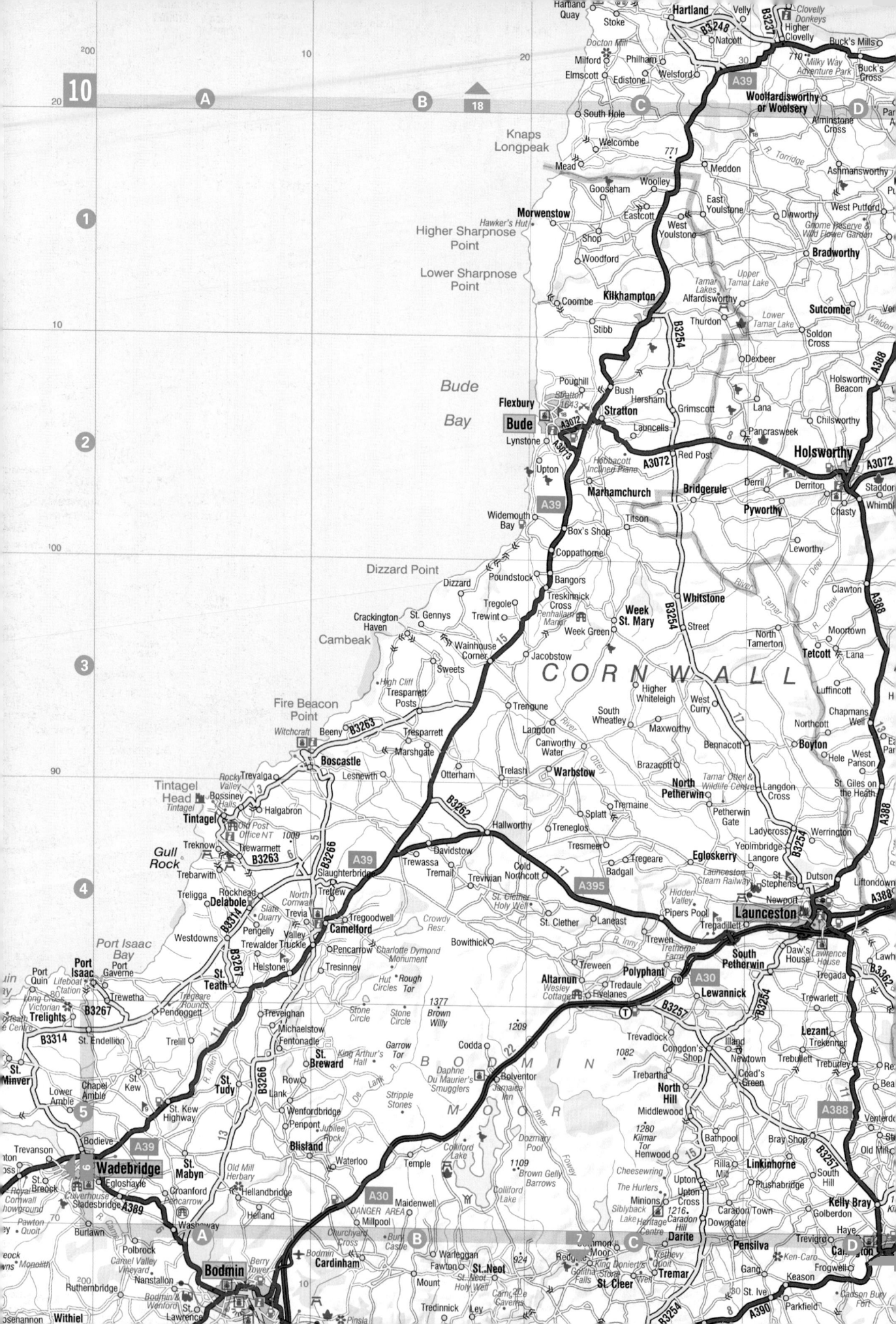

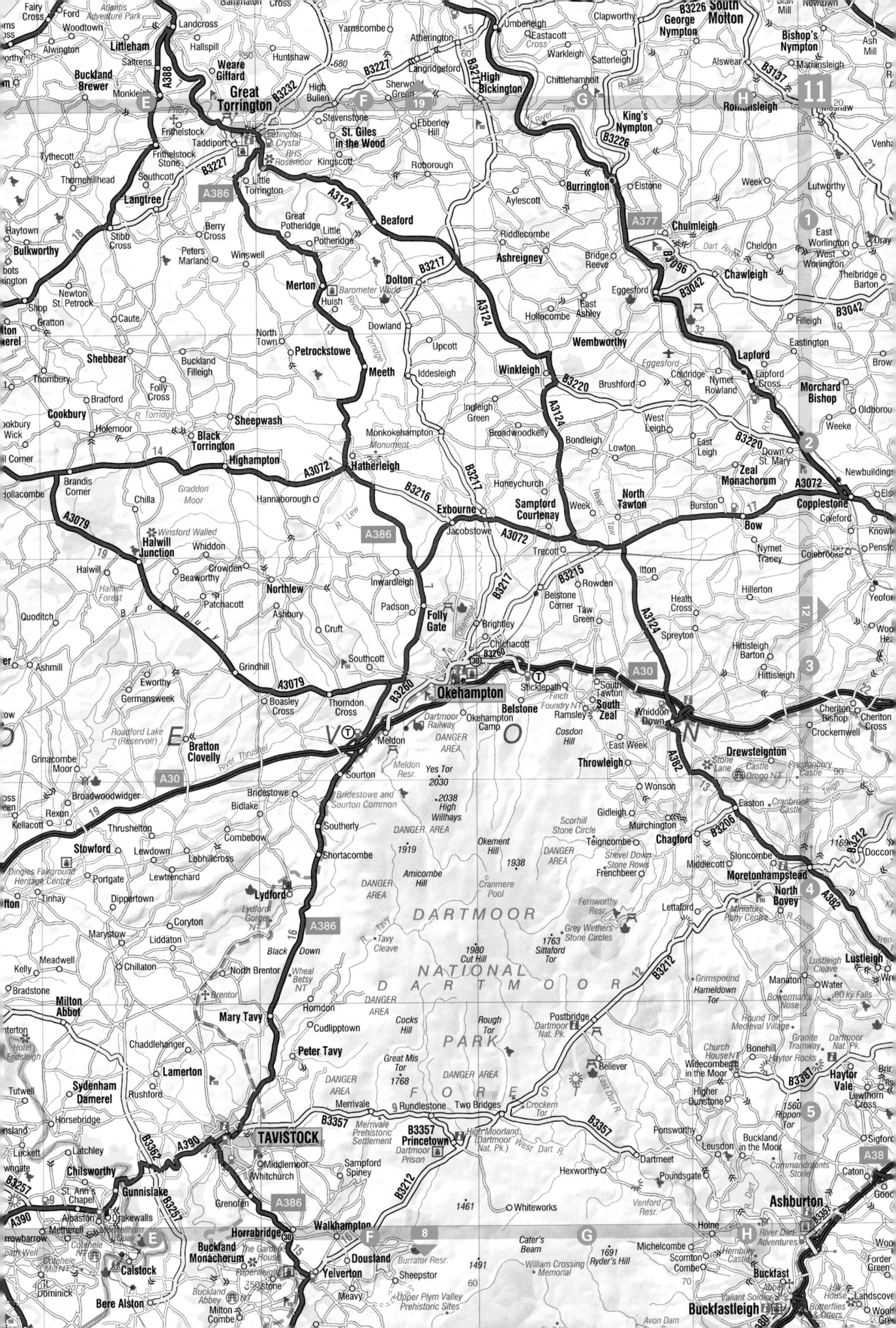

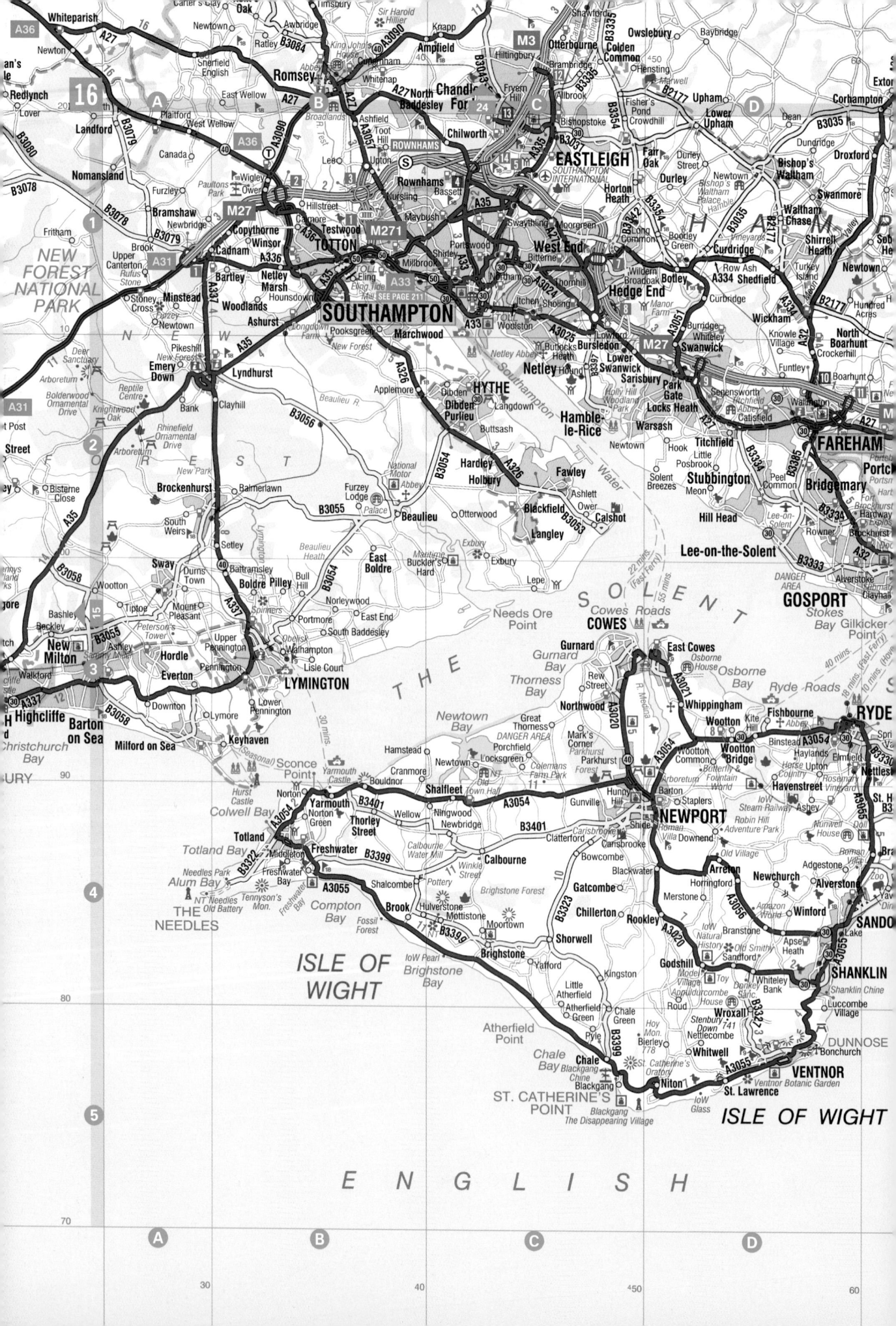

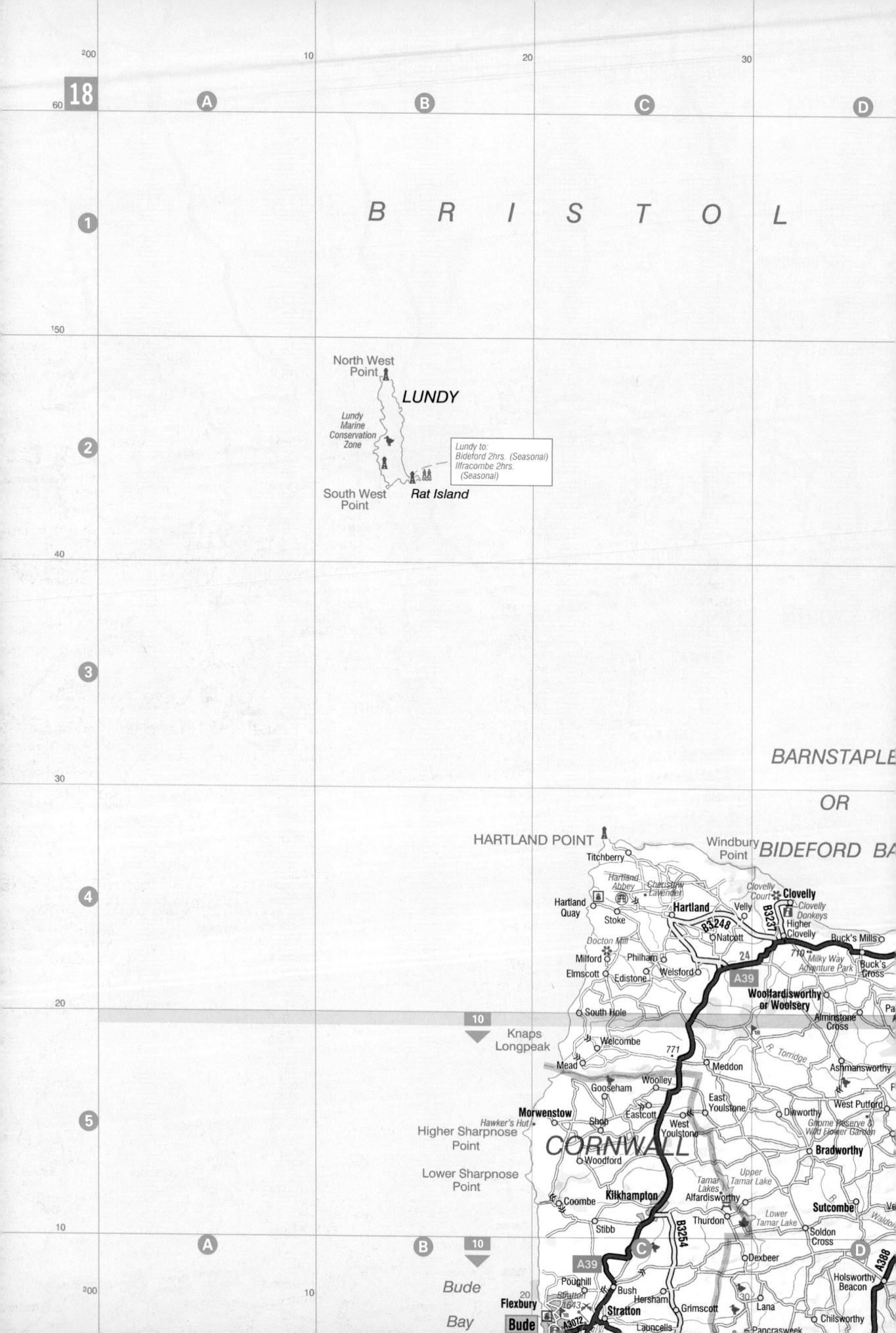

200
60

A   10   B   20   C   30   D

1

B   R   I   S   T   O   L

150

North West
Point

LUNDY

*Lundy
Marine
Conservation
Zone*

2

Lundy to:
Bideford 2hrs. (Seasonal)
Ilfracombe 2hrs.
(Seasonal)

South West
Point

Rat Island

40

3

30

BARNSTAPLE

OR

HARTLAND POINT

Windbury   *BIDEFORD BA*
Point

Titchberry

4

*Hartland
Abbey*   *Cherston
Lavender*

*Clovelly
Court*   **Clovelly**

Hartland
Quay   Stoke   **Hartland**   Velly   *Clovelly
Donkeys*
B3248   B3237   Higher
Clovelly   Buck's Mills

Docton Mill   Natcott   24   710   *Milky Way
Adventure Park*   Buck's
Cross

Milford   Philham   A39   **Woolfardisworthy
or Woolsery**

Elmscott   Edistone   Welsford   Alminstone   Pa
Cross

20

South Hole

10

Knaps   Welcombe   18   *R. Torridge*   Ashmansworthy
Longpeak

Mead   771   Meddon   West Putford

Gooseham   Woolley   East
Youlstone   Dinworthy   *Gnome Reserve &
Wild Flower Garden*

5   **Morwenstow**   Shop   Eastcott   West
Youlstone   **Bradworthy**

Hawker's Hut
Higher Sharpnose   **CORNWALL**   Woodford
Point   *Upper
Tamar Lake*

Lower Sharpnose   *Tamar
Lakes*   **Sutcombe**
Point   **Kilkhampton**   Alfardisworthy

Coombe   *Lower
Tamar Lake*

Stibb   Thurdon   Soldon
Cross

10   B3254   D

A   B   10   A39   C   Dexbeer   D   A388

200   *Bude*   Poughill   Bush   Holsworthy
Beacon

10   Flexbury   Stratton   Hersham   Grimscott   Lana   Chilsworthy
1643   A3072
Bude   18   **Stratton**
Bay   Launcells   Pancrasweek

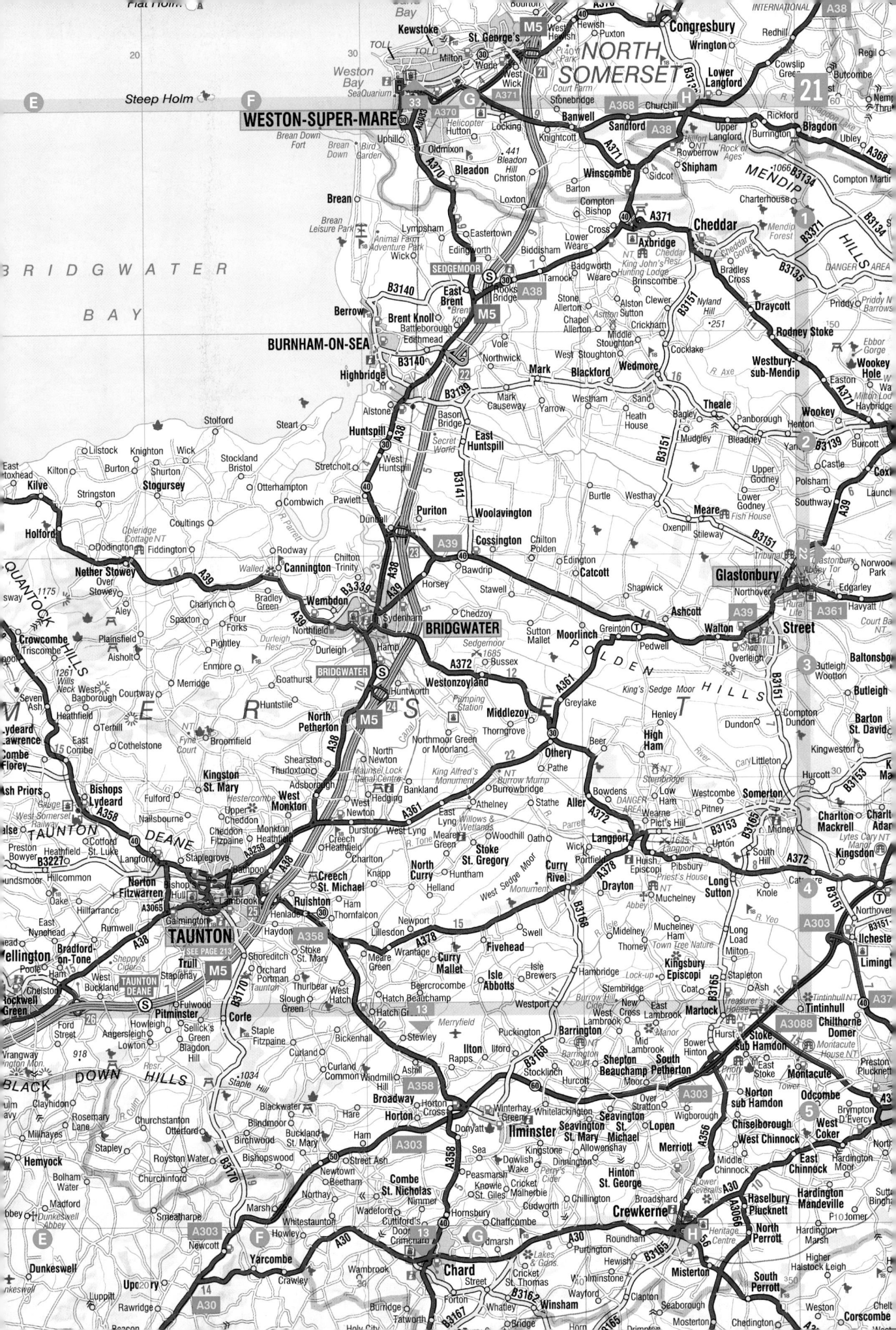

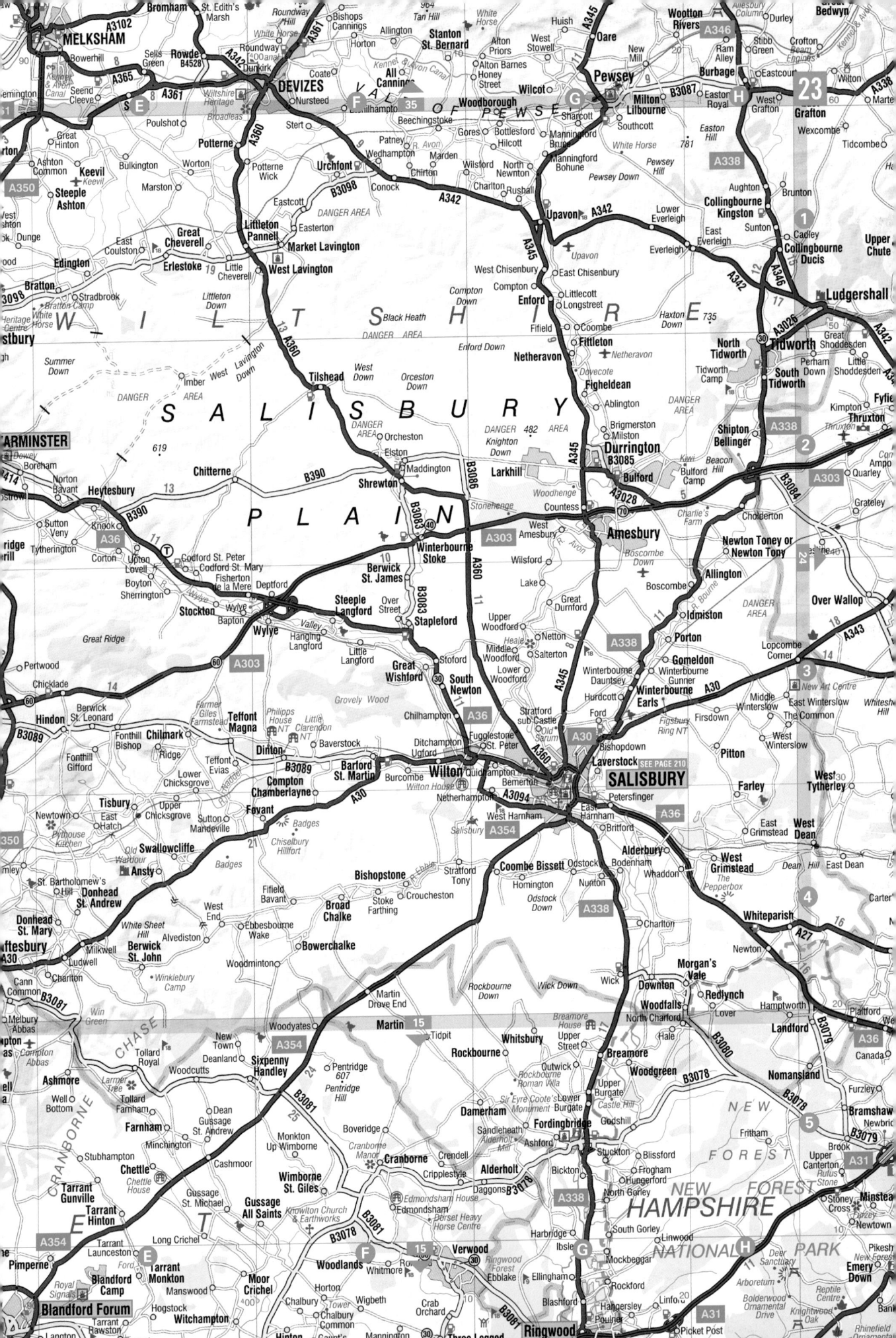

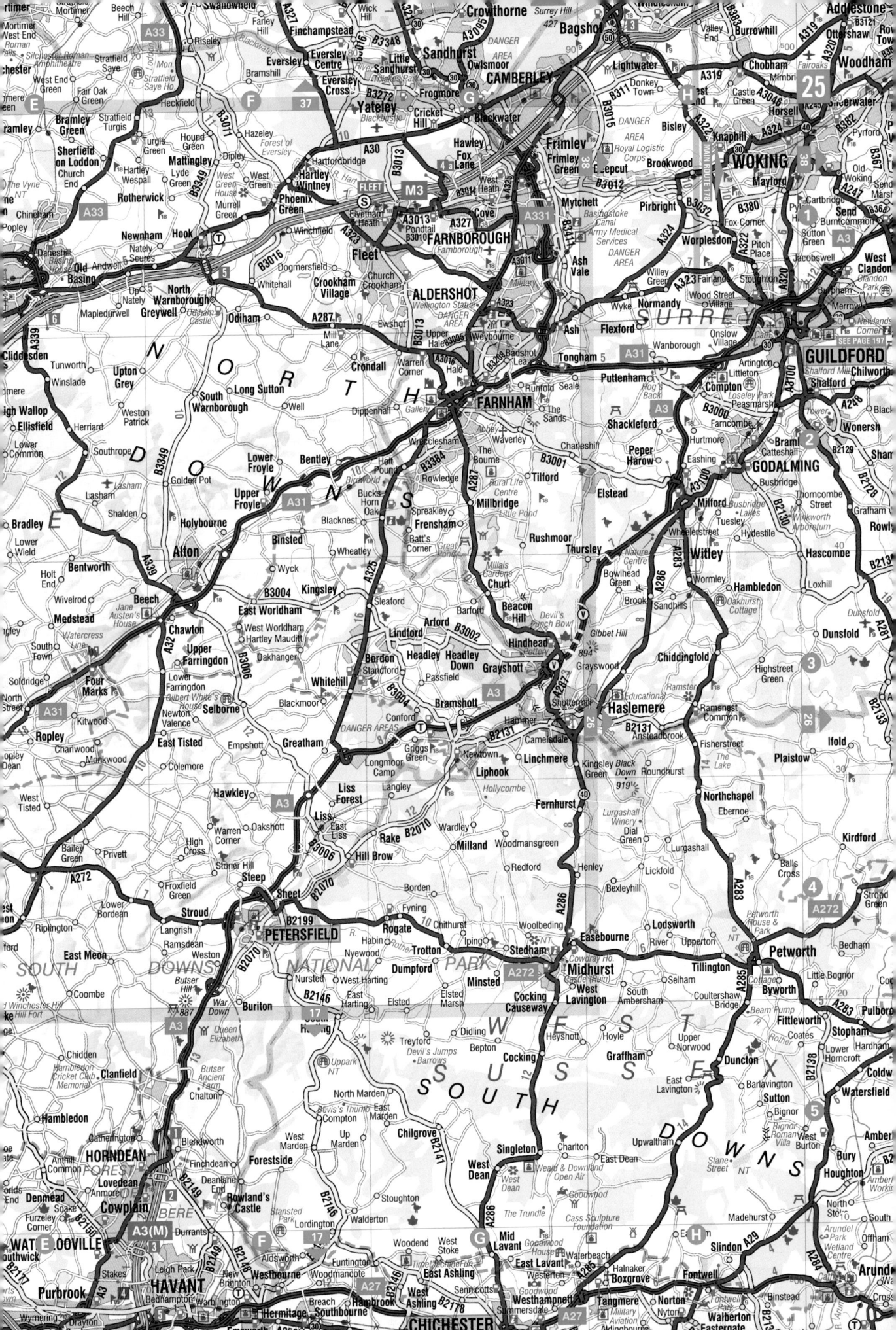

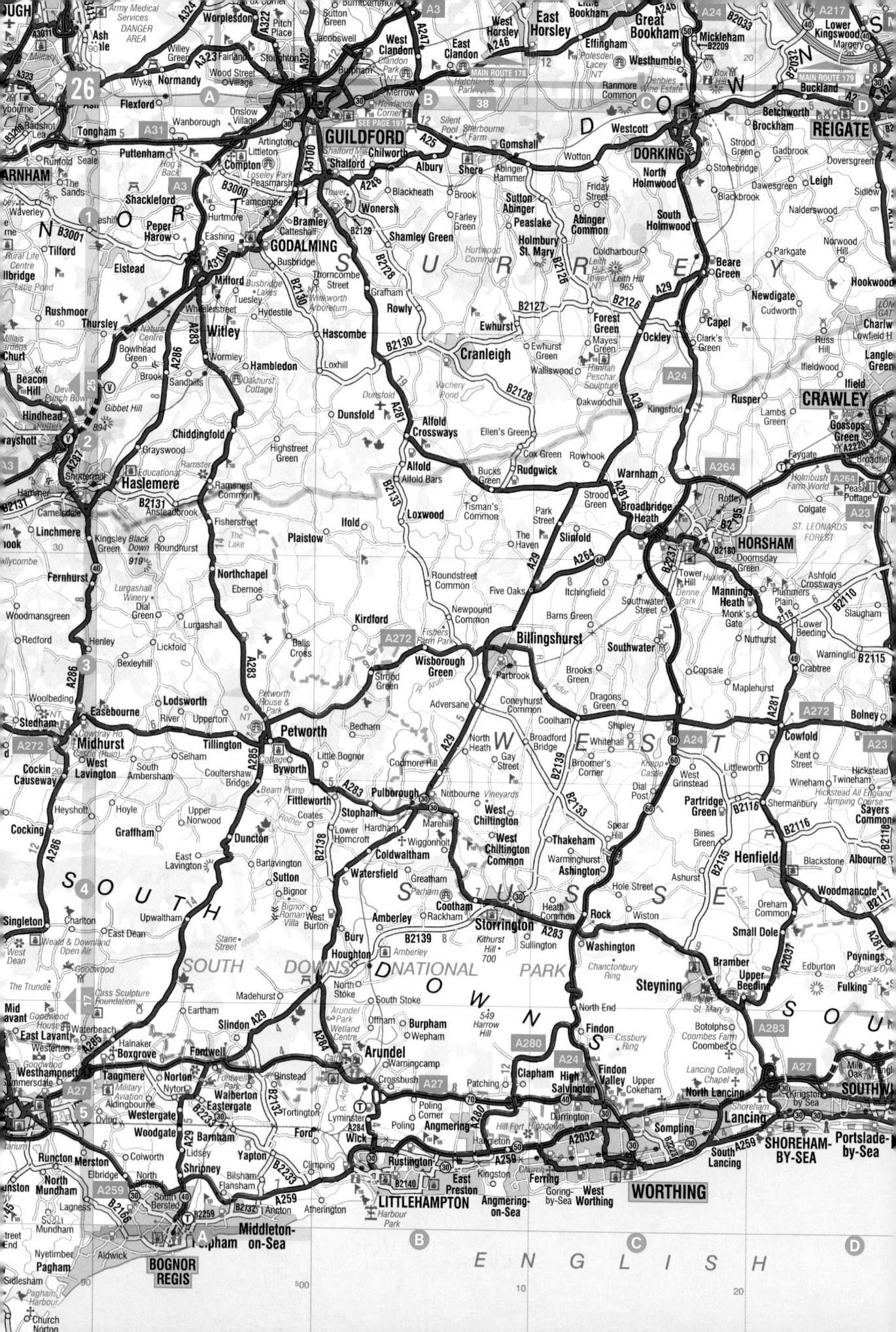

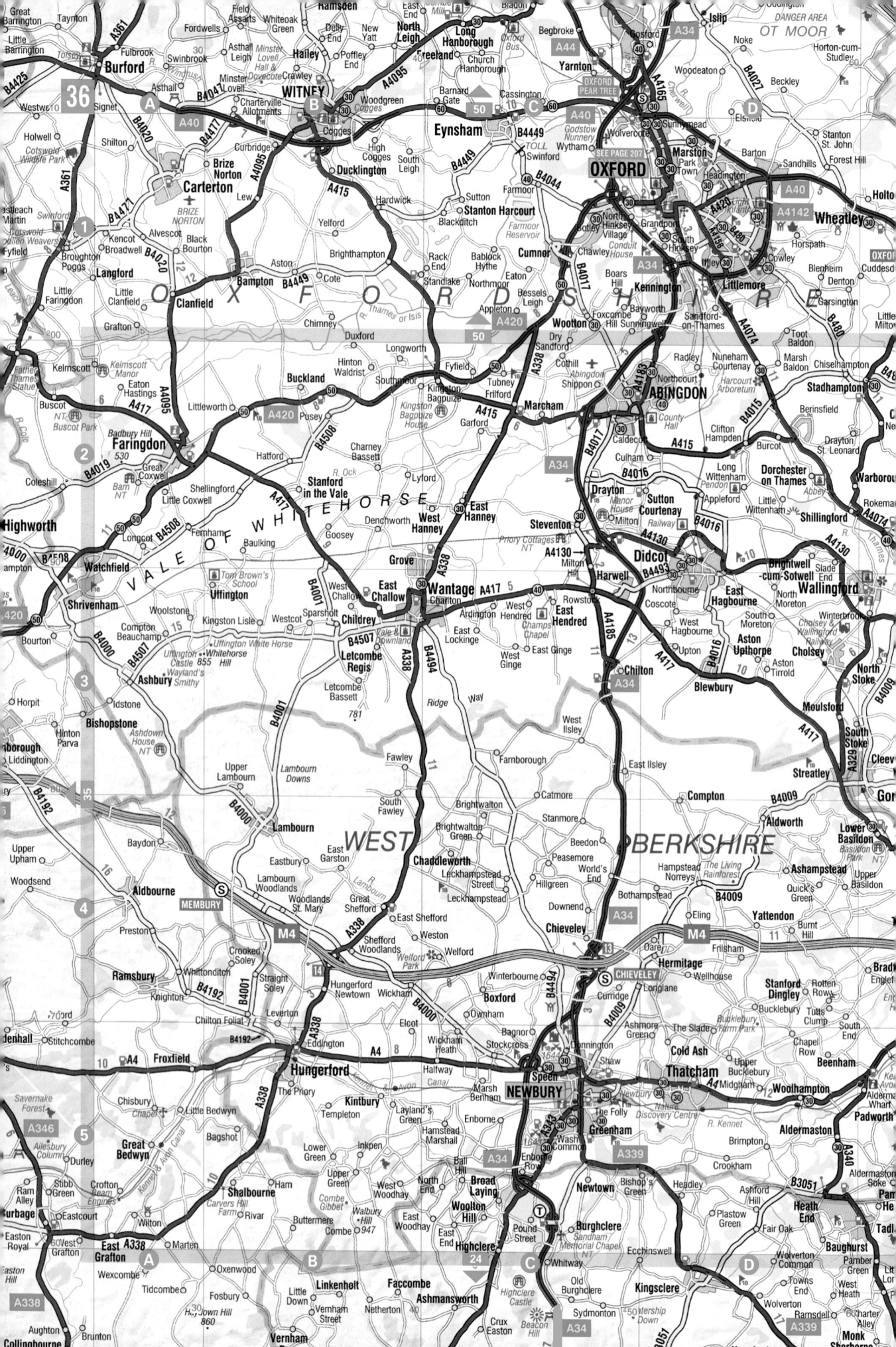

N O R T H

S E A

Holliwell Point
Foulness Sands
Foulness Point
urtsend

lin Sands

den Point

Leysdown-on-Sea

Shell Ness

WHITSTABLE

Whitstable Bay
Seasalter

Graveney
odnestone
A299
Yorkletts
Denstroude
Dargate
Hernhill
odstone
Farming World
Mount Ephraim
Boughton under Blean
Dunkirk
A2
South Street
Overland
Selling
Old Wives Lees
Bagham
Chilham
Shalmsford Street
Chartham
Mountain
Street
Godmersham
Chartham Hatch
Nackington
Thanington Without
Bilt
oughton
buph
A28
Crundale
Sole Street
Kempe's Corner
Wye
Wye Crown
Hassell's Lane
North Leigh
Waltham
Bossingham
Derringstone
29
Stelling Minnis
Stelling Minnis
Denton
Bodsham
Wingmore
Wootton

Herne Bay
HERNE BAY
Hampton
Tankerton
Swalecliffe B2205
A2990
Chestfield
West Street
Radfall
B2205
South Street
5
West End
Greenhill
Eddington
Beltinge
Broomfield
Hunters Forstal
Herne
Herne Common
Wildwood
Hoath
Honey Hill
Druidstone Park
Broad Oak
Calcott
A291
Blean
Tyler Hill
Sturry
Rough Common
A290
Fordwich
Town Hall
Great
Harbledown
30
CANTERBURY
SEE PAGE 190
A2050
A257
Littlebourne
Hewletts
Bramling
Bekesbourne
Patrixbourne
Street End
Lower Hardres
Bridge
A2
Adisham
Garlinge Green
Pett Bottom
Bishopsbourne
Kingston
Petham
Barham
Upper Hardres Court
B2068
Elham Valley Vineyard
Lyddenden Hill
A2
A260
16
Woolage Village
Woolage Green
East Kent Railway
Eythorne
Shepherdswell or Sibertswold
Coldred
West Langdon
East Langdon
A256

Reculver
Reculver Towers
Regulbium Roman Fort
Hillborough
Beltinge
Maypole
Marshside
Boyden Gate
Sarre
Chislet
Upstreet
Hersden
Westbere
Stodmarsh
Grove
Plucks Gutter
West Stourmouth
East Stourmouth
Wickhambreaux
Ickham
11
Wingham
Ash
Staple
Nonington
Knowlton
Chillenden
Heronden
Frogham
Womenswold
Elvington
Tilmanstone
Eastry
Eastling
A260
Wootton

Minnis Bay
Birchington
A299
A28
St. Nicholas at Wade
Acol
B2050
Potten Street
B2190
A253
Monkton
Minster
Due Open Late 2012
A253
A299
Cliffs End
Richborough Port
Westmarsh
Ware
Paramour Street
Elmstone
Goldstone
Richborough Fort
Richborough Amphitheatre
Nash
Hoaden
Cooper Street
Wingham
Woodnesborough
Hammill
Goodnestone
Goodnestone Park
Sandwich
TOLL
Guildhall
Great Stonar
White
Worth
Finglesham
Betteshanger
Northbourne
Sholden
Great Mongeham
Ripple
Sutton
Ashley
Ringwould
Martin
Martin Mill

South Channel
Turner Contemporary
Lifeboat Station
Walpole Bay Hotel
Foreness Point
MARGATE
Westbrook
Cliftonville
B2051
Kingsgate
Westgate on Sea
40
30
ISLE OF THANET
Quex House
Westwood
Lydden
Spitfire & Hurricane
Manston
Manston
30
Northwood
St. Peter's
NORTH FORELAND
Dickens House
BROADSTAIRS
A255
A256
A254
RAMSGATE
Ramsgate to Ostend 4hrs.
Pegwell Bay
A256
R. Stour
Sandwich Bay
Sandown Castle
The Small Downs
Timeball Tower
DEAL
B2056
Walmer
The Downs
150
Kingsdown
DANGER AREA
Dover Patrol Memorial

1
2
3
4
5

90
80
70
60

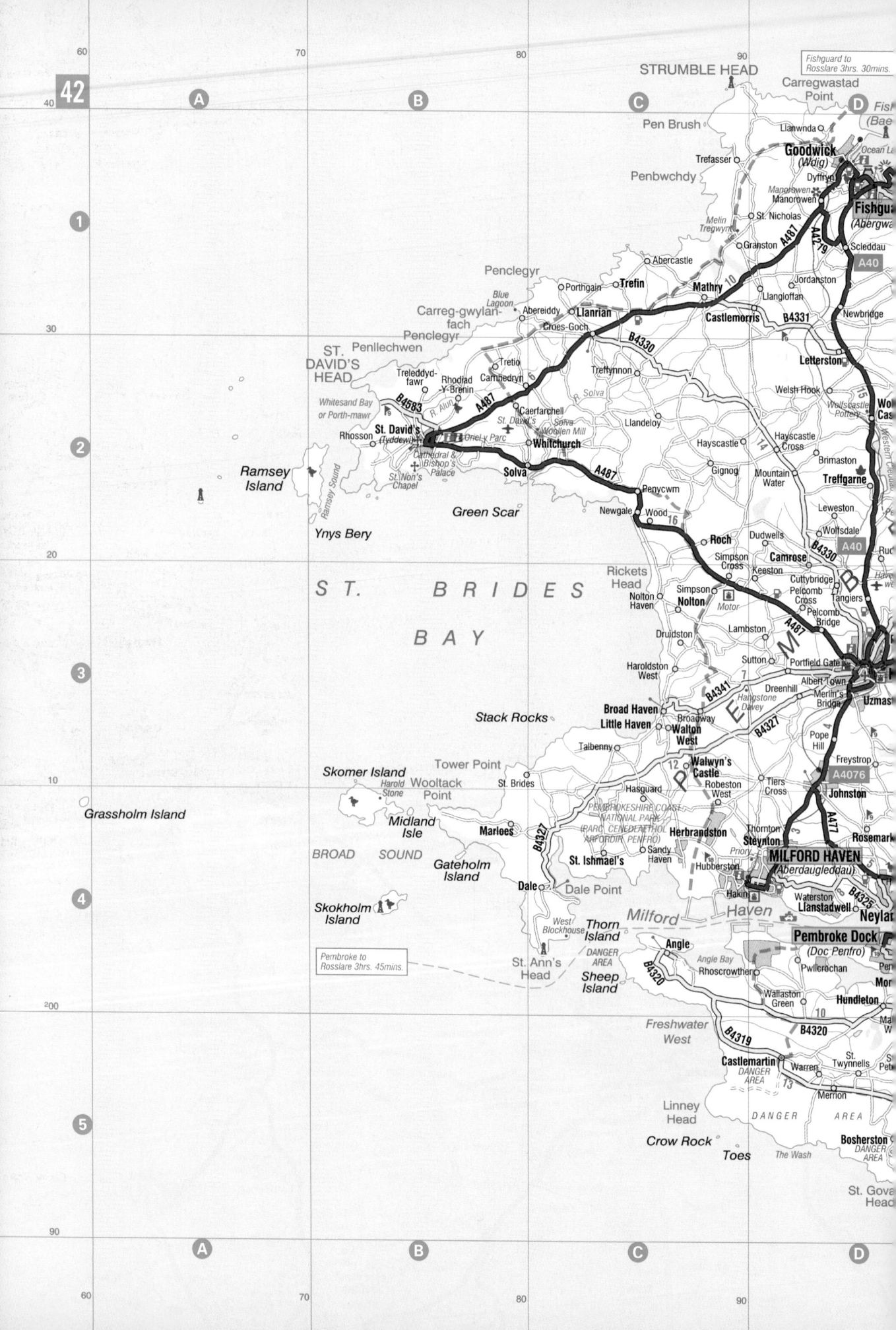

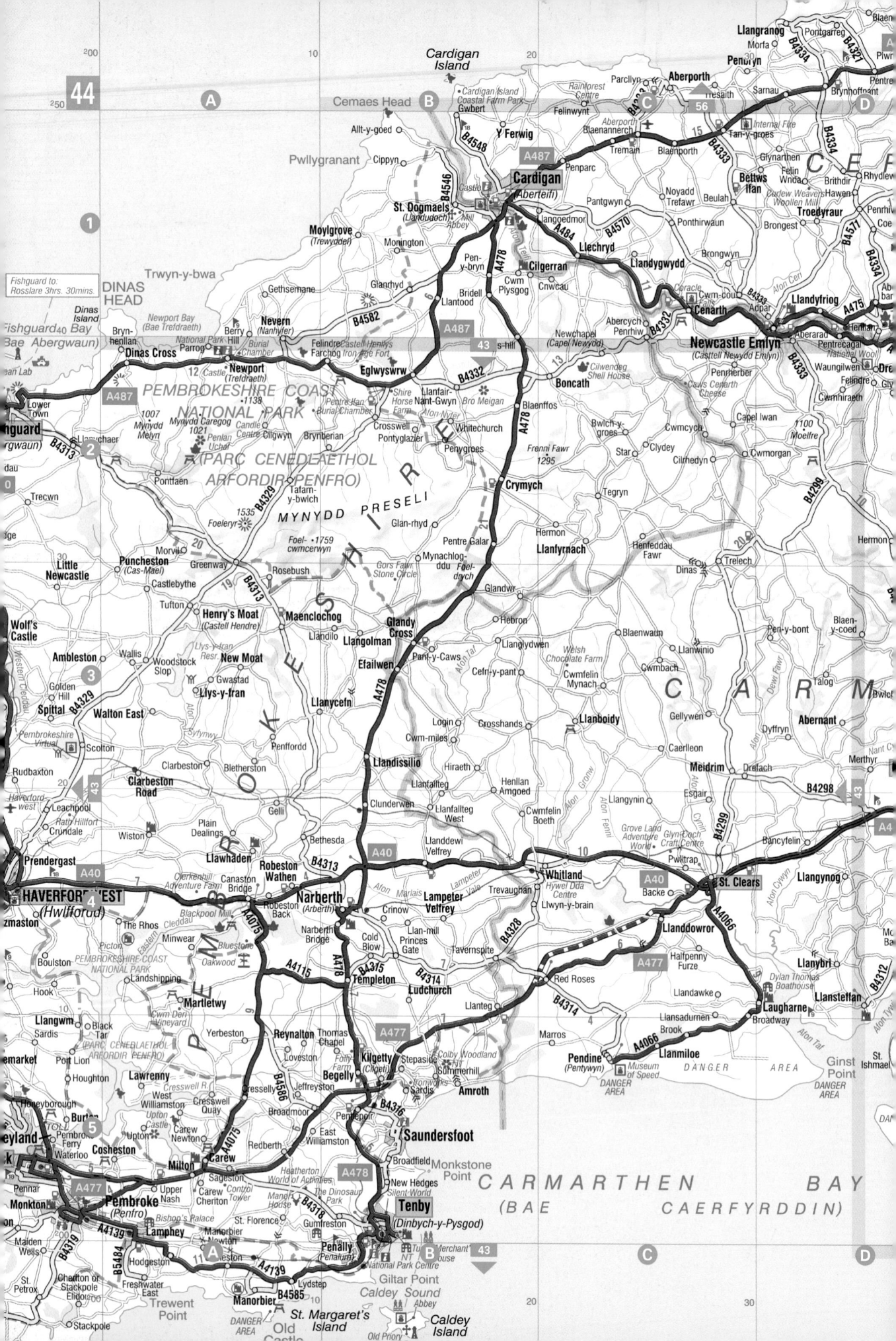

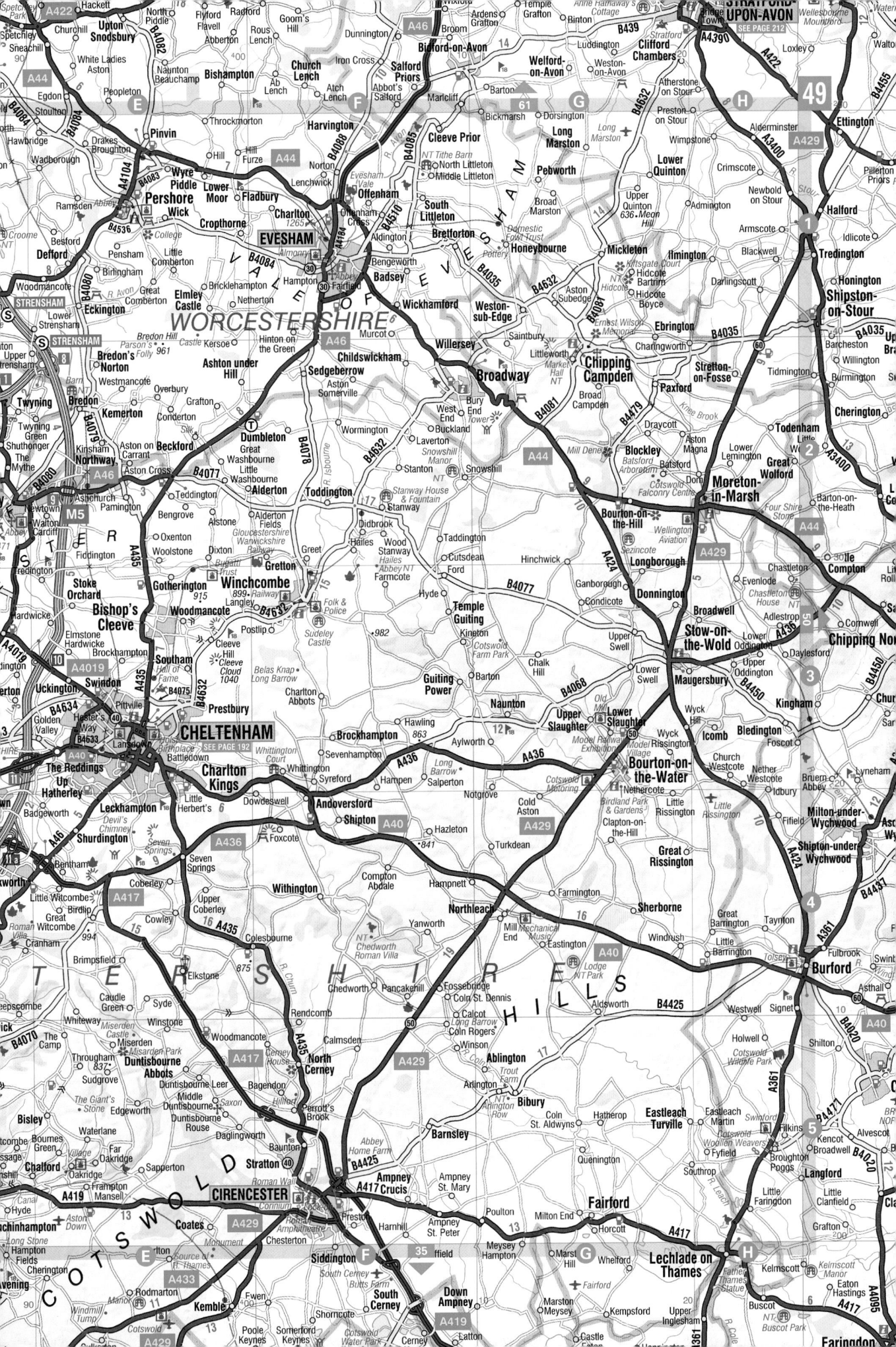

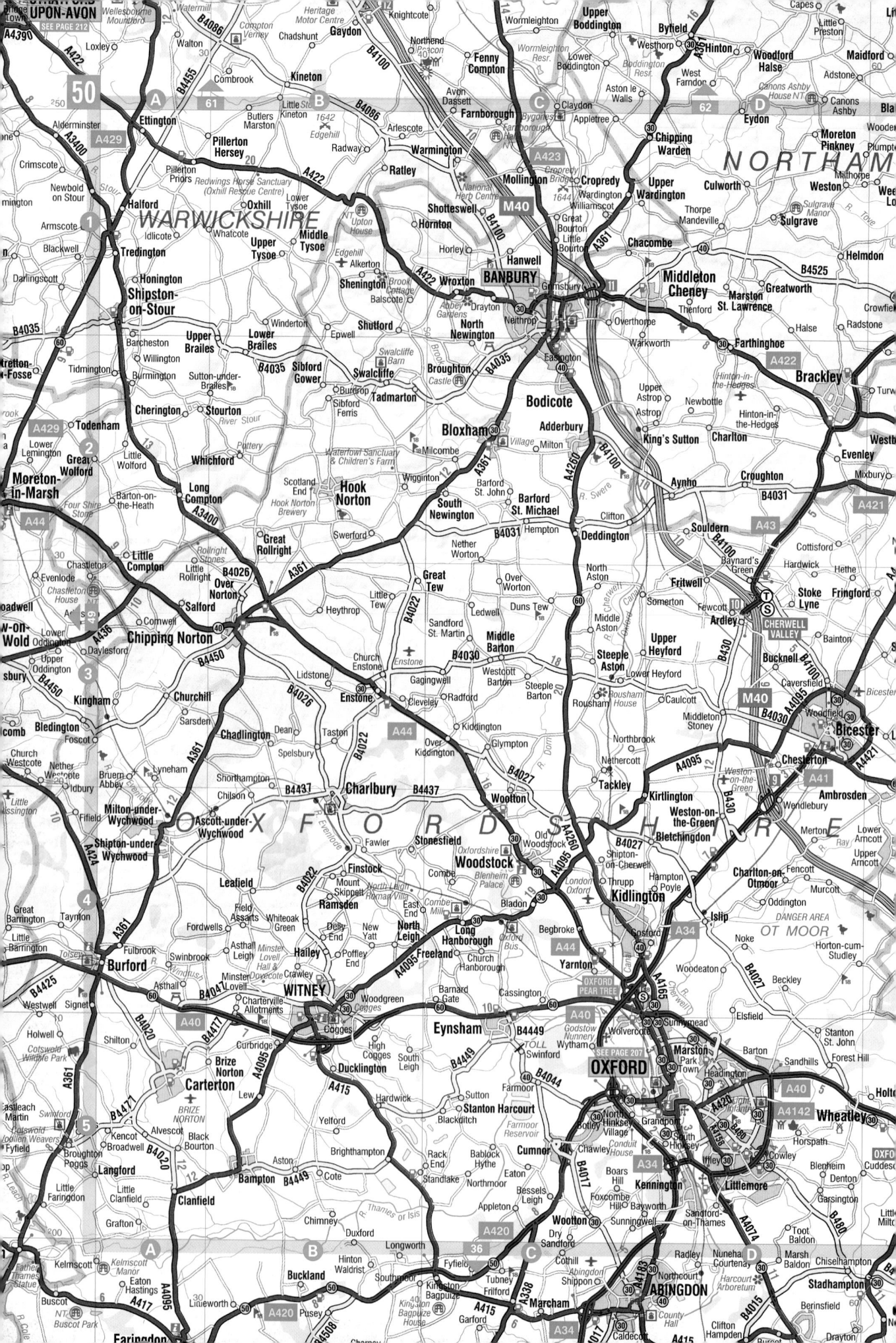

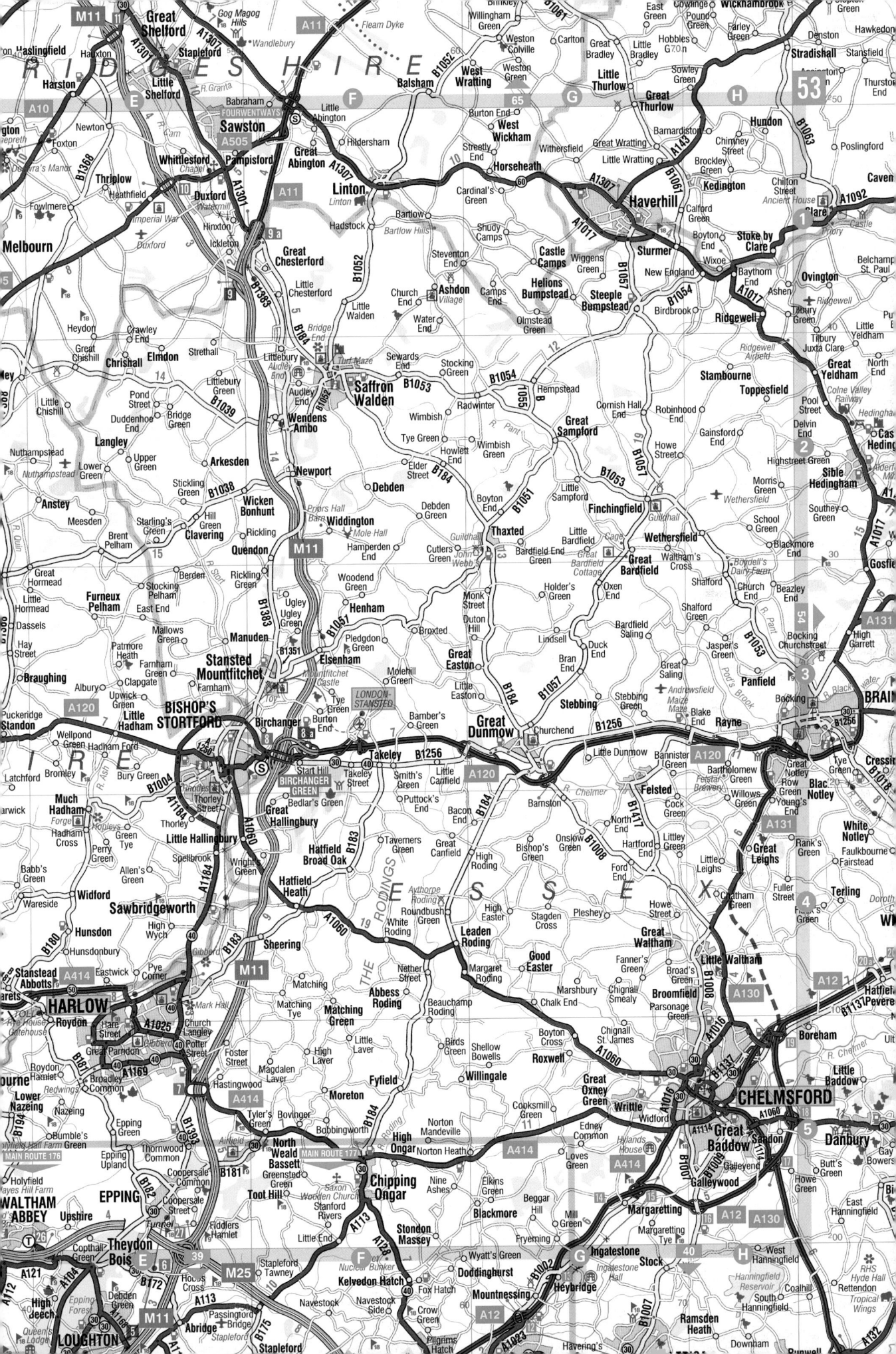

10   20   30   40

300

1

90

2

80

C A R D I G A N   B A Y

(B A E   C E R E D I G I O N)

70

4

Aberaeron

60

New Quay
(Ceinewydd)   Ffos-y-ffin
Marine Wildlife Centre   Llwyncelyn
Gilfachreda
Maen-y-   A486   B4342   Llanarth
groes   Oakford
Cross Inn   New Quay   (Derwen Ga.)
Cwmtudu   Nanternis   Honey Farm   Pen-cae   Geneva
Caerwedros   B4342
Ynys-Lochtyn   Llwyndafydd   Mydroi
Blaen Celyn   Synod Inn
5   (Post-Mawr)
Llangranog   Pontgarreg   A487
Morfa   Plwmp   A486   B4438
Penbryn   Pentregat   Talgarreg
Aberporth   B4334   Brynhoffnant   B4459
Parcllyn   Sarnau   Bwlch-y-fadfa
Rainforest   Felinwynt   Tresaith   Glynarthen   C
Centre   44   Capel
Cardigan Island   berporth   Cynon
Coastal Farm Park   Blaenannerch   15   Internal Fire   Curlew Weavers   Ffostrasol
Gwbert   B   Tan-y-groes   Woollen Mill
Cemaes Head   A   Y Ferwig   Tremain   Blaenporth   B4333   Glynarthen   Rhydlewis
Allt-y-goed   B4548   A487   Bettws   Brithdir   Pont-sian
Pwllygranant   Cippyn   Penparc   Noyadd   Ifan   Felin
250   Cardigan   Trefawr   Beulah   Wnda   Penrhiw-pal
St. Dogmaels   (Aberteifi)   Pantgwyn   Troedyraur
10   Castle

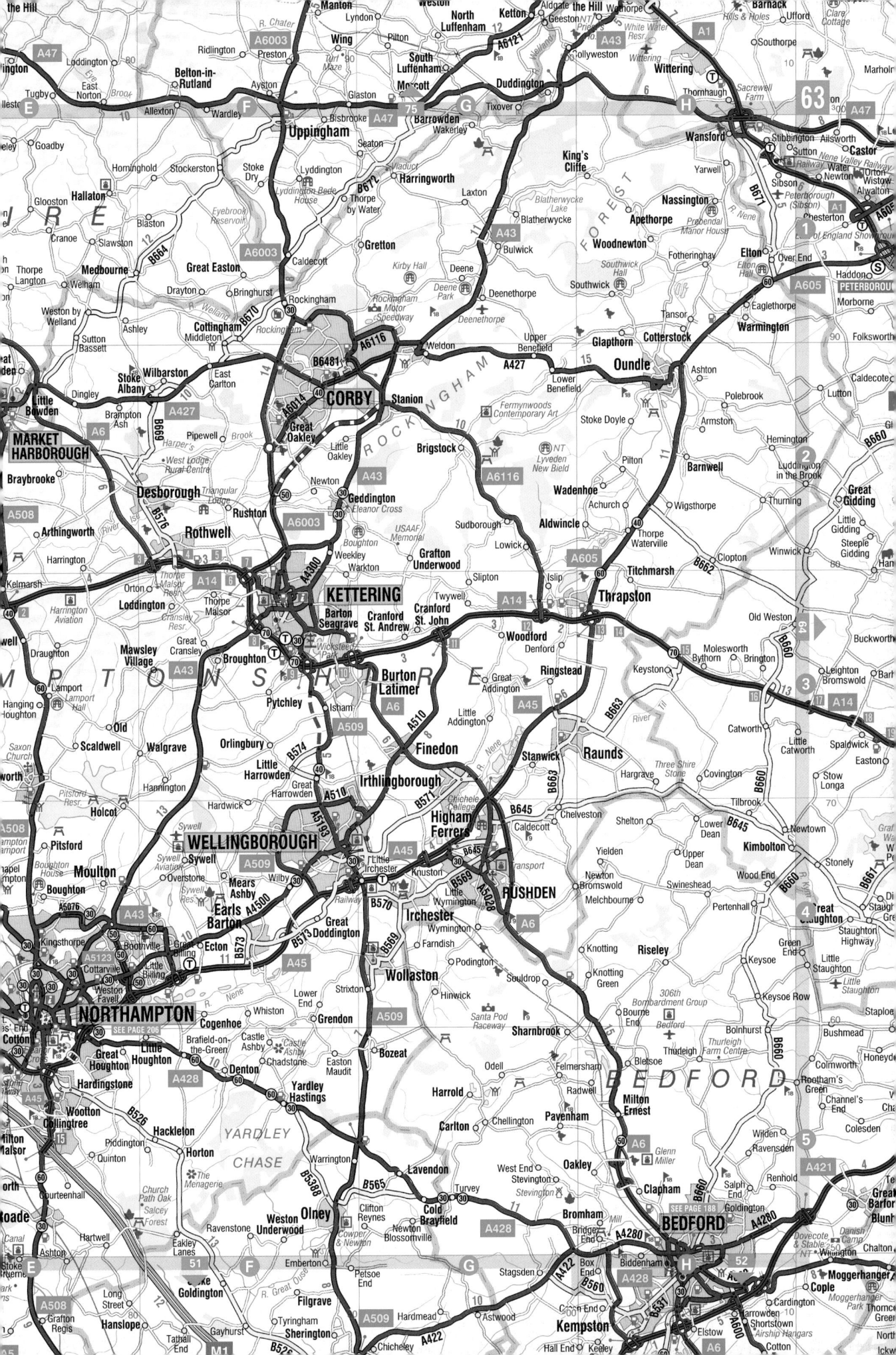

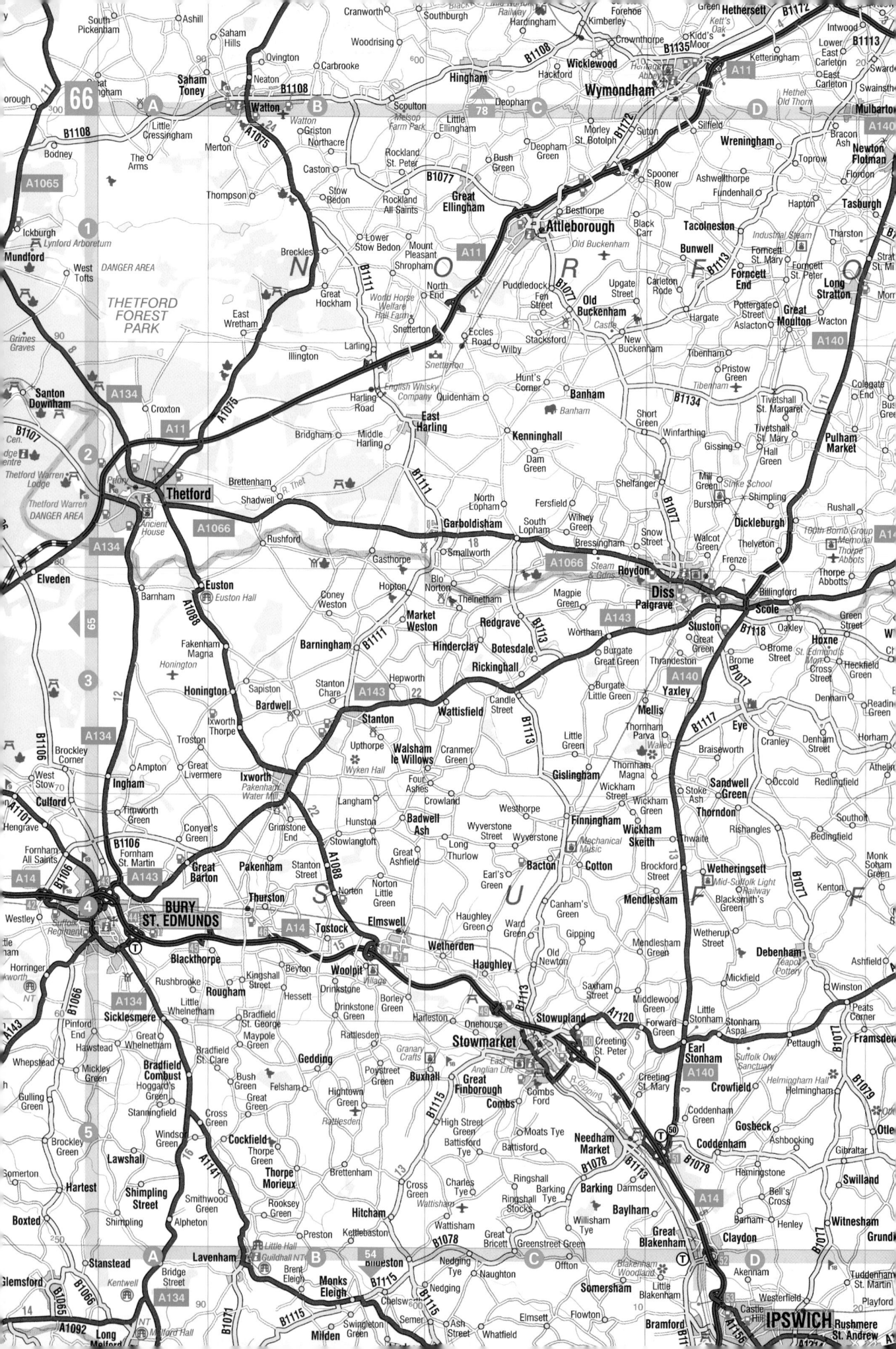

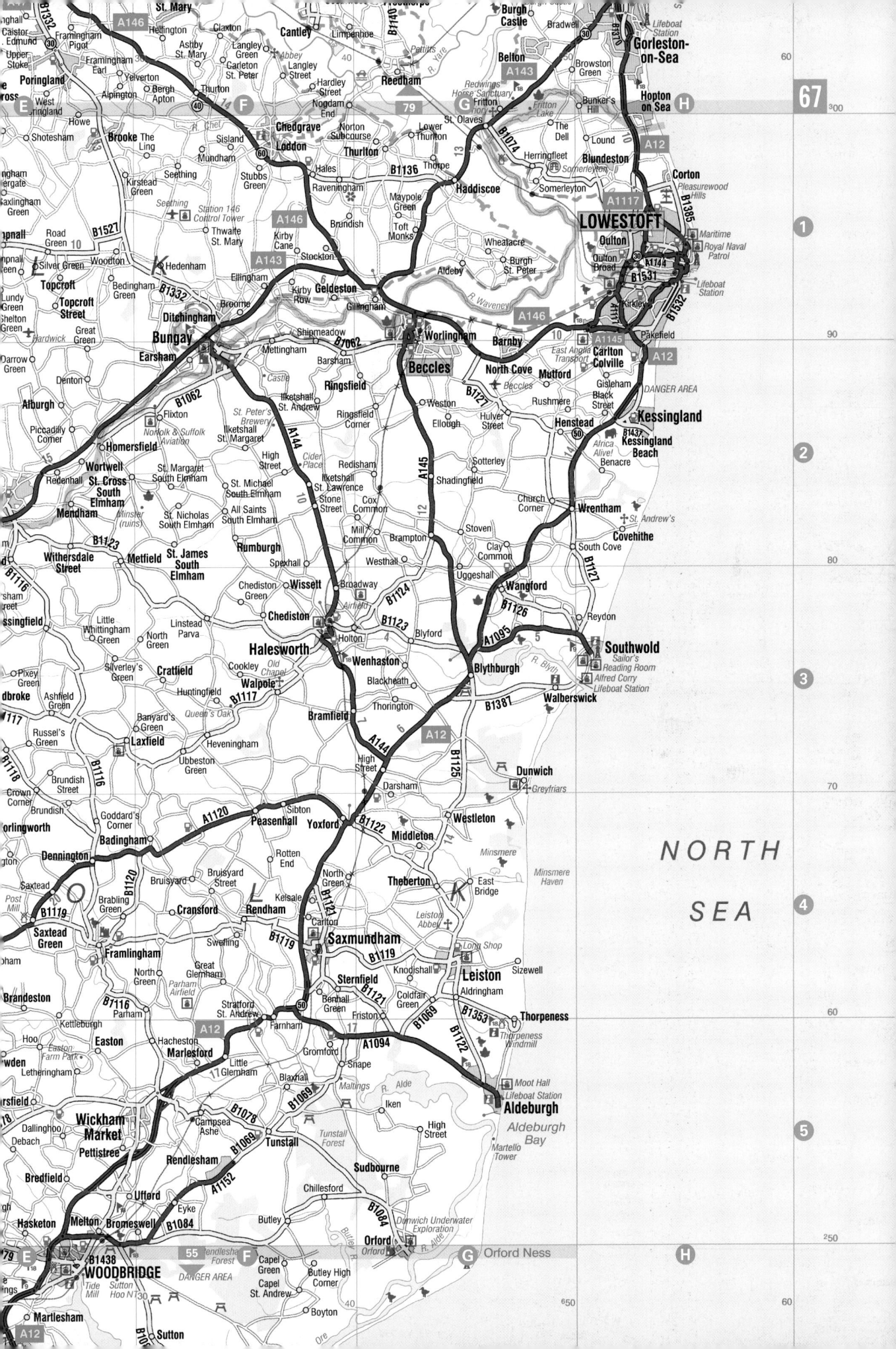

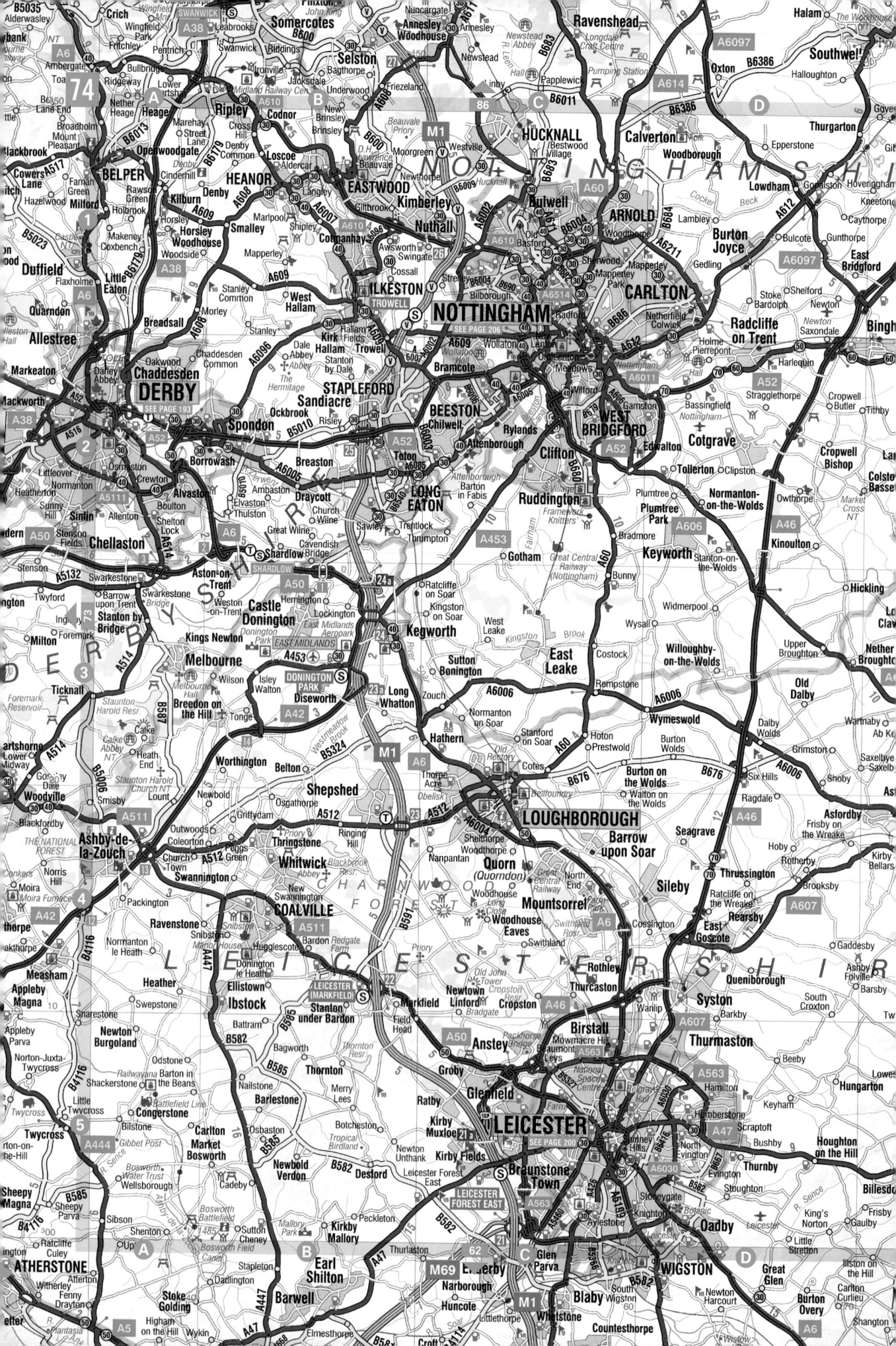

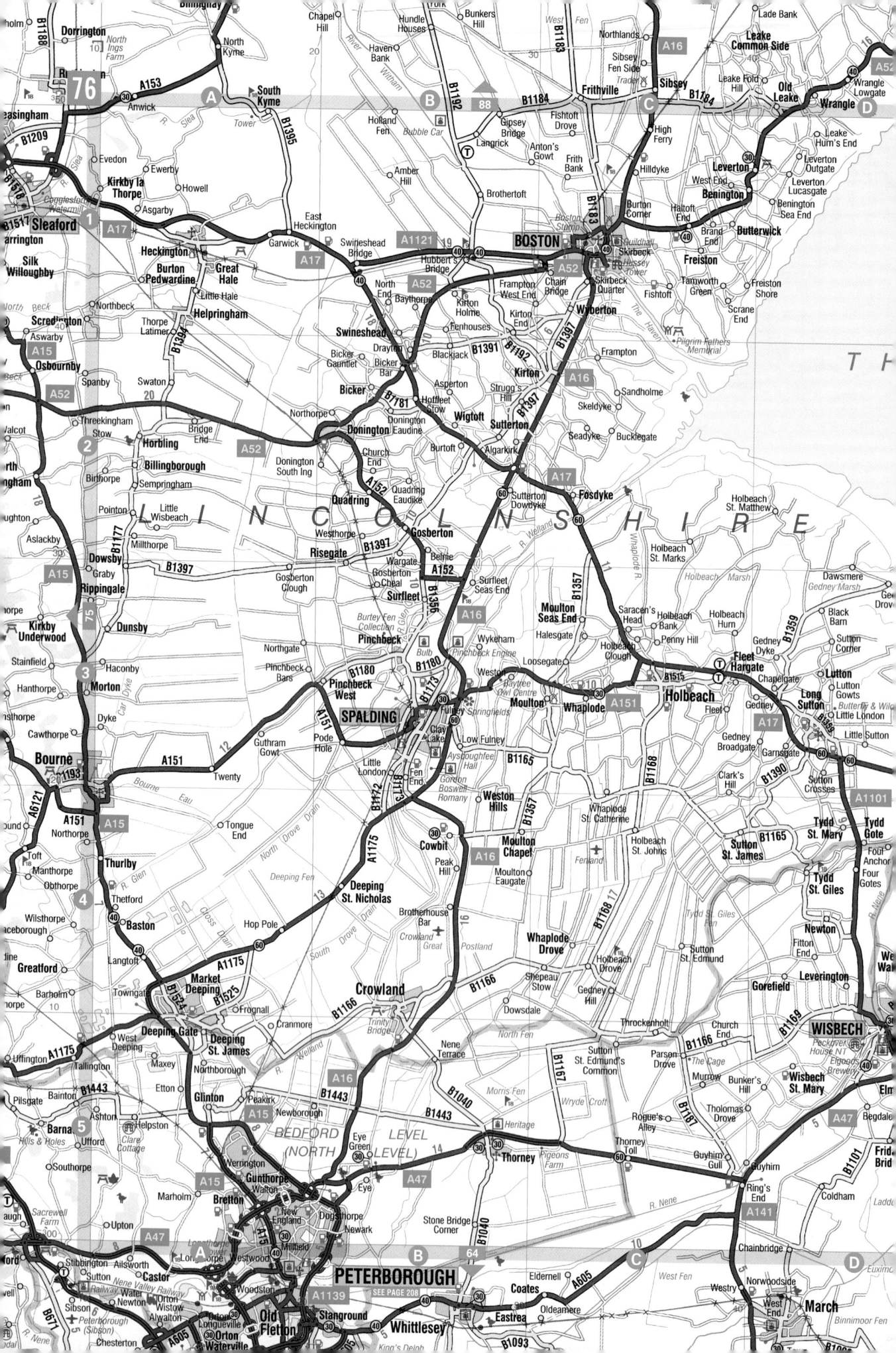

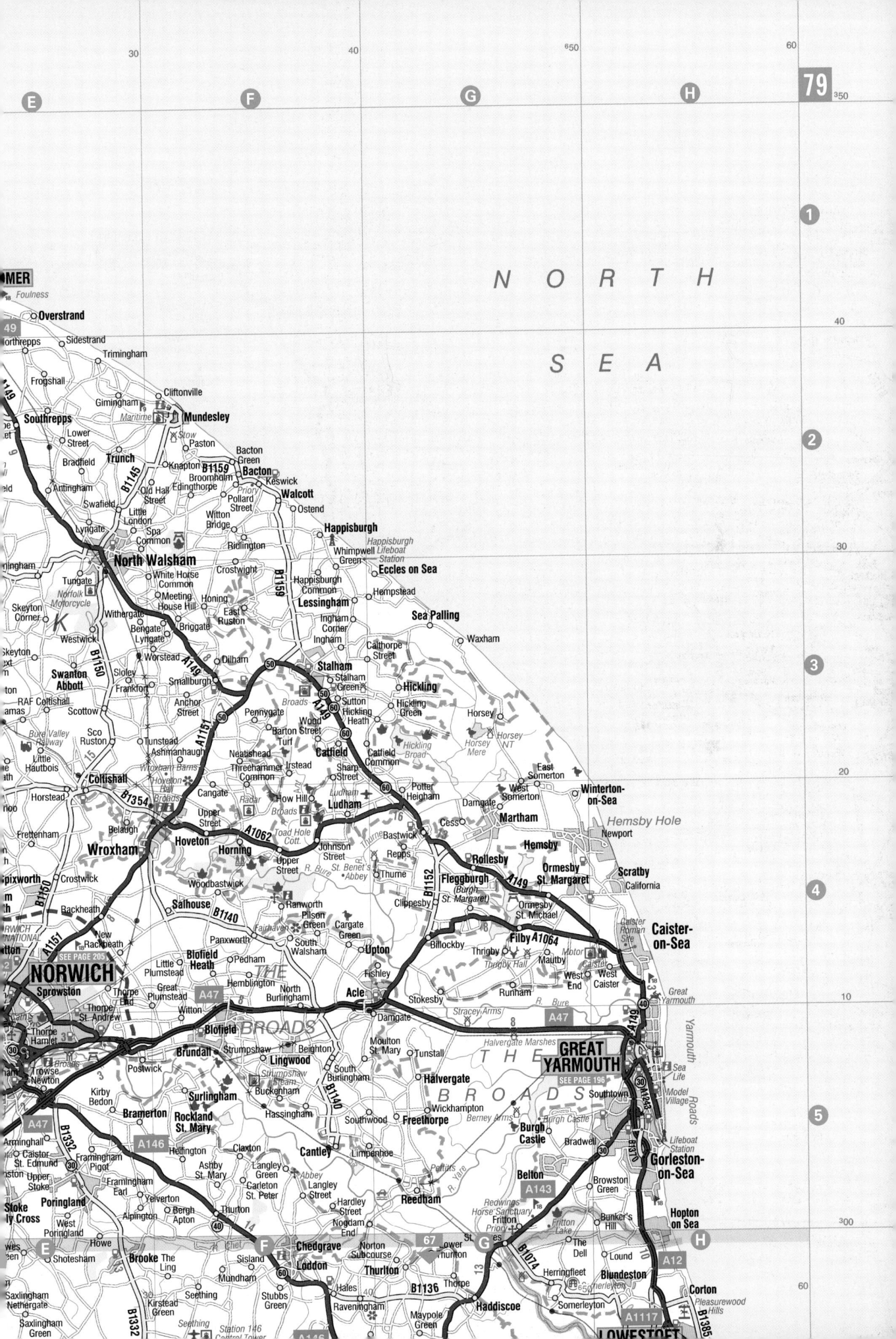

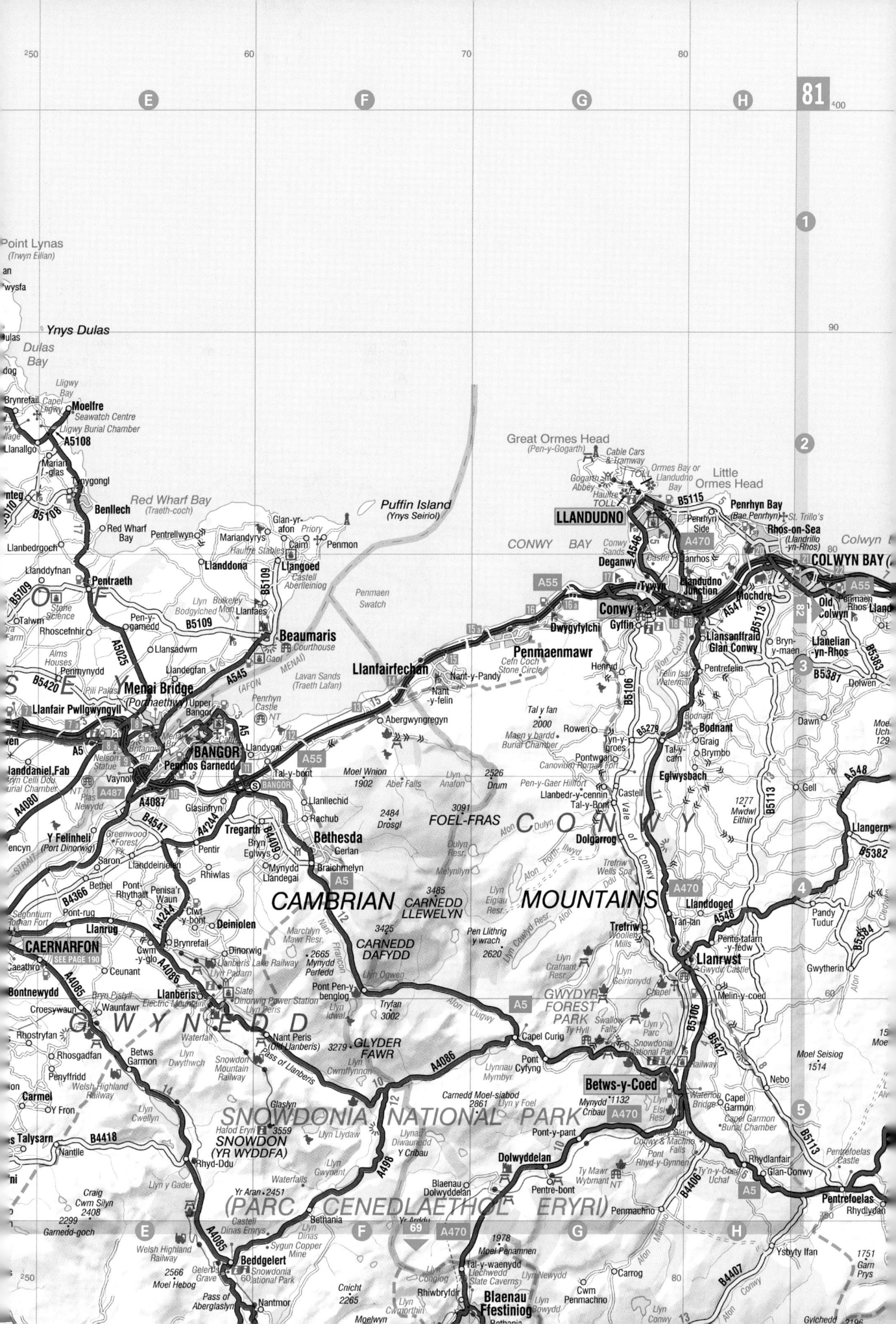

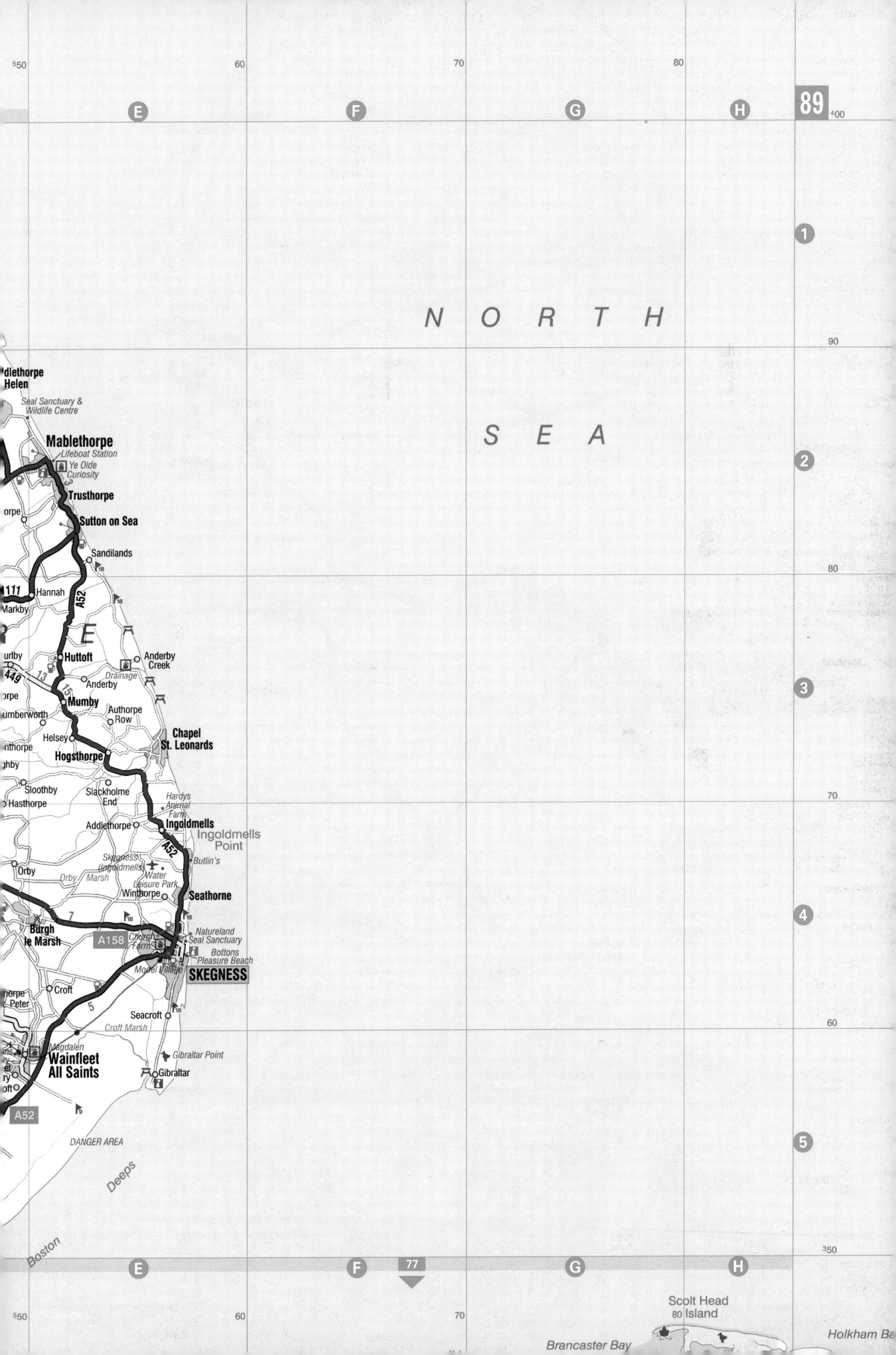

E   F   G   H

N O R T H

S E A

1

2

3

4

5

80

70

60

350

diethorpe
Helen
Seal Sanctuary &
Wildlife Centre
Mablethorpe
Lifeboat Station
Ye Olde
Curiosity
Trusthorpe
Sutton on Sea
orpe
Sandilands
111   Hannah
Markby
A52
urlby   **Huttoft**   Anderby
Creek
449   13   Drainage
orpe   Anderby
15   **Mumby**   Authorpe
umberworth   Row
Helsey   **Chapel
St. Leonards**
nthorpe   **Hogsthorpe**
ghby
Slooby   Slackholme
Hasthorpe   End   Hardys
Animal
Farm
Addlethorpe   **Ingoldmells**
A52   Ingoldmells
Point
Orby   Skegness
(Ingoldmells)   Butlin's
Orby   Marsh   Water
Leisure Park
Winthorpe   **Seathorne**
7   Natureland
Burgh   Seal Sanctuary
le Marsh   Church   Bottons
A158   Farm   Pleasure Beach
Model Village
SKEGNESS
horpe   Croft
Peter
5
Seacroft
Croft Marsh
Magdalen
Wainfleet   Gibraltar Point
ery   **All Saints**   Gibraltar
oft
A52
DANGER AREA

Deeps

Boston

Scolt Head
80 Island
Brancaster Bay   Holkham Ba

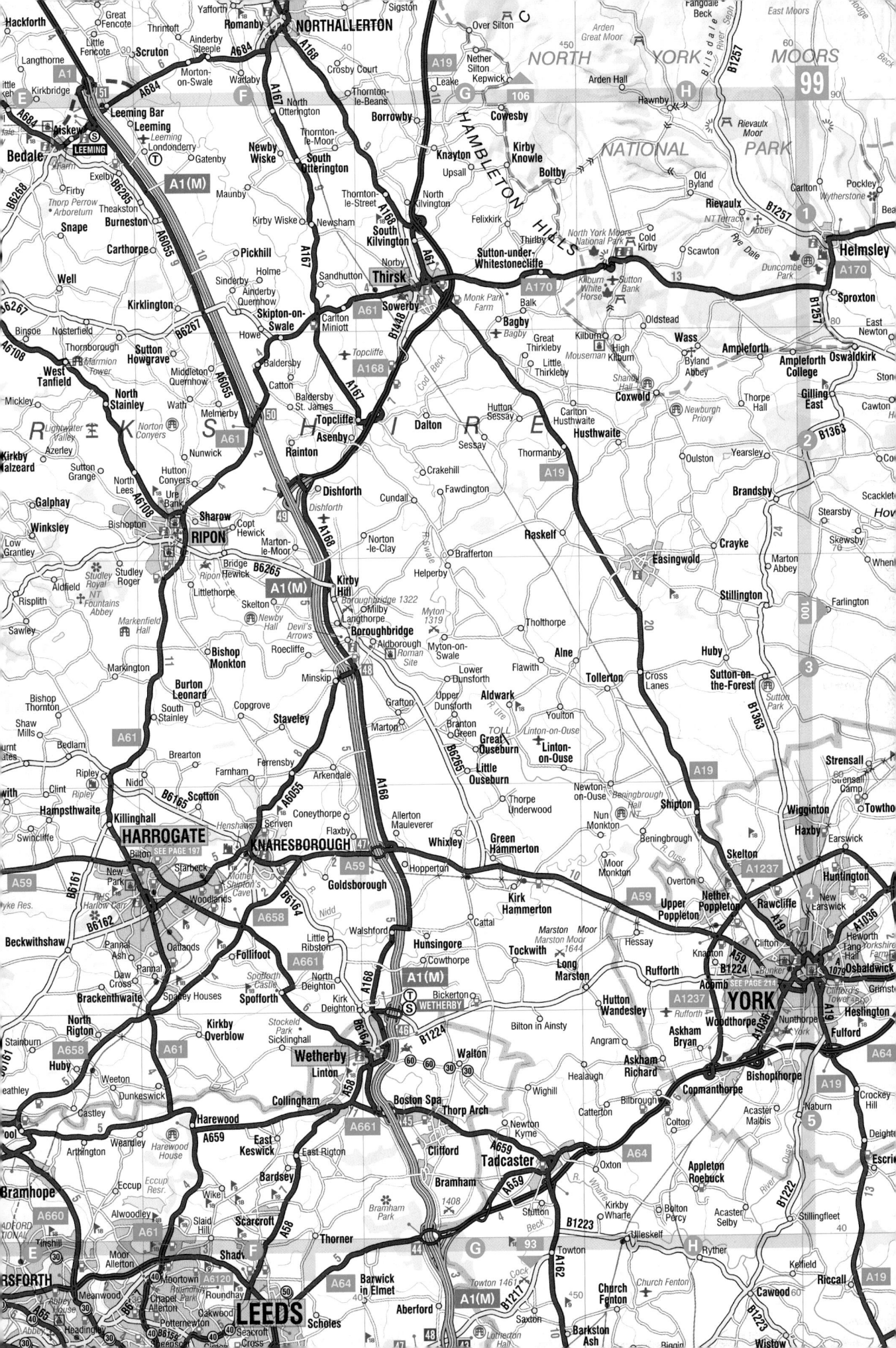

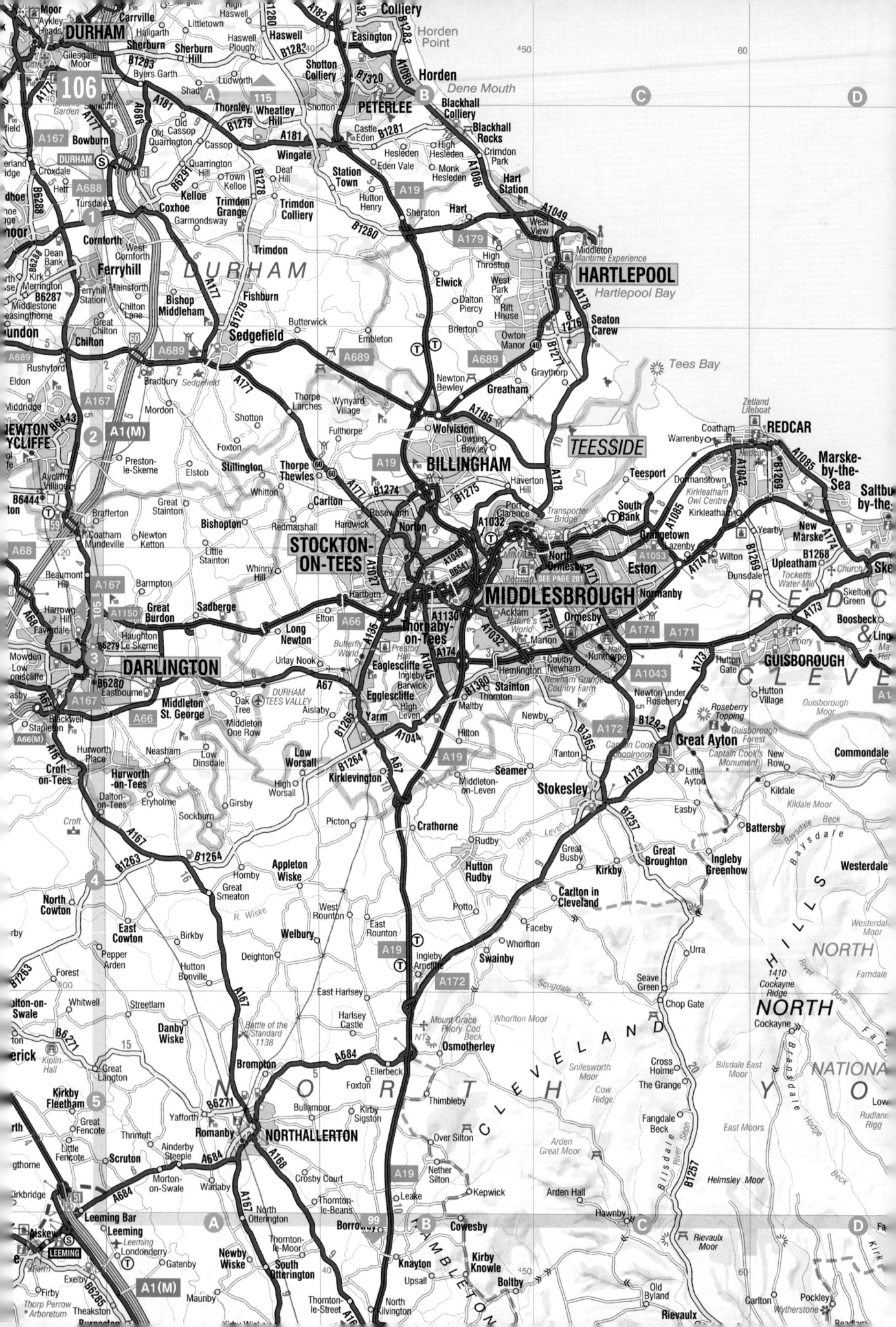

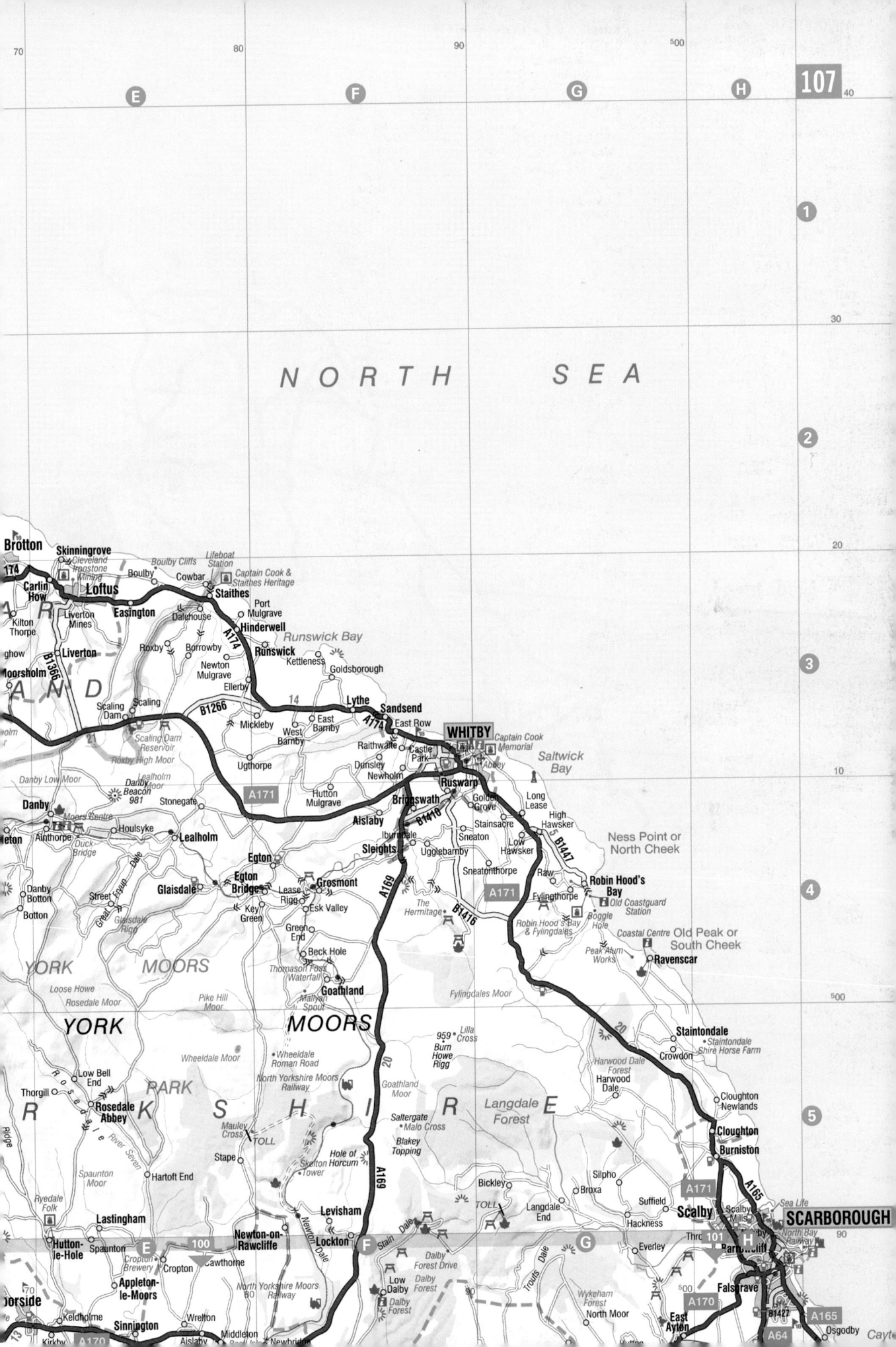

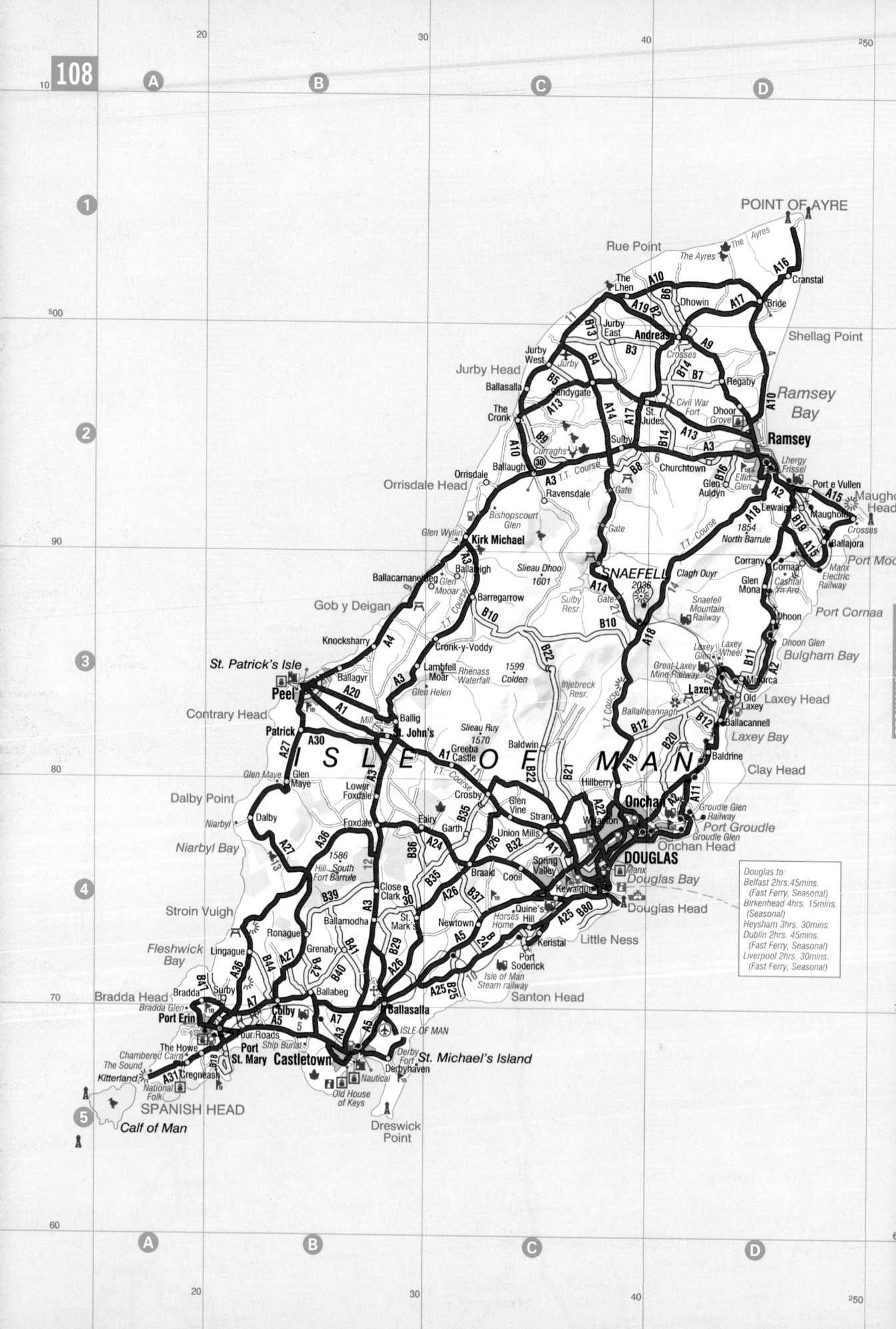

ISLE OF MAN

POINT OF AYRE

Rue Point
The Ayres
The Ayres

The Lhen
A10
A19 B2 Dhowin
B13 Jurby
Jurby East
Andreas
A9
Crosses
Jurby West
B3
B14 B7 Regaby
Jurby Head
B4
Jurby
Ballasalla
Sandygate
The Cronk
A13
A14
St. Judes
Civil War Fort
Dhoor Grove
A10
Orrisdale
Ballaugh
Churchtown
Glen Auldyn
Orrisdale Head
A3 T.T. Course
Ravensdale
Gate
Kirk Michael
Bishopscourt Glen
North Barrule
Glen Wyllin
Ballaleigh
Slieau Dhoo 1601
SNAEFELL 2036
Clagh Ouyr
Glen Mona
Ballacarnane
Glen Mooar
Barregarrow
B10
Snaefell Mountain Railway
Dhoon
Gob y Deigan
B10
Dhoon Glen
Knocksharry
A4
Cronk-y-Voddy
B22
Great Laxey Mine Railway
Bulgham Bay
St. Patrick's Isle
A3
Lambfell Moar
1599 Colden
Laxey Glen
Minorca
Peel
A20
Rhenass Waterfall
Injebreck Resr.
Laxey Wheel
Laxey
Contrary Head
A1
Glen Helen
Old Laxey
Laxey Head
Patrick
A30
Ballig
St. John's
Slieau Ruy 1570
Baldwin
B12
Ballacannell
A27
Mill
Greeba Castle
B21
Laxey Bay
Glen Maye
Glen Maye
T.T. Course
B22
Hillberry
Baldrine
ISLE OF MAN
Clay Head
Dalby Point
Lower Foxdale
Crosby
Glen Vine
Strang
A22
Onchan
Niarbyl
A13
Foxdale
Fairy
B35
Union Mills
A1
Willaston
Groudle Glen Railway
Niarbyl Bay
A36
Garth
A24
B32
Spring Valley
Onchan Head
Groudle Glen
Stroin Vuigh
1586 Hill South Fort Barrule
B36
Braaid
Cooil
DOUGLAS
Fleshwick Bay
B39
Close Clark
B30
A26
B37
Kewaigue
Douglas Bay
Lingague
Ronague
Ballamodha
Newtown
A5
Quine's Home
A25 B80
Douglas Head
Bradda Head
A27
Grenaby
B41
B29
Horse's Home
Keristal
Little Ness
Bradda
A36
B44
B42
B40
A26
Port Soderick
Bradda Glen
Surby
Ballabeg
A25 B25
Santon Head
Port Erin
A7
Colby
A7
A5
Isle of Man Steam railway
The Howe
Four Roads
Ballasalla
ISLE-OF-MAN
Chambered Cairn
Port
Ship Burial
Derby Fort
The Sound
St. Mary
Castletown
Derbyhaven
St. Michael's Island
Kitterland
A31
Cregneash
Nautical
National Folk
Old House of Keys
SPANISH HEAD
Dreswick Point
Calf of Man

Ramsey Bay

Ramsey
Lhergy Frissel
A2
Port e Vullen
A15
Maughold Head
Elfin Glen
A18
Lewaigue
B19 B18
Maughold
Glen Auldyn
A16
Crosses
Ballajora
A15
Port Moc
Corrany
Cornaa
Manx Electric Railway
A18
Glen Mona
Cashtal yn Ard
Port Cornaa
B11
A2
Shellag Point
Cranstal
A17
Bride
B9
A9
Crosses
B16
A10
Civil War Fort

A3

1854

Douglas to:
Belfast 2hrs.45mins.
(Fast Ferry. Seasonal)
Birkenhead 4hrs. 15mins.
(Seasonal)
Heysham 3hrs. 30mins.
Dublin 2hrs. 45mins.
(Fast Ferry, Seasonal)
Liverpool 2hrs. 30mins.
(Fast Ferry, Seasonal)

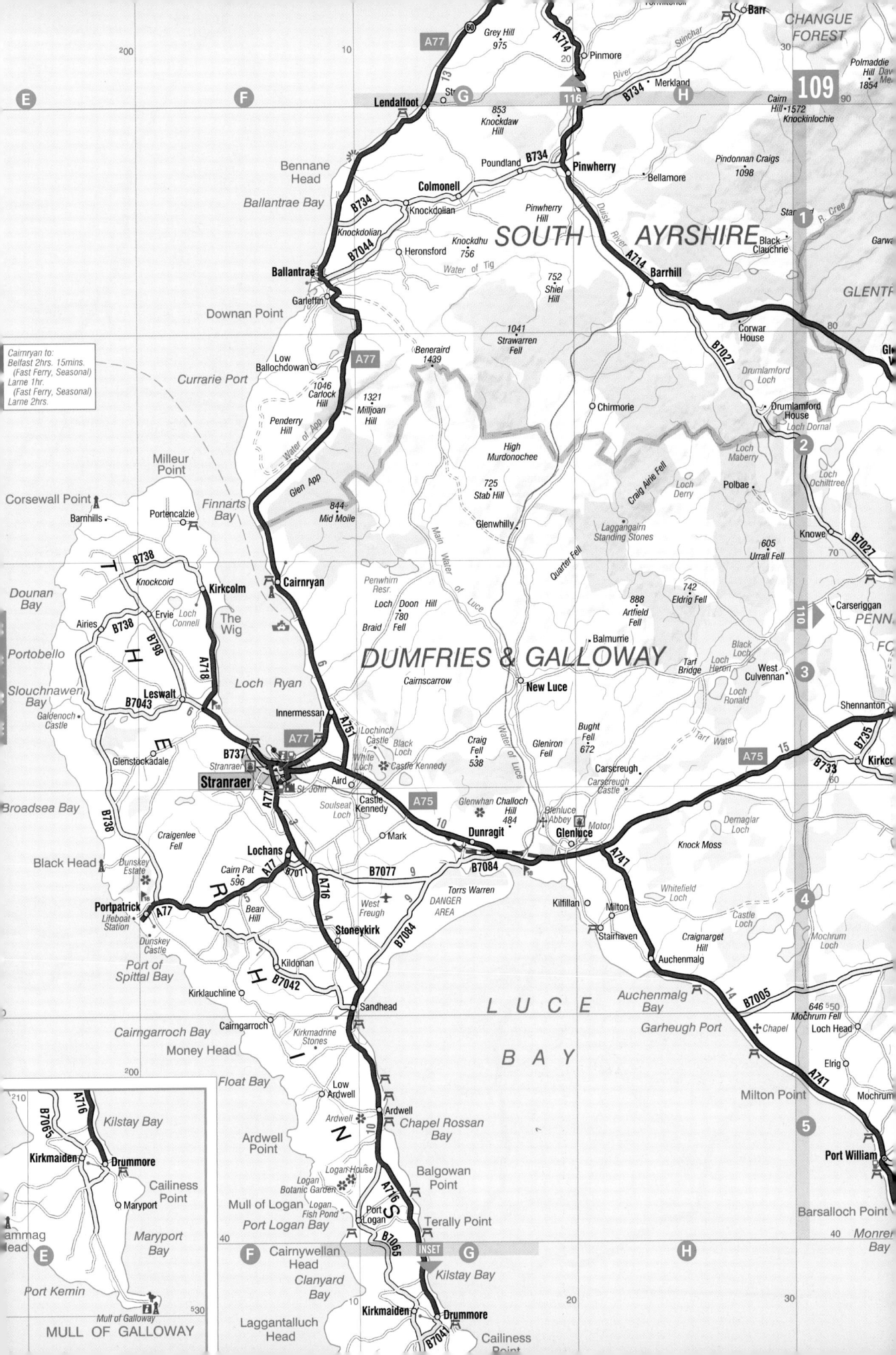

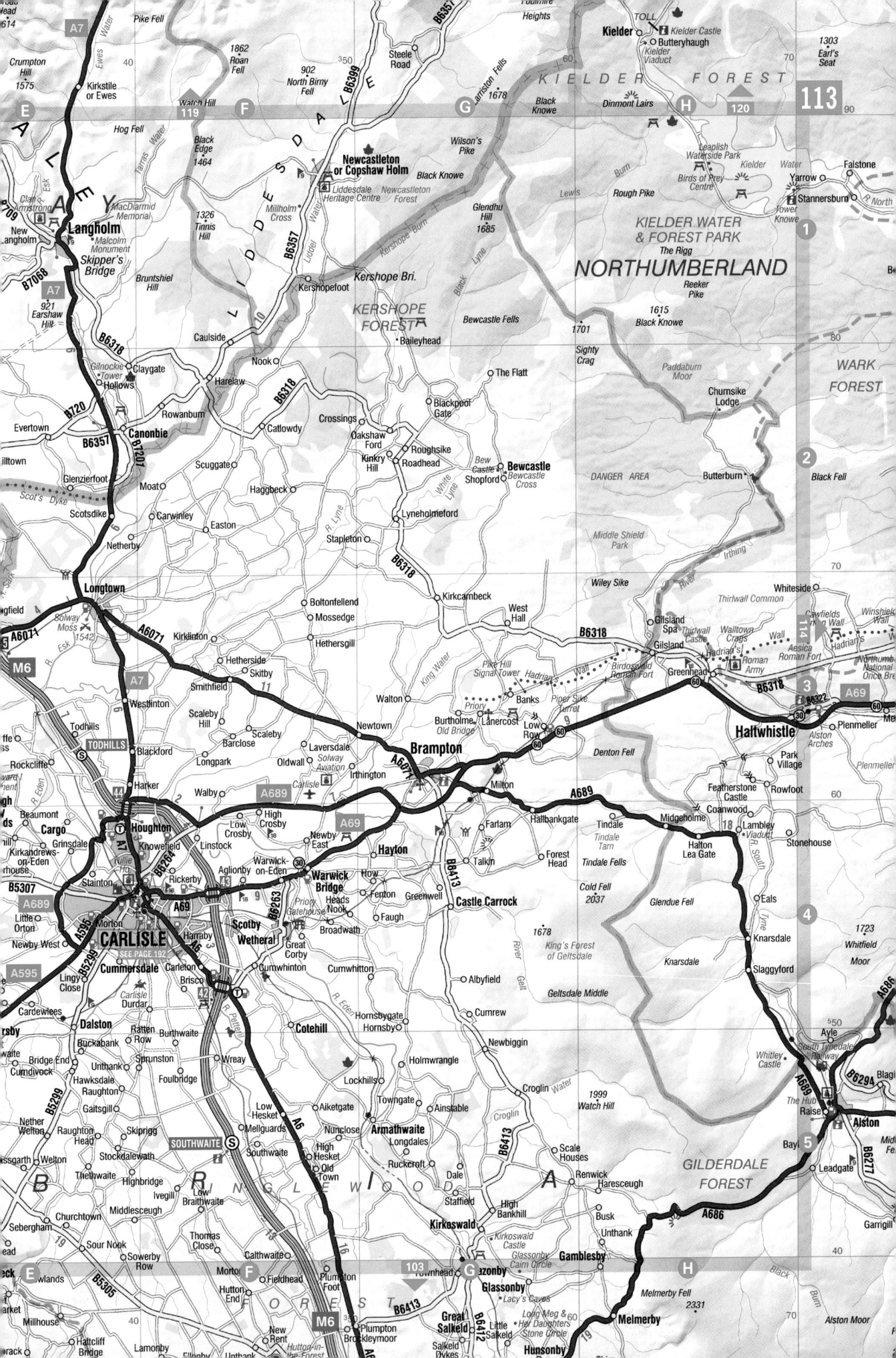

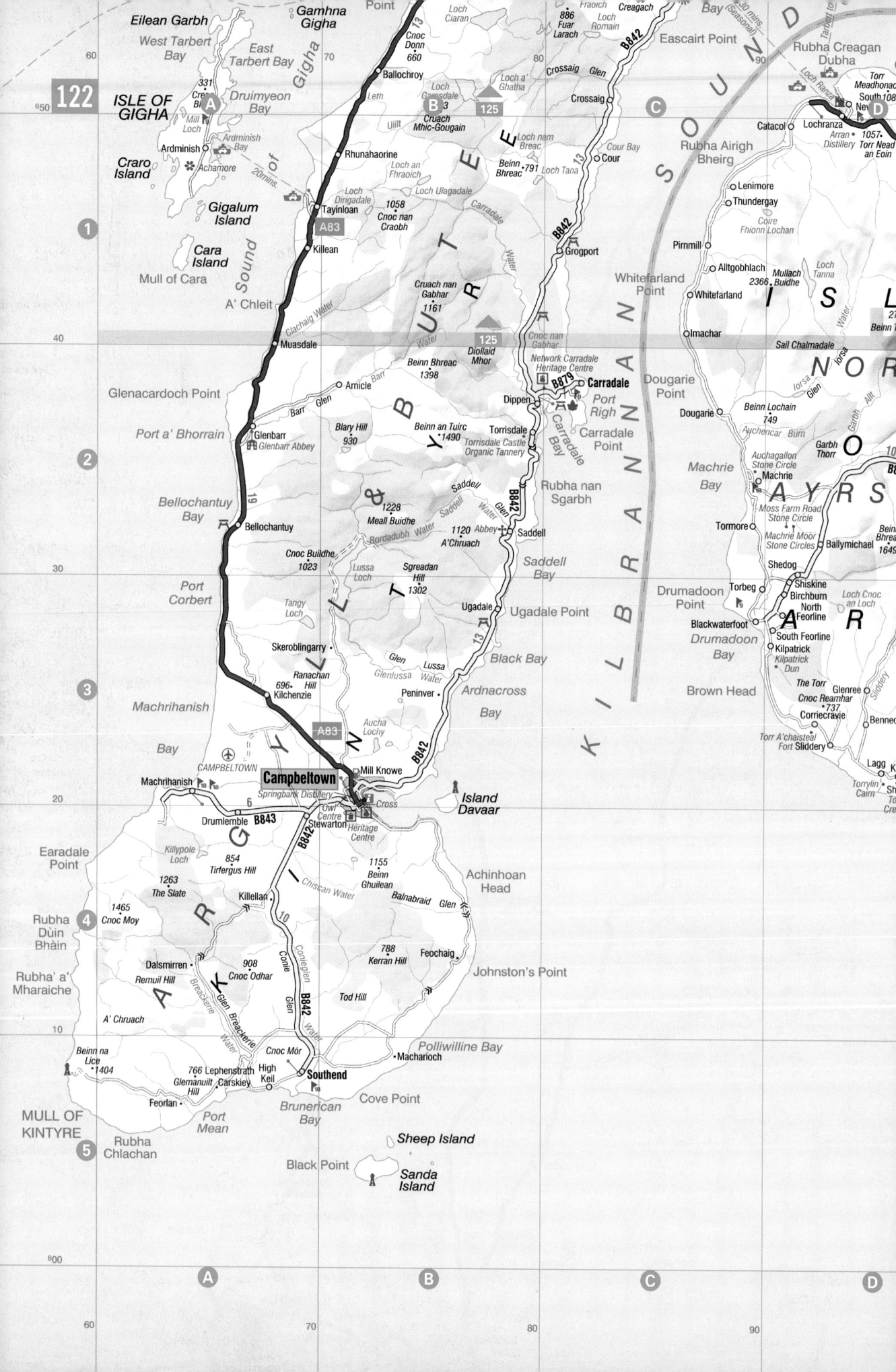

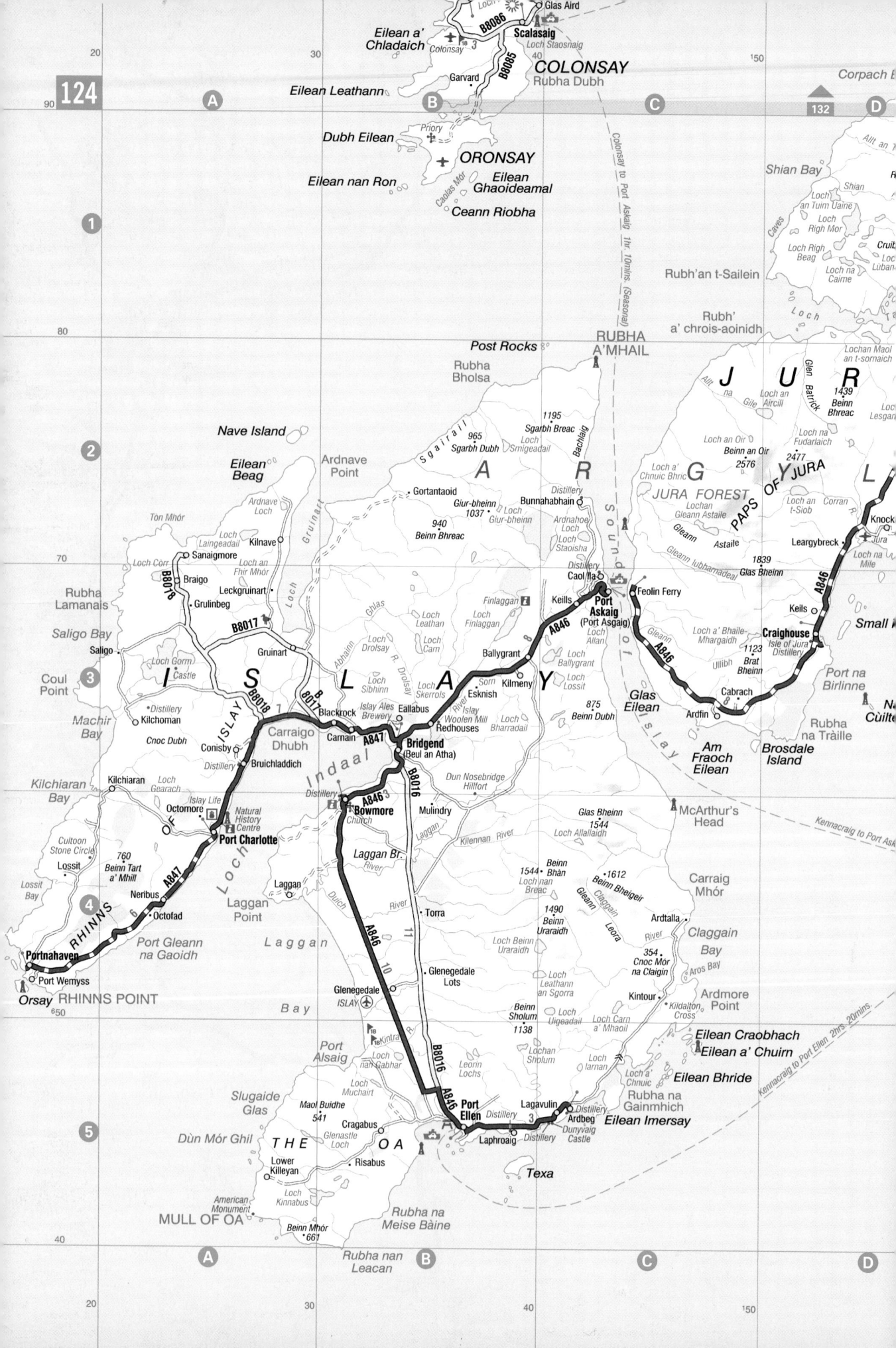

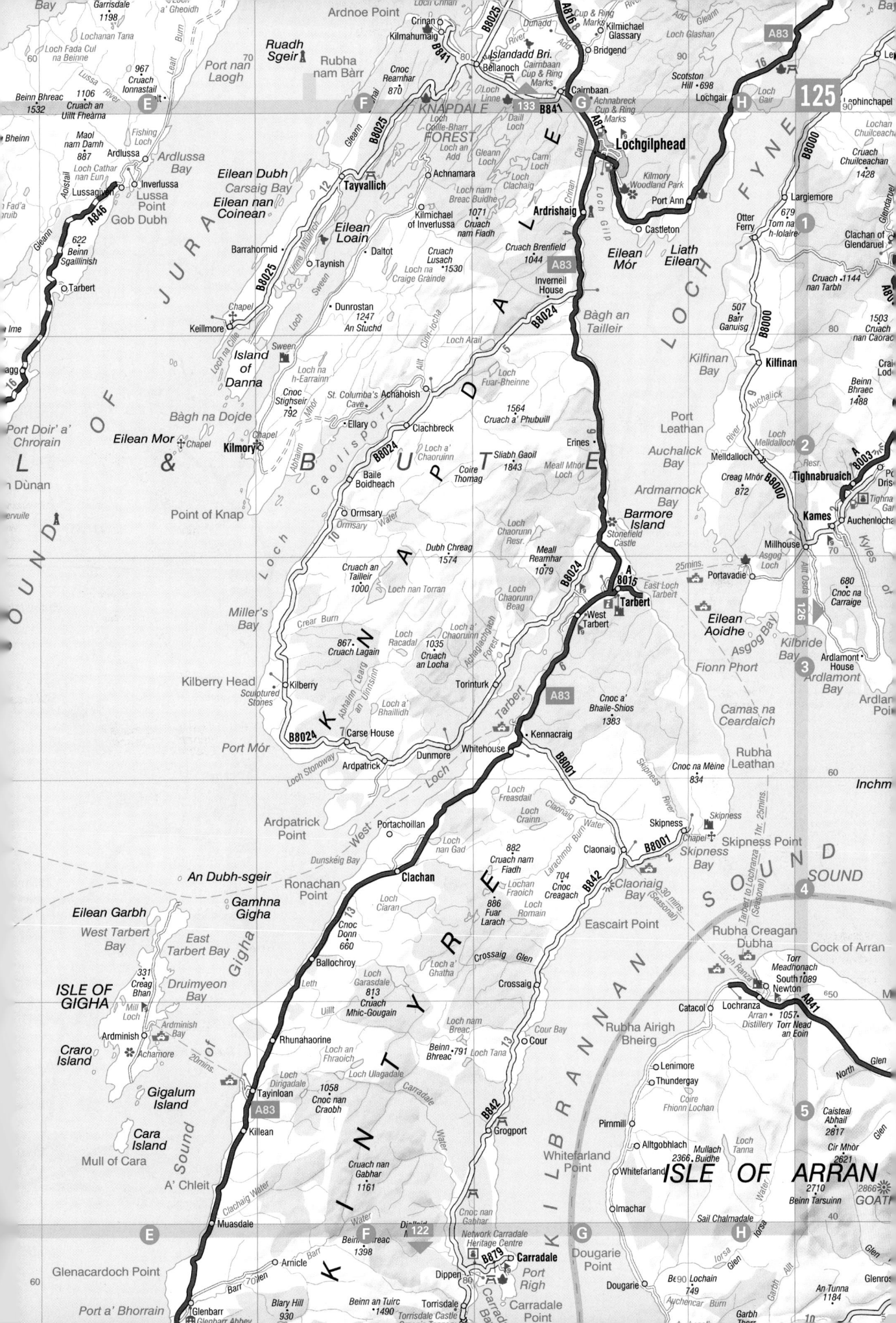

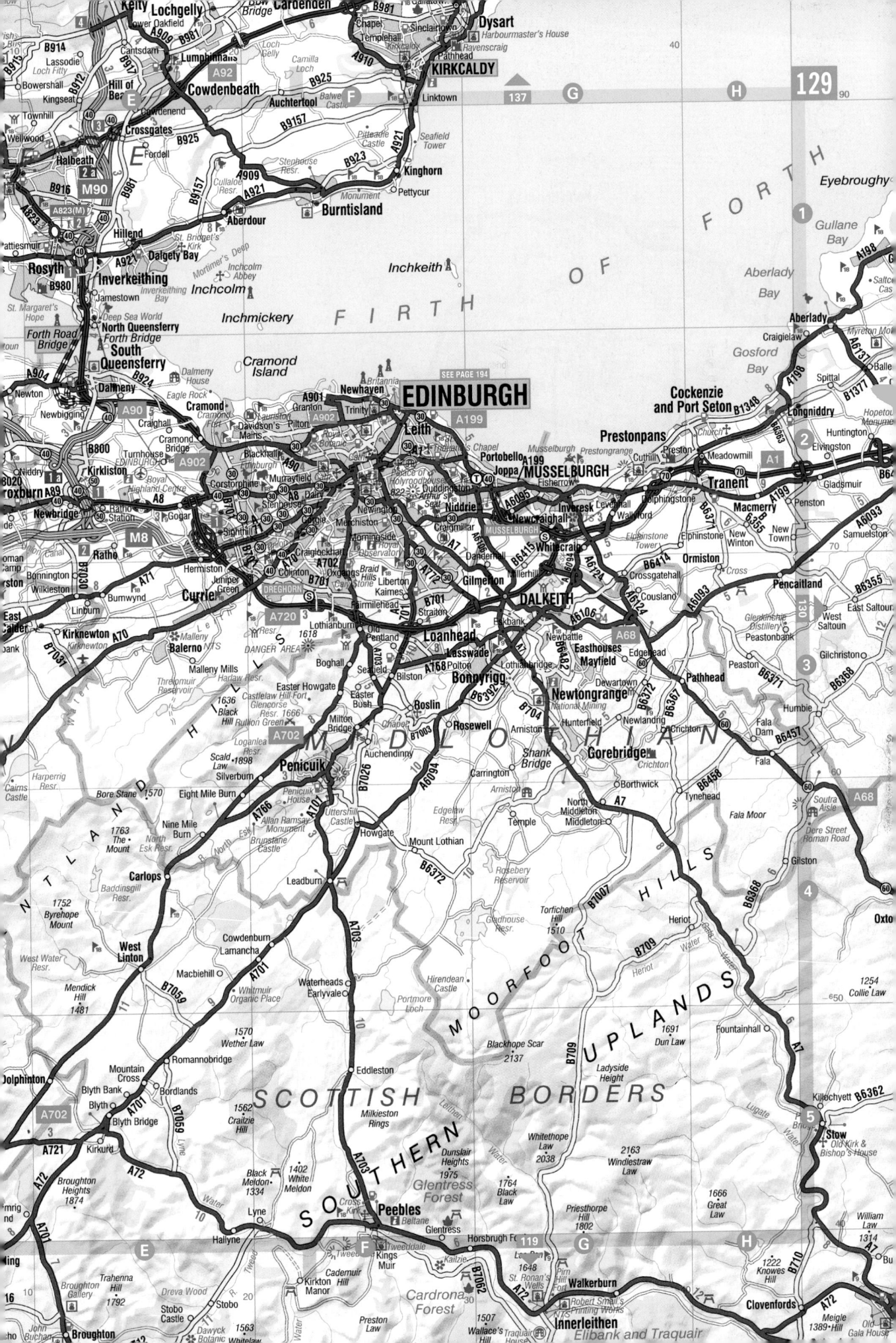

NORTH SEA

Fast Castle Head
Fast Castle
Telegraph Hill
Lumsdaine
Cross Law • 744
ST. ABB'S HEAD
St. Abb's Head
Coldingham Moor
St. Abbs
Lifeboat Station *Coldingham Bay*
Coldingham
Priory
Lifeboat Station
Houndwood
B6438
A1107
Eyemouth
Gunsgreenhill

Water
159
seley Hill
60
60
Reston
18
Ayton
60
Burnmouth
Auchencrow
Ross

B6437
B6355
60
70
Lamberton
Marshall Meadows
Chirnside
Tithe Barn Clappers
12
Conundrum Farm
15
Foulden
Halidon Hill
1333
A6105
A1
Chirnside-bridge
Whiteadder *Water*
Allanton
Hutton
B6460
Paxton
B6461
60
Castle
Bell Tower
BERWICK-UPON-TWEED
A698
Tweedmouth
B6460
Paxton Ho.
Tweed
2
Lifeboat Station
Whitsome
B6461
Fishwick
Chain Bridge
Budge
Loanend
Honey Farm
Spittal
Horncliffe
East Ord
A1167
Pot-a-Doodle Do
Redshin Cove
Horndean
2
Scremerston
Ladykirk
Norham
Murton
Thornton
winton
B6470
B6470
Norham Station
Shoreswood
Cheswick
Upsettlington
Shoresdean
West Allerdean
B6525
Goswick
12
Simprim
B6437
Twizel Bridge
12
Grindon
Felkington
Ancroft
Berrington
Haggerston
Stone Circle
Berrington Law
Beal
LINDISFARNE
HOLY ISLAND
Keel Head
Lindisfarne Centre
Holy Island
Duddo
Bowsden
60
A1
Lindisfarne Priory
NT Lindisfarne
A698
A6112
Castle Heaton
NORTHUMBERLAND
Fenham
Castle Point
Burrows Hole
Lennel
Melkington
ream
Cornhill-on-Tweed
Heatherslaw Light Railway
Etal
Barmoor
Lowick
B6353
West Kyloe
Fenwick
121
West *Barmouth*
A697
Barelees
Crookham
Waterford Hall
Ford
B6353
East Kyloe
G
East Kyloe
H
Buckton
East *Learmouth*
Branxton
B6354
Kyloe Hills
FARNE ISLANDS
Staple Sound
Flodden Field Monument
1513
400
B6525
Holburn
Detchant
Elwick
Ross
Budle Bay
Chapel NT
Pressen
Flodden
B6354
St. Cuthbert's
1342 **Bamburgh**
Inner

80
70
60
650
40
20
90
400
10
20

E
F
G
H
1
2
3
4
5

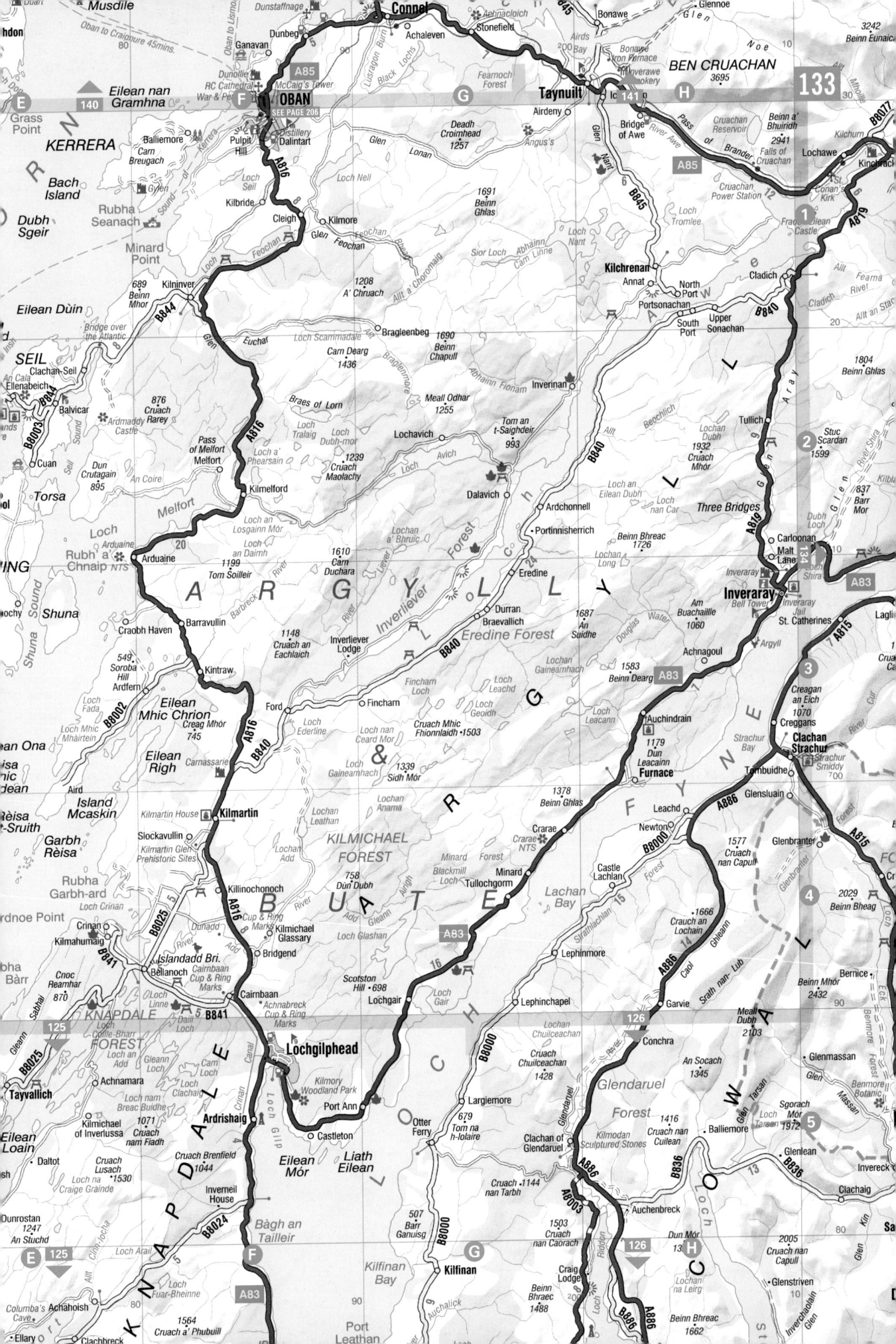

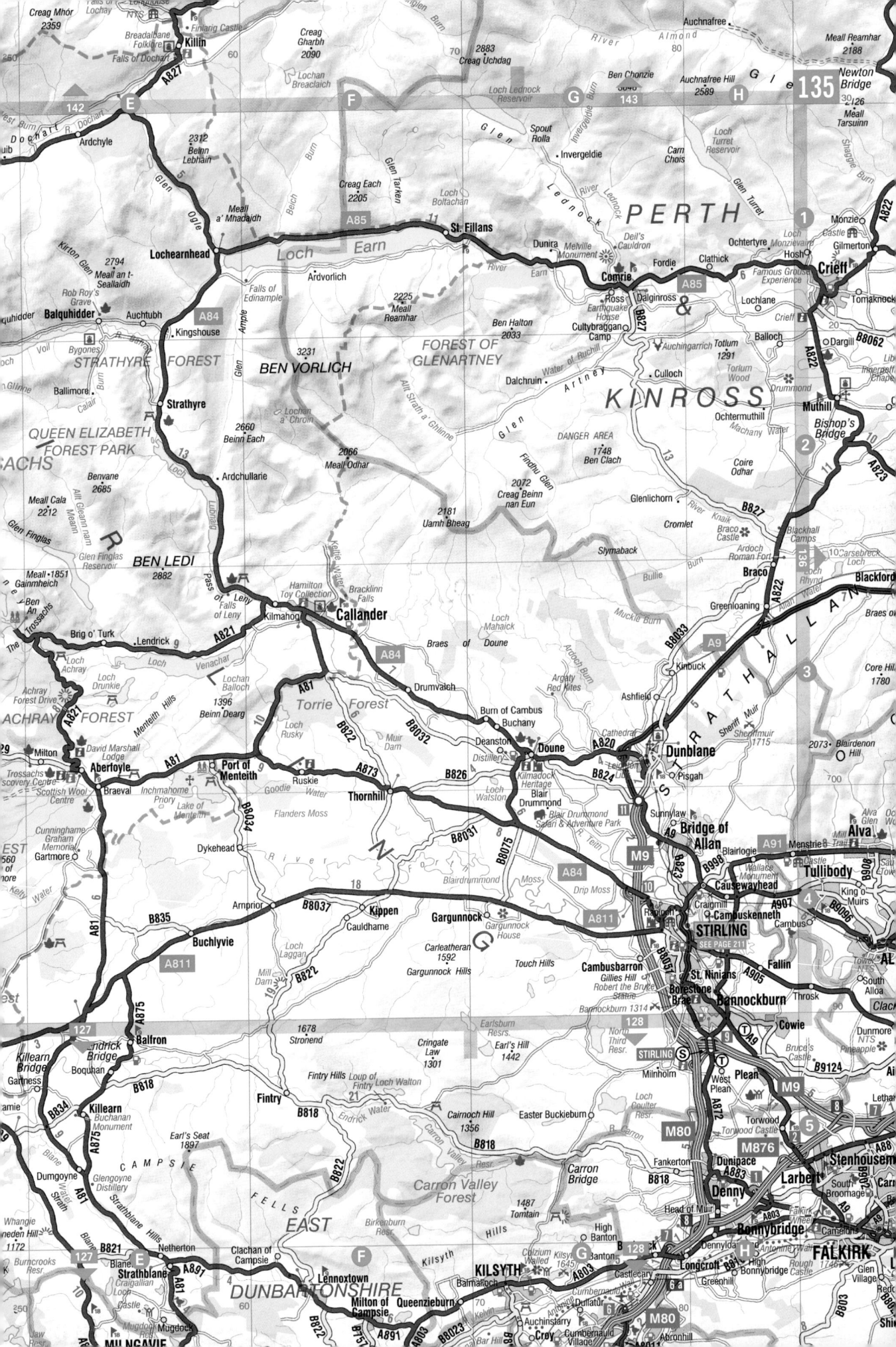

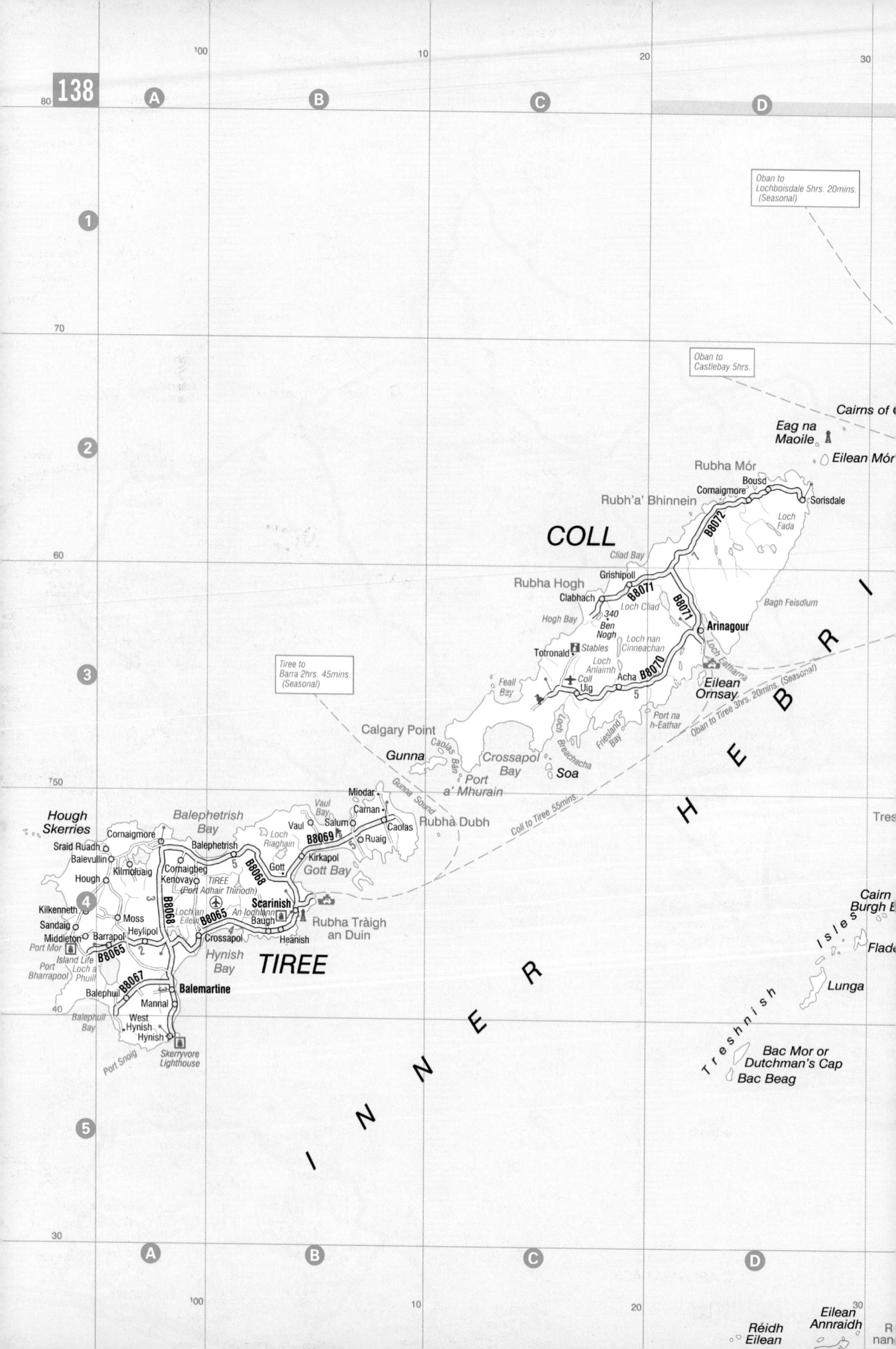

100 10 20 30

80

A B C D

1

Oban to
Lochboisdale 5hrs. 20mins.
(Seasonal)

70

Oban to
Castlebay 5hrs.

Cairns of C

Eag na
Maoile

2

Eilean Mór

Rubha Mór

Bousd
Cornaigmore   Sorisdale

Rubh'a' Bhinnein   B8072   Loch
Fada

60

COLL

Clad Bay

Rubha Hogh   Grishipoll

Clabhach   B8071   Bagh Feisdlum
Loch Clad

340   B8071
Hogh Bay   Ben
Nogh

Tiree to
Barra 2hrs. 45mins.
(Seasonal)

Totronald   Stables   Arinagour

3   Loch   Loch nan
Anlaimh   Cinneachan   B8070

Feall   Coll   Acha   Loch Eatharna
Bay   Uig

Calgary Point   Port na   Eilean
h-Eathar   Ornsay

Oban to Tiree 3hrs. 20mins. (Seasonal)   H
E
Gunna   Crossapol   B
Bay   Soa   R
Port   I
a' Mhurain

750

Coll to Tiree 55mins.   Tres

Hough   Balephetrish   Vaul   Miodar
Skerries   Bay   Bay   Carnan
Cornaigmore   Vaul   Salum   Cairn
Sraid Ruadh   Loch   Caolas   Burgh
Balevullin   Balephetrish   Riaghain   B8069   Ruaig
Hough   Kilmoluaig   Gott   Kirkapol   Rubhà Dubh   Flade
Cornaigbeg   5   Gott Bay
Kenovay   B8068
4   Kilkenneth   TIREE   Lunga
Sandaig   Moss   (Port Adhair Thiríodh)   Scarinish
Middleton   Heylipol   B8065   An Iodhlann   I
Port Mor   Barrapol   Loch an   Baugh   N
Island Life   Eilein   Heanish   Rubha Tràigh   N
Port   B8065   2   Crossapol   an Duin   E
Bharrapool   Loch a'   Hynish   R   Treshnish
Phuill   Bay   TIREE   Isles
Balephuil   B8067
Balephuil   Mannal   Balemartine
Bay   West
40   Hynish   Bac Mor or
Hynish   Dutchman's Cap
Port Snoig   Skerryvore   Bac Beag
Lighthouse

5

30

A B C D
100 10 20 30

Réidh   Eilean
Eilean   Annraidh
R
nan

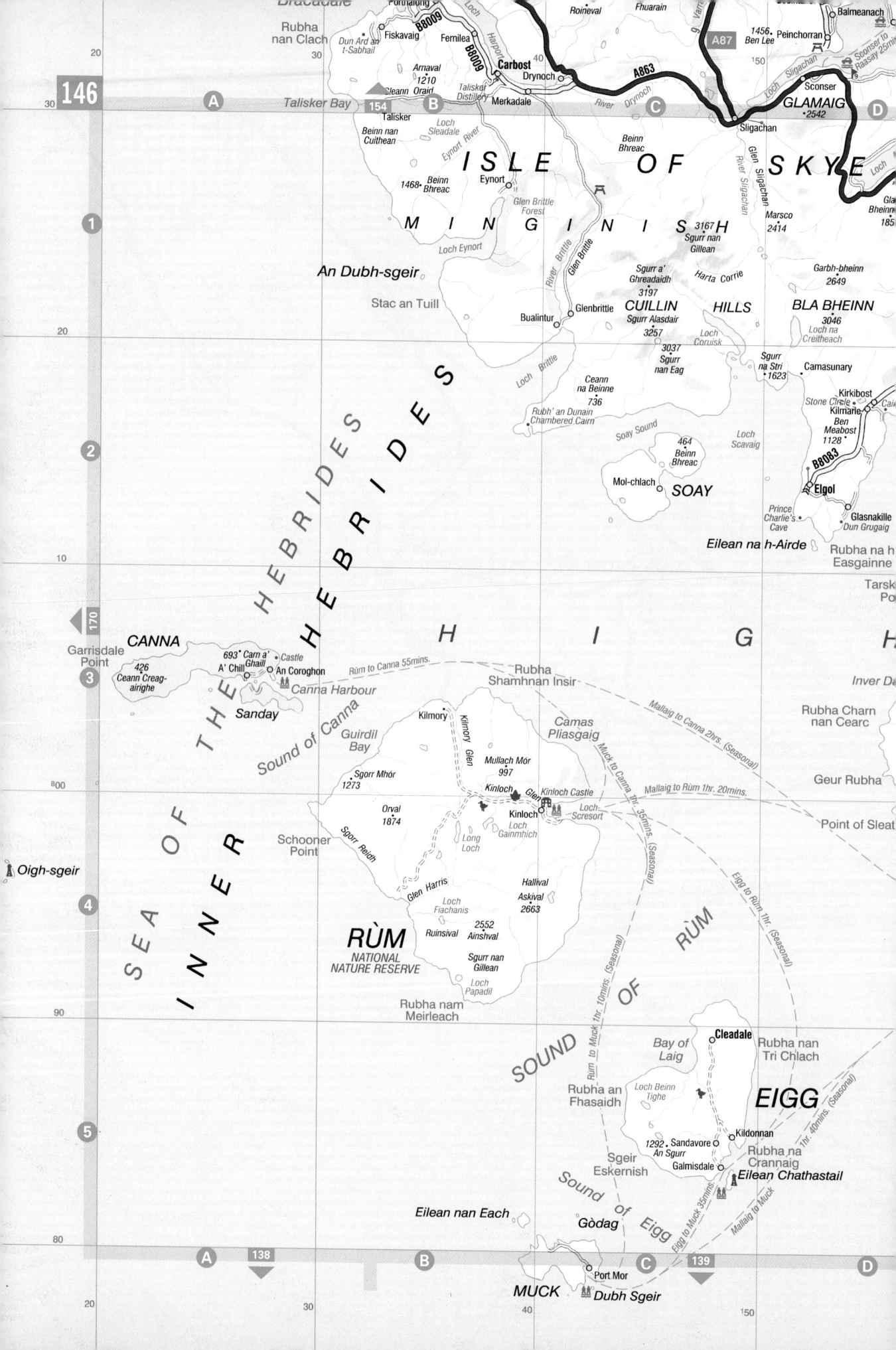

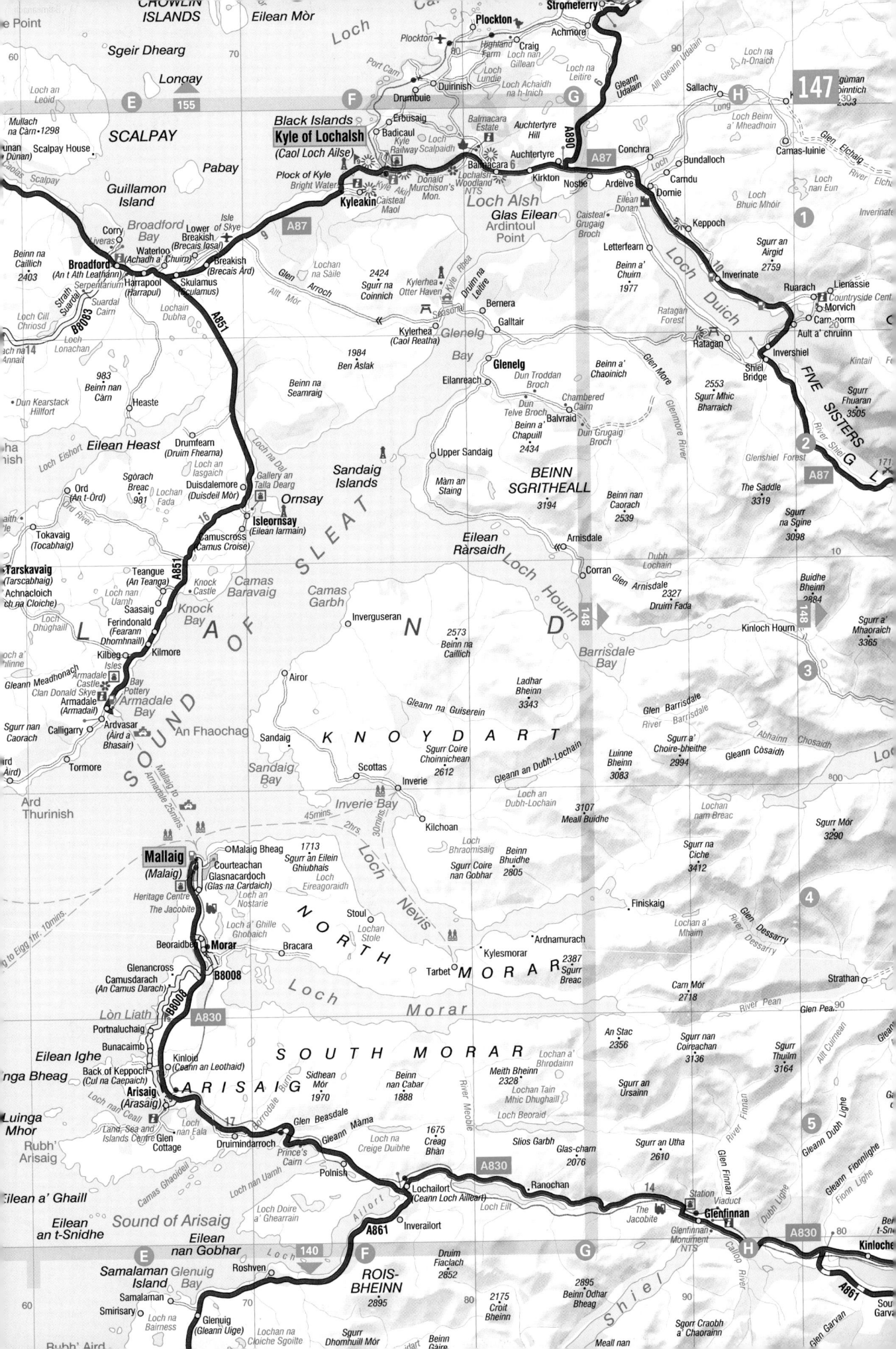

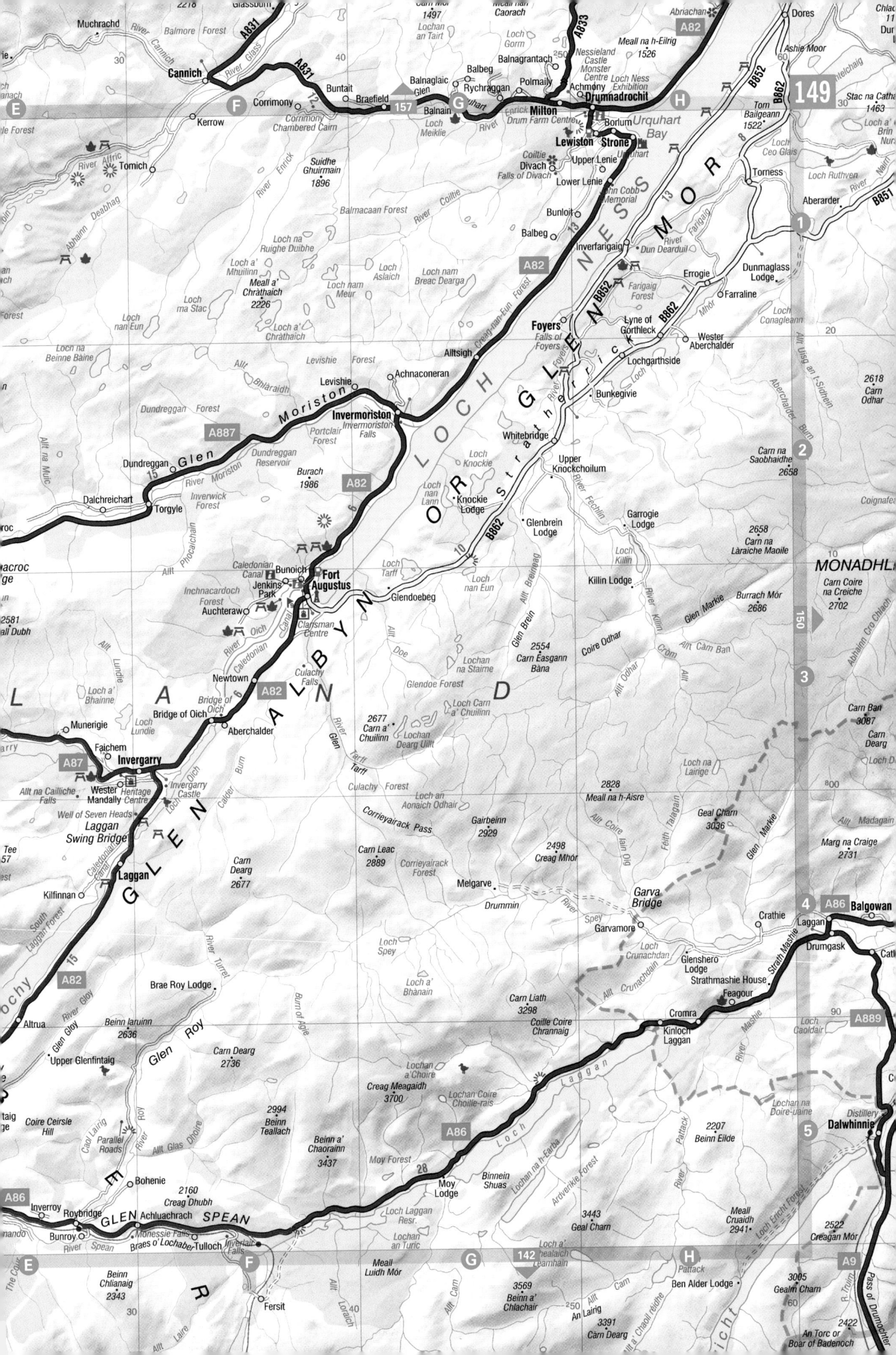

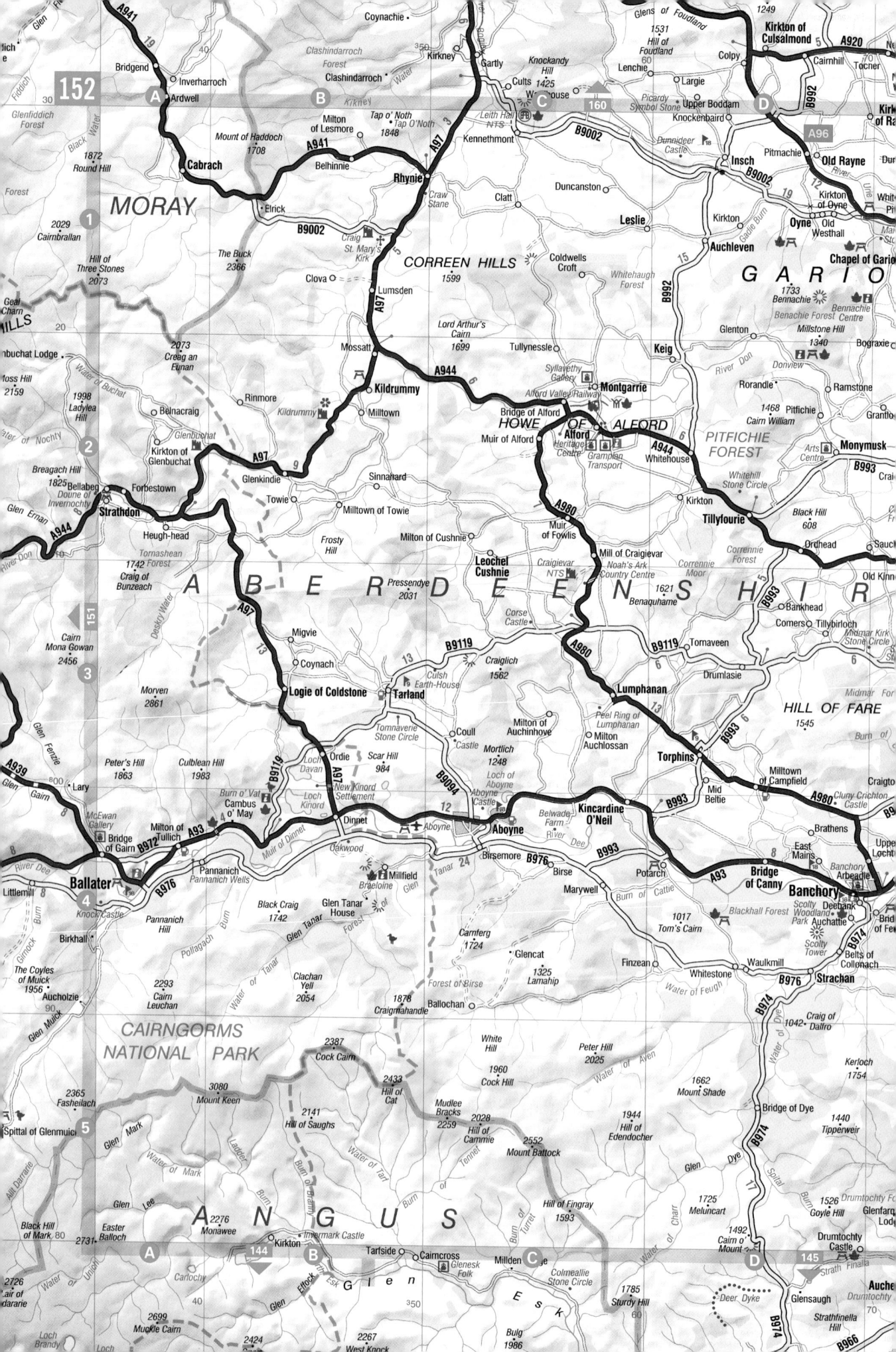

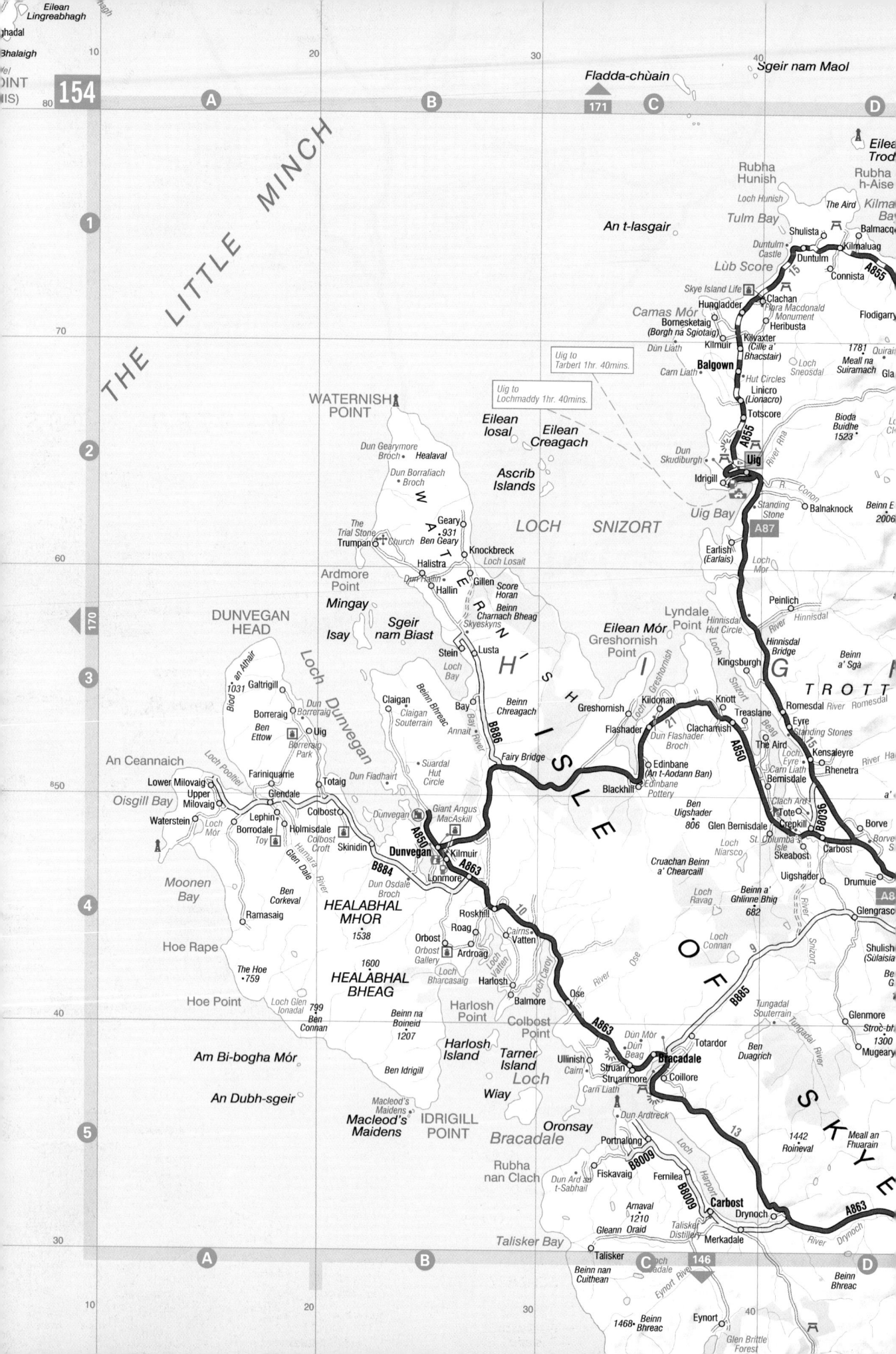

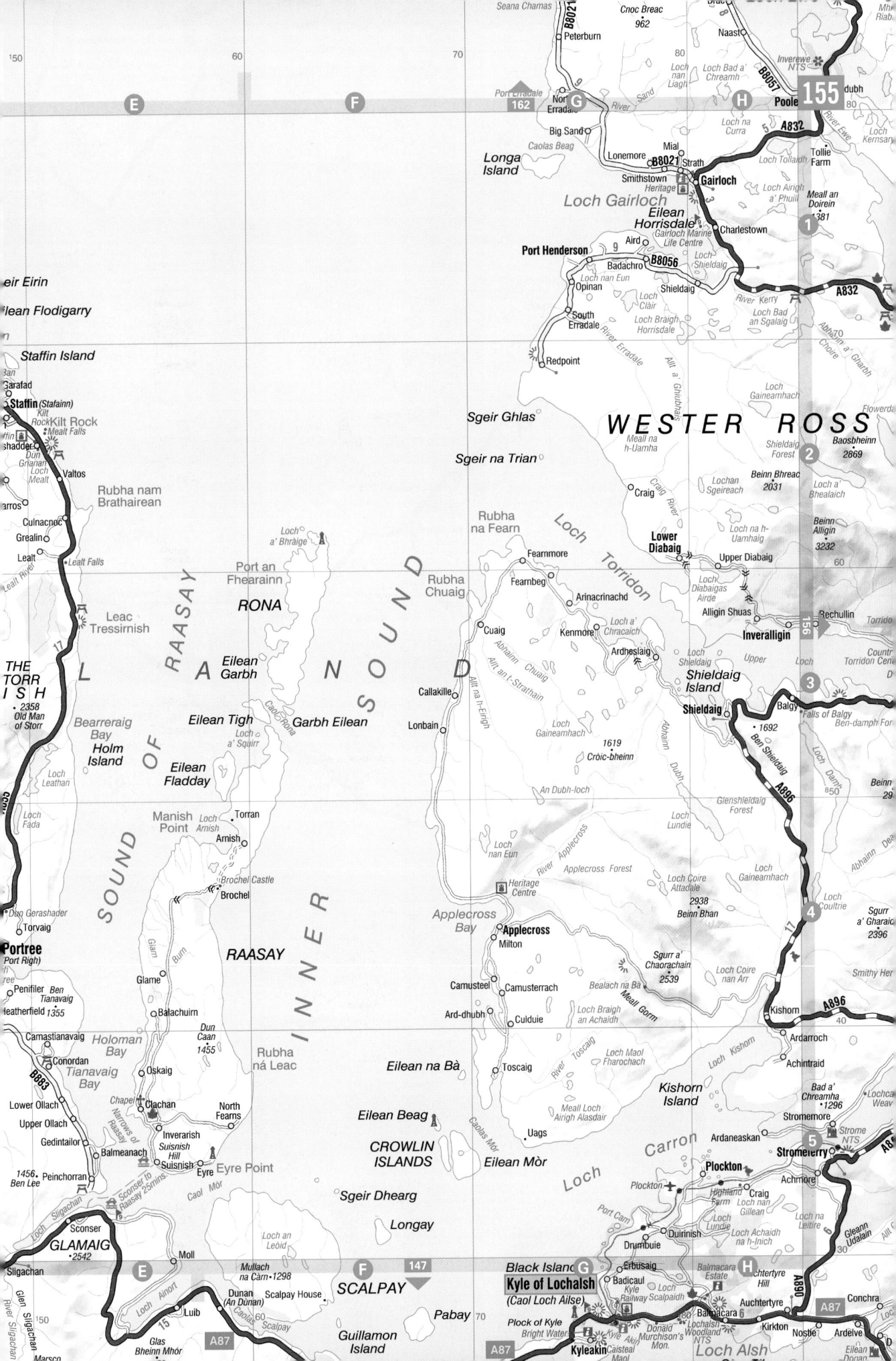

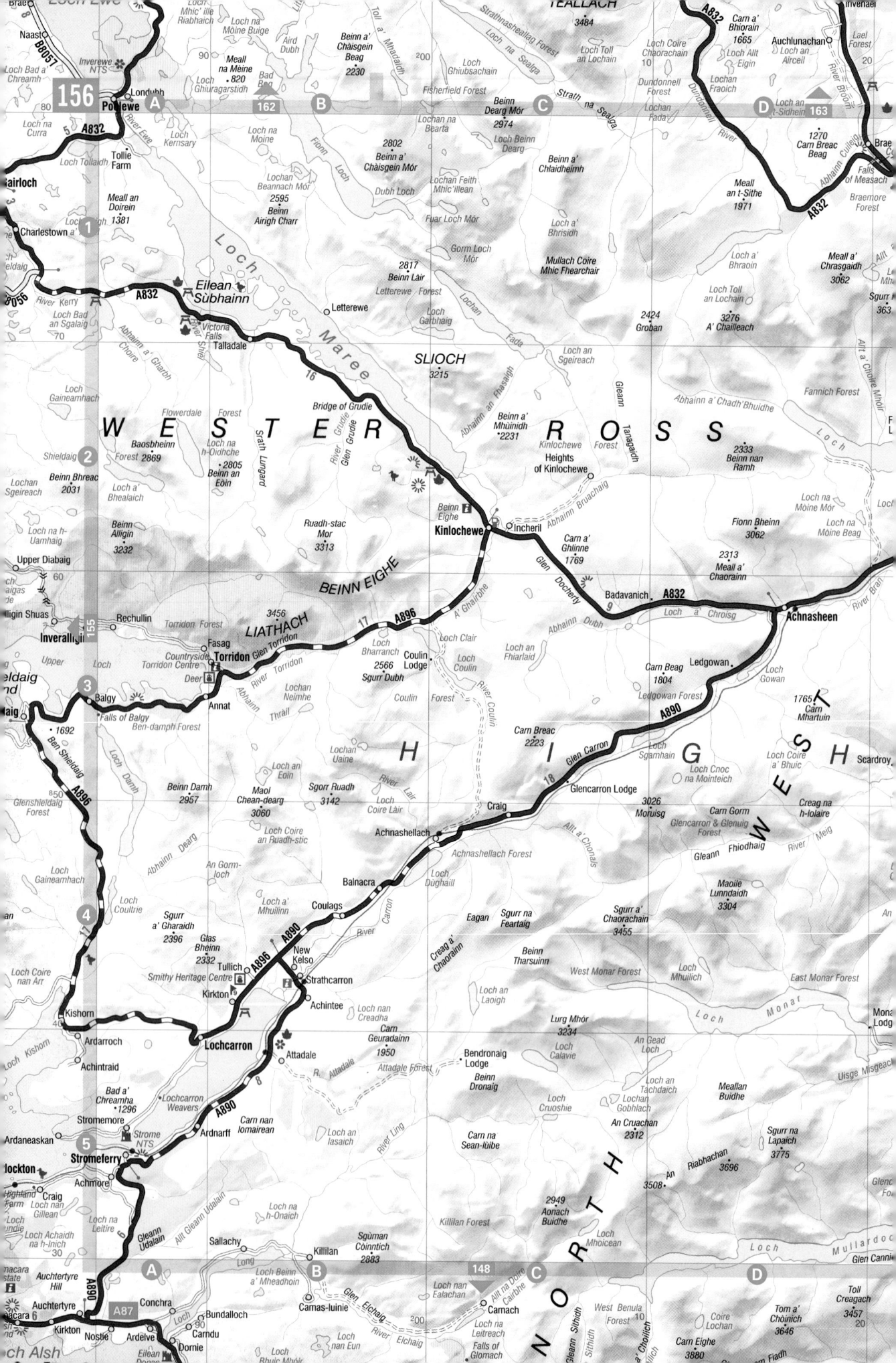

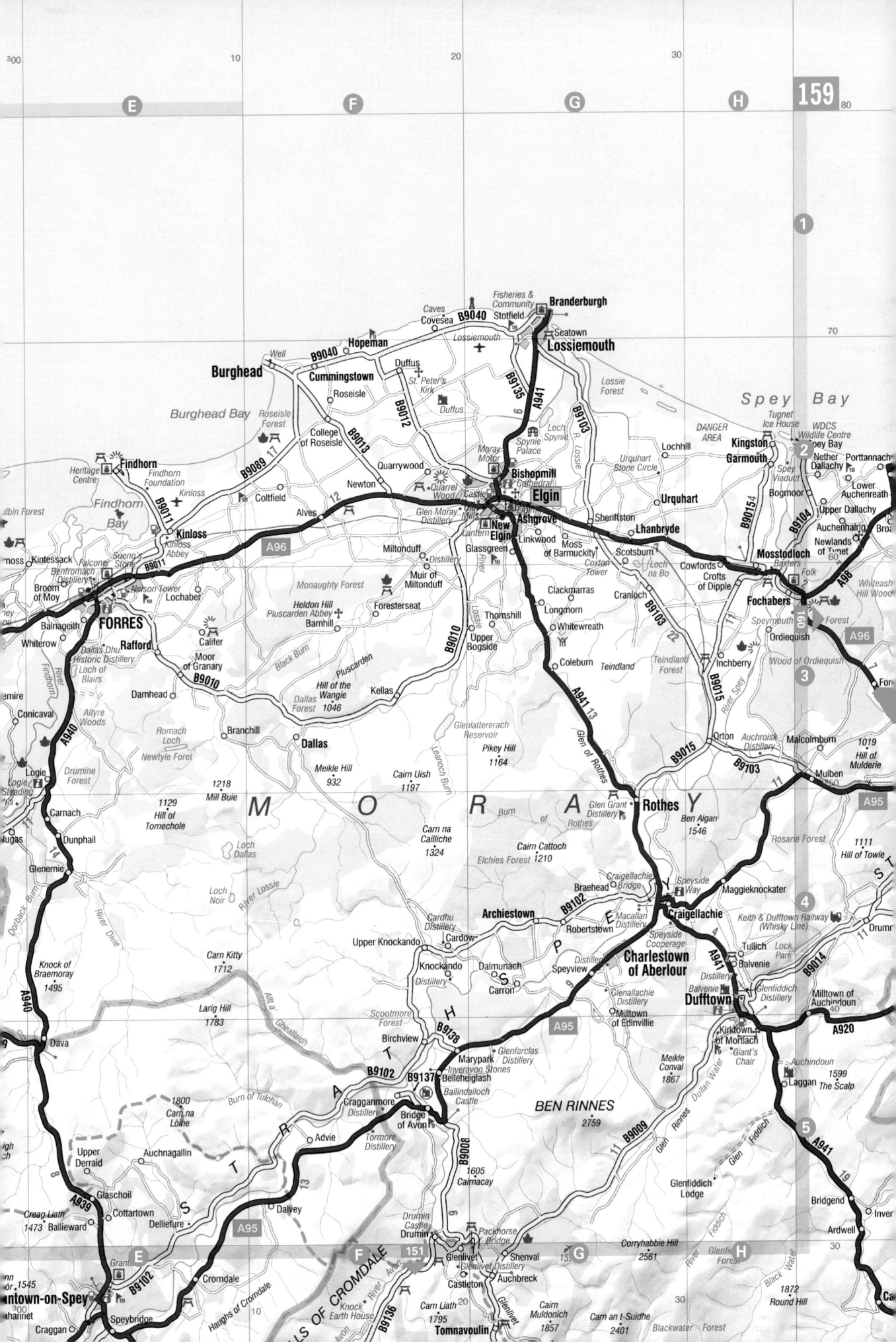

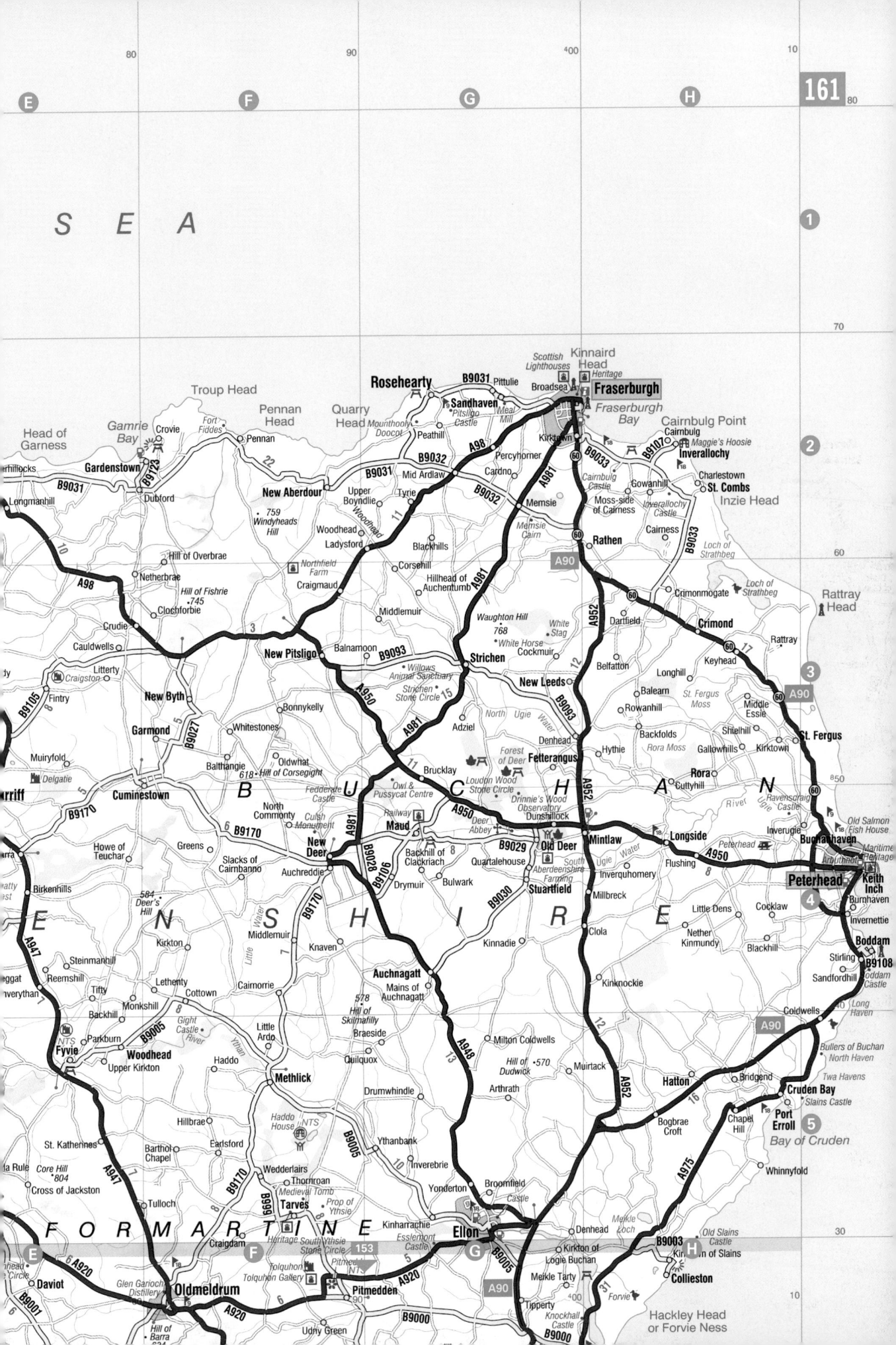

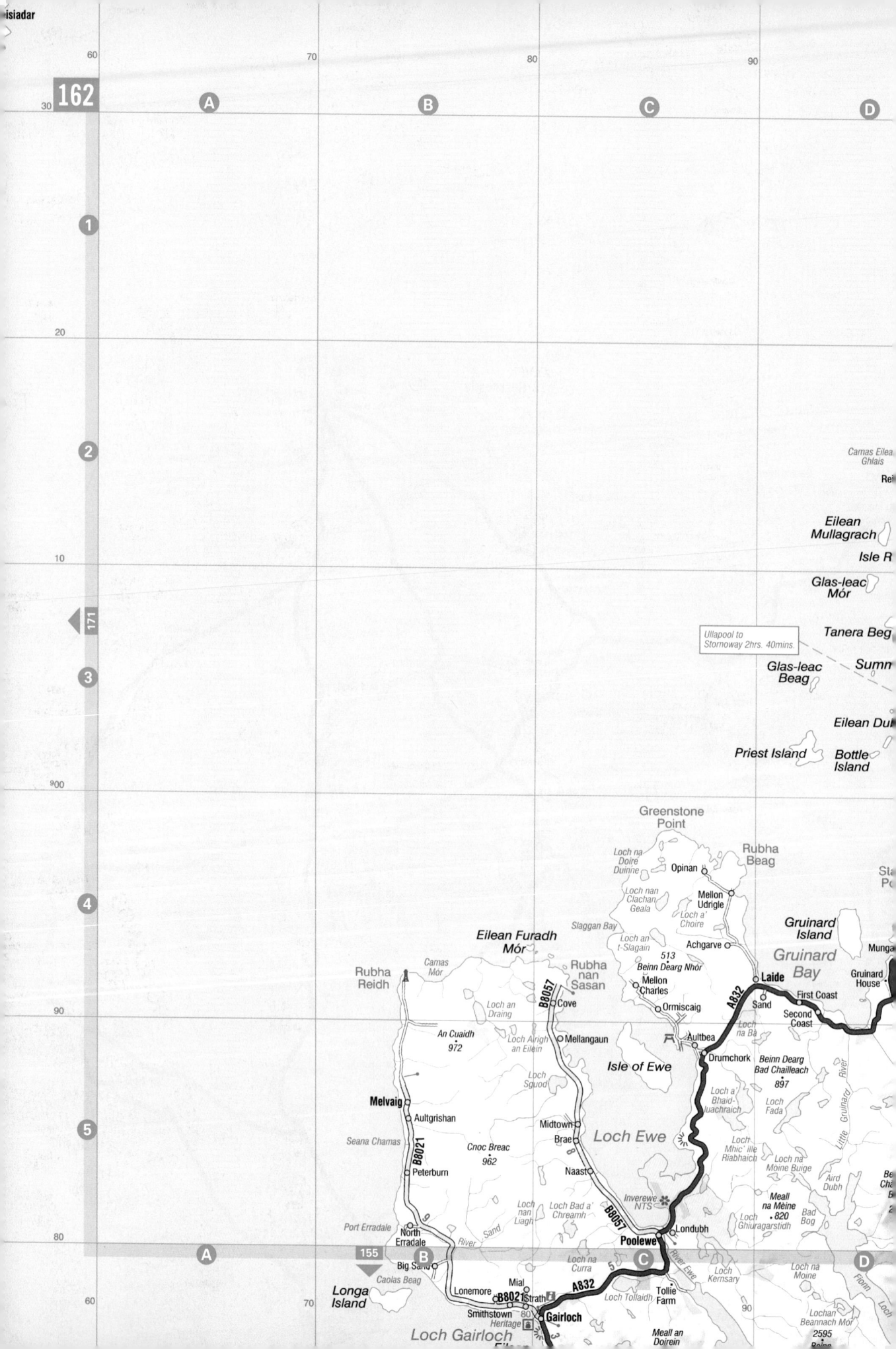

60   70   80   90

A   B   C   D

30

1

20

2

10

171

3

900

4

90

5

80

60

A   B   C   D

Camas Eilea
Ghlais

Rei

Eilean
Mullagrach

Isle R

Glas-leac
Mór

Ullapool to
Stornoway 2hrs. 40mins.

Tanera Beg

Glas-leac
Beag

Summ

Eilean Du

Priest Island

Bottle
Island

Sta
Po

Greenstone
Point

Rubha
Beag

Loch na
Doire
Duinne

Opinan

Mellon
Udrigle

Loch nan
Clachan
Geala

Loch a'
Choire

Gruinard
Island

Slaggan Bay

Loch an
t-Slagain

Achgarve

Gruinard
Bay

Munga

Eilean Furadh
Mór

Rubha
nan
Sasan

Beinn Dearg Nhór
513

Mellon
Charles

Laide

Gruinard
House

Rubha
Reidh

Camas
Mòr

B0057

Cove

Ormiscaig

A832

Sand

First Coast

Second
Coast

Loch an
Draing

Aultbea

Loch
na Ba

Loch Airigh
an Eilein

Mellangaun

Isle of Ewe

Drumchork

Beinn Dearg
Bad Chailleach
897

An Cuaidh
972

Loch
Sguod

Loch a'
Bhaid-
luachraich

Loch
Fada

Little Gruinard River

Melvaig

Aultgrishan

Midtown

Brae

Loch Ewe

Loch
Mhic' ille
Riabhaich

Loch na
Moine Buige

Aird
Dubh

Be
Cha

Seana Chamas

B8021

Cnoc Breac
962

Naast

Meall
na Mèine
820

Bad
Bog

Peterburn

Inverewe
NTS

B0057

Loch
Ghiuragarstidh

Londubh

Port Erradale

North
Erradale

River Sand

Loch
nan
Liagh

Loch Bad a'
Chreamh

Poolewe

River Ewe

Loch na
Moine

Froin

155

Big Sand

Caolas Beag

Lonemore

Mial

B802

Strath

A832

Loch na
Curra

Loch Tollaidh

Tollie
Farm

Loch
Kernsary

Lochan
Beannach Mòr
2595

Longa
Island

Smithstown
Heritage

Gairloch

Loch Gairloch

Meall an
Doirein

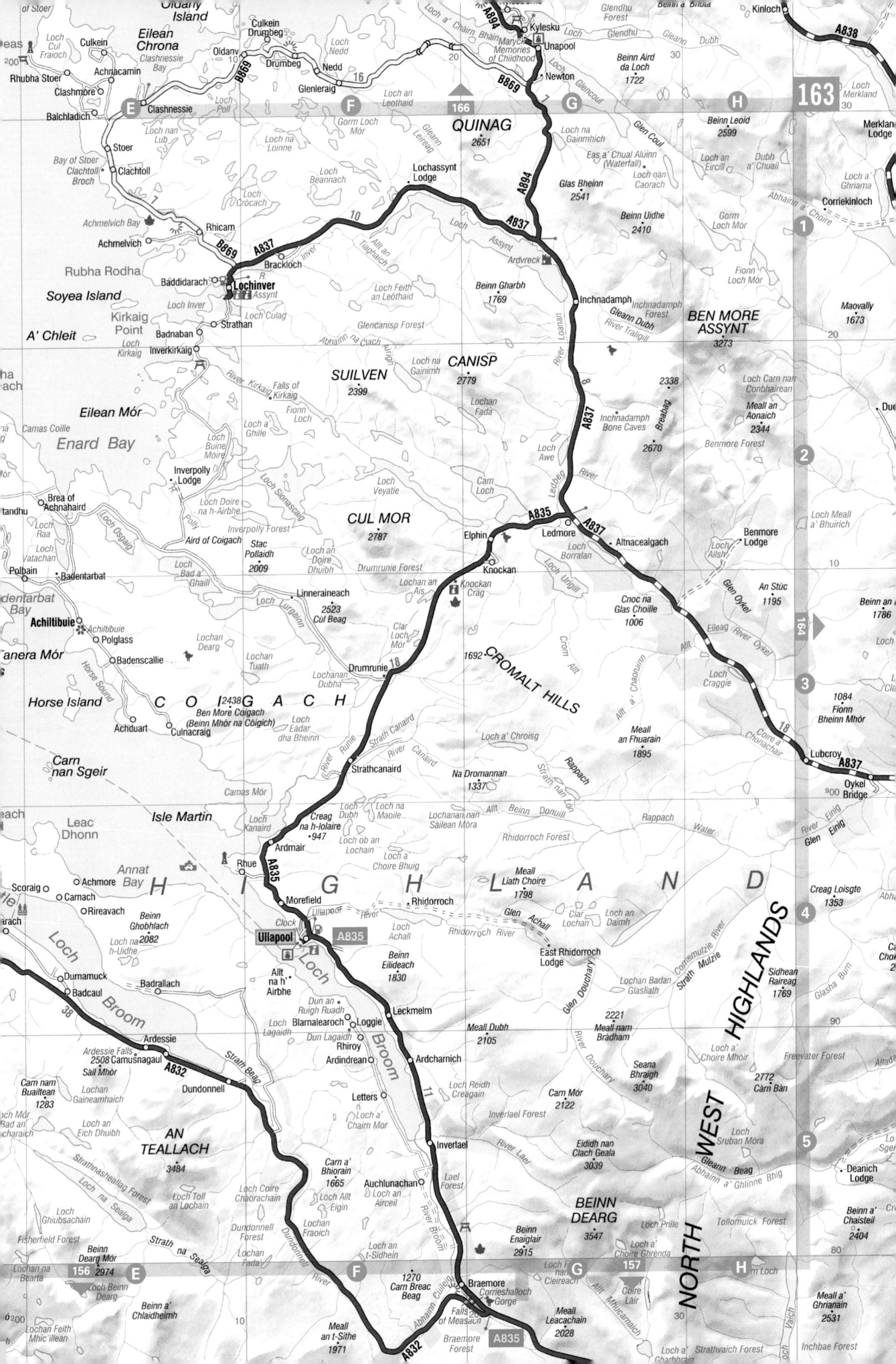

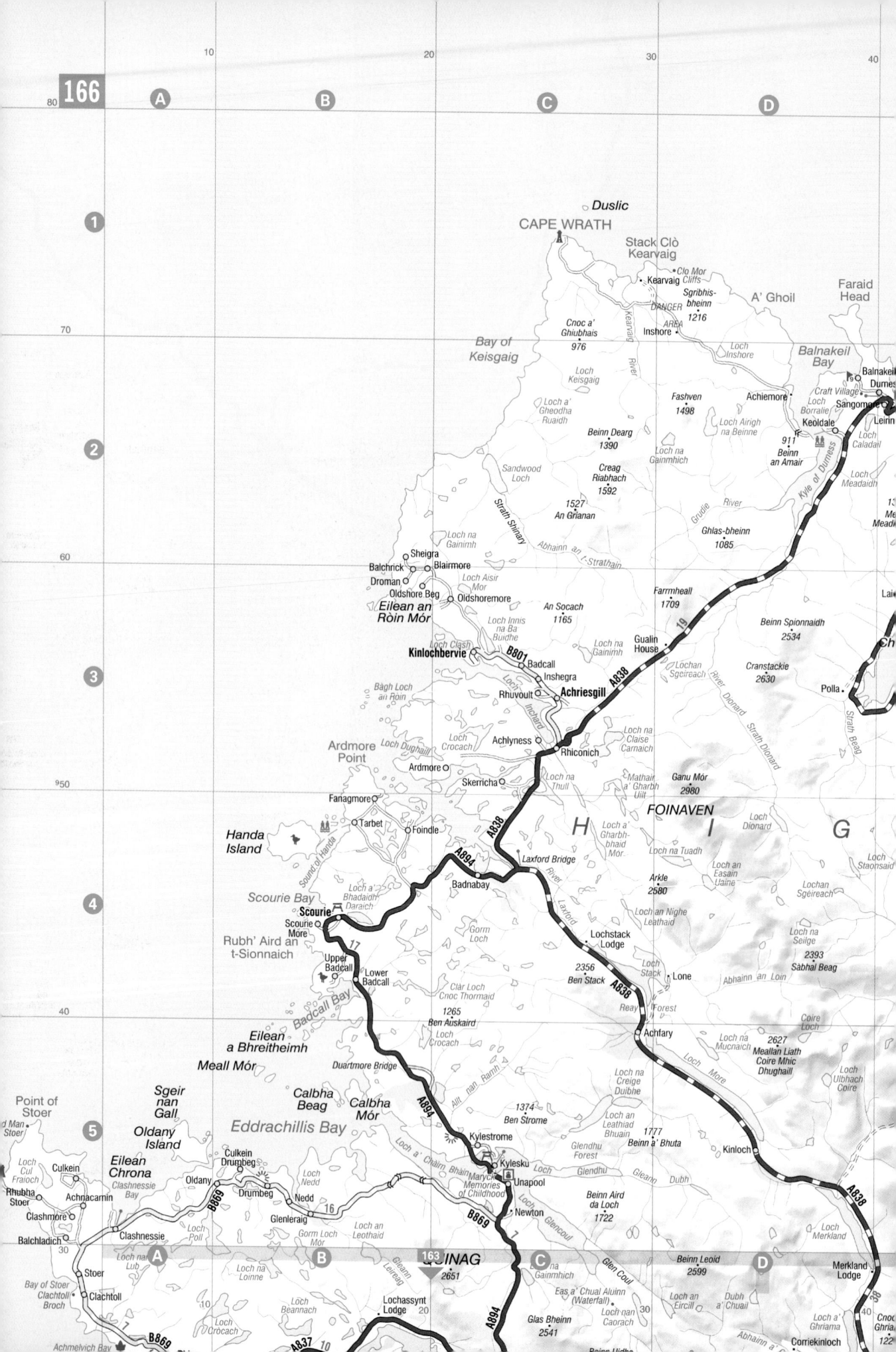

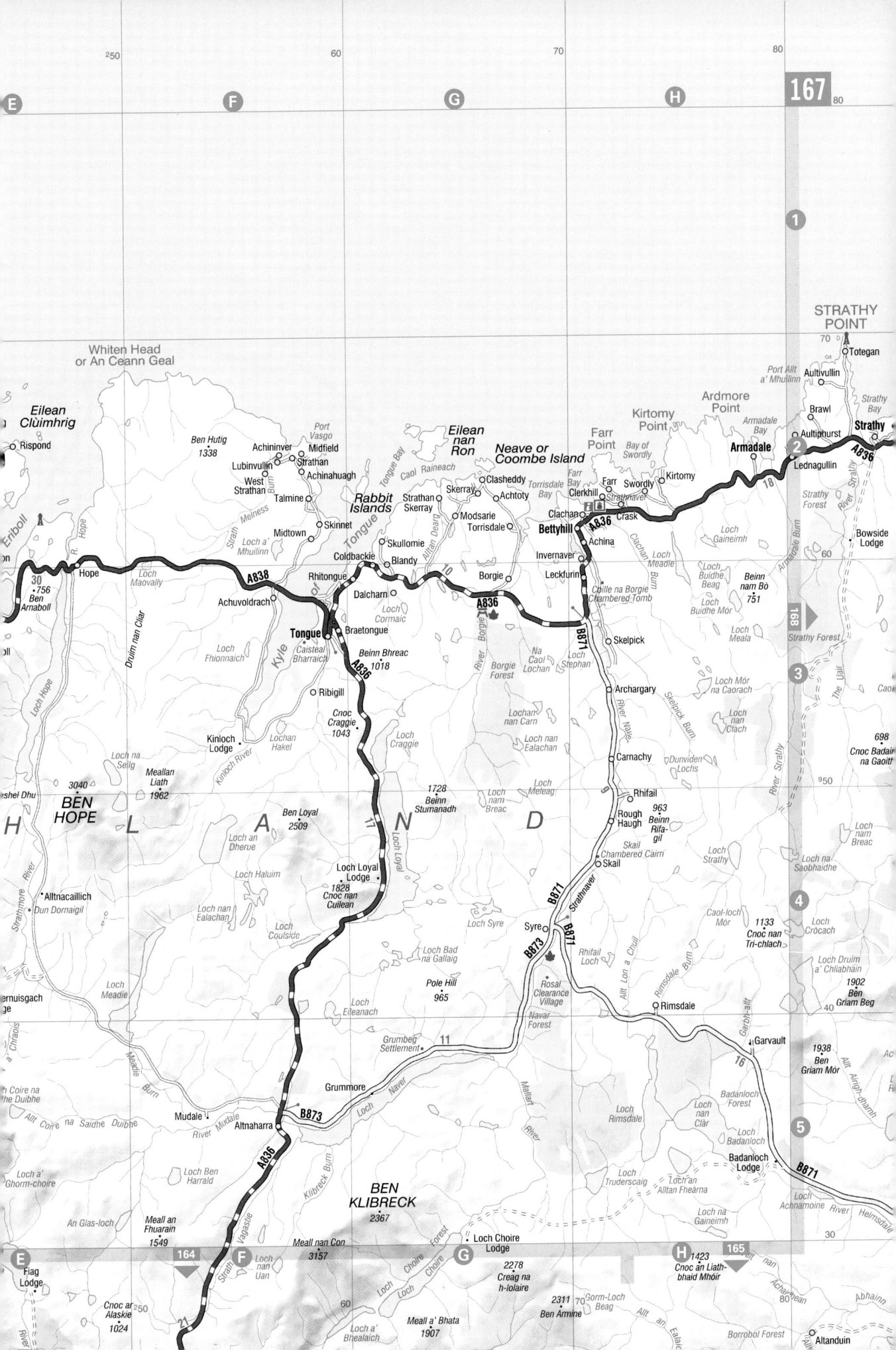

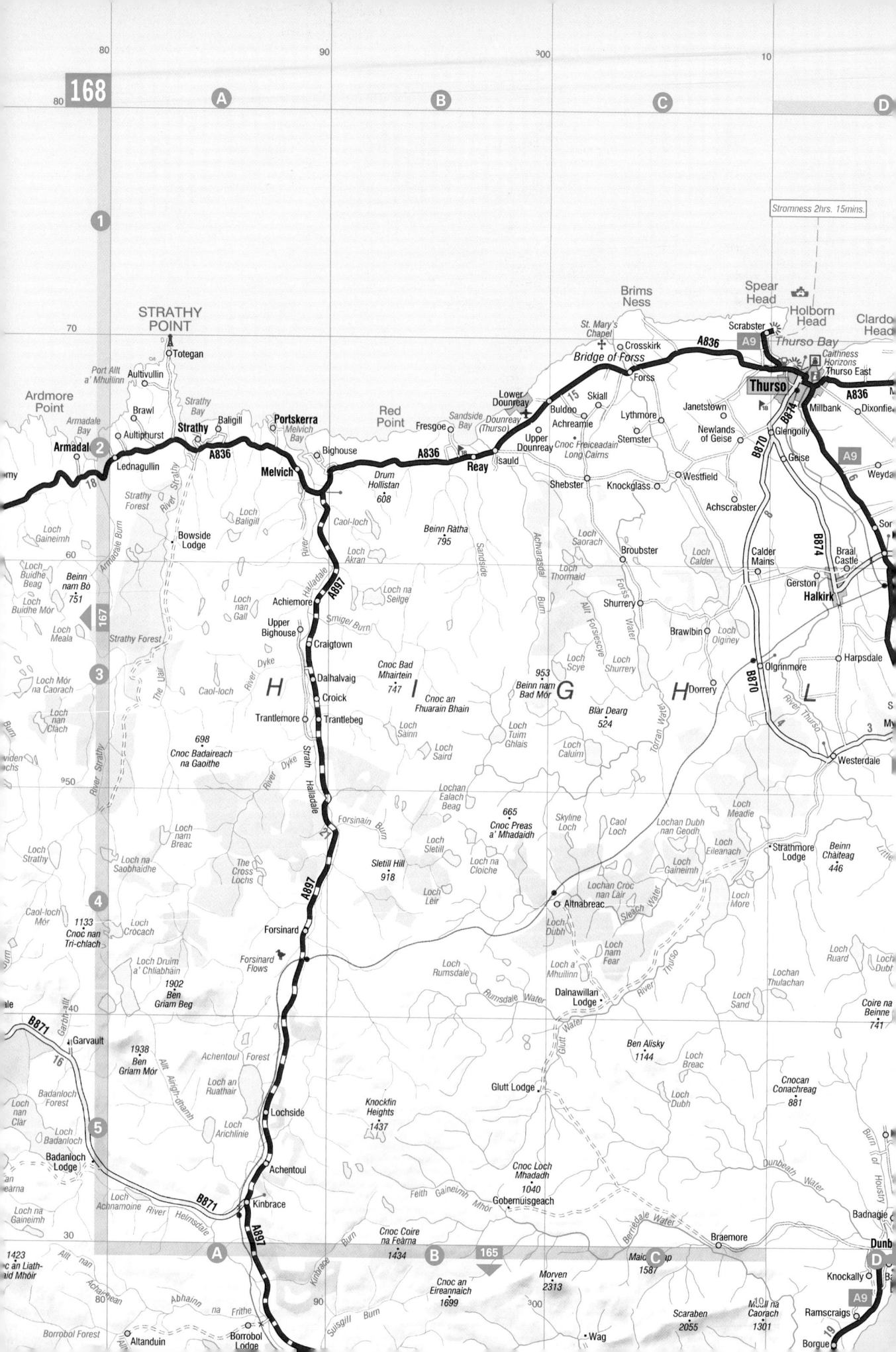

PENTLAND

FIRTH

Burwick
B9041
Cleat
Tomb of the Eagles
Brough
Liddle

20
30
40
350
80

E
172
F
G
H
70

Island of Stroma
Nethertown
Uppertown

Pentland Skerries

NNET HEAD

Long Loch
74
unfa Hill
t Hill
B855 4
Brough
Ham
Rattar
Scarfskerry
Tang Head
St. John's Point
Castle of Mey
East Mey
Gills Bay
Huna
Last Ho.
DUNCANSBY HEAD
Boars of Duncansby

Hunspow
West Dunnet
y-Ann's ottage
St. John's Loch
Corsback
A836
Mey
Barrock
Dunnet
Inkstack
11
Loch of Mey
Gills
Warse
Upper Gills
A836
Seater
Canisby
Kirkstyle
John o' Groats
Duncansby Stacks
Stacks of Duncansby

net
Seadrift-Dunnet
Brabster
Warth Hill 406
A99
Skirza
Skirza Head

B876
Greenland Mains
Lochend
Slickly
Gill Burn
Tofts
Freswick
Freswick Bay
Ness Head

Greenland
Tain
Reaster
Alterwall
Kirk Burn
Caithness Broch Centre
Auckengill
Brough Head

Durran
Bowermadden
Sortat
Lyth Arts Centre
Nybster

Bowertower
Lyth
Howe
A99
Keiss
14
Keiss Castle
Tang Head

B874
Corsback
Halcro
Hastigrow
Burn of Lyth
Mireland

Gillock
North Watten
B870
Kirk
Myrelandhorn
Loch of Wester
9
Westerloch

el
Knapperfield
Killimster
B876
Sinclair's Bay
Sinclair Girnigoe
Noss Head

Oldhall
Loch Watten
B874
18
Reiss
Ackergillshore

N
Watten
B870
D
Winless
Ackergill
Sealky Head

Sinclair I Centre
Loch of Toftingall
Bilbster
Sibster
A99
WICK
Heritage
Staxigoe
Papigoe
Broadhaven

Acharole
Strath
Wick River
3
Pulteney Distillery

Badlipster
A882
Haster
Milton
Janetstown
Wick
Newton
A99
South Head

Achairn Burn
Whiterow
Loch Hempriggs
Old Wick
Gote o' Tram

Tannach
Hempriggs
Helman Head

Hill of Oliclett 462
Gansclet
Thrumster

Grey Cairns of Camster
Loch of Yarrows
Raggra
Borrowston
Sarclet
Sarclet Head

of ag
wanich
South Yarrows Cairns
Cnoc an Earrannaiche 692
Camster
Cairn o'Get
A99
Ulbster

Loch Stemster Standing Stones
815
Stemster Hill
Sheppardstown
Roster
East Clyth
A99

Crofts of Benachielt
umster Forest
Osclay
Upper Lybster
Hill o' Many Stanes
Mid Clyth
Bruan
Halberry Head

Achow
Clyth
Overton

9
Upper A99
Latheron
Standing Stones
w
Swiney
Lybster
Inveshore
Waterlines
Forse
Burrigill
Forse Castle

Latheron
Clan Gunn Heritage Centre
Latheronwheel

kinnon
y Croft

20
30
40
350
30

E
F
G
H

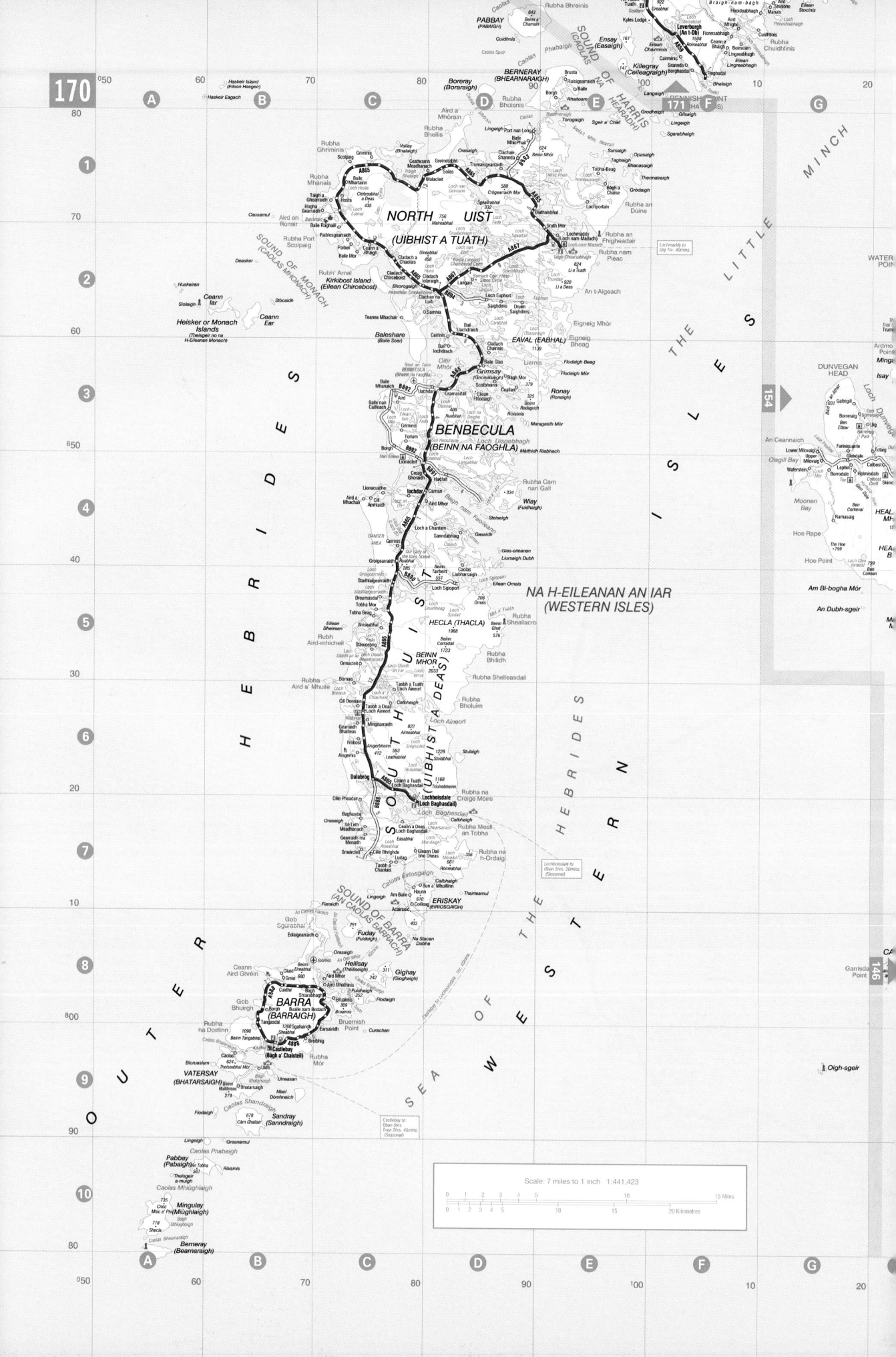

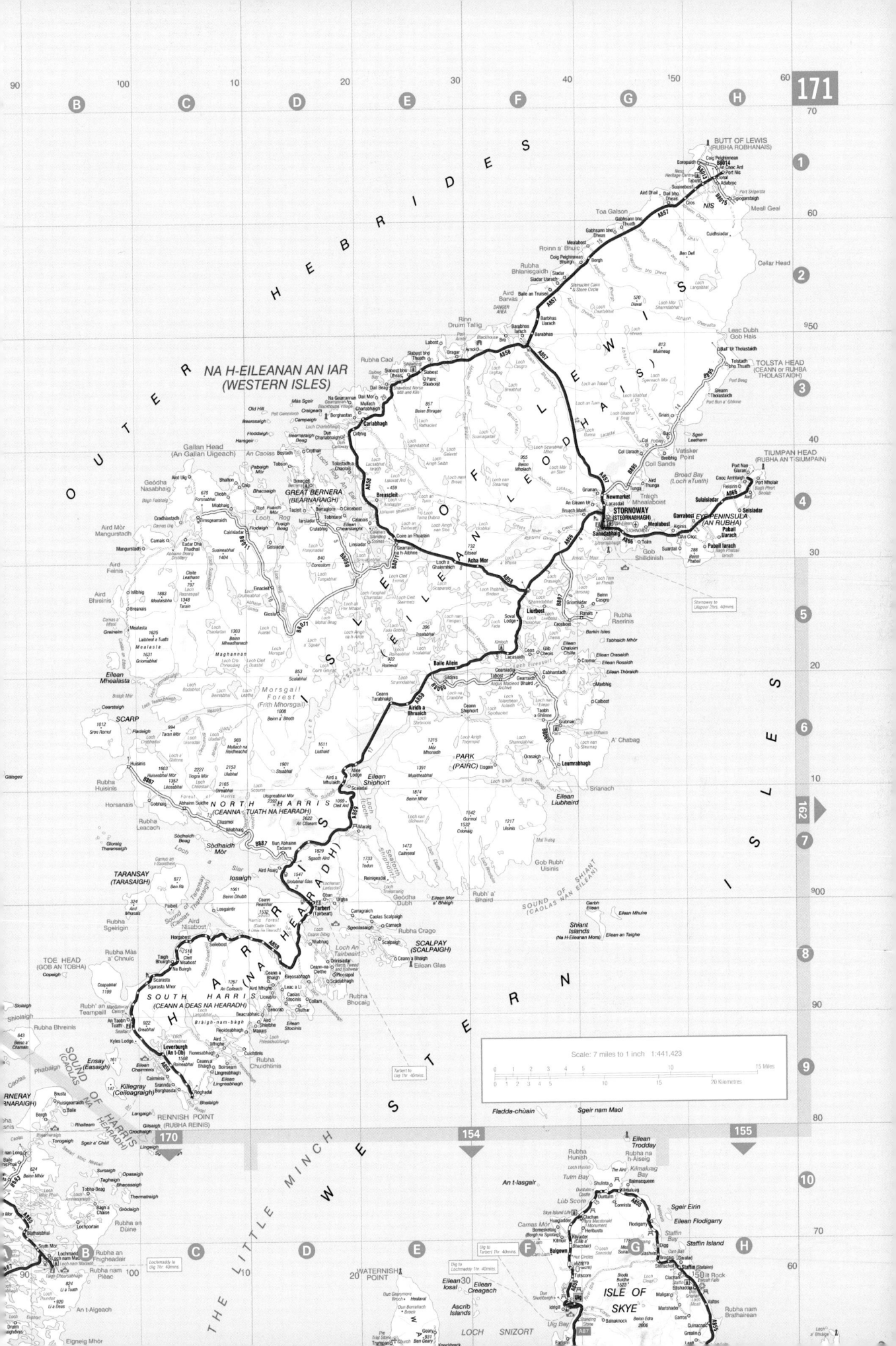

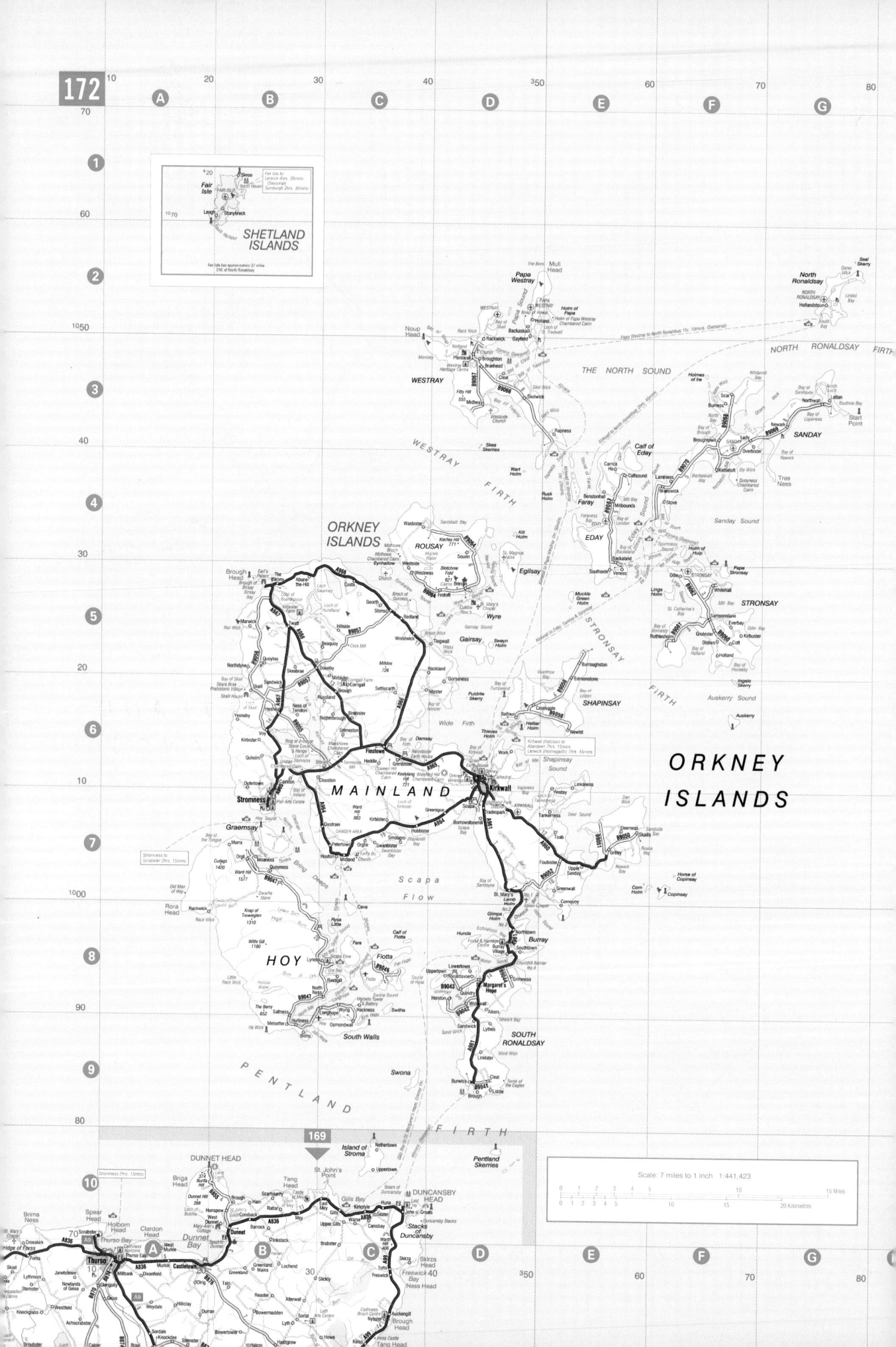

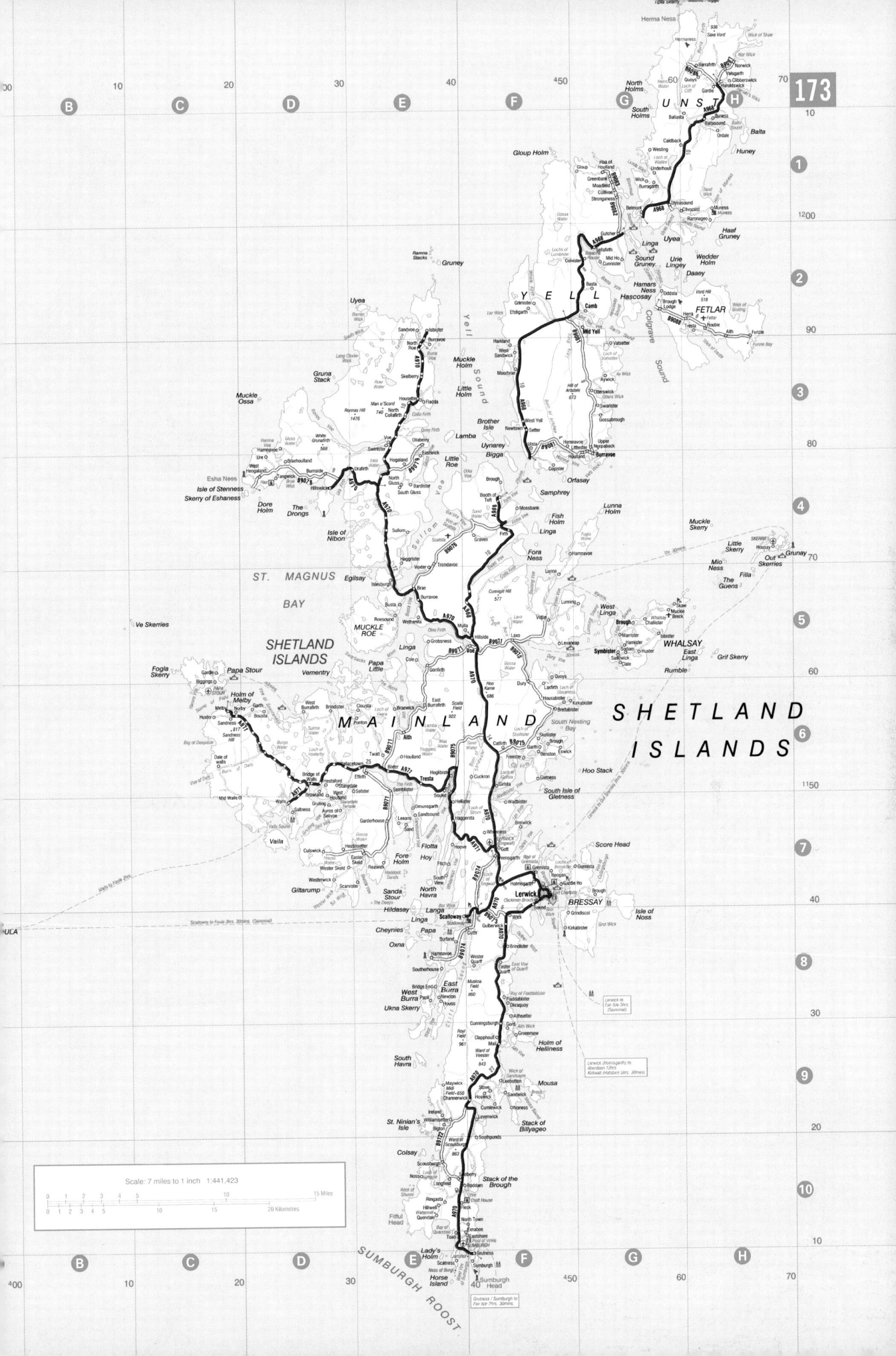

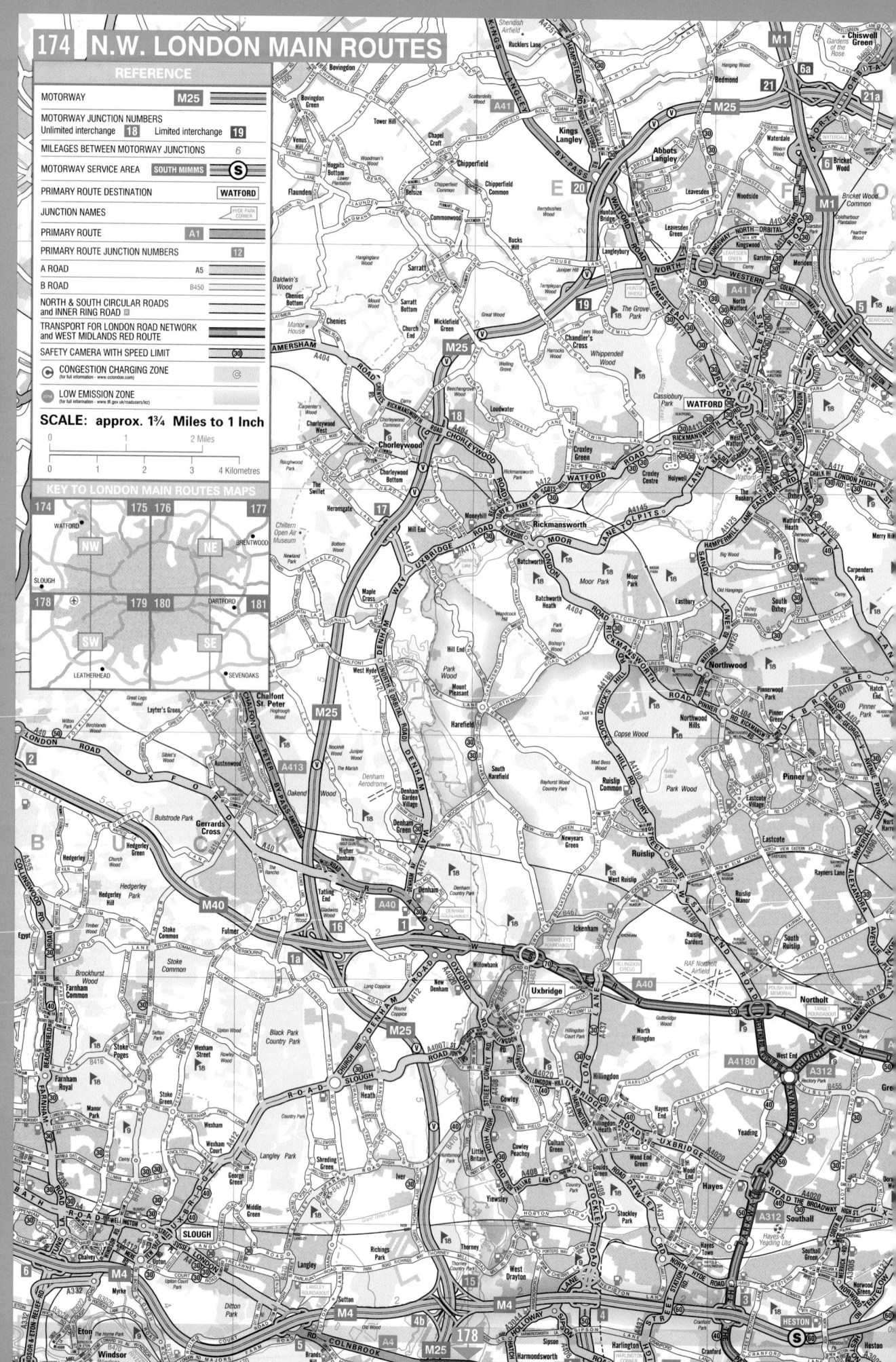

REFERENCE

MOTORWAY	M25
MOTORWAY JUNCTION NUMBERS	
Unlimited interchange **18** Limited interchange **19**	
MILEAGES BETWEEN MOTORWAY JUNCTIONS	6
MOTORWAY SERVICE AREA	SOUTH MIMMS Ⓢ
PRIMARY ROUTE DESTINATION	WATFORD
JUNCTION NAMES	HYDE PARK CORNER
PRIMARY ROUTE	A1
PRIMARY ROUTE JUNCTION NUMBERS	12
A ROAD	A5
B ROAD	B450
NORTH & SOUTH CIRCULAR ROADS and INNER RING ROAD	
TRANSPORT FOR LONDON ROAD NETWORK and WEST MIDLANDS RED ROUTE	
SAFETY CAMERA WITH SPEED LIMIT	30
Ⓒ CONGESTION CHARGING ZONE (for full information - www.cclondon.com)	
LOW EMISSION ZONE (for full information - www.tfl.gov.uk/roadusers/lez)	

SCALE: approx. 1¾ Miles to 1 Inch

0 — 1 — 2 Miles

0 — 1 — 2 — 3 — 4 Kilometres

KEY TO LONDON MAIN ROUTES MAPS

174		175 176		177
WATFORD	NW		NE	BRENTWOOD
SLOUGH				DARTFORD
178		179 180		181
	SW		SE	
	LEATHERHEAD		SEVENOAKS	

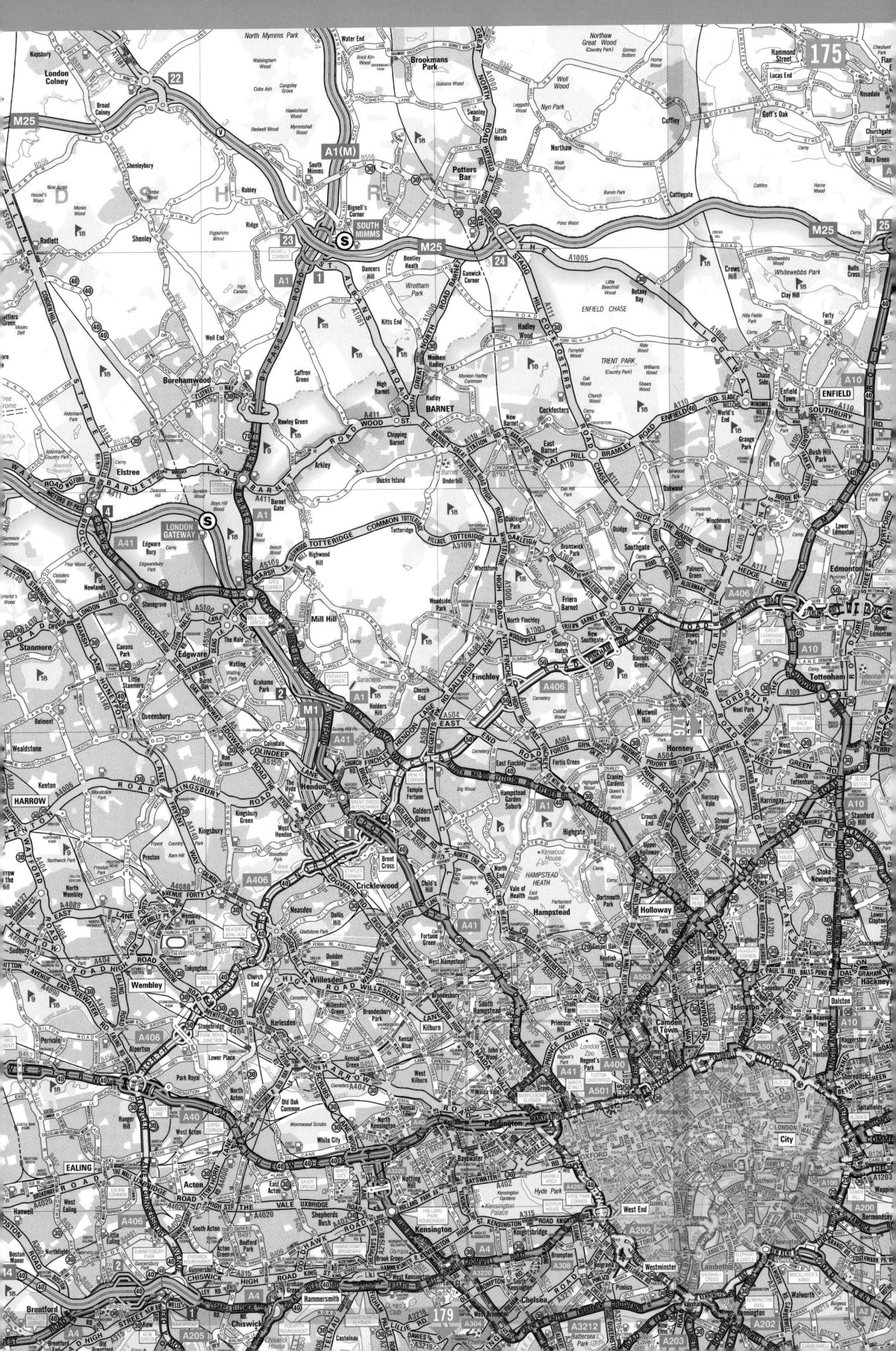

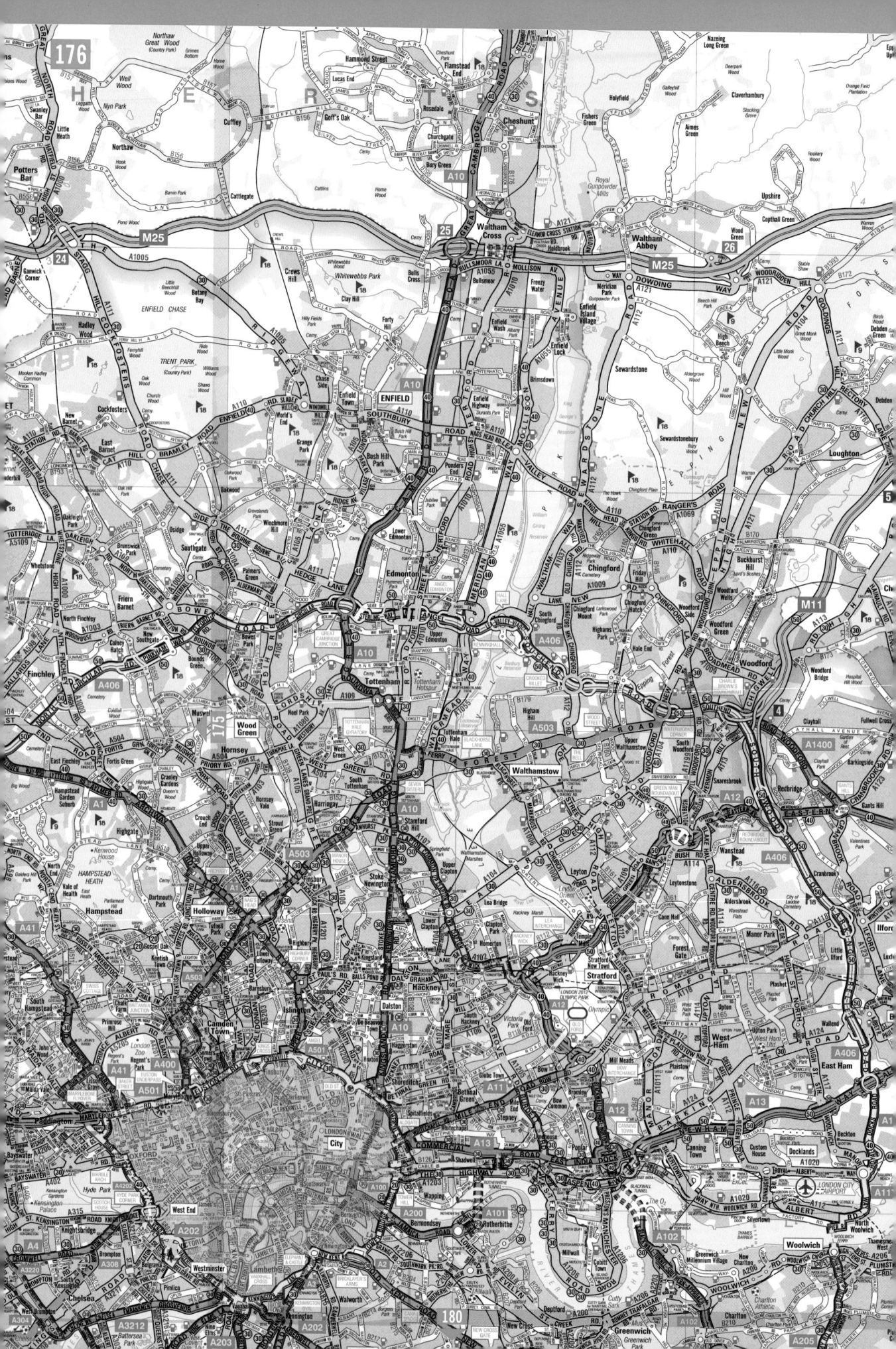

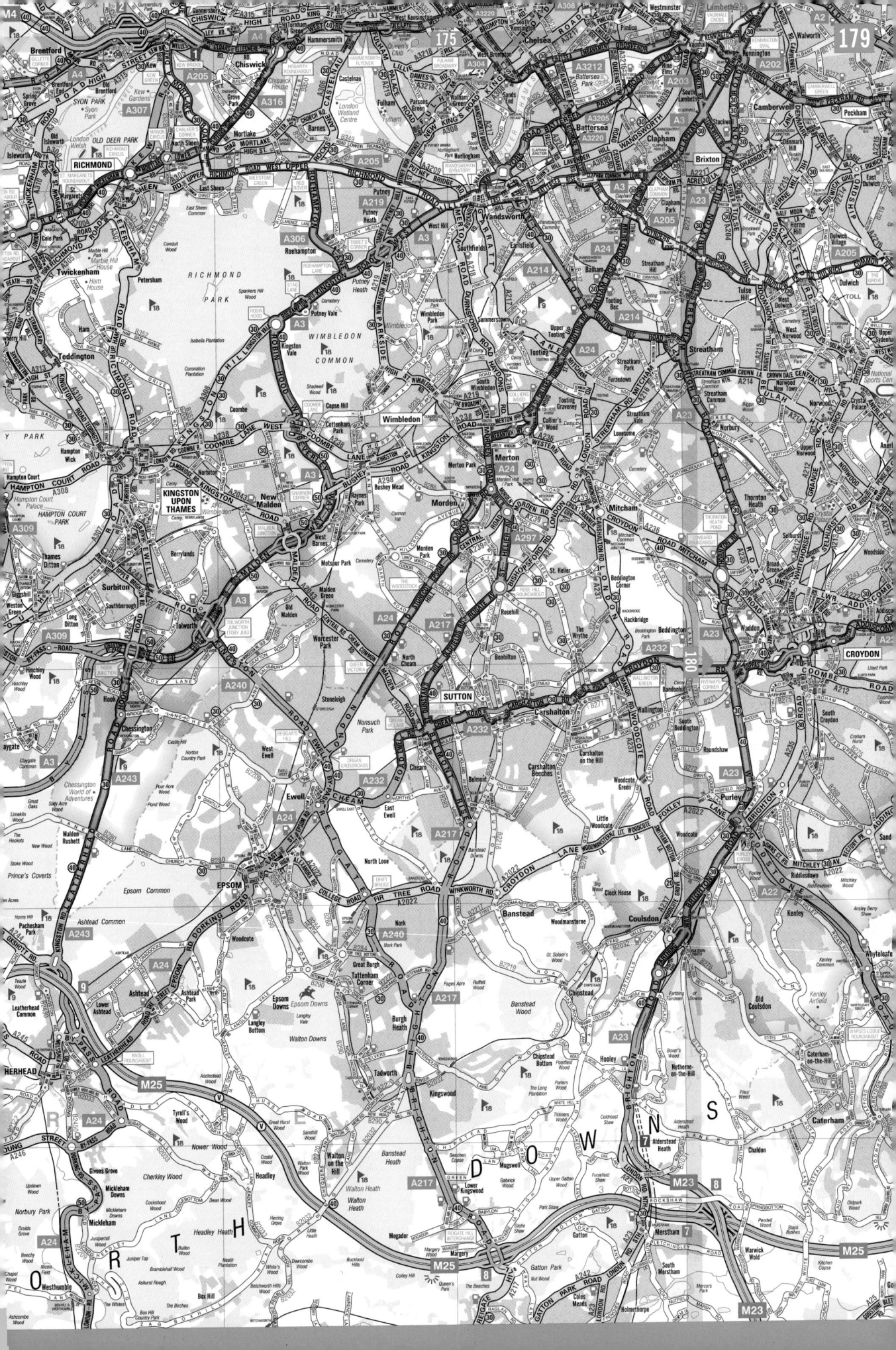

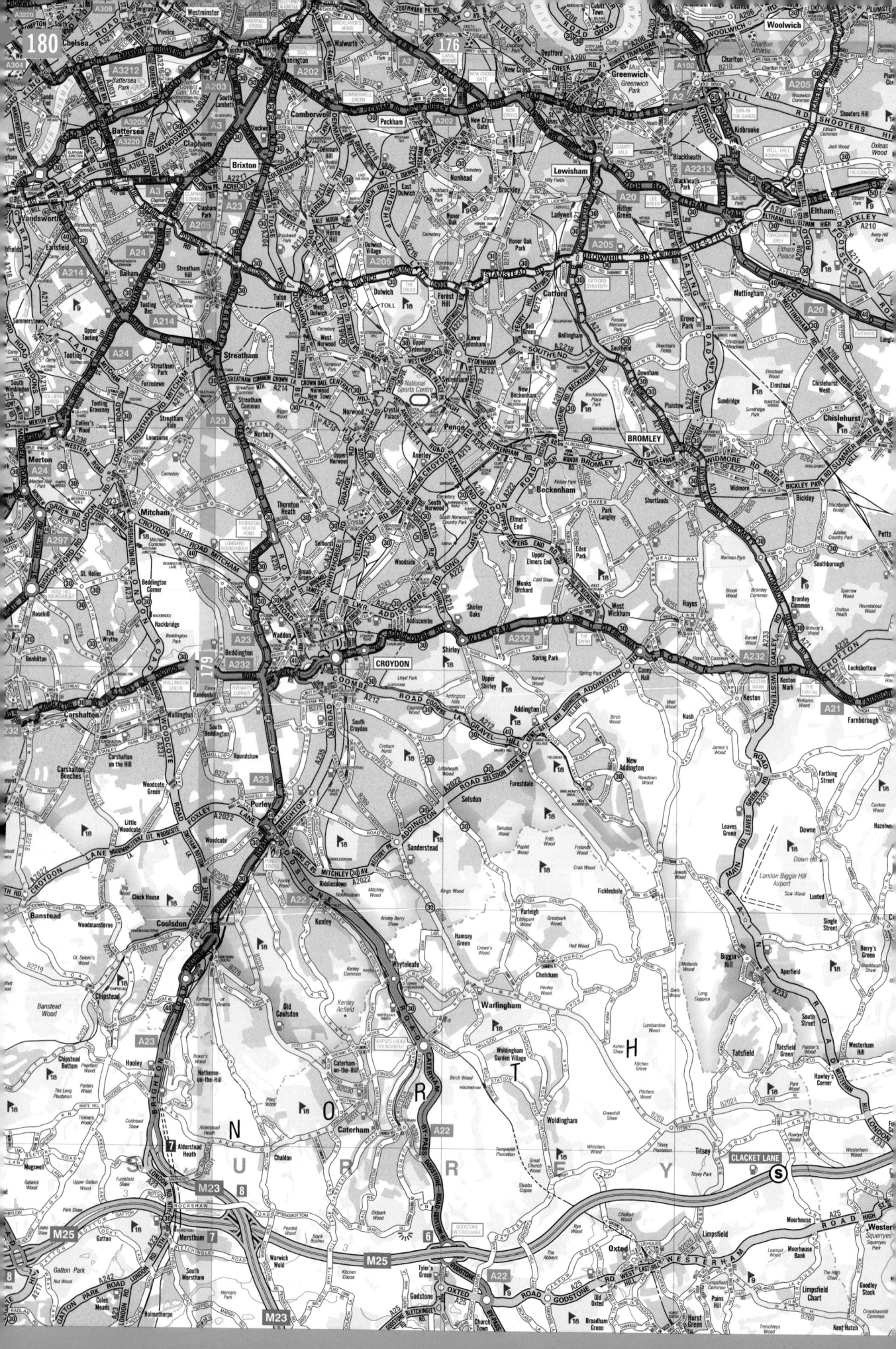

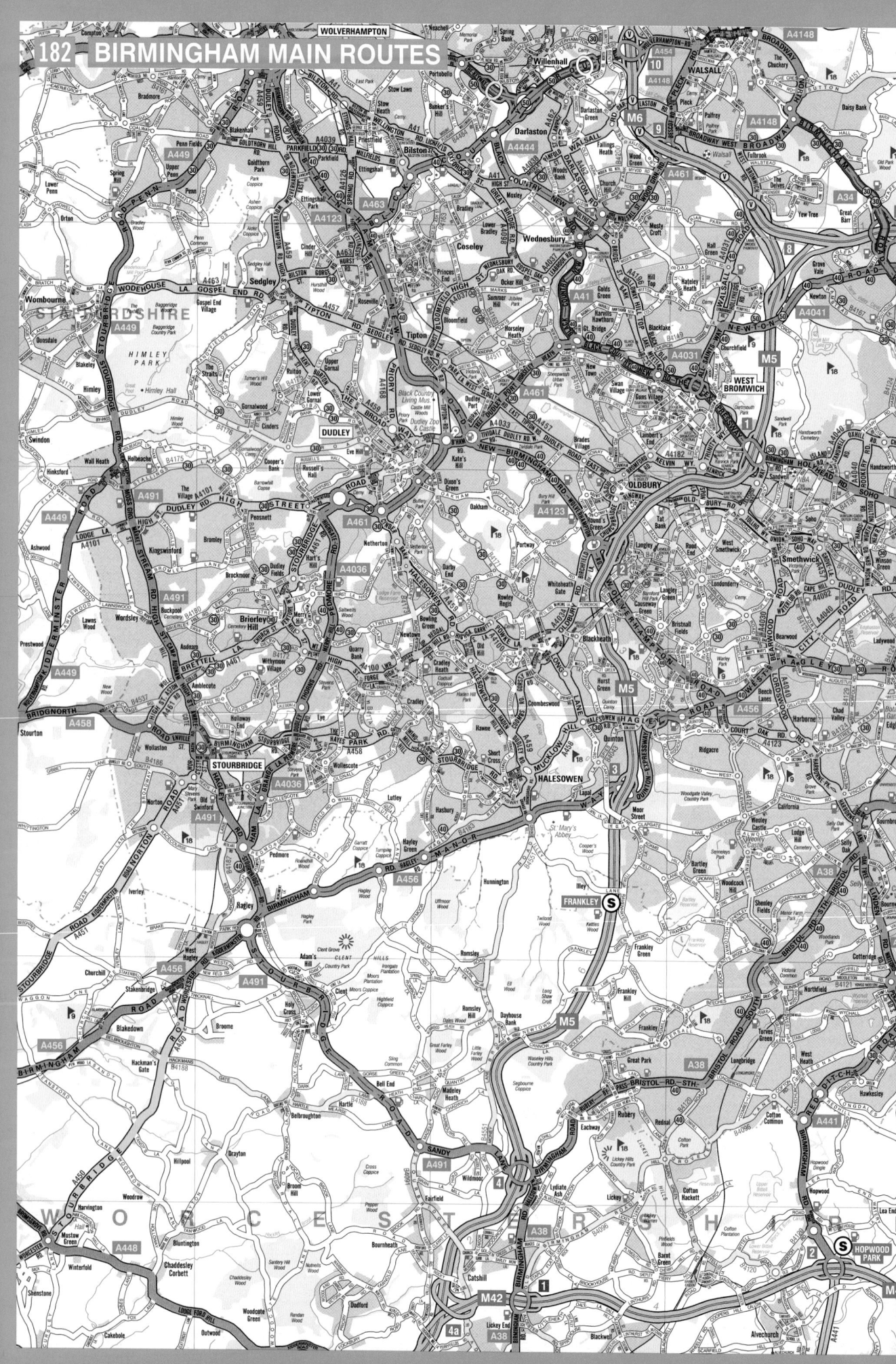

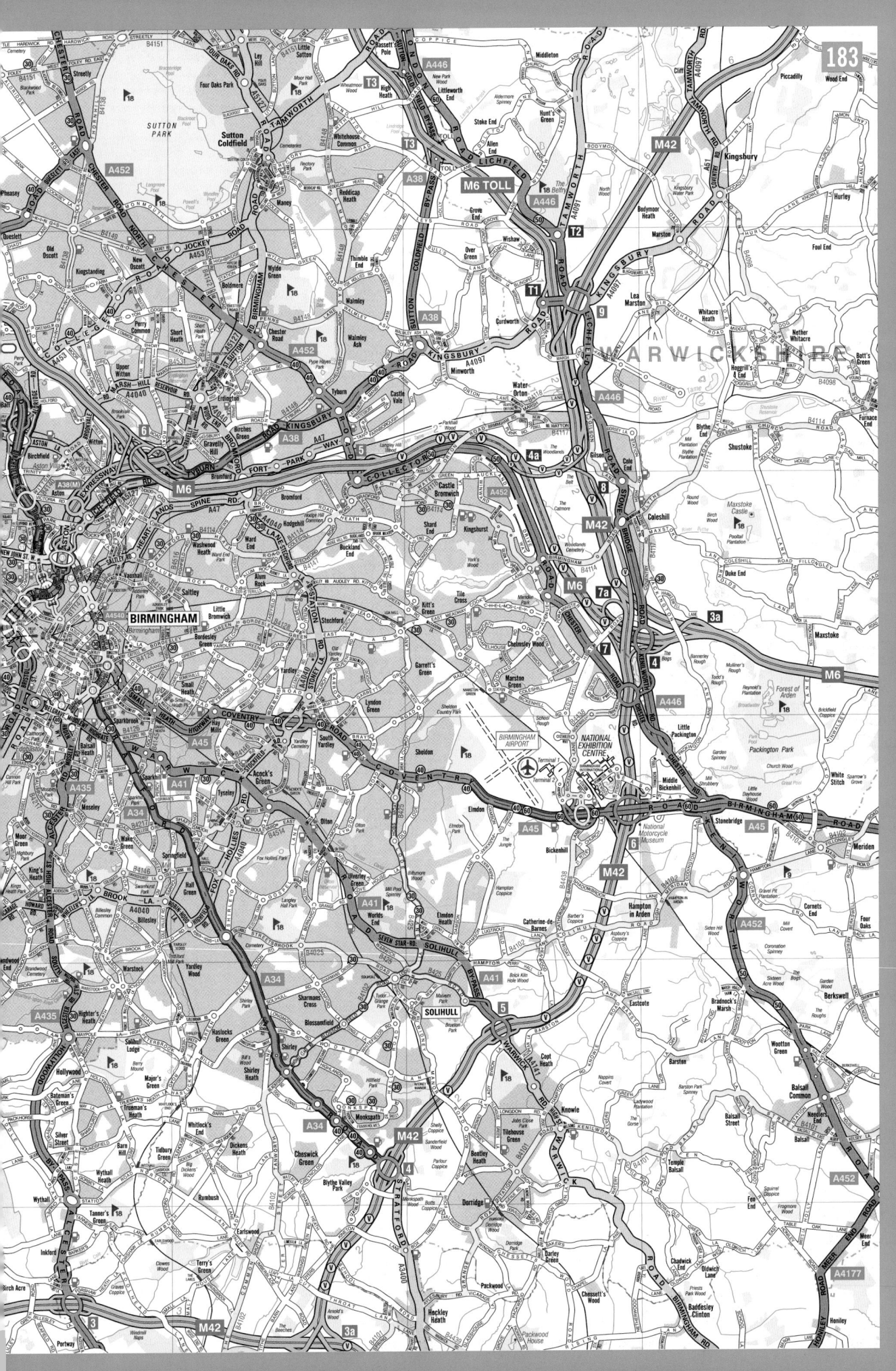

Town Plans

Aberdeen.............................187
Aberystwyth.......................187
Ayr....................................187
Bath..................................187
Bedford.............................188
Birmingham.......................188
Blackpool..........................188
Bournemouth.....................190
Bradford............................190
Brighton & Hove................189
Bristol...............................189
Caernarfon........................190
Cambridge........................191
Canterbury........................190
Cardiff (Caerdydd)..............191
Carlisle.............................192
Cheltenham.......................192
Chester.............................192
Coventry............................192
Derby................................193
Dover................................193
Dumfries...........................193
Dundee.............................194
Durham.............................194
Eastbourne........................195
Edinburgh..........................194
Exeter...............................195
Folkestone.........................195
Glasgow............................196
Gloucester.........................196
Great Yarmouth...................196
Guildford...........................197
Harrogate..........................197
Hereford............................197
Inverness...........................198
Ipswich.............................198
Kilmarnock........................198
Kingston upon Hull..............199
Leeds................................199
Leicester...........................200
Lincoln..............................198
Liverpool...........................200
London.......................202-203
Luton................................201
Manchester........................201
Medway Towns...................204
Middlesbrough....................201
Milton Keynes....................204
Newcastle upon Tyne...........205
Newport (Casnewydd)..........205
Northampton......................206
Norwich............................205
Nottingham........................206
Oban................................206
Oxford..............................207
Paisley..............................207
Perth................................207
Peterborough.....................208
Plymouth...........................208
Portsmouth........................209
Preston.............................208
Reading............................209
St Andrews........................209
Salisbury...........................210
Sheffield............................210
Shrewsbury........................210
Southampton......................211
Stirling..............................211
Stoke-on-Trent...................211
Stratford-upon-Avon............212
Sunderland........................212
Swansea (Abertawe)............212
Swindon............................212
Taunton............................213
Winchester........................213
Windsor.............................213
Wolverhampton...................213
Worcester..........................214
Wrexham (Wrecsam)............214
York..................................214

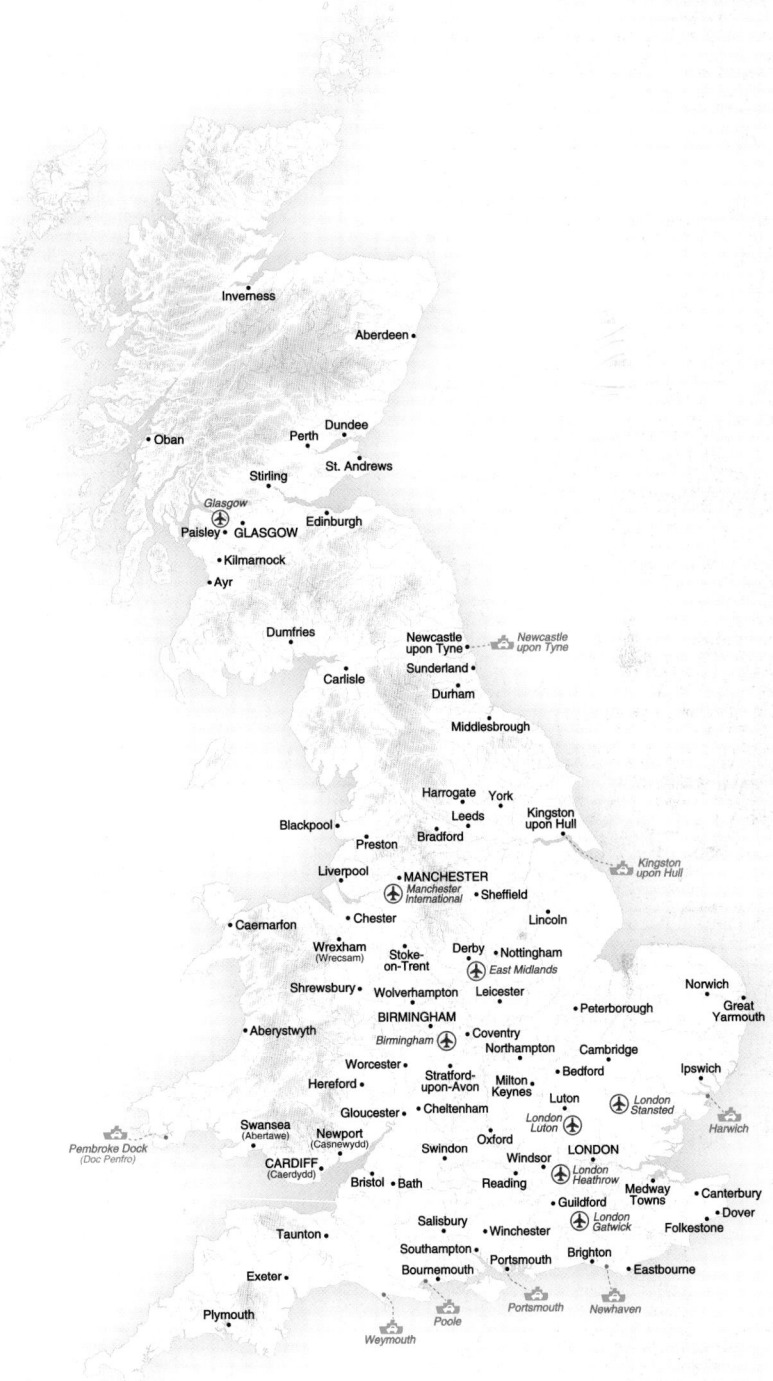

Port Plans

Harwich.............................215
Kingston upon Hull..............215
Newcastle upon Tyne...........215
Newhaven..........................215
Pembroke Dock (Doc Penfro)....215
Poole................................215
Portsmouth........................215
Weymouth..........................215

Airport Plans

Birmingham 216
East Midlands.....................216
Glasgow............................216
London Gatwick..................216
London Heathrow.................216
London Luton......................216
London Stansted..................216
Manchester International........216

Reference to City & Town Centre Plans Légende Zeichenerklärung

Motorway M1
Autoroute
Autobahn

Motorway Under Construction
Autoroute en construction
Autobahn im Bau

Motorway Proposed
Autoroute prévue
Geplante Autobahn

Motorway Junctions with Numbers 4 5
Unlimited Interchange 4
Limited Interchange 5

Autoroute échangeur numéroté
Echangeur complet
Echangeur partiel

Autobahnanschlußstelle mit Nummer
Unbeschränkter Fahrtrichtungswechsel
Beschränkter Fahrtrichtungswechsel

Primary Route A41
Route à grande circulation
Hauptverkehrsstraße

Dual Carriageways (A & B roads)
Route à double chaussées séparées (route A & B)
Zweispurige Schnellstraße (A- und B- Straßen)

Class A Road A129
Route de type A
A-Straße

Class B Road B177
Route de type B
B-Straße

Major Roads Under Construction
Route prioritaire en construction
Hauptverkehrsstaße im Bau

Major Roads Proposed
Route prioritaire prévue
Geplante Hauptverkehrsstaße

Minor Roads
Route secondaire
Nebenstraße

Safety Camera 30
Radars de contrôle de vitesse
Sicherheitskamera

Restricted Access
Accès réglementé
Beschränkte Zufahrt

Pedestrianized Road & Main Footway
Rue piétonne et chemin réservé aux piétons
Fußgängerstraße und Fußweg

One Way Streets
Sens unique
Einbahnstraße

Fuel Station
Station service
Tankstelle

Toll TOLL
Barrière de péage
Gebührenpflichtig

Railway & Station
Voie ferrée et gare
Eisenbahnlinie und Bahnhof

Underground / Metro & DLR Station DLR
Station de métro et DLR
U-Bahnstation und DLR-Station

Level Crossing & Tunnel
Passage à niveau et tunnel
Bahnübergang und Tunnel

Tram Stop & One Way Tram Stop
Arrêt de tramway
Straßenbahnhaltestelle

Built-up Area
Agglomération
Geschloßene Ortschaft

Abbey, Cathedral, Priory etc
Abbaye, cathédrale, prieuré etc
Abtei, Kathedrale, Kloster usw

Airport
Aéroport
Flughafen

Bus Station
Gare routière
Bushaltestelle

Car Park (selection of) P
Sélection de parkings
Auswahl von Parkplatz

Church
Eglise
Kirche

City Wall
Murs d'enceinte
Stadtmauer

Congestion Charging Zone
Zone de péage urbain
City-Maut Zone

Ferry (vehicular)
(foot only)

Bac (véhicules)
(piétons)

Fähre (autos)
(nur für Personen)

Golf Course 9 18
Terrain de golf
Golfplatz

Heliport
Héliport
Hubschrauberlandeplatz

Hospital H
Hôpital
Krankenhaus

Lighthouse
Phare
Leuchtturm

Market
Marché
Markt

National Trust Property
(open) NT
(restricted opening) NT
(National Trust for Scotland) NTS NTS

National Trust Property
(ouvert)
(heures d'ouverture)
(National Trust for Scotland)

National Trust- Eigentum
(geöffnet)
(beschränkte Öffnungszeit)
(National Trust for Scotland)

Park & Ride P+
Parking relais
Auswahl von Parkplatz

Place of Interest
Curiosité
Sehenswürdigkeit

Police Station
Commissariat de police
Polizeirevier

Post Office
Bureau de poste
Postamt

Shopping Area (main street & precinct)
Quartier commerçant (rue et zone principales)
Einkaufsviertel (hauptgeschäftsstraße, fußgängerzone)

Shopmobility
Shopmobility
Shopmobility

Toilet
Toilettes
Toilette

Tourist Information Centre
Syndicat d'initiative
Information

Viewpoint
Vue panoramique
Aussichtspunkt

Visitor Information Centre
Centre d'information touristique
Besucherzentrum

***Please note:** symbols have been enlarged for clarity*

ABERDEEN

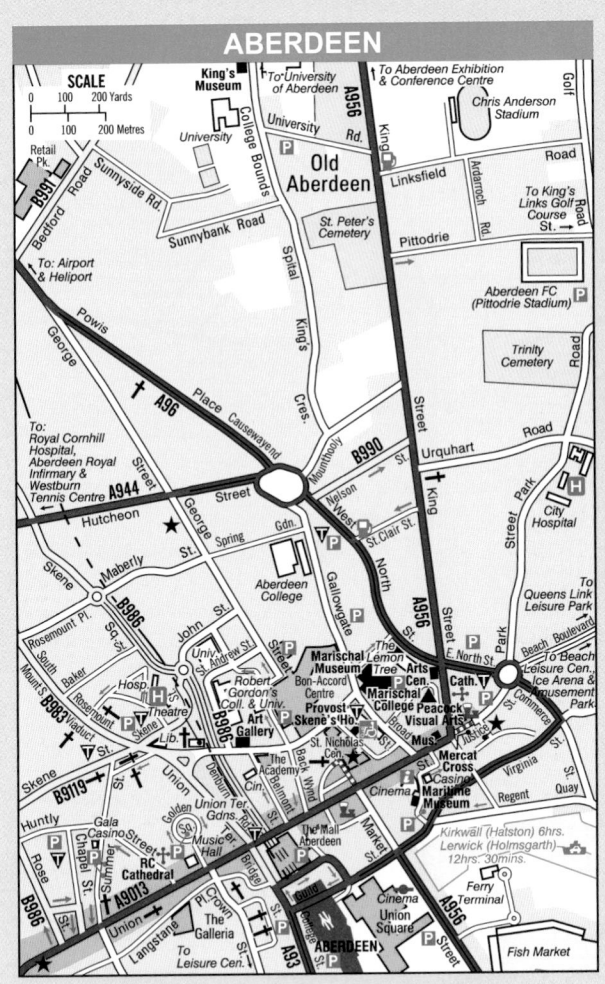

ABERYSTWYTH

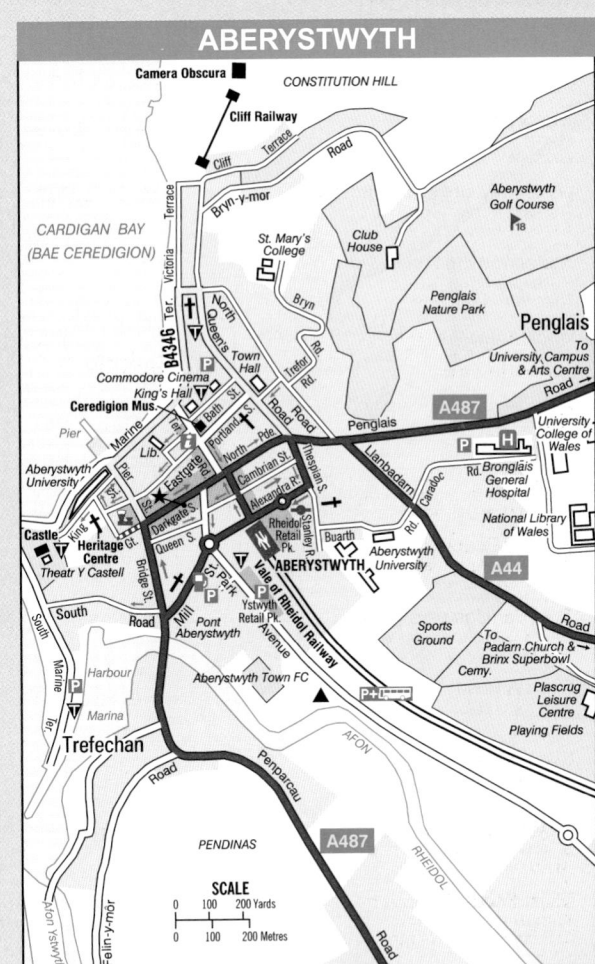

AYR

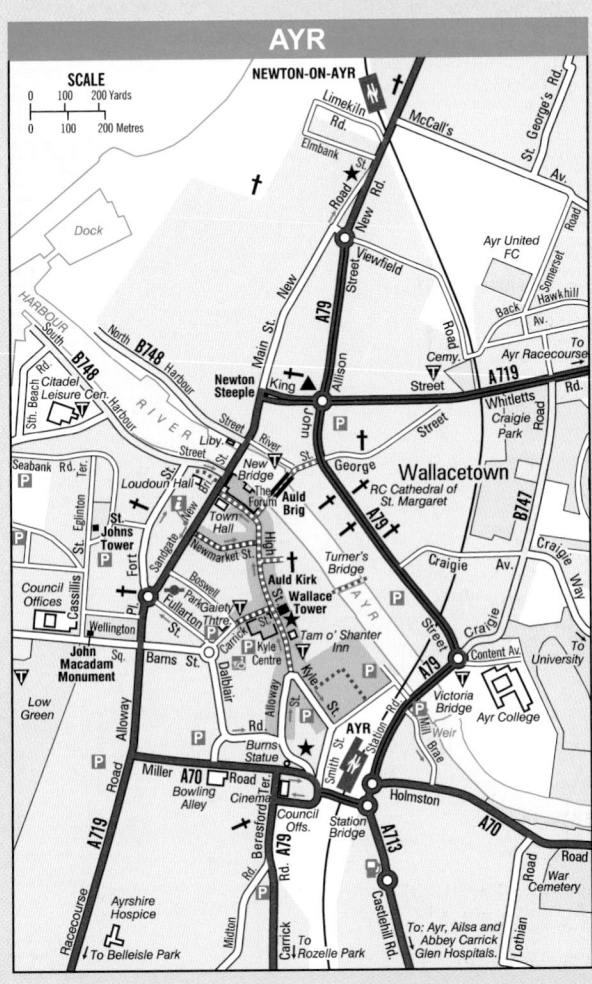

BATH

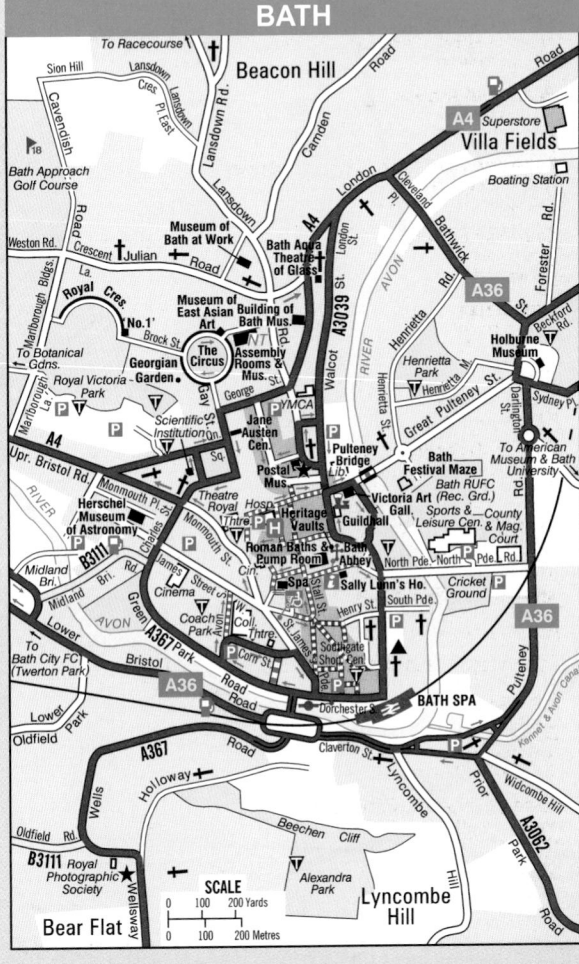

BEDFORD

BLACKPOOL

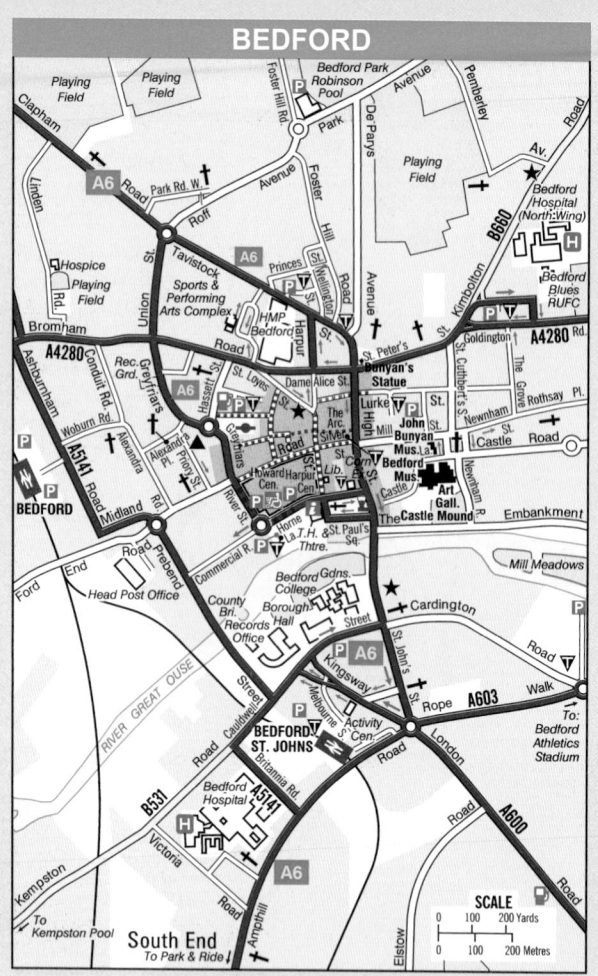

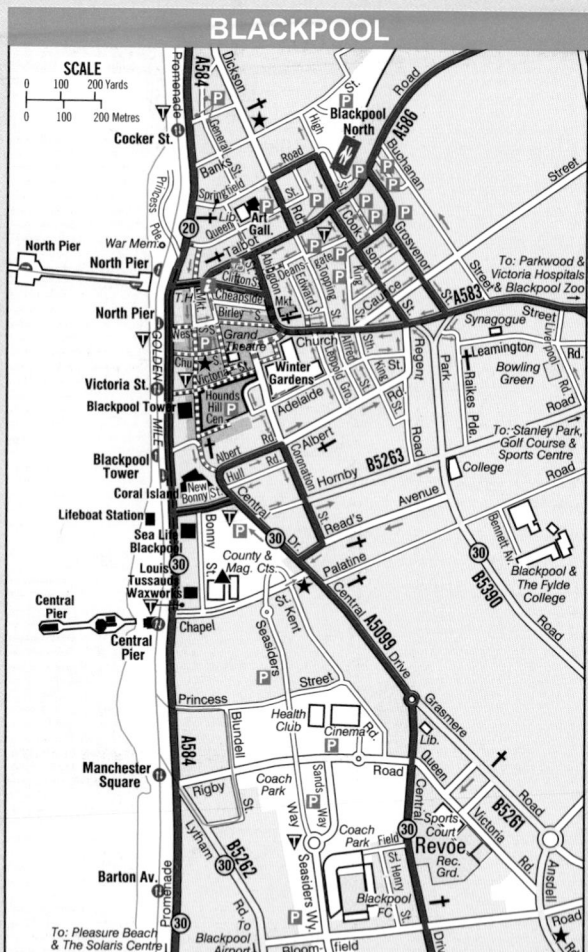

BIRMINGHAM (CITY CENTRE)

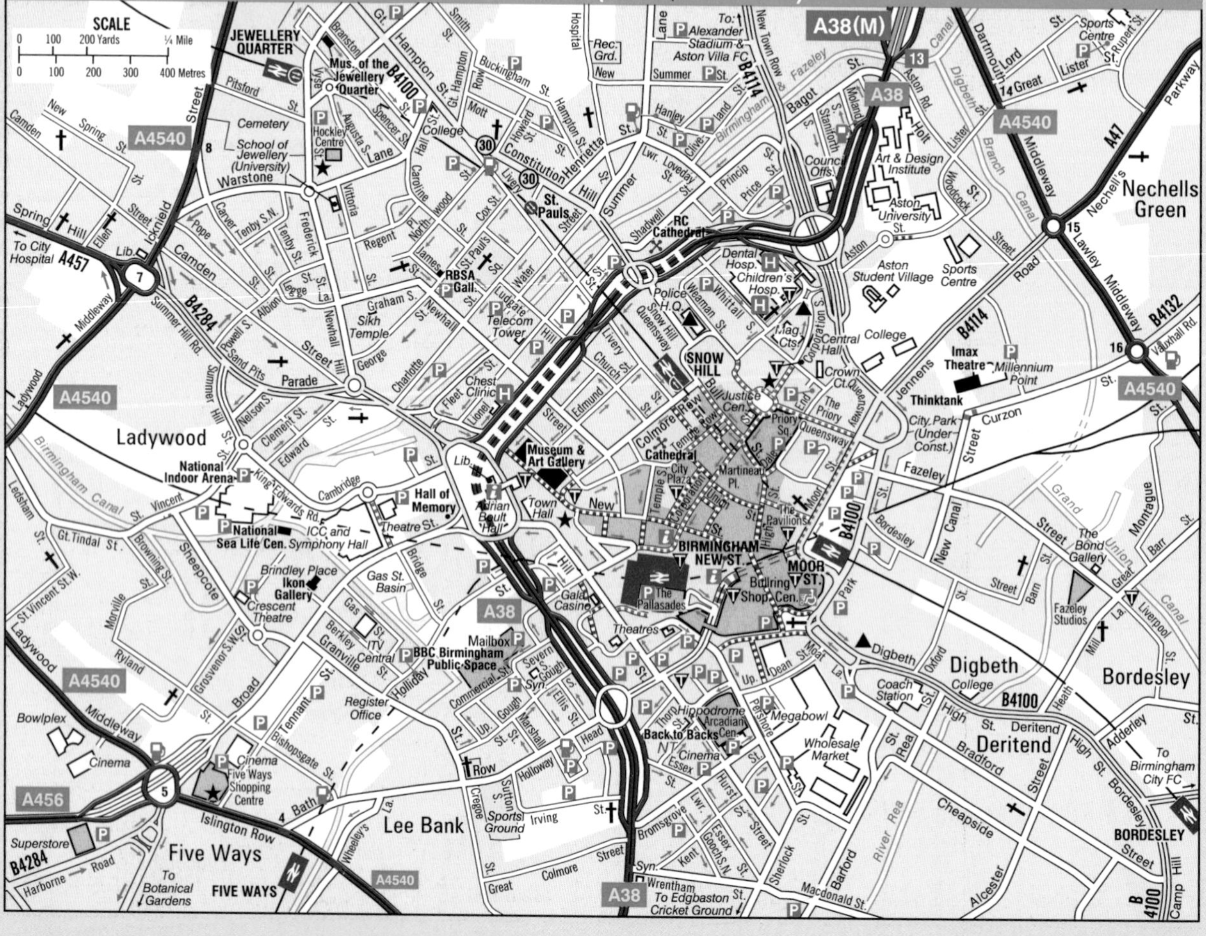

BRIGHTON and HOVE

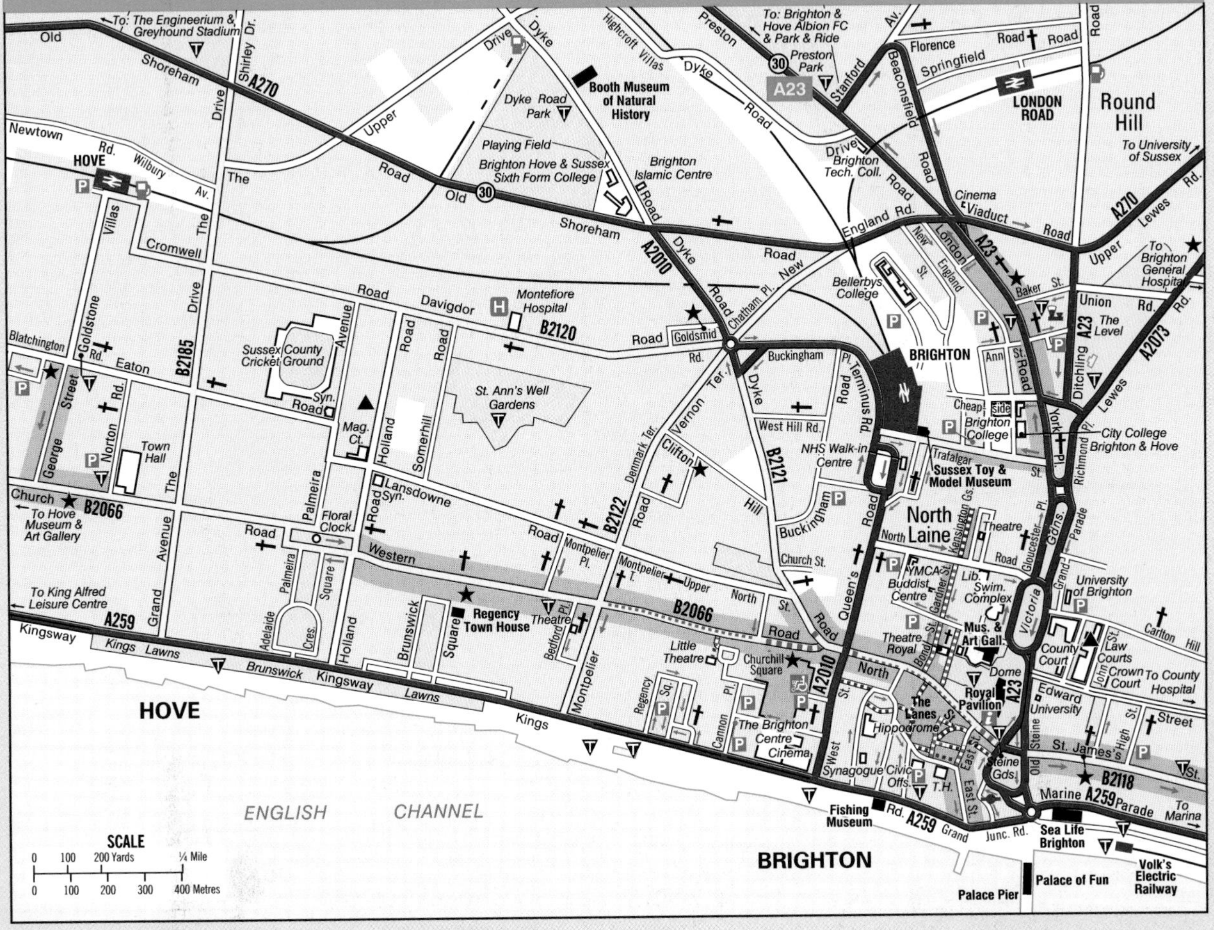

To: The Engineerium & Greyhound Stadium
Old Shoreham Road
Newtown Rd.
Wilbury Dyke Road Drive
HOVE
Booth Museum of Natural History
Dyke Road Park
To: Brighton & Hove Albion FC & Park & Ride
Preston Park
Highcroft Villas
Florence Road
Springfield
LONDON ROAD
Round Hill
Shirley Dr.
A270
Upper Drive
A2010
Dyke Road
A23
Stanford
Beaconsfield
To University of Sussex
Shoreham Road
Playing Field
Brighton Hove & Sussex Sixth Form College
Brighton Islamic Centre
Brighton Tech. Coll.
England Rd.
New England Road
Viaduct
Cinema
A270
Lewes Road
To Brighton General Hospital
Montefiore Hospital
Davigdor Road
B2120
Goldsmid Rd.
Buckingham Road
Bellerbys College
Baker St.
Union Rd.
The Level
Ditchling
A2073
Sussex County Cricket Ground
B2185
Eaton Road
Holland Road
Somerhill
Vernon Ter.
Dyke Rd.
West Hill Rd.
BRIGHTON
Cheapside
Brighton College
City College Brighton & Hove
Richmond
Blatchington Rd.
Norton Rd.
George Street
Town Hall
Palmeira Avenue
St. Ann's Well Gardens
Mag. Ct.
Lansdowne Syn.
Floral Clock
Denmark Ter.
Clifton Hill
NHS Walk-in Centre
Trafalgar St.
Sussex Toy & Model Museum
North Laine
Lib. Swim. Complex
University of Brighton
Carlton Hill
Church Rd.
B2066
To Hove Museum & Art Gallery
Grand Avenue
Western Road
Montpelier Pl.
Montpelier Rd.
Upper North St.
B2066
Church St.
YMCA Buddhist Centre
Theatre Royal
Mus. & Art Gall.
Law Courts
Crown & County Court
To County Hospital
To King Alfred Leisure Centre
A259
Kingsway
Kings Lawns
Brunswick Square
Regency Town House
Theatre
Bedford Sq.
Little Theatre
B2066
Queen's Road
The Brighton Centre Cinema
Dome
Royal Pavilion
Edward Street
University
HOVE
Kingsway
Kings Lawns
Regency Sq.
Cannon St.
West St.
Churchill Square
A2010
North St.
The Lanes
Hippodrome
Synagogue
Civic Offs.
T.H.
St. James's
High St.
Steine Gds.
B2118
Marine
A259
Parade
To Marina

ENGLISH CHANNEL

Fishing Museum
Palace of Fun
Sea Life Brighton
Volk's Electric Railway

BRIGHTON

Palace Pier

SCALE
0 100 200 Yards ¼ Mile
0 100 200 300 400 Metres

BRISTOL

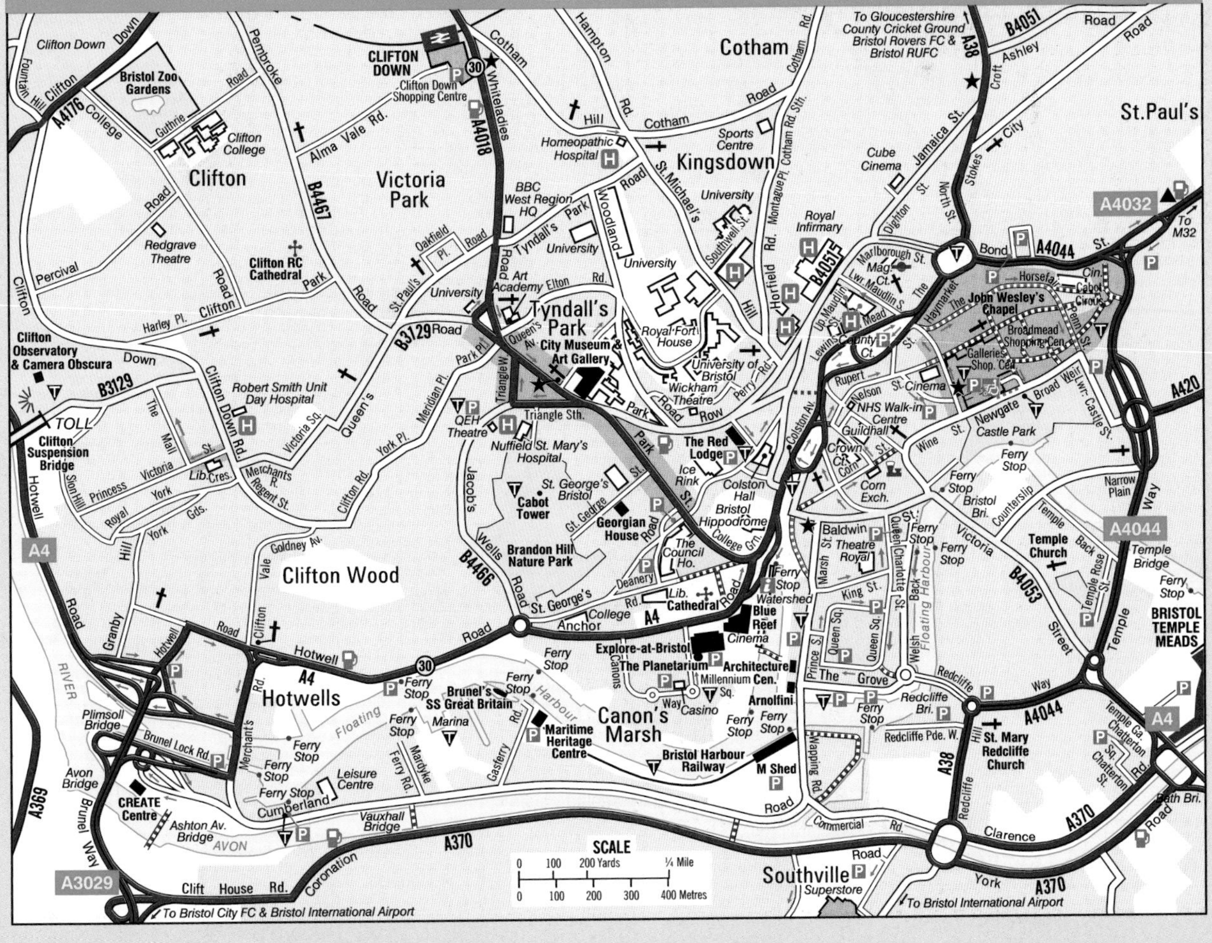

Clifton Down
Bristol Zoo Gardens
CLIFTON DOWN
Clifton Down Shopping Centre
Cotham
To Gloucestershire County Cricket Ground
Bristol Rovers FC & Bristol RUFC
B4051
Ashley Road
St. Paul's
Clifton College
A4176
Pembroke Road
Whiteladies Road
A4018
Cotham Hill
Sports Centre
Kingsdown
Cube Cinema
Jamaica St.
A4032
To M32
Clifton
Victoria Park
Homeopathic Hospital
BBC West Region HQ
St. Michael's
University
Royal Infirmary
A4044
Redgrave Theatre
Clifton RC Cathedral
B4467
Oakfield Rd.
Tyndall's Park
University
Art Academy
John Wesley's Chapel
Broadmead Shopping Cen.
Clifton Observatory & Camera Obscura
B3129
Clifton Down
Robert Smith Unit Day Hospital
Tyndall's Park
City Museum & Art Gallery
Royal Fort House
University of Bristol
Wickham Theatre
Galleries Shop. Cen.
A4044
A420
TOLL
Clifton Suspension Bridge
QEH Theatre
Triangle Sth.
The Red Lodge
Ice Rink
NHS Walk-in Centre
Guildhall
Newgate
Castle Park
Ferry Stop
Lib. Cres.
Merchants Rd.
Nuffield St. Mary's Hospital
St. George's Bristol
Colston Hall
Bristol Hippodrome
College Green
Crown Ct.
Corn Exch.
Narrow Plain
Countership
A4
Clifton Wood
B4466
Cabot Tower
Georgian House
Brandon Hill Nature Park
The Council Ho.
Baldwin St.
Theatre Royal
Temple Church
A4044
Temple Bridge
RIVER
Granby Hill
Hotwell Road
Cathedral
Watershed
Blue Reef Cinema
Queen Sq.
King St.
Victoria St.
B4053
BRISTOL TEMPLE MEADS
Plimsoll Bridge
A4
Hotwells
Brunel's SS Great Britain
Marina
Explore-at-Bristol
The Planetarium
Architecture Centre
Millennium Cen.
Casino
Arnolfini
Redcliffe
A38
St. Mary Redcliffe Church
A4
Avon Bridge
Maritime Heritage Centre
Canon's Marsh
Bristol Harbour Railway
M Shed
Wapping Rd.
Redcliffe Pde. W.
A4044
A369
CREATE Centre
Ashton Av. Bridge
AVON
Leisure Centre
Cumberland Rd.
Vauxhall Bridge
A370
Southville Superstore
Clarence Rd.
A370
A3029
Clift House Rd.
Coronation Road
Commercial Rd.
York Rd.
To Bristol International Airport
To Bristol City FC & Bristol International Airport

SCALE
0 100 200 Yards ¼ Mile
0 100 200 300 400 Metres

BOURNEMOUTH

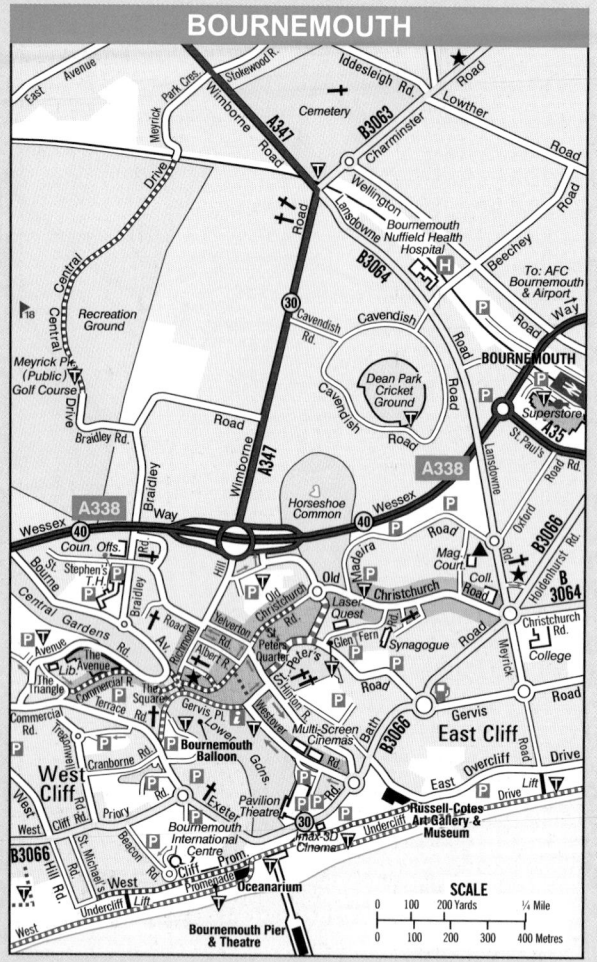

BRADFORD

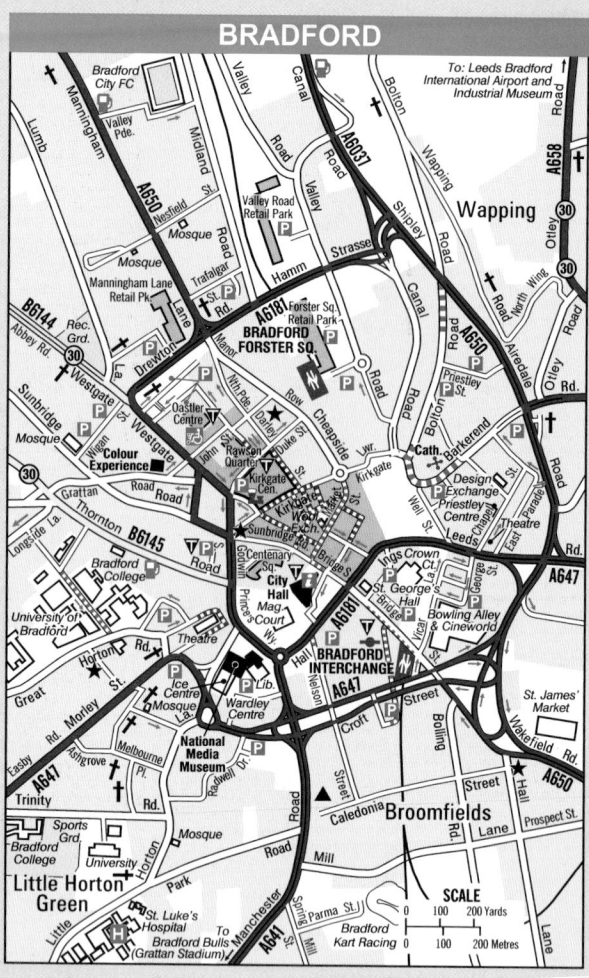

CAERNARFON

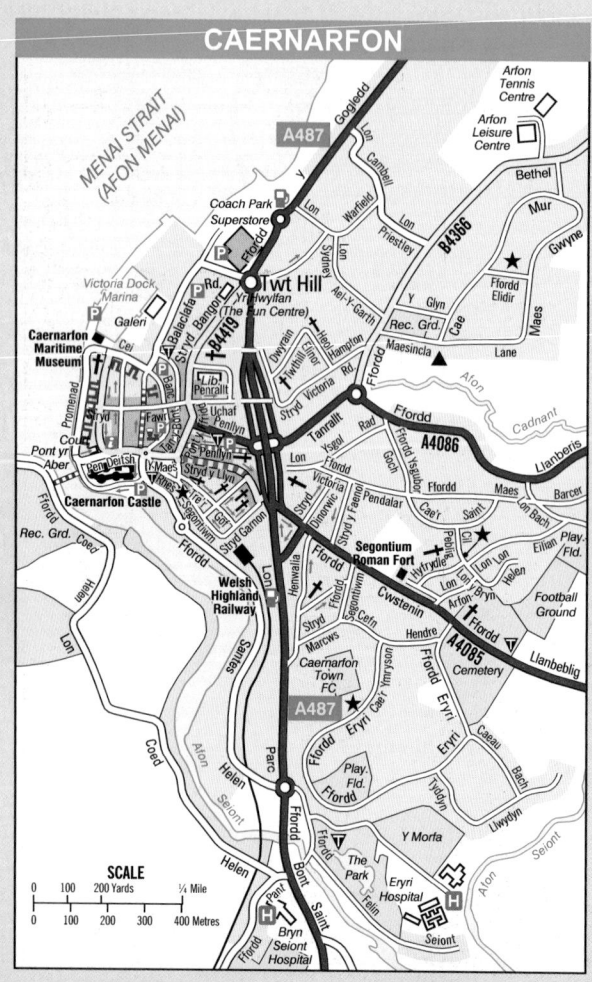

CANTERBURY

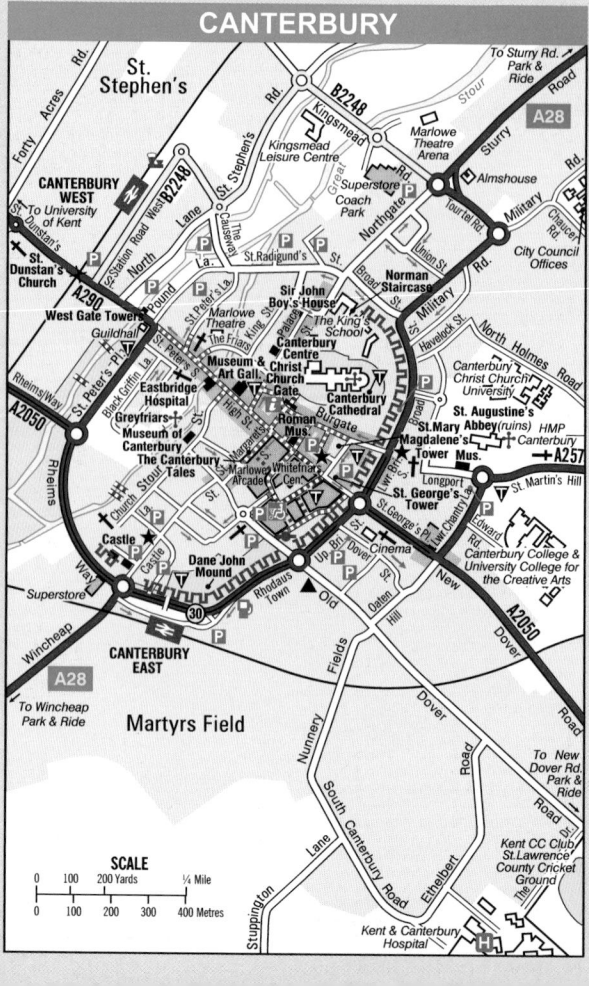

CAMBRIDGE

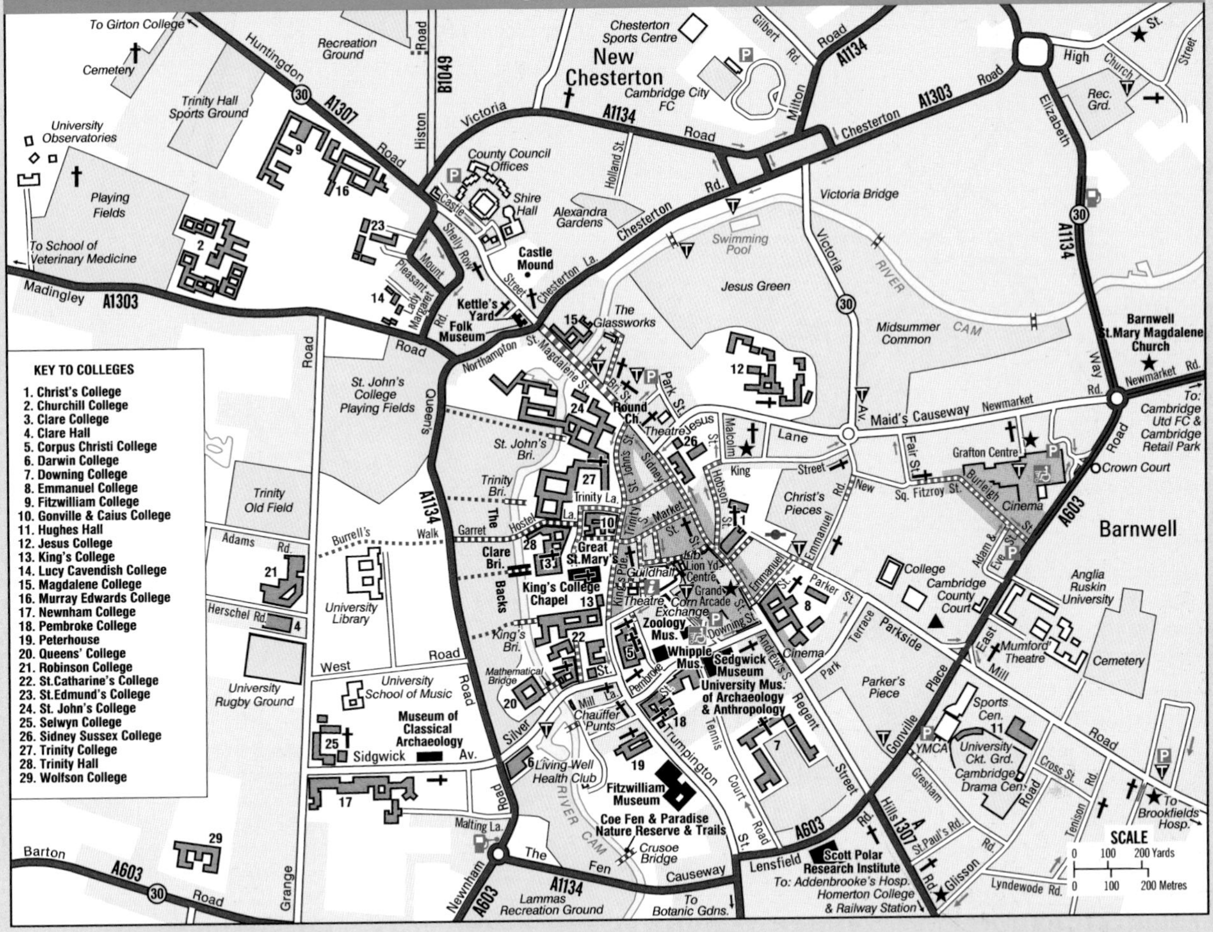
KEY TO COLLEGES
1. Christ's College
2. Churchill College
3. Clare College
4. Clare Hall
5. Corpus Christi College
6. Darwin College
7. Downing College
8. Emmanuel College
9. Fitzwilliam College
10. Gonville & Caius College
11. Hughes Hall
12. Jesus College
13. King's College
14. Lucy Cavendish College
15. Magdalene College
16. Murray Edwards College
17. Newnham College
18. Pembroke College
19. Peterhouse
20. Queens' College
21. Robinson College
22. St.Catharine's College
23. St.Edmund's College
24. St. John's College
25. Selwyn College
26. Sidney Sussex College
27. Trinity College
28. Trinity Hall
29. Wolfson College
To Girton College
Cemetery
Recreation Ground
Huntingdon
A1307
Trinity Hall Sports Ground
University Observatories
Playing Fields
To School of Veterinary Medicine
Madingley
A1303
Chesterton Sports Centre
New Chesterton
Cambridge City FC
Victoria
A1134
Road
Histon
B1049
County Council Offices
Shire Hall
Alexandra Gardens
Holland St.
Castle
Castle Mound
Kettle's Yard
Folk Museum
Chesterton La.
Chesterton
Swimming Pool
Jesus Green
Victoria Bridge
Victoria Av.
RIVER CAM
Midsummer Common
Milton
Gilbert Rd.
Chesterton
A1303
High St.
Church St.
Rec. Grd.
Elizabeth Way
A1134
Barnwell St.Mary Magdalene Church
Newmarket Rd.
To: Cambridge Utd FC & Cambridge Retail Park
Crown Court
Barnwell
The Glassworks
Northampton St.
Magdalene St.
Bridge St.
Park St.
Round Ch.
Theatre
Jesus Lane
Malcolm St.
Maid's Causeway
Newmarket
Grafton Centre
Burleigh St.
Cinema
Fitzroy St.
New Sq.
King Street
Christ's Pieces
Emmanuel Rd.
St. John's College Playing Fields
Queens Road
St. John's Bri.
Trinity Bri.
Trinity La.
Trinity St.
Sidney St.
Hobson St.
The Backs
Clare Bri.
Garret Hostel La.
Great St.Mary's
King's College Chapel
Market
Guildhall
Lion Yd. Centre
Grand Arcade
Corn Exchange
Zoology Mus.
Downing St.
Whipple Mus.
Sedgwick Museum
University Mus. of Archaeology & Anthropology
Parker St.
Parkside
Parker's Piece
Park Terrace
College
Cambridge County Court
Anglia Ruskin University
Mumford Theatre
East Mill Rd.
Cemetery
Trinity Old Field
Burrell's Walk
Adams Rd.
Herschel Rd.
University Library
West Road
University Rugby Ground
University School of Music
Museum of Classical Archaeology
Sidgwick Av.
Mathematical Bridge
King's Bri.
Silver St.
Mill La.
Chauffer Punts
Pembroke St.
Trumpington St.
Living Well Health Club
Fitzwilliam Museum
Coe Fen & Paradise Nature Reserve & Trails
Crusoe Bridge
Tennis Court Road
Regent Street
Gonville Place
YMCA
Sports Cen.
University Ckt. Grd.
Cambridge Drama Cen.
Gresham Rd.
Cross St.
Tenison Rd.
To Brookfields Hosp.
Malting La.
Barton
A603
Grange Road
Newnham
The Fen Causeway
Lammas Recreation Ground
To Botanic Gdns.
Lensfield Rd.
Scott Polar Research Institute
To: Addenbrooke's Hosp. Homerton College & Railway Station
Hills Rd.
A1307
St. Paul's Rd.
Glisson Rd.
Lyndewode Rd.
SCALE
0 100 200 Yards
0 100 200 Metres

CARDIFF (CAERDYDD)

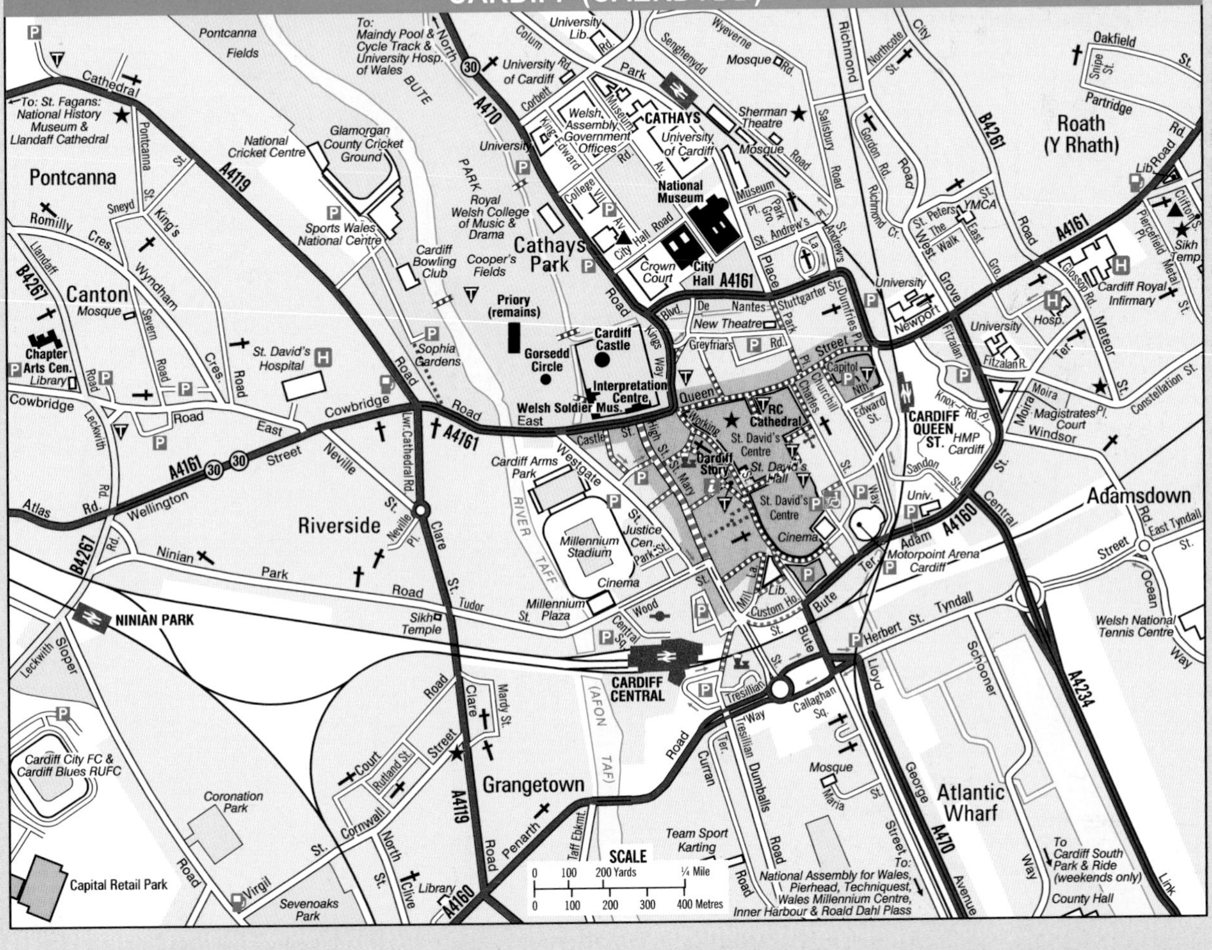
Pontcanna Fields
To: Maindy Pool & Cycle Track & University Hosp. of Wales
North Road
A470
University Lib.
Colum Rd.
University of Cardiff
Corbett Rd.
Park Place
Senghenydd Rd.
Wyeverne Rd.
Mosque
Oakfield St.
Cathedral Rd.
To: St. Fagans: National History Museum & Llandaff Cathedral
Pontcanna St.
Pontcanna
A4119
National Cricket Centre
Glamorgan County Cricket Ground
BUTE PARK
Welsh Assembly Government Offices
CATHAYS
University of Cardiff
Sherman Theatre
Mosque
Salisbury Road
Richmond Rd.
Northcote St.
Partridge Rd.
B4261
Roath (Y Rhath)
Romilly Cres.
Sneyd St.
King's Rd.
Sports Wales National Centre
Royal Welsh College of Music & Drama
Cathays Park
National Museum
City Hall Road
Museum Pl.
Park Gro.
St. Andrew's Pl.
Crown Court
City Hall
A4161
YMCA
Lib.
Road
A4161
Clifton St.
Piercefield Pl.
Sikh Temp.
Cardiff Royal Infirmary
Canton
Mosque
Wyndham Cres.
Severn Road
Cardiff Bowling Club
Cooper's Fields
Priory (remains)
Gorsedd Circle
Cardiff Castle
Interpretation Centre
Welsh Soldier Mus.
Nantes Blvd.
New Theatre
Greyfriars Rd.
Stuttgarter Str.
Dumfries Pl.
University
Newport Rd.
Hosp.
Glossop Rd.
Meteor St.
B4267
Chapter Arts Cen.
Library
St. David's Hospital
Sophia Gardens
Cowbridge Road East
Queen St.
Capitol Ctr.
Churchill Way
Charles St.
RC Cathedral
Edward St.
CARDIFF QUEEN ST.
HMP Cardiff
Moira Ter.
Magistrates Court
Windsor Pl.
Constellation St.
Leckwith Rd.
Lwr.Cathedral Rd.
Neville Street
Atlas Rd.
Wellington St.
Riverside
Castle St.
Westgate St.
Working St.
St. David's Centre
Cardiff Story
St. David's Hall
St. David's Centre
Cinema
Cardiff Arms Park
RIVER TAFF
Millennium Stadium
Justice Cen.
Park St.
Univ.
Adam St.
A4160
Motorpoint Arena Cardiff
Central
Adamsdown
East Tyndall St.
Ninian Park Road
Tudor St.
Sikh Temple
Millennium Plaza
Cinema
Wood St.
Mill La.
Custom Ho. St.
Bute Ter.
Herbert St.
Tyndall St.
Welsh National Tennis Centre
Ocean Way
NINIAN PARK
CARDIFF CENTRAL
Leckwith
Sloper Road
Clare Road
Clare St.
Mardy St.
(AFON TAFF)
Tresillian Way
Callaghan Sq.
Lloyd George Av.
Schooner Way
A4234
Cardiff City FC & Cardiff Blues RUFC
Court Rd.
Rutland St.
Clare Street
A4119
Grangetown
Curran Rd.
Tresillian Ter.
Dumballs Road
Mosque
Maria St.
Atlantic Wharf
A470
Coronation Park
Cornwall St.
North Clive St.
Penarth Rd.
Taff Embkmt.
Team Sport Karting
Capital Retail Park
Virgil St.
Sevenoaks Park
Library
A4160
SCALE
0 100 200 Yards ¼ Mile
0 100 200 300 400 Metres
To: National Assembly for Wales, Pierhead, Techniquest, Wales Millennium Centre, Inner Harbour & Roald Dahl Plass
To Cardiff South Park & Ride (weekends only)
County Hall
Link

CARLISLE

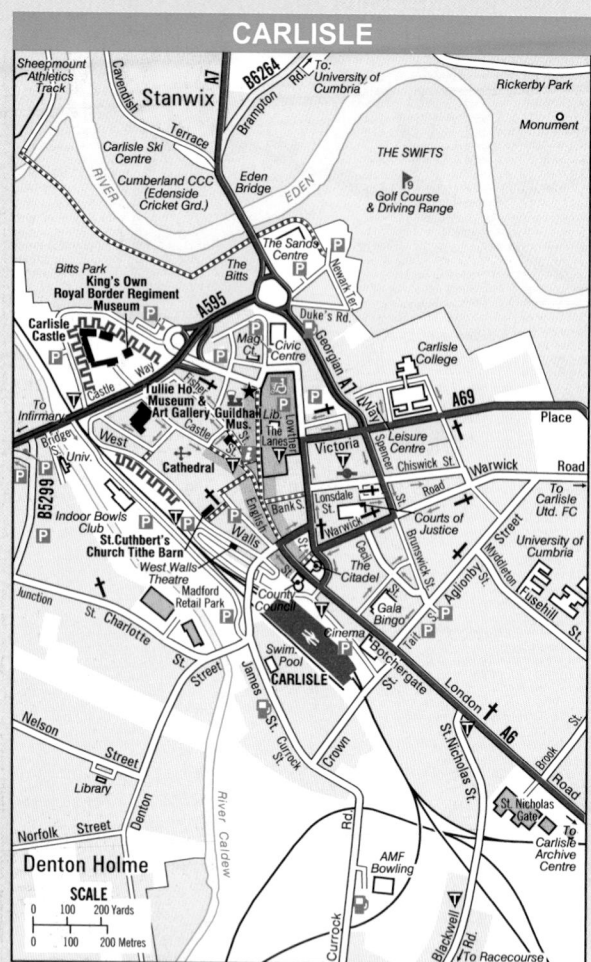

CHELTENHAM

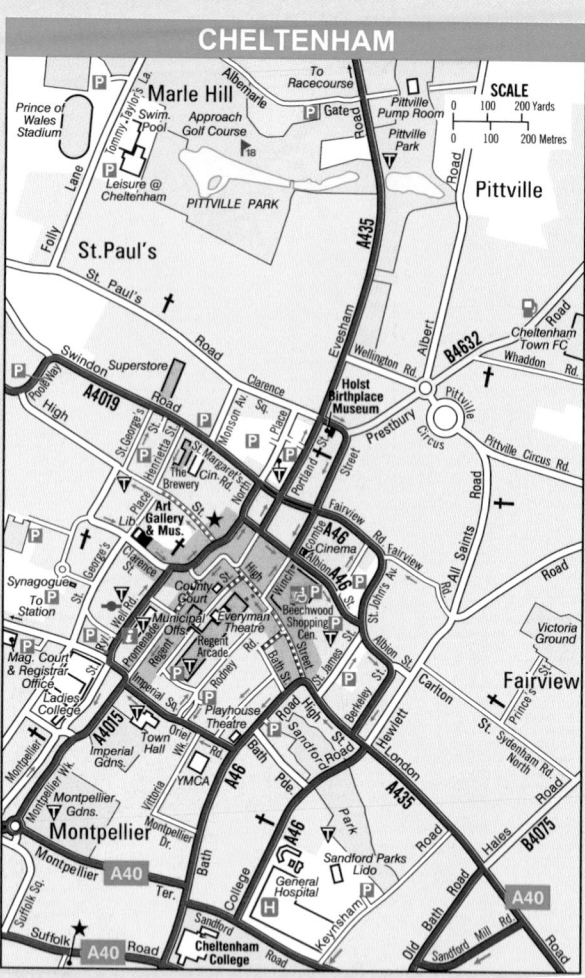

CHESTER

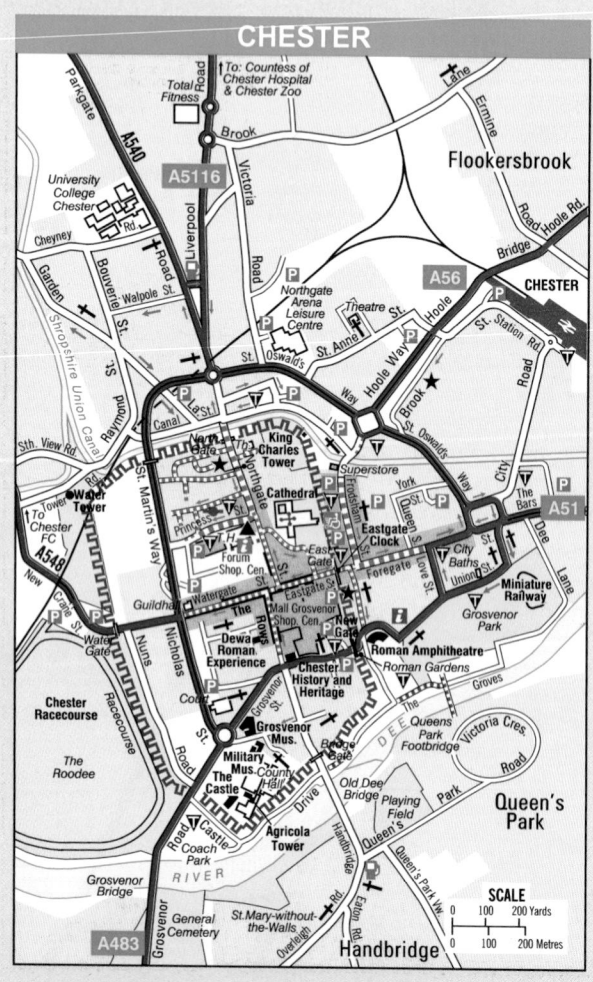

COVENTRY

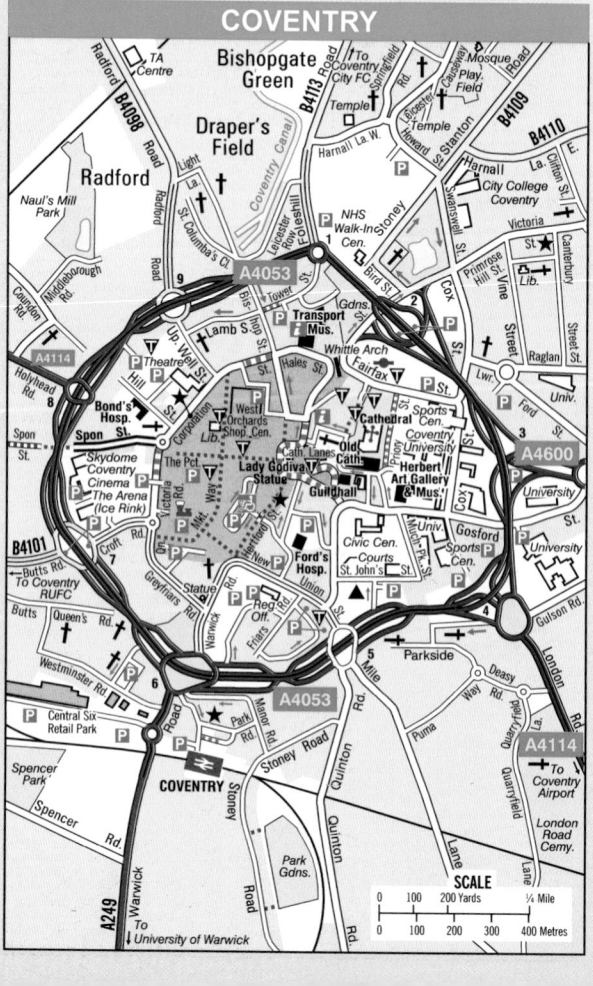

DERBY

DUMFRIES

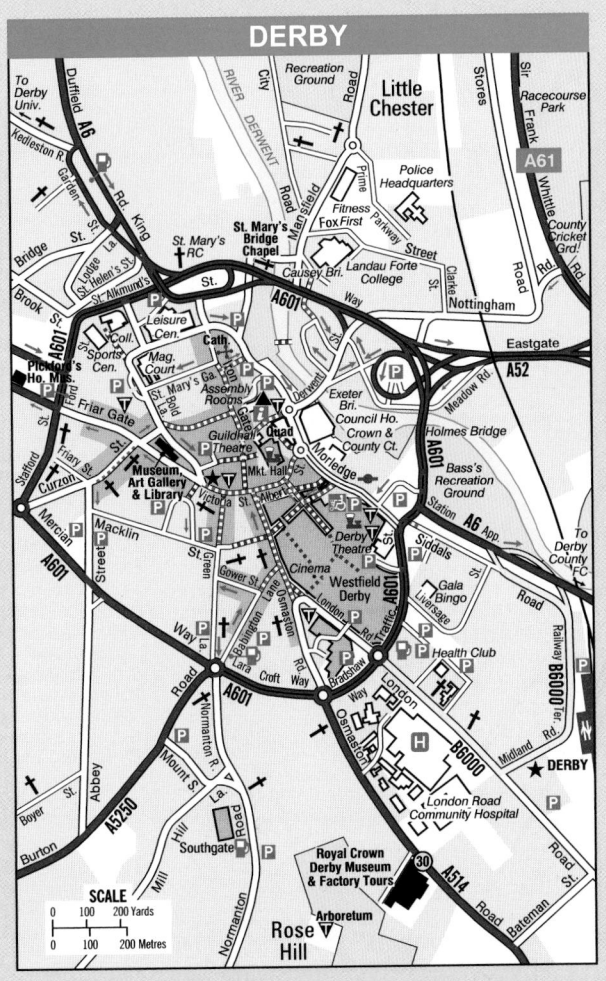

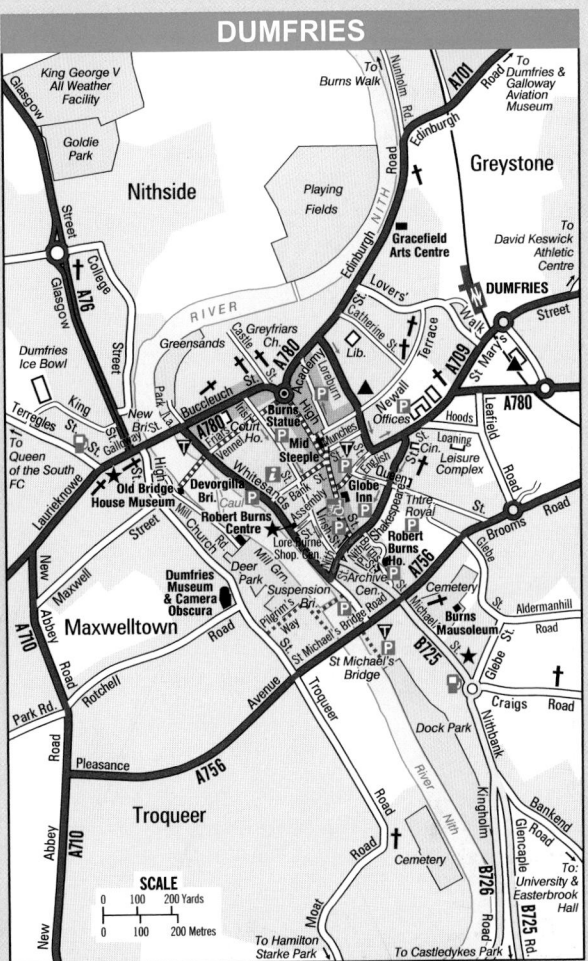

DOVER

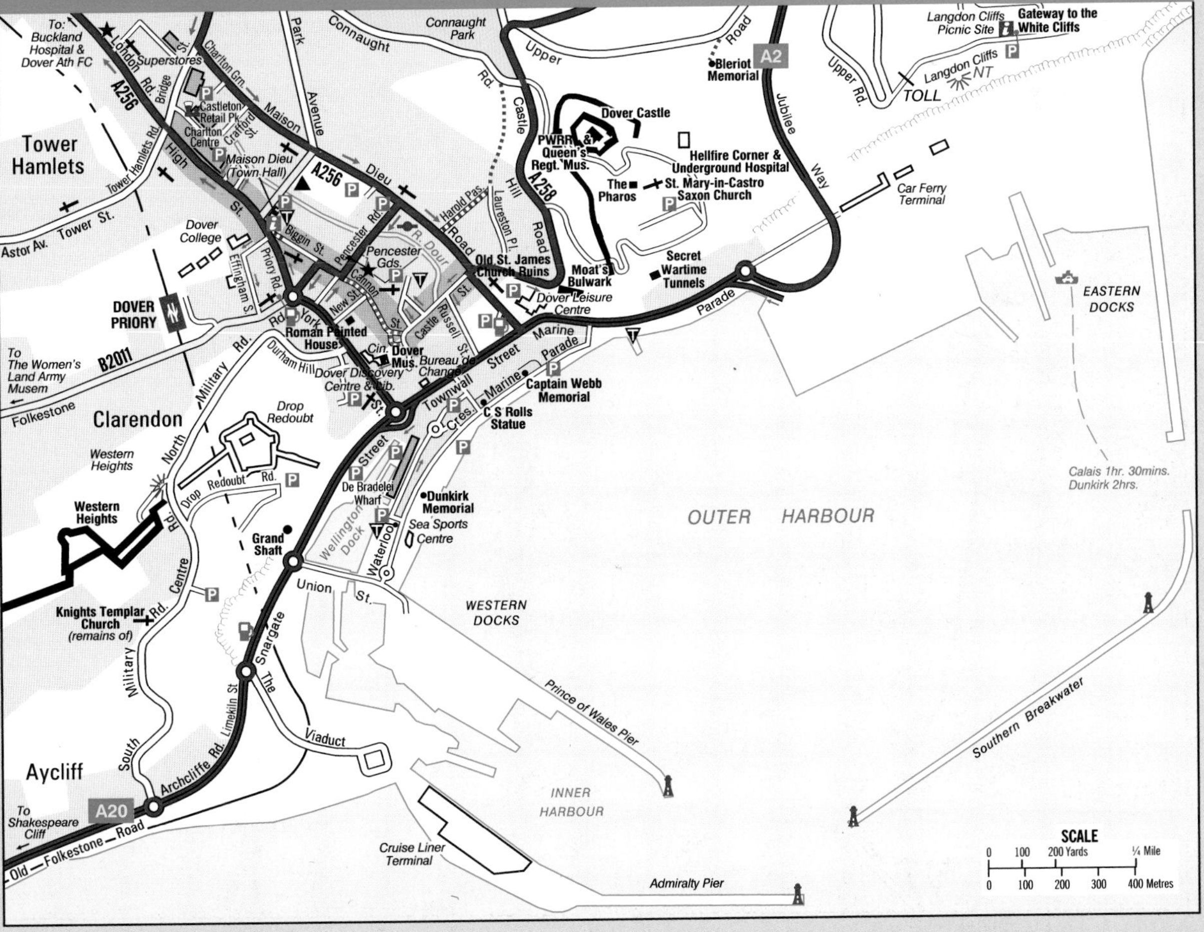

DUNDEE

DURHAM

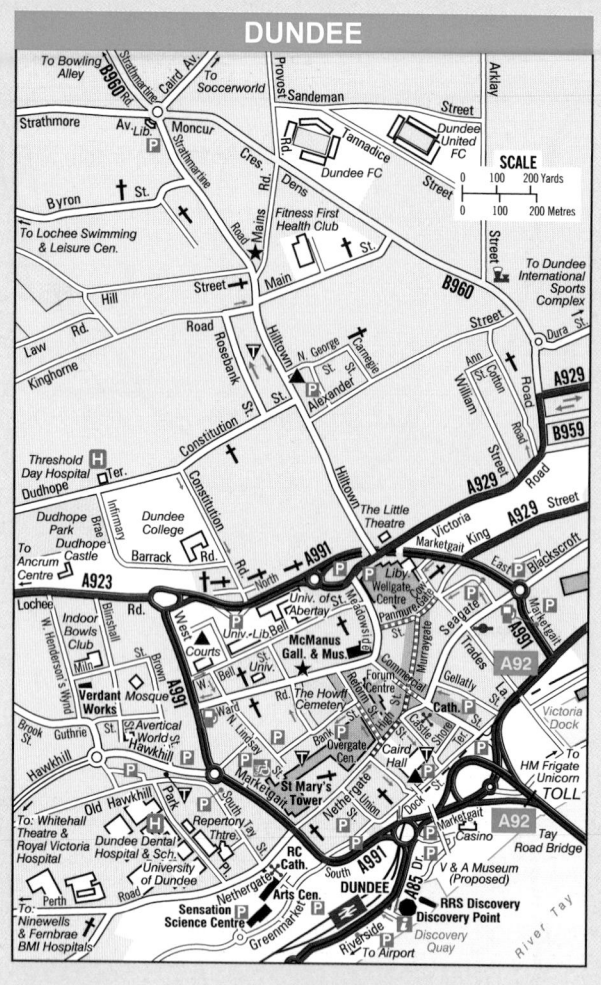

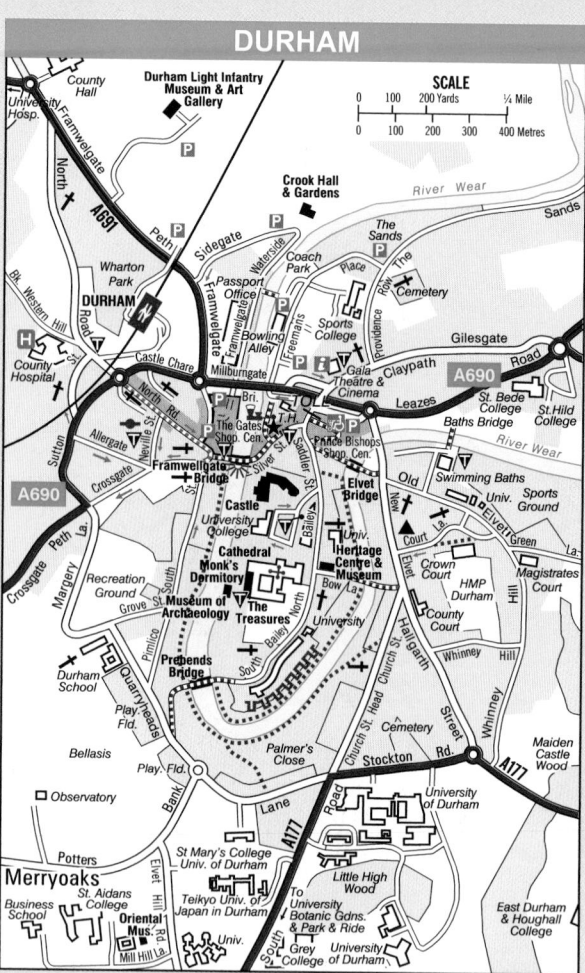

EDINBURGH

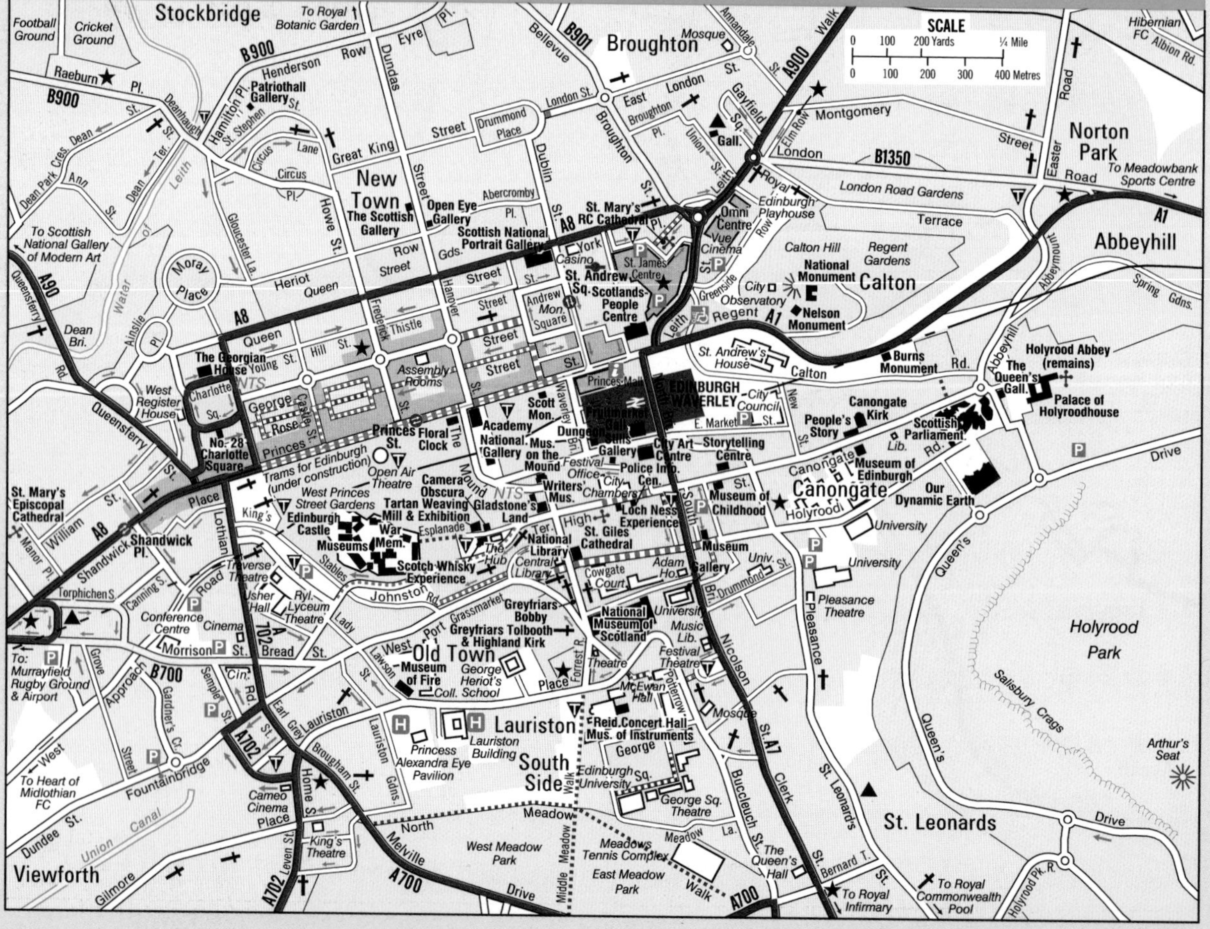

EXETER

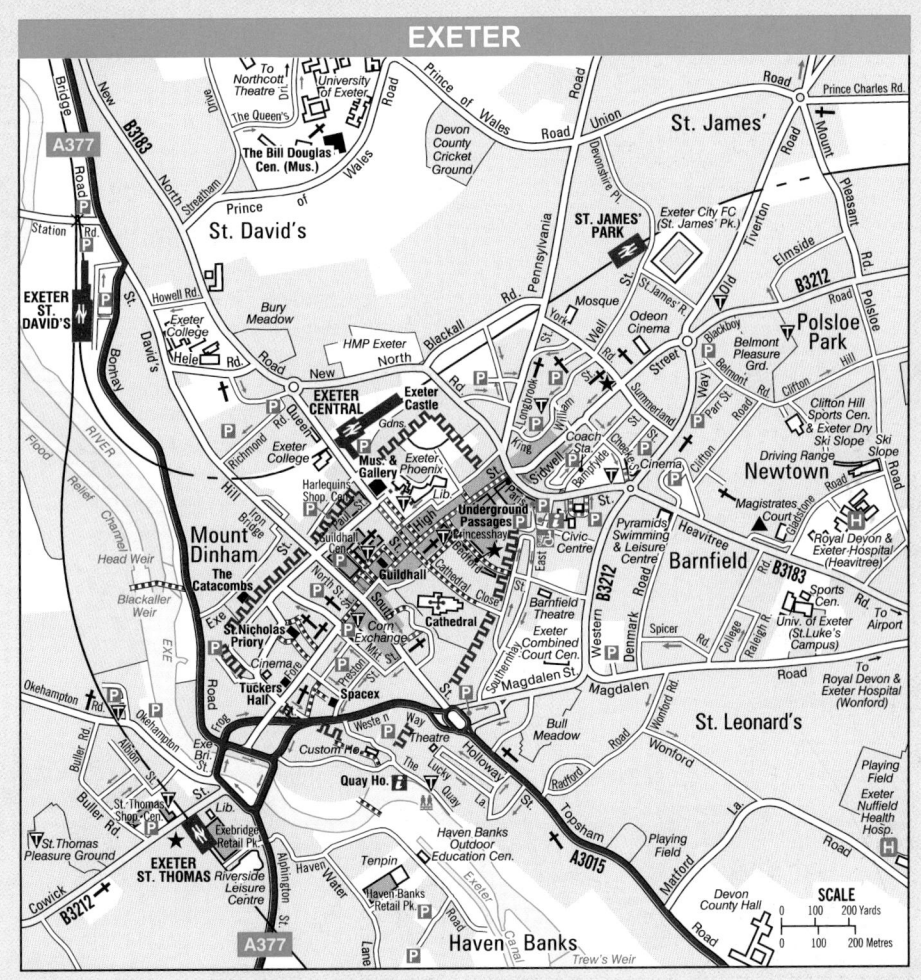

EASTBOURNE

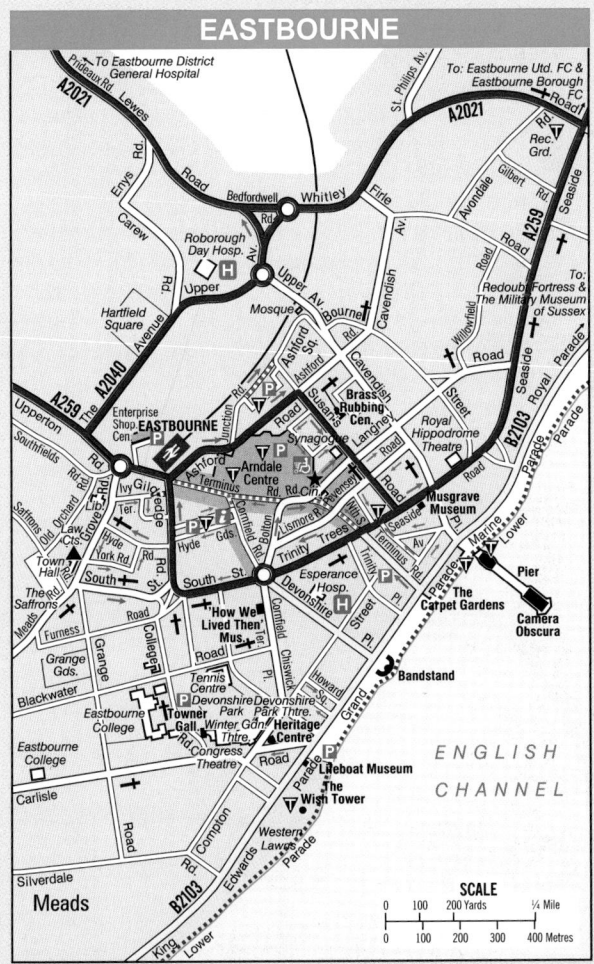

FOLKESTONE

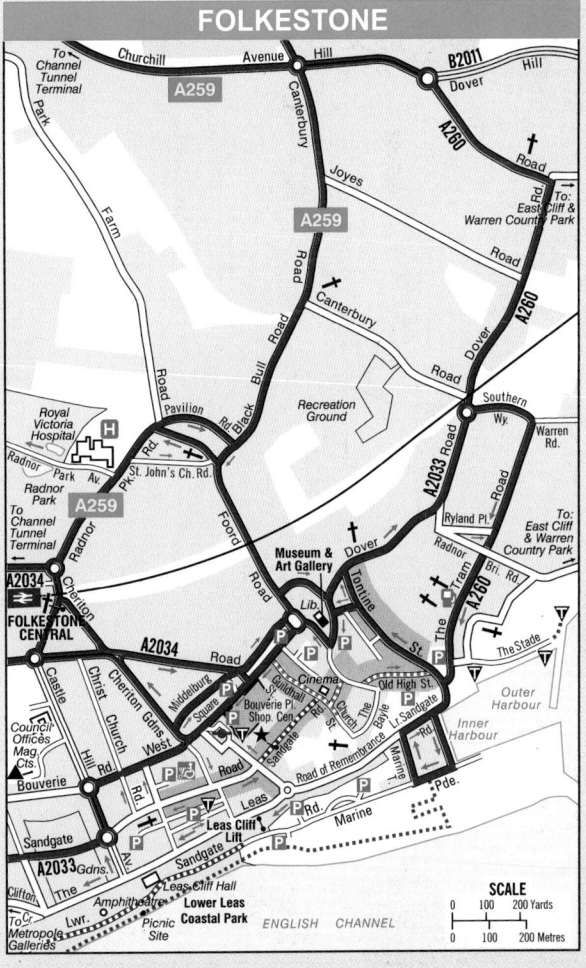

GLASGOW

GLOUCESTER

GREAT YARMOUTH

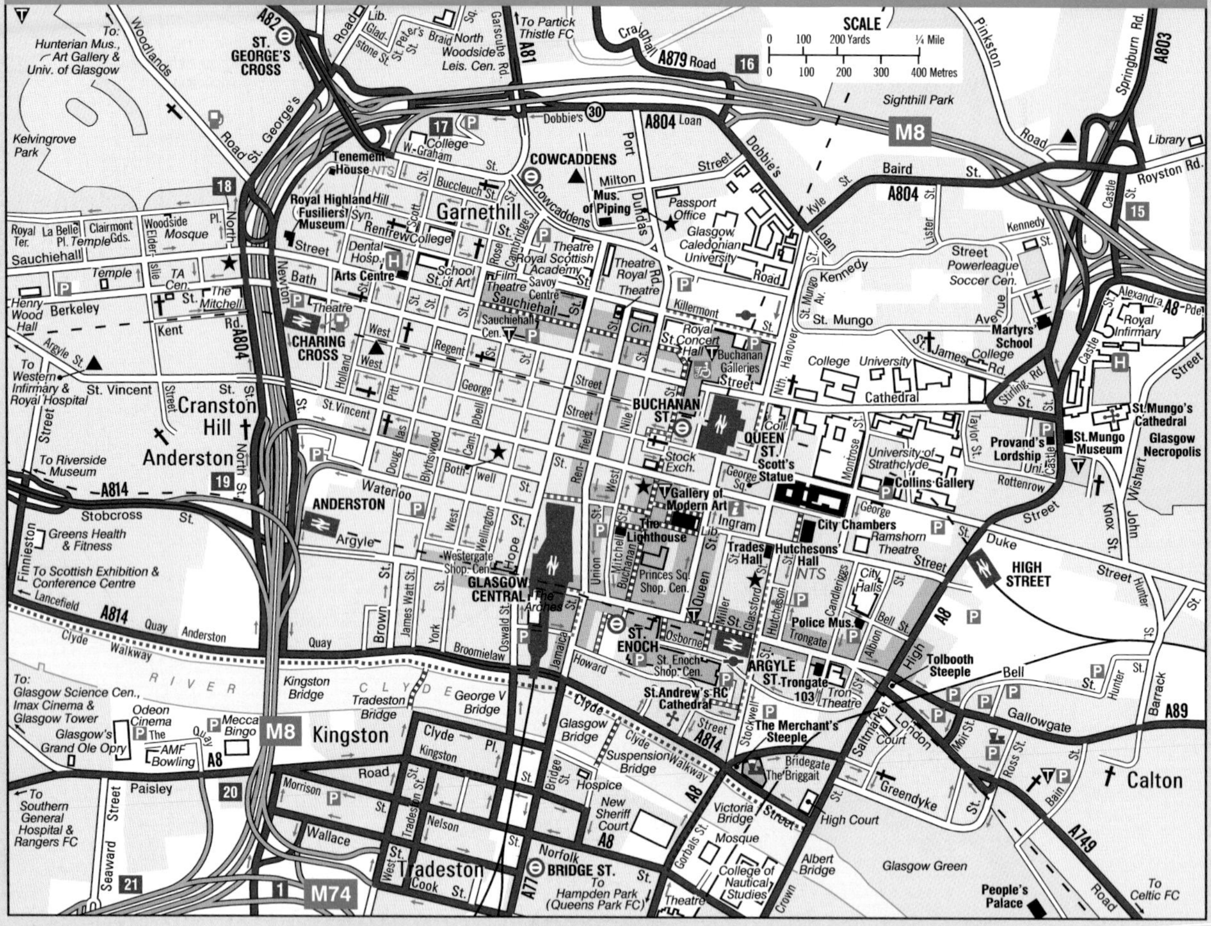

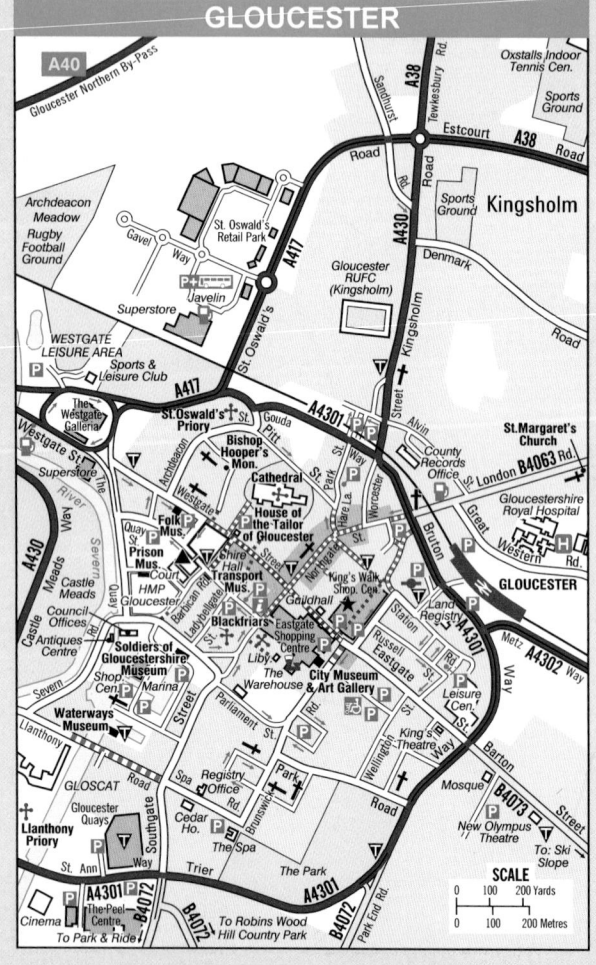

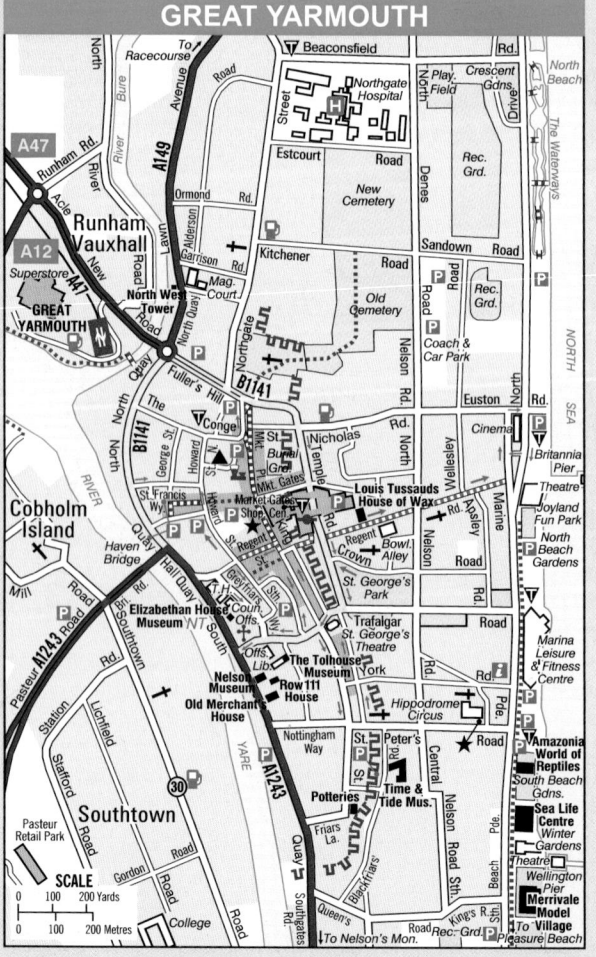

GUILDFORD

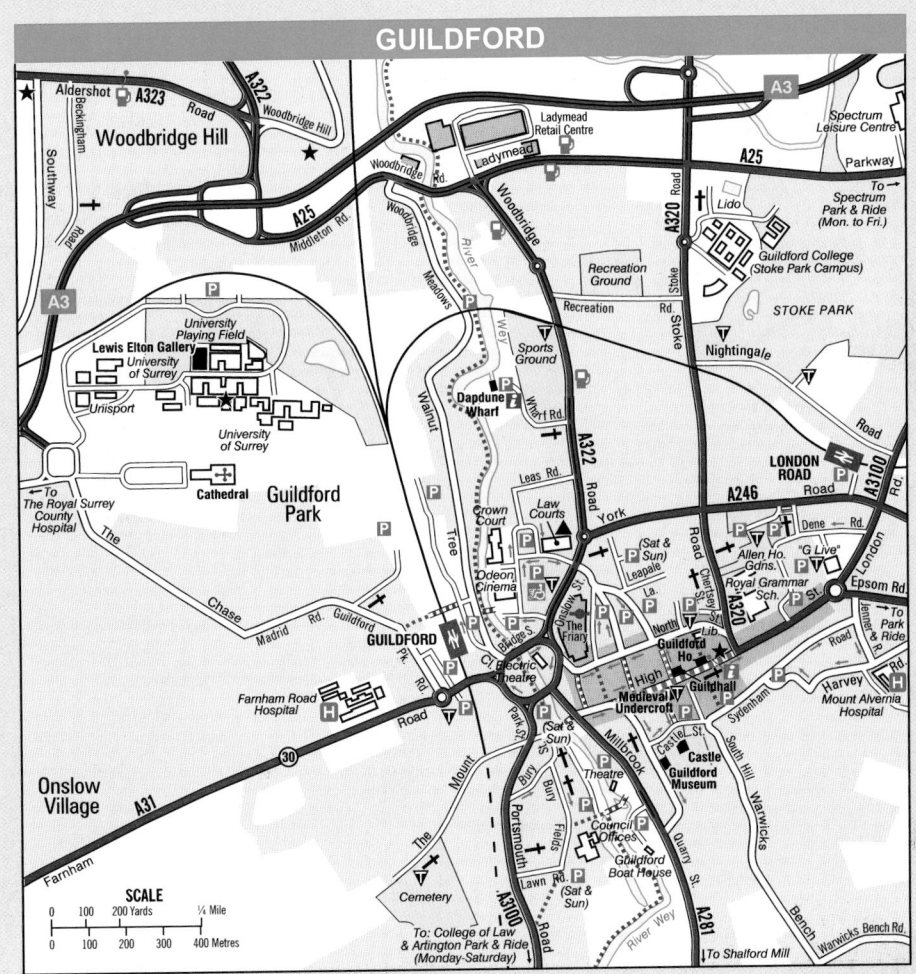

HARROGATE

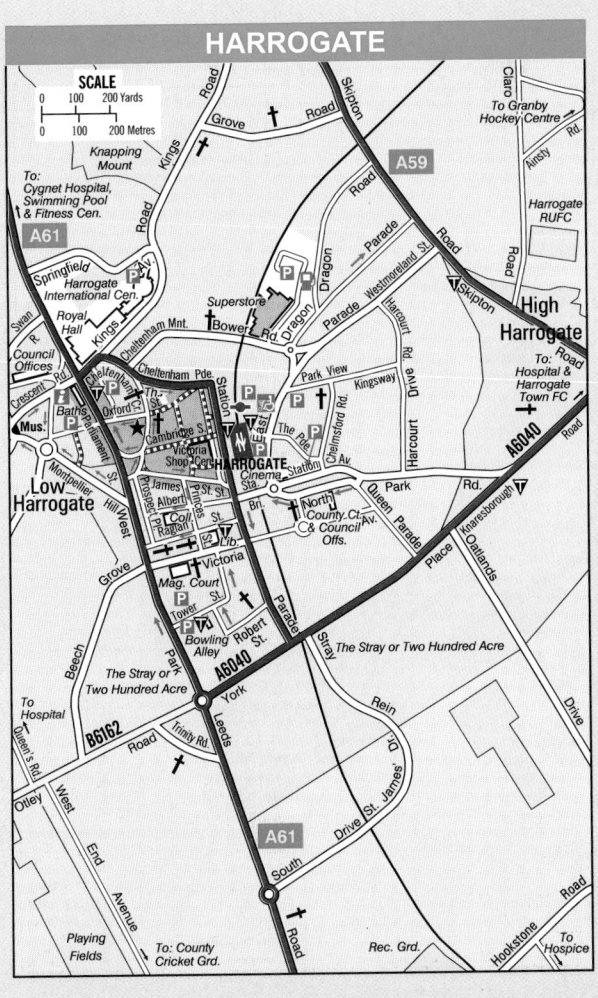

HEREFORD

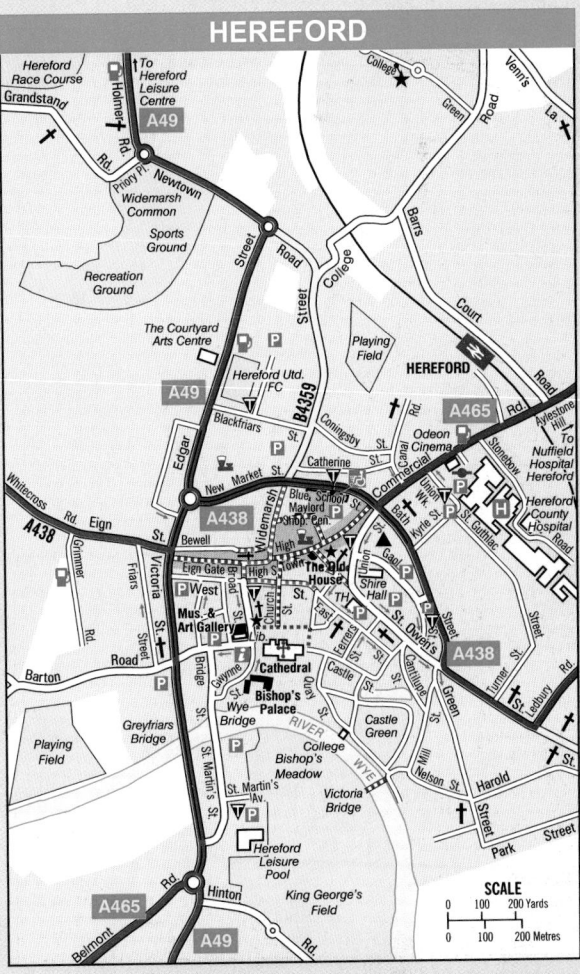

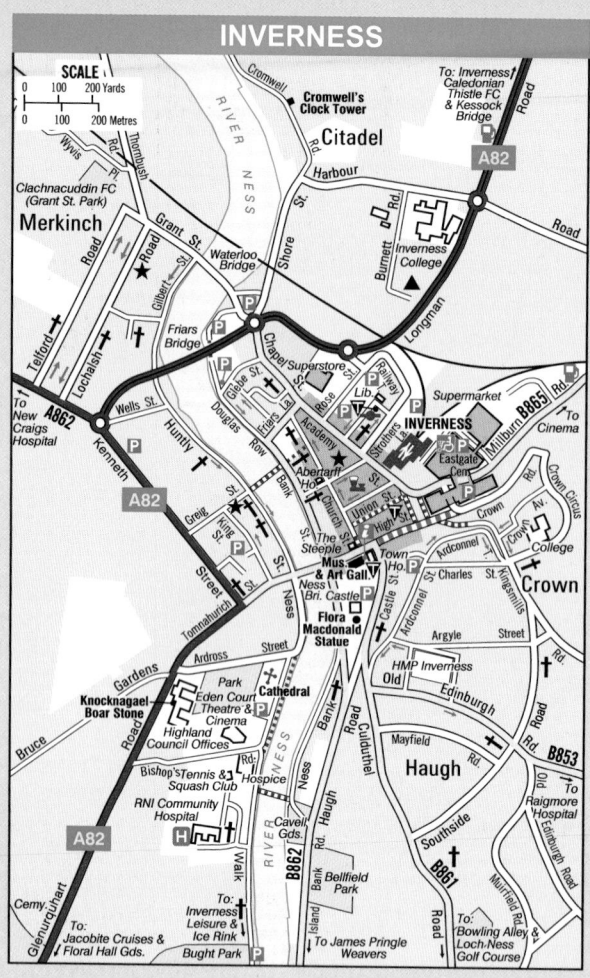

INVERNESS

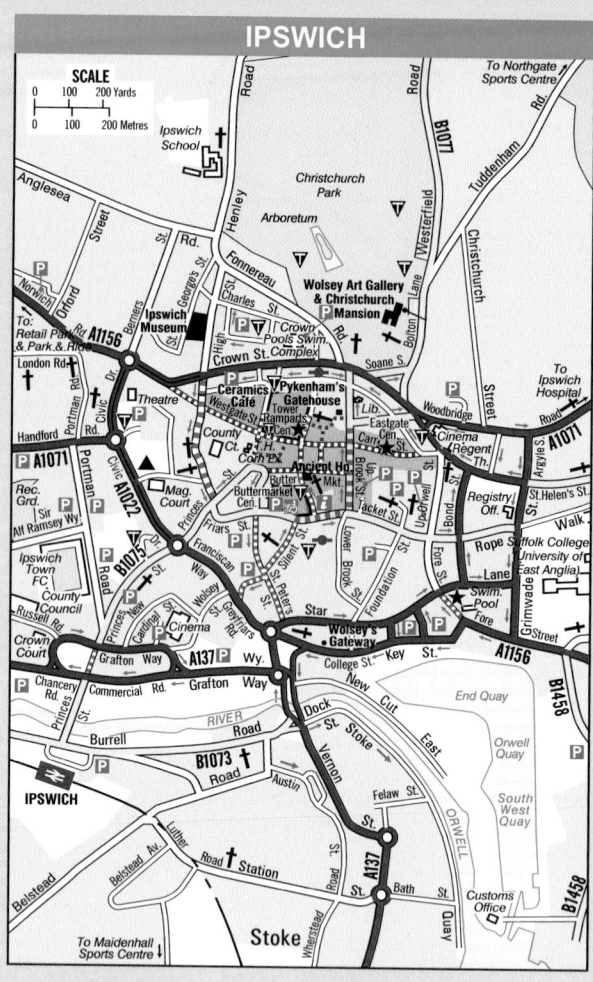

IPSWICH

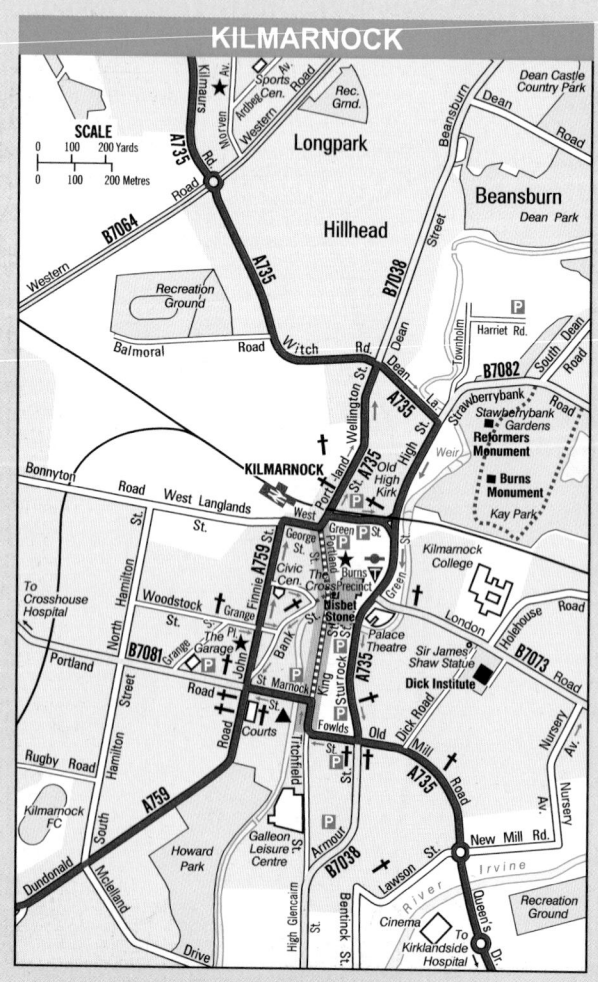

KILMARNOCK

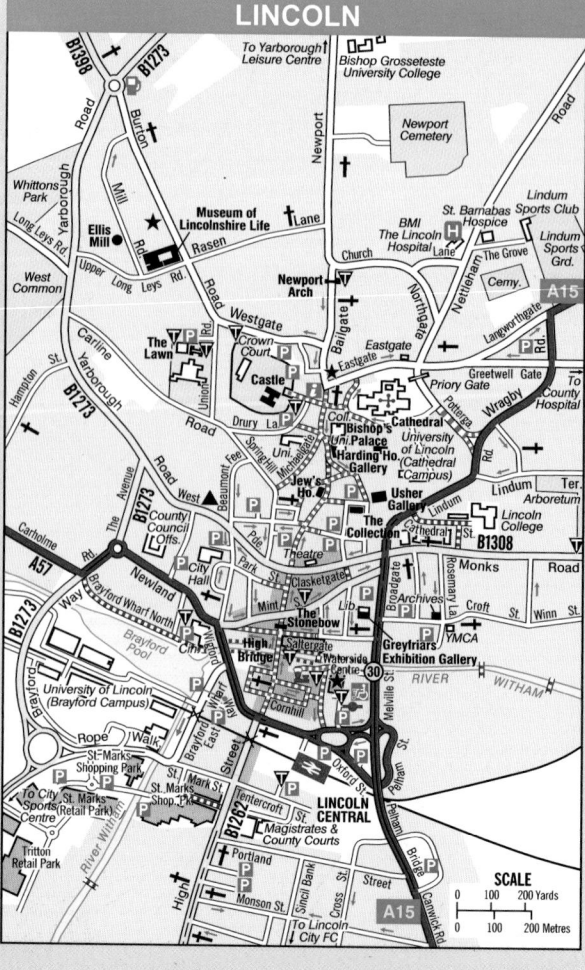

LINCOLN

KINGSTON upon HULL

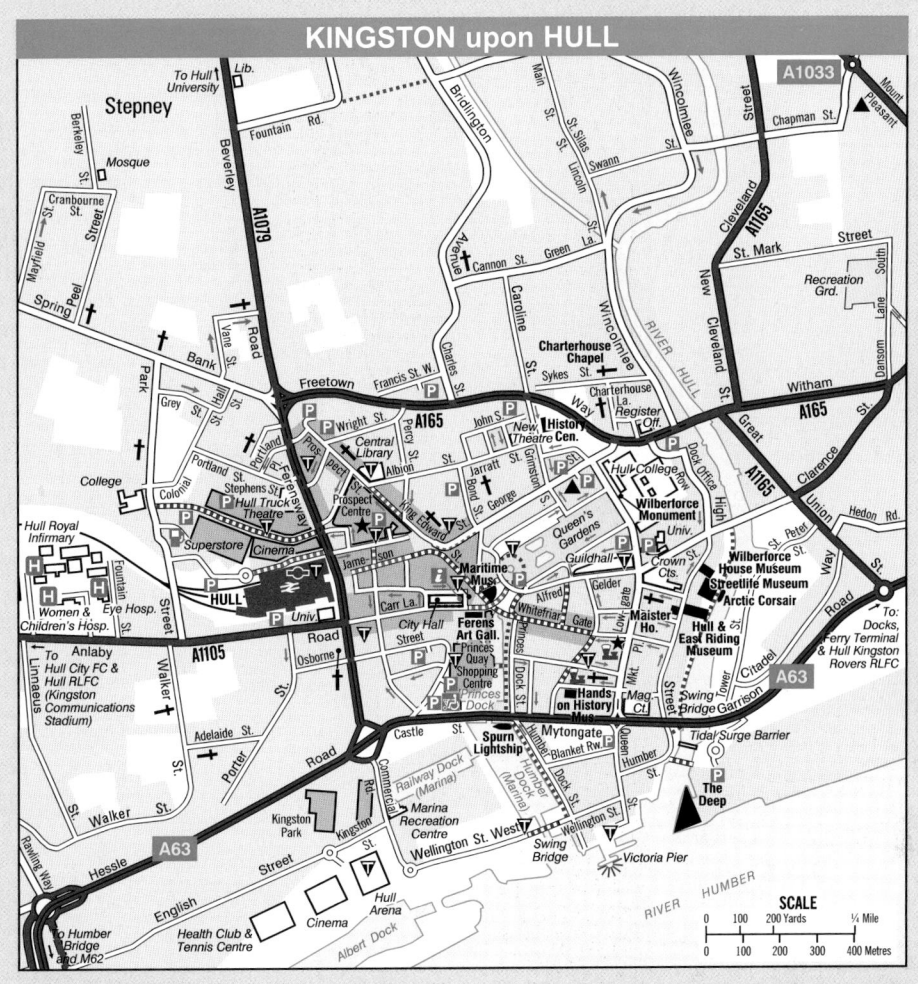

LEEDS

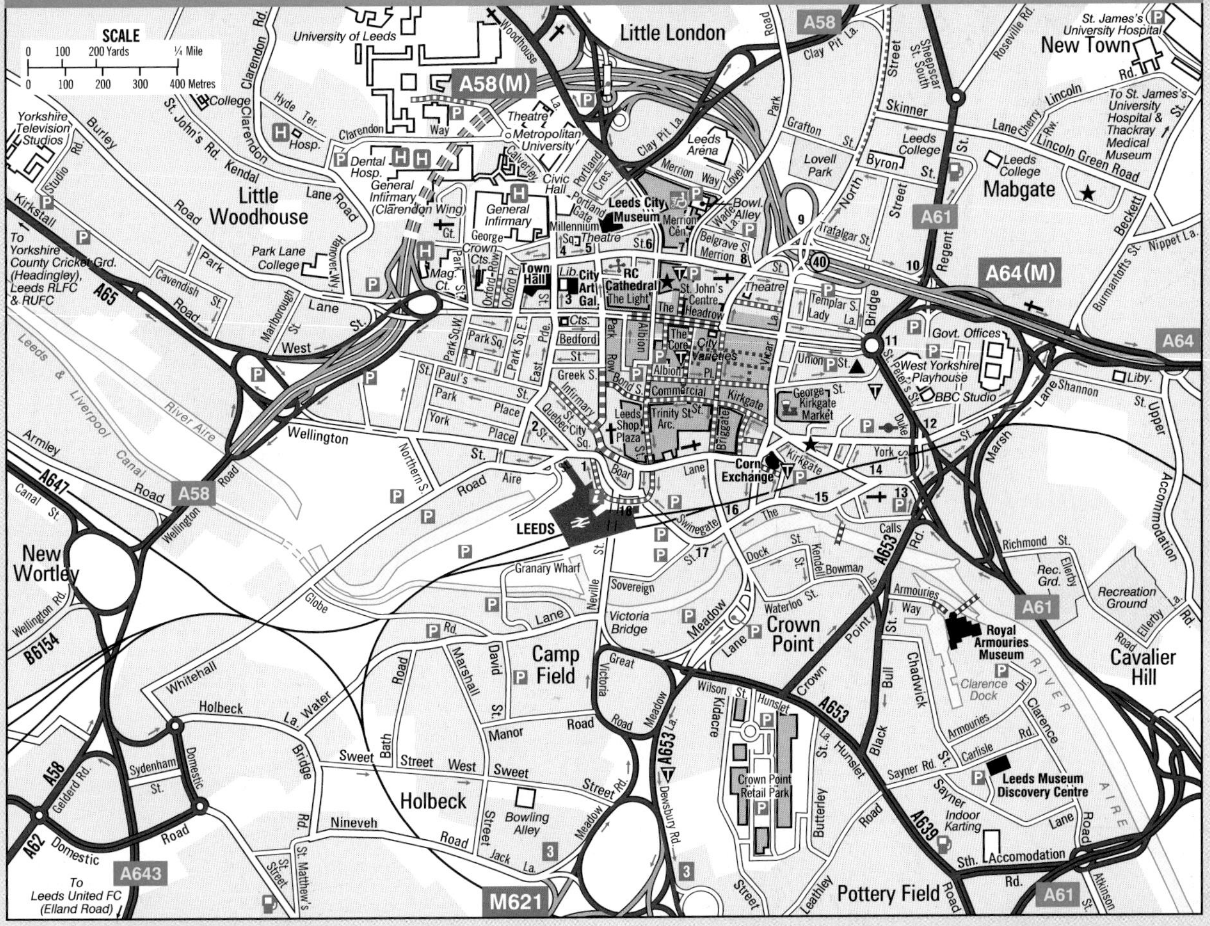

LEICESTER

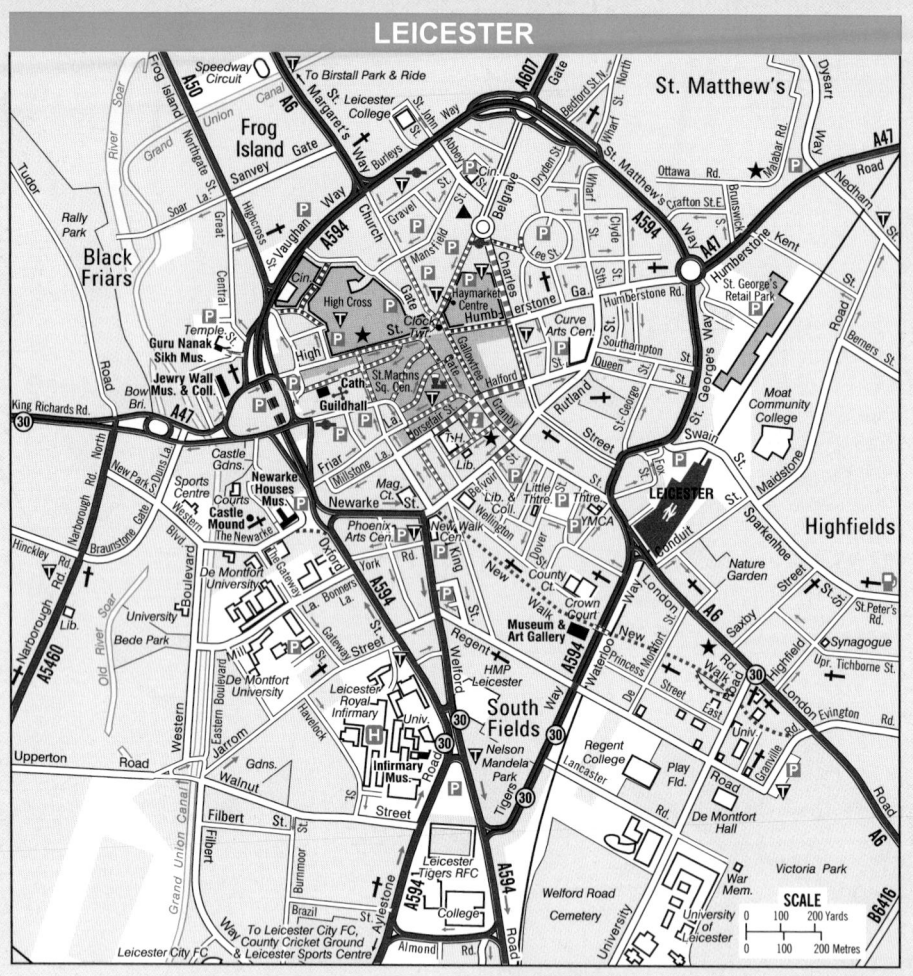

LIVERPOOL

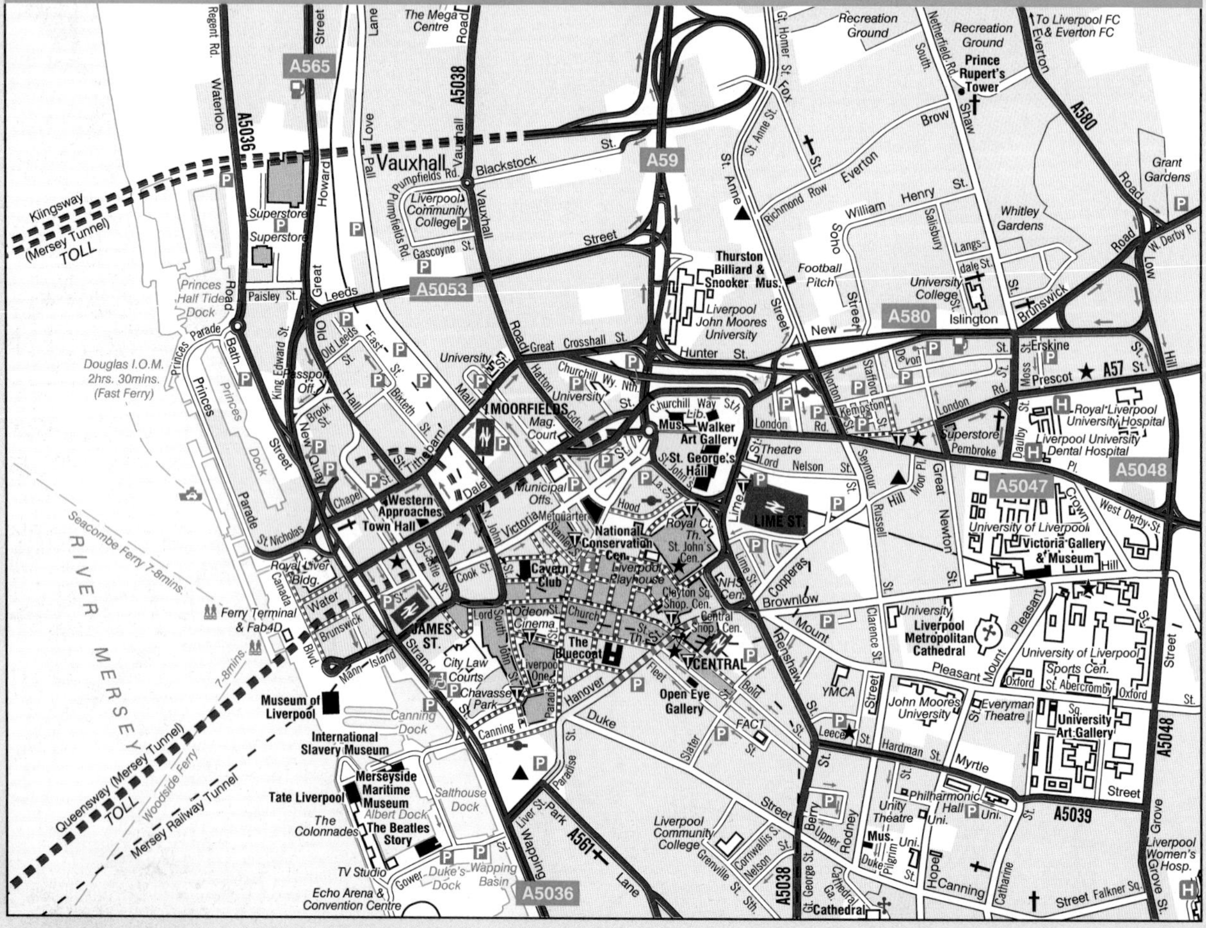

LUTON

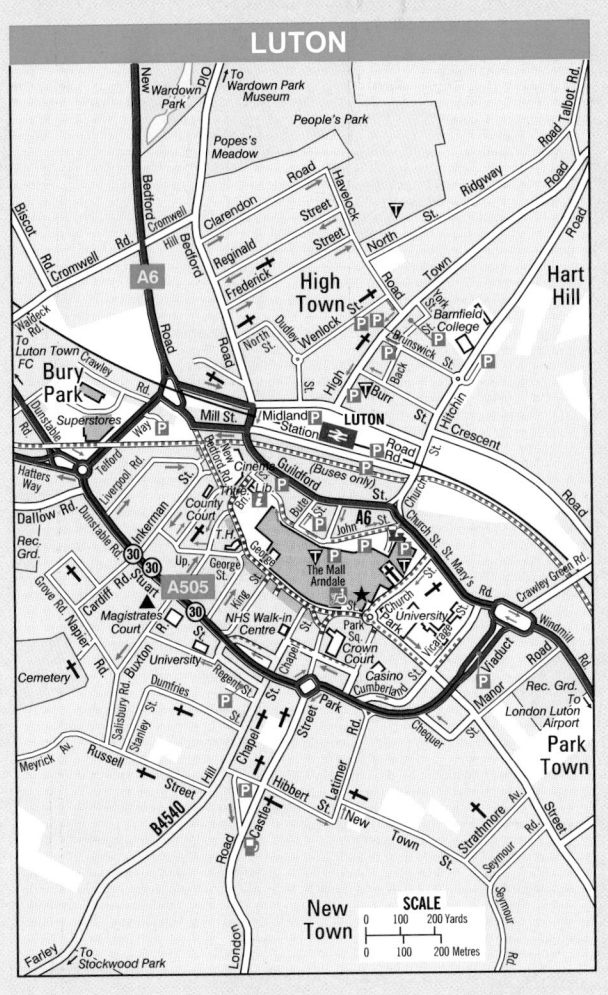

MIDDLESBROUGH

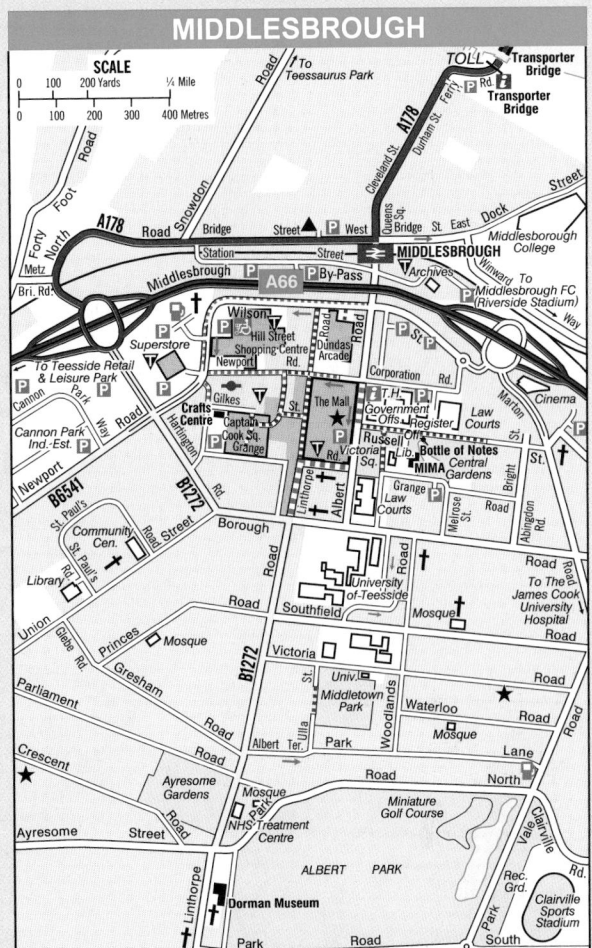

MANCHESTER (CITY CENTRE)

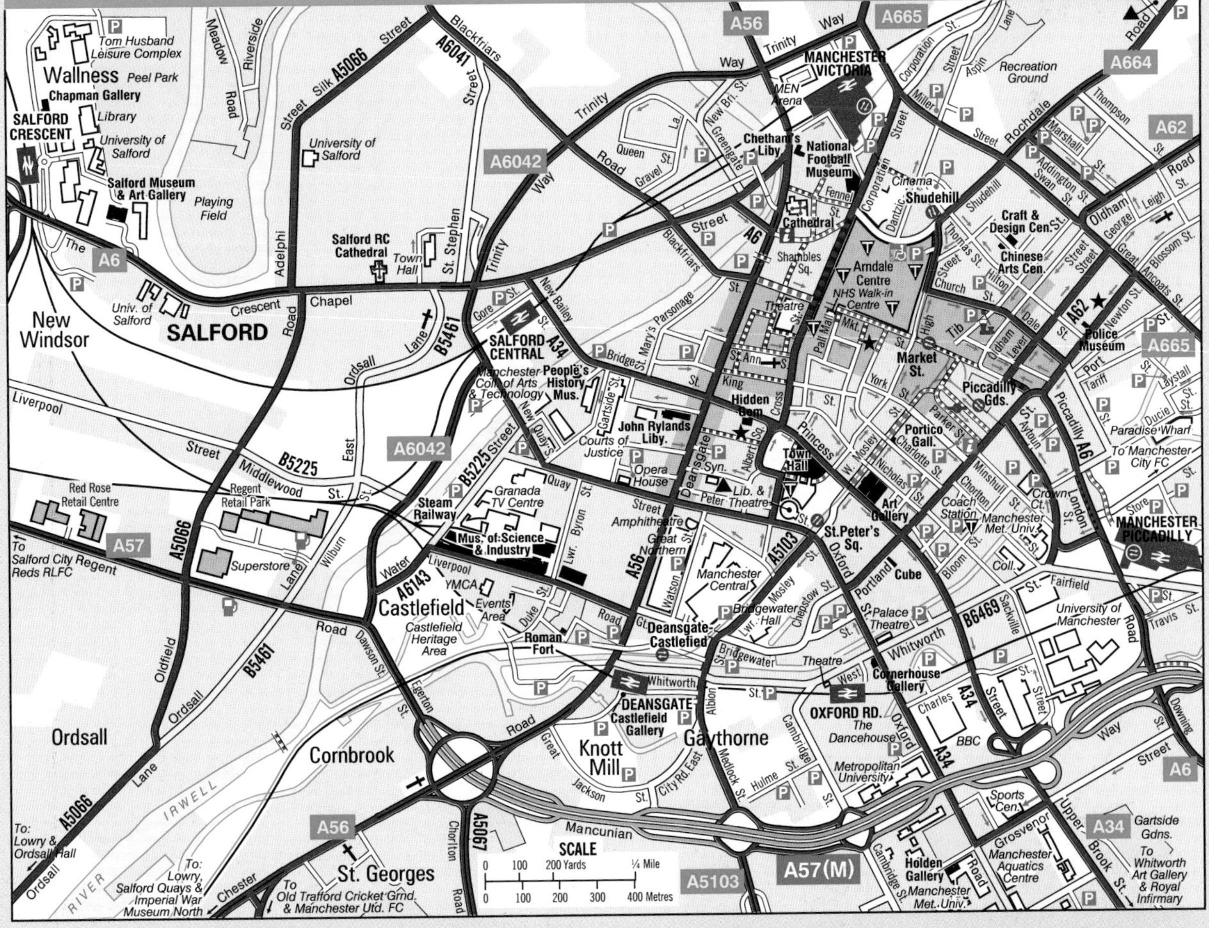

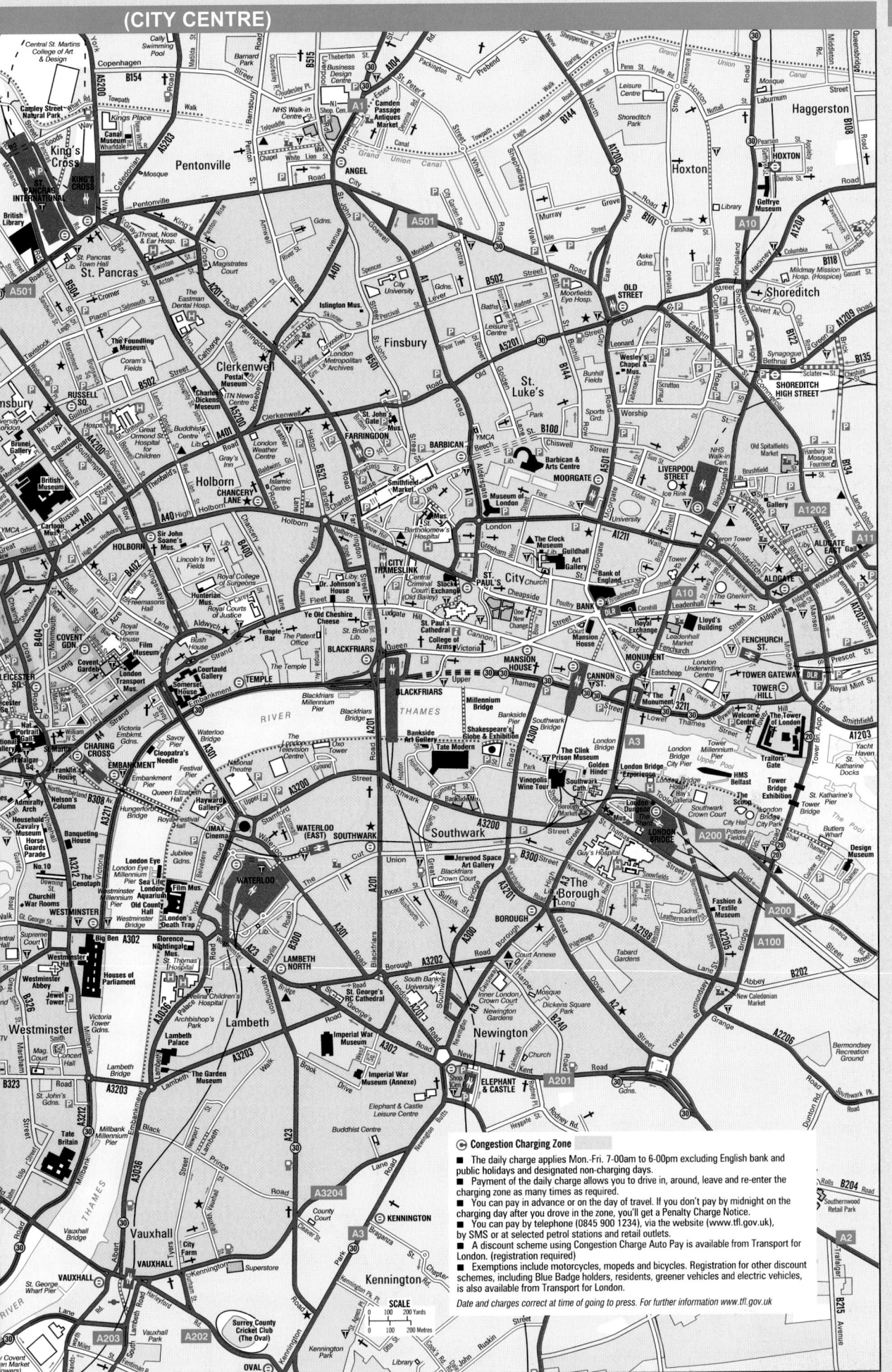

MEDWAY TOWNS

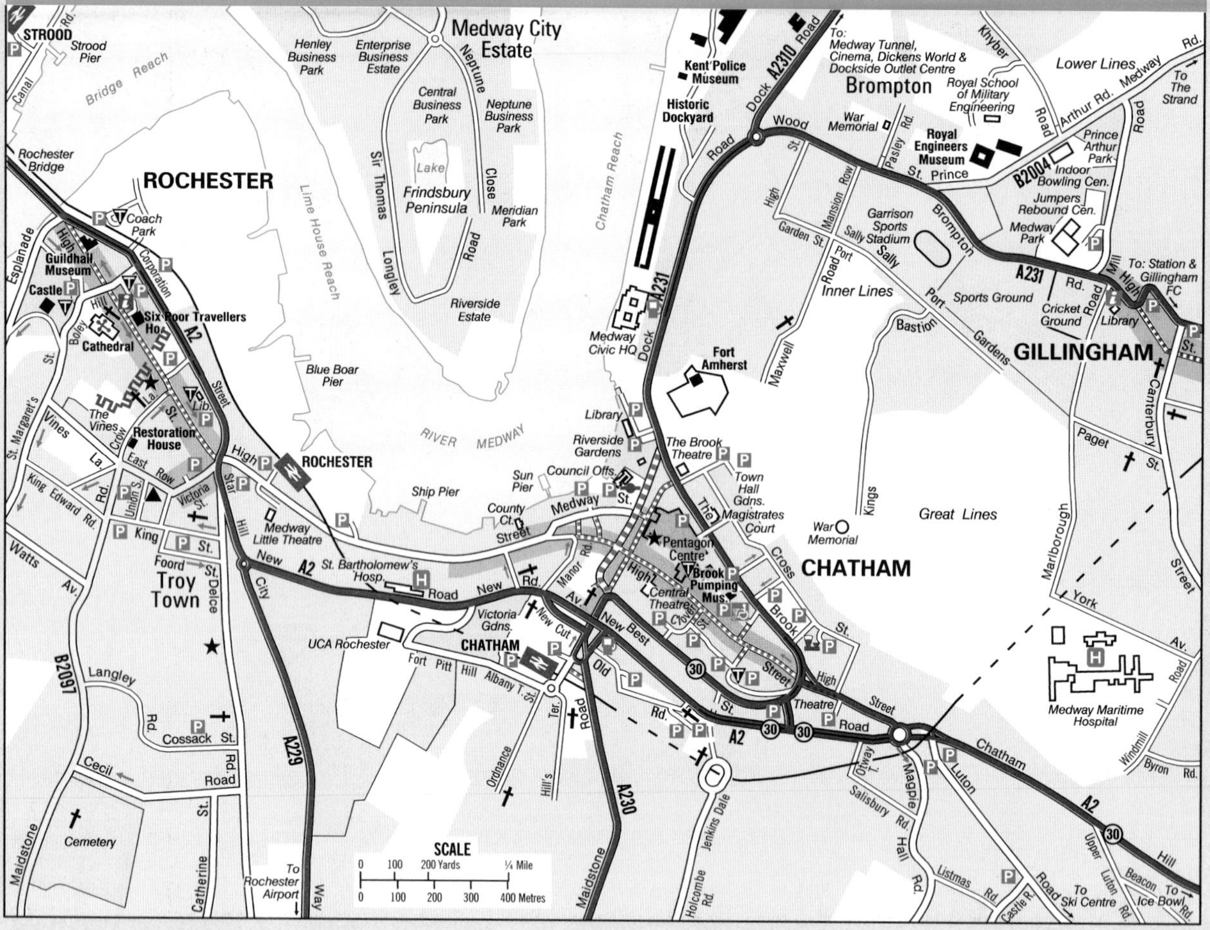
STROOD
Strood Pier
Bridge Reach
Canal
Rochester Bridge
ROCHESTER
Coach Park
Esplanade
High
Guildhall Museum
Castle
Corporation
Six Poor Travellers Ho.
Cathedral
Boley Hill
A2
Street
The Vines
Vines
St. Margaret's
Crow La.
Restoration House
East Row
Victoria St.
King Edward Rd.
Union St.
King St.
Watts Av.
Foord St.
Troy Town
Delce
Star Hill
High
ROCHESTER
Medway Little Theatre
New Rd.
City Way
A229
B2097
Langley
Rd.
Cossack St.
Cecil
Rd.
Road
Cemetery
Maidstone
Catherine St.
To Rochester Airport
Way
Henley Business Park
Enterprise Business Estate
Medway City Estate
Neptune
Central Business Park
Neptune Business Park
Sir Thomas Longley
Lake
Frindsbury Peninsula
Close
Meridian Park
Road
Lime House Reach
Riverside Estate
Blue Boar Pier
RIVER MEDWAY
Ship Pier
Chatham Reach
St. Bartholomew's Hosp.
New Road
UCA Rochester
Victoria Gdns.
CHATHAM
Fort Pitt Hill
Albany T.
New Cut
Manor Rd.
Ordnance
Hill's
Ter.
Road
A230
Maidstone
SCALE
0 100 200 Yards ¼ Mile
0 100 200 300 400 Metres
Kent Police Museum
Historic Dockyard
Dock Road
A2310
Medway Civic HQ
Dock A231
Library
Riverside Gardens
Council Offs.
Sun Pier
County Ct.
Medway St.
Street
Fort Amherst
The Brook Theatre
Town Hall Gdns.
Magistrates Court
Pentagon Centre
Brook Pumping Mus.
Central Theatre
High St.
Best
Old Rd.
30
Brook
The Street
High
Theatre
A2
Rd.
Road
Street
Cross
CHATHAM
War Memorial
Kings
Great Lines
Otway T.
Magpie Hall Rd.
Luton
Salisbury Rd.
Chatham
Holcombe Rd.
Jenkins Dale
Listmas Rd.
Castle R.
Road
To Ski Centre
Upper Luton Rd.
Beacon Rd.
To Ice Bowl
Hill
A2
To: Medway Tunnel, Cinema, Dickens World & Dockside Outlet Centre
Brompton
Wood St.
War Memorial
Pasley Rd.
Royal School of Military Engineering
Royal Engineers Museum
Prince St.
Khyber Road
Lower Lines
Arthur Rd.
Medway Rd.
To The Strand
Prince Arthur Park
Road
B2004
Indoor Bowling Cen.
Jumpers Rebound Cen.
Medway Park
High
Mansion Row
Garden St.
Garrison Sports Stadium
Sally Port
Sally
Brompton
Road
Inner Lines
Maxwell
Bastion
Port
Sports Ground
Gardens
A231
Rd.
Cricket Ground
Library
To: Station & Gillingham FC
Mill Road
High St.
GILLINGHAM
Canterbury St.
Paget St.
Marlborough
York Av.
Street
Road
Medway Maritime Hospital
Windmill
Byron Rd.

MILTON KEYNES

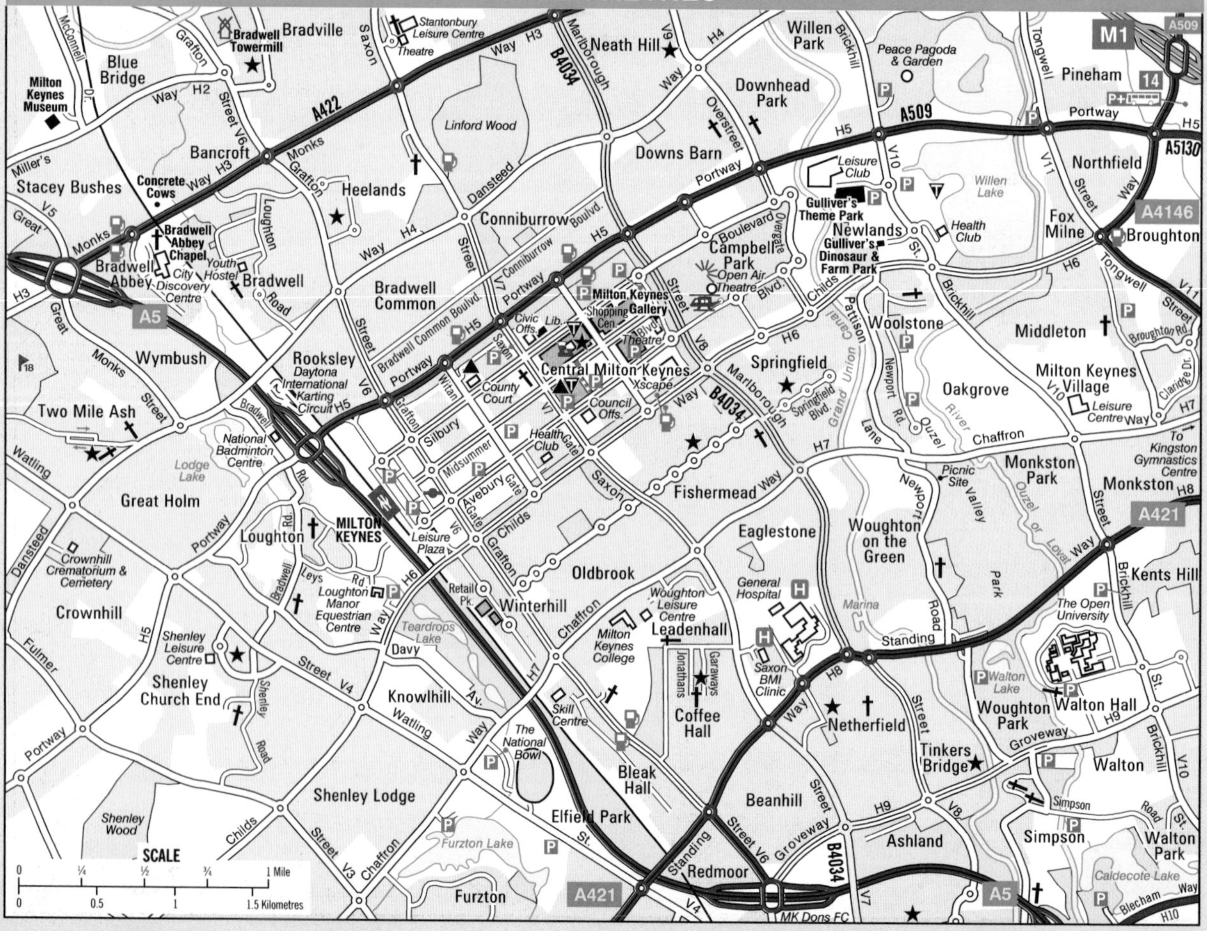
McConnell Dr.
Milton Keynes Museum
Blue Bridge
Grafton
Way H2
Street V6
Bradwell Towermill
Bradville
Stantonbury Leisure Centre
Theatre
Saxon
Way H3
A422
Monks
Bancroft
Miller's
Stacey Bushes
Concrete Cows
Way H3
Great V5
Monks
Bradwell Abbey Chapel
Bradwell Abbey
City Discovery Centre
Youth Hostel
Bradwell
Road
Loughton
Grafton
Heelands
H3
Great
A5
Monks
Wymbush
Two Mile Ash
Street
Watling
National Badminton Centre
Bradwell
Lodge Lake
Great Holm
Portway
Loughton
MILTON KEYNES
Dansteed
Crownhill Crematorium & Cemetery
Crownhill
H5
Fulmer
Shenley Leisure Centre
Shenley Church End
Street V4
Shenley Road
Portway
Shenley Wood
Childs
SCALE
0 ¼ ½ ¾ 1 Mile
0 0.5 1 1.5 Kilometres
Linford Wood
Dansteed
Conniburrow
Boulvd.
Way H4
Street
Bradwell Common
Street V6
Rooksley
Daytona International Karting Circuit H5
Portway
Bradwell Common Boulvd.
H5
Conniburrow Portway
V7
Saxon
Witan
Grafton
Silbury
Midsummer
Avebury
Gate
Leisure Plaza
Childs
Grafton
Leys Rd
Loughton Manor Equestrian Centre
Bradwell
H6
Way
Retail Pk.
Winterhill
Teardrops Lake
Davy
Knowlhill
Av.
Watling
Way
Shenley Lodge
Street V3
Chaffron
Furzton Lake
Furzton
A421
Marlborough
B4034
Neath Hill
V9
Way
H4
Willen Park
Brickhill
Downhead Park
Overstreet
Downs Barn
Portway
H5
Milton Keynes Shopping Cen.
Gallery
Civic Offs.
Lib.
Theatre
Central Milton Keynes
County Court
Council Offs.
Xscape
Health Club
Gate
Saxon
Way
Campbell Park
Boulevard
Overgate
Open Air Theatre
Blvd.
Street
V8
H6
Marlborough
B4034
Springfield
Springfield Blvd.
Fishermead Way
H7
Oldbrook
Chaffron
Woughton Leisure Centre
Milton Keynes College
Leadenhall
Jonathans
Garraways
Coffee Hall
Skill Centre
H7
The National Bowl
Bleak Hall
Elfield Park
St.
Standing
Redmoor
Street V6
Groveway
B4034
Beanhill
Street
Ashland
H9
V8
V7
A5
MK Dons FC
V4
Peace Pagoda & Garden
Leisure Club
Gulliver's Theme Park
Gulliver's Dinosaur & Farm Park
Newlands
Health Club
Willen Lake
V10
A509
Childs
Pattison
Canal
Grand Union
Woolstone
Brickhill
St.
Newport Rd.
Ouzel
River
Oakgrove
Lane
Eaglestone
Woughton on the Green
Newport Road
Picnic Site
Valley
Park
Marina
General Hospital
Saxon BMI Clinic
H8
Way
Netherfield
Standing
Street
Tinkers Bridge
Way
M1
A509
Tongwell
Pineham
14
Portway
H5
A5130
V11
Northfield
Street
Way
Fox Milne
A4146
Broughton
Tongwell
H6
V11 Street
Middleton
Broughton Rd.
Milton Keynes Village
V10
Leisure Centre
Way
Claridge Dr.
H7
Chaffron
To Kingston Gymnastics Centre
Monkston Park
Monkston
H8
Street
Ouzel or Lovat
A421
Way
Kents Hill
Brickhill
The Open University
Walton Lake
Woughton Park
Walton Hall
H9
Groveway
Walton
Brickhill
V10
St.
Simpson
Road
Simpson
Walton Park
Caldecote Lake
Blecham Way
H10

NORWICH

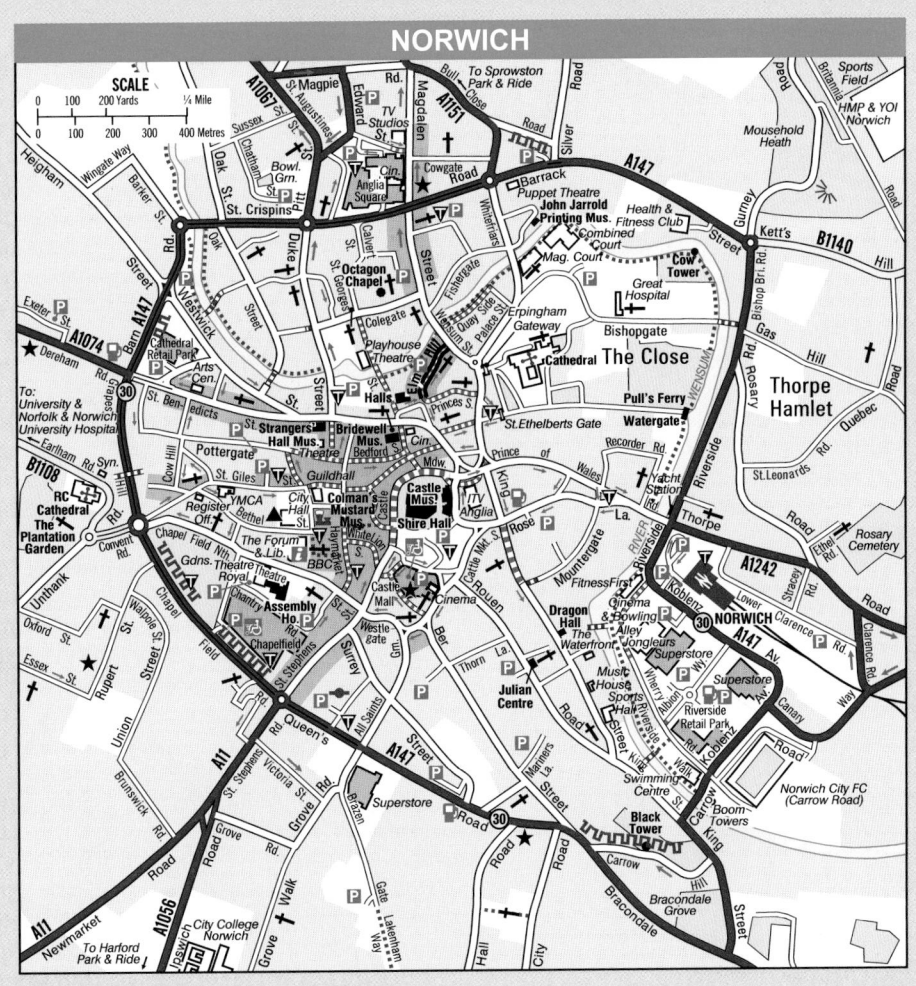

NEWCASTLE UPON TYNE

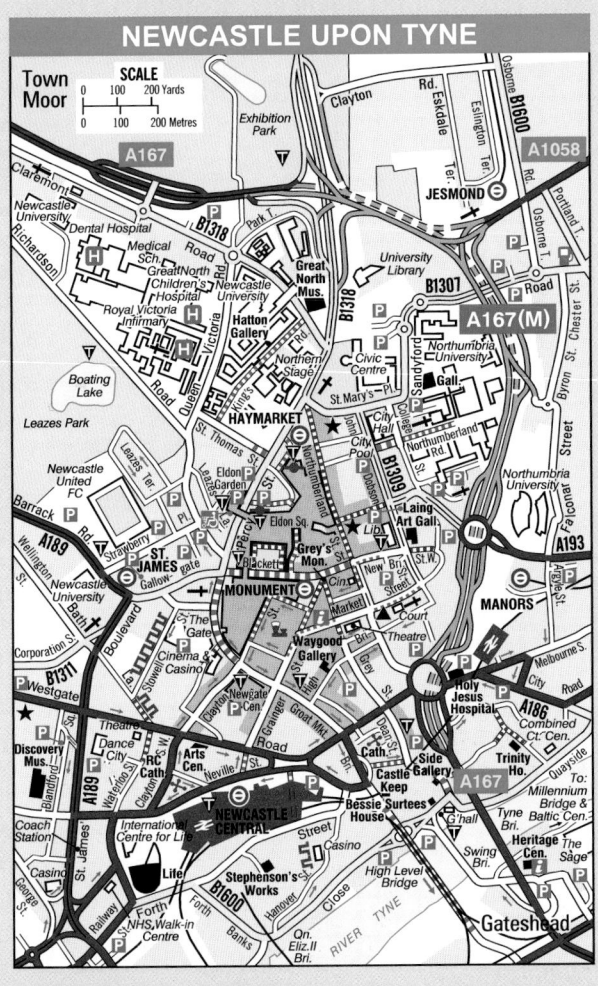

NEWPORT (CASNEWYDD)

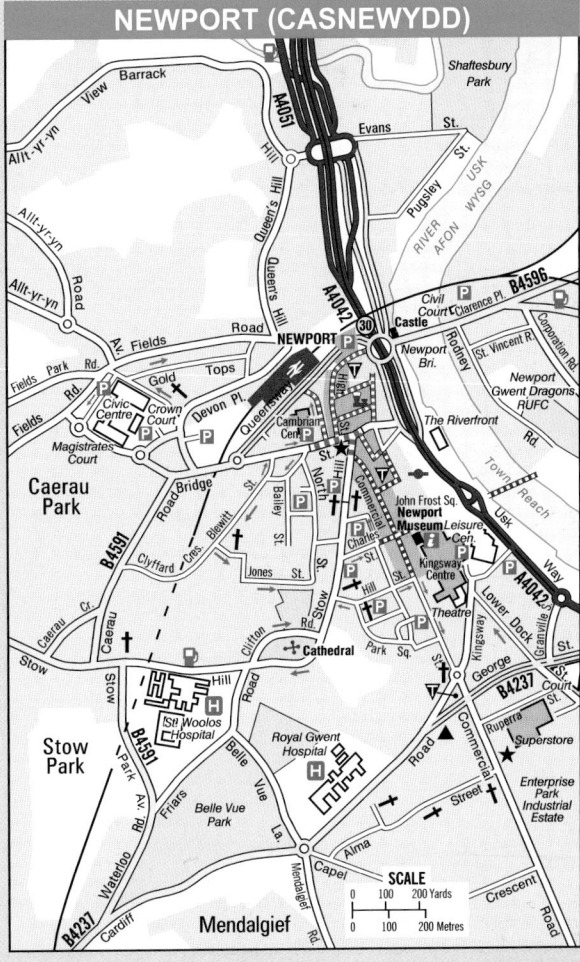

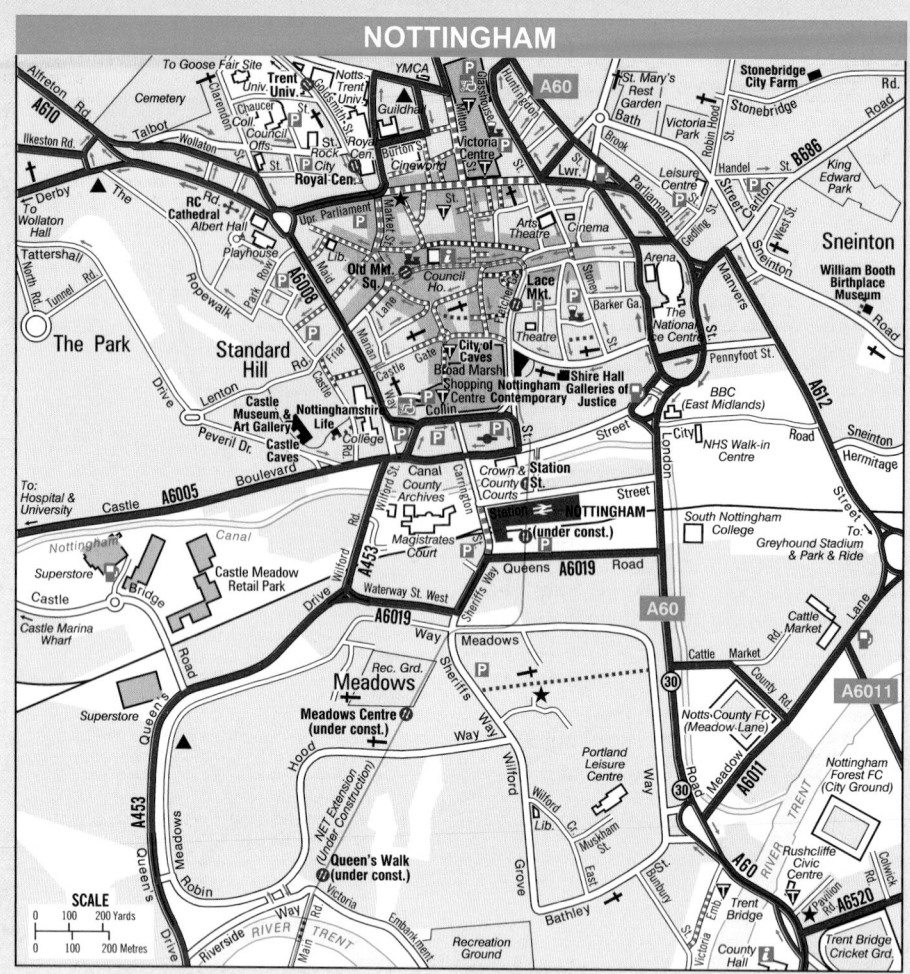

NOTTINGHAM

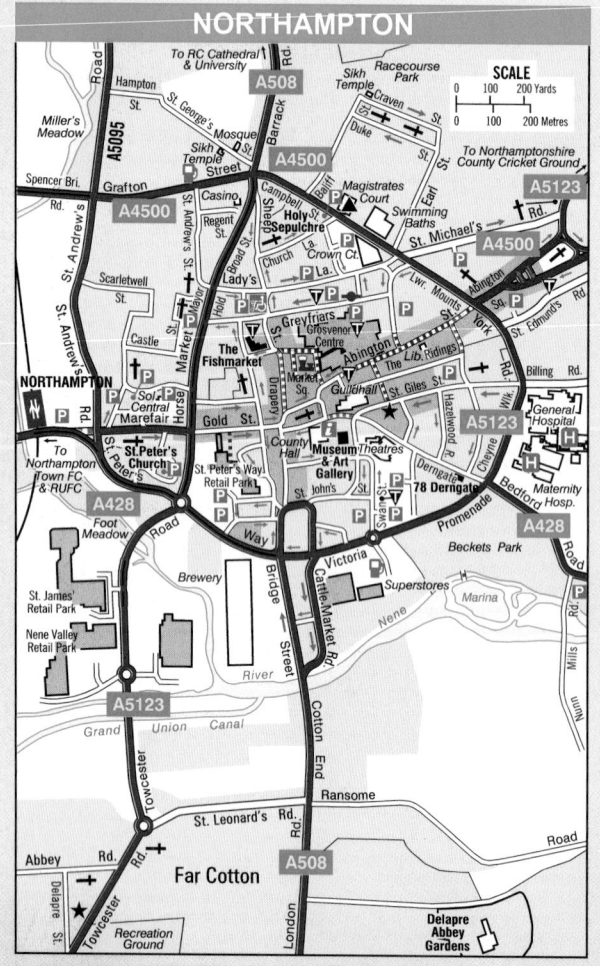

NORTHAMPTON

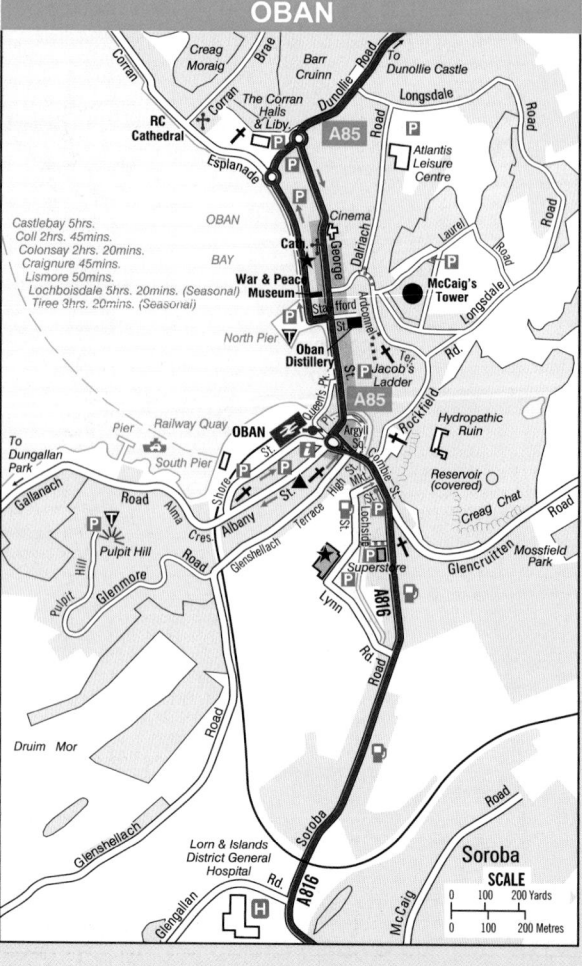

OBAN

OXFORD

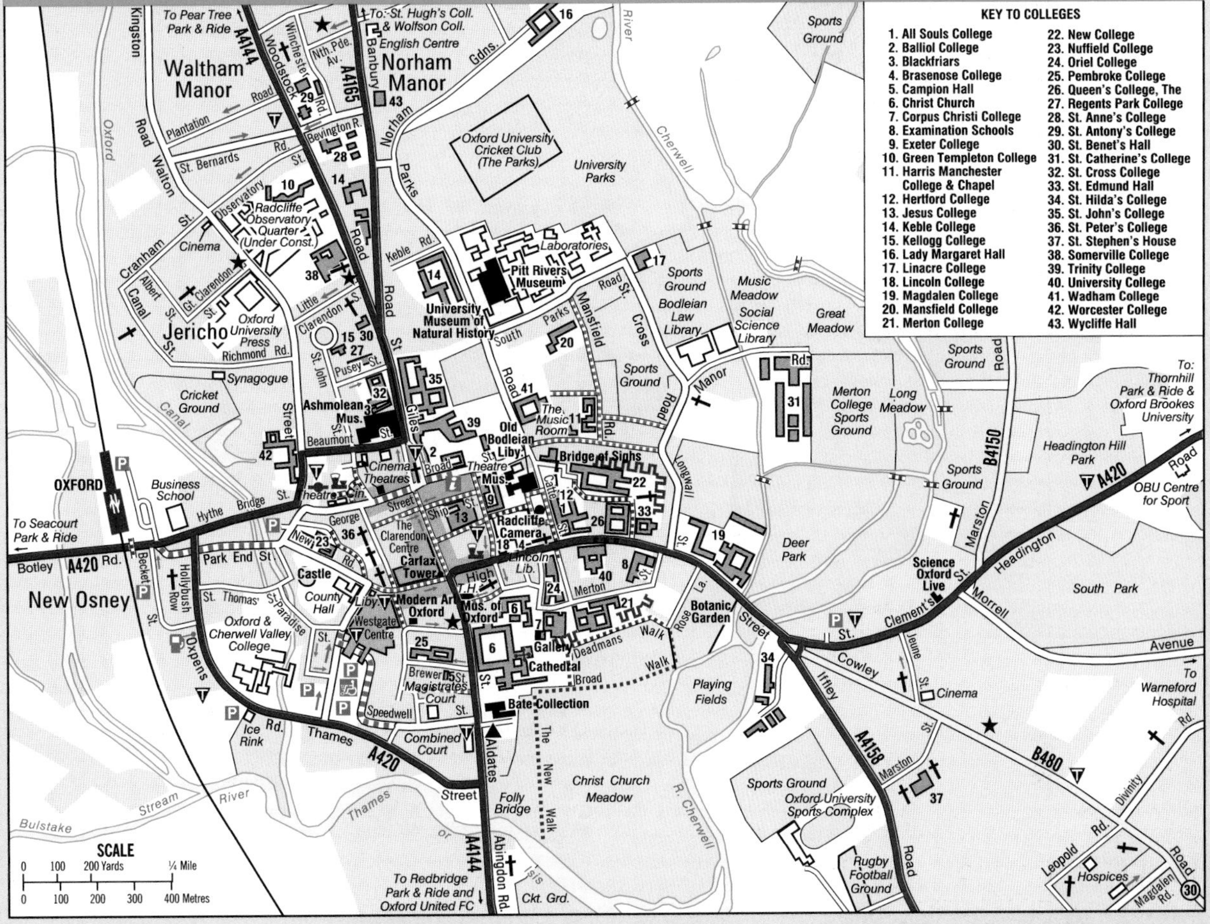
KEY TO COLLEGES
1. All Souls College
2. Balliol College
3. Blackfriars
4. Brasenose College
5. Campion Hall
6. Christ Church
7. Corpus Christi College
8. Examination Schools
9. Exeter College
10. Green Templeton College
11. Harris Manchester College & Chapel
12. Hertford College
13. Jesus College
14. Keble College
15. Kellogg College
16. Lady Margaret Hall
17. Linacre College
18. Lincoln College
19. Magdalen College
20. Mansfield College
21. Merton College
22. New College
23. Nuffield College
24. Oriel College
25. Pembroke College
26. Queen's College, The
27. Regents Park College
28. St. Anne's College
29. St. Antony's College
30. St. Benet's Hall
31. St. Catherine's College
32. St. Cross College
33. St. Edmund Hall
34. St. Hilda's College
35. St. John's College
36. St. Peter's College
37. St. Stephen's House
38. Somerville College
39. Trinity College
40. University College
41. Wadham College
42. Worcester College
43. Wycliffe Hall
To Pear Tree Park & Ride
To: St. Hugh's Coll. & Wolfson Coll.
English Centre
Waltham Manor
Norham Manor
Oxford University Cricket Club (The Parks)
University Parks
Radcliffe Observatory Quarter (Under Const.)
Jericho
Oxford University Press
Pitt Rivers Museum
University Museum of Natural History
Laboratories
Ashmolean Mus.
Old Bodleian Liby.
Bridge of Sighs
Radcliffe Camera
Carfax Tower
Modern Art Oxford
Mus. of Oxford
Cathedral
Bate Collection
Botanic Garden
Christ Church Meadow
Deer Park
Science Oxford Live
Headington Hill Park
OBU Centre for Sport
To: Thornhill Park & Ride & Oxford Brookes University
To Seacourt Park & Ride
New Osney
OXFORD
Business School
Castle
County Hall
Oxford & Cherwell Valley College
Combined Court
Folly Bridge
Playing Fields
Sports Ground Oxford University Sports Complex
Rugby Football Ground
South Park
To Warneford Hospital
Hospices
To Redbridge Park & Ride and Oxford United FC
SCALE
0 100 200 Yards ¼ Mile
0 100 200 300 400 Metres

PAISLEY

To Glasgow Airport
A726
Laigh Park
Reid Kerr College
St. Mirren FC (St. Mirren Park)
Fitness Cen.
Fountain Gardens
Courts
PAISLEY GILMOUR ST.
Paisley Museum & Art Galleries
Coats Observatory
RC Cathedral
Piazza Shop. Cen.
Abbey
District Court
Lagoon Leisure Cen.
East End Park
Paisley Arts Cen.
Abbey Bridge
University
Sma' Shot Cotts.
Paisley Thread Mill Museum
Superstore
PAISLEY CANAL
To: Barshaw Park & Golf Course
To: Elderslie Golf Course & Cinema
Saucel Hill
Saucelhill Park
Castlehead
ROYAL ALEXANDRA HOSPITAL
To Brodie Park
To: Dykebar Hospital & Accord Hospice
SCALE
0 100 200 Yards
0 100 200 Metres

PERTH

SCALE
0 100 200 Yards
0 100 200 Metres
To Perth Racecourse
Supermarket
North Inch Golf Course
Black Watch Regimental Museum (Balhousie Castle)
Bell's Sports Centre
To St. Johnstone FC
Bowling Greens
To Murray Royal Hosp.
St. Catherine's Retail Park
Cathedral
Museum & Art Gall.
Concert Hall
Perth Bridge
Perth Theatre
St. John's Shop. Cen.
St. John's Kirk
Council Chambers
Queen's Bridge
To Perth Royal Infirmary
Dewars Centre
Perth Leisure Pool
PERTH
Bellwood Park
Fergusson Gallery
South Inch
King James VI Golf Course
To M90
HMP Perth

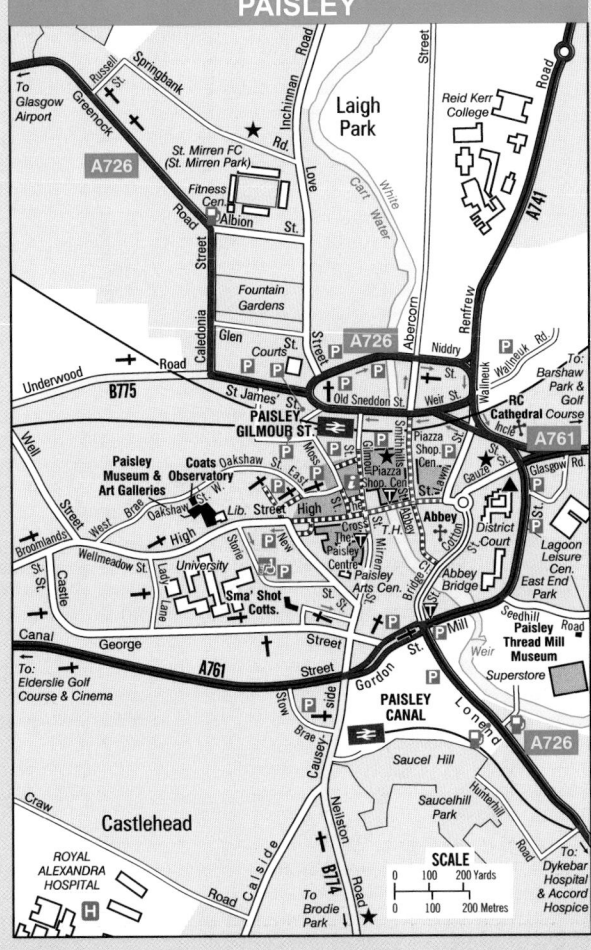

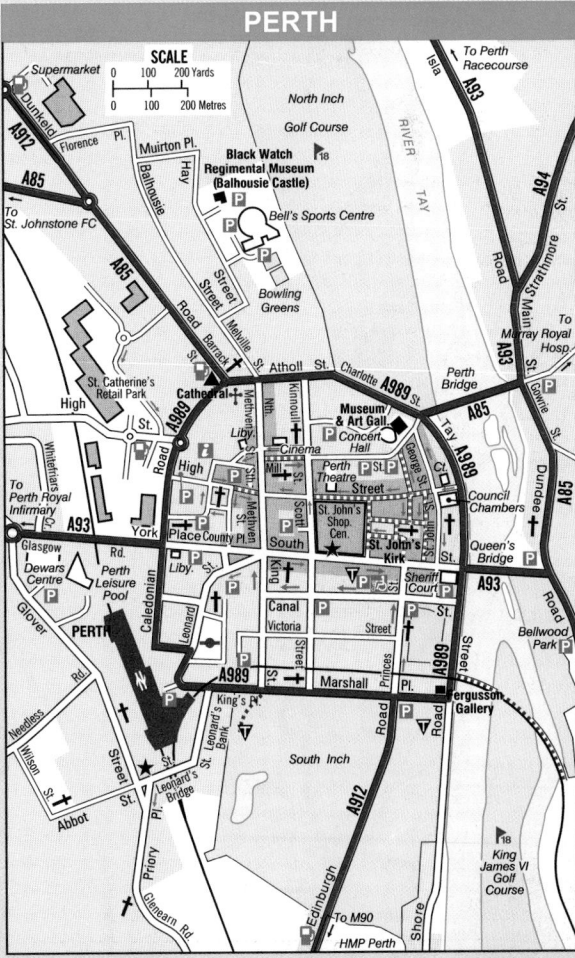

PLYMOUTH

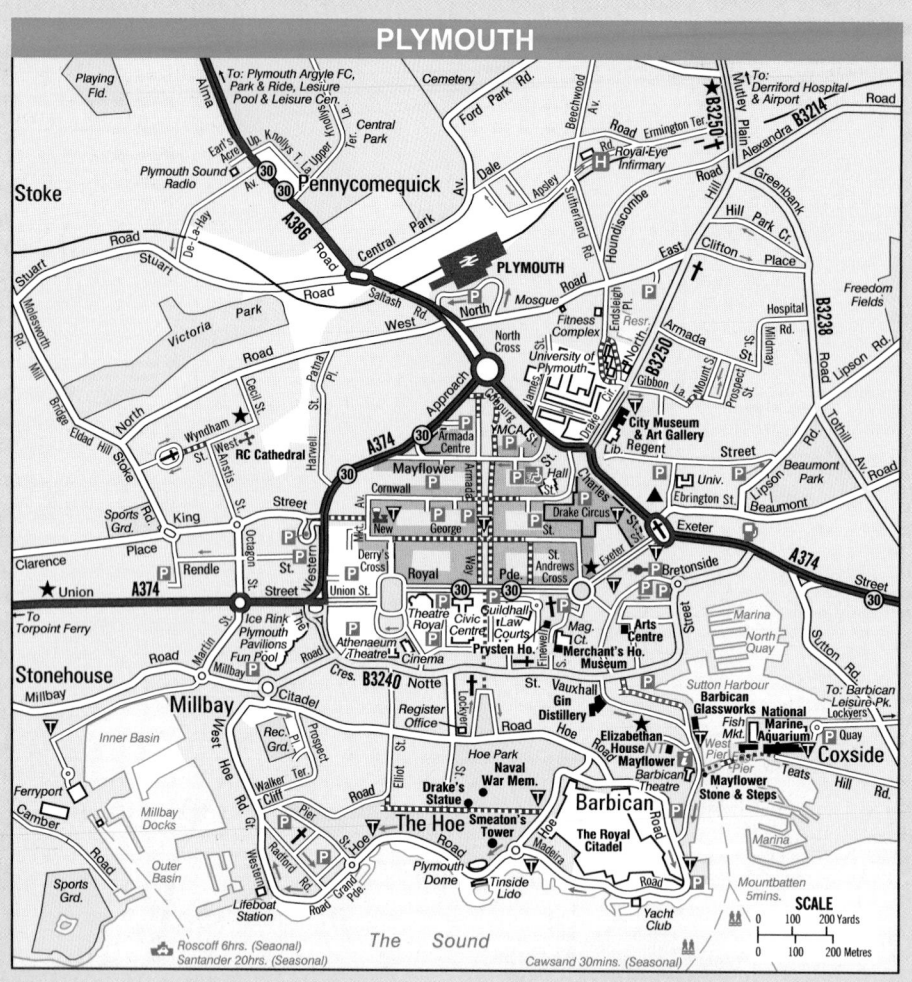

PETERBOROUGH

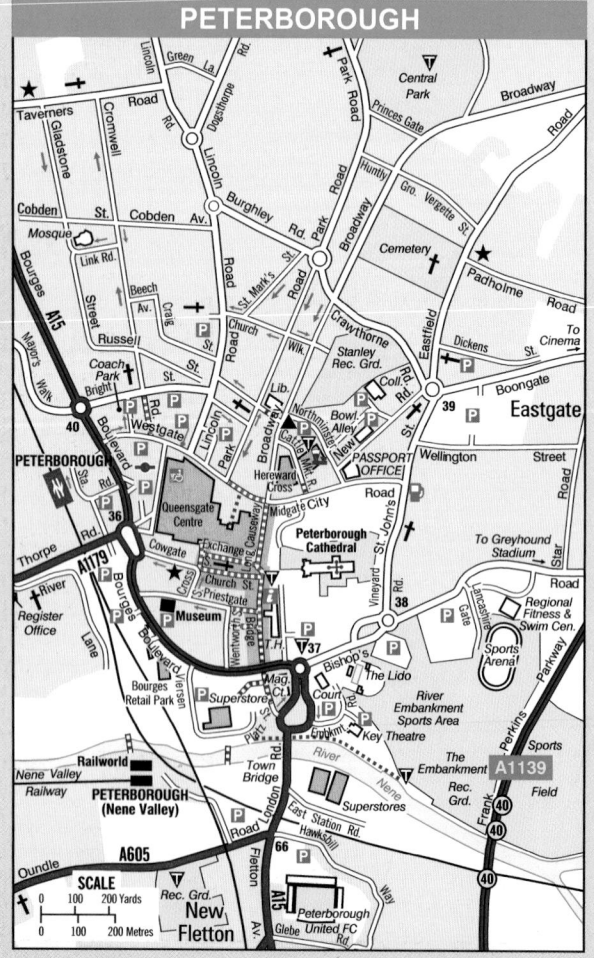

PRESTON

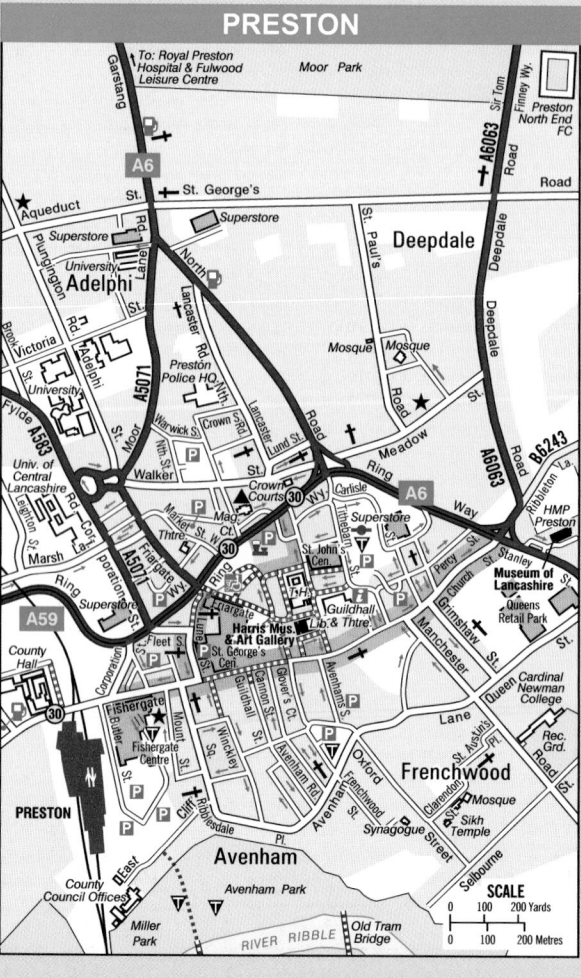

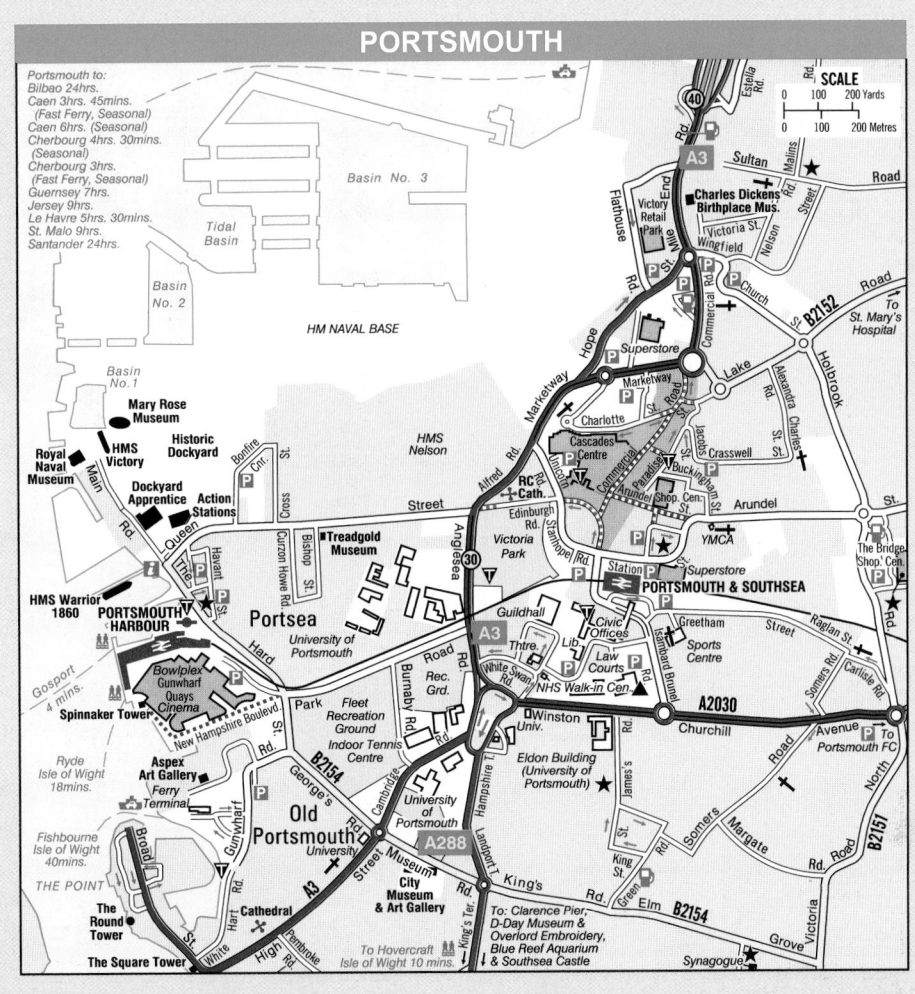

PORTSMOUTH

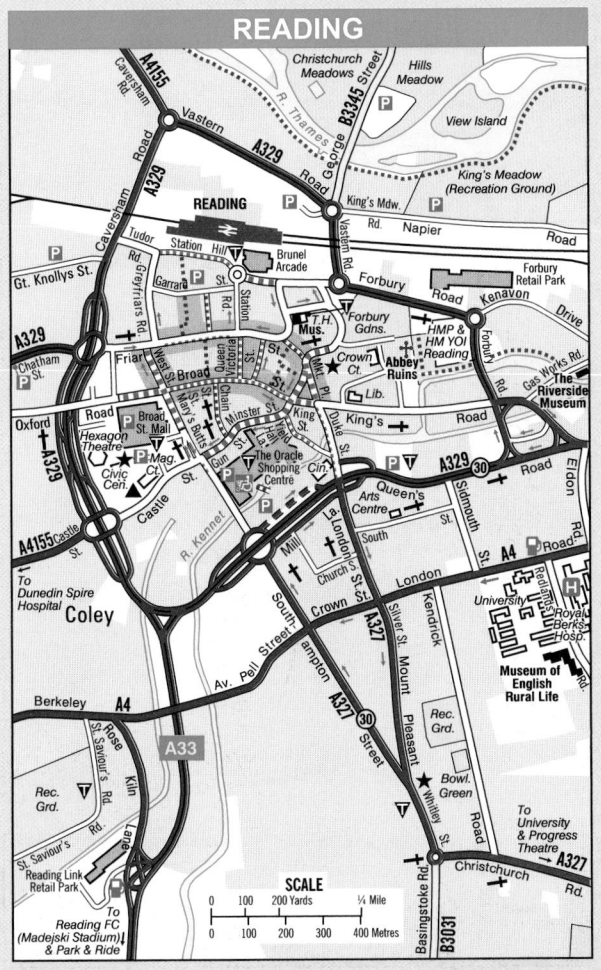

READING

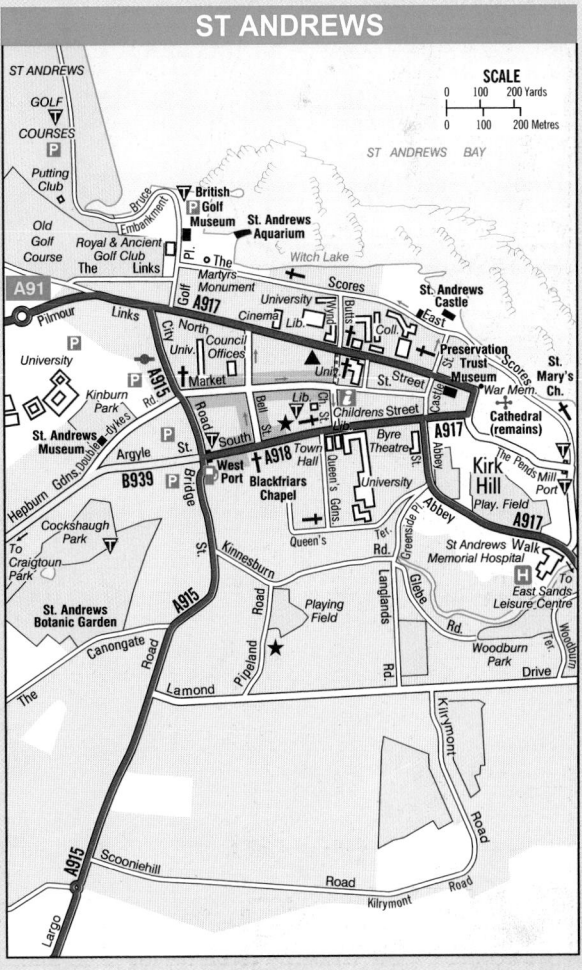

ST ANDREWS

SALISBURY

SHREWSBURY

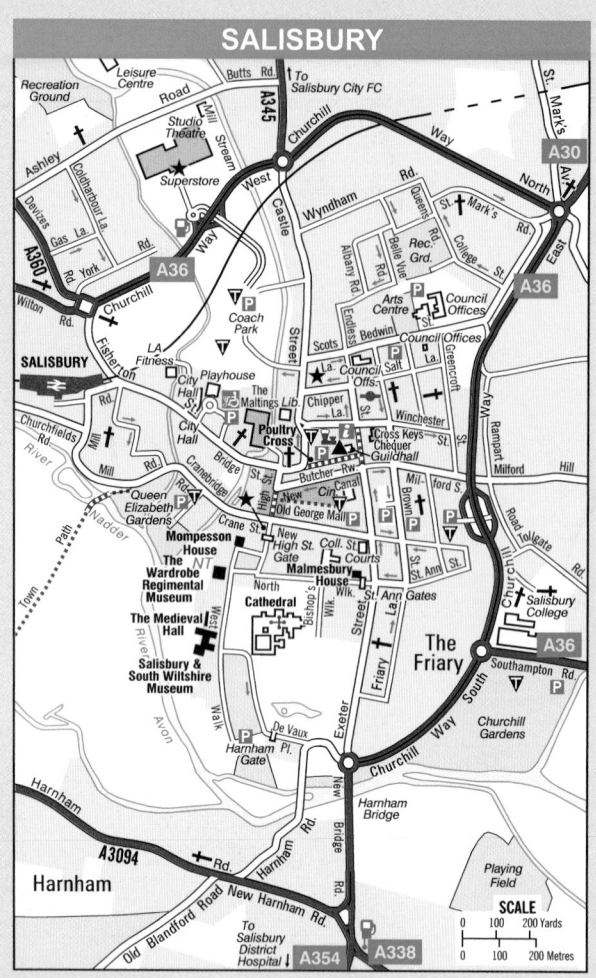
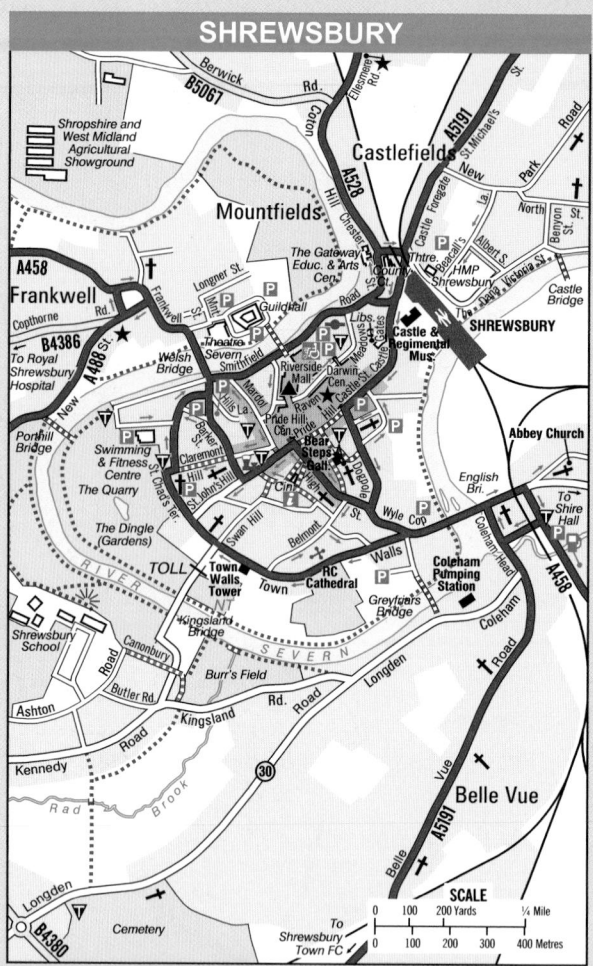

SHEFFIELD

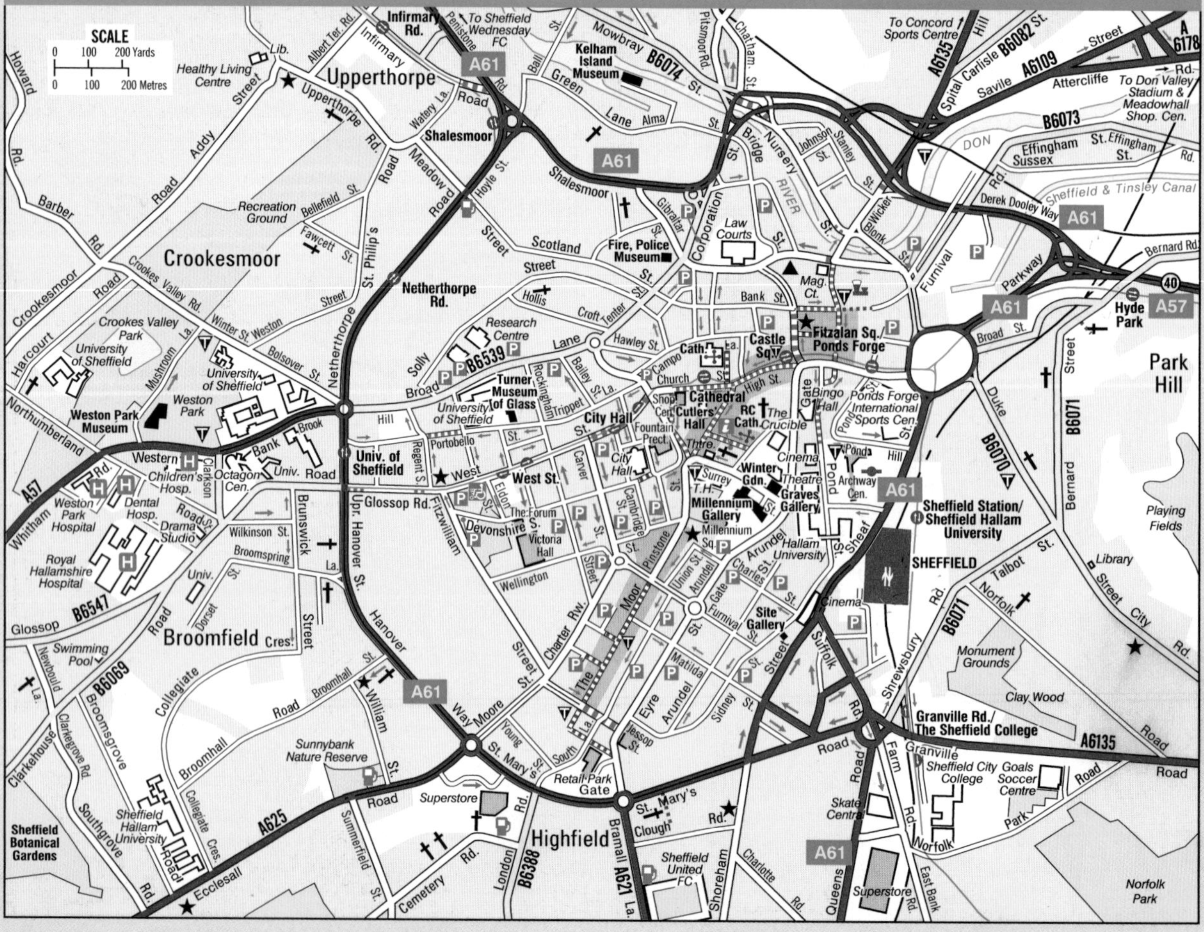

SOUTHAMPTON

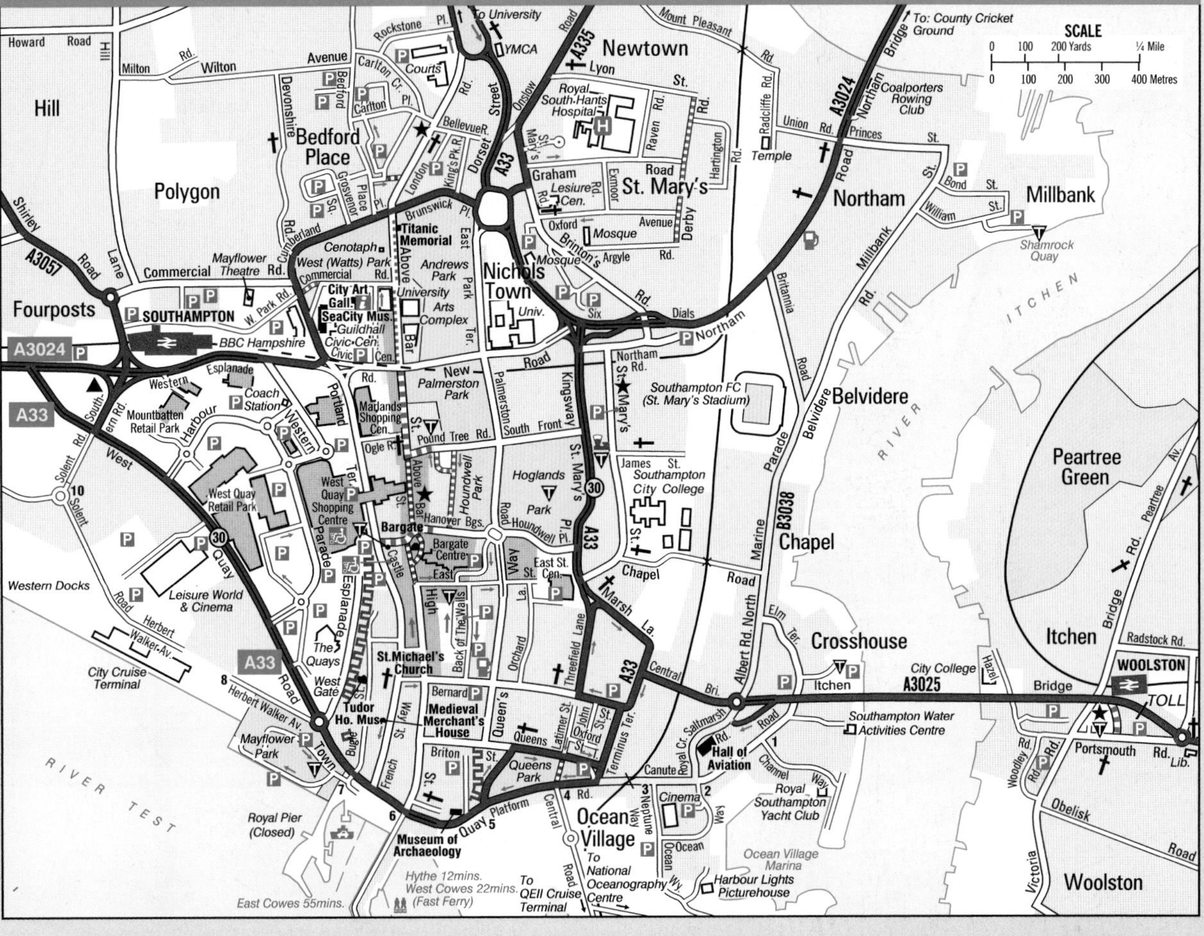

STIRLING

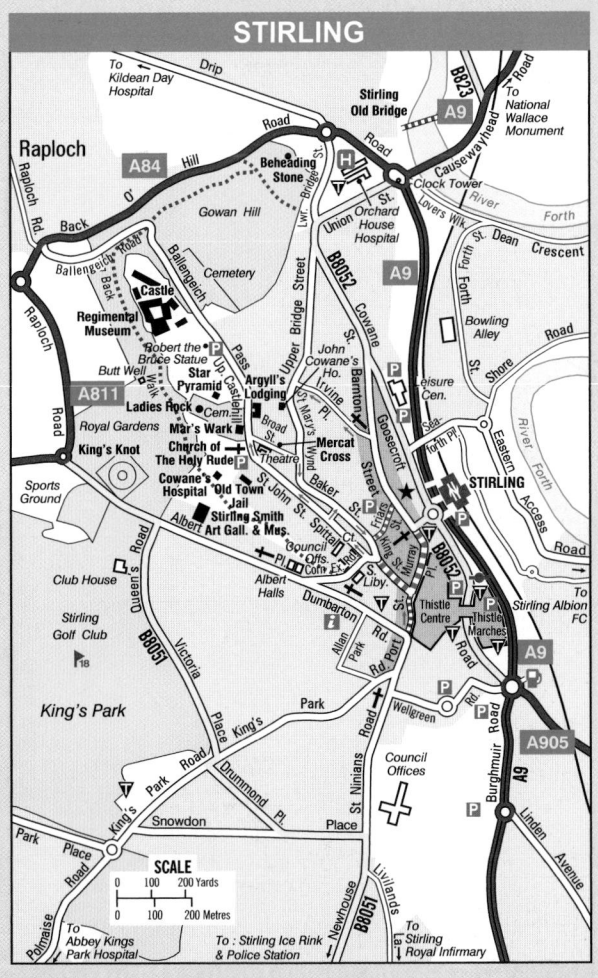

STOKE-ON-TRENT

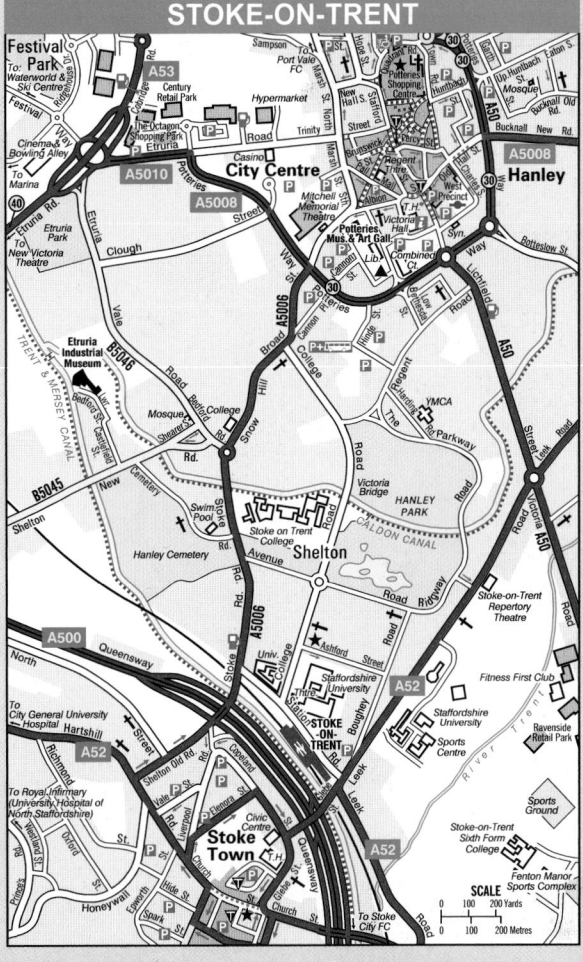

STRATFORD upon AVON

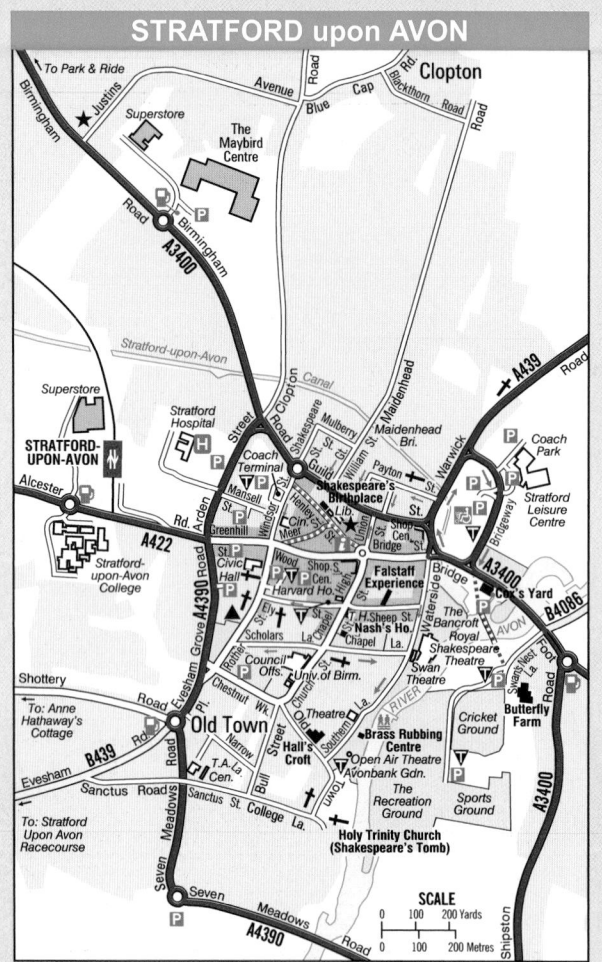

SUNDERLAND

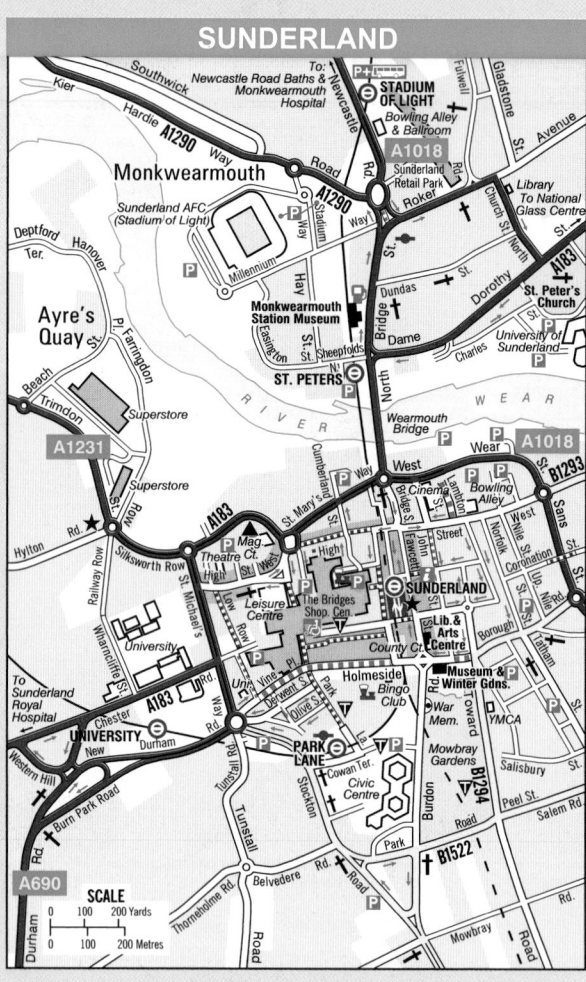

SWANSEA (ABERTAWE)

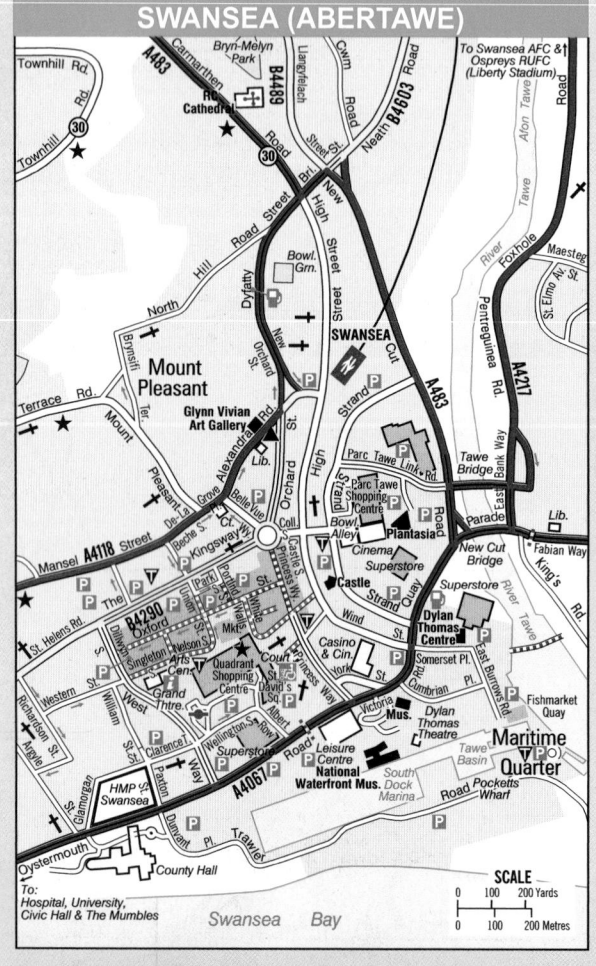

SWINDON

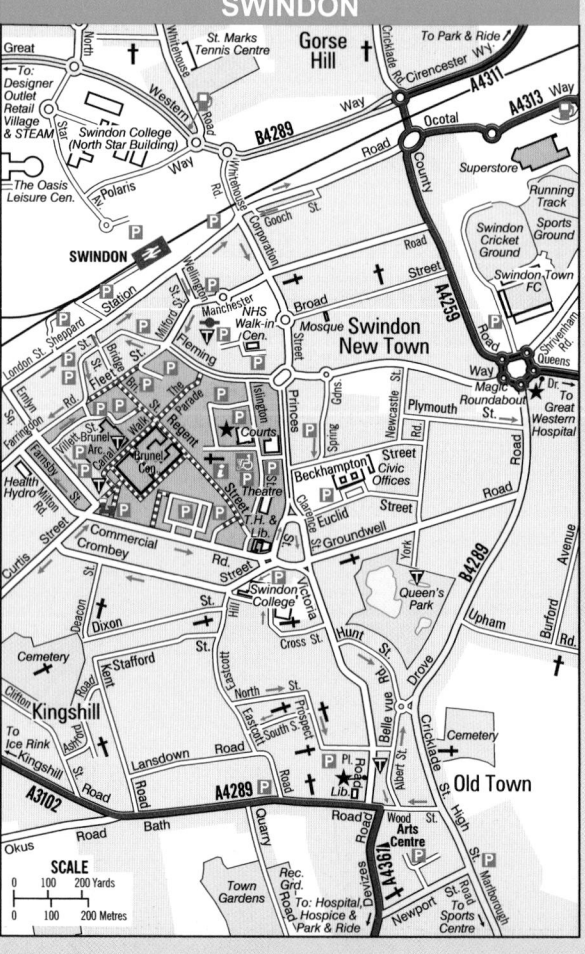

TAUNTON

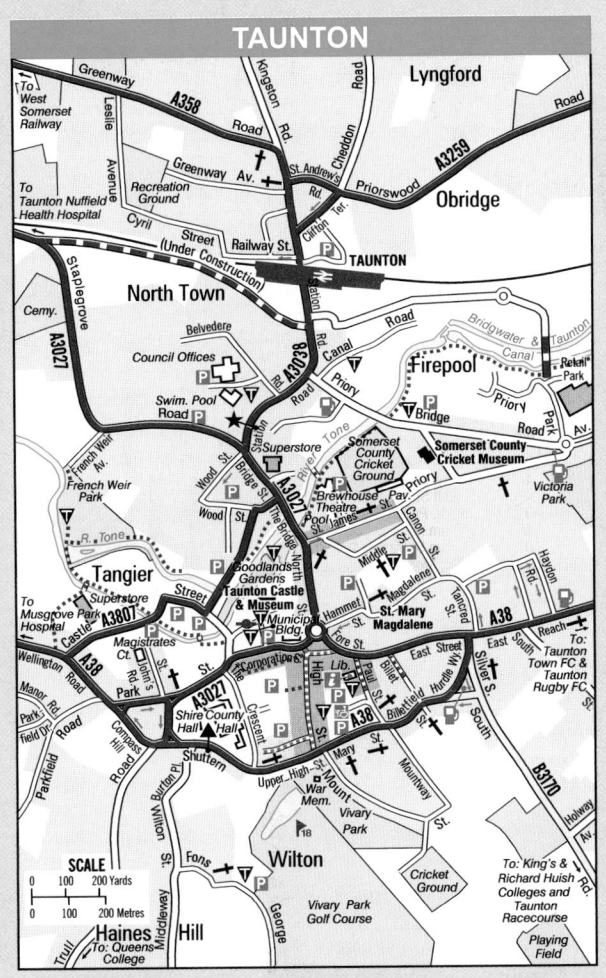

WINCHESTER

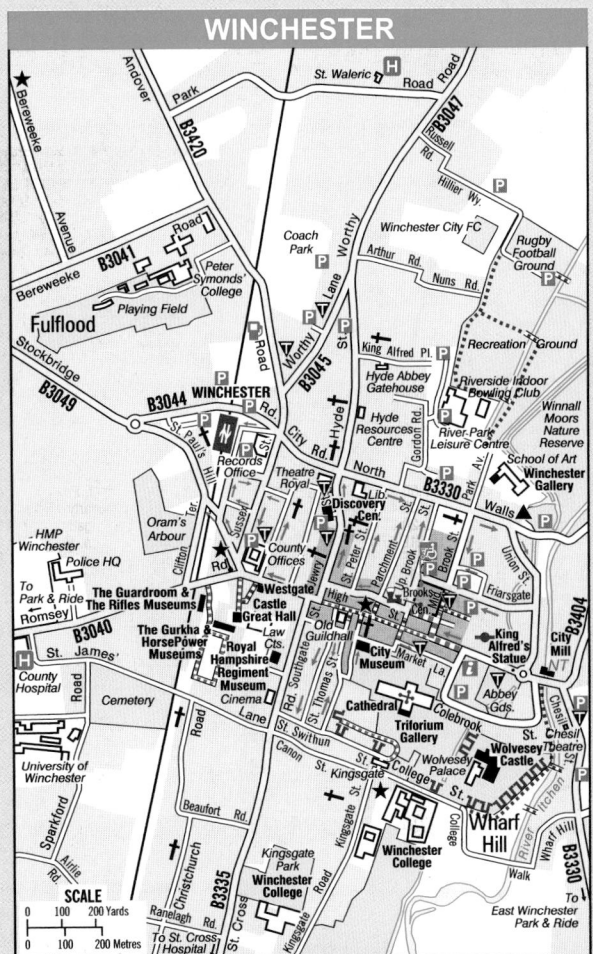

WINDSOR

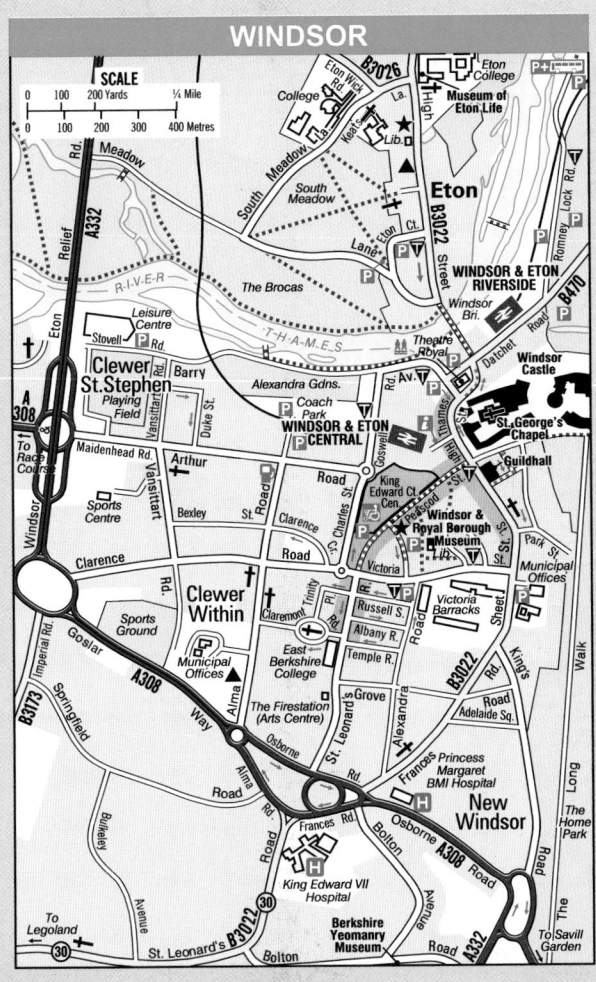

WOLVERHAMPTON

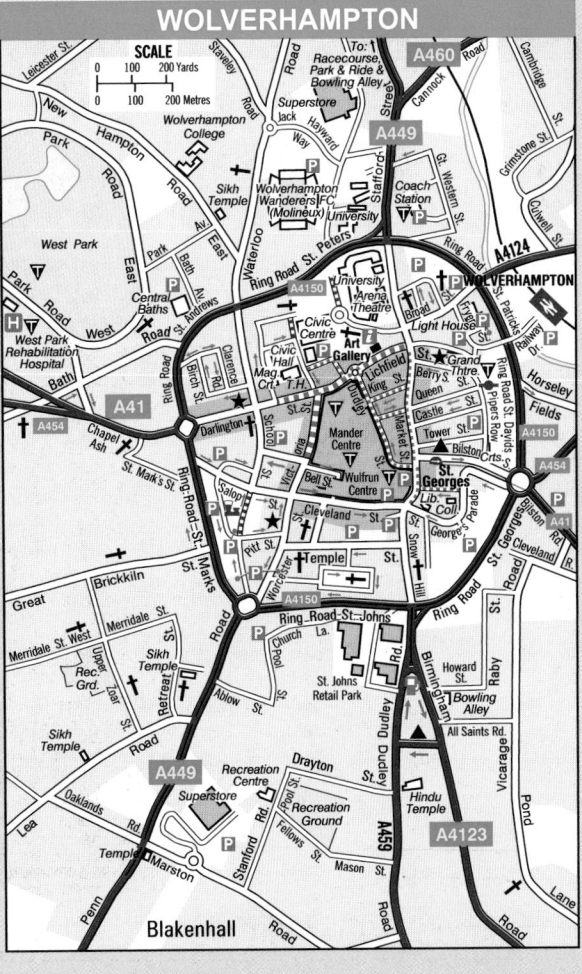

WORCESTER

WREXHAM (WRECSAM)

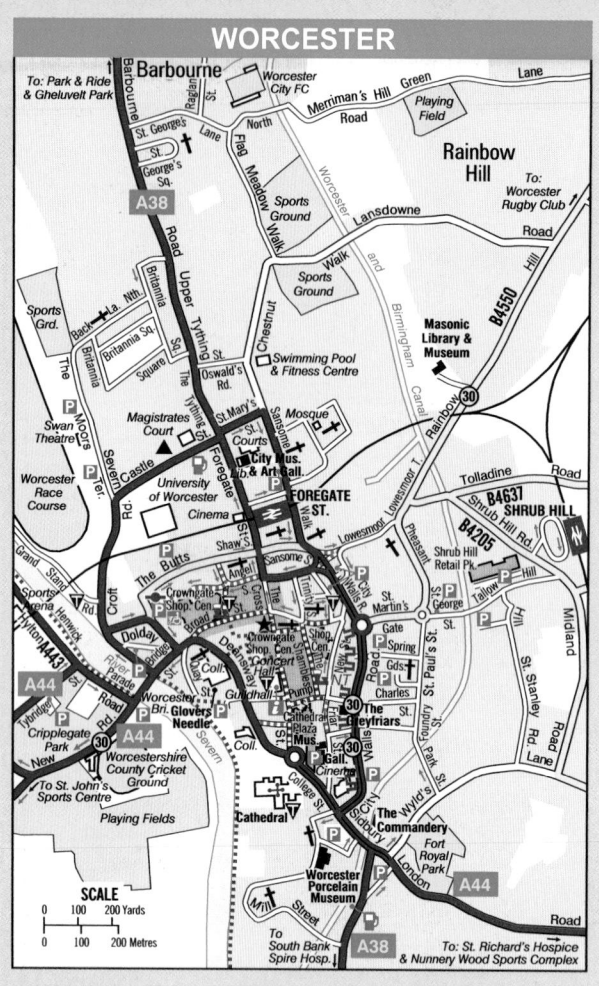

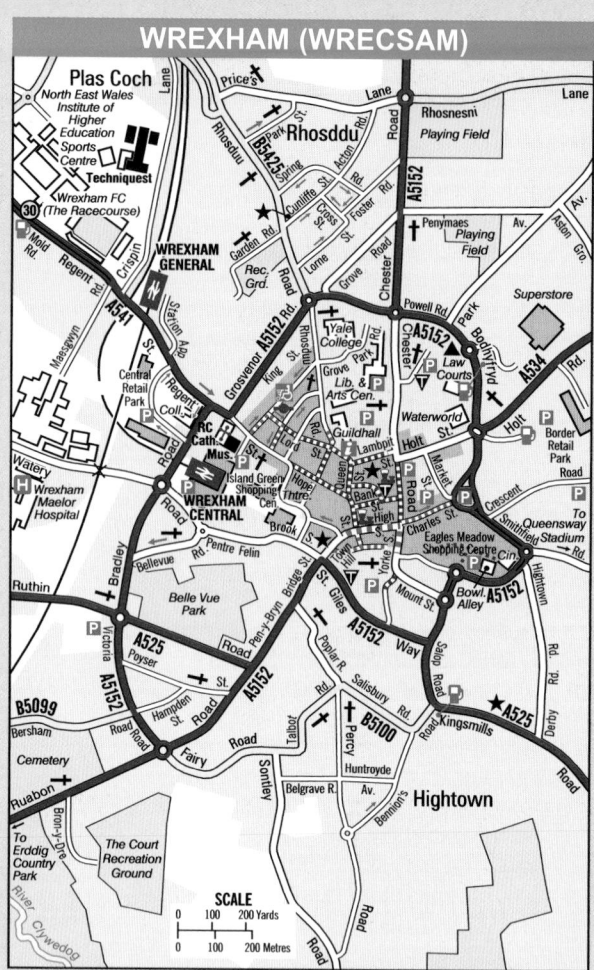

YORK

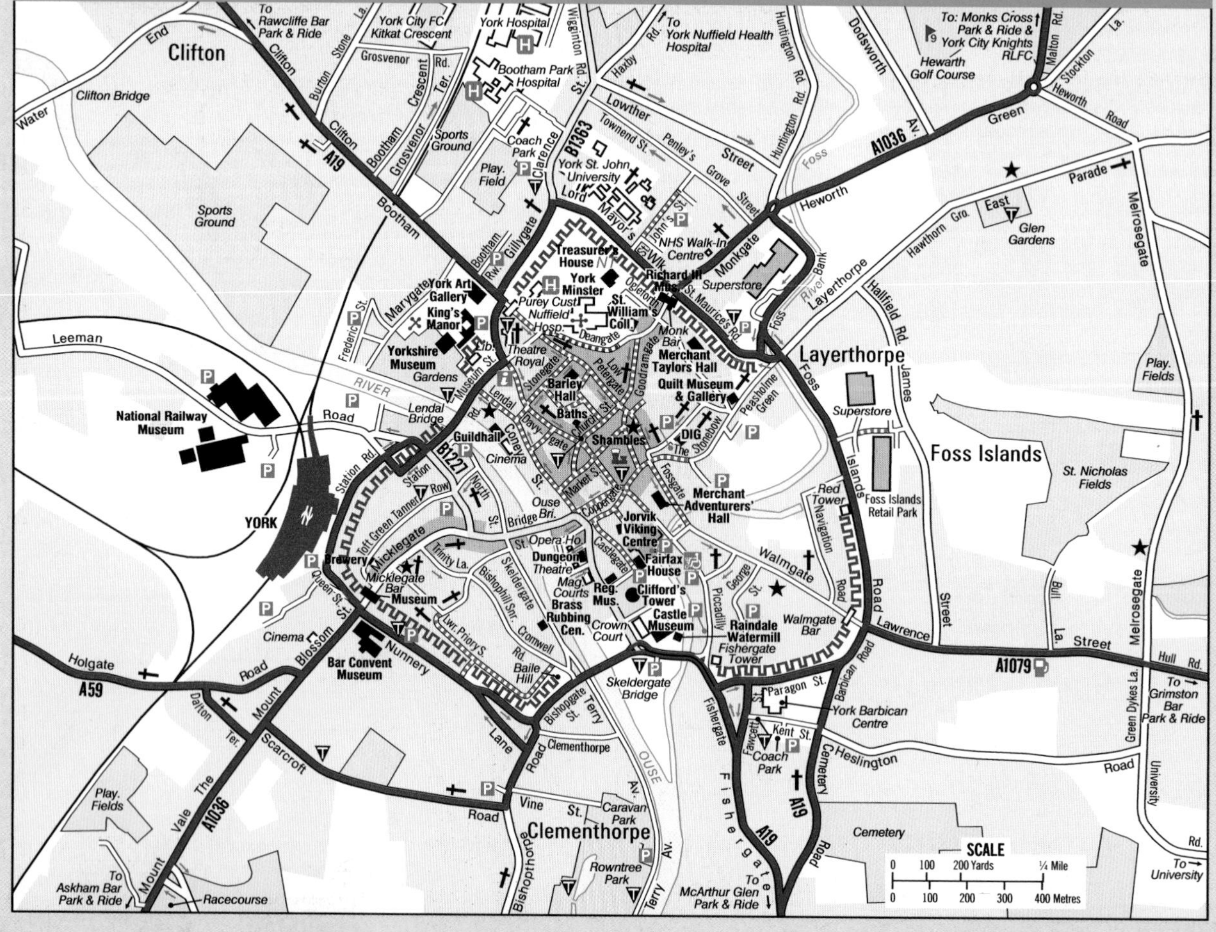

HARWICH

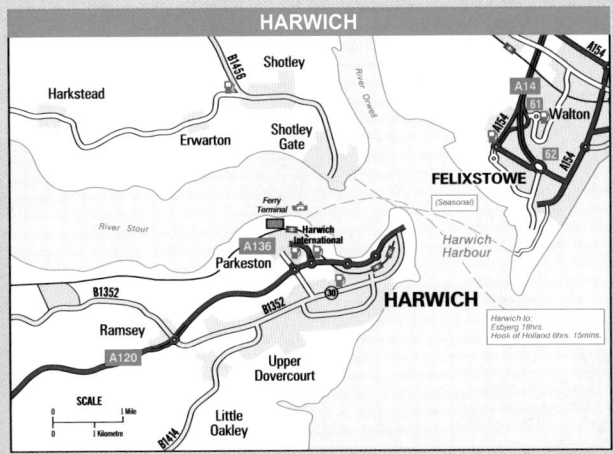

KINGSTON UPON HULL

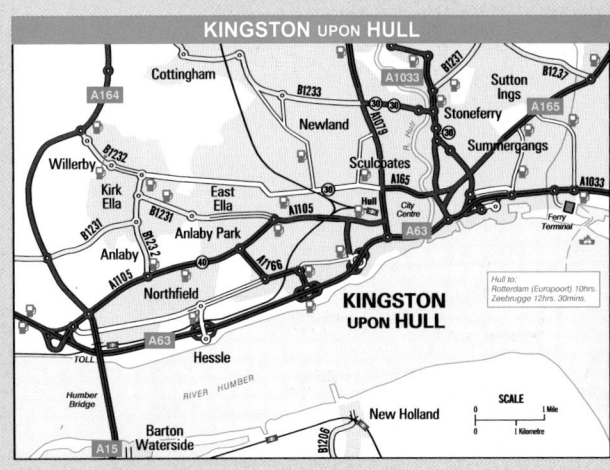

NEWCASTLE UPON TYNE

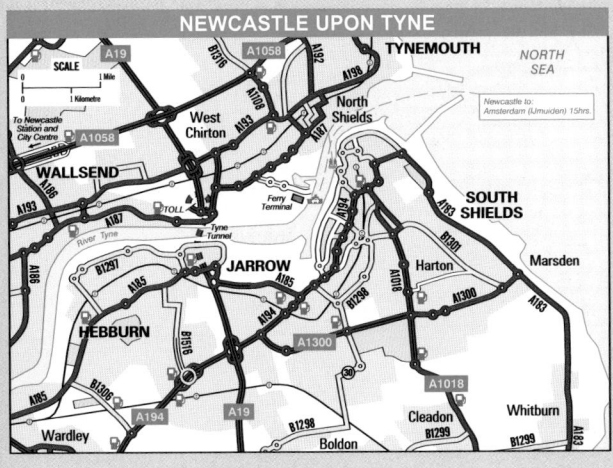

NEWHAVEN

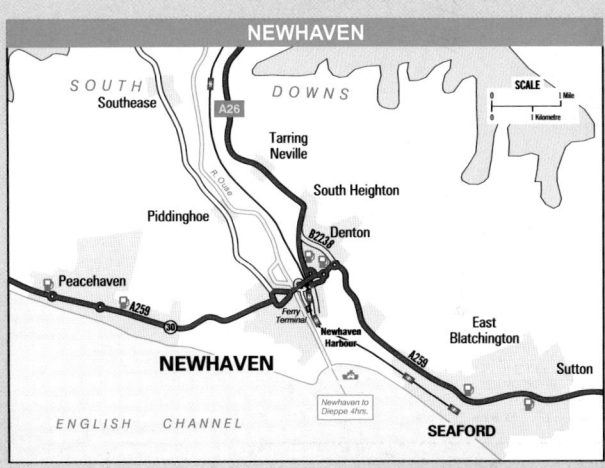

PEMBROKE DOCK (DOC PENFRO)

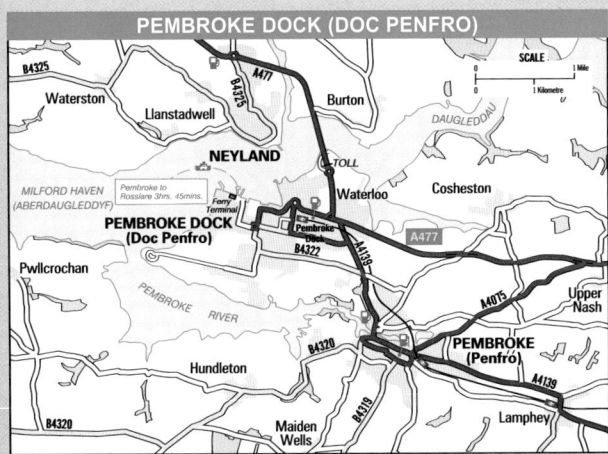

POOLE

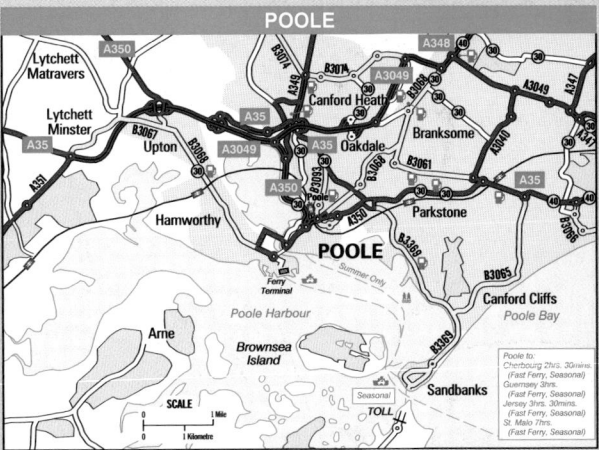

PORTSMOUTH

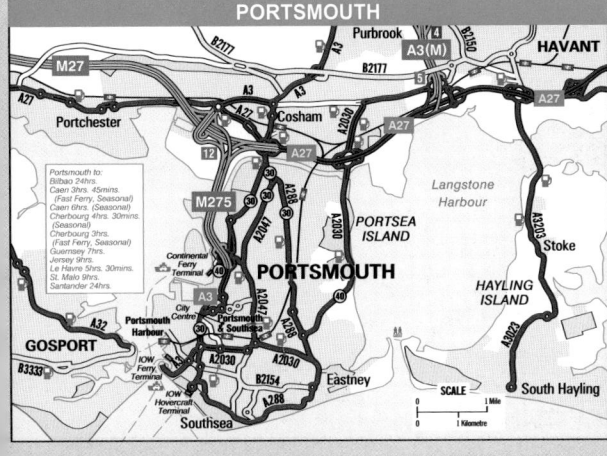

WEYMOUTH

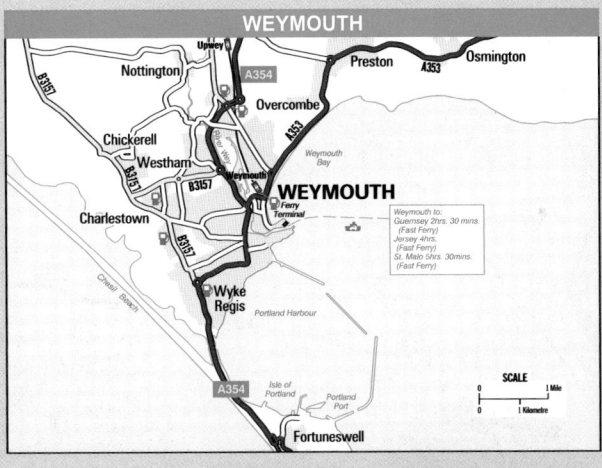

BIRMINGHAM

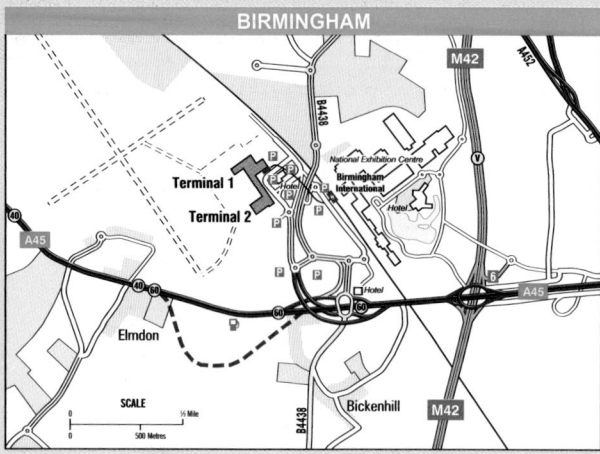

EAST MIDLANDS

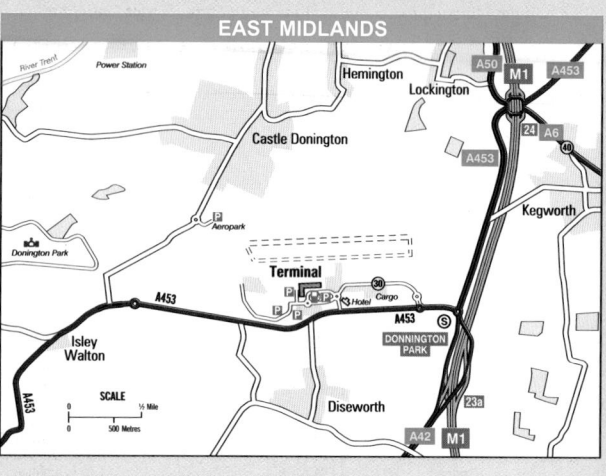

GLASGOW

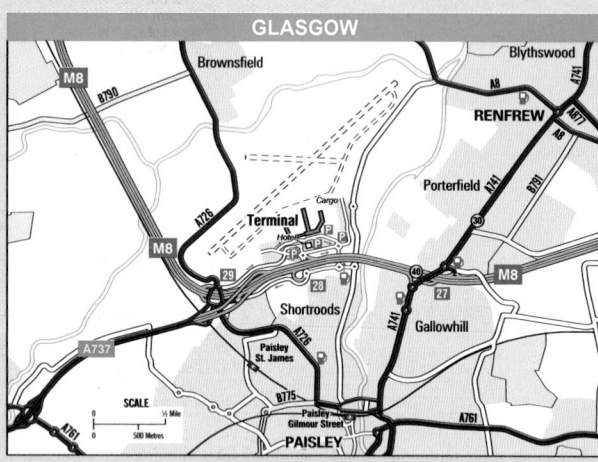

LONDON GATWICK

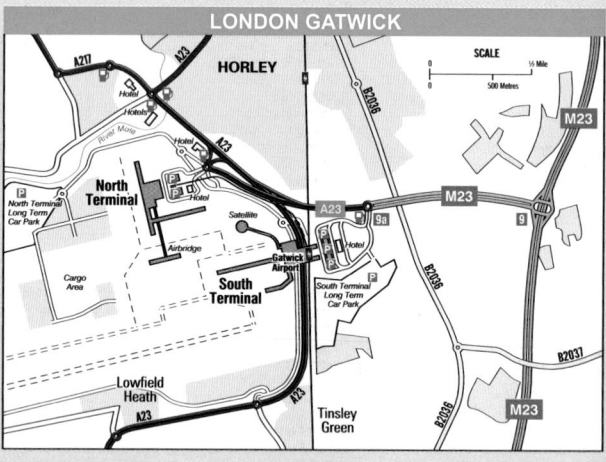

LONDON HEATHROW

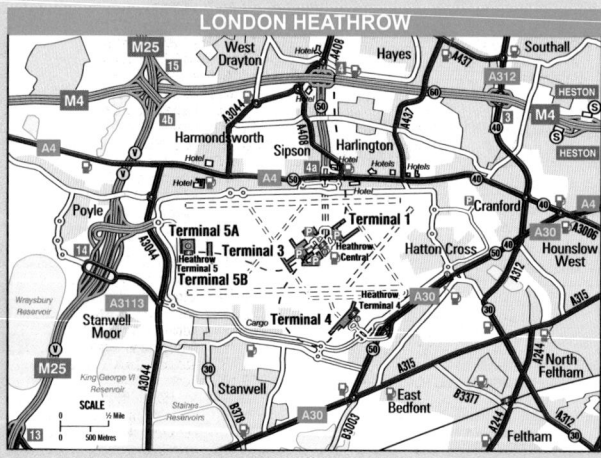

LONDON LUTON

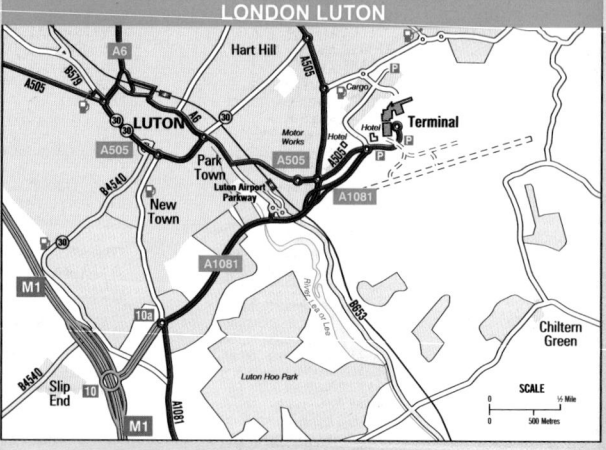

LONDON STANSTED

MANCHESTER INTERNATIONAL

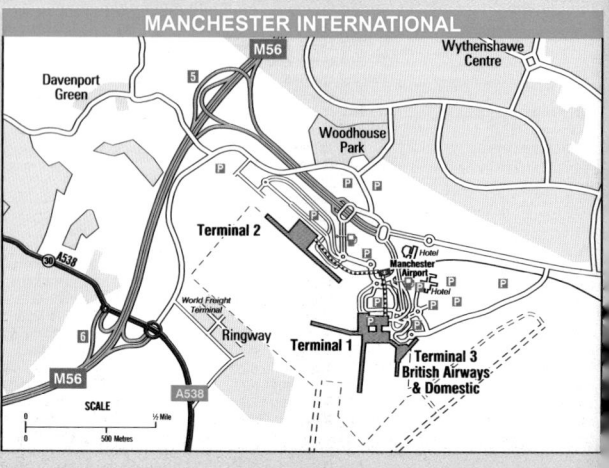

INDEX TO CITIES, TOWNS, VILLAGES, HAMLETS, LOCATIONS, AIRPORTS & PORTS

(1) A strict alphabetical order is used e.g. An Dùnan follows Andreas but precedes Andwell.

(2) The map reference given refers to the actual map square in which the town spot or built-up area is located and not to the place name.

(3) Major towns are shown in bold, i.e. **Aberdeen.** *Aber* . . . .3G **153** & **187**. Where they appear on a Town Plan a second page reference is given.

(4) Where two or more places of the same name occur in the same County or Unitary Authority, the nearest large town is also given; e.g. Achiemore. *High* . . . .2D **166** (nr. Durness) indicates that Achiemore is located in square 2D on page **166** and is situated near Durness in the Unitary Authority of Highland.

(5) Only one reference is given although due to page overlaps the place may appear on more than one page.

COUNTIES and UNITARY AUTHORITIES with the abbreviations used in this index

Aberdeen : *Aber*
Aberdeenshire : *Abers*
Angus : *Ang*
Argyll & Bute : *Arg*
Bath & N E Somerset : *Bath*
Bedford : *Bed*
Blackburn with Darwen : *Bkbn*
Blackpool : *Bkpl*
Blaenau Gwent : *Blae*
Bournemouth : *Bour*
Bracknell Forest : *Brac*
Bridgend : *B'end*
Brighton & Hove : *Brig*
Bristol : *Bris*
Buckinghamshire : *Buck*
Caerphilly : *Cphy*
Cambridgeshire : *Cambs*
Cardiff : *Card*
Carmarthenshire : *Carm*
Central Bedfordshire : *C Beds*
Ceredigion : *Cdgn*
Cheshire East : *Ches E*
Cheshire West & Chester : *Ches W*
Clackmannanshire : *Clac*
Conwy : *Cnwy*
Cornwall : *Corn*
Cumbria : *Cumb*
Darlington : *Darl*
Denbighshire : *Den*
Derby : *Derb*
Derbyshire : *Derbs*
Devon : *Devn*
Dorset : *Dors*
Dumfries & Galloway : *Dum*
Dundee : *D'dee*
Durham : *Dur*
East Ayrshire : *E Ayr*
East Dunbartonshire : *E Dun*
East Lothian : *E Lot*
East Renfrewshire : *E Ren*
East Riding of Yorkshire : *E Yor*
East Sussex : *E Sus*
Edinburgh : *Edin*
Essex : *Essx*
Falkirk : *Falk*
Fife : *Fife*
Flintshire : *Flin*
Glasgow : *Glas*
Gloucestershire : *Glos*
Greater London : *G Lon*
Greater Manchester : *G Man*
Gwynedd : *Gwyn*
Halton : *Hal*
Hampshire : *Hants*
Hartlepool : *Hart*
Herefordshire : *Here*
Hertfordshire : *Herts*
Highland : *High*
Inverclyde : *Inv*
Isle of Anglesey : *IOA*
Isle of Man : *IOM*
Isle of Wight : *IOW*
Isles of Scilly : *IOS*
Kent : *Kent*
Kingston upon Hull : *Hull*
Lancashire : *Lanc*
Leicester : *Leic*
Leicestershire : *Leics*
Lincolnshire : *Linc*
Luton : *Lutn*
Medway : *Medw*
Merseyside : *Mers*
Merthyr Tydfil : *Mer T*
Middlesbrough : *Midd*
Midlothian : *Midl*
Milton Keynes : *Mil*
Monmouthshire : *Mon*
Moray : *Mor*
Neath Port Talbot : *Neat*
Newport : *Newp*
Norfolk : *Norf*
Northamptonshire : *Nptn*
North Ayrshire : *N Ayr*
North East Lincolnshire : *NE Lin*
North Lanarkshire : *N Lan*
North Lincolnshire : *N Lin*
North Somerset : *N Som*
Northumberland : *Nmbd*
North Yorkshire : *N Yor*
Nottingham : *Nott*
Nottinghamshire : *Notts*
Orkney : *Orkn*
Oxfordshire : *Oxon*
Pembrokeshire : *Pemb*
Perth & Kinross : *Per*
Peterborough : *Pet*
Plymouth : *Plym*
Poole : *Pool*
Portsmouth : *Port*
Powys : *Powy*
Reading : *Read*
Redcar & Cleveland : *Red C*
Renfrewshire : *Ren*
Rhondda Cynon Taff : *Rhon*
Rutland : *Rut*
Scottish Borders : *Bord*
Shetland : *Shet*
Shropshire : *Shrp*
Slough : *Slo*
Somerset : *Som*
Southampton : *Sotn*
South Ayrshire : *S Ayr*
Southend-on-Sea : *S'end*
South Gloucestershire : *S Glo*
South Lanarkshire : *S Lan*
South Yorkshire : *S Yor*
Staffordshire : *Staf*
Stirling : *Stir*
Stockton-on-Tees : *Stoc T*
Stoke-on-Trent : *Stoke*
Suffolk : *Suff*
Surrey : *Surr*
Swansea : *Swan*
Swindon : *Swin*
Telford & Wrekin : *Telf*
Thurrock : *Thur*
Torbay : *Torb*
Torfaen : *Torf*
Tyne & Wear : *Tyne*
Vale of Glamorgan, The : *V Glam*
Warrington : *Warr*
Warwickshire : *Warw*
West Berkshire : *W Ber*
West Dunbartonshire : *W Dun*
Western Isles : *W Isl*
West Lothian : *W Lot*
West Midlands : *W Mid*
West Sussex : *W Sus*
West Yorkshire : *W Yor*
Wiltshire : *Wilts*
Windsor & Maidenhead : *Wind*
Wokingham : *Wok*
Worcestershire : *Worc*
Wrexham : *Wrex*
York : *York*

INDEX

A

Abbas Combe. *Som* 4C **22**
Abberley. *Worc* 4B **60**
Abberley Common. *Worc* 4B **60**
Abberton. *Essx* 4D **54**
Abberton. *Worc* 5D **61**
Abberwick. *Nmbd* 3F **121**
Abbess Roding. *Essx* 4F **53**
Abbey. *Devn* 1E **13**
Abbey-cwm-hir. *Powy* 3C **58**
Abbeydale. *S Yor* 2H **85**
Abbeydale Park. *S Yor* 2H **85**
Abbey Dore. *Here* 2G **47**
Abbey Gate. *Devn* 3F **13**
Abbey Hulton. *Stoke* 1D **72**
Abbey St Bathans. *Bord* 3D **130**
Abbeystead. *Lanc* 4E **97**
Abbeytown. *Cumb* 4C **112**
Abbey Village. *Lanc* 2E **91**
Abbey Wood. *G Lon* 3F **39**
Abbots Ann. *Hants* 2B **24**
Abbots Bickington. *Devn* 1D **11**
Abbots Bromley. *Staf* 3E **73**
Abbotsbury. *Dors* 4A **14**
Abbotsham. *Devn* 4E **19**
Abbotskerswell. *Devn* 2E **9**
Abbots Langley. *Herts* 5A **52**
Abbots Leigh. *N Som* 4A **34**
Abbotsley. *Cambs* 5B **64**
Abbots Morton. *Worc* 5E **61**
Abbots Ripton. *Cambs* 3B **64**
Abbot's Salford. *Warw* 5E **61**
Abbotstone. *Hants* 3D **24**
Abbots Worthy. *Hants* 3C **24**
Abcott. *Shrp* 3F **59**
Abdon. *Shrp* 2H **59**
Abenhall. *Glos* 4B **48**
Aber. *Cdgn* 1E **45**
Aberaeron. *Cdgn* 4D **56**
Aberafan. *Neat* 3G **31**
Aberaman. *Rhon* 5D **46**
Aberangell. *Powy* 4H **69**
Aberarad. *Carm* 1H **43**
Aberarder. *High* 1A **150**
Aberargie. *Per* 2D **136**
Aberarth. *Cdgn* 4D **57**
Aberavon. *Neat* 3G **31**
Aber-banc. *Cdgn* 1D **44**
Aberbargoed. *Cphy* 2E **33**
Aberbechan. *Powy* 1D **58**
Aberbeeg. *Blae* 5F **47**
Aberbowlan. *Carm* 2G **45**
Aberbran. *Powy* 3C **46**
Abercanaid. *Mer T* 5D **46**
Abercarn. *Cphy* 2F **33**
Abercastle. *Pemb* 1C **42**
Abercegir. *Powy* 5H **69**
Aberchalder. *High* 3F **149**
Aberchirder. *Abers* 3D **160**
Abercorn. *W Lot* 2D **129**
Abercraf. *Powy* 4B **46**
Abercregan. *Neat* 2B **32**
Abercrombie. *Fife* 3H **137**
Abercwmboi. *Rhon* 2D **32**
Abercych. *Pemb* 1C **44**
Abercynon. *Rhon* 2D **32**
Aber-Cywarch. *Gwyn* 4A **70**
Aberdalgie. *Per* 1C **136**
Aberdar. *Rhon* 5C **46**
Aberdare. *Rhon* 5C **46**
Aberdaron. *Gwyn* 3A **68**
Aberdaugleddau. *Pemb* 4D **42**
Aberdeen. *Aber* . . . . .3G **153** & **187**
Aberdeen (Dyce) Airport. *Aber* 2F **153**
Aberdesach. *Gwyn* 5D **80**
Aberdour. *Fife* 1E **129**
Aberdovey. *Gwyn* 1F **57**
Aberdulais. *Neat* 5A **46**
Aberdyfi. *Gwyn* 1F **57**
Aberedw. *Powy* 1D **46**
Abereiddy. *Pemb* 1B **42**
Abererch. *Gwyn* 2C **68**
Aberfan. *Mer T* 5D **46**
Aberfeldy. *Per* 4F **143**
Aberffraw. *IOA* 4C **80**
Aberffrwd. *Cdgn* 3F **57**
Aberford. *W Yor* 1E **93**
Aberfoyle. *Stir* 3E **135**
Abergarw. *B'end* 3C **32**
Abergarwed. *Neat* 5B **46**
Abergavenny. *Mon* 4G **47**
Abergele. *Cnwy* 3B **82**
Aber-Giar. *Carm* 1F **45**
Abergorlech. *Carm* 2F **45**
Abergwaun. *Pemb* 1D **42**
Abergwesyn. *Powy* 5A **58**
Abergwili. *Carm* 3E **45**
Abergwynfi. *Neat* 2B **32**
Abergwyngregyn. *Gwyn* 3F **81**
Abergynolwyn. *Gwyn* 5F **69**
Aberhafesp. *Powy* 1C **58**
Aberhonddu. *Powy* 3D **46**
Aberhosan. *Powy* 1H **57**
Aberkenfig. *B'end* 3B **32**
Aberlady. *E Lot* 2A **130**
Aberlemno. *Ang* 3E **145**
Aberllefenni. *Gwyn* 5G **69**
Abermaw. *Gwyn* 4F **69**
Abermeurig. *Cdgn* 5E **57**
Aber-miwl. *Powy* 1D **58**
Abermule. *Powy* 1D **58**
Abernant. *Carm* 2H **43**
Abernant. *Rhon* 5D **46**
Abernethy. *Per* 2D **136**
Abernyte. *Per* 5B **144**
Aber-oer. *Wrex* 1E **71**
Aberpennar. *Rhon* 2D **32**
Aberporth. *Cdgn* 5B **56**
Aberriw. *Powy* 5D **70**
Abersoch. *Gwyn* 3C **68**
Abersychan. *Torf* 5F **47**
Abertawe. *Swan* . . . . .3F **31** & **Swansea 212**
Aberteifi. *Cdgn* 1B **44**
Aberthin. *V Glam* 4D **32**
Abertillery. *Blae* 5F **47**
Abertridwr. *Cphy* 3E **32**
Abertridwr. *Powy* 4C **70**
Abertyleri. *Blae* 5F **47**
Abertysswg. *Cphy* 5E **47**
Aberuthven. *Per* 2B **136**
Aber Village. *Powy* 3E **46**
Aberyscir. *Powy* 3D **46**
Aberystwyth. *Cdgn* . . . . .2E **57** & **187**
Abhainn Suidhe. *W Isl* 7C **171**
Abingdon. *Oxon* 2C **36**
Abinger Common. *Surr* 1C **26**
Abinger Hammer. *Surr* 1B **26**
Abington. *S Lan* 2B **118**
Abington Pigotts. *Cambs* 1D **52**
Ab Kettleby. *Leics* 3E **74**
Ab Lench. *Worc* 5E **61**
Ablington. *Glos* 5G **49**
Ablington. *Wilts* 2G **23**
Abney. *Derbs* 3F **85**
Aboyne. *Abers* 4C **152**
Abram. *G Man* 4E **90**
Abriachan. *High* 5H **157**
Abridge. *Essx* 1F **39**
Abronhill. *N Lan* 2A **128**
Abson. *S Glo* 4C **34**
Abthorpe. *Nptn* 1E **51**
Abune-the-Hill. *Orkn* 5B **172**
Aby. *Linc* 3D **88**
Acairseid. *W Isl* 8C **170**
Acaster Malbis. *York* 5H **99**
Acaster Selby. *N Yor* 5H **99**
Accott. *Devn* 3G **19**
Accrington. *Lanc* 2F **91**
Acha. *Arg* 3C **138**
Achachork. *High* 4D **155**
Achadh a' Chuirn. *High* 1E **147**
Achahoish. *Arg* 2F **125**
Achaleven. *Arg* 5D **140**
Achallader. *Arg* 4H **141**
Acha Mor. *W Isl* 5F **171**
Achanalt. *High* 2E **157**
Achandunie. *High* 1A **158**
Ach'an Todhair. *High* 1E **141**
Achany. *High* 3C **164**
Achaphubuil. *High* 1E **141**
Acharacle. *High* 2A **140**
Acharn. *Ang* 1B **144**
Acharn. *Per* 4E **143**
Acharole. *High* 3E **169**
Achateny. *High* 2G **139**
Achavanich. *High* 4D **169**
Achdalieu. *High* 1E **141**
Achduart. *High* 3E **163**
Achentoul. *High* 5A **168**
Achfary. *High* 5C **166**
Achfrish. *High* 2C **164**
Achgarve. *High* 4C **162**
Achiemore. *High* . . . . .2D **166** (nr. Durness)
Achiemore. *High* . . . . .3A **168** (nr. Thurso)
A'Chill. *High* 3A **146**
Achiltibuie. *High* 3E **163**
Achina. *High* 2H **167**
Achinahuagh. *High* 2F **167**
Achindarroch. *High* 3E **141**
Achinduich. *High* 3C **164**
Achinduin. *Arg* 5C **140**
Achininver. *High* 2F **167**
Achintee. *High* 4B **156**
Achintraid. *High* 5H **155**
Achleck. *Arg* 4F **139**
Achlorachan. *High* 3F **157**
Achluachrach. *High* 5E **149**
Achlyness. *High* 3C **166**
Achmelvich. *High* 1E **163**
Achmony. *High* 5H **157**
Achmore. *High* . . . . .5A **156** (nr. Stromeferry)
Achmore. *High* . . . . .4E **163** (nr. Ullapool)
Achnacarnin. *High* 1E **163**
Achnacarry. *High* 5D **148**
Achnaclerach. *High* 2G **157**
Achnacloich. *High* 3D **147**
Ach na Cloiche. *High* 3D **147**
Achnaconeran. *High* 2G **149**
Achnacroish. *Arg* 4C **140**
Achnafalnich. *Arg* 1B **134**
Achnagarron. *High* 1A **158**
Achnaha. *High* 2F **139**
Achnahanat. *High* 4C **164**
Achnahannet. *High* 1D **151**
Achnairn. *High* 2C **164**
Achnamara. *Arg* 1F **125**
Achnanellan. *High* 5C **148**
Achnangoul. *Arg* 3H **133**
Achnasheen. *High* 3D **156**
Achnashellach. *High* 4C **156**
Achosnich. *High* 2F **139**
Achow. *High* 5E **169**
Achranich. *High* 4B **140**
Achreamie. *High* 2C **168**
Achriabhach. *High* 2F **141**
Achriesgill. *High* 3C **166**
Achrimsdale. *High* 3G **165**
Achscrabster. *High* 2C **168**
Achtoty. *High* 2G **167**
Achurch. *Nptn* 2H **63**
Achuvoldrach. *High* 3F **167**
Achvaich. *High* 4E **164**
Achvoan. *High* 3E **165**
Ackenthwaite. *Cumb* 1E **97**
Ackergill. *High* 3F **169**
Ackergillshore. *High* 3F **169**
Acklam. *Midd* 3B **106**
Acklam. *N Yor* 3B **100**
Ackleton. *Shrp* 1B **60**
Acklington. *Nmbd* 4G **121**
Ackton. *W Yor* 2E **93**
Ackworth Moor Top. *W Yor* 3E **93**
Acle. *Norf* 4G **79**
Acocks Green. *W Mid* 2F **61**
Acol. *Kent* 4H **41**
Acomb. *Nmbd* 3C **114**
Acomb. *York* 4H **99**
Aconbury. *Here* 2A **48**
Acre. *G Man* 4H **91**
Acre. *Lanc* 2F **91**
Acrefair. *Wrex* 1E **71**
Acrise. *Kent* 1F **29**
Acton. *Ches E* 5A **84**
Acton. *Dors* 5E **15**
Acton. *G Lon* 2C **38**
Acton. *Shrp* 2F **59**
Acton. *Staf* 1C **72**
Acton. *Suff* 1B **54**
Acton. *Worc* 4C **60**
Acton. *Wrex* 5F **83**
Acton Beauchamp. *Here* 5A **60**
Acton Bridge. *Ches W* 3H **83**
Acton Burnell. *Shrp* 5H **71**
Acton Green. *Here* 5A **60**
Acton Pigott. *Shrp* 5H **71**
Acton Round. *Shrp* 1A **60**
Acton Scott. *Shrp* 2G **59**
Acton Trussell. *Staf* 4D **72**
Acton Turville. *S Glo* 3D **34**
Adabroc. *W Isl* 1H **171**
Adam's Hill. *Worc* 3D **60**
Adbaston. *Staf* 3B **72**
Adber. *Dors* 4B **22**
Adderbury. *Oxon* 2C **50**
Adderley. *Shrp* 2A **72**
Adderstone. *Nmbd* 1F **121**
Addiewell. *W Lot* 3C **128**
Addingham. *W Yor* 5C **98**
Addington. *Buck* 3F **51**
Addington. *G Lon* 4E **39**
Addington. *Kent* 5A **40**
Addinston. *Bord* 4B **130**
Addiscombe. *G Lon* 4E **39**
Addlestone. *Surr* 4B **38**
Addlethorpe. *Linc* 4E **89**
Adeney. *Telf* 4B **72**
Adfa. *Powy* 5C **70**
Adforton. *Here* 3G **59**
Adgestone. *IOW* 4D **16**
Adisham. *Kent* 5G **41**
Adlestrop. *Glos* 3H **49**
Adlingfleet. *E Yor* 2B **94**
Adlington. *Ches E* 2D **84**
Adlington. *Lanc* 3E **90**
Admaston. *Staf* 3E **73**
Admaston. *Telf* 4A **72**
Admington. *Warw* 1G **49**
Adpar. *Cdgn* 1D **44**
Adsborough. *Som* 4F **21**
Adstock. *Buck* 2F **51**
Adstone. *Nptn* 5C **62**
Adversane. *W Sus* 3B **26**
Advie. *High* 5F **159**
Adwalton. *W Yor* 2C **92**
Adwell. *Oxon* 2E **37**
Adwick le Street. *S Yor* 4F **93**
Adwick upon Dearne. *S Yor* 4E **93**
Adziel. *Abers* 3G **161**
Ae. *Dum* 1A **112**
Affleck. *Abers* 1F **153**
Affpuddle. *Dors* 3D **14**
Affric Lodge. *High* 1D **148**
Afon-wen. *Flin* 3D **82**
Agglethorpe. *N Yor* 1C **98**
Aglionby. *Cumb* 4F **113**
Aigburth. *Mers* 2F **83**
Aiginis. *W Isl* 4G **171**
Aike. *E Yor* 5E **101**
Aikers. *Orkn* 8D **172**
Aiketgate. *Cumb* 5F **113**
Aikhead. *Cumb* 5D **112**
Aikton. *Cumb* 4D **112**
Ailey. *Here* 1G **47**
Ailsworth. *Pet* 1A **64**
Ainderby Quernhow. *N Yor* 1F **99**
Ainderby Steeple. *N Yor* 5A **106**
Aingers Green. *Essx* 3E **54**
Ainsdale. *Mers* 3B **90**
Ainsdale-on-Sea. *Mers* 3B **90**
Ainstable. *Cumb* 5G **113**
Ainsworth. *G Man* 3F **91**
Ainthorpe. *N Yor* 4E **107**

Aintree. *Mers* 1F 83
Aird. *Arg* 3E 133
Aird. *Dum* 3F 109
Aird. *High* 1G 155
(nr. Port Henderson)
Aird. *High* 3D 147
(nr. Tarskavaig)
Aird. *W Isl* 3C 170
(on Benbecula)
Aird. *W Isl* 4H 171
(on Isle of Lewis)
Àird a Bhasair. *High* 3E 147
Aird a Mhachair. *W Isl* 4C 170
Aird a Mhulaidh. *W Isl* 6D 171
Aird Asaig. *W Isl* 7D 171
Aird Dhail. *W Isl* 1G 171
Airdens. *High* 4D 164
Airdeny. *Arg* 1G 133
Aird Mhidhinis. *W Isl* 8C 170
Aird Mhighe. *W Isl* 8D 171
(nr. Ceann a Bhaigh)
Aird Mhighe. *W Isl* 9C 171
(nr. Fionnsabhagh)
Aird Mhor. *W Isl* 8C 170
(on Barra)
Aird Mhor. *W Isl* 4D 170
(on South Uist)
Airdrie. *N Lan* 3A 128
Aird Shleibhe. *W Isl* 9D 171
Aird, The. *High* 3D 154
Aird Thunga. *W Isl* 4G 171
Aird Uig. *W Isl* 4C 171
Airedale. *W Yor* 2E 93
Airidh a Bhruaich. *W Isl* 6E 171
Airies. *Dum* 3E 109
Airmyn. *E Yor* 2H 93
Airntully. *Per* 5H 143
Airor. *High* 3F 147
Airth. *Falk* 1C 128
Airton. *N Yor* 4B 98
Aisby. *Linc* 1F 87
(nr. Gainsborough)
Aisby. *Linc* 2H 75
(nr. Grantham)
Aisgernis. *W Isl* 6C 170
Aish. *Devn* 2C 8
(nr. Buckfastleigh)
Aish. *Devn* 3E 9
(nr. Totnes)
Aisholt. *Som* 3E 21
Aiskew. *N Yor* 1E 99
Aislaby. *N Yor* 1B 100
(nr. Pickering)
Aislaby. *N Yor* 4F 107
(nr. Whitby)
Aislaby. *Stoc T* 3B 106
Aisthorpe. *Linc* 2G 87
Aith. *Shet* 2H 173
(on Fetlar)
Aith. *Shet* 6E 173
(on Mainland)
Aithsetter. *Shet* 8F 173
Akeld. *Nmbd* 2D 120
Akeley. *Buck* 2F 51
Akenham. *Suff* 1E 55
Albaston. *Corn* 5E 11
Alberbury. *Shrp* 4F 71
Albert Town. *Pemb* 3D 42
Albert Village. *Leics* 4H 73
Albourne. *W Sus* 4D 26
Albrighton. *Shrp* 4G 71
(nr. Shrewsbury)
Albrighton. *Shrp* 5C 72
(nr. Telford)
Alburgh. *Norf* 2E 67
Albury. *Herts* 3E 53
Albury. *Surr* 1B 26
Albyfield. *Cumb* 4G 113
Alby Hill. *Norf* 2D 78
Alcaig. *High* 3H 157
Alcaston. *Shrp* 2G 59
Alcester. *Warw* 5E 61
Alciston. *E Sus* 5G 27
Alcombe. *Som* 2C 20
Alconbury. *Cambs* 3A 64
Alconbury Weston. *Cambs* 3A 64
Aldborough. *Norf* 2D 78
Aldborough. *N Yor* 3G 99
Aldbourne. *Wilts* 4A 36
Aldbrough. *E Yor* 1F 95
Aldbrough St John. *N Yor* 3F 105
Aldbury. *Herts* 4H 51
Aldcliffe. *Lanc* 3D 96
Aldclune. *Per* 2G 143
Aldeburgh. *Suff* 5G 67
Aldeby. *Norf* 1G 67
Aldenham. *Herts* 1C 38
Alderbury. *Wilts* 4G 23
Aldercar. *Derbs* 1B 74
Alderford. *Norf* 4D 78
Alderholt. *Dors* 1G 15
Alderley. *Glos* 2C 34
Alderley Edge. *Ches E* 3C 84
Aldermaston. *W Ber* 5D 36
Aldermaston Stoke. *W Ber* 5E 36
Aldermaston Wharf. *W Ber* 5E 36
Alderminster. *Warw* 1H 49
Alder Moor. *Staf* 3G 73
Aldersey Green. *Ches W* 5G 83
Aldershot. *Hants* 1G 25
Alderton. *Glos* 2E 49
Alderton. *Nptn* 1F 51
Alderton. *Shrp* 3G 71
Alderton. *Suff* 1G 55
Alderton. *Wilts* 3D 34
Alderton Fields. *Glos* 2F 49
Alderwasley. *Derbs* 5H 85
Aldfield. *N Yor* 3E 99
Aldford. *Ches W* 5G 83
Aldgate. *Rut* 5G 75
Aldham. *Essx* 3C 54
Aldham. *Suff* 1D 54
Aldingbourne. *W Sus* 5A 26
Aldingham. *Cumb* 2B 96
Aldington. *Kent* 2E 29
Aldington. *Worc* 1F 49
Aldington Frith. *Kent* 2E 29
Aldochlay. *Arg* 4C 134
Aldon. *Shrp* 3G 59
Aldoth. *Cumb* 5C 112
Aldreth. *Cambs* 3D 64
Aldridge. *W Mid* 5E 73
Aldringham. *Suff* 4G 67
Aldsworth. *Glos* 4G 49
Aldsworth. *W Sus* 2F 17
Aldwark. *Derbs* 5G 85
Aldwark. *N Yor* 3G 99
Aldwick. *W Sus* 3H 17
Aldwincle. *Nptn* 2H 63
Aldworth. *W Ber* 4D 36
Alexandria. *W Dun* 1E 127
Aley. *Som* 3E 21
Aley Green. *C Beds* 4A 52
Alfardisworthy. *Devn* 1C 10
Alfington. *Devn* 3E 12
Alfold. *Surr* 2B 26
Alfold Bars. *W Sus* 2B 26
Alfold Crossways. *Surr* 2B 26
Alford. *Abers* 2C 152
Alford. *Linc* 3D 88
Alford. *Som* 3B 22
Alfreton. *Derbs* 5B 86
Alfrick. *Worc* 5B 60
Alfrick Pound. *Worc* 5B 60
Alfriston. *E Sus* 5G 27
Algarkirk. *Linc* 2B 76
Alhampton. *Som* 3B 22
Aline Lodge. *W Isl* 6D 171
Alkborough. *N Lin* 2B 94
Alkerton. *Oxon* 1B 50
Alkham. *Kent* 1G 29
Alkington. *Shrp* 2H 71
Alkmonton. *Derbs* 2F 73
Alladale Lodge. *High* 5B 164
Allaleigh. *Devn* 3E 9
Allanbank. *N Lan* 4B 128
Allanton. *N Lan* 4B 128
Allanton. *Bord* 4E 131
Allaston. *Glos* 5B 48
Allbrook. *Hants* 4C 24
All Cannings. *Wilts* 5F 35
Allendale Town. *Nmbd* 4B 114
Allen End. *Warw* 1F 61
Allenheads. *Nmbd* 5B 114
Allensford. *Dur* 5D 115
Allen's Green. *Herts* 4E 53
Allensmore. *Here* 2H 47
Allenton. *Derb* 2A 74
Aller. *Som* 4H 21
Allerby. *Cumb* 1B 102
Allercombe. *Devn* 3D 12
Allerford. *Som* 2C 20
Allerston. *N Yor* 1C 100
Allerthorpe. *E Yor* 5B 100
Allerton. *Mers* 2G 83
Allerton. *W Yor* 1B 92
Allerton Bywater. *W Yor* 2E 93
Allerton Mauleverer. *N Yor* 4G 99
Allesley. *W Mid* 2G 61
Allestree. *Derb* 2H 73
Allet. *Corn* 4B 6
Allexton. *Leics* 5F 75
Allgreave. *Ches E* 4D 84
Allhallows. *Medw* 3C 40
Allhallows-on-Sea. *Medw* 3C 40
Alligin Shuas. *High* 3H 155
Allimore Green. *Staf* 4C 72
Allington. *Kent* 5B 40
Allington. *Linc* 1F 75
Allington. *Wilts* 3H 23
(nr. Amesbury)
Allington. *Wilts* 5F 35
(nr. Devizes)
Allithwaite. *Cumb* 2C 96
Alloa. *Clac* 4A 136
Allonby. *Cumb* 5B 112
Allostock. *Ches W* 3B 84
Alloway. *S Ayr* 3C 116
Allowenshay. *Som* 1G 13
All Saints South Elmham. *Suff* 2F 67
Allscott. *Shrp* 1B 60
Allscott. *Telf* 4A 72
All Stretton. *Shrp* 1G 59
Allt. *Carm* 5F 45
Alltami. *Flin* 4E 83
Alltgobhlach. *N Ayr* 5G 125
Alltmawr. *Powy* 1D 46
Alltnacaillich. *High* 4E 167
Allt na h-Airbhe. *High* 4F 163
Alltour. *High* 5E 148
Alltsigh. *High* 2G 149
Alltwalis. *Carm* 2E 45
Alltwen. *Neat* 5H 45
Alltyblacca. *Cdgn* 1F 45
Allt-y-goed. *Pemb* 1B 44
Almeley. *Here* 5F 59
Almeley Wooton. *Here* 5F 59
Almer. *Dors* 3E 15
Almholme. *S Yor* 4F 93
Almington. *Staf* 2B 72
Alminstone Cross. *Devn* 4D 18
Almodington. *W Sus* 3G 17
Almondbank. *Per* 1C 136
Almondbury. *W Yor* 3B 92
Almondsbury. *S Glo* 3B 34
Alne. *N Yor* 3G 99
Alness. *High* 2A 158
Alnessferry. *High* 2A 158
Alnham. *Nmbd* 3D 121
Alnmouth. *Nmbd* 3G 121
Alnwick. *Nmbd* 3F 121
Alphamstone. *Essx* 2B 54
Alpheton. *Suff* 5A 66
Alphington. *Devn* 3C 12
Alpington. *Norf* 5E 79
Alport. *Derbs* 4G 85
Alport. *Powy* 1E 59
Alpraham. *Ches E* 5H 83
Alresford. *Essx* 3D 54
Alrewas. *Staf* 4F 73
Alsager. *Ches E* 5B 84
Alsagers Bank. *Staf* 1C 72
Alsop en le Dale. *Derbs* 5F 85
Alston. *Cumb* 5A 114
Alston. *Devn* 2G 13
Alstone. *Glos* 2E 49
Alstone. *Som* 2G 21
Alstonefield. *Staf* 5F 85
Alston Sutton. *Som* 1H 21
Alswear. *Devn* 4H 19
Altandhu. *High* 2D 163
Altanduin. *High* 1F 165
Altarnun. *Corn* 4C 10
Altass. *High* 3B 164
Alterwall. *High* 2E 169
Altgaltraig. *Arg* 2B 126
Altham. *Lanc* 1F 91
Althorne. *Essx* 1D 40
Althorpe. *N Lin* 4B 94
Altnabreac. *High* 4C 168
Altnacealgach. *High* 2G 163
Altnafeadh. *High* 3G 141
Altnaharra. *High* 5F 167
Altofts. *W Yor* 2D 92
Alton. *Derbs* 4A 86
Alton. *Hants* 3F 25
Alton. *Staf* 1E 73
Alton Barnes. *Wilts* 5G 35
Altonhill. *E Ayr* 1D 116
Alton Pancras. *Dors* 2C 14
Alton Priors. *Wilts* 5G 35
Altrincham. *G Man* 2B 84
Altrua. *High* 4E 149
Alva. *Clac* 4A 136
Alvanley. *Ches W* 3G 83
Alvaston. *Derb* 2A 74
Alvechurch. *Worc* 3E 61
Alvecote. *Warw* 5G 73
Alvediston. *Wilts* 4E 23
Alveley. *Shrp* 2B 60
Alverdiscott. *Devn* 4F 19
Alverstoke. *Hants* 3D 16
Alverstone. *IOW* 4D 16
Alverthorpe. *W Yor* 2D 92
Alverton. *Notts* 1E 75
Alves. *Mor* 2F 159
Alvescot. *Oxon* 5A 50
Alveston. *S Glo* 3B 34
Alveston. *Warw* 5G 61
Alvie. *High* 3C 150
Alvingham. *Linc* 1C 88
Alvington. *Glos* 5B 48
Alwalton. *Cambs* 1A 64
Alweston. *Dors* 1B 14
Alwington. *Devn* 4E 19
Alwinton. *Nmbd* 4D 120
Alwoodley. *W Yor* 5E 99
Alyth. *Per* 4B 144
Amatnatua. *High* 4B 164
Am Baile. *W Isl* 7C 170
Ambaston. *Derbs* 2B 74
Ambergate. *Derbs* 5H 85
Amber Hill. *Linc* 1B 76
Amberley. *Glos* 5D 48
Amberley. *W Sus* 4B 26
Amble. *Nmbd* 4G 121
Amblecote. *W Mid* 2C 60
Ambler Thorn. *W Yor* 2A 92
Ambleside. *Cumb* 4E 103
Ambleston. *Pemb* 2E 43
Ambrosden. *Oxon* 4E 50
Amcotts. *N Lin* 3B 94
Amersham. *Buck* 1A 38
Amerton. *Staf* 3D 73
Amesbury. *Wilts* 2G 23
Amisfield. *Dum* 1B 112
Amlwch. *IOA* 1D 80
Amlwch Port. *IOA* 1D 80
Ammanford. *Carm* 4G 45
Amotherby. *N Yor* 2B 100
Ampfield. *Hants* 4B 24
Ampleforth. *N Yor* 2H 99
Ampleforth College. *N Yor* 2H 99
Ampney Crucis. *Glos* 5F 49
Ampney St Mary. *Glos* 5F 49
Ampney St Peter. *Glos* 5F 49
Amport. *Hants* 2A 24
Ampthill. *C Beds* 2A 52
Ampton. *Suff* 3A 66
Amroth. *Pemb* 4F 43
Amulree. *Per* 5G 143
Amwell. *Herts* 4B 52
Anaheilt. *High* 2C 140
An Àird. *High* 3D 147
An Camus Darach. *High* 4E 147
Ancaster. *Linc* 1G 75
Anchor. *Shrp* 2D 58
Anchorsholme. *Bkpl* 5C 96
Anchor Street. *Norf* 3F 79
An Cnoc. *W Isl* 4G 171
An Cnoc Ard. *W Isl* 1H 171
An Coroghon. *High* 3A 146
Ancroft. *Nmbd* 5G 131
Ancrum. *Bord* 2A 120
Ancton. *W Sus* 5A 26
Anderby. *Linc* 3E 89
Anderby Creek. *Linc* 3E 89
Anderson. *Dors* 3D 15
Anderton. *Ches W* 3A 84
Andertons Mill. *Lanc* 3D 90
Andover. *Hants* 2B 24
Andover Down. *Hants* 2B 24
Andoversford. *Glos* 4F 49
Andreas. *IOM* 2D 108
An Dùnan. *High* 1D 147
Andwell. *Hants* 1E 25
Anelog. *Gwyn* 3A 68
Anfield. *Mers* 1F 83
Angarrack. *Corn* 3C 4
Angelbank. *Shrp* 3H 59
Angersleigh. *Som* 1F 13
Angerton. *Cumb* 4D 112
Angle. *Pemb* 4C 42
An Gleann Ur. *W Isl* 4G 171
Angmering. *W Sus* 5B 26
Angmering-on-Sea. *W Sus* 5B 26
Angram. *N Yor* 5B 104
(nr. Keld)
Angram. *N Yor* 5H 99
(nr. York)
Anick. *Nmbd* 3C 114
Ankerbold. *Derbs* 4A 86
Ankerville. *High* 1C 158
Anlaby. *E Yor* 2D 94
Anlaby Park. *Hull* 2D 94
An Leth Meadhanach. *W Isl* 7C 170
Anmer. *Norf* 3G 77
Anmore. *Hants* 1E 17
Annan. *Dum* 3D 112
Annaside. *Cumb* 1A 96
Annat. *Arg* 1H 133
Annat. *High* 3A 156
Annathill. *N Lan* 2A 128
Anna Valley. *Hants* 2B 24
Annbank. *S Ayr* 2D 116
Annesley. *Notts* 5C 86
Annesley Woodhouse. *Notts* 5C 86
Annfield Plain. *Dur* 4E 115
Annscroft. *Shrp* 5G 71
An Sailean. *High* 2A 140
Ansdell. *Lanc* 2B 90
Ansford. *Som* 3B 22
Ansley. *Warw* 1G 61
Anslow. *Staf* 3G 73
Anslow Gate. *Staf* 3F 73
Ansteadbrook. *Surr* 2A 26
Anstey. *Herts* 2E 53
Anstey. *Leics* 5C 74
Anston. *S Lan* 5D 128
Anstruther Easter. *Fife* 3H 137
Anstruther Wester. *Fife* 3H 137
Ansty. *Warw* 2A 62
Ansty. *W Sus* 3D 27
Ansty. *Wilts* 4E 23
An Taobh Tuath. *W Isl* 9B 171
An t-Aodann Ban. *High* 3C 154
An t Ath Leathann. *High* 1E 147
An Teanga. *High* 3E 147
Anthill Common. *Hants* 1E 17
Anthorn. *Cumb* 4C 112
Antingham. *Norf* 2E 79
An t-Ob. *W Isl* 9C 171
Anton's Gowt. *Linc* 1B 76
Antony. *Corn* 3A 8
An t-Òrd. *High* 2E 147
Antrobus. *Ches W* 3A 84
Anvil Corner. *Devn* 2D 10
Anwick. *Linc* 5A 88
Anwoth. *Dum* 4C 110
Apethorpe. *Nptn* 1H 63
Apeton. *Staf* 4C 72
Apley. *Linc* 3A 88
Apperknowle. *Derbs* 3A 86
Apperley. *Glos* 3D 48
Apperley Dene. *Nmbd* 4D 114
Appersett. *N Yor* 5B 104
Appin. *Arg* 4D 140
Appleby. *N Lin* 3C 94
Appleby-in-Westmorland. *Cumb* 2H 103
Appleby Magna. *Leics* 5H 73
Appleby Parva. *Leics* 5H 73
Applecross. *High* 4G 155
Appledore. *Devn* 3E 19
(nr. Bideford)
Appledore. *Devn* 1D 12
(nr. Tiverton)
Appledore. *Kent* 3D 28
Appledore Heath. *Kent* 2D 28
Appleford. *Oxon* 2D 36
Applegarthtown. *Dum* 1C 112
Applemore. *Hants* 2B 16
Appleshaw. *Hants* 2B 24
Applethwaite. *Cumb* 2D 102
Appleton. *Hal* 2H 83
Appleton. *Oxon* 5C 50
Appleton-le-Moors. *N Yor* 1B 100
Appleton-le-Street. *N Yor* 2B 100
Appleton Roebuck. *N Yor* 5H 99
Appleton Thorn. *Warr* 2A 84
Appleton Wiske. *N Yor* 4A 106
Appletree. *Nptn* 1C 50
Appletreehall. *Bord* 3H 119
Appletreewick. *N Yor* 3C 98
Appley. *Som* 4D 20
Appley Bridge. *Lanc* 4D 90
Apse Heath. *IOW* 4D 16
Apsley End. *C Beds* 2B 52
Apuldram. *W Sus* 2G 17
Arabella. *High* 1C 158
Arasaig. *High* 5E 147
Arbeadie. *Abers* 4D 152
Arberth. *Pemb* 3F 43
Arbirlot. *Ang* 4F 145
Arborfield. *Wok* 5F 37
Arborfield Cross. *Wok* 5F 37
Arborfield Garrison. *Wok* 5F 37
Arbourthorne. *S Yor* 2A 86
Arbroath. *Ang* 4F 145
Arbuthnott. *Abers* 1H 145
Arcan. *High* 3H 157
Archargary. *High* 3H 167
Archdeacon Newton. *Darl* 3F 105
Archiestown. *Mor* 4G 159
Arclid. *Ches E* 4B 84
Arclid Green. *Ches E* 4B 84
Ardachu. *High* 3D 164
Ardalanish. *Arg* 2A 132
Ardaneaskan. *High* 5H 155
Ardarroch. *High* 5H 155
Ardbeg. *Arg* 1C 126
(nr. Dunoon)
Ardbeg. *Arg* 5C 124
(on Islay)
Ardbeg. *Arg* 3B 126
(on Isle of Bute)
Ardcharnich. *High* 5F 163
Ardchiavaig. *Arg* 2A 132
Ardchonnell. *Arg* 2G 133
Ardchrishnish. *Arg* 1B 132
Ardchronie. *High* 5D 164
Ardchullarie. *Stir* 2E 135
Ardchyle. *Stir* 1E 135
Ard-dhubh. *High* 4G 155
Arddleen. *Powy* 4E 71
Arddlîn. *Powy* 4E 71
Ardechive. *High* 4D 148
Ardeley. *Herts* 3D 52
Ardelve. *High* 1A 148
Arden. *Arg* 1E 127
Ardendrain. *High* 5H 157
Arden Hall. *N Yor* 5C 106
Ardens Grafton. *Warw* 5F 61
Ardentinny. *Arg* 1C 126
Ardeonaig. *Stir* 5D 142
Ardersier. *High* 3B 158
Ardery. *High* 2B 140
Ardessie. *High* 5E 163
Ardfern. *Arg* 3F 133
Ardfernal. *Arg* 2D 124
Ardfin. *Arg* 3C 124
Ardgartan. *Arg* 3B 134
Ardgay. *High* 4C 164
Ardgour. *High* 2E 141
Ardheslaig. *High* 3G 155
Ardindrean. *High* 5F 163
Ardingly. *W Sus* 3E 27
Ardington. *Oxon* 3C 36
Ardlamont House. *Arg* 3A 126
Ardleigh. *Essx* 3D 54
Ardler. *Per* 4B 144
Ardley. *Oxon* 3D 50
Ardlui. *Arg* 2C 134
Ardlussa. *Arg* 1E 125
Ardmair. *High* 4F 163
Ardmay. *Arg* 3B 134
Ardminish. *Arg* 5E 125
Ardmolich. *High* 1B 140
Ardmore. *High* 3C 166
(nr. Kinlochbervie)
Ardmore. *High* 5E 164
(nr. Tain)
Ardnacross. *Arg* 4G 139
Ardnadam. *Arg* 1C 126
Ardnagrask. *High* 4H 157
Ardnamurach. *High* 4G 147
Ardnarff. *High* 5A 156
Ardnastang. *High* 2C 140
Ardoch. *Per* 5H 143
Ardochy House. *High* 3E 148
Ardpatrick. *Arg* 3F 125
Ardrishaig. *Arg* 1G 125
Ardroag. *High* 4B 154
Ardross. *High* 1A 158
Ardrossan. *N Ayr* 5D 126
Ardshealach. *High* 2A 140
Ardsley. *S Yor* 4D 93
Ardslignish. *High* 2G 139

Ardtalla. *Arg* 4C 124
Ardtalnaig. *Per* 5E 142
Ardtoe. *High* 1A 140
Arduaine. *Arg* 2E 133
Ardullie. *High* 2H 157
Ardvasar. *High* 3E 147
Ardvorlich. *Per* 1F 135
Ardwell. *Dum* 5G 109
Ardwell. *Mor* 5A 160
Arean. *High* 1A 140
Areley Common. *Worc* 3C 60
Areley Kings. *Worc* 3B 60
Arford. *Hants* 3G 25
Argoed. *Cphy* 2E 33
Argoed Mill. *Powy* 4B 58
Aridhglas. *Arg* 2B 132
Arinacrinachd. *High* 3G 155
Arinagour. *Arg* 3D 138
Arisaig. *High* 5E 147
Ariundle. *High* 2C 140
Arivegaig. *High* 2A 140
Arkendale. *N Yor* 3F 99
Arkesden. *Essx* 2E 53
Arkholme. *Lanc* 2E 97
Arkle Town. *N Yor* 4D 104
Arkley. *G Lon* 1D 38
Arksey. *S Yor* 4F 93
Arkwright Town. *Derbs* 3B 86
Arlecdon. *Cumb* 3B 102
Arlescote. *Warw* 1B 50
Arlesey. *C Beds* 2B 52
Arleston. *Telf* 4A 72
Arley. *Ches E* 2A 84
Arlingham. *Glos* 4C 48
Arlington. *Devn* 2G 19
Arlington. *E Sus* 5G 27
Arlington. *Glos* 5G 49
Arlington Beccott. *Devn* 2G 19
Armadail. *High* 3E 147
Armadale. *High* 3E 147 (nr. Isleornsay)
Armadale. *High* 2H 167 (nr. Strathy)
Armadale. *W Lot* 3C 128
Armathwaite. *Cumb* 5G 113
Arminghall. *Norf* 5E 79
Armitage. *Staf* 4E 73
Armitage Bridge. *W Yor* 3B 92
Armley. *W Yor* 1C 92
Armscote. *Warw* 1H 49
Arms, The. *Norf* 1A 66
Armston. *Nptn* 2H 63
Armthorpe. *S Yor* 4G 93
Arncliffe. *N Yor* 2B 98
Arncliffe Cote. *N Yor* 2B 98
Arncroach. *Fife* 3H 137
Arne. *Dors* 4E 15
Arnesby. *Leics* 1D 62
Arnicle. *Arg* 2B 122
Arnisdale. *High* 2G 147
Arnish. *High* 4E 155
Arniston. *Midl* 3G 129
Arnol. *W Isl* 3F 171
Arnold. *E Yor* 5F 101
Arnold. *Notts* 1C 74
Arnprior. *Stir* 4F 135
Arnside. *Cumb* 2D 96
Aros Mains. *Arg* 4G 139
Arpafeelie. *High* 3A 158
Arrad Foot. *Cumb* 1C 96
Arram. *E Yor* 5E 101
Arras. *E Yor* 5D 100
Arrathorne. *N Yor* 5E 105
Arreton. *IOW* 4D 16
Arrington. *Cambs* 5C 64
Arrochar. *Arg* 3B 134
Arrow. *Warw* 5E 61
Arscaig. *High* 2C 164
Artafallie. *High* 4A 158
Arthington. *W Yor* 5E 99
Arthingworth. *Nptn* 2E 63
Arthog. *Gwyn* 4F 69
Arthrath. *Abers* 5G 161
Arthurstone. *Per* 4B 144
Artington. *Surr* 1A 26
Arundel. *W Sus* 5B 26
Asby. *Cumb* 2B 102
Ascog. *Arg* 3C 126
Ascot. *Wind* 4A 38
Ascott-under-Wychwood. *Oxon* 4B 50
Asenby. *N Yor* 2F 99
Asfordby. *Leics* 4E 74
Asfordby Hill. *Leics* 4E 74
Asgarby. *Linc* 4C 88 (nr. Horncastle)
Asgarby. *Linc* 1A 76 (nr. Sleaford)
Ash. *Devn* 4E 9
Ash. *Dors* 1D 14
Ash. *Kent* 5G 41 (nr. Sandwich)
Ash. *Kent* 4H 39 (nr. Swanley)
Ash. *Som* 4H 21
Ash. *Surr* 1G 25
Ashampstead. *W Ber* 4D 36
Ashbocking. *Suff* 5D 66
Ashbourne. *Derbs* 1F 73
Ashbrittle. *Som* 4D 20
Ashbrook. *Shrp* 1G 59
Ashburton. *Devn* 2D 8
Ashbury. *Devn* 3F 11
Ashbury. *Oxon* 3A 36
Ashby. *N Lin* 4B 94
Ashby by Partney. *Linc* 4D 88
Ashby cum Fenby. *NE Lin* 4F 95
Ashby de la Launde. *Linc* 5H 87
Ashby-de-la-Zouch. *Leics* 4A 74
Ashby Folville. *Leics* 4E 74
Ashby Magna. *Leics* 1C 62
Ashby Parva. *Leics* 2C 62
Ashby Puerorum. *Linc* 3C 88
Ashby St Ledgars. *Nptn* 4C 62
Ashby St Mary. *Norf* 5F 79
Ashchurch. *Glos* 2E 49
Ashcombe. *Devn* 5C 12
Ashcott. *Som* 3H 21
Ashdon. *Essx* 1F 53
Ashe. *Hants* 1D 24
Asheldham. *Essx* 5C 54
Ashen. *Essx* 1H 53
Ashendon. *Buck* 4F 51
Ashey. *IOW* 4D 16
Ashfield. *Hants* 1B 16
Ashfield. *Here* 3A 48
Ashfield. *Shrp* 2H 59
Ashfield. *Stir* 3G 135
Ashfield. *Suff* 4E 66
Ashfield Green. *Suff* 3E 67
Ashfold Crossways. *W Sus* 3D 26
Ashford. *Devn* 3F 19 (nr. Barnstaple)
Ashford. *Devn* 4C 8 (nr. Kingsbridge)
Ashford. *Hants* 1G 15
Ashford. *Kent* 1E 28
Ashford. *Surr* 3B 38
Ashford Bowdler. *Shrp* 3H 59
Ashford Carbonel. *Shrp* 3H 59
Ashford Hill. *Hants* 5D 36
Ashford in the Water. *Derbs* 4F 85
Ashgill. *S Lan* 5A 128
Ash Green. *Warw* 2H 61
Ashgrove. *Mor* 2G 159
Ashill. *Devn* 1D 12
Ashill. *Norf* 5A 78
Ashill. *Som* 1G 13
Ashingdon. *Essx* 1C 40
Ashington. *Nmbd* 1F 115
Ashington. *W Sus* 4C 26
Ashkirk. *Bord* 2G 119
Ashlett. *Hants* 2C 16
Ashleworth. *Glos* 3D 48
Ashley. *Cambs* 4F 65
Ashley. *Ches E* 2B 84
Ashley. *Dors* 2G 15
Ashley. *Glos* 2E 35
Ashley. *Hants* 3A 16 (nr. New Milton)
Ashley. *Hants* 3B 24 (nr. Winchester)
Ashley. *Kent* 1H 29
Ashley. *Nptn* 1E 63
Ashley. *Staf* 2B 72
Ashley. *Wilts* 5D 34
Ashley Green. *Buck* 5H 51
Ashley Heath. *Dors* 2G 15
Ashley Heath. *Staf* 2B 72
Ashley Moor. *Here* 4G 59
Ash Magna. *Shrp* 2H 71
Ashmanhaugh. *Norf* 3F 79
Ashmansworth. *Hants* 1C 24
Ashmansworthy. *Devn* 1D 10
Ashmead Green. *Glos* 2C 34
Ashmill. *Devn* 3D 11 (nr. Holsworthy)
Ash Mill. *Devn* 4A 20 (nr. South Molton)
Ashmore. *Dors* 1E 15
Ashmore Green. *W Ber* 5D 36
Ashover. *Derbs* 4A 86
Ashow. *Warw* 3H 61
Ash Parva. *Shrp* 2H 71
Ashperton. *Here* 1B 48
Ashprington. *Devn* 3E 9
Ash Priors. *Som* 4E 21
Ashreigney. *Devn* 1G 11
Ash Street. *Suff* 1D 54
Ashtead. *Surr* 5C 38
Ash Thomas. *Devn* 1D 12
Ashton. *Corn* 4D 4
Ashton. *Here* 4H 59
Ashton. *Inv* 2D 126
Ashton. *Nptn* 2H 63 (nr. Oundle)
Ashton. *Nptn* 1F 51 (nr. Roade)
Ashton. *Pet* 5A 76
Ashton Common. *Wilts* 1E 23
Ashton Hayes. *Ches W* 4H 83
Ashton-in-Makerfield. *G Man* 4D 90
Ashton Keynes. *Wilts* 2F 35
Ashton under Hill. *Worc* 2E 49
Ashton-under-Lyne. *G Man* 1D 84
Ashton upon Mersey. *G Man* 1B 84
Ashurst. *Hants* 1B 16
Ashurst. *Kent* 2G 27
Ashurst. *Lanc* 4C 90
Ashurst. *W Sus* 4C 26
Ashurst Wood. *W Sus* 2F 27
Ash Vale. *Surr* 1G 25
Ashwater. *Devn* 3D 11
Ashwell. *Herts* 2C 52
Ashwell. *Rut* 4F 75
Ashwellthorpe. *Norf* 1D 66
Ashwick. *Som* 2B 22
Ashwicken. *Norf* 4G 77
Ashwood. *Staf* 2C 60
Askam in Furness. *Cumb* 2B 96
Askern. *S Yor* 3F 93
Askerswell. *Dors* 3A 14
Askett. *Buck* 5G 51
Askham. *Cumb* 2G 103
Askham. *Notts* 3E 87
Askham Bryan. *York* 5H 99
Askham Richard. *York* 5H 99
Askrigg. *N Yor* 5C 104
Askwith. *N Yor* 5D 98
Aslackby. *Linc* 2H 75
Aslacton. *Norf* 1D 66
Aslockton. *Notts* 1E 75
Aspatria. *Cumb* 5C 112
Aspenden. *Herts* 3D 52
Asperton. *Linc* 2B 76
Aspley Guise. *C Beds* 2H 51
Aspley Heath. *C Beds* 2H 51
Aspull. *G Man* 4E 90
Asselby. *E Yor* 2H 93
Assington. *Suff* 2C 54
Assington Green. *Suff* 5G 65
Astbury. *Ches E* 4C 84
Astcote. *Nptn* 5D 62
Asterby. *Linc* 3B 88
Asterley. *Shrp* 5F 71
Asterton. *Shrp* 1F 59
Asthall. *Oxon* 4A 50
Asthall Leigh. *Oxon* 4B 50
Astle. *High* 4E 165
Astley. *G Man* 4F 91
Astley. *Shrp* 4H 71
Astley. *Warw* 2H 61
Astley. *Worc* 4B 60
Astley Abbotts. *Shrp* 1B 60
Astley Bridge. *G Man* 3F 91
Astley Cross. *Worc* 4C 60
Aston. *Ches E* 1A 72
Aston. *Ches W* 3H 83
Aston. *Derbs* 2F 85 (nr. Hope)
Aston. *Derbs* 2F 73 (nr. Sudbury)
Aston. *Flin* 4F 83
Aston. *Here* 4G 59
Aston. *Herts* 3C 52
Aston. *Oxon* 5B 50
Aston. *Shrp* 1C 60 (nr. Bridgnorth)
Aston. *Shrp* 3H 71 (nr. Wem)
Aston. *S Yor* 2B 86
Aston. *Staf* 1B 72
Aston. *Telf* 5A 72
Aston. *W Mid* 1E 61
Aston. *Wok* 3F 37
Aston Abbotts. *Buck* 3G 51
Aston Botterell. *Shrp* 2A 60
Aston-by-Stone. *Staf* 2D 72
Aston Cantlow. *Warw* 5F 61
Aston Clinton. *Buck* 4G 51
Aston Crews. *Here* 3B 48
Aston Cross. *Glos* 2E 49
Aston End. *Herts* 3C 52
Aston Eyre. *Shrp* 1A 60
Aston Fields. *Worc* 4D 60
Aston Flamville. *Leics* 1B 62
Aston Ingham. *Here* 3B 48
Aston juxta Mondrum. *Ches E* 5A 84
Astonlane. *Shrp* 1A 60
Aston le Walls. *Nptn* 5B 62
Aston Magna. *Glos* 2G 49
Aston Munslow. *Shrp* 2H 59
Aston on Carrant. *Glos* 2E 49
Aston on Clun. *Shrp* 2F 59
Aston-on-Trent. *Derbs* 3B 74
Aston Pigott. *Shrp* 5F 71
Aston Rogers. *Shrp* 5F 71
Aston Rowant. *Oxon* 2F 37
Aston Sandford. *Buck* 5F 51
Aston Somerville. *Worc* 2F 49
Aston Subedge. *Glos* 1G 49
Aston Tirrold. *Oxon* 3D 36
Aston Upthorpe. *Oxon* 3D 36
Astrop. *Nptn* 2D 50
Astwick. *C Beds* 2C 52
Astwood. *Mil* 1H 51
Astwood Bank. *Worc* 4E 61
Aswarby. *Linc* 2H 75
Aswardby. *Linc* 3C 88
Atcham. *Shrp* 5H 71
Atch Lench. *Worc* 5E 61
Athelhampton. *Dors* 3C 14
Athelington. *Suff* 3E 66
Athelney. *Som* 4G 21
Athelstaneford. *E Lot* 2B 130
Atherfield Green. *IOW* 5C 16
Atherington. *Devn* 4F 19
Atherington. *W Sus* 5B 26
Athersley. *S Yor* 4D 92
Atherstone. *Warw* 1H 61
Atherstone on Stour. *Warw* 5G 61
Atherton. *G Man* 4E 91
Ath-Tharracail. *High* 2A 140
Atlow. *Derbs* 1G 73
Attadale. *High* 5B 156
Attenborough. *Notts* 2C 74
Atterby. *Linc* 1G 87
Atterley. *Shrp* 1A 60
Atterton. *Leics* 1A 62
Attleborough. *Norf* 1C 66
Attleborough. *Warw* 1A 62
Attlebridge. *Norf* 4D 78
Atwick. *E Yor* 4F 101
Atworth. *Wilts* 5D 34
Auberrow. *Here* 1H 47
Aubourn. *Linc* 4G 87
Aucharnie. *Abers* 4D 160
Auchattie. *Abers* 4D 152
Auchavan. *Ang* 2A 144
Auchbreck. *Mor* 1G 151
Auchenback. *E Ren* 4G 127
Auchenblae. *Abers* 1G 145
Auchenbrack. *Dum* 5G 117
Auchenbreck. *Arg* 1B 126
Auchencairn. *Dum* 4E 111 (nr. Dalbeattie)
Auchencairn. *Dum* 1A 112 (nr. Dumfries)
Auchencarroch. *W Dun* 1F 127
Auchencrow. *Bord* 3E 131
Auchendennan. *W Dun* 1E 127
Auchendinny. *Midl* 3F 129
Auchengray. *S Lan* 4C 128
Auchenhalrig. *Mor* 2A 160
Auchenheath. *S Lan* 5B 128
Auchenlochan. *Arg* 2A 126
Auchenmade. *N Ayr* 5E 127
Auchenmalg. *Dum* 4H 109
Auchentiber. *N Ayr* 5E 127
Auchenvennel. *Arg* 1D 126
Auchindrain. *Arg* 3H 133
Auchininna. *Abers* 4D 160
Auchinleck. *Dum* 2B 110
Auchinleck. *E Ayr* 2E 117
Auchinloch. *N Lan* 2H 127
Auchinstarry. *N Lan* 2A 128
Auchleven. *Abers* 1D 152
Auchlochan. *S Lan* 1H 117
Auchlunachan. *High* 5F 163
Auchmillan. *E Ayr* 2E 117
Auchmithie. *Ang* 4F 145
Auchmuirbridge. *Per* 3E 136
Auchmull. *Ang* 1E 145
Auchnacree. *Ang* 4G 161
Auchnafree. *Per* 5F 143
Auchnagallin. *High* 5E 159
Auchnagatt. *Abers* 4G 161
Aucholzie. *Abers* 4H 151
Auchreddie. *Abers* 4F 161
Auchterarder. *Per* 2B 136
Auchteraw. *High* 3F 149
Auchterderran. *Fife* 4E 136
Auchterhouse. *Ang* 5C 144
Auchtermuchty. *Fife* 2E 137
Auchterneed. *High* 3G 157
Auchtertool. *Fife* 4E 136
Auchtertyre. *High* 1G 147
Auchtubh. *Stir* 1E 135
Auckengill. *High* 2F 169
Auckley. *S Yor* 4G 93
Audenshaw. *G Man* 1D 84
Audlem. *Ches E* 1A 72
Audley. *Staf* 5B 84
Audley End. *Essx* 2F 53
Audmore. *Staf* 3C 72
Auds. *Abers* 2D 160
Aughertree. *Cumb* 1D 102
Aughton. *E Yor* 1H 93
Aughton. *Lanc* 3E 97 (nr. Lancaster)
Aughton. *Lanc* 4B 90 (nr. Ormskirk)
Aughton. *S Yor* 2B 86
Aughton. *Wilts* 1H 23
Aughton Park. *Lanc* 4C 90
Auldearn. *High* 3D 158
Aulden. *Here* 5G 59
Auldgirth. *Dum* 1G 111
Auldhouse. *S Lan* 4H 127
Ault a' chruinn. *High* 1B 148
Aultbea. *High* 5C 162
Aultdearg. *High* 2E 157
Aultgrishan. *High* 5B 162
Aultguish Inn. *High* 1F 157
Ault Hucknall. *Derbs* 4B 86
Aultibea. *High* 1H 165
Aultiphurst. *High* 2A 168
Aultivullin. *High* 2A 168
Aultmore. *Mor* 3B 160
Aultnamain Inn. *High* 5D 164
Aunby. *Linc* 4H 75
Aunsby. *Linc* 2H 75
Aust. *S Glo* 3A 34
Austerfield. *S Yor* 1D 86
Austin Fen. *Linc* 1C 88
Austrey. *Warw* 5G 73
Austwick. *N Yor* 3G 97
Authorpe. *Linc* 2D 88
Authorpe Row. *Linc* 3E 89
Avebury. *Wilts* 5G 35
Avebury Trusloe. *Wilts* 5F 35
Aveley. *Thur* 2G 39
Avening. *Glos* 2D 35
Averham. *Notts* 5E 87
Aveton Gifford. *Devn* 4C 8
Avielochan. *High* 2D 150
Aviemore. *High* 2C 150
Avington. *Hants* 3D 24
Avoch. *High* 3B 158
Avon. *Hants* 3G 15
Avonbridge. *Falk* 2C 128
Avon Dassett. *Warw* 5B 62
Avonmouth. *Bris* 4A 34
Avonwick. *Devn* 3D 8
Awbridge. *Hants* 4B 24
Awliscombe. *Devn* 2E 13
Awre. *Glos* 5C 48
Awsworth. *Notts* 1B 74
Axbridge. *Som* 1H 21
Axford. *Hants* 2E 24
Axford. *Wilts* 5H 35
Axminster. *Devn* 3F 13
Axmouth. *Devn* 3F 13
Aycliffe Village. *Dur* 2F 105
Aydon. *Nmbd* 3D 114
Aykley Heads. *Dur* 5F 115
Aylburton. *Glos* 5B 48
Aylburton Common. *Glos* 5B 48
Ayle. *Nmbd* 5A 114
Aylesbeare. *Devn* 3D 12
Aylesbury. *Buck* 4G 51
Aylesby. *NE Lin* 4F 95
Aylescott. *Devn* 1G 11
Aylesford. *Kent* 5B 40
Aylesham. *Kent* 5G 41
Aylestone. *Leic* 5C 74
Aylmerton. *Norf* 2D 78
Aylsham. *Norf* 3D 78
Aylton. *Here* 2B 48
Aylworth. *Glos* 3G 49
Aymestrey. *Here* 4G 59
Aynho. *Nptn* 2D 50
Ayot Green. *Herts* 4C 52
Ayot St Lawrence. *Herts* 4B 52
Ayot St Peter. *Herts* 4C 52
Ayr. *S Ayr* 2C 116 & 187
Ayres of Selivoe. *Shet* 7D 173
Ayreville. *Torb* 2E 9
Aysgarth. *N Yor* 1C 98
Ayshford. *Devn* 1D 12
Ayside. *Cumb* 1C 96
Ayston. *Rut* 5F 75
Ayton. *Bord* 3F 131
Aywick. *Shet* 3G 173
Azerley. *N Yor* 2E 99

B

Babbacombe. *Torb* 2F 9
Babbinswood. *Shrp* 3F 71
Babb's Green. *Herts* 4D 53
Babcary. *Som* 4A 22
Babel. *Carm* 2B 46
Babell. *Flin* 3D 82
Babingley. *Norf* 3F 77
Bablock Hythe. *Oxon* 5C 50
Babraham. *Cambs* 5E 65
Babworth. *Notts* 2D 86
Bac. *W Isl* 3G 171
Bachau. *IOA* 2D 80
Bacheldre. *Powy* 1E 59
Bachymbyd Fawr. *Den* 4C 82
Backaland. *Orkn* 4E 172
Backaskaill. *Orkn* 2D 172
Backbarrow. *Cumb* 1C 96
Backe. *Carm* 3G 43
Backfolds. *Abers* 3H 161
Backford. *Ches W* 3G 83
Backhill. *Abers* 5E 161
Backhill of Clackriach. *Abers* 4G 161
Backies. *High* 3F 165
Backmuir of New Gilston. *Fife* 3G 137
Back of Keppoch. *High* 5E 147
Back Street. *Suff* 5G 65
Backwell. *N Som* 5H 33
Backworth. *Tyne* 2G 115
Bacon End. *Essx* 4G 53
Baconsthorpe. *Norf* 2D 78
Bacton. *Here* 2G 47
Bacton. *Norf* 2F 79
Bacton. *Suff* 4C 66
Bacton Green. *Norf* 2F 79
Bacup. *Lanc* 2G 91
Badachonacher. *High* 1A 158
Badachro. *High* 1G 155
Badanloch Lodge. *High* 5H 167
Badavanich. *High* 3D 156
Badbury. *Swin* 3G 35
Badby. *Nptn* 5C 62
Badcall. *High* 3C 166
Badcaul. *High* 4E 163
Baddeley Green. *Stoke* 5D 84
Baddesley Clinton. *W Mid* 3G 61
Baddesley Ensor. *Warw* 1G 61
Baddidarach. *High* 1E 163
Baddoch. *Abers* 5F 151
Badenscallie. *High* 3E 163
Badenscoth. *Abers* 5E 160
Badentarbat. *High* 2E 163
Badgall. *Corn* 4C 10
Badgers Mount. *Kent* 4F 39
Badgeworth. *Glos* 4E 49
Badgworth. *Som* 1G 21

Badicaul. *High* 1F 147
Badingham. *Suff* 4F 67
Badlesmere. *Kent* 5E 40
Badlipster. *High* 4E 169
Badluarach. *High* 4D 163
Badminton. *S Glo* 3D 34
Badnaban. *High* 1E 163
Badnabay. *High* 4C 166
Badnagie. *High* 5D 168
Badnellan. *High* 3F 165
Badninish. *High* 4E 165
Badrallach. *High* 4E 163
Badsey. *Worc* 1F 49
Badshot Lea. *Surr* 2G 25
Badsworth. *W Yor* 3E 93
Badwell Ash. *Suff* 4B 66
Bae Cinmel. *Cnwy* 2B 82
Bae Colwyn. *Cnwy* 3A 82
Bae Penrhyn. *Cnwy* 2H 81
Bagby. *N Yor* 1G 99
Bag Enderby. *Linc* 3C 88
Bagendon. *Glos* 5F 49
Bagginswood. *Shrp* 2A 60
Bàgh a Chàise. *W Isl* 1E 170
Bàgh a' Chaisteil. *W Isl* 9B 170
Bagham. *Kent* 5E 41
Baghasdal. *W Isl* 7C 170
Bagh Mor. *W Isl* 3D 170
Bagh Shiarabhagh. *W Isl* 8C 170
Bagillt. *Flin* 3E 83
Baginton. *Warw* 3H 61
Baglan. *Neat* 2A 32
Bagley. *Shrp* 3G 71
Bagley. *Som* 2H 21
Bagnall. *Staf* 5D 84
Bagnor. *W Ber* 5C 36
Bagshot. *Surr* 4A 38
Bagshot. *Wilts* 5B 36
Bagstone. *S Glo* 3B 34
Bagthorpe. *Norf* 2G 77
Bagthorpe. *Notts* 5B 86
Bagworth. *Leics* 5B 74
Bagwy Llydiart. *Here* 3H 47
Baildon. *W Yor* 1B 92
Baildon Green. *W Yor* 1B 92
Baile. *W Isl* 1E 170
Baile Ailein. *W Isl* 5E 171
Baile an Truiseil. *W Isl* 2F 171
Baile Boidheach. *Arg* 2F 125
Baile Glas. *W Isl* 3D 170
Bailemeonach. *Arg* 4A 140
Baile Mhanaich. *W Isl* 3C 170
Baile Mhartainn. *W Isl* 1C 170
Baile MhicPhail. *W Isl* 1D 170
Baile Mor. *Arg* 2A 132
Baile Mor. *W Isl* 2C 170
Baile nan Cailleach. *W Isl* 3C 170
Baile Raghaill. *W Isl* 2C 170
Bailey Green. *Hants* 4E 25
Baileyhead. *Cumb* 1G 113
Bailiesward. *Abers* 5B 160
Bail' Iochdrach. *W Isl* 3D 170
Baillieston. *Glas* 3H 127
Bailrigg. *Lanc* 4D 97
Bail' Uachdraich. *W Isl* 2D 170
Bail Ur Tholastaidh. *W Isl* 3H 171
Bainbridge. *N Yor* 5C 104
Bainsford. *Falk* 1B 128
Bainshole. *Abers* 5D 160
Bainton. *E Yor* 4D 100
Bainton. *Oxon* 3D 50
Bainton. *Pet* 5H 75
Baintown. *Fife* 3F 137
Baker Street. *Thur* 2H 39
Bakewell. *Derbs* 4G 85
Bala. *Gwyn* 2B 70
Balachuirn. *High* 4E 155
Balbeg. *High* 5G 157
(nr. Cannich)
Balbeg. *High* 1G 149
(nr. Loch Ness)
Balbeggie. *Per* 1D 136
Balblair. *High* 4C 164
(nr. Bonar Bridge)
Balblair. *High* 2B 158
(nr. Invergordon)
Balblair. *High* 4H 157
(nr. Inverness)
Balby. *S Yor* 4F 93
Balcathie. *Ang* 5F 145
Balchladich. *High* 1E 163
Balchraggan. *High* 4H 157
Balchrick. *High* 3B 166
Balcombe. *W Sus* 2E 27
Balcombe Lane. *W Sus* 2E 27
Balcurvie. *Fife* 3F 137
Baldersby. *N Yor* 2F 99
Baldersby St James. *N Yor* 2F 99
Balderstone. *Lanc* 1E 91
Balderton. *Ches W* 4F 83
Balderton. *Notts* 5F 87
Baldinnie. *Fife* 2G 137
Baldock. *Herts* 2C 52
Baldrine. *IOM* 3D 108
Baldslow. *E Sus* 4C 28
Baldwin. *IOM* 3C 108
Baldwinholme. *Cumb* 4E 113
Baldwin's Gate. *Staf* 2B 72
Bale. *Norf* 2C 78
Balearn. *Abers* 3H 161
Balemartine. *Arg* 4A 138
Balephretrish. *Arg* 4B 138
Balephuil. *Arg* 4A 138
Balerno. *Edin* 3E 129
Balevullin. *Arg* 4A 138
Balfield. *Ang* 2E 145
Balfour. *Orkn* 6D 172
Balfron. *Stir* 1G 127
Balgaveny. *Abers* 4D 160
Balgonar. *Fife* 4C 136
Balgowan. *High* 4A 150
Balgown. *High* 2C 154
Balgrochan. *E Dun* 2H 127
Balgy. *High* 3H 155
Balhalgardy. *Abers* 1E 153
Baliasta. *Shet* 1H 173
Baligill. *High* 2A 168
Balintore. *Ang* 3B 144
Balintore. *High* 1C 158
Balintraid. *High* 1B 158
Balk. *N Yor* 1G 99
Balkeerie. *Ang* 4C 144
Balkholme. *E Yor* 2A 94
Ball. *Shrp* 3F 71
Ballabeg. *IOM* 4B 108
Ballacannell. *IOM* 3D 108
Ballacarnane Beg. *IOM* 3C 108
Ballachulish. *High* 3E 141
Ballagyr. *IOM* 3B 108
Ballajora. *IOM* 2D 108
Ballaleigh. *IOM* 3C 108
Ballamodha. *IOM* 4B 108
Ballantrae. *S Ayr* 1F 109
Ballards Gore. *Essx* 1D 40
Ballasalla. *IOM* 4B 108
(nr. Castletown)
Ballasalla. *IOM* 2C 108
(nr. Kirk Michael)
Ballater. *Abers* 4A 152
Ballaugh. *IOM* 2C 108
Ballencrieff. *E Lot* 2A 130
Ballencrieff Toll. *W Lot* 2C 128
Ballentoul. *Per* 2F 143
Ball Hill. *Hants* 5C 36
Ballidon. *Derbs* 5G 85
Balliemore. *Arg* 1B 126
(nr. Dunoon)
Balliemore. *Arg* 1F 133
(nr. Oban)
Ballieward. *High* 5E 159
Ballig. *IOM* 3B 108
Ballimore. *Stir* 2E 135
Ballingdon. *Suff* 1B 54
Ballinger Common. *Buck* 5H 51
Ballingham. *Here* 2A 48
Ballingry. *Fife* 4D 136
Ballinluig. *Per* 3G 143
Ballintuim. *Per* 3A 144
Balliveolan. *Arg* 4C 140
Balloan. *High* 3C 164
Balloch. *High* 4B 158
Balloch. *N Lan* 2A 128
Balloch. *Per* 2H 135
Balloch. *W Dun* 1E 127
Ballochan. *Abers* 4C 152
Ballochgoy. *Arg* 3B 126
Ballochmyle. *E Ayr* 2E 117
Ballochroy. *Arg* 4F 125
Balls Cross. *W Sus* 3A 26
Ball's Green. *E Sus* 2F 27
Ballygown. *Arg* 4F 139
Ballygrant. *Arg* 3B 124
Ballymichael. *N Ayr* 2D 122
Balmacara. *High* 1G 147
Balmaclellan. *Dum* 2D 110
Balmacqueen. *High* 1D 154
Balmaha. *Stir* 4D 134
Balmalcolm. *Fife* 3F 137
Balmalloch. *N Lan* 2A 128
Balmeanach. *High* 5E 155
Balmedie. *Abers* 2G 153
Balmerino. *Fife* 1F 137
Balmerlawn. *Hants* 2B 16
Balmore. *E Dun* 2H 127
Balmore. *High* 4B 154
Balmuir. *Ang* 5D 144
Balmullo. *Fife* 1G 137
Balmurrie. *Dum* 3H 109
Balnaboth. *Ang* 2C 144
Balnabruaich. *High* 1B 158
Balnabruich. *High* 5D 168
Balnacoil. *High* 2F 165
Balnacra. *High* 4B 156
Balnacroft. *Abers* 4G 151
Balnageith. *Mor* 3E 159
Balnaglaic. *High* 5G 157
Balnagrantach. *High* 5G 157
Balnaguard. *Per* 3G 143
Balnahard. *Arg* 4B 132
Balnain. *High* 5G 157
Balnakeil. *High* 2D 166
Balnaknock. *High* 2D 154
Balnamoon. *Abers* 3G 161
Balnamoon. *Ang* 2E 145
Balnapaling. *High* 2B 158
Balornock. *Glas* 3H 127
Balquhidder. *Stir* 1E 135
Balsall. *W Mid* 3G 61
Balsall Common. *W Mid* 3G 61
Balscote. *Oxon* 1B 50
Balsham. *Cambs* 5E 65
Balstonia. *Thur* 2A 40
Baltasound. *Shet* 1H 173
Balterley. *Staf* 5B 84
Baltersan. *Dum* 3B 110
Balthangie. *Abers* 3F 161
Baltonsborough. *Som* 3A 22
Balvaird. *High* 3H 157
Balvaird. *Per* 2D 136
Balvenie. *Mor* 4H 159
Balvicar. *Arg* 2E 133
Balvraid. *High* 2G 147
Balvraid Lodge. *High* 5C 158
Bamber Bridge. *Lanc* 2D 90
Bamber's Green. *Essx* 3F 53
Bamburgh. *Nmbd* 1F 121
Bamford. *Derbs* 2G 85
Bamfurlong. *G Man* 4D 90
Bampton. *Cumb* 3G 103
Bampton. *Devn* 4C 20
Bampton. *Oxon* 5B 50
Bampton Grange. *Cumb* 3G 103
Banavie. *High* 1F 141
Banbury. *Oxon* 1C 50
Bancffosfelen. *Carm* 4E 45
Banchory. *Abers* 4D 152
Banchory-Devenick. *Abers* 3G 153
Bancycapel. *Carm* 4E 45
Bancyfelin. *Carm* 3H 43
Banc-y-ffordd. *Carm* 2E 45
Banff. *Abers* 2D 160
Bangor. *Gwyn* 3E 81
Bangor-is-y-coed. *Wrex* 1F 71
Bangors. *Corn* 3C 10
Bangor's Green. *Lanc* 4B 90
Banham. *Norf* 2C 66
Bank. *Hants* 2A 16
Bankend. *Dum* 3B 112
Bankfoot. *Per* 5H 143
Bankglen. *E Ayr* 3E 117
Bankhead. *Aber* 2F 153
Bankhead. *Abers* 3D 152
Bankhead. *S Lan* 5B 128
Bankland. *Som* 4G 21
Bank Newton. *N Yor* 4B 98
Banknock. *Falk* 2A 128
Banks. *Cumb* 3G 113
Banks. *Lanc* 2B 90
Bankshill. *Dum* 1C 112
Bank Street. *Worc* 4A 60
Bank, The. *Ches E* 5C 84
Bank, The. *Shrp* 1A 60
Bank Top. *Lanc* 4D 90
Banners Gate. *W Mid* 1E 61
Banningham. *Norf* 3E 78
Banniskirk. *High* 3D 168
Bannister Green. *Essx* 3G 53
Bannockburn. *Stir* 4H 135
Banstead. *Surr* 5D 38
Bantham. *Devn* 4C 8
Banton. *N Lan* 2A 128
Banwell. *N Som* 1G 21
Banyard's Green. *Suff* 3F 67
Bapchild. *Kent* 4D 40
Bapton. *Wilts* 3E 23
Barabhas. *W Isl* 2F 171
Barabhas Iarach. *W Isl* 3F 171
Baramore. *High* 1A 140
Barassie. *S Ayr* 1C 116
Baravullin. *Arg* 4D 140
Barbaraville. *High* 1B 158
Barber Booth. *Derbs* 2F 85
Barber Green. *Cumb* 1C 96
Barbhas Uarach. *W Isl* 2F 171
Barbieston. *S Ayr* 3D 116
Barbon. *Cumb* 1F 97
Barbourne. *Worc* 5C 60
Barbridge. *Ches E* 5A 84
Barbrook. *Devn* 2H 19
Barby. *Nptn* 3C 62
Barby Nortoft. *Nptn* 3C 62
Barcaldine. *Arg* 4D 140
Barcheston. *Warw* 1A 50
Barclose. *Cumb* 3F 113
Barcombe. *E Sus* 4F 27
Barcombe Cross. *E Sus* 4F 27
Barden. *N Yor* 5E 105
Barden Scale. *N Yor* 4C 98
Bardfield End Green. *Essx* 2G 53
Bardfield Saling. *Essx* 3G 53
Bardister. *Shet* 4E 173
Bardnabeinne. *High* 4E 164
Bardney. *Linc* 4A 88
Bardon. *Leics* 4B 74
Bardon Mill. *Nmbd* 3A 114
Bardowie. *E Dun* 2G 127
Bardrainney. *Inv* 2E 127
Bardsea. *Cumb* 2C 96
Bardsey. *W Yor* 5F 99
Bardsley. *G Man* 4H 91
Bardwell. *Suff* 3B 66
Bare. *Lanc* 3D 96
Barelees. *Nmbd* 1C 120
Barewood. *Here* 5F 59
Barford. *Hants* 3G 25
Barford. *Norf* 5D 78
Barford. *Warw* 4G 61
Barford St John. *Oxon* 2C 50
Barford St Martin. *Wilts* 3F 23
Barford St Michael. *Oxon* 2C 50
Barfrestone. *Kent* 5G 41
Bargeddie. *N Lan* 3A 128
Bargod. *Cphy* 2E 33
Bargoed. *Cphy* 2E 33
Bargrennan. *Dum* 2A 110
Barham. *Cambs* 3A 64
Barham. *Kent* 5G 41
Barham. *Suff* 5D 66
Barharrow. *Dum* 4D 110
Bar Hill. *Cambs* 4C 64
Barholm. *Linc* 4H 75
Barkby. *Leics* 4D 74
Barkestone-le-Vale. *Leics* 2E 75
Barkham. *Wok* 5F 37
Barking. *G Lon* 2F 39
Barking. *Suff* 5C 66
Barkingside. *G Lon* 2F 39
Barking Tye. *Suff* 5C 66
Barkisland. *W Yor* 3A 92
Barkston. *Linc* 1G 75
Barkston Ash. *N Yor* 1E 93
Barkway. *Herts* 2D 53
Barlanark. *Glas* 3H 127
Barlaston. *Staf* 2C 72
Barlavington. *W Sus* 4A 26
Barlborough. *Derbs* 3B 86
Barlby. *N Yor* 1G 93
Barlestone. *Leics* 5B 74
Barley. *Herts* 2D 53
Barley. *Lanc* 5H 97
Barley Mow. *Tyne* 4F 115
Barleythorpe. *Rut* 5F 75
Barling. *Essx* 2D 40
Barlings. *Linc* 3H 87
Barlow. *Derbs* 3H 85
Barlow. *N Yor* 2G 93
Barlow. *Tyne* 3E 115
Barmby Moor. *E Yor* 5B 100
Barmby on the Marsh. *E Yor* 2G 93
Barmer. *Norf* 2H 77
Barming. *Kent* 5B 40
Barming Heath. *Kent* 5B 40
Barmoor. *Nmbd* 1E 121
Barmouth. *Gwyn* 4F 69
Barmpton. *Darl* 3A 106
Barmston. *E Yor* 4F 101
Barmulloch. *Glas* 3H 127
Barnack. *Pet* 5H 75
Barnacle. *Warw* 2A 62
Barnard Castle. *Dur* 3D 104
Barnard Gate. *Oxon* 4C 50
Barnardiston. *Suff* 1H 53
Barnbarroch. *Dum* 4F 111
Barnburgh. *S Yor* 4E 93
Barnby. *Suff* 2G 67
Barnby Dun. *S Yor* 4G 93
Barnby in the Willows. *Notts* 5F 87
Barnby Moor. *Notts* 2D 86
Barnes. *G Lon* 3D 38
Barnes Street. *Kent* 1H 27
Barnet. *G Lon* 1D 38
Barnetby le Wold. *N Lin* 4D 94
Barney. *Norf* 2B 78
Barnham. *Suff* 3A 66
Barnham. *W Sus* 5A 26
Barnham Broom. *Norf* 5C 78
Barnhead. *Ang* 3F 145
Barnhill. *D'dee* 5D 145
Barnhill. *Mor* 3F 159
Barnhill. *Per* 1D 136
Barnhills. *Dum* 2E 109
Barningham. *Dur* 3D 105
Barningham. *Suff* 3B 66
Barnoldby le Beck. *NE Lin* 4F 95
Barnoldswick. *Lanc* 5A 98
Barns Green. *W Sus* 3C 26
Barnsley. *Glos* 5F 49
Barnsley. *Shrp* 1B 60
Barnsley. *S Yor* 4D 92
Barnstaple. *Devn* 3F 19
Barnston. *Essx* 4G 53
Barnston. *Mers* 2E 83
Barnstone. *Notts* 2E 75
Barnt Green. *Worc* 3E 61
Barnton. *Ches W* 3A 84
Barnwell. *Cambs* 5D 64
Barnwell. *Nptn* 2H 63
Barnwood. *Glos* 4D 48
Barons Cross. *Here* 5G 59
Barony, The. *Orkn* 5B 172
Barr. *Dum* 4G 117
Barr. *S Ayr* 5B 116
Barra Airport. *W Isl* 8C 170
Barrachan. *Dum* 5A 110
Barraglom. *W Isl* 4D 171
Barrahormid. *Arg* 1F 125
Barrapol. *Arg* 4A 138
Barrasford. *Nmbd* 2C 114
Barravullin. *Arg* 3F 133
Barregarrow. *IOM* 3C 108
Barrhead. *E Ren* 4G 127
Barrhill. *S Ayr* 1H 109
Barri. *V Glam* 5E 32
Barrington. *Cambs* 1D 53
Barrington. *Som* 1G 13
Barripper. *Corn* 3D 4
Barrmill. *N Ayr* 4E 127
Barrock. *High* 1E 169
Barrow. *Lanc* 1F 91
Barrow. *Rut* 4F 75
Barrow. *Shrp* 5A 72
Barrow. *Som* 3C 22
Barrow. *Suff* 4G 65
Barroway Drove. *Norf* 5E 77
Barrow Bridge. *G Man* 3E 91
Barrowburn. *Nmbd* 3C 120
Barrowby. *Linc* 2F 75
Barrowcliff. *N Yor* 1E 101
Barrow Common. *N Som* 5A 34
Barrowden. *Rut* 5G 75
Barrowford. *Lanc* 1G 91
Barrow Gurney. *N Som* 5A 34
Barrow Haven. *N Lin* 2D 94
Barrow Hill. *Derbs* 3B 86
Barrow-in-Furness. *Cumb* 3B 96
Barrow Nook. *Lanc* 4C 90
Barrows Green. *Cumb* 1E 97
Barrow's Green. *Hal* 2H 83
Barrow Street. *Wilts* 3D 22
Barrow upon Humber. *N Lin* 2D 94
Barrow upon Soar. *Leics* 4C 74
Barrow upon Trent. *Derbs* 3A 74
Barry. *Ang* 5E 145
Barry. *V Glam* 5E 32
Barry Island. *V Glam* 5E 32
Barsby. *Leics* 4D 74
Barsham. *Suff* 2F 67
Barston. *W Mid* 3G 61
Bartestree. *Here* 1A 48
Barthol Chapel. *Abers* 5F 161
Bartholomew Green. *Essx* 3H 53
Barthomley. *Ches E* 5B 84
Bartley. *Hants* 1B 16
Bartley Green. *W Mid* 2E 61
Bartlow. *Cambs* 1F 53
Barton. *Cambs* 5D 64
Barton. *Ches W* 5G 83
Barton. *Cumb* 2F 103
Barton. *Glos* 3F 49
Barton. *IOW* 4D 16
Barton. *Lanc* 4B 90
(nr. Ormskirk)
Barton. *Lanc* 1D 90
(nr. Preston)
Barton. *N Som* 1G 21
Barton. *N Yor* 4F 105
Barton. *Oxon* 5D 50
Barton. *Torb* 2F 9
Barton. *Warw* 5F 61
Barton Bendish. *Norf* 5G 77
Barton Gate. *Staf* 4F 73
Barton Green. *Staf* 4F 73
Barton Hartsthorn. *Buck* 2E 51
Barton Hill. *N Yor* 3B 100
Barton in Fabis. *Notts* 2C 74
Barton in the Beans. *Leics* 5A 74
Barton-le-Clay. *C Beds* 2A 52
Barton-le-Street. *N Yor* 2B 100
Barton-le-Willows. *N Yor* 3B 100
Barton Mills. *Suff* 3G 65
Barton on Sea. *Hants* 3H 15
Barton-on-the-Heath. *Warw* 2A 50
Barton St David. *Som* 3A 22
Barton Seagrave. *Nptn* 3F 63
Barton Stacey. *Hants* 2C 24
Barton Town. *Devn* 2G 19
Barton Turf. *Norf* 3F 79
Barton-under-Needwood. *Staf* 4F 73
Barton-upon-Humber. *N Lin* 2D 94
Barton Waterside. *N Lin* 2D 94
Barugh Green. *S Yor* 4D 92
Barway. *Cambs* 3E 65
Barwell. *Leics* 1B 62
Barwick. *Herts* 4D 53
Barwick. *Som* 1A 14
Barwick in Elmet. *W Yor* 1D 93
Baschurch. *Shrp* 3G 71
Bascote. *Warw* 4B 62
Basford Green. *Staf* 5D 85
Bashall Eaves. *Lanc* 5F 97
Bashall Town. *Lanc* 5G 97
Bashley. *Hants* 3H 15
Basildon. *Essx* 2B 40
Basingstoke. *Hants* 1E 25
Baslow. *Derbs* 3G 85
Bason Bridge. *Som* 2G 21
Bassaleg. *Newp* 3F 33
Bassendean. *Bord* 5C 130
Bassenthwaite. *Cumb* 1D 102
Bassett. *Sotn* 1C 16
Bassingbourn. *Cambs* 1D 52
Bassingfield. *Notts* 2D 74
Bassingham. *Linc* 5G 87
Bassingthorpe. *Linc* 3G 75
Bassus Green. *Herts* 3D 52
Basta. *Shet* 2G 173
Baston. *Linc* 4A 76
Bastonford. *Worc* 5C 60
Bastwick. *Norf* 4G 79
Batchley. *Worc* 4E 61
Batchworth. *Herts* 1B 38
Batcombe. *Dors* 2B 14
Batcombe. *Som* 3B 22
Bate Heath. *Ches E* 3A 84
Bath. *Bath* 5C 34 & 187
Bathampton. *Bath* 5C 34
Bathealton. *Som* 4D 20
Batheaston. *Bath* 5C 34
Bathford. *Bath* 5C 34
Bathgate. *W Lot* 3C 128
Bathley. *Notts* 5E 87
Bathpool. *Corn* 5C 10
Bathpool. *Som* 4F 21
Bathville. *W Lot* 3C 128
Bathway. *Som* 1A 22
Batley. *W Yor* 2C 92
Batsford. *Glos* 2G 49
Batson. *Devn* 5D 8

Battersby. *N Yor* 4C **106**
Battersea. *G Lon* 3D **39**
Battisborough Cross. *Devn* 4C **8**
Battisford. *Suff* 5C **66**
Battisford Tye. *Suff* 5C **66**
Battle. *E Sus* 4B **28**
Battle. *Powy* 2D **46**
Battleborough. *Som* 1G **21**
Battledown. *Glos* 3E **49**
Battlefield. *Shrp* 4H **71**
Battlesbridge. *Essx* 1B **40**
Battlesden. *C Beds* 3H **51**
Battlesea Green. *Suff* 3E **66**
Battleton. *Som* 4C **20**
Battram. *Leic* 5B **74**
Battramsley. *Hants* 3B **16**
Batt's Corner. *Surr* 2G **25**
Bauds of Cullen. *Mor* 2B **160**
Baugh. *Arg* 4B **138**
Baughton. *Worc* 1D **49**
Baughurst. *Hants* 5D **36**
Baulking. *Oxon* 2B **36**
Baumber. *Linc* 3B **88**
Baunton. *Glos* 5F **49**
Baverstock. *Wilts* 3F **23**
Bawburgh. *Norf* 5D **78**
Bawdeswell. *Norf* 3C **78**
Bawdrip. *Som* 3G **21**
Bawdsey. *Suff* 1G **55**
Bawdsey Manor. *Suff* 2G **55**
Bawsey. *Norf* 4F **77**
Bawtry. *S Yor* 1D **86**
Baxenden. *Lanc* 2F **91**
Baxterley. *Warw* 1G **61**
Baxter's Green. *Suff* 5G **65**
Baybridge. *Hants* 4D **24**
Baybridge. *Nmbd* 4C **114**
Baycliff. *Cumb* 2B **96**
Baydon. *Wilts* 4A **36**
Bayford. *Herts* 5D **52**
Bayford. *Som* 4C **22**
Bayles. *Cumb* 5A **114**
Baylham. *Suff* 5D **66**
Baynard's Green. *Oxon* 3D **50**
Bayston Hill. *Shrp* 5G **71**
Baythorn End. *Essx* 1H **53**
Baythorpe. *Linc* 1B **76**
Bayton. *Worc* 3A **60**
Bayton Common. *Worc* 3B **60**
Bayworth. *Oxon* 5D **50**
Beach. *S Glo* 4C **34**
Beachampton. *Buck* 2F **51**
Beachamwell. *Norf* 5G **77**
Beachley. *Glos* 2A **34**
Beacon. *Devn* 2E **13**
Beacon End. *Essx* 3C **54**
Beacon Hill. *Surr* 3G **25**
Beacon's Bottom. *Buck* 2F **37**
Beaconsfield. *Buck* 1A **38**
Beacontree. *G Lon* 2F **39**
Beacrabhaicg. *W Isl* 8D **171**
Beadlam. *N Yor* 1A **100**
Beadnell. *Nmbd* 2G **121**
Beaford. *Devn* 1F **11**
Beal. *Nmbd* 5G **131**
Beal. *N Yor* 2F **93**
Bealsmill. *Corn* 5D **10**
Beam Hill. *Staf* 3G **73**
Beamhurst. *Staf* 2E **73**
Beaminster. *Dors* 2H **13**
Beamish. *Dur* 4F **115**
Beamond End. *Buck* 1A **38**
Beamsley. *N Yor* 4C **98**
Bean. *Kent* 3G **39**
Beanacre. *Wilts* 5E **35**
Beanley. *Nmbd* 3E **121**
Beanshanger. *Nptn* 2F **51**
Beaquoy. *Orkn* 5C **172**
Beardwood. *Bkbn* 2E **91**
Beare Green. *Surr* 1C **26**
Bearley. *Warw* 4F **61**
Bearpark. *Dur* 5F **115**
Bearsbridge. *Nmbd* 4A **114**
Bearsden. *E Dun* 2G **127**
Bearsted. *Kent* 5B **40**
Bearstone. *Shrp* 2B **72**
Bearwood. *Pool* 3F **15**
Bearwood. *W Mid* 2E **61**
Beattock. *Dum* 4C **118**
Beauchamp Roding. *Essx* 5F **53**
Beauchief. *S Yor* 2H **85**
Beaufort. *Blae* 4E **47**
Beaulieu. *Hants* 2B **16**
Beauly. *High* 4H **157**
Beaumaris. *IOA* 3F **81**
Beaumont. *Cumb* 4E **113**
Beaumont. *Essx* 3E **55**
Beaumont Hill. *Darl* 3F **105**
Beaumont Leys. *Leic* 5C **74**
Beausale. *Warw* 3G **61**
Beauvale. *Notts* 1B **74**
Beauworth. *Hants* 4D **24**
Beaworthy. *Devn* 3E **11**
Beazley End. *Essx* 3H **53**
Bebington. *Mers* 2F **83**
Bebside. *Nmbd* 1F **115**
Beccles. *Suff* 2G **67**
Becconsall. *Lanc* 2C **90**
Beckbury. *Shrp* 5B **72**
Beckenham. *G Lon* 4E **39**
Beckermet. *Cumb* 4B **102**
Beckett End. *Norf* 1G **65**
Beckfoot. *Cumb* 1A **96**
(nr. Broughton in Furness)
Beck Foot. *Cumb* 5H **103**
(nr. Kendal)
Beckfoot. *Cumb* 4C **102**
(nr. Seascale)
Beckfoot. *Cumb* 5B **112**
(nr. Silloth)
Beckford. *Worc* 2E **49**
Beckhampton. *Wilts* 5F **35**
Beck Hole. *N Yor* 4F **107**
Beckingham. *Linc* 5F **87**
Beckingham. *Notts* 1E **87**
Beckington. *Som* 1D **22**
Beckley. *E Sus* 3C **28**
Beckley. *Hants* 3H **15**
Beckley. *Oxon* 4D **50**
Beck Row. *Suff* 3F **65**
Beck Side. *Cumb* 1C **96**
(nr. Cartmel)
Beckside. *Cumb* 1F **97**
(nr. Sedbergh)
Beck Side. *Cumb* 1B **96**
(nr. Ulverston)
Beckton. *G Lon* 2F **39**
Beckwithshaw. *N Yor* 4E **99**
Becontree. *G Lon* 2F **39**
Bedale. *N Yor* 1E **99**
Bedburn. *Dur* 1E **105**
Bedchester. *Dors* 1D **14**
Beddau. *Rhon* 3D **32**
Beddgelert. *Gwyn* 1E **69**
Beddingham. *E Sus* 5F **27**
Beddington. *G Lon* 4D **39**
Bedfield. *Suff* 4E **66**
Bedford. *Bed* 1A **52** & **188**
Bedford. *G Man* 4E **91**
Bedham. *W Sus* 3B **26**
Bedhampton. *Hants* 2F **17**
Bedingfield. *Suff* 4D **66**
Bedingham Green. *Norf* 1E **67**
Bedlam. *N Yor* 3E **99**
Bedlar's Green. *Essx* 3F **53**
Bedlington. *Nmbd* 1F **115**
Bedlinog. *Mer T* 5D **46**
Bedminster. *Bris* 4A **34**
Bedmond. *Herts* 5A **52**
Bednall. *Staf* 4D **72**
Bedrule. *Bord* 3A **120**
Bedstone. *Shrp* 3F **59**
Bedwas. *Cphy* 3E **33**
Bedwellty. *Cphy* 5E **47**
Bedworth. *Warw* 2A **62**
Beeby. *Leics* 5D **74**
Beech. *Hants* 3E **25**
Beech. *Staf* 2C **72**
Beechcliffe. *W Yor* 5C **98**
Beech Hill. *W Ber* 5E **37**
Beechingstoke. *Wilts* 1F **23**
Beedon. *W Ber* 4C **36**
Beeford. *E Yor* 4F **101**
Beeley. *Derbs* 4G **85**
Beelsby. *NE Lin* 4F **95**
Beenham. *W Ber* 5D **36**
Beeny. *Corn* 3B **10**
Beer. *Devn* 4F **13**
Beer. *Som* 3H **21**
Beercrocombe. *Som* 4G **21**
Beer Hackett. *Dors* 1B **14**
Beesands. *Devn* 4E **9**
Beesby. *Linc* 2D **88**
Beeson. *Devn* 4E **9**
Beeston. *C Beds* 1B **52**
Beeston. *Ches W* 5H **83**
Beeston. *Norf* 4B **78**
Beeston. *Notts* 2C **74**
Beeston. *W Yor* 1C **92**
Beeston Regis. *Norf* 1D **78**
Beeswing. *Dum* 3F **111**
Beetham. *Cumb* 2D **97**
Beetham. *Som* 1F **13**
Beetley. *Norf* 4B **78**
Beffcote. *Staf* 4C **72**
Began. *Card* 3F **33**
Begbroke. *Oxon* 4C **50**
Begdale. *Cambs* 5D **76**
Begelly. *Pemb* 4F **43**
Beggar Hill. *Essx* 5G **53**
Beggar's Bush. *Powy* 4E **59**
Beggearn Huish. *Som* 3D **20**
Beguildy. *Powy* 3D **58**
Beighton. *Norf* 5F **79**
Beighton. *S Yor* 2B **86**
Beighton Hill. *Derbs* 5G **85**
Beinn Casgro. *W Isl* 5G **171**
Beith. *N Ayr* 4E **127**
Bekesbourne. *Kent* 5F **41**
Belaugh. *Norf* 4E **79**
Belbroughton. *Worc* 3D **60**
Belchalwell. *Dors* 2C **14**
Belchalwell Street. *Dors* 2C **14**
Belchamp Otten. *Essx* 1B **54**
Belchamp St Paul. *Essx* 1A **54**
Belchamp Walter. *Essx* 1B **54**
Belchford. *Linc* 3B **88**
Belfatton. *Abers* 3H **161**
Belford. *Nmbd* 1F **121**
Belgrano. *Cnwy* 3B **82**
Belhaven. *E Lot* 2C **130**
Belhelvie. *Abers* 2G **153**
Belhinnie. *Abers* 1B **152**
Bellabeg. *Abers* 2A **152**
Belladrum. *High* 4H **157**
Bellamore. *S Ayr* 1H **109**
Bellanoch. *Arg* 4F **133**
Bell Busk. *N Yor* 4B **98**
Belleau. *Linc* 3D **88**
Belleheiglash. *Mor* 5F **159**
Bell End. *Worc* 3D **60**
Bellerby. *N Yor* 5E **105**
Bellerby Camp. *N Yor* 5D **105**
Bellever. *Devn* 5G **11**
Belle Vue. *Cumb* 1C **102**
Belle Vue. *Shrp* 4G **71**
Bellfield. *S Lan* 1H **117**
Belliehill. *Ang* 2E **145**
Bellingdon. *Buck* 5H **51**
Bellingham. *Nmbd* 1B **114**
Bellmount. *Norf* 3E **77**
Bellochantuy. *Arg* 2A **122**
Bellsbank. *E Ayr* 4D **117**
Bell's Cross. *Suff* 5D **66**
Bellshill. *N Lan* 4A **128**
Bellshill. *Nmbd* 1F **121**
Bellside. *N Lan* 4B **128**
Bellspool. *Bord* 1D **118**
Bellsquarry. *W Lot* 3D **128**
Bells Yew Green. *E Sus* 2H **27**
Belmaduthy. *High* 3A **158**
Belmesthorpe. *Rut* 4H **75**
Belmont. *Bkbn* 3E **91**
Belmont. *Shet* 1G **173**
Belmont. *S Ayr* 3C **116**
Belnacraig. *Abers* 2A **152**
Belnie. *Linc* 2B **76**
Belowda. *Corn* 2D **6**
Belper. *Derbs* 1A **74**
Belper Lane End. *Derbs* 1H **73**
Belph. *Derbs* 3C **86**
Belsay. *Nmbd* 2E **115**
Belsford. *Devn* 3D **8**
Belsize. *Herts* 5A **52**
Belstead. *Suff* 1E **55**
Belston. *S Ayr* 2C **116**
Belstone. *Devn* 3G **11**
Belstone Corner. *Devn* 3G **11**
Belthorn. *Lanc* 2F **91**
Beltinge. *Kent* 4F **41**
Beltoft. *N Lin* 4B **94**
Belton. *Leics* 3B **74**
Belton. *Linc* 2G **75**
Belton. *Norf* 5G **79**
Belton. *N Lin* 4A **94**
Belton-in-Rutland. *Rut* 5F **75**
Beltring. *Kent* 1A **28**
Belts of Collonach. *Abers* 4D **152**
Belvedere. *G Lon* 3F **39**
Belvoir. *Leics* 2F **75**
Bembridge. *IOW* 4E **17**
Bemersyde. *Bord* 1H **119**
Bemerton. *Wilts* 3G **23**
Bempton. *E Yor* 2F **101**
Benacre. *Suff* 2H **67**
Ben Alder Lodge. *High* 1C **142**
Ben Armine Lodge. *High* 2E **164**
Benbecula Airport. *W Isl* 3C **170**
Benbuie. *Dum* 5G **117**
Benchill. *G Man* 2C **84**
Benderloch. *Arg* 5D **140**
Bendish. *Herts* 3B **52**
Bendronaig Lodge. *High* 5C **156**
Benenden. *Kent* 2C **28**
Benera. *High* 1G **147**
Benfieldside. *Dur* 4D **115**
Bengate. *Norf* 3F **79**
Bengeworth. *Worc* 1F **49**
Bengrove. *Glos* 2E **49**
Benhall Green. *Suff* 4F **67**
Benholm. *Abers* 2H **145**
Beningbrough. *N Yor* 4H **99**
Benington. *Herts* 3C **52**
Benington. *Linc* 1C **76**
Benington Sea End. *Linc* 1D **76**
Benllech. *IOA* 2E **81**
Benmore Lodge. *High* 2H **163**
Bennacott. *Corn* 3D **10**
Bennah. *Devn* 4B **12**
Bennecarrigan. *N Ayr* 3D **122**
Bennethead. *Cumb* 2F **103**
Benniworth. *Linc* 2B **88**
Benover. *Kent* 1B **28**
Benson. *Oxon* 2E **36**
Benston. *Shet* 6F **173**
Benstonhall. *Orkn* 4E **172**
Bent. *Abers* 1F **145**
Benthall. *Shrp* 5A **72**
Bentham. *Glos* 4E **49**
Benthoul. *Aber* 3F **153**
Bentlawnt. *Shrp* 5F **71**
Bentley. *E Yor* 1D **94**
Bentley. *Hants* 2F **25**
Bentley. *S Yor* 4F **93**
Bentley. *Suff* 2E **54**
Bentley. *Warw* 1G **61**
Bentley. *W Mid* 1D **61**
Bentley Heath. *Herts* 1D **38**
Bentley Heath. *W Mid* 3F **61**
Bentpath. *Dum* 5F **119**
Bents. *W Lot* 3C **128**
Bentworth. *Hants* 2E **25**
Benvie. *D'dee* 5C **144**
Benville. *Dors* 2A **14**
Benwell. *Tyne* 3F **115**
Benwick. *Cambs* 1C **64**
Beoley. *Worc* 4E **61**
Beoraidbeg. *High* 4E **147**
Bepton. *W Sus* 1G **17**
Berden. *Essx* 3E **53**
Bere Alston. *Devn* 2A **8**
Bere Ferrers. *Devn* 2A **8**
Berepper. *Corn* 4D **4**
Bere Regis. *Dors* 3D **14**
Bergh Apton. *Norf* 5F **79**
Berinsfield. *Oxon* 2D **36**
Berkeley. *Glos* 2B **34**
Berkhamsted. *Herts* 5H **51**
Berkley. *Som* 2D **22**
Berkswell. *W Mid* 3G **61**
Bermondsey. *G Lon* 3E **39**
Bernice. *Arg* 4A **134**
Bernisdale. *High* 3D **154**
Berrick Salome. *Oxon* 2E **36**
Berriedale. *High* 1H **165**
Berrier. *Cumb* 2F **103**
Berriew. *Powy* 5D **70**
Berrington. *Nmbd* 5G **131**
Berrington. *Shrp* 5H **71**
Berrington. *Worc* 4H **59**
Berrington Green. *Worc* 4H **59**
Berrington Law. *Nmbd* 5F **131**
Berrow. *Som* 1G **21**
Berrow Green. *Worc* 5B **60**
Berry Cross. *Devn* 1E **11**
Berry Down Cross. *Devn* 2F **19**
Berry Hill. *Glos* 4A **48**
Berry Hill. *Pemb* 1A **44**
Berryhillock. *Mor* 2C **160**
Berrynarbor. *Devn* 2F **19**
Berry Pomeroy. *Devn* 2E **9**
Berryscaur. *Dum* 5D **118**
Berry's Green. *G Lon* 5F **39**
Bersham. *Wrex* 1F **71**
Berthengam. *Flin* 3D **82**
Berwick. *E Sus* 5G **27**
Berwick Bassett. *Wilts* 4G **35**
Berwick Hill. *Nmbd* 2E **115**
Berwick St James. *Wilts* 3F **23**
Berwick St John. *Wilts* 4E **23**
Berwick St Leonard. *Wilts* 3E **23**
Berwick-upon-Tweed.
Nmbd 4G **131**
Berwyn. *Den* 1D **70**
Bescaby. *Leics* 3F **75**
Bescar. *Lanc* 3B **90**
Besford. *Worc* 1E **49**
Bessacarr. *S Yor* 4G **93**
Bessels Leigh. *Oxon* 5C **50**
Bessingby. *E Yor* 3F **101**
Bessingham. *Norf* 2D **78**
Best Beech Hill. *E Sus* 2H **27**
Besthorpe. *Norf* 1C **66**
Besthorpe. *Notts* 4F **87**
Bestwood Village. *Notts* 1C **74**
Beswick. *E Yor* 5E **101**
Betchworth. *Surr* 5D **38**
Bethania. *Cdgn* 4E **57**
Bethania. *Gwyn* 1G **69**
(nr. Blaenau Ffestiniog)
Bethania. *Gwyn* 5F **81**
(nr. Caernarfon)
Bethel. *Gwyn* 2B **70**
(nr. Bala)
Bethel. *Gwyn* 4E **81**
(nr. Caernarfon)
Bethel. *IOA* 3C **80**
Bethersden. *Kent* 1D **28**
Bethesda. *Gwyn* 4F **81**
Bethesda. *Pemb* 3E **43**
Bethlehem. *Carm* 3G **45**
Bethnal Green. *G Lon* 2E **39**
Betishill. *N Lan* 3A **128**
Betley. *Staf* 1B **72**
Betsham. *Kent* 3H **39**
Betteshanger. *Kent* 5H **41**
Bettiscombe. *Dors* 3H **13**
Bettisfield. *Wrex* 2G **71**
Betton. *Shrp* 2A **72**
Betton Strange. *Shrp* 5H **71**
Bettws. *B'end* 3C **32**
Bettws. *Newp* 2F **33**
Bettws Bledrws. *Cdgn* 5E **57**
Bettws Cedewain. *Powy* 1D **58**
Bettws Gwerfil Goch. *Den* 1C **70**
Bettws Ifan. *Cdgn* 1D **44**
Bettws Newydd. *Mon* 5G **47**
Bettyhill. *High* 2H **167**
Betws. *Carm* 4G **45**
Betws Garmon. *Gwyn* 5E **81**
Betws-y-Coed. *Cnwy* 5G **81**
Betws-yn-Rhos. *Cnwy* 3B **82**
Beulah. *Cdgn* 1C **44**
Beulah. *Powy* 5B **58**
Beul an Atha. *Arg* 3B **124**
Bevendean. *Brig* 5E **27**
Bevercotes. *Notts* 3E **86**
Beverley. *E Yor* 1D **94**
Beverston. *Glos* 2D **34**
Bevington. *Glos* 2B **34**
Bewaldeth. *Cumb* 1D **102**
Bewcastle. *Cumb* 2G **113**
Bewdley. *Worc* 3B **60**
Bewerley. *N Yor* 3D **98**
Bewholme. *E Yor* 4F **101**
Bexfield. *Norf* 3C **78**
Bexhill. *E Sus* 5B **28**
Bexley. *G Lon* 3F **39**
Bexleyheath. *G Lon* 3F **39**
Bexleyhill. *W Sus* 3A **26**
Bexwell. *Norf* 5F **77**
Beyton. *Suff* 4B **66**
Bhalton. *W Isl* 4C **171**
Bhatarsaigh. *W Isl* 9B **170**
Bibbington. *Derbs* 3E **85**
Bibury. *Glos* 5G **49**
Bicester. *Oxon* 3D **50**
Bickenhall. *Som* 1F **13**
Bickenhill. *W Mid* 2F **61**
Bicker. *Linc* 2B **76**
Bicker Bar. *Linc* 2B **76**
Bicker Gauntlet. *Linc* 2B **76**
Bickershaw. *G Man* 4E **91**
Bickerstaffe. *Lanc* 4C **90**
Bickerton. *Ches E* 5H **83**
Bickerton. *Nmbd* 4D **121**
Bickerton. *N Yor* 4G **99**
Bickford. *Staf* 4C **72**
Bickington. *Devn* 3F **19**
(nr. Barnstaple)
Bickington. *Devn* 5B **12**
(nr. Newton Abbot)
Bickleigh. *Devn* 2B **8**
(nr. Plymouth)
Bickleigh. *Devn* 2C **12**
(nr. Tiverton)
Bickleton. *Devn* 3F **19**
Bickley. *N Yor* 5G **107**
Bickley Moss. *Ches W* 1H **71**
Bickmarsh. *Warw* 5F **61**
Bicknacre. *Essx* 5A **54**
Bicknoller. *Som* 3E **20**
Bicknor. *Kent* 5C **40**
Bickton. *Hants* 1G **15**
Bicton. *Here* 4G **59**
Bicton. *Shrp* 2E **59**
(nr. Bishop's Castle)
Bicton. *Shrp* 4G **71**
(nr. Shrewsbury)
Bicton Heath. *Shrp* 4G **71**
Bidborough. *Kent* 1G **27**
Biddenden. *Kent* 2C **28**
Biddenden Green. *Kent* 1C **28**
Biddenham. *Bed* 1A **52**
Biddestone. *Wilts* 4D **34**
Biddisham. *Som* 1G **21**
Biddlesden. *Buck* 1E **51**
Biddlestone. *Nmbd* 4D **120**
Biddulph. *Staf* 5C **84**
Biddulph Moor. *Staf* 5D **84**
Bideford. *Devn* 4E **19**
Bidford-on-Avon. *Warw* 5E **61**
Bidlake. *Devn* 4F **11**
Bidston. *Mers* 2E **83**
Bielby. *E Yor* 5B **100**
Bieldside. *Aber* 3F **153**
Bierley. *IOW* 5D **16**
Bierley. *W Yor* 1B **92**
Bierton. *Buck* 4G **51**
Bigbury. *Devn* 4C **8**
Bigbury-on-Sea. *Devn* 4C **8**
Bigby. *Linc* 4D **94**
Biggar. *Cumb* 3A **96**
Biggar. *S Lan* 1C **118**
Biggin. *Derbs* 5F **85**
(nr. Hartington)
Biggin. *Derbs* 1G **73**
(nr. Hulland)
Biggin. *N Yor* 1F **93**
Biggings. *Shet* 5C **173**
Biggin Hill. *G Lon* 5F **39**
Biggleswade. *C Beds* 1B **52**
Bighouse. *High* 2A **168**
Bighton. *Hants* 3E **24**
Biglands. *Cumb* 4D **112**
Bignall End. *Staf* 5C **84**
Bignor. *W Sus* 4A **26**
Bigrigg. *Cumb* 3B **102**
Big Sand. *High* 1G **155**
Bigton. *Shet* 9E **173**
Bilberry. *Corn* 2E **6**
Bilborough. *Nott* 1C **74**
Bilbrook. *Som* 2D **20**
Bilbrook. *Staf* 5C **72**
Bilbrough. *N Yor* 5H **99**
Bilbster. *High* 3E **169**
Bilby. *Notts* 2D **86**
Bildershaw. *Dur* 2F **105**
Bildeston. *Suff* 1C **54**
Billericay. *Essx* 1A **40**
Billesdon. *Leics* 5E **74**
Billesley. *Warw* 5F **61**
Billingborough. *Linc* 2A **76**
Billinge. *Mers* 4D **90**
Billingford. *Norf* 3C **78**
(nr. Dereham)
Billingford. *Norf* 3D **66**
(nr. Diss)
Billingham. *Stoc T* 2B **106**
Billinghay. *Linc* 5A **88**
Billingley. *S Yor* 4E **93**
Billingshurst. *W Sus* 3B **26**
Billingsley. *Shrp* 2B **60**
Billington. *C Beds* 3H **51**
Billington. *Lanc* 1F **91**
Billington. *Staf* 3C **72**
Billockby. *Norf* 4G **79**
Billy Row. *Dur* 1E **105**
Bilsborrow. *Lanc* 5E **97**
Bilsby. *Linc* 3D **88**

Bilsham. W Sus 5A 26
Bilsington. Kent 2E 29
Bilson Green. Glos 4B 48
Bilsthorpe. Notts 4D 86
Bilston. Midl 3F 129
Bilston. W Mid 1D 60
Bilstone. Leics 5A 74
Bilting. Kent 1E 29
Bilton. E Yor 1E 95
Bilton. Nmbd 3G 121
Bilton. N Yor 4E 99
Bilton. Warw 3B 62
Bilton in Ainsty. N Yor 5G 99
Bimbister. Orkn 6C 172
Binbrook. Linc 1B 88
Binchester. Dur 1F 105
Bincombe. Dors 4B 14
Bindal. High 5G 165
Binegar. Som 2B 22
Bines Green. W Sus 4C 26
Binfield. Brac 4G 37
Binfield Heath. Oxon 4F 37
Bingfield. Nmbd 2C 114
Bingham. Notts 1E 74
Bingham's Melcombe. Dors 2C 14
Bingley. W Yor 1B 92
Bings Heath. Shrp 4H 71
Binham. Norf 2B 78
Binley. Hants 1C 24
Binley. W Mid 3A 62
Binnegar. Dors 4D 15
Binniehill. Falk 2B 128
Binsoe. N Yor 2E 99
Binstead. IOW 3D 16
Binstead. W Sus 5A 26
Binsted. Hants 2F 25
Binton. Warw 5F 61
Bintree. Norf 3C 78
Binweston. Shrp 5F 71
Birch. Essx 4C 54
Birchall. Staf 5D 85
Bircham Newton. Norf 2G 77
Bircham Tofts. Norf 2G 77
Birchanger. Essx 3F 53
Birchburn. N Ayr 3D 122
Birch Cross. Staf 2F 73
Bircher. Here 4G 59
Birch Green. Essx 4C 54
Birchgrove. Card 4E 33
Birchgrove. Swan 3G 31
Birch Heath. Ches W 4H 83
Birch Hill. Ches W 3H 83
Birchill. Devn 2G 13
Birchington. Kent 4G 41
Birch Langley. G Man 4G 91
Birchley Heath. Warw 1G 61
Birchmoor. Warw 5G 73
Birchmoor Green. C Beds 2H 51
Birchover. Derbs 4G 85
Birch Vale. Derbs 2E 85
Birchview. Mor 5F 159
Birchwood. Linc 4G 87
Birchwood. Som 1F 13
Birchwood. Warr 1A 84
Bircotes. Notts 1D 86
Birdbrook. Essx 1H 53
Birdham. W Sus 2G 17
Birdholme. Derbs 4A 86
Birdingbury. Warw 4B 62
Birdlip. Glos 4E 49
Birdsall. N Yor 3C 100
Birds Edge. W Yor 4C 92
Birds Green. Essx 5F 53
Birdsgreen. Shrp 2B 60
Birdsmoorgate. Dors 2G 13
Birdston. E Dun 2H 127
Birdwell. S Yor 4D 92
Birdwood. Glos 4C 48
Birgham. Bord 1B 120
Birichen. High 4E 165
Birkby. Cumb 1B 102
Birkby. N Yor 4A 106
Birkdale. Mers 3B 90
Birkenhead. Mers 2F 83
Birkenhills. Abers 4E 161
Birkenshaw. N Lan 3H 127
Birkenshaw. W Yor 2C 92
Birkhall. Abers 4H 151
Birkhill. Ang 5C 144
Birkholme. Linc 3G 75
Birkin. N Yor 2F 93
Birley. Here 5G 59
Birling. Kent 4A 40
Birling. Nmbd 4G 121
Birling Gap. E Sus 5G 27
Birlingham. Worc 1E 49
Birmingham. W Mid 2E 61 & 188
Birmingham Airport. W Mid 2F 61 & 216
Birnam. Per 4H 143
Birsay. Orkn 5B 172
Birse. Abers 4C 152
Birsemore. Abers 4C 152
Birstall. Leics 5C 74
Birstall. W Yor 2C 92
Birstall Smithies. W Yor 2C 92
Birstwith. N Yor 4E 99
Birthorpe. Linc 2A 76
Birtle. Lanc 3G 91
Birtley. Here 4F 59
Birtley. Nmbd 2B 114
Birtley. Tyne 4F 115
Birtsmorton. Worc 2D 48
Birts Street. Worc 2C 48
Bisbrooke. Rut 1F 63
Bisham. Wind 3G 37
Bishampton. Worc 5D 61
Bish Mill. Devn 4H 19
Bishop Auckland. Dur 2F 105
Bishopbridge. Linc 1H 87
Bishopbriggs. E Dun 2H 127
Bishop Burton. E Yor 1C 94
Bishopdown. Wilts 3G 23
Bishop Middleham. Dur 1A 106
Bishopmill. Mor 2G 159
Bishop Monkton. N Yor 3F 99
Bishop Norton. Linc 1G 87
Bishopsbourne. Kent 5F 41
Bishops Cannings. Wilts 5F 35
Bishop's Castle. Shrp 2F 59
Bishop's Caundle. Dors 1B 14
Bishop's Cleeve. Glos 3E 49
Bishop's Down. Dors 1B 14
Bishop's Frome. Here 1B 48
Bishop's Green. Essx 4G 53
Bishop's Green. Hants 5D 36
Bishop's Hull. Som 4F 21
Bishop's Itchington. Warw 5A 62
Bishops Lydeard. Som 4E 21
Bishop's Norton. Glos 3D 48
Bishop's Nympton. Devn 4A 20
Bishop's Offley. Staf 3B 72
Bishop's Stortford. Herts 3E 53
Bishops Sutton. Hants 3E 24
Bishop's Tachbrook. Warw 4H 61
Bishop's Tawton. Devn 3F 19
Bishopsteignton. Devn 5C 12
Bishopstoke. Hants 1C 16
Bishopston. Swan 4E 31
Bishopstone. Buck 4G 51
Bishopstone. E Sus 5F 27
Bishopstone. Here 1H 47
Bishopstone. Swin 3H 35
Bishopstone. Wilts 4F 23
Bishopstrow. Wilts 2D 23
Bishop Sutton. Bath 1A 22
Bishop's Waltham. Hants 1D 16
Bishopswood. Som 1F 13
Bishops Wood. Staf 5C 72
Bishopsworth. Bris 5A 34
Bishop Thornton. N Yor 3E 99
Bishopthorpe. York 5H 99
Bishopton. Darl 2A 106
Bishopton. Dum 5B 110
Bishopton. N Yor 2F 99
Bishopton. Ren 2F 127
Bishopton. Warw 5F 61
Bishop Wilton. E Yor 4B 100
Bishton. Newp 3G 33
Bishton. Staf 3E 73
Bisley. Glos 5E 49
Bisley. Surr 5A 38
Bispham. Bkpl 5C 96
Bispham Green. Lanc 3C 90
Bissoe. Corn 4B 6
Bisterne. Hants 2G 15
Bisterne Close. Hants 2H 15
Bitchfield. Linc 3G 75
Bittadon. Devn 2F 19
Bittaford. Devn 3C 8
Bittering. Norf 4B 78
Bitterley. Shrp 3H 59
Bitterne. Sotn 1C 16
Bitteswell. Leics 2C 62
Bitton. S Glo 5B 34
Bix. Oxon 3F 37
Bixter. Shet 6E 173
Blaby. Leics 1C 62
Blackawton. Devn 3E 9
Black Bank. Cambs 2E 65
Black Barn. Linc 3D 76
Blackborough. Devn 2D 12
Blackborough. Norf 4F 77
Blackborough End. Norf 4F 77
Black Bourton. Oxon 5A 50
Blackboys. E Sus 3G 27
Blackbrook. Derbs 1H 73
Blackbrook. Mers 1H 83
Blackbrook. Staf 2B 72
Blackbrook. Surr 1C 26
Blackburn. Abers 2F 153
Blackburn. Bkbn 2E 91
Blackburn. W Lot 3C 128
Black Callerton. Tyne 3E 115
Black Carr. Norf 1C 66
Black Clauchrie. S Ayr 1H 109
Black Corries. High 3G 141
Black Crofts. Arg 5D 140
Black Cross. Corn 2D 6
Blackden Heath. Ches E 3B 84
Blackditch. Oxon 5C 50
Blackdog. Abers 2G 153
Black Dog. Devn 2B 12
Blackdown. Dors 2G 13
Blackdyke. Cumb 4C 112
Blacker Hill. S Yor 4D 92
Blackfen. G Lon 3F 39
Blackfield. Hants 2C 16
Blackford. Cumb 3E 113
Blackford. Per 3A 136
Blackford. Shrp 2H 59
Blackford. Som 2H 21 (nr. Burnham-on-Sea)
Blackford. Som 4B 22 (nr. Wincanton)
Blackfordby. Leics 4H 73
Blackgang. IOW 5C 16
Blackhall. Edin 2F 129
Blackhall. Ren 3F 127
Blackhall Colliery. Dur 1B 106
Blackhall Mill. Tyne 4E 115
Blackhall Rocks. Dur 1B 106
Blackham. E Sus 2F 27
Blackheath. Essx 3D 54
Blackheath. G Lon 3E 39
Blackheath. Suff 3G 67
Blackheath. Surr 1B 26
Blackheath. W Mid 2D 61
Black Heddon. Nmbd 2D 115
Blackhill. Abers 4H 161
Blackhill. High 3C 154
Black Hill. Warw 5G 61
Blackhills. Abers 2G 161
Blackhills. High 3D 158
Blackjack. Linc 2B 76
Blackland. Wilts 5F 35
Black Lane. G Man 4F 91
Blackleach. Lanc 1C 90
Blackley. G Man 4G 91
Blackley. W Yor 3B 92
Blacklunans. Per 2A 144
Blackmill. B'end 3C 32
Blackmoor. G Man 4E 91
Blackmoor. Hants 3F 25
Blackmoor Gate. Devn 2G 19
Blackmore. Essx 5G 53
Blackmore End. Essx 2H 53
Blackmore End. Herts 4B 52
Black Mount. Arg 4G 141
Blackness. Falk 2D 128
Blacknest. Hants 2F 25
Blackney. Dors 3H 13
Blacknoll. Dors 4D 14
Black Notley. Essx 3A 54
Blacko. Lanc 5A 98
Black Pill. Swan 3F 31
Blackpool. Bkpl 1B 90 & 188
Blackpool. Devn 4E 9
Blackpool Airport. Lanc 1B 90
Blackpool Corner. Devn 3G 13
Blackpool Gate. Cumb 2G 113
Blackridge. W Lot 3C 128
Blackrock. Arg 3B 124
Blackrock. Mon 4F 47
Blackrod. G Man 3E 90
Blackshaw. Dum 3B 112
Blackshaw Head. W Yor 2H 91
Blackshaw Moor. Staf 5E 85
Blacksmith's Green. Suff 4D 66
Blacksnape. Bkbn 2F 91
Blackstone. W Sus 4D 26
Black Street. Suff 2H 67
Black Tar. Pemb 4D 43
Blackthorn. Oxon 4E 50
Blackthorpe. Suff 4B 66
Blacktoft. E Yor 2B 94
Blacktop. Aber 3F 153
Black Torrington. Devn 2E 11
Blacktown. Newp 3F 33
Blackwall Tunnel. G Lon 2E 39
Blackwater. Corn 4B 6
Blackwater. Hants 1G 25
Blackwater. IOW 4D 16
Blackwater. Som 1F 13
Blackwaterfoot. N Ayr 3C 122
Blackwell. Darl 3F 105
Blackwell. Derbs 5B 86 (nr. Alfreton)
Blackwell. Derbs 3F 85 (nr. Buxton)
Blackwell. Som 4D 20
Blackwell. Warw 1H 49
Blackwell. Worc 3D 61
Blackwood. Cphy 2E 33
Blackwood. Dum 1G 111
Blackwood. S Lan 5A 128
Blackwood Hill. Staf 5D 84
Blacon. Ches W 4F 83
Bladnoch. Dum 4B 110
Bladon. Oxon 4C 50
Blaenannerch. Cdgn 1C 44
Blaenau Dolwyddelan. Cnwy 5F 81
Blaenau Ffestiniog. Gwyn 1G 69
Blaenavon. Torf 5F 47
Blaenawey. Mon 4F 47
Blaen Celyn. Cdgn 5C 56
Blaen Clydach. Rhon 2C 32
Blaendulais. Neat 5B 46
Blaenffos. Pemb 1F 43
Blaengarw. B'end 2C 32
Blaen-geuffordd. Cdgn 2F 57
Blaengwrach. Neat 5B 46
Blaengwynfi. Neat 2B 32
Blaenllechau. Rhon 2D 32
Blaenpennal. Cdgn 4F 57
Blaenplwyf. Cdgn 3E 57
Blaenporth. Cdgn 1C 44
Blaenrhondda. Rhon 2C 32
Blaenwaun. Carm 2G 43
Blaen-y-coed. Carm 2H 43
Blaenycwm. Rhon 2C 32
Blagdon. N Som 1A 22
Blagdon. Torb 2E 9
Blagdon Hill. Som 1F 13
Blagill. Cumb 5A 114
Blaguegate. Lanc 4C 90
Blaich. High 1E 141
Blain. High 2A 140
Blaina. Blae 5F 47
Blair Atholl. Per 2F 143
Blair Drummond. Stir 4G 135
Blairgowrie. Per 4A 144
Blairhall. Fife 1D 128
Blairingone. Per 4B 136
Blairlogie. Stir 4H 135
Blairmore. Abers 5B 160
Blairmore. Arg 1C 126
Blairmore. High 3B 166
Blairquhanan. W Dun 1F 127
Blaisdon. Glos 4C 48
Blakebrook. Worc 3C 60
Blakedown. Worc 3C 60
Blake End. Essx 3H 53
Blakemere. Here 1G 47
Blakeney. Glos 5B 48
Blakeney. Norf 1C 78
Blakenhall. Ches E 1B 72
Blakenhall. W Mid 1C 60
Blakeshall. Worc 2C 60
Blakesley. Nptn 5D 62
Blanchland. Nmbd 4C 114
Blandford Camp. Dors 2E 15
Blandford Forum. Dors 2D 15
Blandford St Mary. Dors 2D 15
Bland Hill. N Yor 4E 98
Blandy. High 3G 167
Blanefield. Stir 2G 127
Blankney. Linc 4H 87
Blantyre. S Lan 4H 127
Blarmachfoldach. High 2E 141
Blarnalearoch. High 4F 163
Blashford. Hants 2G 15
Blaston. Leics 1F 63
Blatchbridge. Som 2C 22
Blathaisbhal. W Isl 1D 170
Blatherwycke. Nptn 1G 63
Blawith. Cumb 1B 96
Blaxhall. Suff 5F 67
Blaxton. S Yor 4G 93
Blaydon. Tyne 3E 115
Bleadney. Som 2H 21
Bleadon. N Som 1G 21
Blean. Kent 4F 41
Bleasby. Linc 2A 88
Bleasby. Notts 1E 74
Bleasby Moor. Linc 2A 88
Blebocraigs. Fife 2G 137
Bleddfa. Powy 4E 58
Bledington. Glos 3H 49
Bledlow. Buck 5F 51
Bledlow Ridge. Buck 2F 37
Blencarn. Cumb 1H 103
Blencogo. Cumb 5C 112
Blendworth. Hants 1F 17
Blenheim. Oxon 5D 50
Blennerhasset. Cumb 5C 112
Bletchingdon. Oxon 4D 50
Bletchingley. Surr 5E 39
Bletchley. Mil 2G 51
Bletchley. Shrp 2A 72
Bletherston. Pemb 2E 43
Bletsoe. Bed 5H 63
Blewbury. Oxon 3D 36
Blickling. Norf 3D 78
Blidworth. Notts 5C 86
Blindburn. Nmbd 3C 120
Blindcrake. Cumb 1C 102
Blindley Heath. Surr 1E 27
Blindmoor. Som 1F 13
Blisland. Corn 5A 10
Blissford. Hants 1G 15
Bliss Gate. Worc 3B 60
Blists Hill. Telf 5A 72
Blisworth. Nptn 5E 63
Blithbury. Staf 3E 73
Blitterlees. Cumb 4C 112
Blockley. Glos 2G 49
Blofield. Norf 5F 79
Blofield Heath. Norf 4F 79
Blo' Norton. Norf 3C 66
Bloomfield. Bord 2H 119
Blore. Staf 1F 73
Blount's Green. Staf 2E 73
Bloxham. Oxon 2C 50
Bloxholm. Linc 5H 87
Bloxwich. W Mid 5E 73
Bloxworth. Dors 3D 15
Blubberhouses. N Yor 4D 98
Blue Anchor. Som 2D 20
Blue Anchor. Swan 3E 31
Blue Bell Hill. Kent 4B 40
Blue Row. Essx 4D 54
Bluetown. Kent 5D 40
Blundeston. Suff 1H 67
Blunham. C Beds 5A 64
Blunsdon St Andrew. Swin 3G 35
Bluntington. Worc 3C 60
Bluntisham. Cambs 3C 64
Blunts. Corn 2H 7
Blurton. Stoke 1C 72
Blyborough. Linc 1G 87
Blyford. Suff 3G 67
Blymhill. Staf 4C 72
Blymhill Lawns. Staf 4C 72
Blyth. Nmbd 1G 115
Blyth. Notts 2D 86
Blyth. Bord 5E 129
Blyth Bank. Bord 5E 129
Blyth Bridge. Bord 5E 129
Blythburgh. Suff 3G 67
Blythe Bridge. Staf 1D 72
Blythe Marsh. Staf 1D 72
Blythe, The. Staf 3E 73
Blyton. Linc 1F 87
Boarhills. Fife 2H 137
Boarhunt. Hants 2E 16
Boarshead. E Sus 2G 27
Boar's Head. G Man 4D 90
Boars Hill. Oxon 5C 50
Boarstall. Buck 4E 51
Boasley Cross. Devn 3F 11
Boath. High 1H 157
Boat of Garten. High 2D 150
Bobbing. Kent 4C 40
Bobbington. Staf 1C 60
Bobbingworth. Essx 5F 53
Bocaddon. Corn 3F 7
Bocking. Essx 3A 54
Bocking Churchstreet. Essx 3A 54
Boddam. Abers 4H 161
Boddam. Shet 10E 173
Boddington. Glos 3D 49
Bodedern. IOA 2C 80
Bodelwyddan. Den 3C 82
Bodenham. Here 5H 59
Bodenham. Wilts 4G 23
Bodewryd. IOA 1C 80
Bodfari. Den 3C 82
Bodffordd. IOA 3D 80
Bodham. Norf 1D 78
Bodiam. E Sus 3B 28
Bodicote. Oxon 2C 50
Bodieve. Corn 1D 6
Bodinnick. Corn 3F 7
Bodle Street Green. E Sus 4A 28
Bodmin. Corn 2E 7
Bodnant. Cnwy 3H 81
Bodney. Norf 1H 65
Bodorgan. IOA 4C 80
Bodrane. Corn 2G 7
Bodsham. Kent 1F 29
Boduan. Gwyn 2C 68
Bodymoor Heath. Warw 1F 61
Bogallan. High 3A 158
Bogbrae Croft. Abers 5H 161
Bogend. S Ayr 1C 116
Boghall. Midl 3F 129
Boghall. W Lot 3C 128
Boghead. S Lan 5A 128
Bogindollo. Ang 3D 144
Bogmoor. Mor 2A 160
Bogniebrae. Abers 4C 160
Bognor Regis. W Sus 3H 17
Bograxie. Abers 2E 152
Bogside. N Lan 4B 128
Bog, The. Shrp 1F 59
Bogton. Abers 3D 160
Bogue. Dum 1D 110
Bohenie. High 5E 149
Bohortha. Corn 5C 6
Boirseam. W Isl 9C 171
Bokiddick. Corn 2E 7
Bolam. Dur 2E 105
Bolam. Nmbd 1D 115
Bolberry. Devn 5C 8
Bold Heath. Mers 2H 83
Boldon. Tyne 3G 115
Boldon Colliery. Tyne 3G 115
Boldre. Hants 3B 16
Boldron. Dur 3D 104
Bole. Notts 2E 87
Bolehall. Staf 5G 73
Bolehill. Derbs 5G 85
Bolenowe. Corn 5A 6
Boleside. Bord 1G 119
Bolham. Devn 1C 12
Bolham Water. Devn 1E 13
Bolingey. Corn 3B 6
Bollington. Ches E 3D 84
Bolney. W Sus 3D 26
Bolnhurst. Bed 5H 63
Bolshan. Ang 3F 145
Bolsover. Derbs 3B 86
Bolsterstone. S Yor 1G 85
Bolstone. Here 2A 48
Boltachan. Per 3F 143
Boltby. N Yor 1G 99
Bolton. Cumb 2H 103
Bolton. E Lot 2B 130
Bolton. E Yor 4B 100
Bolton. G Man 4F 91
Bolton. Nmbd 3F 121
Bolton Abbey. N Yor 4C 98
Bolton-by-Bowland. Lanc 5G 97
Boltonfellend. Cumb 3F 113
Boltongate. Cumb 5D 112
Bolton Green. Lanc 3D 90
Bolton-le-Sands. Lanc 3D 97
Bolton Low Houses. Cumb 5D 112
Bolton New Houses. Cumb 5D 112
Bolton-on-Swale. N Yor 5F 105
Bolton Percy. N Yor 5H 99
Bolton Town End. Lanc 3D 97
Bolton upon Dearne. S Yor 4E 93
Bolton Wood Lane. Cumb 5D 112
Bolventor. Corn 5B 10
Bomarsund. Nmbd 1F 115

Bomere Heath. Shrp 4G 71
Bonar Bridge. High 4D 164
Bonawe. Arg 5E 141
Bonby. N Lin 3D 94
Boncath. Pemb 1G 43
Bonchester Bridge. Bord 3H 119
Bonchurch. IOW 5D 16
Bond End. Staf 4F 73
Bondleigh. Devn 2G 11
Bonds. Lanc 5D 97
Bonehill. Devn 5H 11
Bonehill. Staf 5F 73
Bo'ness. Falk 1C 128
Boney Hay. Staf 4E 73
Bonham. Wilts 3C 22
Bonhill. W Dun 2E 127
Boningale. Shrp 5C 72
Bonjedward. Bord 2A 120
Bonkle. N Lan 4B 128
Bonnington. Ang 5E 145
Bonnington. Edin 3E 129
Bonnington. Kent 2E 29
Bonnybank. Fife 3F 137
Bonnybridge. Falk 1B 128
Bonnykelly. Abers 3F 161
Bonnyrigg. Midl 3G 129
Bonnyton. Ang 5C 144
Bonnytown. Fife 2H 137
Bonsall. Derbs 5G 85
Bont. Mon 4G 47
Bontddu. Gwyn 4F 69
Bont Dolgadfan. Powy 5A 70
Bontgoch. Cdgn 2F 57
Bonthorpe. Linc 3D 89
Bontnewydd. Cdgn 4F 57
Bont-newydd. Cnwy 3C 82
Bontnewydd. Gwyn 4D 81
(nr. Caernarfon)
Bont Newydd. Gwyn 1G 69
(nr. Llan Ffestiniog)
Bontuchel. Den 5C 82
Bonvilston. V Glam 4D 32
Bon-y-maen. Swan 3F 31
Booker. Buck 2G 37
Booley. Shrp 3H 71
Boorley Green. Hants 1D 16
Boosbeck. Red C 3D 106
Boot. Cumb 4C 102
Booth. W Yor 2A 92
Boothby Graffoe. Linc 5G 87
Boothby Pagnell. Linc 2G 75
Booth Green. Ches E 2D 84
Booth of Toft. Shet 4F 173
Boothstown. G Man 4F 91
Boothville. Nptn 4E 63
Booth Wood. W Yor 3A 92
Bootle. Cumb 1A 96
Bootle. Mers 1F 83
Booton. Norf 3D 78
Booze. N Yor 4D 104
Boquhan. Stir 1G 127
Boraston. Shrp 3A 60
Borden. Kent 4C 40
Borden. W Sus 4G 25
Bordlands. Bord 5E 129
Bordley. N Yor 3B 98
Bordon. Hants 3G 25
Boreham. Essx 5A 54
Boreham. Wilts 2D 23
Boreham Street. E Sus 4A 28
Borehamwood. Herts 1C 38
Boreland. Dum 5D 118
Boreston. Devn 3D 8
Borestone Brae. Stir 4H 135
Boreton. Shrp 5H 71
Borgh. W Isl 8B 170
(on Barra)
Borgh. W Isl 3C 170
(on Benbecula)
Borgh. W Isl 1E 170
(on Berneray)
Borgh. W Isl 2G 171
(on Isle of Lewis)
Borghasdal. W Isl 9C 171
Borghastan. W Isl 3D 171
Borgh na Sgiotaig. High 1C 154
Borgie. High 3G 167
Borgue. Dum 5D 110
Borgue. High 1H 165
Borley. Essx 1B 54
Borley Green. Essx 1B 54
Borley Green. Suff 4B 66
Borlum. High 1H 149
Bornais. W Isl 6C 170
Bornesketaig. High 1C 154
Boroughbridge. N Yor 3F 99
Borough Green. Kent 5H 39
Borras Head. Wrex 5F 83
Borreraig. High 3A 154
Borrobol Lodge. High 1F 165
Borrodale. High 4A 154
Borrowash. Derb 2B 74
Borrowby. N Yor 1G 99
(nr. Northallerton)
Borrowby. N Yor 3E 107
(nr. Whitby)
Borrowston. High 4F 169
Borrowstonehill. Orkn 7D 172
Borrowstoun. Falk 1C 128
Borstal. Medw 4B 40
Borth. Cdgn 2F 57
Borthwick. Midl 4G 129
Borth-y-Gest. Gwyn 2E 69
Borve. High 4D 154
Borwick. Lanc 2E 97
Bosbury. Here 1B 48
Boscastle. Corn 3A 10
Boscombe. Bour 3G 15
Boscombe. Wilts 3H 23
Boscoppa. Corn 3E 7
Bosham. W Sus 2G 17
Bosherston. Pemb 5D 42
Bosley. Ches E 4D 84
Bossall. N Yor 3B 100
Bossiney. Corn 4A 10
Bossingham. Kent 1F 29
Bossington. Som 2B 20
Bostadh. W Isl 3D 171
Bostock Green. Ches W 4A 84
Boston. Linc 1C 76
Boston Spa. W Yor 5G 99
Boswarthen. Corn 3B 4
Boswinger. Corn 4D 6
Botallack. Corn 3A 4
Botany Bay. G Lon 1D 39
Botcheston. Leics 5B 74
Botesdale. Suff 3C 66
Bothal. Nmbd 1F 115
Bothampstead. W Ber 4D 36
Bothamsall. Notts 3D 86
Bothel. Cumb 1C 102
Bothenhampton. Dors 3H 13
Bothwell. S Lan 4H 127
Botley. Buck 5H 51
Botley. Hants 1D 16
Botley. Oxon 5C 50
Botloe's Green. Glos 3C 48
Botolph Claydon. Buck 3F 51
Botolphs. W Sus 5C 26
Bottacks. High 2G 157
Bottesford. Leics 2F 75
Bottesford. N Lin 4B 94
Bottisham. Cambs 4E 65
Bottlesford. Wilts 1G 23
Bottomcraig. Fife 1F 137
Bottom o' th' Moor. G Man 3E 91
Botton. N Yor 4D 107
Botton Head. Lanc 3F 97
Bottreaux Mill. Devn 4B 20
Botus Fleming. Corn 2A 8
Botwnnog. Gwyn 2B 68
Bough Beech. Kent 1F 27
Boughrood. Powy 2E 47
Boughspring. Glos 2A 34
Boughton. Norf 5F 77
Boughton. Nptn 4E 63
Boughton. Notts 4D 86
Boughton Aluph. Kent 1E 29
Boughton Green. Kent 5B 40
Boughton Lees. Kent 1E 28
Boughton Malherbe. Kent 1C 28
Boughton Monchelsea. Kent 5B 40
Boughton under Blean. Kent 5E 41
Boulby. Red C 3E 107
Bouldnor. IOW 4B 16
Bouldon. Shrp 2H 59
Boulmer. Nmbd 3G 121
Boulston. Pemb 3D 42
Boultham. Linc 4G 87
Boulton. Derb 2A 74
Boundary. Staf 1D 73
Bounds. Here 2B 48
Bourn. Cambs 5C 64
Bournbrook. W Mid 2E 61
Bourne. Linc 3H 75
Bourne End. Bed 4H 63
Bourne End. Buck 3G 37
Bourne End. C Beds 1H 51
Bourne End. Herts 5A 52
Bournemouth. Bour 3F 15 & 190
Bournemouth Airport. Dors 3G 15
Bournes Green. Glos 5E 49
Bournes Green. S'end 2D 40
Bourne, The. Surr 2G 25
Bournheath. Worc 3D 60
Bournmoor. Dur 4G 115
Bournville. W Mid 2E 61
Bourton. Dors 3C 22
Bourton. N Som 5G 33
Bourton. Oxon 3H 35
Bourton. Shrp 1H 59
Bourton. Wilts 5F 35
Bourton on Dunsmore. Warw 3B 62
Bourton-on-the-Hill. Glos 2G 49
Bourton-on-the-Water. Glos 3G 49
Bousd. Arg 2D 138
Bousta. Shet 6D 173
Boustead Hill. Cumb 4D 112
Bouth. Cumb 1C 96
Bouthwaite. N Yor 2D 98
Boveney. Buck 3A 38
Boveridge. Dors 1F 15
Boverton. V Glam 5C 32
Bovey Tracey. Devn 5B 12
Bovingdon. Herts 5A 52
Bovingdon Green. Buck 3G 37
Bovinger. Essx 5F 53
Bovington Camp. Dors 4D 14
Bow. Devn 2H 11
Bowbank. Dur 2C 104
Bow Brickhill. Mil 2H 51
Bowbridge. Glos 5D 48
Bowburn. Dur 1A 106
Bowcombe. IOW 4C 16
Bowd. Devn 4E 12
Bowden. Devn 4E 9
Bowden. Bord 1H 119
Bowden Hill. Wilts 5E 35
Bowdens. Som 4H 21
Bowderdale. Cumb 4H 103
Bowdon. G Man 2B 84
Bower. Nmbd 1A 114
Bowerchalke. Wilts 4F 23
Bowerhill. Wilts 5E 35
Bower Hinton. Som 1H 13
Bowermadden. High 2E 169
Bowers. Staf 2C 72
Bowers Gifford. Essx 2B 40
Bowershall. Fife 4C 136
Bowertower. High 2E 169
Bowes. Dur 3C 104
Bowgreave. Lanc 5D 97
Bowhousebog. N Lan 4B 128
Bowithick. Corn 4B 10
Bowland Bridge. Cumb 1D 96
Bowlees. Dur 2C 104
Bowley. Here 5H 59
Bowlhead Green. Surr 2A 26
Bowling. W Dun 2F 127
Bowling. W Yor 1B 92
Bowling Bank. Wrex 1F 71
Bowling Green. Worc 5C 60
Bowlish. Som 2B 22
Bowmanstead. Cumb 5E 102
Bowmore. Arg 4B 124
Bowness-on-Solway. Cumb 3D 112
Bowness-on-Windermere.
Cumb 5F 103
Bow of Fife. Fife 2F 137
Bowriefauld. Ang 4E 145
Bowscale. Cumb 1E 103
Bowsden. Nmbd 5F 131
Bowside Lodge. High 2A 168
Bowston. Cumb 5F 103
Bow Street. Cdgn 2F 57
Bowthorpe. Norf 5D 78
Box. Glos 5D 48
Box. Wilts 5D 34
Boxbush. Glos 3B 48
Box End. Bed 1A 52
Boxford. Suff 1C 54
Boxford. W Ber 4C 36
Boxgrove. W Sus 5A 26
Boxley. Kent 5B 40
Boxmoor. Herts 5A 52
Box's Shop. Corn 2C 10
Boxted. Essx 2C 54
Boxted. Suff 5H 65
Boxted Cross. Essx 2D 54
Boxworth. Cambs 4C 64
Boxworth End. Cambs 4C 64
Boyden End. Suff 5G 65
Boyden Gate. Kent 4G 41
Boylestone. Derbs 2F 73
Boylestonfield. Derbs 2F 73
Boyndlie. Abers 2D 160
Boynton. E Yor 3F 101
Boys Hill. Dors 1B 14
Boythorpe. Derbs 4A 86
Boyton. Corn 3D 10
Boyton. Suff 1G 55
Boyton. Wilts 3E 23
Boyton Cross. Essx 5G 53
Boyton End. Essx 2G 53
Boyton End. Suff 1H 53
Bozeat. Nptn 5G 63
Braaid. IOM 4C 108
Braal Castle. High 2D 168
Brabling Green. Suff 4E 67
Brabourne. Kent 1F 29
Brabourne Lees. Kent 1E 29
Brabster. High 2F 169
Bracadale. High 5C 154
Bracara. High 4F 147
Braceborough. Linc 4H 75
Bracebridge. Linc 4G 87
Bracebridge Heath. Linc 4G 87
Braceby. Linc 2H 75
Bracewell. Lanc 5A 98
Brackenber. Cumb 3A 104
Brackenfield. Derbs 5A 86
Brackenlands. Cumb 5D 112
Brackenthwaite. Cumb 5D 112
Brackenthwaite. N Yor 4E 99
Brackla. B'end 4C 32
Brackla. High 3C 158
Bracklesham. W Sus 3G 17
Brackletter. High 5D 148
Brackley. Nptn 2D 50
Brackley Hatch. Nptn 1E 51
Brackloch. High 1F 163
Bracknell. Brac 5G 37
Braco. Per 3H 135
Bracobrae. Mor 3C 160
Bracon. N Lin 4A 94
Bracon Ash. Norf 1D 66
Bradbourne. Derbs 5G 85
Bradbury. Dur 2A 106
Bradda. IOM 4A 108
Bradden. Nptn 1E 51
Bradenham. Buck 2G 37
Bradenham. Norf 5B 78
Bradenstoke. Wilts 4F 35
Bradfield. Essx 2E 55
Bradfield. Norf 2E 79
Bradfield. W Ber 4E 36
Bradfield Combust. Suff 5A 66
Bradfield Green. Ches E 5A 84
Bradfield Heath. Essx 3E 55
Bradfield St Clare. Suff 5B 66
Bradfield St George. Suff 4B 66
Bradford. Derbs 4G 85
Bradford. Devn 2E 11
Bradford. Nmbd 1F 121
Bradford. W Yor 1B 92 & 190
Bradford Abbas. Dors 1A 14
Bradford Barton. Devn 1B 12
Bradford Leigh. Wilts 5D 34
Bradford-on-Avon. Wilts 5D 34
Bradford-on-Tone. Som 4E 21
Bradford Peverell. Dors 3B 14
Bradiford. Devn 3F 19
Brading. IOW 4E 16
Bradley. Ches W 3H 83
Bradley. Derbs 1G 73
Bradley. Glos 2C 34
Bradley. Hants 2E 25
Bradley. NE Lin 4F 95
Bradley. N Yor 1C 98
Bradley. Staf 4C 72
Bradley. W Mid 1D 60
Bradley. W Yor 2B 92
Bradley. Wrex 5F 83
Bradley Cross. Som 1H 21
Bradley Green. Ches W 1H 71
Bradley Green. Som 3F 21
Bradley Green. Warw 5G 73
Bradley Green. Worc 4D 61
Bradley in the Moors. Staf 1E 73
Bradley Mount. Ches E 3D 84
Bradley Stoke. S Glo 3B 34
Bradlow. Here 2C 48
Bradmore. Notts 2C 74
Bradmore. W Mid 1C 60
Bradninch. Devn 2D 12
Bradnop. Staf 5E 85
Bradpole. Dors 3H 13
Bradshaw. G Man 3F 91
Bradstone. Devn 4D 11
Bradwall Green. Ches E 4B 84
Bradway. S Yor 2H 85
Bradwell. Derbs 2F 85
Bradwell. Essx 3B 54
Bradwell. Mil 2G 51
Bradwell. Norf 5H 79
Bradwell-on-Sea. Essx 5D 54
Bradwell Waterside. Essx 5C 54
Bradworthy. Devn 1D 10
Brae. High 5C 162
Brae. Shet 5E 173
Braeantra. High 1H 157
Braefield. High 5G 157
Braefindon. High 3A 158
Braegrum. Per 1C 136
Braehead. Ang 3F 145
Braehead. Dum 4B 110
Braehead. Mor 4G 159
Braehead. Orkn 3D 172
Braehead. S Lan 1H 117
(nr. Coalburn)
Braehead. S Lan 4C 128
(nr. Forth)
Braehoulland. Shet 4D 173
Braemar. Abers 4F 151
Braemore. High 5C 168
(nr. Dunbeath)
Braemore. High 1D 156
(nr. Ullapool)
Brae of Achnahaird. High 2E 163
Brae Roy Lodge. High 4F 149
Braeside. Abers 5G 161
Braeside. Inv 2D 126
Braes of Coul. Ang 3B 144
Braeswick. Orkn 4F 172
Braetongue. High 3F 167
Braeval. Stir 3E 135
Braevallich. Arg 3G 133
Braewick. Shet 6E 173
Brafferton. Darl 2F 105
Brafferton. N Yor 2G 99
Brafield-on-the-Green. Nptn 5F 63
Bragar. W Isl 3E 171
Bragbury End. Herts 3C 52
Bragleenbeg. Arg 1G 133
Braichmelyn. Gwyn 4F 81
Braides. Lanc 4D 96
Braidwood. S Lan 5B 128
Braigo. Arg 3A 124
Brailsford. Derbs 1G 73
Braintree. Essx 3A 54
Braiseworth. Suff 3D 66
Braishfield. Hants 4B 24
Braithwaite. Cumb 2D 102
Braithwaite. S Yor 3G 93
Braithwaite. W Yor 5C 98
Braithwell. S Yor 1C 86
Brakefield Green. Norf 5C 78
Bramber. W Sus 4C 26
Brambledown. Kent 3D 40
Brambridge. Hants 4C 24
Bramcote. Notts 2C 74
Bramcote. Warw 2B 62
Bramdean. Hants 4E 24
Bramerton. Norf 5E 79
Bramfield. Herts 4C 52
Bramfield. Suff 3F 67
Bramford. Suff 1E 54
Bramhall. G Man 2C 84
Bramham. W Yor 5G 99
Bramhope. W Yor 5E 99
Bramley. Hants 1E 25
Bramley. S Yor 1B 86
Bramley. Surr 1B 26
Bramley. W Yor 1C 92
Bramley Green. Hants 1E 25
Bramley Head. N Yor 4D 98
Bramley Vale. Derbs 4B 86
Bramling. Kent 5G 41
Brampford Speke. Devn 3C 12
Brampton. Cambs 3B 64
Brampton. Cumb 2H 103
(nr. Appleby-in-Westmorland)
Brampton. Cumb 3G 113
(nr. Carlisle)
Brampton. Linc 3F 87
Brampton. Norf 3E 78
Brampton. S Yor 4E 93
Brampton. Suff 2G 67
Brampton Abbotts. Here 3B 48
Brampton Ash. Nptn 2E 63
Brampton Bryan. Here 3F 59
Brampton en le Morthen.
S Yor 2B 86
Bramshall. Staf 2E 73
Bramshaw. Hants 1A 16
Bramshill. Hants 5F 37
Bramshott. Hants 3G 25
Branault. High 2G 139
Brancaster. Norf 1G 77
Brancaster Staithe. Norf 1G 77
Brancepeth. Dur 1F 105
Branch End. Nmbd 3D 114
Branchill. Mor 3E 159
Brand End. Linc 1C 76
Branderburgh. Mor 1G 159
Brandesburton. E Yor 5F 101
Brandeston. Suff 4E 67
Brand Green. Glos 3C 48
Brandhill. Shrp 3G 59
Brandis Corner. Devn 2E 11
Brandish Street. Som 2C 20
Brandiston. Norf 3D 78
Brandon. Dur 1F 105
Brandon. Linc 1G 75
Brandon. Nmbd 3E 121
Brandon. Suff 2G 65
Brandon. Warw 3B 62
Brandon Bank. Cambs 2F 65
Brandon Creek. Norf 1F 65
Brandon Parva. Norf 5C 78
Brandsby. N Yor 2H 99
Brandy Wharf. Linc 1H 87
Brane. Corn 4B 4
Bran End. Essx 3G 53
Branksome. Pool 3F 15
Bransbury. Hants 2C 24
Bransby. Linc 3G 87
Branscombe. Devn 4E 13
Bransford. Worc 5B 60
Bransgore. Hants 3G 15
Bransholme. Hull 1D 94
Bransley. Shrp 3A 60
Branston. Leics 3F 75
Branston. Linc 4H 87
Branston. Staf 3G 73
Branston Booths. Linc 4H 87
Branstone. IOW 4D 16
Bransty. Cumb 3A 102
Brant Broughton. Linc 5G 87
Brantham. Suff 2E 54
Branthwaite. Cumb 1D 102
(nr. Caldbeck)
Branthwaite. Cumb 2B 102
(nr. Workington)
Brantingham. E Yor 2C 94
Branton. Nmbd 3E 121
Branton. S Yor 4G 93
Branton Green. N Yor 3G 99
Branxholme. Bord 3G 119
Branxton. Nmbd 1C 120
Brassington. Derbs 5G 85
Brasted. Kent 5F 39
Brasted Chart. Kent 5F 39
Bratch, The. Staf 1C 60
Brathens. Abers 4D 152
Bratoft. Linc 4D 88
Brattleby. Linc 2G 87
Bratton. Som 2C 20
Bratton. Telf 4A 72
Bratton. Wilts 1E 23
Bratton Clovelly. Devn 3E 11
Bratton Fleming. Devn 3G 19
Bratton Seymour. Som 4B 22
Braughing. Herts 3D 53
Braulen Lodge. High 5E 157
Braunston. Nptn 4C 62
Braunstone Town. Leic 5C 74
Braunston-in-Rutland.
Rut 5F 75
Braunton. Devn 3E 19
Brawby. N Yor 2B 100
Brawl. High 2A 168
Brawlbin. High 3C 168
Bray. Wind 3A 38
Braybrooke. Nptn 2E 63
Brayford. Devn 3G 19
Bray Shop. Corn 5D 10
Braystones. Cumb 4B 102
Brayton. N Yor 1G 93
Bray Wick. Wind 4G 37

Brazacott. *Corn* 3C 10
Brea. *Corn* 4A 6
Breach. *W Sus* 2F 17
Breachwood Green. *Herts* 3B 52
Breacleit. *W Isl* 4D 171
Breaden Heath. *Shrp* 2G 71
Breadsall. *Derbs* 1A 74
Breadstone. *Glos* 5C 48
Breage. *Corn* 4D 4
Breakachy. *High* 4G 157
Breakish. *High* 1E 147
Bream. *Glos* 5B 48
Breamore. *Hants* 1G 15
Bream's Meend. *Glos* 5B 48
Brean. *Som* 1F 21
Breanais. *W Isl* 5B 171
Brearton. *N Yor* 3F 99
Breascleit. *W Isl* 4E 171
Breaston. *Derbs* 2B 74
Brecais Àrd. *High* 1E 147
Brecais Iosal. *High* 1E 147
Brechfa. *Carm* 2F 45
Brechin. *Ang* 3F 145
Breckles. *Norf* 1B 66
Brecon. *Powy* 3D 46
Brecon Beacons. *Powy* 3C 46
Bredbury. *G Man* 1D 84
Brede. *E Sus* 4C 28
Bredenbury. *Here* 5A 60
Breden's Norton. *Worc* 2E 49
Bredfield. *Suff* 5E 67
Bredgar. *Kent* 4C 40
Bredhurst. *Kent* 4B 40
Bredicot. *Worc* 5D 60
Bredon. *Worc* 2E 49
Bredwardine. *Here* 1G 47
Breedon on the Hill. *Leics* 3B 74
Breibhig. *W Isl* 9B 170 (on Barra)
Breibhig. *W Isl* 4G 171 (on Isle of Lewis)
Breich. *W Lot* 3C 128
Breightmet. *G Man* 3F 91
Breighton. *E Yor* 1H 93
Breinton. *Here* 2H 47
Breinton Common. *Here* 2H 47
Breiwick. *Shet* 7F 173
Brelston Green. *Here* 3A 48
Bremhill. *Wilts* 4E 35
Brenachie. *High* 1B 158
Brenchley. *Kent* 1A 28
Brendon. *Devn* 2A 20
Brent Cross. *G Lon* 2D 38
Brent Eleigh. *Suff* 1C 54
Brentford. *G Lon* 3C 38
Brentingby. *Leics* 4E 75
Brent Knoll. *Som* 1G 21
Brent Pelham. *Herts* 2E 53
Brentwood. *Essx* 1H 39
Brenzett. *Kent* 3E 28
Brereton. *Staf* 4E 73
Brereton Cross. *Staf* 4E 73
Brereton Green. *Ches E* 4B 84
Brereton Heath. *Ches E* 4C 84
Bressingham. *Norf* 2C 66
Bretby. *Derbs* 3G 73
Bretford. *Warw* 3B 62
Bretforton. *Worc* 1F 49
Bretherdale Head. *Cumb* 4G 103
Bretherton. *Lanc* 2C 90
Brettabister. *Shet* 6F 173
Brettenham. *Norf* 2B 66
Brettenham. *Suff* 5B 66
Bretton. *Flin* 4F 83
Bretton. *Pet* 5A 76
Brewer Street. *Surr* 5E 39
Brewlands Bridge. *Ang* 2A 144
Brewood. *Staf* 5C 72
Briantspuddle. *Dors* 3D 14
Bricket Wood. *Herts* 5B 52
Bricklehampton. *Worc* 1E 49
Bride. *IOM* 1D 108
Bridekirk. *Cumb* 1C 102
Bridell. *Pemb* 1B 44
Bridestowe. *Devn* 4F 11
Brideswell. *Abers* 5C 160
Bridford. *Devn* 4B 12
Bridge. *Corn* 4A 6
Bridge. *Kent* 5F 41
Bridge. *Som* 2G 13
Bridge End. *Bed* 5H 63
Bridge End. *Cumb* 5D 102 (nr. Broughton in Furness)
Bridge End. *Cumb* 5E 113 (nr. Dalston)
Bridge End. *Linc* 2A 76
Bridge End. *Shet* 8E 173
Bridgefoot. *Ang* 5C 144
Bridgefoot. *Cumb* 2B 102
Bridge Green. *Essx* 2E 53
Bridgehampton. *Som* 4A 22
Bridge Hewick. *N Yor* 2F 99
Bridgehill. *Dur* 4D 115
Bridgemary. *Hants* 2D 16
Bridgemere. *Ches E* 1B 72
Bridgemont. *Derbs* 2E 85
Bridgend. *Abers* 5C 160 (nr. Huntly)
Bridgend. *Abers* 5H 161 (nr. Peterhead)
Bridgend. *Ang* 2E 145 (nr. Brechin)
Bridgend. *Ang* 4C 144 (nr. Kirriemuir)
Bridgend. *Arg* 4F 133 (nr. Lochgilphead)
Bridgend. *Arg* 3B 124 (on Islay)
Bridgend. *B'end* 3C 32
Bridgend. *Cumb* 3F 103
Bridgend. *Devn* 4B 8
Bridgend. *Fife* 2F 137
Bridgend. *High* 3F 157
Bridgend. *Mor* 5A 160
Bridgend. *Per* 1D 136
Bridgend. *W Lot* 2D 128
Bridgend of Lintrathen. *Ang* 3B 144
Bridgeness. *Falk* 1D 128
Bridge of Alford. *Abers* 2C 152
Bridge of Allan. *Stir* 4G 135
Bridge of Avon. *Mor* 5F 159
Bridge of Awe. *Arg* 1H 133
Bridge of Balgie. *Per* 4C 142
Bridge of Brown. *High* 1F 151
Bridge of Cally. *Per* 3A 144
Bridge of Canny. *Abers* 4D 152
Bridge of Dee. *Dum* 3E 111
Bridge of Don. *Aber* 2G 153
Bridge of Dun. *Ang* 3F 145
Bridge of Dye. *Abers* 5D 152
Bridge of Earn. *Per* 2D 136
Bridge of Ericht. *Per* 3C 142
Bridge of Feugh. *Abers* 4E 152
Bridge of Forss. *High* 2C 168
Bridge of Gairn. *Abers* 4A 152
Bridge of Gaur. *Per* 3C 142
Bridge of Muchalls. *Abers* 4F 153
Bridge of Oich. *High* 3F 149
Bridge of Orchy. *Arg* 5H 141
Bridge of Walls. *Shet* 6D 173
Bridge of Weir. *Ren* 3E 127
Bridge Reeve. *Devn* 1G 11
Bridgerule. *Devn* 2C 10
Bridge Sollers. *Here* 1H 47
Bridge Street. *Suff* 1B 54
Bridgetown. *Devn* 2E 9
Bridgetown. *Som* 3C 20
Bridge Town. *Warw* 5G 61
Bridge Trafford. *Ches W* 3G 83
Bridgeyate. *S Glo* 4B 34
Bridgham. *Norf* 2B 66
Bridgnorth. *Shrp* 1B 60
Bridgtown. *Staf* 5D 73
Bridgwater. *Som* 3G 21
Bridister. *Shet* 6D 173
Bridlington. *E Yor* 3F 101
Bridport. *Dors* 3H 13
Bridstow. *Here* 3A 48
Brierfield. *Lanc* 1G 91
Brierley. *Glos* 4B 48
Brierley. *Here* 5G 59
Brierley. *S Yor* 3E 93
Brierley Hill. *W Mid* 2D 60
Brierton. *Hart* 1B 106
Briestfield. *W Yor* 3C 92
Brigg. *N Lin* 4D 94
Briggate. *Norf* 3F 79
Briggswath. *N Yor* 4F 107
Brigham. *Cumb* 1B 102
Brigham. *E Yor* 4E 101
Brighouse. *W Yor* 2B 92
Brighstone. *IOW* 4C 16
Brightgate. *Derbs* 5G 85
Brighthampton. *Oxon* 5B 50
Brightholmlee. *S Yor* 1G 85
Brightley. *Devn* 3G 11
Brightling. *E Sus* 3A 28
Brightlingsea. *Essx* 4D 54
Brighton. *Brig* 5E 27 & 189
Brighton. *Corn* 3D 6
Brighton Hill. *Hants* 2E 24
Brightons. *Falk* 2C 128
Brightwalton. *W Ber* 4C 36
Brightwalton Green. *W Ber* 4C 36
Brightwell. *Suff* 1F 55
Brightwell Baldwin. *Oxon* 2E 37
Brightwell-cum-Sotwell. *Oxon* 2D 36
Brigmerston. *Wilts* 2G 23
Brignall. *Dur* 3D 104
Brig o'Turk. *Stir* 3E 135
Brigsley. *NE Lin* 4F 95
Brigsteer. *Cumb* 1D 97
Brigstock. *Nptn* 2G 63
Brill. *Buck* 4E 51
Brill. *Corn* 4E 5
Brilley. *Here* 1F 47
Brimaston. *Pemb* 2D 42
Brimfield. *Here* 4H 59
Brimington. *Derbs* 3B 86
Brimley. *Devn* 5B 12
Brimpsfield. *Glos* 4E 49
Brimpton. *W Ber* 5D 36
Brims. *Orkn* 9B 172
Brimscombe. *Glos* 5D 48
Brimstage. *Mers* 2F 83
Brincliffe. *S Yor* 2H 85
Brind. *E Yor* 1H 93
Brindister. *Shet* 8F 173
Brindle. *Lanc* 2E 90
Brindley. *Ches E* 5H 83
Brindley Ford. *Stoke* 5C 84
Brineton. *Staf* 4C 72
Bringhurst. *Leics* 1F 63
Brington. *Cambs* 3H 63
Brinian. *Orkn* 5D 172
Briningham. *Norf* 2C 78
Brinkhill. *Linc* 3C 88
Brinkley. *Cambs* 5F 65
Brinklow. *Warw* 3B 62
Brinkworth. *Wilts* 3F 35
Brinscall. *Lanc* 2E 91
Brinscombe. *Som* 1H 21
Brinsley. *Notts* 1B 74
Brinsty Common. *Here* 5A 60
Brinsworth. *S Yor* 2B 86
Brinton. *Norf* 2C 78
Brisco. *Cumb* 4F 113
Brisley. *Norf* 3B 78
Brislington. *Bris* 4B 34
Brissenden Green. *Kent* 2D 28
Bristol. *Bris* 4A 34 & 189
Bristol International Airport. *N Som* 5A 34
Briston. *Norf* 2C 78
Britannia. *Lanc* 2G 91
Britford. *Wilts* 4G 23
Brithdir. *Cphy* 5E 47
Brithdir. *Cdgn* 1D 44
Brithdir. *Gwyn* 4G 69
Briton Ferry. *Neat* 3G 31
Britwell Salome. *Oxon* 2E 37
Brixham. *Torb* 3F 9
Brixton. *Devn* 3B 8
Brixton. *G Lon* 3E 39
Brixton Deverill. *Wilts* 3D 22
Brixworth. *Nptn* 3E 63
Brize Norton. *Oxon* 5B 50
Broad Alley. *Worc* 4C 60
Broad Blunsdon. *Swin* 2G 35
Broadbottom. *G Man* 1D 85
Broadbridge. *W Sus* 2G 17
Broadbridge Heath. *W Sus* 2C 26
Broad Campden. *Glos* 2G 49
Broad Chalke. *Wilts* 4F 23
Broadclyst. *Devn* 3C 12
Broadfield. *Inv* 2E 127
Broadfield. *Pemb* 4F 43
Broadfield. *W Sus* 2D 26
Broadford. *High* 1E 147
Broadford Bridge. *W Sus* 3B 26
Broadgate. *Cumb* 1A 96
Broad Green. *Cambs* 5F 65
Broad Green. *C Beds* 1H 51
Broad Green. *Worc* 3D 61 (nr. Bromsgrove)
Broad Green. *Worc* 5B 60 (nr. Worcester)
Broadhaven. *High* 3F 169
Broad Haven. *Pemb* 3C 42
Broadheath. *G Man* 2B 84
Broad Heath. *Staf* 3C 72
Broadheath. *Worc* 4A 60
Broadhembury. *Devn* 2E 12
Broadhempston. *Devn* 2E 9
Broad Hill. *Cambs* 3E 65
Broad Hinton. *Wilts* 4G 35
Broadholm. *Derbs* 1A 74
Broadholme. *Linc* 3F 87
Broadlay. *Carm* 5D 44
Broad Laying. *Hants* 5C 36
Broadley. *Lanc* 3G 91
Broadley. *Mor* 2A 160
Broadley Common. *Essx* 5E 53
Broad Marston. *Worc* 1G 49
Broadmayne. *Dors* 4C 14
Broadmere. *Hants* 2E 24
Broadmoor. *Pemb* 4E 43
Broad Oak. *Carm* 3F 45
Broad Oak. *Cumb* 5C 102
Broad Oak. *Devn* 3D 12
Broadoak. *Dors* 3H 13 (nr. Bridport)
Broad Oak. *Dors* 1C 14 (nr. Sturminster Newton)
Broad Oak. *E Sus* 4C 28 (nr. Hastings)
Broad Oak. *E Sus* 3H 27 (nr. Heathfield)
Broadoak. *Glos* 4B 48
Broadoak. *Hants* 1C 16
Broad Oak. *Here* 3H 47
Broad Oak. *Kent* 4F 41
Broadrashes. *Mor* 3B 160
Broads. *Norf* 5G 79
Broadsea. *Abers* 2G 161
Broad's Green. *Essx* 4G 53
Broadshard. *Som* 1H 13
Broadstairs. *Kent* 4H 41
Broadstone. *Pool* 3F 15
Broadstone. *Shrp* 2H 59
Broad Street. *E Sus* 4C 28
Broad Street. *Kent* 1F 29 (nr. Ashford)
Broad Street. *Kent* 5C 40 (nr. Maidstone)
Broad Street Green. *Essx* 5B 54
Broad, The. *Here* 4G 59
Broad Town. *Wilts* 4F 35
Broadwas. *Worc* 5B 60
Broadwath. *Cumb* 4F 113
Broadway. *Carm* 5D 45 (nr. Kidwelly)
Broadway. *Carm* 3G 43 (nr. Laugharne)
Broadway. *Pemb* 3C 42
Broadway. *Som* 1G 13
Broadway. *Suff* 3F 67
Broadway. *Worc* 2G 49
Broadwell. *Glos* 4A 48 (nr. Cinderford)
Broadwell. *Glos* 3H 49 (nr. Stow-on-the-Wold)
Broadwell. *Oxon* 5A 50
Broadwell. *Warw* 4B 62
Broadwell House. *Nmbd* 4C 114
Broadwey. *Dors* 4B 14
Broadwindsor. *Dors* 2H 13
Broadwoodkelly. *Devn* 2G 11
Broadwoodwidger. *Devn* 4E 11
Broallan. *High* 4G 157
Brobury. *Here* 1G 47
Brochel. *High* 4E 155
Brockamin. *Worc* 5B 60
Brockbridge. *Hants* 1E 16
Brockdish. *Norf* 3E 66
Brockencote. *Worc* 3C 60
Brockenhurst. *Hants* 2A 16
Brocketsbrae. *S Lan* 1H 117
Brockford Street. *Suff* 4D 66
Brockhall. *Nptn* 4D 62
Brockham. *Surr* 1C 26
Brockhampton. *Glos* 3E 49 (nr. Bishop's Cleeve)
Brockhampton. *Glos* 3F 49 (nr. Sevenhampton)
Brockhampton. *Here* 2A 48
Brockhill. *Bord* 2F 119
Brockholes. *W Yor* 3B 92
Brockhouse. *S Yor* 2C 86
Brockhurst. *Hants* 2D 16
Brocklesby. *Linc* 3E 95
Brockley. *N Som* 5H 33
Brockley Corner. *Suff* 3H 65
Brockley Green. *Suff* 1H 53 (nr. Bury St Edmunds)
Brockley Green. *Suff* 5H 65 (nr. Haverhill)
Brockleymoor. *Cumb* 1F 103
Brockmoor. *W Mid* 2C 60
Brockton. *Shrp* 2F 59 (nr. Bishop's Castle)
Brockton. *Shrp* 5B 72 (nr. Madeley)
Brockton. *Shrp* 1H 59 (nr. Much Wenlock)
Brockton. *Shrp* 5F 71 (nr. Pontesbury)
Brockton. *Staf* 2C 72
Brockton. *Telf* 4B 72
Brockweir. *Glos* 5A 48
Brockworth. *Glos* 4D 49
Brocton. *Staf* 4D 72
Brodick. *N Ayr* 2E 123
Brodie. *Mor* 3D 159
Brodiesord. *Abers* 3C 160
Brodsworth. *S Yor* 4F 93
Brogaig. *High* 2D 154
Brogborough. *C Beds* 2H 51
Brokenborough. *Wilts* 3E 35
Broken Cross. *Ches E* 3C 84
Bromborough. *Mers* 2F 83
Bromdon. *Shrp* 2A 60
Brome. *Suff* 3D 66
Brome Street. *Suff* 3D 66
Bromeswell. *Suff* 5F 67
Bromfield. *Cumb* 5C 112
Bromfield. *Shrp* 3G 59
Bromford. *W Mid* 1F 61
Bromham. *Bed* 5H 63
Bromham. *Wilts* 5E 35
Bromley. *G Lon* 4F 39
Bromley. *Herts* 3E 53
Bromley. *Shrp* 1B 60
Bromley Cross. *G Man* 3F 91
Bromley Green. *Kent* 2D 28
Bromley Wood. *Staf* 3F 73
Brompton. *Medw* 4B 40
Brompton. *N Yor* 5A 106 (nr. Northallerton)
Brompton. *N Yor* 1D 100 (nr. Scarborough)
Brompton. *Shrp* 5H 71
Brompton-on-Swale. *N Yor* 5F 105
Brompton Ralph. *Som* 3D 20
Brompton Regis. *Som* 3C 20
Bromsash. *Here* 3B 48
Bromsberrow. *Glos* 2C 48
Bromsberrow Heath. *Glos* 2C 48
Bromsgrove. *Worc* 3D 60
Bromstead Heath. *Staf* 4B 72
Bromyard. *Here* 5A 60
Bromyard Downs. *Here* 5A 60
Bronaber. *Gwyn* 2G 69
Broncroft. *Shrp* 2H 59
Brongest. *Cdgn* 1D 44
Brongwyn. *Cdgn* 1C 44
Bronington. *Wrex* 2G 71
Bronllys. *Powy* 2E 47
Bronnant. *Cdgn* 4F 57
Bronwydd Arms. *Carm* 3E 45
Bronydd. *Powy* 1F 47
Bronygarth. *Shrp* 2E 71
Brook. *Carm* 4G 43
Brook. *Hants* 1A 16 (nr. Cadnam)
Brook. *Hants* 4B 24 (nr. Romsey)
Brook. *IOW* 4B 16
Brook. *Kent* 1E 29
Brook. *Surr* 1B 26 (nr. Guildford)
Brook. *Surr* 2A 26 (nr. Haslemere)
Brooke. *Norf* 1E 67
Brooke. *Rut* 5F 75
Brookenby. *Linc* 1B 88
Brookend. *Glos* 5B 48
Brook End. *Worc* 1D 48
Brookfield. *Lanc* 1D 90
Brookfield. *Ren* 3F 127
Brookhouse. *Lanc* 3E 97
Brookhouse Green. *Ches E* 4C 84
Brookhouses. *Staf* 1D 73
Brookhurst. *Mers* 2F 83
Brookland. *Kent* 3D 28
Brooklands. *G Man* 1B 84
Brooklands. *Shrp* 1H 71
Brookmans Park. *Herts* 5C 52
Brooks. *Powy* 1D 58
Brooksby. *Leics* 4D 74
Brooks Green. *W Sus* 3C 26
Brook Street. *Essx* 1G 39
Brook Street. *Kent* 2D 28
Brook Street. *W Sus* 3E 27
Brookthorpe. *Glos* 4D 48
Brookville. *Norf* 1G 65
Brookwood. *Surr* 5A 38
Broom. *C Beds* 1B 52
Broom. *Fife* 3F 137
Broom. *Warw* 5E 61
Broome. *Norf* 1F 67
Broome. *Shrp* 1H 59 (nr. Cardington)
Broome. *Shrp* 2G 59 (nr. Craven Arms)
Broome. *Worc* 3D 60
Broomedge. *Warr* 2B 84
Broomend. *Abers* 2E 153
Broome Park. *Nmbd* 3F 121
Broomer's Corner. *W Sus* 3C 26
Broomfield. *Abers* 5G 161
Broomfield. *Essx* 4H 53
Broomfield. *Kent* 4F 41 (nr. Herne Bay)
Broomfield. *Kent* 5C 40 (nr. Maidstone)
Broomfield. *Som* 3F 21
Broomfleet. *E Yor* 2B 94
Broom Green. *Norf* 3B 78
Broomhall. *Ches E* 1A 72
Broomhall. *Wind* 4A 38
Broomhaugh. *Nmbd* 3D 114
Broomhill. *Bris* 4B 34
Broom Hill. *Dors* 2F 15
Broomhill. *High* 1D 151 (nr. Grantown-on-Spey)
Broomhill. *High* 1B 158 (nr. Invergordon)
Broomhill. *Norf* 5F 77
Broomhill. *S Yor* 4E 93
Broom Hill. *Worc* 3D 60
Broomhillbank. *Dum* 5D 118
Broomholm. *Norf* 2F 79
Broomlands. *Dum* 4C 118
Broomley. *Nmbd* 3D 114
Broom of Moy. *Mor* 3E 159
Broompark. *Dur* 5F 115
Broom's Green. *Glos* 2C 48
Brora. *High* 3G 165
Broseley. *Shrp* 5A 72
Brotherhouse Bar. *Linc* 4B 76
Brotheridge Green. *Worc* 1D 48
Brotherlee. *Dur* 1C 104
Brothertoft. *Linc* 1B 76
Brotherton. *N Yor* 2E 93
Brotton. *Red C* 2D 107
Broubster. *High* 2C 168
Brough. *Cumb* 3A 104
Brough. *Derbs* 2F 85
Brough. *E Yor* 2C 94
Brough. *High* 1E 169
Brough. *Notts* 5F 87
Brough. *Orkn* 6C 172 (nr. Finstown)
Brough. *Orkn* 9D 172 (nr. St Margaret's Hope)
Brough. *Shet* 6F 173 (nr. Benston)
Brough. *Shet* 4F 173 (nr. Booth of Toft)
Brough. *Shet* 7G 173 (on Bressay)
Brough. *Shet* 5G 173 (on Whalsay)
Broughall. *Shrp* 1H 71
Brougham. *Cumb* 2G 103
Brough Lodge. *Shet* 2G 173
Brough Sowerby. *Cumb* 3A 104
Broughton. *Cambs* 3B 64
Broughton. *Flin* 4F 83
Broughton. *Hants* 3B 24

Broughton. *Lanc* 1D 90
Broughton. *Mil* 2G 51
Broughton. *Nptn* 3F 63
Broughton. *N Lin* 4C 94
Broughton. *N Yor* 2B 100
(nr. Malton)
Broughton. *N Yor* 4B 98
(nr. Skipton)
Broughton. *Orkn* 3D 172
Broughton. *Oxon* 2C 50
Broughton. *Bord* 1D 118
Broughton. *Staf* 2B 72
Broughton. *V Glam* 4C 32
Broughton Astley. *Leics* 1C 62
Broughton Beck. *Cumb* 1B 96
Broughton Cross. *Cumb* 1B 102
Broughton Gifford. *Wilts* 5D 35
Broughton Green. *Worc* 4D 60
Broughton Hackett. *Worc* 5D 60
Broughton in Furness. *Cumb* 1B 96
Broughton Mills. *Cumb* 5D 102
Broughton Moor. *Cumb* 1B 102
Broughton Park. *G Man* 4G 91
Broughton Poggs. *Oxon* 5H 49
Broughtown. *Orkn* 3F 172
Broughty Ferry. *D'dee* 5D 144
Browland. *Shet* 6D 173
Brownbread Street. *E Sus* 4A 28
Brown Candover. *Hants* 3D 24
Brown Edge. *Lanc* 3B 90
Brown Edge. *Staf* 5D 84
Brownhill. *Bkbn* 1E 91
Brownhill. *Shrp* 3G 71
Brownhills. *Shrp* 2A 72
Brownhills. *W Mid* 5E 73
Brown Knowl. *Ches W* 5G 83
Brownlow. *Ches E* 4C 84
Brownlow Heath. *Ches E* 4C 84
Brown's Green. *W Mid* 1E 61
Brownshill. *Glos* 5D 49
Brownston. *Devn* 3C 8
Brownstone. *Devn* 2A 12
Browston Green. *Norf* 5G 79
Broxa. *N Yor* 5G 107
Broxbourne. *Herts* 5D 52
Broxburn. *E Lot* 2C 130
Broxburn. *W Lot* 2D 129
Broxholme. *Linc* 3G 87
Broxted. *Essx* 3F 53
Broxton. *Ches W* 5G 83
Broxwood. *Here* 5F 59
Broyle Side. *E Sus* 4F 27
Brù. *W Isl* 3F 171
Bruach Mairi. *W Isl* 4G 171
Bruairnis. *W Isl* 8C 170
Bruan. *High* 5F 169
Bruar Lodge. *Per* 1F 143
Brucehill. *W Dun* 2E 127
Brucklay. *Abers* 3G 161
Bruera. *Ches W* 4G 83
Bruern Abbey. *Oxon* 3A 50
Bruichladdich. *Arg* 3A 124
Bruisyard. *Suff* 4F 67
Bruisyard Street. *Suff* 4F 67
Brumby. *N Lin* 4B 94
Brund. *Staf* 4F 85
Brundall. *Norf* 5F 79
Brundish. *Norf* 1F 67
Brundish. *Suff* 4E 67
Brundish Street. *Suff* 3E 67
Brunery. *High* 1B 140
Brunswick Village. *Tyne* 2F 115
Brunthwaite. *W Yor* 5C 98
Bruntingthorpe. *Leics* 1D 62
Brunton. *Fife* 1F 137
Brunton. *Nmbd* 2G 121
Brunton. *Wilts* 1H 23
Brushford. *Devn* 2G 11
Brushford. *Som* 4C 20
Brusta. *W Isl* 1E 170
Bruton. *Som* 3B 22
Bryanston. *Dors* 2D 15
Bryant's Bottom. *Buck* 2G 37
Brydekirk. *Dum* 2C 112
Brymbo. *Cnwy* 3H 81
Brymbo. *Wrex* 5E 83
Brympton D'Evercy. *Som* 1A 14
Bryn. *Carm* 5F 45
Bryn. *G Man* 4D 90
Bryn. *Neat* 2B 32
Bryn. *Shrp* 2E 59
Brynamman. *Carm* 4H 45
Brynberian. *Pemb* 1F 43
Brynbryddan. *Neat* 2A 32
Bryncae. *Rhon* 3C 32
Bryncethin. *B'end* 3C 32
Bryncir. *Gwyn* 1D 69
Bryn-coch. *Neat* 3G 31
Bryncroes. *Gwyn* 2B 68
Bryncrug. *Gwyn* 5F 69
Bryn Du. *IOA* 3C 80
Bryn Eden. *Gwyn* 3G 69
Bryneglwys. *Den* 1D 70
Bryn Eglwys. *Gwyn* 4F 81
Brynford. *Flin* 3D 82
Bryn Gates. *G Man* 4D 90
Bryn Golau. *Rhon* 3D 32
Bryngwran. *IOA* 3C 80
Bryngwyn. *Mon* 5G 47
Bryngwyn. *Powy* 1E 47
Bryn-henllan. *Pemb* 1E 43
Brynhoffnant. *Cdgn* 5C 56
Bryn-llwyn. *Flin* 2C 82
Brynllywarch. *Powy* 2D 58
Brynmawr. *Blae* 4E 47
Bryn-mawr. *Gwyn* 2B 68
Brynmenyn. *B'end* 3C 32
Brynmill. *Swan* 3F 31
Brynna. *Rhon* 3C 32
Brynrefail. *Gwyn* 4E 81
Brynrefail. *IOA* 2D 81
Brynsadler. *Rhon* 3D 32
Bryn-Saith Marchog. *Den* 5C 82
Brynsiencyn. *IOA* 4D 81
Brynteg. *IOA* 2D 81
Brynteg. *Wrex* 5F 83
Brynygwenyn. *Mon* 4G 47
Bryn-y-maen. *Cnwy* 3H 81
Buaile nam Bodach. *W Isl* 8C 170
Bualintur. *High* 1C 146
Bubbenhall. *Warw* 3A 62
Bubwith. *E Yor* 1H 93
Buccleuch. *Bord* 3F 119
Buchanan Smithy. *Stir* 1F 127
Buchanhaven. *Abers* 4H 161
Buchanty. *Per* 1B 136
Buchany. *Stir* 3G 135
Buchley. *E Dun* 2G 127
Buchlyvie. *Stir* 4E 135
Buckabank. *Cumb* 5E 113
Buckden. *Cambs* 4A 64
Buckden. *N Yor* 2B 98
Buckenham. *Norf* 5F 79
Buckerell. *Devn* 2E 13
Buckfast. *Devn* 2D 8
Buckfastleigh. *Devn* 2D 8
Buckhaven. *Fife* 4F 137
Buckholm. *Bord* 1G 119
Buckholt. *Here* 4A 48
Buckhorn Weston. *Dors* 4C 22
Buckhurst Hill. *Essx* 1F 39
Buckie. *Mor* 2B 160
Buckingham. *Buck* 2E 51
Buckland. *Buck* 4G 51
Buckland. *Glos* 2F 49
Buckland. *Here* 5H 59
Buckland. *Herts* 2D 52
Buckland. *Kent* 1H 29
Buckland. *Oxon* 2B 36
Buckland. *Surr* 5D 38
Buckland Brewer. *Devn* 4E 19
Buckland Common. *Buck* 5H 51
Buckland Dinham. *Som* 1C 22
Buckland Filleigh. *Devn* 2E 11
Buckland in the Moor. *Devn* 5H 11
Buckland Monachorum. *Devn* 2A 8
Buckland Newton. *Dors* 2B 14
Buckland Ripers. *Dors* 4B 14
Buckland St Mary. *Som* 1F 13
Buckland-tout-Saints. *Devn* 4D 8
Bucklebury. *W Ber* 4D 36
Bucklegate. *Linc* 2C 76
Buckleigh. *Devn* 4E 19
Buckler's Hard. *Hants* 3C 16
Bucklesham. *Suff* 1F 55
Buckley. *Flin* 4E 83
Buckley Green. *Warw* 4F 61
Buckley Hill. *Mers* 1F 83
Bucklow Hill. *Ches E* 2B 84
Buckminster. *Leics* 3F 75
Bucknall. *Linc* 4A 88
Bucknall. *Stoke* 1D 72
Bucknell. *Oxon* 3D 50
Bucknell. *Shrp* 3F 59
Buckpool. *Mor* 2B 160
Bucksburn. *Aber* 3F 153
Buck's Cross. *Devn* 4D 18
Bucks Green. *W Sus* 2B 26
Buckshaw Village. *Lanc* 2D 90
Bucks Hill. *Herts* 5A 52
Bucks Horn Oak. *Hants* 2G 25
Buck's Mills. *Devn* 4D 18
Buckton. *E Yor* 2F 101
Buckton. *Here* 3F 59
Buckton. *Nmbd* 1E 121
Buckton Vale. *G Man* 4H 91
Buckworth. *Cambs* 3A 64
Budby. *Notts* 4D 86
Bude. *Corn* 2C 10
Budge's Shop. *Corn* 3H 7
Budlake. *Devn* 2C 12
Budle. *Nmbd* 1F 121
Budleigh Salterton. *Devn* 4D 12
Budock Water. *Corn* 5B 6
Buerton. *Ches E* 1A 72
Buffler's Holt. *Buck* 2E 51
Bugbrooke. *Nptn* 5D 62
Buglawton. *Ches E* 4C 84
Bugle. *Corn* 3E 6
Bugthorpe. *E Yor* 4B 100
Buildwas. *Shrp* 5A 72
Builth Road. *Powy* 5C 58
Builth Wells. *Powy* 5C 58
Bulbourne. *Herts* 4H 51
Bulby. *Linc* 3H 75
Bulcote. *Notts* 1D 74
Buldoo. *High* 2B 168
Bulford. *Wilts* 2G 23
Bulford Camp. *Wilts* 2G 23
Bulkeley. *Ches E* 5H 83
Bulkington. *Warw* 2A 62
Bulkington. *Wilts* 1E 23
Bulkworthy. *Devn* 1D 11
Bullamoor. *N Yor* 5A 106
Bull Bay. *IOA* 1D 80
Bullbridge. *Derbs* 5A 86
Bullgill. *Cumb* 1B 102
Bull Hill. *Hants* 3B 16
Bullinghope. *Here* 2A 48
Bull's Green. *Herts* 4C 52
Bullwood. *Arg* 2C 126
Bulmer. *Essx* 1B 54
Bulmer. *N Yor* 3A 100
Bulmer Tye. *Essx* 2B 54
Bulphan. *Thur* 2H 39
Bulverhythe. *E Sus* 5B 28
Bulwark. *Abers* 4G 161
Bulwell. *Nott* 1C 74
Bulwick. *Nptn* 1G 63
Bumble's Green. *Essx* 5E 53
Bun Abhainn Eadarra. *W Isl* 7D 171
Bunacaimb. *High* 5E 147
Bun a' Mhuillinn. *W Isl* 7C 170
Bunarkaig. *High* 5D 148
Bunbury. *Ches E* 5H 83
Bunchrew. *High* 4A 158
Bundalloch. *High* 1A 148
Buness. *Shet* 1H 173
Bunessan. *Arg* 1A 132
Bungay. *Suff* 2F 67
Bunkegivie. *High* 2H 149
Bunker's Hill. *Cambs* 5D 76
Bunkers Hill. *Linc* 5B 88
Bunker's Hill. *Norf* 5H 79
Bunloit. *High* 1H 149
Bunnahabhain. *Arg* 2C 124
Bunny. *Notts* 3C 74
Bunoich. *High* 3F 149
Bunree. *High* 2E 141
Bunroy. *High* 5E 149
Buntait. *High* 5F 157
Buntingford. *Herts* 3D 52
Buntings Green. *Essx* 2B 54
Bunwell. *Norf* 1D 66
Burbage. *Derbs* 3E 85
Burbage. *Leics* 1B 62
Burbage. *Wilts* 5H 35
Burcher. *Here* 4F 59
Burchett's Green. *Wind* 3G 37
Burcombe. *Wilts* 3F 23
Burcot. *Oxon* 2D 36
Burcot. *Worc* 3D 61
Burcote. *Shrp* 1B 60
Burcott. *Buck* 3G 51
Burcott. *Som* 2A 22
Burdale. *N Yor* 3C 100
Burdrop. *Oxon* 2B 50
Bures. *Suff* 2C 54
Burford. *Oxon* 4A 50
Burford. *Shrp* 4H 59
Burf, The. *Worc* 4C 60
Burg. *Arg* 4E 139
Burgate Great Green. *Suff* 3C 66
Burgate Little Green. *Suff* 3C 66
Burgess Hill. *W Sus* 4E 27
Burgh. *Suff* 5E 67
Burgh by Sands. *Cumb* 4E 113
Burgh Castle. *Norf* 5G 79
Burghclere. *Hants* 5C 36
Burghead. *Mor* 2F 159
Burghfield. *W Ber* 5E 37
Burghfield Common. *W Ber* 5E 37
Burghfield Hill. *W Ber* 5E 37
Burgh Heath. *Surr* 5D 38
Burghill. *Here* 1H 47
Burgh le Marsh. *Linc* 4E 89
Burgh Muir. *Abers* 2E 153
Burgh next Aylsham. *Norf* 3E 78
Burgh on Bain. *Linc* 2B 88
Burgh St Margaret. *Norf* 4G 79
Burgh St Peter. *Norf* 1G 67
Burghwallis. *S Yor* 3F 93
Burgie. *Mor* 3E 159
Burham. *Kent* 4B 40
Buriton. *Hants* 4F 25
Burland. *Ches E* 5A 84
Burland. *Shet* 8E 173
Burlawn. *Corn* 2D 6
Burleigh. *Brac* 3A 38
Burleigh. *Glos* 5D 48
Burlescombe. *Devn* 1D 12
Burleston. *Dors* 3C 14
Burlestone. *Devn* 4E 9
Burley. *Hants* 2H 15
Burley. *Rut* 4F 75
Burley. *W Yor* 1C 92
Burley Gate. *Here* 1A 48
Burley in Wharfedale. *W Yor* 5D 98
Burley Street. *Hants* 2H 15
Burley Woodhead. *W Yor* 5D 98
Burlingjobb. *Powy* 5E 59
Burlington. *Shrp* 4B 72
Burlton. *Shrp* 3G 71
Burmantofts. *W Yor* 1D 92
Burmarsh. *Kent* 2F 29
Burmington. *Warw* 2A 50
Burn. *N Yor* 2F 93
Burnage. *G Man* 1C 84
Burnaston. *Derbs* 2G 73
Burnbanks. *Cumb* 3G 103
Burnby. *E Yor* 5C 100
Burncross. *S Yor* 1H 85
Burneside. *Cumb* 5G 103
Burness. *Orkn* 3F 172
Burneston. *N Yor* 1F 99
Burnett. *Bath* 5B 34
Burnfoot. *E Ayr* 4D 116
Burnfoot. *Per* 3B 136
Burnfoot. *Bord* 3H 119
(nr. Hawick)
Burnfoot. *Bord* 3G 119
(nr. Roberton)
Burngreave. *S Yor* 2A 86
Burnham. *Buck* 2A 38
Burnham. *N Lin* 3D 94
Burnham Deepdale. *Norf* 1H 77
Burnham Green. *Herts* 4C 52
Burnham Market. *Norf* 1H 77
Burnham Norton. *Norf* 1H 77
Burnham-on-Crouch. *Essx* 1D 40
Burnham-on-Sea. *Som* 2G 21
Burnham Overy Staithe. *Norf* 1H 77
Burnham Overy Town. *Norf* 1H 77
Burnham Thorpe. *Norf* 1A 78
Burnhaven. *Abers* 4H 161
Burnhead. *Dum* 5A 118
Burnhervie. *Abers* 2E 153
Burnhill Green. *Staf* 5B 72
Burnhope. *Dur* 5E 115
Burnhouse. *N Ayr* 4E 127
Burniston. *N Yor* 5H 107
Burnlee. *W Yor* 4B 92
Burnley. *Lanc* 1G 91
Burnleydam. *Ches E* 1A 72
Burnmouth. *Bord* 3F 131
Burn Naze. *Lanc* 5C 96
Burn of Cambus. *Stir* 3G 135
Burnopfield. *Dur* 4E 115
Burnsall. *N Yor* 3C 98
Burnside. *Ang* 3E 145
Burnside. *E Ayr* 3E 117
Burnside. *Per* 3D 136
Burnside. *Shet* 4D 173
Burnside. *S Lan* 4H 127
Burnside. *W Lot* 2D 129
(nr. Broxburn)
Burnside. *W Lot* 2D 128
(nr. Winchburgh)
Burntcommon. *Surr* 5B 38
Burntheath. *Derbs* 2G 73
Burnt Heath. *Essx* 3D 54
Burnt Hill. *W Ber* 4D 36
Burnt Houses. *Dur* 2E 105
Burntisland. *Fife* 1F 129
Burnt Oak. *G Lon* 1D 38
Burnton. *E Ayr* 4D 117
Burntstalk. *Norf* 2G 77
Burntwood. *Staf* 5E 73
Burntwood Green. *Staf* 5E 73
Burnt Yates. *N Yor* 3E 99
Burnwynd. *Edin* 3E 129
Burpham. *Surr* 5B 38
Burpham. *W Sus* 5B 26
Burradon. *Nmbd* 4D 121
Burradon. *Tyne* 2F 115
Burrafirth. *Shet* 1H 173
Burragarth. *Shet* 1G 173
Burras. *Corn* 5A 6
Burraton. *Corn* 3A 8
Burravoe. *Shet* 3E 173
(nr. North Roe)
Burravoe. *Shet* 5E 173
(on Mainland)
Burravoe. *Shet* 4G 173
(on Yell)
Burray Village. *Orkn* 8D 172
Burrells. *Cumb* 3H 103
Burrelton. *Per* 5A 144
Burridge. *Devn* 2G 13
Burridge. *Hants* 1D 16
Burrigill. *High* 5E 169
Burrill. *N Yor* 1E 99
Burringham. *N Lin* 4B 94
Burrington. *Devn* 1G 11
Burrington. *Here* 3G 59
Burrington. *N Som* 1H 21
Burrough End. *Cambs* 5F 65
Burrough Green. *Cambs* 5F 65
Burrough on the Hill. *Leics* 4E 75
Burroughston. *Orkn* 5E 172
Burrow. *Devn* 4D 12
Burrow. *Som* 2C 20
Burrowbridge. *Som* 4G 21
Burrowhill. *Surr* 4A 38
Burry. *Swan* 3D 30
Burry Green. *Swan* 3D 30
Burry Port. *Carm* 5E 45
Burscough. *Lanc* 3C 90
Burscough Bridge. *Lanc* 3C 90
Bursea. *E Yor* 1B 94
Burshill. *E Yor* 5E 101
Bursledon. *Hants* 2C 16
Burslem. *Stoke* 1C 72
Burstall. *Suff* 1D 54
Burstock. *Dors* 2H 13
Burston. *Devn* 2H 11
Burston. *Norf* 2D 66
Burston. *Staf* 2D 72
Burstow. *Surr* 1E 27
Burstwick. *E Yor* 2F 95
Burtersett. *N Yor* 1A 98
Burtholme. *Cumb* 3G 113
Burthorpe. *Suff* 4G 65
Burthwaite. *Cumb* 5F 113
Burtle. *Som* 2H 21
Burtoft. *Linc* 2B 76
Burton. *Ches W* 4H 83
(nr. Kelsall)
Burton. *Ches W* 3F 83
(nr. Neston)
Burton. *Dors* 3G 15
(nr. Christchurch)
Burton. *Dors* 3B 14
(nr. Dorchester)
Burton. *Nmbd* 1F 121
Burton. *Pemb* 4D 43
Burton. *Som* 2E 21
Burton. *Wilts* 4D 34
(nr. Chippenham)
Burton. *Wilts* 3D 22
(nr. Warminster)
Burton. *Wrex* 5F 83
Burton Agnes. *E Yor* 3F 101
Burton Bradstock. *Dors* 4H 13
Burton-by-Lincoln. *Linc* 3G 87
Burton Coggles. *Linc* 3G 75
Burton Constable. *E Yor* 1E 95
Burton Corner. *Linc* 1C 76
Burton End. *Cambs* 1G 53
Burton End. *Essx* 3F 53
Burton Fleming. *E Yor* 2E 101
Burton Green. *W Mid* 3G 61
Burton Green. *Wrex* 5F 83
Burton Hastings. *Warw* 2B 62
Burton-in-Kendal. *Cumb* 2E 97
Burton in Lonsdale. *N Yor* 2F 97
Burton Joyce. *Notts* 1D 74
Burton Latimer. *Nptn* 3G 63
Burton Lazars. *Leics* 4E 75
Burton Leonard. *N Yor* 3F 99
Burton on the Wolds. *Leics* 3C 74
Burton Overy. *Leics* 1D 62
Burton Pedwardine. *Linc* 1A 76
Burton Pidsea. *E Yor* 1F 95
Burton Salmon. *N Yor* 2E 93
Burton's Green. *Essx* 3B 54
Burton Stather. *N Lin* 3B 94
Burton upon Stather. *N Lin* 3B 94
Burton upon Trent. *Staf* 3G 73
Burton Wolds. *Leics* 3D 74
Burtonwood. *Warr* 1H 83
Burwardsley. *Ches W* 5H 83
Burwarton. *Shrp* 2A 60
Burwash. *E Sus* 3A 28
Burwash Common. *E Sus* 3H 27
Burwash Weald. *E Sus* 3A 28
Burwell. *Cambs* 4E 65
Burwell. *Linc* 3C 88
Burwen. *IOA* 1D 80
Burwick. *Orkn* 9D 172
Bury. *Cambs* 2B 64
Bury. *G Man* 3G 91
Bury. *Som* 4C 20
Bury. *W Sus* 4B 26
Burybank. *Staf* 2C 72
Bury End. *Worc* 2F 49
Bury Green. *Herts* 3E 53
Bury Hill. *S Glo* 3C 34
Bury St Edmunds. *Suff* 4A 66
Burythorpe. *N Yor* 3B 100
Busbridge. *Surr* 1A 26
Busby. *E Ren* 4G 127
Busby. *Per* 1C 136
Buscot. *Oxon* 2H 35
Bush. *Corn* 2C 10
Bush Bank. *Here* 5G 59
Bushbury. *W Mid* 5D 72
Bushby. *Leics* 5D 74
Bushey. *Dors* 4E 15
Bushey. *Herts* 1C 38
Bushey Heath. *Herts* 1C 38
Bush Green. *Norf* 1C 66
(nr. Attleborough)
Bush Green. *Norf* 2E 66
(nr. Harleston)
Bush Green. *Suff* 5B 66
Bushley. *Worc* 2D 48
Bushley Green. *Worc* 2D 48
Bushmead. *Bed* 4A 64
Bushmoor. *Shrp* 2G 59
Bushton. *Wilts* 4F 35
Bushy Common. *Norf* 4B 78
Busk. *Cumb* 5H 113
Buslingthorpe. *Linc* 2H 87
Bussage. *Glos* 5D 49
Bussex. *Som* 3G 21
Busta. *Shet* 5E 173
Bustard Green. *Essx* 3G 53
Butcher's Cross. *E Sus* 3G 27
Butcombe. *N Som* 5A 34
Bute Town. *Cphy* 5E 46
Butleigh. *Som* 3A 22
Butleigh Wootton. *Som* 3A 22
Butlers Marston. *Warw* 5H 61
Butley. *Suff* 5F 67
Butley High Corner. *Suff* 1G 55
Butlocks Heath. *Hants* 2C 16
Butterburn. *Cumb* 2H 113
Buttercrambe. *N Yor* 4B 100
Butterknowle. *Dur* 2E 105
Butterleigh. *Devn* 2C 12
Buttermere. *Cumb* 3C 102
Buttermere. *Wilts* 5B 36
Buttershaw. *W Yor* 2B 92
Butterstone. *Per* 4H 143

Butterton. *Staf* 5E **85**
(nr. Leek)
Butterton. *Staf* 1C **72**
(nr. Stoke-on-Trent)
Butterwick. *Dur* 2A **106**
Butterwick. *Linc* 1C **76**
Butterwick. *N Yor* 2B **100**
(nr. Malton)
Butterwick. *N Yor* 2D **101**
(nr. Weaverthorpe)
Butteryhaugh. *Nmbd* 5A **120**
Butt Green. *Ches E* 5A **84**
Buttington. *Powy* 5E **71**
Buttonbridge. *Shrp* 3B **60**
Buttonoak. *Shrp* 3B **60**
Buttsash. *Hants* 2C **16**
Butt's Green. *Essx* 5A **54**
Butt Yeats. *Lanc* 3E **97**
Buxhall. *Suff* 5C **66**
Buxted. *E Sus* 3F **27**
Buxton. *Derbs* 3E **85**
Buxton. *Norf* 3E **79**
Buxworth. *Derbs* 2E **85**
Bwcle. *Flin* 4E **83**
Bwlch. *Powy* 3E **47**
Bwlchderwin. *Gwyn* 1D **68**
Bwlchgwyn. *Wrex* 5E **83**
Bwlch-Llan. *Cdgn* 5E **57**
Bwlchnewydd. *Carm* 3D **44**
Bwlchtocyn. *Gwyn* 3C **68**
Bwlch-y-cibau. *Powy* 4D **70**
Bwlchyddar. *Powy* 3D **70**
Bwlch-y-fadfa. *Cdgn* 1E **45**
Bwlch-y-ffridd. *Powy* 1C **58**
Bwlch y Garreg. *Powy* 1C **58**
Bwlch-y-groes. *Pemb* 1G **43**
Bwlch-y-sarnau. *Powy* 3C **58**
Bybrook. *Kent* 1E **28**
Byermoor. *Tyne* 4E **115**
Byers Garth. *Dur* 5G **115**
Byers Green. *Dur* 1F **105**
Byfield. *Nptn* 5C **62**
Byfleet. *Surr* 4B **38**
Byford. *Here* 1G **47**
Bygrave. *Herts* 2C **52**
Byker. *Tyne* 3F **115**
Byland Abbey. *N Yor* 2H **99**
Bylchau. *Cnwy* 4B **82**
Byley. *Ches W* 4B **84**
Bynea. *Carm* 3E **31**
Byram. *N Yor* 2E **93**
Byrness. *Nmbd* 4B **120**
Bystock. *Devn* 4D **12**
Bythorn. *Cambs* 3H **63**
Byton. *Here* 4F **59**
Bywell. *Nmbd* 3D **114**
Byworth. *W Sus* 3A **26**

C

Cabharstadh. *W Isl* 6F **171**
Cabourne. *Linc* 4E **95**
Cabrach. *Arg* 3C **124**
Cabrach. *Mor* 1A **152**
Cabus. *Lanc* 5D **97**
Cadbury. *Devn* 2C **12**
Cadder. *E Dun* 2H **127**
Caddington. *C Beds* 4A **52**
Caddonfoot. *Bord* 1G **119**
Cadeby. *Leics* 5B **74**
Cadeby. *S Yor* 4F **93**
Cadeleigh. *Devn* 2C **12**
Cade Street. *E Sus* 3H **27**
Cadgwith. *Corn* 5E **5**
Cadham. *Fife* 3E **137**
Cadishead. *G Man* 1B **84**
Cadle. *Swan* 3F **31**
Cadley. *Lanc* 1D **90**
Cadley. *Wilts* 1H **23**
(nr. Ludgershall)
Cadley. *Wilts* 5H **35**
(nr. Marlborough)
Cadmore End. *Buck* 2F **37**
Cadnam. *Hants* 1A **16**
Cadney. *N Lin* 4D **94**
Cadole. *Flin* 4E **82**
Cadoxton-Juxta-Neath. *Neat* 2A **32**
Cadwell. *Herts* 2B **52**
Cadwst. *Den* 2C **70**
Caeathro. *Gwyn* 4E **81**
Caehopkin. *Powy* 4B **46**
Caenby. *Linc* 2H **87**
Caenn-na-Cleithe. *W Isl* 8D **171**
Caerau. *B'end* 2B **32**
Caerau. *Card* 4E **33**
Cae'r-bont. *Powy* 4B **46**
Cae'r-bryn. *Carm* 4F **45**
Caerdeon. *Gwyn* 4F **69**
Caerdydd.
Card 4E **33** & **Cardiff 191**
Caerfarchell. *Pemb* 2B **42**
Caerffili. *Cphy* 3E **33**
Caerfyrddin. *Carm* 4E **45**
Caergeiliog. *IOA* 3C **80**
Caergwrle. *Flin* 5F **83**
Caergybi. *IOA* 2B **80**
Caerlaverock. *Per* 2A **136**
Caerleon. *Newp* 2G **33**
Caerlleon. *Carm* 2G **43**
Caerllion. *Newp* 2G **33**
Caernarfon. *Gwyn* 4D **81** & **190**
Caerphilly. *Cphy* 3E **33**
Caersws. *Powy* 1C **58**
Caerwedros. *Cdgn* 5C **56**
Caerwent. *Mon* 2H **33**
Caerwys. *Flin* 3D **82**
Caim. *IOA* 2F **81**
Caio. *Carm* 2G **45**
Cairinis. *W Isl* 2D **170**
Cairisiadar. *W Isl* 4D **171**
Cairminis. *W Isl* 9C **171**
Cairnbaan. *Arg* 4F **133**
Cairnbulg. *Abers* 2H **161**
Cairncross. *Ang* 1D **145**
Cairndow. *Arg* 2A **134**
Cairness. *Abers* 2H **161**
Cairneyhill. *Fife* 1D **128**
Cairngarroch. *Dum* 5F **109**
Cairngorms. *High* 3D **151**
Cairnhill. *Abers* 5D **160**
Cairnie. *Abers* 4B **160**
Cairnorrie. *Abers* 4F **161**
Cairnryan. *Dum* 3F **109**
Cairston. *Orkn* 6B **172**
Caister-on-Sea. *Norf* 4H **79**
Caistor. *Linc* 4E **95**
Caistor St Edmund. *Norf* 5E **79**
Caistron. *Nmbd* 4D **121**
Cakebole. *Worc* 3C **60**
Calais Street. *Suff* 1C **54**
Calanais. *W Isl* 4E **171**
Calbost. *W Isl* 6G **171**
Calbourne. *IOW* 4C **16**
Calceby. *Linc* 3C **88**
Calcot. *Glos* 4F **49**
Calcot Row. *W Ber* 4E **37**
Calcott. *Kent* 4F **41**
Calcott. *Shrp* 4G **71**
Caldback. *Shet* 1H **173**
Caldbeck. *Cumb* 1E **102**
Caldbergh. *N Yor* 1C **98**
Caldecote. *Cambs* 5C **64**
(nr. Cambridge)
Caldecote. *Cambs* 2A **64**
(nr. Peterborough)
Caldecote. *Herts* 2C **52**
Caldecote. *Warw* 1A **62**
Caldecott. *Nptn* 4G **63**
Caldecott. *Oxon* 2C **36**
Caldecott. *Rut* 1F **63**
Calderbank. *N Lan* 3A **128**
Calder Bridge. *Cumb* 4B **102**
Calderbrook. *G Man* 3H **91**
Caldercruix. *N Lan* 3B **128**
Calder Grove. *W Yor* 3D **92**
Calder Mains. *High* 3C **168**
Caldermill. *S Lan* 5H **127**
Calder Vale. *Lanc* 5E **97**
Calderwood. *S Lan* 4H **127**
Caldescote. *Nptn* 5D **62**
Caldicot. *Mon* 3H **33**
Caldwell. *Derbs* 4G **73**
Caldwell. *N Yor* 3E **105**
Caldy. *Mers* 2E **83**
Calebrack. *Cumb* 1E **103**
Caledfwlch. *Carm* 3G **45**
Calf Heath. *Staf* 5D **72**
Calford Green. *Suff* 1G **53**
Calfsound. *Orkn* 4E **172**
Calgary. *Arg* 3E **139**
Califer. *Mor* 3E **159**
California. *Cambs* 2E **65**
California. *Falk* 2C **128**
California. *Norf* 4H **79**
California. *Suff* 1E **55**
Calke. *Derbs* 3A **74**
Callakille. *High* 3F **155**
Callaly. *Nmbd* 4E **121**
Callander. *Stir* 3F **135**
Callaughton. *Shrp* 1A **60**
Callendoun. *Arg* 1E **127**
Callestick. *Corn* 3B **6**
Calligarry. *High* 3E **147**
Callington. *Corn* 2H **7**
Callingwood. *Staf* 3F **73**
Callow. *Here* 2H **47**
Callowell. *Glos* 5D **48**
Callow End. *Worc* 1D **48**
Callow Hill. *Wilts* 3F **35**
Callow Hill. *Worc* 3B **60**
(nr. Bewdley)
Callow Hill. *Worc* 4E **61**
(nr. Redditch)
Calmore. *Hants* 1B **16**
Calmsden. *Glos* 5F **49**
Calne. *Wilts* 4E **35**
Calow. *Derbs* 3B **86**
Calshot. *Hants* 2C **16**
Calstock. *Corn* 2A **8**
Calstone Wellington. *Wilts* 5F **35**
Calthorpe. *Norf* 2D **78**
Calthorpe Street. *Norf* 3G **79**
Calthwaite. *Cumb* 5F **113**
Calton. *N Yor* 4B **98**
Calton. *Staf* 5F **85**
Calveley. *Ches E* 5H **83**
Calver. *Derbs* 3G **85**
Calverhall. *Shrp* 2A **72**
Calverleigh. *Devn* 1C **12**
Calverley. *W Yor* 1C **92**
Calvert. *Buck* 3E **51**
Calverton. *Mil* 2F **51**
Calverton. *Notts* 1D **74**
Calvine. *Per* 2F **143**
Calvo. *Cumb* 4C **112**
Cam. *Glos* 2C **34**
Camaghael. *High* 1F **141**
Camas-luinie. *High* 1B **148**
Camasnacroise. *High* 3C **140**
Camastianavaig. *High* 5E **155**
Camasunary. *High* 2D **146**
Camault Muir. *High* 4H **157**
Camb. *Shet* 2G **173**
Camber. *E Sus* 4D **28**
Camberley. *Surr* 5G **37**
Camberwell. *G Lon* 3E **39**
Camblesforth. *N Yor* 2G **93**
Cambo. *Nmbd* 1D **114**
Cambois. *Nmbd* 1G **115**
Camborne. *Corn* 3D **4**
Cambourne. *Cambs* 5C **64**
Cambridge. *Cambs* 5D **64** & **191**
Cambridge. *Glos* 5C **48**
Cambrose. *Corn* 4A **6**
Cambus. *Clac* 4A **136**
Cambusbarron. *Stir* 4G **135**
Cambuskenneth. *Stir* 4H **135**
Cambuslang. *S Lan* 3H **127**
Cambusnethan. *N Lan* 4B **128**
Cambus o'May. *Abers* 4B **152**
Camden Town. *G Lon* 2D **39**
Cameley. *Bath* 1B **22**
Camelford. *Corn* 4B **10**
Camelon. *Falk* 1B **128**
Camelsdale. *Surr* 2A **26**
Camer's Green. *Worc* 2C **48**
Camerton. *Bath* 1B **22**
Camerton. *Cumb* 1B **102**
Camerton. *E Yor* 2F **95**
Camghouran. *Per* 3C **142**
Cammachmore. *Abers* 4G **153**
Cammeringham. *Linc* 2G **87**
Camore. *High* 4E **165**
Campbelton. *N Ayr* 4C **126**
Campbeltown. *Arg* 3B **122**
Campbeltown Airport. *Arg* 3A **122**
Cample. *Dum* 5B **118**
Campmuir. *Per* 5B **144**
Campsall. *S Yor* 3F **93**
Campsea Ashe. *Suff* 5F **67**
Camps End. *Cambs* 1G **53**
Camp, The. *Glos* 5E **49**
Campton. *C Beds* 2B **52**
Camptoun. *E Lot* 2B **130**
Camptown. *Bord* 3A **120**
Camrose. *Pemb* 2D **42**
Camserney. *Per* 4F **143**
Camster. *High* 4E **169**
Camus Croise. *High* 2E **147**
Camuscross. *High* 2E **147**
Camusdarach. *High* 4E **147**
Camusnagaul. *High* 1E **141**
(nr. Fort William)
Camusnagaul. *High* 5E **163**
(nr. Little Loch Broom)
Camusteel. *High* 4G **155**
Camusterrach. *High* 4G **155**
Camusvrachan. *Per* 4D **142**
Canada. *Hants* 1A **16**
Canadia. *E Sus* 4B **28**
Canaston Bridge. *Pemb* 3E **43**
Candlesby. *Linc* 4D **88**
Candle Street. *Suff* 3C **66**
Candy Mill. *S Lan* 5D **128**
Cane End. *Oxon* 4E **37**
Canewdon. *Essx* 1C **40**
Canford Cliffs. *Pool* 4F **15**
Canford Heath. *Pool* 3F **15**
Canford Magna. *Pool* 3F **15**
Cangate. *Norf* 3F **79**
Canham's Green. *Suff* 4C **66**
Canholes. *Derbs* 3E **85**
Canisbay. *High* 1F **169**
Canley. *W Mid* 3H **61**
Cann. *Dors* 4D **22**
Cann Common. *Dors* 4D **23**
Cannich. *High* 5F **157**
Cannington. *Som* 3F **21**
Cannock. *Staf* 4D **73**
Cannock Wood. *Staf* 4E **73**
Canonbie. *Dum* 2E **113**
Canon Bridge. *Here* 1H **47**
Canon Frome. *Here* 1B **48**
Canon Pyon. *Here* 1H **47**
Canons Ashby. *Nptn* 5C **62**
Canonstown. *Corn* 3C **4**
Canterbury. *Kent* 5F **41** & **190**
Cantley. *Norf* 5F **79**
Cantley. *S Yor* 4G **93**
Cantlop. *Shrp* 5H **71**
Canton. *Card* 4E **33**
Cantray. *High* 4B **158**
Cantraybruich. *High* 4B **158**
Cantraywood. *High* 4B **158**
Cantsdam. *Fife* 4D **136**
Cantsfield. *Lanc* 2F **97**
Canvey Island. *Essx* 2B **40**
Canwick. *Linc* 4G **87**
Canworthy Water. *Corn* 3C **10**
Caol. *High* 1F **141**
Caolas. *W Isl* 9B **170**
Caolas Liubharsaigh. *W Isl* 4D **170**
Caolas Scalpaigh. *W Isl* 8E **171**
Caolas Stocinis. *W Isl* 8D **171**
Caoles. *Arg* 4B **138**
Caol Ila. *Arg* 3C **124**
Caol Loch Ailse. *High* 1F **147**
Caol Reatha. *High* 1F **147**
Capel. *Kent* 1H **27**
Capel. *Surr* 1C **26**
Capel Bangor. *Cdgn* 2F **57**
Capel Betws Lleucu. *Cdgn* 5F **57**
Capel Coch. *IOA* 2D **80**
Capel Curig. *Cnwy* 5G **81**
Capel Cynon. *Cdgn* 1D **45**
Capel Dewi. *Carm* 3E **45**
Capel Dewi. *Cdgn* 2F **57**
(nr. Aberystwyth)
Capel Dewi. *Cdgn* 1E **45**
(nr. Llandysul)
Capel Garmon. *Cnwy* 5H **81**
Capel Green. *Suff* 1G **55**
Capel Gwyn. *IOA* 3C **80**
Capel Gwynfe. *Carm* 3H **45**
Capel Hendre. *Carm* 4F **45**
Capel Isaac. *Carm* 3F **45**
Capel Iwan. *Carm* 1G **43**
Capel-le-Ferne. *Kent* 2G **29**
Capel Llanilterne. *Card* 4D **32**
Capel Mawr. *IOA* 3D **80**
Capel Newydd. *Pemb* 1G **43**
Capel St Andrew. *Suff* 1G **55**
Capel St Mary. *Suff* 2D **54**
Capel Seion. *Carm* 4F **45**
Capel Seion. *Cdgn* 3F **57**
Capel Uchaf. *Gwyn* 1D **68**
Capel-y-ffin. *Powy* 2F **47**
Capenhurst. *Ches W* 3F **83**
Capernwray. *Lanc* 2E **97**
Capheaton. *Nmbd* 1D **114**
Cappercleuch. *Bord* 2E **119**
Capplegill. *Dum* 4D **118**
Capton. *Devn* 3E **9**
Capton. *Som* 3D **20**
Caputh. *Per* 5H **143**
Caradon Town. *Corn* 5C **10**
Carbis Bay. *Corn* 3C **4**
Carbost. *High* 5C **154**
(nr. Loch Harport)
Carbost. *High* 4D **154**
(nr. Portree)
Carbrook. *S Yor* 2A **86**
Carbrooke. *Norf* 5B **78**
Carburton. *Notts* 3D **86**
Carcluie. *S Ayr* 3C **116**
Car Colston. *Notts* 1E **74**
Carcroft. *S Yor* 3F **93**
Cardenden. *Fife* 4E **136**
Cardeston. *Shrp* 4F **71**
Cardewlees. *Cumb* 4E **113**
Cardiff. *Card* 4E **33** & **191**
Cardiff International Airport.
V Glam 5D **32**
Cardigan. *Cdgn* 1B **44**
Cardinal's Green. *Cambs* 1G **53**
Cardington. *Bed* 1A **52**
Cardington. *Shrp* 1H **59**
Cardinham. *Corn* 2F **7**
Cardno. *Abers* 2G **161**
Cardow. *Mor* 4F **159**
Cardross. *Arg* 2E **127**
Cardurnock. *Cumb* 4C **112**
Careby. *Linc* 4H **75**
Careston. *Ang* 2E **145**
Carew. *Pemb* 4E **43**
Carew Cheriton. *Pemb* 4E **43**
Carew Newton. *Pemb* 4E **43**
Carey. *Here* 2A **48**
Carfin. *N Lan* 4A **128**
Carfrae. *Bord* 4B **130**
Cargate Green. *Norf* 4F **79**
Cargenbridge. *Dum* 2G **111**
Cargill. *Per* 5A **144**
Cargo. *Cumb* 4E **113**
Cargreen. *Corn* 2A **8**
Carham. *Nmbd* 1B **120**
Carhampton. *Som* 2D **20**
Carharrack. *Corn* 4B **6**
Carie. *Per* 3D **142**
(nr. Loch Rannah)
Carie. *Per* 5D **142**
(nr. Loch Tay)
Carisbrooke. *IOW* 4C **16**
Cark. *Cumb* 2C **96**
Carkeel. *Corn* 2A **8**
Carlabhagh. *W Isl* 3E **171**
Carland Cross. *Corn* 3C **6**
Carlbury. *Darl* 3F **105**
Carlby. *Linc* 4H **75**
Carlecotes. *S Yor* 4B **92**
Carleen. *Corn* 4D **4**
Carlesmoor. *N Yor* 2D **98**
Carleton. *Cumb* 4F **113**
(nr. Carlisle)
Carleton. *Cumb* 4B **102**
(nr. Egremont)
Carleton. *Cumb* 2G **103**
(nr. Penrith)
Carleton. *Lanc* 1B **90**
Carleton. *N Yor* 5B **98**
Carleton. *W Yor* 2E **93**
Carleton Forehoe. *Norf* 5C **78**
Carleton Rode. *Norf* 1D **66**
Carleton St Peter. *Norf* 5F **79**
Carlidnack. *Corn* 4E **5**
Carlingcott. *Bath* 1B **22**
Carlin How. *Red C* 3E **107**
Carlisle. *Cumb* 4F **113** & **192**
Carloonan. *Arg* 2H **133**
Carlops. *Bord* 4E **129**
Carlton. *Bed* 5G **63**
Carlton. *Cambs* 5F **65**
Carlton. *Leics* 5A **74**
Carlton. *N Yor* 1A **100**
(nr. Helmsley)
Carlton. *N Yor* 1C **98**
(nr. Middleham)
Carlton. *N Yor* 2G **93**
(nr. Selby)
Carlton. *Notts* 1D **74**
Carlton. *S Yor* 3D **92**
Carlton. *Stoc T* 2A **106**
Carlton. *Suff* 4F **67**
Carlton. *W Yor* 2D **92**
Carlton Colville. *Suff* 1H **67**
Carlton Curlieu. *Leics* 1D **62**
Carlton Husthwaite. *N Yor* 2G **99**
Carlton in Cleveland. *N Yor* 4C **106**
Carlton in Lindrick. *Notts* 2C **86**
Carlton-le-Moorland. *Linc* 5G **87**
Carlton Miniott. *N Yor* 1F **99**
Carlton-on-Trent. *Notts* 4F **87**
Carlton Scroop. *Linc* 1G **75**
Carluke. *S Lan* 4B **128**
Carlyon Bay. *Corn* 3E **7**
Carmarthen. *Carm* 4E **45**
Carmel. *Carm* 4F **45**
Carmel. *Flin* 3D **82**
Carmel. *Gwyn* 5D **81**
Carmel. *IOA* 2C **80**
Carmichael. *S Lan* 1B **118**
Carmunnock. *Glas* 4H **127**
Carmyle. *S Lan* 3H **127**
Carmyllie. *Ang* 4E **145**
Carnaby. *E Yor* 3F **101**
Carnach. *High* 1C **148**
(nr. Lochcarron)
Carnach. *High* 4E **163**
(nr. Ullapool)
Carnach. *Mor* 4E **159**
Carnach. *W Isl* 8E **171**
Carnachy. *High* 3H **167**
Carnain. *Arg* 3B **124**
Carnais. *W Isl* 4C **171**
Carnan. *Arg* 4B **138**
Carnan. *W Isl* 4C **170**
Carnbee. *Fife* 3H **137**
Carnbo. *Per* 3C **136**
Carn Brea Village. *Corn* 4A **6**
Carndu. *High* 1A **148**
Carne. *Corn* 5D **6**
Carnell. *S Ayr* 1D **116**
Carnforth. *Lanc* 2E **97**
Carn-gorm. *High* 1B **148**
Carnhedryn. *Pemb* 2B **42**
Carnhell Green. *Corn* 3D **4**
Carnie. *Abers* 3F **153**
Carnkie. *Corn* 5B **6**
(nr. Falmouth)
Carnkie. *Corn* 5A **6**
(nr. Redruth)
Carnkief. *Corn* 3B **6**
Carno. *Powy* 1B **58**
Carnock. *Fife* 1D **128**
Carnon Downs. *Corn* 4B **6**
Carnoustie. *Ang* 5E **145**
Carntyne. *Glas* 3H **127**
Carnwath. *S Lan* 5C **128**
Carnyorth. *Corn* 3A **4**
Carol Green. *W Mid* 3G **61**
Carpalla. *Corn* 3D **6**
Carperby. *N Yor* 1C **98**
Carradale. *Arg* 2C **122**
Carragraich. *W Isl* 8D **171**
Carrbridge. *High* 1D **150**
Carr Cross. *Lanc* 3B **90**
Carreglefn. *IOA* 2C **80**
Carrhouse. *N Lin* 4A **94**
Carrick Castle. *Arg* 4A **134**
Carrick Ho. *Orkn* 4E **172**
Carriden. *Falk* 1D **128**
Carrington. *G Man* 1B **84**
Carrington. *Linc* 5C **88**
Carrington. *Midl* 3G **129**
Carrog. *Cnwy* 1G **69**
Carrog. *Den* 1D **70**
Carron. *Falk* 1B **128**
Carron. *Mor* 4G **159**
Carronbridge. *Dum* 5A **118**
Carronshore. *Falk* 1B **128**
Carrow Hill. *Mon* 2H **33**
Carr Shield. *Nmbd* 5B **114**
Carrutherstown. *Dum* 2C **112**
Carr Vale. *Derbs* 4B **86**
Carrville. *Dur* 5G **115**
Carrycoats Hall. *Nmbd* 2C **114**
Carsaig. *Arg* 1C **132**
Carscreugh. *Dum* 3H **109**
Carsegowan. *Dum* 4B **110**
Carse House. *Arg* 3F **125**
Carseriggan. *Dum* 3A **110**
Carsethorn. *Dum* 4A **112**
Carshalton. *G Lon* 4D **38**
Carsington. *Derbs* 5G **85**
Carskiey. *Arg* 5A **122**
Carsluith. *Dum* 4B **110**
Carsphairn. *Dum* 5E **117**
Carstairs. *S Lan* 5C **128**
Carstairs Junction. *S Lan* 5C **128**

Cartbridge. Surr 5B 38
Carterhaugh. Ang 4D 144
Carter's Clay. Hants 4B 24
Carterton. Oxon 5A 50
Carterway Heads. Nmbd 4D 114
Carthew. Corn 3E 6
Carthorpe. N Yor 1F 99
Cartington. Nmbd 4E 121
Cartland. S Lan 5B 128
Cartmel. Cumb 2C 96
Cartmel Fell. Cumb 1D 96
Cartworth. W Yor 4B 92
Carwath. Cumb 5E 112
Carway. Carm 5E 45
Carwinley. Cumb 2F 113
Cascob. Powy 4E 59
Cas-gwent. Mon 2A 34
Cash Feus. Fife 3E 136
Cashlie. Per 4B 142
Cashmoor. Dors 1E 15
Cas-Mael. Pemb 2E 43
Casnewydd.
Newp 3G 33 & **Newport 205**
Cassington. Oxon 4C 50
Cassop. Dur 1A 106
Castell. Cnwy 4G 81
Castell. Den 4D 82
Castell Hendre. Pemb 2E 43
Castell-nedd. Neat 2A 32
Castell Newydd Emlyn. Carm 1D 44
Castell-y-bwch. Torf 2F 33
Casterton. Cumb 2F 97
Castle. Som 2A 22
Castle Acre. Norf 4H 77
Castle Ashby. Nptn 5F 63
Castlebay. W Isl 9B 170
Castle Bolton. N Yor 5D 104
Castle Bromwich. W Mid 2F 61
Castle Bytham. Linc 4G 75
Castlebythe. Pemb 2E 43
Castle Caereinion. Powy 5D 70
Castle Camps. Cambs 1G 53
Castle Carrock. Cumb 4G 113
Castlecary. N Lan 2A 128
Castle Cary. Som 3B 22
Castle Combe. Wilts 4D 34
Castlecraig. High 2C 158
Castle Donington. Leics 3B 74
Castle Douglas. Dum 3E 111
Castle Eaton. Swin 2G 35
Castle Eden. Dur 1B 106
Castleford. W Yor 2E 93
Castle Frome. Here 1B 48
Castle Green. Surr 4A 38
Castle Green. Warw 3G 61
Castle Gresley. Derbs 4G 73
Castle Heaton. Nmbd 5F 131
Castle Hedingham. Essx 2A 54
Castle Hill. Kent 1A 28
Castlehill. Per 5B 144
Castlehill. S Lan 4B 128
Castle Hill. Suff 1E 55
Castlehill. W Dun 2E 127
Castle Kennedy. Dum 4G 109
Castle Lachlan. Arg 4H 133
Castlemartin. Pemb 5D 42
Castlemilk. Glas 4H 127
Castlemorris. Pemb 1D 42
Castlemorton. Worc 2C 48
Castle O'er. Dum 5E 119
Castle Park. N Yor 3F 107
Castlerigg. Cumb 2D 102
Castle Rising. Norf 3F 77
Castleside. Dur 5D 115
Castlethorpe. Mil 1F 51
Castleton. Abers 4F 151
Castleton. Arg 1G 125
Castleton. Derbs 2F 85
Castleton. G Man 3G 91
Castleton. Mor 1F 151
Castleton. Newp 3F 33
Castleton. N Yor 4D 107
Castleton. Per 2B 136
Castletown. Cumb 1G 103
Castletown. Dors 5B 14
Castletown. High 2D 169
Castletown. IOM 5B 108
Castletown. Tyne 4G 115
Castley. N Yor 5E 99
Caston. Norf 1B 66
Castor. Pet 1A 64
Caswell. Swan 4E 31
Catacol. N Ayr 5H 125
Catbrook. Mon 5A 48
Catchems End. Worc 3B 60
Catchgate. Dur 4E 115
Catcleugh. Nmbd 4B 120
Catcliffe. S Yor 2B 86
Catcott. Som 3G 21
Caterham. Surr 5E 39
Catfield. Norf 3F 79
Catfield Common. Norf 3F 79
Catfirth. Shet 6F 173
Catford. G Lon 3E 39
Catforth. Lanc 1C 90
Cathcart. Glas 3G 127
Cathedine. Powy 3E 47
Catherine-de-Barnes. W Mid 2F 61
Catherington. Hants 1E 17
Catherston Leweston. Dors 3G 13
Catherton. Shrp 3A 60
Catisfield. Hants 2D 16
Catlodge. High 4A 150
Catlowdy. Cumb 2F 113
Catmore. W Ber 3C 36
Caton. Devn 5A 12
Caton. Lanc 3E 97
Catrine. E Ayr 2E 117
Cat's Ash. Newp 2G 33
Catsfield. E Sus 4B 28
Catsgore. Som 4A 22
Catshill. Worc 3D 60
Cattal. N Yor 4G 99
Cattawade. Suff 2E 54
Catterall. Lanc 5D 97
Catterick. N Yor 5F 105
Catterick Bridge. N Yor 5F 105
Catterick Garrison. N Yor 5E 105
Catterlen. Cumb 1F 103
Catterline. Abers 1H 145
Catterton. N Yor 5H 99
Catteshall. Surr 1A 26
Catthorpe. Leics 3C 62
Cattistock. Dors 3A 14
Catton. Nmbd 4B 114
Catton. N Yor 2F 99
Catwick. E Yor 5F 101
Catworth. Cambs 3H 63
Caudle Green. Glos 4E 49
Caulcott. Oxon 3D 50
Cauldhame. Stir 4F 135
Cauldmill. Bord 3H 119
Cauldon. Staf 1E 73
Cauldon Lowe. Staf 1E 73
Cauldwells. Abers 3E 161
Caulkerbush. Dum 4G 111
Caulside. Dum 1F 113
Caunsall. Worc 2C 60
Caunton. Notts 4E 87
Causewayend. S Lan 1C 118
Causewayhead. Stir 4H 135
Causey Park. Nmbd 5F 121
Caute. Devn 1E 11
Cautley. Cumb 5H 103
Cavendish. Suff 1B 54
Cavendish Bridge. Derbs 2B 74
Cavenham. Suff 4G 65
Caversfield. Oxon 3D 50
Caversham. Read 4F 37
Caversham Heights. Read 4E 37
Caverswall. Staf 1D 72
Cawdor. High 4C 158
Cawkwell. Linc 2B 88
Cawood. N Yor 1F 93
Cawsand. Corn 3A 8
Cawston. Norf 3D 78
Cawston. Warw 3B 62
Cawthorne. N Yor 1B 100
Cawthorne. S Yor 4C 92
Cawthorpe. Linc 3H 75
Cawton. N Yor 2A 100
Caxton. Cambs 5C 64
Caynham. Shrp 3H 59
Caythorpe. Linc 1G 75
Caythorpe. Notts 1D 74
Cayton. N Yor 1E 101
Ceallan. W Isl 3D 170
Ceann a Bhàigh. W Isl 9C 171
(on Harris)
Ceann a Bhaigh. W Isl 2C 170
(on North Uist)
Ceann a Bhaigh. W Isl 8E 171
(on Scalpay)
Ceann a Bhaigh. W Isl 8D 171
(on South Harris)
Ceannacroc Lodge. High 2E 149
Ceann a Deas Loch Baghasdail.
W Isl 7C 170
Ceann an Leothaid. High 5E 147
Ceann a Tuath Loch Baghasdail.
W Isl 6C 170
Ceann Loch Ailleart. High 5F 147
Ceann Loch Muideirt. High 1B 140
Ceann Shiphoirt. W Isl 6E 171
Ceann Tarabhaigh. W Isl 6E 171
Cearsiadar. W Isl 5F 171
Ceathramh Meadhanach.
W Isl 1C 170
Cefn Berain. Cnwy 4B 82
Cefn-brith. Cnwy 5B 82
Cefn-bryn-brain. Carm 4H 45
Cefn Bychan. Cphy 2F 33
Cefn-bychan. Flin 4D 82
Cefncaeau. Carm 3E 31
Cefn Canol. Powy 2E 71
Cefn Coch. Powy 5C 70
(nr. Llanfair Caereinion)
Cefn-coch. Powy 3D 70
(nr. Llanrhaeadr-ym-Mochnant)
Cefn-coed-y-cymmer. Mer T 5D 46
Cefn Cribwr. B'end 3B 32
Cefn-ddwysarn. Gwyn 2B 70
Cefn Einion. Shrp 2E 59
Cefneithin. Carm 4F 45
Cefn Glas. B'end 3B 32
Cefngorwydd. Powy 1C 46
Cefn Llwyd. Cdgn 2F 57
Cefn-mawr. Wrex 1E 71
Cefn-y-bedd. Flin 5F 83
Cefn-y-coed. Powy 1D 58
Cefn-y-pant. Carm 2F 43
Cegidfa. Powy 4E 70
Ceinewydd. Cdgn 5C 56
Cellan. Cdgn 1G 45
Cellardyke. Fife 3H 137
Cellarhead. Staf 1D 72
Cemaes. IOA 1C 80
Cemmaes. Powy 5H 69
Cemmaes Road. Powy 5H 69
Cenarth. Carm 1C 44
Cenin. Gwyn 1D 68
Ceos. W Isl 5F 171
Ceres. Fife 2G 137
Ceri. Powy 2D 58
Cerist. Powy 2B 58
Cerne Abbas. Dors 2B 14
Cerney Wick. Glos 2F 35
Cerrigceinwen. IOA 3D 80
Cerrigydrudion. Cnwy 1B 70
Cess. Norf 4G 79
Cessford. Bord 2B 120
Ceunant. Gwyn 4E 81
Chaceley. Glos 2D 48
Chacewater. Corn 4B 6
Chackmore. Buck 2E 51
Chacombe. Nptn 1C 50
Chadderton. G Man 4H 91
Chaddesden. Derb 2A 74
Chaddesden Common. Derb 2A 74
Chaddesley Corbett. Worc 3C 60
Chaddlehanger. Devn 5E 11
Chaddleworth. W Ber 4C 36
Chadlington. Oxon 3B 50
Chadshunt. Warw 5H 61
Chadstone. Nptn 5F 63
Chad Valley. W Mid 2E 61
Chadwell. Leics 3E 75
Chadwell. Shrp 4B 72
Chadwell Heath. G Lon 2F 39
Chadwell St Mary. Thur 3H 39
Chadwick End. W Mid 3G 61
Chadwick Green. Mers 1H 83
Chaffcombe. Som 1G 13
Chafford Hundred. Thur 3H 39
Chagford. Devn 4H 11
Chailey. E Sus 4E 27
Chainbridge. Cambs 5D 76
Chain Bridge. Linc 1C 76
Chainhurst. Kent 1B 28
Chalbury. Dors 2F 15
Chalbury Common. Dors 2F 15
Chaldon. Surr 5E 39
Chaldon Herring. Dors 4C 14
Chale. IOW 5C 16
Chale Green. IOW 5C 16
Chalfont Common. Buck 1B 38
Chalfont St Giles. Buck 1A 38
Chalfont St Peter. Buck 2B 38
Chalford. Glos 5D 49
Chalgrove. Oxon 2E 37
Chalk. Kent 3A 40
Chalk End. Essx 4G 53
Chalk Hill. Glos 3G 49
Challaborough. Devn 4C 8
Challacombe. Devn 2G 19
Challister. Shet 5G 173
Challoch. Dum 3A 110
Challock. Kent 5E 40
Chalton. C Beds 5A 64
(nr. Bedford)
Chalton. C Beds 3A 52
(nr. Luton)
Chalton. Hants 1F 17
Chalvington. E Sus 5G 27
Champany. Falk 2D 128
Chance Inn. Fife 2F 137
Chancery. Cdgn 3E 57
Chandler's Cross. Herts 1B 38
Chandler's Cross. Worc 2C 48
Chandler's Ford. Hants 4C 24
Chanlockfoot. Dum 4G 117
Channel's End. Bed 5A 64
Channel Tunnel. Kent 2F 29
Channerwick. Shet 9F 173
Chantry. Som 2C 22
Chantry. Suff 1E 55
Chapel. Cumb 1D 102
Chapel. Fife 4E 137
Chapel Allerton. Som 1H 21
Chapel Allerton. W Yor 1D 92
Chapel Amble. Corn 1D 6
Chapel Brampton. Nptn 4E 63
Chapelbridge. Cambs 1B 64
Chapel Chorlton. Staf 2C 72
Chapel Cleeve. Som 2D 20
Chapel End. C Beds 1A 52
Chapel-en-le-Frith. Derbs 2E 85
Chapelfield. Abers 2G 145
Chapelgate. Linc 3D 76
Chapel Green. Warw 2G 61
(nr. Coventry)
Chapel Green. Warw 4B 62
(nr. Southam)
Chapel Haddlesey. N Yor 2F 93
Chapelhall. N Lan 3A 128
Chapel Hill. Abers 5H 161
Chapel Hill. Linc 5B 88
Chapel Hill. Mon 5A 48
Chapelhill. Per 1E 136
(nr. Glencarse)
Chapelhill. Per 5H 143
(nr. Harrietfield)
Chapelknowe. Dum 2E 112
Chapel Lawn. Shrp 3F 59
Chapel le Dale. N Yor 2G 97
Chapel Milton. Derbs 2E 85
Chapel of Garioch. Abers 1E 152
Chapel Row. W Ber 5D 36
Chapels. Cumb 1B 96
Chapel St Leonards. Linc 3E 89
Chapel Stile. Cumb 4E 102
Chapelthorne. W Yor 3D 92
Chapelton. Ang 4F 145
Chapelton. Devn 4F 19
Chapelton. High 2D 150
(nr. Grantown-on-Spey)
Chapelton. High 3H 157
(nr. Inverness)
Chapelton. S Lan 5H 127
Chapeltown. Bkbn 3F 91
Chapel Town. Corn 3C 6
Chapeltown. Mor 1G 151
Chapeltown. S Yor 1H 85
Chapmanslade. Wilts 2D 22
Chapmans Well. Devn 3D 10
Chapmore End. Herts 4D 52
Chappel. Essx 3B 54
Chard. Som 2G 13
Chard Junction. Dors 2G 13
Chardstock. Devn 2G 13
Charfield. S Glo 2C 34
Charing. Kent 1D 28
Charing Heath. Kent 1D 28
Charing Hill. Kent 5D 40
Charingworth. Glos 2G 49
Charlbury. Oxon 4B 50
Charlcombe. Bath 5C 34
Charlcutt. Wilts 4E 35
Charlecote. Warw 5G 61
Charles. Devn 3G 19
Charlesfield. Dum 3C 112
Charleshill. Surr 2G 25
Charleston. Ang 4C 144
Charleston. Ren 3F 127
Charlestown. Aber 3G 153
Charlestown. Abers 2H 161
Charlestown. Corn 3E 7
Charlestown. Dors 5B 14
Charlestown. Fife 1D 128
Charlestown. G Man 4G 91
Charlestown. High 1H 155
(nr. Gairloch)
Charlestown. High 4A 158
(nr. Inverness)
Charlestown. W Yor 2H 91
Charlestown of Aberlour.
Mor 4G 159
Charles Tye. Suff 5C 66
Charlesworth. Derbs 1E 85
Charlton. G Lon 3F 39
Charlton. Hants 2B 24
Charlton. Herts 3B 52
Charlton. Nptn 2D 50
Charlton. Nmbd 1B 114
Charlton. Oxon 3C 36
Charlton. Som 1B 22
(nr. Radstock)
Charlton. Som 2B 22
(nr. Shepton Mallet)
Charlton. Som 4F 21
(nr. Taunton)
Charlton. Telf 4H 71
Charlton. W Sus 1G 17
Charlton. Wilts 3E 35
(nr. Malmesbury)
Charlton. Wilts 1G 23
(nr. Pewsey)
Charlton. Wilts 4G 23
(nr. Salisbury)
Charlton. Wilts 4E 23
(nr. Shaftesbury)
Charlton. Worc 1F 49
(nr. Evesham)
Charlton. Worc 3C 60
(nr. Stourport-on-Severn)
Charlton Abbots. Glos 3F 49
Charlton Adam. Som 4A 22
Charlton Down. Dors 3B 14
Charlton Horethorne. Som 4B 22
Charlton Kings. Glos 3E 49
Charlton Mackrell. Som 4A 22
Charlton Marshall. Dors 2E 15
Charlton Musgrove. Som 4C 22
Charlton-on-Otmoor. Oxon 4D 50
Charlton on the Hill. Dors 2D 15
Charlwood. Hants 3E 25
Charlwood. Surr 1D 26
Charlynch. Som 3F 21
Charminster. Dors 3B 14
Charmouth. Dors 3G 13
Charndon. Buck 3E 51
Charney Bassett. Oxon 2B 36
Charnock Green. Lanc 3D 90
Charnock Richard. Lanc 3D 90
Charsfield. Suff 5E 67
Chart Corner. Kent 5B 40
Charter Alley. Hants 1D 24
Charterhouse. Som 1H 21
Charterville Allotments. Oxon 4B 50
Chartham. Kent 5F 41
Chartham Hatch. Kent 5F 41
Chartridge. Buck 5H 51
Chart Sutton. Kent 5B 40
Chart, The. Kent 5F 39
Charvil. Wok 4F 37
Charwelton. Nptn 5C 62
Chase Terrace. Staf 5E 73
Chasetown. Staf 5E 73
Chastleton. Oxon 3H 49
Chasty. Devn 2D 10
Chatburn. Lanc 5G 97
Chatcull. Staf 2B 72
Chatham.
Medw 4B 40 & **Medway 204**
Chatham Green. Essx 4H 53
Chathill. Nmbd 2F 121
Chatley. Worc 4C 60
Chattenden. Medw 3B 40
Chatteris. Cambs 2C 64
Chattisham. Suff 1D 54
Chatton. Nmbd 2E 121
Chatwall. Shrp 1H 59
Chaulden. Herts 5A 52
Chaul End. C Beds 3A 52
Chawleigh. Devn 1H 11
Chawley. Oxon 5C 50
Chawston. Bed 5A 64
Chawton. Hants 3F 25
Chaxhill. Glos 4C 48
Cheadle. G Man 2C 84
Cheadle. Staf 1E 73
Cheadle Hulme. G Man 2C 84
Cheam. Surr 4D 38
Cheapside. Wind 4A 38
Chearsley. Buck 4F 51
Chebsey. Staf 3C 72
Checkendon. Oxon 3E 37
Checkley. Ches E 1B 72
Checkley. Here 2A 48
Checkley. Staf 2E 73
Chedburgh. Suff 5G 65
Cheddar. Som 1H 21
Cheddington. Buck 4H 51
Cheddleton. Staf 5D 84
Cheddon Fitzpaine. Som 4F 21
Chedglow. Wilts 2E 35
Chedgrave. Norf 1F 67
Chedington. Dors 2H 13
Chediston. Suff 3F 67
Chediston Green. Suff 3F 67
Chedworth. Glos 4F 49
Chedzoy. Som 3G 21
Cheeseman's Green. Kent 2E 29
Cheetham Hill. G Man 4G 91
Cheglinch. Devn 2F 19
Cheldon. Devn 1H 11
Chelford. Ches E 3C 84
Chellaston. Derb 2A 74
Chellington. Bed 5G 63
Chelmarsh. Shrp 2B 60
Chelmick. Shrp 1G 59
Chelmondiston. Suff 2F 55
Chelmorton. Derbs 4F 85
Chelmsford. Essx 5H 53
Chelsea. G Lon 3D 39
Chelsfield. G Lon 4F 39
Chelsham. Surr 5E 39
Chelston. Som 4E 21
Chelsworth. Suff 1C 54
Cheltenham. Glos 3E 49 & 192
Chelveston. Nptn 4G 63
Chelvey. N Som 5H 33
Chelwood. Bath 5B 34
Chelwood Common. E Sus 3F 27
Chelwood Gate. E Sus 3F 27
Chelworth. Wilts 2E 35
Chelworth Lower Green.
Wilts 2F 35
Chelworth Upper Green.
Wilts 2F 35
Chelynch. Som 2B 22
Cheney Longville. Shrp 2G 59
Chenies. Buck 1B 38
Chepstow. Mon 2A 34
Chequerfield. W Yor 2E 93
Chequers Corner. Norf 5D 77
Cherhill. Wilts 4F 35
Cherington. Glos 2E 35
Cherington. Warw 2A 50
Cheriton. Devn 2H 19
Cheriton. Hants 4D 24
Cheriton. Kent 2G 29
Cheriton. Pemb 5D 43
Cheriton. Swan 3D 30
Cheriton Bishop. Devn 3A 12
Cheriton Cross. Devn 3A 12
Cheriton Fitzpaine. Devn 2B 12
Cherrington. Telf 3A 72
Cherrybank. Per 1D 136
Cherry Burton. E Yor 5D 101
Cherry Green. Herts 3D 52
Cherry Hinton. Cambs 5D 65
Cherry Willingham. Linc 3H 87
Chertsey. Surr 4B 38
Cheselbourne. Dors 3C 14
Chesham. Buck 5H 51
Chesham. G Man 3G 91
Chesham Bois. Buck 1A 38
Cheshunt. Herts 5D 52
Cheslyn Hay. Staf 5D 73
Chessetts Wood. Warw 3F 61
Chessington. G Lon 4C 38
Chester. Ches W 4G 83 & 192
Chesterblade. Som 2B 22
Chesterfield. Derbs 3A 86
Chesterfield. Staf 5F 73
Chesterhope. Nmbd 1C 114
Chester-le-Street. Dur 4F 115
Chester Moor. Dur 5F 115
Chesters. Bord 3A 120

Chesterton. *Cambs* 4D 64 (nr. Cambridge)
Chesterton. *Cambs* 1A 64 (nr. Peterborough)
Chesterton. *Glos* 5F 49
Chesterton. *Oxon* 3D 50
Chesterton. *Shrp* 1B 60
Chesterton. *Staf* 1C 72
Chesterton Green. *Warw* 5H 61
Chesterwood. *Nmbd* 3B 114
Chestfield. *Kent* 4F 41
Cheston. *Devn* 3C 8
Cheswardine. *Shrp* 2B 72
Cheswell. *Telf* 4B 72
Cheswick. *Nmbd* 5G 131
Cheswick Green. *W Mid* 3F 61
Chetnole. *Dors* 2B 14
Chettiscombe. *Devn* 1C 12
Chettisham. *Cambs* 2E 65
Chettle. *Dors* 1E 15
Chetton. *Shrp* 1A 60
Chetwode. *Buck* 3E 51
Chetwynd Aston. *Telf* 4B 72
Cheveley. *Cambs* 4F 65
Chevening. *Kent* 5F 39
Chevington. *Suff* 5G 65
Chevithorne. *Devn* 1C 12
Chew Magna. *Bath* 5A 34
Chew Moor. *G Man* 4E 91
Chew Stoke. *Bath* 5A 34
Chewton Keynsham. *Bath* 5B 34
Chewton Mendip. *Som* 1A 22
Chichacott. *Devn* 3G 11
Chicheley. *Mil* 1H 51
Chichester. *W Sus* 2G 17
Chickerell. *Dors* 4B 14
Chickering. *Suff* 3E 66
Chicklade. *Wilts* 3E 23
Chicksands. *C Beds* 2B 52
Chickward. *Here* 5E 59
Chidden. *Hants* 1E 17
Chiddingfold. *Surr* 2A 26
Chiddingly. *E Sus* 4G 27
Chiddingstone. *Kent* 1G 27
Chiddingstone Causeway. *Kent* 1G 27
Chiddingstone Hoath. *Kent* 1F 27
Chideock. *Dors* 3H 13
Chidgley. *Som* 3D 20
Chidham. *W Sus* 2F 17
Chieveley. *W Ber* 4C 36
Chignall St James. *Essx* 5G 53
Chignall Smealy. *Essx* 4G 53
Chigwell. *Essx* 1F 39
Chigwell Row. *Essx* 1F 39
Chilbolton. *Hants* 2B 24
Chilcomb. *Hants* 4D 24
Chilcombe. *Dors* 3A 14
Chilcompton. *Som* 1B 22
Chilcote. *Leics* 4G 73
Childer Thornton. *Ches W* 3F 83
Child Okeford. *Dors* 1D 14
Childrey. *Oxon* 3B 36
Child's Ercall. *Shrp* 3A 72
Childswickham. *Worc* 2F 49
Childwall. *Mers* 2G 83
Childwick Green. *Herts* 4B 52
Chilfrome. *Dors* 3A 14
Chilgrove. *W Sus* 1G 17
Chilham. *Kent* 5E 41
Chilhampton. *Wilts* 3F 23
Chilla. *Devn* 2E 11
Chilland. *Hants* 3D 24
Chillaton. *Devn* 4E 11
Chillenden. *Kent* 5G 41
Chillerton. *IOW* 4C 16
Chillesford. *Suff* 5F 67
Chillingham. *Nmbd* 2E 121
Chillington. *Devn* 4D 9
Chillington. *Som* 1G 13
Chilmark. *Wilts* 3E 23
Chilmington Green. *Kent* 1D 28
Chilson. *Oxon* 4B 50
Chilsworthy. *Corn* 5E 11
Chilsworthy. *Devn* 2D 10
Chiltern Green. *C Beds* 4B 52
Chilthorne Domer. *Som* 1A 14
Chilton. *Buck* 4E 51
Chilton. *Devn* 2B 12
Chilton. *Dur* 2F 105
Chilton. *Oxon* 3C 36
Chilton Candover. *Hants* 2D 24
Chilton Cantelo. *Som* 4A 22
Chilton Foliat. *Wilts* 4B 36
Chilton Lane. *Dur* 1A 106
Chilton Polden. *Som* 3G 21
Chilton Street. *Suff* 1A 54
Chilton Trinity. *Som* 3F 21
Chilwell. *Notts* 2C 74
Chilworth. *Hants* 1C 16
Chilworth. *Surr* 1B 26
Chimney. *Oxon* 5B 50
Chimney Street. *Suff* 1H 53
Chineham. *Hants* 1E 25
Chingford. *G Lon* 1E 39
Chinley. *Derbs* 2E 85
Chinnor. *Oxon* 5F 51
Chipley. *Som* 4E 20
Chipnall. *Shrp* 2B 72
Chippenham. *Cambs* 4F 65
Chippenham. *Wilts* 4E 35
Chipperfield. *Herts* 5A 52
Chipping. *Herts* 2D 52
Chipping. *Lanc* 5F 97
Chipping Campden. *Glos* 2G 49
Chipping Hill. *Essx* 4B 54
Chipping Norton. *Oxon* 3B 50
Chipping Ongar. *Essx* 5F 53
Chipping Sodbury. *S Glo* 3C 34
Chipping Warden. *Nptn* 1C 50
Chipstable. *Som* 4D 20
Chipstead. *Kent* 5G 39
Chipstead. *Surr* 5D 38
Chirbury. *Shrp* 1E 59
Chirk. *Wrex* 2E 71
Chirmorie. *S Ayr* 2H 109
Chirnside. *Bord* 4E 131
Chirnsidebridge. *Bord* 4E 131
Chirton. *Wilts* 1F 23
Chisbridge Cross. *Buck* 3G 37
Chisbury. *Wilts* 5A 36
Chiselborough. *Som* 1H 13
Chiseldon. *Swin* 4G 35
Chiselhampton. *Oxon* 2D 36
Chiserley. *W Yor* 2A 92
Chislehurst. *G Lon* 4F 39
Chislet. *Kent* 4G 41
Chiswell. *Dors* 5B 14
Chiswell Green. *Herts* 5B 52
Chiswick. *G Lon* 3D 38
Chisworth. *Derbs* 1D 85
Chitcombe. *E Sus* 3C 28
Chithurst. *W Sus* 4G 25
Chittering. *Cambs* 4D 65
Chitterley. *Devn* 2C 12
Chitterne. *Wilts* 2E 23
Chittlehamholt. *Devn* 4G 19
Chittlehampton. *Devn* 4G 19
Chittoe. *Wilts* 5E 35
Chivelstone. *Devn* 5D 9
Chivenor. *Devn* 3F 19
Chobham. *Surr* 4A 38
Cholderton. *Wilts* 2H 23
Cholesbury. *Buck* 5H 51
Chollerford. *Nmbd* 2C 114
Chollerton. *Nmbd* 2C 114
Cholsey. *Oxon* 3D 36
Cholstrey. *Here* 5G 59
Chop Gate. *N Yor* 5C 106
Choppington. *Nmbd* 1F 115
Chopwell. *Tyne* 4E 115
Chorley. *Ches E* 5H 83
Chorley. *Lanc* 3D 90
Chorley. *Shrp* 2A 60
Chorley. *Staf* 4E 73
Chorleywood. *Herts* 1B 38
Chorlton. *Ches E* 5B 84
Chorlton-cum-Hardy. *G Man* 1C 84
Chorlton Lane. *Ches W* 1G 71
Choulton. *Shrp* 2F 59
Chrishall. *Essx* 2E 53
Christchurch. *Cambs* 1D 65
Christchurch. *Dors* 3G 15
Christchurch. *Glos* 4A 48
Christian Malford. *Wilts* 4E 35
Christleton. *Ches W* 4G 83
Christmas Common. *Oxon* 2F 37
Christon. *N Som* 1G 21
Christon Bank. *Nmbd* 2G 121
Christow. *Devn* 4B 12
Chryston. *N Lan* 2H 127
Chuck Hatch. *E Sus* 2F 27
Chudleigh. *Devn* 5B 12
Chudleigh Knighton. *Devn* 5B 12
Chulmleigh. *Devn* 1G 11
Chunal. *Derbs* 1E 85
Church. *Lanc* 2F 91
Churcham. *Glos* 4C 48
Church Aston. *Telf* 4B 72
Church Brampton. *Nptn* 4E 62
Church Brough. *Cumb* 3A 104
Church Broughton. *Derbs* 2G 73
Church Corner. *Suff* 2G 67
Church Crookham. *Hants* 1G 25
Churchdown. *Glos* 4D 48
Church Eaton. *Staf* 4C 72
Church End. *Cambs* 5D 65 (nr. Cambridge)
Church End. *Cambs* 2B 64 (nr. Sawtry)
Church End. *Cambs* 3C 64 (nr. Willingham)
Church End. *Cambs* 5C 76 (nr. Wisbech)
Church End. *C Beds* 3H 51 (nr. Dunstable)
Church End. *C Beds* 2B 52 (nr. Stotfold)
Church End. *E Yor* 4E 101
Church End. *Essx* 3H 53 (nr. Braintree)
Churchend. *Essx* 3G 53 (nr. Great Dunmow)
Church End. *Essx* 1F 53 (nr. Saffron Walden)
Churchend. *Essx* 1E 40 (nr. Southend-on-Sea)
Church End. *Glos* 5C 48
Church End. *Hants* 1E 25
Church End. *Linc* 2B 76 (nr. Donington)
Church End. *Linc* 1D 88 (nr. North Somercotes)
Church End. *Norf* 4E 77
Church End. *Warw* 1G 61 (nr. Coleshill)
Church End. *Warw* 1G 61 (nr. Nuneaton)
Church End. *Wilts* 4F 35
Church Enstone. *Oxon* 3B 50
Church Fenton. *N Yor* 1F 93
Church Green. *Devn* 3E 13
Church Gresley. *Derbs* 4G 73
Church Hanborough. *Oxon* 4C 50
Church Hill. *Ches W* 4A 84
Church Hill. *Worc* 4E 61
Church Hougham. *Kent* 1G 29
Church Houses. *N Yor* 5D 106
Churchill. *Devn* 2G 13 (nr. Axminster)
Churchill. *Devn* 2F 19 (nr. Barnstaple)
Churchill. *N Som* 1H 21
Churchill. *Oxon* 3A 50
Churchill. *Worc* 3C 60 (nr. Kidderminster)
Churchill. *Worc* 5D 60 (nr. Worcester)
Churchinford. *Som* 1F 13
Church Knowle. *Dors* 4E 15
Church Laneham. *Notts* 3F 87
Church Langley. *Essx* 5E 53
Church Langton. *Leics* 1E 62
Church Lawford. *Warw* 3B 62
Church Lawton. *Ches E* 5C 84
Church Leigh. *Staf* 2E 73
Church Lench. *Worc* 5E 61
Church Mayfield. *Staf* 1F 73
Church Minshull. *Ches E* 4A 84
Church Norton. *W Sus* 3G 17
Churchover. *Warw* 2C 62
Church Preen. *Shrp* 1H 59
Church Pulverbatch. *Shrp* 5G 71
Churchstanton. *Som* 1E 13
Church Stoke. *Powy* 1E 59
Churchstow. *Devn* 4D 8
Church Stowe. *Nptn* 5D 62
Church Street. *Kent* 3B 40
Church Stretton. *Shrp* 1G 59
Churchthorpe. *Linc* 1C 88
Churchtown. *Cumb* 5E 113
Churchtown. *Derbs* 4G 85
Churchtown. *Devn* 2G 19
Churchtown. *IOM* 2D 108
Churchtown. *Lanc* 5D 97
Church Town. *Leics* 4A 74
Churchtown. *Mers* 3B 90
Church Town. *N Lin* 4A 94
Churchtown. *Shrp* 2E 59
Church Village. *Rhon* 3D 32
Church Warsop. *Notts* 4C 86
Church Westcote. *Glos* 3H 49
Church Wilne. *Derbs* 2B 74
Churnsike Lodge. *Nmbd* 2H 113
Churston Ferrers. *Torb* 3F 9
Churt. *Surr* 3G 25
Churton. *Ches W* 5G 83
Churwell. *W Yor* 2C 92
Chute Standen. *Wilts* 1B 24
Chwilog. *Gwyn* 2D 68
Chwittffordd. *Flin* 3D 82
Chyandour. *Corn* 3B 4
Cilan Uchaf. *Gwyn* 3B 68
Cilcain. *Flin* 4D 82
Cilcennin. *Cdgn* 4E 57
Cilfrew. *Neat* 5A 46
Cilfynydd. *Rhon* 2D 32
Cilgerran. *Pemb* 1B 44
Cilgeti. *Pemb* 4F 43
Cilgwyn. *Carm* 3H 45
Cilgwyn. *Pemb* 1E 43
Ciliau Aeron. *Cdgn* 5D 57
Cill Amhlaidh. *W Isl* 4C 170
Cill Donnain. *High* 1G 165
Cill Donnain. *W Isl* 6C 170
Cille a' Bhacstair. *High* 2C 154
Cille Bhrighde. *W Isl* 7C 170
Cille Pheadair. *W Isl* 7C 170
Cilmaengwyn. *Neat* 5H 45
Cilmeri. *Powy* 5C 58
Cilmery. *Powy* 5C 58
Cilrhedyn. *Pemb* 1G 43
Cilsan. *Carm* 3F 45
Ciltalgarth. *Gwyn* 1A 70
Ciltwrch. *Powy* 1E 47
Cilybebyll. *Neat* 5H 45
Cilycwm. *Carm* 2A 46
Cimla. *Neat* 2A 32
Cinderford. *Glos* 4B 48
Cinderhill. *Derbs* 1A 74
Cippenham. *Slo* 2A 38
Cippyn. *Pemb* 1B 44
Cirbhig. *W Isl* 3D 171
Circebost. *W Isl* 4D 171
Cirencester. *Glos* 5F 49
City. *Powy* 1E 58
City. *V Glam* 4C 32
City Centre. *Stoke* 1C 72 & Stoke 211
City Dulas. *IOA* 2D 80
City (London) Airport. *G Lon* 2F 39
City of London. *G Lon* 2E 39
City, The. *Buck* 2F 37
Clabhach. *Arg* 3C 138
Clachaig. *Arg* 1C 126
Clachaig. *High* 3F 141 (nr. Kinlochleven)
Clachaig. *High* 2E 151 (nr. Nethy Bridge)
Clachamish. *High* 3C 154
Clachan. *Arg* 4F 125 (on Kintyre)
Clachan. *Arg* 4C 140 (on Lismore)
Clachan. *High* 2H 167 (nr. Bettyhill)
Clachan. *High* 2D 155 (nr. Staffin)
Clachan. *High* 1C 154 (nr. Uig)
Clachan. *High* 5E 155 (on Raasay)
Clachan Farm. *Arg* 2A 134
Clachan na Luib. *W Isl* 2D 170
Clachan of Campsie. *E Dun* 2H 127
Clachan of Glendaruel. *Arg* 1A 126
Clachan-Seil. *Arg* 2E 133
Clachan Shannda. *W Isl* 1D 170
Clachan Strachur. *Arg* 3H 133
Clachbreck. *Arg* 2F 125
Clachnaharry. *High* 4A 158
Clachtoll. *High* 1E 163
Clackmannan. *Clac* 4B 136
Clackmarras. *Mor* 3G 159
Clacton-on-Sea. *Essx* 4E 55
Cladach a Chaolais. *W Isl* 2C 170
Cladach Chairinis. *W Isl* 3D 170
Cladach Chirceboist. *W Isl* 2C 170
Cladach Iolaraigh. *W Isl* 2C 170
Cladich. *Arg* 1H 133
Cladswell. *Worc* 5E 61
Claggan. *High* 1F 141 (nr. Fort William)
Claggan. *High* 4A 140 (nr. Lochaline)
Claigan. *High* 3B 154
Clandown. *Bath* 1B 22
Clanfield. *Hants* 1E 17
Clanfield. *Oxon* 5A 50
Clanville. *Hants* 2B 24
Clanville. *Som* 3B 22
Claonaig. *Arg* 4G 125
Clapgate. *Dors* 2F 15
Clapgate. *Herts* 3E 53
Clapham. *Bed* 5H 63
Clapham. *Devn* 4B 12
Clapham. *G Lon* 3D 39
Clapham. *N Yor* 3G 97
Clapham. *W Sus* 5B 26
Clap Hill. *Kent* 2E 29
Clappers. *Bord* 4F 131
Clappersgate. *Cumb* 4E 103
Clapphoull. *Shet* 9F 173
Clapton. *Som* 2H 13 (nr. Crewkerne)
Clapton. *Som* 1B 22 (nr. Radstock)
Clapton-in-Gordano. *N Som* 4H 33
Clapton-on-the-Hill. *Glos* 4G 49
Clapworthy. *Devn* 4G 19
Clara Vale. *Tyne* 3E 115
Clarbeston. *Pemb* 2E 43
Clarbeston Road. *Pemb* 2E 43
Clarborough. *Notts* 2E 87
Clare. *Suff* 1A 54
Clarebrand. *Dum* 3E 111
Clarencefield. *Dum* 3B 112
Clarilaw. *Bord* 3H 119
Clark's Green. *Surr* 2C 26
Clark's Hill. *Linc* 3C 76
Clarkston. *E Ren* 4G 127
Clasheddy. *High* 2G 167
Clashindarroch. *Abers* 5B 160
Clashmore. *High* 5E 165 (nr. Dornoch)
Clashmore. *High* 1E 163 (nr. Stoer)
Clashnessie. *High* 5A 166
Clashnoir. *Mor* 1G 151
Clate. *Shet* 5G 173
Clathick. *Per* 1H 135
Clathy. *Per* 2B 136
Clatt. *Abers* 1C 152
Clatter. *Powy* 1B 58
Clatterford. *IOW* 4C 16
Clatworthy. *Som* 3D 20
Claughton. *Lanc* 3E 97 (nr. Caton)
Claughton. *Lanc* 5E 97 (nr. Garstang)
Claughton. *Mers* 2F 83
Claverdon. *Warw* 4F 61
Claverham. *N Som* 5H 33
Clavering. *Essx* 2E 53
Claverley. *Shrp* 1B 60
Claverton. *Bath* 5C 34
Clawdd-coch. *V Glam* 4D 32
Clawdd-newydd. *Den* 5C 82
Clawson Hill. *Leics* 3E 75
Clawton. *Devn* 3D 10
Claxby. *Linc* 3D 88 (nr. Alford)
Claxby. *Linc* 1A 88 (nr. Market Rasen)
Claxton. *Norf* 5F 79
Claxton. *N Yor* 4A 100
Claybrooke Magna. *Leics* 2B 62
Claybrooke Parva. *Leics* 2B 62
Clay Common. *Suff* 2G 67
Clay Coton. *Nptn* 3C 62
Clay Cross. *Derbs* 4A 86
Claydon. *Oxon* 5B 62
Claydon. *Suff* 5D 66
Clay End. *Herts* 3D 52
Claygate. *Dum* 2E 113
Claygate. *Kent* 1B 28
Claygate. *Surr* 4C 38
Claygate Cross. *Kent* 5H 39
Clayhall. *Hants* 3E 16
Clayhanger. *Devn* 4D 20
Clayhanger. *W Mid* 5E 73
Clayhidon. *Devn* 1E 13
Clay Hill. *Bris* 4B 34
Clayhill. *E Sus* 3C 28
Clayhill. *Hants* 2B 16
Clayhithe. *Cambs* 4E 65
Clayholes. *Ang* 5E 145
Clay Lake. *Linc* 3B 76
Clayock. *High* 3D 168
Claypits. *Glos* 5C 48
Claypole. *Linc* 1F 75
Claythorpe. *Linc* 3D 88
Clayton. *G Man* 1C 84
Clayton. *S Yor* 4E 93
Clayton. *Staf* 1C 72
Clayton. *W Sus* 4E 27
Clayton. *W Yor* 1B 92
Clayton Green. *Lanc* 2D 90
Clayton-le-Moors. *Lanc* 1F 91
Clayton-le-Woods. *Lanc* 2D 90
Clayton West. *W Yor* 3C 92
Clayworth. *Notts* 2E 87
Cleadale. *High* 5C 146
Cleadon. *Tyne* 3G 115
Clearbrook. *Devn* 2B 8
Clearwell. *Glos* 5A 48
Cleasby. *N Yor* 3F 105
Cleat. *Orkn* 3D 172 (nr. Braehead)
Cleat. *Orkn* 9D 172 (nr. St Margaret's Hope)
Cleatlam. *Dur* 3E 105
Cleator. *Cumb* 3B 102
Cleator Moor. *Cumb* 3B 102
Cleckheaton. *W Yor* 2B 92
Cleedownton. *Shrp* 2H 59
Cleehill. *Shrp* 3H 59
Cleekhimin. *N Lan* 4A 128
Clee St Margaret. *Shrp* 2H 59
Cleestanton. *Shrp* 3H 59
Cleethorpes. *NE Lin* 4G 95
Cleeton St Mary. *Shrp* 3A 60
Cleeve. *N Som* 5H 33
Cleeve. *Oxon* 3E 36
Cleeve Hill. *Glos* 3E 49
Cleeve Prior. *Worc* 1F 49
Clehonger. *Here* 2H 47
Cleigh. *Arg* 1F 133
Cleish. *Per* 4C 136
Cleland. *N Lan* 4B 128
Clench Common. *Wilts* 5G 35
Clenchwarton. *Norf* 3E 77
Clennell. *Nmbd* 4D 120
Clent. *Worc* 3D 60
Cleobury Mortimer. *Shrp* 3A 60
Cleobury North. *Shrp* 2A 60
Clephanton. *High* 3C 158
Clerkhill. *High* 2H 167
Clestrain. *Orkn* 7C 172
Clevancy. *Wilts* 4F 35
Clevedon. *N Som* 4H 33
Cleveley. *Oxon* 3B 50
Cleveleys. *Lanc* 5C 96
Clevelode. *Worc* 1D 48
Cleverton. *Wilts* 3E 35
Clewer. *Som* 1H 21
Cley next the Sea. *Norf* 1C 78
Cliaid. *W Isl* 8B 170
Cliasmol. *W Isl* 7C 171
Clibberswick. *Shet* 1H 173
Cliburn. *Cumb* 2G 103
Cliddesden. *Hants* 2E 25
Clieves Hills. *Lanc* 4B 90
Cliff. *Warw* 1G 61
Cliffburn. *Ang* 4F 145
Cliffe. *Medw* 3B 40
Cliffe. *N Yor* 3F 105 (nr. Darlington)
Cliffe. *N Yor* 1G 93 (nr. Selby)
Cliff End. *E Sus* 4C 28
Cliffe Woods. *Medw* 3B 40
Clifford. *Here* 1F 47
Clifford. *W Yor* 5G 99
Clifford Chambers. *Warw* 5F 61
Clifford's Mesne. *Glos* 3B 48
Cliffs End. *Kent* 4H 41
Clifton. *Bris* 4A 34
Clifton. *C Beds* 2B 52
Clifton. *Cumb* 2G 103
Clifton. *Derbs* 1F 73
Clifton. *Devn* 2G 19
Clifton. *G Man* 4F 91
Clifton. *Lanc* 1C 90
Clifton. *Nmbd* 1F 115
Clifton. *N Yor* 5D 98
Clifton. *Nott* 2C 74
Clifton. *Oxon* 2C 50
Clifton. *S Yor* 1C 86

Clifton. Stir 5H 141
Clifton. W Yor 2B 92
Clifton. Worc 1D 48
Clifton. York 4H 99
Clifton Campville. Staf 4G 73
Clifton Hampden. Oxon 2D 36
Clifton Hill. Worc 4B 60
Clifton Reynes. Mil 5G 63
Clifton upon Dunsmore. Warw 3C 62
Clifton upon Teme. Worc 4B 60
Cliftonville. Kent 3H 41
Cliftonville. Norf 2F 79
Climping. W Sus 5A 26
Climpy. S Lan 4C 128
Clint. N Yor 4E 99
Clint Green. Norf 4C 78
Clintmains. Bord 1A 120
Cliobh. W Isl 4C 171
Clipiau. Gwyn 4H 69
Clippesby. Norf 4G 79
Clippings Green. Norf 4C 78
Clipsham. Rut 4G 75
Clipston. Nptn 2E 62
Clipston. Notts 2D 74
Clipstone. Notts 4C 86
Clitheroe. Lanc 5G 97
Cliuthar. W Isl 8D 171
Clive. Shrp 3H 71
Clivocast. Shet 1H 173
Clixby. Linc 4D 94
Clocaenog. Den 5C 82
Clochan. Mor 2B 160
Clochforbie. Abers 3F 161
Clock Face. Mers 1H 83
Cloddiau. Powy 5E 70
Cloddymoss. Mor 2D 159
Clodock. Here 3G 47
Cloford. Som 2C 22
Clola. Abers 4H 161
Clophill. C Beds 2A 52
Clopton. Nptn 2H 63
Clopton Corner. Suff 5E 66
Clopton Green. Suff 5G 65
Closeburn. Dum 5A 118
Close Clark. IOM 4B 108
Closworth. Som 1A 14
Clothall. Herts 2C 52
Clotton. Ches W 4H 83
Clough. G Man 3H 91
Clough. W Yor 3A 92
Clough Foot. W Yor 2H 91
Cloughton. N Yor 5H 107
Cloughton Newlands. N Yor 5H 107
Clousta. Shet 6E 173
Clouston. Orkn 6B 172
Clova. Abers 1B 152
Clova. Ang 1C 144
Clovelly. Devn 4D 18
Clovenfords. Bord 1G 119
Clovenstone. Abers 2E 153
Clovullin. High 2E 141
Clowne. Derbs 3B 86
Clows Top. Worc 3B 60
Cloy. Wrex 1F 71
Cluanie Inn. High 2C 148
Cluanie Lodge. High 2C 148
Cluddley. Telf 5A 72
Clun. Shrp 2F 59
Clunas. High 4C 158
Clunbury. Shrp 2F 59
Clunderwen. Pemb 3F 43
Clune. High 1B 150
Clunes. High 5E 148
Clungunford. Shrp 3F 59
Clunie. Per 4A 144
Clunton. Shrp 2F 59
Cluny. Fife 4E 137
Clutton. Bath 1B 22
Clutton. Ches W 5G 83
Clwt-y-bont. Gwyn 4E 81
Clwydfagwyr. Mer T 5D 46
Clydach. Mon 4F 47
Clydach. Swan 5G 45
Clydach Vale. Rhon 2C 32
Clydebank. W Dun 2G 127
Clydey. Pemb 1G 43
Clyffe Pypard. Wilts 4F 35
Clynder. Arg 1D 126
Clyne. Neat 5B 46
Clynelish. High 3F 165
Clynnog-fawr. Gwyn 1D 68
Clyro. Powy 1F 47
Clyst Honiton. Devn 3C 12
Clyst Hydon. Devn 2D 12
Clyst St George. Devn 4C 12
Clyst St Lawrence. Devn 2D 12
Clyst St Mary. Devn 3C 12
Clyth. High 5E 169
Cnip. W Isl 4C 171
Cnoc Amhlaigh. W Isl 4H 171
Cnwcau. Pemb 1C 44
Cnwch Coch. Cdgn 3F 57
Coad's Green. Corn 5C 10
Coal Aston. Derbs 3A 86
Coalbrookdale. Telf 5A 72
Coalbrookvale. Blae 5E 47
Coalburn. S Lan 1H 117
Coalburns. Tyne 3E 115
Coalcleugh. Nmbd 5B 114
Coaley. Glos 5C 48
Coalford. Abers 4F 153
Coalhall. E Ayr 3D 116
Coalhill. Essx 1B 40
Coalpit Heath. S Glo 3B 34
Coal Pool. W Mid 5E 73
Coalport. Telf 5B 72
Coalsnaughton. Clac 4B 136
Coaltown of Balgonie. Fife 4F 137
Coaltown of Wemyss. Fife 4F 137
Coalville. Leics 4B 74
Coalville. Mil 5F 63
Coalway. Glos 4A 48
Coanwood. Nmbd 4H 113
Coat. Som 4H 21
Coatbridge. N Lan 3A 128
Coatdyke. N Lan 3A 128
Coate. Swin 3G 35
Coate. Wilts 5F 35
Coates. Cambs 1C 64
Coates. Glos 5E 49
Coates. Linc 2G 87
Coates. W Sus 4A 26
Coatham. Red C 2C 106
Coatham Mundeville. Darl 2F 105
Cobbaton. Devn 4G 19
Coberley. Glos 4E 49
Cobhall Common. Here 2H 47
Cobham. Kent 4A 40
Cobham. Surr 4C 38
Cobnash. Here 4G 59
Coburg. Devn 5B 12
Cockayne. N Yor 5D 106
Cockayne Hatley. C Beds 1C 52
Cock Bank. Wrex 1F 71
Cock Bridge. Abers 3G 151
Cockburnspath. Bord 2D 130
Cock Clarks. Essx 5B 54
Cockenzie and Port Seton. E Lot 2H 129
Cockerham. Lanc 4D 96
Cockermouth. Cumb 1C 102
Cockernhoe. Herts 3B 52
Cockfield. Dur 2E 105
Cockfield. Suff 5B 66
Cockfosters. G Lon 1D 39
Cock Gate. Here 4G 59
Cock Green. Essx 4G 53
Cocking. W Sus 1G 17
Cocking Causeway. W Sus 1G 17
Cockington. Torb 2F 9
Cocklake. Som 2H 21
Cocklaw. Abers 4H 161
Cocklaw. Nmbd 2C 114
Cockley Beck. Cumb 4D 102
Cockley Cley. Norf 5G 77
Cockmuir. Abers 3G 161
Cockpole Green. Wind 3G 37
Cockshutford. Shrp 2H 59
Cockshutt. Shrp 3G 71
Cockthorpe. Norf 1B 78
Cockwood. Devn 4C 12
Cockyard. Derbs 3E 85
Cockyard. Here 2H 47
Codda. Corn 5B 10
Coddenham. Suff 5D 66
Coddenham Green. Suff 5D 66
Coddington. Ches W 5G 83
Coddington. Here 1C 48
Coddington. Notts 5F 87
Codford St Mary. Wilts 3E 23
Codford St Peter. Wilts 3E 23
Codicote. Herts 4C 52
Codmore Hill. W Sus 3B 26
Codnor. Derbs 1B 74
Codrington. S Glo 4C 34
Codsall. Staf 5C 72
Codsall Wood. Staf 5C 72
Coed Duon. Cphy 2E 33
Coedely. Rhon 3D 32
Coedglasson. Powy 4C 58
Coedkernew. Newp 3F 33
Coed Morgan. Mon 4G 47
Coedpoeth. Wrex 5E 83
Coedway. Powy 4F 71
Coed-y-bryn. Cdgn 1D 44
Coed-y-paen. Mon 2G 33
Coed-yr-ynys. Powy 3E 47
Coed Ystumgwern. Gwyn 3E 69
Coelbren. Powy 4B 46
Coffinswell. Devn 2E 9
Cofton Hackett. Worc 3E 61
Cogan. V Glam 4E 33
Cogenhoe. Nptn 4F 63
Cogges. Oxon 5B 50
Coggeshall. Essx 3B 54
Coggeshall Hamlet. Essx 3B 54
Coggins Mill. E Sus 3G 27
Coignafearn Lodge. High 2A 150
Coig Peighinnean. W Isl 1H 171
Coig Peighinnean Bhuirgh. W Isl 2G 171
Coilleag. W Isl 7C 170
Coilliemore. High 1A 158
Coillore. High 5C 154
Coire an Fhuarain. W Isl 4E 171
Coity. B'end 3C 32
Cokhay Green. Derbs 3G 73
Col. W Isl 3G 171
Colaboll. High 2C 164
Colan. Corn 2C 6
Colaton Raleigh. Devn 4D 12
Colbost. High 4B 154
Colburn. N Yor 5E 105
Colby. Cumb 2H 103
Colby. IOM 4B 108
Colby. Norf 2E 78
Colchester. Essx 3D 54
Cold Ash. W Ber 5D 36
Cold Ashby. Nptn 3D 62
Cold Ashton. S Glo 4C 34
Cold Aston. Glos 4G 49
Coldbackie. High 3G 167
Cold Blow. Pemb 3F 43
Cold Brayfield. Mil 5G 63
Cold Cotes. N Yor 2G 97
Coldean. Brig 5E 27
Coldeast. Devn 5B 12
Colden. W Yor 2H 91
Colden Common. Hants 4C 24
Coldfair Green. Suff 4G 67
Coldham. Cambs 5D 76
Coldham. Staf 5C 72
Cold Hanworth. Linc 2H 87
Coldharbour. Corn 4B 6
Cold Harbour. Dors 3E 15
Coldharbour. Glos 5A 48
Coldharbour. Kent 5G 39
Coldharbour. Surr 1C 26
Cold Hatton. Telf 3A 72
Cold Hatton Heath. Telf 3A 72
Cold Hesledon. Dur 5H 115
Cold Hiendley. W Yor 3D 92
Cold Higham. Nptn 5D 62
Coldingham. Bord 3F 131
Cold Kirby. N Yor 1H 99
Coldmeece. Staf 2C 72
Cold Northcott. Corn 4C 10
Cold Norton. Essx 5B 54
Cold Overton. Leics 4F 75
Coldrain. Per 3C 136
Coldred. Kent 1G 29
Coldridge. Devn 2G 11
Cold Row. Lanc 5C 96
Coldstream. Bord 5E 131
Coldwaltham. W Sus 4B 26
Coldwell. Here 2H 47
Coldwells. Abers 5H 161
Coldwells Croft. Abers 1C 152
Cole. Shet 5E 173
Cole. Som 3B 22
Colebatch. Shrp 2F 59
Colebrook. Devn 2D 12
Colebrooke. Devn 2A 12
Coleburn. Mor 3G 159
Coleby. Linc 4G 87
Coleby. N Lin 3B 94
Cole End. Warw 2G 61
Coleford. Devn 2A 12
Coleford. Glos 4A 48
Coleford. Som 2B 22
Colegate End. Norf 2D 66
Cole Green. Herts 4C 52
Cole Henley. Hants 1C 24
Colehill. Dors 2F 15
Coleman Green. Herts 4B 52
Coleman's Hatch. E Sus 2F 27
Colemere. Shrp 2G 71
Colemore. Hants 3F 25
Colemore Green. Shrp 1B 60
Coleorton. Leics 4B 74
Colerne. Wilts 4D 34
Colesbourne. Glos 4E 49
Colesden. Bed 5A 64
Coles Green. Worc 5B 60
Coleshill. Buck 1A 38
Coleshill. Oxon 2H 35
Coleshill. Warw 2G 61
Colestocks. Devn 2D 12
Colethrop. Glos 4D 48
Coley. Bath 1A 22
Colgate. W Sus 2D 26
Colinsburgh. Fife 3G 137
Colinton. Edin 3F 129
Colintraive. Arg 2B 126
Colkirk. Norf 3B 78
Collace. Per 5B 144
Collam. W Isl 8D 171
Collaton. Devn 5D 8
Collaton St Mary. Torb 2E 9
College of Roseisle. Mor 2F 159
Collessie. Fife 2E 137
Collier Row. G Lon 1F 39
Colliers End. Herts 3D 52
Collier Street. Kent 1B 28
Colliery Row. Tyne 5G 115
Collieston. Abers 1H 153
Collin. Dum 2B 112
Collingbourne Ducis. Wilts 1H 23
Collingbourne Kingston. Wilts 1H 23
Collingham. Notts 4F 87
Collingham. W Yor 5F 99
Collingtree. Nptn 5E 63
Collins Green. Warr 1H 83
Collins Green. Worc 5B 60
Colliston. Ang 4F 145
Colliton. Devn 2D 12
Collydean. Fife 3E 137
Collyweston. Nptn 5G 75
Colmonell. S Ayr 1G 109
Colmworth. Bed 5A 64
Colnbrook. Slo 3B 38
Colne. Cambs 3C 64
Colne. Lanc 5A 98
Colne Engaine. Essx 2B 54
Colney. Norf 5D 78
Colney Heath. Herts 5C 52
Colney Street. Herts 5B 52
Coln Rogers. Glos 5F 49
Coln St Aldwyns. Glos 5G 49
Coln St Dennis. Glos 4F 49
Colpitts Grange. Nmbd 4C 114
Colpy. Abers 5D 160
Colscott. Devn 1D 10
Colsterdale. N Yor 1D 98
Colsterworth. Linc 3G 75
Colston Bassett. Notts 2D 74
Colstoun House. E Lot 2B 130
Coltfield. Mor 2F 159
Colthouse. Cumb 5E 103
Coltishall. Norf 4E 79
Coltness. N Lan 4A 128
Colton. Cumb 1C 96
Colton. Norf 5D 78
Colton. N Yor 5H 99
Colton. Staf 3E 73
Colton. W Yor 1D 92
Colt's Hill. Kent 1H 27
Col Uarach. W Isl 4G 171
Colvend. Dum 4F 111
Colvister. Shet 2G 173
Colwall. Here 1C 48
Colwall Green. Here 1C 48
Colwell. Nmbd 2C 114
Colwich. Staf 3E 73
Colwick. Notts 1D 74
Colwinston. V Glam 4C 32
Colworth. W Sus 5A 26
Colwyn Bay. Cnwy 3A 82
Colyford. Devn 3F 13
Colyton. Devn 3F 13
Combe. Devn 2D 8
Combe. Here 4F 59
Combe. Oxon 4C 50
Combe. W Ber 5B 36
Combe Almer. Dors 3E 15
Combebow. Devn 4E 11
Combe Down. Bath 5C 34
Combe Fishacre. Devn 2E 9
Combe Florey. Som 3E 21
Combe Hay. Bath 1C 22
Combeinteignhead. Devn 5C 12
Combe Martin. Devn 2F 19
Combe Moor. Here 4F 59
Combe Raleigh. Devn 2E 13
Comberbach. Ches W 3A 84
Comberford. Staf 5F 73
Comberton. Cambs 5C 64
Comberton. Here 4G 59
Combe St Nicholas. Som 1G 13
Combpyne. Devn 3F 13
Combridge. Staf 2E 73
Combrook. Warw 5H 61
Combs. Derbs 3E 85
Combs. Suff 5C 66
Combs Ford. Suff 5C 66
Combwich. Som 2F 21
Comers. Abers 3D 152
Comhampton. Worc 4C 60
Comins Coch. Cdgn 2F 57
Comley. Shrp 1G 59
Commercial End. Cambs 4E 65
Commins. Powy 3D 70
Commins Coch. Powy 5H 69
Commondale. N Yor 3D 106
Common End. Cumb 2B 102
Common Hill. Here 2A 48
Common Moor. Corn 2G 7
Commonside. Ches W 3H 83
Common Side. Derbs 3H 85 (nr. Chesterfield)
Commonside. Derbs 1G 73 (nr. Derby)
Common, The. Wilts 3H 23 (nr. Salisbury)
Common, The. Wilts 3F 35 (nr. Swindon)
Compstall. G Man 1D 84
Compton. Devn 2E 9
Compton. Hants 4C 24
Compton. Staf 2C 60
Compton. Surr 1A 26
Compton. W Ber 3D 36
Compton. W Sus 1F 17
Compton. Wilts 1G 23
Compton Abbas. Dors 1D 14
Compton Abdale. Glos 4F 49
Compton Bassett. Wilts 4F 35
Compton Beauchamp. Oxon 3A 36
Compton Bishop. Som 1G 21
Compton Chamberlayne. Wilts 4F 23
Compton Dando. Bath 5B 34
Compton Dundon. Som 3H 21
Compton Greenfield. S Glo 3A 34
Compton Martin. Bath 1A 22
Compton Pauncefoot. Som 4B 22
Compton Valence. Dors 3A 14
Comrie. Fife 1D 128
Comrie. Per 1G 135
Conaglen. High 2E 141
Conchra. Arg 1B 126
Conchra. High 1A 148
Conder Green. Lanc 4D 96
Conderton. Worc 2E 49
Condicote. Glos 3G 49
Condorrat. N Lan 2A 128
Condover. Shrp 5G 71
Coneyhurst Common. W Sus 3C 26
Coneysthorpe. N Yor 2B 100
Coneythorpe. N Yor 4F 99
Coney Weston. Suff 3B 66
Conford. Hants 3G 25
Congdon's Shop. Corn 5C 10
Congerstone. Leics 5A 74
Congham. Norf 3G 77
Congleton. Ches E 4C 84
Congl-y-wal. Gwyn 1G 69
Congresbury. N Som 5H 33
Congreve. Staf 4D 72
Conham. S Glo 4B 34
Conicaval. Mor 3D 159
Coningsby. Linc 5B 88
Conington. Cambs 4C 64 (nr. Fenstanton)
Conington. Cambs 2A 64 (nr. Sawtry)
Conisbrough. S Yor 1C 86
Conisby. Arg 3A 124
Conisholme. Linc 1D 88
Coniston. Cumb 5E 102
Coniston. E Yor 1E 95
Coniston Cold. N Yor 4B 98
Conistone. N Yor 3B 98
Connah's Quay. Flin 4E 83
Connel. Arg 5D 140
Connel Park. E Ayr 3F 117
Connista. High 1D 154
Connor Downs. Corn 3C 4
Conock. Wilts 1F 23
Conon Bridge. High 3H 157
Cononley. N Yor 5B 98
Cononsyth. Ang 4E 145
Conordan. High 5E 155
Consall. Staf 1D 73
Consett. Dur 4E 115
Constable Burton. N Yor 5E 105
Constantine. Corn 4E 5
Constantine Bay. Corn 1C 6
Contin. High 3G 157
Contullich. High 1A 158
Conwy. Cnwy 3G 81
Conyer. Kent 4D 40
Conyer's Green. Suff 4A 66
Cooden. E Sus 5B 28
Cooil. IOM 4C 108
Cookbury. Devn 2E 11
Cookbury Wick. Devn 2D 11
Cookham. Wind 3G 37
Cookham Dean. Wind 3G 37
Cookham Rise. Wind 3G 37
Cookhill. Worc 5E 61
Cookley. Suff 3F 67
Cookley. Worc 2C 60
Cookley Green. Oxon 2E 37
Cookney. Abers 4F 153
Cooksbridge. E Sus 4F 27
Cooksey Green. Worc 4D 60
Cookshill. Staf 1D 72
Cooksmill Green. Essx 5G 53
Coolham. W Sus 3C 26
Cooling. Medw 3B 40
Cooling Street. Medw 3B 40
Coombe. Corn 1C 10 (nr. Bude)
Coombe. Corn 3D 6 (nr. St Austell)
Coombe. Corn 4C 6 (nr. Truro)
Coombe. Devn 3E 12 (nr. Sidmouth)
Coombe. Devn 5C 12 (nr. Teignmouth)
Coombe. Glos 2C 34
Coombe. Hants 4E 25
Coombe. Wilts 1G 23
Coombe Bissett. Wilts 4G 23
Coombe Hill. Glos 3D 49
Coombe Keynes. Dors 4D 14
Coombes. W Sus 5C 26
Coopersale Common. Essx 5E 53
Coopersale Street. Essx 5E 53
Cooper's Corner. Kent 1F 27
Cooper Street. Kent 5H 41
Cootham. W Sus 4B 26
Copalder Corner. Cambs 1C 64
Copdock. Suff 1E 54
Copford. Essx 3C 54
Copford Green. Essx 3C 54
Copgrove. N Yor 3F 99
Copister. Shet 4F 173
Cople. Bed 1B 52
Copley. Dur 2D 105
Coplow Dale. Derbs 3F 85
Copmanthorpe. York 5H 99
Copp. Lanc 1C 90
Coppathorne. Corn 2C 10
Coppenhall. Ches E 5B 84
Coppenhall. Staf 4D 72
Coppenhall Moss. Ches E 5B 84
Copperhouse. Corn 3C 4
Coppicegate. Shrp 2B 60
Coppingford. Cambs 2A 64
Copplestone. Devn 2A 12
Coppull. Lanc 3D 90
Coppull Moor. Lanc 3D 90
Copsale. W Sus 3C 26
Copster Green. Lanc 1E 91
Copston Magna. Warw 2B 62

Copt Green. *Warw* 4F **61**
Copthall Green. *Essx* 5E **53**
Copt Heath. *W Mid* 3F **61**
Copt Hewick. *N Yor* 2F **99**
Copthill. *Dur* 5B **114**
Copthorne. *W Sus* 2E **27**
Coptiviney. *Shrp* 2G **71**
Copy's Green. *Norf* 2B **78**
Copythorne. *Hants* 1B **16**
Corbridge. *Nmbd* 3C **114**
Corby. *Nptn* 2F **63**
Corby Glen. *Linc* 3H **75**
Cordon. *N Ayr* 2E **123**
Coreley. *Shrp* 3A **60**
Corfe. *Som* 1F **13**
Corfe Castle. *Dors* 4E **15**
Corfe Mullen. *Dors* 3E **15**
Corfton. *Shrp* 2G **59**
Corgarff. *Abers* 3G **151**
Corhampton. *Hants* 4E **24**
Corlae. *Dum* 5F **117**
Corlannau. *Neat* 2A **32**
Corley. *Warw* 2H **61**
Corley Ash. *Warw* 2G **61**
Corley Moor. *Warw* 2G **61**
Cormiston. *S Lan* 1C **118**
Cornaa. *IOM* 3D **108**
Cornaigbeg. *Arg* 4A **138**
Cornaigmore. *Arg* 2D **138** (on Coll)
Cornaigmore. *Arg* 4A **138** (on Tiree)
Corner Row. *Lanc* 1C **90**
Corney. *Cumb* 5C **102**
Cornforth. *Dur* 1A **106**
Cornhill. *Abers* 3C **160**
Cornhill. *High* 4C **164**
Cornhill-on-Tweed. *Nmbd* 1C **120**
Cornholme. *W Yor* 2H **91**
Cornish Hall End. *Essx* 2G **53**
Cornquoy. *Orkn* 7E **172**
Cornriggs. *Dur* 5B **114**
Cornsay. *Dur* 5E **115**
Cornsay Colliery. *Dur* 5E **115**
Corntown. *High* 3H **157**
Corntown. *V Glam* 4C **32**
Cornwell. *Oxon* 3A **50**
Cornwood. *Devn* 3C **8**
Cornworthy. *Devn* 3E **9**
Corpach. *High* 1E **141**
Corpusty. *Norf* 3D **78**
Corra. *Dum* 3F **111**
Corran. *High* 2E **141** (nr. Arnisdale)
Corran. *High* 3A **148** (nr. Fort William)
Corrany. *IOM* 3D **108**
Corribeg. *High* 1D **141**
Corrie. *N Ayr* 5B **126**
Corrie Common. *Dum* 1D **112**
Corriecravie. *N Ayr* 3D **122**
Corriekinloch. *High* 1A **164**
Corriemoillie. *High* 2F **157**
Corrievarkie Lodge. *Per* 1C **142**
Corrievorrie. *High* 1B **150**
Corrigall. *Orkn* 6C **172**
Corrimony. *High* 5F **157**
Corringham. *Linc* 1F **87**
Corringham. *Thur* 2B **40**
Corris. *Gwyn* 5G **69**
Corris Uchaf. *Gwyn* 5G **69**
Corrour Shooting Lodge. *High* 2B **142**
Corry. *High* 1E **147**
Corrybrough. *High* 1C **150**
Corrygills. *N Ayr* 2E **123**
Corry of Ardnagrask. *High* 4H **157**
Corsback. *High* 1E **169** (nr. Dunnet)
Corsback. *High* 3E **169** (nr. Halkirk)
Corscombe. *Dors* 2A **14**
Corse. *Abers* 4D **160**
Corse. *Glos* 3C **48**
Corsehill. *Abers* 3G **161**
Corse Lawn. *Worc* 2D **48**
Corse of Kinnoir. *Abers* 4C **160**
Corsham. *Wilts* 4D **34**
Corsley. *Wilts* 2D **22**
Corsley Heath. *Wilts* 2D **22**
Corsock. *Dum* 2E **111**
Corston. *Bath* 5B **34**
Corston. *Wilts* 3E **35**
Corstorphine. *Edin* 2F **129**
Cortachy. *Ang* 3C **144**
Corton. *Suff* 1H **67**
Corton. *Wilts* 2E **23**
Corton Denham. *Som* 4B **22**
Corwar House. *S Ayr* 1H **109**
Corwen. *Den* 1C **70**
Coryates. *Dors* 4B **14**
Coryton. *Devn* 4E **11**
Coryton. *Thur* 2B **40**
Cosby. *Leics* 1C **62**
Coscote. *Oxon* 3D **36**
Coseley. *W Mid* 1D **60**
Cosgrove. *Nptn* 1F **51**
Cosham. *Port* 2E **17**
Cosheston. *Pemb* 4E **43**
Coskills. *N Lin* 3D **94**
Cosmeston. *V Glam* 5E **33**
Cossall. *Notts* 1B **74**
Cossington. *Leics* 4D **74**
Cossington. *Som* 2G **21**
Costa. *Orkn* 5C **172**
Costessey. *Norf* 4D **78**
Costock. *Notts* 3C **74**
Coston. *Leics* 3F **75**
Coston. *Norf* 5C **78**
Cote. *Oxon* 5B **50**
Cotebrook. *Ches W* 4H **83**
Cotehill. *Cumb* 4F **113**
Cotes. *Cumb* 1D **97**
Cotes. *Leics* 3C **74**
Cotes. *Staf* 2C **72**
Cotesbach. *Leics* 2C **62**
Cotes Heath. *Staf* 2C **72**
Cotford St Luke. *Som* 4E **21**
Cotgrave. *Notts* 2D **74**
Cothall. *Abers* 2F **153**
Cotham. *Notts* 1E **75**
Cothelstone. *Som* 3E **21**
Cotheridge. *Worc* 5B **60**
Cotherstone. *Dur* 3D **104**
Cothill. *Oxon* 2C **36**
Cotland. *Mon* 5A **48**
Cotleigh. *Devn* 2F **13**
Cotmanhay. *Derbs* 1B **74**
Coton. *Cambs* 5D **64**
Coton. *Nptn* 3D **62**
Coton. *Staf* 3C **72** (nr. Gnosall)
Coton. *Staf* 2D **73** (nr. Stone)
Coton. *Staf* 5F **73** (nr. Tamworth)
Coton Clanford. *Staf* 3C **72**
Coton Hayes. *Staf* 2D **73**
Coton Hill. *Shrp* 4G **71**
Coton in the Clay. *Staf* 3F **73**
Coton in the Elms. *Derbs* 4G **73**
Cotonwood. *Shrp* 2H **71**
Cotonwood. *Staf* 3C **72**
Cott. *Devn* 2D **9**
Cott. *Orkn* 5F **172**
Cottam. *E Yor* 3D **101**
Cottam. *Lanc* 1D **90**
Cottam. *Notts* 3F **87**
Cottartown. *High* 5E **159**
Cottarville. *Nptn* 4E **63**
Cottenham. *Cambs* 4D **64**
Cotterdale. *N Yor* 5B **104**
Cottered. *Herts* 3D **52**
Cotterstock. *Nptn* 1H **63**
Cottesbrooke. *Nptn* 3E **62**
Cottesmore. *Rut* 4G **75**
Cotteylands. *Devn* 1C **12**
Cottingham. *E Yor* 1D **94**
Cottingham. *Nptn* 1F **63**
Cottingley. *W Yor* 1B **92**
Cottisford. *Oxon* 2D **50**
Cotton. *Staf* 1E **73**
Cotton. *Suff* 4C **66**
Cotton End. *Bed* 1A **52**
Cottown. *Abers* 4F **161**
Cotts. *Devn* 2A **8**
Cotwalton. *Staf* 2D **72**
Couch's Mill. *Corn* 3F **7**
Coughton. *Here* 3A **48**
Coughton. *Warw* 4E **61**
Coulags. *High* 4B **156**
Coulby Newham. *Midd* 3C **106**
Coulderton. *Cumb* 4A **102**
Coulin Lodge. *High* 3C **156**
Coull. *Abers* 3C **152**
Coulport. *Arg* 1D **126**
Coulsdon. *Surr* 5D **39**
Coulter. *S Lan* 1C **118**
Coultershaw Bridge. *W Sus* 4A **26**
Coultings. *Som* 2F **21**
Coulton. *N Yor* 2A **100**
Cound. *Shrp* 5H **71**
Coundon. *Dur* 2F **105**
Coundon Grange. *Dur* 2F **105**
Countersett. *N Yor* 1B **98**
Countess. *Wilts* 2G **23**
Countess Cross. *Essx* 2B **54**
Countesthorpe. *Leics* 1C **62**
Countisbury. *Devn* 2H **19**
Coupar Angus. *Per* 4B **144**
Coupe Green. *Lanc* 2D **90**
Coupland. *Cumb* 3A **104**
Coupland. *Nmbd* 1D **120**
Cour. *Arg* 5G **125**
Courance. *Dum* 5C **118**
Court-at-Street. *Kent* 2E **29**
Courteachan. *High* 4E **147**
Courteenhall. *Nptn* 5E **63**
Court Henry. *Carm* 3F **45**
Courtsend. *Essx* 1E **41**
Courtway. *Som* 3F **21**
Cousland. *Midl* 3G **129**
Cousley Wood. *E Sus* 2A **28**
Coustonn. *Arg* 2B **126**
Cove. *Arg* 1D **126**
Cove. *Devn* 1C **12**
Cove. *Hants* 1G **25**
Cove. *High* 4C **162**
Cove. *Bord* 2D **130**
Cove Bay. *Aber* 3G **153**
Covehithe. *Suff* 2H **67**
Coven. *Staf* 5D **72**
Coveney. *Cambs* 2D **65**
Covenham St Bartholomew. *Linc* 1C **88**
Covenham St Mary. *Linc* 1C **88**
Coven Heath. *Staf* 5D **72**
Coventry. *W Mid* 3H **61** & **192**
Coverack. *Corn* 5E **5**
Coverham. *N Yor* 1D **98**
Covesea. *Mor* 1F **159**
Covingham. *Swin* 3G **35**
Covington. *Cambs* 3H **63**
Covington. *S Lan* 1B **118**
Cowan Bridge. *Lanc* 2F **97**
Cowan Head. *Cumb* 5F **103**
Cowbar. *Red C* 3E **107**
Cowbeech. *E Sus* 4H **27**
Cowbit. *Linc* 4B **76**
Cowbridge. *V Glam* 4C **32**
Cowden. *Kent* 1F **27**
Cowdenbeath. *Fife* 4D **136**
Cowdenburn. *Bord* 4F **129**
Cowdenend. *Fife* 4D **136**
Cowers Lane. *Derbs* 1H **73**
Cowes. *IOW* 3C **16**
Cowesby. *N Yor* 1G **99**
Cowfold. *W Sus* 3D **26**
Cowfords. *Mor* 3H **159**
Cowgill. *Cumb* 1G **97**
Cowie. *Abers* 5F **153**
Cowie. *Stir* 1B **128**
Cowlam. *E Yor* 3D **100**
Cowley. *Devn* 3C **12**
Cowley. *Glos* 4E **49**
Cowley. *G Lon* 2B **38**
Cowley. *Oxon* 5D **50**
Cowley. *Staf* 4C **72**
Cowleymoor. *Devn* 1C **12**
Cowling. *Lanc* 3D **90**
Cowling. *N Yor* 1E **99** (nr. Bedale)
Cowling. *N Yor* 5B **98** (nr. Glusburn)
Cowlinge. *Suff* 5G **65**
Cowmes. *W Yor* 3B **92**
Cowpe. *Lanc* 2G **91**
Cowpen. *Nmbd* 1F **115**
Cowpen Bewley. *Stoc T* 2B **106**
Cowplain. *Hants* 1E **17**
Cowshill. *Dur* 5B **114**
Cowslip Green. *N Som* 5H **33**
Cowstrandburn. *Fife* 4C **136**
Cowthorpe. *N Yor* 4G **99**
Coxall. *Here* 3F **59**
Coxbank. *Ches E* 1A **72**
Coxbench. *Derbs* 1A **74**
Cox Common. *Suff* 2G **67**
Coxford. *Norf* 3H **77**
Coxgreen. *Staf* 2C **60**
Cox Green. *Surr* 2B **26**
Cox Green. *Tyne* 4G **115**
Coxheath. *Kent* 5B **40**
Coxhoe. *Dur* 1A **106**
Coxley. *Som* 2A **22**
Coxwold. *N Yor* 2H **99**
Coychurch. *V Glam* 3C **32**
Coylton. *S Ayr* 3D **116**
Coylumbridge. *High* 2D **150**
Coynach. *Abers* 3B **152**
Coynachie. *Abers* 5B **160**
Coytrahen. *B'end* 3B **32**
Crabbs Cross. *Worc* 4E **61**
Crabgate. *Norf* 3C **78**
Crab Orchard. *Dors* 2F **15**
Crabtree. *W Sus* 3D **26**
Crabtree Green. *Wrex* 1F **71**
Crackaig. *High* 2G **165**
Crackenthorpe. *Cumb* 2H **103**
Crackington Haven. *Corn* 3B **10**
Crackley. *Staf* 5C **84**
Crackley. *Warw* 3G **61**
Crackleybank. *Shrp* 4B **72**
Crackpot. *N Yor* 5C **104**
Cracoe. *N Yor* 3B **98**
Craddock. *Devn* 1D **12**
Cradhlastadh. *W Isl* 4C **171**
Cradley. *Here* 1C **48**
Cradley. *W Mid* 2D **60**
Cradoc. *Powy* 2D **46**
Crafthole. *Corn* 3H **7**
Crafton. *Buck* 4G **51**
Cragabus. *Arg* 5B **124**
Crag Foot. *Lanc* 2D **97**
Craggan. *High* 1E **151**
Cragganmore. *Mor* 5F **159**
Cragganvallie. *High* 5H **157**
Craggie. *High* 1F **165**
Craggiemore. *High* 5B **158**
Cragg Vale. *W Yor* 2A **92**
Craghead. *Dur* 4F **115**
Crai. *Powy* 3B **46**
Craibstone. *Aber* 2F **153**
Craichie. *Ang* 4E **145**
Craig. *Arg* 5E **141**
Craig. *Dum* 2D **111**
Craig. *High* 4C **156** (nr. Achnashellach)
Craig. *High* 2G **155** (nr. Lower Diabaig)
Craig. *High* 5H **155** (nr. Stromeferry)
Craiganour Lodge. *Per* 3D **142**
Craigbrack. *Arg* 4A **134**
Craig-cefn-parc. *Swan* 5G **45**
Craigdallie. *Per* 1E **137**
Craigdam. *Abers* 5F **161**
Craigdarroch. *E Ayr* 4F **117**
Craigdarroch. *High* 3G **157**
Craigdhu. *High* 4G **157**
Craigearn. *Abers* 2E **152**
Craigellachie. *Mor* 4G **159**
Craigend. *Per* 1D **136**
Craigendoran. *Arg* 1E **126**
Craigends. *Ren* 3F **127**
Craigenputtock. *Dum* 1E **111**
Craigens. *E Ayr* 3E **117**
Craighall. *Edin* 2E **129**
Craighead. *Fife* 2H **137**
Craighouse. *Arg* 3D **124**
Craigie. *Abers* 2G **153**
Craigie. *D'dee* 5D **144**
Craigie. *Per* 4A **144** (nr. Blairgowrie)
Craigie. *Per* 1D **136** (nr. Perth)
Craigie. *S Ayr* 1D **116**
Craigielaw. *E Lot* 2A **130**
Craiglemine. *Dum* 5B **110**
Craig-llwyn. *Shrp* 3E **71**
Craiglockhart. *Edin* 2F **129**
Craig Lodge. *Arg* 2B **126**
Craigmalloch. *E Ayr* 5D **117**
Craigmaud. *Abers* 3F **161**
Craigmill. *Stir* 4H **135**
Craigmillar. *Edin* 2F **129**
Craigmore. *Arg* 3C **126**
Craigmuie. *Dum* 1E **111**
Craignair. *Dum* 3F **111**
Craignant. *Shrp* 2E **71**
Craigneuk. *N Lan* 3A **128** (nr. Airdrie)
Craigneuk. *N Lan* 4A **128** (nr. Motherwell)
Craignure. *Arg* 5B **140**
Craigo. *Abers* 2F **145**
Craigrory. *High* 4A **158**
Craigrothie. *Fife* 2F **137**
Craigs. *Dum* 2D **112**
Craigshill. *W Lot* 3D **128**
Craigs, The. *High* 4B **164**
Craigton. *Aber* 3F **153**
Craigton. *Abers* 3E **152**
Craigton. *Ang* 5E **145** (nr. Carnoustie)
Craigton. *Ang* 3C **144** (nr. Kirriemuir)
Craigton. *High* 4A **158**
Craigtown. *High* 3A **168**
Craig-y-Duke. *Neat* 5H **45**
Craigyloch. *Ang* 3B **144**
Craig-y-nos. *Powy* 4B **46**
Craik. *Bord* 4F **119**
Crail. *Fife* 3H **137**
Crailing. *Bord* 2A **120**
Crailinghall. *Bord* 2A **120**
Crakehill. *N Yor* 2G **99**
Crakemarsh. *Staf* 2E **73**
Crambe. *N Yor* 3B **100**
Crambeck. *N Yor* 3B **100**
Cramlington. *Nmbd* 2F **115**
Cramond. *Edin* 2E **129**
Cramond Bridge. *Edin* 2E **129**
Cranage. *Ches E* 4B **84**
Cranberry. *Staf* 2C **72**
Cranborne. *Dors* 1F **15**
Cranbourne. *Brac* 3A **38**
Cranbrook. *Devn* 3D **12**
Cranbrook. *Kent* 2B **28**
Cranbrook Common. *Kent* 2B **28**
Crane Moor. *S Yor* 4D **92**
Crane's Corner. *Norf* 4B **78**
Cranfield. *C Beds* 1H **51**
Cranford. *G Lon* 3B **38**
Cranford St Andrew. *Nptn* 3G **63**
Cranford St John. *Nptn* 3G **63**
Cranham. *Glos* 4D **49**
Cranham. *G Lon* 2G **39**
Crank. *Mers* 1H **83**
Cranleigh. *Surr* 2B **26**
Cranley. *Suff* 3D **66**
Cranloch. *Mor* 3G **159**
Cranmer Green. *Suff* 3C **66**
Cranmore. *IOW* 3B **16**
Cranmore. *Linc* 5A **76**
Crannich. *Arg* 4G **139**
Crannoch. *Mor* 3B **160**
Cranoe. *Leics* 1E **63**
Cransford. *Suff* 4F **67**
Cranshaws. *Bord* 3C **130**
Cranstal. *IOM* 1D **108**
Crantock. *Corn* 2B **6**
Cranwell. *Linc* 5H **87**
Cranwich. *Norf* 1G **65**
Cranworth. *Norf* 5B **78**
Craobh Haven. *Arg* 3E **133**
Craobhnaclag. *High* 4G **157**
Crapstone. *Devn* 2B **8**
Crarae. *Arg* 4G **133**
Crask. *High* 2H **167**
Crask Inn. *High* 1C **164**
Crask of Aigas. *High* 4G **157**
Craster. *Nmbd* 3G **121**
Cratfield. *Suff* 3F **67**
Crathes. *Abers* 4E **153**
Crathie. *Abers* 4G **151**
Crathie. *High* 4H **149**
Crathorne. *N Yor* 4B **106**
Craven Arms. *Shrp* 2G **59**
Crawcrook. *Tyne* 3E **115**
Crawford. *Lanc* 4D **90**
Crawford. *S Lan* 2B **118**
Crawforddyke. *S Lan* 4B **128**
Crawfordjohn. *S Lan* 2A **118**
Crawick. *Dum* 3G **117**
Crawley. *Devn* 2F **13**
Crawley. *Hants* 3C **24**
Crawley. *Oxon* 4B **50**
Crawley. *W Sus* 2D **26**
Crawley Down. *W Sus* 2E **27**
Crawley Side. *Dur* 5C **114**
Crawshawbooth. *Lanc* 2G **91**
Crawton. *Abers* 5F **153**
Cray. *N Yor* 2B **98**
Cray. *Per* 2A **144**
Crayford. *G Lon* 3G **39**
Crayke. *N Yor* 2H **99**
Craymere Beck. *Norf* 2C **78**
Crays Hill. *Essx* 1B **40**
Cray's Pond. *Oxon* 3E **37**
Crazies Hill. *Wok* 3F **37**
Creacombe. *Devn* 1B **12**
Creagan. *Arg* 4D **141**
Creag Aoil. *High* 1F **141**
Creag Ghoraidh. *W Isl* 4C **170**
Creaguaineach Lodge. *High* 2H **141**
Creamore Bank. *Shrp* 2H **71**
Creaton. *Nptn* 3E **62**
Creca. *Dum* 2D **112**
Credenhill. *Here* 1H **47**
Crediton. *Devn* 2B **12**
Creebridge. *Dum* 3B **110**
Creech. *Dors* 4E **15**
Creech Heathfield. *Som* 4F **21**
Creech St Michael. *Som* 4F **21**
Creed. *Corn* 4D **6**
Creekmoor. *Pool* 3E **15**
Creekmouth. *G Lon* 2F **39**
Creeting St Mary. *Suff* 5C **66**
Creeting St Peter. *Suff* 5C **66**
Creeton. *Linc* 3H **75**
Creetown. *Dum* 4B **110**
Creggans. *Arg* 3H **133**
Cregneash. *IOM* 5A **108**
Cregrina. *Powy* 5D **58**
Creich. *Arg* 2B **132**
Creich. *Fife* 1F **137**
Creighton. *Staf* 2E **73**
Creigiau. *Card* 3D **32**
Cremyll. *Corn* 3A **8**
Crendell. *Dors* 1F **15**
Crepkill. *High* 4D **154**
Cressage. *Shrp* 5H **71**
Cressbrook. *Derbs* 3F **85**
Cresselly. *Pemb* 4E **43**
Cressing. *Essx* 3A **54**
Cresswell. *Nmbd* 5G **121**
Cresswell. *Staf* 2D **73**
Cresswell Quay. *Pemb* 4E **43**
Creswell. *Derbs* 3C **86**
Creswell Green. *Staf* 4E **73**
Cretingham. *Suff* 4E **67**
Crewe. *Ches E* 5B **84**
Crewe-by-Farndon. *Ches W* 5G **83**
Crewgreen. *Powy* 4F **71**
Crewkerne. *Som* 2H **13**
Crews Hill. *G Lon* 5D **52**
Crewton. *Derb* 2A **74**
Crianlarich. *Stir* 1C **134**
Cribbs Causeway. *S Glo* 3A **34**
Cribyn. *Cdgn* 5E **57**
Criccieth. *Gwyn* 2D **69**
Crich. *Derbs* 5A **86**
Crichton. *Midl* 3G **129**
Crick. *Mon* 2H **33**
Crick. *Nptn* 3C **62**
Crickadarn. *Powy* 1D **46**
Cricket Hill. *Hants* 5G **37**
Cricket Malherbie. *Som* 1G **13**
Cricket St Thomas. *Som* 2G **13**
Crickham. *Som* 2H **21**
Crickheath. *Shrp* 3E **71**
Crickhowell. *Powy* 4F **47**
Cricklade. *Wilts* 2F **35**
Cricklewood. *G Lon* 2D **38**
Cridling Stubbs. *N Yor* 2F **93**
Crieff. *Per* 1A **136**
Criftins. *Shrp* 2F **71**
Criggion. *Powy* 4E **71**
Crigglestone. *W Yor* 3D **92**
Crimchard. *Som* 2G **13**
Crimdon Park. *Dur* 1B **106**
Crimond. *Abers* 3H **161**
Crimonmogate. *Abers* 3H **161**
Crimplesham. *Norf* 5F **77**
Crimscote. *Warw* 1H **49**
Crinan. *Arg* 4E **133**
Cringleford. *Norf* 5D **78**
Crinow. *Pemb* 3F **43**
Cripplesease. *Corn* 3C **4**
Cripplestyle. *Dors* 1F **15**
Cripp's Corner. *E Sus* 3B **28**
Croanford. *Corn* 5A **10**
Crockenhill. *Kent* 4G **39**
Crocker End. *Oxon* 3F **37**
Crockerhill. *Hants* 2D **16**
Crockernwell. *Devn* 3A **12**
Crocker's Ash. *Here* 4A **48**

Crockerton. Wilts . . . 2D 22
Crocketford. Dum . . . 2F 111
Crockey Hill. York . . . 5A 100
Crockham Hill. Kent . . . 5F 39
Crockhurst Street. Kent . . . 1H 27
Crockleford Heath. Essx . . . 3D 54
Croeserw. Neat . . . 2B 32
Croes-Goch. Pemb . . . 1C 42
Croes Hywel. Mon . . . 4G 47
Croes-lan. Cdgn . . . 1D 45
Croesor. Gwyn . . . 1F 69
Croesoswallt. Shrp . . . 3E 71
Croesyceiliog. Carm . . . 4E 45
Croesyceiliog. Torf . . . 2F 33
Croes-y-mwyalch. Torf . . . 2G 33
Croesywaun. Gwyn . . . 5E 81
Croford. Som . . . 4E 20
Croft. Leics . . . 1C 62
Croft. Linc . . . 4E 89
Croft. Warr . . . 1A 84
Croftamie. Stir . . . 1F 127
Croftfoot. Glas . . . 3G 127
Croftmill. Per . . . 5F 143
Crofton. Cumb . . . 4E 112
Crofton. W Yor . . . 3D 93
Crofton. Wilts . . . 5A 36
Croft-on-Tees. N Yor . . . 4F 105
Crofts. Dum . . . 2E 111
Crofts of Benachielt. High . . . 5D 169
Crofts of Dipple. Mor . . . 3H 159
Crofty. Swan . . . 3E 31
Croggan. Arg . . . 1E 132
Croglin. Cumb . . . 5G 113
Croich. High . . . 4B 164
Croick. High . . . 3A 168
Croig. Arg . . . 3E 139
Cromarty. High . . . 2B 158
Crombie. Fife . . . 1D 128
Cromdale. High . . . 1E 151
Cromer. Herts . . . 3C 52
Cromer. Norf . . . 1E 79
Cromford. Derbs . . . 5G 85
Cromhall. S Glo . . . 2B 34
Cromhall Common. S Glo . . . 3B 34
Cromor. W Isl . . . 5G 171
Cromra. High . . . 5H 149
Cromwell. Notts . . . 4E 87
Cronberry. E Ayr . . . 2F 117
Crondall. Hants . . . 2F 25
Cronk, The. IOM . . . 2C 108
Cronk-y-Voddy. IOM . . . 3C 108
Cronton. Mers . . . 2G 83
Crook. Cumb . . . 5F 103
Crook. Dur . . . 1E 105
Crookdake. Cumb . . . 5C 112
Crooke. G Man . . . 4D 90
Crookedholm. E Ayr . . . 1D 116
Crooked Soley. Wilts . . . 4B 36
Crookes. S Yor . . . 2H 85
Crookgate Bank. Dur . . . 4E 115
Crookhall. Dur . . . 4E 115
Crookham. Nmbd . . . 1D 120
Crookham. W Ber . . . 5D 36
Crookham Village. Hants . . . 1F 25
Crooklands. Cumb . . . 1E 97
Crook of Devon. Per . . . 3C 136
Crookston. Ren . . . 3G 127
Cropredy. Oxon . . . 1C 50
Cropston. Leics . . . 4C 74
Cropthorne. Worc . . . 1E 49
Cropton. N Yor . . . 1B 100
Cropwell Bishop. Notts . . . 2D 74
Cropwell Butler. Notts . . . 2D 74
Cros. W Isl . . . 1H 171
Crosbie. N Ayr . . . 5D 126
Crosbost. W Isl . . . 5F 171
Crosby. Cumb . . . 1B 102
Crosby. IOM . . . 4C 108
Crosby. Mers . . . 1F 83
Crosby. N Lin . . . 3B 94
Crosby Court. N Yor . . . 5A 106
Crosby Garrett. Cumb . . . 4A 104
Crosby Ravensworth. Cumb . . . 3H 103
Crosby Villa. Cumb . . . 1B 102
Croscombe. Som . . . 2A 22
Crosland Moor. W Yor . . . 3B 92
Cross. Som . . . 1H 21
Crossaig. Arg . . . 4G 125
Crossapol. Arg . . . 4A 138
Cross Ash. Mon . . . 4H 47
Cross-at-Hand. Kent . . . 1B 28
Crossbush. W Sus . . . 5B 26
Crosscanonby. Cumb . . . 1B 102
Crossdale Street. Norf . . . 2E 79
Cross End. Essx . . . 2B 54
Crossens. Mers . . . 3B 90
Crossford. Fife . . . 1D 128
Crossford. S Lan . . . 5B 128
Cross Foxes. Gwyn . . . 4G 69
Crossgate. Orkn . . . 6D 172
Crossgate. Staf . . . 2D 72
Crossgatehall. E Lot . . . 3G 129
Crossgates. Fife . . . 1E 129
Crossgates. N Yor . . . 1E 101
Crossgates. Powy . . . 4C 58
Cross Gates. W Yor . . . 1D 92
Crossgill. Lanc . . . 3E 97
Cross Green. Devn . . . 4D 11
Cross Green. Staf . . . 5D 72
Cross Green. Suff . . . 5A 66 (nr. Cockfield)
Cross Green. Suff . . . 5B 66 (nr. Hitcham)
Cross Hands. Carm . . . 4F 45 (nr. Ammanford)
Crosshands. Carm . . . 2F 43 (nr. Whitland)
Crosshands. E Ayr . . . 1D 117
Cross Hill. Derbs . . . 1B 74
Crosshill. E Ayr . . . 2D 117
Crosshill. Fife . . . 4D 136
Cross Hill. Glos . . . 2A 34
Crosshill. S Ayr . . . 4C 116
Crosshills. High . . . 1A 158
Cross Hills. N Yor . . . 5C 98
Cross Holme. N Yor . . . 5C 106
Crosshouse. E Ayr . . . 1C 116
Cross Houses. Shrp . . . 5H 71
Crossings. Cumb . . . 2G 113
Cross in Hand. E Sus . . . 3G 27
Cross Inn. Cdgn . . . 4E 57 (nr. Aberaeron)
Cross Inn. Cdgn . . . 5C 56 (nr. New Quay)
Cross Inn. Rhon . . . 3D 32
Crosskeys. Cphy . . . 2F 33
Crosskirk. High . . . 2C 168
Crosslands. Cumb . . . 1C 96
Cross Lane Head. Shrp . . . 1B 60
Cross Lanes. Corn . . . 4D 5
Cross Lanes. Dur . . . 3D 104
Cross Lanes. N Yor . . . 3H 99
Crosslanes. Shrp . . . 4F 71
Cross Lanes. Wrex . . . 1F 71
Crosslee. Ren . . . 3F 127
Crossmichael. Dum . . . 3E 111
Crossmoor. Lanc . . . 1C 90
Cross Oak. Powy . . . 3E 46
Cross of Jackston. Abers . . . 5E 161
Cross o' th' Hands. Derbs . . . 1G 73
Crossroads. Abers . . . 3G 153 (nr. Aberdeen)
Crossroads. Abers . . . 4E 153 (nr. Banchory)
Crossroads. E Ayr . . . 1D 116
Cross Side. Devn . . . 4B 20
Cross Street. Suff . . . 3D 66
Crosston. Ang . . . 3E 145
Cross Town. Ches E . . . 3B 84
Crossway. Mon . . . 4H 47
Crossway. Powy . . . 5C 58
Crossway Green. Mon . . . 2A 34
Crossway Green. Worc . . . 4C 60
Crossways. Dors . . . 4C 14
Crosswell. Pemb . . . 1F 43
Crosswood. Cdgn . . . 3F 57
Crosthwaite. Cumb . . . 5F 103
Croston. Lanc . . . 3C 90
Crostwick. Norf . . . 4E 79
Crostwight. Norf . . . 3F 79
Crothair. W Isl . . . 4D 171
Crouch. Kent . . . 5H 39
Croucheston. Wilts . . . 4F 23
Crouch Hill. Dors . . . 1C 14
Croughton. Nptn . . . 2D 50
Crovie. Abers . . . 2F 161
Crow. Hants . . . 2G 15
Crowan. Corn . . . 3D 4
Crowborough. E Sus . . . 2G 27
Crowcombe. Som . . . 3E 21
Crowcroft. Worc . . . 5B 60
Crowdecote. Derbs . . . 4F 85
Crowden. Derbs . . . 1E 85
Crowden. Devn . . . 3E 11
Crowdhill. Hants . . . 1C 16
Crowdon. N Yor . . . 5G 107
Crow Edge. S Yor . . . 4B 92
Crow End. Cambs . . . 5C 64
Crowfield. Nptn . . . 1E 50
Crowfield. Suff . . . 5D 66
Crow Green. Essx . . . 1G 39
Crow Hill. Here . . . 3B 48
Crowhurst. E Sus . . . 4B 28
Crowhurst. Surr . . . 1E 27
Crowhurst Lane End. Surr . . . 1E 27
Crowland. Linc . . . 4B 76
Crowland. Suff . . . 3C 66
Crowlas. Corn . . . 3C 4
Crowle. N Lin . . . 3A 94
Crowle. Worc . . . 5D 60
Crowle Green. Worc . . . 5D 60
Crowmarsh Gifford. Oxon . . . 3E 36
Crown Corner. Suff . . . 3E 67
Crownthorpe. Norf . . . 5C 78
Crowntown. Corn . . . 3D 4
Crows-an-wra. Corn . . . 4A 4
Crowshill. Norf . . . 5B 78
Crowthorne. Brac . . . 5G 37
Crowton. Ches W . . . 3H 83
Croxall. Staf . . . 4F 73
Croxby. Linc . . . 1A 88
Croxdale. Dur . . . 1F 105
Croxden. Staf . . . 2E 73
Croxley Green. Herts . . . 1B 38
Croxton. Cambs . . . 4B 64
Croxton. Norf . . . 2B 78 (nr. Fakenham)
Croxton. Norf . . . 2A 66 (nr. Thetford)
Croxton. N Lin . . . 3D 94
Croxton. Staf . . . 2B 72
Croxtonbank. Staf . . . 2B 72
Croxton Green. Ches E . . . 5H 83
Croxton Kerrial. Leics . . . 3F 75
Croy. High . . . 4B 158
Croy. N Lan . . . 2A 128
Croyde. Devn . . . 3E 19
Croydon. Cambs . . . 1D 52
Croydon. G Lon . . . 4E 39
Crubenbeg. High . . . 4A 150
Crubenmore Lodge. High . . . 4A 150
Cruckmeole. Shrp . . . 5G 71
Cruckton. Shrp . . . 4G 71
Cruden Bay. Abers . . . 5H 161
Crudgington. Telf . . . 4A 72
Crudie. Abers . . . 3E 161
Crudwell. Wilts . . . 2E 35
Cruft. Devn . . . 3F 11
Crug. Powy . . . 3D 58
Crughywel. Powy . . . 4F 47
Crugmeer. Corn . . . 1D 6
Crugybar. Carm . . . 2G 45
Crug-y-byddar. Powy . . . 2D 58
Crulabhig. W Isl . . . 4D 171
Crumlin. Cphy . . . 2F 33
Crumpsall. G Man . . . 4G 91
Crumpsbrook. Shrp . . . 3A 60
Crundale. Kent . . . 1E 29
Crundale. Pemb . . . 3D 42
Cruwys Morchard. Devn . . . 1B 12
Crux Easton. Hants . . . 1C 24
Cruxton. Dors . . . 3B 14
Crwbin. Carm . . . 4E 45
Cryers Hill. Buck . . . 2G 37
Crymych. Pemb . . . 1F 43
Crynant. Neat . . . 5A 46
Crystal Palace. G Lon . . . 3E 39
Cuaich. High . . . 5A 150
Cuaig. High . . . 3G 155
Cuan. Arg . . . 2E 133
Cubbington. Warw . . . 4H 61
Cubert. Corn . . . 3B 6
Cubley. S Yor . . . 4C 92
Cubley Common. Derbs . . . 2F 73
Cublington. Buck . . . 3G 51
Cublington. Here . . . 2H 47
Cuckfield. W Sus . . . 3E 27
Cucklington. Som . . . 4C 22
Cuckney. Notts . . . 3C 86
Cuckron. Shet . . . 6F 173
Cuddesdon. Oxon . . . 5E 50
Cuddington. Buck . . . 4F 51
Cuddington. Ches W . . . 3A 84
Cuddington Heath. Ches W . . . 1G 71
Cuddy Hill. Lanc . . . 1C 90
Cudham. G Lon . . . 5F 39
Cudlipptown. Devn . . . 5F 11
Cudworth. Som . . . 1G 13
Cudworth. S Yor . . . 4D 93
Cudworth. Surr . . . 1D 26
Cuerdley Cross. Warr . . . 2H 83
Cuffley. Herts . . . 5D 52
Cuidhir. W Isl . . . 8B 170
Cuidhsiadar. W Isl . . . 2H 171
Cuidhtinis. W Isl . . . 9C 171
Culbo. High . . . 2A 158
Culbokie. High . . . 3A 158
Culburnie. High . . . 4G 157
Culcabock. High . . . 4A 158
Culcharry. High . . . 3C 158
Culcheth. Warr . . . 1A 84
Culduie. High . . . 4G 155
Culeave. High . . . 4C 164
Culford. Suff . . . 4H 65
Culgaith. Cumb . . . 2H 103
Culham. Oxon . . . 2D 36
Culkein. High . . . 1E 163
Culkein Drumbeg. High . . . 5B 166
Culkerton. Glos . . . 2E 35
Cullen. Mor . . . 2C 160
Cullercoats. Tyne . . . 2G 115
Cullicudden. High . . . 2A 158
Cullingworth. W Yor . . . 1A 92
Cullipool. Arg . . . 2E 133
Cullivoe. Shet . . . 1G 173
Culloch. Per . . . 2G 135
Culloden. High . . . 4B 158
Cullompton. Devn . . . 2D 12
Culm Davy. Devn . . . 1E 13
Culmington. Shrp . . . 2G 59
Culmstock. Devn . . . 1E 12
Cul na Caepaich. High . . . 5E 147
Culnacnoc. High . . . 2E 155
Culnacraig. High . . . 3E 163
Culrain. High . . . 4C 164
Culross. Fife . . . 1C 128
Culroy. S Ayr . . . 3C 116
Culswick. Shet . . . 7D 173
Cults. Aber . . . 3F 153
Cults. Abers . . . 5C 160
Cults. Fife . . . 3F 137
Cultybraggan Camp. Per . . . 1G 135
Culver. Devn . . . 3B 12
Culverlane. Devn . . . 2D 8
Culverstone Green. Kent . . . 4H 39
Culverthorpe. Linc . . . 1H 75
Culworth. Nptn . . . 1D 50
Culzie Lodge. High . . . 1H 157
Cumberlow Green. Herts . . . 2D 52
Cumbernauld. N Lan . . . 2A 128
Cumbernauld Village. N Lan . . . 2A 128
Cumberworth. Linc . . . 3E 89
Cumdivock. Cumb . . . 5E 113
Cuminestown. Abers . . . 3F 161
Cumledge Mill. Bord . . . 4D 130
Cumlewick. Shet . . . 9F 173
Cummersdale. Cumb . . . 4E 113
Cummertrees. Dum . . . 3C 112
Cummingstown. Mor . . . 2F 159
Cumnock. E Ayr . . . 3E 117
Cumnor. Oxon . . . 5C 50
Cumrew. Cumb . . . 4G 113
Cumwhinton. Cumb . . . 4F 113
Cumwhitton. Cumb . . . 4G 113
Cundall. N Yor . . . 2G 99
Cunninghamhead. N Ayr . . . 5E 127
Cunning Park. S Ayr . . . 3C 116
Cunningsburgh. Shet . . . 9F 173
Cunnister. Shet . . . 2G 173
Cupar. Fife . . . 2F 137
Cupar Muir. Fife . . . 2F 137
Cupernham. Hants . . . 4B 24
Curbar. Derbs . . . 3G 85
Curborough. Staf . . . 4F 73
Curbridge. Hants . . . 1D 16
Curbridge. Oxon . . . 5B 50
Curdridge. Hants . . . 1D 16
Curdworth. Warw . . . 1F 61
Curland. Som . . . 1F 13
Curland Common. Som . . . 1F 13
Curridge. W Ber . . . 4C 36
Currie. Edin . . . 3E 129
Curry Mallet. Som . . . 4G 21
Curry Rivel. Som . . . 4G 21
Curtisden Green. Kent . . . 1B 28
Curtisknowle. Devn . . . 3D 8
Cury. Corn . . . 4D 5
Cusgarne. Corn . . . 4B 6
Cusop. Here . . . 1F 47
Cusworth. S Yor . . . 4F 93
Cutcombe. Som . . . 3C 20
Cuthill. E Lot . . . 2G 129
Cutiau. Gwyn . . . 4F 69
Cutlers Green. Essx . . . 2F 53
Cutmadoc. Corn . . . 2E 7
Cutnall Green. Worc . . . 4C 60
Cutsdean. Glos . . . 2F 49
Cutthorpe. Derbs . . . 3H 85
Cuttiford's Door. Som . . . 1G 13
Cuttivett. Corn . . . 2H 7
Cutts. Shet . . . 8F 173
Cuttybridge. Pemb . . . 3D 42
Cuttyhill. Abers . . . 3H 161
Cuxham. Oxon . . . 2E 37
Cuxton. Medw . . . 4B 40
Cuxwold. Linc . . . 4E 95
Cwm. Blae . . . 5E 47
Cwm. Den . . . 3C 82
Cwm. Powy . . . 1E 59
Cwmafan. Neat . . . 2A 32
Cwmaman. Rhon . . . 2C 32
Cwmann. Carm . . . 1F 45
Cwmbach. Carm . . . 2G 43
Cwmbach. Powy . . . 2E 47
Cwmbach. Rhon . . . 5D 46
Cwmbach Llechryd. Powy . . . 5C 58
Cwmbelan. Powy . . . 2B 58
Cwmbran. Torf . . . 2F 33
Cwmbrwyno. Cdgn . . . 2G 57
Cwm Capel. Carm . . . 5E 45
Cwmcarn. Cphy . . . 2F 33
Cwmcarvan. Mon . . . 5H 47
Cwm-celyn. Blae . . . 5F 47
Cwmcerdinen. Swan . . . 5G 45
Cwm-Cewydd. Gwyn . . . 4A 70
Cwmcoy. Cdgn . . . 1C 44
Cwmcrawnon. Powy . . . 4E 47
Cwmcych. Pemb . . . 1G 43
Cwmdare. Rhon . . . 5C 46
Cwmdu. Carm . . . 2G 45
Cwmdu. Powy . . . 3E 47
Cwmduad. Carm . . . 2D 45
Cwm Dulais. Swan . . . 5G 45
Cwmerfyn. Cdgn . . . 2F 57
Cwmfelin. B'end . . . 3B 32
Cwmfelin Boeth. Carm . . . 3F 43
Cwmfelinfach. Cphy . . . 2E 33
Cwmfelin Mynach. Carm . . . 2G 43
Cwmffrwd. Carm . . . 4E 45
Cwmgiedd. Powy . . . 4A 46
Cwmgors. Neat . . . 4H 45
Cwmgwili. Carm . . . 4F 45
Cwmgwrach. Neat . . . 5B 46
Cwmhiraeth. Carm . . . 1H 43
Cwmifor. Carm . . . 3G 45
Cwmisfael. Carm . . . 4E 45
Cwm-Llinau. Powy . . . 5H 69
Cwmllynfell. Neat . . . 4H 45
Cwm-mawr. Carm . . . 4F 45
Cwm-miles. Carm . . . 2F 43
Cwmorgan. Carm . . . 1G 43
Cwmparc. Rhon . . . 2C 32
Cwm Penmachno. Cnwy . . . 1G 69
Cwmpennar. Rhon . . . 5D 46
Cwm Plysgog. Pemb . . . 1B 44
Cwmrhos. Powy . . . 3E 47
Cwmsychpant. Cdgn . . . 1E 45
Cwmsyfiog. Cphy . . . 5E 47
Cwmsymlog. Cdgn . . . 2F 57
Cwmtillery. Blae . . . 5F 47
Cwm-twrch Isaf. Powy . . . 5A 46
Cwm-twrch Uchaf. Powy . . . 4A 46
Cwmwysg. Powy . . . 3B 46
Cwm-y-glo. Gwyn . . . 4E 81
Cwmyoy. Mon . . . 3G 47
Cwmystwyth. Cdgn . . . 3G 57
Cwrt. Gwyn . . . 1F 57
Cwrtnewydd. Cdgn . . . 1E 45
Cwrt-y-Cadno. Carm . . . 1G 45
Cydweli. Carm . . . 5E 45
Cyffylliog. Den . . . 5C 82
Cymau. Flin . . . 5E 83
Cymer. Neat . . . 2B 32
Cymmer. Neat . . . 2B 32
Cymmer. Rhon . . . 2D 32
Cyncoed. Card . . . 3E 33
Cynghordy. Carm . . . 2B 46
Cynghordy. Swan . . . 5G 45
Cynheidre. Carm . . . 5E 45
Cynonville. Neat . . . 2B 32
Cynwyd. Den . . . 1C 70
Cynwyl Elfed. Carm . . . 3D 44
Cywarch. Gwyn . . . 4A 70

D

Dacre. Cumb . . . 2F 103
Dacre. N Yor . . . 3D 98
Dacre Banks. N Yor . . . 3D 98
Daddry Shield. Dur . . . 1B 104
Dadford. Buck . . . 2E 51
Dadlington. Leics . . . 1B 62
Dafen. Carm . . . 5F 45
Daffy Green. Norf . . . 5B 78
Dagdale. Staf . . . 2E 73
Dagenham. G Lon . . . 2F 39
Daggons. Dors . . . 1G 15
Daglingworth. Glos . . . 5E 49
Dagnall. Buck . . . 4H 51
Dagtail End. Worc . . . 4E 61
Dail. Arg . . . 5E 141
Dail Beag. W Isl . . . 3E 171
Dail bho Dheas. W Isl . . . 1G 171
Dailly. S Ayr . . . 4B 116
Dail Mor. W Isl . . . 3E 171
Dairsie. Fife . . . 2G 137
Daisy Bank. W Mid . . . 1E 61
Daisy Hill. G Man . . . 4E 91
Daisy Hill. W Yor . . . 1B 92
Dalabrog. W Isl . . . 6C 170
Dalavich. Arg . . . 2G 133
Dalbeattie. Dum . . . 3F 111
Dalblair. E Ayr . . . 3F 117
Dalbury. Derbs . . . 2G 73
Dalby. IOM . . . 4B 108
Dalby Wolds. Leics . . . 3D 74
Dalchalm. High . . . 3G 165
Dalcharn. High . . . 3G 167
Dalchork. High . . . 2C 164
Dalchreichart. High . . . 2E 149
Dalchruin. Per . . . 2G 135
Dalcross. High . . . 4B 158
Dalderby. Linc . . . 4B 88
Dale. Cumb . . . 5G 113
Dale. Pemb . . . 4C 42
Dale Abbey. Derbs . . . 2B 74
Dalebank. Derbs . . . 4A 86
Dale Bottom. Cumb . . . 2D 102
Dale Head. Cumb . . . 3F 103
Dalehouse. N Yor . . . 3E 107
Dalelia. High . . . 2B 140
Dale of Walls. Shet . . . 6C 173
Dalgarven. N Ayr . . . 5D 126
Dalgety Bay. Fife . . . 1E 129
Dalginross. Per . . . 1G 135
Dalguise. Per . . . 4G 143
Dalhalvaig. High . . . 3A 168
Dalham. Suff . . . 4G 65
Dalintart. Arg . . . 1F 133
Dalkeith. Midl . . . 3G 129
Dallas. Mor . . . 3F 159
Dalleagles. E Ayr . . . 3E 117
Dall House. Per . . . 3C 142
Dallinghoo. Suff . . . 5E 67
Dallington. E Sus . . . 4A 28
Dallow. N Yor . . . 2D 98
Dalmally. Arg . . . 1A 134
Dalmarnock. Glas . . . 3H 127
Dalmellington. E Ayr . . . 4D 117
Dalmeny. Edin . . . 2E 129
Dalmigavie. High . . . 2B 150
Dalmilling. S Ayr . . . 2C 116
Dalmore. High . . . 2A 158 (nr. Alness)
Dalmore. High . . . 3E 164 (nr. Rogart)
Dalmuir. W Dun . . . 2F 127
Dalmunach. Mor . . . 4G 159
Dalnabreck. High . . . 2B 140
Dalnacardoch Lodge. Per . . . 1E 142
Dalnamein Lodge. Per . . . 2E 143
Dalnaspidal Lodge. Per . . . 1D 142
Dalnatrat. High . . . 3D 140
Dalnavie. High . . . 1A 158
Dalnawillan Lodge. High . . . 4C 168
Dalness. High . . . 3F 141
Dalnessie. High . . . 2D 164
Dalqueich. Per . . . 3C 136
Dalquhairn. S Ayr . . . 5C 116
Dalreavoch. High . . . 3E 165
Dalreoch. Per . . . 2C 136
Dalry. Edin . . . 2F 129
Dalry. N Ayr . . . 5D 126
Dalrymple. E Ayr . . . 3C 116
Dalscote. Nptn . . . 5D 62
Dalserf. S Lan . . . 4A 128

Dalsmirren. Arg 4A 122
Dalston. Cumb 4E 113
Dalswinton. Dum 1G 111
Dalton. Dum 2C 112
Dalton. Lanc 4C 90
Dalton. Nmbd 4C 114
(nr. Hexham)
Dalton. Nmbd 2E 115
(nr. Ponteland)
Dalton. N Yor 4E 105
(nr. Richmond)
Dalton. N Yor 2G 99
(nr. Thirsk)
Dalton. S Lan 4H 127
Dalton. S Yor 1B 86
Dalton-in-Furness. Cumb 2B 96
Dalton-le-Dale. Dur 5H 115
Dalton Magna. S Yor 1B 86
Dalton-on-Tees. N Yor 4F 105
Dalton Piercy. Hart 1B 106
Daltot. Arg 1F 125
Dalvey. High 5F 159
Dalwhinnie. High 5A 150
Dalwood. Devn 2F 13
Damerham. Hants 1G 15
Damgate. Norf 5G 79
(nr. Acle)
Damgate. Norf 4G 79
(nr. Martham)
Dam Green. Norf 2C 66
Damhead. Mor 3E 159
Danaway. Kent 4C 40
Danbury. Essx 5A 54
Danby. N Yor 4E 107
Danby Botton. N Yor 4D 107
Danby Wiske. N Yor 5A 106
Danderhall. Midl 3G 129
Danebank. Ches E 2D 85
Danebridge. Ches E 4D 84
Dane End. Herts 3D 52
Danehill. E Sus 3F 27
Danesford. Shrp 1B 60
Daneshill. Hants 1E 25
Danesmoor. Derbs 4A 86
Danestone. Aber 2G 153
Dangerous Corner. Lanc 3D 90
Daniel's Water. Kent 1D 28
Dan's Castle. Dur 1E 105
Danzey Green. Warw 4F 61
Dapple Heath. Staf 3E 73
Daren. Powy 4F 47
Darenth. Kent 3G 39
Daresbury. Hal 2H 83
Darfield. S Yor 4E 93
Dargate. Kent 4E 41
Dargill. Per 2A 136
Darite. Corn 2G 7
Darlaston. W Mid 1D 60
Darley. N Yor 4E 98
Darley Abbey. Derb 2A 74
Darley Bridge. Derbs 4G 85
Darley Dale. Derbs 4G 85
Darley Head. N Yor 4D 98
Darlingscott. Warw 1H 49
Darlington. Darl 3F 105
Darliston. Shrp 2H 71
Darlton. Notts 3E 87
Darmsden. Suff 5C 66
Darnall. S Yor 2A 86
Darnford. Abers 4E 153
Darnford. Staf 5F 73
Darnhall. Ches W 4A 84
Darnick. Bord 1H 119
Darowen. Powy 5H 69
Darra. Abers 4E 161
Darracott. Devn 3E 19
Darras Hall. Nmbd 2E 115
Darrington. W Yor 3E 93
Darrow Green. Norf 2E 67
Darsham. Suff 4G 67
Dartfield. Abers 3H 161
Dartford. Kent 3G 39
Dartford-Thurrock River Crossing. Kent 3G 39
Dartington. Devn 2D 9
Dartmeet. Devn 5G 11
Dartmoor. Devn 4F 11
Dartmouth. Devn 3E 9
Darton. S Yor 3D 92
Darvel. E Ayr 1E 117
Darwen. Bkbn 2E 91
Dassels. Herts 3D 53
Datchet. Wind 3A 38
Datchworth. Herts 4C 52
Datchworth Green. Herts 4C 52
Daubhill. G Man 4F 91
Dauntsey. Wilts 3E 35
Dauntsey Green. Wilts 3E 35
Dauntsey Lock. Wilts 3E 35
Dava. Mor 5E 159
Davenham. Ches W 3A 84
Daventry. Nptn 4C 62
Davidson's Mains. Edin 2F 129
Davidston. High 2B 158
Davidstow. Corn 4B 10
David's Well. Powy 3C 58
Davington. Dum 4E 119
Daviot. Abers 1E 153
Daviot. High 5B 158
Davyhulme. G Man 1B 84
Daw Cross. N Yor 4E 99
Dawdon. Dur 5H 115
Dawesgreen. Surr 1D 26
Dawley. Telf 5A 72
Dawlish. Devn 5C 12
Dawlish Warren. Devn 5C 12
Dawn. Cnwy 3A 82
Daws Heath. Essx 2C 40
Dawshill. Worc 5C 60
Daw's House. Corn 4D 10
Dawsmere. Linc 2D 76
Dayhills. Staf 2D 72
Dayhouse Bank. Worc 3D 60
Daylesford. Glos 3H 49
Daywall. Shrp 2E 71
Ddol. Flin 3D 82
Ddol Cownwy. Powy 4C 70
Deadman's Cross. C Beds 1B 52
Deadwater. Nmbd 5A 120
Deaf Hill. Dur 1A 106
Deal. Kent 5H 41
Dean. Cumb 2B 102
Dean. Devn 2G 19
(nr. Combe Martin)
Dean. Devn 2H 19
(nr. Lynton)
Dean. Dors 1E 15
Dean. Hants 1D 16
(nr. Bishop's Waltham)
Dean. Hants 3C 24
(nr. Winchester)
Dean. Oxon 3B 50
Dean. Som 2B 22
Dean Bank. Dur 1F 105
Deanburnhaugh. Bord 3F 119
Dean Cross. Devn 2F 19
Deane. Hants 1D 24
Deanich Lodge. High 5A 164
Deanland. Dors 1E 15
Deanlane End. W Sus 1F 17
Dean Park. Shrp 4H 59
Dean Prior. Devn 2D 8
Dean Row. Ches E 2C 84
Deans. W Lot 3D 128
Deanscales. Cumb 2B 102
Deanshanger. Nptn 2F 51
Deanston. Stir 3G 135
Dearham. Cumb 1B 102
Dearne. S Yor 4E 93
Dearne Valley. S Yor 4D 93
Debach. Suff 5E 67
Debden. Essx 2F 53
Debden Green. Essx 1F 39
(nr. Loughton)
Debden Green. Essx 2F 53
(nr. Saffron Walden)
Debenham. Suff 4D 66
Dechmont. W Lot 2D 128
Deddington. Oxon 2C 50
Dedham. Essx 2D 54
Dedham Heath. Essx 2D 54
Deebank. Abers 4D 152
Deene. Nptn 1G 63
Deenethorpe. Nptn 1G 63
Deepcar. S Yor 1G 85
Deepcut. Surr 5A 38
Deepdale. Cumb 1G 97
Deepdale. N Lin 3D 94
Deepdale. N Yor 2A 98
Deeping Gate. Pet 5A 76
Deeping St James. Linc 5A 76
Deeping St Nicholas. Linc 4B 76
Deerhill. Mor 3B 160
Deerhurst. Glos 3D 48
Deerhurst Walton. Glos 3D 49
Deerness. Orkn 7E 172
Defford. Worc 1E 49
Defynnog. Powy 3C 46
Deganwy. Cnwy 3G 81
Deighton. N Yor 4A 106
Deighton. W Yor 3B 92
Deighton. York 5A 100
Deiniolen. Gwyn 4E 81
Delabole. Corn 4A 10
Delamere. Ches W 4H 83
Delfour. High 3C 150
Dellieture. High 5E 159
Dell, The. Suff 1G 67
Delly End. Oxon 4B 50
Delny. High 1B 158
Delph. G Man 4H 91
Delves. Dur 5E 115
Delves, The. W Mid 1E 61
Delvin End. Essx 2A 54
Dembleby. Linc 2H 75
Demelza. Corn 2D 6
Denaby Main. S Yor 1B 86
Denbeath. Fife 4F 137
Denbigh. Den 4C 82
Denbury. Devn 2E 9
Denby. Derbs 1A 74
Denby Common. Derbs 1B 74
Denby Dale. W Yor 4C 92
Denchworth. Oxon 2B 36
Dendron. Cumb 2B 96
Deneside. Dur 5H 115
Denford. Nptn 3G 63
Dengie. Essx 5C 54
Denham. Buck 2B 38
Denham. Suff 4G 65
(nr. Bury St Edmunds)
Denham. Suff 3D 66
(nr. Eye)
Denham Green. Buck 2B 38
Denham Street. Suff 3D 66
Denhead. Abers 5G 161
(nr. Ellon)
Denhead. Abers 3G 161
(nr. Strichen)
Denhead. Fife 2G 137
Denholm. Bord 3H 119
Denholme. W Yor 1A 92
Denholme Clough. W Yor 1A 92
Denholme Gate. W Yor 1A 92
Denio. Gwyn 2C 68
Denmead. Hants 1E 17
Dennington. Suff 4E 67
Denny. Falk 1B 128
Denny End. Cambs 4D 65
Dennyloanhead. Falk 1B 128
Den of Lindores. Fife 2E 137
Denshaw. G Man 3H 91
Denside. Abers 4F 153
Densole. Kent 1G 29
Denston. Suff 5G 65
Denstone. Staf 1F 73
Denstroude. Kent 4F 41
Dent. Cumb 1G 97
Den, The. N Ayr 4E 127
Denton. Cambs 2A 64
Denton. Darl 3F 105
Denton. E Sus 5F 27
Denton. G Man 1D 84
Denton. Kent 1G 29
Denton. Linc 2F 75
Denton. Norf 2E 67
Denton. Nptn 5F 63
Denton. N Yor 5D 98
Denton. Oxon 5D 50
Denver. Norf 5F 77
Denwick. Nmbd 3G 121
Deopham. Norf 5C 78
Deopham Green. Norf 1C 66
Depden. Suff 5G 65
Depden Green. Suff 5G 65
Deptford. G Lon 3E 39
Deptford. Wilts 3F 23
Derby. Derb 2A 74 & 193
Derbyhaven. IOM 5B 108
Derculich. Per 3F 143
Dereham. Norf 4B 78
Deri. Cphy 5E 47
Derril. Devn 2D 10
Derringstone. Kent 1G 29
Derrington. Shrp 1A 60
Derrington. Staf 3C 72
Derriton. Devn 2D 10
Derryguaig. Arg 5F 139
Derry Hill. Wilts 4E 35
Derrythorpe. N Lin 4B 94
Dersingham. Norf 2F 77
Dervaig. Arg 3F 139
Derwen. Den 5C 82
Derwen Gam. Cdgn 5D 56
Derwenlas. Powy 1G 57
Desborough. Nptn 2F 63
Desford. Leics 5B 74
Detchant. Nmbd 1E 121
Dethick. Derbs 5H 85
Detling. Kent 5B 40
Deuchar. Ang 2D 144
Deuddwr. Powy 4E 71
Devauden. Mon 2H 33
Devil's Bridge. Cdgn 3G 57
Devitts Green. Warw 1G 61
Devizes. Wilts 5F 35
Devonport. Plym 3A 8
Devonside. Clac 4B 136
Devoran. Corn 5B 6
Dewartown. Midl 3G 129
Dewlish. Dors 3C 14
Dewsbury. W Yor 2C 92
Dewshall Court. Here 2H 47
Dexbeer. Devn 2C 10
Dhoon. IOM 3D 108
Dhoor. IOM 2D 108
Dhowin. IOM 1D 108
Dial Green. W Sus 3A 26
Dial Post. W Sus 4C 26
Dibberford. Dors 2H 13
Dibden. Hants 2C 16
Dibden Purlieu. Hants 2C 16
Dickleburgh. Norf 2D 66
Didbrook. Glos 2F 49
Didcot. Oxon 2D 36
Diddington. Cambs 4A 64
Diddlebury. Shrp 2H 59
Didley. Here 2H 47
Didling. W Sus 1G 17
Didmarton. Glos 3D 34
Didsbury. G Man 1C 84
Didworthy. Devn 2C 8
Digby. Linc 5H 87
Digg. High 2D 154
Diggle. G Man 4A 92
Digmoor. Lanc 4C 90
Digswell. Herts 4C 52
Dihewyd. Cdgn 5D 57
Dilham. Norf 3F 79
Dilhorne. Staf 1D 72
Dillarburn. S Lan 5B 128
Dillington. Cambs 4A 64
Dilston. Nmbd 3C 114
Dilton Marsh. Wilts 2D 22
Dilwyn. Here 5G 59
Dimmer. Som 3B 22
Dimple. G Man 3F 91
Dinas. Carm 1G 43
Dinas. Gwyn 5D 81
(nr. Caernarfon)
Dinas. Gwyn 2B 68
(nr. Tudweiliog)
Dinas Cross. Pemb 1E 43
Dinas Dinlle. Gwyn 5D 80
Dinas Mawddwy. Gwyn 4A 70
Dinas Powys. V Glam 4E 33
Dinbych. Den 4C 82
Dinbych-y-Pysgod. Pemb 4F 43
Dinckley. Lanc 1E 91
Dinder. Som 2A 22
Dinedor. Here 2A 48
Dinedor Cross. Here 2A 48
Dingestow. Mon 4H 47
Dingle. Mers 2F 83
Dingleden. Kent 2C 28
Dingleton. Bord 1H 119
Dingley. Nptn 2E 63
Dingwall. High 3H 157
Dinmael. Cnwy 1C 70
Dinnet. Abers 4B 152
Dinnington. Som 1H 13
Dinnington. S Yor 2C 86
Dinnington. Tyne 2F 115
Dinorwig. Gwyn 4E 81
Dinton. Buck 4F 51
Dinton. Wilts 3F 23
Dinworthy. Devn 1D 10
Dipley. Hants 1F 25
Dippen. Arg 2B 122
Dippenhall. Surr 2G 25
Dippertown. Devn 4E 11
Dippin. N Ayr 3E 123
Dipple. S Ayr 4B 116
Diptford. Devn 3D 8
Dipton. Dur 4E 115
Dirleton. E Lot 1B 130
Dirt Pot. Nmbd 5B 114
Discoed. Powy 4E 59
Diseworth. Leics 3B 74
Dishes. Orkn 5F 172
Dishforth. N Yor 2F 99
Disley. Ches E 2D 85
Diss. Norf 3D 66
Disserth. Powy 5C 58
Distington. Cumb 2B 102
Ditchampton. Wilts 3F 23
Ditcheat. Som 3B 22
Ditchingham. Norf 1F 67
Ditchling. E Sus 4E 27
Ditteridge. Wilts 5D 34
Dittisham. Devn 3E 9
Ditton. Hal 2G 83
Ditton. Kent 5B 40
Ditton Green. Cambs 5F 65
Ditton Priors. Shrp 2A 60
Divach. High 1G 149
Dixonfield. High 2D 168
Dixton. Glos 2E 49
Dixton. Mon 4A 48
Dizzard. Corn 3B 10
Dobcross. G Man 4H 91
Dobs Hill. Flin 4F 83
Dobson's Bridge. Shrp 2G 71
Dobwalls. Corn 2G 7
Doccombe. Devn 4A 12
Dochgarroch. High 4A 158
Docking. Norf 2G 77
Docklow. Here 5H 59
Dockray. Cumb 2E 103
Doc Penfro. Pemb 4D 42 & 215
Dodbrooke. Devn 4D 8
Doddenham. Worc 5B 60
Doddinghurst. Essx 1G 39
Doddington. Cambs 1C 64
Doddington. Kent 5D 40
Doddington. Linc 4G 87
Doddington. Nmbd 1D 121
Doddington. Shrp 3A 60
Doddiscombsleigh. Devn 4B 12
Doddshill. Norf 2G 77
Dodford. Nptn 4D 62
Dodford. Worc 3D 60
Dodington. Som 2E 21
Dodington. S Glo 4C 34
Dodleston. Ches W 4F 83
Dods Leigh. Staf 2E 73
Dodworth. S Yor 4D 92
Doe Lea. Derbs 4B 86
Dogdyke. Linc 5B 88
Dogmersfield. Hants 1F 25
Dogsthorpe. Pet 5B 76
Dog Village. Devn 3C 12
Dolanog. Powy 4C 70
Dolau. Powy 4D 58
Dolau. Rhon 3D 32
Dolbenmaen. Gwyn 1E 69
Doley. Staf 3B 72
Dol-fach. Powy 5B 70
(nr. Llanbrynmair)
Dolfach. Powy 3B 58
(nr. Llanidloes)
Dolfor. Powy 2D 58
Dolgarrog. Cnwy 4G 81
Dolgellau. Gwyn 4G 69
Dolgoch. Gwyn 5F 69
Dol-gran. Carm 2E 45
Dolhelfa. Powy 3B 58
Doll. High 3F 165
Dollar. Clac 4B 136
Dolley Green. Powy 4E 59
Dollwen. Cdgn 2F 57
Dolphin. Flin 3D 82
Dolphingstone. E Lot 2G 129
Dolphinholme. Lanc 4E 97
Dolphinton. S Lan 5E 129
Dolton. Devn 1F 11
Dolwen. Cnwy 3A 82
Dolwyddelan. Cnwy 5G 81
Dol-y-Bont. Cdgn 2F 57
Dolyhir. Powy 5E 59
Domgay. Powy 4E 71
Doncaster. S Yor 4F 93
Donhead St Andrew. Wilts 4E 23
Donhead St Mary. Wilts 4E 23
Doniford. Som 2D 20
Donington. Linc 2B 76
Donington. Shrp 5C 72
Donington Eaudike. Linc 2B 76
Donington le Heath. Leics 4B 74
Donington on Bain. Linc 2B 88
Donington South Ing. Linc 2B 76
Donisthorpe. Leics 4H 73
Donkey Street. Kent 2F 29
Donkey Town. Surr 4A 38
Donna Nook. Linc 1D 88
Donnington. Glos 3G 49
Donnington. Here 2C 48
Donnington. Shrp 5H 71
Donnington. Telf 4B 72
Donnington. W Ber 5C 36
Donnington. W Sus 2G 17
Donyatt. Som 1G 13
Doomsday Green. W Sus 2C 26
Doonfoot. S Ayr 3C 116
Doonholm. S Ayr 3C 116
Dorback Lodge. High 2E 151
Dorchester. Dors 3B 14
Dorchester on Thames. Oxon 2D 36
Dordon. Warw 5G 73
Dore. S Yor 2H 85
Dores. High 5H 157
Dorking. Surr 1C 26
Dorking Tye. Suff 2C 54
Dormansland. Surr 1F 27
Dormans Park. Surr 1E 27
Dormanstown. Red C 2C 106
Dormington. Here 1A 48
Dormston. Worc 5D 61
Dorn. Glos 2H 49
Dorney. Buck 3A 38
Dornie. High 1A 148
Dornoch. High 5E 165
Dornock. Dum 3D 112
Dorrery. High 3C 168
Dorridge. W Mid 3F 61
Dorrington. Linc 5H 87
Dorrington. Shrp 5G 71
Dorsington. Warw 1G 49
Dorstone. Here 1G 47
Dorton. Buck 4E 51
Dotham. IOA 3C 80
Dottery. Dors 3H 13
Doublebois. Corn 2F 7
Dougarie. N Ayr 2C 122
Doughton. Glos 2D 35
Douglas. IOM 4C 108
Douglas. S Lan 1H 117
Douglastown. Ang 4D 144
Douglas Water. S Lan 1A 118
Doulting. Som 2B 22
Dounby. Orkn 5B 172
Doune. High 3C 150
(nr. Kingussie)
Doune. High 3B 164
(nr. Lairg)
Doune. Stir 3G 135
Dounie. High 4C 164
(nr. Bonar Bridge)
Dounie. High 5D 164
(nr. Tain)
Dounreay. High 2B 168
Doura. N Ayr 5E 127
Dousland. Devn 2B 8
Dovaston. Shrp 3F 71
Dove Holes. Derbs 3E 85
Dovenby. Cumb 1B 102
Dover. Kent 1H 29 & 193
Dovercourt. Essx 2F 55
Doverdale. Worc 4C 60
Doveridge. Derbs 2F 73
Doversgreen. Surr 1D 26
Dowally. Per 4H 143
Dowbridge. Lanc 1C 90
Dowdeswell. Glos 4F 49
Dowlais. Mer T 5D 46
Dowland. Devn 1F 11
Dowlands. Devn 3F 13
Dowles. Worc 3B 60
Dowlesgreen. Wok 5G 37
Dowlish Wake. Som 1G 13
Downall Green. Mers 4D 90
Down Ampney. Glos 2F 35
Downderry. Corn 3H 7
(nr. Looe)
Downderry. Corn 3D 6
(nr. St Austell)
Downe. G Lon 4F 39
Downend. IOW 4D 16
Downend. S Glo 4B 34
Downend. W Ber 4C 36

Down Field. *Cambs* 3F 65
Downfield. *D'dee* 5C 144
Downgate. *Corn* 5D 10
(nr. Kelly Bray)
Downgate. *Corn* 5C 10
(nr. Upton Cross)
Downham. *Essx* 1B 40
Downham. *Lanc* 5G 97
Downham. *Nmbd* 1C 120
Downham Market. *Norf* 5F 77
Down Hatherley. *Glos* 3D 48
Downhead. *Som* 2B 22
(nr. Frome)
Downhead. *Som* 4A 22
(nr. Yeovil)
Downholland Cross. *Lanc* 4B 90
Downholme. *N Yor* 5E 105
Downies. *Abers* 4G 153
Downley. *Buck* 2G 37
Down St Mary. *Devn* 2H 11
Downside. *Som* 1B 22
(nr. Chilcompton)
Downside. *Som* 2B 22
(nr. Shepton Mallet)
Downside. *Surr* 5C 38
Down, The. *Shrp* 1A 60
Down Thomas. *Devn* 3B 8
Downton. *Hants* 3A 16
Downton. *Wilts* 4G 23
Downton on the Rock. *Here* 3G 59
Dowsby. *Linc* 3A 76
Dowsdale. *Linc* 4B 76
Dowthwaitehead. *Cumb* 2E 103
Doxey. *Staf* 3D 72
Doxford. *Nmbd* 2F 121
Doynton. *S Glo* 4C 34
Drabblegate. *Norf* 3E 78
Draethen. *Cphy* 3F 33
Draffan. *S Lan* 5A 128
Dragonby. *N Lin* 3C 94
Dragons Green. *W Sus* 3C 26
Drakelow. *Worc* 2C 60
Drakemyre. *N Ayr* 4D 126
Drakes Broughton. *Worc* 1E 49
Drakes Cross. *Worc* 3E 61
Drakewalls. *Corn* 5E 11
Draughton. *Nptn* 3E 63
Draughton. *N Yor* 4C 98
Drax. *N Yor* 2G 93
Draycot. *Oxon* 5E 51
Draycote. *Warw* 4B 62
Draycot Foliat. *Swin* 4G 35
Draycott. *Derbs* 2B 74
Draycott. *Glos* 2G 49
Draycott. *Shrp* 1C 60
Draycott. *Som* 1H 21
(nr. Cheddar)
Draycott. *Som* 4A 22
(nr. Yeovil)
Draycott. *Worc* 1D 48
Draycott in the Clay. *Staf* 3F 73
Draycott in the Moors. *Staf* 1D 73
Drayford. *Devn* 1A 12
Drayton. *Leics* 1F 63
Drayton. *Linc* 2B 76
Drayton. *Norf* 4D 78
Drayton. *Nptn* 4C 62
Drayton. *Oxon* 2C 36
(nr. Abingdon)
Drayton. *Oxon* 1C 50
(nr. Banbury)
Drayton. *Port* 2E 17
Drayton. *Som* 4H 21
Drayton. *Warw* 5F 61
Drayton. *Worc* 3D 60
Drayton Bassett. *Staf* 5F 73
Drayton Beauchamp. *Buck* 4H 51
Drayton Parslow. *Buck* 3G 51
Drayton St Leonard. *Oxon* 2D 36
Drebley. *N Yor* 4C 98
Dreenhill. *Pemb* 3D 42
Drefach. *Carm* 4F 45
(nr. Meidrim)
Drefach. *Carm* 2D 44
(nr. Newcastle Emlyn)
Drefach. *Carm* 2G 43
(nr. Tumble)
Drefach. *Cdgn* 1E 45
Dreghorn. *N Ayr* 1C 116
Drellingore. *Kent* 1G 29
Drem. *E Lot* 2B 130
Dreumasdal. *W Isl* 5C 170
Drewsteignton. *Devn* 3H 11
Driby. *Linc* 3C 88
Driffield. *E Yor* 4E 101
Driffield. *Glos* 2F 35
Drift. *Corn* 4B 4
Drigg. *Cumb* 5B 102
Drighlington. *W Yor* 2C 92
Drimnin. *High* 3G 139
Drimpton. *Dors* 2H 13
Dringhoe. *E Yor* 4F 101
Drinisiadar. *W Isl* 8D 171
Drinkstone. *Suff* 4B 66
Drinkstone Green. *Suff* 4B 66
Drointon. *Staf* 3E 73
Droitwich Spa. *Worc* 4C 60
Droman. *High* 3B 166
Dron. *Per* 2D 136
Dronfield. *Derbs* 3A 86
Dronfield Woodhouse. *Derbs* 3H 85
Drongan. *E Ayr* 3D 116
Dronley. *Ang* 5C 144
Droop. *Dors* 2C 14
Drope. *V Glam* 4E 32
Droxford. *Hants* 1E 16
Droylsden. *G Man* 1C 84
Druggers End. *Worc* 2C 48
Druid. *Den* 1C 70
Druid's Heath. *W Mid* 5E 73
Druidston. *Pemb* 3C 42
Druim. *High* 3D 158
Druimarbin. *High* 1E 141
Druim Fhearna. *High* 2E 147
Druimindarroch. *High* 5E 147
Druim Saighdinis. *W Isl* 2D 170
Drum. *Per* 3C 136
Drumbeg. *High* 5B 166
Drumblade. *Abers* 4C 160
Drumbuie. *Dum* 1C 110
Drumbuie. *High* 5G 155
Drumburgh. *Cumb* 4D 112
Drumburn. *Dum* 3A 112
Drumchapel. *Glas* 2G 127
Drumchardine. *High* 4H 157
Drumchork. *High* 5C 162
Drumclog. *S Lan* 1F 117
Drumeldrie. *Fife* 3G 137
Drumelzier. *Bord* 1D 118
Drumfearn. *High* 2E 147
Drumgask. *High* 4A 150
Drumgelloch. *N Lan* 3A 128
Drumgley. *Ang* 3D 144
Drumguish. *High* 4B 150
Drumin. *Mor* 5F 159
Druminadrochit. *High* 4G 157
Drumlamford House. *S Ayr* 2H 109
Drumlasie. *Abers* 3D 152
Drumlemble. *Arg* 4A 122
Drumlithie. *Abers* 5E 153
Drummoddie. *Dum* 5A 110
Drummond. *High* 2A 158
Drummore. *Dum* 5E 109
Drummuir. *Mor* 4A 160
Drumnadrochit. *High* 5H 157
Drumnagorrach. *Mor* 3C 160
Drumoak. *Abers* 4E 153
Drumrunie. *High* 3F 163
Drumry. *W Dun* 2G 127
Drums. *Abers* 1G 153
Drumsleet. *Dum* 2G 111
Drumsmittal. *High* 4A 158
Drums of Park. *Abers* 3C 160
Drumsturdy. *Ang* 5D 145
Drumtochty Castle. *Abers* 5D 152
Drumuie. *High* 4D 154
Drumuillie. *High* 1D 150
Drumvaich. *Stir* 3F 135
Drumwhindle. *Abers* 5G 161
Drunkendub. *Ang* 4F 145
Drury. *Flin* 4E 83
Drury Square. *Norf* 4B 78
Drybeck. *Cumb* 3H 103
Drybridge. *Mor* 2B 160
Drybridge. *N Ayr* 1C 116
Drybrook. *Glos* 4B 48
Drybrook. *Here* 4A 48
Dryburgh. *Bord* 1H 119
Dry Doddington. *Linc* 1F 75
Dry Drayton. *Cambs* 4C 64
Drym. *Corn* 3D 4
Drymen. *Stir* 1F 127
Drymuir. *Abers* 4G 161
Drynachan Lodge. *High* 5C 158
Drynie Park. *High* 3H 157
Drynoch. *High* 5D 154
Dry Sandford. *Oxon* 5C 50
Dryslwyn. *Carm* 3F 45
Dry Street. *Essx* 2A 40
Dryton. *Shrp* 5H 71
Dubford. *Abers* 2E 161
Dubiton. *Abers* 3D 160
Dubton. *Ang* 3E 145
Duchally. *High* 2A 164
Duck End. *Essx* 3G 53
Duckington. *Ches W* 5G 83
Ducklington. *Oxon* 5B 50
Duckmanton. *Derbs* 3B 86
Duck Street. *Hants* 2B 24
Dudbridge. *Glos* 5D 48
Duddenhoe End. *Essx* 2E 53
Duddingston. *Edin* 2F 129
Duddington. *Nptn* 5G 75
Duddleswell. *E Sus* 3F 27
Duddo. *Nmbd* 5F 131
Duddon. *Ches W* 4H 83
Duddon Bridge. *Cumb* 1A 96
Dudleston. *Shrp* 2F 71
Dudleston Heath. *Shrp* 2F 71
Dudley. *Tyne* 2F 115
Dudley. *W Mid* 2D 60
Dudston. *Shrp* 1E 59
Dudwells. *Pemb* 2D 42
Duffield. *Derbs* 1H 73
Duffryn. *Neat* 2B 32
Dufftown. *Mor* 4H 159
Duffus. *Mor* 2F 159
Dufton. *Cumb* 2H 103
Duggleby. *N Yor* 3C 100
Duirinish. *High* 5G 155
Duisdalemore. *High* 2E 147
Duisdeil Mòr. *High* 2E 147
Duisky. *High* 1E 141
Dukesfield. *Nmbd* 4C 114
Dukestown. *Blae* 5E 47
Dukinfield. *G Man* 1D 84
Dulas. *IOA* 2D 81
Dulcote. *Som* 2A 22
Dulford. *Devn* 2D 12
Dull. *Per* 4F 143
Dullatur. *N Lan* 2A 128
Dullingham. *Cambs* 5F 65
Dullingham Ley. *Cambs* 5F 65
Dulnain Bridge. *High* 1D 151
Duloe. *Bed* 4A 64
Duloe. *Corn* 3G 7
Dulverton. *Som* 4C 20
Dulwich. *G Lon* 3E 39
Dumbarton. *W Dun* 2F 127
Dumbleton. *Glos* 2F 49
Dumfin. *Arg* 1E 127
Dumfries. *Dum* 2A 112 & 193
Dumgoyne. *Stir* 1G 127
Dummer. *Hants* 2D 24
Dumpford. *W Sus* 4G 25
Dun. *Ang* 2F 145
Dunagoil. *Arg* 4B 126
Dunalastair. *Per* 3E 142
Dunan. *High* 1D 147
Dunball. *Som* 2G 21
Dunbar. *E Lot* 2C 130
Dunbeath. *High* 5D 168
Dunbeg. *Arg* 5C 140
Dunblane. *Stir* 3G 135
Dunbog. *Fife* 2E 137
Dunbridge. *Hants* 4B 24
Duncanston. *Abers* 1C 152
Duncanston. *High* 3H 157
Dun Charlabhaigh. *W Isl* 3D 171
Dunchideock. *Devn* 4B 12
Dunchurch. *Warw* 3B 62
Duncote. *Nptn* 5D 62
Duncow. *Dum* 1A 112
Duncrievie. *Per* 3D 136
Duncton. *W Sus* 4A 26
Dundee. *D'dee* 5D 144 & 194
Dundee Airport. *D'dee* 1F 137
Dundon. *Som* 3H 21
Dundonald. *S Ayr* 1C 116
Dundonnell. *High* 5E 163
Dundraw. *Cumb* 5D 112
Dundreggan. *High* 2F 149
Dundrennan. *Dum* 5E 111
Dundridge. *Hants* 1D 16
Dundry. *N Som* 5A 34
Dunecht. *Abers* 3E 153
Dunfermline. *Fife* 1D 129
Dunford Bridge. *S Yor* 4B 92
Dungate. *Kent* 5D 40
Dunge. *Wilts* 1D 23
Dungeness. *Kent* 4E 29
Dungworth. *S Yor* 2G 85
Dunham-on-the-Hill. *Ches W* 3G 83
Dunham-on-Trent. *Notts* 3F 87
Dunhampton. *Worc* 4C 60
Dunham Town. *G Man* 2B 84
Dunham Woodhouses. *G Man* 2B 84
Dunholme. *Linc* 3H 87
Dunino. *Fife* 2H 137
Dunipace. *Falk* 1B 128
Dunira. *Per* 1G 135
Dunkeld. *Per* 4H 143
Dunkerton. *Bath* 1C 22
Dunkeswell. *Devn* 2E 13
Dunkeswick. *N Yor* 5F 99
Dunkirk. *Kent* 5E 41
Dunkirk. *S Glo* 3C 34
Dunkirk. *Staf* 5C 84
Dunkirk. *Wilts* 5E 35
Dunk's Green. *Kent* 5H 39
Dunlappie. *Ang* 2E 145
Dunley. *Hants* 1C 24
Dunley. *Worc* 4B 60
Dunlichity Lodge. *High* 5A 158
Dunlop. *E Ayr* 5F 127
Dunmaglass Lodge. *High* 1H 149
Dunmore. *Arg* 3F 125
Dunmore. *Falk* 1B 128
Dunmore. *High* 4H 157
Dunnet. *High* 1E 169
Dunnichen. *Ang* 4E 145
Dunning. *Per* 2C 136
Dunnington. *E Yor* 4F 101
Dunnington. *Warw* 5E 61
Dunnington. *York* 4A 100
Dunningwell. *Cumb* 1A 96
Dunnockshaw. *Lanc* 2G 91
Dunoon. *Arg* 2C 126
Dunphail. *Mor* 4E 159
Dunragit. *Dum* 4G 109
Dunrostan. *Arg* 1F 125
Duns. *Bord* 4D 130
Dunsby. *Linc* 3A 76
Dunscar. *G Man* 3F 91
Dunscore. *Dum* 1F 111
Dunscroft. *S Yor* 4G 93
Dunsdale. *Red C* 3D 106
Dunsden Green. *Oxon* 4F 37
Dunsfold. *Surr* 2B 26
Dunsford. *Devn* 4B 12
Dunshalt. *Fife* 2E 137
Dunshillock. *Abers* 4G 161
Dunsley. *N Yor* 3F 107
Dunsley. *Staf* 2C 60
Dunsmore. *Buck* 5G 51
Dunsop Bridge. *Lanc* 4F 97
Dunstable. *C Beds* 3A 52
Dunstal. *Staf* 3E 73
Dunstall. *Staf* 3F 73
Dunstall Green. *Suff* 4G 65
Dunstall Hill. *W Mid* 1D 60
Dunstan. *Nmbd* 3G 121
Dunster. *Som* 2C 20
Duns Tew. *Oxon* 3C 50
Dunston. *Linc* 4H 87
Dunston. *Norf* 5E 79
Dunston. *Staf* 4D 72
Dunston. *Tyne* 3F 115
Dunstone. *Devn* 3B 8
Dunston Heath. *Staf* 4D 72
Dunsville. *S Yor* 4G 93
Dunswell. *E Yor* 1D 94
Dunsyre. *S Lan* 5D 128
Dunterton. *Devn* 5D 11
Duntisbourne Abbots. *Glos* 5E 49
Duntisbourne Leer. *Glos* 5E 49
Duntisbourne Rouse. *Glos* 5E 49
Duntish. *Dors* 2B 14
Duntocher. *W Dun* 2F 127
Dunton. *Buck* 3G 51
Dunton. *C Beds* 1C 52
Dunton. *Norf* 2A 78
Dunton Bassett. *Leics* 1C 62
Dunton Green. *Kent* 5G 39
Dunton Patch. *Norf* 2A 78
Duntulm. *High* 1D 154
Dunure. *S Ayr* 3B 116
Dunvant. *Swan* 3E 31
Dunvegan. *High* 4B 154
Dunwich. *Suff* 3G 67
Dunwood. *Staf* 5D 84
Durdar. *Cumb* 4F 113
Durgates. *E Sus* 2H 27
Durham. *Dur* 5F 115 & 194
Durham Tees Valley Airport. *Darl* 3A 106
Durisdeer. *Dum* 4A 118
Durisdeermill. *Dum* 4A 118
Durkar. *W Yor* 3D 92
Durleigh. *Som* 3F 21
Durley. *Hants* 1D 16
Durley. *Wilts* 5H 35
Durley Street. *Hants* 1D 16
Durlow Common. *Here* 2B 48
Durnamuck. *High* 4E 163
Durness. *High* 2E 166
Durno. *Abers* 1E 152
Durns Town. *Hants* 3A 16
Duror. *High* 3D 141
Durran. *Arg* 3G 133
Durran. *High* 2D 169
Durrant Green. *Kent* 2C 28
Durrants. *Hants* 1F 17
Durrington. *W Sus* 5C 26
Durrington. *Wilts* 2G 23
Dursley. *Glos* 2C 34
Dursley Cross. *Glos* 4B 48
Durston. *Som* 4F 21
Durweston. *Dors* 2D 14
Dury. *Shet* 6F 173
Duston. *Nptn* 4E 62
Duthil. *High* 1D 150
Dutlas. *Powy* 3E 58
Duton Hill. *Essx* 3G 53
Dutson. *Corn* 4D 10
Dutton. *Ches W* 3H 83
Duxford. *Cambs* 1E 53
Duxford. *Oxon* 2B 36
Dwygyfylchi. *Cnwy* 3G 81
Dwyran. *IOA* 4D 80
Dyce. *Aber* 2F 153
Dyffryn. *B'end* 2B 32
Dyffryn. *Carm* 2H 43
Dyffryn. *Pemb* 1D 42
Dyffryn. *V Glam* 4D 32
Dyffryn Ardudwy. *Gwyn* 3E 69
Dyffryn Castell. *Cdgn* 2G 57
Dyffryn Ceidrych. *Carm* 3H 45
Dyffryn Cellwen. *Neat* 5B 46
Dyke. *Linc* 3A 76
Dyke. *Mor* 3D 159
Dykehead. *Ang* 2C 144
Dykehead. *N Lan* 3B 128
Dykehead. *Stir* 4E 135
Dykend. *Ang* 3B 144
Dykesfield. *Cumb* 4E 112
Dylife. *Powy* 1A 58
Dymchurch. *Kent* 3F 29
Dymock. *Glos* 2C 48
Dyrham. *S Glo* 4C 34
Dysart. *Fife* 4F 137
Dyserth. *Den* 3C 82

E

Eachwick. *Nmbd* 2E 115
Eadar Dha Fhadhail. *W Isl* 4C 171
Eagland Hill. *Lanc* 5D 96
Eagle. *Linc* 4F 87
Eagle Barnsdale. *Linc* 4F 87
Eagle Moor. *Linc* 4F 87
Eaglescliffe. *Stoc T* 3B 106
Eaglesfield. *Cumb* 2B 102
Eaglesfield. *Dum* 2D 112
Eaglesham. *E Ren* 4G 127
Eaglethorpe. *Nptn* 1H 63
Eagley. *G Man* 3F 91
Eairy. *IOM* 4B 108
Eakley Lanes. *Mil* 5F 63
Eakring. *Notts* 4D 86
Ealand. *N Lin* 3A 94
Ealing. *G Lon* 2C 38
Eallabus. *Arg* 3B 124
Eals. *Nmbd* 4H 113
Eamont Bridge. *Cumb* 2G 103
Earby. *Lanc* 5B 98
Earcroft. *Bkbn* 2E 91
Eardington. *Shrp* 1B 60
Eardisland. *Here* 5G 59
Eardisley. *Here* 1G 47
Eardiston. *Shrp* 3F 71
Eardiston. *Worc* 4A 60
Earith. *Cambs* 3C 64
Earlais. *High* 2C 154
Earle. *Nmbd* 2D 121
Earlesfield. *Linc* 2G 75
Earlestown. *Mers* 1H 83
Earley. *Wok* 4F 37
Earlham. *Norf* 5D 78
Earlish. *High* 2C 154
Earls Barton. *Nptn* 4F 63
Earls Colne. *Essx* 3B 54
Earls Common. *Worc* 5D 60
Earl's Croome. *Worc* 1D 48
Earlsdon. *W Mid* 3H 61
Earlsferry. *Fife* 3G 137
Earlsford. *Abers* 5F 161
Earl's Green. *Suff* 4C 66
Earlsheaton. *W Yor* 2C 92
Earl Shilton. *Leics* 1B 62
Earl Soham. *Suff* 4E 67
Earl Sterndale. *Derbs* 4E 85
Earlston. *E Ayr* 1D 116
Earlston. *Bord* 1H 119
Earl Stonham. *Suff* 5D 66
Earlstoun. *Dum* 1D 110
Earlswood. *Mon* 2H 33
Earlswood. *Warw* 3F 61
Earlyvale. *Bord* 4F 129
Earnley. *W Sus* 3G 17
Earsairidh. *W Isl* 9C 170
Earsdon. *Tyne* 2G 115
Earsham. *Norf* 2F 67
Earsham Street. *Suff* 3E 67
Earswick. *York* 4A 100
Eartham. *W Sus* 5A 26
Earthcott Green. *S Glo* 3B 34
Easby. *N Yor* 4C 106
(nr. Great Ayton)
Easby. *N Yor* 4E 105
(nr. Richmond)
Easdale. *Arg* 2E 133
Easebourne. *W Sus* 4G 25
Easenhall. *Warw* 3B 62
Eashing. *Surr* 1A 26
Easington. *Buck* 4E 51
Easington. *Dur* 5H 115
Easington. *E Yor* 3G 95
Easington. *Nmbd* 1F 121
Easington. *Oxon* 2C 50
(nr. Banbury)
Easington. *Oxon* 2E 37
(nr. Watlington)
Easington. *Red C* 3E 107
Easington Colliery. *Dur* 5H 115
Easington Lane. *Tyne* 5G 115
Easingwold. *N Yor* 3H 99
Easole Street. *Kent* 5G 41
Eassie. *Ang* 4C 144
Eassie and Nevay. *Ang* 4C 144
East Aberthaw. *V Glam* 5D 32
Eastacombe. *Devn* 4F 19
Eastacott. *Devn* 4G 19
East Allington. *Devn* 4D 8
East Anstey. *Devn* 4B 20
East Anton. *Hants* 2B 24
East Appleton. *N Yor* 5F 105
East Ardsley. *W Yor* 2D 92
East Ashley. *Devn* 1G 11
East Ashling. *W Sus* 2G 17
East Aston. *Hants* 2C 24
East Ayton. *N Yor* 1D 101
East Barkwith. *Linc* 2A 88
East Barnby. *N Yor* 3F 107
East Barnet. *G Lon* 1D 39
East Barns. *E Lot* 2D 130
East Barsham. *Norf* 2B 78
East Beach. *W Sus* 3G 17
East Beckham. *Norf* 1D 78
East Bedfont. *G Lon* 3B 38
East Bennan. *N Ayr* 3D 123
East Bergholt. *Suff* 2D 54
East Bierley. *W Yor* 2B 92
East Blatchington. *E Sus* 5F 27
East Bliney. *Norf* 4B 78
East Bloxworth. *Dors* 3D 15
East Boldre. *Hants* 2B 16
East Bolton. *Nmbd* 3F 121
Eastbourne. *Darl* 3F 105
Eastbourne. *E Sus* 5H 27 & 195
East Brent. *Som* 1G 21
East Bridge. *Suff* 4G 67
East Bridgford. *Notts* 1D 74
East Briscoe. *Dur* 3C 104
East Buckland. *Devn* 3G 19
(nr. Barnstaple)
East Buckland. *Devn* 4C 8
(nr. Thurlestone)

East Budleigh. *Devn* 4D 12
Eastburn. *W Yor* 5C 98
East Burnham. *Buck* 2A 38
East Burrafirth. *Shet* 6E 173
East Burton. *Dors* 4D 14
Eastbury. *Herts* 1B 38
Eastbury. *W Ber* 4B 36
East Butsfield. *Dur* 5E 115
East Butterleigh. *Devn* 2C 12
East Butterwick. *N Lin* 4B 94
Eastby. *N Yor* 4C 98
East Calder. *W Lot* 3D 129
East Carleton. *Norf* 5D 78
East Carlton. *Nptn* 2F 63
East Carlton. *W Yor* 5E 98
East Chaldon. *Dors* 4C 14
East Challow. *Oxon* 3B 36
East Charleton. *Devn* 4D 8
East Chelborough. *Dors* 2A 14
East Chiltington. *E Sus* 4E 27
East Chinnock. *Som* 1H 13
East Chisenbury. *Wilts* 1G 23
Eastchurch. *Kent* 3D 40
East Clandon. *Surr* 5B 38
East Claydon. *Buck* 3F 51
East Clevedon. *N Som* 4H 33
East Clyne. *High* 3F 165
East Clyth. *High* 5E 169
East Coker. *Som* 1A 14
Eastcombe. *Glos* 5D 49
East Combe. *Som* 3E 21
East Common. *N Yor* 1G 93
East Compton. *Som* 2B 22
East Cornworthy. *Devn* 3E 9
Eastcote. *G Lon* 2C 38
Eastcote. *Nptn* 5D 62
Eastcote. *W Mid* 3F 61
Eastcott. *Corn* 1C 10
Eastcott. *Wilts* 1F 23
East Cottingwith. *E Yor* 5B 100
East Coulston. *Wilts* 1E 23
Eastcourt. *Wilts* 5H 35
(nr. Pewsey)
Eastcourt. *Wilts* 2E 35
(nr. Tetbury)
East Cowes. *IOW* 3D 16
East Cowick. *E Yor* 2G 93
East Cowton. *N Yor* 4A 106
East Cramlington. *Nmbd* 2F 115
East Cranmore. *Som* 2B 22
East Creech. *Dors* 4E 15
East Croachy. *High* 1A 150
East Dean. *E Sus* 5G 27
East Dean. *Glos* 3B 48
East Dean. *Hants* 4A 24
East Dean. *W Sus* 4A 26
East Down. *Devn* 2G 19
East Drayton. *Notts* 3E 87
East Dundry. *N Som* 5A 34
East Ella. *Hull* 2D 94
East End. *Cambs* 3C 64
East End. *Dors* 3E 15
East End. *E Yor* 4F 101
(nr. Ulrome)
East End. *E Yor* 2F 95
(nr. Withernsea)
East End. *Hants* 3B 16
(nr. Lymington)
East End. *Hants* 5C 36
(nr. Newbury)
East End. *Herts* 3E 53
East End. *Kent* 3D 40
(nr. Minster)
East End. *Kent* 2C 28
(nr. Tenterden)
East End. *N Som* 4H 33
East End. *Oxon* 4B 50
East End. *Som* 1A 22
East End. *Suff* 2E 54
Easter Ardross. *High* 1A 158
Easter Balgedie. *Per* 3D 136
Easter Balmoral. *Abers* 4G 151
Easter Brae. *High* 2A 158
Easter Buckieburn. *Stir* 1A 128
Easter Bush. *Midl* 3F 129
Easter Compton. *S Glo* 3A 34
Easter Fearn. *High* 5D 164
Easter Galcantray. *High* 4C 158
Eastergate. *W Sus* 5A 26
Easterhouse. *Glas* 3H 127
Easter Howgate. *Midl* 3F 129
Easter Kinkell. *High* 3H 157
Easter Lednathie. *Ang* 2C 144
Easter Ogil. *Ang* 2D 144
Easter Ord. *Abers* 3F 153
Easter Quarff. *Shet* 8F 173
Easter Rhynd. *Per* 2D 136
Easter Skeld. *Shet* 7E 173
Easter Suddie. *High* 3A 158
Easterton. *Wilts* 1F 23
Eastertown. *Som* 1G 21
Easter Tulloch. *Abers* 1G 145
East Everleigh. *Wilts* 1H 23
East Farleigh. *Kent* 5B 40
East Farndon. *Nptn* 2E 62
East Ferry. *Linc* 1F 87
Eastfield. *N Lan* 3B 128
(nr. Caldercruix)
Eastfield. *N Lan* 3B 128
(nr. Harthill)
Eastfield. *N Yor* 1E 101
Eastfield. *S Lan* 3H 127
Eastfield Hall. *Nmbd* 4G 121
East Fortune. *E Lot* 2B 130
East Garforth. *W Yor* 1E 93
East Garston. *W Ber* 4B 36
Eastgate. *Dur* 1C 104
Eastgate. *Norf* 3D 78
East Ginge. *Oxon* 3C 36
East Gores. *Essx* 3B 54
East Goscote. *Leics* 4D 74
East Grafton. *Wilts* 5A 36
East Green. *Suff* 5F 65
East Grimstead. *Wilts* 4H 23
East Grinstead. *W Sus* 2E 27
East Guldeford. *E Sus* 3D 28
East Haddon. *Nptn* 4D 62
East Hagbourne. *Oxon* 3D 36
East Halton. *N Lin* 2E 95
East Ham. *G Lon* 2F 39
Eastham. *Mers* 2F 83
Eastham. *Worc* 4A 60
Eastham Ferry. *Mers* 2F 83
Easthampstead. *Brac* 5G 37
Easthampton. *Here* 4G 59
East Hanney. *Oxon* 2C 36
East Hanningfield. *Essx* 5A 54
East Hardwick. *W Yor* 3E 93
East Harling. *Norf* 2B 66
East Harlsey. *N Yor* 5B 106
East Harnham. *Wilts* 4G 23
East Harptree. *Bath* 1A 22
East Hartford. *Nmbd* 2F 115
East Harting. *W Sus* 1G 17
East Hatch. *Wilts* 4E 23
East Hatley. *Cambs* 5B 64
Easthaugh. *Norf* 4C 78
East Hauxwell. *N Yor* 5E 105
East Haven. *Ang* 5E 145
Eastheath. *Wok* 5G 37
East Heckington. *Linc* 1A 76
East Hedleyhope. *Dur* 5E 115
East Helmsdale. *High* 2H 165
East Hendred. *Oxon* 3C 36
East Heslerton. *N Yor* 2D 100
East Hoathly. *E Sus* 4G 27
East Holme. *Dors* 4D 15
Easthope. *Shrp* 1H 59
Easthorpe. *Essx* 3C 54
Easthorpe. *Leics* 2F 75
East Horrington. *Som* 2A 22
East Horsley. *Surr* 5B 38
East Horton. *Nmbd* 1E 121
Easthouses. *Midl* 3G 129
East Howe. *Bour* 3F 15
East Huntspill. *Som* 2G 21
East Hyde. *C Beds* 4B 52
East Ilsley. *W Ber* 3C 36
Eastington. *Devn* 2H 11
Eastington. *Glos* 4G 49
(nr. Northleach)
Eastington. *Glos* 5C 48
(nr. Stonehouse)
East Keal. *Linc* 4C 88
East Kennett. *Wilts* 5G 35
East Keswick. *W Yor* 5F 99
East Kilbride. *S Lan* 4H 127
East Kirkby. *Linc* 4C 88
East Knapton. *N Yor* 2C 100
East Knighton. *Dors* 4D 14
East Knowstone. *Devn* 4B 20
East Knoyle. *Wilts* 3D 23
East Kyloe. *Nmbd* 1E 121
East Lambrook. *Som* 1H 13
East Langdon. *Kent* 1H 29
East Langton. *Leics* 1E 63
East Langwell. *High* 3E 164
East Lavant. *W Sus* 2G 17
East Lavington. *W Sus* 4A 26
East Layton. *N Yor* 4E 105
Eastleach Martin. *Glos* 5H 49
Eastleach Turville. *Glos* 5G 49
East Leake. *Notts* 3C 74
East Learmouth. *Nmbd* 1C 120
Eastleigh. *Devn* 4E 19
(nr. Bideford)
East Leigh. *Devn* 2H 11
(nr. Crediton)
East Leigh. *Devn* 3C 8
(nr. Modbury)
Eastleigh. *Hants* 1C 16
East Lexham. *Norf* 4A 78
East Lilburn. *Nmbd* 2E 121
Eastling. *Kent* 5D 40
East Linton. *E Lot* 2B 130
East Liss. *Hants* 4F 25
East Lockinge. *Oxon* 3C 36
East Looe. *Corn* 3G 7
East Lound. *N Lin* 1E 87
East Lulworth. *Dors* 4D 14
East Lutton. *N Yor* 3D 100
East Lydford. *Som* 3A 22
East Lyng. *Som* 4G 21
East Mains. *Abers* 4D 152
East Malling. *Kent* 5B 40
East Marden. *W Sus* 1G 17
East Markham. *Notts* 3E 87
East Marton. *N Yor* 4B 98
East Meon. *Hants* 4E 25
East Mersea. *Essx* 4D 54
East Mey. *High* 1F 169
East Midlands Airport.
Leics 3B 74 & 216
East Molesey. *Surr* 4C 38
Eastmoor. *Norf* 5G 77
East Morden. *Dors* 3E 15
East Morton. *W Yor* 5D 98
East Ness. *N Yor* 2A 100
East Newton. *E Yor* 1F 95
East Newton. *N Yor* 2A 100
Eastney. *Port* 3E 17
Eastnor. *Here* 2C 48
East Norton. *Leics* 5E 75
East Nynehead. *Som* 4E 21
East Oakley. *Hants* 1D 24
Eastoft. *N Lin* 3B 94
East Ogwell. *Devn* 5B 12
Easton. *Cambs* 3A 64
Easton. *Cumb* 4D 112
(nr. Burgh by Sands)
Easton. *Cumb* 2F 113
(nr. Longtown)
Easton. *Devn* 4H 11
Easton. *Dors* 5B 14
Easton. *Hants* 3D 24
Easton. *Linc* 3G 75
Easton. *Norf* 4D 78
Easton. *Som* 2A 22
Easton. *Suff* 5E 67
Easton. *Wilts* 4D 35
Easton Grey. *Wilts* 3D 35
Easton-in-Gordano. *N Som* 4A 34
Easton Maudit. *Nptn* 5F 63
Easton on the Hill. *Nptn* 5H 75
Easton Royal. *Wilts* 5H 35
East Orchard. *Dors* 1D 14
East Ord. *Nmbd* 4F 131
East Panson. *Devn* 3D 10
East Peckham. *Kent* 1A 28
East Pennard. *Som* 3A 22
East Perry. *Cambs* 4A 64
East Pitcorthie. *Fife* 3H 137
East Portlemouth. *Devn* 5D 8
East Prawle. *Devn* 5D 9
East Preston. *W Sus* 5B 26
East Putford. *Devn* 1D 10
East Quantoxhead. *Som* 2E 21
East Rainton. *Tyne* 5G 115
East Ravendale. *NE Lin* 1B 88
East Raynham. *Norf* 3A 78
Eastrea. *Cambs* 1B 64
East Rhidorroch Lodge.
High 4G 163
Eastriggs. *Dum* 3D 112
East Rigton. *W Yor* 5F 99
Eastrington. *E Yor* 1A 94
East Rounton. *N Yor* 4B 106
East Row. *N Yor* 3F 107
East Rudham. *Norf* 3H 77
East Runton. *Norf* 1D 78
East Ruston. *Norf* 3F 79
Eastry. *Kent* 5H 41
East Saltoun. *E Lot* 3A 130
East Shaws. *Dur* 3D 105
East Shefford. *W Ber* 4B 36
Eastshore. *Shet* 10E 173
East Sleekburn. *Nmbd* 1F 115
East Somerton. *Norf* 4G 79
East Stockwith. *Linc* 1E 87
East Stoke. *Dors* 4D 14
East Stoke. *Notts* 1E 75
East Stoke. *Som* 1H 13
East Stour. *Dors* 4D 22
East Stourmouth. *Kent* 4G 41
East Stowford. *Devn* 4G 19
East Stratton. *Hants* 2D 24
East Studdal. *Kent* 1H 29
East Taphouse. *Corn* 2F 7
East-the-Water. *Devn* 4E 19
East Thirston. *Nmbd* 5F 121
East Tilbury. *Thur* 3A 40
East Tisted. *Hants* 3F 25
East Torrington. *Linc* 2A 88
East Tuddenham. *Norf* 4C 78
East Tytherley. *Hants* 4A 24
East Tytherton. *Wilts* 4E 35
East Village. *Devn* 2B 12
Eastville. *Linc* 5D 88
East Wall. *Shrp* 1H 59
East Walton. *Norf* 4G 77
East Week. *Devn* 3G 11
Eastwell. *Leics* 3E 75
East Wellow. *Hants* 4B 24
East Wemyss. *Fife* 4F 137
East Whitburn. *W Lot* 3C 128
Eastwick. *Herts* 4E 53
Eastwick. *Shet* 4E 173
East Williamston. *Pemb* 4E 43
East Winch. *Norf* 4F 77
East Winterslow. *Wilts* 3H 23
East Wittering. *W Sus* 3F 17
East Witton. *N Yor* 1D 98
Eastwood. *Notts* 1B 74
Eastwood. *S'end* 2C 40
East Woodburn. *Nmbd* 1C 114
Eastwood End. *Cambs* 1D 64
East Woodhay. *Hants* 5C 36
East Woodlands. *Som* 2C 22
East Worldham. *Hants* 3F 25
East Worlington. *Devn* 1A 12
East Wretham. *Norf* 1B 66
East Youlstone. *Devn* 1C 10
Eathorpe. *Warw* 4A 62
Eaton. *Ches E* 4C 84
Eaton. *Ches W* 4H 83
Eaton. *Leics* 3E 75
Eaton. *Norf* 2F 77
(nr. Heacham)
Eaton. *Norf* 5E 78
(nr. Norwich)
Eaton. *Notts* 3E 86
Eaton. *Oxon* 5C 50
Eaton. *Shrp* 2F 59
(nr. Bishop's Castle)
Eaton. *Shrp* 1H 59
(nr. Church Stretton)
Eaton Bishop. *Here* 2H 47
Eaton Bray. *C Beds* 3H 51
Eaton Constantine. *Shrp* 5H 71
Eaton Hastings. *Oxon* 2A 36
Eaton Socon. *Cambs* 5A 64
Eaton upon Tern. *Shrp* 3A 72
Eau Brink. *Norf* 4E 77
Eaves Green. *W Mid* 2G 61
Ebberley Hill. *Devn* 1F 11
Ebberston. *N Yor* 1C 100
Ebbesbourne Wake. *Wilts* 4E 23
Ebblake. *Dors* 2G 15
Ebbsfleet. *Kent* 3H 39
Ebbw Vale. *Blae* 5E 47
Ebchester. *Dur* 4E 115
Ebernoe. *W Sus* 3A 26
Ebford. *Devn* 4C 12
Ebley. *Glos* 5D 48
Ebnal. *Ches W* 1G 71
Ebrington. *Glos* 1G 49
Ecchinswell. *Hants* 1D 24
Ecclefechan. *Dum* 2C 112
Eccles. *G Man* 1B 84
Eccles. *Kent* 4B 40
Eccles. *Bord* 5D 130
Ecclesall. *S Yor* 2H 85
Ecclesfield. *S Yor* 1A 86
Eccles Green. *Here* 1G 47
Eccleshall. *Staf* 3C 72
Eccleshill. *W Yor* 1B 92
Ecclesmachan. *W Lot* 2D 128
Eccles on Sea. *Norf* 3G 79
Eccles Road. *Norf* 1C 66
Eccleston. *Ches W* 4G 83
Eccleston. *Lanc* 3D 90
Eccleston. *Mers* 1G 83
Eccup. *W Yor* 5E 99
Echt. *Abers* 3E 153
Eckford. *Bord* 2B 120
Eckington. *Derbs* 3B 86
Eckington. *Worc* 1E 49
Ecton. *Nptn* 4F 63
Edale. *Derbs* 2F 85
Eday Airport. *Orkn* 4E 172
Edburton. *W Sus* 4D 26
Edderside. *Cumb* 5C 112
Edderton. *High* 5E 164
Eddington. *Kent* 4F 41
Eddington. *W Ber* 5B 36
Eddleston. *Bord* 5F 129
Eddlewood. *S Lan* 4A 128
Edenbridge. *Kent* 1F 27
Edendonich. *Arg* 1A 134
Edenfield. *Lanc* 3G 91
Edenhall. *Cumb* 1G 103
Edenham. *Linc* 3H 75
Edensor. *Derbs* 4G 85
Edentaggart. *Arg* 4C 134
Edenthorpe. *S Yor* 4G 93
Eden Vale. *Dur* 1B 106
Edern. *Gwyn* 2B 68
Edgarley. *Som* 3A 22
Edgbaston. *W Mid* 2E 61
Edgcott. *Buck* 3E 51
Edgcott. *Som* 3B 20
Edge. *Glos* 5D 48
Edge. *Shrp* 5F 71
Edgebolton. *Shrp* 3H 71
Edge End. *Glos* 4A 48
Edgefield. *Norf* 2C 78
Edgefield Street. *Norf* 2C 78
Edge Green. *Ches W* 5G 83
Edgehead. *Midl* 3G 129
Edgeley. *Shrp* 1H 71
Edgeside. *Lanc* 2G 91
Edgeworth. *Glos* 5E 49
Edgiock. *Worc* 4E 61
Edgmond. *Telf* 4B 72
Edgmond Marsh. *Telf* 3B 72
Edgton. *Shrp* 2F 59
Edgware. *G Lon* 1C 38
Edgworth. *Bkbn* 3F 91
Edinbane. *High* 3C 154
Edinburgh. *Edin* 2F 129 & 194
Edinburgh Airport. *Edin* 2E 129
Edingale. *Staf* 4G 73
Edingley. *Notts* 5D 86
Edingthorpe. *Norf* 2F 79
Edington. *Som* 3G 21
Edington. *Wilts* 1E 23
Edingworth. *Som* 1G 21
Edistone. *Devn* 4C 18
Edithmead. *Som* 2G 21
Edith Weston. *Rut* 5G 75
Edlaston. *Derbs* 1F 73
Edlesborough. *Buck* 4H 51
Edlingham. *Nmbd* 4F 121
Edlington. *Linc* 3B 88
Edmondsham. *Dors* 1F 15
Edmondsley. *Dur* 5F 115
Edmondthorpe. *Leics* 4F 75
Edmonstone. *Orkn* 5E 172
Edmonton. *Corn* 1D 6
Edmonton. *G Lon* 1E 39
Edmundbyers. *Dur* 4D 114
Ednam. *Bord* 1B 120
Ednaston. *Derbs* 1G 73
Edney Common. *Essx* 5G 53
Edrom. *Bord* 4E 131
Edstaston. *Shrp* 2H 71
Edstone. *Warw* 4F 61
Edwalton. *Notts* 2D 74
Edwardstone. *Suff* 1C 54
Edwardsville. *Mer T* 2D 32
Edwinsford. *Carm* 2G 45
Edwinstowe. *Notts* 4D 86
Edworth. *C Beds* 1C 52
Edwyn Ralph. *Here* 5A 60
Edzell. *Ang* 2F 145
Efail-fach. *Neat* 2A 32
Efail Isaf. *Rhon* 3D 32
Efailnewydd. *Gwyn* 2C 68
Efail-rhyd. *Powy* 3D 70
Efailwen. *Carm* 2F 43
Efenechtyd. *Den* 5D 82
Effingham. *Surr* 5C 38
Effingham Common. *Surr* 5C 38
Effirth. *Shet* 6E 173
Efflinch. *Staf* 4F 73
Efford. *Devn* 2B 12
Efstigarth. *Shet* 2F 173
Egbury. *Hants* 1C 24
Egdon. *Worc* 5D 60
Egerton. *G Man* 3F 91
Egerton. *Kent* 1D 28
Egerton Forstal. *Kent* 1C 28
Eggborough. *N Yor* 2F 93
Eggbuckland. *Plym* 3A 8
Eggesford. *Devn* 1G 11
Eggington. *C Beds* 3H 51
Egginton. *Derbs* 3G 73
Egglescliffe. *Stoc T* 3B 106
Eggleston. *Dur* 2C 104
Egham. *Surr* 3B 38
Egham Hythe. *Surr* 3B 38
Egleton. *Rut* 5F 75
Eglingham. *Nmbd* 3F 121
Egloshayle. *Corn* 5A 10
Egloskerry. *Corn* 4C 10
Eglwysbach. *Cnwy* 3H 81
Eglwys Brewis. *V Glam* 5D 32
Eglwys Fach. *Cdgn* 1F 57
Eglwyswrw. *Pemb* 1F 43
Egmanton. *Notts* 4E 87
Egmere. *Norf* 2B 78
Egremont. *Cumb* 3B 102
Egremont. *Mers* 1F 83
Egton. *N Yor* 4F 107
Egton Bridge. *N Yor* 4F 107
Egypt. *Buck* 2A 38
Egypt. *Hants* 2C 24
Eight Ash Green. *Essx* 3C 54
Eight Mile Burn. *Midl* 4E 129
Eignaig. *High* 4B 140
Eilanreach. *High* 2G 147
Eildon. *Bord* 1H 119
Eileanach Lodge. *High* 2H 157
Eilean Fhlodaigh. *W Isl* 3D 170
Eilean Iarmain. *High* 2F 147
Einacleit. *W Isl* 5D 171
Eisgein. *W Isl* 6F 171
Eisingrug. *Gwyn* 2F 69
Elan Village. *Powy* 4B 58
Elberton. *S Glo* 3B 34
Elbridge. *W Sus* 5A 26
Elburton. *Plym* 3B 8
Elcho. *Per* 1D 136
Elcombe. *Swin* 3G 35
Elcot. *W Ber* 5B 36
Eldernell. *Cambs* 1C 64
Eldersfield. *Worc* 2D 48
Elderslie. *Ren* 3F 127
Elder Street. *Essx* 2F 53
Eldon. *Dur* 2F 105
Eldroth. *N Yor* 3G 97
Eldwick. *W Yor* 5D 98
Elfhowe. *Cumb* 5F 103
Elford. *Nmbd* 1F 121
Elford. *Staf* 4F 73
Elford Closes. *Cambs* 3D 65
Elgin. *Mor* 2G 159
Elgol. *High* 2D 146
Elham. *Kent* 1F 29
Elie. *Fife* 3G 137
Eling. *Hants* 1B 16
Eling. *W Ber* 4D 36
Elishaw. *Nmbd* 5C 120
Elizafield. *Dum* 2B 112
Elkesley. *Notts* 3D 86
Elkington. *Nptn* 3D 62
Elkins Green. *Essx* 5G 53
Elkstone. *Glos* 4E 49
Ellan. *High* 1C 150
Elland. *W Yor* 2B 92
Ellary. *Arg* 2F 125
Ellastone. *Staf* 1F 73
Ellbridge. *Corn* 2A 8
Ellel. *Lanc* 4D 97
Ellemford. *Bord* 3D 130
Ellenabeich. *Arg* 2E 133
Ellenborough. *Cumb* 1B 102
Ellenbrook. *Herts* 5C 52
Ellenhall. *Staf* 3C 72
Ellen's Green. *Surr* 2B 26

Ellerbec. N Yor 5B 106
Ellerburn. N Yor 1C 100
Ellerby. N Yor 3E 107
Ellerdine. Telf 3A 72
Ellerdine Heath. Telf 3A 72
Ellerhayes. Devn 2C 12
Elleric. Arg 4E 141
Ellerker. E Yor 2C 94
Ellerton. E Yor 1H 93
Ellerton. N Yor 5F 105
Ellerton. Shrp 3B 72
Ellesborough. Buck 5G 51
Ellesmere. Shrp 2F 71
Ellesmere Port. Ches W 3G 83
Ellingham. Hants 2G 15
Ellingham. Norf 1F 67
Ellingham. Nmbd 2F 121
Ellingstring. N Yor 1D 98
Ellington. Cambs 3A 64
Ellington. Nmbd 5G 121
Ellington Thorpe. Cambs 3A 64
Elliot. Ang 5F 145
Ellisfield. Hants 2E 25
Ellishadder. High 2E 155
Ellistown. Leics 4B 74
Ellon. Abers 5G 161
Ellonby. Cumb 1F 103
Ellough. Suff 2G 67
Elloughton. E Yor 2C 94
Ellwood. Glos 5A 48
Elm. Cambs 5D 76
Elmbridge. Glos 4D 48
Elmbridge. Worc 4D 60
Elmdon. Essx 2E 53
Elmdon. W Mid 2F 61
Elmdon Heath. W Mid 2F 61
Elmesthorpe. Leics 1B 62
Elmfield. IOW 3D 16
Elm Hill. Dors 4D 22
Elmhurst. Staf 4F 73
Elmley Castle. Worc 1E 49
Elmley Lovett. Worc 4C 60
Elmore. Glos 4C 48
Elmore Back. Glos 4C 48
Elm Park. G Lon 2G 39
Elmscott. Devn 4C 18
Elmsett. Suff 1D 54
Elmstead. Essx 3D 54
Elmstead Heath. Essx 3D 54
Elmstead Market. Essx 3D 54
Elmsted. Kent 1F 29
Elmstone. Kent 4G 41
Elmstone Hardwicke. Glos 3E 49
Elmswell. E Yor 4D 101
Elmswell. Suff 4B 66
Elmton. Derbs 3C 86
Elphin. High 2G 163
Elphinstone. E Lot 2G 129
Elrick. Abers 3F 153
Elrick. Mor 1B 152
Elrig. Dum 5A 110
Elsdon. Nmbd 5D 120
Elsecar. S Yor 1A 86
Elsenham. Essx 3F 53
Elsfield. Oxon 4D 50
Elsham. N Lin 3D 94
Elsing. Norf 4C 78
Elslack. N Yor 5B 98
Elsrickle. S Lan 5D 128
Elstead. Surr 1A 26
Elsted. W Sus 1G 17
Elsted Marsh. W Sus 4G 25
Elsthorpe. Linc 3H 75
Elstob. Dur 2A 106
Elston. Devn 2A 12
Elston. Lanc 1E 90
Elston. Notts 1E 75
Elston. Wilts 2F 23
Elstone. Devn 1G 11
Elstow. Bed 1A 52
Elstree. Herts 1C 38
Elstronwick. E Yor 1F 95
Elswick. Lanc 1C 90
Elswick. Tyne 3F 115
Elsworth. Cambs 4C 64
Elterwater. Cumb 4E 103
Eltham. G Lon 3F 39
Eltisley. Cambs 5B 64
Elton. Cambs 1H 63
Elton. Ches W 3G 83
Elton. Derbs 4G 85
Elton. Glos 4C 48
Elton. G Man 3F 91
Elton. Here 3G 59
Elton. Notts 2E 75
Elton. Stoc T 3B 106
Elton Green. Ches W 3G 83
Eltringham. Nmbd 3D 115
Elvanfoot. S Lan 3B 118
Elvaston. Derbs 2B 74
Elveden. Suff 3H 65
Elvetham Heath. Hants 1F 25
Elvingston. E Lot 2A 130
Elvington. Kent 5G 41
Elvington. York 5B 100
Elwick. Hart 1B 106
Elwick. Nmbd 1F 121
Elworth. Ches E 4B 84
Elworth. Dors 4A 14
Elworthy. Som 3D 20
Ely. Cambs 2E 65
Ely. Card 4E 33
Emberton. Mil 1G 51
Embleton. Cumb 1C 102
Embleton. Dur 2B 106
Embleton. Nmbd 2G 121
Embo. High 4F 165
Emborough. Som 1B 22
Embo Street. High 4F 165
Embsay. N Yor 4C 98
Emery Down. Hants 2A 16
Emley. W Yor 3C 92
Emmbrook. Wok 5F 37
Emmer Green. Read 4F 37
Emmington. Oxon 5F 51
Emneth. Norf 5D 77
Emneth Hungate. Norf 5E 77
Empingham. Rut 5G 75
Empshott. Hants 3F 25
Emsworth. Hants 2F 17
Enborne. W Ber 5C 36
Enborne Row. W Ber 5C 36
Enchmarsh. Shrp 1H 59
Enderby. Leics 1C 62
Endmoor. Cumb 1E 97
Endon. Staf 5D 84
Endon Bank. Staf 5D 84
Enfield. G Lon 1E 39
Enfield Wash. G Lon 1E 39
Enford. Wilts 1G 23
Engine Common. S Glo 3B 34
Englefield. W Ber 4E 36
Englefield Green. Surr 3A 38
Engleseabrook. Ches E 5B 84
English Bicknor. Glos 4A 48
Englishcombe. Bath 5C 34
English Frankton. Shrp 3G 71
Enham Alamein. Hants 2B 24
Enmore. Som 3F 21
Ennerdale Bridge. Cumb 3B 102
Enniscaven. Corn 3D 6
Enoch. Dum 4A 118
Enochdhu. Per 2H 143
Ensay. Arg 4E 139
Ensbury. Bour 3F 15
Ensdon. Shrp 4G 71
Ensis. Devn 4F 19
Enson. Staf 3D 72
Enstone. Oxon 3B 50
Enterkinfoot. Dum 4A 118
Enville. Staf 2C 60
Eolaigearraidh. W Isl 8C 170
Eorabus. Arg 1A 132
Eoropaidh. W Isl 1H 171
Epney. Glos 4C 48
Epperstone. Notts 1D 74
Epping. Essx 5E 53
Epping Green. Essx 5E 53
Epping Green. Herts 5C 52
Epping Upland. Essx 5E 53
Eppleby. N Yor 3E 105
Eppleworth. E Yor 1D 94
Epsom. Surr 4D 38
Epwell. Oxon 1B 50
Epworth. N Lin 4A 94
Epworth Turbary. N Lin 4A 94
Erbistock. Wrex 1F 71
Erbusaig. High 1F 147
Erchless Castle. High 4G 157
Erdington. W Mid 1F 61
Eredine. Arg 3G 133
Eriboll. High 3E 167
Ericstane. Dum 3C 118
Eridge Green. E Sus 2G 27
Erines. Arg 2G 125
Eriswell. Suff 3G 65
Erith. G Lon 3G 39
Erlestoke. Wilts 1E 23
Ermine. Linc 3G 87
Ermington. Devn 3C 8
Ernesettle. Plym 3A 8
Erpingham. Norf 2D 78
Erriottwood. Kent 5D 40
Errogie. High 1H 149
Errol. Per 1E 137
Errol Station. Per 1E 137
Erskine. Ren 2F 127
Erskine Bridge. Ren 2F 127
Ervie. Dum 3F 109
Erwarton. Suff 2F 55
Erwood. Powy 1D 46
Eryholme. N Yor 4A 106
Eryrys. Den 5E 82
Escalls. Corn 4A 4
Escomb. Dur 1E 105
Escrick. N Yor 5A 100
Esgair. Carm 3D 45
(nr. Carmarthen)
Esgair. Carm 3G 43
(nr. St Clears)
Esgairgeiliog. Powy 5G 69
Esh. Dur 5E 115
Esher. Surr 4C 38
Esholt. W Yor 5D 98
Eshott. Nmbd 5G 121
Eshton. N Yor 4B 98
Esh Winning. Dur 5E 115
Eskadale. High 5G 157
Eskbank. Midl 3G 129
Eskdale Green. Cumb 4C 102
Eskdalemuir. Dum 5E 119
Eskham. Linc 1C 88
Esknish. Arg 3B 124
Esk Valley. N Yor 4F 107
Eslington Hall. Nmbd 3E 121
Espley Hall. Nmbd 5F 121
Esprick. Lanc 1C 90
Essendine. Rut 4H 75
Essendon. Herts 5C 52
Essich. High 5A 158
Essington. Staf 5D 72
Eston. Red C 3C 106
Estover. Plym 3B 8
Eswick. Shet 6F 173
Etal. Nmbd 1D 120
Etchilhampton. Wilts 5F 35
Etchingham. E Sus 3B 28
Etchinghill. Kent 2F 29
Etchinghill. Staf 4E 73
Etherley Dene. Dur 2E 105
Ethie Haven. Ang 4F 145
Etling Green. Norf 4C 78
Etloe. Glos 5B 48
Eton. Wind 3A 38
Eton Wick. Wind 3A 38
Etteridge. High 4A 150
Ettersgill. Dur 2B 104
Ettiley Heath. Ches E 4B 84
Ettington. Warw 1A 50
Etton. E Yor 5D 101
Etton. Pet 5A 76
Ettrick. Bord 3E 119
Ettrickbridge. Bord 2F 119
Etwall. Derbs 2G 73
Eudon Burnell. Shrp 2B 60
Eudon George. Shrp 2A 60
Euston. Suff 3A 66
Euxton. Lanc 3D 90
Evanstown. B'end 3C 32
Evanton. High 2A 158
Evedon. Linc 1H 75
Evelix. High 4E 165
Evendine. Here 1C 48
Evenjobb. Powy 4E 59
Evenley. Nptn 2D 50
Evenlode. Glos 3H 49
Even Swindon. Swin 3G 35
Evenwood. Dur 2E 105
Evenwood Gate. Dur 2E 105
Everbay. Orkn 5F 172
Evercreech. Som 3B 22
Everdon. Nptn 5C 62
Everingham. E Yor 5C 100
Everleigh. Wilts 1H 23
Everley. N Yor 1D 100
Eversholt. C Beds 2H 51
Evershot. Dors 2A 14
Eversley. Hants 5F 37
Eversley Centre. Hants 5F 37
Eversley Cross. Hants 5F 37
Everthorpe. E Yor 1C 94
Everton. C Beds 5B 64
Everton. Hants 3A 16
Everton. Mers 1F 83
Everton. Notts 1D 86
Evertown. Dum 2E 113
Evesbatch. Here 1B 48
Evesham. Worc 1F 49
Evington. Leic 5D 74
Ewden Village. S Yor 1G 85
Ewdness. Shrp 1B 60
Ewell. Surr 4D 38
Ewell Minnis. Kent 1G 29
Ewelme. Oxon 2E 37
Ewen. Glos 2F 35
Ewenny. V Glam 4C 32
Ewerby. Linc 1A 76
Ewes. Dum 5F 119
Ewesley. Nmbd 5E 121
Ewhurst. Surr 1B 26
Ewhurst Green. E Sus 3B 28
Ewhurst Green. Surr 2B 26
Ewlo. Flin 4F 83
Ewloe. Flin 4F 83
Ewood Bridge. Lanc 2F 91
Eworthy. Devn 3E 11
Ewshot. Hants 1G 25
Ewyas Harold. Here 3G 47
Exbourne. Devn 2G 11
Exbury. Hants 2C 16
Exceat. E Sus 5G 27
Exebridge. Som 4C 20
Exelby. N Yor 1E 99
Exeter. Devn 3C 12 & 195
Exeter International Airport. Devn 3D 12
Exford. Som 3B 20
Exfords Green. Shrp 5G 71
Exhall. Warw 5F 61
Exlade Street. Oxon 3E 37
Exminster. Devn 4C 12
Exmoor. Som 3B 20
Exmouth. Devn 4D 12
Exnaboe. Shet 10E 173
Exning. Suff 4F 65
Exton. Devn 4C 12
Exton. Hants 4E 24
Exton. Rut 4G 75
Exton. Som 3C 20
Exwick. Devn 3C 12
Eyam. Derbs 3G 85
Eydon. Nptn 5C 62
Eye. Here 4G 59
Eye. Pet 5B 76
Eye. Suff 3D 66
Eye Green. Pet 5B 76
Eyemouth. Bord 3F 131
Eyeworth. C Beds 1C 52
Eyhorne Street. Kent 5C 40
Eyke. Suff 5F 67
Eynesbury. Cambs 5A 64
Eynort. High 1B 146
Eynsford. Kent 4G 39
Eynsham. Oxon 5C 50
Eyre. High 3D 154
(on Isle of Skye)
Eyre. High 5E 155
(on Raasay)
Eythorne. Kent 1G 29
Eyton. Here 4G 59
Eyton. Shrp 2F 59
(nr. Bishop's Castle)
Eyton. Shrp 4F 71
(nr. Shrewsbury)
Eyton. Wrex 1F 71
Eyton on Severn. Shrp 5H 71
Eyton upon the Weald Moors. Telf 4A 72

F

Faccombe. Hants 1B 24
Faceby. N Yor 4B 106
Faddiley. Ches E 5H 83
Fadmoor. N Yor 1A 100
Fagwyr. Swan 5G 45
Faichem. High 3E 149
Faifley. W Dun 2G 127
Fail. S Ayr 2D 116
Failand. N Som 4A 34
Failford. S Ayr 2D 116
Failsworth. G Man 4H 91
Fairbourne. Gwyn 4F 69
Fairbourne Heath. Kent 5C 40
Fairburn. N Yor 2E 93
Fairfield. Derbs 3E 85
Fairfield. Kent 3D 28
Fairfield. Worc 3D 60
(nr. Bromsgrove)
Fairfield. Worc 1F 49
(nr. Evesham)
Fairford. Glos 5G 49
Fair Green. Norf 4F 77
Fair Hill. Cumb 1G 103
Fairhill. S Lan 4A 128
Fair Isle Airport. Shet 1B 172
Fairlands. Surr 5A 38
Fairlie. N Ayr 4D 126
Fairlight. E Sus 4C 28
Fairlight Cove. E Sus 4C 28
Fairmile. Devn 3D 12
Fairmile. Surr 4C 38
Fairmilehead. Edin 3F 129
Fair Oak. Devn 1D 12
Fair Oak. Hants 1C 16
(nr. Eastleigh)
Fair Oak. Hants 5D 36
(nr. Kingsclere)
Fairoak. Staf 2B 72
Fair Oak Green. Hants 5E 37
Fairseat. Kent 4H 39
Fairstead. Essx 4A 54
Fairstead. Norf 4F 77
Fairwarp. E Sus 3F 27
Fairwater. Card 4E 33
Fairy Cross. Devn 4E 19
Fakenham. Norf 3B 78
Fakenham Magna. Suff 3B 66
Fala. Midl 3H 129
Fala Dam. Midl 3H 129
Falcon. Here 2B 48
Faldingworth. Linc 2H 87
Falfield. S Glo 2B 34
Falkenham. Suff 2F 55
Falkirk. Falk 2B 128
Falkland. Fife 3E 137
Fallin. Stir 4H 135
Fallowfield. G Man 1C 84
Falmer. E Sus 5E 27
Falmouth. Corn 5C 6
Falsgrave. N Yor 1E 101
Falstone. Nmbd 1A 114
Fanagmore. High 4B 166
Fancott. C Beds 3A 52
Fanellan. High 4G 157
Fangdale Beck. N Yor 5C 106
Fangfoss. E Yor 4B 100
Fankerton. Falk 1A 128
Fanmore. Arg 4F 139
Fanner's Green. Essx 4G 53
Fannich Lodge. High 2E 156
Fans. Bord 5C 130
Farcet. Cambs 1B 64
Far Cotton. Nptn 5E 63
Fareham. Hants 2D 16
Farewell. Staf 4E 73
Far Forest. Worc 3B 60
Farforth. Linc 3C 88
Far Green. Glos 5C 48
Far Hoarcross. Staf 3F 73
Faringdon. Oxon 2A 36
Farington. Lanc 2D 90
Farlam. Cumb 4G 113
Farleigh. N Som 5H 33
Farleigh. Surr 4E 39
Farleigh Hungerford. Som 1D 22
Farleigh Wallop. Hants 2E 24
Farleigh Wick. Wilts 5D 34
Farlesthorpe. Linc 3D 88
Farleton. Cumb 1E 97
Farleton. Lanc 3E 97
Farley. High 4G 157
Farley. N Som 4H 33
Farley. Shrp 5F 71
(nr. Shrewsbury)
Farley. Shrp 5A 72
(nr. Telford)
Farley. Staf 1E 73
Farley. Wilts 4H 23
Farley Green. Suff 5G 65
Farley Green. Surr 1B 26
Farley Hill. Wok 5F 37
Farley's End. Glos 4C 48
Farlington. N Yor 3A 100
Farlington. Port 2E 17
Farlow. Shrp 2A 60
Farmborough. Bath 5B 34
Farmcote. Glos 3F 49
Farmcote. Shrp 1B 60
Farmington. Glos 4G 49
Far Moor. G Man 4D 90
Farmoor. Oxon 5C 50
Farmtown. Mor 3C 160
Farnah Green. Derbs 1H 73
Farnborough. G Lon 4F 39
Farnborough. Hants 1G 25
Farnborough. Warw 1C 50
Farnborough. W Ber 3C 36
Farncombe. Surr 1A 26
Farndish. Bed 4G 63
Farndon. Ches W 5G 83
Farndon. Notts 5E 87
Farnell. Ang 3F 145
Farnham. Dors 1E 15
Farnham. Essx 3E 53
Farnham. N Yor 3F 99
Farnham. Suff 4F 67
Farnham. Surr 2G 25
Farnham Common. Buck 2A 38
Farnham Green. Essx 3E 53
Farnham Royal. Buck 2A 38
Farnhill. N Yor 5C 98
Farningham. Kent 4G 39
Farnley. N Yor 5E 98
Farnley Tyas. W Yor 3B 92
Farnsfield. Notts 5D 86
Farnworth. G Man 4F 91
Farnworth. Hal 2H 83
Far Oakridge. Glos 5E 49
Farr. High 2H 167
(nr. Bettyhill)
Farr. High 5A 158
(nr. Inverness)
Farr. High 3C 150
(nr. Kingussie)
Farraline. High 1H 149
Farringdon. Devn 3D 12
Farrington. Dors 1D 14
Farrington Gurney. Bath 1B 22
Far Sawrey. Cumb 5E 103
Farsley. W Yor 1C 92
Farthinghoe. Nptn 2D 50
Farthingstone. Nptn 5D 62
Farthorpe. Linc 3B 88
Fartown. W Yor 3B 92
Farway. Devn 3E 13
Fasag. High 3A 156
Fascadale. High 1G 139
Fasnacloich. Arg 4E 141
Fassfern. High 1E 141
Fatfield. Tyne 4G 115
Faugh. Cumb 4G 113
Fauld. Staf 3F 73
Fauldhouse. W Lot 3C 128
Faulkbourne. Essx 4A 54
Faulkland. Som 1C 22
Fauls. Shrp 2H 71
Faverdale. Darl 3F 105
Faversham. Kent 4E 40
Fawdington. N Yor 2G 99
Fawfieldhead. Staf 4E 85
Fawkham Green. Kent 4G 39
Fawler. Oxon 4B 50
Fawley. Buck 3F 37
Fawley. Hants 2C 16
Fawley. W Ber 3B 36
Fawley Chapel. Here 3A 48
Fawton. Corn 2F 7
Faxfleet. E Yor 2B 94
Faygate. W Sus 2D 26
Fazakerley. Mers 1F 83
Fazeley. Staf 5F 73
Feabuie. High 4B 158
Feagour. High 4H 149
Fearann Dhomhnaill. High 3E 147
Fearby. N Yor 1D 98
Fearn. High 1C 158
Fearnan. Per 4E 142
Fearnbeg. High 3G 155
Fearnhead. Warr 1A 84
Fearnmore. High 2G 155
Featherstone. Staf 5D 72
Featherstone. W Yor 2E 93
Featherstone Castle. Nmbd 3H 113
Feckenham. Worc 4E 61
Feering. Essx 3B 54
Feetham. N Yor 5C 104

Feizor. N Yor 3G 97
Felbridge. Surr 2E 27
Felbrigg. Norf 2E 78
Felcourt. Surr 1E 27
Felden. Herts 5A 52
Felhampton. Shrp 2G 59
Felindre. Carm 3F 45 (nr. Llandeilo)
Felindre. Carm 2G 45 (nr. Llandovery)
Felindre. Carm 2D 44 (nr. Newcastle Emlyn)
Felindre. Powy 2D 58
Felindre. Swan 5G 45
Felindre Farchog. Pemb 1F 43
Felinfach. Cdgn 5E 57
Felinfach. Powy 2D 46
Felinfoel. Carm 5F 45
Felingwmisaf. Carm 3F 45
Felingwmuchaf. Carm 3F 45
Felin Newydd. Powy 5C 70 (nr. Newtown)
Felin Newydd. Powy 3E 70 (nr. Oswestry)
Felin Wnda. Cdgn 1D 44
Felinwynt. Cdgn 5B 56
Felixkirk. N Yor 1G 99
Felixstowe. Suff 2F 55
Felixstowe Ferry. Suff 2G 55
Felkington. Nmbd 5F 131
Fell End. Cumb 5A 104
Felling. Tyne 3F 115
Fell Side. Cumb 1E 102
Felmersham. Bed 5G 63
Felmingham. Norf 3E 79
Felpham. W Sus 3H 17
Felsham. Suff 5B 66
Felsted. Essx 3G 53
Feltham. G Lon 3C 38
Felthamhill. Surr 3B 38
Felthorpe. Norf 4D 78
Felton. Here 1A 48
Felton. N Som 5A 34
Felton. Nmbd 4F 121
Felton Butler. Shrp 4F 71
Feltwell. Norf 1G 65
Fenay Bridge. W Yor 3B 92
Fence. Lanc 1G 91
Fence Houses. Tyne 4G 115
Fencott. Oxon 4D 50
Fen Ditton. Cambs 4D 65
Fen Drayton. Cambs 4C 64
Fen End. Linc 3B 76
Fen End. W Mid 3G 61
Fenham. Nmbd 5G 131
Fenham. Tyne 3F 115
Fenhouses. Linc 1B 76
Feniscowles. Bkbn 2E 91
Feniton. Devn 3D 12
Fenn Green. Shrp 2B 60
Fenn's Bank. Wrex 2H 71
Fenn Street. Medw 3B 40
Fenny Bentley. Derbs 5F 85
Fenny Bridges. Devn 3E 12
Fenny Compton. Warw 5B 62
Fenny Drayton. Leics 1A 62
Fenny Stratford. Mil 2G 51
Fenrother. Nmbd 5F 121
Fenstanton. Cambs 4C 64
Fen Street. Norf 1C 66
Fenton. Cambs 3C 64
Fenton. Cumb 4G 113
Fenton. Linc 5F 87 (nr. Caythorpe)
Fenton. Linc 3F 87 (nr. Saxilby)
Fenton. Nmbd 1D 120
Fenton. Notts 2E 87
Fenton. Stoke 1C 72
Fentonadle. Corn 5A 10
Fenton Barns. E Lot 1B 130
Fenwick. E Ayr 5F 127
Fenwick. Nmbd 5G 131 (nr. Berwick-upon-Tweed)
Fenwick. Nmbd 2D 114 (nr. Hexham)
Fenwick. S Yor 3F 93
Feochaig. Arg 4B 122
Feock. Corn 5C 6
Feolin Ferry. Arg 3C 124
Feorlan. Arg 5A 122
Ferindonald. High 3E 147
Feriniquarrie. High 3A 154
Fern. Ang 2D 145
Ferndale. Rhon 2C 32
Ferndown. Dors 2F 15
Ferness. High 4D 158
Fernham. Oxon 2A 36
Fernhill. W Sus 1D 27
Fernhill Heath. Worc 5C 60
Fernhurst. W Sus 4G 25
Fernieflatt. Abers 1H 145
Ferniegair. S Lan 4A 128
Fernilea. High 5C 154
Fernilee. Derbs 3E 85
Ferrensby. N Yor 3F 99
Ferriby Sluice. N Lin 2C 94
Ferring. W Sus 5C 26
Ferrybridge. W Yor 2E 93
Ferryden. Ang 3G 145
Ferryhill. Aber 3G 153
Ferry Hill. Cambs 2C 64
Ferryhill. Dur 1F 105
Ferryhill Station. Dur 1F 105
Ferryside. Carm 4D 44
Ferryton. High 2A 158
Fersfield. Norf 2C 66
Fersit. High 1A 142
Feshiebridge. High 3C 150
Fetcham. Surr 5C 38
Fetterangus. Abers 3G 161
Fettercairn. Abers 1F 145
Fewcott. Oxon 3D 50
Fewston. N Yor 4D 98
Ffairfach. Carm 3G 45
Ffair Rhos. Cdgn 4G 57
Ffaldybrenin. Carm 1G 45
Ffarmers. Carm 1G 45
Ffawyddog. Powy 4F 47
Ffodun. Powy 5E 71
Ffont-y-gari. V Glam 5D 32
Fforest. Carm 5F 45
Fforest-fach. Swan 3F 31
Fforest Goch. Neat 5H 45
Ffostrasol. Cdgn 1D 44
Ffos-y-ffin. Cdgn 4D 56
Ffrith. Flin 5E 83
Ffrwdgrech. Powy 3D 46
Ffwl-y-mwn. V Glam 5D 32
Ffynnon-ddrain. Carm 3E 45
Ffynnongroyw. Flin 2D 82
Ffynnon Gynydd. Powy 1E 47
Ffynnonoer. Cdgn 5E 57
Fiag Lodge. High 1B 164
Fidden. Arg 2B 132
Fiddington. Glos 2E 49
Fiddington. Som 2F 21
Fiddleford. Dors 1D 14
Fiddlers Hamlet. Essx 5E 53
Field. Staf 2E 73
Field Assarts. Oxon 4B 50
Field Broughton. Cumb 1C 96
Field Dalling. Norf 2C 78
Fieldhead. Cumb 1F 103
Field Head. Leics 5B 74
Fifehead Magdalen. Dors 4C 22
Fifehead Neville. Dors 1C 14
Fifehead St Quintin. Dors 1C 14
Fife Keith. Mor 3B 160
Fifield. Oxon 4H 49
Fifield. Wilts 1G 23
Fifield. Wind 3A 38
Fifield Bavant. Wilts 4F 23
Figheldean. Wilts 2G 23
Filby. Norf 4G 79
Filey. N Yor 1F 101
Filford. Dors 3H 13
Filgrave. Mil 1G 51
Filkins. Oxon 5H 49
Filleigh. Devn 1H 11 (nr. Crediton)
Filleigh. Devn 4G 19 (nr. South Molton)
Fillingham. Linc 2G 87
Fillongley. Warw 2G 61
Filton. S Glo 4B 34
Fimber. E Yor 3C 100
Finavon. Ang 3D 145
Fincham. Norf 5F 77
Finchampstead. Wok 5F 37
Fincharn. Arg 3G 133
Finchdean. Hants 1F 17
Finchingfield. Essx 2G 53
Finchley. G Lon 1D 38
Findern. Derbs 2H 73
Findhorn. Mor 2E 159
Findhorn Bridge. High 1C 150
Findochty. Mor 2B 160
Findo Gask. Per 1C 136
Findon. Abers 4G 153
Findon. W Sus 5C 26
Findon Mains. High 2A 158
Findon Valley. W Sus 5C 26
Finedon. Nptn 3G 63
Fingal Street. Suff 3E 66
Fingest. Buck 2F 37
Finghall. N Yor 1D 98
Fingland. Cumb 4D 112
Fingland. Dum 3G 117
Finglesham. Kent 5H 41
Fingringhoe. Essx 3D 54
Finiskaig. High 4A 148
Finmere. Oxon 2E 51
Finnart. Per 3C 142
Finningham. Suff 4C 66
Finningley. S Yor 1D 86
Finnyguad. Abers 3D 160
Finsbury. G Lon 2E 39
Finstall. Worc 3D 61
Finsthwaite. Cumb 1C 96
Finstock. Oxon 4B 50
Finstown. Orkn 6C 172
Fintry. Abers 3E 161
Fintry. D'dee 5D 144
Fintry. Stir 1H 127
Finwood. Warw 4F 61
Finzean. Abers 4D 152
Fionnphort. Arg 2B 132
Fionnsabhagh. W Isl 9C 171
Firbeck. S Yor 2C 86
Firby. N Yor 1E 99 (nr. Bedale)
Firby. N Yor 3B 100 (nr. Malton)
Firgrove. G Man 3H 91
Firle. E Sus 5F 27
Firsdown. Wilts 3H 23
First Coast. High 4D 162
Firth. Shet 4F 173
Fir Tree. Dur 1E 105
Fishbourne. IOW 3D 16
Fishbourne. W Sus 2G 17
Fishburn. Dur 1A 106
Fishcross. Clac 4B 136
Fisherford. Abers 5D 160
Fisherrow. E Lot 2G 129
Fisher's Pond. Hants 4C 24
Fisher's Row. Lanc 5D 96
Fisherstreet. W Sus 2A 26
Fisherton. High 3B 158
Fisherton. S Ayr 3B 116
Fisherton de la Mere. Wilts 3E 23
Fishguard. Pemb 1D 42
Fishlake. S Yor 3G 93
Fishley. Norf 4G 79
Fishnish. Arg 4A 140
Fishpond Bottom. Dors 3G 13
Fishponds. Bris 4B 34
Fishpool. Glos 3B 48
Fishpool. G Man 4G 91
Fishpools. Powy 4D 58
Fishtoft. Linc 1C 76
Fishtoft Drove. Linc 1C 76
Fishwick. Bord 4F 131
Fiskavaig. High 5C 154
Fiskerton. Linc 3H 87
Fiskerton. Notts 5E 87
Fitch. Shet 7E 173
Fitling. E Yor 1F 95
Fittleton. Wilts 2G 23
Fittleworth. W Sus 4B 26
Fitton End. Cambs 4D 76
Fitz. Shrp 4G 71
Fitzhead. Som 4E 20
Fitzwilliam. W Yor 3E 93
Fiunary. High 4A 140
Five Ash Down. E Sus 3F 27
Five Ashes. E Sus 3G 27
Five Bells. Som 2D 20
Five Bridges. Here 1B 48
Fivehead. Som 4G 21
Five Lane Ends. Lanc 4E 97
Fivelanes. Corn 4C 10
Five Oak Green. Kent 1H 27
Five Oaks. W Sus 3B 26
Five Roads. Carm 5E 45
Five Ways. Warw 3G 61
Flack's Green. Essx 4A 54
Flackwell Heath. Buck 3G 37
Fladbury. Worc 1E 49
Fladda. Shet 3E 173
Fladdabister. Shet 8F 173
Flagg. Derbs 4F 85
Flamborough. E Yor 2G 101
Flamstead. Herts 4A 52
Flansham. W Sus 5A 26
Flasby. N Yor 4B 98
Flash. Staf 4E 85
Flashader. High 3C 154
Flatt, The. Cumb 2G 113
Flaunden. Herts 5A 52
Flawborough. Notts 1E 75
Flawith. N Yor 3G 99
Flax Bourton. N Som 5A 34
Flaxby. N Yor 4F 99
Flaxholme. Derbs 1H 73
Flaxley. Glos 4B 48
Flaxley Green. Staf 4E 73
Flaxpool. Som 3E 21
Flaxton. N Yor 3A 100
Fleck. Shet 10E 173
Fleckney. Leics 1D 62
Flecknoe. Warw 4C 62
Fledborough. Notts 3F 87
Fleet. Dors 4B 14
Fleet. Hants 1G 25 (nr. Farnborough)
Fleet. Hants 2F 17 (nr. South Hayling)
Fleet. Linc 3C 76
Fleet Hargate. Linc 3C 76
Fleetville. Herts 5B 52
Fleetwood. Lanc 5C 96
Fleggburgh. Norf 4G 79
Fleisirin. W Isl 4H 171
Flemingston. V Glam 4D 32
Flemington. S Lan 3H 127 (nr. Glasgow)
Flemington. S Lan 5A 128 (nr. Strathaven)
Flempton. Suff 4H 65
Fleoideabhagh. W Isl 9C 171
Fletcher's Green. Kent 1G 27
Fletchertown. Cumb 5D 112
Fletching. E Sus 3F 27
Fleuchary. High 4E 165
Flexbury. Corn 2C 10
Flexford. Surr 5A 38
Flimby. Cumb 1B 102
Flimwell. E Sus 2B 28
Flint. Flin 3E 83
Flintham. Notts 1E 75
Flint Mountain. Flin 3E 83
Flinton. E Yor 1F 95
Flintsham. Here 5F 59
Flishinghurst. Kent 2B 28
Flitcham. Norf 3G 77
Flitton. C Beds 2A 52
Flitwick. C Beds 2A 52
Flixborough. N Lin 3B 94
Flixton. G Man 1B 84
Flixton. N Yor 2E 101
Flixton. Suff 2F 67
Flockton. W Yor 3C 92
Flodden. Nmbd 1D 120
Flodigarry. High 1D 154
Flood's Ferry. Cambs 1C 64
Flookburgh. Cumb 2C 96
Flordon. Norf 1D 66
Flore. Nptn 4D 62
Flotterton. Nmbd 4E 121
Flowton. Suff 1D 54
Flushing. Abers 4H 161
Flushing. Corn 5C 6
Fluxton. Devn 3D 12
Flyford Flavell. Worc 5D 61
Fobbing. Thur 2B 40
Fochabers. Mor 3H 159
Fochriw. Cphy 5E 46
Fockerby. N Lin 3B 94
Fodderty. High 3H 157
Foddington. Som 4A 22
Foel. Powy 4B 70
Foffarty. Ang 4D 144
Foggathorpe. E Yor 1A 94
Fogo. Bord 5D 130
Fogorig. Bord 5D 130
Foindle. High 4B 166
Folda. Ang 2A 144
Fole. Staf 2E 73
Foleshill. W Mid 2A 62
Foley Park. Worc 3C 60
Folke. Dors 1B 14
Folkestone. Kent 2G 29 & 195
Folkingham. Linc 2H 75
Folkington. E Sus 5G 27
Folksworth. Cambs 1A 64
Folkton. N Yor 2E 101
Folla Rule. Abers 5E 161
Follifoot. N Yor 4F 99
Folly Cross. Devn 2E 11
Folly Gate. Devn 3F 11
Folly, The. Herts 4B 52
Folly, The. W Ber 5C 36
Fonmon. V Glam 5D 32
Fonthill Bishop. Wilts 3E 23
Fonthill Gifford. Wilts 3E 23
Fontmell Magna. Dors 1D 14
Fontwell. W Sus 5A 26
Font-y-gary. V Glam 5D 32
Foodieash. Fife 2F 137
Foolow. Derbs 3F 85
Footdee. Aber 3G 153
Footherley. Staf 5F 73
Foots Cray. G Lon 3F 39
Forbestown. Abers 2A 152
Force Forge. Cumb 5E 103
Force Mills. Cumb 5E 103
Forcett. N Yor 3E 105
Ford. Arg 3F 133
Ford. Buck 5F 51
Ford. Derbs 2B 86
Ford. Devn 4E 19 (nr. Bideford)
Ford. Devn 3C 8 (nr. Holbeton)
Ford. Devn 4D 9 (nr. Salcombe)
Ford. Glos 3F 49
Ford. Nmbd 1D 120
Ford. Plym 3A 8
Ford. Shrp 4G 71
Ford. Som 1A 22 (nr. Wells)
Ford. Som 4D 20 (nr. Wiveliscombe)
Ford. Staf 5E 85
Ford. W Sus 5B 26
Ford. Wilts 4D 34 (nr. Chippenham)
Ford. Wilts 3G 23 (nr. Salisbury)
Forda. Devn 3E 19
Ford Barton. Devn 1C 12
Fordcombe. Kent 1G 27
Fordell. Fife 1E 129
Forden. Powy 5E 71
Ford End. Essx 4G 53
Forder Green. Devn 2D 9
Ford Green. Lanc 5D 97
Fordham. Cambs 3F 65
Fordham. Essx 3C 54
Fordham. Norf 1F 65
Fordham Heath. Essx 3C 54
Ford Heath. Shrp 4G 71
Fordhouses. W Mid 5D 72
Fordie. Per 1G 135
Fordingbridge. Hants 1G 15
Fordington. Linc 3D 88
Fordon. E Yor 2E 101
Fordoun. Abers 1G 145
Ford Street. Essx 3C 54
Ford Street. Som 1E 13
Fordton. Devn 3B 12
Fordwells. Oxon 4B 50
Fordwich. Kent 5F 41
Fordyce. Abers 2C 160
Forebridge. Staf 3D 72
Foremark. Derbs 3H 73
Forest. N Yor 4F 105
Forestburn Gate. Nmbd 5E 121
Foresterseat. Mor 3F 159
Forest Green. Glos 2D 34
Forest Green. Surr 1C 26
Forest Hall. Cumb 4G 103
Forest Head. Cumb 4G 113
Forest Hill. Oxon 5D 50
Forest-in-Teesdale. Dur 2B 104
Forest Lodge. Per 1G 143
Forest Mill. Clac 4B 136
Forest Row. E Sus 2F 27
Forestside. W Sus 1F 17
Forest Town. Notts 4C 86
Forfar. Ang 3D 144
Forgandenny. Per 2C 136
Forge. Powy 1G 57
Forge Side. Torf 5F 47
Forge, The. Here 5F 59
Forgewood. N Lan 4A 128
Forgie. Mor 3A 160
Forgue. Abers 4D 160
Formby. Mers 4A 90
Forncett End. Norf 1D 66
Forncett St Mary. Norf 1D 66
Forncett St Peter. Norf 1D 66
Forneth. Per 4H 143
Fornham All Saints. Suff 4H 65
Fornham St Martin. Suff 4A 66
Forres. Mor 3E 159
Forrestfield. N Lan 3B 128
Forrest Lodge. Dum 1C 110
Forsbrook. Staf 1D 72
Forse. High 5E 169
Forsinard. High 4A 168
Forss. High 2C 168
Forstal, The. Kent 2E 29
Forston. Dors 3B 14
Fort Augustus. High 3F 149
Forteviot. Per 2C 136
Fort George. High 3B 158
Forth. S Lan 4C 128
Forthampton. Glos 2D 48
Forthay. Glos 2C 34
Forth Road Bridge. Fife 2E 129
Fortingall. Per 4E 143
Fort Matilda. Inv 2D 126
Forton. Hants 2C 24
Forton. Lanc 4D 97
Forton. Shrp 4G 71
Forton. Som 2G 13
Forton. Staf 3B 72
Forton Heath. Shrp 4G 71
Fortrie. Abers 4D 160
Fortrose. High 3B 158
Fortuneswell. Dors 5B 14
Fort William. High 1F 141
Forty Green. Buck 1A 38
Forty Hill. G Lon 1E 39
Forward Green. Suff 5C 66
Fosbury. Wilts 1B 24
Foscot. Oxon 3H 49
Fosdyke. Linc 2C 76
Foss. Per 3E 143
Fossebridge. Glos 4F 49
Foster Street. Essx 5E 53
Foston. Derbs 2F 73
Foston. Leics 1D 62
Foston. Linc 1F 75
Foston. N Yor 3A 100
Foston on the Wolds. E Yor 4F 101
Fotherby. Linc 1C 88
Fothergill. Cumb 1B 102
Fotheringhay. Nptn 1H 63
Foubister. Orkn 7E 172
Foula Airport. Shet 8A 173
Foul Anchor. Cambs 4D 76
Foulbridge. Cumb 5F 113
Foulden. Norf 1G 65
Foulden. Bord 4F 131
Foul Mile. E Sus 4H 27
Foulridge. Lanc 5A 98
Foulsham. Norf 3C 78
Fountainhall. Bord 5H 129
Four Alls, The. Shrp 2A 72
Four Ashes. Staf 5D 72 (nr. Cannock)
Four Ashes. Staf 2C 60 (nr. Kinver)
Four Ashes. Suff 3C 66
Four Crosses. Powy 5C 70 (nr. Llanerfyl)
Four Crosses. Powy 4E 71 (nr. Llanymynech)
Four Crosses. Staf 5D 72
Four Elms. Kent 1F 27
Four Forks. Som 3F 21
Four Gotes. Cambs 4D 76
Four Lane End. S Yor 4C 92
Four Lane Ends. Lanc 4E 97
Four Lanes. Corn 5A 6
Fourlanes End. Ches E 5B 84
Four Marks. Hants 3E 25
Four Mile Bridge. IOA 3B 80
Four Oaks. E Sus 3C 28
Four Oaks. Glos 3B 48
Four Oaks. W Mid 2G 61
Four Roads. Carm 5E 45
Four Roads. IOM 5B 108
Fourstones. Nmbd 3B 114
Four Throws. Kent 3B 28

Fovant. *Wilts* 4F **23**
Foveran. *Abers* 1G **153**
Fowey. *Corn* 3F **7**
Fowlershill. *Abers* 2G **153**
Fowley Common. *Warr* 1A **84**
Fowlis. *Ang* 5C **144**
Fowlis Wester. *Per* 1B **136**
Fowlmere. *Cambs* 1E **53**
Fownhope. *Here* 2A **48**
Foxcombe Hill. *Oxon* 5C **50**
Fox Corner. *Surr* 5A **38**
Foxcote. *Glos* 4F **49**
Foxcote. *Som* 1C **22**
Foxdale. *IOM* 4B **108**
Foxearth. *Essx* 1B **54**
Foxfield. *Cumb* 1B **96**
Foxham. *Wilts* 4E **35**
Fox Hatch. *Essx* 1G **39**
Foxhole. *Corn* 3D **6**
Foxholes. *N Yor* 2E **101**
Foxhunt Green. *E Sus* 4G **27**
Fox Lane. *Hants* 1G **25**
Foxley. *Norf* 3C **78**
Foxley. *Nptn* 5D **62**
Foxley. *Wilts* 3D **35**
Foxlydiate. *Worc* 4E **61**
Fox Street. *Essx* 3D **54**
Foxt. *Staf* 1E **73**
Foxton. *Cambs* 1E **53**
Foxton. *Dur* 2A **106**
Foxton. *Leics* 2D **62**
Foxton. *N Yor* 5B **106**
Foxup. *N Yor* 2A **98**
Foxwist Green. *Ches W* 4A **84**
Foxwood. *Shrp* 3A **60**
Foy. *Here* 3A **48**
Foyers. *High* 1G **149**
Foynesfield. *High* 3C **158**
Fraddam. *Corn* 3C **4**
Fraddon. *Corn* 3D **6**
Fradley. *Staf* 4F **73**
Fradley South. *Staf* 4F **73**
Fradswell. *Staf* 2D **73**
Fraisthorpe. *E Yor* 3F **101**
Framfield. *E Sus* 3F **27**
Framingham Earl. *Norf* 5E **79**
Framingham Pigot. *Norf* 5E **79**
Framlingham. *Suff* 4E **67**
Frampton. *Dors* 3B **14**
Frampton. *Linc* 2C **76**
Frampton Cotterell. *S Glo* 3B **34**
Frampton Mansell. *Glos* 5E **49**
Frampton on Severn. *Glos* 5C **48**
Frampton West End. *Linc* 1B **76**
Framsden. *Suff* 5D **66**
Framwellgate Moor. *Dur* 5F **115**
Franche. *Worc* 3C **60**
Frandley. *Ches W* 3A **84**
Frankby. *Mers* 2E **83**
Frankfort. *Norf* 3F **79**
Frankley. *Worc* 2D **61**
Frank's Bridge. *Powy* 5D **58**
Frankton. *Warw* 3B **62**
Frankwell. *Shrp* 4G **71**
Frant. *E Sus* 2G **27**
Fraserburgh. *Abers* 2G **161**
Frating Green. *Essx* 3D **54**
Fratton. *Port* 2E **17**
Freathy. *Corn* 3A **8**
Freckenham. *Suff* 3F **65**
Freckleton. *Lanc* 2C **90**
Freeby. *Leics* 3F **75**
Freefolk Priors. *Hants* 2C **24**
Freehay. *Staf* 1E **73**
Freeland. *Oxon* 4C **50**
Freester. *Shet* 6F **173**
Freethorpe. *Norf* 5G **79**
Freiston. *Linc* 1C **76**
Freiston Shore. *Linc* 1C **76**
Fremington. *Devn* 3F **19**
Fremington. *N Yor* 5D **104**
Frenchbeer. *Devn* 4G **11**
French Street. *Kent* 5F **39**
Frenich. *Stir* 3D **134**
Frensham. *Surr* 2G **25**
Frenze. *Norf* 2D **66**
Fresgoe. *High* 2B **168**
Freshfield. *Mers* 4A **90**
Freshford. *Bath* 5C **34**
Freshwater. *IOW* 4B **16**
Freshwater Bay. *IOW* 4B **16**
Freshwater East. *Pemb* 5E **43**
Fressingfield. *Suff* 3E **67**
Freston. *Suff* 2E **55**
Freswick. *High* 2F **169**
Fretherne. *Glos* 5C **48**
Frettenham. *Norf* 4E **79**
Freuchie. *Fife* 3E **137**
Freystrop. *Pemb* 3D **42**
Friar's Gate. *E Sus* 2F **27**
Friar Waddon. *Dors* 4B **14**
Friday Bridge. *Cambs* 5D **76**
Friday Street. *E Sus* 5H **27**
Friday Street. *Surr* 1C **26**
Fridaythorpe. *E Yor* 4C **100**
Friden. *Derbs* 4F **85**
Friern Barnet. *G Lon* 1D **39**
Friesthorpe. *Linc* 2H **87**
Frieston. *Linc* 1G **75**
Frieth. *Buck* 2F **37**
Friezeland. *Notts* 5B **86**
Frilford. *Oxon* 2C **36**
Frilsham. *W Ber* 4D **36**
Frimley. *Surr* 1G **25**
Frimley Green. *Surr* 1G **25**
Frindsbury. *Medw* 4B **40**
Fring. *Norf* 2G **77**
Fringford. *Oxon* 3E **50**
Frinsted. *Kent* 5C **40**
Frinton-on-Sea. *Essx* 4F **55**
Friockheim. *Ang* 4E **145**
Friog. *Gwyn* 4F **69**
Frisby. *Leics* 5E **75**
Frisby. *Linc* 4D **88**
Frisby on the Wreake. *Leics* 4D **74**
Friskney. *Linc* 5D **88**
Friskney Eaudyke. *Linc* 5D **88**
Friston. *E Sus* 5G **27**
Friston. *Suff* 4G **67**
Fritchley. *Derbs* 5A **86**
Fritham. *Hants* 1H **15**
Frith Bank. *Linc* 1C **76**
Frith Common. *Worc* 4A **60**
Frithelstock. *Devn* 1E **11**
Frithelstock Stone. *Devn* 1E **11**
Frithsden. *Herts* 5A **52**
Frithville. *Linc* 5C **88**
Frittenden. *Kent* 1C **28**
Frittiscombe. *Devn* 4E **9**
Fritton. *Norf* 5G **79**
(nr. Great Yarmouth)
Fritton. *Norf* 1E **67**
(nr. Long Stratton)
Fritwell. *Oxon* 3D **50**
Frizinghall. *W Yor* 1B **92**
Frizington. *Cumb* 3B **102**
Frobost. *W Isl* 6C **170**
Frocester. *Glos* 5C **48**
Frochas. *Powy* 5D **70**
Frodesley. *Shrp* 5H **71**
Frodingham. *N Lin* 3C **94**
Frodsham. *Ches W* 3H **83**
Froggat. *Derbs* 3G **85**
Froghall. *Staf* 1E **73**
Frogham. *Hants* 1G **15**
Frogham. *Kent* 5G **41**
Frogmore. *Devn* 4D **8**
Frogmore. *Hants* 5G **37**
Frogmore. *Herts* 5B **52**
Frognall. *Linc* 4A **76**
Frogshall. *Norf* 2E **79**
Frogwell. *Corn* 2H **7**
Frolesworth. *Leics* 1C **62**
Frome. *Som* 2C **22**
Fromefield. *Som* 2C **22**
Frome St Quintin. *Dors* 2A **14**
Fromes Hill. *Here* 1B **48**
Fron. *Carm* 2A **46**
Fron. *Gwyn* 2C **68**
Fron. *Powy* 4C **58**
(nr. Llandrindod Wells)
Fron. *Powy* 1D **58**
(nr. Newtown)
Fron. *Powy* 5E **71**
(nr. Welshpool)
Froncysyllte. *Wrex* 1E **71**
Frongoch. *Gwyn* 2B **70**
Fron Isaf. *Wrex* 1E **71**
Fronoleu. *Gwyn* 2G **69**
Frosterley. *Dur* 1D **104**
Frotoft. *Orkn* 5D **172**
Froxfield. *C Beds* 2H **51**
Froxfield. *Wilts* 5A **36**
Froxfield Green. *Hants* 4F **25**
Fryern Hill. *Hants* 4C **24**
Fryerning. *Essx* 5G **53**
Fryton. *N Yor* 2A **100**
Fugglestone St Peter. *Wilts* 3G **23**
Fulbeck. *Linc* 5G **87**
Fulbourn. *Cambs* 5E **65**
Fulbrook. *Oxon* 4A **50**
Fulflood. *Hants* 3C **24**
Fulford. *Som* 4F **21**
Fulford. *Staf* 2D **72**
Fulford. *York* 5A **100**
Fulham. *G Lon* 3D **38**
Fulking. *W Sus* 4D **26**
Fuller's Moor. *Ches W* 5G **83**
Fuller Street. *Essx* 4H **53**
Fullerton. *Hants* 3B **24**
Fulletby. *Linc* 3B **88**
Full Sutton. *E Yor* 4B **100**
Fullwood. *E Ayr* 4F **127**
Fulmer. *Buck* 2A **38**
Fulmodestone. *Norf* 2B **78**
Fulnetby. *Linc* 3H **87**
Fulney. *Linc* 3B **76**
Fulstow. *Linc* 1C **88**
Fulthorpe. *Stoc T* 2B **106**
Fulwell. *Tyne* 4G **115**
Fulwood. *Lanc* 1D **90**
Fulwood. *Notts* 5B **86**
Fulwood. *Som* 1F **13**
Fulwood. *S Yor* 2G **85**
Fundenhall. *Norf* 1D **66**
Funtington. *W Sus* 2G **17**
Funtley. *Hants* 2D **16**
Funzie. *Shet* 2H **173**
Furley. *Devn* 2F **13**
Furnace. *Arg* 3H **133**
Furnace. *Carm* 5F **45**
Furnace. *Cdgn* 1F **57**
Furner's Green. *E Sus* 3F **27**
Furness Vale. *Derbs* 2E **85**
Furneux Pelham. *Herts* 3E **53**
Furzebrook. *Dors* 4E **15**
Furzehill. *Devn* 2H **19**
Furzehill. *Dors* 2F **15**
Furzeley Corner. *Hants* 1E **17**
Furzey Lodge. *Hants* 2B **16**
Furzley. *Hants* 1A **16**
Fyfield. *Essx* 5F **53**
Fyfield. *Glos* 5H **49**
Fyfield. *Hants* 2A **24**
Fyfield. *Oxon* 2C **36**
Fyfield. *Wilts* 5G **35**
Fylde, The. *Lanc* 1B **90**
Fylingthorpe. *N Yor* 4G **107**
Fyning. *W Sus* 4G **25**
Fyvie. *Abers* 5E **161**

G

Gabhsann bho Dheas. *W Isl* 2G **171**
Gabhsann bho Thuath. *W Isl* 2G **171**
Gabroc Hill. *E Ayr* 4F **127**
Gadbrook. *Surr* 1D **26**
Gaddesby. *Leics* 4D **74**
Gadfa. *IOA* 2D **80**
Gadgirth. *S Ayr* 2D **116**
Gaer. *Powy* 3E **47**
Gaerwen. *IOA* 3D **81**
Gagingwell. *Oxon* 3C **50**
Gaick Lodge. *High* 5B **150**
Gailey. *Staf* 4D **72**
Gainford. *Dur* 3E **105**
Gainsborough. *Linc* 1F **87**
Gainsborough. *Suff* 1E **55**
Gainsford End. *Essx* 2H **53**
Gairletter. *Arg* 1C **126**
Gairloch. *Abers* 3E **153**
Gairloch. *High* 1H **155**
Gairlochy. *High* 5D **148**
Gairney Bank. *Per* 4D **136**
Gairnshiel Lodge. *Abers* 3G **151**
Gaisgill. *Cumb* 4H **103**
Gaitsgill. *Cumb* 5E **113**
Galashiels. *Bord* 1G **119**
Galgate. *Lanc* 4D **97**
Galhampton. *Som* 4B **22**
Gallatown. *Fife* 4E **137**
Galley Common. *Warw* 1H **61**
Galleyend. *Essx* 5H **53**
Galleywood. *Essx* 5H **53**
Gallin. *Per* 4C **142**
Gallowfauld. *Ang* 4D **144**
Gallowhill. *E Dun* 2H **127**
Gallowhill. *Per* 5A **144**
Gallowhill. *Ren* 3F **127**
Gallowhills. *Abers* 3H **161**
Gallows Green. *Staf* 1E **73**
Gallows Green. *Worc* 4D **60**
Gallowstree Common. *Oxon* 3E **37**
Galltair. *High* 1G **147**
Gallt Melyd. *Den* 2C **82**
Galmington. *Som* 4F **21**
Galmisdale. *High* 5C **146**
Galmpton. *Devn* 4C **8**
Galmpton. *Torb* 3E **9**
Galmpton Warborough. *Torb* 3E **9**
Galphay. *N Yor* 2E **99**
Galston. *E Ayr* 1D **117**
Galton. *Dors* 4C **14**
Galtrigill. *High* 3A **154**
Gamblesby. *Cumb* 1H **103**
Gamelsby. *Cumb* 4D **112**
Gamesley. *Derbs* 1E **85**
Gamlingay. *Cambs* 5B **64**
Gamlingay Cinques. *Cambs* 5B **64**
Gamlingay Great Heath. *C Beds* 5B **64**
Gammaton. *Devn* 4E **19**
Gammersgill. *N Yor* 1C **98**
Gamston. *Notts* 2D **74**
(nr. Nottingham)
Gamston. *Notts* 3E **86**
(nr. Retford)
Ganarew. *Here* 4A **48**
Ganavan. *Arg* 5C **140**
Ganborough. *Glos* 3G **49**
Gang. *Corn* 2H **7**
Ganllwyd. *Gwyn* 3G **69**
Gannochy. *Ang* 1E **145**
Gannochy. *Per* 1D **136**
Gansclet. *High* 4F **169**
Ganstead. *E Yor* 1E **95**
Ganthorpe. *N Yor* 2A **100**
Ganton. *N Yor* 2D **101**
Gants Hill. *G Lon* 2F **39**
Gappah. *Devn* 5B **12**
Garafad. *High* 2D **155**
Garboldisham. *Norf* 2C **66**
Garden City. *Flin* 4F **83**
Gardeners Green. *Wok* 5G **37**
Gardenstown. *Abers* 2F **161**
Garden Village. *S Yor* 1G **85**
Garden Village. *Swan* 3E **31**
Garderhouse. *Shet* 7E **173**
Gardham. *E Yor* 5D **100**
Gardie. *Shet* 5C **173**
(on Papa Stour)
Gardie. *Shet* 1H **173**
(on Unst)
Gardie Ho. *Shet* 7F **173**
Gare Hill. *Som* 2C **22**
Garelochhead. *Arg* 4B **134**
Garford. *Oxon* 2C **36**
Garforth. *W Yor* 1E **93**
Gargrave. *N Yor* 4B **98**
Gargunnock. *Stir* 4G **135**
Garleffin. *S Ayr* 1F **109**
Garlieston. *Dum* 5B **110**
Garlinge Green. *Kent* 5F **41**
Garlogie. *Abers* 3E **153**
Garmelow. *Staf* 3B **72**
Garmond. *Abers* 3F **161**
Garmondsway. *Dur* 1A **106**
Garmony. *Arg* 4A **140**
Garmouth. *Mor* 2H **159**
Garmston. *Shrp* 5A **72**
Garnant. *Carm* 4G **45**
Garndiffaith. *Torf* 5F **47**
Garndolbenmaen. *Gwyn* 1D **69**
Garnett Bridge. *Cumb* 5G **103**
Garnfadryn. *Gwyn* 2B **68**
Garnkirk. *N Lan* 3H **127**
Garnlydan. *Blae* 4E **47**
Garnsgate. *Linc* 3D **76**
Garnswllt. *Swan* 5G **45**
Garn-yr-erw. *Torf* 4F **47**
Garrabost. *W Isl* 4H **171**
Garrallan. *E Ayr* 3E **117**
Garras. *Corn* 4E **5**
Garreg. *Gwyn* 1F **69**
Garrigill. *Cumb* 5A **114**
Garriston. *N Yor* 5E **105**
Garrogie Lodge. *High* 2H **149**
Garros. *High* 2D **155**
Garrow. *Per* 4F **143**
Garsdale. *Cumb* 1G **97**
Garsdale Head. *Cumb* 5A **104**
Garsdon. *Wilts* 3E **35**
Garshall Green. *Staf* 2D **72**
Garsington. *Oxon* 5D **50**
Garstang. *Lanc* 5D **97**
Garston. *Mers* 2G **83**
Garswood. *Mers* 1H **83**
Gartcosh. *N Lan* 3H **127**
Garth. *B'end* 2B **32**
Garth. *Cdgn* 2F **57**
Garth. *Gwyn* 2E **69**
Garth. *IOM* 4C **108**
Garth. *Powy* 1C **46**
(nr. Builth Wells)
Garth. *Powy* 3E **59**
(nr. Knighton)
Garth. *Shet* 6D **173**
(nr. Sandness)
Garth. *Shet* 6F **173**
(nr. Skellister)
Garth. *Wrex* 1E **71**
Garthamlock. *Glas* 3H **127**
Garthbrengy. *Powy* 2D **46**
Gartheli. *Cdgn* 5E **57**
Garthmyl. *Powy* 1D **58**
Garthorpe. *Leics* 3F **75**
Garthorpe. *N Lin* 3B **94**
Garth Owen. *Powy* 1D **58**
Garth Row. *Cumb* 5G **103**
Gartly. *Abers* 5C **160**
Gartmore. *Stir* 4E **135**
Gartness. *N Lan* 3A **128**
Gartness. *Stir* 1G **127**
Gartocharn. *W Dun* 1F **127**
Garton. *E Yor* 1F **95**
Garton-on-the-Wolds. *E Yor* 4D **101**
Gartsherrie. *N Lan* 3A **128**
Gartymore. *High* 2H **165**
Garvald. *E Lot* 2B **130**
Garvamore. *High* 4H **149**
Garvard. *Arg* 4A **132**
Garvault. *High* 5H **167**
Garve. *High* 2F **157**
Garvestone. *Norf* 5C **78**
Garvie. *Arg* 4H **133**
Garvock. *Abers* 1G **145**
Garvock. *Inv* 2D **126**
Garway. *Here* 3H **47**
Garway Common. *Here* 3H **47**
Garway Hill. *Here* 3H **47**
Gaskan. *High* 1C **140**
Gasper. *Wilts* 3C **22**
Gastard. *Wilts* 5D **35**
Gasthorpe. *Norf* 2B **66**
Gatcombe. *IOW* 4C **16**
Gateacre. *Mers* 2G **83**
Gatebeck. *Cumb* 1E **97**
Gate Burton. *Linc* 2F **87**
Gateforth. *N Yor* 2F **93**
Gatehead. *E Ayr* 1C **116**
Gate Helmsley. *N Yor* 4A **100**
Gatehouse. *Nmbd* 1A **114**
Gatehouse of Fleet. *Dum* 4D **110**
Gatelawbridge. *Dum* 5B **118**
Gateley. *Norf* 3B **78**
Gatenby. *N Yor* 1F **99**
Gatesgarth. *Cumb* 3C **102**
Gateshead. *Tyne* 3F **115**
Gatesheath. *Ches W* 4G **83**
Gateside. *Ang* 4D **144**
(nr. Forfar)
Gateside. *Ang* 4C **144**
(nr. Kirriemuir)
Gateside. *Fife* 3D **136**
Gateside. *N Ayr* 4E **127**
Gathurst. *G Man* 4D **90**
Gatley. *G Man* 2C **84**
Gatton. *Surr* 5D **39**
Gattonside. *Bord* 1H **119**
Gatwick (London) Airport. *W Sus* 1D **27** & **216**
Gaufron. *Powy* 4B **58**
Gaulby. *Leics* 5D **74**
Gauldry. *Fife* 1F **137**
Gaultree. *Norf* 5D **77**
Gaunt's Common. *Dors* 2F **15**
Gaunt's Earthcott. *S Glo* 3B **34**
Gautby. *Linc* 3A **88**
Gavinton. *Bord* 4D **130**
Gawber. *S Yor* 4D **92**
Gawcott. *Buck* 2E **51**
Gawsworth. *Ches E* 4C **84**
Gawthorpe. *W Yor* 2C **92**
Gawthrop. *Cumb* 1F **97**
Gawthwaite. *Cumb* 1B **96**
Gay Bowers. *Essx* 5A **54**
Gaydon. *Warw* 5A **62**
Gayfield. *Orkn* 2D **172**
Gayhurst. *Mil* 1G **51**
Gayle. *N Yor* 1A **98**
Gayles. *N Yor* 4E **105**
Gay Street. *W Sus* 3B **26**
Gayton. *Mers* 2E **83**
Gayton. *Norf* 4G **77**
Gayton. *Nptn* 5E **62**
Gayton. *Staf* 3D **73**
Gayton le Marsh. *Linc* 2D **88**
Gayton le Wold. *Linc* 2B **88**
Gayton Thorpe. *Norf* 4G **77**
Gaywood. *Norf* 3F **77**
Gazeley. *Suff* 4G **65**
Geanies. *High* 1C **158**
Gearraidh Bhailteas. *W Isl* 6C **170**
Gearraidh Bhaird. *W Isl* 6F **171**
Gearraidh ma Monadh. *W Isl* 7C **170**
Gearraidh na h-Aibhne. *W Isl* 4E **171**
Geary. *High* 2B **154**
Geddes. *High* 3C **158**
Gedding. *Suff* 5B **66**
Geddington. *Nptn* 2F **63**
Gedintailor. *High* 5E **155**
Gedling. *Notts* 1D **74**
Gedney. *Linc* 3D **76**
Gedney Broadgate. *Linc* 3D **76**
Gedney Drove End. *Linc* 3D **76**
Gedney Dyke. *Linc* 3D **76**
Gedney Hill. *Linc* 4C **76**
Gee Cross. *G Man* 1D **84**
Geeston. *Rut* 5G **75**
Geilston. *Arg* 2E **127**
Geirinis. *W Isl* 4C **170**
Geise. *High* 2D **168**
Geisiadar. *W Isl* 4D **171**
Gelder Shiel. *Abers* 5G **151**
Geldeston. *Norf* 1F **67**
Gell. *Cnwy* 4A **82**
Gelli. *Pemb* 3E **43**
Gelli. *Rhon* 2C **32**
Gellifor. *Den* 4D **82**
Gelligaer. *Cphy* 2E **33**
Gellilydan. *Gwyn* 2F **69**
Gellinudd. *Neat* 5H **45**
Gellyburn. *Per* 5H **143**
Gellywen. *Carm* 2G **43**
Gelston. *Dum* 4E **111**
Gelston. *Linc* 1G **75**
Gembling. *E Yor* 4F **101**
Geneva. *Cdgn* 5D **56**
Gentleshaw. *Staf* 4E **73**
Geocrab. *W Isl* 8D **171**
George Green. *Buck* 2A **38**
Georgeham. *Devn* 3E **19**
George Nympton. *Devn* 4H **19**
Georgetown. *Blae* 5E **47**
Georgetown. *Ren* 3F **127**
Georth. *Orkn* 5C **172**
Gerlan. *Gwyn* 4F **81**
Germansweek. *Devn* 3E **11**
Germoe. *Corn* 4C **4**
Gerrans. *Corn* 5C **6**
Gerrard's Bromley. *Staf* 2B **72**
Gerrards Cross. *Buck* 2A **38**
Gerston. *High* 3D **168**
Gestingthorpe. *Essx* 2B **54**
Gethsemane. *Pemb* 1A **44**
Geuffordd. *Powy* 4E **70**
Gibraltar. *Buck* 4F **51**
Gibraltar. *Linc* 5E **89**
Gibraltar. *Suff* 5D **66**
Gibsmere. *Notts* 1E **74**
Giddeahall. *Wilts* 4D **34**
Gidea Park. *G Lon* 2G **39**
Gidleigh. *Devn* 4G **11**
Giffnock. *E Ren* 4G **127**
Gifford. *E Lot* 3B **130**
Giffordtown. *Fife* 2E **137**
Giggetty. *Staf* 1C **60**
Giggleswick. *N Yor* 3H **97**
Gignog. *Pemb* 2C **42**
Gilberdyke. *E Yor* 2B **94**
Gilbert's End. *Worc* 1D **48**
Gilbert's Green. *Warw* 3F **61**
Gilchriston. *E Lot* 3A **130**

Gilcrux. Cumb 1C 102
Gildersome. W Yor 2C 92
Gildingwells. S Yor 2C 86
Gilesgate Moor. Dur 5F 115
Gileston. V Glam 5D 32
Gilfach. Cphy 2E 33
Gilfach Goch. Rhon 2C 32
Gilfachreda. Cdgn 5D 56
Gilgarran. Cumb 2B 102
Gillamoor. N Yor 5D 107
Gillan. Corn 4E 5
Gillar's Green. Mers 1G 83
Gillen. High 3B 154
Gilling East. N Yor 2A 100
Gillingham. Dors 4D 22
Gillingham. Medw 4B 40 & **Medway 204**
Gillingham. Norf 1G 67
Gilling West. N Yor 4E 105
Gillock. High 3E 169
Gillow Heath. Staf 5C 84
Gills. High 1F 169
Gill's Green. Kent 2B 28
Gilmanscleuch. Bord 2F 119
Gilmerton. Edin 3F 129
Gilmerton. Per 1A 136
Gilmonby. Dur 3C 104
Gilmorton. Leics 2C 62
Gilsland. Nmbd 3H 113
Gilsland Spa. Cumb 3H 113
Gilston. Midl 4H 129
Giltbrook. Notts 1B 74
Gilwern. Mon 4F 47
Gimingham. Norf 2E 79
Giosla. W Isl 5D 171
Gipping. Suff 4C 66
Gipsey Bridge. Linc 1B 76
Gipton. W Yor 1D 92
Girdle Toll. N Ayr 5E 127
Girlsta. Shet 6F 173
Girsby. N Yor 4A 106
Girthon. Dum 4D 110
Girton. Cambs 4D 64
Girton. Notts 4F 87
Girvan. S Ayr 5A 116
Gisburn. Lanc 5H 97
Gisleham. Suff 2H 67
Gislingham. Suff 3C 66
Gissing. Norf 2D 66
Gittisham. Devn 3E 13
Gladestry. Powy 5E 59
Gladsmuir. E Lot 2A 130
Glaichbea. High 5H 157
Glais. Swan 5H 45
Glaisdale. N Yor 4E 107
Glame. High 4E 155
Glamis. Ang 4C 144
Glamisdale. High 5C 146
Glanaman. Carm 4G 45
Glan-Conwy. Cnwy 5H 81
Glandford. Norf 1C 78
Glan Duar. Carm 1F 45
Glandwr. Blae 5F 47
Glandwr. Pemb 2F 43
Glan-Dwyfach. Gwyn 1D 69
Glandy Cross. Carm 2F 43
Glandyfi. Cdgn 1F 57
Glangrwyney. Powy 4F 47
Glanmule. Powy 1D 58
Glanrhyd. Gwyn 2B 68
Glanrhyd. Pemb 1B 44 (nr. Cardigan)
Glan-rhyd. Pemb 1F 43 (nr. Crymych)
Glan-rhyd. Powy 5A 46
Glanton. Nmbd 3E 121
Glanton Pyke. Nmbd 3E 121
Glanvilles Wootton. Dors 2B 14
Glan-y-don. Flin 3D 82
Glan-y-nant. Powy 2B 58
Glan-yr-afon. Gwyn 1C 70
Glan-yr-afon. IOA 2F 81
Glan-yr-afon. Powy 5C 70
Glan-y-wern. Gwyn 2F 69
Glapthorn. Nptn 1H 63
Glapwell. Derbs 4B 86
Glas Aird. Arg 4A 132
Glas-allt Shiel. Abers 5G 151
Glasbury. Powy 2E 47
Glaschoil. Mor 5E 159
Glascoed. Den 3B 82
Glascoed. Mon 5G 47
Glascote. Staf 5G 73
Glascwm. Powy 5D 58
Glasfryn. Cnwy 5B 82
Glasgow. Glas 3G 127 & 196
Glasgow Airport. Ren 3F 127 & 216
Glasgow Prestwick International Airport. S Ayr 2C 116
Glashvin. High 2D 154
Glasinfryn. Gwyn 4E 81
Glas na Cardaich. High 4E 147
Glasnacardoch. High 4E 147
Glasnakille. High 2D 146
Glaspwll. Cdgn 1G 57
Glassburn. High 5F 157
Glassenbury. Kent 2B 28
Glasserton. Dum 5B 110
Glassford. S Lan 5A 128
Glassgreen. Mor 2G 159
Glasshouse. Glos 3C 48
Glasshouses. N Yor 3D 98
Glasson. Cumb 3D 112
Glasson. Lanc 4D 96
Glassonby. Cumb 1G 103
Glasterlaw. Ang 3E 145
Glaston. Rut 5F 75
Glastonbury. Som 3H 21
Glatton. Cambs 2A 64
Glazebrook. Warr 1A 84
Glazebury. Warr 1A 84
Glazeley. Shrp 2B 60
Gleadless. S Yor 2A 86
Gleadsmoss. Ches E 4C 84
Gleann Dail bho Dheas. W Isl 7C 170
Gleann Tholastaidh. W Isl 3H 171
Gleann Uige. High 1A 140
Gleaston. Cumb 2B 96
Glecknabae. Arg 3B 126
Gledrid. Shrp 2E 71
Gleiniant. Powy 1B 58
Glemsford. Suff 1B 54
Glen. Dum 4C 110
Glenancross. High 4E 147
Glen Audlyn. IOM 2D 108
Glenbarr. Arg 2A 122
Glenbeg. High 2G 139
Glen Bernisdale. High 4D 154
Glenbervie. Abers 5E 153
Glenboig. N Lan 3A 128
Glenborrodale. High 2A 140
Glenbranter. Arg 4A 134
Glenbreck. Bord 2C 118
Glenbrein Lodge. High 2G 149
Glenbrittle. High 1C 146
Glenbuchat Lodge. Abers 2H 151
Glenbuck. E Ayr 2G 117
Glenburn. Ren 3F 127
Glencalvie Lodge. High 5B 164
Glencaple. Dum 3A 112
Glencarron Lodge. High 3C 156
Glencarse. Per 1D 136
Glencassley Castle. High 3B 164
Glencat. Abers 4C 152
Glencoe. High 3F 141
Glen Cottage. High 5E 147
Glencraig. Fife 4D 136
Glendale. High 4A 154
Glendevon. Per 3B 136
Glendoebeg. High 3G 149
Glendoick. Per 1E 136
Glendoune. S Ayr 5A 116
Glenduckie. Fife 2E 137
Gleneagles. Per 3B 136
Glenegedale. Arg 4B 124
Glenegedale Lots. Arg 4B 124
Glenelg. High 2G 147
Glenernie. Mor 4E 159
Glenesslin. Dum 1F 111
Glenfarg. Per 2D 136
Glenfarquhar Lodge. Abers 5E 152
Glenferness Mains. High 4D 158
Glenfeshie Lodge. High 4C 150
Glenfiddich Lodge. Mor 5H 159
Glenfield. Leics 5C 74
Glenfinnan. High 5B 148
Glenfintaig Lodge. High 5E 149
Glenfoot. Per 2D 136
Glenfyne Lodge. Arg 2B 134
Glengap. Dum 4D 110
Glengarnock. N Ayr 4E 126
Glengolly. High 2D 168
Glengorm Castle. Arg 3F 139
Glengrasco. High 4D 154
Glenhead Farm. Ang 2B 144
Glenholm. Bord 1D 118
Glen House. Bord 1E 119
Glenhurich. High 2C 140
Glenkerry. Bord 3E 119
Glenkiln. Dum 2F 111
Glenkindie. Abers 2B 152
Glenkinglass Lodge. Arg 5F 141
Glenkirk. Bord 2C 118
Glenlean. Arg 1B 126
Glenlee. Dum 1D 110
Glenleraig. High 5B 166
Glenlichorn. Per 2G 135
Glenlivet. Mor 1F 151
Glenlochar. Dum 3E 111
Glenlochsie Lodge. Per 1H 143
Glenluce. Dum 4G 109
Glenmarskie. High 3F 157
Glenmassan. Arg 1C 126
Glenmavis. N Lan 3A 128
Glen Maye. IOM 4B 108
Glenmazeran Lodge. High 1B 150
Glenmidge. Dum 1F 111
Glen Mona. IOM 3D 108
Glenmore. High 2G 139 (nr. Glenborrodale)
Glenmore. High 3D 151 (nr. Kingussie)
Glenmore. High 4D 154 (on Isle of Skye)
Glenmoy. Ang 2D 144
Glennoe. Arg 5E 141
Glen of Coachford. Abers 4B 160
Glenogil. Ang 2D 144
Glen Parva. Leics 1C 62
Glenprosen Village. Ang 2C 144
Glenree. N Ayr 3D 122
Glenridding. Cumb 3E 103
Glenrosa. N Ayr 2E 123
Glenrothes. Fife 3E 137
Glensanda. High 4C 140
Glensaugh. Abers 1F 145
Glenshero Lodge. High 4H 149
Glensluain. Arg 4H 133
Glenstockadale. Dum 3F 109
Glenstriven. Arg 2B 126
Glen Tanar House. Abers 4B 152
Glentham. Linc 1H 87
Glenton. Abers 1D 152
Glentress. Bord 1E 119
Glentromie Lodge. High 4B 150
Glentrool Lodge. Dum 1B 110
Glentrool Village. Dum 2A 110
Glentruim House. High 4A 150
Glentworth. Linc 2G 87
Glenuig. High 1A 140
Glen Village. Falk 2B 128
Glen Vine. IOM 4C 108
Glenwhilly. Dum 2G 109
Glenzierfoot. Dum 2E 113
Glespin. S Lan 2H 117
Gletness. Shet 6F 173
Glewstone. Here 3A 48
Glib Cheois. W Isl 5F 171
Glinton. Pet 5A 76
Glooston. Leics 1E 63
Glossop. Derbs 1E 85
Gloster Hill. Nmbd 4G 121
Gloucester. Glos 4D 48 & 196
Gloucestershire Airport. Glos 3D 49
Gloup. Shet 1G 173
Glusburn. N Yor 5C 98
Glutt Lodge. High 5B 168
Glutton Bridge. Staf 4E 85
Gluvian. Corn 2D 6
Glympton. Oxon 3C 50
Glyn. Cnwy 3A 82
Glynarthen. Cdgn 1D 44
Glynbrochan. Powy 2B 58
Glyn Ceiriog. Wrex 2E 70
Glyncoch. Rhon 2D 32
Glyncorrwg. Neat 2B 32
Glynde. E Sus 5F 27
Glyndebourne. E Sus 4F 27
Glyndyfrdwy. Den 1D 70
Glyn Ebwy. Blae 5E 47
Glynllan. B'end 3C 32
Glyn-neath. Neat 5B 46
Glynogwr. B'end 3C 32
Glyntaff. Rhon 3D 32
Glyntawe. Powy 4B 46
Glynteg. Carm 2D 44
Gnosall. Staf 3C 72
Gnosall Heath. Staf 3C 72
Goadby. Leics 1E 63
Goadby Marwood. Leics 3E 75
Goatacre. Wilts 4F 35
Goathill. Dors 1B 14
Goathland. N Yor 4F 107
Goathurst. Som 3F 21
Goathurst Common. Kent 5F 39
Goat Lees. Kent 1E 28
Gobernuisgach Lodge. High 4E 167
Gobernuisgeach. High 5B 168
Gobhaig. W Isl 7C 171
Gobowen. Shrp 2F 71
Godalming. Surr 1A 26
Goddard's Corner. Suff 4E 67
Goddard's Green. Kent 2C 28 (nr. Benenden)
Goddard's Green. Kent 2B 28 (nr. Cranbrook)
Goddards Green. W Sus 3D 27
Godford Cross. Devn 2E 13
Godleybrook. Staf 1D 73
Godmanchester. Cambs 3B 64
Godmanstone. Dors 3B 14
Godmersham. Kent 5E 41
Godolphin Cross. Corn 3D 4
Godre'r-graig. Neat 5A 46
Godshill. Hants 1G 15
Godshill. IOW 4D 16
Godstone. Staf 2E 73
Godstone. Surr 5E 39
Goetre. Mon 5G 47
Goff's Oak. Herts 5D 52
Gogar. Edin 2E 129
Goginan. Cdgn 2F 57
Golan. Gwyn 1E 69
Golant. Corn 3F 7
Golberdon. Corn 5D 10
Golborne. G Man 1A 84
Golcar. W Yor 3A 92
Goldcliff. Newp 3G 33
Golden Cross. E Sus 4G 27
Golden Green. Kent 1H 27
Golden Grove. Carm 4F 45
Golden Grove. N Yor 4F 107
Golden Hill. Pemb 2D 43
Goldenhill. Stoke 5C 84
Golden Pot. Hants 2F 25
Golden Valley. Glos 3E 49
Golders Green. G Lon 2D 38
Goldhanger. Essx 5C 54
Gold Hill. Norf 1E 65
Golding. Shrp 5H 71
Goldington. Bed 5H 63
Goldsborough. N Yor 4F 99 (nr. Harrogate)
Goldsborough. N Yor 3F 107 (nr. Whitby)
Goldsithney. Corn 3C 4
Goldstone. Kent 4G 41
Goldstone. Shrp 3B 72
Goldthorpe. S Yor 4E 93
Goldworthy. Devn 4D 19
Golfa. Powy 3D 70
Gollanfield. High 3C 158
Gollinglith Foot. N Yor 1D 98
Golsoncott. Som 3D 20
Golspie. High 4F 165
Gomeldon. Wilts 3G 23
Gomersal. W Yor 2C 92
Gometra House. Arg 4E 139
Gomshall. Surr 1B 26
Gonalston. Notts 1D 74
Gonerby Hill Foot. Linc 2G 75
Gonfirth. Shet 5E 173
Good Easter. Essx 4G 53
Gooderstone. Norf 5G 77
Goodleigh. Devn 3G 19
Goodmanham. E Yor 5C 100
Goodmayes. G Lon 2F 39
Goodnestone. Kent 5G 41 (nr. Aylesham)
Goodnestone. Kent 4E 41 (nr. Faversham)
Goodrich. Here 4A 48
Goodrington. Torb 3E 9
Goodshaw. Lanc 2G 91
Goodshaw Fold. Lanc 2G 91
Goodstone. Devn 5A 12
Goodwick. Pemb 1D 42
Goodworth Clatford. Hants 2B 24
Goole. E Yor 2H 93
Goom's Hill. Worc 5E 61
Goonabarn. Corn 3D 6
Goonbell. Corn 4B 6
Goonhavern. Corn 3B 6
Goonvrea. Corn 4B 6
Goose Green. Cumb 1E 97
Goose Green. S Glo 3C 34
Gooseham. Corn 1C 10
Goosewell. Plym 3B 8
Goosey. Oxon 2B 36
Goosnargh. Lanc 1D 90
Goostrey. Ches E 3B 84
Gorcott Hill. Warw 4E 61
Gord. Shet 9F 173
Gordon. Bord 5C 130
Gordonbush. High 3F 165
Gordonstown. Abers 3C 160 (nr. Cornhill)
Gordonstown. Abers 5E 160 (nr. Fyvie)
Gorebridge. Midl 3G 129
Gorefield. Cambs 4D 76
Gores. Wilts 1G 23
Gorgie. Edin 2F 129
Goring. Oxon 3E 36
Goring-by-Sea. W Sus 5C 26
Goring Heath. Oxon 4E 37
Gorleston-on-Sea. Norf 5H 79
Gornalwood. W Mid 1D 60
Gorran Churchtown. Corn 4D 6
Gorran Haven. Corn 4E 6
Gorran High Lanes. Corn 4D 6
Gors. Cdgn 3F 57
Gorsedd. Flin 3D 82
Gorseinon. Swan 3E 31
Gorseness. Orkn 6D 172
Gorseybank. Derbs 5G 85
Gorsgoch. Cdgn 5D 57
Gorslas. Carm 4F 45
Gorsley. Glos 3B 48
Gorsley Common. Here 3B 48
Gorstan. High 2F 157
Gorstella. Ches W 4F 83
Gorsty Common. Here 2H 47
Gorsty Hill. Staf 3E 73
Gortantaoid. Arg 2B 124
Gorteneorn. High 2A 140
Gortenfern. High 2A 140
Gorton. G Man 1C 84
Gosbeck. Suff 5D 66
Gosberton. Linc 2B 76
Gosberton Cheal. Linc 3B 76
Gosberton Clough. Linc 3A 76
Goseley Dale. Derbs 3H 73
Gosfield. Essx 3A 54
Gosford. Oxon 4D 50
Gosforth. Cumb 4B 102
Gosforth. Tyne 3F 115
Gosmore. Herts 3B 52
Gospel End Village. Staf 1C 60
Gosport. Hants 2E 16
Gossabrough. Shet 3G 173
Gossington. Glos 5C 48
Gossops Green. W Sus 2D 26
Goswick. Nmbd 5G 131
Gotham. Notts 2C 74
Gotherington. Glos 3E 49
Gott. Arg 4B 138
Gott. Shet 7F 173
Goudhurst. Kent 2B 28
Goulceby. Linc 3B 88
Gourdon. Abers 1H 145
Gourock. Inv 2D 126
Govan. Glas 3G 127
Govanhill. Glas 3G 127
Goverton. Notts 1E 74
Goveton. Devn 4D 8
Govilon. Mon 4F 47
Gowanhill. Abers 2H 161
Gowdall. E Yor 2G 93
Gowerton. Swan 3E 31
Gowkhall. Fife 1D 128
Gowthorpe. E Yor 4B 100
Goxhill. E Yor 5F 101
Goxhill. N Lin 2E 94
Goxhill Haven. N Lin 2E 94
Goytre. Neat 3A 32
Grabhair. W Isl 6F 171
Graby. Linc 3H 75
Graffham. W Sus 4A 26
Grafham. Cambs 4A 64
Grafham. Surr 1B 26
Grafton. Here 2H 47
Grafton. N Yor 3G 99
Grafton. Oxon 5A 50
Grafton. Shrp 4G 71
Grafton. Worc 2E 49 (nr. Evesham)
Grafton. Worc 4H 59 (nr. Leominster)
Grafton Flyford. Worc 5D 60
Grafton Regis. Nptn 1F 51
Grafton Underwood. Nptn 2G 63
Grafty Green. Kent 1C 28
Graianrhyd. Den 5E 82
Graig. Carm 5E 45
Graig. Cnwy 3H 81
Graig. Den 3C 82
Graig-fechan. Den 5D 82
Graig Penllyn. V Glam 4C 32
Grain. Medw 3C 40
Grainsby. Linc 1B 88
Grainthorpe. Linc 1C 88
Grainthorpe Fen. Linc 1C 88
Graiselound. N Lin 1E 87
Gramasdail. W Isl 3D 170
Grampound. Corn 4D 6
Grampound Road. Corn 3D 6
Granborough. Buck 3F 51
Granby. Notts 2E 75
Grandborough. Warw 4B 62
Grandpont. Oxon 5D 50
Grandtully. Per 3G 143
Grange. Cumb 3D 102
Grange. E Ayr 1D 116
Grange. Here 3G 59
Grange. Mers 2E 83
Grange. Per 1E 137
Grange Crossroads. Mor 3B 160
Grange Hill. G Lon 1F 39
Grangemill. Derbs 5G 85
Grange Moor. W Yor 3C 92
Grangemouth. Falk 1C 128
Grange of Lindores. Fife 2E 137
Grange-over-Sands. Cumb 2D 96
Grangepans. Falk 1D 128
Grange, The. N Yor 5C 106
Grangetown. Card 4E 33
Grangetown. Red C 2C 106
Grange Villa. Dur 4F 115
Granish. High 2C 150
Gransmoor. E Yor 4F 101
Granston. Pemb 1C 42
Grantchester. Cambs 5D 64
Grantham. Linc 2G 75
Grantley. N Yor 3E 99
Grantlodge. Abers 2E 152
Granton. Edin 2F 129
Grantown-on-Spey. High 1E 151
Grantshouse. Bord 3E 130
Grappenhall. Warr 2A 84
Grasby. Linc 4D 94
Grasmere. Cumb 4E 103
Grasscroft. G Man 4H 91
Grassendale. Mers 2F 83
Grassgarth. Cumb 5E 113
Grassholme. Dur 2C 104
Grassington. N Yor 3C 98
Grassmoor. Derbs 4B 86
Grassthorpe. Notts 4E 87
Grateley. Hants 2A 24
Gratton. Devn 1D 11
Gratton. Staf 5D 84
Gratwich. Staf 2E 73
Graveley. Cambs 4B 64
Graveley. Herts 3C 52
Gravelhill. Shrp 4G 71
Gravel Hole. G Man 4H 91
Gravelly Hill. W Mid 1F 61
Graven. Shet 4F 173
Graveney. Kent 4E 41
Gravesend. Kent 3H 39
Grayingham. Linc 1G 87
Grayrigg. Cumb 5G 103
Grays. Thur 3H 39
Grayshott. Hants 3G 25
Grayson Green. Cumb 2A 102
Grayswood. Surr 2A 26
Graythorp. Hart 2C 106
Grazeley. Wok 5E 37
Grealin. High 2E 155
Greasbrough. S Yor 1B 86
Greasby. Mers 2E 83
Great Abington. Cambs 1F 53
Great Addington. Nptn 3G 63
Great Alne. Warw 5F 61

Great Altcar. *Lanc* 4B 90
Great Amwell. *Herts* 4D 52
Great Asby. *Cumb* 3H 103
Great Ashfield. *Suff* 4B 66
Great Ayton. *N Yor* 3C 106
Great Baddow. *Essx* 5H 53
Great Bardfield. *Essx* 2G 53
Great Barford. *Bed* 5A 64
Great Barr. *W Mid* 1E 61
Great Barrington. *Glos* 4H 49
Great Barrow. *Ches W* 4G 83
Great Barton. *Suff* 4A 66
Great Barugh. *N Yor* 2B 100
Great Bavington. *Nmbd* 1C 114
Great Bealings. *Suff* 1F 55
Great Bedwyn. *Wilts* 5A 36
Great Bentley. *Essx* 3E 54
Great Billing. *Nptn* 4F 63
Great Bircham. *Norf* 2G 77
Great Blakenham. *Suff* 5D 66
Great Blencow. *Cumb* 1F 103
Great Bolas. *Telf* 3A 72
Great Bookham. *Surr* 5C 38
Great Bosullow. *Corn* 3B 4
Great Bourton. *Oxon* 1C 50
Great Bowden. *Leics* 2E 63
Great Bradley. *Suff* 5F 65
Great Braxted. *Essx* 4B 54
Great Bricett. *Suff* 5C 66
Great Brickhill. *Buck* 2H 51
Great Bridgeford. *Staf* 3C 72
Great Brington. *Nptn* 4D 62
Great Bromley. *Essx* 3D 54
Great Broughton. *Cumb* 1B 102
Great Broughton. *N Yor* 4C 106
Great Budworth. *Ches W* 3A 84
Great Burdon. *Darl* 3A 106
Great Burstead. *Essx* 1A 40
Great Busby. *N Yor* 4C 106
Great Canfield. *Essx* 4F 53
Great Carlton. *Linc* 2D 88
Great Casterton. *Rut* 5H 75
Great Chalfield. *Wilts* 5D 34
Great Chart. *Kent* 1D 28
Great Chatwell. *Staf* 4B 72
Great Chesterford. *Essx* 1F 53
Great Cheverell. *Wilts* 1E 23
Great Chilton. *Dur* 1F 105
Great Chishill. *Cambs* 2E 53
Great Clacton. *Essx* 4E 55
Great Cliff. *W Yor* 3D 92
Great Clifton. *Cumb* 2B 102
Great Coates. *NE Lin* 3F 95
Great Comberton. *Worc* 1E 49
Great Corby. *Cumb* 4F 113
Great Cornard. *Suff* 1B 54
Great Cowden. *E Yor* 5G 101
Great Coxwell. *Oxon* 2A 36
Great Crakehall. *N Yor* 1E 99
Great Cransley. *Nptn* 3F 63
Great Cressingham. *Norf* 5H 77
Great Crosby. *Mers* 1F 83
Great Cubley. *Derbs* 2F 73
Great Dalby. *Leics* 4E 75
Great Doddington. *Nptn* 4F 63
Great Doward. *Here* 4A 48
Great Dunham. *Norf* 4A 78
Great Dunmow. *Essx* 3G 53
Great Durnford. *Wilts* 3G 23
Great Easton. *Essx* 3G 53
Great Easton. *Leics* 1F 63
Great Eccleston. *Lanc* 5D 96
Great Edstone. *N Yor* 1B 100
Great Ellingham. *Norf* 1C 66
Great Elm. *Som* 2C 22
Great Eppleton. *Tyne* 5G 115
Great Eversden. *Cambs* 5C 64
Great Fencote. *N Yor* 5F 105
Great Finborough. *Suff* 5C 66
Greatford. *Linc* 4H 75
Great Fransham. *Norf* 4A 78
Great Gaddesden. *Herts* 4A 52
Great Gate. *Staf* 1E 73
Great Gidding. *Cambs* 2A 64
Great Givendale. *E Yor* 4C 100
Great Glemham. *Suff* 4F 67
Great Glen. *Leics* 1D 62
Great Gonerby. *Linc* 2G 75
Great Gransden. *Cambs* 5B 64
Great Green. *Norf* 2E 67
Great Green. *Suff* 5B 66
(nr. Lavenham)
Great Green. *Suff* 3D 66
(nr. Palgrave)
Great Habton. *N Yor* 2B 100
Great Hale. *Linc* 1A 76
Great Hallingbury. *Essx* 4F 53
Greatham. *Hants* 3F 25
Greatham. *Hart* 2B 106
Greatham. *W Sus* 4B 26
Great Hampden. *Buck* 5G 51
Great Harrowden. *Nptn* 3F 63
Great Harwood. *Lanc* 1F 91
Great Haseley. *Oxon* 5E 51
Great Hatfield. *E Yor* 5F 101
Great Haywood. *Staf* 3D 73
Great Heath. *W Mid* 2H 61
Great Heck. *N Yor* 2F 93
Great Henny. *Essx* 2B 54
Great Hinton. *Wilts* 1E 23
Great Hockham. *Norf* 1B 66
Great Holland. *Essx* 4F 55
Great Horkesley. *Essx* 2C 54
Great Hormead. *Herts* 2E 53
Great Horton. *W Yor* 1B 92
Great Horwood. *Buck* 2F 51
Great Houghton. *Nptn* 5E 63
Great Houghton. *S Yor* 4E 93
Great Hucklow. *Derbs* 3F 85
Great Kelk. *E Yor* 4F 101
Great Kendale. *E Yor* 3E 101
Great Kimble. *Buck* 5G 51
Great Kingshill. *Buck* 2G 37
Great Langdale. *Cumb* 4D 102
Great Langton. *N Yor* 5F 105
Great Leighs. *Essx* 4H 53
Great Limber. *Linc* 4E 95
Great Linford. *Mil* 1G 51
Great Livermere. *Suff* 3A 66
Great Longstone. *Derbs* 3G 85
Great Lumley. *Dur* 5F 115
Great Lyth. *Shrp* 5G 71
Great Malvern. *Worc* 1C 48
Great Maplestead. *Essx* 2B 54
Great Marton. *Bkpl* 1B 90
Great Massingham. *Norf* 3G 77
Great Melton. *Norf* 5D 78
Great Milton. *Oxon* 5E 51
Great Missenden. *Buck* 5G 51
Great Mitton. *Lanc* 1F 91
Great Mongeham. *Kent* 5H 41
Great Moulton. *Norf* 1D 66
Great Munden. *Herts* 3D 52
Great Musgrave. *Cumb* 3A 104
Great Ness. *Shrp* 4F 71
Great Notley. *Essx* 3H 53
Great Oak. *Mon* 5G 47
Great Oakley. *Essx* 3E 55
Great Oakley. *Nptn* 2F 63
Great Offley. *Herts* 3B 52
Great Ormside. *Cumb* 3A 104
Great Orton. *Cumb* 4E 113
Great Ouseburn. *N Yor* 3G 99
Great Oxendon. *Nptn* 2E 63
Great Oxney Green. *Essx* 5G 53
Great Parndon. *Essx* 5E 53
Great Paxton. *Cambs* 4B 64
Great Plumpton. *Lanc* 1B 90
Great Plumstead. *Norf* 4F 79
Great Ponton. *Linc* 2G 75
Great Potheridge. *Devn* 1F 11
Great Preston. *W Yor* 2E 93
Great Raveley. *Cambs* 2B 64
Great Rissington. *Glos* 4G 49
Great Rollright. *Oxon* 2B 50
Great Ryburgh. *Norf* 3B 78
Great Ryle. *Nmbd* 3E 121
Great Ryton. *Shrp* 5G 71
Great Saling. *Essx* 3G 53
Great Salkeld. *Cumb* 1G 103
Great Sampford. *Essx* 2G 53
Great Sankey. *Warr* 2H 83
Great Saredon. *Staf* 5D 72
Great Saxham. *Suff* 4G 65
Great Shefford. *W Ber* 4B 36
Great Shelford. *Cambs* 5D 64
Great Shoddesden. *Hants* 2A 24
Great Smeaton. *N Yor* 4A 106
Great Snoring. *Norf* 2B 78
Great Somerford. *Wilts* 3E 35
Great Stainton. *Darl* 2A 106
Great Stambridge. *Essx* 1C 40
Great Staughton. *Cambs* 4A 64
Great Steeping. *Linc* 4D 88
Great Stonar. *Kent* 5H 41
Greatstone-on-Sea. *Kent* 3E 29
Great Strickland. *Cumb* 2G 103
Great Stukeley. *Cambs* 3B 64
Great Sturton. *Linc* 3B 88
Great Sutton. *Ches W* 3F 83
Great Sutton. *Shrp* 2H 59
Great Swinburne. *Nmbd* 2C 114
Great Tew. *Oxon* 3B 50
Great Tey. *Essx* 3B 54
Great Thirkleby. *N Yor* 2G 99
Great Thorness. *IOW* 3C 16
Great Thurlow. *Suff* 5F 65
Great Torr. *Devn* 4C 8
Great Torrington. *Devn* 1E 11
Great Tosson. *Nmbd* 4E 121
Great Totham North. *Essx* 4B 54
Great Totham South. *Essx* 4B 54
Great Tows. *Linc* 1B 88
Great Urswick. *Cumb* 2B 96
Great Wakering. *Essx* 2D 40
Great Waldingfield. *Suff* 1C 54
Great Walsingham. *Norf* 2B 78
Great Waltham. *Essx* 4G 53
Great Warley. *Essx* 1G 39
Great Washbourne. *Glos* 2E 49
Great Wenham. *Suff* 2D 54
Great Whelnetham. *Suff* 5A 66
Great Whittington. *Nmbd* 2D 114
Great Wigborough. *Essx* 4C 54
Great Wilbraham. *Cambs* 5E 65
Great Wilne. *Derbs* 2B 74
Great Wishford. *Wilts* 3F 23
Great Witchingham. *Norf* 3D 78
Great Witcombe. *Glos* 4E 49
Great Witley. *Worc* 4B 60
Great Wolford. *Warw* 2H 49
Greatworth. *Nptn* 1D 50
Great Wratting. *Suff* 1G 53
Great Wymondley. *Herts* 3C 52
Great Wyrley. *Staf* 5D 73
Great Wytheford. *Shrp* 4H 71
Great Yarmouth. *Norf* 5H 79 & 196
Great Yeldham. *Essx* 2A 54
Grebby. *Linc* 4D 88
Greeba Castle. *IOM* 3C 108
Greenbank. *Shet* 1G 173
Greenbottom. *Corn* 4B 6
Greenburn. *W Lot* 3C 128
Greencroft. *Dur* 4E 115
Greencroft Park. *Dur* 5E 115
Greendown. *Som* 1A 22
Greendykes. *Nmbd* 2E 121
Green End. *Bed* 1A 52
(nr. Bedford)
Green End. *Bed* 4A 64
(nr. St Neots)
Green End. *Herts* 2D 52
(nr. Buntingford)
Green End. *Herts* 3D 52
(nr. Stevenage)
Green End. *N Yor* 4F 107
Green End. *Warw* 2G 61
Greenfield. *Arg* 4B 134
Greenfield. *C Beds* 2A 52
Greenfield. *Flin* 3D 82
Greenfield. *G Man* 4H 91
Greenfield. *Oxon* 2F 37
Greenfoot. *N Lan* 3A 128
Greenford. *G Lon* 2C 38
Greengairs. *N Lan* 2A 128
Greengate. *Norf* 4C 78
Greengill. *Cumb* 1C 102
Greenhalgh. *Lanc* 1C 90
Greenham. *Dors* 2H 13
Greenham. *Som* 4D 20
Greenham. *W Ber* 5C 36
Green Hammerton. *N Yor* 4G 99
Greenhaugh. *Nmbd* 1A 114
Greenhead. *Nmbd* 3H 113
Green Heath. *Staf* 4D 73
Greenhill. *Dum* 2C 112
Greenhill. *Falk* 2B 128
Greenhill. *Kent* 4F 41
Greenhill. *S Yor* 2H 85
Greenhill. *Worc* 3C 60
Greenhills. *N Ayr* 4E 127
Greenhithe. *Kent* 3G 39
Greenholm. *E Ayr* 1E 117
Greenhow Hill. *N Yor* 3D 98
Greenigoe. *Orkn* 7D 172
Greenland. *High* 2E 169
Greenland Mains. *High* 2E 169
Greenlands. *Worc* 4E 61
Green Lane. *Shrp* 3A 72
Green Lane. *Warw* 4E 61
Greenlaw. *Bord* 5D 130
Greenlea. *Dum* 2B 112
Greenloaning. *Per* 3H 135
Greenmount. *G Man* 3F 91
Greenmow. *Shet* 9F 173
Greenock. *Inv* 2D 126
Greenock Mains. *E Ayr* 2F 117
Greenodd. *Cumb* 1C 96
Green Ore. *Som* 1A 22
Greenrow. *Cumb* 4C 112
Greens. *Abers* 4F 161
Greensgate. *Norf* 4D 78
Greenside. *Tyne* 3E 115
Greensidehill. *Nmbd* 3D 121
Greens Norton. *Nptn* 1E 51
Greenstead Green. *Essx* 3B 54
Greensted Green. *Essx* 5F 53
Green Street. *Herts* 1C 38
Green Street. *Suff* 3D 66
Green Street Green. *G Lon* 4F 39
Green Street Green. *Kent* 3G 39
Greenstreet Green. *Suff* 1D 54
Green, The. *Cumb* 1A 96
Green, The. *Wilts* 3D 22
Green Tye. *Herts* 4E 53
Greenwall. *Orkn* 7E 172
Greenway. *Pemb* 2E 43
Greenway. *V Glam* 4D 32
Greenwell. *Cumb* 4G 113
Greenwich. *G Lon* 3E 39
Greet. *Glos* 2F 49
Greete. *Shrp* 3H 59
Greetham. *Linc* 3C 88
Greetham. *Rut* 4G 75
Greetland. *W Yor* 2A 92
Gregson Lane. *Lanc* 2D 90
Grein. *W Isl* 8B 170
Greinetobht. *W Isl* 1D 170
Greinton. *Som* 3H 21
Gremista. *Shet* 7F 173
Grenaby. *IOM* 4B 108
Grendon. *Nptn* 4F 63
Grendon. *Warw* 1G 61
Grendon Common. *Warw* 1G 61
Grendon Green. *Here* 5H 59
Grendon Underwood. *Buck* 3E 51
Grenofen. *Devn* 5E 11
Grenoside. *S Yor* 1H 85
Greosabhagh. *W Isl* 8D 171
Gresford. *Wrex* 5F 83
Gresham. *Norf* 2D 78
Greshornish. *High* 3C 154
Gressenhall. *Norf* 4B 78
Gressingham. *Lanc* 2E 97
Greta Bridge. *Dur* 3D 105
Gretna. *Dum* 3E 112
Gretna Green. *Dum* 3E 112
Gretton. *Glos* 2F 49
Gretton. *Nptn* 1G 63
Gretton. *Shrp* 1H 59
Grewelthorpe. *N Yor* 2E 99
Greygarth. *N Yor* 2D 98
Grey Green. *N Lin* 4A 94
Greylake. *Som* 3G 21
Greysouthen. *Cumb* 2B 102
Greystoke. *Cumb* 1F 103
Greystoke Gill. *Cumb* 2F 103
Greystone. *Ang* 4E 145
Greystones. *S Yor* 2H 85
Greywell. *Hants* 1F 25
Griais. *W Isl* 3G 171
Grianan. *W Isl* 4G 171
Gribthorpe. *E Yor* 1A 94
Gribun. *Arg* 5F 139
Griff. *Warw* 2A 62
Griffithstown. *Torf* 2F 33
Griffydam. *Leics* 4B 74
Griggs Green. *Hants* 3G 25
Grimbister. *Orkn* 6C 172
Grimeford Village. *Lanc* 3E 90
Grimeston. *Orkn* 6C 172
Grimethorpe. *S Yor* 4E 93
Griminis. *W Isl* 3C 170
(on Benbecula)
Griminis. *W Isl* 1C 170
(on North Uist)
Grimister. *Shet* 2F 173
Grimley. *Worc* 4C 60
Grimness. *Orkn* 8D 172
Grimoldby. *Linc* 2C 88
Grimpo. *Shrp* 3F 71
Grimsargh. *Lanc* 1D 90
Grimsbury. *Oxon* 1C 50
Grimsby. *NE Lin* 3F 95
Grimscote. *Nptn* 5D 62
Grimscott. *Corn* 2C 10
Grimshaw. *Bkbn* 2F 91
Grimshaw Green. *Lanc* 3C 90
Grimsthorpe. *Linc* 3H 75
Grimston. *E Yor* 1F 95
Grimston. *Leics* 3D 74
Grimston. *Norf* 3G 77
Grimston. *York* 4A 100
Grimstone. *Dors* 3B 14
Grimstone End. *Suff* 4B 66
Grinacombe Moor. *Devn* 3E 11
Grindale. *E Yor* 2F 101
Grindhill. *Devn* 3E 11
Grindiscol. *Shet* 8F 173
Grindle. *Shrp* 5B 72
Grindleford. *Derbs* 3G 85
Grindleton. *Lanc* 5G 97
Grindley. *Staf* 3E 73
Grindley Brook. *Shrp* 1H 71
Grindlow. *Derbs* 3F 85
Grindon. *Nmbd* 5F 131
Grindon. *Staf* 5E 85
Gringley on the Hill. *Notts* 1E 87
Grinsdale. *Cumb* 4E 113
Grinshill. *Shrp* 3H 71
Grinton. *N Yor* 5D 104
Griomsidar. *W Isl* 5G 171
Grishipoll. *Arg* 3C 138
Grisling Common. *E Sus* 3F 27
Gristhorpe. *N Yor* 1E 101
Griston. *Norf* 1B 66
Gritley. *Orkn* 7E 172
Grittenham. *Wilts* 3F 35
Grittleton. *Wilts* 4D 34
Grizebeck. *Cumb* 1B 96
Grizedale. *Cumb* 5E 103
Grobister. *Orkn* 5F 172
Grobsness. *Shet* 5E 173
Groby. *Leics* 5C 74
Groes. *Cnwy* 4C 82
Groes. *Neat* 3A 32
Groes-faen. *Rhon* 3D 32
Groesffordd. *Gwyn* 2B 68
Groesffordd. *Powy* 3D 46
Groeslon. *Gwyn* 5D 81
Groes-lwyd. *Powy* 4E 70
Groes-wen. *Cphy* 3E 33
Grogport. *Arg* 5G 125
Groigearraidh. *W Isl* 4C 170
Gromford. *Suff* 5F 67
Gronant. *Flin* 2C 82
Groombridge. *E Sus* 2G 27
Grosmont. *Mon* 3H 47
Grosmont. *N Yor* 4F 107
Groton. *Suff* 1C 54
Grove. *Dors* 5C 14
Grove. *Kent* 4G 41
Grove. *Notts* 3E 87
Grove. *Oxon* 2B 36
Grovehill. *E Yor* 1D 94
Grove Park. *G Lon* 3F 39
Grovesend. *Swan* 5F 45
Grove, The. *Dum* 2A 112
Grove, The. *Worc* 1D 48
Grub Street. *Staf* 3B 72
Grudie. *High* 2F 157
Gruids. *High* 3C 164
Gruinard House. *High* 4D 162
Gruinart. *Arg* 3A 124
Grulinbeg. *Arg* 3A 124
Gruline. *Arg* 4G 139
Grummore. *High* 5G 167
Grundisburgh. *Suff* 5E 66
Gruting. *Shet* 7D 173
Grutness. *Shet* 10F 173
Gualachulain. *High* 4F 141
Gualin House. *High* 3D 166
Guardbridge. *Fife* 2G 137
Guarlford. *Worc* 1D 48
Guay. *Per* 4H 143
Gubblecote. *Herts* 4H 51
Guestling Green. *E Sus* 4C 28
Guestling Thorn. *E Sus* 4C 28
Guestwick. *Norf* 3C 78
Guestwick Green. *Norf* 3C 78
Guide. *Bkbn* 2F 91
Guide Post. *Nmbd* 1F 115
Guilden Down. *Shrp* 2F 59
Guilden Morden. *Cambs* 1C 52
Guilden Sutton. *Ches W* 4G 83
Guildford. *Surr* 1A 26 & 197
Guildtown. *Per* 5A 144
Guilsborough. *Nptn* 3D 62
Guilsfield. *Powy* 4E 70
Guineaford. *Devn* 3F 19
Guisborough. *Red C* 3D 106
Guiseley. *W Yor* 5D 98
Guist. *Norf* 3B 78
Guiting Power. *Glos* 3F 49
Gulberwick. *Shet* 8F 173
Gullane. *E Lot* 1A 130
Gulling Green. *Suff* 5H 65
Gulval. *Corn* 3B 4
Gumfreston. *Pemb* 4F 43
Gumley. *Leics* 1D 62
Gunby. *E Yor* 1H 93
Gunby. *Linc* 3G 75
Gundleton. *Hants* 3E 24
Gun Green. *Kent* 2B 28
Gun Hill. *E Sus* 4G 27
Gunn. *Devn* 3G 19
Gunnerside. *N Yor* 5C 104
Gunnerton. *Nmbd* 2C 114
Gunness. *N Lin* 3B 94
Gunnislake. *Corn* 5E 11
Gunnista. *Shet* 7F 173
Gunsgreenhill. *Bord* 3F 131
Gunstone. *Staf* 5C 72
Gunthorpe. *Norf* 2C 78
Gunthorpe. *N Lin* 1F 87
Gunthorpe. *Notts* 1D 74
Gunthorpe. *Pet* 5A 76
Gunville. *IOW* 4C 16
Gupworthy. *Som* 3C 20
Gurnard. *IOW* 3C 16
Gurney Slade. *Som* 2B 22
Gurnos. *Powy* 5A 46
Gussage All Saints. *Dors* 1F 15
Gussage St Andrew. *Dors* 1E 15
Gussage St Michael. *Dors* 1E 15
Guston. *Kent* 1H 29
Gutcher. *Shet* 2G 173
Guthram Gowt. *Linc* 3A 76
Guthrie. *Ang* 3E 145
Guyhirn. *Cambs* 5D 76
Guyhirn Gull. *Cambs* 5C 76
Guy's Head. *Linc* 3D 77
Guy's Marsh. *Dors* 4D 22
Guyzance. *Nmbd* 4G 121
Gwaelod-y-garth. *Card* 3E 32
Gwaenynog Bach. *Den* 4C 82
Gwaenysgor. *Flin* 2C 82
Gwalchmai. *IOA* 3C 80
Gwastad. *Pemb* 2E 43
Gwaun-Cae-Gurwen. *Neat* 4H 45
Gwaun-y-bara. *Cphy* 3E 33
Gwbert. *Cdgn* 1B 44
Gweek. *Corn* 4E 5
Gwehelog. *Mon* 5G 47
Gwenddwr. *Powy* 1D 46
Gwennap. *Corn* 4B 6
Gwenter. *Corn* 5E 5
Gwernaffield. *Flin* 4E 82
Gwernesney. *Mon* 5H 47
Gwernogle. *Carm* 2F 45
Gwern-y-go. *Powy* 1E 58
Gwernymynydd. *Flin* 4E 82
Gwersyllt. *Wrex* 5F 83
Gwespyr. *Flin* 2D 82
Gwinear. *Corn* 3C 4
Gwithian. *Corn* 2C 4
Gwredog. *IOA* 2D 80
Gwyddelwern. *Den* 1C 70
Gwyddgrug. *Carm* 2E 45
Gwynfryn. *Wrex* 5E 83
Gwystre. *Powy* 4C 58
Gwytherin. *Cnwy* 4A 82
Gyfelia. *Wrex* 1F 71
Gyffin. *Cnwy* 3G 81

H

Haa of Houlland. *Shet* 1G 173
Habberley. *Shrp* 5F 71
Habblesthorpe. *Notts* 2E 87
Habergham. *Lanc* 1G 91
Habin. *W Sus* 4G 25
Habrough. *NE Lin* 3E 95
Haceby. *Linc* 2H 75
Hacheston. *Suff* 5F 67
Hackenthorpe. *S Yor* 2B 86
Hackford. *Norf* 5C 78
Hackforth. *N Yor* 5F 105

Hackland. *Orkn* 5C 172
Hackleton. *Nptn* 5F 63
Hackman's Gate. *Worc* 3C 60
Hackness. *N Yor* 5G 107
Hackness. *Orkn* 8C 172
Hackney. *G Lon* 2E 39
Hackthorn. *Linc* 2G 87
Hackthorpe. *Cumb* 2G 103
Haclait. *W Isl* 4D 170
Haconby. *Linc* 3A 76
Hadden. *Bord* 1B 120
Haddenham. *Buck* 5F 51
Haddenham. *Cambs* 3D 64
Haddenham End. *Cambs* 3D 64
Haddington. *E Lot* 2B 130
Haddington. *Linc* 4G 87
Haddiscoe. *Norf* 1G 67
Haddo. *Abers* 5F 161
Haddon. *Cambs* 1A 64
Hademore. *Staf* 5F 73
Hadfield. *Derbs* 1E 85
Hadham Cross. *Herts* 4E 53
Hadham Ford. *Herts* 3E 53
Hadleigh. *Essx* 2C 40
Hadleigh. *Suff* 1D 54
Hadleigh Heath. *Suff* 1C 54
Hadley. *Telf* 4A 72
Hadley. *Worc* 4C 60
Hadley End. *Staf* 3F 73
Hadley Wood. *G Lon* 1D 38
Hadlow. *Kent* 1H 27
Hadlow Down. *E Sus* 3G 27
Hadnall. *Shrp* 3H 71
Hadstock. *Essx* 1F 53
Hadston. *Nmbd* 5G 121
Hady. *Derbs* 3A 86
Hadzor. *Worc* 4D 60
Haffenden Quarter. *Kent* 1C 28
Haggate. *Lanc* 1G 91
Haggbeck. *Cumb* 2F 113
Haggersta. *Shet* 7E 173
Haggerston. *Nmbd* 5G 131
Haggrister. *Shet* 4E 173
Hagley. *Here* 1A 48
Hagley. *Worc* 2D 60
Hagnaby. *Linc* 4C 88
Hagworthingham. *Linc* 4C 88
Haigh. *G Man* 4E 90
Haigh Moor. *W Yor* 2C 92
Haighton Green. *Lanc* 1D 90
Haile. *Cumb* 4B 102
Hailes. *Glos* 2F 49
Hailey. *Herts* 4D 52
Hailey. *Oxon* 4B 50
Hailsham. *E Sus* 5G 27
Hail Weston. *Cambs* 4A 64
Hainault. *G Lon* 1F 39
Hainford. *Norf* 4E 78
Hainton. *Linc* 2A 88
Hainworth. *W Yor* 1A 92
Haisthorpe. *E Yor* 3F 101
Hakin. *Pemb* 4C 42
Halam. *Notts* 5D 86
Halbeath. *Fife* 1E 129
Halberton. *Devn* 1D 12
Halcro. *High* 2E 169
Hale. *Cumb* 2E 97
Hale. *G Man* 2B 84
Hale. *Hal* 2G 83
Hale. *Hants* 1G 15
Hale. *Surr* 2G 25
Hale Bank. *Hal* 2G 83
Halebarns. *G Man* 2B 84
Hales. *Norf* 1F 67
Hales. *Staf* 2B 72
Halesgate. *Linc* 3C 76
Hales Green. *Derbs* 1F 73
Halesowen. *W Mid* 2D 60
Hale Street. *Kent* 1A 28
Halesworth. *Suff* 3F 67
Halewood. *Mers* 2G 83
Halford. *Shrp* 2G 59
Halford. *Warw* 1A 50
Halfpenny. *Cumb* 1E 97
Halfpenny Furze. *Carm* 3G 43
Halfpenny Green. *Shrp* 1C 60
Halfway. *Carm* 2G 45
Halfway. *Powy* 2B 46
Halfway. *S Yor* 2B 86
Halfway. *W Ber* 5C 36
Halfway House. *Shrp* 4F 71
Halfway Houses. *Kent* 3D 40
Halgabron. *Corn* 4A 10
Halifax. *W Yor* 2A 92
Halistra. *High* 3B 154
Halket. *E Ayr* 4F 127
Halkirk. *High* 3D 168
Halkyn. *Flin* 3E 82
Hall. *E Ren* 4F 127
Hallam Fields. *Derbs* 1B 74
Halland. *E Sus* 4G 27
Hallands, The. *N Lin* 2D 94
Hallaton. *Leics* 1E 63
Hallatrow. *Bath* 1B 22
Hallbank. *Cumb* 5H 103
Hallbankgate. *Cumb* 4G 113
Hall Dunnerdale. *Cumb* 5D 102
Hallen. *S Glo* 3A 34
Hall End. *Bed* 1A 52
Hallgarth. *Dur* 5G 115
Hall Green. *Ches E* 5C 84
Hall Green. *Norf* 2D 66
Hall Green. *W Mid* 2F 61
Hall Green. *W Yor* 3D 92
Hall Green. *Wrex* 1G 71
Halliburton. *Bord* 5C 130
Hallin. *High* 3B 154
Halling. *Medw* 4B 40
Hallington. *Linc* 2C 88
Hallington. *Nmbd* 2C 114
Halloughton. *Notts* 5D 86
Hallow. *Worc* 5C 60
Hallow Heath. *Worc* 5C 60
Hallowsgate. *Ches W* 4H 83
Hallsands. *Devn* 5E 9
Hall's Green. *Herts* 3C 52
Hallspill. *Devn* 4E 19
Hallthwaites. *Cumb* 1A 96
Hall Waberthwaite. *Cumb* 5C 102
Hallwood Green. *Glos* 2B 48
Hallworthy. *Corn* 4B 10
Hallyne. *Bord* 5E 129
Halmer End. *Staf* 1C 72
Halmond's Frome. *Here* 1B 48
Halmore. *Glos* 5B 48
Halnaker. *W Sus* 5A 26
Halsall. *Lanc* 3B 90
Halse. *Nptn* 1D 50
Halse. *Som* 4E 21
Halsetown. *Corn* 3C 4
Halsham. *E Yor* 2F 95
Halsinger. *Devn* 3F 19
Halstead. *Essx* 2B 54
Halstead. *Kent* 4F 39
Halstead. *Leics* 5E 75
Halstock. *Dors* 2A 14
Halsway. *Som* 3E 21
Haltcliff Bridge. *Cumb* 1E 103
Haltham. *Linc* 4B 88
Haltoft End. *Linc* 1C 76
Halton. *Buck* 5G 51
Halton. *Hal* 2H 83
Halton. *Lanc* 3E 97
Halton. *Nmbd* 3C 114
Halton. *W Yor* 1D 92
Halton. *Wrex* 2F 71
Halton East. *N Yor* 4C 98
Halton Fenside. *Linc* 4D 88
Halton Gill. *N Yor* 2A 98
Halton Holegate. *Linc* 4D 88
Halton Lea Gate. *Nmbd* 4H 113
Halton Moor. *W Yor* 1D 92
Halton Shields. *Nmbd* 3D 114
Halton West. *N Yor* 4H 97
Haltwhistle. *Nmbd* 3A 114
Halvergate. *Norf* 5G 79
Halwell. *Devn* 3D 9
Halwill. *Devn* 3E 11
Halwill Junction. *Devn* 3E 11
Ham. *Devn* 2F 13
Ham. *Glos* 2B 34
Ham. *G Lon* 3C 38
Ham. *High* 1E 169
Ham. *Kent* 5H 41
Ham. *Plym* 3A 8
Ham. *Shet* 8A 173
Ham. *Som* 1F 13
(nr. Ilminster)
Ham. *Som* 4F 21
(nr. Taunton)
Ham. *Som* 4E 21
(nr. Wellington)
Ham. *Wilts* 5B 36
Hambleden. *Buck* 3F 37
Hambledon. *Hants* 1E 17
Hambledon. *Surr* 2A 26
Hamble-le-Rice. *Hants* 2C 16
Hambleton. *Lanc* 5C 96
Hambleton. *N Yor* 1F 93
Hambridge. *Som* 4G 21
Hambrook. *S Glo* 4B 34
Hambrook. *W Sus* 2F 17
Ham Common. *Dors* 4D 22
Hameringham. *Linc* 4C 88
Hamerton. *Cambs* 3A 64
Ham Green. *Here* 1C 48
Ham Green. *Kent* 4C 40
Ham Green. *N Som* 4A 34
Ham Green. *Worc* 4E 61
Ham Hill. *Kent* 4A 40
Hamilton. *Leics* 5D 74
Hamilton. *S Lan* 4A 128
Hamister. *Shet* 5G 173
Hammer. *W Sus* 3G 25
Hammersmith. *G Lon* 3D 38
Hammerwich. *Staf* 5E 73
Hammerwood. *E Sus* 2F 27
Hammill. *Kent* 5G 41
Hammond Street. *Herts* 5D 52
Hammoon. *Dors* 1D 14
Hamnavoe. *Shet* 8E 173
(nr. Braehoulland)
Hamnavoe. *Shet* 8E 173
(nr. Burland)
Hamnavoe. *Shet* 4F 173
(nr. Lunna)
Hamnavoe. *Shet* 3F 173
(on Yell)
Hamp. *Som* 3G 21
Hampden Park. *E Sus* 5H 27
Hampen. *Glos* 3F 49
Hamperden End. *Essx* 2F 53
Hamperley. *Shrp* 2G 59
Hampnett. *Glos* 4F 49
Hampole. *S Yor* 3F 93
Hampreston. *Dors* 3F 15
Hampstead. *G Lon* 2D 38
Hampstead Norreys. *W Ber* 4D 36
Hampsthwaite. *N Yor* 4E 99
Hampton. *Devn* 3F 13
Hampton. *G Lon* 3C 38
Hampton. *Kent* 4F 41
Hampton. *Shrp* 2B 60
Hampton. *Swin* 2G 35
Hampton. *Worc* 1F 49
Hampton Bishop. *Here* 2A 48
Hampton Fields. *Glos* 2D 35
Hampton Hargate. *Pet* 1A 64
Hampton Heath. *Ches W* 1H 71
Hampton in Arden. *W Mid* 2G 61
Hampton Loade. *Shrp* 2B 60
Hampton Lovett. *Worc* 4C 60
Hampton Lucy. *Warw* 5G 61
Hampton Magna. *Warw* 4G 61
Hampton on the Hill. *Warw* 4G 61
Hampton Poyle. *Oxon* 4D 50
Hampton Wick. *G Lon* 4C 38
Hamptworth. *Wilts* 1H 15
Hamrow. *Norf* 3B 78
Hamsey. *E Sus* 4F 27
Hamsey Green. *Surr* 5E 39
Hamstall Ridware. *Staf* 4F 73
Hamstead. *IOW* 3C 16
Hamstead. *W Mid* 1E 61
Hamstead Marshall. *W Ber* 5C 36
Hamsterley. *Dur* 4E 115
(nr. Consett)
Hamsterley. *Dur* 1E 105
(nr. Wolsingham)
Hamsterley Mill. *Dur* 4E 115
Hamstreet. *Kent* 2E 28
Ham Street. *Som* 3A 22
Hamworthy. *Pool* 3E 15
Hanbury. *Staf* 3F 73
Hanbury. *Worc* 4D 60
Hanbury Woodend. *Staf* 3F 73
Hanby. *Linc* 2H 75
Hanchurch. *Staf* 1C 72
Hand and Pen. *Devn* 3D 12
Handbridge. *Ches W* 4G 83
Handcross. *W Sus* 3D 26
Handforth. *Ches E* 2C 84
Handley. *Ches W* 5G 83
Handley. *Derbs* 4A 86
Handsacre. *Staf* 4E 73
Handsworth. *S Yor* 2B 86
Handsworth. *W Mid* 1E 61
Handy Cross. *Buck* 2G 37
Hanford. *Dors* 1D 14
Hanford. *Stoke* 1C 72
Hangersley. *Hants* 2G 15
Hanging Houghton. *Nptn* 3E 63
Hanging Langford. *Wilts* 3F 23
Hangleton. *Brig* 5D 26
Hangleton. *W Sus* 5B 26
Hanham. *S Glo* 4B 34
Hanham Green. *S Glo* 4B 34
Hankelow. *Ches E* 1A 72
Hankerton. *Wilts* 2E 35
Hankham. *E Sus* 5H 27
Hanley. *Stoke* 1C 72 & **Stoke** 211
Hanley Castle. *Worc* 1D 48
Hanley Childe. *Worc* 4A 60
Hanley Swan. *Worc* 1D 48
Hanley William. *Worc* 4A 60
Hanlith. *N Yor* 3B 98
Hanmer. *Wrex* 2G 71
Hannaborough. *Devn* 2F 11
Hannaford. *Devn* 4G 19
Hannah. *Linc* 3E 89
Hannington. *Hants* 1D 24
Hannington. *Nptn* 3F 63
Hannington. *Swin* 2G 35
Hannington Wick. *Swin* 2G 35
Hanscombe End. *C Beds* 2B 52
Hanslope. *Mil* 1G 51
Hanthorpe. *Linc* 3H 75
Hanwell. *G Lon* 2C 38
Hanwell. *Oxon* 1C 50
Hanwood. *Shrp* 5G 71
Hanworth. *G Lon* 3C 38
Hanworth. *Norf* 2D 78
Happas. *Ang* 4D 144
Happendon. *S Lan* 1A 118
Happisburgh. *Norf* 2F 79
Happisburgh Common. *Norf* 3F 79
Hapsford. *Ches W* 3G 83
Hapton. *Lanc* 1F 91
Hapton. *Norf* 1D 66
Harberton. *Devn* 3D 9
Harbertonford. *Devn* 3D 9
Harbledown. *Kent* 5F 41
Harborne. *W Mid* 2E 61
Harborough Magna. *Warw* 3B 62
Harbottle. *Nmbd* 4D 120
Harbourneford. *Devn* 2D 8
Harbours Hill. *Worc* 4D 60
Harbridge. *Hants* 1G 15
Harbury. *Warw* 4A 62
Harby. *Leics* 2E 75
Harby. *Notts* 3F 87
Harcombe. *Devn* 3E 13
Harcombe Bottom. *Devn* 3G 13
Harcourt. *Corn* 5C 6
Harden. *W Yor* 1A 92
Hardenhuish. *Wilts* 4E 35
Hardgate. *Abers* 3E 153
Hardgate. *Dum* 3F 111
Hardham. *W Sus* 4B 26
Hardingham. *Norf* 5C 78
Hardingstone. *Nptn* 5E 63
Hardings Wood. *Ches E* 5C 84
Hardington. *Som* 1C 22
Hardington Mandeville. *Som* 1A 14
Hardington Marsh. *Som* 2A 14
Hardington Moor. *Som* 1A 14
Hardley. *Hants* 2C 16
Hardley Street. *Norf* 5F 79
Hardmead. *Mil* 1H 51
Hardraw. *N Yor* 5B 104
Hardstoft. *Derbs* 4B 86
Hardway. *Hants* 2E 16
Hardway. *Som* 3C 22
Hardwick. *Buck* 4G 51
Hardwick. *Cambs* 5C 64
Hardwick. *Norf* 2E 66
Hardwick. *Nptn* 4F 63
Hardwick. *Oxon* 3D 50
(nr. Bicester)
Hardwick. *Oxon* 5B 50
(nr. Witney)
Hardwick. *Shrp* 1F 59
Hardwick. *S Yor* 2B 86
Hardwick. *Stoc T* 2B 106
Hardwick. *W Mid* 1E 61
Hardwicke. *Glos* 3E 49
(nr. Cheltenham)
Hardwicke. *Glos* 4C 48
(nr. Gloucester)
Hardwicke. *Here* 1F 47
Hardwick Village. *Notts* 3D 86
Hardy's Green. *Essx* 3C 54
Hare. *Som* 1F 13
Hareby. *Linc* 4C 88
Hareden. *Lanc* 4F 97
Harefield. *G Lon* 1B 38
Hare Green. *Essx* 3D 54
Hare Hatch. *Wok* 4G 37
Harehill. *Derbs* 2F 73
Harehills. *W Yor* 1D 92
Harehope. *Nmbd* 2E 121
Harelaw. *Dum* 2F 113
Harelaw. *Dur* 4E 115
Hareplain. *Kent* 2C 28
Haresceugh. *Cumb* 5H 113
Harescombe. *Glos* 4D 48
Haresfield. *Glos* 4D 48
Haresfinch. *Mers* 1H 83
Hareshaw. *N Lan* 3B 128
Hare Street. *Essx* 5E 53
Hare Street. *Herts* 3D 53
Harewood. *W Yor* 5F 99
Harewood End. *Here* 3A 48
Harford. *Devn* 3C 8
Hargate. *Norf* 1D 66
Hargatewall. *Derbs* 3F 85
Hargrave. *Ches W* 4G 83
Hargrave. *Nptn* 3H 63
Hargrave. *Suff* 5G 65
Harker. *Cumb* 3E 113
Harkland. *Shet* 3F 173
Harkstead. *Suff* 2E 55
Harlaston. *Staf* 4G 73
Harlaxton. *Linc* 2F 75
Harlech. *Gwyn* 2E 69
Harlequin. *Notts* 2D 74
Harlescott. *Shrp* 4H 71
Harleston. *Devn* 4D 9
Harleston. *Norf* 2E 67
Harleston. *Suff* 4C 66
Harlestone. *Nptn* 4E 62
Harley. *Shrp* 5H 71
Harley. *S Yor* 1A 86
Harling Road. *Norf* 2B 66
Harlington. *C Beds* 2A 52
Harlington. *G Lon* 3B 38
Harlington. *S Yor* 4E 93
Harlosh. *High* 4B 154
Harlow. *Essx* 4E 53
Harlow Hill. *Nmbd* 3D 115
Harlsey Castle. *N Yor* 5B 106
Harlthorpe. *E Yor* 1H 93
Harlton. *Cambs* 5C 64
Harlyn Bay. *Corn* 1C 6
Harman's Cross. *Dors* 4E 15
Harmby. *N Yor* 1D 98
Harmer Green. *Herts* 4C 52
Harmer Hill. *Shrp* 3G 71
Harmondsworth. *G Lon* 3B 38
Harmston. *Linc* 4G 87
Harnage. *Shrp* 5H 71
Harnham. *Nmbd* 1D 115
Harnhill. *Glos* 5F 49
Harold Hill. *G Lon* 1G 39
Haroldston West. *Pemb* 3C 42
Haroldswick. *Shet* 1H 173
Harold Wood. *G Lon* 1G 39
Harome. *N Yor* 1A 100
Harpenden. *Herts* 4B 52
Harpford. *Devn* 3D 12
Harpham. *E Yor* 3E 101
Harpley. *Norf* 3G 77
Harpley. *Worc* 4A 60
Harpole. *Nptn* 4D 62
Harpsdale. *High* 3D 168
Harpsden. *Oxon* 3F 37
Harpswell. *Linc* 2G 87
Harpurhey. *G Man* 4G 91
Harpur Hill. *Derbs* 3E 85
Harraby. *Cumb* 4F 113
Harracott. *Devn* 4F 19
Harrapool. *High* 1E 147
Harrapul. *High* 1E 147
Harrietfield. *Per* 1B 136
Harrietsham. *Kent* 5C 40
Harrington. *Cumb* 2A 102
Harrington. *Linc* 3C 88
Harrington. *Nptn* 2E 63
Harringworth. *Nptn* 1G 63
Harriseahead. *Staf* 5C 84
Harriston. *Cumb* 5C 112
Harrogate. *N Yor* 4F 99 & 197
Harrold. *Bed* 5G 63
Harrop Dale. *G Man* 4A 92
Harrow. *G Lon* 2C 38
Harrowbarrow. *Corn* 2H 7
Harrowden. *Bed* 1A 52
Harrowgate Hill. *Darl* 3F 105
Harrow on the Hill. *G Lon* 2C 38
Harrow Weald. *G Lon* 1C 38
Harry Stoke. *S Glo* 4B 34
Harston. *Cambs* 5D 64
Harston. *Leics* 2F 75
Harswell. *E Yor* 5C 100
Hart. *Hart* 1B 106
Hartburn. *Nmbd* 1D 115
Hartburn. *Stoc T* 3B 106
Hartest. *Suff* 5H 65
Hartfield. *E Sus* 2F 27
Hartford. *Cambs* 3B 64
Hartford. *Ches W* 3A 84
Hartford. *Som* 4C 20
Hartfordbridge. *Hants* 1F 25
Hartford End. *Essx* 4G 53
Harthill. *Ches W* 5H 83
Harthill. *N Lan* 3C 128
Harthill. *S Yor* 2B 86
Hartington. *Derbs* 4F 85
Hartland. *Devn* 4C 18
Hartland Quay. *Devn* 4C 18
Hartle. *Worc* 3D 60
Hartlebury. *Worc* 3C 60
Hartlepool. *Hart* 1C 106
Hartley. *Cumb* 4A 104
Hartley. *Kent* 2B 28
(nr. Cranbrook)
Hartley. *Kent* 4H 39
(nr. Dartford)
Hartley. *Nmbd* 2G 115
Hartley Green. *Staf* 2D 73
Hartley Mauditt. *Hants* 3F 25
Hartley Wespall. *Hants* 1E 25
Hartley Wintney. *Hants* 1F 25
Hartlip. *Kent* 4C 40
Hartmount. *High* 1B 158
Hartoft End. *N Yor* 5E 107
Harton. *N Yor* 3B 100
Harton. *Shrp* 2G 59
Harton. *Tyne* 3G 115
Hartpury. *Glos* 3C 48
Hartshead. *W Yor* 2B 92
Hartshill. *Warw* 1H 61
Hartshorne. *Derbs* 3H 73
Hartsop. *Cumb* 3F 103
Hart Station. *Hart* 1B 106
Hartswell. *Som* 4D 20
Hartwell. *Nptn* 5E 63
Hartwood. *Lanc* 3D 90
Hartwood. *N Lan* 4B 128
Harvel. *Kent* 4A 40
Harvington. *Worc* 1F 49
(nr. Evesham)
Harvington. *Worc* 3C 60
(nr. Kidderminster)
Harwell. *Oxon* 3C 36
Harwich. *Essx* 2F 55 & 215
Harwood. *Dur* 1B 104
Harwood. *G Man* 3F 91
Harwood Dale. *N Yor* 5G 107
Harworth. *Notts* 1D 86
Hascombe. *Surr* 2A 26
Haselbech. *Nptn* 3E 62
Haselbury Plucknett. *Som* 1H 13
Haseley. *Warw* 4G 61
Haselor. *Warw* 5F 61
Hasfield. *Glos* 3D 48
Hasguard. *Pemb* 4C 42
Haskayne. *Lanc* 4B 90
Hasketon. *Suff* 5E 67
Hasland. *Derbs* 4A 86
Haslemere. *Surr* 2A 26
Haslingden. *Lanc* 2F 91
Haslingden Grane. *Lanc* 2F 91
Haslingfield. *Cambs* 5D 64
Haslington. *Ches E* 5B 84
Hassall. *Ches E* 5B 84
Hassall Green. *Ches E* 5B 84
Hassell Street. *Kent* 1E 29
Hassendean. *Bord* 2H 119
Hassingham. *Norf* 5F 79
Hassness. *Cumb* 3C 102
Hassocks. *W Sus* 4E 27
Hassop. *Derbs* 3G 85
Haster. *High* 3F 169
Hasthorpe. *Linc* 4D 89
Hastigrow. *High* 2E 169

Hastingleigh. Kent 1E 29
Hastings. E Sus 5C 28
Hastingwood. Essx 5E 53
Hastoe. Herts 5H 51
Haston. Shrp 3H 71
Haswell. Dur 5G 115
Haswell Plough. Dur 5G 115
Hatch. C Beds 1B 52
Hatch Beauchamp. Som 4G 21
Hatch End. G Lon 1C 38
Hatch Green. Som 1G 13
Hatching Green. Herts 4B 52
Hatchmere. Ches W 3H 83
Hatch Warren. Hants 2E 24
Hatcliffe. NE Lin 4F 95
Hatfield. Here 5H 59
Hatfield. Herts 5C 52
Hatfield. S Yor 4G 93
Hatfield. Worc 5C 60
Hatfield Broad Oak. Essx 4F 53
Hatfield Garden Village. Herts 5C 52
Hatfield Heath. Essx 4F 53
Hatfield Hyde. Herts 4C 52
Hatfield Peverel. Essx 4A 54
Hatfield Woodhouse. S Yor 4G 93
Hatford. Oxon 2B 36
Hatherden. Hants 1B 24
Hatherleigh. Devn 2F 11
Hathern. Leics 3C 74
Hatherop. Glos 5G 49
Hathersage. Derbs 2G 85
Hathersage Booths. Derbs 2G 85
Hatherton. Ches E 1A 72
Hatherton. Staf 4D 72
Hatley St George. Cambs 5B 64
Hatt. Corn 2H 7
Hattersley. G Man 1D 85
Hattingley. Hants 3E 25
Hatton. Abers 5H 161
Hatton. Derbs 2G 73
Hatton. G Lon 3B 38
Hatton. Linc 3A 88
Hatton. Shrp 1G 59
Hatton. Warr 2H 83
Hatton. Warw 4G 61
Hattoncrook. Abers 1F 153
Hatton Heath. Ches W 4G 83
Hatton of Fintray. Abers 2F 153
Haugh. E Ayr 2D 117
Haugh. Linc 3D 88
Haugham. Linc 2C 88
Haugh Head. Nmbd 2E 121
Haughley. Suff 4C 66
Haughley Green. Suff 4C 66
Haugh of Ballechin. Per 3G 143
Haugh of Glass. Mor 5B 160
Haugh of Urr. Dum 3F 111
Haughton. Ches E 5H 83
Haughton. Notts 3D 86
Haughton. Shrp 1A 60
(nr. Bridgnorth)
Haughton. Shrp 3F 71
(nr. Oswestry)
Haughton. Shrp 5B 72
(nr. Shifnal)
Haughton. Shrp 4H 71
(nr. Shrewsbury)
Haughton. Staf 3C 72
Haughton Green. G Man 1D 84
Haughton le Skerne. Darl 3A 106
Haultwick. Herts 3D 52
Haunn. Arg 4E 139
Haunn. W Isl 7C 170
Haunton. Staf 4G 73
Hauxton. Cambs 5D 64
Havannah. Ches E 4C 84
Havant. Hants 2F 17
Haven. Here 5G 59
Haven Bank. Linc 5B 88
Havenside. E Yor 2E 95
Havenstreet. IOW 3D 16
Haven, The. W Sus 2B 26
Havercroft. W Yor 3D 93
Haverfordwest. Pemb 3D 42
Haverhill. Suff 1G 53
Haverigg. Cumb 2A 96
Havering-atte-Bower. G Lon 1G 39
Havering's Grove. Essx 1A 40
Haversham. Mil 1G 51
Haverthwaite. Cumb 1C 96
Haverton Hill. Stoc T 2B 106
Havyatt. Som 3A 22
Hawarden. Flin 4F 83
Hawbridge. Worc 1E 49
Hawcoat. Cumb 2B 96
Hawcross. Glos 2C 48
Hawen. Cdgn 1D 44
Hawes. N Yor 1A 98
Hawes Green. Norf 1E 67
Hawick. Bord 3H 119
Hawkchurch. Devn 2G 13
Hawkedon. Suff 5G 65
Hawkenbury. Kent 1C 28
Hawkeridge. Wilts 1D 22
Hawkerland. Devn 4D 12
Hawkesbury. S Glo 3C 34
Hawkesbury. W Mid 2A 62
Hawkesbury Upton. S Glo 3C 34
Hawkes End. W Mid 2G 61
Hawk Green. G Man 2D 84
Hawkhurst. Kent 2B 28
Hawkhurst Common. E Sus 4G 27
Hawkinge. Kent 1G 29
Hawkley. Hants 4F 25
Hawkridge. Som 3B 20
Hawksdale. Cumb 5E 113
Hawkshaw. G Man 3F 91
Hawkshead. Cumb 5E 103
Hawkshead Hill. Cumb 5E 103
Hawkswick. N Yor 2B 98
Hawksworth. Notts 1E 75
Hawksworth. W Yor 5D 98
Hawkwell. Essx 1C 40
Hawley. Hants 1G 25
Hawley. Kent 3G 39
Hawling. Glos 3F 49
Hawnby. N Yor 1H 99
Haworth. W Yor 1A 92
Hawstead. Suff 5A 66
Hawthorn. Dur 5H 115
Hawthorn Hill. Brac 4G 37
Hawthorn Hill. Linc 5B 88
Hawthorpe. Linc 3H 75
Hawton. Notts 5E 87
Haxby. York 4A 100
Haxey. N Lin 1E 87
Haybridge. Shrp 3A 60
Haybridge. Som 2A 22
Haydock. Mers 1H 83
Haydon. Bath 1B 22
Haydon. Dors 1B 14
Haydon. Som 4F 21
Haydon Bridge. Nmbd 3B 114
Haydon Wick. Swin 3G 35
Haye. Corn 2H 7
Hayes. G Lon 4F 39
(nr. Bromley)
Hayes. G Lon 2B 38
(nr. Uxbridge)
Hayfield. Derbs 2E 85
Hay Green. Norf 4E 77
Hayhill. E Ayr 3D 116
Haylands. IOW 3D 16
Hayle. Corn 3C 4
Hayley Green. W Mid 2D 60
Hayling Island. Hants 3F 17
Hayne. Devn 2B 12
Haynes. C Beds 1A 52
Haynes West End. C Beds 1A 52
Hay-on-Wye. Powy 1F 47
Hayscastle. Pemb 2C 42
Hayscastle Cross. Pemb 2D 42
Haysden. Kent 1G 27
Hayshead. Ang 4F 145
Hay Street. Herts 3D 53
Hayton. Aber 3G 153
Hayton. Cumb 5C 112
(nr. Aspatria)
Hayton. Cumb 4G 113
(nr. Brampton)
Hayton. E Yor 5C 100
Hayton. Notts 2E 87
Hayton's Bent. Shrp 2H 59
Haytor Vale. Devn 5A 12
Haytown. Devn 1D 11
Haywards Heath. W Sus 3E 27
Haywood. S Lan 4C 128
Hazelbank. S Lan 5B 128
Hazelbury Bryan. Dors 2C 14
Hazeleigh. Essx 5B 54
Hazeley. Hants 1F 25
Hazel Grove. G Man 2D 84
Hazelhead. S Yor 4B 92
Hazelslade. Staf 4E 73
Hazel Street. Kent 2A 28
Hazelton Walls. Fife 1F 137
Hazelwood. Derbs 1H 73
Hazlemere. Buck 2G 37
Hazler. Shrp 1G 59
Hazlerigg. Tyne 2F 115
Hazles. Staf 1E 73
Hazleton. Glos 4F 49
Hazon. Nmbd 4F 121
Heacham. Norf 2F 77
Headbourne Worthy. Hants 3C 24
Headcorn. Kent 1C 28
Headingley. W Yor 1C 92
Headington. Oxon 5D 50
Headlam. Dur 3E 105
Headless Cross. Worc 4E 61
Headley. Hants 3G 25
(nr. Haslemere)
Headley. Hants 5D 36
(nr. Kingsclere)
Headley. Surr 5D 38
Headley Down. Hants 3G 25
Headley Heath. Worc 3E 61
Headley Park. Bris 5A 34
Head of Muir. Falk 1B 128
Headon. Notts 3E 87
Heads Nook. Cumb 4F 113
Heage. Derbs 5A 86
Healaugh. N Yor 5D 104
(nr. Grinton)
Healaugh. N Yor 5H 99
(nr. York)
Heald Green. G Man 2C 84
Heale. Devn 2G 19
Healey. G Man 3G 91
Healey. Nmbd 4D 114
Healey. N Yor 1D 98
Healeyfield. Dur 5D 114
Healey Hall. Nmbd 4D 114
Healing. NE Lin 3F 95
Heamoor. Corn 3B 4
Heanish. Arg 4B 138
Heanor. Derbs 1B 74
Heanton Punchardon. Devn 3F 19
Heapham. Linc 2F 87
Heartsease. Powy 4D 58
Heasley Mill. Devn 3H 19
Heaste. High 2E 147
Heath. Derbs 4B 86
Heath and Reach. C Beds 3H 51
Heath Common. W Sus 4C 26
Heathcote. Derbs 4F 85
Heath Cross. Devn 3H 11
Heathencote. Nptn 1F 51
Heath End. Derbs 3A 74
Heath End. Hants 5D 36
Heath End. W Mid 5E 73
Heather. Leics 4A 74
Heatherfield. High 4D 155
Heatherton. Derb 2H 73
Heathfield. Cambs 1E 53
Heathfield. Cumb 5C 112
Heathfield. Devn 5B 12
Heathfield. E Sus 3G 27
Heathfield. Ren 3E 126
Heathfield. Som 3E 21
(nr. Lydeard St Lawrence)
Heathfield. Som 4E 21
(nr. Norton Fitzwarren)
Heath Green. Worc 3E 61
Heathhall. Dum 2A 112
Heath Hayes. Staf 4E 73
Heath Hill. Shrp 4B 72
Heath House. Som 2H 21
Heathrow (London) Airport.
G Lon 3B 38 & 216
Heathstock. Devn 2F 13
Heath, The. Norf 3E 79
(nr. Buxton)
Heath, The. Norf 3B 78
(nr. Fakenham)
Heath, The. Norf 3D 78
(nr. Hevingham)
Heath, The. Staf 2E 73
Heath, The. Suff 2E 55
Heathton. Shrp 1C 60
Heathtop. Derbs 2F 73
Heath Town. W Mid 1D 60
Heatley. G Man 2B 84
Heatley. Staf 3E 73
Heaton. Lanc 3D 96
Heaton. Staf 4D 84
Heaton. Tyne 3F 115
Heaton. W Yor 1B 92
Heaton Moor. G Man 1C 84
Heaton's Bridge. Lanc 3C 90
Heaverham. Kent 5G 39
Heavitree. Devn 3C 12
Hebburn. Tyne 3G 115
Hebden. N Yor 3C 98
Hebden Bridge. W Yor 2H 91
Hebden Green. Ches W 4A 84
Hebing End. Herts 3D 52
Hebron. Carm 2F 43
Hebron. Nmbd 1E 115
Heck. Dum 1B 112
Heckdyke. Notts 1E 87
Heckfield. Hants 5F 37
Heckfield Green. Suff 3D 66
Heckfordbridge. Essx 3C 54
Heckington. Linc 1A 76
Heckmondwike. W Yor 2C 92
Heddington. Wilts 5E 35
Heddle. Orkn 6C 172
Heddon. Devn 4G 19
Heddon-on-the-Wall. Nmbd 3E 115
Hedenham. Norf 1F 67
Hedge End. Hants 1C 16
Hedgerley. Buck 2A 38
Hedging. Som 4G 21
Hedley on the Hill. Nmbd 4D 115
Hednesford. Staf 4E 73
Hedon. E Yor 2E 95
Hegdon Hill. Here 5H 59
Heglibister. Shet 6E 173
Heighington. Darl 2F 105
Heighington. Linc 4H 87
Heightington. Worc 3B 60
Heights of Brae. High 2H 157
Heights of Fodderty. High 2H 157
Heights of Kinlochewe. High 2C 156
Heiton. Bord 1B 120
Hele. Devn 2C 12
(nr. Exeter)
Hele. Devn 3D 10
(nr. Holsworthy)
Hele. Devn 2F 19
(nr. Ilfracombe)
Hele. Torb 2F 9
Helensburgh. Arg 1D 126
Helford. Corn 4E 5
Helhoughton. Norf 3A 78
Helions Bumpstead. Essx 1G 53
Helland. Corn 5A 10
Helland. Som 4G 21
Hellandbridge. Corn 5A 10
Hellesdon. Norf 4E 78
Hellesveor. Corn 2C 4
Hellidon. Nptn 5C 62
Hellifield. N Yor 4A 98
Hellingly. E Sus 4G 27
Hellington. Norf 5F 79
Hellister. Shet 7E 173
Helmdon. Nptn 1D 50
Helmingham. Suff 5D 66
Helmington Row. Dur 1E 105
Helmsdale. High 2H 165
Helmshore. Lanc 2F 91
Helmsley. N Yor 1A 100
Helperby. N Yor 3G 99
Helperthorpe. N Yor 2D 100
Helpringham. Linc 1A 76
Helpston. Pet 5A 76
Helsby. Ches W 3G 83
Helsey. Linc 3E 89
Helston. Corn 4D 4
Helstone. Corn 4A 10
Helton. Cumb 2G 103
Helwith. N Yor 4D 105
Helwith Bridge. N Yor 3H 97
Helygain. Flin 3E 82
Hemblington. Norf 4F 79
Hemel Hempstead. Herts 5A 52
Hemerdon. Devn 3B 8
Hemingbrough. N Yor 1G 93
Hemingby. Linc 3B 88
Hemingfield. S Yor 4D 93
Hemingford Abbots. Cambs 3B 64
Hemingford Grey. Cambs 3B 64
Hemingstone. Suff 5D 66
Hemington. Leics 3B 74
Hemington. Nptn 2H 63
Hemington. Som 1C 22
Hemley. Suff 1F 55
Hemlington. Midd 3B 106
Hempholme. E Yor 4E 101
Hempnall. Norf 1E 67
Hempnall Green. Norf 1E 67
Hempriggs. High 4F 169
Hemp's Green. Essx 3C 54
Hempstead. Essx 2G 53
Hempstead. Medw 4B 40
Hempstead. Norf 2D 78
(nr. Holt)
Hempstead. Norf 3G 79
(nr. Stalham)
Hempsted. Glos 4D 48
Hempton. Norf 3B 78
Hempton. Oxon 2C 50
Hemsby. Norf 4G 79
Hemswell. Linc 1G 87
Hemswell Cliff. Linc 2G 87
Hemsworth. Dors 2E 15
Hemsworth. W Yor 3E 93
Hem, The. Shrp 5B 72
Hemyock. Devn 1E 13
Henallt. Carm 3E 45
Henbury. Bris 4A 34
Henbury. Ches E 3C 84
Hendomen. Powy 1E 58
Hendon. G Lon 2D 38
Hendon. Tyne 4H 115
Hendra. Corn 3D 6
Hendre. B'end 3C 32
Hendreforgan. Rhon 3C 32
Hendy. Carm 5F 45
Heneglwys. IOA 3D 80
Henfeddau Fawr. Pemb 1G 43
Henfield. S Glo 4B 34
Henfield. W Sus 4D 26
Henford. Devn 3D 10
Hengoed. Cphy 2E 33
Hengoed. Shrp 2E 71
Hengrave. Suff 4H 65
Henham. Essx 3F 53
Heniarth. Powy 5D 70
Henlade. Som 4F 21
Henley. Dors 2B 14
Henley. Shrp 2G 59
(nr. Church Stretton)
Henley. Shrp 3H 59
(nr. Ludlow)
Henley. Som 3H 21
Henley. Suff 5D 66
Henley. W Sus 4G 25
Henley-in-Arden. Warw 4F 61
Henley-on-Thames. Oxon 3F 37
Henley's Down. E Sus 4B 28
Henley Street. Kent 4A 40
Henllan. Cdgn 1D 44
Henllan. Den 4C 82
Henllan. Mon 3F 47
Henllan Amgoed. Carm 3F 43
Henllys. Torf 2F 33
Henlow. C Beds 2B 52
Hennock. Devn 4B 12
Henny Street. Essx 2B 54
Henryd. Cnwy 3G 81
Henry's Moat. Pemb 2E 43
Hensall. N Yor 2F 93
Henshaw. Nmbd 3A 114
Hensingham. Cumb 3A 102
Henstead. Suff 2G 67
Hensting. Hants 4C 24
Henstridge. Som 1C 14
Henstridge Ash. Som 4C 22
Henstridge Bowden. Som 4B 22
Henstridge Marsh. Som 4C 22
Henton. Oxon 5F 51
Henton. Som 2H 21
Henwood. Corn 5C 10
Heogan. Shet 7F 173
Heol Senni. Powy 3C 46
Heol-y-Cyw. B'end 3C 32
Hepburn. Nmbd 2E 121
Hepple. Nmbd 4D 121
Hepscott. Nmbd 1F 115
Heptonstall. W Yor 2H 91
Hepworth. Suff 3B 66
Hepworth. W Yor 4B 92
Herbrandston. Pemb 4C 42
Hereford. Here 2A 48 & 197
Heribusta. High 1D 154
Heriot. Bord 4H 129
Hermiston. Edin 2E 129
Hermitage. Dors 2B 14
Hermitage. Bord 5H 119
Hermitage. W Ber 4D 36
Hermitage. W Sus 2F 17
Hermon. Carm 3G 45
(nr. Llandeilo)
Hermon. Carm 2D 44
(nr. Newcastle Emlyn)
Hermon. IOA 4C 80
Hermon. Pemb 1G 43
Herne. Kent 4F 41
Herne Bay. Kent 4F 41
Herne Common. Kent 4F 41
Herne Pound. Kent 5A 40
Herner. Devn 4F 19
Hernhill. Kent 4E 41
Herodsfoot. Corn 2G 7
Heronden. Kent 5G 41
Herongate. Essx 1H 39
Heronsford. S Ayr 1G 109
Heronsgate. Herts 1B 38
Heron's Ghyll. E Sus 3F 27
Herra. Shet 2H 173
Herriard. Hants 2E 25
Herringfleet. Suff 1G 67
Herringswell. Suff 4G 65
Herrington. Tyne 4G 115
Hersden. Kent 4G 41
Hersham. Corn 2C 10
Hersham. Surr 4C 38
Herstmonceux. E Sus 4H 27
Herston. Dors 5F 15
Herston. Orkn 8D 172
Hertford. Herts 4D 52
Hertford Heath. Herts 4D 52
Hertingfordbury. Herts 4D 52
Hesketh. Lanc 2C 90
Hesketh Bank. Lanc 2C 90
Hesketh Lane. Lanc 5F 97
Hesket Newmarket. Cumb 1E 103
Heskin Green. Lanc 3D 90
Hesleden. Dur 1B 106
Hesleyside. Nmbd 1B 114
Heslington. York 4A 100
Hessay. York 4H 99
Hessenford. Corn 3H 7
Hessett. Suff 4B 66
Hessilhead. N Ayr 4E 127
Hessle. Hull 2D 94
Hestaford. Shet 6D 173
Hest Bank. Lanc 3D 96
Hester's Way. Glos 3E 49
Hestinsetter. Shet 7D 173
Heston. G Lon 3C 38
Hestwall. Orkn 6B 172
Heswall. Mers 2E 83
Hethe. Oxon 3D 50
Hethelpit Cross. Glos 3C 48
Hethersett. Norf 5D 78
Hethersgill. Cumb 3F 113
Hetherside. Cumb 3F 113
Hethpool. Nmbd 2C 120
Hett. Dur 1F 105
Hetton. N Yor 4B 98
Hetton-le-Hole. Tyne 5G 115
Hetton Steads. Nmbd 1E 121
Heugh. Nmbd 2D 115
Heugh-head. Abers 2A 152
Heveningham. Suff 3F 67
Hever. Kent 1F 27
Heversham. Cumb 1D 97
Hevingham. Norf 3D 78
Hewas Water. Corn 4D 6
Hewelsfield. Glos 5A 48
Hewish. N Som 5G 33
Hewish. Som 2H 13
Hewood. Dors 2G 13
Heworth. York 4A 100
Hexham. Nmbd 3C 114
Hextable. Kent 3G 39
Hexton. Herts 2B 52
Hexworthy. Devn 5G 11
Heybridge. Essx 1H 39
(nr. Brentwood)
Heybridge. Essx 5B 54
(nr. Maldon)
Heybridge Basin. Essx 5B 54
Heybrook Bay. Devn 4A 8
Heydon. Cambs 1E 53
Heydon. Norf 3D 78
Heydour. Linc 2H 75
Heylipol. Arg 4A 138
Heyop. Powy 3E 59
Heysham. Lanc 3D 96
Heyshott. W Sus 1G 17
Heytesbury. Wilts 2E 23
Heythrop. Oxon 3B 50
Heywood. G Man 3G 91
Heywood. Wilts 1D 22
Hibaldstow. N Lin 4C 94
Hickleton. S Yor 4E 93

Hickling. *Norf* 3G **79**
Hickling. *Notts* 3D **74**
Hickling Green. *Norf* 3G **79**
Hickling Heath. *Norf* 3G **79**
Hickstead. *W Sus* 3D **26**
Hidcote Bartrim. *Glos* 1G **49**
Hidcote Boyce. *Glos* 1G **49**
Higford. *Shrp* 5B **72**
High Ackworth. *W Yor* 3E **93**
Higham. *Derbs* 5A **86**
Higham. *Kent* 3B **40**
Higham. *Lanc* 1G **91**
Higham. *S Yor* 4D **92**
Higham. *Suff* 2D **54**
(nr. Ipswich)
Higham. *Suff* 4G **65**
(nr. Newmarket)
Higham Dykes. *Nmbd* 2E **115**
Higham Ferrers. *Nptn* 4G **63**
Higham Gobion. *C Beds* 2B **52**
Higham on the Hill. *Leics* 1A **62**
Highampton. *Devn* 2E **11**
Higham Wood. *Kent* 1G **27**
High Angerton. *Nmbd* 1D **115**
High Auldgirth. *Dum* 1G **111**
High Bankhill. *Cumb* 5G **113**
High Banton. *N Lan* 1A **128**
High Barnet. *G Lon* 1D **38**
High Beech. *Essx* 1F **39**
High Bentham. *N Yor* 3F **97**
High Bickington. *Devn* 4G **19**
High Biggins. *Cumb* 2F **97**
High Birkwith. *N Yor* 2H **97**
High Blantyre. *S Lan* 4H **127**
High Bonnybridge. *Falk* 2B **128**
High Borrans. *Cumb* 4F **103**
High Bradfield. *S Yor* 1G **85**
High Bray. *Devn* 3G **19**
Highbridge. *Cumb* 5E **113**
Highbridge. *High* 5D **148**
Highbridge. *Som* 2G **21**
Highbrook. *W Sus* 2E **27**
High Brooms. *Kent* 1G **27**
High Bullen. *Devn* 4F **19**
Highburton. *W Yor* 3B **92**
Highbury. *Som* 2B **22**
High Buston. *Nmbd* 4G **121**
High Callerton. *Nmbd* 2E **115**
High Carlingill. *Cumb* 4H **103**
High Catton. *E Yor* 4B **100**
High Church. *Nmbd* 1E **115**
Highclere. *Hants* 5C **36**
Highcliffe. *Dors* 3H **15**
High Cogges. *Oxon* 5B **50**
High Common. *Norf* 5B **78**
High Coniscliffe. *Darl* 3F **105**
High Crosby. *Cumb* 4F **113**
High Cross. *Hants* 4F **25**
High Cross. *Herts* 4D **52**
High Dougarie. *N Ayr* 2C **122**
High Easter. *Essx* 4G **53**
High Eggborough. *N Yor* 2F **93**
High Ellington. *N Yor* 1D **98**
Higher Alham. *Som* 2B **22**
Higher Ansty. *Dors* 2C **14**
Higher Ashton. *Devn* 4B **12**
Higher Ballam. *Lanc* 1B **90**
Higher Bartle. *Lanc* 1D **90**
Higher Bockhampton. *Dors* 3C **14**
Higher Bojewyan. *Corn* 3A **4**
High Ercall. *Telf* 4H **71**
Higher Cheriton. *Devn* 2E **12**
Higher Clovelly. *Devn* 4D **18**
Higher Compton. *Plym* 3A **8**
Higher Dinting. *Derbs* 1E **85**
Higher Dunstone. *Devn* 5H **11**
Higher End. *G Man* 4D **90**
Higher Gabwell. *Devn* 2F **9**
Higher Halstock Leigh. *Dors* 2A **14**
Higher Heysham. *Lanc* 3D **96**
Higher Hurdsfield. *Ches E* 3D **84**
Higher Kingcombe. *Dors* 3A **14**
Higher Kinnerton. *Flin* 4F **83**
Higher Melcombe. *Dors* 2C **14**
Higher Penwortham. *Lanc* 2D **90**
Higher Porthpean. *Corn* 3E **7**
Higher Poynton. *Ches E* 2D **84**
Higher Shotton. *Flin* 4F **83**
Higher Shurlach. *Ches W* 3A **84**
Higher Slade. *Devn* 2F **19**
Higher Tale. *Devn* 2D **12**
Highertown. *Corn* 4C **6**
Higher Town. *IOS* 1B **4**
Higher Town. *Som* 2C **20**
Higher Vexford. *Som* 3E **20**
Higher Walton. *Lanc* 2D **90**
Higher Walton. *Warr* 2H **83**
Higher Whatcombe. *Dors* 2D **14**
Higher Wheelton. *Lanc* 2E **90**
Higher Whiteleigh. *Corn* 3C **10**
Higher Whitley. *Ches W* 3A **84**
Higher Wincham. *Ches W* 3A **84**
Higher Wraxall. *Dors* 2A **14**
Higher Wych. *Wrex* 1G **71**
Higher Yalberton. *Torb* 3E **9**
High Etherley. *Dur* 2E **105**
High Ferry. *Linc* 1C **76**
Highfield. *E Yor* 1H **93**
Highfield. *N Ayr* 4E **126**
Highfield. *Tyne* 4E **115**
Highfields Caldecote. *Cambs* 5C **64**
High Garrett. *Essx* 3A **54**
Highgate. *G Lon* 2D **39**
Highgate. *N Ayr* 4E **127**
Highgate. *Powy* 1D **58**
High Grange. *Dur* 1E **105**
High Green. *Cumb* 4F **103**
High Green. *Norf* 5D **78**
High Green. *Shrp* 2B **60**
High Green. *S Yor* 1H **85**
High Green. *W Yor* 3B **92**
High Green. *Worc* 1D **49**
Highgreen Manor. *Nmbd* 5C **120**
High Halden. *Kent* 2C **28**
High Halstow. *Medw* 3B **40**
High Ham. *Som* 3H **21**
High Harrington. *Cumb* 2B **102**
High Haswell. *Dur* 5G **115**
High Hatton. *Shrp* 3A **72**
High Hawkser. *N Yor* 4G **107**
High Hesket. *Cumb* 5F **113**
High Hesleden. *Dur* 1B **106**
High Hoyland. *S Yor* 3C **92**
High Hunsley. *E Yor* 1C **94**
High Hurstwood. *E Sus* 3F **27**
High Hutton. *N Yor* 3B **100**
High Ireby. *Cumb* 1D **102**
High Keil. *Arg* 5A **122**
High Kelling. *Norf* 1D **78**
High Kilburn. *N Yor* 2H **99**
High Knipe. *Cumb* 3G **103**
High Lands. *Dur* 2E **105**
Highlands, The. *Shrp* 2A **60**
Highlane. *Ches E* 4C **84**
Highlane. *Derbs* 2B **86**
High Lane. *G Man* 2D **84**
High Lane. *Here* 4A **60**
High Laver. *Essx* 5F **53**
Highlaws. *Cumb* 5C **112**
Highleadon. *Glos* 3C **48**
High Legh. *Ches E* 2A **84**
Highleigh. *W Sus* 3G **17**
High Leven. *Stoc T* 3B **106**
Highley. *Shrp* 2B **60**
High Littleton. *Bath* 1B **22**
High Longthwaite. *Cumb* 5D **112**
High Lorton. *Cumb* 2C **102**
High Marishes. *N Yor* 2C **100**
High Marnham. *Notts* 3F **87**
High Melton. *S Yor* 4F **93**
High Mickley. *Nmbd* 3D **115**
Highmoor. *Cumb* 5D **112**
High Moor. *Lanc* 3D **90**
Highmoor. *Oxon* 3F **37**
Highmoor Cross. *Oxon* 3F **37**
Highmoor Hill. *Mon* 3H **33**
High Mowthorpe. *N Yor* 3C **100**
Highnam. *Glos* 4C **48**
High Newport. *Tyne* 4G **115**
High Newton. *Cumb* 1D **96**
High Newton-by-the-Sea.
Nmbd 2G **121**
High Nibthwaite. *Cumb* 1B **96**
High Offley. *Staf* 3B **72**
High Ongar. *Essx* 5F **53**
High Onn. *Staf* 4C **72**
High Orchard. *Glos* 4D **48**
High Park. *Mers* 3B **90**
High Roding. *Essx* 4G **53**
High Row. *Cumb* 1E **103**
High Salvington. *W Sus* 5C **26**
High Scales. *Cumb* 5C **112**
High Shaw. *N Yor* 5B **104**
High Shincliffe. *Dur* 5F **115**
High Side. *Cumb* 1D **102**
High Spen. *Tyne* 3E **115**
Highsted. *Kent* 4D **40**
High Stoop. *Dur* 5E **115**
High Street. *Corn* 3D **6**
High Street. *Suff* 5G **67**
(nr. Aldeburgh)
High Street. *Suff* 2F **67**
(nr. Bungay)
High Street. *Suff* 3G **67**
(nr. Yoxford)
Highstreet Green. *Essx* 2A **54**
High Street Green. *Suff* 5C **66**
Highstreet Green. *Surr* 2A **26**
Hightae. *Dum* 2B **112**
High Throston. *Hart* 1B **106**
Hightown. *Ches E* 4C **84**
Hightown. *Mers* 4A **90**
High Town. *Staf* 4D **73**
Hightown Green. *Suff* 5B **66**
High Toynton. *Linc* 4B **88**
High Trewhitt. *Nmbd* 4E **121**
High Valleyfield. *Fife* 1D **128**
Highway. *Here* 1H **47**
Highweek. *Devn* 5B **12**
High Westwood. *Dur* 4E **115**
Highwood. *Staf* 2E **73**
Highwood. *Worc* 4A **60**
High Worsall. *N Yor* 4A **106**
Highworth. *Swin* 2H **35**
High Wray. *Cumb* 5E **103**
High Wych. *Herts* 4E **53**
High Wycombe. *Buck* 2G **37**
Hilborough. *Norf* 5H **77**
Hilcott. *Wilts* 1G **23**
Hildenborough. *Kent* 1G **27**
Hildersham. *Cambs* 1F **53**
Hilderstone. *Staf* 2D **72**
Hilderthorpe. *E Yor* 3F **101**
Hilfield. *Dors* 2B **14**
Hilgay. *Norf* 1F **65**
Hill. *S Glo* 2B **34**
Hill. *Warw* 4B **62**
Hill. *Worc* 1E **49**
Hillam. *N Yor* 2F **93**
Hillbeck. *Cumb* 3A **104**
Hillberry. *IOM* 4C **108**
Hillborough. *Kent* 4G **41**
Hillbourne. *Pool* 3F **15**
Hillbrae. *Abers* 4D **160**
(nr. Aberchirder)
Hillbrae. *Abers* 1E **153**
(nr. Inverurie)
Hillbrae. *Abers* 5F **161**
(nr. Methlick)
Hill Brow. *Hants* 4F **25**
Hillbutts. *Dors* 2E **15**
Hillclifflane. *Derbs* 1G **73**
Hillcommon. *Som* 4E **21**
Hill Deverill. *Wilts* 2D **22**
Hilldyke. *Linc* 1C **76**
Hill End. *Dur* 1D **104**
Hillend. *Fife* 1E **129**
(nr. Inverkeithing)
Hill End. *Fife* 4C **136**
(nr. Saline)
Hillend. *N Lan* 3B **128**
Hill End. *N Yor* 4C **98**
Hillend. *Shrp* 1C **60**
Hillend. *Swan* 3D **30**
Hillersland. *Glos* 4A **48**
Hillerton. *Devn* 3H **11**
Hillesden. *Buck* 3E **51**
Hillesley. *Glos* 3C **34**
Hillfarrance. *Som* 4E **21**
Hill Furze. *Worc* 1E **49**
Hill Gate. *Here* 3H **47**
Hill Green. *Essx* 2E **53**
Hillgreen. *W Ber* 4C **36**
Hillhead. *Abers* 5C **160**
Hill Head. *Hants* 2D **16**
Hillhead. *S Ayr* 3D **116**
Hillhead. *Torb* 3F **9**
Hillhead of Auchentumb.
Abers 3G **161**
Hilliard's Cross. *Staf* 4F **73**
Hilliclay. *High* 2D **168**
Hillingdon. *G Lon* 2B **38**
Hillington. *Norf* 3G **77**
Hillington. *Ren* 3G **127**
Hillmorton. *Warw* 3C **62**
Hill of Beath. *Fife* 4D **136**
Hill of Fearn. *High* 1C **158**
Hill of Fiddes. *Abers* 1G **153**
Hill of Keillor. *Ang* 4B **144**
Hill of Overbrae. *Abers* 2F **161**
Hill Ridware. *Staf* 4E **73**
Hillsborough. *S Yor* 1H **85**
Hillside. *Abers* 4G **153**
Hillside. *Ang* 2G **145**
Hillside. *Devn* 2D **8**
Hillside. *Mers* 3B **90**
Hillside. *Orkn* 5C **172**
Hillside. *Shet* 5F **173**
Hillside. *Shrp* 2A **60**
Hill Side. *W Yor* 3B **92**
Hillside. *Worc* 4B **60**
Hillside of Prieston. *Ang* 5C **144**
Hill Somersal. *Derbs* 2F **73**
Hillstown. *Derbs* 4B **86**
Hillstreet. *Hants* 1B **16**
Hillswick. *Shet* 4D **173**
Hill, The. *Cumb* 1A **96**
Hill Top. *Dur* 2C **104**
(nr. Barnard Castle)
Hill Top. *Dur* 5F **115**
(nr. Durham)
Hill Top. *Dur* 4E **115**
(nr. Stanley)
Hill Top. *Hants* 2C **16**
Hill View. *Dors* 3E **15**
Hillwell. *Shet* 10E **173**
Hill Wootton. *Warw* 4H **61**
Hillyland. *Per* 1C **136**
Hilmarton. *Wilts* 4F **35**
Hilperton. *Wilts* 1D **22**
Hilperton Marsh. *Wilts* 1D **22**
Hilsea. *Port* 2E **17**
Hilston. *E Yor* 1F **95**
Hiltingbury. *Hants* 4C **24**
Hilton. *Cambs* 4B **64**
Hilton. *Cumb* 2A **104**
Hilton. *Derbs* 2G **73**
Hilton. *Dors* 2C **14**
Hilton. *Dur* 2E **105**
Hilton. *High* 5E **165**
Hilton. *Shrp* 1B **60**
Hilton. *Staf* 5E **73**
Hilton. *Stoc T* 3B **106**
Hilton of Cadboll. *High* 1C **158**
Himbleton. *Worc* 5D **60**
Himley. *Staf* 1C **60**
Hincaster. *Cumb* 1E **97**
Hinchcliffe Mill. *W Yor* 4B **92**
Hinchwick. *Glos* 2G **49**
Hinckley. *Leics* 1B **62**
Hinderclay. *Suff* 3C **66**
Hinderwell. *N Yor* 3E **107**
Hindford. *Shrp* 2F **71**
Hindhead. *Surr* 3G **25**
Hindley. *G Man* 4E **90**
Hindley. *Nmbd* 4D **114**
Hindley Green. *G Man* 4E **91**
Hindlip. *Worc* 5C **60**
Hindolveston. *Norf* 3C **78**
Hindon. *Wilts* 3E **23**
Hindringham. *Norf* 2B **78**
Hingham. *Norf* 5C **78**
Hinksford. *Staf* 2C **60**
Hinstock. *Shrp* 3A **72**
Hintlesham. *Suff* 1D **54**
Hinton. *Hants* 3H **15**
Hinton. *Here* 2G **47**
Hinton. *Nptn* 5C **62**
Hinton. *Shrp* 5G **71**
Hinton. *S Glo* 4C **34**
Hinton Ampner. *Hants* 4D **24**
Hinton Blewett. *Bath* 1A **22**
Hinton Charterhouse. *Bath* 1C **22**
Hinton-in-the-Hedges. *Nptn* 2D **50**
Hinton Martell. *Dors* 2F **15**
Hinton on the Green. *Worc* 1F **49**
Hinton Parva. *Swin* 3H **35**
Hinton St George. *Som* 1H **13**
Hinton St Mary. *Dors* 1C **14**
Hinton Waldrist. *Oxon* 2B **36**
Hints. *Shrp* 3A **60**
Hints. *Staf* 5F **73**
Hinwick. *Bed* 4G **63**
Hinxhill. *Kent* 1E **29**
Hinxton. *Cambs* 1E **53**
Hinxworth. *Herts* 1C **52**
Hipley. *Hants* 1E **16**
Hipperholme. *W Yor* 2B **92**
Hipsburn. *Nmbd* 3G **121**
Hipswell. *N Yor* 5E **105**
Hiraeth. *Carm* 2F **43**
Hirn. *Abers* 3E **153**
Hirnant. *Powy* 3C **70**
Hirst. *N Lan* 3B **128**
Hirst. *Nmbd* 1F **115**
Hirst Courtney. *N Yor* 2G **93**
Hirwaen. *Den* 4D **82**
Hirwaun. *Rhon* 5C **46**
Hiscott. *Devn* 4F **19**
Histon. *Cambs* 4D **64**
Hitcham. *Suff* 5B **66**
Hitchin. *Herts* 3B **52**
Hittisleigh. *Devn* 3H **11**
Hittisleigh Barton. *Devn* 3H **11**
Hive. *E Yor* 1B **94**
Hixon. *Staf* 3E **73**
Hoaden. *Kent* 5G **41**
Hoar Cross. *Staf* 3F **73**
Hoarwithy. *Here* 3A **48**
Hoath. *Kent* 4G **41**
Hobarris. *Shrp* 3F **59**
Hobbister. *Orkn* 7C **172**
Hobbles Green. *Suff* 5G **65**
Hobbs Cross. *Essx* 1F **39**
Hobkirk. *Bord* 3H **119**
Hobson. *Dur* 4E **115**
Hoby. *Leics* 4D **74**
Hockering. *Norf* 4C **78**
Hockering Heath. *Norf* 4C **78**
Hockerton. *Notts* 5E **86**
Hockley. *Essx* 1C **40**
Hockley. *Staf* 5G **73**
Hockley. *W Mid* 3G **61**
Hockley Heath. *W Mid* 3F **61**
Hockliffe. *C Beds* 3H **51**
Hockwold cum Wilton. *Norf* 2G **65**
Hockworthy. *Devn* 1D **12**
Hoddesdon. *Herts* 5D **52**
Hoddlesden. *Bkbn* 2F **91**
Hoddomcross. *Dum* 2C **112**
Hodgeston. *Pemb* 5E **43**
Hodley. *Powy* 1D **58**
Hodnet. *Shrp* 3A **72**
Hodsoll Street. *Kent* 4H **39**
Hodson. *Swin* 3G **35**
Hodthorpe. *Derbs* 3C **86**
Hoe. *Norf* 4B **78**
Hoe Gate. *Hants* 1E **17**
Hoe, The. *Plym* 3A **8**
Hoff. *Cumb* 3H **103**
Hoffleet Stow. *Linc* 2B **76**
Hogaland. *Shet* 4E **173**
Hogben's Hill. *Kent* 5E **41**
Hoggard's Green. *Suff* 5A **66**
Hoggeston. *Buck* 3G **51**
Hoggrill's End. *Warw* 1G **61**
Hogha Gearraidh. *W Isl* 1C **170**
Hoghton. *Lanc* 2E **90**
Hoghton Bottoms. *Lanc* 2E **91**
Hognaston. *Derbs* 5G **85**
Hogsthorpe. *Linc* 3E **89**
Hogstock. *Dors* 2E **15**
Holbeach. *Linc* 3C **76**
Holbeach Bank. *Linc* 3C **76**
Holbeach Clough. *Linc* 3C **76**
Holbeach Drove. *Linc* 4C **76**
Holbeach Hurn. *Linc* 3C **76**
Holbeach St Johns. *Linc* 4C **76**
Holbeach St Marks. *Linc* 2C **76**
Holbeach St Matthew. *Linc* 2D **76**
Holbeck. *Notts* 3C **86**
Holbeck. *W Yor* 1C **92**
Holbeck Woodhouse. *Notts* 3C **86**
Holberrow Green. *Worc* 5E **61**
Holbeton. *Devn* 3C **8**
Holborn. *G Lon* 2E **39**
Holbrook. *Derbs* 1A **74**
Holbrook. *S Yor* 2B **86**
Holbrook. *Suff* 2E **55**
Holburn. *Nmbd* 1E **121**
Holbury. *Hants* 2C **16**
Holcombe. *Devn* 5C **12**
Holcombe. *G Man* 3F **91**
Holcombe. *Som* 2B **22**
Holcombe Brook. *G Man* 3F **91**
Holcombe Rogus. *Devn* 1D **12**
Holcot. *Nptn* 4E **63**
Holden. *Lanc* 5G **97**
Holdenby. *Nptn* 4D **62**
Holder's Green. *Essx* 3G **53**
Holdgate. *Shrp* 2H **59**
Holdingham. *Linc* 1H **75**
Holditch. *Dors* 2G **13**
Holemoor. *Devn* 2E **11**
Hole Street. *W Sus* 4C **26**
Holford. *Som* 2E **21**
Holker. *Cumb* 2C **96**
Holkham. *Norf* 1A **78**
Hollacombe. *Devn* 2D **11**
Holland. *Orkn* 2D **172**
(on Papa Westray)
Holland. *Orkn* 5F **172**
(on Stronsay)
Holland Fen. *Linc* 1B **76**
Holland Lees. *Lanc* 4D **90**
Holland-on-Sea. *Essx* 4F **55**
Holland Park. *W Mid* 5E **73**
Hollandstoun. *Orkn* 2G **172**
Hollesley. *Suff* 1G **55**
Hollinfare. *Warr* 1A **84**
Hollingbourne. *Kent* 5C **40**
Hollingbury. *Brig* 5E **27**
Hollingdon. *Buck* 3G **51**
Hollingrove. *E Sus* 3A **28**
Hollington. *Derbs* 1G **73**
Hollington. *E Sus* 4B **28**
Hollington. *Staf* 2E **73**
Hollington Grove. *Derbs* 2G **73**
Hollingworth. *G Man* 1E **85**
Hollins. *Derbs* 3H **85**
Hollins. *G Man* 4G **91**
(nr. Bury)
Hollins. *G Man* 4G **91**
(nr. Middleton)
Hollinsclough. *Staf* 4E **85**
Hollinswood. *Telf* 5A **72**
Hollinthorpe. *W Yor* 1D **93**
Hollinwood. *G Man* 4H **91**
Hollinwood. *Shrp* 2H **71**
Hollocombe. *Devn* 1G **11**
Holloway. *Derbs* 5H **85**
Hollow Court. *Worc* 5D **61**
Hollowell. *Nptn* 3D **62**
Hollow Meadows. *S Yor* 2G **85**
Hollows. *Dum* 2E **113**
Hollybush. *Cphy* 5E **47**
Hollybush. *E Ayr* 3C **116**
Hollybush. *Worc* 2C **48**
Holly End. *Norf* 5D **77**
Holly Hill. *N Yor* 4E **105**
Hollyhurst. *Ches E* 1H **71**
Hollym. *E Yor* 2G **95**
Hollywood. *Worc* 3E **61**
Holmacott. *Devn* 4F **19**
Holmbridge. *W Yor* 4B **92**
Holmbury St Mary. *Surr* 1C **26**
Holmbush. *Corn* 3E **7**
Holmcroft. *Staf* 3D **72**
Holme. *Cambs* 2A **64**
Holme. *Cumb* 2E **97**
Holme. *N Lin* 4C **94**
Holme. *N Yor* 1F **99**
Holme. *Notts* 5F **87**
Holme. *W Yor* 4B **92**
Holmebridge. *Dors* 4D **15**
Holme Chapel. *Lanc* 2G **91**
Holme Hale. *Norf* 5A **78**
Holme Lacy. *Here* 2A **48**
Holme Marsh. *Here* 5F **59**
Holmend. *Dum* 4C **118**
Holme next the Sea. *Norf* 1G **77**
Holme-on-Spalding-Moor.
E Yor 1B **94**
Holme on the Wolds. *E Yor* 5D **100**
Holme Pierrepont. *Notts* 2D **74**
Holmer. *Here* 1A **48**
Holmer Green. *Buck* 1A **38**
Holmes. *Lanc* 3C **90**
Holme St Cuthbert. *Cumb* 5C **112**
Holmes Chapel. *Ches E* 4B **84**
Holmesfield. *Derbs* 3H **85**
Holmeswood. *Lanc* 3C **90**
Holmewood. *Derbs* 4B **86**
Holmfirth. *W Yor* 4B **92**
Holmhead. *E Ayr* 2E **117**
Holmisdale. *High* 4A **154**
Holm of Drumlanrig. *Dum* 5H **117**
Holmpton. *E Yor* 2G **95**
Holmrook. *Cumb* 5B **102**
Holmsgarth. *Shet* 7F **173**
Holmside. *Dur* 5F **115**
Holmwrangle. *Cumb* 5G **113**
Holne. *Devn* 2D **8**
Holsworthy. *Devn* 2D **10**
Holsworthy Beacon. *Devn* 2D **10**
Holt. *Dors* 2F **15**
Holt. *Norf* 2C **78**
Holt. *Wilts* 5D **34**
Holt. *Worc* 4C **60**
Holt. *Wrex* 5G **83**

Holtby. *York* 4A **100**
Holt End. *Hants* 3E **25**
Holt End. *Worc* 4E **61**
Holt Fleet. *Worc* 4C **60**
Holt Green. *Lanc* 4B **90**
Holt Heath. *Dors* 2F **15**
Holt Heath. *Worc* 4C **60**
Holton. *Oxon* 5E **50**
Holton. *Som* 4B **22**
Holton. *Suff* 3F **67**
Holton cum Beckering. *Linc* 2A **88**
Holton Heath. *Dors* 3E **15**
Holton le Clay. *Linc* 4F **95**
Holton le Moor. *Linc* 1H **87**
Holton St Mary. *Suff* 2D **54**
Holt Pound. *Hants* 2G **25**
Holtsmere End. *Herts* 4A **52**
Holtye. *E Sus* 2F **27**
Holwell. *Dors* 1C **14**
Holwell. *Herts* 2B **52**
Holwell. *Leics* 3E **75**
Holwell. *Oxon* 5H **49**
Holwell. *Som* 2C **22**
Holwick. *Dur* 2C **104**
Holworth. *Dors* 4C **14**
Holybourne. *Hants* 2F **25**
Holy City. *Devn* 2G **13**
Holy Cross. *Worc* 3D **60**
Holyfield. *Essx* 5D **53**
Holyhead. *IOA* 2B **80**
Holy Island. *Nmbd* 5H **131**
Holymoorside. *Derbs* 4H **85**
Holyport. *Wind* 4G **37**
Holystone. *Nmbd* 4D **120**
Holytown. *N Lan* 3A **128**
Holywell. *Cambs* 3C **64**
Holywell. *Dors* 2A **14**
Holywell. *Flin* 3D **82**
Holywell. *Glos* 2C **34**
Holywell. *Nmbd* 2G **115**
Holywell. *Warw* 4F **61**
Holywell Bay. *Corn* 3B **6**
Holywell Green. *W Yor* 3A **92**
Holywell Lake. *Som* 4E **20**
Holywell Row. *Suff* 3G **65**
Holywood. *Dum* 1G **111**
Homer. *Shrp* 5A **72**
Homer Green. *Mers* 4B **90**
Homersfield. *Suff* 2E **67**
Hom Green. *Here* 3A **48**
Homington. *Wilts* 4G **23**
Honeyborough. *Pemb* 4D **42**
Honeybourne. *Worc* 1G **49**
Honeychurch. *Devn* 2G **11**
Honeydon. *Bed* 5A **64**
Honey Hill. *Kent* 4F **41**
Honey Street. *Wilts* 5G **35**
Honey Tye. *Suff* 2C **54**
Honeywick. *C Beds* 3H **51**
Honiley. *Warw* 3G **61**
Honing. *Norf* 3F **79**
Honingham. *Norf* 4D **78**
Honington. *Linc* 1G **75**
Honington. *Suff* 3B **66**
Honington. *Warw* 1A **50**
Honiton. *Devn* 2E **13**
Honley. *W Yor* 3B **92**
Honnington. *Telf* 4B **72**
Hoo. *Suff* 5E **67**
Hoobrook. *Worc* 3C **60**
Hood Green. *S Yor* 4D **92**
Hooe. *E Sus* 5A **28**
Hooe. *Plym* 3B **8**
Hooe Common. *E Sus* 4A **28**
Hoohill. *Bkpl* 1B **90**
Hook. *Cambs* 1D **64**
Hook. *E Yor* 2A **94**
Hook. *G Lon* 4C **38**
Hook. *Hants* 1F **25**
(nr. Basingstoke)
Hook. *Hants* 2D **16**
(nr. Fareham)
Hook. *Pemb* 3D **43**
Hook. *Wilts* 3F **35**
Hook-a-Gate. *Shrp* 5G **71**
Hook Bank. *Worc* 1D **48**
Hooke. *Dors* 2A **14**
Hooker Gate. *Tyne* 4E **115**
Hookgate. *Staf* 2B **72**
Hook Green. *Kent* 2A **28**
(nr. Lamberhurst)
Hook Green. *Kent* 3H **39**
(nr. Longfield)
Hook Green. *Kent* 4H **39**
(nr. Meopham)
Hook Norton. *Oxon* 2B **50**
Hook's Cross. *Herts* 3C **52**
Hook Street. *Glos* 2B **34**
Hookway. *Devn* 3B **12**
Hookwood. *Surr* 1D **26**
Hoole. *Ches W* 4G **83**
Hooley. *Surr* 5D **39**
Hooley Bridge. *G Man* 3G **91**
Hooley Brow. *G Man* 3G **91**
Hoo St Werburgh. *Medw* 3B **40**
Hooton. *Ches W* 3F **83**
Hooton Levitt. *S Yor* 1C **86**
Hooton Pagnell. *S Yor* 4E **93**
Hooton Roberts. *S Yor* 1B **86**
Hoove. *Shet* 7E **173**
Hope. *Derbs* 2F **85**
Hope. *Flin* 5F **83**
Hope. *High* 2E **167**
Hope. *Powy* 5E **71**
Hope. *Shrp* 5F **71**
Hope. *Staf* 5F **85**
Hope Bagot. *Shrp* 3H **59**
Hope Bowdler. *Shrp* 1G **59**
Hopedale. *Staf* 5F **85**
Hope Green. *Ches E* 2D **84**
Hopeman. *Mor* 2F **159**
Hope Mansell. *Here* 4B **48**
Hopesay. *Shrp* 2F **59**
Hope's Green. *Essx* 2B **40**
Hopetown. *W Yor* 2D **93**
Hope under Dinmore. *Here* 5H **59**
Hopley's Green. *Here* 5F **59**
Hopperton. *N Yor* 4G **99**
Hop Pole. *Linc* 4A **76**
Hopstone. *Shrp* 1B **60**
Hopton. *Derbs* 5G **85**
Hopton. *Powy* 1E **59**
Hopton. *Shrp* 3F **71**
(nr. Oswestry)
Hopton. *Shrp* 3H **71**
(nr. Wem)
Hopton. *Staf* 3D **72**
Hopton. *Suff* 3B **66**
Hopton Cangeford. *Shrp* 2H **59**
Hopton Castle. *Shrp* 3F **59**
Hoptonheath. *Shrp* 3F **59**
Hopton Heath. *Staf* 3D **72**
Hopton on Sea. *Norf* 5H **79**
Hopton Wafers. *Shrp* 3A **60**
Hopwas. *Staf* 5F **73**
Hopwood. *Worc* 3E **61**
Horam. *E Sus* 4G **27**
Horbling. *Linc* 2A **76**
Horbury. *W Yor* 3C **92**
Horcott. *Glos* 5G **49**
Horden. *Dur* 5H **115**
Horderley. *Shrp* 2G **59**
Hordle. *Hants* 3A **16**
Hordley. *Shrp* 2F **71**
Horeb. *Carm* 3F **45**
(nr. Brechfa)
Horeb. *Carm* 5E **45**
(nr. Llanelli)
Horeb. *Cdgn* 1D **45**
Horfield. *Bris* 4B **34**
Horgabost. *W Isl* 8C **171**
Horham. *Suff* 3E **66**
Horkesley Heath. *Essx* 3C **54**
Horkstow. *N Lin* 3C **94**
Horley. *Oxon* 1C **50**
Horley. *Surr* 1D **27**
Horn Ash. *Dors* 2G **13**
Hornblotton Green. *Som* 3A **22**
Hornby. *Lanc* 2E **97**
Hornby. *N Yor* 4A **106**
(nr. Appleton Wiske)
Hornby. *N Yor* 5F **105**
(nr. Catterick Garrison)
Horncastle. *Linc* 4B **88**
Hornchurch. *G Lon* 2G **39**
Horncliffe. *Nmbd* 5F **131**
Horndean. *Hants* 1E **17**
Horndean. *Bord* 5E **131**
Horndon. *Devn* 4F **11**
Horndon on the Hill. *Thur* 2A **40**
Horne. *Surr* 1E **27**
Horner. *Som* 2C **20**
Horning. *Norf* 4F **79**
Horninghold. *Leics* 1F **63**
Horninglow. *Staf* 3G **73**
Horningsea. *Cambs* 4D **65**
Horningsham. *Wilts* 2D **22**
Horningtoft. *Norf* 3B **78**
Hornsbury. *Som* 1G **13**
Hornsby. *Cumb* 4G **113**
Hornsbygate. *Cumb* 4G **113**
Horns Corner. *Kent* 3B **28**
Horns Cross. *Devn* 4D **19**
Hornsea. *E Yor* 5G **101**
Hornsea Burton. *E Yor* 5G **101**
Hornsey. *G Lon* 2E **39**
Hornton. *Oxon* 1B **50**
Horpit. *Swin* 3H **35**
Horrabridge. *Devn* 2B **8**
Horringer. *Suff* 4H **65**
Horringford. *IOW* 4D **16**
Horrocks Fold. *G Man* 3F **91**
Horrocksford. *Lanc* 5G **97**
Horsbrugh Ford. *Bord* 1E **119**
Horsebridge. *Devn* 5E **11**
Horsebridge. *E Sus* 4G **27**
Horsebridge. *Hants* 3B **24**
Horse Bridge. *Staf* 5D **84**
Horsebrook. *Staf* 4C **72**
Horsecastle. *N Som* 5H **33**
Horsehay. *Telf* 5A **72**
Horseheath. *Cambs* 1G **53**
Horsehouse. *N Yor* 1C **98**
Horsell. *Surr* 5A **38**
Horseman's Green. *Wrex* 1G **71**
Horsenden. *Buck* 5F **51**
Horseway. *Cambs* 2D **64**
Horsey. *Norf* 3G **79**
Horsey. *Som* 3G **21**
Horsford. *Norf* 4D **78**
Horsforth. *W Yor* 1C **92**
Horsham. *W Sus* 2C **26**
Horsham. *Worc* 5B **60**
Horsham St Faith. *Norf* 4E **78**
Horsington. *Linc* 4A **88**
Horsington. *Som* 4C **22**
Horsley. *Derbs* 1A **74**
Horsley. *Glos* 2D **34**
Horsley. *Nmbd* 3D **115**
(nr. Prudhoe)
Horsley. *Nmbd* 5C **120**
(nr. Rochester)
Horsley Cross. *Essx* 3E **54**
Horsleycross Street.
Essx 3E **54**
Horsleyhill. *Bord* 3H **119**
Horsleyhope. *Dur* 5D **114**
Horsley Woodhouse.
Derbs 1A **74**
Horsmonden. *Kent* 1A **28**
Horspath. *Oxon* 5D **50**
Horstead. *Norf* 4E **79**
Horsted Keynes. *W Sus* 3E **27**
Horton. *Buck* 4H **51**
Horton. *Dors* 2F **15**
Horton. *Lanc* 4A **98**
Horton. *Nptn* 5F **63**
Horton. *Shrp* 2G **71**
Horton. *Som* 1G **13**
Horton. *S Glo* 3C **34**
Horton. *Staf* 5D **84**
Horton. *Swan* 4D **30**
Horton. *Wilts* 5F **35**
Horton. *Wind* 3B **38**
Horton Cross. *Som* 1G **13**
Horton-cum-Studley. *Oxon* 4D **50**
Horton Grange. *Nmbd* 2F **115**
Horton Green. *Ches W* 1G **71**
Horton Heath. *Hants* 1C **16**
Horton in Ribblesdale. *N Yor* 2H **97**
Horton Kirby. *Kent* 4G **39**
Hortonwood. *Telf* 4A **72**
Horwich. *G Man* 3E **91**
Horwich End. *Derbs* 2E **85**
Horwood. *Devn* 4F **19**
Hoscar. *Lanc* 3C **90**
Hose. *Leics* 3E **75**
Hosh. *Per* 1A **136**
Hosta. *W Isl* 1C **170**
Hoswick. *Shet* 9F **173**
Hotham. *E Yor* 1B **94**
Hothfield. *Kent* 1D **28**
Hoton. *Leics* 3C **74**
Houbie. *Shet* 2H **173**
Hough. *Arg* 4A **138**
Hough. *Ches E* 5B **84**
(nr. Crewe)
Hough. *Ches E* 3C **84**
(nr. Wilmslow)
Hougham. *Linc* 1F **75**
Hough Green. *Hal* 2G **83**
Hough-on-the-Hill. *Linc* 1G **75**
Houghton. *Cambs* 3B **64**
Houghton. *Cumb* 4F **113**
Houghton. *Hants* 3B **24**
Houghton. *Nmbd* 3E **115**
Houghton. *Pemb* 4D **43**
Houghton. *W Sus* 4B **26**
Houghton Bank. *Darl* 2F **105**
Houghton Conquest. *C Beds* 1A **52**
Houghton Green. *E Sus* 3D **28**
Houghton-le-Side. *Darl* 2F **105**
Houghton-le-Spring. *Tyne* 5G **115**
Houghton on the Hill. *Leics* 5D **74**
Houghton Regis. *C Beds* 3A **52**
Houghton St Giles. *Norf* 2B **78**
Houlland. *Shet* 6E **173**
(on Mainland)
Houlland. *Shet* 4G **173**
(on Yell)
Houlsyke. *N Yor* 4E **107**
Hound. *Hants* 2C **16**
Hound Green. *Hants* 1F **25**
Houndslow. *Bord* 5C **130**
Houndsmoor. *Som* 4E **21**
Houndwood. *Bord* 3E **131**
Hounsdown. *Hants* 1B **16**
Hounslow. *G Lon* 3C **38**
Housabister. *Shet* 6F **173**
Housay. *Shet* 4H **173**
Househill. *High* 3C **158**
Housetter. *Shet* 3E **173**
Houss. *Shet* 8E **173**
Houston. *Ren* 3F **127**
Housty. *High* 5D **168**
Houton. *Orkn* 7C **172**
Hove. *Brig* 5D **27** & **189**
Hoveringham. *Notts* 1E **74**
Hoveton. *Norf* 4F **79**
Hovingham. *N Yor* 2A **100**
How. *Cumb* 4G **113**
How Caple. *Here* 2B **48**
Howden. *E Yor* 2H **93**
Howden-le-Wear. *Dur* 1E **105**
Howe. *High* 2F **169**
Howe. *Norf* 5E **79**
Howe. *N Yor* 1F **99**
Howe Green. *Essx* 5H **53**
(nr. Chelmsford)
Howegreen. *Essx* 5B **54**
(nr. Maldon)
Howe Green. *Warw* 2H **61**
Howell. *Linc* 1A **76**
How End. *C Beds* 1A **52**
Howe of Teuchar. *Abers* 4E **161**
Howes. *Dum* 3C **112**
Howe Street. *Essx* 4G **53**
(nr. Chelmsford)
Howe Street. *Essx* 2G **53**
(nr. Finchingfield)
Howe, The. *Cumb* 1D **96**
Howe, The. *IOM* 5A **108**
Howey. *Powy* 5C **58**
Howgate. *Midl* 4F **129**
Howgill. *Lanc* 5H **97**
Howgill. *N Yor* 4C **98**
How Green. *Kent* 1F **27**
How Hill. *Norf* 4F **79**
Howick. *Nmbd* 3G **121**
Howle. *Telf* 3A **72**
Howle Hill. *Here* 3B **48**
Howleigh. *Som* 1F **13**
Howlett End. *Essx* 2F **53**
Howley. *Som* 2F **13**
Howley. *Warr* 2A **84**
Hownam. *Bord* 3B **120**
Howsham. *N Lin* 4D **94**
Howsham. *N Yor* 3B **100**
Howtel. *Nmbd* 1C **120**
Howt Green. *Kent* 4C **40**
Howton. *Here* 3H **47**
Howwood. *Ren* 3E **127**
Hoxne. *Suff* 3D **66**
Hoylake. *Mers* 2E **82**
Hoyland. *S Yor* 4D **92**
Hoylandswaine. *S Yor* 4C **92**
Hoyle. *W Sus* 4A **26**
Hubberholme. *N Yor* 2B **98**
Hubberston. *Pemb* 4C **42**
Hubbert's Bridge. *Linc* 1B **76**
Huby. *N Yor* 5E **99**
(nr. Harrogate)
Huby. *N Yor* 3H **99**
(nr. York)
Hucclecote. *Glos* 4D **48**
Hucking. *Kent* 5C **40**
Hucknall. *Notts* 1C **74**
Huddersfield. *W Yor* 3B **92**
Huddington. *Worc* 5D **60**
Huddlesford. *Staf* 5F **73**
Hudswell. *N Yor* 4E **105**
Huggate. *E Yor* 4C **100**
Hugglescote. *Leics* 4B **74**
Hughenden Valley. *Buck* 2G **37**
Hughley. *Shrp* 1H **59**
Hughton. *High* 4G **157**
Hugh Town. *IOS* 1B **4**
Hugus. *Corn* 4B **6**
Huish. *Devn* 1F **11**
Huish. *Wilts* 5G **35**
Huish Champflower. *Som* 4D **20**
Huish Episcopi. *Som* 4H **21**
Huisinis. *W Isl* 6B **171**
Hulcote. *Nptn* 5E **62**
Hulcott. *Buck* 4G **51**
Hulham. *Devn* 4D **12**
Hull. *Hull* 2D **94** & **199**
Hulland. *Derbs* 1G **73**
Hulland Moss. *Derbs* 1G **73**
Hulland Ward. *Derbs* 1G **73**
Hullavington. *Wilts* 3D **35**
Hullbridge. *Essx* 1C **40**
Hulme. *G Man* 1C **84**
Hulme. *Staf* 1D **72**
Hulme End. *Staf* 5F **85**
Hulme Walfield. *Ches E* 4C **84**
Hulverstone. *IOW* 4B **16**
Hulver Street. *Suff* 2G **67**
Humber. *Devn* 5C **12**
Humber. *Here* 5H **59**
Humber Bridge. *N Lin* 2D **94**
Humberside International Airport.
N Lin 3D **94**
Humberston. *NE Lin* 4G **95**
Humberstone. *Leic* 5D **74**
Humbie. *E Lot* 3A **130**
Humbleton. *E Yor* 1F **95**
Humbleton. *Nmbd* 2D **121**
Humby. *Linc* 2H **75**
Hume. *Bord* 5D **130**
Humshaugh. *Nmbd* 2C **114**
Huna. *High* 1F **169**
Huncoat. *Lanc* 1F **91**
Huncote. *Leics* 1C **62**
Hundall. *Derbs* 3A **86**
Hunderthwaite. *Dur* 2C **104**
Hundleby. *Linc* 4C **88**
Hundle Houses. *Linc* 5B **88**
Hundleton. *Pemb* 4D **42**
Hundon. *Suff* 1H **53**
Hundred Acres. *Hants* 1D **16**
Hundred House. *Powy* 5D **58**
Hundred, The. *Here* 4H **59**
Hungarton. *Leics* 5D **74**
Hungerford. *Hants* 1G **15**
Hungerford. *Shrp* 2H **59**
Hungerford. *Som* 2D **20**
Hungerford. *W Ber* 5B **36**
Hungerford Newtown. *W Ber* 4B **36**
Hunger Hill. *G Man* 4E **91**
Hungerton. *Linc* 2F **75**
Hungladder. *High* 1C **154**
Hungryhatton. *Shrp* 3A **72**
Hunmanby. *N Yor* 2E **101**
Hunmanby Sands. *N Yor* 2F **101**
Hunningham. *Warw* 4A **62**
Hunnington. *Worc* 2D **60**
Hunny Hill. *IOW* 4C **16**
Hunsdon. *Herts* 4E **53**
Hunsdonbury. *Herts* 4E **53**
Hunsingore. *N Yor* 4G **99**
Hunslet. *W Yor* 1D **92**
Hunslet Carr. *W Yor* 2D **92**
Hunsonby. *Cumb* 1G **103**
Hunspow. *High* 1E **169**
Hunstanton. *Norf* 1F **77**
Hunstanworth. *Dur* 5C **114**
Hunston. *Suff* 4B **66**
Hunston. *W Sus* 2G **17**
Hunstrete. *Bath* 5B **34**
Hunt End. *Worc* 4E **61**
Hunterfield. *Midl* 3G **129**
Hunters Forstal. *Kent* 4F **41**
Hunter's Quay. *Arg* 2C **126**
Huntham. *Som* 4G **21**
Hunthill Lodge. *Ang* 1D **144**
Huntingdon. *Cambs* 3B **64**
Huntingfield. *Suff* 3F **67**
Huntingford. *Wilts* 3D **22**
Huntington. *Ches W* 4G **83**
Huntington. *E Lot* 2A **130**
Huntington. *Here* 5E **59**
Huntington. *Staf* 4D **72**
Huntington. *Telf* 5A **72**
Huntington. *York* 4A **100**
Huntingtower. *Per* 1C **136**
Huntley. *Glos* 4C **48**
Huntley. *Staf* 1E **73**
Huntly. *Abers* 4C **160**
Huntlywood. *Bord* 5C **130**
Hunton. *Hants* 3C **24**
Hunton. *Kent* 1B **28**
Hunton. *N Yor* 5E **105**
Hunton Bridge. *Herts* 5A **52**
Hunt's Corner. *Norf* 2C **66**
Huntscott. *Som* 2C **20**
Hunt's Cross. *Mers* 2G **83**
Hunts Green. *Warw* 1F **61**
Huntsham. *Devn* 4D **20**
Huntshaw. *Devn* 4F **19**
Huntspill. *Som* 2G **21**
Huntstile. *Som* 3F **21**
Huntstrete. *Bath* 5B **34**
Huntworth. *Som* 3G **21**
Hunwick. *Dur* 1E **105**
Hunworth. *Norf* 2C **78**
Hurcott. *Som* 1G **13**
(nr. Ilminster)
Hurcott. *Som* 4A **22**
(nr. Somerton)
Hurdcott. *Wilts* 3G **23**
Hurdley. *Powy* 1E **59**
Hurdsfield. *Ches E* 3D **84**
Hurlet. *Glas* 3G **127**
Hurley. *Warw* 1G **61**
Hurley. *Wind* 3G **37**
Hurlford. *E Ayr* 1D **116**
Hurliness. *Orkn* 9B **172**
Hurlston Green. *Lanc* 3B **90**
Hurn. *Dors* 3G **15**
Hursey. *Dors* 2H **13**
Hursley. *Hants* 4C **24**
Hurst. *G Man* 4H **91**
Hurst. *N Yor* 4D **104**
Hurst. *Som* 1H **13**
Hurst. *Wok* 4F **37**
Hurstbourne Priors. *Hants* 2C **24**
Hurstbourne Tarrant. *Hants* 1B **24**
Hurst Green. *Ches E* 1H **71**
Hurst Green. *E Sus* 3B **28**
Hurst Green. *Essx* 4D **54**
Hurst Green. *Lanc* 1E **91**
Hurst Green. *Surr* 5E **39**
Hurstley. *Here* 1G **47**
Hurstpierpoint. *W Sus* 4D **27**
Hurstway Common. *Here* 1F **47**
Hurst Wickham. *W Sus* 4D **27**
Hurstwood. *Lanc* 1G **91**
Hurtmore. *Surr* 1A **26**
Hurworth-on-Tees. *Darl* 3A **106**
Hurworth Place. *Darl* 3F **105**
Hury. *Dur* 3C **104**
Husbands Bosworth. *Leics* 2D **62**
Husborne Crawley.
C Beds 2H **51**
Husthwaite. *N Yor* 2H **99**
Hutcherleigh. *Devn* 3D **9**
Hut Green. *N Yor* 2F **93**
Huthwaite. *Notts* 5B **86**
Huttoft. *Linc* 3E **89**
Hutton. *Cumb* 2F **103**
Hutton. *E Yor* 4E **101**
Hutton. *Essx* 1H **39**
Hutton. *Lanc* 2C **90**
Hutton. *N Som* 1G **21**
Hutton. *Bord* 4F **131**
Hutton Bonville. *N Yor* 4A **106**
Hutton Buscel. *N Yor* 1D **100**
Hutton Conyers. *N Yor* 2F **99**
Hutton Cranswick. *E Yor* 4E **101**
Hutton End. *Cumb* 1F **103**
Hutton Gate. *Red C* 3C **106**
Hutton Henry. *Dur* 1B **106**
Hutton-le-Hole. *N Yor* 1B **100**
Hutton Magna. *Dur* 3E **105**
Hutton Mulgrave. *N Yor* 4F **107**
Hutton Roof. *Cumb* 2E **97**
(nr. Kirkby Lonsdale)
Hutton Roof. *Cumb* 1E **103**
(nr. Penrith)

Hutton Rudby. *N Yor* 4B **106**
Huttons Ambo. *N Yor* 3B **100**
Hutton Sessay. *N Yor* 2G **99**
Hutton Village. *Red C* 3D **106**
Hutton Wandesley. *N Yor* 4H **99**
Huxham. *Devn* 3C **12**
Huxham Green. *Som* 3A **22**
Huxley. *Ches W* 4H **83**
Huxter. *Shet* 6C **173** (on Mainland)
Huxter. *Shet* 5G **173** (on Whalsay)
Huyton. *Mers* 1G **83**
Hwlffordd. *Pemb* 3D **42**
Hycemoor. *Cumb* 1A **96**
Hyde. *Glos* 5D **49** (nr. Stroud)
Hyde. *Glos* 3F **49** (nr. Winchcombe)
Hyde. *G Man* 1D **84**
Hyde Heath. *Buck* 5H **51**
Hyde Lea. *Staf* 3D **72**
Hyde Park. *S Yor* 4F **93**
Hydestile. *Surr* 1A **26**
Hyndford Bridge. *S Lan* 5C **128**
Hynish. *Arg* 5A **138**
Hyssington. *Powy* 1F **59**
Hythe. *Hants* 2C **16**
Hythe. *Kent* 2F **29**
Hythe End. *Wind* 3B **38**
Hythie. *Abers* 3H **161**
Hyton. *Cumb* 1A **96**

I

Ianstown. *Mor* 2B **160**
Iarsiadar. *W Isl* 4D **171**
Ibberton. *Dors* 2C **14**
Ible. *Derbs* 5G **85**
Ibrox. *Glas* 3G **127**
Ibsley. *Hants* 2G **15**
Ibstock. *Leics* 4B **74**
Ibstone. *Buck* 2F **37**
Ibthorpe. *Hants* 1B **24**
Iburndale. *N Yor* 4F **107**
Ibworth. *Hants* 1D **24**
Icelton. *N Som* 5G **33**
Ichrachan. *Arg* 5E **141**
Ickburgh. *Norf* 1H **65**
Ickenham. *G Lon* 2B **38**
Ickenthwaite. *Cumb* 1C **96**
Ickford. *Buck* 5E **51**
Ickham. *Kent* 5G **41**
Ickleford. *Herts* 2B **52**
Icklesham. *E Sus* 4C **28**
Ickleton. *Cambs* 1E **53**
Icklingham. *Suff* 3G **65**
Ickwell. *C Beds* 1B **52**
Icomb. *Glos* 3H **49**
Idbury. *Oxon* 3H **49**
Iddesleigh. *Devn* 2F **11**
Ide. *Devn* 3B **12**
Ideford. *Devn* 5B **12**
Ide Hill. *Kent* 5F **39**
Iden. *E Sus* 3D **28**
Iden Green. *Kent* 2C **28** (nr. Benenden)
Iden Green. *Kent* 2B **28** (nr. Goudhurst)
Idle. *W Yor* 1B **92**
Idless. *Corn* 4C **6**
Idlicote. *Warw* 1A **50**
Idmiston. *Wilts* 3G **23**
Idole. *Carm* 4E **45**
Idridgehay. *Derbs* 1G **73**
Idrigill. *High* 2C **154**
Idstone. *Oxon* 3A **36**
Iffley. *Oxon* 5D **50**
Ifield. *W Sus* 2D **26**
Ifieldwood. *W Sus* 2D **26**
Ifold. *W Sus* 2B **26**
Iford. *E Sus* 5F **27**
Ifton Heath. *Shrp* 2F **71**
Ightfield. *Shrp* 2H **71**
Ightham. *Kent* 5G **39**
Iken. *Suff* 5G **67**
Ilam. *Staf* 5F **85**
Ilchester. *Som* 4A **22**
Ilderton. *Nmbd* 2E **121**
Ilford. *G Lon* 2F **39**
Ilford. *Som* 1G **13**
Ilfracombe. *Devn* 2F **19**
Ilkeston. *Derbs* 1B **74**
Ilketshall St Andrew. *Suff* 2F **67**
Ilketshall St Lawrence. *Suff* 2F **67**
Ilketshall St Margaret. *Suff* 2F **67**
Ilkley. *W Yor* 5D **98**
Illand. *Corn* 5C **10**
Illey. *W Mid* 2D **61**
Illidge Green. *Ches E* 4B **84**
Illington. *Norf* 2B **66**
Illingworth. *W Yor* 2A **92**
Illogan. *Corn* 4A **6**
Illogan Highway. *Corn* 4A **6**
Illston on the Hill. *Leics* 1E **62**
Ilmer. *Buck* 5F **51**
Ilmington. *Warw* 1H **49**
Ilminster. *Som* 1G **13**
Ilsington. *Devn* 5A **12**
Ilsington. *Dors* 3C **14**
Ilston. *Swan* 3E **31**
Ilton. *N Yor* 2D **98**
Ilton. *Som* 1G **13**
Imachar. *N Ayr* 5G **125**
Imber. *Wilts* 2E **23**
Immingham. *NE Lin* 3E **95**
Immingham Dock. *NE Lin* 3E **95**
Impington. *Cambs* 4D **64**
Ince. *Ches W* 3G **83**
Ince Blundell. *Mers* 4B **90**
Ince-in-Makerfield. *G Man* 4D **90**
Inchbae Lodge. *High* 2G **157**
Inchbare. *Ang* 2F **145**
Inchberry. *Mor* 3H **159**
Inchbraoch. *Ang* 3G **145**
Inchbrook. *Glos* 5D **48**
Incheril. *High* 2C **156**
Inchinnan. *Ren* 3F **127**
Inchlaggan. *High* 3D **148**
Inchmichael. *Per* 1E **137**
Inchnadamph. *High* 1G **163**
Inchree. *High* 2E **141**
Inchture. *Per* 1E **137**
Inchyra. *Per* 1D **136**
Indian Queens. *Corn* 3D **6**
Ingatestone. *Essx* 1H **39**
Ingbirchworth. *S Yor* 4C **92**
Ingestre. *Staf* 3D **73**
Ingham. *Linc* 2G **87**
Ingham. *Norf* 3F **79**
Ingham. *Suff* 3A **66**
Ingham Corner. *Norf* 3F **79**
Ingleborough. *Norf* 4D **76**
Ingleby. *Derbs* 3H **73**
Ingleby Arncliffe. *N Yor* 4B **106**
Ingleby Barwick. *Stoc T* 3B **106**
Ingleby Greenhow. *N Yor* 4C **106**
Ingleigh Green. *Devn* 2G **11**
Inglemire. *Hull* 1D **94**
Inglesbatch. *Bath* 5C **34**
Ingleton. *Dur* 2E **105**
Ingleton. *N Yor* 2F **97**
Inglewhite. *Lanc* 5E **97**
Ingoe. *Nmbd* 2D **114**
Ingol. *Lanc* 1D **90**
Ingoldisthorpe. *Norf* 2F **77**
Ingoldmells. *Linc* 4E **89**
Ingoldsby. *Linc* 2H **75**
Ingon. *Warw* 5G **61**
Ingram. *Nmbd* 3E **121**
Ingrave. *Essx* 1H **39**
Ingrow. *W Yor* 1A **92**
Ings. *Cumb* 5F **103**
Ingst. *S Glo* 3A **34**
Ingthorpe. *Rut* 5G **75**
Ingworth. *Norf* 3D **78**
Inkberrow. *Worc* 5E **61**
Inkford. *Worc* 3E **61**
Inkpen. *W Ber* 5B **36**
Inkstack. *High* 1E **169**
Innellan. *Arg* 3C **126**
Inner Hope. *Devn* 5C **8**
Innerleith. *Fife* 2E **137**
Innerleithen. *Bord* 1F **119**
Innerleven. *Fife* 3F **137**
Innermessan. *Dum* 3F **109**
Innerwick. *E Lot* 2D **130**
Innerwick. *Per* 4C **142**
Innsworth. *Glos* 3D **48**
Insch. *Abers* 1D **152**
Insh. *High* 3C **150**
Inshegra. *High* 3C **166**
Inshore. *High* 1D **166**
Inskip. *Lanc* 1C **90**
Instow. *Devn* 3E **19**
Intwood. *Norf* 5D **78**
Inver. *Abers* 4G **151**
Inver. *High* 5F **165**
Inver. *Per* 4H **143**
Inverailort. *High* 5F **147**
Inveralligin. *High* 3H **155**
Inverallochy. *Abers* 2H **161**
Inveramsay. *Abers* 1E **153**
Inveran. *High* 4C **164**
Inveraray. *Arg* 3H **133**
Inverarish. *High* 5E **155**
Inverarity. *Ang* 4D **144**
Inverarnan. *Arg* 2C **134**
Inverarnie. *High* 5A **158**
Inverbeg. *Arg* 4C **134**
Inverbervie. *Abers* 1H **145**
Inverboyndie. *Abers* 2D **160**
Invercassley. *High* 3B **164**
Invercharnan. *High* 4F **141**
Inverchoran. *High* 3E **157**
Invercreran. *Arg* 4E **141**
Inverdruie. *High* 2D **150**
Inverebrie. *Abers* 5G **161**
Invereck. *Arg* 1C **126**
Inveresk. *E Lot* 2G **129**
Inveresragan. *Arg* 5D **140**
Inverey. *Abers* 5E **151**
Inverfarigaig. *High* 1H **149**
Invergarry. *High* 3F **149**
Invergeldie. *Per* 1G **135**
Invergordon. *High* 2B **158**
Invergowrie. *Per* 5C **144**
Inverguseran. *High* 3F **147**
Inverharroch. *Mor* 5A **160**
Inverie. *High* 3F **147**
Inverinan. *Arg* 2G **133**
Inverinate. *High* 1B **148**
Inverkeilor. *Ang* 4F **145**
Inverkeithing. *Fife* 1E **129**
Inverkeithny. *Abers* 4D **160**
Inverkip. *Inv* 2D **126**
Inverkirkaig. *High* 2E **163**
Inverlael. *High* 5F **163**
Inverliever Lodge. *Arg* 3F **133**
Inverliver. *Arg* 5E **141**
Inverloch. *High* 1F **141**
Inverlochlarig. *Stir* 2D **134**
Inverlussa. *Arg* 1E **125**
Inver Mallie. *High* 5D **148**
Invermarkie. *Abers* 5B **160**
Invermoriston. *High* 2G **149**
Invernaver. *High* 2H **167**
Inverneil House. *Arg* 1G **125**
Inverness. *High* 4A **158** & **198**
Inverness Airport. *High* 3B **158**
Invernettie. *Abers* 4H **161**
Inverpolly Lodge. *High* 2E **163**
Inverquhomery. *Abers* 4H **161**
Inverroy. *High* 5E **149**
Inversanda. *High* 3D **140**
Invershiel. *High* 2B **148**
Invershin. *High* 4C **164**
Invershore. *High* 5E **169**
Inversnaid. *Stir* 3C **134**
Inverugie. *Abers* 4H **161**
Inveruglas. *Arg* 3C **134**
Inverurie. *Abers* 1E **153**
Invervar. *Per* 4D **142**
Inverythan. *Abers* 4E **161**
Inwardleigh. *Devn* 3F **11**
Inworth. *Essx* 4B **54**
Iochdar. *W Isl* 4C **170**
Iping. *W Sus* 4G **25**
Ipplepen. *Devn* 2E **9**
Ipsden. *Oxon* 3E **37**
Ipstones. *Staf* 1E **73**
Ipswich. *Suff* 1E **55** & **198**
Irby. *Mers* 2E **83**
Irby in the Marsh. *Linc* 4D **88**
Irby upon Humber. *NE Lin* 4E **95**
Irchester. *Nptn* 4G **63**
Ireby. *Cumb* 1D **102**
Ireby. *Lanc* 2F **97**
Ireland. *Shet* 9E **173**
Ireleth. *Cumb* 2B **96**
Ireshopeburn. *Dur* 1B **104**
Ireton Wood. *Derbs* 1G **73**
Irlam. *G Man* 1B **84**
Irnham. *Linc* 3H **75**
Iron Acton. *S Glo* 3B **34**
Iron Bridge. *Cambs* 1D **65**
Ironbridge. *Telf* 5A **72**
Iron Cross. *Warw* 5E **61**
Ironville. *Derbs* 5B **86**
Irstead. *Norf* 3F **79**
Irthington. *Cumb* 3F **113**
Irthlingborough. *Nptn* 3G **63**
Irton. *N Yor* 1E **101**
Irvine. *N Ayr* 1C **116**
Irvine Mains. *N Ayr* 1C **116**
Isabella Pit. *Nmbd* 1G **115**
Isauld. *High* 2B **168**
Isbister. *Orkn* 6C **172**
Isbister. *Shet* 2E **173** (on Mainland)
Isbister. *Shet* 5G **173** (on Whalsay)
Isfield. *E Sus* 4F **27**
Isham. *Nptn* 3F **63**
Island Carr. *N Lin* 4C **94**
Islay Airport. *Arg* 4B **124**
Isle Abbotts. *Som* 4G **21**
Isle Brewers. *Som* 4G **21**
Isleham. *Cambs* 3F **65**
Isle of Man Airport. *IOM* 5B **108**
Isle of Thanet. *Kent* 4H **41**
Isle of Whithorn. *Dum* 5B **110**
Isleornsay. *High* 2F **147**
Islesburgh. *Shet* 5E **173**
Isles of Scilly (St Mary's) Airport. *IOS* 1B **4**
Islesteps. *Dum* 2A **112**
Isleworth. *G Lon* 3C **38**
Isley Walton. *Leics* 3B **74**
Islibhig. *W Isl* 5B **171**
Islington. *G Lon* 2E **39**
Islington. *Telf* 3B **72**
Islip. *Nptn* 3G **63**
Islip. *Oxon* 4D **50**
Islwyn. *Cphy* 2F **33**
Isombridge. *Telf* 4A **72**
Istead Rise. *Kent* 4H **39**
Itchen. *Sotn* 1C **16**
Itchen Abbas. *Hants* 3D **24**
Itchen Stoke. *Hants* 3D **24**
Itchingfield. *W Sus* 3C **26**
Itchington. *S Glo* 3B **34**
Itlaw. *Abers* 3D **160**
Itteringham. *Norf* 2D **78**
Itteringham Common. *Norf* 3D **78**
Itton. *Devn* 3G **11**
Itton Common. *Mon* 2H **33**
Ivegill. *Cumb* 5F **113**
Ivelet. *N Yor* 5C **104**
Iverchaolain. *Arg* 2B **126**
Iver Heath. *Buck* 2B **38**
Iveston. *Dur* 4E **115**
Ivetsey Bank. *Staf* 4C **72**
Ivinghoe. *Buck* 4H **51**
Ivinghoe Aston. *Buck* 4H **51**
Ivington. *Here* 5G **59**
Ivington Green. *Here* 5G **59**
Ivybridge. *Devn* 3C **8**
Ivychurch. *Kent* 3E **29**
Ivy Hatch. *Kent* 5G **39**
Ivy Todd. *Norf* 5A **78**
Iwade. *Kent* 4D **40**
Iwerne Courtney. *Dors* 1D **14**
Iwerne Minster. *Dors* 1D **14**
Ixworth. *Suff* 3B **66**
Ixworth Thorpe. *Suff* 3B **66**

J

Jackfield. *Shrp* 5A **72**
Jack Hill. *N Yor* 4E **98**
Jacksdale. *Notts* 5B **86**
Jackton. *S Lan* 4G **127**
Jacobstow. *Corn* 3B **10**
Jacobstowe. *Devn* 2F **11**
Jacobswell. *Surr* 5A **38**
Jameston. *Pemb* 5E **43**
Jamestown. *Dum* 5F **119**
Jamestown. *Fife* 1E **129**
Jamestown. *High* 3G **157**
Jamestown. *W Dun* 1E **127**
Janetstown. *High* 2C **168** (nr. Thurso)
Janetstown. *High* 3F **169** (nr. Wick)
Jarrow. *Tyne* 3G **115**
Jarvis Brook. *E Sus* 3G **27**
Jasper's Green. *Essx* 3H **53**
Jaywick. *Essx* 4E **55**
Jedburgh. *Bord* 2A **120**
Jeffreyston. *Pemb* 4E **43**
Jemimaville. *High* 2B **158**
Jenkins Park. *High* 3F **149**
Jersey Marine. *Neat* 3G **31**
Jesmond. *Tyne* 3F **115**
Jevington. *E Sus* 5G **27**
Jingle Street. *Mon* 4H **47**
Jockey End. *Herts* 4A **52**
Jodrell Bank. *Ches E* 3B **84**
Johnby. *Cumb* 1F **103**
John o' Gaunts. *W Yor* 2D **92**
John o' Groats. *High* 1F **169**
John's Cross. *E Sus* 3B **28**
Johnshaven. *Abers* 2G **145**
Johnson Street. *Norf* 4F **79**
Johnston. *Pemb* 3D **42**
Johnstone. *Ren* 3F **127**
Johnstonebridge. *Dum* 5C **118**
Johnstown. *Carm* 4D **45**
Johnstown. *Wrex* 1F **71**
Joppa. *Edin* 2G **129**
Joppa. *S Ayr* 3D **116**
Jordan Green. *Norf* 3C **78**
Jordans. *Buck* 1A **38**
Jordanston. *Pemb* 1D **42**
Jump. *S Yor* 4D **93**
Jumpers Common. *Dors* 3G **15**
Juniper. *Nmbd* 4C **114**
Juniper Green. *Edin* 3E **129**
Jurby East. *IOM* 2C **108**
Jurby West. *IOM* 2C **108**
Jury's Gap. *E Sus* 4D **28**

K

Kaber. *Cumb* 3A **104**
Kaimend. *S Lan* 5C **128**
Kaimes. *Edin* 3F **129**
Kaimrig End. *Bord* 5D **129**
Kames. *Arg* 2A **126**
Kames. *E Ayr* 2F **117**
Kea. *Corn* 4C **6**
Keadby. *N Lin* 3B **94**
Keal Cotes. *Linc* 4C **88**
Kearsley. *G Man* 4F **91**
Kearsney. *Kent* 1G **29**
Kearstwick. *Cumb* 1F **97**
Kearton. *N Yor* 5C **104**
Kearvaig. *High* 1C **166**
Keasden. *N Yor* 3G **97**
Keason. *Corn* 2H **7**
Keckwick. *Hal* 2H **83**
Keddington. *Linc* 2C **88**
Keddington Corner. *Linc* 2C **88**
Kedington. *Suff* 1H **53**
Kedleston. *Derbs* 1H **73**
Kedlock Feus. *Fife* 2F **137**
Keekle. *Cumb* 3B **102**
Keelby. *Linc* 3E **95**
Keele. *Staf* 1C **72**
Keeley Green. *Bed* 1A **52**
Keeston. *Pemb* 3D **42**
Keevil. *Wilts* 1E **23**
Kegworth. *Leics* 3B **74**
Kehelland. *Corn* 2D **4**
Keig. *Abers* 2D **152**
Keighley. *W Yor* 5C **98**
Keilarsbrae. *Clac* 4A **136**
Keillmore. *Arg* 1E **125**
Keillor. *Per* 4B **144**
Keillour. *Per* 1B **136**
Keills. *Arg* 3C **124**
Keiloch. *Abers* 4F **151**
Keils. *Arg* 3D **124**
Keinton Mandeville. *Som* 3A **22**
Keir Mill. *Dum* 5A **118**
Keirsleywell Row. *Nmbd* 4A **114**
Keisby. *Linc* 3H **75**
Keisley. *Cumb* 2A **104**
Keiss. *High* 2F **169**
Keith. *Mor* 3B **160**
Keith Inch. *Abers* 4H **161**
Kelbrook. *Lanc* 5B **98**
Kelby. *Linc* 1H **75**
Keld. *Cumb* 3G **103**
Keld. *N Yor* 4B **104**
Keldholme. *N Yor* 1B **100**
Kelfield. *N Lin* 4B **94**
Kelfield. *N Yor* 1F **93**
Kelham. *Notts* 5E **87**
Kellacott. *Devn* 4E **11**
Kellan. *Arg* 4G **139**
Kellas. *Ang* 5D **144**
Kellas. *Mor* 3F **159**
Kellaton. *Devn* 5E **9**
Kelleth. *Cumb* 4H **103**
Kelling. *Norf* 1C **78**
Kellingley. *N Yor* 2F **93**
Kellington. *N Yor* 2F **93**
Kelloe. *Dur* 1A **106**
Kelloholm. *Dum* 3G **117**
Kells. *Cumb* 3A **102**
Kelly. *Devn* 4D **11**
Kelly Bray. *Corn* 5D **10**
Kelmarsh. *Nptn* 3E **63**
Kelmscott. *Oxon* 2A **36**
Kelsale. *Suff* 4F **67**
Kelsall. *Ches W* 4H **83**
Kelshall. *Herts* 2D **52**
Kelsick. *Cumb* 4C **112**
Kelso. *Bord* 1B **120**
Kelstedge. *Derbs* 4H **85**
Kelstern. *Linc* 1B **88**
Kelsterton. *Flin* 3E **83**
Kelston. *Bath* 5C **34**
Keltneyburn. *Per* 4E **143**
Kelton. *Dum* 2A **112**
Kelton Hill. *Dum* 4E **111**
Kelty. *Fife* 4D **136**
Kelvedon. *Essx* 4B **54**
Kelvedon Hatch. *Essx* 1G **39**
Kelvinside. *Glas* 3G **127**
Kelynack. *Corn* 3A **4**
Kemback. *Fife* 2G **137**
Kemberton. *Shrp* 5B **72**
Kemble. *Glos* 2E **35**
Kemerton. *Worc* 2E **49**
Kemeys Commander. *Mon* 5G **47**
Kemnay. *Abers* 2E **153**
Kempe's Corner. *Kent* 1E **29**
Kempley. *Glos* 3B **48**
Kempley Green. *Glos* 3B **48**
Kempsey. *Worc* 1D **48**
Kempsford. *Glos* 2G **35**
Kemps Green. *Warw* 3F **61**
Kempshott. *Hants* 1E **24**
Kempston. *Bed* 1A **52**
Kempston Hardwick. *Bed* 1A **52**
Kempton. *Shrp* 2F **59**
Kemp Town. *Brig* 5E **27**
Kemsing. *Kent* 5G **39**
Kemsley. *Kent* 4D **40**
Kenardington. *Kent* 2D **28**
Kenchester. *Here* 1H **47**
Kencot. *Oxon* 5A **50**
Kendal. *Cumb* 5G **103**
Kendleshire. *S Glo* 4B **34**
Kendray. *S Yor* 4D **92**
Kenfig. *B'end* 3B **32**
Kenfig Hill. *B'end* 3B **32**
Kengharair. *Arg* 4F **139**
Kenilworth. *Warw* 3G **61**
Kenknock. *Stir* 5B **142**
Kenley. *G Lon* 5E **39**
Kenley. *Shrp* 5H **71**
Kenmore. *High* 3G **155**
Kenmore. *Per* 4E **143**
Kenn. *Devn* 4C **12**
Kenn. *N Som* 5H **33**
Kennacraig. *Arg* 3G **125**
Kenneggy Downs. *Corn* 4C **4**
Kennerleigh. *Devn* 2B **12**
Kennet. *Clac* 4B **136**
Kennethmont. *Abers* 1C **152**
Kennett. *Cambs* 4G **65**
Kennford. *Devn* 4C **12**
Kenninghall. *Norf* 2C **66**
Kennington. *Kent* 1E **29**
Kennington. *Oxon* 5D **50**
Kennoway. *Fife* 3F **137**
Kennyhill. *Suff* 3F **65**
Kennythorpe. *N Yor* 3B **100**
Kenovay. *Arg* 4A **138**
Kensaleyre. *High* 3D **154**
Kensington. *G Lon* 3D **38**
Kenstone. *Shrp* 3H **71**
Kensworth. *C Beds* 4A **52**
Kensworth Common. *C Beds* 4A **52**
Kentallen. *High* 3E **141**
Kentchurch. *Here* 3H **47**
Kentford. *Suff* 4G **65**
Kentisbeare. *Devn* 2D **12**
Kentisbury. *Devn* 2G **19**
Kentisbury Ford. *Devn* 2G **19**
Kentmere. *Cumb* 4F **103**

Kenton. Devn 4C 12
Kenton. G Lon 2C 38
Kenton. Suff 4D 66
Kenton Bankfoot. Tyne 3F 115
Kentra. High 2A 140
Kentrigg. Cumb 5G 103
Kents Bank. Cumb 2C 96
Kent's Green. Glos 3C 48
Kent's Oak. Hants 4B 24
Kent Street. E Sus 4B 28
Kent Street. Kent 5A 40
Kent Street. W Sus 3D 26
Kenwick. Shrp 2G 71
Kenwyn. Corn 4C 6
Kenyon. Warr 1A 84
Keoldale. High 2D 166
Keppoch. High 1B 148
Kepwick. N Yor 5B 106
Keresley. W Mid 2H 61
Keresley Newland. Warw 2H 61
Keristal. IOM 4C 108
Kerne Bridge. Here 4A 48
Kerridge. Ches E 3D 84
Kerris. Corn 4B 4
Kerrow. High 5F 157
Kerry. Powy 2D 58
Kerrycroy. Arg 3C 126
Kerry's Gate. Here 2G 47
Kersall. Notts 4E 86
Kersbrook. Devn 4D 12
Kerse. Ren 4E 127
Kersey. Suff 1D 54
Kershopefoot. Cumb 1F 113
Kersoe. Worc 2E 49
Kerswell. Devn 2D 12
Kerswell Green. Worc 1D 48
Kesgrave. Suff 1F 55
Kessingland. Suff 2H 67
Kessingland Beach. Suff 2H 67
Kestle. Corn 4D 6
Kestle Mill. Corn 3C 6
Keston. G Lon 4F 39
Keswick. Cumb 2D 102
Keswick. Norf 2F 79
(nr. North Walsham)
Keswick. Norf 5E 78
(nr. Norwich)
Ketsby. Linc 3C 88
Kettering. Nptn 3F 63
Ketteringham. Norf 5D 78
Kettins. Per 5B 144
Kettlebaston. Suff 5B 66
Kettlebridge. Fife 3F 137
Kettlebrook. Staf 5G 73
Kettleburgh. Suff 4E 67
Kettleholm. Dum 2C 112
Kettleness. N Yor 3F 107
Kettleshulme. Ches E 3D 85
Kettlesing. N Yor 4E 99
Kettlesing Bottom. N Yor 4E 99
Kettlestone. Norf 2B 78
Kettlethorpe. Linc 3F 87
Kettletoft. Orkn 4F 172
Kettlewell. N Yor 2B 98
Ketton. Rut 5G 75
Kew. G Lon 3C 38
Kewaigue. IOM 4C 108
Kewstoke. N Som 5G 33
Kexbrough. S Yor 4D 92
Kexby. Linc 2F 87
Kexby. York 4B 100
Keyford. Som 2C 22
Key Green. Ches E 4C 84
Key Green. N Yor 4F 107
Keyham. Leics 5D 74
Keyhaven. Hants 3B 16
Keyhead. Abers 3H 161
Keyingham. E Yor 2F 95
Keymer. W Sus 4E 27
Keynsham. Bath 5B 34
Keysoe. Bed 4H 63
Keysoe Row. Bed 4H 63
Key's Toft. Linc 5D 89
Keyston. Cambs 3H 63
Key Street. Kent 4C 40
Keyworth. Notts 2D 74
Kibblesworth. Tyne 4F 115
Kibworth Beauchamp. Leics 1D 62
Kibworth Harcourt. Leics 1D 62
Kidbrooke. G Lon 3F 39
Kidburngill. Cumb 2B 102
Kiddemore Green. Staf 5C 72
Kidderminster. Worc 3C 60
Kiddington. Oxon 3C 50
Kidd's Moor. Norf 5D 78
Kidlington. Oxon 4C 50
Kidmore End. Oxon 4E 37
Kidnal. Ches W 1G 71
Kidsgrove. Staf 5C 84
Kidstones. N Yor 1B 98
Kidwelly. Carm 5E 45
Kiel Crofts. Arg 5D 140
Kielder. Nmbd 5A 120
Kilbagie. Fife 4B 136
Kilbarchan. Ren 3F 127
Kilbeg. High 3E 147
Kilberry. Arg 3F 125
Kilbirnie. N Ayr 4E 126
Kilbride. Arg 1F 133
Kilbride. High 1D 147
Kilbucho Place. Bord 1C 118
Kilburn. Derbs 1A 74
Kilburn. G Lon 2D 38
Kilburn. N Yor 2H 99
Kilby. Leics 1D 62
Kilchattan. Arg 4A 132
(on Colonsay)
Kilchattan. Arg 4C 126
(on Isle of Bute)
Kilchattan Bay. Arg 4B 126
Kilchenzie. Arg 3A 122
Kilcheran. Arg 5C 140
Kilchiaran. Arg 3A 124
Kilchoan. High 4F 147
(nr. Inverie)
Kilchoan. High 2F 139
(nr. Tobermory)
Kilchoman. Arg 3A 124
Kilchrenan. Arg 1H 133
Kilconquhar. Fife 3G 137
Kilcot. Glos 3B 48
Kilcoy. High 3H 157
Kilcreggan. Arg 1D 126
Kildale. N Yor 4D 106
Kildary. High 1B 158
Kildermorie Lodge. High 1H 157
Kildonan. Dum 4F 109
Kildonan. High 1G 165
(nr. Helmsdale)
Kildonan. High 3C 154
(on Isle of Skye)
Kildonan. N Ayr 3E 123
Kildonnan. High 5C 146
Kildrummy. Abers 2B 152
Kildwick. N Yor 5C 98
Kilfillan. Dum 4H 109
Kilfinan. Arg 2H 125
Kilfinnan. High 4E 149
Kilgetty. Pemb 4F 43
Kilgour. Fife 3E 136
Kilgrammie. S Ayr 4B 116
Kilham. E Yor 3E 101
Kilham. Nmbd 1C 120
Kilkenneth. Arg 4A 138
Kilkhampton. Corn 1C 10
Killamarsh. Derbs 2B 86
Killandrist. Arg 4C 140
Killay. Swan 3F 31
Killean. Arg 5E 125
Killearn. Stir 1G 127
Killellan. Arg 4A 122
Killen. High 3A 158
Killerby. Darl 3E 105
Killichonan. Per 3C 142
Killiechronan. Arg 4G 139
Killiecrankie. Per 2G 143
Killilan. High 5B 156
Killimster. High 3F 169
Killin. Stir 5C 142
Killinghall. N Yor 4E 99
Killington. Cumb 1F 97
Killingworth. Tyne 2F 115
Killin Lodge. High 3H 149
Killinochonoch. Arg 4F 133
Killochyett. Bord 5A 130
Killundine. High 4G 139
Kilmacolm. Inv 3E 127
Kilmahog. Stir 3F 135
Kilmahumaig. Arg 4E 133
Kilmalieu. High 3C 140
Kilmaluag. High 1D 154
Kilmany. Fife 1F 137
Kilmarie. High 2D 146
Kilmarnock. E Ayr 1D 116 & 198
Kilmaron. Fife 2F 137
Kilmartin. Arg 4F 133
Kilmaurs. E Ayr 5F 127
Kilmelford. Arg 2F 133
Kilmeny. Arg 3B 124
Kilmersdon. Som 1B 22
Kilmeston. Hants 4D 24
Kilmichael Glassary. Arg 4F 133
Kilmichael of Inverlussa. Arg 1F 125
Kilmington. Devn 3F 13
Kilmington. Wilts 3C 22
Kilmoluag. Arg 4A 138
Kilmorack. High 4G 157
Kilmore. Arg 1F 133
Kilmore. High 3E 147
Kilmory. Arg 2F 125
Kilmory. High 1G 139
(nr. Kilchoan)
Kilmory. High 3B 146
(on Rùm)
Kilmory. N Ayr 3D 122
Kilmory Lodge. Arg 3E 132
Kilmote. High 2G 165
Kilmuir. High 4B 154
(nr. Dunvegan)
Kilmuir. High 1B 158
(nr. Invergordon)
Kilmuir. High 4A 158
(nr. Inverness)
Kilmuir. High 1C 154
(nr. Uig)
Kilmun. Arg 1C 126
Kilnave. Arg 2A 124
Kilncadzow. S Lan 5B 128
Kilndown. Kent 2B 28
Kiln Green. Here 4B 48
Kiln Green. Wind 4G 37
Kilnhill. Cumb 1D 102
Kilnhurst. S Yor 1B 86
Kilninian. Arg 4E 139
Kilninver. Arg 1F 133
Kiln Pit Hill. Nmbd 4D 114
Kilnsea. E Yor 3H 95
Kilnsey. N Yor 3B 98
Kilnwick. E Yor 5D 101
Kiloran. Arg 4A 132
Kilpatrick. N Ayr 3D 122
Kilpeck. Here 2H 47
Kilpin. E Yor 2A 94
Kilpin Pike. E Yor 2A 94
Kilrenny. Fife 3H 137
Kilsby. Nptn 3C 62
Kilspindie. Per 1E 136
Kilsyth. N Lan 2A 128
Kiltarlity. High 4H 157
Kilton. Som 2E 21
Kilton Thorpe. Red C 3D 107
Kilvaxter. High 2C 154
Kilve. Som 2E 21
Kilvington. Notts 1F 75
Kilwinning. N Ayr 5D 126
Kimberley. Norf 5C 78
Kimberley. Notts 1B 74
Kimblesworth. Dur 5F 115
Kimble Wick. Buck 5G 51
Kimbolton. Cambs 4H 63
Kimbolton. Here 4H 59
Kimcote. Leics 2C 62
Kimmeridge. Dors 5E 15
Kimmerston. Nmbd 1D 120
Kimpton. Hants 2A 24
Kimpton. Herts 4B 52
Kinbeachie. High 2A 158
Kinbrace. High 5A 168
Kinbuck. Stir 3G 135
Kincaple. Fife 2G 137
Kincardine. Fife 1C 128
Kincardine. High 5D 164
Kincardine Bridge. Fife 1C 128
Kincardine O'Neil. Abers 4C 152
Kinchrackine. Arg 1A 134
Kincorth. Aber 3G 153
Kincraig. High 3C 150
Kincraigie. Per 4G 143
Kindallachan. Per 3G 143
Kineton. Glos 3F 49
Kineton. Warw 5H 61
Kinfauns. Per 1D 136
Kingairloch. High 3C 140
Kingarth. Arg 4B 126
Kingcoed. Mon 5H 47
King Edward. Abers 3E 160
Kingerby. Linc 1H 87
Kingham. Oxon 3A 50
Kingholm Quay. Dum 2A 112
Kinghorn. Fife 1F 129
Kingie. High 3D 148
Kinglassie. Fife 4E 137
Kingledores. Bord 2D 118
Kingodie. Per 1F 137
King o' Muirs. Clac 4A 136
King's Acre. Here 1H 47
Kingsand. Corn 3A 8
Kingsash. Buck 5G 51
Kingsbarns. Fife 2H 137
Kingsbridge. Devn 4D 8
Kingsbridge. Som 3C 20
King's Bromley. Staf 4F 73
Kingsburgh. High 3C 154
Kingsbury. G Lon 2C 38
Kingsbury. Warw 1G 61
Kingsbury Episcopi. Som 4H 21
Kings Caple. Here 3A 48
Kingscavil. W Lot 2D 128
Kingsclere. Hants 1D 24
King's Cliffe. Nptn 1H 63
Kings Clipstone. Notts 4D 86
Kingscote. Glos 2D 34
Kingscott. Devn 1F 11
Kings Coughton. Warw 5E 61
Kingscross. N Ayr 3E 123
Kingsdon. Som 4A 22
Kingsdown. Kent 1H 29
Kingsdown. Swin 3G 35
Kingsdown. Wilts 5D 34
Kingseat. Fife 4D 136
Kingsey. Buck 5F 51
Kingsfold. Lanc 2D 90
Kingsfold. W Sus 2C 26
Kingsford. E Ayr 5F 127
Kingsford. Worc 2C 60
Kingsforth. N Lin 3D 94
Kingsgate. Kent 3H 41
King's Green. Glos 2C 48
Kingshall Street. Suff 4B 66
Kingsheanton. Devn 3F 19
King's Heath. W Mid 2E 61
Kings Hill. Kent 5A 40
Kingsholm. Glos 4D 48
Kingshouse. High 3G 141
Kingshouse. Stir 1E 135
Kingshurst. W Mid 2F 61
Kingskerswell. Devn 2E 9
Kingskettle. Fife 3F 137
Kingsland. Here 4G 59
Kingsland. IOA 2B 80
Kings Langley. Herts 5A 52
Kingsley. Ches W 3H 83
Kingsley. Hants 3F 25
Kingsley. Staf 1E 73
Kingsley Green. W Sus 3G 25
Kingsley Holt. Staf 1E 73
King's Lynn. Norf 3F 77
King's Meaburn. Cumb 2H 103
Kings Moss. Mers 4D 90
Kingsmuir. Ang 4D 145
Kingsmuir. Fife 3H 137
Kings Muir. Bord 1E 119
King's Newnham. Warw 3B 62
Kings Newton. Derbs 3A 74
Kingsnorth. Kent 2E 28
Kingsnorth. Medw 3C 40
King's Norton. Leics 5D 74
King's Norton. W Mid 3E 61
King's Nympton. Devn 1G 11
King's Pyon. Here 5G 59
Kings Ripton. Cambs 3B 64
King's Somborne.
Hants 3B 24
King's Stag. Dors 1C 14
King's Stanley. Glos 5D 48
King's Sutton. Nptn 2C 50
Kingstanding. W Mid 1E 61
Kingsteignton. Devn 5B 12
Kingsteps. High 3D 158
King Sterndale. Derbs 3E 85
King's Thorn. Here 2A 48
Kingsthorpe. Nptn 4E 63
Kingston. Cambs 5C 64
Kingston. Devn 4C 8
Kingston. Dors 2C 14
(nr. Sturminster Newton)
Kingston. Dors 5E 15
(nr. Swanage)
Kingston. E Lot 1B 130
Kingston. Hants 2G 15
Kingston. IOW 4C 16
Kingston. Kent 5F 41
Kingston. Mor 2H 159
Kingston. W Sus 5B 26
Kingston Bagpuize.
Oxon 2C 36
Kingston Blount. Oxon 2F 37
Kingston by Sea. W Sus 5D 26
Kingston Deverill. Wilts 3D 22
Kingstone. Here 2H 47
Kingstone. Som 1G 13
Kingstone. Staf 3E 73
Kingston Lisle. Oxon 3B 36
Kingston Maurward. Dors 3C 14
Kingston near Lewes.
E Sus 5E 27
Kingston on Soar. Notts 3C 74
Kingston Russell. Dors 3A 14
Kingston St Mary. Som 4F 21
Kingston Seymour. N Som 5H 33
Kingston Stert. Oxon 5F 51
Kingston upon Hull.
Hull 2D 94 & 199
Kingston upon Thames.
G Lon 4C 38
King's Walden. Herts 3B 52
Kingswear. Devn 3E 9
Kingswells. Aber 3F 153
Kingswinford. W Mid 2C 60
Kingswood. Buck 4E 51
Kingswood. Glos 2C 34
Kingswood. Here 5E 59
Kingswood. Kent 5C 40
Kingswood. Per 5H 143
Kingswood. Powy 5E 71
Kingswood. Som 3E 20
Kingswood. S Glo 4B 34
Kingswood. Surr 5D 38
Kingswood. Warw 3F 61
Kingswood Common. Staf 5C 72
Kings Worthy. Hants 3C 24
Kingthorpe. Linc 3A 88
Kington. Here 5F 59
Kington. S Glo 2B 34
Kington. Worc 5D 61
Kington Langley. Wilts 4E 35
Kington Magna. Dors 4C 22
Kington St Michael. Wilts 4E 35
Kingussie. High 3B 150
Kingweston. Som 3A 22
Kinharrachie. Abers 5G 161
Kinhrive. High 1B 158
Kinkell Bridge. Per 2B 136
Kinknockie. Abers 4H 161
Kinkry Hill. Cumb 2G 113
Kinlet. Shrp 2B 60
Kinloch. High 5D 166
(nr. Loch More)
Kinloch. High 3A 140
(nr. Lochaline)
Kinloch. High 4C 146
(on Rùm)
Kinloch. Per 4A 144
Kinlochard. Stir 3D 134
Kinlochbervie. High 3C 166
Kinlocheil. High 1D 141
Kinlochewe. High 2C 156
Kinloch Hourn. High 3B 148
Kinloch Laggan. High 5H 149
Kinlochleven. High 2F 141
Kinloch Lodge. High 3F 167
Kinlochmoidart. High 1B 140
Kinlochmore. High 2F 141
Kinloch Rannoch. Per 3D 142
Kinlochspelve. Arg 1D 132
Kinloid. High 5E 147
Kinloss. Mor 2E 159
Kinmel Bay. Cnwy 2B 82
Kinmuck. Abers 2F 153
Kinnadie. Abers 4G 161
Kinnaird. Per 1E 137
Kinneff. Abers 1H 145
Kinnelhead. Dum 4C 118
Kinnell. Ang 3F 145
Kinnerley. Shrp 3F 71
Kinnernie. Abers 2E 152
Kinnersley. Here 1G 47
Kinnersley. Worc 1D 48
Kinnerton. Powy 4E 59
Kinnerton. Shrp 1F 59
Kinnesswood. Per 3D 136
Kinninvie. Dur 2D 104
Kinnordy. Ang 3C 144
Kinoulton. Notts 2D 74
Kinross. Per 3D 136
Kinrossie. Per 5A 144
Kinsbourne Green. Herts 4B 52
Kinsey Heath. Ches E 1A 72
Kinsham. Here 4F 59
Kinsham. Worc 2E 49
Kinsley. W Yor 3E 93
Kinson. Bour 3F 15
Kintbury. W Ber 5B 36
Kintessack. Mor 2E 159
Kintillo. Per 2D 136
Kinton. Here 3G 59
Kinton. Shrp 4F 71
Kintore. Abers 2E 153
Kintour. Arg 4C 124
Kintra. Arg 2B 132
Kintraw. Arg 3F 133
Kinveachy. High 2D 150
Kinver. Staf 2C 60
Kinwarton. Warw 5F 61
Kiplingcotes. E Yor 5D 100
Kippax. W Yor 1E 93
Kippen. Stir 4F 135
Kippford. Dum 4F 111
Kipping's Cross. Kent 1H 27
Kirbister. Orkn 7C 172
(nr. Hobbister)
Kirbister. Orkn 6B 172
(nr. Quholm)
Kirbuster. Orkn 5F 172
Kirby Bedon. Norf 5E 79
Kirby Bellars. Leics 4E 74
Kirby Cane. Norf 1F 67
Kirby Cross. Essx 3F 55
Kirby Fields. Leics 5C 74
Kirby Grindalythe. N Yor 3D 100
Kirby Hill. N Yor 4E 105
(nr. Richmond)
Kirby Hill. N Yor 3F 99
(nr. Ripon)
Kirby Knowle. N Yor 1G 99
Kirby-le-Soken. Essx 3F 55
Kirby Misperton. N Yor 2B 100
Kirby Muxloe. Leics 5C 74
Kirby Row. Norf 1F 67
Kirby Sigston. N Yor 5B 106
Kirby Underdale. E Yor 4C 100
Kirby Wiske. N Yor 1F 99
Kirdford. W Sus 3B 26
Kirk. High 3E 169
Kirkabister. Shet 8F 173
(on Bressay)
Kirkabister. Shet 6F 173
(on Mainland)
Kirkandrews. Dum 5D 110
Kirkandrews-on-Eden.
Cumb 4E 113
Kirkapol. Arg 4B 138
Kirkbampton. Cumb 4E 112
Kirkbean. Dum 4A 112
Kirk Bramwith. S Yor 3G 93
Kirkbride. Cumb 4D 112
Kirkbridge. N Yor 5F 105
Kirkbuddo. Ang 4E 145
Kirkburn. E Yor 4D 101
Kirkburton. W Yor 3B 92
Kirkby. Linc 1H 87
Kirkby. Mers 1G 83
Kirkby. N Yor 4C 106
Kirkby Fenside. Linc 4C 88
Kirkby Fleetham. N Yor 5F 105
Kirkby Green. Linc 5H 87
Kirkby-in-Ashfield. Notts 5C 86
Kirkby Industrial Estate.
Mers 1G 83
Kirkby-in-Furness. Cumb 1B 96
Kirkby la Thorpe. Linc 1A 76
Kirkby Lonsdale. Cumb 2F 97
Kirkby Malham. N Yor 3A 98
Kirkby Mallory. Leics 5B 74
Kirkby Malzeard. N Yor 2E 99
Kirkby Mills. N Yor 1B 100
Kirkbymoorside. N Yor 1A 100
Kirkby on Bain. Linc 4B 88
Kirkby Overblow. N Yor 5F 99
Kirkby Stephen. Cumb 4A 104
Kirkby Thore. Cumb 2H 103
Kirkby Underwood. Linc 3H 75
Kirkby Wharfe. N Yor 5H 99
Kirkcaldy. Fife 4E 137
Kirkcambeck. Cumb 3G 113
Kirkcolm. Dum 3F 109
Kirkconnel. Dum 3G 117
Kirkconnell. Dum 3A 112
Kirkcowan. Dum 3A 110
Kirkcudbright. Dum 4D 111

Kirkdale. *Mers* 1F 83
Kirk Deighton. *N Yor* 4F 99
Kirk Ella. *E Yor* 2D 94
Kirkfieldbank. *S Lan* 5B 128
Kirkforthar Feus. *Fife* 3E 137
Kirkgunzeon. *Dum* 3F 111
Kirk Hallam. *Derbs* 1B 74
Kirkham. *Lanc* 1C 90
Kirkham. *N Yor* 3B 100
Kirkhamgate. *W Yor* 2C 92
Kirk Hammerton. *N Yor* 4G 99
Kirkharle. *Nmbd* 1D 114
Kirkheaton. *Nmbd* 2D 114
Kirkheaton. *W Yor* 3B 92
Kirkhill. *Ang* 2F 145
Kirkhill. *High* 4H 157
Kirkhope. *S Lan* 4B 118
Kirkhouse. *Bord* 1F 119
Kirkibost. *High* 2D 146
Kirkinch. *Ang* 4C 144
Kirkinner. *Dum* 4B 110
Kirkintilloch. *E Dun* 2H 127
Kirk Ireton. *Derbs* 5G 85
Kirkland. *Cumb* 3B 102
(nr. Cleator Moor)
Kirkland. *Cumb* 1H 103
(nr. Penrith)
Kirkland. *Cumb* 5D 112
(nr. Wigton)
Kirkland. *Dum* 3G 117
(nr. Kirkconnel)
Kirkland. *Dum* 5H 117
(nr. Moniaive)
Kirkland Guards. *Cumb* 5C 112
Kirk Langley. *Derbs* 2G 73
Kirklauchline. *Dum* 4F 109
Kirkleatham. *Red C* 2C 106
Kirklevington. *Stoc T* 4B 106
Kirkley. *Suff* 1H 67
Kirklington. *N Yor* 1F 99
Kirklington. *Notts* 5D 86
Kirklinton. *Cumb* 3F 113
Kirkliston. *Edin* 2E 129
Kirkmabreck. *Dum* 4B 110
Kirkmaiden. *Dum* 5E 109
Kirk Merrington. *Dur* 1F 105
Kirk Michael. *IOM* 2C 108
Kirkmichael. *Per* 2H 143
Kirkmichael. *S Ayr* 4C 116
Kirkmuirhill. *S Lan* 5A 128
Kirknewton. *Nmbd* 1D 120
Kirknewton. *W Lot* 3E 129
Kirkney. *Abers* 5C 160
Kirk of Shotts. *N Lan* 3B 128
Kirkoswald. *Cumb* 5G 113
Kirkoswald. *S Ayr* 4B 116
Kirkpatrick. *Dum* 5B 118
Kirkpatrick Durham. *Dum* 2E 111
Kirkpatrick-Fleming. *Dum* 2D 112
Kirk Sandall. *S Yor* 4G 93
Kirksanton. *Cumb* 1A 96
Kirk Smeaton. *N Yor* 3F 93
Kirkstall. *W Yor* 1C 92
Kirkstile. *Dum* 5F 119
Kirkstyle. *High* 1F 169
Kirkthorpe. *W Yor* 2D 92
Kirkton. *Abers* 2D 152
(nr. Alford)
Kirkton. *Abers* 1D 152
(nr. Insch)
Kirkton. *Abers* 4F 161
(nr. Turriff)
Kirkton. *Ang* 5D 144
(nr. Dundee)
Kirkton. *Ang* 4D 144
(nr. Forfar)
Kirkton. *Ang* 5B 152
(nr. Tarfside)
Kirkton. *Dum* 1A 112
Kirkton. *Fife* 1F 137
Kirkton. *High* 4E 165
(nr. Golspie)
Kirkton. *High* 1G 147
(nr. Kyle of Lochalsh)
Kirkton. *High* 4B 156
(nr. Lochcarron)
Kirkton. *Bord* 3H 119
Kirkton. *S Lan* 2B 118
Kirktonhill. *W Dun* 2E 127
Kirkton Manor. *Bord* 1E 118
Kirkton of Airlie. *Ang* 3C 144
Kirkton of Auchterhouse.
Ang 5C 144
Kirkton of Bourtie. *Abers* 1F 153
Kirkton of Collace. *Per* 5A 144
Kirkton of Craig. *Ang* 3G 145
Kirkton of Culsalmond.
Abers 5D 160
Kirkton of Durris. *Abers* 4E 153
Kirkton of Glenbuchat.
Abers 2A 152
Kirkton of Glenisla. *Ang* 2B 144
Kirkton of Kingoldrum. *Ang* 3C 144
Kirkton of Largo. *Fife* 3G 137
Kirkton of Lethendy. *Per* 4A 144
Kirkton of Logie Buchan.
Abers 1G 153
Kirkton of Maryculter. *Abers* 4F 153
Kirkton of Menmuir. *Ang* 2E 145
Kirkton of Monikie. *Ang* 5E 145
Kirkton of Oyne. *Abers* 1D 152
Kirkton of Rayne. *Abers* 5D 160
Kirkton of Skene. *Abers* 3F 153
Kirktown. *Abers* 2G 161
(nr. Fraserburgh)
Kirktown. *Abers* 3H 161
(nr. Peterhead)
Kirktown of Alvah. *Abers* 2D 160
Kirktown of Auchterless.
Abers 4E 160
Kirktown of Deskford. *Mor* 2C 160
Kirktown of Fetteresso.
Abers 5F 153
Kirktown of Mortlach. *Mor* 5H 159
Kirktown of Slains. *Abers* 1H 153
Kirkurd. *Bord* 5E 129
Kirkwall. *Orkn* 6D 172
Kirkwall Airport. *Orkn* 7D 172
Kirkwhelpington. *Nmbd* 1C 114
Kirk Yetholm. *Bord* 2C 120
Kirmington. *N Lin* 3E 94
Kirmond le Mire. *Linc* 1A 88
Kirn. *Arg* 2C 126
Kirriemuir. *Ang* 3C 144
Kirstead Green. *Norf* 1E 67
Kirtlebridge. *Dum* 2D 112
Kirtleton. *Dum* 2D 112
Kirtling. *Cambs* 5F 65
Kirtling Green. *Cambs* 5F 65
Kirtlington. *Oxon* 4D 50
Kirtomy. *High* 2H 167
Kirton. *Linc* 2C 76
Kirton. *Notts* 4D 86
Kirton. *Suff* 2F 55
Kirton End. *Linc* 1B 76
Kirton Holme. *Linc* 1B 76
Kirton in Lindsey. *N Lin* 1G 87
Kishorn. *High* 4H 155
Kislingbury. *Nptn* 5D 62
Kite Hill. *IOW* 3D 16
Kites Hardwick. *Warw* 4B 62
Kittisford. *Som* 4D 20
Kittle. *Swan* 4E 31
Kittybrewster. *Aber* 3G 153
Kitwood. *Hants* 3E 25
Kivernoll. *Here* 2H 47
Kiveton Park. *S Yor* 2B 86
Knaith. *Linc* 2F 87
Knaith Park. *Linc* 2F 87
Knaphill. *Surr* 5A 38
Knapp. *Hants* 4C 24
Knapp. *Per* 5B 144
Knapp. *Som* 4G 21
Knapperfield. *High* 3E 169
Knapton. *Norf* 2F 79
Knapton. *York* 4H 99
Knapton Green. *Here* 5G 59
Knapwell. *Cambs* 4C 64
Knaresborough. *N Yor* 4F 99
Knarsdale. *Nmbd* 4H 113
Knatts Valley. *Kent* 4G 39
Knaven. *Abers* 4F 161
Knayton. *N Yor* 1G 99
Knebworth. *Herts* 3C 52
Knedlington. *E Yor* 2H 93
Kneesall. *Notts* 4E 86
Kneesworth. *Cambs* 1D 52
Kneeton. *Notts* 1E 74
Knelston. *Swan* 4D 30
Knenhall. *Staf* 2D 72
Knightacott. *Devn* 3G 19
Knightcote. *Warw* 5B 62
Knightcott. *N Som* 1G 21
Knightley. *Staf* 3C 72
Knightley Dale. *Staf* 3C 72
Knightlow Hill. *Warw* 3B 62
Knighton. *Devn* 4B 8
Knighton. *Dors* 1B 14
Knighton. *Leic* 5D 74
Knighton. *Powy* 3E 59
Knighton. *Som* 2E 21
Knighton. *Staf* 3B 72
(nr. Eccleshall)
Knighton. *Staf* 1B 72
(nr. Woore)
Knighton. *Warw* 5H 61
Knighton. *Wilts* 4A 36
Knighton. *Worc* 5E 61
Knighton Common. *Worc* 3A 60
Knight's End. *Cambs* 1D 64
Knightswood. *Glas* 3G 127
Knightwick. *Worc* 5B 60
Knill. *Here* 4E 59
Knipton. *Leics* 2F 75
Knitsley. *Dur* 5E 115
Kniveton. *Derbs* 5G 85
Knock. *Arg* 5G 139
Knock. *Cumb* 2H 103
Knock. *Mor* 3C 160
Knockally. *High* 5D 168
Knockan. *Arg* 1B 132
Knockan. *High* 2G 163
Knockandhu. *Mor* 1G 151
Knockando. *Mor* 4F 159
Knockarthur. *High* 3E 165
Knockbain. *High* 3A 158
Knockbreck. *High* 2B 154
Knockdee. *High* 2D 168
Knockdolian. *S Ayr* 1G 109
Knockdon. *S Ayr* 3C 116
Knockdown. *Glos* 3D 34
Knockenbaird. *Abers* 1D 152
Knockenkelly. *N Ayr* 3E 123
Knockentiber. *E Ayr* 1C 116
Knockfarrel. *High* 3H 157
Knockglass. *High* 2C 168
Knockholt. *Kent* 5F 39
Knockholt Pound. *Kent* 5F 39
Knockie Lodge. *High* 2G 149
Knockin. *Shrp* 3F 71
Knockinlaw. *E Ayr* 1D 116
Knockinnon. *High* 5D 169
Knockrome. *Arg* 2D 124
Knocksharry. *IOM* 3B 108
Knockshinnoch. *E Ayr* 3D 116
Knockvennie. *Dum* 2E 111
Knockvologan. *Arg* 3B 132
Knodishall. *Suff* 4G 67
Knole. *Som* 4H 21
Knollbury. *Mon* 3H 33
Knolls Green. *Ches E* 3C 84
Knolton. *Wrex* 2F 71
Knook. *Wilts* 2E 23
Knossington. *Leics* 5F 75
Knott. *High* 3C 154
Knott End-on-Sea. *Lanc* 5C 96
Knotting. *Bed* 4H 63
Knotting Green. *Bed* 4H 63
Knottingley. *W Yor* 2E 93
Knotts. *Cumb* 2F 103
Knotty Ash. *Mers* 1G 83
Knotty Green. *Buck* 1A 38
Knowbury. *Shrp* 3H 59
Knowe. *Dum* 2A 110
Knowefield. *Cumb* 4F 113
Knowehead. *Dum* 5F 117
Knowes. *E Lot* 2C 130
Knowesgate. *Nmbd* 1C 114
Knoweside. *S Ayr* 3B 116
Knowle. *Bris* 4A 34
Knowle. *Devn* 3E 19
(nr. Braunton)
Knowle. *Devn* 4D 12
(nr. Budleigh Salterton)
Knowle. *Devn* 2A 12
(nr. Crediton)
Knowle. *Shrp* 3H 59
Knowle. *W Mid* 3F 61
Knowle Green. *Lanc* 1E 91
Knowle St Giles. *Som* 1G 13
Knowlesands. *Shrp* 1B 60
Knowles of Elrick. *Abers* 3D 160
Knowle Village. *Hants* 2D 16
Knowl Hill. *Wind* 4G 37
Knowlton. *Kent* 5G 41
Knowsley. *Mers* 1G 83
Knowstone. *Devn* 4B 20
Knucklas. *Powy* 3E 59
Knuston. *Nptn* 4G 63
Knutsford. *Ches E* 3B 84
Knypersley. *Staf* 5C 84
Krumlin. *W Yor* 3A 92
Kuggar. *Corn* 5E 5
Kyleakin. *High* 1F 147
Kyle of Lochalsh. *High* 1F 147
Kylerhea. *High* 1F 147
Kylesku. *High* 5C 166
Kyles Lodge. *W Isl* 9B 171
Kylesmorar. *High* 4G 147
Kylestrome. *High* 5C 166
Kymin. *Mon* 4A 48
Kynaston. *Here* 2B 48
Kynaston. *Shrp* 3F 71
Kynnersley. *Telf* 4A 72
Kyre Green. *Worc* 4A 60
Kyre Park. *Worc* 4A 60
Kyrewood. *Worc* 4A 60

L

Labost. *W Isl* 3E 171
Lacasaidh. *W Isl* 5F 171
Lacasdail. *W Isl* 4G 171
Laceby. *NE Lin* 4F 95
Lacey Green. *Buck* 5G 51
Lach Dennis. *Ches W* 3B 84
Lache. *Ches W* 4F 83
Lackford. *Suff* 3G 65
Lacock. *Wilts* 5E 35
Ladbroke. *Warw* 5B 62
Laddingford. *Kent* 1A 28
Lade Bank. *Linc* 5C 88
Ladock. *Corn* 3C 6
Lady. *Orkn* 3F 172
Ladybank. *Fife* 2F 137
Ladycross. *Corn* 4D 10
Lady Green. *Mers* 4B 90
Lady Hall. *Cumb* 1A 96
Ladykirk. *Bord* 5E 131
Ladysford. *Abers* 2G 161
Ladywood. *W Mid* 2E 61
Ladywood. *Worc* 4C 60
Laga. *High* 2A 140
Lagavulin. *Arg* 5C 124
Lagg. *Arg* 2D 125
Lagg. *N Ayr* 3D 122
Laggan. *Arg* 4A 124
Laggan. *High* 4E 149
(nr. Fort Augustus)
Laggan. *High* 4A 150
(nr. Newtonmore)
Laggan. *Mor* 5H 159
Lagganlia. *High* 3C 150
Lagganulva. *Arg* 4F 139
Laglingarten. *Arg* 3A 134
Lagness. *W Sus* 2G 17
Laid. *High* 3E 166
Laide. *High* 4D 162
Laigh Fenwick. *E Ayr* 5F 127
Laindon. *Essx* 2A 40
Lairg. *High* 3C 164
Lairg Muir. *High* 3C 164
Laithes. *Cumb* 1F 103
Laithkirk. *Dur* 2C 104
Lake. *Devn* 3F 19
Lake. *IOW* 4D 16
Lake. *Wilts* 3G 23
Lake District. *Cumb* 3E 103
Lakenham. *Norf* 5E 79
Lakenheath. *Suff* 2G 65
Lakesend. *Norf* 1E 65
Lakeside. *Cumb* 1C 96
Laleham. *Surr* 4B 38
Laleston. *B'end* 3B 32
Lamancha. *Bord* 4F 129
Lamarsh. *Essx* 2B 54
Lamas. *Norf* 3E 79
Lamb Corner. *Essx* 2D 54
Lambden. *Bord* 5D 130
Lamberhead Green. *G Man* 4D 90
Lamberhurst. *Kent* 2A 28
Lamberhurst Quarter. *Kent* 2A 28
Lamberton. *Bord* 4F 131
Lambeth. *G Lon* 3E 39
Lambfell Moar. *IOM* 3B 108
Lambhill. *Glas* 3G 127
Lambley. *Nmbd* 4H 113
Lambley. *Notts* 1D 74
Lambourn. *W Ber* 4B 36
Lambourne End. *Essx* 1F 39
Lambourn Woodlands. *W Ber* 4B 36
Lambrook. *Som* 4F 21
Lambs Green. *Dors* 3E 15
Lambs Green. *W Sus* 2D 26
Lambston. *Pemb* 3D 42
Lamellion. *Corn* 2G 7
Lamerton. *Devn* 5E 11
Lamesley. *Tyne* 4F 115
Laminess. *Orkn* 4F 172
Lamington. *High* 1B 158
Lamington. *S Lan* 1B 118
Lamlash. *N Ayr* 2E 123
Lamonby. *Cumb* 1F 103
Lamorick. *Corn* 2E 7
Lamorna. *Corn* 4B 4
Lamorran. *Corn* 4C 6
Lampeter. *Cdgn* 1F 45
Lampeter Velfrey. *Pemb* 3F 43
Lamphey. *Pemb* 4E 43
Lamplugh. *Cumb* 2B 102
Lamport. *Nptn* 3E 63
Lamyatt. *Som* 3B 22
Lana. *Devn* 3D 10
(nr. Ashwater)
Lana. *Devn* 2D 10
(nr. Holsworthy)
Lanark. *S Lan* 5B 128
Lanarth. *Corn* 4E 5
Lancaster. *Lanc* 3D 97
Lanchester. *Dur* 5E 115
Lancing. *W Sus* 5C 26
Landbeach. *Cambs* 4D 64
Landcross. *Devn* 4E 19
Landerberry. *Abers* 3E 153
Landford. *Wilts* 1A 16
Land Gate. *G Man* 4D 90
Landhallow. *High* 5D 169
Landimore. *Swan* 3D 30
Landkey. *Devn* 3F 19
Landkey Newland. *Devn* 3F 19
Landore. *Swan* 3F 31
Landport. *Port* 2E 17
Landrake. *Corn* 2H 7
Landscove. *Devn* 2D 9
Land's End (St Just) Airport.
Corn 4A 4
Landshipping. *Pemb* 3E 43
Landulph. *Corn* 2A 8
Landywood. *Staf* 5D 73
Lane. *Corn* 2C 6
Laneast. *Corn* 4C 10
Lane Bottom. *Lanc* 1G 91
Lane End. *Buck* 2G 37
Lane End. *Hants* 4D 24
Lane End. *IOW* 4E 17
Lane End. *Wilts* 2D 22
Lane Ends. *Derbs* 2G 73
Lane Ends. *Dur* 1E 105
Lane Ends. *Lanc* 4G 97
Laneham. *Notts* 3F 87
Lanehead. *Dur* 5B 114
(nr. Cowshill)
Lane Head. *Dur* 3E 105
(nr. Hutton Magna)
Lane Head. *Dur* 2D 105
(nr. Woodland)
Lane Head. *G Man* 1A 84
Lanehead. *Nmbd* 1A 114
Lane Head. *W Yor* 4B 92
Lane Heads. *Lanc* 1C 90
Lanercost. *Cumb* 3G 113
Laneshaw Bridge. *Lanc* 5B 98
Laney Green. *Staf* 5D 72
Langais. *W Isl* 2D 170
Langal. *High* 2B 140
Langar. *Notts* 2E 74
Langbank. *Ren* 2E 127
Langbar. *N Yor* 4C 98
Langburnshiels. *Bord* 4H 119
Langcliffe. *N Yor* 3H 97
Langdale End. *N Yor* 5G 107
Langdon. *Corn* 3C 10
Langdon Beck. *Dur* 1B 104
Langdon Cross. *Corn* 4D 10
Langdon Hills. *Essx* 2A 40
Langdown. *Hants* 2C 16
Langdyke. *Fife* 3F 137
Langenhoe. *Essx* 4D 54
Langford. *C Beds* 1B 52
Langford. *Devn* 2D 12
Langford. *Essx* 5B 54
Langford. *Notts* 5F 87
Langford. *Oxon* 5H 49
Langford. *Som* 4F 21
Langford Budville. *Som* 4E 20
Langham. *Dors* 4C 22
Langham. *Essx* 2D 54
Langham. *Norf* 1C 78
Langham. *Rut* 4F 75
Langham. *Suff* 4B 66
Langho. *Lanc* 1F 91
Langholm. *Dum* 1E 113
Langland. *Swan* 4F 31
Langleeford. *Nmbd* 2D 120
Langley. *Ches E* 3D 84
Langley. *Derbs* 1B 74
Langley. *Essx* 2E 53
Langley. *Glos* 3F 49
Langley. *Hants* 2C 16
Langley. *Herts* 3C 52
Langley. *Kent* 5C 40
Langley. *Nmbd* 3B 114
Langley. *Slo* 3B 38
Langley. *Som* 4D 20
Langley. *Warw* 4F 61
Langley. *W Sus* 4G 25
Langley Burrell. *Wilts* 4E 35
Langleybury. *Herts* 5A 52
Langley Common. *Derbs* 2G 73
Langley Green. *Derbs* 2G 73
Langley Green. *Norf* 5F 79
Langley Green. *Warw* 4F 61
Langley Green. *W Sus* 2D 26
Langley Heath. *Kent* 5C 40
Langley Marsh. *Som* 4D 20
Langley Moor. *Dur* 5F 115
Langley Park. *Dur* 5F 115
Langley Street. *Norf* 5F 79
Langney. *E Sus* 5H 27
Langold. *Notts* 2C 86
Langore. *Corn* 4D 10
Langport. *Som* 4H 21
Langrick. *Linc* 1B 76
Langridge. *Bath* 5C 34
Langridgeford. *Devn* 4F 19
Langrigg. *Cumb* 5C 112
Langrish. *Hants* 4F 25
Langsett. *S Yor* 4C 92
Langshaw. *Bord* 1H 119
Langstone. *Hants* 2F 17
Langthorne. *N Yor* 5F 105
Langthorpe. *N Yor* 3F 99
Langthwaite. *N Yor* 4D 104
Langtoft. *E Yor* 3E 101
Langtoft. *Linc* 4A 76
Langton. *Dur* 3E 105
Langton. *Linc* 4B 88
(nr. Horncastle)
Langton. *Linc* 3C 88
(nr. Spilsby)
Langton. *N Yor* 3B 100
Langton by Wragby. *Linc* 3A 88
Langton Green. *Kent* 2G 27
Langton Herring. *Dors* 4B 14
Langton Long Blandford.
Dors 2E 15
Langton Matravers. *Dors* 5F 15
Langtree. *Devn* 1E 11
Langwathby. *Cumb* 1G 103
Langwith. *Derbs* 4C 86
Langworth. *Linc* 3H 87
Lanivet. *Corn* 2E 7
Lanjeth. *Corn* 3D 6
Lank. *Corn* 5A 10
Lanlivery. *Corn* 3E 7
Lanner. *Corn* 5B 6
Lanreath. *Corn* 3F 7
Lansallos. *Corn* 3F 7
Lansdown. *Bath* 5C 34
Lansdown. *Glos* 3E 49
Lanteglos Highway. *Corn* 3F 7
Lanton. *Nmbd* 1D 120
Lanton. *Bord* 2A 120
Lapford. *Devn* 2H 11
Lapford Cross. *Devn* 2H 11
Laphroaig. *Arg* 5B 124
Lapley. *Staf* 4C 72
Lapworth. *Warw* 3F 61
Larachbeg. *High* 4A 140
Larbert. *Falk* 1B 128
Larden Green. *Ches E* 5H 83
Larel. *High* 3D 169
Largie. *Abers* 5D 160
Largiemore. *Arg* 1H 125
Largoward. *Fife* 3G 137
Largs. *N Ayr* 4D 126
Largue. *Abers* 4D 160
Largybeg. *N Ayr* 3E 123
Largymeanoch. *N Ayr* 3E 123

Largymore. N Ayr 3E 123
Larkfield. Inv 2D 126
Larkfield. Kent 5A 40
Larkhall. Bath 5C 34
Larkhall. S Lan 4A 128
Larkhill. Wilts 2G 23
Larling. Norf 2B 66
Larport. Here 2A 48
Lartington. Dur 3D 104
Lary. Abers 3H 151
Lasham. Hants 2E 25
Lashenden. Kent 1C 28
Lassodie. Fife 4D 136
Lasswade. Midl 3G 129
Lastingham. N Yor 5E 107
Latchford. Herts 3D 53
Latchford. Oxon 5E 51
Latchingdon. Essx 5B 54
Latchley. Corn 5E 11
Latchmere Green. Hants 5E 37
Lathbury. Mil 1G 51
Latheron. High 5D 169
Latheronwheel. High 5D 169
Lathom. Lanc 4C 90
Lathones. Fife 3G 137
Latimer. Buck 1B 38
Latteridge. S Glo 3B 34
Lattiford. Som 4B 22
Latton. Wilts 2F 35
Laudale House. High 3B 140
Lauder. Bord 5B 130
Laugharne. Carm 3H 43
Laughterton. Linc 3F 87
Laughton. E Sus 4G 27
Laughton. Leics 2D 62
Laughton. Linc 1F 87
(nr. Gainsborough)
Laughton. Linc 2H 75
(nr. Grantham)
Laughton Common. S Yor 2C 86
Laughton en le Morthen. S Yor 2C 86
Launcells. Corn 2C 10
Launceston. Corn 4D 10
Launcherley. Som 2A 22
Launton. Oxon 3E 50
Laurencekirk. Abers 1G 145
Laurieston. Dum 3D 111
Laurieston. Falk 2C 128
Lavendon. Mil 5G 63
Lavenham. Suff 1C 54
Laverhay. Dum 5D 118
Laversdale. Cumb 3F 113
Laverstock. Wilts 3G 23
Laverstoke. Hants 2C 24
Laverton. Glos 2F 49
Laverton. N Yor 2E 99
Laverton. Som 1C 22
Lavister. Wrex 5F 83
Law. S Lan 4B 128
Lawers. Per 5D 142
Lawford. Essx 2D 54
Lawhitton. Corn 4D 10
Lawkland. N Yor 3G 97
Lawley. Shrp 5A 72
Lawnhead. Staf 3C 72
Lawrenny. Pemb 4E 43
Lawshall. Suff 5A 66
Lawton. Here 5G 59
Laxey. IOM 3D 108
Laxfield. Suff 3E 67
Laxfirth. Shet 6F 173
Laxo. Shet 5F 173
Laxton. E Yor 2A 94
Laxton. Nptn 1G 63
Laxton. Notts 4E 86
Laycock. W Yor 5C 98
Layer Breton. Essx 4C 54
Layer-de-la-Haye. Essx 3C 54
Layer Marney. Essx 4C 54
Layland's Green. W Ber 5B 36
Laymore. Dors 2G 13
Laysters Pole. Here 4H 59
Layter's Green. Buck 1A 38
Laytham. E Yor 1H 93
Lazenby. Red C 3C 106
Lazonby. Cumb 1G 103
Lea. Derbs 5H 85
Lea. Here 3B 48
Lea. Linc 2F 87
Lea. Shrp 2F 59
(nr. Bishop's Castle)
Lea. Shrp 5G 71
(nr. Shrewsbury)
Lea. Wilts 3E 35
Leabrooks. Derbs 5B 86
Leac a Li. W Isl 8D 171
Leachd. Arg 4H 133
Leachkin. High 4A 158
Leachpool. Pemb 3D 42
Leadburn. Midl 4F 129
Leadenham. Linc 5G 87
Leaden Roding. Essx 4F 53
Leaderfoot. Bord 1H 119
Leadgate. Cumb 5A 114
Leadgate. Dur 4E 115
Leadgate. Nmbd 4E 115
Leadhills. S Lan 3A 118
Leadingcross Green. Kent 5C 40
Lea End. Worc 3E 61
Leafield. Oxon 4B 50
Leagrave. Lutn 3A 52
Lea Hall. W Mid 2F 61
Lea Heath. Staf 3E 73
Leake. N Yor 5B 106
Leake Common Side. Linc 5C 88
Leake Fold Hill. Linc 5D 88
Leake Hurn's End. Linc 1D 76
Lealholm. N Yor 4E 107
Lealt. Arg 4D 132
Lealt. High 2E 155
Leam. Derbs 3G 85
Lea Marston. Warw 1G 61
Leamington Hastings. Warw 4B 62
Leamington Spa, Royal. Warw 4H 61
Leamonsley. Staf 5F 73
Leamside. Dur 5G 115
Leargybreck. Arg 2D 124
Lease Rigg. N Yor 4F 107
Leasgill. Cumb 1D 97
Leasingham. Linc 1H 75
Leasingthorne. Dur 1F 105
Leasowe. Mers 1E 83
Leatherhead. Surr 5C 38
Leathley. N Yor 5E 99
Leaths. Dum 3E 111
Leaton. Shrp 4G 71
Leaton. Telf 4A 72
Lea Town. Lanc 1C 90
Leaveland. Kent 5E 40
Leavenheath. Suff 2C 54
Leavening. N Yor 3B 100
Leaves Green. G Lon 4F 39
Lea Yeat. Cumb 1G 97
Leazes. Dur 4E 115
Lebberston. N Yor 1E 101
Lechlade on Thames. Glos 2H 35
Leck. Lanc 2F 97
Leckford. Hants 3B 24
Leckfurin. High 3H 167
Leckgruinart. Arg 3A 124
Leckhampstead. Buck 2F 51
Leckhampstead. W Ber 4C 36
Leckhampstead Street. W Ber 4C 36
Leckhampton. Glos 4E 49
Leckmelm. High 4F 163
Leckwith. V Glam 4E 33
Leconfield. E Yor 5E 101
Ledaig. Arg 5D 140
Ledburn. Buck 3H 51
Ledbury. Here 2C 48
Ledgemoor. Here 5G 59
Ledgowan. High 3D 156
Ledicot. Here 4G 59
Ledmore. High 2G 163
Lednabirichen. High 4E 165
Lednagullin. High 2A 168
Ledsham. Ches W 3F 83
Ledsham. W Yor 2E 93
Ledston. W Yor 2E 93
Ledstone. Devn 4D 8
Ledwell. Oxon 3C 50
Lee. Devn 2E 19
(nr. Ilfracombe)
Lee. Devn 4B 20
(nr. South Molton)
Lee. G Lon 3F 39
Lee. Hants 1B 16
Lee. Lanc 4E 97
Lee. Shrp 2G 71
Leeans. Shet 7E 173
Leebotten. Shet 9F 173
Leebotwood. Shrp 1G 59
Lee Brockhurst. Shrp 3H 71
Leece. Cumb 3B 96
Leechpool. Mon 3A 34
Lee Clump. Buck 5H 51
Leeds. Kent 5C 40
Leeds. W Yor 1C 92 & 199
Leeds Bradford International Airport. W Yor 5E 98
Leedstown. Corn 3D 4
Leegomery. Telf 4A 72
Lee Head. Derbs 1E 85
Leek. Staf 5D 85
Leekbrook. Staf 5D 85
Leek Wootton. Warw 4G 61
Lee Mill. Devn 3B 8
Leeming. N Yor 1E 99
Leeming Bar. N Yor 5F 105
Lee Moor. Devn 2B 8
Lee Moor. W Yor 2D 92
Lee-on-the-Solent. Hants 2D 16
Lees. Derbs 2G 73
Lees. G Man 4H 91
Lees. W Yor 1A 92
Lees, The. Kent 5E 40
Leeswood. Flin 4E 83
Lee, The. Buck 5H 51
Leetown. Per 1E 136
Leftwich. Ches W 3A 84
Legbourne. Linc 2C 88
Legburthwaite. Cumb 3E 102
Legerwood. Bord 5B 130
Legsby. Linc 2A 88
Leicester. Leic 5C 74 & 200
Leicester Forest East. Leics 5C 74
Leigh. Dors 2B 14
Leigh. G Man 4E 91
Leigh. Kent 1G 27
Leigh. Shrp 5F 71
Leigh. Surr 1D 26
Leigh. Wilts 2F 35
Leigh. Worc 5B 60
Leigham. Plym 3B 8
Leigh Beck. Essx 2C 40
Leigh Common. Som 4C 22
Leigh Delamere. Wilts 4D 35
Leigh Green. Kent 2D 28
Leighland Chapel. Som 3D 20
Leigh-on-Sea. S'end 2C 40
Leigh Park. Hants 2F 17
Leigh Sinton. Worc 5B 60
Leighterton. Glos 2D 34
Leigh, The. Glos 3D 48
Leighton. N Yor 2D 98
Leighton. Powy 5E 71
Leighton. Shrp 5A 72
Leighton. Som 2C 22
Leighton Bromswold. Cambs 3A 64
Leighton Buzzard. C Beds 3H 51
Leigh-upon-Mendip. Som 2B 22
Leinthall Earls. Here 4G 59
Leinthall Starkes. Here 4G 59
Leintwardine. Here 3G 59
Leire. Leics 1C 62
Leirinmore. High 2E 166
Leishmore. High 4G 157
Leiston. Suff 4G 67
Leitfie. Per 4B 144
Leith. Edin 2F 129
Leitholm. Bord 5D 130
Lelant. Corn 3C 4
Lelant Downs. Corn 3C 4
Lelley. E Yor 1F 95
Lem Hill. Worc 3B 60
Lemington. Tyne 3E 115
Lemmington Hall. Nmbd 3F 121
Lempitlaw. Bord 1B 120
Lemsford. Herts 4C 52
Lenacre. Cumb 1F 97
Lenchie. Abers 5C 160
Lenchwick. Worc 1F 49
Lendalfoot. S Ayr 5A 116
Lendrick. Stir 3E 135
Lenham. Kent 5C 40
Lenham Heath. Kent 1D 28
Lenimore. N Ayr 5G 125
Lennel. Bord 5E 131
Lennoxtown. E Dun 2H 127
Lenton. Linc 2H 75
Lentran. High 4H 157
Lenwade. Norf 4C 78
Lenzie. E Dun 2H 127
Leochel Cushnie. Abers 2C 152
Leogh. Shet 1B 172
Leominster. Here 5G 59
Leonard Stanley. Glos 5D 48
Lepe. Hants 3C 16
Lephenstrath. Arg 5A 122
Lephin. High 4A 154
Lephinchapel. Arg 4G 133
Lephinmore. Arg 4G 133
Leppington. N Yor 3B 100
Lepton. W Yor 3C 92
Lerryn. Corn 3F 7
Lerwick. Shet 7F 173
Lerwick (Tingwall) Airport. Shet 7F 173
Lesbury. Nmbd 3G 121
Leslie. Abers 1C 152
Leslie. Fife 3E 137
Lesmahagow. S Lan 1H 117
Lesnewth. Corn 3B 10
Lessingham. Norf 3F 79
Lessonhall. Cumb 4D 112
Leswalt. Dum 3F 109
Letchmore Heath. Herts 1C 38
Letchworth Garden City. Herts 2C 52
Letcombe Bassett. Oxon 3B 36
Letcombe Regis. Oxon 3B 36
Letham. Ang 4E 145
Letham. Falk 1B 128
Letham. Fife 2F 137
Lethanhill. E Ayr 3D 116
Lethenty. Abers 4F 161
Letheringham. Suff 5E 67
Letheringsett. Norf 2C 78
Lettaford. Devn 4H 11
Lettan. Orkn 3G 172
Letter. Abers 2E 153
Letterewe. High 1B 156
Letterfearn. High 1A 148
Lettermore. Arg 4F 139
Letters. High 5F 163
Letterston. Pemb 2D 42
Letton. Here 1G 47
(nr. Kington)
Letton. Here 3F 59
(nr. Leintwardine)
Letty Green. Herts 4C 52
Letwell. S Yor 2C 86
Leuchars. Fife 1G 137
Leumrabhagh. W Isl 6F 171
Leusdon. Devn 5H 11
Levaneap. Shet 5F 173
Levedale. Staf 4C 72
Leven. E Yor 5F 101
Leven. Fife 3F 137
Levencorroch. N Ayr 3E 123
Levenhall. E Lot 2G 129
Levens. Cumb 1D 97
Levens Green. Herts 3D 52
Levenshulme. G Man 1C 84
Levenwick. Shet 9F 173
Leverburgh. W Isl 9C 171
Leverington. Cambs 4D 76
Leverton. Linc 1C 76
Leverton. W Ber 4B 36
Leverton Lucasgate. Linc 1D 76
Leverton Outgate. Linc 1D 76
Levington. Suff 2F 55
Levisham. N Yor 5F 107
Levishie. High 2G 149
Lew. Oxon 5B 50
Lewaigue. IOM 2D 108
Lewannick. Corn 4C 10
Lewdown. Devn 4E 11
Lewes. E Sus 4F 27
Leweston. Pemb 2D 42
Lewisham. G Lon 3E 39
Lewiston. High 1H 149
Lewistown. B'end 3C 32
Lewknor. Oxon 2F 37
Leworthy. Devn 3G 19
(nr. Barnstaple)
Leworthy. Devn 2D 10
(nr. Holsworthy)
Lewson Street. Kent 4D 40
Lewthorn Cross. Devn 5A 12
Lewtrenchard. Devn 4E 11
Ley. Corn 2F 7
Leybourne. Kent 5A 40
Leyburn. N Yor 5E 105
Leycett. Staf 1B 72
Leyfields. Staf 5G 73
Ley Green. Herts 3B 52
Ley Hill. Buck 5H 51
Leyland. Lanc 2D 90
Leylodge. Abers 2E 153
Leymoor. W Yor 3B 92
Leys. Per 5B 144
Leysdown-on-Sea. Kent 3E 41
Leysmill. Ang 4F 145
Leyton. G Lon 2E 39
Leytonstone. G Lon 2F 39
Lezant. Corn 5D 10
Leziate. Norf 4F 77
Lhanbryde. Mor 2G 159
Lhen, The. IOM 1C 108
Liatrie. High 5E 157
Libanus. Powy 3C 46
Libberton. S Lan 5C 128
Libbery. Worc 5D 60
Liberton. Edin 3F 129
Liceasto. W Isl 8D 171
Lichfield. Staf 5F 73
Lickey. Worc 3D 61
Lickey End. Worc 3D 61
Lickfold. W Sus 3A 26
Liddaton. Devn 4E 11
Liddington. Swin 3H 35
Liddle. Orkn 9D 172
Lidgate. Suff 5G 65
Lidgett. Notts 4D 86
Lidham Hill. E Sus 4C 28
Lidlington. C Beds 2H 51
Lidsey. W Sus 5A 26
Lidstone. Oxon 3B 50
Lienassie. High 1B 148
Liff. Ang 5C 144
Lifford. W Mid 2E 61
Lifton. Devn 4D 11
Liftondown. Devn 4D 10
Lighthorne. Warw 5H 61
Light Oaks. Staf 5D 84
Lightwater. Surr 4A 38
Lightwood. Staf 1E 73
Lightwood. Stoke 1D 72
Lightwood Green. Ches E 1A 72
Lightwood Green. Wrex 1F 71
Lilbourne. Nptn 3C 62
Lilburn Tower. Nmbd 2E 121
Lillesdon. Som 4G 21
Lilleshall. Telf 4B 72
Lilley. Herts 3B 52
Lilliesleaf. Bord 2H 119
Lillingstone Dayrell. Buck 2F 51
Lillingstone Lovell. Buck 1F 51
Lillington. Dors 1B 14
Lilstock. Som 2E 21
Lilybank. Inv 2E 126
Lilyhurst. Shrp 4B 72
Limbrick. Lanc 3E 90
Limbury. Lutn 3A 52
Limekilnburn. S Lan 4A 128
Limekilns. Fife 1D 129
Limerigg. Falk 2B 128
Limestone Brae. Nmbd 5A 114
Lime Street. Worc 2D 48
Limington. Som 4A 22
Limpenhoe. Norf 5F 79
Limpley Stoke. Wilts 5C 34
Limpsfield. Surr 5E 39
Limpsfield Chart. Surr 5F 39
Linburn. W Lot 3E 129
Linby. Notts 5C 86
Linchmere. W Sus 3G 25
Lincluden. Dum 2A 112
Lincoln. Linc 3G 87 & 198
Lincomb. Worc 4C 60
Lindale. Cumb 1D 96
Lindal in Furness. Cumb 2B 96
Lindean. Bord 1G 119
Linden. Glos 4D 48
Lindfield. W Sus 3E 27
Lindford. Hants 3G 25
Lindores. Fife 2E 137
Lindridge. Worc 4A 60
Lindsell. Essx 3G 53
Lindsey. Suff 1C 54
Lindsey Tye. Suff 1C 54
Linford. Hants 2G 15
Linford. Thur 3A 40
Lingague. IOM 4B 108
Lingdale. Red C 3D 106
Lingen. Here 4F 59
Lingfield. Surr 1E 27
Lingoed. Mon 3G 47
Lingreabhagh. W Isl 9C 171
Ling, The. Norf 1F 67
Lingwood. Norf 5F 79
Lingy Close. Cumb 4E 113
Linicro. High 2C 154
Linkend. Worc 2D 48
Linkenholt. Hants 1B 24
Linkinhorne. Corn 5D 10
Linklater. Orkn 9D 172
Linksness. Orkn 6E 172
Linktown. Fife 4E 137
Linkwood. Mor 2G 159
Linley. Shrp 1F 59
(nr. Bishop's Castle)
Linley. Shrp 1A 60
(nr. Bridgnorth)
Linley Green. Here 5A 60
Linlithgow. W Lot 2C 128
Linlithgow Bridge. Falk 2C 128
Linneraineach. High 3F 163
Linshiels. Nmbd 4C 120
Linsiadar. W Isl 4E 171
Linsidemore. High 4C 164
Linslade. C Beds 3H 51
Linstead Parva. Suff 3F 67
Linstock. Cumb 4F 113
Linthwaite. W Yor 3B 92
Lintlaw. Bord 4E 131
Lintmill. Mor 2C 160
Linton. Cambs 1F 53
Linton. Derbs 4G 73
Linton. Here 3B 48
Linton. Kent 5B 40
Linton. N Yor 3B 98
Linton. Bord 2B 120
Linton. W Yor 5F 99
Linton Colliery. Nmbd 5G 121
Linton Hill. Here 3B 48
Linton-on-Ouse. N Yor 3G 99
Lintzford. Tyne 4E 115
Lintzgarth. Dur 5C 114
Linwood. Hants 2G 15
Linwood. Linc 2A 88
Linwood. Ren 3F 127
Lionacleit. W Isl 4C 170
Lionacro. High 2C 154
Lionacuidhe. W Isl 4C 170
Lional. W Isl 1H 171
Liphook. Hants 3G 25
Lipley. Shrp 2B 72
Lipyeate. Som 1B 22
Liquo. N Lan 4B 128
Liscard. Mers 1F 83
Liscombe. Som 3B 20
Liskeard. Corn 2G 7
Lisle Court. Hants 3B 16
Liss. Hants 4F 25
Lissett. E Yor 4F 101
Liss Forest. Hants 4F 25
Lissington. Linc 2A 88
Liston. Essx 1B 54
Lisvane. Card 3E 33
Liswerry. Newp 3G 33
Litcham. Norf 4A 78
Litchard. B'end 3C 32
Litchborough. Nptn 5D 62
Litchfield. Hants 1C 24
Litherland. Mers 1F 83
Litlington. Cambs 1D 52
Litlington. E Sus 5G 27
Littemill. Nmbd 3G 121
Litterty. Abers 3E 161
Little Abington. Cambs 1F 53
Little Addington. Nptn 3G 63
Little Airmyn. N Yor 2H 93
Little Alne. Warw 4F 61
Little Ardo. Abers 5F 161
Little Asby. Cumb 4H 103
Little Aston. Staf 5E 73
Little Atherfield. IOW 4C 16
Little Ayton. N Yor 3C 106
Little Baddow. Essx 5A 54
Little Badminton. S Glo 3D 34
Little Ballinluig. Per 3G 143
Little Bampton. Cumb 4D 112
Little Bardfield. Essx 2G 53
Little Barford. Bed 5A 64
Little Barningham. Norf 2D 78
Little Barrington. Glos 4H 49
Little Barrow. Ches W 4G 83
Little Barugh. N Yor 2B 100
Little Bavington. Nmbd 2C 114
Little Bealings. Suff 1F 55
Littlebeck. Cumb 3H 103
Little Bedwyn. Wilts 5A 36
Little Bentley. Essx 3E 54
Little Berkhamsted. Herts 5C 52
Little Billing. Nptn 4F 63
Little Billington. C Beds 3H 51

Little Birch. Here 2A 48
Little Bispham. Bkpl 5C 96
Little Blakenham. Suff 1E 54
Little Blencow. Cumb 1F 103
Little Bognor. W Sus 3B 26
Little Bolas. Shrp 3A 72
Little Bollington. Ches E 2B 84
Little Bookham. Surr 5C 38
Littleborough. Devn 1B 12
Littleborough. G Man 3H 91
Littleborough. Notts 2F 87
Littlebourne. Kent 5G 41
Little Bourton. Oxon 1C 50
Little Bowden. Leics 2E 63
Little Bradley. Suff 5F 65
Little Brampton. Shrp 2F 59
Little Brechin. Ang 2E 145
Littlebredy. Dors 4A 14
Little Brickhill. Mil 2H 51
Little Bridgeford. Staf 3C 72
Little Brington. Nptn 4D 62
Little Bromley. Essx 3D 54
Little Broughton. Cumb 1B 102
Little Budworth. Ches W 4H 83
Little Burstead. Essx 1A 40
Little Burton. E Yor 5F 101
Littlebury. Essx 2F 53
Littlebury Green. Essx 2E 53
Little Bytham. Linc 4H 75
Little Canfield. Essx 3F 53
Little Canford. Dors 3F 15
Little Carlton. Linc 2C 88
Little Carlton. Notts 5E 87
Little Casterton. Rut 5H 75
Little Catwick. E Yor 5F 101
Little Catworth. Cambs 3A 64
Little Cawthorpe. Linc 2C 88
Little Chalfont. Buck 1A 38
Little Chart. Kent 1D 28
Little Chesterford. Essx 1F 53
Little Cheverell. Wilts 1E 23
Little Chishill. Cambs 2E 53
Little Clacton. Essx 4E 55
Little Clanfield. Oxon 5A 50
Little Clifton. Cumb 2B 102
Little Coates. NE Lin 4F 95
Little Comberton. Worc 1E 49
Little Common. E Sus 5B 28
Little Compton. Warw 2A 50
Little Cornard. Suff 2B 54
Littlecote. Buck 3G 51
Littlecott. Wilts 1G 23
Little Cowarne. Here 5A 60
Little Coxwell. Oxon 2A 36
Little Crakehall. N Yor 5F 105
Little Crawley. Mil 1H 51
Little Creich. High 5D 164
Little Cressingham. Norf 5A 78
Little Crosby. Mers 4B 90
Little Crosthwaite. Cumb 2D 102
Little Cubley. Derbs 2F 73
Little Dalby. Leics 4E 75
Little Dawley. Telf 5A 72
Littledean. Glos 4B 48
Little Dens. Abers 4H 161
Little Dewchurch. Here 2A 48
Little Ditton. Cambs 5F 65
Little Down. Hants 1B 24
Little Downham. Cambs 2E 65
Little Drayton. Shrp 2A 72
Little Driffield. E Yor 4E 101
Little Dunham. Norf 4A 78
Little Dunkeld. Per 4H 143
Little Dunmow. Essx 3G 53
Little Easton. Essx 3G 53
Little Eaton. Derbs 1A 74
Little Eccleston. Lanc 5D 96
Little Ellingham. Norf 1C 66
Little Elm. Som 2C 22
Little End. Essx 5F 53
Little Everdon. Nptn 5C 62
Little Eversden. Cambs 5C 64
Little Faringdon. Oxon 5H 49
Little Fencote. N Yor 5F 105
Little Fenton. N Yor 1F 93
Littleferry. High 4F 165
Little Fransham. Norf 4B 78
Little Gaddesden. Herts 4H 51
Little Garway. Here 3H 47
Little Gidding. Cambs 2A 64
Little Glemham. Suff 5F 67
Little Glenshee. Per 5G 143
Little Gransden. Cambs 5B 64
Little Green. Suff 3C 66
Little Green. Wrex 1G 71
Little Grimsby. Linc 1C 88
Little Habton. N Yor 2B 100
Little Hadham. Herts 3E 53
Little Hale. Linc 1A 76
Little Hallingbury. Essx 4E 53
Littleham. Devn 4E 19
(nr. Bideford)
Littleham. Devn 4D 12
(nr. Exmouth)
Little Hampden. Buck 5G 51
Littlehampton. W Sus 5B 26
Little Haresfield. Glos 5D 48
Little Harrowden. Nptn 3F 63
Little Haseley. Oxon 5E 51
Little Hatfield. E Yor 5F 101
Little Hautbois. Norf 3E 79
Little Haven. Pemb 3C 42
Little Hay. Staf 5F 73
Little Hayfield. Derbs 2E 85
Little Haywood. Staf 3E 73
Little Heath. W Mid 2H 61
Little Heck. N Yor 2F 93
Littlehempston. Devn 2E 9
Little Herbert's. Glos 3E 49
Little Hereford. Here 4H 59
Little Horkesley. Essx 2C 54
Little Hormead. Herts 3E 53
Little Horsted. E Sus 4F 27
Little Horton. W Yor 1B 92
Little Horwood. Buck 2F 51
Little Houghton. Nptn 5F 63
Littlehoughton. Nmbd 3G 121
Little Houghton. S Yor 4E 93
Little Hucklow. Derbs 3F 85
Little Hulton. G Man 4F 91
Little Irchester. Nptn 4G 63
Little Kelk. E Yor 3E 101
Little Kimble. Buck 5G 51
Little Kineton. Warw 5H 61
Little Kingshill. Buck 2G 37
Little Langdale. Cumb 4E 102
Little Langford. Wilts 3F 23
Little Laver. Essx 5F 53
Little Lawford. Warw 3B 62
Little Leigh. Ches W 3A 84
Little Leighs. Essx 4H 53
Little Leven. E Yor 5E 101
Little Lever. G Man 4F 91
Little Linford. Mil 1G 51
Little London. Buck 4E 51
Little London. E Sus 4G 27
Little London. Hants 2B 24
(nr. Andover)
Little London. Hants 1E 24
(nr. Basingstoke)
Little London. Linc 3D 76
(nr. Long Sutton)
Little London. Linc 3B 76
(nr. Spalding)
Little London. Norf 2E 79
(nr. North Walsham)
Little London. Norf 1G 65
(nr. Northwold)
Little London. Norf 2D 78
(nr. Saxthorpe)
Little London. Norf 1F 65
(nr. Southery)
Little London. Powy 2C 58
Little Longstone. Derbs 3F 85
Little Malvern. Worc 1C 48
Little Maplestead. Essx 2B 54
Little Marcle. Here 2B 48
Little Marlow. Buck 3G 37
Little Massingham. Norf 3G 77
Little Melton. Norf 5D 78
Littlemill. Abers 4H 151
Littlemill. E Ayr 3D 116
Littlemill. High 4D 158
Little Mill. Mon 5G 47
Little Milton. Oxon 5E 50
Little Missenden. Buck 1A 38
Littlemoor. Derbs 4A 86
Littlemoor. Dors 4B 14
Littlemore. Oxon 5D 50
Little Mountain. Flin 4E 83
Little Musgrave. Cumb 3A 104
Little Ness. Shrp 4G 71
Little Neston. Ches W 3F 83
Little Newcastle. Pemb 2D 43
Little Newsham. Dur 3E 105
Little Oakley. Essx 3F 55
Little Oakley. Nptn 2F 63
Little Onn. Staf 4C 72
Little Ormside. Cumb 3A 104
Little Orton. Cumb 4E 113
Little Orton. Leics 5H 73
Little Ouse. Norf 2F 65
Little Ouseburn. N Yor 3G 99
Littleover. Derb 2H 73
Little Packington. Warw 2G 61
Little Paxton. Cambs 4A 64
Little Petherick. Corn 1D 6
Little Plumpton. Lanc 1B 90
Little Plumstead. Norf 4F 79
Little Ponton. Linc 2G 75
Littleport. Cambs 2E 65
Little Posbrook. Hants 2D 16
Little Potheridge. Devn 1F 11
Little Preston. Nptn 5C 62
Little Raveley. Cambs 3B 64
Little Reynoldston. Swan 4D 31
Little Ribston. N Yor 4F 99
Little Rissington. Glos 4G 49
Little Rogart. High 3E 165
Little Rollright. Oxon 2A 50
Little Ryburgh. Norf 3B 78
Little Ryle. Nmbd 3E 121
Little Ryton. Shrp 5G 71
Little Salkeld. Cumb 1G 103
Little Sampford. Essx 2G 53
Little Sandhurst. Brac 5G 37
Little Saredon. Staf 5D 72
Little Saxham. Suff 4G 65
Little Scatwell. High 3F 157
Little Shelford. Cambs 5D 64
Little Shoddesden. Hants 2A 24
Little Singleton. Lanc 1B 90
Little Smeaton. N Yor 3F 93
Little Snoring. Norf 2B 78
Little Sodbury. S Glo 3C 34
Little Somborne. Hants 3B 24
Little Somerford. Wilts 3E 35
Little Soudley. Shrp 3B 72
Little Stainforth. N Yor 3H 97
Little Stainton. Darl 2A 106
Little Stanney. Ches W 3G 83
Little Staughton. Bed 4A 64
Little Steeping. Linc 4D 88
Littlester. Shet 3G 173
Little Stoke. Staf 2D 72
Littlestone-on-Sea. Kent 3E 29
Little Stonham. Suff 4D 66
Little Stretton. Leics 5D 74
Little Stretton. Shrp 1G 59
Little Strickland. Cumb 3G 103
Little Stukeley. Cambs 3B 64
Little Sugnall. Staf 2C 72
Little Sutton. Ches W 3F 83
Little Sutton. Linc 3D 76
Little Swinburne. Nmbd 2C 114
Little Tew. Oxon 3B 50
Little Tey. Essx 3B 54
Little Thetford. Cambs 3E 65
Little Thirkleby. N Yor 2G 99
Little Thornage. Norf 2C 78
Little Thornton. Lanc 5C 96
Littlethorpe. Leics 1C 62
Littlethorpe. N Yor 3F 99
Little Thorpe. W Yor 2B 92
Little Thurlow. Suff 5F 65
Little Thurrock. Thur 3H 39
Littleton. Ches W 4G 83
Littleton. Hants 3C 24
Littleton. Som 3H 21
Littleton. Surr 1A 26
(nr. Guildford)
Littleton. Surr 4B 38
(nr. Staines)
Littleton Drew. Wilts 3D 34
Littleton Pannell. Wilts 1E 23
Littleton-upon-Severn. S Glo 3A 34
Little Torboll. High 4E 165
Little Torrington. Devn 1E 11
Little Totham. Essx 4B 54
Little Town. Cumb 3D 102
Littletown. Dur 5G 115
Littletown. High 5E 165
Little Town. Lanc 1E 91
Little Twycross. Leics 5H 73
Little Urswick. Cumb 2B 96
Little Wakering. Essx 2D 40
Little Walden. Essx 1F 53
Little Waldingfield. Suff 1C 54
Little Walsingham. Norf 2B 78
Little Waltham. Essx 4H 53
Little Warley. Essx 1H 39
Little Washbourne. Glos 2E 49
Little Weighton. E Yor 1C 94
Little Wenham. Suff 2D 54
Little Wenlock. Telf 5A 72
Little Whelnetham. Suff 5A 66
Little Whittingham Green.
Suff 3E 67
Littlewick Green. Wind 4G 37
Little Wilbraham. Cambs 5E 65
Littlewindsor. Dors 2H 13
Little Wisbeach. Linc 2A 76
Little Witcombe. Glos 4E 49
Little Witley. Worc 4B 60
Little Wittenham. Oxon 2D 36
Little Wolford. Warw 2A 50
Littleworth. Bed 1A 52
Littleworth. Glos 2G 49
Littleworth. Oxon 2B 36
Littleworth. Staf 4E 73
(nr. Cannock)
Littleworth. Staf 3B 72
(nr. Eccleshall)
Littleworth. Staf 3D 72
(nr. Stafford)
Littleworth. W Sus 3C 26
Littleworth. Worc 4D 61
(nr. Redditch)
Littleworth. Worc 1D 49
(nr. Worcester)
Little Wratting. Suff 1G 53
Little Wymington. Nptn 4G 63
Little Wymondley. Herts 3C 52
Little Wyrley. Staf 5E 73
Little Yeldham. Essx 2A 54
Littley Green. Essx 4G 53
Litton. Derbs 3F 85
Litton. N Yor 2B 98
Litton. Som 1A 22
Litton Cheney. Dors 3A 14
Liurbost. W Isl 5F 171
Liverpool. Mers 1F 83 & 200
Liverpool John Lennon Airport.
Mers 2G 83
Liversedge. W Yor 2B 92
Liverton. Devn 5B 12
Liverton. Red C 3E 107
Liverton Mines. Red C 3E 107
Livingston. W Lot 3D 128
Livingston Village. W Lot 3D 128
Lixwm. Flin 3D 82
Lizard. Corn 5E 5
Llaingoch. IOA 2B 80
Llaithddu. Powy 2C 58
Llampha. V Glam 4C 32
Llan. Powy 5A 70
Llanaber. Gwyn 4F 69
Llanaelhaearn. Gwyn 1C 68
Llanaeron. Cdgn 4D 57
Llanafan. Cdgn 3F 57
Llanafan-fawr. Powy 5B 58
Llanafan-fechan. Powy 5B 58
Llanallgo. IOA 2D 81
Llanandras. Powy 4F 59
Llananno. Powy 3C 58
Llanarmon. Gwyn 2D 68
Llanarmon Dyffryn Ceiriog.
Wrex 2D 70
Llanarmon-yn-Ial. Den 5D 82
Llanarth. Cdgn 5D 56
Llanarth. Mon 4G 47
Llanarthne. Carm 3F 45
Llanasa. Flin 2D 82
Llanbabo. IOA 2C 80
Llanbadarn Fawr. Cdgn 2F 57
Llanbadarn Fynydd. Powy 3C 58
Llanbadarn-y-garreg.
Powy 1E 46
Llanbadoc. Mon 5G 47
Llanbadrig. IOA 1C 80
Llanbeder. Newp 2G 33
Llanbedr. Gwyn 3E 69
Llanbedr. Powy 3F 47
(nr. Crickhowell)
Llanbedr. Powy 1E 47
(nr. Hay-on-Wye)
Llanbedr-Dyffryn-Clwyd. Den 5D 82
Llanbedrgoch. IOA 2E 81
Llanbedrog. Gwyn 2C 68
Llanbedr Pont Steffan.
Cdgn 1F 45
Llanbedr-y-cennin. Cnwy 4G 81
Llanberis. Gwyn 4E 81
Llanbethery. V Glam 5D 32
Llanbister. Powy 3D 58
Llanblethian. V Glam 4C 32
Llanboidy. Carm 2G 43
Llanbradach. Cphy 2E 33
Llanbrynmair. Powy 5A 70
Llanbydderi. V Glam 5D 32
Llancadle. V Glam 5D 32
Llancarfan. V Glam 4D 32
Llancatal. V Glam 5D 32
Llancayo. Mon 5G 47
Llancloudy. Here 3H 47
Llancoch. Powy 3E 58
Llancynfelyn. Cdgn 1F 57
Llandaff. Card 4E 33
Llandanwg. Gwyn 3E 69
Llandarcy. Neat 3G 31
Llandawke. Carm 3G 43
Llanddaniel-Fab. IOA 3D 81
Llanddarog. Carm 4F 45
Llanddeiniol. Cdgn 3E 57
Llanddeiniolen. Gwyn 4E 81
Llandderfel. Gwyn 2B 70
Llanddeusant. Carm 3A 46
Llanddeusant. IOA 2C 80
Llanddew. Powy 2D 46
Llanddewi. Swan 4D 30
Llanddewi Brefi. Cdgn 5F 57
Llanddewi'r Cwm. Powy 1D 46
Llanddewi Rhydderch. Mon 4G 47
Llanddewi Velfrey. Pemb 3F 43
Llanddewi Ystradenni. Powy 4D 58
Llanddoged. Cnwy 4H 81
Llanddona. IOA 3E 81
Llanddowror. Carm 3G 43
Llanddulas. Cnwy 3B 82
Llanddwywe. Gwyn 3E 69
Llanddyfnan. IOA 3E 81
Llandecwyn. Gwyn 2F 69
Llandefaelog Fach. Powy 2D 46
Llandefaelog-tre'r-graig.
Powy 2E 47
Llandefalle. Powy 2E 46
Llandegfan. IOA 3E 81
Llandegla. Den 5D 82
Llandegley. Powy 4D 58
Llandegveth. Mon 2G 33
Llandeilo. Carm 3G 45
Llandeilo Graban. Powy 1D 46
Llandeilo'r Fan. Powy 2B 46
Llandeloy. Pemb 2C 42
Llandenny. Mon 5H 47
Llandevaud. Newp 2H 33
Llandevenny. Mon 3G 33
Llandilo. Pemb 2F 43
Llandinabo. Here 3A 48
Llandinam. Powy 2C 58
Llandissilio. Pemb 2F 43
Llandogo. Mon 5A 48
Llandough. V Glam 4C 32
(nr. Cowbridge)
Llandough. V Glam 4E 33
(nr. Penarth)
Llandovery. Carm 2A 46
Llandow. V Glam 4C 32
Llandre. Cdgn 2F 57
Llandrillo. Den 2C 70
Llandrillo-yn-Rhos. Cnwy 2H 81
Llandrindod. Powy 4C 58
Llandrindod Wells. Powy 4C 58
Llandrinio. Powy 4E 71
Llandsadwrn. Carm 2G 45
Llandudno. Cnwy 2G 81
Llandudno Junction. Cnwy 3G 81
Llandudoch. Pemb 1B 44
Llandw. V Glam 4C 32
Llandwrog. Gwyn 5D 80
Llandybie. Carm 4G 45
Llandyfaelog. Carm 4E 45
Llandyfan. Carm 4G 45
Llandyfriog. Cdgn 1D 44
Llandyfrydog. IOA 2D 80
Llandygai. Gwyn 3E 81
Llandygwydd. Cdgn 1C 44
Llandynan. Den 1D 70
Llandyrnog. Den 4D 82
Llandysilio. Powy 4E 71
Llandyssil. Powy 1D 58
Llandysul. Cdgn 1E 45
Llanedeyrn. Card 3F 33
Llaneglwys. Powy 2D 46
Llanegryn. Gwyn 5F 69
Llanegwad. Carm 3F 45
Llaneilian. IOA 1D 80
Llanelian-yn-Rhos. Cnwy 3A 82
Llanelidan. Den 5D 82
Llanelieu. Powy 2E 47
Llanellen. Mon 4G 47
Llanelli. Carm 3E 31
Llanelltyd. Gwyn 4G 69
Llanelly. Mon 4F 47
Llanelly Hill. Mon 4F 47
Llanelwedd. Powy 5C 58
Llanelwy. Den 3C 82
Llanenddwyn. Gwyn 3E 69
Llanengan. Gwyn 3B 68
Llanerch. Powy 1F 59
Llanerchymedd. IOA 2D 80
Llanerfyl. Powy 5C 70
Llaneuddog. IOA 2D 80
Llanfachraeth. IOA 2C 80
Llanfaelog. IOA 3C 80
Llanfaelrhys. Gwyn 3B 68
Llanfaenor. Mon 4H 47
Llanfaes. IOA 3F 81
Llanfaes. Powy 3D 46
Llanfaethlu. IOA 2C 80
Llanfaglan. Gwyn 4E 80
Llanfair. Gwyn 3E 69
Llanfair. Here 1F 47
Llanfair Caereinion. Powy 5D 70
Llanfair Clydogau. Cdgn 5F 57
Llanfair Dyffryn Clwyd. Den 5D 82
Llanfairfechan. Cnwy 3F 81
Llanfair-Nant-Gwyn. Pemb 1F 43
Llanfair Pwllgwyngyll. IOA 3E 81
Llanfair Talhaiarn. Cnwy 3B 82
Llanfair Waterdine. Shrp 3E 59
Llanfair-ym-Muallt. Powy 5C 58
Llanfairyneubwll. IOA 3C 80
Llanfairynghornwy. IOA 1C 80
Llanfallteg. Carm 3F 43
Llanfallteg West. Carm 3F 43
Llanfaredd. Powy 5C 58
Llanfarian. Cdgn 3E 57
Llanfechain. Powy 3D 70
Llanfechell. IOA 1C 80
Llanfechreth. Gwyn 3G 69
Llanfendigaid. Gwyn 5E 69
Llanferres. Den 4D 82
Llan Ffestiniog. Gwyn 1G 69
Llanfflewyn. IOA 2C 80
Llanfihangel Glyn Myfyr.
Cnwy 1B 70
Llanfihangel Nant Bran. Powy 2C 46
Llanfihangel-Nant-Melan.
Powy 5D 58
Llanfihangel Rhydithon.
Powy 4D 58
Llanfihangel Rogiet. Mon 3H 33
Llanfihangel Tal-y-llyn. Powy 3E 46
Llanfihangel-uwch-Gwili.
Carm 3E 45
Llanfihangel-yng-Ngwynfa.
Powy 4C 70
Llanfihangel yn Nhowyn. IOA 3C 80
Llanfihangel-y-pennant. Gwyn 1E 69
(nr. Golan)
Llanfihangel-y-pennant. Gwyn 5F 69
(nr. Tywyn)
Llanfilo. Powy 2E 46
Llanfinhangel-ar-Arth. Carm 2E 45
Llanfinhangel-y-Creuddyn.
Cdgn 3F 57
Llanfinhangel-y-traethau.
Gwyn 2E 69
Llanfleiddan. V Glam 4C 32
Llanfoist. Mon 4F 47
Llanfor. Gwyn 2B 70
Llanfrechfa. Torf 2G 33
Llanfrothen. Gwyn 1F 69
Llanfrynach. Powy 3D 46
Llanfwrog. Den 5D 82
Llanfwrog. IOA 2C 80
Llanfyllin. Powy 4D 70
Llanfynydd. Carm 3F 45
Llanfynydd. Flin 5E 83
Llanfyrnach. Pemb 1G 43
Llangadfan. Powy 4C 70
Llangadog. Carm 3H 45
(nr. Llandovery)
Llangadog. Carm 5E 45
(nr. Llanelli)
Llangadwaladr. IOA 4C 80
Llangadwaladr. Powy 2D 70
Llangaffo. IOA 4D 80
Llangain. Carm 4D 45

Llangammarch Wells. Powy 1C 46
Llangan. V Glam 4C 32
Llangarron. Here 3A 48
Llangasty-Talyllyn. Powy 3E 47
Llangathen. Carm 3F 45
Llangattock. Powy 4F 47
Llangattock Lingoed. Mon 3G 47
Llangattock-Vibon-Avel. Mon 4H 47
Llangedwyn. Powy 3D 70
Llangefni. IOA 3D 80
Llangeinor. B'end 3C 32
Llangeitho. Cdgn 5F 57
Llangeler. Carm 2D 44
Llangelynin. Gwyn 5E 69
Llangendeirne. Carm 4E 45
Llangennech. Carm 5F 45
Llangennith. Swan 3D 30
Llangenny. Powy 4F 47
Llangernyw. Cnwy 4A 82
Llangian. Gwyn 3B 68
Llangiwg. Neat 5H 45
Llangloffan. Pemb 1D 42
Llanglydwen. Carm 2F 43
Llangoed. IOA 3F 81
Llangoedmor. Cdgn 1B 44
Llangollen. Den 1E 70
Llangolman. Pemb 2F 43
Llangorse. Powy 3E 47
Llangorwen. Cdgn 2F 57
Llangovan. Mon 5H 47
Llangower. Gwyn 2B 70
Llangranog. Cdgn 5C 56
Llangristiolus. IOA 3D 80
Llangrove. Here 4A 48
Llangua. Mon 3G 47
Llangunllo. Powy 3E 58
Llangunnor. Carm 3E 45
Llangurig. Powy 3B 58
Llangwm. Cnwy 1B 70
Llangwm. Mon 5H 47
Llangwm. Pemb 4D 43
Llangwm-isaf. Mon 5H 47
Llangwnnadl. Gwyn 2B 68
Llangwyfan. Den 4D 82
Llangwyfan-isaf. IOA 4C 80
Llangwyllog. IOA 3D 80
Llangwyryfon. Cdgn 3E 57
Llangybi. Cdgn 5F 57
Llangybi. Gwyn 1D 68
Llangybi. Mon 2G 33
Llangyfelach. Swan 3F 31
Llangynhafal. Den 4D 82
Llangynidr. Powy 4E 47
Llangynin. Carm 3G 43
Llangynog. Carm 3H 43
Llangynog. Powy 3C 70
Llangynwyd. B'end 3B 32
Llanhamlach. Powy 3D 46
Llanharan. Rhon 3D 32
Llanharry. Rhon 3D 32
Llanhennock. Mon 2G 33
Llanhilleth. Blae 5F 47
Llanidloes. Powy 2B 58
Llaniestyn. Gwyn 2B 68
Llanigon. Powy 1F 47
Llanilar. Cdgn 3F 57
Llanilid. Rhon 3C 32
Llanilltud Fawr. V Glam 5C 32
Llanishen. Card 3E 33
Llanishen. Mon 5H 47
Llanllawddog. Carm 3E 45
Llanllechid. Gwyn 4F 81
Llanllowell. Mon 2G 33
Llanllugan. Powy 5C 70
Llanllwch. Carm 4D 45
Llanllwchaiarn. Powy 1D 58
Llanllwni. Carm 2E 45
Llanllyfni. Gwyn 5D 80
Llanmadoc. Swan 3D 30
Llanmaes. V Glam 5C 32
Llanmartin. Newp 3G 33
Llanmerwig. Powy 1D 58
Llanmihangel. V Glam 4C 32
Llan-mill. Pemb 3F 43
Llanmiloe. Carm 4G 43
Llanmorlais. Swan 3E 31
Llannefydd. Cnwy 3B 82
Llannon. Carm 5F 45
Llan-non. Cdgn 4E 57
Llannor. Gwyn 2C 68
Llanpumsaint. Carm 3E 45
Llanrhaeadr. Den 4C 82
Llanrhaeadr-ym-Mochnant. Powy 3D 70
Llanrhidian. Swan 3D 31
Llanrhos. Cnwy 2G 81
Llanrhyddlad. IOA 2C 80
Llanrhystud. Cdgn 4E 57
Llanrian. Pemb 1C 42
Llanrothal. Here 4H 47
Llanrug. Gwyn 4E 81
Llanrumney. Card 3F 33
Llanrwst. Cnwy 4G 81
Llansadurnen. Carm 3G 43
Llansadwrn. IOA 3E 81
Llansaint. Carm 5D 45
Llansamlet. Swan 3F 31
Llansanffraid Glan Conwy. Cnwy 3H 81
Llansannan. Cnwy 4B 82
Llansannor. V Glam 4C 32
Llansantffraed. Cdgn 4E 57
Llansantffraed. Powy 3E 46
Llansantffraed Cwmdeuddwr. Powy 4B 58
Llansantffraed in Elwel. Powy 5C 58
Llansantffraid-ym-Mechain. Powy 3E 70
Llansawel. Carm 2G 45
Llansawel. Neat 3G 31
Llansilin. Powy 3E 70
Llansoy. Mon 5H 47
Llanspyddid. Powy 3D 46
Llanstadwell. Pemb 4D 42
Llansteffan. Carm 3H 43
Llanstephan. Powy 1E 46
Llantarnam. Torf 2F 33
Llanteg. Pemb 3F 43
Llanthony. Mon 3F 47
Llantilio Crossenny. Mon 4G 47
Llantilio Pertholey. Mon 4G 47
Llantood. Pemb 1B 44
Llantrisant. Mon 2G 33
Llantrisant. Rhon 3D 32
Llantrithyd. V Glam 4D 32
Llantwit Fardre. Rhon 3D 32
Llantwit Major. V Glam 5C 32
Llanuwchllyn. Gwyn 2A 70
Llanvaches. Newp 2H 33
Llanvair Discoed. Mon 2H 33
Llanvapley. Mon 4G 47
Llanvetherine. Mon 4G 47
Llanveynoe. Here 2G 47
Llanvihangel Crucorney. Mon 3G 47
Llanvihangel Gobion. Mon 5G 47
Llanvihangel Ystern-Llewern. Mon 4H 47
Llanwarne. Here 3A 48
Llanwddyn. Powy 4C 70
Llanwenarth. Mon 4F 47
Llanwenog. Cdgn 1E 45
Llanwern. Newp 3G 33
Llanwinio. Carm 2G 43
Llanwnda. Gwyn 5D 81
Llanwnda. Pemb 1D 42
Llanwnnen. Cdgn 1F 45
Llanwnog. Powy 1C 58
Llanwrda. Carm 2H 45
Llanwrin. Powy 5G 69
Llanwrthwl. Powy 4B 58
Llanwrtud. Powy 1B 46
Llanwrtyd. Powy 1B 46
Llanwrtyd Wells. Powy 1B 46
Llanwyddelan. Powy 5C 70
Llanyblodwel. Shrp 3E 71
Llanybri. Carm 3H 43
Llanybydder. Carm 1F 45
Llanycefn. Pemb 2E 43
Llanychaer. Pemb 1D 43
Llanycil. Gwyn 2B 70
Llanymawddwy. Gwyn 4B 70
Llanymddyfri. Carm 2A 46
Llanymynech. Shrp 3E 71
Llanynghenedl. IOA 2C 80
Llanynys. Den 4D 82
Llan-y-pwll. Wrex 5F 83
Llanyrafon. Torf 2G 33
Llanyre. Powy 4C 58
Llanystumdwy. Gwyn 2D 68
Llanywern. Powy 3E 46
Llawhaden. Pemb 3E 43
Llawndy. Flin 2D 82
Llawnt. Shrp 2E 71
Llawr Dref. Gwyn 3B 68
Llawryglyn. Powy 1B 58
Llay. Wrex 5F 83
Llechfaen. Powy 3D 46
Llechryd. Cphy 5E 46
Llechryd. Cdgn 1C 44
Llechrydau. Wrex 2E 71
Lledrod. Cdgn 3F 57
Llethrid. Swan 3E 31
Llidiad-Nenog. Carm 2F 45
Llidiardau. Gwyn 2A 70
Llidiart y Parc. Den 1D 70
Llithfaen. Gwyn 1C 68
Lloc. Flin 3D 82
Llong. Flin 4E 83
Llowes. Powy 1E 47
Lloyney. Powy 3E 59
Llundain-fach. Cdgn 5E 57
Llwydcoed. Rhon 5C 46
Llwyncelyn. Cdgn 5D 56
Llwyncelyn. Swan 5G 45
Llwyndaffydd. Cdgn 5C 56
Llwynderw. Powy 5E 70
Llwyn-du. Mon 4F 47
Llwyngwril. Gwyn 5E 69
Llwynhendy. Carm 3E 31
Llwynmawr. Wrex 2E 71
Llwyn-on Village. Mer T 4D 46
Llwyn-teg. Carm 5F 45
Llwyn-y-brain. Carm 3F 43
Llwynygog. Powy 1A 58
Llwyn-y-groes. Cdgn 5E 57
Llwynypia. Rhon 2C 32
Llynclys. Shrp 3E 71
Llynfaes. IOA 3D 80
Llysfaen. Cnwy 3A 82
Llyswen. Powy 2E 47
Llysworney. V Glam 4C 32
Llys-y-fran. Pemb 2E 43
Llywel. Powy 2B 46
Llywernog. Cdgn 2G 57
Loan. Falk 2C 128
Loanend. Nmbd 4F 131
Loanhead. Midl 3F 129
Loaningfoot. Dum 4A 112
Loanreoch. High 1A 158
Loans. S Ayr 1C 116
Loansdean. Nmbd 1F 115
Lobb. Devn 3E 19
Lobhillcross. Devn 4E 11
Lochaber. Mor 3E 159
Loch a Charnain. W Isl 4D 170
Loch a Ghainmhich. W Isl 5E 171
Lochailort. High 5F 147
Lochaline. High 4A 140
Lochans. Dum 4F 109
Locharbriggs. Dum 1A 112
Lochardil. High 4A 158
Lochassynt Lodge. High 1F 163
Lochavich. Arg 2G 133
Lochawe. Arg 1A 134
Loch Baghasdail. W Isl 7C 170
Lochboisdale. W Isl 7C 170
Lochbuie. Arg 1D 132
Lochcarron. High 5A 156
Loch Choire Lodge. High 5G 167
Lochdar. W Isl 4C 170
Lochdochart House. Stir 1D 134
Lochdon. Arg 5B 140
Lochearnhead. Stir 1E 135
Lochee. D'dee 5C 144
Lochend. High 5H 157
(nr. Inverness)
Lochend. High 2E 169
(nr. Thurso)
Locherben. Dum 5B 118
Loch Euphort. W Isl 2D 170
Lochfoot. Dum 2F 111
Lochgair. Arg 4G 133
Lochgarthside. High 2H 149
Lochgelly. Fife 4D 136
Lochgilphead. Arg 1G 125
Lochgoilhead. Arg 3A 134
Loch Head. Dum 5A 110
Lochhill. Mor 2G 159
Lochindorb Lodge. High 5D 158
Lochinver. High 1E 163
Lochlane. Per 1H 135
Loch Lomond. Arg 3C 134
Loch Loyal Lodge. High 4G 167
Lochluichart. High 2F 157
Lochmaben. Dum 1B 112
Lochmaddy. W Isl 2E 170
Loch nam Madadh. W Isl 2E 170
Lochore. Fife 4D 136
Lochportain. W Isl 1E 170
Lochranza. N Ayr 4H 125
Loch Sgioport. W Isl 5D 170
Lochside. Abers 2G 145
Lochside. High 5A 168
(nr. Achentoul)
Lochside. High 3C 158
(nr. Nairn)
Lochslin. High 5F 165
Lochstack Lodge. High 4C 166
Lochton. Abers 4E 153
Lochty. Fife 3H 137
Lochuisge. High 3B 140
Lochussie. High 3G 157
Lochwinnoch. Ren 4E 127
Lochyside. High 1F 141
Lockengate. Corn 2E 7
Lockerbie. Dum 1C 112
Lockeridge. Wilts 5G 35
Lockerley. Hants 4A 24
Lockhills. Cumb 5G 113
Locking. N Som 1G 21
Lockington. E Yor 5D 101
Lockington. Leics 3B 74
Lockleywood. Shrp 3A 72
Locksgreen. IOW 3C 16
Locks Heath. Hants 2D 16
Lockton. N Yor 5F 107
Loddington. Leics 5E 75
Loddington. Nptn 3F 63
Loddiswell. Devn 4D 8
Loddon. Norf 1F 67
Lode. Cambs 4E 65
Loders. Dors 3H 13
Lodsworth. W Sus 3A 26
Lofthouse. N Yor 2D 98
Lofthouse. W Yor 2D 92
Lofthouse Gate. W Yor 2D 92
Loftus. Red C 3E 107
Logan. E Ayr 2E 117
Loganlea. W Lot 3C 128
Logaston. Here 5F 59
Loggerheads. Staf 2B 72
Loggie. High 4F 163
Logie. Ang 2F 145
Logie. Fife 1G 137
Logie. Mor 3E 159
Logie Coldstone. Abers 3B 152
Logie Pert. Ang 2F 145
Logierait. Per 3G 143
Login. Carm 2F 43
Lolworth. Cambs 4C 64
Lonbain. High 3F 155
Londesborough. E Yor 5C 100
London. G Lon 2E 39 & 202-203
London Apprentice. Corn 3E 6
London Ashford (Lydd) Airport. Kent 3E 29
London City Airport. G Lon 2F 39
London Colney. Herts 5B 52
Londonderry. N Yor 1F 99
London Gatwick Airport. W Sus 1D 27 & 216
London Heathrow Airport. G Lon 3B 38 & 216
London Luton Airport. Lutn 3B 52 & 216
London Southend Airport. Essx 2C 40
London Stansted Airport. Essx 3F 53 & 216
Londonthorpe. Linc 2G 75
Londubh. High 5C 162
Lone. High 4D 166
Lonemore. High 5E 165
(nr. Dornoch)
Lonemore. High 1G 155
(nr. Gairloch)
Long Ashton. N Som 4A 34
Long Bank. Worc 3B 60
Longbar. N Ayr 4E 127
Long Bennington. Linc 1F 75
Longbenton. Tyne 3F 115
Longborough. Glos 3G 49
Long Bredy. Dors 3A 14
Longbridge. Warw 4G 61
Longbridge. W Mid 3E 61
Longbridge Deverill. Wilts 2D 22
Long Buckby. Nptn 4D 62
Long Buckby Wharf. Nptn 4D 62
Longburgh. Cumb 4E 112
Longburton. Dors 1B 14
Long Clawson. Leics 3E 74
Longcliffe. Derbs 5G 85
Long Common. Hants 1D 16
Long Compton. Staf 3C 72
Long Compton. Warw 2A 50
Longcot. Oxon 2A 36
Long Crendon. Buck 5E 51
Long Crichel. Dors 1E 15
Longcroft. Cumb 4D 112
Longcroft. Falk 2A 128
Longcross. Surr 4A 38
Longdale. Cumb 4H 103
Longdales. Cumb 5G 113
Longden. Shrp 5G 71
Longden Common. Shrp 5G 71
Long Ditton. Surr 4C 38
Longdon. Staf 4E 73
Longdon. Worc 2D 48
Longdon Green. Staf 4E 73
Longdon on Tern. Telf 4A 72
Longdown. Devn 3B 12
Longdowns. Corn 5B 6
Long Drax. N Yor 2G 93
Long Duckmanton. Derbs 3B 86
Long Eaton. Derbs 2B 74
Longfield. Kent 4H 39
Longfield. Shet 10E 173
Longfield Hill. Kent 4H 39
Longford. Derbs 2G 73
Longford. Glos 3D 48
Longford. G Lon 3B 38
Longford. Shrp 2A 72
Longford. Telf 4B 72
Longford. W Mid 2H 61
Longforgan. Per 1F 137
Longformacus. Bord 4C 130
Longframlington. Nmbd 4F 121
Long Gardens. Essx 2B 54
Long Green. Ches W 3G 83
Long Green. Worc 2D 48
Longham. Dors 3F 15
Longham. Norf 4B 78
Long Hanborough. Oxon 4C 50
Longhedge. Wilts 2D 22
Longhill. Abers 3H 161
Longhirst. Nmbd 1F 115
Longhope. Glos 4B 48
Longhope. Orkn 8C 172
Longhorsley. Nmbd 5F 121
Longhoughton. Nmbd 3G 121
Long Itchington. Warw 4B 62
Longlands. Cumb 1D 102
Longlane. Derbs 2G 73
Long Lane. Telf 4A 72
Longlane. W Ber 4C 36
Long Lawford. Warw 3B 62
Long Lease. N Yor 4G 107
Longley Green. Worc 5B 60
Long Load. Som 4H 21
Longmanhill. Abers 2E 161
Long Marston. Herts 4G 51
Long Marston. N Yor 4H 99
Long Marston. Warw 1G 49
Long Marton. Cumb 2H 103
Long Meadow. Cambs 4E 65
Long Meadowend. Shrp 2G 59
Long Melford. Suff 1B 54
Longmoor Camp. Hants 3F 25
Longmorn. Mor 3G 159
Longmoss. Ches E 3C 84
Long Newnton. Glos 2E 35
Longnewton. Bord 2H 119
Long Newton. Stoc T 3A 106
Longney. Glos 4C 48
Longniddry. E Lot 2H 129
Longnor. Shrp 5G 71
Longnor. Staf 4E 85
(nr. Leek)
Longnor. Staf 4C 72
(nr. Stafford)
Longparish. Hants 2C 24
Longpark. Cumb 3F 113
Long Preston. N Yor 4H 97
Longridge. Lanc 1E 90
Longridge. Staf 4D 72
Longridge. W Lot 3C 128
Longriggend. N Lan 2B 128
Long Riston. E Yor 5F 101
Longrock. Corn 3C 4
Longsdon. Staf 5D 84
Longshaw. G Man 4D 90
Longshaw. Staf 1E 73
Longside. Abers 4H 161
Longslow. Shrp 2A 72
Longstanton. Cambs 4C 64
Longstock. Hants 3B 24
Longstowe. Cambs 5C 64
Long Stratton. Norf 1D 66
Long Street. Mil 1F 51
Longstreet. Wilts 1G 23
Long Sutton. Hants 2F 25
Long Sutton. Linc 3D 76
Long Sutton. Som 4H 21
Longthorpe. Pet 1A 64
Long Thurlow. Suff 4C 66
Longthwaite. Cumb 2F 103
Longton. Lanc 2C 90
Longton. Stoke 1D 72
Longtown. Cumb 3E 113
Longtown. Here 3G 47
Longville in the Dale. Shrp 1H 59
Long Whatton. Leics 3B 74
Longwick. Buck 5F 51
Long Wittenham. Oxon 2D 36
Longwitton. Nmbd 1D 115
Longworth. Oxon 2B 36
Longyester. E Lot 3B 130
Lonmore. High 4B 154
Looe. Corn 3G 7
Loose. Kent 5B 40
Loosegate. Linc 3C 76
Loosley Row. Buck 5G 51
Lopcombe Corner. Wilts 3A 24
Lopen. Som 1H 13
Loppington. Shrp 3G 71
Lorbottle. Nmbd 4E 121
Lorbottle Hall. Nmbd 4E 121
Lordington. W Sus 2F 17
Loscoe. Derbs 1B 74
Loscombe. Dors 3A 14
Losgaintir. W Isl 8C 171
Lossiemouth. Mor 2G 159
Lossit. Arg 4A 124
Lostock Gralam. Ches W 3A 84
Lostock Green. Ches W 3A 84
Lostock Hall. Lanc 2D 90
Lostock Junction. G Man 4E 91
Lostwithiel. Corn 3F 7
Lothbeg. High 2G 165
Lothersdale. N Yor 5B 98
Lothianbridge. Midl 3G 129
Lothianburn. Edin 3F 129
Lothmore. High 2G 165
Lottisham. Som 3A 22
Loudwater. Buck 1A 38
Loughborough. Leics 4C 74
Loughor. Swan 3E 31
Loughton. Essx 1F 39
Loughton. Mil 2G 51
Loughton. Shrp 2A 60
Lound. Linc 4H 75
Lound. Notts 2D 86
Lound. Suff 1H 67
Lount. Leics 4A 74
Louth. Linc 2C 88
Love Clough. Lanc 2G 91
Lovedean. Hants 1E 17
Lover. Wilts 4H 23
Loversall. S Yor 1C 86
Loves Green. Essx 5G 53
Loveston. Pemb 4E 43
Lovington. Som 3A 22
Low Ackworth. W Yor 3E 93
Low Angerton. Nmbd 1D 115
Low Ardwell. Dum 5F 109
Low Ballochdoan. S Ayr 2F 109
Lowbands. Glos 2C 48
Low Barlings. Linc 3H 87
Low Bell End. N Yor 5E 107
Low Bentham. N Yor 3F 97
Low Borrowbridge. Cumb 4H 103
Low Bradfield. S Yor 1G 85
Low Bradley. N Yor 5C 98
Low Braithwaite. Cumb 5F 113
Low Brunton. Nmbd 2C 114
Low Burnham. N Lin 4A 94
Lowca. Cumb 2A 102
Low Catton. E Yor 4B 100
Low Coniscliffe. Darl 3F 105
Low Coylton. S Ayr 3D 116
Low Crosby. Cumb 4F 113
Low Dalby. N Yor 1C 100
Lowdham. Notts 1D 74
Low Dinsdale. Darl 3A 106
Lowe. Shrp 2G 71
Low Ellington. N Yor 1E 98
Lower Amble. Corn 1D 6

Lower Ansty. *Dors* 2C **14**
Lower Arboll. *High* 5F **165**
Lower Arncott. *Oxon* 4E **50**
Lower Ashton. *Devn* 4B **12**
Lower Assendon. *Oxon* 3F **37**
Lower Auchenreath. *Mor* 2A **160**
Lower Badcall. *High* 4B **166**
Lower Ballam. *Lanc* 1B **90**
Lower Basildon. *W Ber* 4E **36**
Lower Beeding. *W Sus* 3D **26**
Lower Benefield. *Nptn* 2G **63**
Lower Bentley. *Worc* 4D **61**
Lower Beobridge. *Shrp* 1B **60**
Lower Bockhampton. *Dors* 3C **14**
Lower Boddington. *Nptn* 5B **62**
Lower Bordean. *Hants* 4E **25**
Lower Brailes. *Warw* 2B **50**
Lower Breakish. *High* 1E **147**
Lower Broadheath. *Worc* 5C **60**
Lower Brynamman. *Neat* 4H **45**
Lower Bullingham. *Here* 2A **48**
Lower Bullington. *Hants* 2C **24**
Lower Burgate. *Hants* 1G **15**
Lower Cam. *Glos* 5C **48**
Lower Catesby. *Nptn* 5C **62**
Lower Chapel. *Powy* 2D **46**
Lower Cheriton. *Devn* 2E **12**
Lower Chicksgrove. *Wilts* 3E **23**
Lower Chute. *Wilts* 1B **24**
Lower Clopton. *Warw* 5F **61**
Lower Common. *Hants* 2E **25**
Lower Cumberworth. *W Yor* 4C **92**
Lower Darwen. *Bkbn* 2E **91**
Lower Dean. *Bed* 4H **63**
Lower Dean. *Devn* 2D **8**
Lower Diabaig. *High* 2G **155**
Lower Dicker. *E Sus* 4G **27**
Lower Dounreay. *High* 2B **168**
Lower Down. *Shrp* 2F **59**
Lower Dunsforth. *N Yor* 3G **99**
Lower East Carleton. *Norf* 5D **78**
Lower Egleton. *Here* 1B **48**
Lower Ellastone. *Derbs* 1F **73**
Lower End. *Nptn* 4F **63**
Lower Everleigh. *Wilts* 1G **23**
Lower Eype. *Dors* 3H **13**
Lower Failand. *N Som* 4A **34**
Lower Faintree. *Shrp* 2A **60**
Lower Farringdon. *Hants* 3F **25**
Lower Foxdale. *IOM* 4B **108**
Lower Frankton. *Shrp* 2F **71**
Lower Froyle. *Hants* 2F **25**
Lower Gabwell. *Devn* 2F **9**
Lower Gledfield. *High* 4C **164**
Lower Godney. *Som* 2H **21**
Lower Gravenhurst. *C Beds* 2B **52**
Lower Green. *Essx* 2E **53**
Lower Green. *Norf* 2B **78**
Lower Green. *Staf* 5D **72**
Lower Green. *W Ber* 5B **36**
Lower Halstow. *Kent* 4C **40**
Lower Hardres. *Kent* 5F **41**
Lower Hardwick. *Here* 5G **59**
Lower Hartshay. *Derbs* 5A **86**
Lower Hawthwaite. *Cumb* 1B **96**
Lower Hayton. *Shrp* 2H **59**
Lower Hergest. *Here* 5E **59**
Lower Heyford. *Oxon* 3C **50**
Lower Heysham. *Lanc* 3D **96**
Lower Higham. *Kent* 3B **40**
Lower Holbrook. *Suff* 2E **55**
Lower Holditch. *Dors* 2G **13**
Lower Hordley. *Shrp* 3F **71**
Lower Horncroft. *W Sus* 4B **26**
Lower Kilcott. *Glos* 3C **34**
Lower Killeyan. *Arg* 5A **124**
Lower Kingcombe. *Dors* 3A **14**
Lower Kingswood. *Surr* 5D **38**
Lower Kinnerton. *Ches W* 4F **83**
Lower Langford. *N Som* 5H **33**
Lower Largo. *Fife* 3G **137**
Lower Layham. *Suff* 1D **54**
Lower Ledwyche. *Shrp* 3H **59**
Lower Leigh. *Staf* 2E **73**
Lower Lemington. *Glos* 2H **49**
Lower Lenie. *High* 1H **149**
Lower Ley. *Glos* 4C **48**
Lower Llanfadog. *Powy* 4B **58**
Lower Lode. *Glos* 2D **49**
Lower Lovacott. *Devn* 4F **19**
Lower Loxhore. *Devn* 3G **19**
Lower Loxley. *Staf* 2E **73**
Lower Lydbrook. *Glos* 4A **48**
Lower Lye. *Here* 4G **59**
Lower Machen. *Newp* 3F **33**
Lower Maes-coed. *Here* 2G **47**
Lower Meend. *Glos* 5A **48**
Lower Milovaig. *High* 3A **154**
Lower Moor. *Worc* 1E **49**
Lower Morton. *S Glo* 2B **34**
Lower Mountain. *Flin* 5F **83**
Lower Nazeing. *Essx* 5D **53**
Lower Netchwood. *Shrp* 1A **60**
Lower Nyland. *Dors* 4C **22**
Lower Oakfield. *Fife* 4D **136**
Lower Oddington. *Glos* 3H **49**
Lower Ollach. *High* 5E **155**
Lower Penarth. *V Glam* 5E **33**
Lower Penn. *Staf* 1C **60**
Lower Pennington. *Hants* 3B **16**
Lower Peover. *Ches W* 3B **84**
Lower Pilsley. *Derbs* 4B **86**
Lower Pitkerrie. *High* 1C **158**
Lower Place. *G Man* 3H **91**
Lower Quinton. *Warw* 1G **49**
Lower Rainham. *Medw* 4C **40**
Lower Raydon. *Suff* 2D **54**
Lower Seagry. *Wilts* 3E **35**
Lower Shelton. *C Beds* 1H **51**
Lower Shiplake. *Oxon* 4F **37**
Lower Shuckburgh. *Warw* 4B **62**
Lower Sketty. *Swan* 3F **31**
Lower Slade. *Devn* 2F **19**
Lower Slaughter. *Glos* 3G **49**
Lower Soudley. *Glos* 4B **48**
Lower Stanton St Quintin. *Wilts* 3E **35**
Lower Stoke. *Medw* 3C **40**
Lower Stondon. *C Beds* 2B **52**
Lower Stonnall. *Staf* 5E **73**
Lower Stow Bedon. *Norf* 1B **66**
Lower Street. *Norf* 2E **79**
Lower Strensham. *Worc* 1E **49**
Lower Sundon. *C Beds* 3A **52**
Lower Swanwick. *Hants* 2C **16**
Lower Swell. *Glos* 3G **49**
Lower Tale. *Devn* 2D **12**
Lower Tean. *Staf* 2E **73**
Lower Thurlton. *Norf* 1G **67**
Lower Thurnham. *Lanc* 4D **96**
Lower Thurvaston. *Derbs* 2G **73**
Lowertown. *Corn* 4D **4**
Lower Town. *Here* 1B **48**
Lower Town. *IOS* 1B **4**
Lowertown. *Orkn* 8D **172**
Lower Town. *Pemb* 1D **42**
Lower Tysoe. *Warw* 1B **50**
Lower Upham. *Hants* 1D **16**
Lower Upnor. *Medw* 3B **40**
Lower Vexford. *Som* 3E **20**
Lower Walton. *Warr* 2A **84**
Lower Wear. *Devn* 4C **12**
Lower Weare. *Som* 1H **21**
Lower Welson. *Here* 5E **59**
Lower Whatcombe. *Dors* 2D **14**
Lower Whitley. *Ches W* 3A **84**
Lower Wield. *Hants* 2E **25**
Lower Withington. *Ches E* 4C **84**
Lower Woodend. *Buck* 3G **37**
Lower Woodford. *Wilts* 3G **23**
Lower Wraxall. *Dors* 2A **14**
Lower Wych. *Ches W* 1G **71**
Lower Wyche. *Worc* 1C **48**
Lowesby. *Leics* 5E **74**
Lowestoft. *Suff* 1H **67**
Loweswater. *Cumb* 2C **102**
Low Etherley. *Dur* 2E **105**
Lowfield Heath. *W Sus* 1D **26**
Lowford. *Hants* 1C **16**
Low Fulney. *Linc* 3B **76**
Low Gate. *Nmbd* 3C **114**
Lowgill. *Cumb* 5H **103**
Lowgill. *Lanc* 3F **97**
Low Grantley. *N Yor* 2E **99**
Low Green. *N Yor* 4E **98**
Low Habberley. *Worc* 3C **60**
Low Ham. *Som* 4H **21**
Low Hameringham. *Linc* 4C **88**
Low Hawkser. *N Yor* 4G **107**
Low Hesket. *Cumb* 5F **113**
Low Hesleyhurst. *Nmbd* 5E **121**
Lowick. *Cumb* 1B **96**
Lowick. *Nptn* 2G **63**
Lowick. *Nmbd* 1E **121**
Lowick Bridge. *Cumb* 1B **96**
Lowick Green. *Cumb* 1B **96**
Low Knipe. *Cumb* 3G **103**
Low Leighton. *Derbs* 2E **85**
Low Lorton. *Cumb* 2C **102**
Low Marishes. *N Yor* 2C **100**
Low Marnham. *Notts* 4F **87**
Low Mill. *N Yor* 5D **106**
Low Moor. *Lanc* 5G **97**
Low Moor. *W Yor* 2B **92**
Low Moorsley. *Tyne* 5G **115**
Low Newton-by-the-Sea. *Nmbd* 2G **121**
Lownie Moor. *Ang* 4D **145**
Lowood. *Bord* 1H **119**
Low Row. *Cumb* 3G **113** (nr. Brampton)
Low Row. *Cumb* 5C **112** (nr. Wigton)
Low Row. *N Yor* 5C **104**
Lowsonford. *Warw* 4F **61**
Low Street. *Norf* 5C **78**
Lowther. *Cumb* 2G **103**
Lowthorpe. *E Yor* 3E **101**
Lowton. *Devn* 2G **11**
Lowton. *G Man* 1A **84**
Lowton. *Som* 1E **13**
Lowton Common. *G Man* 1A **84**
Low Torry. *Fife* 1D **128**
Low Toynton. *Linc* 3B **88**
Low Valleyfield. *Fife* 1C **128**
Low Westwood. *Dur* 4E **115**
Low Whinnow. *Cumb* 4E **112**
Low Wood. *Cumb* 1C **96**
Low Worsall. *N Yor* 4A **106**
Low Wray. *Cumb* 4E **103**
Loxbeare. *Devn* 1C **12**
Loxhill. *Surr* 2B **26**
Loxhore. *Devn* 3G **19**
Loxley. *S Yor* 2H **85**
Loxley. *Warw* 5G **61**
Loxley Green. *Staf* 2E **73**
Loxton. *N Som* 1G **21**
Loxwood. *W Sus* 2B **26**
Lubcroy. *High* 3A **164**
Lubenham. *Leics* 2E **62**
Lubinvullin. *High* 2F **167**
Luccombe. *Som* 2C **20**
Luccombe Village. *IOW* 4D **16**
Lucker. *Nmbd* 1F **121**
Luckett. *Corn* 5D **11**
Luckington. *Wilts* 3D **34**
Lucklawhill. *Fife* 1G **137**
Luckwell Bridge. *Som* 3C **20**
Lucton. *Here* 4G **59**
Ludag. *W Isl* 7C **170**
Ludborough. *Linc* 1B **88**
Ludchurch. *Pemb* 3F **43**
Luddenden. *W Yor* 2A **92**
Luddenden Foot. *W Yor* 2A **92**
Luddenham. *Kent* 4D **40**
Ludderburn. *Cumb* 5F **103**
Luddesdown. *Kent* 4A **40**
Luddington. *N Lin* 3B **94**
Luddington. *Warw* 5F **61**
Luddington in the Brook. *Nptn* 2A **64**
Ludford. *Linc* 2A **88**
Ludford. *Shrp* 3H **59**
Ludgershall. *Buck* 4E **51**
Ludgershall. *Wilts* 1A **24**
Ludgvan. *Corn* 3C **4**
Ludham. *Norf* 4F **79**
Ludlow. *Shrp* 3H **59**
Ludstone. *Shrp* 1C **60**
Ludwell. *Wilts* 4E **23**
Ludworth. *Dur* 5G **115**
Luffenhall. *Herts* 3C **52**
Luffincott. *Devn* 3D **10**
Lugar. *E Ayr* 2E **117**
Luggate Burn. *E Lot* 2C **130**
Lugg Green. *Here* 4G **59**
Luggiebank. *N Lan* 2A **128**
Lugton. *E Ayr* 4F **127**
Lugwardine. *Here* 1A **48**
Luib. *High* 1D **146**
Luib. *Stir* 1D **135**
Lulham. *Here* 1H **47**
Lullington. *Derbs* 4G **73**
Lullington. *E Sus* 5G **27**
Lullington. *Som* 1C **22**
Lulsgate Bottom. *N Som* 5A **34**
Lulsley. *Worc* 5B **60**
Lulworth Camp. *Dors* 4D **14**
Lumb. *Lanc* 2G **91**
Lumb. *W Yor* 2A **92**
Lumby. *N Yor* 1E **93**
Lumphanan. *Abers* 3C **152**
Lumphinnans. *Fife* 4D **136**
Lumsdaine. *Bord* 3E **131**
Lumsden. *Abers* 1B **152**
Lunan. *Ang* 3F **145**
Lunanhead. *Ang* 3D **145**
Luncarty. *Per* 1C **136**
Lund. *E Yor* 5D **100**
Lund. *N Yor* 1G **93**
Lundie. *Ang* 5B **144**
Lundin Links. *Fife* 3G **137**
Lundy Green. *Norf* 1E **67**
Lunna. *Shet* 5F **173**
Lunning. *Shet* 5G **173**
Lunnon. *Swan* 4E **31**
Lunsford. *Kent* 5B **40**
Lunsford's Cross. *E Sus* 4B **28**
Lunt. *Mers* 4B **90**
Luppitt. *Devn* 2E **13**
Lupridge. *Devn* 3D **8**
Lupset. *W Yor* 3D **92**
Lupton. *Cumb* 1E **97**
Lurgashall. *W Sus* 3A **26**
Lurley. *Devn* 1C **12**
Lusby. *Linc* 4C **88**
Luscombe. *Devn* 3D **9**
Luson. *Devn* 4C **8**
Luss. *Arg* 4C **134**
Lussagiven. *Arg* 1E **125**
Lusta. *High* 3B **154**
Lustleigh. *Devn* 4A **12**
Luston. *Here* 4G **59**
Luthermuir. *Abers* 2F **145**
Luthrie. *Fife* 2F **137**
Lutley. *Staf* 2C **60**
Luton. *Devn* 2D **12** (nr. Honiton)
Luton. *Devn* 5C **12** (nr. Teignmouth)
Luton. *Lutn* 3A **52** & **201**
Luton (London) Airport. *Lutn* 3B **52** & **216**
Lutterworth. *Leics* 2C **62**
Lutton. *Devn* 3B **8** (nr. Ivybridge)
Lutton. *Devn* 2C **8** (nr. South Brent)
Lutton. *Linc* 3D **76**
Lutton. *Nptn* 2A **64**
Lutton Gowts. *Linc* 3D **76**
Lutworthy. *Devn* 1A **12**
Luxborough. *Som* 3C **20**
Luxley. *Glos* 3B **48**
Luxulyan. *Corn* 3E **7**
Lybster. *High* 5E **169**
Lydbury North. *Shrp* 2F **59**
Lydcott. *Devn* 3G **19**
Lydd. *Kent* 3E **29**
Lydden. *Kent* 1G **29** (nr. Dover)
Lydden. *Kent* 4H **41** (nr. Margate)
Lyddington. *Rut* 1F **63**
Lydd (London Ashford) Airport. *Kent* 3E **29**
Lydd-on-Sea. *Kent* 3E **29**
Lydeard St Lawrence. *Som* 3E **21**
Lyde Green. *Hants* 1F **25**
Lydford. *Devn* 4F **11**
Lydford Fair Place. *Som* 3A **22**
Lydgate. *G Man* 4H **91**
Lydgate. *W Yor* 2H **91**
Lydham. *Shrp* 1F **59**
Lydiard Millicent. *Wilts* 3F **35**
Lydiate. *Mers* 4B **90**
Lydiate Ash. *Worc* 3D **61**
Lydlinch. *Dors* 1C **14**
Lydmarsh. *Som* 2G **13**
Lydney. *Glos* 5B **48**
Lydstep. *Pemb* 5E **43**
Lye. *W Mid* 2D **60**
Lye Green. *Buck* 5H **51**
Lye Green. *E Sus* 2G **27**
Lye Head. *Worc* 3B **60**
Lye, The. *Shrp* 1A **60**
Lyford. *Oxon* 2B **36**
Lyham. *Nmbd* 1E **121**
Lylestone. *N Ayr* 5E **127**
Lymbridge Green. *Kent* 1F **29**
Lyme Regis. *Dors* 3G **13**
Lyminge. *Kent* 1F **29**
Lymington. *Hants* 3B **16**
Lyminster. *W Sus* 5B **26**
Lymm. *Warr* 2A **84**
Lymore. *Hants* 3A **16**
Lympne. *Kent* 2F **29**
Lympsham. *Som* 1G **21**
Lympstone. *Devn* 4C **12**
Lynaberack Lodge. *High* 4B **150**
Lynbridge. *Devn* 2H **19**
Lynch. *Som* 2C **20**
Lynchat. *High* 3B **150**
Lynch Green. *Norf* 5D **78**
Lyndhurst. *Hants* 2B **16**
Lyndon. *Rut* 5G **75**
Lyne. *Bord* 5F **129**
Lyne. *Surr* 4B **38**
Lyneal. *Shrp* 2G **71**
Lyne Down. *Here* 2B **48**
Lyneham. *Oxon* 3A **50**
Lyneham. *Wilts* 4F **35**
Lyneholmeford. *Cumb* 2G **113**
Lynemouth. *Nmbd* 5G **121**
Lyne of Gorthleck. *High* 1H **149**
Lyne of Skene. *Abers* 2E **153**
Lynesack. *Dur* 2D **105**
Lyness. *Orkn* 8C **172**
Lyng. *Norf* 4C **78**
Lyngate. *Norf* 2E **79** (nr. North Walsham)
Lyngate. *Norf* 3F **79** (nr. Worstead)
Lynmouth. *Devn* 2H **19**
Lynn. *Staf* 5E **73**
Lynn. *Telf* 4B **72**
Lynsted. *Kent* 4D **40**
Lynstone. *Corn* 2C **10**
Lynton. *Devn* 2H **19**
Lynwilg. *High* 2C **150**
Lyon's Gate. *Dors* 2B **14**
Lyonshall. *Here* 5F **59**
Lytchett Matravers. *Dors* 3E **15**
Lytchett Minster. *Dors* 3E **15**
Lyth. *High* 2E **169**
Lytham. *Lanc* 2B **90**
Lytham St Anne's. *Lanc* 2B **90**
Lythe. *N Yor* 3F **107**
Lythes. *Orkn* 9D **172**
Lythmore. *High* 2C **168**

M

Mabe Burnthouse. *Corn* 5B **6**
Mabie. *Dum* 2A **112**
Mablethorpe. *Linc* 2E **89**
Macbiehill. *Bord* 4E **129**
Macclesfield. *Ches E* 3D **84**
Macclesfield Forest. *Ches E* 3D **85**
Macduff. *Abers* 2E **160**
Machan. *S Lan* 4A **128**
Macharioch. *Arg* 5B **122**
Machen. *Cphy* 3F **33**
Machrie. *N Ayr* 2C **122**
Machrihanish. *Arg* 3A **122**
Machroes. *Gwyn* 3C **68**
Machynlleth. *Powy* 5G **69**
Mackerye End. *Herts* 4B **52**
Mackworth. *Derb* 2H **73**
Macmerry. *E Lot* 2H **129**
Madderty. *Per* 1B **136**
Maddington. *Wilts* 2F **23**
Maddiston. *Falk* 2C **128**
Madehurst. *W Sus* 4A **26**
Madeley. *Staf* 1B **72**
Madeley. *Telf* 5A **72**
Madeley Heath. *Staf* 1B **72**
Madeley Heath. *Worc* 3D **60**
Madford. *Devn* 1E **13**
Madingley. *Cambs* 4C **64**
Madley. *Here* 2H **47**
Madresfield. *Worc* 1D **48**
Madron. *Corn* 3B **4**
Maenaddwyn. *IOA* 2D **80**
Maenclochog. *Pemb* 2E **43**
Maendy. *V Glam* 4D **32**
Maenporth. *Corn* 4E **5**
Maentwrog. *Gwyn* 1F **69**
Maen-y-groes. *Cdgn* 5C **56**
Maer. *Staf* 2B **72**
Maerdy. *Carm* 3G **45**
Maerdy. *Cnwy* 1C **70**
Maerdy. *Rhon* 2C **32**
Maesbrook. *Shrp* 3F **71**
Maesbury. *Shrp* 3F **71**
Maesbury Marsh. *Shrp* 3F **71**
Maes-glas. *Flin* 3D **82**
Maesgwyn-Isaf. *Powy* 4D **70**
Maeshafn. *Den* 4E **82**
Maes Llyn. *Cdgn* 1D **44**
Maesmynis. *Powy* 1D **46**
Maesteg. *B'end* 2B **32**
Maestir. *Cdgn* 1F **45**
Maesybont. *Carm* 4F **45**
Maesycrugiau. *Carm* 1E **45**
Maesycwmmer. *Cphy* 2E **33**
Maesyrhandir. *Powy* 1C **58**
Magdalen Laver. *Essx* 5F **53**
Maggieknockater. *Mor* 4H **159**
Magham Down. *E Sus* 4H **27**
Maghull. *Mers* 4B **90**
Magna Park. *Leics* 2C **62**
Magor. *Mon* 3H **33**
Magpie Green. *Suff* 3C **66**
Magwyr. *Mon* 3H **33**
Maidenbower. *W Sus* 2D **27**
Maiden Bradley. *Wilts* 3D **22**
Maidencombe. *Torb* 2F **9**
Maidenhayne. *Devn* 3F **13**
Maidenhead. *Wind* 3G **37**
Maiden Law. *Dur* 5E **115**
Maiden Newton. *Dors* 3A **14**
Maidens. *S Ayr* 4B **116**
Maiden's Green. *Brac* 4G **37**
Maidensgrove. *Oxon* 3F **37**
Maidenwell. *Corn* 5B **10**
Maidenwell. *Linc* 3C **88**
Maiden Wells. *Pemb* 5D **42**
Maidford. *Nptn* 5D **62**
Maids Moreton. *Buck* 2F **51**
Maidstone. *Kent* 5B **40**
Maidwell. *Nptn* 3E **63**
Mail. *Shet* 9F **173**
Maindee. *Newp* 3G **33**
Mainsforth. *Dur* 1A **106**
Mains of Auchindachy. *Mor* 4B **160**
Mains of Auchnagatt. *Abers* 4G **161**
Mains of Drum. *Abers* 4F **153**
Mains of Edingight. *Mor* 3C **160**
Mainsriddle. *Dum* 4G **111**
Mainstone. *Shrp* 2E **59**
Maisemore. *Glos* 3D **48**
Major's Green. *Worc* 3F **61**
Makeney. *Derbs* 1A **74**
Makerstoun. *Bord* 1A **120**
Malacleit. *W Isl* 1C **170**
Malaig. *High* 4E **147**
Malaig Bheag. *High* 4E **147**
Malborough. *Devn* 5D **8**
Malcoff. *Derbs* 2E **85**
Malcolmburn. *Mor* 3A **160**
Malden Rushett. *G Lon* 4C **38**
Maldon. *Essx* 5B **54**
Malham. *N Yor* 3B **98**
Maligar. *High* 2D **155**
Malinslee. *Telf* 5A **72**
Mallaig. *High* 4E **147**
Malleny Mills. *Edin* 3E **129**
Mallows Green. *Essx* 3E **53**
Malltraeth. *IOA* 4D **80**
Mallwyd. *Gwyn* 4A **70**
Malmesbury. *Wilts* 3E **35**
Malmsmead. *Devn* 2A **20**
Malpas. *Ches W* 1G **71**
Malpas. *Corn* 4C **6**
Malpas. *Newp* 2F **33**
Malswick. *Glos* 3C **48**
Maltby. *S Yor* 1C **86**
Maltby. *Stoc T* 3B **106**
Maltby le Marsh. *Linc* 2D **88**
Malt Lane. *Arg* 3H **133**
Maltman's Hill. *Kent* 1D **28**
Malton. *N Yor* 2B **100**
Malvern Link. *Worc* 1C **48**
Malvern Wells. *Worc* 1C **48**
Mamble. *Worc* 3A **60**
Mamhilad. *Mon* 5G **47**
Manaccan. *Corn* 4E **5**
Manafon. *Powy* 5D **70**
Manais. *W Isl* 9D **171**
Manaton. *Devn* 4A **12**
Manby. *Linc* 2C **88**
Mancetter. *Warw* 1H **61**
Manchester. *G Man* 1C **84** & **201**
Manchester International Airport. *G Man* 2C **84** & **216**
Mancot. *Flin* 4F **83**
Manea. *Cambs* 2D **65**
Maney. *W Mid* 1F **61**

Manfield. *N Yor* ... 3F 105
Mangotsfield. *S Glo* ... 4B 34
Mangurstadh. *W Isl* ... 4C 171
Mankinholes. *W Yor* ... 2H 91
Manley. *Ches W* ... 3H 83
Manmoel. *Cphy* ... 5E 47
Mannal. *Arg* ... 4A 138
Mannerston. *Falk* ... 2D 128
Manningford Bohune. *Wilts* ... 1G 23
Manningford Bruce. *Wilts* ... 1G 23
Manningham. *W Yor* ... 1B 92
Mannings Heath. *W Sus* ... 3D 26
Mannington. *Dors* ... 2F 15
Manningtree. *Essx* ... 2E 54
Mannofield. *Aber* ... 3G 153
Manorbier. *Pemb* ... 5E 43
Manorbier Newton. *Pemb* ... 5E 43
Manorowen. *Pemb* ... 1D 42
Manor Park. *G Lon* ... 2F 39
Mansell Gamage. *Here* ... 1G 47
Mansell Lacy. *Here* ... 1H 47
Mansergh. *Cumb* ... 1F 97
Mansewood. *Glas* ... 3G 127
Mansfield. *E Ayr* ... 3F 117
Mansfield. *Notts* ... 4C 86
Mansfield Woodhouse. *Notts* ... 4C 86
Mansriggs. *Cumb* ... 1B 96
Manston. *Dors* ... 1D 14
Manston. *Kent* ... 4H 41
Manston. *W Yor* ... 1D 92
Manswood. *Dors* ... 2E 15
Manthorpe. *Linc* ... 4H 75
(nr. Bourne)
Manthorpe. *Linc* ... 2G 75
(nr. Grantham)
Manton. *N Lin* ... 4C 94
Manton. *Notts* ... 3C 86
Manton. *Rut* ... 5F 75
Manton. *Wilts* ... 5G 35
Manuden. *Essx* ... 3E 53
Maperton. *Som* ... 4B 22
Maplebeck. *Notts* ... 4E 86
Maple Cross. *Herts* ... 1B 38
Mapledurham. *Oxon* ... 4E 37
Mapledurwell. *Hants* ... 1E 25
Maplehurst. *W Sus* ... 3C 26
Maplescombe. *Kent* ... 4G 39
Mapperley. *Derbs* ... 1B 74
Mapperley. *Notts* ... 1C 74
Mapperley Park. *Notts* ... 1C 74
Mapperton. *Dors* ... 3A 14
(nr. Beaminster)
Mapperton. *Dors* ... 3E 15
(nr. Poole)
Mappleborough Green. *Warw* ... 4E 61
Mappleton. *Derbs* ... 1F 73
Mappleton. *E Yor* ... 5G 101
Mapplewell. *S Yor* ... 4D 92
Mappowder. *Dors* ... 2C 14
Maraig. *W Isl* ... 7E 171
Marazion. *Corn* ... 3C 4
Marbhig. *W Isl* ... 6G 171
Marbury. *Ches E* ... 1H 71
March. *Cambs* ... 1D 64
Marcham. *Oxon* ... 2C 36
Marchamley. *Shrp* ... 3H 71
Marchington. *Staf* ... 2F 73
Marchington Woodlands. *Staf* ... 3F 73
Marchwiel. *Wrex* ... 1F 71
Marchwood. *Hants* ... 1B 16
Marcross. *V Glam* ... 5C 32
Marden. *Here* ... 1A 48
Marden. *Kent* ... 1B 28
Marden. *Wilts* ... 1F 23
Marden Beech. *Kent* ... 1B 28
Marden Thorn. *Kent* ... 1B 28
Mardu. *Shrp* ... 2E 59
Mardy. *Mon* ... 4G 47
Marefield. *Leics* ... 5E 75
Mareham le Fen. *Linc* ... 4B 88
Mareham on the Hill. *Linc* ... 4B 88
Marehay. *Derbs* ... 1A 74
Marehill. *W Sus* ... 4B 26
Maresfield. *E Sus* ... 3F 27
Marfleet. *Hull* ... 2E 95
Marford. *Wrex* ... 5F 83
Margam. *Neat* ... 3A 32
Margaret Marsh. *Dors* ... 1D 14
Margaret Roding. *Essx* ... 4F 53
Margaretting. *Essx* ... 5G 53
Margaretting Tye. *Essx* ... 5G 53
Margate. *Kent* ... 3H 41
Margery. *Surr* ... 5D 38
Margnaheglish. *N Ayr* ... 2E 123
Marham. *Norf* ... 5G 77
Marhamchurch. *Corn* ... 2C 10
Marholm. *Pet* ... 5A 76
Marian Cwm. *Den* ... 3C 82
Mariandyrys. *IOA* ... 2F 81
Marian-glas. *IOA* ... 2E 81
Mariansleigh. *Devn* ... 4H 19
Marian-y-de. *Gwyn* ... 2C 68
Marine Town. *Kent* ... 3D 40
Marion-y-mor. *Gwyn* ... 2C 68
Marishader. *High* ... 2D 155
Marjoriebanks. *Dum* ... 1B 112
Mark. *Dum* ... 4G 109
Mark. *Som* ... 2G 21
Markbeech. *Kent* ... 1F 27
Markby. *Linc* ... 3D 89
Mark Causeway. *Som* ... 2G 21
Mark Cross. *E Sus* ... 2G 27
Markeaton. *Derb* ... 2H 73
Market Bosworth. *Leics* ... 5B 74
Market Deeping. *Linc* ... 4A 76
Market Drayton. *Shrp* ... 2A 72
Market End. *Warw* ... 2H 61
Market Harborough.
Leics ... 2E 63
Markethill. *Per* ... 5B 144
Market Lavington. *Wilts* ... 1F 23
Market Overton. *Rut* ... 4F 75
Market Rasen. *Linc* ... 2A 88
Market Stainton. *Linc* ... 2B 88
Market Weighton. *E Yor* ... 5C 100
Market Weston. *Suff* ... 3B 66
Markfield. *Leics* ... 4B 74
Markham. *Cphy* ... 5E 47
Markinch. *Fife* ... 3E 137
Markington. *N Yor* ... 3E 99
Marksbury. *Bath* ... 5B 34
Mark's Corner. *IOW* ... 3C 16
Marks Tey. *Essx* ... 3C 54
Markwell. *Corn* ... 3H 7
Markyate. *Herts* ... 4A 52
Marlborough. *Wilts* ... 5G 35
Marlcliff. *Warw* ... 5E 61
Marldon. *Devn* ... 2E 9
Marle Green. *E Sus* ... 4G 27
Marlesford. *Suff* ... 5F 67
Marley Green. *Ches E* ... 1H 71
Marley Hill. *Tyne* ... 4F 115
Marlingford. *Norf* ... 5D 78
Mar Lodge. *Abers* ... 5E 151
Marloes. *Pemb* ... 4B 42
Marlow. *Buck* ... 3G 37
Marlow. *Here* ... 3G 59
Marlow Bottom. *Buck* ... 3G 37
Marlow Common. *Buck* ... 3G 37
Marlpit Hill. *Kent* ... 1F 27
Marlpits. *E Sus* ... 3F 27
Marlpool. *Derbs* ... 1B 74
Marnhull. *Dors* ... 1C 14
Marnoch. *Abers* ... 3C 160
Marnock. *N Lan* ... 3A 128
Marple. *G Man* ... 2D 84
Marr. *S Yor* ... 4F 93
Marrel. *High* ... 2H 165
Marrick. *N Yor* ... 5D 105
Marrister. *Shet* ... 5G 173
Marros. *Carm* ... 4G 43
Marsden. *Tyne* ... 3G 115
Marsden. *W Yor* ... 3A 92
Marsett. *N Yor* ... 1B 98
Marsh. *Buck* ... 5G 51
Marsh. *Devn* ... 1F 13
Marshall Meadows. *Nmbd* ... 4F 131
Marshalsea. *Dors* ... 2G 13
Marshalswick. *Herts* ... 5B 52
Marsham. *Norf* ... 3D 78
Marshaw. *Lanc* ... 4E 97
Marsh Baldon. *Oxon* ... 2D 36
Marsh Benham. *W Ber* ... 5C 36
Marshborough. *Kent* ... 5H 41
Marshbrook. *Shrp* ... 2G 59
Marshbury. *Essx* ... 4G 53
Marshchapel. *Linc* ... 1C 88
Marshfield. *Newp* ... 3F 33
Marshfield. *S Glo* ... 4C 34
Marshgate. *Corn* ... 3B 10
Marsh Gibbon. *Buck* ... 3E 51
Marsh Green. *Devn* ... 3D 12
Marsh Green. *Kent* ... 1F 27
Marsh Green. *Staf* ... 5C 84
Marsh Green. *Telf* ... 4A 72
Marsh Lane. *Derbs* ... 3B 86
Marshside. *Kent* ... 4G 41
Marshside. *Mers* ... 3B 90
Marsh Side. *Norf* ... 1G 77
Marsh Street. *Som* ... 2C 20
Marsh, The. *Powy* ... 1F 59
Marsh, The. *Shrp* ... 3A 72
Marshwood. *Dors* ... 3G 13
Marske. *N Yor* ... 4E 105
Marske-by-the-Sea. *Red C* ... 2D 106
Marston. *Ches W* ... 3A 84
Marston. *Here* ... 5F 59
Marston. *Linc* ... 1F 75
Marston. *Oxon* ... 5D 50
Marston. *Staf* ... 3D 72
(nr. Stafford)
Marston. *Staf* ... 4C 72
(nr. Wheaton Aston)
Marston. *Warw* ... 1G 61
Marston. *Wilts* ... 1E 23
Marston Doles. *Warw* ... 5B 62
Marston Green. *W Mid* ... 2F 61
Marston Hill. *Glos* ... 2G 35
Marston Jabbett. *Warw* ... 2A 62
Marston Magna. *Som* ... 4A 22
Marston Meysey. *Wilts* ... 2G 35
Marston Montgomery. *Derbs* ... 2F 73
Marston Moretaine. *C Beds* ... 1H 51
Marston on Dove. *Derbs* ... 3G 73
Marston St Lawrence. *Nptn* ... 1D 50
Marston Stannett. *Here* ... 5H 59
Marston Trussell. *Nptn* ... 2D 62
Marstow. *Here* ... 4A 48
Marsworth. *Buck* ... 4H 51
Marten. *Wilts* ... 5A 36
Marthall. *Ches E* ... 3C 84
Martham. *Norf* ... 4G 79
Marthwaite. *Cumb* ... 5H 103
Martin. *Hants* ... 1F 15
Martin. *Kent* ... 1H 29
Martin. *Linc* ... 4B 88
(nr. Horncastle)
Martin. *Linc* ... 5A 88
(nr. Metheringham)
Martindale. *Cumb* ... 3F 103
Martin Dales. *Linc* ... 4A 88
Martin Drove End. *Hants* ... 4F 23
Martinhoe. *Devn* ... 2G 19
Martinhoe Cross. *Devn* ... 2G 19
Martin Hussingtree. *Worc* ... 4C 60
Martin Mill. *Kent* ... 1H 29
Martinscroft. *Warr* ... 2A 84
Martin's Moss. *Ches E* ... 4C 84
Martinstown. *Dors* ... 4B 14
Martlesham. *Suff* ... 1F 55
Martlesham Heath. *Suff* ... 1F 55
Martletwy. *Pemb* ... 3E 43
Martley. *Worc* ... 5B 60
Martock. *Som* ... 1H 13
Marton. *Ches E* ... 4C 84
Marton. *Cumb* ... 2B 96
Marton. *E Yor* ... 3G 101
(nr. Bridlington)
Marton. *E Yor* ... 1E 95
(nr. Hull)
Marton. *Linc* ... 2F 87
Marton. *Midd* ... 3C 106
Marton. *N Yor* ... 3G 99
(nr. Boroughbridge)
Marton. *N Yor* ... 1B 100
(nr. Pickering)
Marton. *Shrp* ... 3G 71
(nr. Myddle)
Marton. *Shrp* ... 5E 71
(nr. Worthen)
Marton. *Warw* ... 4B 62
Marton Abbey. *N Yor* ... 3H 99
Marton-le-Moor. *N Yor* ... 2F 99
Martyr's Green. *Surr* ... 5B 38
Martyr Worthy. *Hants* ... 3D 24
Marwick. *Orkn* ... 5B 172
Marwood. *Devn* ... 3F 19
Marybank. *High* ... 3G 157
(nr. Dingwall)
Marybank. *High* ... 1B 158
(nr. Invergordon)
Maryburgh. *High* ... 3H 157
Maryfield. *Corn* ... 3A 8
Maryhill. *Glas* ... 3G 127
Marykirk. *Abers* ... 2F 145
Marylebone. *G Lon* ... 2D 39
Marylebone. *G Man* ... 4D 90
Marypark. *Mor* ... 5F 159
Maryport. *Cumb* ... 1B 102
Maryport. *Dum* ... 5E 109
Marystow. *Devn* ... 4E 11
Mary Tavy. *Devn* ... 5F 11
Maryton. *Ang* ... 3C 144
(nr. Kirriemuir)
Maryton. *Ang* ... 3F 145
(nr. Montrose)
Marywell. *Abers* ... 4C 152
Marywell. *Ang* ... 4F 145
Masham. *N Yor* ... 1E 98
Mashbury. *Essx* ... 4G 53
Masongill. *N Yor* ... 2F 97
Masons Lodge. *Abers* ... 3F 153
Mastin Moor. *Derbs* ... 3B 86
Mastrick. *Aber* ... 3G 153
Matching. *Essx* ... 4F 53
Matching Green. *Essx* ... 4F 53
Matching Tye. *Essx* ... 4F 53
Matfen. *Nmbd* ... 2D 114
Matfield. *Kent* ... 1A 28
Mathern. *Mon* ... 2A 34
Mathon. *Here* ... 1C 48
Mathry. *Pemb* ... 1C 42
Matlaske. *Norf* ... 2D 78
Matlock. *Derbs* ... 4G 85
Matlock Bath. *Derbs* ... 5G 85
Matterdale End. *Cumb* ... 2E 103
Mattersey. *Notts* ... 2D 86
Mattersey Thorpe.
Notts ... 2D 86
Mattingley. *Hants* ... 1F 25
Mattishall. *Norf* ... 4C 78
Mattishall Burgh. *Norf* ... 4C 78
Mauchline. *E Ayr* ... 2D 117
Maud. *Abers* ... 4G 161
Maudlin. *Corn* ... 2E 7
Maugersbury. *Glos* ... 3G 49
Maughold. *IOM* ... 2D 108
Maulden. *C Beds* ... 2A 52
Maulds Meaburn. *Cumb* ... 3H 103
Maunby. *N Yor* ... 1F 99
Maund Bryan. *Here* ... 5H 59
Mautby. *Norf* ... 4G 79
Mavesyn Ridware.
Staf ... 4E 73
Mavis Enderby. *Linc* ... 4C 88
Mawbray. *Cumb* ... 5B 112
Mawdesley. *Lanc* ... 3C 90
Mawdlam. *B'end* ... 3B 32
Mawgan. *Corn* ... 4E 5
Mawgan Porth. *Corn* ... 2C 6
Maw Green. *Ches E* ... 5B 84
Mawla. *Corn* ... 4B 6
Mawnan. *Corn* ... 4E 5
Mawnan Smith. *Corn* ... 4E 5
Mawsley Village. *Nptn* ... 3F 63
Mawthorpe. *Linc* ... 3D 88
Maxey. *Pet* ... 5A 76
Maxstoke. *Warw* ... 2G 61
Maxted Street. *Kent* ... 1F 29
Maxton. *Kent* ... 1G 29
Maxton. *Bord* ... 1A 120
Maxwellheugh. *Bord* ... 1B 120
Maxwelltown. *Dum* ... 2A 112
Maxworthy. *Corn* ... 3C 10
Mayals. *Swan* ... 4F 31
Maybole. *S Ayr* ... 4C 116
Maybush. *Sotn* ... 1B 16
Mayes Green. *Surr* ... 2C 26
Mayfield. *E Sus* ... 3G 27
Mayfield. *Midl* ... 3G 129
Mayfield. *Per* ... 1C 136
Mayfield. *Staf* ... 1F 73
Mayford. *Surr* ... 5A 38
Mayhill. *Swan* ... 3F 31
Mayland. *Essx* ... 5C 54
Maylandsea. *Essx* ... 5C 54
Maynard's Green. *E Sus* ... 4G 27
Maypole. *IOS* ... 1B 4
Maypole. *Kent* ... 4G 41
Maypole. *Mon* ... 4H 47
Maypole Green. *Norf* ... 1G 67
Maypole Green. *Suff* ... 5B 66
Mayshill. *S Glo* ... 3B 34
Maywick. *Shet* ... 9E 173
Mead. *Devn* ... 1C 10
Meadgate. *Bath* ... 1B 22
Meadle. *Buck* ... 5G 51
Meadowbank. *Ches W* ... 4A 84
Meadowfield. *Dur* ... 1F 105
Meadow Green. *Here* ... 5B 60
Meadowmill. *E Lot* ... 2H 129
Meadows. *Nott* ... 2C 74
Meadowtown. *Shrp* ... 5F 71
Meadwell. *Devn* ... 4E 11
Meaford. *Staf* ... 2C 72
Mealabost. *W Isl* ... 2G 171
(nr. Borgh)
Mealabost. *W Isl* ... 4G 171
(nr. Stornoway)
Mealasta. *W Isl* ... 5B 171
Meal Bank. *Cumb* ... 5G 103
Mealrigg. *Cumb* ... 5C 112
Mealsgate. *Cumb* ... 5D 112
Meanwood. *W Yor* ... 1C 92
Mearbeck. *N Yor* ... 3H 97
Meare. *Som* ... 2H 21
Meare Green. *Som* ... 4F 21
(nr. Curry Mallet)
Meare Green. *Som* ... 4G 21
(nr. Stoke St Gregory)
Mears Ashby. *Nptn* ... 4F 63
Measham. *Leics* ... 4H 73
Meath Green. *Surr* ... 1D 27
Meathop. *Cumb* ... 1D 96
Meaux. *E Yor* ... 1D 94
Meavy. *Devn* ... 2B 8
Medbourne. *Leics* ... 1E 63
Medburn. *Nmbd* ... 2E 115
Meddon. *Devn* ... 1C 10
Meden Vale. *Notts* ... 4C 86
Medlam. *Linc* ... 5C 88
Medlicott. *Shrp* ... 1G 59
Medmenham. *Buck* ... 3G 37
Medomsley. *Dur* ... 4E 115
Medstead. *Hants* ... 3E 25
Medway Towns.
Medw ... 4B 40 & 204
Meerbrook. *Staf* ... 4D 85
Meer End. *W Mid* ... 3G 61
Meers Bridge. *Linc* ... 2D 89
Meesden. *Herts* ... 2E 53
Meeson. *Telf* ... 3A 72
Meeth. *Devn* ... 2F 11
Meeting Green. *Suff* ... 5G 65
Meeting House Hill. *Norf* ... 3F 79
Meidrim. *Carm* ... 2G 43
Meifod. *Powy* ... 4D 70
Meigle. *Per* ... 4B 144
Meikle Earnock. *S Lan* ... 4A 128
Meikle Kilchattan Butts. *Arg* ... 4B 126
Meikleour. *Per* ... 5A 144
Meikle Tarty. *Abers* ... 1G 153
Meikle Wartle. *Abers* ... 5E 160
Meinciau. *Carm* ... 4E 45
Meir. *Stoke* ... 1D 72
Meir Heath. *Staf* ... 1D 72
Melbourn. *Cambs* ... 1D 53
Melbourne. *Derbs* ... 3A 74
Melbourne. *E Yor* ... 5B 100
Melbury Abbas. *Dors* ... 4D 23
Melbury Bubb. *Dors* ... 2A 14
Melbury Osmond. *Dors* ... 2A 14
Melbury Sampford. *Dors* ... 2A 14
Melby. *Shet* ... 6C 173
Melchbourne. *Bed* ... 4H 63
Melcombe Bingham. *Dors* ... 2C 14
Melcombe Regis. *Dors* ... 4B 14
Meldon. *Devn* ... 3F 11
Meldon. *Nmbd* ... 1E 115
Meldreth. *Cambs* ... 1D 53
Melfort. *Arg* ... 2F 133
Melgarve. *High* ... 4G 149
Meliden. *Den* ... 2C 82
Melinbyrhedyn. *Powy* ... 1H 57
Melincourt. *Neat* ... 5B 46
Melin-y-coed. *Cnwy* ... 4H 81
Melin-y-ddol. *Powy* ... 5C 70
Melin-y-wig. *Den* ... 1C 70
Melkington. *Nmbd* ... 5E 131
Melkinthorpe. *Cumb* ... 2G 103
Melkridge. *Nmbd* ... 3A 114
Melksham. *Wilts* ... 5E 35
Mellangaun. *High* ... 5C 162
Melldalloch. *Arg* ... 2H 125
Mellguards. *Cumb* ... 5F 113
Melling. *Lanc* ... 2E 97
Melling. *Mers* ... 4B 90
Melling Mount. *Mers* ... 4C 90
Mellis. *Suff* ... 3C 66
Mellon Charles. *High* ... 4C 162
Mellon Udrigle. *High* ... 4C 162
Mellor. *G Man* ... 2D 85
Mellor. *Lanc* ... 1E 91
Mellor Brook. *Lanc* ... 1E 91
Mells. *Som* ... 2C 22
Melmerby. *Cumb* ... 1H 103
Melmerby. *N Yor* ... 1C 98
(nr. Middleham)
Melmerby. *N Yor* ... 2F 99
(nr. Ripon)
Melplash. *Dors* ... 3H 13
Melrose. *Bord* ... 1H 119
Melsetter. *Orkn* ... 9B 172
Melsonby. *N Yor* ... 4E 105
Meltham. *W Yor* ... 3A 92
Meltham Mills. *W Yor* ... 3B 92
Melton. *E Yor* ... 2C 94
Melton. *Suff* ... 5E 67
Meltonby. *E Yor* ... 4B 100
Melton Constable. *Norf* ... 2C 78
Melton Mowbray. *Leics* ... 4E 75
Melton Ross. *N Lin* ... 3D 94
Melvaig. *High* ... 5B 162
Melverley. *Shrp* ... 4F 71
Melverley Green. *Shrp* ... 4F 71
Melvich. *High* ... 2A 168
Membury. *Devn* ... 2F 13
Memsie. *Abers* ... 2G 161
Memus. *Ang* ... 3D 144
Menabilly. *Corn* ... 3E 7
Menai Bridge. *IOA* ... 3E 81
Mendham. *Suff* ... 2E 67
Mendlesham. *Suff* ... 4D 66
Mendlesham Green.
Suff ... 4C 66
Menethorpe. *N Yor* ... 3B 100
Menheniot. *Corn* ... 2G 7
Menithwood. *Worc* ... 4B 60
Menna. *Corn* ... 3D 6
Mennock. *Dum* ... 4H 117
Menston. *W Yor* ... 5D 98
Menstrie. *Clac* ... 4H 135
Menthorpe. *N Yor* ... 1H 93
Mentmore. *Buck* ... 4H 51
Meole Brace. *Shrp* ... 4G 71
Meols. *Mers* ... 2E 83
Meon. *Hants* ... 2D 16
Meonstoke. *Hants* ... 4E 24
Meopham. *Kent* ... 4H 39
Meopham Green. *Kent* ... 4H 39
Meopham Station. *Kent* ... 4H 39
Mepal. *Cambs* ... 2D 64
Meppershall. *C Beds* ... 2B 52
Merbach. *Here* ... 1G 47
Mercaston. *Derbs* ... 1G 73
Merchiston. *Edin* ... 2F 129
Mere. *Ches E* ... 2B 84
Mere. *Wilts* ... 3D 22
Mere Brow. *Lanc* ... 3C 90
Mereclough. *Lanc* ... 1G 91
Mere Green. *W Mid* ... 1F 61
Mere Green. *Worc* ... 4D 60
Mere Heath. *Ches W* ... 3A 84
Mereside. *Bkpl* ... 1B 90
Meretown. *Staf* ... 3B 72
Mereworth. *Kent* ... 5A 40
Meriden. *W Mid* ... 2G 61
Merkadale. *High* ... 5C 154
Merkland. *S Ayr* ... 5B 116
Merkland Lodge. *High* ... 1A 164
Merley. *Pool* ... 3F 15
Merlin's Bridge. *Pemb* ... 3D 42
Merridge. *Som* ... 3F 21
Merrington. *Shrp* ... 3G 71
Merrion. *Pemb* ... 5D 42
Merriott. *Som* ... 1H 13
Merrivale. *Devn* ... 5F 11
Merrow. *Surr* ... 5B 38
Merrybent. *Darl* ... 3F 105
Merry Lees. *Leics* ... 5B 74
Merrymeet. *Corn* ... 2G 7
Mersham. *Kent* ... 2E 29
Merstham. *Surr* ... 5D 39
Merston. *W Sus* ... 2G 17
Merstone. *IOW* ... 4D 16
Merther. *Corn* ... 4C 6
Merthyr. *Carm* ... 3D 44
Merthyr Cynog. *Powy* ... 2C 46
Merthyr Dyfan. *V Glam* ... 4E 32
Merthyr Mawr. *B'end* ... 4B 32
Merthyr Tudful. *Mer T* ... 5D 46
Merthyr Tydfil. *Mer T* ... 5D 46
Merthyr Vale. *Mer T* ... 5D 46
Merton. *Devn* ... 1F 11
Merton. *G Lon* ... 4D 38
Merton. *Norf* ... 1B 66
Merton. *Oxon* ... 4D 50
Meshaw. *Devn* ... 1A 12
Messing. *Essx* ... 4B 54
Messingham. *N Lin* ... 4B 94

Metcombe. Devn 3D 12
Metfield. Suff 2E 67
Metherell. Corn 2A 8
Metheringham. Linc 4H 87
Methil. Fife 4F 137
Methilhill. Fife 4F 137
Methley. W Yor 2D 93
Methley Junction. W Yor 2D 93
Methlick. Abers 5F 161
Methven. Per 1C 136
Methwold. Norf 1G 65
Methwold Hythe. Norf 1G 65
Mettingham. Suff 1F 67
Metton. Norf 2D 78
Mevagissey. Corn 4E 6
Mexborough. S Yor 4E 93
Mey. High 1E 169
Meysey Hampton. Glos 2G 35
Miabhag. W Isl 8D 171
Miabhaig. W Isl 7C 171
(nr. Cliasmol)
Miabhaig. W Isl 4C 171
(nr. Timsgearraidh)
Mial. High 1G 155
Michaelchurch. Here 3A 48
Michaelchurch Escley. Here 2G 47
Michaelchurch-on-Arrow. Powy 5E 59
Michaelston-le-Pit. V Glam 4E 33
Michaelston-y-Fedw. Newp 3F 33
Michaelstow. Corn 5A 10
Michelcombe. Devn 2C 8
Micheldever. Hants 3D 24
Micheldever Station. Hants 2D 24
Michelmersh. Hants 4B 24
Mickfield. Suff 4D 66
Micklebring. S Yor 1C 86
Mickleby. N Yor 3F 107
Micklefield. W Yor 1E 93
Micklefield Green. Herts 1B 38
Mickleham. Surr 5C 38
Mickleover. Derb 2H 73
Micklethwaite. Cumb 4D 112
Micklethwaite. W Yor 5D 98
Mickleton. Dur 2C 104
Mickleton. Glos 1G 49
Mickletown. W Yor 2D 93
Mickle Trafford. Ches W 4G 83
Mickley. N Yor 2E 99
Mickley Green. Suff 5H 65
Mickley Square. Nmbd 3D 115
Mid Ardlaw. Abers 2G 161
Midbea. Orkn 3D 172
Mid Beltie. Abers 3D 152
Mid Calder. W Lot 3D 129
Mid Clyth. High 5E 169
Middle Assendon. Oxon 3F 37
Middle Aston. Oxon 3C 50
Middle Barton. Oxon 3C 50
Middlebie. Dum 2D 112
Middle Chinnock. Som 1H 13
Middle Claydon. Buck 3F 51
Middlecliffe. S Yor 4E 93
Middlecott. Devn 4H 11
Middle Drums. Ang 3E 145
Middle Duntisbourne. Glos 5E 49
Middle Essie. Abers 3H 161
Middleforth Green. Lanc 2D 90
Middleham. N Yor 1D 98
Middle Handley. Derbs 3B 86
Middle Harling. Norf 2B 66
Middlehope. Shrp 2G 59
Middle Littleton. Worc 1F 49
Middle Maes-coed. Here 2G 47
Middlemarsh. Dors 2B 14
Middle Marwood. Devn 3F 19
Middle Mayfield. Staf 1F 73
Middlemoor. Devn 5E 11
Middlemuir. Abers 4F 161
(nr. New Deer)
Middlemuir. Abers 3G 161
(nr. Strichen)
Middle Rainton. Tyne 5G 115
Middle Rasen. Linc 2H 87
Middlesbrough. Midd 3B 106 & 201
Middlesceugh. Cumb 5E 113
Middleshaw. Cumb 1E 97
Middlesmoor. N Yor 2C 98
Middles, The. Dur 4F 115
Middlestone. Dur 1F 105
Middlestone Moor. Dur 1F 105
Middle Stoughton. Som 2H 21
Middlestown. W Yor 3C 92
Middle Street. Glos 5C 48
Middle Taphouse. Corn 2F 7
Middleton. Ang 4E 145
Middleton. Arg 4A 138
Middleton. Cumb 1F 97
Middleton. Derbs 4F 85
(nr. Bakewell)
Middleton. Derbs 5G 85
(nr. Wirksworth)
Middleton. Essx 2B 54
Middleton. G Man 4G 91
Middleton. Hants 2C 24
Middleton. Hart 1C 106
Middleton. Here 4H 59
Middleton. IOW 4B 16
Middleton. Lanc 4D 96
Middleton. Midl 4G 129
Middleton. Norf 4F 77
Middleton. Nptn 1F 63
Middleton. Nmbd 1F 121
(nr. Belford)
Middleton. Nmbd 1D 114
(nr. Morpeth)
Middleton. N Yor 5D 98
(nr. Ilkley)
Middleton. N Yor 1B 100
(nr. Pickering)
Middleton. Per 3D 136
Middleton. Shrp 3H 59
(nr. Ludlow)
Middleton. Shrp 3F 71
(nr. Oswestry)
Middleton. Suff 4G 67
Middleton. Swan 4D 30
Middleton. Warw 1F 61
Middleton. W Yor 2D 92
Middleton Cheney. Nptn 1D 50
Middleton Green. Staf 2D 73
Middleton Hall. Nmbd 2D 121
Middleton-in-Teesdale. Dur 2C 104
Middleton One Row. Darl 3A 106
Middleton-on-Leven. N Yor 4B 106
Middleton-on-Sea. W Sus 5A 26
Middleton on the Hill. Here 4H 59
Middleton-on-the-Wolds. E Yor 5D 100
Middleton Priors. Shrp 1A 60
Middleton Quernhow. N Yor 2F 99
Middleton St George. Darl 3A 106
Middleton Scriven. Shrp 2A 60
Middleton Stoney. Oxon 3D 50
Middleton Tyas. N Yor 4F 105
Middletown. Cumb 4A 102
Middle Town. IOS 1B 4
Middletown. Powy 4F 71
Middle Tysoe. Warw 1B 50
Middle Wallop. Hants 3A 24
Middlewich. Ches E 4B 84
Middle Winterslow. Wilts 3H 23
Middlewood. Corn 5C 10
Middlewood. S Yor 1H 85
Middle Woodford. Wilts 3G 23
Middlewood Green. Suff 4C 66
Middleyard. Glos 5D 48
Middlezoy. Som 3G 21
Middridge. Dur 2F 105
Midelney. Som 4H 21
Midfield. High 2F 167
Midford. Bath 5C 34
Mid Garrary. Dum 2C 110
Midge Hall. Lanc 2D 90
Midgeholme. Cumb 4H 113
Midgham. W Ber 5D 36
Midgley. W Yor 2A 92
(nr. Halifax)
Midgley. W Yor 3C 92
(nr. Horbury)
Mid Ho. Shet 2G 173
Midhopestones. S Yor 1G 85
Midhurst. W Sus 4G 25
Mid Kirkton. N Ayr 4C 126
Mid Lambrook. Som 1H 13
Midland. Orkn 7C 172
Mid Lavant. W Sus 2G 17
Midlem. Bord 2H 119
Midney. Som 4A 22
Midsomer Norton. Bath 1B 22
Midton. Inv 2D 126
Midtown. High 5C 162
(nr. Poolewe)
Midtown. High 2F 167
(nr. Tongue)
Midville. Linc 5C 88
Mid Walls. Shet 7C 173
Midway. Derbs 3H 73
Mid Yell. Shet 2G 173
Migdale. High 4D 164
Migvie. Abers 3B 152
Milborne Port. Som 1B 14
Milborne St Andrew. Dors 3D 14
Milborne Wick. Som 4B 22
Milbourne. Nmbd 2E 115
Milbourne. Wilts 3E 35
Milburn. Cumb 2H 103
Milbury Heath. S Glo 2B 34
Milby. N Yor 3G 99
Milcombe. Oxon 2C 50
Milden. Suff 1C 54
Mildenhall. Suff 3G 65
Mildenhall. Wilts 5H 35
Milebrook. Powy 3F 59
Milebush. Kent 1B 28
Mile End. Cambs 2F 65
Mile End. Essx 3C 54
Mileham. Norf 4B 78
Mile Oak. Brig 5D 26
Miles Green. Staf 5C 84
Miles Hope. Here 4H 59
Milesmark. Fife 1D 128
Mile Town. Kent 3D 40
Milfield. Nmbd 1D 120
Milford. Derbs 1A 74
Milford. Devn 4C 18
Milford. Powy 1C 58
Milford. Staf 3D 72
Milford. Surr 1A 26
Milford Haven. Pemb 4D 42
Milford on Sea. Hants 3A 16
Milkwall. Glos 5A 48
Milkwell. Wilts 4E 23
Milland. W Sus 4G 25
Millbank. High 2D 168
Mill Bank. W Yor 2A 92
Millbeck. Cumb 2D 102
Millbounds. Orkn 4E 172
Millbreck. Abers 4H 161
Millbridge. Surr 2G 25
Millbrook. C Beds 2A 52
Millbrook. Corn 3A 8
Millbrook. G Man 1D 85
Millbrook. Sotn 1B 16
Mill Common. Suff 2G 67
Mill Corner. E Sus 3C 28
Milldale. Staf 5F 85
Millden Lodge. Ang 1E 145
Milldens. Ang 3E 145
Millearn. Per 2B 136
Mill End. Buck 3F 37
Mill End. Cambs 5F 65
Millend. Glos 2C 34
(nr. Dursley)
Mill End. Glos 4G 49
(nr. Northleach)
Mill End. Herts 2D 52
Millerhill. Midl 3G 129
Miller's Dale. Derbs 3F 85
Millers Green. Derbs 5G 85
Millerston. N Lan 3H 127
Millfield. Abers 4B 152
Millfield. Pet 1A 64
Millgate. Lanc 3G 91
Mill Green. Essx 5G 53
Mill Green. Norf 2D 66
Mill Green. Shrp 3A 72
Mill Green. Staf 3E 73
Mill Green. Suff 1C 54
Millhalf. Here 1F 47
Millhall. E Ren 4G 127
Millhayes. Devn 2F 13
(nr. Honiton)
Millhayes. Devn 1E 13
(nr. Wellington)
Millhead. Lanc 2D 97
Millheugh. S Lan 4A 128
Mill Hill. Bkbn 2E 91
Mill Hill. G Lon 1D 38
Millholme. Cumb 5G 103
Millhouse. Arg 2A 126
Millhouse. Cumb 1E 103
Millhousebridge. Dum 1C 112
Millhouses. S Yor 2H 85
Millikenpark. Ren 3F 127
Millington. E Yor 4C 100
Millington Green. Derbs 1G 73
Mill Knowe. Arg 3B 122
Mill Lane. Hants 1F 25
Millmeece. Staf 2C 72
Mill of Craigievar. Abers 2C 152
Mill of Fintray. Abers 2F 153
Mill of Haldane. W Dun 1F 127
Millom. Cumb 1A 96
Millow. C Beds 1C 52
Millpool. Corn 5B 10
Millport. N Ayr 4C 126
Mill Side. Cumb 1D 96
Mill Street. Norf 4C 78
(nr. Lyng)
Mill Street. Norf 4C 78
(nr. Swanton Morley)
Millthorpe. Derbs 3H 85
Millthorpe. Linc 2A 76
Millthrop. Cumb 5H 103
Milltimber. Aber 3F 153
Milltown. Abers 3G 151
(nr. Corgarff)
Milltown. Abers 2B 152
(nr. Lumsden)
Milltown. Corn 3F 7
Milltown. Derbs 4A 86
Milltown. Devn 3F 19
Milltown. Dum 2E 113
Milltown. Mor 4C 160
Milltown of Aberdalgie. Per 1C 136
Milltown of Auchindoun. Mor 4A 160
Milltown of Campfield. Abers 3D 152
Milltown of Edinville. Mor 4G 159
Milltown of Towie. Abers 2B 152
Milnacraig. Ang 3B 144
Milnathort. Per 3D 136
Milngavie. E Dun 2G 127
Milnholm. Stir 1A 128
Milnrow. G Man 3H 91
Milnthorpe. Cumb 1D 97
Milnthorpe. W Yor 3D 92
Milson. Shrp 3A 60
Milstead. Kent 5D 40
Milston. Wilts 2G 23
Milthorpe. Nptn 1D 50
Milton. Ang 4C 144
Milton. Cambs 4D 65
Milton. Cumb 2C 50
(nr. Banbury)
Milton. Cumb 3G 113
(nr. Brampton)
Milton. Cumb 1E 97
(nr. Crooklands)
Milton. Derbs 3H 73
Milton. Dum 2F 111
(nr. Crocketford)
Milton. Dum 4H 109
(nr. Glenluce)
Milton. E Ayr 2D 116
Milton. Glas 2G 127
Milton. High 3F 157
(nr. Achnasheen)
Milton. High 4G 155
(nr. Applecross)
Milton. High 5G 157
(nr. Drumnadrochit)
Milton. High 1B 158
(nr. Invergordon)
Milton. High 4H 157
(nr. Inverness)
Milton. High 3F 169
(nr. Wick)
Milton. Mor 2C 160
(nr. Cullen)
Milton. Mor 2F 151
(nr. Tomintoul)
Milton. N Som 5G 33
Milton. Notts 3E 86
Milton. Oxon 2C 36
Milton. Pemb 4E 43
Milton. Port 3E 17
Milton. Som 4H 21
Milton. Stir 3E 135
(nr. Aberfoyle)
Milton. Stir 4D 134
(nr. Drymen)
Milton. Stoke 5D 84
Milton. W Dun 2F 127
Milton Abbas. Dors 2D 14
Milton Abbot. Devn 5E 11
Milton Auchlossan. Abers 3C 152
Milton Bridge. Midl 3F 129
Milton Bryan. C Beds 2H 51
Milton Clevedon. Som 3B 22
Milton Coldwells. Abers 5G 161
Milton Combe. Devn 2A 8
Milton Common. Oxon 5E 51
Milton Damerel. Devn 1D 11
Miltonduff. Mor 2F 159
Milton End. Glos 5G 49
Milton Ernest. Bed 5H 63
Milton Green. Ches W 5G 83
Milton Hill. Devn 5C 12
Milton Hill. Oxon 2C 36
Milton Keynes. Mil 2G 51 & 204
Milton Keynes Village. Mil 2G 51
Milton Lilbourne. Wilts 5G 35
Milton Malsor. Nptn 5E 63
Milton Morenish. Per 5D 142
Milton of Auchinhove. Abers 3C 152
Milton of Balgonie. Fife 3F 137
Milton of Barras. Abers 1H 145
Milton of Campsie. E Dun 2H 127
Milton of Cultoquhey. Per 1A 136
Milton of Cushnie. Abers 2C 152
Milton of Finavon. Ang 3D 145
Milton of Gollanfield. High 3B 158
Milton of Lesmore. Abers 1B 152
Milton of Tullich. Abers 4A 152
Milton on Stour. Dors 4C 22
Milton Regis. Kent 4C 40
Milton Street. E Sus 5G 27
Milton-under-Wychwood. Oxon 4A 50
Milverton. Som 4E 20
Milverton. Warw 4H 61
Milwich. Staf 2D 72
Mimbridge. Surr 4A 38
Minard. Arg 4G 133
Minchington. Dors 1E 15
Minchinhampton. Glos 5D 49
Mindrum. Nmbd 1C 120
Minehead. Som 2C 20
Minera. Wrex 5E 83
Minety. Wilts 2F 35
Minffordd. Gwyn 2E 69
Mingarrypark. High 2A 140
Mingary. High 2G 139
Mingearraidh. W Isl 6C 170
Miningsby. Linc 4C 88
Minions. Corn 5C 10
Minishant. S Ayr 3C 116
Minllyn. Gwyn 4A 70
Minnigaff. Dum 3B 110
Minorca. IOM 3D 108
Minskip. N Yor 3F 99
Minstead. Hants 1A 16
Minsted. W Sus 4G 25
Minster. Kent 4H 41
(nr. Ramsgate)
Minster. Kent 3D 40
(nr. Sheerness)
Minsteracres. Nmbd 4D 114
Minsterley. Shrp 5F 71
Minster Lovell. Oxon 4B 50
Minsterworth. Glos 4C 48
Minterne Magna. Dors 2B 14
Minterne Parva. Dors 2B 14
Minting. Linc 3A 88
Mintlaw. Abers 4H 161
Minto. Bord 2H 119
Minton. Shrp 1G 59
Minwear. Pemb 3E 43
Minworth. W Mid 1F 61
Miodar. Arg 4B 138
Mirbister. Orkn 5C 172
Mirehouse. Cumb 3A 102
Mireland. High 2F 169
Mirfield. W Yor 3C 92
Miserden. Glos 5E 49
Miskin. Rhon 3D 32
Misson. Notts 1D 86
Misterton. Leics 2C 62
Misterton. Notts 1E 87
Misterton. Som 2H 13
Mistley. Essx 2E 54
Mistley Heath. Essx 2E 55
Mitcham. G Lon 4D 39
Mitcheldean. Glos 4B 48
Mitchell. Corn 3C 6
Mitchel Troy. Mon 4H 47
Mitcheltroy Common. Mon 5H 47
Mitford. Nmbd 1E 115
Mithian. Corn 3B 6
Mitton. Staf 4C 72
Mixbury. Oxon 2E 50
Mixenden. W Yor 2A 92
Mixon. Staf 5E 85
Moaness. Orkn 7B 172
Moarfield. Shet 1G 173
Moat. Cumb 2F 113
Moats Tye. Suff 5C 66
Mobberley. Ches E 3B 84
Mobberley. Staf 1E 73
Moccas. Here 1G 47
Mochdre. Cnwy 3H 81
Mochdre. Powy 2C 58
Mochrum. Dum 5A 110
Mockbeggar. Hants 2G 15
Mockerkin. Cumb 2B 102
Modbury. Devn 3C 8
Moddershall. Staf 2D 72
Modsarie. High 2G 167
Moelfre. Cnwy 3B 82
Moelfre. IOA 2E 81
Moelfre. Powy 3D 70
Moffat. Dum 4C 118
Moggerhanger. C Beds 1B 52
Mogworthy. Devn 1B 12
Moira. Leics 4H 73
Molash. Kent 5E 41
Mol-chlach. High 2C 146
Mold. Flin 4E 83
Molehill Green. Essx 3F 53
Molescroft. E Yor 5E 101
Molesden. Nmbd 1E 115
Molesworth. Cambs 3H 63
Moll. High 5E 155
Molland. Devn 4B 20
Mollington. Ches W 3F 83
Mollington. Oxon 1C 50
Mollinsburn. N Lan 2A 128
Monachty. Cdgn 4E 57
Monachyle. Stir 2D 134
Monar Lodge. High 4E 156
Monaughty. Powy 4E 59
Monewden. Suff 5E 67
Moneydie. Per 1C 136
Moneyrow Green. Wind 4G 37
Moniaive. Dum 5G 117
Monifieth. Ang 5E 145
Monikie. Ang 5E 145
Monimail. Fife 2E 137
Monington. Pemb 1B 44
Monk Bretton. S Yor 4D 92
Monken Hadley. G Lon 1D 38
Monk Fryston. N Yor 2F 93
Monk Hesleden. Dur 1B 106
Monkhide. Here 1B 48
Monkhill. Cumb 4E 113
Monkhopton. Shrp 1A 60
Monkland. Here 5G 59
Monkleigh. Devn 4E 19
Monknash. V Glam 4C 32
Monkokehampton. Devn 2F 11
Monkseaton. Tyne 2G 115
Monks Eleigh. Suff 1C 54
Monk's Gate. W Sus 3D 26
Monk's Heath. Ches E 3C 84
Monk Sherborne. Hants 1E 24
Monkshill. Abers 4E 161
Monksilver. Som 3D 20
Monks Kirby. Warw 2B 62
Monk Soham. Suff 4E 66
Monk Soham Green. Suff 4E 66
Monkspath. W Mid 3F 61
Monks Risborough. Buck 5G 51
Monksthorpe. Linc 4D 88
Monk Street. Essx 3G 53
Monkswood. Mon 5G 47
Monkton. Devn 2E 13
Monkton. Kent 4G 41
Monkton. Pemb 4D 42
Monkton. S Ayr 2C 116
Monkton Combe. Bath 5C 34
Monkton Deverill. Wilts 3D 22
Monkton Farleigh. Wilts 5D 34
Monkton Heathfield. Som 4F 21
Monktonhill. S Ayr 2C 116
Monkton Up Wimborne. Dors 1F 15
Monkton Wyld. Dors 3G 13
Monkwearmouth. Tyne 4H 115
Monkwood. Dors 3H 13
Monkwood. Hants 3E 25
Monmarsh. Here 1A 48
Monmouth. Mon 4A 48
Monnington on Wye. Here 1G 47

Monreith. Dum 5A 110
Montacute. Som 1H 13
Montford. Arg 3C 126
Montford. Shrp 4G 71
Montford Bridge. Shrp 4G 71
Montgarrie. Abers 2C 152
Montgarswood. E Ayr 2E 117
Montgomery. Powy 1E 58
Montgreenan. N Ayr 5E 127
Montrave. Fife 3F 137
Montrose. Ang 3G 145
Monxton. Hants 2B 24
Monyash. Derbs 4F 85
Monymusk. Abers 2D 152
Monzie. Per 1A 136
Moodiesburn. N Lan 2H 127
Moon's Green. Kent 3C 28
Moonzie. Fife 2F 137
Moor. Som 1H 13
Moor Allerton. W Yor 1C 92
Moorbath. Dors 3H 13
Moorbrae. Shet 3F 173
Moorby. Linc 4B 88
Moorcot. Here 5F 59
Moor Crichel. Dors 2E 15
Moor Cross. Devn 3C 8
Moordown. Bour 3F 15
Moore. Hal 2H 83
Moorend. Dum 2D 112
Moor End. E Yor 1B 94
Moorend. Glos 5C 48
(nr. Dursley)
Moorend. Glos 4D 48
(nr. Gloucester)
Moorends. S Yor 3G 93
Moorgate. S Yor 1B 86
Moorgreen. Hants 1C 16
Moorgreen. Notts 1B 74
Moor Green. Wilts 5D 34
Moorhaigh. Notts 4C 86
Moorhall. Derbs 3H 85
Moorhampton. Here 1G 47
Moorhouse. Cumb 4E 113
(nr. Carlisle)
Moorhouse. Cumb 4D 112
(nr. Wigton)
Moorhouse. Notts 4E 87
Moorhouse. Surr 5F 39
Moorhouses. Linc 5B 88
Moorland. Som 3G 21
Moorlinch. Som 3H 21
Moor Monkton. N Yor 4H 99
Moor of Granary. Mor 3E 159
Moor Row. Cumb 3B 102
(nr. Whitehaven)
Moor Row. Cumb 5D 112
(nr. Wigton)
Moorsholm. Red C 3D 107
Moorside. Dors 1C 14
Moorside. G Man 4H 91
Moor, The. Kent 3B 28
Moortown. Devn 3D 10
Moortown. Hants 2G 15
Moortown. IOW 4C 16
Moortown. Linc 1H 87
Moortown. Telf 4A 72
Moortown. W Yor 1D 92
Morangie. High 5E 165
Morar. High 4E 147
Morborne. Cambs 1A 64
Morchard Bishop. Devn 2A 12
Morcombelake. Dors 3H 13
Morcott. Rut 5G 75
Morda. Shrp 3E 71
Morden. G Lon 4D 38
Mordiford. Here 2A 48
Mordon. Dur 2A 106
More. Shrp 1F 59
Morebath. Devn 4C 20
Morebattle. Bord 2B 120
Morecambe. Lanc 3D 96
Morefield. High 4F 163
Moreleigh. Devn 3D 8
Morenish. Per 5C 142
Moresby Parks. Cumb 3A 102
Morestead. Hants 4D 24
Moreton. Dors 4D 14
Moreton. Essx 5F 53
Moreton. Here 4H 59
Moreton. Mers 1E 83
Moreton. Oxon 5E 51
Moreton. Staf 4B 72
Moreton Corbet. Shrp 3H 71
Moretonhampstead. Devn 4A 12
Moreton-in-Marsh. Glos 2H 49
Moreton Jeffries. Here 1B 48
Moreton Morrell. Warw 5H 61
Moreton on Lugg. Here 1A 48
Moreton Pinkney. Nptn 1D 50
Moreton Say. Shrp 2A 72
Moreton Valence. Glos 5C 48
Morfa. Cdgn 5C 56
Morfa Bach. Carm 4D 44
Morfa Bychan. Gwyn 2E 69
Morfa Glas. Neat 5B 46
Morfa Nefyn. Gwyn 1B 68
Morganstown. Card 3E 33
Morgan's Vale. Wilts 4G 23
Morham. E Lot 2B 130
Moriah. Cdgn 3F 57
Morland. Cumb 2G 103
Morley. Ches E 2C 84
Morley. Derbs 1A 74
Morley. Dur 2E 105
Morley. W Yor 2C 92
Morley St Botolph. Norf 1C 66
Morningside. Edin 2F 129
Morningside. N Lan 4B 128
Morningthorpe. Norf 1E 66
Morpeth. Nmbd 1F 115
Morrey. Staf 4F 73
Morridge Side. Staf 5E 85
Morridge Top. Staf 4E 85
Morrington. Dum 1F 111
Morris Green. Essx 2H 53
Morriston. Swan 3F 31
Morston. Norf 1C 78
Mortehoe. Devn 2E 19
Morthen. S Yor 2B 86
Mortimer. W Ber 5E 37
Mortimer's Cross. Here 4G 59
Mortimer West End. Hants 5E 37
Mortomley. S Yor 1H 85
Morton. Cumb 1F 103
(nr. Calthwaite)
Morton. Cumb 4E 113
(nr. Carlisle)
Morton. Derbs 4B 86
Morton. Linc 3H 75
(nr. Bourne)
Morton. Linc 1F 87
(nr. Gainsborough)
Morton. Linc 4F 87
(nr. Lincoln)
Morton. Norf 4D 78
Morton. Notts 5E 87
Morton. Shrp 3E 71
Morton. S Glo 2B 34
Morton Bagot. Warw 4F 61
Morton Mill. Shrp 3H 71
Morton-on-Swale. N Yor 5A 106
Morton Tinmouth. Dur 2E 105
Morvah. Corn 3B 4
Morval. Corn 3G 7
Morvich. High 3E 165
(nr. Golspie)
Morvich. High 1B 148
(nr. Shiel Bridge)
Morvil. Pemb 1E 43
Morville. Shrp 1A 60
Morwenstow. Corn 1C 10
Morwick Hall. Nmbd 4G 121
Mosborough. S Yor 2B 86
Moscow. E Ayr 5F 127
Mose. Shrp 1B 60
Mosedale. Cumb 1E 103
Moseley. W Mid 2E 61
(nr. Birmingham)
Moseley. W Mid 5D 72
(nr. Wolverhampton)
Moseley. Worc 5C 60
Moss. Arg 4A 138
Moss. High 2A 140
Moss. S Yor 3F 93
Moss. Wrex 5F 83
Mossatt. Abers 2B 152
Moss Bank. Mers 1H 83
Mossbank. Shet 4F 173
Mossblown. S Ayr 2D 116
Mossbrow. G Man 2B 84
Mossburnford. Bord 3A 120
Mossdale. Dum 2D 110
Mossedge. Cumb 3F 113
Mossend. N Lan 3A 128
Mossgate. Staf 2D 72
Moss Lane. Ches E 3D 84
Mossley. Ches E 4C 84
Mossley. G Man 4H 91
Mossley Hill. Mers 2F 83
Moss of Barmuckity. Mor 2G 159
Mosspark. Glas 3G 127
Mosspaul. Bord 5G 119
Moss Side. Cumb 4C 112
Moss Side. G Man 1C 84
Moss-side. High 3C 158
Moss Side. Lanc 1B 90
(nr. Blackpool)
Moss Side. Lanc 2D 90
(nr. Preston)
Moss Side. Mers 4B 90
Moss-side of Cairness. Abers 2H 161
Mosstodloch. Mor 2H 159
Mosswood. Nmbd 4D 114
Mossy Lea. Lanc 3D 90
Mosterton. Dors 2H 13
Moston. Shrp 3H 71
Moston Green. Ches E 4B 84
Mostyn. Flin 2D 82
Mostyn Quay. Flin 2D 82
Motcombe. Dors 4D 22
Mothecombe. Devn 4C 8
Motherby. Cumb 2F 103
Motherwell. N Lan 4A 128
Mottingham. G Lon 3F 39
Mottisfont. Hants 4B 24
Mottistone. IOW 4C 16
Mottram in Longdendale. G Man 1D 85
Mottram St Andrew. Ches E 3C 84
Mott's Mill. E Sus 2G 27
Mouldsworth. Ches W 3H 83
Moulin. Per 3G 143
Moulsecoomb. Brig 5E 27
Moulsford. Oxon 3D 36
Moulsoe. Mil 1H 51
Moulton. Ches W 4A 84
Moulton. Linc 3C 76
Moulton. Nptn 4E 63
Moulton. N Yor 4F 105
Moulton. Suff 4F 65
Moulton. V Glam 4D 32
Moulton Chapel. Linc 4B 76
Moulton Eugate. Linc 4B 76
Moulton St Mary. Norf 5F 79
Moulton Seas End. Linc 3C 76
Mount. Corn 2F 7
(nr. Bodmin)
Mount. Corn 3B 6
(nr. Newquay)
Mountain Ash. Rhon 2D 32
Mountain Cross. Bord 5E 129
Mountain Street. Kent 5E 41
Mountain Water. Pemb 2D 42
Mount Ambrose. Corn 4B 6
Mountbenger. Bord 2F 119
Mountblow. W Dun 2F 127
Mount Bures. Essx 2C 54
Mountfield. E Sus 3B 28
Mountgerald. High 2H 157
Mount Hawke. Corn 4B 6
Mount High. High 2A 158
Mountjoy. Corn 2C 6
Mount Lothian. Midl 4F 129
Mountnessing. Essx 1H 39
Mounton. Mon 2A 34
Mount Pleasant. Buck 2E 51
Mount Pleasant. Ches E 5C 84
Mount Pleasant. Derbs 1H 73
(nr. Derby)
Mount Pleasant. Derbs 4G 73
(nr. Swadlincote)
Mount Pleasant. E Sus 4F 27
Mount Pleasant. Fife 2E 137
Mount Pleasant. Hants 3A 16
Mount Pleasant. Norf 1B 66
Mount Skippett. Oxon 4B 50
Mountsorrel. Leics 4C 74
Mount Stuart. Arg 4C 126
Mousehole. Corn 4B 4
Mouswald. Dum 2B 112
Mow Cop. Ches E 5C 84
Mowden. Darl 3F 105
Mowhaugh. Bord 2C 120
Mowmacre Hill. Leic 5C 74
Mowsley. Leics 2D 62
Moy. High 5B 158
Moylgrove. Pemb 1B 44
Moy Lodge. High 5G 149
Muasdale. Arg 5E 125
Muchalls. Abers 4G 153
Much Birch. Here 2A 48
Much Cowarne. Here 1B 48
Much Dewchurch. Here 2H 47
Muchelney. Som 4H 21
Muchelney Ham. Som 4H 21
Much Hadham. Herts 4E 53
Much Hoole. Lanc 2C 90
Muchlarnick. Corn 3G 7
Much Marcle. Here 2B 48
Muchrachd. High 5E 157
Much Wenlock. Shrp 1A 60
Mucking. Thur 2A 40
Muckle Breck. Shet 5G 173
Muckleford. Dors 3B 14
Mucklestone. Staf 2B 72
Muckleton. Norf 2H 77
Muckleton. Shrp 3H 71
Muckley. Shrp 1A 60
Muckley Corner. Staf 5E 73
Muckton. Linc 2C 88
Mudale. High 5F 167
Muddiford. Devn 3F 19
Mudeford. Dors 3G 15
Mudford. Som 1A 14
Mudgley. Som 2H 21
Mugdock. Stir 2G 127
Mugeary. High 5D 154
Mugginton. Derbs 1G 73
Muggintonlane End. Derbs 1G 73
Muggleswick. Dur 4D 114
Mugswell. Surr 5D 38
Muie. High 3D 164
Muirden. Abers 3E 160
Muirdrum. Ang 5E 145
Muiredge. Per 1E 137
Muirend. Glas 3G 127
Muirhead. Ang 5C 144
Muirhead. Fife 3E 137
Muirhead. N Lan 3H 127
Muirhouses. Falk 1D 128
Muirkirk. E Ayr 2F 117
Muir of Alford. Abers 2C 152
Muir of Fairburn. High 3G 157
Muir of Fowlis. Abers 2C 152
Muir of Miltonduff. Mor 3F 159
Muir of Ord. High 3H 157
Muir of Tarradale. High 3H 157
Muirshearlich. High 5D 148
Muirtack. Abers 5G 161
Muirton. High 2B 158
Muirton. Per 1D 136
Muirton of Ardblair. Per 4A 144
Muirtown. Per 2B 136
Muiryfold. Abers 3E 161
Muker. N Yor 5C 104
Mulbarton. Norf 5D 78
Mulben. Mor 3A 160
Mulindry. Arg 4B 124
Mulla. Shet 5F 173
Mullach Charlabhaigh. W Isl 3E 171
Mullacott. Devn 2F 19
Mullion. Corn 5D 5
Mullion Cove. Corn 5D 4
Mumbles. Swan 4F 31
Mumby. Linc 3E 89
Munderfield Row. Here 5A 60
Munderfield Stocks. Here 5A 60
Mundesley. Norf 2F 79
Mundford. Norf 1H 65
Mundham. Norf 1F 67
Mundon. Essx 5B 54
Munerigie. High 3E 149
Muness. Shet 1H 173
Mungasdale. High 4D 162
Mungrisdale. Cumb 1E 103
Munlochy. High 3A 158
Munsley. Here 1B 48
Munslow. Shrp 2H 59
Murchington. Devn 4G 11
Murcot. Worc 1F 49
Murcott. Oxon 4D 50
Murdishaw. Hal 2H 83
Murieston. W Lot 3D 128
Murkle. High 2D 168
Murlaggan. High 4C 148
Murra. Orkn 7B 172
Murrayfield. Edin 2F 129
Murray, The. S Lan 4H 127
Murrell Green. Hants 1F 25
Murroes. Ang 5D 144
Murrow. Cambs 5C 76
Mursley. Buck 3G 51
Murthly. Per 5H 143
Murton. Cumb 2A 104
Murton. Dur 5G 115
Murton. Nmbd 5F 131
Murton. Swan 4E 31
Murton. York 4A 100
Musbury. Devn 3F 13
Muscoates. N Yor 1A 100
Muscott. Nptn 4D 62
Musselburgh. E Lot 2G 129
Muston. Leics 2F 75
Muston. N Yor 2E 101
Mustow Green. Worc 3C 60
Muswell Hill. G Lon 2D 39
Mutehill. Dum 5D 111
Mutford. Suff 2G 67
Muthill. Per 2A 136
Mutterton. Devn 2D 12
Muxton. Telf 4B 72
Mwmbwls. Swan 4F 31
Mybster. High 3D 168
Myddfai. Carm 2A 46
Myddle. Shrp 3G 71
Mydroilyn. Cdgn 5D 56
Myerscough. Lanc 1C 90
Mylor Bridge. Corn 5C 6
Mylor Churchtown. Corn 5C 6
Mynachlog-ddu. Pemb 1F 43
Mynydd-bach. Mon 2H 33
Mynydd Isa. Flin 4E 83
Mynyddislwyn. Cphy 2E 33
Mynydd Llandegai. Gwyn 4F 81
Mynydd Mechell. IOA 1C 80
Mynydd-y-briw. Powy 3D 70
Mynyddygarreg. Carm 5E 45
Mynytho. Gwyn 2C 68
Myrebird. Abers 4E 153
Myrelandhorn. High 3E 169
Mytchett. Surr 1G 25
Mythe, The. Glos 2D 49
Mytholmroyd. W Yor 2A 92
Myton-on-Swale. N Yor 3G 99
Mytton. Shrp 4G 71

N

Naast. High 5C 162
Na Buirgh. W Isl 8C 171
Naburn. York 5H 99
Nab Wood. W Yor 1B 92
Nackington. Kent 5F 41
Nacton. Suff 1F 55
Nafferton. E Yor 4E 101
Na Gearrannan. W Isl 3D 171
Nailbridge. Glos 4B 48
Nailsbourne. Som 4F 21
Nailsea. N Som 4H 33
Nailstone. Leics 5B 74
Nailsworth. Glos 2D 34
Nairn. High 3C 158
Nalderswood. Surr 1D 26
Nancegollan. Corn 3D 4
Nancledra. Corn 3B 4
Nangreaves. G Man 3G 91
Nanhyfer. Pemb 1E 43
Nannerch. Flin 4D 82
Nanpantan. Leics 4C 74
Nanpean. Corn 3D 6
Nanstallon. Corn 2E 7
Nant-ddu. Powy 4D 46
Nanternis. Cdgn 5C 56
Nantgaredig. Carm 3E 45
Nantgarw. Rhon 3E 33
Nant Glas. Powy 4B 58
Nantglyn. Den 4C 82
Nantgwyn. Powy 3B 58
Nantlle. Gwyn 5E 81
Nantmawr. Shrp 3E 71
Nantmel. Powy 4C 58
Nantmor. Gwyn 1F 69
Nant Peris. Gwyn 5F 81
Nantwich. Ches E 5A 84
Nant-y-bai. Carm 1A 46
Nant-y-bwch. Blae 4E 47
Nant-y-Derry. Mon 5G 47
Nant-y-dugoed. Powy 4B 70
Nant-y-felin. Cnwy 3F 81
Nantyffyllon. B'end 2B 32
Nantyglo. Blae 4E 47
Nant-y-meichiaid. Powy 4D 70
Nant-y-moel. B'end 2C 32
Nant-y-Pandy. Cnwy 3F 81
Naphill. Buck 2G 37
Nappa. Lanc 4A 98
Napton on the Hill. Warw 4B 62
Narberth. Pemb 3F 43
Narberth Bridge. Pemb 3F 43
Narborough. Leics 1C 62
Narborough. Norf 4G 77
Narkurs. Corn 3H 7
Narth, The. Mon 5A 48
Narthwaite. Cumb 5A 104
Nasareth. Gwyn 1D 68
Naseby. Nptn 3D 62
Nash. Buck 2F 51
Nash. Here 4F 59
Nash. Kent 5G 41
Nash. Newp 3G 33
Nash. Shrp 3A 60
Nash Lee. Buck 5G 51
Nassington. Nptn 1H 63
Nasty. Herts 3D 52
Natcott. Devn 4C 18
Nateby. Cumb 4A 104
Nateby. Lanc 5D 96
Nately Scures. Hants 1F 25
Natland. Cumb 1E 97
Naughton. Suff 1D 54
Naunton. Glos 3G 49
Naunton. Worc 2D 49
Naunton Beauchamp. Worc 5D 60
Navenby. Linc 5G 87
Navestock Heath. Essx 1G 39
Navestock Side. Essx 1G 39
Navidale. High 2H 165
Nawton. N Yor 1A 100
Nayland. Suff 2C 54
Nazeing. Essx 5E 53
Neacroft. Hants 3G 15
Nealhouse. Cumb 4E 113
Neal's Green. W Mid 2H 61
Neap House. N Lin 3B 94
Near Sawrey. Cumb 5E 103
Neasden. G Lon 2D 38
Neasham. Darl 3A 106
Neath. Neat 2A 32
Neath Abbey. Neat 3G 31
Neatishead. Norf 3F 79
Neaton. Norf 5B 78
Nebo. Cdgn 4E 57
Nebo. Cnwy 5H 81
Nebo. Gwyn 5D 81
Nebo. IOA 1D 80
Necton. Norf 5A 78
Nedd. High 5B 166
Nedderton. Nmbd 1F 115
Nedging. Suff 1D 54
Nedging Tye. Suff 1D 54
Needham. Norf 2E 67
Needham Market. Suff 5C 66
Needham Street. Suff 4G 65
Needingworth. Cambs 3C 64
Needwood. Staf 3F 73
Neen Savage. Shrp 3A 60
Neen Sollars. Shrp 3A 60
Neenton. Shrp 2A 60
Nefyn. Gwyn 1C 68
Neilston. E Ren 4F 127
Neithrop. Oxon 1C 50
Nelly Andrews Green. Powy 5E 71
Nelson. Cphy 2E 32
Nelson. Lanc 1G 91
Nelson Village. Nmbd 2F 115
Nemphlar. S Lan 5B 128
Nempnett Thrubwell. Bath 5A 34
Nene Terrace. Linc 5B 76
Nenthall. Cumb 5A 114
Nenthead. Cumb 5A 114
Nenthorn. Bord 1A 120
Nercwys. Flin 4E 83
Neribus. Arg 4A 124
Nerston. S Lan 4H 127
Nesbit. Nmbd 1D 121
Nesfield. N Yor 5C 98
Ness. Ches W 3F 83
Nesscliffe. Shrp 4F 71
Ness of Tenston. Orkn 6B 172
Neston. Ches W 3E 83
Neston. Wilts 5D 34
Nethanfoot. S Lan 5B 128
Nether Alderley. Ches E 3C 84

Netheravon. Wilts 2G 23
Nether Blainslie. Bord 5B 130
Netherbrae. Abers 3E 161
Netherbrough. Orkn 6C 172
Nether Broughton. Leics 3E 74
Netherburn. S Lan 5B 128
Nether Burrow. Lanc 2F 97
Netherbury. Dors 3H 13
Netherby. Cumb 2E 113
Nether Careston. Ang 3E 145
Nether Cerne. Dors 3B 14
Nether Compton. Dors 1A 14
Nethercote. Glos 3G 49
Nethercote. Warw 4C 62
Nethercott. Devn 3E 19
Nethercott. Oxon 3C 50
Nether Dallachy. Mor 2A 160
Nether Durdie. Per 1E 136
Nether End. Derbs 3G 85
Netherend. Glos 5A 48
Nether Exe. Devn 2C 12
Netherfield. E Sus 4B 28
Netherfield. Notts 1D 74
Nethergate. Norf 3C 78
Netherhampton. Wilts 4G 23
Nether Handley. Derbs 3B 86
Nether Haugh. S Yor 1B 86
Nether Heage. Derbs 5A 86
Nether Heyford. Nptn 5D 62
Netherhouses. Cumb 1B 96
Nether Howcleugh. Dum 3C 118
Nether Kellet. Lanc 3E 97
Nether Kinmundy. Abers 4H 161
Netherland Green. Staf 2F 73
Nether Langwith. Notts 3C 86
Netherlaw. Dum 5E 111
Netherley. Abers 4F 153
Nethermill. Dum 1B 112
Nethermills. Mor 3C 160
Nether Moor. Derbs 4A 86
Nether Padley. Derbs 3G 85
Netherplace. E Ren 4G 127
Nether Poppleton. York 4H 99
Netherseal. Derbs 4G 73
Nether Silton. N Yor 5B 106
Nether Stowey. Som 3E 21
Nether Street. Essx 4F 53
Netherstreet. Wilts 5E 35
Netherthird. E Ayr 3E 117
Netherthong. W Yor 4B 92
Netherton. Ang 3E 145
Netherton. Cumb 1B 102
Netherton. Devn 5B 12
Netherton. Hants 1B 24
Netherton. Here 3A 48
Netherton. Mers 1F 83
Netherton. N Lan 4A 128
Netherton. Nmbd 4D 121
Netherton. Per 3A 144
Netherton. Shrp 2B 60
Netherton. Stir 2G 127
Netherton. W Mid 2D 60
Netherton. W Yor 3C 92 (nr. Horbury)
Netherton. W Yor 3B 92 (nr. Huddersfield)
Netherton. Worc 1E 49
Nethertown. Cumb 4A 102
Nethertown. High 1F 169
Nethertown. Staf 4F 73
Nether Urquhart. Fife 3D 136
Nether Wallop. Hants 3B 24
Nether Wasdale. Cumb 4C 102
Nether Welton. Cumb 5E 113
Nether Westcote. Glos 3H 49
Nether Whitacre. Warw 1G 61
Netherwhitton. Nmbd 5F 121
Nether Winchendon. Buck 4F 51
Nether Worton. Oxon 2C 50
Nethy Bridge. High 1E 151
Netley. Hants 2C 16
Netley. Shrp 5G 71
Netley Marsh. Hants 1B 16
Nettlebed. Oxon 3F 37
Nettlebridge. Som 2B 22
Nettlecombe. Dors 3A 14
Nettlecombe. IOW 5D 16
Nettleden. Herts 4A 52
Nettleham. Linc 3H 87
Nettlestead. Kent 5A 40
Nettlestead Green. Kent 5A 40
Nettlestone. IOW 3E 16
Nettlesworth. Dur 5F 115
Nettleton. Linc 4E 94
Nettleton. Wilts 4D 34
Netton. Devn 4B 8
Netton. Wilts 3G 23
Neuadd. Carm 3H 45
Neuadd. Powy 5C 70
Neuk, The. Abers 4E 153
Nevendon. Essx 1B 40
Nevern. Pemb 1A 44
New Abbey. Dum 3A 112
New Aberdour. Abers 2F 161
New Addington. G Lon 4E 39
Newall. W Yor 5D 98
New Alresford. Hants 3D 24
New Alyth. Per 4B 144
Newark. Orkn 3G 172
Newark. Pet 5B 76
Newark-on-Trent. Notts 5E 87
New Arley. Warw 2G 61
Newarthill. N Lan 4A 128
New Ash Green. Kent 4H 39
New Balderton. Notts 5F 87
New Barn. Kent 4H 39
New Barnetby. N Lin 3D 94
Newbattle. Midl 3G 129
New Bewick. Nmbd 2E 121
Newbie. Dum 3C 112
Newbiggin. Cumb 2H 103 (nr. Appleby)
Newbiggin. Cumb 3B 96 (nr. Barrow-in-Furness)
Newbiggin. Cumb 5G 113 (nr. Cumrew)
Newbiggin. Cumb 2F 103 (nr. Penrith)
Newbiggin. Cumb 5B 102 (nr. Seascale)
Newbiggin. Dur 5E 115 (nr. Consett)
Newbiggin. Dur 2C 104 (nr. Holwick)
Newbiggin. Nmbd 5C 114
Newbiggin. N Yor 5C 104 (nr. Askrigg)
Newbiggin. N Yor 1F 101 (nr. Filey)
Newbiggin. N Yor 1B 98 (nr. Thoralby)
Newbiggin-by-the-Sea. Nmbd 1G 115
Newbigging. Ang 5D 145 (nr. Monikie)
Newbigging. Ang 4B 144 (nr. Newtyle)
Newbigging. Ang 5D 144 (nr. Tealing)
Newbigging. Edin 2E 129
Newbigging. S Lan 5D 128
Newbiggin-on-Lune. Cumb 4A 104
Newbold. Derbs 3A 86
Newbold. Leics 4B 74
Newbold on Avon. Warw 3B 62
Newbold on Stour. Warw 1H 49
Newbold Pacey. Warw 5G 61
Newbold Verdon. Leics 5B 74
New Bolingbroke. Linc 5C 88
Newborough. IOA 4D 80
Newborough. Pet 5B 76
Newborough. Staf 3F 73
Newbottle. Nptn 2D 50
Newbottle. Tyne 4G 115
New Boultham. Linc 3G 87
Newbourne. Suff 1F 55
New Brancepeth. Dur 5F 115
Newbridge. Cphy 2F 33
Newbridge. Cdgn 5E 57
Newbridge. Corn 3B 4
Newbridge. Dum 2G 111
Newbridge. Edin 2E 129
Newbridge. Hants 1A 16
Newbridge. IOW 4C 16
Newbridge. N Yor 1C 100
Newbridge. Pemb 1D 42
Newbridge. Wrex 1E 71
Newbridge Green. Worc 2D 48
Newbridge-on-Usk. Mon 2G 33
Newbridge on Wye. Powy 5C 58
New Brighton. Flin 4E 83
New Brighton. Hants 2F 17
New Brighton. Mers 1F 83
New Brinsley. Notts 5B 86
Newbrough. Nmbd 3B 114
New Broughton. Wrex 5F 83
New Buckenham. Norf 1C 66
Newbuildings. Devn 2A 12
Newburgh. Abers 1G 153
Newburgh. Fife 2E 137
Newburgh. Lanc 3C 90
Newburn. Tyne 3E 115
Newbury. W Ber 5C 36
Newbury. Wilts 2D 22
Newby. Cumb 2G 103
Newby. N Yor 2G 97 (nr. Ingleton)
Newby. N Yor 1E 101 (nr. Scarborough)
Newby. N Yor 3C 106 (nr. Stokesley)
Newby Bridge. Cumb 1C 96
Newby Cote. N Yor 2G 97
Newby East. Cumb 4F 113
Newby Head. Cumb 2G 103
New Byth. Abers 3F 161
Newby West. Cumb 4E 113
Newby Wiske. N Yor 1F 99
Newcastle. B'end 3B 32
Newcastle. Mon 4H 47
Newcastle. Shrp 2E 59
Newcastle Emlyn. Carm 1D 44
Newcastle International Airport. Tyne 2E 115
Newcastleton. Bord 1F 113
Newcastle-under-Lyme. Staf 1C 72
Newcastle Upon Tyne. Tyne 3F 115 & 205
Newchapel. Pemb 1G 43
Newchapel. Powy 2B 58
Newchapel. Staf 5C 84
Newchapel. Surr 1E 27
New Cheriton. Hants 4D 24
Newchurch. Carm 3D 45
Newchurch. Here 5F 59
Newchurch. IOW 4D 16
Newchurch. Kent 2E 29
Newchurch. Lanc 1G 91 (nr. Nelson)
Newchurch. Lanc 2G 91 (nr. Rawtenstall)
Newchurch. Mon 2H 33
Newchurch. Powy 5E 58
Newchurch. Staf 3F 73
New Costessey. Norf 4D 78
Newcott. Devn 2F 13
New Cowper. Cumb 5C 112
Newcraighall. Edin 2G 129
New Crofton. W Yor 3D 93
New Cross. Cdgn 3F 57
New Cross. Som 1H 13
New Cumnock. E Ayr 3F 117
New Deer. Abers 4F 161
New Denham. Buck 2B 38
Newdigate. Surr 1C 26
New Duston. Nptn 4E 62
New Earswick. York 4A 100
New Edlington. S Yor 1C 86
New Elgin. Mor 2G 159
New Ellerby. E Yor 1E 95
Newell Green. Brac 4G 37
New Eltham. G Lon 3F 39
New End. Warw 4F 61
New End. Worc 5E 61
Newenden. Kent 3C 28
New England. Essx 1H 53
New England. Pet 5A 76
Newent. Glos 3C 48
New Ferry. Mers 2F 83
Newfield. Dur 4F 115 (nr. Chester-le-Street)
Newfield. Dur 1F 105 (nr. Willington)
New Forest. Hants 1H 15
Newfound. Hants 1D 24
New Fryston. W Yor 2E 93
New Galloway. Dum 2D 110
Newgate. Norf 1C 78
Newgate. Pemb 2C 42
Newgate Street. Herts 5D 52
New Greens. Herts 5B 52
New Grimsby. IOS 1A 4
New Hainford. Norf 4E 78
Newhall. Ches E 1A 72
Newhall. Staf 3G 73
Newham. Nmbd 2F 121
New Hartley. Nmbd 2G 115
Newhaven. Derbs 4F 85
Newhaven. E Sus 5F 27 & 215
Newhaven. Edin 2F 129
New Haw. Surr 4B 38
New Hedges. Pemb 4F 43
New Herrington. Tyne 4G 115
Newhey. G Man 3H 91
New Holkham. Norf 2A 78
New Holland. N Lin 2D 94
Newholm. N Yor 3F 107
New Houghton. Derbs 4C 86
New Houghton. Norf 3G 77
Newhouse. N Lan 3A 128
New Houses. N Yor 2H 97
New Hutton. Cumb 5G 103
New Hythe. Kent 5B 40
Newick. E Sus 3F 27
Newingreen. Kent 2F 29
Newington. Edin 2F 129
Newington. Kent 2F 29 (nr. Folkestone)
Newington. Kent 4C 40 (nr. Sittingbourne)
Newington. Notts 1D 86
Newington. Oxon 2E 36
Newington Bagpath. Glos 2D 34
New Inn. Carm 2E 45
New Inn. Mon 5H 47
New Inn. N Yor 2H 97
New Inn. Torf 5G 47
New Invention. Shrp 3E 59
New Kelso. High 4B 156
New Lanark. S Lan 5B 128
Newland. Glos 5A 48
Newland. Hull 1D 94
Newland. N Yor 2G 93
Newland. Som 3B 20
Newland. Worc 1C 48
Newlandrig. Midl 3G 129
Newlands. Cumb 1E 103
Newlands. Essx 2C 40
Newlands. High 4B 158
Newlands. Nmbd 4D 115
Newlands. Staf 3E 73
Newlands of Geise. High 2C 168
Newlands of Tynet. Mor 2A 160
Newlands Park. IOA 2B 80
New Lane. Lanc 3C 90
New Lane End. Warr 1A 84
New Langholm. Dum 1E 113
New Leake. Linc 5D 88
New Leeds. Abers 3G 161
New Lenton. Nott 2C 74
New Longton. Lanc 2D 90
Newlot. Orkn 6E 172
New Luce. Dum 3G 109
Newlyn. Corn 4B 4
Newmachar. Abers 2F 153
Newmains. N Lan 4B 128
New Mains of Ury. Abers 5F 153
New Malden. G Lon 4D 38
Newman's Green. Suff 1B 54
Newmarket. Suff 4F 65
Newmarket. W Isl 4G 171
New Marske. Red C 2D 106
New Marton. Shrp 2F 71
New Micklefield. W Yor 1E 93
New Mill. Abers 4E 160
New Mill. Corn 3B 4
New Mill. Herts 4H 51
Newmill. Mor 3B 160
Newmill. Bord 3G 119
New Mill. W Yor 4B 92
New Mill. Wilts 5G 35
Newmillerdam. W Yor 3D 92
New Mills. Corn 3C 6
New Mills. Derbs 2E 85
Newmills. Fife 1D 128
Newmills. High 2A 158
New Mills. Mon 5A 48
New Mills. Powy 5C 70
Newmiln. Per 5A 144
Newmilns. E Ayr 1E 117
New Milton. Hants 3H 15
New Mistley. Essx 2E 54
New Moat. Pemb 2E 43
Newmore. High 3H 157 (nr. Dingwall)
Newmore. High 1A 158 (nr. Invergordon)
Newnham. Cambs 5D 64
Newnham. Glos 4B 48
Newnham. Hants 1F 25
Newnham. Herts 2C 52
Newnham. Kent 5D 40
Newnham. Nptn 5C 62
Newnham. Warw 4F 61
Newnham Bridge. Worc 4A 60
New Ollerton. Notts 4D 86
New Oscott. W Mid 1F 61
Newpark. Fife 2G 137
New Park. N Yor 4E 99
New Pitsligo. Abers 3F 161
New Polzeath. Corn 1D 6
Newport. Corn 4D 10
Newport. Devn 3F 19
Newport. E Yor 1B 94
Newport. Essx 2F 53
Newport. Glos 2B 34
Newport. High 1H 165
Newport. IOW 4D 16
Newport. Newp 3G 33 & 205
Newport. Norf 4H 79
Newport. Pemb 1E 43
Newport. Som 4G 21
Newport. Telf 4B 72
Newport-on-Tay. Fife 1G 137
Newport Pagnell. Mil 1G 51
Newpound Common. W Sus 3B 26
New Prestwick. S Ayr 2C 116
New Quay. Cdgn 5C 56
Newquay. Corn 2C 6
Newquay Cornwall Airport. Corn 2C 6
New Rackheath. Norf 4E 79
New Radnor. Powy 4E 58
New Rent. Cumb 1F 103
New Ridley. Nmbd 4D 114
New Romney. Kent 3E 29
New Rossington. S Yor 1D 86
New Row. Cdgn 3G 57
New Row. Lanc 1E 91
New Row. N Yor 3D 106
New Sauchie. Clac 4A 136
Newsbank. Ches E 4C 84
Newseat. Abers 5E 160
Newsham. Lanc 1D 90
Newsham. Nmbd 2G 115
Newsham. N Yor 3E 105 (nr. Richmond)
Newsham. N Yor 1F 99 (nr. Thirsk)
New Sharlston. W Yor 3D 93
Newsholme. E Yor 2H 93
Newsholme. Lanc 4H 97
New Shoreston. Nmbd 1F 121
New Springs. G Man 4D 90
Newstead. Notts 5C 86
Newstead. Bord 1H 119
New Stevenston. N Lan 4A 128
New Street. Here 5F 59
Newstreet Lane. Shrp 2A 72
New Swanage. Dors 4F 15
New Swannington. Leics 4B 74
Newthorpe. N Yor 1E 93
Newthorpe. Notts 1B 74
Newton. Arg 4H 133
Newton. B'end 4B 32
Newton. Cambs 1E 53 (nr. Cambridge)
Newton. Cambs 4D 76 (nr. Wisbech)
Newton. Ches W 4G 83 (nr. Chester)
Newton. Ches W 5H 83 (nr. Tattenhall)
Newton. Cumb 2B 96
Newton. Derbs 5B 86
Newton. Dors 1C 14
Newton. Dum 2D 112 (nr. Annan)
Newton. Dum 5D 118 (nr. Moffat)
Newton. G Man 1D 84
Newton. Here 2G 47 (nr. Ewyas Harold)
Newton. Here 5H 59 (nr. Leominster)
Newton. High 2B 158 (nr. Cromarty)
Newton. High 4B 158 (nr. Inverness)
Newton. High 5C 166 (nr. Kylestrome)
Newton. High 4F 169 (nr. Wick)
Newton. Lanc 2E 97 (nr. Carnforth)
Newton. Lanc 4F 97 (nr. Clitheroe)
Newton. Lanc 1C 90 (nr. Kirkham)
Newton. Linc 2H 75
Newton. Mers 2E 83
Newton. Mor 2F 159
Newton. Norf 4H 77
Newton. Nptn 2F 63
Newton. Nmbd 3D 114
Newton. Notts 1D 74
Newton. Bord 2A 120
Newton. Shet 8E 173
Newton. Shrp 1B 60 (nr. Bridgnorth)
Newton. Shrp 2G 71 (nr. Wem)
Newton. Som 3E 20
Newton. S Lan 3H 127 (nr. Glasgow)
Newton. S Lan 1B 118 (nr. Lanark)
Newton. Staf 3E 73
Newton. Suff 1C 54
Newton. Swan 4F 31
Newton. Warw 3C 62
Newton. W Lot 2D 129
Newton. Wilts 4H 23
Newton Abbot. Devn 5B 12
Newtonairds. Dum 1F 111
Newton Arlosh. Cumb 4D 112
Newton Aycliffe. Dur 2F 105
Newton Bewley. Hart 2B 106
Newton Blossomville. Mil 5G 63
Newton Bromswold. Bed 4G 63
Newton Burgoland. Leics 5A 74
Newton by Toft. Linc 2H 87
Newton Ferrers. Devn 4B 8
Newton Flotman. Norf 1E 66
Newtongrange. Midl 3G 129
Newton Green. Mon 2A 34
Newton Hall. Dur 5F 115
Newton Hall. Nmbd 3D 114
Newton Harcourt. Leics 1D 62
Newton Heath. G Man 4G 91
Newtonhill. Abers 4G 153
Newtonhill. High 4H 157
Newton Hill. W Yor 2D 92
Newton Ketton. Darl 2A 106
Newton Kyme. N Yor 5G 99
Newton-le-Willows. Mers 1H 83
Newton-le-Willows. N Yor 1E 98
Newton Longville. Buck 2G 51
Newton Mearns. E Ren 4G 127
Newtonmore. High 4B 150
Newton Morrell. N Yor 4F 105
Newton Mulgrave. N Yor 3E 107
Newton of Ardtoe. High 1A 140
Newton of Balcanquhal. Per 2D 136
Newton of Beltrees. Ren 4E 127
Newton of Falkland. Fife 3E 137
Newton of Mountblairy. Abers 3E 160
Newton of Pitcairns. Per 2C 136
Newton-on-Ouse. N Yor 4H 99
Newton-on-Rawcliffe. N Yor 5F 107
Newton on the Hill. Shrp 3G 71
Newton-on-the-Moor. Nmbd 4F 121
Newton on Trent. Linc 3F 87
Newton Poppleford. Devn 4D 12
Newton Purcell. Oxon 2E 51
Newton Regis. Warw 5G 73
Newton Reigny. Cumb 1F 103
Newton Rigg. Cumb 1F 103
Newton St Cyres. Devn 3B 12
Newton St Faith. Norf 4E 78
Newton St Loe. Bath 5C 34
Newton St Petrock. Devn 1E 11
Newton Solney. Derbs 3G 73
Newton Stacey. Hants 2C 24
Newton Stewart. Dum 3B 110
Newton Toney. Wilts 2H 23
Newton Tony. Wilts 2H 23
Newton Tracey. Devn 4F 19
Newton under Roseberry. Red C 3C 106
Newton Unthank. Leics 5B 74
Newton upon Ayr. S Ayr 2C 116
Newton upon Derwent. E Yor 5B 100
Newton Valence. Hants 3F 25
Newton-with-Scales. Lanc 1B 90

Newtown. *Abers* 2E **160**
Newtown. *Cambs* 4H **63**
Newtown. *Corn* 5C **10**
Newtown. *Cumb* 5B **112**
(nr. Aspatria)
Newtown. *Cumb* 3G **113**
(nr. Brampton)
Newtown. *Cumb* 2G **103**
(nr. Penrith)
Newtown. *Derbs* 2D **85**
Newtown. *Devn* 4A **20**
Newtown. *Dors* 2H **13**
(nr. Beaminster)
New Town. *Dors* 1E **15**
(nr. Sixpenny Handley)
New Town. *E Lot* 2H **129**
Newtown. *Falk* 1C **128**
Newtown. *Glos* 5B **48**
(nr. Lydney)
Newtown. *Glos* 2E **49**
(nr. Tewkesbury)
Newtown. *Hants* 1D **16**
(nr. Bishop's Waltham)
Newtown. *Hants* 3G **25**
(nr. Liphook)
Newtown. *Hants* 1A **16**
(nr. Lyndhurst)
Newtown. *Hants* 5C **36**
(nr. Newbury)
Newtown. *Hants* 4B **24**
(nr. Romsey)
Newtown. *Hants* 2C **16**
(nr. Warsash)
Newtown. *Hants* 1E **16**
(nr. Wickham)
Newtown. *Here* 2A **48**
(nr. Little Dewchurch)
Newtown. *Here* 1B **48**
(nr. Stretton Grandison)
Newtown. *High* 3F **149**
Newtown. *IOM* 4C **108**
Newtown. *IOW* 3C **16**
Newtown. *Lanc* 3D **90**
New Town. *Lutn* 3A **52**
Newtown. *Nmbd* 4E **121**
(nr. Rothbury)
Newtown. *Nmbd* 2E **121**
(nr. Wooler)
Newtown. *Pool* 3F **15**
Newtown. *Powy* 1D **58**
Newtown. *Rhon* 2D **32**
Newtown. *Shet* 3F **173**
Newtown. *Shrp* 2G **71**
Newtown. *Som* 1F **13**
Newtown. *Staf* 4D **84**
(nr. Biddulph)
Newtown. *Staf* 5D **73**
(nr. Cannock)
Newtown. *Staf* 4E **85**
(nr. Longnor)
New Town. *W Yor* 2E **93**
Newtown. *Wilts* 4E **23**
Newtown-in-St Martin.
Corn 4E **5**
Newtown Linford. *Leics* 4C **74**
Newtown St Boswells.
Bord 1H **119**
New Tredegar. *Cphy* 5E **47**
Newtyle. *Ang* 4B **144**
New Village. *E Yor* 1D **94**
New Village. *S Yor* 4F **93**
New Walsoken. *Cambs* 5D **76**
New Waltham. *NE Lin* 4F **95**
New Winton. *E Lot* 2H **129**
New World. *Cambs* 1C **64**
New Yatt. *Oxon* 4B **50**
Newyears Green. *G Lon* 2B **38**
New York. *Linc* 5B **88**
New York. *Tyne* 2G **115**
Nextend. *Here* 5F **59**
Neyland. *Pemb* 4D **42**
Nib Heath. *Shrp* 4G **71**
Nicholashayne. *Devn* 1E **12**
Nicholaston. *Swan* 4E **31**
Nidd. *N Yor* 3F **99**
Niddrie. *Edin* 2F **129**
Niddry. *Edin* 2D **129**
Nigg. *Aber* 3G **153**
Nigg. *High* 1C **158**
Nigg Ferry. *High* 2B **158**
Nightcott. *Som* 4B **20**
Nimmer. *Som* 1G **13**
Nine Ashes. *Essx* 5F **53**
Ninebanks. *Nmbd* 4A **114**
Nine Elms. *Swin* 3G **35**
Ninemile Bar. *Dum* 2F **111**
Nine Mile Burn. *Midl* 4E **129**
Ninfield. *E Sus* 4B **28**
Ningwood. *IOW* 4C **16**
Nisbet. *Bord* 2A **120**
Nisbet Hill. *Bord* 4D **130**
Niton. *IOW* 5D **16**
Nitshill. *E Ren* 4G **127**
Niwbwrch. *IOA* 4D **80**
Noak Hill. *G Lon* 1G **39**
Nobold. *Shrp* 4G **71**
Nobottle. *Nptn* 4D **62**
Nocton. *Linc* 4H **87**
Nogdam End. *Norf* 5F **79**
Noke. *Oxon* 4D **50**
Nolton. *Pemb* 3C **42**
Nolton Haven. *Pemb* 3C **42**
No Man's Heath.
Ches W 1H **71**
No Man's Heath. *Warw* 5G **73**
Nomansland. *Devn* 1B **12**
Nomansland. *Wilts* 1A **16**
Noneley. *Shrp* 3G **71**
Noness. *Shet* 9F **173**
Nonikiln. *High* 1A **158**
Nonington. *Kent* 5G **41**
Nook. *Cumb* 2F **113**
(nr. Longtown)
Nook. *Cumb* 1E **97**
(nr. Milnthorpe)
Noranside. *Ang* 2D **144**
Norbreck. *Bkpl* 5C **96**
Norbridge. *Here* 1C **48**
Norbury. *Ches E* 1H **71**
Norbury. *Derbs* 1F **73**
Norbury. *Shrp* 1F **59**
Norbury. *Staf* 3B **72**
Norby. *N Yor* 1G **99**
Norby. *Shet* 6C **173**
Norcross. *Lanc* 5C **96**
Nordelph. *Norf* 5E **77**
Norden. *G Man* 3G **91**
Nordley. *Shrp* 1A **60**
Norfolk Broads. *Norf* 5G **79**
Norham. *Nmbd* 5F **131**
Norland Town. *W Yor* 2A **92**
Norley. *Ches W* 3H **83**
Norleywood. *Hants* 3B **16**
Normanby. *N Lin* 3B **94**
Normanby. *N Yor* 1B **100**
Normanby. *Red C* 3C **106**
Normanby-by-Spital. *Linc* 2H **87**
Normanby le Wold. *Linc* 1A **88**
Norman Cross. *Cambs* 1A **64**
Normandy. *Surr* 5A **38**
Norman's Bay. *E Sus* 5A **28**
Norman's Green. *Devn* 2D **12**
Normanton. *Derb* 2H **73**
Normanton. *Leics* 1F **75**
Normanton. *Linc* 1G **75**
Normanton. *Notts* 5E **86**
Normanton. *W Yor* 2D **93**
Normanton le Heath. *Leics* 4A **74**
Normanton on Soar. *Notts* 3C **74**
Normanton-on-the-Wolds.
Notts 2D **74**
Normanton on Trent. *Notts* 4E **87**
Normoss. *Lanc* 1B **90**
Norrington Common. *Wilts* 5D **35**
Norris Green. *Mers* 1F **83**
Norris Hill. *Leics* 4H **73**
Norristhorpe. *W Yor* 2C **92**
Northacre. *Norf* 1B **66**
Northall. *Buck* 3H **51**
Northallerton. *N Yor* 5A **106**
Northam. *Devn* 4E **19**
Northam. *Sotn* 1C **16**
Northampton. *Nptn* 4E **63** & **206**
North Anston. *S Yor* 2C **86**
North Ascot. *Brac* 4A **38**
North Aston. *Oxon* 3C **50**
Northaw. *Herts* 5C **52**
Northay. *Som* 1F **13**
North Baddesley. *Hants* 4B **24**
North Balfern. *Dum* 4B **110**
North Ballachulish. *High* 2E **141**
North Barrow. *Som* 4B **22**
North Barsham. *Norf* 2B **78**
Northbeck. *Linc* 1H **75**
North Benfleet. *Essx* 2B **40**
North Bersted. *W Sus* 5A **26**
North Berwick. *E Lot* 1B **130**
North Bitchburn. *Dur* 1E **105**
North Blyth. *Nmbd* 1G **115**
North Boarhunt. *Hants* 1E **16**
North Bockhampton. *Dors* 3G **15**
Northborough. *Pet* 5A **76**
Northbourne. *Kent* 5H **41**
Northbourne. *Oxon* 3D **36**
North Bovey. *Devn* 4H **11**
North Bowood. *Dors* 3H **13**
North Bradley. *Wilts* 1D **22**
North Brentor. *Devn* 4E **11**
North Brewham. *Som* 3C **22**
Northbrook. *Oxon* 3C **50**
North Brook End. *Cambs* 1C **52**
North Broomhill. *Nmbd* 4G **121**
North Buckland. *Devn* 2E **19**
North Burlingham. *Norf* 4F **79**
North Cadbury. *Som* 4B **22**
North Carlton. *Linc* 3G **87**
North Cave. *E Yor* 1B **94**
North Cerney. *Glos* 5F **49**
North Chailey. *E Sus* 3E **27**
Northchapel. *W Sus* 3A **26**
North Charford. *Hants* 1G **15**
North Charlton. *Nmbd* 2F **121**
North Cheriton. *Som* 4B **22**
North Chideock. *Dors* 3H **13**
Northchurch. *Herts* 5H **51**
North Cliffe. *E Yor* 1B **94**
North Clifton. *Notts* 3F **87**
North Close. *Dur* 1F **105**
North Cockerington. *Linc* 1C **88**
North Coker. *Som* 1A **14**
North Collafirth. *Shet* 3E **173**
North Common. *E Sus* 3E **27**
North Commonty. *Abers* 4F **161**
North Coombe. *Devn* 1B **12**
North Cornelly. *B'end* 3B **32**
North Cotes. *Linc* 4G **95**
Northcott. *Devn* 3D **10**
(nr. Boyton)
Northcott. *Devn* 1D **12**
(nr. Culmstock)
Northcourt. *Oxon* 2D **36**
North Cove. *Suff* 2G **67**
North Cowton. *N Yor* 4F **105**
North Craigo. *Ang* 2F **145**
North Crawley. *Mil* 1H **51**
North Cray. *G Lon* 3F **39**
North Creake. *Norf* 2A **78**
North Curry. *Som* 4G **21**
North Dalton. *E Yor* 4D **100**
North Deighton. *N Yor* 4F **99**
North Dronley. *Ang* 5C **144**
North Duffield. *N Yor* 1G **93**
Northdyke. *Orkn* 5B **172**
Northedge. *Derbs* 4A **86**
North Elkington. *Linc* 1B **88**
North Elmham. *Norf* 3B **78**
North Elmsall. *W Yor* 3E **93**
Northend. *Buck* 2F **37**
North End. *E Yor* 1F **95**
North End. *Essx* 4G **53**
(nr. Great Dunmow)
North End. *Essx* 2A **54**
(nr. Great Yeldham)
North End. *Hants* 5C **36**
North End. *Leics* 4C **74**
North End. *Linc* 1B **76**
North End. *Norf* 1B **66**
North End. *N Som* 5H **33**
North End. *Port* 2E **17**
Northend. *Warw* 5A **62**
North End. *W Sus* 5C **26**
North End. *Wilts* 2F **35**
North Erradale. *High* 5B **162**
North Evington. *Leic* 5D **74**
North Fambridge. *Essx* 1C **40**
North Fearns. *High* 5E **155**
North Featherstone. *W Yor* 2E **93**
North Feorline. *N Ayr* 3D **122**
North Ferriby. *E Yor* 2C **94**
Northfield. *Aber* 3F **153**
Northfield. *Hull* 2D **94**
Northfield. *Som* 3F **21**
Northfield. *W Mid* 3E **61**
Northfleet. *Kent* 3H **39**
North Frodingham. *E Yor* 4F **101**
Northgate. *Linc* 3A **76**
North Gluss. *Shet* 4E **173**
North Gorley. *Hants* 1G **15**
North Green. *Norf* 2E **66**
North Green. *Suff* 4F **67**
(nr. Framlingham)
North Green. *Suff* 3F **67**
(nr. Halesworth)
North Green. *Suff* 4F **67**
(nr. Saxmundham)
North Greetwell. *Linc* 3H **87**
North Grimston. *N Yor* 3C **100**
North Halling. *Medw* 4B **40**
North Hayling. *Hants* 2F **17**
North Hazelrigg. *Nmbd* 1E **121**
North Heasley. *Devn* 3H **19**
North Heath. *W Sus* 3B **26**
North Hill. *Corn* 5C **10**
North Hinksey Village. *Oxon* 5C **50**
North Holmwood. *Surr* 1C **26**
North Huish. *Devn* 3D **8**
North Hykeham. *Linc* 4G **87**
Northiam. *E Sus* 3C **28**
Northill. *C Beds* 1B **52**
Northington. *Hants* 3D **24**
North Kelsey. *Linc* 4D **94**
North Kelsey Moor. *Linc* 4D **94**
North Kessock. *High* 4A **158**
North Killingholme. *N Lin* 3E **95**
North Kilvington. *N Yor* 1G **99**
North Kilworth. *Leics* 2D **62**
North Kyme. *Linc* 5A **88**
North Lancing. *W Sus* 5C **26**
Northlands. *Linc* 5C **88**
Northleach. *Glos* 4G **49**
North Lee. *Buck* 5G **51**
North Lees. *N Yor* 2E **99**
Northleigh. *Devn* 3G **19**
(nr. Barnstaple)
Northleigh. *Devn* 3E **13**
(nr. Honiton)
North Leigh. *Kent* 1F **29**
North Leigh. *Oxon* 4B **50**
North Leverton. *Notts* 2E **87**
Northlew. *Devn* 3F **11**
North Littleton. *Worc* 1F **49**
North Lopham. *Norf* 2C **66**
North Luffenham. *Rut* 5G **75**
North Marden. *W Sus* 1G **17**
North Marston. *Buck* 3F **51**
North Middleton. *Midl* 4G **129**
North Middleton. *Nmbd* 2E **121**
North Molton. *Devn* 4H **19**
North Moor. *N Yor* 1D **100**
Northmoor. *Oxon* 5C **50**
Northmoor Green. *Som* 3G **21**
North Moreton. *Oxon* 3D **36**
Northmuir. *Ang* 3C **144**
North Mundham. *W Sus* 2G **17**
North Murie. *Per* 1E **137**
North Muskham. *Notts* 5E **87**
North Ness. *Orkn* 8C **172**
North Newbald. *E Yor* 1C **94**
North Newington. *Oxon* 2C **50**
North Newnton. *Wilts* 1G **23**
North Newton. *Som* 3F **21**
Northney. *Hants* 2F **17**
North Nibley. *Glos* 2C **34**
North Oakley. *Hants* 1D **24**
North Ockendon. *G Lon* 2G **39**
Northolt. *G Lon* 2C **38**
Northop. *Flin* 4E **83**
Northop Hall. *Flin* 4E **83**
North Ormesby. *Midd* 3C **106**
North Ormsby. *Linc* 1B **88**
Northorpe. *Linc* 4H **75**
(nr. Bourne)
Northorpe. *Linc* 2B **76**
(nr. Donington)
Northorpe. *Linc* 1F **87**
(nr. Gainsborough)
North Otterington. *N Yor* 1F **99**
Northover. *Som* 3H **21**
(nr. Glastonbury)
Northover. *Som* 4A **22**
(nr. Yeovil)
North Owersby. *Linc* 1H **87**
Northowram. *W Yor* 2B **92**
North Perrott. *Som* 2H **13**
North Petherton. *Som* 3F **21**
North Petherwin. *Corn* 4C **10**
North Pickenham. *Norf* 5A **78**
North Piddle. *Worc* 5D **60**
North Poorton. *Dors* 3A **14**
North Port. *Arg* 1H **133**
Northport. *Dors* 4E **15**
North Queensferry. *Fife* 1E **129**
North Radworthy. *Devn* 3A **20**
North Rauceby. *Linc* 1H **75**
Northrepps. *Norf* 2E **79**
North Rigton. *N Yor* 5E **99**
North Rode. *Ches E* 4C **84**
North Roe. *Shet* 3E **173**
North Ronaldsay Airport.
Orkn 2G **172**
North Row. *Cumb* 1D **102**
North Runcton. *Norf* 4F **77**
North Sannox. *N Ayr* 5B **126**
North Scale. *Cumb* 2A **96**
North Scarle. *Linc* 4F **87**
North Seaton. *Nmbd* 1F **115**
North Seaton Colliery. *Nmbd* 1F **115**
North Sheen. *G Lon* 3C **38**
North Shian. *Arg* 4D **140**
North Shields. *Tyne* 3G **115**
North Shoebury. *S'end* 2D **40**
North Shore. *Bkpl* 1B **90**
North Side. *Cumb* 2B **102**
North Skelton. *Red C* 3D **106**
North Somercotes. *Linc* 1D **88**
North Stainley. *N Yor* 2E **99**
North Stainmore. *Cumb* 3B **104**
North Stifford. *Thur* 2H **39**
North Stoke. *Bath* 5C **34**
North Stoke. *Oxon* 3E **36**
North Stoke. *W Sus* 4B **26**
Northstowe. *Cambs* 4D **64**
North Street. *Hants* 3E **25**
North Street. *Kent* 5E **40**
North Street. *Medw* 3C **40**
North Street. *W Ber* 4E **37**
North Sunderland. *Nmbd* 1G **121**
North Tamerton. *Corn* 3D **10**
North Tawton. *Devn* 2G **11**
North Thoresby. *Linc* 1B **88**
North Town. *Devn* 2F **11**
Northtown. *Orkn* 8D **172**
North Town. *Shet* 10E **173**
North Tuddenham. *Norf* 4C **78**
North Walbottle. *Tyne* 3E **115**
Northwall. *Orkn* 3G **172**
North Walney. *Cumb* 3A **96**
North Walsham. *Norf* 2E **79**
North Waltham. *Hants* 2D **24**
North Warnborough.
Hants 1F **25**
North Water Bridge.
Ang 2F **145**
North Watten. *High* 3E **169**
Northway. *Glos* 2E **49**
Northway. *Swan* 4E **31**
North Weald Bassett. *Essx* 5F **53**
North Weston. *N Som* 4H **33**
North Weston. *Oxon* 5E **51**
North Wheatley. *Notts* 2E **87**
North Whilborough. *Devn* 2E **9**
Northwich. *Ches W* 3A **84**
North Wick. *Bath* 5A **34**
Northwick. *Som* 2G **21**
Northwick. *S Glo* 3A **34**
North Widcombe. *Bath* 1A **22**
North Willingham. *Linc* 2A **88**
North Wingfield. *Derbs* 4B **86**
North Witham. *Linc* 3G **75**
Northwold. *Norf* 1G **65**
Northwood. *Derbs* 4G **85**
Northwood. *G Lon* 1B **38**
Northwood. *IOW* 3C **16**
Northwood. *Kent* 4H **41**
Northwood. *Shrp* 2G **71**
Northwood. *Stoke* 1C **72**
Northwood Green. *Glos* 4C **48**
North Wootton. *Dors* 1B **14**
North Wootton. *Norf* 3F **77**
North Wootton. *Som* 2A **22**
North Wraxall. *Wilts* 4D **34**
North Wroughton. *Swin* 3G **35**
North Yardhope. *Nmbd* 4D **120**
North York Moors. *N Yor* 5D **107**
Norton. *Devn* 3E **9**
Norton. *Glos* 3D **48**
Norton. *Hal* 2H **83**
Norton. *Herts* 2C **52**
Norton. *IOW* 4B **16**
Norton. *Mon* 3H **47**
Norton. *Nptn* 4D **62**
Norton. *Notts* 3C **86**
Norton. *Powy* 4F **59**
Norton. *Shrp* 2G **59**
(nr. Ludlow)
Norton. *Shrp* 5B **72**
(nr. Madeley)
Norton. *Shrp* 5H **71**
(nr. Shrewsbury)
Norton. *S Yor* 3F **93**
(nr. Askern)
Norton. *S Yor* 2A **86**
(nr. Sheffield)
Norton. *Stoc T* 2B **106**
Norton. *Suff* 4B **66**
Norton. *Swan* 4F **31**
Norton. *W Sus* 5A **26**
(nr. Arundel)
Norton. *W Sus* 3G **17**
(nr. Selsey)
Norton. *Wilts* 3D **35**
Norton. *Worc* 1F **49**
(nr. Evesham)
Norton. *Worc* 5C **60**
(nr. Worcester)
Norton Bavant. *Wilts* 2E **23**
Norton Bridge. *Staf* 2C **72**
Norton Canes. *Staf* 5E **73**
Norton Canon. *Here* 1G **47**
Norton Corner. *Norf* 3C **78**
Norton Disney. *Linc* 5F **87**
Norton East. *Staf* 5E **73**
Norton Ferris. *Wilts* 3C **22**
Norton Fitzwarren. *Som* 4F **21**
Norton Green. *IOW* 4B **16**
Norton Green. *Stoke* 5D **84**
Norton Hawkfield. *Bath* 5A **34**
Norton Heath. *Essx* 5G **53**
Norton in Hales. *Shrp* 2B **72**
Norton in the Moors. *Stoke* 5C **84**
Norton-Juxta-Twycross. *Leics* 5H **73**
Norton-le-Clay. *N Yor* 2G **99**
Norton Lindsey. *Warw* 4G **61**
Norton Little Green. *Suff* 4B **66**
Norton Malreward. *Bath* 5B **34**
Norton Mandeville. *Essx* 5F **53**
Norton-on-Derwent. *N Yor* 2B **100**
Norton St Philip. *Som* 1C **22**
Norton Subcourse. *Norf* 1G **67**
Norton sub Hamdon.
Som 1H **13**
Norton Woodseats. *S Yor* 2A **86**
Norwell. *Notts* 4E **87**
Norwell Woodhouse. *Notts* 4E **87**
Norwich. *Norf* 5E **79** & **205**
Norwich International Airport.
Norf 4E **79**
Norwick. *Shet* 1H **173**
Norwood. *Derbs* 2B **86**
Norwood Green. *W Yor* 2B **92**
Norwood Hill. *Surr* 1D **26**
Norwood Park. *Som* 3A **22**
Norwoodside. *Cambs* 1D **64**
Noseley. *Leics* 1E **63**
Noss. *Shet* 10E **173**
Noss Mayo. *Devn* 4B **8**
Nosterfield. *N Yor* 1E **99**
Nostie. *High* 1A **148**
Notgrove. *Glos* 3G **49**
Nottage. *B'end* 4B **32**
Nottingham. *Nott* 1C **74** & **206**
Nottington. *Dors* 4B **14**
Notton. *Dors* 3B **14**
Notton. *W Yor* 3D **92**
Notton. *Wilts* 5E **35**
Nounsley. *Essx* 4A **54**
Noutard's Green. *Worc* 4B **60**
Nox. *Shrp* 4G **71**
Noyadd Trefawr. *Cdgn* 1C **44**
Nuffield. *Oxon* 3E **37**
Nunburnholme. *E Yor* 5C **100**
Nuncargate. *Notts* 5C **86**
Nunclose. *Cumb* 5F **113**
Nuneaton. *Warw* 1A **62**
Nuneham Courtenay. *Oxon* 2D **36**
Nun Monkton. *N Yor* 4H **99**
Nunnerie. *S Lan* 3B **118**
Nunney. *Som* 2C **22**
Nunnington. *N Yor* 2A **100**
Nunnykirk. *Nmbd* 5E **121**
Nunsthorpe. *NE Lin* 4F **95**
Nunthorpe. *Red C* 3C **106**
Nunthorpe. *York* 5H **99**
Nunton. *Wilts* 4G **23**
Nunwick. *Nmbd* 2B **114**
Nunwick. *N Yor* 2F **99**
Nupend. *Glos* 5C **48**
Nursling. *Hants* 1B **16**
Nursted. *W Sus* 4F **25**
Nursteed. *Wilts* 5F **35**

Nurston. *V Glam* 5D 32
Nutbourne. *W Sus* 2F 17
(nr. Chichester)
Nutbourne. *W Sus* 4B 26
(nr. Pulborough)
Nutfield. *Surr* 5E 39
Nuthall. *Notts* 1C 74
Nuthampstead. *Herts* 2E 53
Nuthurst. *Warw* 3F 61
Nuthurst. *W Sus* 3C 26
Nutley. *E Sus* 3F 27
Nuttall. *G Man* 3F 91
Nutwell. *S Yor* 4G 93
Nybster. *High* 2F 169
Nyetimber. *W Sus* 3G 17
Nyewood. *W Sus* 4G 25
Nymet Rowland. *Devn* 2H 11
Nymet Tracey. *Devn* 2H 11
Nympsfield. *Glos* 5D 48
Nynehead. *Som* 4E 21
Nyton. *W Sus* 5A 26

O

Oadby. *Leics* 5D 74
Oad Street. *Kent* 4C 40
Oakamoor. *Staf* 1E 73
Oakbank. *Arg* 5B 140
Oakbank. *W Lot* 3D 129
Oakdale. *Cphy* 2E 33
Oakdale. *Pool* 3F 15
Oake. *Som* 4E 21
Oaken. *Staf* 5C 72
Oakenclough. *Lanc* 5E 97
Oakengates. *Telf* 4B 72
Oakenholt. *Flin* 3E 83
Oakenshaw. *Dur* 1F 105
Oakenshaw. *W Yor* 2B 92
Oakerthorpe. *Derbs* 5A 86
Oakford. *Cdgn* 5D 56
Oakford. *Devn* 4C 20
Oakfordbridge. *Devn* 4C 20
Oakgrove. *Ches E* 4D 84
Oakham. *Rut* 5F 75
Oakhanger. *Ches E* 5B 84
Oakhanger. *Hants* 3F 25
Oakhill. *Som* 2B 22
Oakington. *Cambs* 4D 64
Oaklands. *Powy* 5C 58
Oakle Street. *Glos* 4C 48
Oakley. *Bed* 5H 63
Oakley. *Buck* 4E 51
Oakley. *Fife* 1D 128
Oakley. *Hants* 1D 24
Oakley. *Suff* 3D 66
Oakley Green. *Wind* 3A 38
Oakley Park. *Powy* 2B 58
Oakmere. *Ches W* 4H 83
Oakridge. *Glos* 5E 49
Oaks. *Shrp* 5G 71
Oaksey. *Wilts* 2E 35
Oaks Green. *Derbs* 2F 73
Oakshaw Ford. *Cumb* 2G 113
Oakshott. *Hants* 4F 25
Oakthorpe. *Leics* 4H 73
Oak Tree. *Darl* 3A 106
Oakwood. *Derb* 2A 74
Oakwood. *W Yor* 1D 92
Oakwoodhill. *Surr* 2C 26
Oakworth. *W Yor* 1A 92
Oape. *High* 3B 164
Oare. *Kent* 4E 40
Oare. *Som* 2B 20
Oare. *W Ber* 4D 36
Oare. *Wilts* 5G 35
Oareford. *Som* 2B 20
Oasby. *Linc* 2H 75
Oath. *Som* 4G 21
Oathlaw. *Ang* 3D 145
Oatlands. *N Yor* 4F 99
Oban. *Arg* 1F 133 & 206
Oban. *W Isl* 7D 171
Oborne. *Dors* 1B 14
Obsdale. *High* 2A 158
Obthorpe. *Linc* 4H 75
Occlestone Green. *Ches W* 4A 84
Occold. *Suff* 3D 66
Ochiltree. *E Ayr* 2E 117
Ochtermuthill. *Per* 2H 135
Ochtertyre. *Per* 1H 135
Ockbrook. *Derbs* 2B 74
Ockeridge. *Worc* 4B 60
Ockham. *Surr* 5B 38
Ockle. *High* 1G 139
Ockley. *Surr* 1C 26
Ocle Pychard. *Here* 1A 48
Octofad. *Arg* 4A 124
Octomore. *Arg* 4A 124
Octon. *E Yor* 3E 101
Odcombe. *Som* 1A 14
Odd Down. *Bath* 5C 34
Oddingley. *Worc* 5D 60
Oddington. *Oxon* 4D 50
Oddsta. *Shet* 2G 173
Odell. *Bed* 5G 63
Odie. *Orkn* 5F 172
Odiham. *Hants* 1F 25
Odsey. *Cambs* 2C 52
Odstock. *Wilts* 4G 23
Odstone. *Leics* 5A 74
Offchurch. *Warw* 4A 62
Offenham. *Worc* 1F 49
Offenham Cross. *Worc* 1F 49
Offerton. *G Man* 2D 84
Offerton. *Tyne* 4G 115
Offham. *E Sus* 4F 27
Offham. *Kent* 5A 40
Offham. *W Sus* 5B 26
Offleyhay. *Staf* 3C 72
Offley Hoo. *Herts* 3B 52
Offleymarsh. *Staf* 3B 72
Offord Cluny. *Cambs* 4B 64
Offord D'Arcy. *Cambs* 4B 64
Offton. *Suff* 1D 54
Offwell. *Devn* 3E 13
Ogbourne Maizey. *Wilts* 4G 35
Ogbourne St Andrew. *Wilts* 4G 35
Ogbourne St George. *Wilts* 4H 35
Ogden. *G Man* 3H 91
Ogle. *Nmbd* 2E 115
Ogmore. *V Glam* 4B 32
Ogmore-by-Sea. *V Glam* 4B 32
Ogmore Vale. *B'end* 2C 32
Okeford Fitzpaine. *Dors* 1D 14
Okehampton. *Devn* 3F 11
Okehampton Camp. *Devn* 3F 11
Okraquoy. *Shet* 8F 173
Okus. *Swin* 3G 35
Old. *Nptn* 3E 63
Old Aberdeen. *Aber* 3G 153
Old Alresford. *Hants* 3D 24
Oldany. *High* 5B 166
Old Arley. *Warw* 1G 61
Old Basford. *Nott* 1C 74
Old Basing. *Hants* 1E 25
Oldberrow. *Warw* 4F 61
Old Bewick. *Nmbd* 2E 121
Old Bexley. *G Lon* 3F 39
Old Blair. *Per* 2F 143
Old Bolingbroke. *Linc* 4C 88
Oldborough. *Devn* 2A 12
Old Brampton. *Derbs* 3H 85
Old Bridge of Tilt. *Per* 2F 143
Old Bridge of Urr. *Dum* 3E 111
Old Buckenham. *Norf* 1C 66
Old Burghclere. *Hants* 1C 24
Oldbury. *Shrp* 1B 60
Oldbury. *Warw* 1H 61
Oldbury. *W Mid* 2D 61
Oldbury-on-Severn. *S Glo* 2B 34
Oldbury on the Hill. *Glos* 3D 34
Old Byland. *N Yor* 1H 99
Old Cassop. *Dur* 1A 106
Oldcastle. *Mon* 3G 47
Oldcastle Heath. *Ches W* 1G 71
Old Catton. *Norf* 4E 79
Old Clee. *NE Lin* 4F 95
Old Cleeve. *Som* 2D 20
Old Colwyn. *Cnwy* 3A 82
Oldcotes. *Notts* 2C 86
Old Coulsdon. *G Lon* 5E 39
Old Dailly. *S Ayr* 5B 116
Old Dalby. *Leics* 3D 74
Old Dam. *Derbs* 3F 85
Old Deer. *Abers* 4G 161
Old Dilton. *Wilts* 2D 22
Old Down. *S Glo* 3B 34
Oldeamere. *Cambs* 1C 64
Old Edlington. *S Yor* 1C 86
Old Eldon. *Dur* 2F 105
Old Ellerby. *E Yor* 1E 95
Old Fallings. *W Mid* 5D 72
Oldfallow. *Staf* 4D 72
Old Felixstowe. *Suff* 2G 55
Oldfield. *Shrp* 2A 60
Oldfield. *Worc* 4C 60
Old Fletton. *Pet* 1A 64
Oldford. *Som* 1C 22
Old Forge. *Here* 4A 48
Old Glossop. *Derbs* 1E 85
Old Goole. *E Yor* 2H 93
Old Gore. *Here* 3B 48
Old Graitney. *Dum* 3E 112
Old Grimsby. *IOS* 1A 4
Oldhall. *High* 3E 169
Old Hall Street. *Norf* 2F 79
Oldham. *G Man* 4H 91
Oldhamstocks. *E Lot* 2D 130
Old Heathfield. *E Sus* 3G 27
Old Hill. *W Mid* 2D 60
Old Hunstanton. *Norf* 1F 77
Old Hurst. *Cambs* 3B 64
Old Hutton. *Cumb* 1E 97
Old Kea. *Corn* 4C 6
Old Kilpatrick. *W Dun* 2F 127
Old Kinnernie. *Abers* 3E 152
Old Knebworth. *Herts* 3C 52
Oldland. *S Glo* 4B 34
Old Laxey. *IOM* 3D 108
Old Leake. *Linc* 5D 88
Old Lenton. *Nott* 2C 74
Old Llanberis. *Gwyn* 5F 81
Old Malton. *N Yor* 2B 100
Oldmeldrum. *Abers* 1F 153
Old Micklefield. *W Yor* 1E 93
Old Mill. *Corn* 5D 10
Oldmixon. *N Som* 1G 21
Old Monkland. *N Lan* 3A 128
Old Newton. *Suff* 4C 66
Old Park. *Telf* 5A 72
Old Pentland. *Midl* 3F 129
Old Philpstoun. *W Lot* 2D 128
Old Quarrington. *Dur* 1A 106
Old Radnor. *Powy* 5E 59
Old Rayne. *Abers* 1D 152
Oldridge. *Devn* 3B 12
Old Romney. *Kent* 3E 29
Old Scone. *Per* 1D 136
Oldshore Beg. *High* 3B 166
Oldshoremore. *High* 3C 166
Old Snydale. *W Yor* 2E 93
Old Sodbury. *S Glo* 3C 34
Old Somerby. *Linc* 2G 75
Old Spital. *Dur* 3C 104
Oldstead. *N Yor* 1H 99
Old Stratford. *Nptn* 1F 51
Old Swan. *Mers* 1F 83
Old Swarland. *Nmbd* 4F 121
Old Tebay. *Cumb* 4H 103
Old Town. *Cumb* 5F 113
Old Town. *E Sus* 5G 27
Oldtown. *High* 5C 164
Old Town. *IOS* 1B 4
Old Town. *Nmbd* 5C 120
Oldtown of Ord. *Abers* 3D 160
Old Trafford. *G Man* 1C 84
Old Tupton. *Derbs* 4A 86
Oldwall. *Cumb* 3F 113
Oldwalls. *Swan* 3D 31
Old Warden. *C Beds* 1B 52
Oldways End. *Som* 4B 20
Old Westhall. *Abers* 1D 152
Old Weston. *Cambs* 3H 63
Oldwhat. *Abers* 3F 161
Old Windsor. *Wind* 3A 38
Old Wives Lees. *Kent* 5E 41
Old Woking. *Surr* 5B 38
Oldwood Common. *Worc* 4H 59
Old Woodstock. *Oxon* 4C 50
Olgrinmore. *High* 3C 168
Oliver's Battery. *Hants* 4C 24
Ollaberry. *Shet* 3E 173
Ollerton. *Ches E* 3B 84
Ollerton. *Notts* 4D 86
Ollerton. *Shrp* 3A 72
Olmarch. *Cdgn* 5F 57
Olmstead Green. *Cambs* 1G 53
Olney. *Mil* 5F 63
Olrig. *High* 2D 169
Olton. *W Mid* 2F 61
Olveston. *S Glo* 3B 34
Ombersley. *Worc* 4C 60
Ompton. *Notts* 4D 86
Omunsgarth. *Shet* 7E 173
Onchan. *IOM* 4D 108
Onecote. *Staf* 5E 85
Onehouse. *Suff* 5C 66
Onen. *Mon* 4H 47
Ongar Hill. *Norf* 3E 77
Ongar Street. *Here* 4F 59
Onibury. *Shrp* 3G 59
Onich. *High* 2E 141
Onllwyn. *Neat* 4B 46
Onneley. *Shrp* 1B 72
Onslow Green. *Essx* 4G 53
Onslow Village. *Surr* 1A 26
Onthank. *E Ayr* 1D 116
Openwoodgate. *Derbs* 1A 74
Opinan. *High* 1G 155
(nr. Gairloch)
Opinan. *High* 4C 162
(nr. Laide)
Orasaigh. *W Isl* 6F 171
Orbost. *High* 4B 154
Orby. *Linc* 4D 89
Orchard Hill. *Devn* 4E 19
Orchard Portman. *Som* 4F 21
Orcheston. *Wilts* 2F 23
Orcop. *Here* 3H 47
Orcop Hill. *Here* 3H 47
Ord. *High* 2E 147
Ordale. *Shet* 1H 173
Ordhead. *Abers* 2D 152
Ordie. *Abers* 3B 152
Ordiquish. *Mor* 3H 159
Ordley. *Nmbd* 4C 114
Ordsall. *Notts* 3E 86
Ore. *E Sus* 4C 28
Oreham Common. *W Sus* 4D 26
Oreton. *Shrp* 2A 60
Orford. *Suff* 1H 55
Orford. *Warr* 1A 84
Organford. *Dors* 3E 15
Orgil. *Orkn* 7B 172
Orgreave. *Staf* 4F 73
Oridge Street. *Glos* 3C 48
Orlestone. *Kent* 2D 28
Orleton. *Here* 4G 59
Orleton. *Worc* 4A 60
Orleton Common. *Here* 4G 59
Orlingbury. *Nptn* 3F 63
Ormacleit. *W Isl* 5C 170
Ormathwaite. *Cumb* 2D 102
Ormesby. *Midd* 3C 106
Ormesby St Margaret. *Norf* 4G 79
Ormesby St Michael. *Norf* 4G 79
Ormiscaig. *High* 4C 162
Ormiston. *E Lot* 3H 129
Ormsaigbeg. *High* 2F 139
Ormsaigmore. *High* 2F 139
Ormsary. *Arg* 2F 125
Ormsgill. *Cumb* 2A 96
Ormskirk. *Lanc* 4C 90
Orphir. *Orkn* 7C 172
Orpington. *G Lon* 4F 39
Orrell. *Lanc* 4D 90
Orrell. *Mers* 1F 83
Orrisdale. *IOM* 2C 108
Orsett. *Thur* 2H 39
Orslow. *Staf* 4C 72
Orston. *Notts* 1E 75
Orthwaite. *Cumb* 1D 102
Orton. *Cumb* 4H 103
Orton. *Mor* 3H 159
Orton. *Nptn* 3F 63
Orton. *Staf* 1C 60
Orton Longueville. *Pet* 1A 64
Orton-on-the-Hill. *Leics* 5H 73
Orton Waterville. *Pet* 1A 64
Orton Wistow. *Pet* 1A 64
Orwell. *Cambs* 5C 64
Osbaldeston. *Lanc* 1E 91
Osbaldwick. *York* 4A 100
Osbaston. *Leics* 5B 74
Osbaston. *Shrp* 3F 71
Osbournby. *Linc* 2H 75
Osclay. *High* 5E 169
Oscroft. *Ches W* 4H 83
Ose. *High* 4C 154
Osgathorpe. *Leics* 4B 74
Osgodby. *Linc* 1H 87
Osgodby. *N Yor* 1E 101
(nr. Scarborough)
Osgodby. *N Yor* 1G 93
(nr. Selby)
Oskaig. *High* 5E 155
Oskamull. *Arg* 4F 139
Osleston. *Derbs* 2G 73
Osmaston. *Derb* 2A 74
Osmaston. *Derbs* 1G 73
Osmington. *Dors* 4C 14
Osmington Mills. *Dors* 4C 14
Osmondthorpe. *W Yor* 1D 92
Osmondwall. *Orkn* 9C 172
Osmotherley. *N Yor* 5B 106
Osnaburgh. *Fife* 2G 137
Ospisdale. *High* 5E 164
Ospringe. *Kent* 4E 40
Ossett. *W Yor* 2C 92
Ossington. *Notts* 4E 87
Ostend. *Essx* 1D 40
Ostend. *Norf* 2F 79
Osterley. *G Lon* 3C 38
Oswaldkirk. *N Yor* 2A 100
Oswaldtwistle. *Lanc* 2F 91
Oswestry. *Shrp* 3E 71
Otby. *Linc* 1A 88
Otford. *Kent* 5G 39
Otham. *Kent* 5B 40
Otherton. *Staf* 4D 72
Othery. *Som* 3G 21
Otley. *Suff* 5E 66
Otley. *W Yor* 5E 98
Otterbourne. *Hants* 4C 24
Otterburn. *Nmbd* 5C 120
Otterburn. *N Yor* 4A 98
Otterburn Camp. *Nmbd* 5C 120
Otterburn Hall. *Nmbd* 5C 120
Otter Ferry. *Arg* 1H 125
Otterford. *Som* 1F 13
Otterham. *Corn* 3B 10
Otterhampton. *Som* 2F 21
Otterham Quay. *Kent* 4C 40
Ottershaw. *Surr* 4B 38
Otterspool. *Mers* 2F 83
Otterswick. *Shet* 3G 173
Otterton. *Devn* 4D 12
Otterwood. *Hants* 2C 16
Ottery St Mary. *Devn* 3E 12
Ottinge. *Kent* 1F 29
Ottringham. *E Yor* 2F 95
Oughterby. *Cumb* 4D 112
Oughtershaw. *N Yor* 1A 98
Oughterside. *Cumb* 5C 112
Oughtibridge. *S Yor* 1H 85
Oughtrington. *Warr* 2A 84
Oulston. *N Yor* 2H 99
Oulton. *Cumb* 4D 112
Oulton. *Norf* 3D 78
Oulton. *Staf* 3B 72
(nr. Gnosall Heath)
Oulton. *Staf* 2D 72
(nr. Stone)
Oulton. *Suff* 1H 67
Oulton. *W Yor* 2D 92
Oulton Broad. *Suff* 1H 67
Oulton Street. *Norf* 3D 78
Oundle. *Nptn* 2H 63
Ousby. *Cumb* 1H 103
Ousdale. *High* 1H 165
Ousden. *Suff* 5G 65
Ousefleet. *E Yor* 2B 94
Ouston. *Dur* 4F 115
Ouston. *Nmbd* 4A 114
(nr. Bearsbridge)
Ouston. *Nmbd* 2D 114
(nr. Stamfordham)
Outer Hope. *Devn* 4C 8
Outertown. *Orkn* 6B 172
Outgate. *Cumb* 5E 103
Outhgill. *Cumb* 4A 104
Outlands. *Staf* 2B 72
Outlane. *W Yor* 3A 92
Out Newton. *E Yor* 2G 95
Out Rawcliffe. *Lanc* 5D 96
Outwell. *Norf* 5E 77
Outwick. *Hants* 1G 15
Outwood. *Surr* 1E 27
Outwood. *W Yor* 2D 92
Outwood. *Worc* 3D 60
Outwoods. *Leics* 4B 74
Outwoods. *Staf* 4B 72
Ouzlewell Green. *W Yor* 2D 92
Ovenden. *W Yor* 2A 92
Over. *Cambs* 3C 64
Over. *Ches W* 4A 84
Over. *Glos* 4D 48
Over. *S Glo* 3A 34
Overbister. *Orkn* 3F 172
Over Burrows. *Derbs* 2G 73
Overbury. *Worc* 2E 49
Overcombe. *Dors* 4B 14
Over Compton. *Dors* 1A 14
Over End. *Cambs* 1H 63
Over Finlarg. *Ang* 4D 144
Overgreen. *Derbs* 3H 85
Over Green. *W Mid* 1F 61
Over Haddon. *Derbs* 4G 85
Over Hulton. *G Man* 4E 91
Over Kellet. *Lanc* 2E 97
Over Kiddington. *Oxon* 3C 50
Overleigh. *Som* 3H 21
Overley. *Staf* 4F 73
Over Monnow. *Mon* 4A 48
Over Norton. *Oxon* 3B 50
Over Peover. *Ches E* 3B 84
Overpool. *Ches W* 3F 83
Overscaig. *High* 1B 164
Overseal. *Derbs* 4G 73
Over Silton. *N Yor* 5B 106
Oversland. *Kent* 5E 41
Overstone. *Nptn* 4F 63
Over Stowey. *Som* 3E 21
Overstrand. *Norf* 1E 79
Over Stratton. *Som* 1H 13
Over Street. *Wilts* 3F 23
Overthorpe. *Nptn* 1C 50
Overton. *Aber* 2F 153
Overton. *Ches W* 3H 83
Overton. *Hants* 2D 24
Overton. *High* 5E 169
Overton. *Lanc* 4D 96
Overton. *N Yor* 4H 99
Overton. *Shrp* 2A 60
(nr. Bridgnorth)
Overton. *Shrp* 3H 59
(nr. Ludlow)
Overton. *Swan* 4D 30
Overton. *W Yor* 3C 92
Overton. *Wrex* 1F 71
Overtown. *Lanc* 2F 97
Overtown. *N Lan* 4B 128
Overtown. *Swin* 4G 35
Over Wallop. *Hants* 3A 24
Over Whitacre. *Warw* 1G 61
Over Worton. *Oxon* 3C 50
Oving. *Buck* 3F 51
Oving. *W Sus* 5A 26
Ovingdean. *Brig* 5E 27
Ovingham. *Nmbd* 3D 115
Ovington. *Dur* 3E 105
Ovington. *Essx* 1A 54
Ovington. *Hants* 3D 24
Ovington. *Norf* 5B 78
Ovington. *Nmbd* 3D 114
Owen's Bank. *Staf* 3G 73
Ower. *Hants* 2C 16
(nr. Holbury)
Ower. *Hants* 1B 16
(nr. Totton)
Owermoigne. *Dors* 4C 14
Owlbury. *Shrp* 1F 59
Owler Bar. *Derbs* 3G 85
Owlerton. *S Yor* 2H 85
Owlsmoor. *Brac* 5G 37
Owlswick. *Buck* 5F 51
Owmby. *Linc* 4D 94
Owmby-by-Spital. *Linc* 2H 87
Ownham. *W Ber* 4C 36
Owrytn. *Wrex* 1F 71
Owslebury. *Hants* 4D 24
Owston. *Leics* 5E 75
Owston. *S Yor* 3F 93
Owston Ferry. *N Lin* 4B 94
Owstwick. *E Yor* 1F 95
Owthorne. *E Yor* 2G 95
Owthorpe. *Notts* 2D 74
Owton Manor. *Hart* 2B 106
Oxborough. *Norf* 5G 77
Oxbridge. *Dors* 3H 13
Oxcombe. *Linc* 3C 88
Oxen End. *Essx* 3G 53
Oxenhall. *Glos* 3C 48
Oxenholme. *Cumb* 5G 103
Oxenhope. *W Yor* 1A 92
Oxen Park. *Cumb* 1C 96
Oxenpill. *Som* 2H 21
Oxenton. *Glos* 2E 49
Oxenwood. *Wilts* 1B 24
Oxford. *Oxon* 5D 50 & 207
Oxgangs. *Edin* 3F 129
Oxhey. *Herts* 1C 38
Oxhill. *Warw* 1B 50
Oxley. *W Mid* 5C 72
Oxley Green. *Essx* 4C 54
Oxley's Green. *E Sus* 3A 28
Oxlode. *Cambs* 2D 65
Oxnam. *Bord* 3B 120
Oxshott. *Surr* 4C 38

Oxspring. S Yor 4C 92
Oxted. Surr 5E 39
Oxton. Mers 2E 83
Oxton. N Yor 5H 99
Oxton. Notts 5D 86
Oxton. Bord 4A 130
Oxwich. Swan 4D 31
Oxwich Green. Swan 4D 31
Oxwick. Norf 3B 78
Oykel Bridge. High 3A 164
Oyne. Abers 1D 152
Oystermouth. Swan 4F 31
Ozleworth. Glos 2C 34

P

Pabail Iarach. W Isl 4H 171
Pabail Uarach. W Isl 4H 171
Pachesham. Surr 5C 38
Packers Hill. Dors 1C 14
Packington. Leics 4A 74
Packmoor. Stoke 5C 84
Packmores. Warw 4G 61
Packwood. W Mid 3F 61
Packwood Gullett. W Mid 3F 61
Padanaram. Ang 3D 144
Padbury. Buck 2F 51
Paddington. G Lon 2D 38
Paddington. Warr 2A 84
Paddlesworth. Kent 2F 29
Paddock. Kent 5D 40
Paddockhole. Dum 1D 112
Paddock Wood. Kent 1A 28
Paddolgreen. Shrp 2H 71
Padeswood. Flin 4E 83
Padiham. Lanc 1F 91
Padside. N Yor 4D 98
Padson. Devn 3F 11
Padstow. Corn 1D 6
Padworth. W Ber 5E 36
Page Bank. Dur 1F 105
Pagham. W Sus 3G 17
Paglesham Churchend. Essx 1D 40
Paglesham Eastend. Essx 1D 40
Paibeil. W Isl 2C 170 (on North Uist)
Paibeil. W Isl 8C 171 (on Taransay)
Paiblesgearraidh. W Isl 2C 170
Paignton. Torb 2E 9
Pailton. Warw 2B 62
Paine's Corner. E Sus 3H 27
Painleyhill. Staf 2E 73
Painscastle. Powy 1E 47
Painshawfield. Nmbd 3D 114
Painsthorpe. E Yor 4C 100
Painswick. Glos 5D 48
Painter's Forstal. Kent 5D 40
Painthorpe. W Yor 3D 92
Pairc Shiaboist. W Isl 3E 171
Paisley. Ren 3F 127 & 207
Pakefield. Suff 1H 67
Pakenham. Suff 4B 66
Pale. Gwyn 2B 70
Palehouse Common. E Sus 4F 27
Palestine. Hants 2A 24
Paley Street. Wind 4G 37
Palgowan. Dum 1A 110
Palgrave. Suff 3D 66
Pallington. Dors 3C 14
Palmarsh. Kent 2F 29
Palmer Moor. Derbs 2F 73
Palmers Cross. W Mid 5C 72
Palmerstown. V Glam 5E 33
Palnackie. Dum 4F 111
Palnure. Dum 3B 110
Palterton. Derbs 4B 86
Pamber End. Hants 1E 24
Pamber Green. Hants 1E 24
Pamber Heath. Hants 5E 36
Pamington. Glos 2E 49
Pamphill. Dors 2E 15
Pampisford. Cambs 1E 53
Panborough. Som 2H 21
Panbride. Ang 5E 145
Pancakehill. Glos 4F 49
Pancrasweek. Devn 2C 10
Pandy. Gwyn 3A 70 (nr. Bala)
Pandy. Gwyn 5F 69 (nr. Tywyn)
Pandy. Mon 3G 47
Pandy. Powy 5B 70
Pandy. Wrex 2D 70
Pandy Tudur. Cnwy 4A 82
Panfield. Essx 3H 53
Pangbourne. W Ber 4E 37
Pannal. N Yor 4F 99
Pannal Ash. N Yor 4E 99
Pannanich. Abers 4A 152
Pant. Shrp 3E 71
Pant. Wrex 1F 71
Pantasaph. Flin 3D 82
Pant Glas. Gwyn 1D 68
Pant-glas. Shrp 2E 71
Pantgwyn. Carm 3F 45
Pantgwyn. Cdgn 1C 44
Pant-lasau. Swan 3F 31
Panton. Linc 3A 88
Pant-pastynog. Den 4C 82
Pantperthog. Gwyn 5G 69
Pant-teg. Carm 3E 45
Pant-y-Caws. Carm 2F 43
Pant-y-dwr. Powy 3B 58
Pant-y-ffridd. Powy 5D 70
Pantyffynnon. Carm 4G 45
Pantygasseg. Torf 5F 47
Pant-y-llyn. Carm 4G 45
Pant-yr-awel. B'end 3C 32
Pant y Wacco. Flin 3D 82
Panxworth. Norf 4F 79
Papa Stour Airport. Shet 6C 173
Papa Westray Airport. Orkn 2D 172
Papcastle. Cumb 1C 102
Papigoe. High 3F 169
Papil. Shet 8E 173
Papple. E Lot 2B 130
Papplewick. Notts 5C 86
Papworth Everard. Cambs 4B 64
Papworth St Agnes. Cambs 4B 64
Par. Corn 3E 7
Paramour Street. Kent 4G 41
Parbold. Lanc 3C 90
Parbrook. Som 3A 22
Parbrook. W Sus 3B 26
Parc. Gwyn 2A 70
Parcllyn. Cdgn 5B 56
Parc-Seymour. Newp 2H 33
Pardown. Hants 2D 24
Pardshaw. Cumb 2B 102
Parham. Suff 4F 67
Park. Abers 4E 153
Park. Arg 4D 140
Park. Dum 5B 118
Park Bottom. Corn 4A 6
Parkburn. Abers 5E 161
Park Corner. E Sus 2G 27
Park Corner. Oxon 3E 37
Parkend. Glos 5B 48
Park End. Nmbd 2B 114
Parkeston. Essx 2F 55
Parkfield. Corn 2H 7
Parkgate. Ches W 3E 83
Parkgate. Cumb 5D 112
Parkgate. Dum 1B 112
Park Gate. Hants 2D 16
Parkgate. Surr 1D 26
Park Gate. Worc 3D 60
Parkhall. W Dun 2F 127
Parkham. Devn 4D 19
Parkham Ash. Devn 4D 18
Parkhead. Cumb 5E 113
Parkhead. Glas 3H 127
Park Hill. Mers 4C 90
Parkhouse. Mon 5H 47
Parkhurst. IOW 3C 16
Park Lane. G Man 4F 91
Park Lane. Staf 5C 72
Parkmill. Swan 4E 31
Park Mill. W Yor 3C 92
Parkneuk. Abers 1G 145
Parkside. N Lan 4B 128
Parkstone. Pool 3F 15
Park Street. Herts 5B 52
Park Street. W Sus 2C 26
Park Town. Oxon 5D 50
Park Village. Nmbd 3H 113
Parkway. Here 2C 48
Parley Cross. Dors 3F 15
Parmoor. Buck 3F 37
Parr. Mers 1H 83
Parracombe. Devn 2G 19
Parrog. Pemb 1E 43
Parsonage Green. Essx 4H 53
Parsonby. Cumb 1C 102
Parson Cross. S Yor 1A 86
Parson Drove. Cambs 5C 76
Partick. Glas 3G 127
Partington. G Man 1B 84
Partney. Linc 4D 88
Parton. Cumb 2A 102 (nr. Whitehaven)
Parton. Cumb 4D 112 (nr. Wigton)
Parton. Dum 2D 111
Partridge Green. W Sus 4C 26
Parwich. Derbs 5F 85
Passenham. Nptn 2F 51
Passfield. Hants 3G 25
Passingford Bridge. Essx 1G 39
Paston. Norf 2F 79
Pasturefields. Staf 3D 73
Patchacott. Devn 3E 11
Patcham. Brig 5E 27
Patchetts Green. Herts 1C 38
Patching. W Sus 5B 26
Patchole. Devn 2G 19
Patchway. S Glo 3B 34
Pateley Bridge. N Yor 3D 98
Pathe. Som 3G 21
Pathfinder Village. Devn 3B 12
Pathhead. Abers 2G 145
Pathhead. E Ayr 3F 117
Pathhead. Fife 4E 137
Pathhead. Midl 3G 129
Pathlow. Warw 5F 61
Path of Condie. Per 2C 136
Pathstruie. Per 2C 136
Patmore Heath. Herts 3E 53
Patna. E Ayr 3D 116
Patney. Wilts 1F 23
Patrick. IOM 3B 108
Patrick Brompton. N Yor 5F 105
Patrington. E Yor 2G 95
Patrington Haven. E Yor 2G 95
Patrixbourne. Kent 5F 41
Patterdale. Cumb 3E 103
Pattiesmuir. Fife 1D 129
Pattingham. Staf 1C 60
Pattishall. Nptn 5D 62
Pattiswick. Essx 3B 54
Patton Bridge. Cumb 5G 103
Paul. Corn 4B 4
Paulerspury. Nptn 1F 51
Paull. E Yor 2E 95
Paulton. Bath 1B 22
Pauperhaugh. Nmbd 5F 121
Pave Lane. Telf 4B 72
Pavenham. Bed 5G 63
Pawlett. Som 2G 21
Pawston. Nmbd 1C 120
Paxford. Glos 2G 49
Paxton. Bord 4F 131
Payhembury. Devn 2D 12
Paythorne. Lanc 4H 97
Payton. Som 4E 20
Peacehaven. E Sus 5F 27
Peak Dale. Derbs 3E 85
Peak District. Derbs 2F 85
Peak Forest. Derbs 3F 85
Peak Hill. Linc 4B 76
Peakirk. Pet 5A 76
Pearsie. Ang 3C 144
Peasedown St John. Bath 1C 22
Peaseland Green. Norf 4C 78
Peasemore. W Ber 4C 36
Peasenhall. Suff 4F 67
Pease Pottage. W Sus 2D 26
Peaslake. Surr 1B 26
Peasley Cross. Mers 1H 83
Peasmarsh. E Sus 3C 28
Peasmarsh. Som 1G 13
Peasmarsh. Surr 1A 26
Peaston. E Lot 3H 129
Peastonbank. E Lot 3H 129
Peathill. Abers 2G 161
Peat Inn. Fife 3G 137
Peatling Magna. Leics 1C 62
Peatling Parva. Leics 2C 62
Peaton. Arg 1D 126
Peaton. Shrp 2H 59
Peats Corner. Suff 4D 66
Pebmarsh. Essx 2B 54
Pebworth. Worc 1G 49
Pecket Well. W Yor 2H 91
Peckforton. Ches E 5H 83
Peckham Bush. Kent 5A 40
Peckleton. Leics 5B 74
Pedair-ffordd. Powy 3D 70
Pedham. Norf 4F 79
Pedlinge. Kent 2F 29
Pedmore. W Mid 2D 60
Pedwell. Som 3H 21
Peebles. Bord 5F 129
Peel. IOM 3B 108
Peel. Bord 1G 119
Peel Common. Hants 2D 16
Peening Quarter. Kent 3C 28
Peggs Green. Leics 4B 74
Pegsdon. C Beds 2B 52
Pegswood. Nmbd 1F 115
Peinchorran. High 5E 155
Peinlich. High 3D 154
Pelaw. Tyne 3G 115
Pelcomb Bridge. Pemb 3D 42
Pelcomb Cross. Pemb 3D 42
Peldon. Essx 4C 54
Pelsall. W Mid 5E 73
Pelton. Dur 4F 115
Pelutho. Cumb 5C 112
Pelynt. Corn 3G 7
Pemberton. Carm 5F 45
Pembrey. Carm 5E 45
Pembridge. Here 5F 59
Pembroke. Pemb 4D 43
Pembroke Dock. Pemb 4D 42 & 215
Pembroke Ferry. Pemb 4D 43
Pembury. Kent 1H 27
Penallt. Mon 4A 48
Penally. Pemb 5F 43
Penalt. Here 3A 48
Penalum. Pemb 5F 43
Penare. Corn 4D 6
Penarth. V Glam 4E 33
Penbeagle. Corn 3C 4
Penberth. Corn 4B 4
Pen-bont Rhydybeddau. Cdgn 2F 57
Penbryn. Cdgn 5B 56
Pencader. Carm 2E 45
Pen-cae. Cdgn 5D 56
Pencaenewydd. Gwyn 1D 68
Pencaerau. Neat 3G 31
Pencaitland. E Lot 3H 129
Pencarnisiog. IOA 3C 80
Pencarreg. Carm 1F 45
Pencarrow. Corn 4B 10
Pencelli. Powy 3D 46
Pen-clawdd. Swan 3E 31
Pencoed. B'end 3C 32
Pencombe. Here 5H 59
Pencraig. Here 3A 48
Pencraig. Powy 3C 70
Pendeen. Corn 3A 4
Pendeford. W Mid 5D 72
Penderyn. Rhon 5C 46
Pendine. Carm 4G 43
Pendlebury. G Man 4F 91
Pendleton. G Man 1C 84
Pendleton. Lanc 1F 91
Pendock. Worc 2C 48
Pendoggett. Corn 5A 10
Pendomer. Som 1A 14
Pendoylan. V Glam 4D 32
Pendre. B'end 3C 32
Penegoes. Powy 5G 69
Penelewey. Corn 4C 6
Penffordd. Pemb 2E 43
Penffordd-Lâs. Powy 1A 58
Penfro. Pemb 4D 43
Pengam. Cphy 2E 33
Pengam. Card 4F 33
Penge. G Lon 3E 39
Pengelly. Corn 4A 10
Pengenffordd. Powy 2E 47
Pengorffwysfa. IOA 1D 80
Pengover Green. Corn 2G 7
Pengwern. Den 3C 82
Penhale. Corn 5D 5 (nr. Mullion)
Penhale. Corn 3D 6 (nr. St Austell)
Penhale Camp. Corn 3B 6
Penhallow. Corn 3B 6
Penhalvean. Corn 5B 6
Penhelig. Gwyn 1F 57
Penhill. Swin 3G 35
Penhow. Newp 2H 33
Penhurst. E Sus 4A 28
Peniarth. Gwyn 5F 69
Penicuik. Midl 3F 129
Peniel. Carm 3E 45
Penifiler. High 4D 155
Peninver. Arg 3B 122
Penisa'r Waun. Gwyn 4E 81
Penistone. S Yor 4C 92
Penketh. Warr 2H 83
Penkill. S Ayr 5B 116
Penkridge. Staf 4D 72
Penley. Wrex 2G 71
Penllech. Gwyn 2B 68
Penllergaer. Swan 3F 31
Pen-llyn. IOA 2C 80
Penmachno. Cnwy 5G 81
Penmaen. Swan 4E 31
Penmaenmawr. Cnwy 3G 81
Penmaenpool. Gwyn 4F 69
Penmaen Rhos. Cnwy 3A 82
Pen-marc. V Glam 5D 32
Penmark. V Glam 5D 32
Penmarth. Corn 5B 6
Penmon. IOA 2F 81
Penmorfa. Gwyn 1E 69
Penmynydd. IOA 3E 81
Penn. Buck 1A 38
Penn. Dors 3G 13
Penn. W Mid 1C 60
Pennal. Gwyn 5G 69
Pennan. Abers 2F 161
Pennant. Cdgn 4E 57
Pennant. Den 2C 70
Pennant. Gwyn 3B 70
Pennant. Powy 1A 58
Pennant Melangell. Powy 3C 70
Pennar. Pemb 4D 42
Pennard. Swan 4E 31
Pennerley. Shrp 1F 59
Pennington. Cumb 2B 96
Pennington. G Man 1A 84
Pennington. Hants 3B 16
Pennorth. Powy 3E 46
Penn Street. Buck 1A 38
Pennsylvania. Devn 3C 12
Pennsylvania. S Glo 4C 34
Penny Bridge. Cumb 1C 96
Pennycross. Plym 3A 8
Pennygate. Norf 3F 79
Pennyghael. Arg 1C 132
Penny Hill. Linc 3C 76
Pennylands. Lanc 4C 90
Pennymoor. Devn 1B 12
Pennyvenie. E Ayr 4D 117
Pennywell. Tyne 4G 115
Penparc. Cdgn 1C 44
Penparcau. Cdgn 2E 57
Penpedairheol. Cphy 2E 33
Penperlleni. Mon 5G 47
Penpillick. Corn 3E 7
Penpol. Corn 5C 6
Penpoll. Corn 3F 7
Penponds. Corn 3D 4
Penpont. Corn 5A 10
Penpont. Dum 5H 117
Penpont. Powy 3C 46
Penprysg. B'end 3C 32
Penquit. Devn 3C 8
Penrherber. Carm 1G 43
Penrhiw. Pemb 1C 44
Penrhiwceiber. Rhon 2D 32
Pen Rhiwfawr. Neat 4H 45
Penrhiw-llan. Cdgn 1D 44
Penrhiw-pal. Cdgn 1D 44
Penrhos. Gwyn 2C 68
Penrhos. Here 5F 59
Penrhos. IOA 2B 80
Penrhos. Mon 4H 47
Penrhos. Powy 4A 46
Penrhos Garnedd. Gwyn 3E 81
Penrhyn. IOA 1C 80
Penrhyn Bay. Cnwy 2H 81
Penrhyn-coch. Cdgn 2F 57
Penrhyndeudraeth. Gwyn 2F 69
Penrhyn Side. Cnwy 2H 81
Penrice. Swan 4D 31
Penrith. Cumb 2G 103
Penrose. Corn 1C 6
Penruddock. Cumb 2F 103
Penryn. Corn 5B 6
Pensarn. Carm 4E 45
Pen-sarn. Gwyn 3E 69
Pensax. Worc 4B 60
Pensby. Mers 2E 83
Penselwood. Som 3C 22
Pensford. Bath 5B 34
Pensham. Worc 1E 49
Penshaw. Tyne 4G 115
Penshurst. Kent 1G 27
Pensilva. Corn 2G 7
Pensnett. W Mid 2D 60
Penston. E Lot 2H 129
Penstone. Devn 2A 12
Pente-tafarn-y-fedw. Cnwy 4H 81
Pentewan. Corn 4E 6
Pentir. Gwyn 4E 81
Pentire. Corn 2B 6
Pentlepoir. Pemb 4F 43
Pentlow. Essx 1B 54
Pentney. Norf 4G 77
Penton Mewsey. Hants 2B 24
Pentraeth. IOA 3E 81
Pentre. Powy 1E 59 (nr. Church Stoke)
Pentre. Powy 2D 58 (nr. Kerry)
Pentre. Powy 2C 58 (nr. Mochdre)
Pentre. Rhon 2C 32
Pentre. Shrp 4F 71
Pentre. Wrex 2D 70 (nr. Llanfyllin)
Pentre. Wrex 1E 71 (nr. Rhosllanerchrugog)
Pentrebach. Carm 2B 46
Pentre-bach. Cdgn 1F 45
Pentrebach. Mer T 5D 46
Pentre-bach. Powy 2C 46
Pentrebach. Swan 5G 45
Pentre Berw. IOA 3D 80
Pentre-bont. Cnwy 5G 81
Pentrecagal. Carm 1D 44
Pentre-celyn. Den 5D 82
Pentre-clawdd. Shrp 2E 71
Pentreclwydau. Neat 5B 46
Pentre-cwrt. Carm 2D 45
Pentre Dolau Honddu. Powy 1C 46
Pentre-dwr. Swan 3F 31
Pentrefelin. Carm 3F 45
Pentrefelin. Cdgn 1G 45
Pentrefelin. Cnwy 3H 81
Pentrefelin. Gwyn 2E 69
Pentrefoelas. Cnwy 5A 82
Pentre Galar. Pemb 1F 43
Pentregat. Cdgn 5C 56
Pentre Gwenlais. Carm 4G 45
Pentre Gwynfryn. Gwyn 3E 69
Pentre Halkyn. Flin 3E 82
Pentre Hodre. Shrp 3F 59
Pentre-Llanrhaeadr. Den 4C 82
Pentre Llifior. Powy 1D 58
Pentrellwyn. IOA 2E 81
Pentre-llwyn-llwyd. Powy 5B 58
Pentre-llyn-cymmer. Cnwy 5B 82
Pentre Meyrick. V Glam 4C 32
Pentre-piod. Gwyn 2A 70
Pentre-poeth. Newp 3F 33
Pentre'r Beirdd. Powy 4D 70
Pentre'r-felin. Powy 2C 46
Pentre-ty-gwyn. Carm 2B 46
Pentre-uchaf. Gwyn 2C 68
Pentrich. Derbs 5A 86
Pentridge. Dors 1F 15
Pen-twyn. Cphy 5F 47 (nr. Oakdale)
Pentwyn. Cphy 5E 46 (nr. Rhymney)
Pentwyn. Card 3F 33
Pentyrch. Card 3E 32
Pentywyn. Carm 4G 43
Penuwch. Cdgn 4E 57
Penwithick. Corn 3E 7
Penwyllt. Powy 4B 46
Penybanc. Carm 4G 45 (nr. Ammanford)
Pen-y-banc. Carm 3G 45 (nr. Llandeilo)
Pen-y-bont. Carm 2H 43
Penybont. Powy 4D 58 (nr. Llandrindod Wells)
Pen-y-bont. Powy 3E 70 (nr. Llanfyllin)
Pen-y-Bont Ar Ogwr. B'end 3C 32
Penybontfawr. Powy 3C 70
Penybryn. Cphy 2E 33
Pen-y-bryn. Pemb 1B 44
Pen-y-bryn. Wrex 1E 71
Pen-y-cae. Powy 4B 46
Penycae. Wrex 1E 71

Pen-y-cae-mawr. *Mon* 2H 33
Penycaerau. *Gwyn* 3A 68
Pen-y-cefn. *Flin* 3D 82
Pen-y-clawdd. *Mon* 5H 47
Pen-y-coedcae. *Rhon* 3D 32
Penycwm. *Pemb* 2C 42
Pen-y-Darren. *Mer T* 5D 46
Pen-y-fai. *B'end* 3B 32
Penyffordd. *Flin* 4F 83 (nr. Mold)
Pen-y-ffordd. *Flin* 2D 82 (nr. Prestatyn)
Penyffridd. *Gwyn* 5E 81
Pen-y-garn. *Cdgn* 2F 57
Pen-y-garnedd. *IOA* 3E 81
Penygarnedd. *Powy* 3D 70
Pen-y-graig. *Gwyn* 2B 68
Penygraig. *Rhon* 2C 32
Penygraigwen. *IOA* 2D 80
Pen-y-groes. *Carm* 4F 45
Penygroes. *Gwyn* 5D 80
Penygroes. *Pemb* 1F 43
Pen-y-Mynydd. *Carm* 5E 45
Penymynydd. *Flin* 4F 83
Penyrheol. *Cphy* 3E 33
Pen-yr-heol. *Mon* 4H 47
Penyrheol. *Swan* 3E 31
Pen-yr-Heolgerrig. *Mer T* 5D 46
Penysarn. *IOA* 1D 80
Pen-y-stryt. *Den* 5E 82
Penywaun. *Rhon* 5C 46
Penzance. *Corn* 3B 4
Peopleton. *Worc* 5D 60
Peover Heath. *Ches E* 3B 84
Peper Harow. *Surr* 1A 26
Peplow. *Shrp* 3A 72
Pepper Arden. *N Yor* 4F 105
Perceton. *N Ayr* 5E 127
Percyhorner. *Abers* 2G 161
Perham Down. *Wilts* 2A 24
Periton. *Som* 2C 20
Perkinsville. *Dur* 4F 115
Perlethorpe. *Notts* 3D 86
Perranarworthal. *Corn* 5B 6
Perranporth. *Corn* 3B 6
Perranuthnoe. *Corn* 4C 4
Perranwell. *Corn* 5B 6
Perranzabuloe. *Corn* 3B 6
Perrott's Brook. *Glos* 5F 49
Perry. *W Mid* 1E 61
Perry Barr. *W Mid* 1E 61
Perry Crofts. *Staf* 5G 73
Perry Green. *Essx* 3B 54
Perry Green. *Herts* 4E 53
Perry Green. *Wilts* 3E 35
Perry Street. *Kent* 3H 39
Perry Street. *Som* 2G 13
Perrywood. *Kent* 5E 41
Pershall. *Staf* 3C 72
Pershore. *Worc* 1E 49
Pertenhall. *Bed* 4H 63
Perth. *Per* 1D 136 & 207
Perthy. *Shrp* 2F 71
Perton. *Staf* 1C 60
Pertwood. *Wilts* 3D 23
Peterborough. *Pet* 1A 64 & 208
Peterburn. *High* 5B 162
Peterchurch. *Here* 2G 47
Peterculter. *Aber* 3F 153
Peterhead. *Abers* 4H 161
Peterlee. *Dur* 5H 115
Petersfield. *Hants* 4F 25
Petersfinger. *Wilts* 4G 23
Peter's Green. *Herts* 4B 52
Peters Marland. *Devn* 1E 11
Peterstone Wentlooge. *Newp* 3F 33
Peterston-super-Ely. *V Glam* 4D 32
Peterstow. *Here* 3A 48
Peter Tavy. *Devn* 5F 11
Petertown. *Orkn* 7C 172
Petham. *Kent* 5F 41
Petherwin Gate. *Corn* 4C 10
Petrockstowe. *Devn* 2F 11
Petsoe End. *Mil* 1G 51
Pett. *E Sus* 4C 28
Pettaugh. *Suff* 5D 66
Pett Bottom. *Kent* 5F 41
Petteridge. *Kent* 1A 28
Pettinain. *S Lan* 5C 128
Pettistree. *Suff* 5E 67
Petton. *Devn* 4D 20
Petton. *Shrp* 3G 71
Petts Wood. *G Lon* 4F 39
Pettycur. *Fife* 1F 129
Pettywell. *Norf* 3C 78
Petworth. *W Sus* 3A 26
Pevensey. *E Sus* 5A 28
Pevensey Bay. *E Sus* 5A 28
Pewsey. *Wilts* 5G 35
Pheasants Hill. *Buck* 3F 37
Philadelphia. *Tyne* 4G 115
Philham. *Devn* 4C 18
Philiphaugh. *Bord* 2G 119
Phillack. *Corn* 3C 4
Philleigh. *Corn* 5C 6
Philpstoun. *W Lot* 2D 128
Phocle Green. *Here* 3B 48
Phoenix Green. *Hants* 1F 25
Pibsbury. *Som* 4H 21
Pibwrlwyd. *Carm* 4E 45
Pica. *Cumb* 2B 102
Piccadilly. *Warw* 1G 61
Piccadilly Corner. *Norf* 2E 67
Piccotts End. *Herts* 5A 52
Pickering. *N Yor* 1B 100
Picket Piece. *Hants* 2B 24
Picket Post. *Hants* 2G 15
Pickford. *W Mid* 2G 61
Pickhill. *N Yor* 1F 99
Picklenash. *Glos* 3C 48
Picklescott. *Shrp* 1G 59
Pickletillem. *Fife* 1G 137
Pickmere. *Ches E* 3A 84
Pickstock. *Telf* 3B 72
Pickwell. *Devn* 2E 19
Pickwell. *Leics* 4E 75
Pickworth. *Linc* 2H 75
Pickworth. *Rut* 4G 75
Picton. *Ches W* 3G 83
Picton. *Flin* 2D 82
Picton. *N Yor* 4B 106
Pict's Hill. *Som* 4H 21
Piddinghoe. *E Sus* 5F 27
Piddington. *Buck* 2G 37
Piddington. *Nptn* 5F 63
Piddington. *Oxon* 4E 51
Piddlehinton. *Dors* 3C 14
Piddletrenthide. *Dors* 2C 14
Pidley. *Cambs* 3C 64
Pidney. *Dors* 2C 14
Pie Corner. *Here* 4A 60
Piercebridge. *Darl* 3F 105
Pierowall. *Orkn* 3D 172
Pigdon. *Nmbd* 1E 115
Pightley. *Som* 3F 21
Pikehall. *Derbs* 5F 85
Pikeshill. *Hants* 2A 16
Pilford. *Dors* 2F 15
Pilgrims Hatch. *Essx* 1G 39
Pilham. *Linc* 1F 87
Pill. *N Som* 4A 34
Pillaton. *Corn* 2H 7
Pillaton. *Staf* 4D 72
Pillerton Hersey. *Warw* 1A 50
Pillerton Priors. *Warw* 1A 50
Pilleth. *Powy* 4E 59
Pilley. *Hants* 3B 16
Pilley. *S Yor* 4D 92
Pillgwenlly. *Newp* 3G 33
Pilling. *Lanc* 5D 96
Pilling Lane. *Lanc* 5C 96
Pillowell. *Glos* 5B 48
Pill, The. *Mon* 3H 33
Pillwell. *Dors* 1C 14
Pilning. *S Glo* 3A 34
Pilsbury. *Derbs* 4F 85
Pilsdon. *Dors* 3H 13
Pilsgate. *Pet* 5H 75
Pilsley. *Derbs* 3G 85 (nr. Bakewell)
Pilsley. *Derbs* 4B 86 (nr. Clay Cross)
Pilson Green. *Norf* 4F 79
Piltdown. *E Sus* 3F 27
Pilton. *Edin* 2F 129
Pilton. *Nptn* 2H 63
Pilton. *Rut* 5G 75
Pilton. *Som* 2A 22
Pilton Green. *Swan* 4D 30
Pimperne. *Dors* 2E 15
Pinchbeck. *Linc* 3B 76
Pinchbeck Bars. *Linc* 3A 76
Pinchbeck West. *Linc* 3B 76
Pinfold. *Lanc* 3B 90
Pinford End. *Suff* 5H 65
Pinged. *Carm* 5E 45
Pinhoe. *Devn* 3C 12
Pinkerton. *E Lot* 2D 130
Pinkneys Green. *Wind* 3G 37
Pinley. *W Mid* 3A 62
Pinley Green. *Warw* 4G 61
Pinmill. *Suff* 2F 55
Pinmore. *S Ayr* 5B 116
Pinner. *G Lon* 2C 38
Pins Green. *Worc* 1C 48
Pinsley Green. *Ches E* 1H 71
Pinvin. *Worc* 1E 49
Pinwherry. *S Ayr* 1G 109
Pinxton. *Derbs* 5B 86
Pipe and Lyde. *Here* 1A 48
Pipe Aston. *Here* 3G 59
Pipe Gate. *Shrp* 1B 72
Pipehill. *Staf* 5E 73
Piperhill. *High* 3C 158
Pipe Ridware. *Staf* 4E 73
Pipers Pool. *Corn* 4C 10
Pipewell. *Nptn* 2F 63
Pippacott. *Devn* 3F 19
Pipton. *Powy* 2E 47
Pirbright. *Surr* 5A 38
Pirnmill. *N Ayr* 5G 125
Pirton. *Herts* 2B 52
Pirton. *Worc* 1D 49
Pisgah. *Stir* 3G 135
Pishill. *Oxon* 3F 37
Pistyll. *Gwyn* 1C 68
Pitagowan. *Per* 2F 143
Pitcairn. *Per* 3F 143
Pitcairngreen. *Per* 1C 136
Pitcalnie. *High* 1C 158
Pitcaple. *Abers* 1E 152
Pitchcombe. *Glos* 5D 48
Pitchcott. *Buck* 3F 51
Pitchford. *Shrp* 5H 71
Pitch Green. *Buck* 5F 51
Pitch Place. *Surr* 5A 38
Pitcombe. *Som* 3B 22
Pitcox. *E Lot* 2C 130
Pitcur. *Per* 5B 144
Pitfichie. *Abers* 2D 152
Pitgrudy. *High* 4E 165
Pitkennedy. *Ang* 3E 145
Pitlessie. *Fife* 3F 137
Pitlochry. *Per* 3G 143
Pitmachie. *Abers* 1D 152
Pitmaduthy. *High* 1B 158
Pitmedden. *Abers* 1F 153
Pitminster. *Som* 1F 13
Pitnacree. *Per* 3G 143
Pitney. *Som* 4H 21
Pitroddie. *Per* 1E 136
Pitscottie. *Fife* 2G 137
Pitsea. *Essx* 2B 40
Pitsford. *Nptn* 4E 63
Pitsford Hill. *Som* 3E 20
Pitsmoor. *S Yor* 2A 86
Pitstone. *Buck* 4H 51
Pitt. *Hants* 4C 24
Pitt Court. *Glos* 2C 34
Pittentrail. *High* 3E 164
Pittenweem. *Fife* 3H 137
Pittington. *Dur* 5G 115
Pitton. *Swan* 4D 30
Pitton. *Wilts* 3H 23
Pittswood. *Kent* 1H 27
Pittulie. *Abers* 2G 161
Pittville. *Glos* 3E 49
Pitversie. *Per* 2D 136
Pityme. *Corn* 1D 6
Pity Me. *Dur* 5F 115
Pixey Green. *Suff* 3E 67
Pixley. *Here* 2B 48
Place Newton. *N Yor* 2C 100
Plaidy. *Abers* 3E 161
Plaidy. *Corn* 3G 7
Plain Dealings. *Pemb* 3E 43
Plains. *N Lan* 3A 128
Plainsfield. *Som* 3E 21
Plaish. *Shrp* 1H 59
Plaistow. *Here* 2B 48
Plaistow. *W Sus* 2B 26
Plaitford. *Wilts* 1A 16
Plas Llwyd. *Cnwy* 3B 82
Plastow Green. *Hants* 5D 36
Plas yn Cefn. *Den* 3C 82
Platt. *Kent* 5H 39
Platt Bridge. *G Man* 4E 90
Platt Lane. *Shrp* 2H 71
Platts Common. *S Yor* 4D 92
Platt's Heath. *Kent* 5C 40
Platt, The. *E Sus* 2G 27
Plawsworth. *Dur* 5F 115
Plaxtol. *Kent* 5H 39
Playden. *E Sus* 3D 28
Playford. *Suff* 1F 55
Play Hatch. *Oxon* 4F 37
Playing Place. *Corn* 4C 6
Playley Green. *Glos* 2C 48
Plealey. *Shrp* 5G 71
Plean. *Stir* 1B 128
Pleasington. *Bkbn* 2E 91
Pleasley. *Derbs* 4C 86
Pledgdon Green. *Essx* 3F 53
Plenmeller. *Nmbd* 3A 114
Pleshey. *Essx* 4G 53
Plockton. *High* 5H 155
Plocrapol. *W Isl* 8D 171
Ploughfield. *Here* 1G 47
Plowden. *Shrp* 2F 59
Ploxgreen. *Shrp* 5F 71
Pluckley. *Kent* 1D 28
Plucks Gutter. *Kent* 4G 41
Plumbland. *Cumb* 1C 102
Plumgarths. *Cumb* 5F 103
Plumley. *Ches E* 3B 84
Plummers Plain. *W Sus* 3D 26
Plumpton. *Cumb* 1F 103
Plumpton. *E Sus* 4E 27
Plumpton. *Nptn* 1D 50
Plumpton Foot. *Cumb* 1F 103
Plumpton Green. *E Sus* 4E 27
Plumpton Head. *Cumb* 1G 103
Plumstead. *G Lon* 3F 39
Plumstead. *Norf* 2D 78
Plumtree. *Notts* 2D 74
Plumtree Park. *Notts* 2D 74
Plungar. *Leics* 2E 75
Plush. *Dors* 2C 14
Plushabridge. *Corn* 5D 10
Plwmp. *Cdgn* 5C 56
Plymouth. *Plym* 3A 8 & 208
Plympton. *Plym* 3B 8
Plymstock. *Plym* 3B 8
Plymtree. *Devn* 2D 12
Pockley. *N Yor* 1A 100
Pocklington. *E Yor* 5C 100
Pode Hole. *Linc* 3B 76
Podimore. *Som* 4A 22
Podington. *Bed* 4G 63
Podmore. *Staf* 2B 72
Poffley End. *Oxon* 4B 50
Point Clear. *Essx* 4D 54
Pointon. *Linc* 2A 76
Pokesdown. *Bour* 3G 15
Polbae. *Dum* 2H 109
Polbain. *High* 3E 163
Polbathic. *Corn* 3H 7
Polbeth. *W Lot* 3D 128
Polbrock. *Corn* 2E 6
Polchar. *High* 3C 150
Polebrook. *Nptn* 2H 63
Pole Elm. *Worc* 1D 48
Polegate. *E Sus* 5G 27
Pole Moor. *W Yor* 3A 92
Poles. *High* 4E 165
Polesworth. *Warw* 5G 73
Polglass. *High* 3E 163
Polgooth. *Corn* 3D 6
Poling. *W Sus* 5B 26
Poling Corner. *W Sus* 5B 26
Polio. *High* 1B 158
Polkerris. *Corn* 3E 7
Polla. *High* 3D 166
Pollard Street. *Norf* 2F 79
Pollicott. *Buck* 4F 51
Pollington. *E Yor* 3G 93
Polloch. *High* 2B 140
Pollok. *Glas* 3G 127
Pollokshaws. *Glas* 3G 127
Pollokshields. *Glas* 3G 127
Polmaily. *High* 5G 157
Polmassick. *Corn* 4D 6
Polmont. *Falk* 2C 128
Polnessan. *E Ayr* 3D 116
Polnish. *High* 5F 147
Polperro. *Corn* 3G 7
Polruan. *Corn* 3F 7
Polscoe. *Corn* 2F 7
Polsham. *Som* 2A 22
Polskeoch. *Dum* 4F 117
Polstead. *Suff* 2C 54
Polstead Heath. *Suff* 1C 54
Poltesco. *Corn* 5E 5
Poltimore. *Devn* 3C 12
Polton. *Midl* 3G 129
Polwarth. *Bord* 4D 130
Polyphant. *Corn* 4C 10
Polzeath. *Corn* 1D 6
Ponde. *Powy* 2E 46
Pondersbridge. *Cambs* 1B 64
Ponders End. *G Lon* 1E 39
Pond Street. *Essx* 2E 53
Pondtail. *Hants* 1G 25
Ponsanooth. *Corn* 5B 6
Ponsongath. *Corn* 5E 5
Ponsworthy. *Devn* 5H 11
Pontamman. *Carm* 4G 45
Pontantwn. *Carm* 4E 45
Pontardawe. *Neat* 5H 45
Pontarddulais. *Swan* 5F 45
Pontarfynach. *Cdgn* 3G 57
Pont-ar-gothi. *Carm* 3F 45
Pont ar Hydfer. *Powy* 3B 46
Pontarllechau. *Carm* 3H 45
Pontarsais. *Carm* 3E 45
Pontblyddyn. *Flin* 4E 83
Pontbren Llwyd. *Rhon* 5C 46
Pont Cyfyng. *Cnwy* 5G 81
Pontdolgoch. *Powy* 1C 58
Pontefract. *W Yor* 2E 93
Ponteland. *Nmbd* 2E 115
Ponterwyd. *Cdgn* 2G 57
Pontesbury. *Shrp* 5G 71
Pontesford. *Shrp* 5G 71
Pontfadog. *Wrex* 2E 71
Pontfaen. *Pemb* 1E 43
Pont-faen. *Powy* 2C 46
Pont-Faen. *Shrp* 2E 71
Pontgarreg. *Cdgn* 5C 56
Pont-Henri. *Carm* 5E 45
Ponthir. *Torf* 2G 33
Ponthirwaun. *Cdgn* 1C 44
Pont-iets. *Carm* 5E 45
Pontllanfraith. *Cphy* 2E 33
Pontlliw. *Swan* 5G 45
Pont Llogel. *Powy* 4C 70
Pontllyfni. *Gwyn* 5D 80
Pontlottyn. *Cphy* 5E 46
Pontneddfechan. *Neat* 5C 46
Pont-newydd. *Carm* 5E 45
Pont-newydd. *Flin* 4D 82
Pontnewydd. *Torf* 2F 33
Ponton. *Shet* 6E 173
Pont Pen-y-benglog. *Gwyn* 4F 81
Pontrhydfendigaid. *Cdgn* 4G 57
Pont Rhyd-y-cyff. *B'end* 3B 32
Pontrhydyfen. *Neat* 2A 32
Pont-rhyd-y-groes. *Cdgn* 3G 57
Pontrhydyrun. *Torf* 2F 33
Pont Rhythallt. *Gwyn* 4E 81
Pontrilas. *Here* 3G 47
Pontrilas Road. *Here* 3G 47
Pontrobert. *Powy* 4D 70
Pont-rug. *Gwyn* 4E 81
Ponts Green. *E Sus* 4A 28
Pontshill. *Here* 3B 48
Pont-Sian. *Cdgn* 1E 45
Pontsticill. *Mer T* 4D 46
Pont-Walby. *Neat* 5B 46
Pontwelly. *Carm* 2E 45
Pontwgan. *Cnwy* 3G 81
Pontyates. *Carm* 5E 45
Pontyberem. *Carm* 4F 45
Pontybodkin. *Flin* 5E 83
Pontyclun. *Rhon* 3D 32
Pontycymer. *B'end* 2C 32
Pontyglazier. *Pemb* 1F 43
Pontygwaith. *Rhon* 2D 32
Pont-y-pant. *Cnwy* 5G 81
Pontypool. *Torf* 2G 33
Pontypridd. *Rhon* 2D 32
Pontypwl. *Torf* 2G 33
Pontywaun. *Cphy* 2F 33
Pooksgreen. *Hants* 1B 16
Pool. *Corn* 4A 6
Pool. *W Yor* 5E 99
Poole. *N Yor* 2E 93
Poole. *Pool* 3F 15 & 215
Poole. *Som* 4E 21
Poole Keynes. *Glos* 2E 35
Poolend. *Staf* 5D 84
Poolewe. *High* 5C 162
Pooley Bridge. *Cumb* 2F 103
Poolfold. *Staf* 5C 84
Pool Head. *Here* 5H 59
Pool Hey. *Lanc* 3B 90
Poolhill. *Glos* 3C 48
Poolmill. *Here* 3A 48
Pool o' Muckhart. *Clac* 3C 136
Pool Quay. *Powy* 4E 71
Poolsbrook. *Derbs* 3B 86
Pool Street. *Essx* 2A 54
Pootings. *Kent* 1F 27
Pope Hill. *Pemb* 3D 42
Pope's Hill. *Glos* 4B 48
Popeswood. *Brac* 5G 37
Popham. *Hants* 2D 24
Poplar. *G Lon* 2E 39
Popley. *Hants* 1E 25
Porchfield. *IOW* 3C 16
Porin. *High* 3F 157
Poringland. *Norf* 5E 79
Porkellis. *Corn* 5A 6
Porlock. *Som* 2B 20
Porlock Weir. *Som* 2B 20
Portachoillan. *Arg* 4F 125
Port Adhair Bheinn na Faoghla. *W Isl* 3C 170
Port Adhair Thirlodh. *Arg* 4B 138
Port Ann. *Arg* 1H 125
Port Appin. *Arg* 4D 140
Port Asgaig. *Arg* 3C 124
Port Askaig. *Arg* 3C 124
Portavadie. *Arg* 3H 125
Port Bannatyne. *Arg* 3B 126
Portbury. *N Som* 4A 34
Port Carlisle. *Cumb* 3D 112
Port Charlotte. *Arg* 4A 124
Portchester. *Hants* 2E 16
Port Clarence. *Stoc T* 2B 106
Port Dinorwig. *Gwyn* 4E 81
Port Driseach. *Arg* 2A 126
Port Dundas. *Glas* 3H 127
Port Ellen. *Arg* 5B 124
Port Elphinstone. *Abers* 1E 153
Portencalzie. *Dum* 2F 109
Portencross. *N Ayr* 5C 126
Port Erin. *IOM* 5A 108
Port Erroll. *Abers* 5H 161
Porter's Fen Corner. *Norf* 5E 77
Portesham. *Dors* 4B 14
Portessie. *Mor* 2B 160
Port e Vullen. *IOM* 2D 108
Port-Eynon. *Swan* 4D 30
Portfield. *Som* 4H 21
Portfield Gate. *Pemb* 3D 42
Portgate. *Devn* 4E 11
Port Gaverne. *Corn* 4A 10
Port Glasgow. *Inv* 2E 127
Portgordon. *Mor* 2A 160
Portgower. *High* 2H 165
Porth. *Corn* 2C 6
Porth. *Rhon* 2D 32
Porthaethwy. *IOA* 3E 81
Porthallow. *Corn* 3G 7 (nr. Looe)
Porthallow. *Corn* 4E 5 (nr. St Keverne)
Porthalong. *High* 5C 154
Porthcawl. *B'end* 4B 32
Porthceri. *V Glam* 5D 32
Porthcothan. *Corn* 1C 6
Porthcurno. *Corn* 4A 4
Port Henderson. *High* 1G 155
Porthgain. *Pemb* 1C 42
Porthgwarra. *Corn* 4A 4
Porthill. *Shrp* 4G 71
Porthkerry. *V Glam* 5D 32
Porthleven. *Corn* 4D 4
Porthllechog. *IOA* 1D 80
Porthmadog. *Gwyn* 2E 69
Porthmeirion. *Gwyn* 2E 69
Porthmeor. *Corn* 3B 4
Porth Navas. *Corn* 4E 5
Porthoustock. *Corn* 4F 5
Porthtowan. *Corn* 4A 6
Porth Tywyn. *Carm* 5E 45
Porth-y-felin. *IOA* 2B 80
Porthyrhyd. *Carm* 4F 45 (nr. Carmarthen)
Porthyrhyd. *Carm* 2H 45 (nr. Llandovery)
Porth-y-waen. *Shrp* 3E 71
Portincaple. *Arg* 4B 134
Portington. *E Yor* 1A 94
Portinnisherrich. *Arg* 2G 133
Portinscale. *Cumb* 2D 102
Port Isaac. *Corn* 1D 6
Portishead. *N Som* 4H 33

Portknockie. *Mor* 2B **160**
Port Lamont. *Arg* 2B **126**
Portlethen. *Abers* 4G **153**
Portlethen Village. *Abers* 4G **153**
Portling. *Dum* 4F **111**
Port Lion. *Pemb* 4D **43**
Portloe. *Corn* 5D **6**
Port Logan. *Dum* 5F **109**
Portmahomack. *High* 5G **165**
Port Mead. *Swan* 3F **31**
Portmellon. *Corn* 4E **6**
Port Mholair. *W Isl* 4H **171**
Port Mor. *High* 1F **139**
Portmore. *Hants* 3B **16**
Port Mulgrave. *N Yor* 3E **107**
Portnacroish. *Arg* 4D **140**
Portnahaven. *Arg* 4A **124**
Portnalong. *High* 5C **154**
Portnaluchaig. *High* 5E **147**
Portnancon. *High* 2E **167**
Port Nan Giuran. *W Isl* 4H **171**
Port nan Long. *W Isl* 1D **170**
Port Nis. *W Isl* 1H **171**
Portobello. *Edin* 2G **129**
Portobello. *W Yor* 3D **92**
Port of Menteith. *Stir* 3E **135**
Porton. *Wilts* 3G **23**
Portormin. *High* 5D **168**
Portpatrick. *Dum* 4F **109**
Port Quin. *Corn* 1D **6**
Port Ramsay. *Arg* 4C **140**
Portreath. *Corn* 4A **6**
Portree. *High* 4D **155**
Port Righ. *High* 4D **155**
Port St Mary. *IOM* 5B **108**
Portscatho. *Corn* 5C **6**
Portsea. *Port* 2E **17**
Portskerra. *High* 2A **168**
Portskewett. *Mon* 3A **34**
Portslade-by-Sea. *Brig* 5D **26**
Portsmouth. *Port* 3E **17 & 209**
Portsmouth. *W Yor* 2H **91**
Port Soderick. *IOM* 4C **108**
Port Solent. *Port* 2E **17**
Portsonachan. *Arg* 1H **133**
Portsoy. *Abers* 2C **160**
Port Sunlight. *Mers* 2F **83**
Portswood. *Sotn* 1C **16**
Port Talbot. *Neat* 4G **31**
Porttannachy. *Mor* 2A **160**
Port Tennant. *Swan* 3F **31**
Portuairk. *High* 2F **139**
Portway. *Here* 1H **47**
Portway. *Worc* 3E **61**
Port Wemyss. *Arg* 4A **124**
Port William. *Dum* 5A **110**
Portwrinkle. *Corn* 3H **7**
Poslingford. *Suff* 1A **54**
Postbridge. *Devn* 5G **11**
Postcombe. *Oxon* 2F **37**
Post Green. *Dors* 3E **15**
Posthill. *Staf* 5G **73**
Postling. *Kent* 2F **29**
Postlip. *Glos* 3F **49**
Post-Mawr. *Cdgn* 5D **56**
Postwick. *Norf* 5E **79**
Potarch. *Abers* 4D **152**
Potsgrove. *C Beds* 3H **51**
Potten End. *Herts* 5A **52**
Potter Brompton. *N Yor* 2D **101**
Pottergate Street. *Norf* 1D **66**
Potterhanworth. *Linc* 4H **87**
Potterhanworth Booths. *Linc* 4H **87**
Potter Heigham. *Norf* 4G **79**
Potter Hill. *Leics* 3E **75**
Potteries, The. *Stoke* 1C **72**
Potterne. *Wilts* 1E **23**
Potterne Wick. *Wilts* 1E **23**
Potternewton. *W Yor* 1D **92**
Potters Bar. *Herts* 5C **52**
Potters Brook. *Lanc* 4D **97**
Potter's Cross. *Staf* 2C **60**
Potters Crouch. *Herts* 5B **52**
Potter Somersal. *Derbs* 2F **73**
Potterspury. *Nptn* 1F **51**
Potter Street. *Essx* 5E **53**
Potterton. *Abers* 2G **153**
Potthorpe. *Norf* 3B **78**
Pottle Street. *Wilts* 2D **22**
Potto. *N Yor* 4B **106**
Potton. *C Beds* 1C **52**
Pott Row. *Norf* 3G **77**
Pott Shrigley. *Ches E* 3D **84**
Poughill. *Corn* 2C **10**
Poughill. *Devn* 2B **12**
Poulner. *Hants* 2G **15**
Poulshot. *Wilts* 1E **23**
Poulton. *Glos* 5G **49**
Poulton-le-Fylde. *Lanc* 1B **90**
Pound Bank. *Worc* 3B **60**
Poundbury. *Dors* 3B **14**
Poundfield. *E Sus* 2G **27**
Poundgate. *E Sus* 3F **27**
Pound Green. *E Sus* 3G **27**
Pound Green. *Suff* 5G **65**
Pound Hill. *W Sus* 2D **27**
Poundland. *S Ayr* 1G **109**
Poundon. *Buck* 3E **51**
Poundsgate. *Devn* 5H **11**
Poundstock. *Corn* 3C **10**
Pound Street. *Hants* 5C **36**
Pounsley. *E Sus* 3G **27**
Powburn. *Nmbd* 3E **121**
Powderham. *Devn* 4C **12**
Powerstock. *Dors* 3A **14**
Powfoot. *Dum* 3C **112**
Powick. *Worc* 5C **60**
Powmill. *Per* 4C **136**
Poxwell. *Dors* 4C **14**
Poyle. *Slo* 3B **38**
Poynings. *W Sus* 4D **26**
Poyntington. *Dors* 4B **22**
Poynton. *Ches E* 2D **84**
Poynton. *Telf* 4H **71**
Poynton Green. *Telf* 4H **71**
Poystreet Green. *Suff* 5B **66**
Praa Sands. *Corn* 4C **4**
Pratt's Bottom. *G Lon* 4F **39**
Praze-an-Beeble. *Corn* 3D **4**
Prees. *Shrp* 2H **71**
Preesall. *Lanc* 5C **96**
Preesall Park. *Lanc* 5C **96**
Prees Green. *Shrp* 2H **71**
Prees Higher Heath. *Shrp* 2H **71**
Prendergast. *Pemb* 3D **42**
Prendwick. *Nmbd* 3E **121**
Pren-gwyn. *Cdgn* 1E **45**
Prenteg. *Gwyn* 1E **69**
Prenton. *Mers* 2F **83**
Prescot. *Mers* 1G **83**
Prescott. *Devn* 1D **12**
Prescott. *Shrp* 3G **71**
Preshute. *Wilts* 5G **35**
Pressen. *Nmbd* 1C **120**
Prestatyn. *Den* 2C **82**
Prestbury. *Ches E* 3D **84**
Prestbury. *Glos* 3E **49**
Presteigne. *Powy* 4F **59**
Presthope. *Shrp* 1H **59**
Prestleigh. *Som* 2B **22**
Preston. *Brig* 5E **27**
Preston. *Devn* 5B **12**
Preston. *Dors* 4C **14**
Preston. *E Lot* 2B **130**
(nr. East Linton)
Preston. *E Lot* 2G **129**
(nr. Prestonpans)
Preston. *E Yor* 1E **95**
Preston. *Glos* 5F **49**
Preston. *Herts* 3B **52**
Preston. *Kent* 4G **41**
(nr. Canterbury)
Preston. *Kent* 4E **40**
(nr. Faversham)
Preston. *Lanc* 2D **90 & 208**
Preston. *Nmbd* 2F **121**
Preston. *Rut* 5F **75**
Preston. *Bord* 4D **130**
Preston. *Shrp* 4H **71**
Preston. *Suff* 5B **66**
Preston. *Wilts* 4A **36**
(nr. Aldbourne)
Preston. *Wilts* 4F **35**
(nr. Lyneham)
Preston Bagot. *Warw* 4F **61**
Preston Bissett. *Buck* 3E **51**
Preston Bowyer. *Som* 4E **21**
Preston Brockhurst. *Shrp* 3H **71**
Preston Brook. *Hal* 3H **83**
Preston Candover. *Hants* 2E **24**
Preston Capes. *Nptn* 5C **62**
Preston Cross. *Glos* 2B **48**
Preston Gubbals. *Shrp* 4G **71**
Preston-le-Skerne. *Dur* 2A **106**
Preston Marsh. *Here* 1A **48**
Prestonmill. *Dum* 4A **112**
Preston on Stour. *Warw* 5G **61**
Preston on the Hill. *Hal* 2H **83**
Preston on Wye. *Here* 1G **47**
Prestonpans. *E Lot* 2G **129**
Preston Plucknett. *Som* 1A **14**
Preston-under-Scar. *N Yor* 5D **104**
Preston upon the Weald Moors. *Telf* 4A **72**
Preston Wynne. *Here* 1A **48**
Prestwich. *G Man* 4G **91**
Prestwick. *Nmbd* 2E **115**
Prestwick. *S Ayr* 2C **116**
Prestwold. *Leics* 3C **74**
Prestwood. *Buck* 5G **51**
Prestwood. *Staf* 1E **73**
Price Town. *B'end* 2C **32**
Prickwillow. *Cambs* 2E **65**
Priddy. *Som* 1A **22**
Priestcliffe. *Derbs* 3F **85**
Priesthill. *Glas* 3G **127**
Priest Hutton. *Lanc* 2E **97**
Priestland. *E Ayr* 1E **117**
Priest Weston. *Shrp* 1E **59**
Priestwood. *Brac* 4G **37**
Priestwood. *Kent* 4A **40**
Primethorpe. *Leics* 1C **62**
Primrose Green. *Norf* 4C **78**
Primrose Hill. *Derbs* 5B **86**
Primrose Hill. *Glos* 5B **48**
Primrose Hill. *Lanc* 4B **90**
Primrose Valley. *N Yor* 2F **101**
Primsidemill. *Bord* 2C **120**
Princes Gate. *Pemb* 3F **43**
Princes Risborough. *Buck* 5G **51**
Princethorpe. *Warw* 3B **62**
Princetown. *Devn* 5F **11**
Prinsted. *W Sus* 2F **17**
Prion. *Den* 4C **82**
Prior Muir. *Fife* 2H **137**
Prior's Frome. *Here* 2A **48**
Priors Halton. *Shrp* 3G **59**
Priors Hardwick. *Warw* 5B **62**
Priorslee. *Telf* 4B **72**
Priors Marston. *Warw* 5B **62**
Prior's Norton. *Glos* 3D **48**
Priory, The. *W Ber* 5B **36**
Priory Wood. *Here* 1F **47**
Priston. *Bath* 5B **34**
Pristow Green. *Norf* 2D **66**
Prittlewell. *S'end* 2C **40**
Privett. *Hants* 4E **25**
Prixford. *Devn* 3F **19**
Probus. *Corn* 4D **6**
Prospect. *Cumb* 5C **112**
Prospect Village. *Staf* 4E **73**
Provanmill. *Glas* 3H **127**
Prudhoe. *Nmbd* 3D **115**
Publow. *Bath* 5B **34**
Puckeridge. *Herts* 3D **53**
Puckington. *Som* 1G **13**
Pucklechurch. *S Glo* 4B **34**
Puckrup. *Glos* 2D **49**
Puddinglake. *Ches W* 4B **84**
Puddington. *Ches W* 3F **83**
Puddington. *Devn* 1B **12**
Puddlebrook. *Glos* 4B **48**
Puddledock. *Norf* 1C **66**
Puddletown. *Dors* 3C **14**
Pudleston. *Here* 5H **59**
Pudsey. *W Yor* 1C **92**
Pulborough. *W Sus* 4B **26**
Puleston. *Telf* 3B **72**
Pulford. *Ches W* 5F **83**
Pulham. *Dors* 2C **14**
Pulham Market. *Norf* 2D **66**
Pulham St Mary. *Norf* 2E **66**
Pulley. *Shrp* 5G **71**
Pulloxhill. *C Beds* 2A **52**
Pulpit Hill. *Arg* 1F **133**
Pulverbatch. *Shrp* 5G **71**
Pumpherston. *W Lot* 3D **128**
Pumsaint. *Carm* 1G **45**
Puncheston. *Pemb* 2E **43**
Puncknowle. *Dors* 4A **14**
Punnett's Town. *E Sus* 3H **27**
Purbrook. *Hants* 2E **17**
Purfleet. *Thur* 3G **39**
Puriton. *Som* 2G **21**
Purleigh. *Essx* 5B **54**
Purley. *G Lon* 4E **39**
Purley on Thames. *W Ber* 4E **37**
Purlogue. *Shrp* 3E **59**
Purl's Bridge. *Cambs* 2D **65**
Purse Caundle. *Dors* 1B **14**
Purslow. *Shrp* 2F **59**
Purston Jaglin. *W Yor* 3E **93**
Purtington. *Som* 2G **13**
Purton. *Glos* 5B **48**
(nr. Lydney)
Purton. *Glos* 5B **48**
(nr. Sharpness)
Purton. *Wilts* 3F **35**
Purton Stoke. *Wilts* 2F **35**
Pury End. *Nptn* 1F **51**
Pusey. *Oxon* 2B **36**
Putley. *Here* 2B **48**
Putney. *G Lon* 3D **38**
Putsborough. *Devn* 2E **19**
Puttenham. *Herts* 4G **51**
Puttenham. *Surr* 1A **26**
Puttock End. *Essx* 1B **54**
Puttock's End. *Essx* 4F **53**
Puxey. *Dors* 1C **14**
Puxton. *N Som* 5H **33**
Pwll. *Carm* 5E **45**
Pwll. *Powy* 5D **70**
Pwllcrochan. *Pemb* 4D **42**
Pwll-glas. *Den* 5D **82**
Pwllgloyw. *Powy* 2D **46**
Pwllheli. *Gwyn* 2C **68**
Pwllmeyric. *Mon* 2A **34**
Pwlltrap. *Carm* 3G **43**
Pwll-y-glaw. *Neat* 2A **32**
Pyecombe. *W Sus* 4D **27**
Pye Corner. *Herts* 4E **53**
Pye Corner. *Newp* 3G **33**
Pye Green. *Staf* 4D **73**
Pyewipe. *NE Lin* 3F **95**
Pyle. *B'end* 3B **32**
Pyle. *IOW* 5C **16**
Pylle. *Som* 3B **22**
Pymoor. *Cambs* 2D **65**
Pymoor. *Dors* 3H **13**
Pyrford. *Surr* 5B **38**
Pyrford Village. *Surr* 5B **38**
Pyrton. *Oxon* 2E **37**
Pytchley. *Nptn* 3F **63**
Pyworthy. *Devn* 2D **10**

Q

Quabbs. *Shrp* 2E **58**
Quadring. *Linc* 2B **76**
Quadring Eaudike. *Linc* 2B **76**
Quainton. *Buck* 3F **51**
Quaking Houses. *Dur* 4E **115**
Quarley. *Hants* 2A **24**
Quarndon. *Derbs* 1H **73**
Quarrendon. *Buck* 4G **51**
Quarrier's Village. *Inv* 3E **127**
Quarrington. *Linc* 1H **75**
Quarrington Hill. *Dur* 1A **106**
Quarry Bank. *W Mid* 2D **60**
Quarry, The. *Glos* 2C **34**
Quarrywood. *Mor* 2F **159**
Quartalehouse. *Abers* 4G **161**
Quarter. *N Ayr* 3C **126**
Quarter. *S Lan* 4A **128**
Quatford. *Shrp* 1B **60**
Quatt. *Shrp* 2B **60**
Quebec. *Dur* 5E **115**
Quedgeley. *Glos* 4D **48**
Queen Adelaide. *Cambs* 2E **65**
Queenborough. *Kent* 3D **40**
Queen Camel. *Som* 4A **22**
Queen Charlton. *Bath* 5B **34**
Queen Dart. *Devn* 1B **12**
Queenhill. *Worc* 2D **48**
Queen Oak. *Dors* 3C **22**
Queensbury. *W Yor* 2B **92**
Queensferry. *Flin* 4F **83**
Queenstown. *Bkpl* 1B **90**
Queen Street. *Kent* 1A **28**
Queenzieburn. *N Lan* 2H **127**
Quemerford. *Wilts* 5F **35**
Quendale. *Shet* 10E **173**
Quendon. *Essx* 2F **53**
Queniborough. *Leics* 4D **74**
Quenington. *Glos* 5G **49**
Quernmore. *Lanc* 3E **97**
Quethiock. *Corn* 2H **7**
Quholm. *Orkn* 6B **172**
Quick's Green. *W Ber* 4D **36**
Quidenham. *Norf* 2C **66**
Quidhampton. *Hants* 1D **24**
Quidhampton. *Wilts* 3G **23**
Quilquox. *Abers* 5G **161**
Quina Brook. *Shrp* 2H **71**
Quindry. *Orkn* 8D **172**
Quine's Hill. *IOM* 4C **108**
Quinton. *Nptn* 5E **63**
Quinton. *W Mid* 2D **61**
Quintrell Downs. *Corn* 2C **6**
Quixhill. *Staf* 1F **73**
Quoditch. *Devn* 3E **11**
Quorn. *Leics* 4C **74**
Quorndon. *Leics* 4C **74**
Quothquan. *S Lan* 1B **118**
Quoyloo. *Orkn* 5B **172**
Quoyness. *Orkn* 7B **172**
Quoys. *Shet* 5F **173**
(on Mainland)
Quoys. *Shet* 1H **173**
(on Unst)

R

Rableyheath. *Herts* 4C **52**
Raby. *Cumb* 4C **112**
Raby. *Mers* 3F **83**
Rachan Mill. *Bord* 1D **118**
Rachub. *Gwyn* 4F **81**
Rack End. *Oxon* 5C **50**
Rackenford. *Devn* 1B **12**
Rackham. *W Sus* 4B **26**
Rackheath. *Norf* 4E **79**
Racks. *Dum* 2B **112**
Rackwick. *Orkn* 8A **172**
(on Hoy)
Rackwick. *Orkn* 3D **172**
(on Westray)
Radbourne. *Derbs* 2G **73**
Radcliffe. *G Man* 4F **91**
Radcliffe. *Nmbd* 4G **121**
Radcliffe on Trent. *Notts* 2D **74**
Radclive. *Buck* 2E **51**
Radernie. *Fife* 2G **137**
Radfall. *Kent* 4F **41**
Radford. *Bath* 1B **22**
Radford. *Nott* 1C **74**
Radford. *Oxon* 3C **50**
Radford. *W Mid* 2H **61**
Radford. *Worc* 5E **61**
Radford Semele. *Warw* 4H **61**
Radipole. *Dors* 4B **14**
Radlett. *Herts* 1C **38**
Radley. *Oxon* 2D **36**
Radnage. *Buck* 2F **37**
Radstock. *Bath* 1B **22**
Radstone. *Nptn* 1D **50**
Radway. *Warw* 1B **50**
Radway Green. *Ches E* 5B **84**
Radwell. *Bed* 5H **63**
Radwell. *Herts* 2C **52**
Radwinter. *Essx* 2G **53**
Radyr. *Card* 3E **33**
RAF Coltishall. *Norf* 3E **79**
Rafford. *Mor* 3E **159**
Ragdale. *Leics* 4D **74**
Ragdon. *Shrp* 1G **59**
Ragged Appleshaw. *Hants* 2B **24**
Raggra. *High* 4F **169**
Raglan. *Mon* 5H **47**
Ragnall. *Notts* 3F **87**
Raigbeg. *High* 1C **150**
Rainford. *Mers* 4C **90**
Rainford Junction. *Mers* 4C **90**
Rainham. *G Lon* 2G **39**
Rainham. *Medw* 4C **40**
Rainhill. *Mers* 1G **83**
Rainow. *Ches E* 3D **84**
Rainton. *N Yor* 2F **99**
Rainworth. *Notts* 5C **86**
Raisbeck. *Cumb* 4H **103**
Raise. *Cumb* 5A **114**
Rait. *Per* 1E **137**
Raithby. *Linc* 2C **88**
Raithby by Spilsby. *Linc* 4C **88**
Raithwaite. *N Yor* 3F **107**
Rake. *W Sus* 4G **25**
Rake End. *Staf* 4E **73**
Rakeway. *Staf* 1E **73**
Rakewood. *G Man* 3H **91**
Ralia. *High* 4B **150**
Ram Alley. *Wilts* 5H **35**
Ramasaig. *High* 4A **154**
Rame. *Corn* 4A **8**
(nr. Millbrook)
Rame. *Corn* 5B **6**
(nr. Penryn)
Ram Lane. *Kent* 1D **28**
Ramnageo. *Shet* 1H **173**
Rampisham. *Dors* 2A **14**
Rampside. *Cumb* 3B **96**
Rampton. *Cambs* 4D **64**
Rampton. *Notts* 3E **87**
Ramsbottom. *G Man* 3F **91**
Ramsburn. *Mor* 3C **160**
Ramsbury. *Wilts* 4A **36**
Ramscraigs. *High* 1H **165**
Ramsdean. *Hants* 4F **25**
Ramsdell. *Hants* 1D **24**
Ramsden. *Oxon* 4B **50**
Ramsden. *Worc* 1E **49**
Ramsden Bellhouse. *Essx* 1B **40**
Ramsden Heath. *Essx* 1B **40**
Ramsey. *Cambs* 2B **64**
Ramsey. *Essx* 2F **55**
Ramsey. *IOM* 2D **108**
Ramsey Forty Foot. *Cambs* 2C **64**
Ramsey Heights. *Cambs* 2B **64**
Ramsey Island. *Essx* 5C **54**
Ramsey Mereside. *Cambs* 2B **64**
Ramsey St Mary's. *Cambs* 2B **64**
Ramsgate. *Kent* 4H **41**
Ramsgill. *N Yor* 2D **98**
Ramshaw. *Dur* 5C **114**
Ramshorn. *Staf* 1E **73**
Ramsley. *Devn* 3G **11**
Ramsnest Common. *Surr* 2A **26**
Ramstone. *Abers* 2D **152**
Ranais. *W Isl* 5G **171**
Ranby. *Linc* 3B **88**
Ranby. *Notts* 2D **86**
Rand. *Linc* 3A **88**
Randwick. *Glos* 5D **48**
Ranfurly. *Ren* 3E **127**
Rangag. *High* 4D **168**
Rangemore. *Staf* 3F **73**
Rangeworthy. *S Glo* 3B **34**
Rankinston. *E Ayr* 3D **116**
Rank's Green. *Essx* 4H **53**
Ranmore Common. *Surr* 5C **38**
Rannoch Station. *Per* 3B **142**
Ranochan. *High* 5G **147**
Ranskill. *Notts* 2D **86**
Ranton. *Staf* 3C **72**
Ranton Green. *Staf* 3C **72**
Ranworth. *Norf* 4F **79**
Raploch. *Stir* 4G **135**
Rapness. *Orkn* 3E **172**
Rapps. *Som* 1G **13**
Rascal Moor. *E Yor* 1B **94**
Rascarrel. *Dum* 5E **111**
Rashfield. *Arg* 1C **126**
Rashwood. *Worc* 4D **60**
Raskelf. *N Yor* 2G **99**
Rassau. *Blae* 4E **47**
Rastrick. *W Yor* 2B **92**
Ratagan. *High* 2B **148**
Ratby. *Leics* 5C **74**
Ratcliffe Culey. *Leics* 1H **61**
Ratcliffe on Soar. *Notts* 3B **74**
Ratcliffe on the Wreake. *Leics* 4D **74**
Rathen. *Abers* 2H **161**
Rathillet. *Fife* 1F **137**
Rathmell. *N Yor* 4H **97**
Ratho. *Edin* 2E **129**
Ratho Station. *Edin* 2E **129**
Rathven. *Mor* 2B **160**
Ratley. *Hants* 4B **24**
Ratley. *Warw* 1B **50**
Ratlinghope. *Shrp* 1G **59**
Rattar. *High* 1E **169**
Ratten Row. *Cumb* 5E **113**
Ratten Row. *Lanc* 5D **96**
Rattery. *Devn* 2D **8**
Rattlesden. *Suff* 5B **66**
Ratton Village. *E Sus* 5G **27**
Rattray. *Abers* 3H **161**
Rattray. *Per* 4A **144**
Raughton. *Cumb* 5E **113**
Raughton Head. *Cumb* 5E **113**
Raunds. *Nptn* 3G **63**
Ravenfield. *S Yor* 1B **86**
Ravenfield Common. *S Yor* 1B **86**
Ravenglass. *Cumb* 5B **102**
Ravenhills Green. *Worc* 5B **60**
Raveningham. *Norf* 1F **67**
Ravenscar. *N Yor* 4G **107**

Ravensdale. IOM 2C 108
Ravensden. Bed 5H 63
Ravenseat. N Yor 4B 104
Ravenshead. Notts 5C 86
Ravensmoor. Ches E 5A 84
Ravensthorpe. Nptn 3D 62
Ravensthorpe. W Yor 2C 92
Ravenstone. Leics 4B 74
Ravenstonedale. Cumb 4A 104
Ravenstown. Cumb 2C 96
Ravenstruther. S Lan 5C 128
Ravensworth. N Yor 4E 105
Raw. N Yor 4G 107
Rawcliffe. E Yor 2G 93
Rawcliffe. York 4H 99
Rawcliffe Bridge. E Yor 2G 93
Rawdon. W Yor 1C 92
Rawgreen. Nmbd 4C 114
Rawmarsh. S Yor 1B 86
Rawnsley. Staf 4E 73
Rawreth. Essx 1B 40
Rawridge. Devn 2F 13
Rawson Green. Derbs 1A 74
Rawtenstall. Lanc 2F 91
Raydon. Suff 2D 54
Raylees. Nmbd 5D 120
Rayleigh. Essx 1C 40
Raymond's Hill. Devn 3G 13
Rayne. Essx 3H 53
Rayners Lane. G Lon 2C 38
Reach. Cambs 4E 65
Read. Lanc 1F 91
Reading. Read 4F 37 & 209
Reading Green. Suff 3D 66
Reading Street. Kent 2D 28
Readymoney. Corn 3F 7
Reagill. Cumb 3H 103
Rea Hill. Torb 3F 9
Rearquhar. High 4E 165
Rearsby. Leics 4D 74
Reasby. Linc 3H 87
Reaseheath. Ches E 5A 84
Reaster. High 2E 169
Reawick. Shet 7E 173
Reay. High 2B 168
Rechullin. High 3A 156
Reculver. Kent 4G 41
Redberth. Pemb 4E 43
Redbourn. Herts 4B 52
Redbourne. N Lin 4C 94
Redbrook. Glos 4A 48
Redbrook. Wrex 1H 71
Redburn. High 4D 158
Redburn. Nmbd 3A 114
Redcar. Red C 2D 106
Redcastle. High 4H 157
Redcliff Bay. N Som 4H 33
Red Dial. Cumb 5D 112
Redding. Falk 2C 128
Reddingmuirhead. Falk 2C 128
Reddings, The. Glos 3E 49
Reddish. G Man 1C 84
Redditch. Worc 4E 61
Rede. Suff 5H 65
Redenhall. Norf 2E 67
Redesdale Camp. Nmbd 5C 120
Redesmouth. Nmbd 1B 114
Redford. Ang 4E 145
Redford. Dur 1D 105
Redford. W Sus 4G 25
Redfordgreen. Bord 3F 119
Redgate. Corn 2G 7
Redgrave. Suff 3C 66
Redhill. Abers 3E 153
Redhill. Herts 2C 52
Redhill. N Som 5H 33
Redhill. Shrp 4B 72
Redhill. Surr 5D 39
Red Hill. Warw 5F 61
Red Hill. W Yor 2E 93
Redhouses. Arg 3B 124
Redisham. Suff 2G 67
Redland. Bris 4A 34
Redland. Orkn 5C 172
Redlingfield. Suff 3D 66
Red Lodge. Suff 3F 65
Redlynch. Som 3C 22
Redlynch. Wilts 4H 23
Redmain. Cumb 1C 102
Redmarley. Worc 4B 60
Redmarley D'Abitot. Glos 2C 48
Redmarshall. Stoc T 2A 106
Redmile. Leics 2E 75
Redmire. N Yor 5D 104
Rednal. Shrp 3F 71
Redpath. Bord 1H 119
Redpoint. High 2G 155
Red Post. Corn 2C 10
Red Rock. G Man 4D 90
Red Roses. Carm 3G 43
Red Row. Nmbd 5G 121
Redruth. Corn 4B 6
Red Street. Staf 5C 84
Redvales. G Man 4F 91
Red Wharf Bay. IOA 2E 81
Redwick. Newp 3H 33
Redwick. S Glo 3A 34
Redworth. Darl 2F 105
Reed. Herts 2D 52
Reed End. Herts 2D 52
Reedham. Linc 5B 88
Reedham. Norf 5G 79
Reedness. E Yor 2B 94
Reeds Beck. Linc 4B 88
Reemshill. Abers 4E 161
Reepham. Linc 3H 87
Reepham. Norf 3C 78
Reeth. N Yor 5D 104
Regaby. IOM 2D 108
Regil. N Som 5A 34
Regoul. High 3C 158
Reiff. High 2D 162
Reigate. Surr 5D 38
Reighton. N Yor 2F 101
Reilth. Shrp 2E 59
Reinigeadal. W Isl 7E 171
Reisque. Abers 1F 153
Reiss. High 3F 169
Rejerrah. Corn 3B 6
Releath. Corn 5A 6
Relubbus. Corn 3C 4
Relugas. Mor 4D 159
Remenham. Wok 3F 37
Remenham Hill. Wok 3F 37
Rempstone. Notts 3C 74
Rendcomb. Glos 5F 49
Rendham. Suff 4F 67
Rendlesham. Suff 5F 67
Renfrew. Ren 3G 127
Renhold. Bed 5H 63
Renishaw. Derbs 3B 86
Rennington. Nmbd 3G 121
Renton. W Dun 2E 127
Renwick. Cumb 5G 113
Repps. Norf 4G 79
Repton. Derbs 3H 73
Resaurie. High 4B 158
Rescassa. Corn 4D 6
Rescobie. Ang 3E 145
Rescorla. Corn 3E 7 (nr. Rosevean)
Rescorla. Corn 4D 6 (nr. St Ewe)
Resipole. High 2B 140
Resolfen. Neat 5B 46
Resolis. High 2A 158
Resolven. Neat 5B 46
Rest and be thankful. Arg 3B 134
Reston. Bord 3E 131
Restrop. Wilts 3F 35
Retford. Notts 2E 86
Retire. Corn 2E 6
Rettendon. Essx 1B 40
Revesby. Linc 4C 88
Rew. Devn 5D 8
Rewe. Devn 3C 12
Rew Street. IOW 3C 16
Rexon. Devn 4E 11
Reybridge. Wilts 5E 35
Reydon. Suff 3H 67
Reymerston. Norf 5C 78
Reynalton. Pemb 4E 43
Reynoldston. Swan 4D 31
Rezare. Corn 5D 10
Rhadyr. Mon 5G 47
Rhaeadr Gwy. Powy 4B 58
Rhandirmwyn. Carm 1A 46
Rhayader. Powy 4B 58
Rheindown. High 4H 157
Rhemore. High 3G 139
Rhenetra. High 3D 154
Rhewl. Den 1D 70 (nr. Llangollen)
Rhewl. Den 4D 82 (nr. Ruthin)
Rhewl. Shrp 2F 71
Rhewl-Mostyn. Flin 3D 82
Rhian. High 2C 164
Rhian Breck. High 3C 164
Rhicarn. High 1E 163
Rhiconich. High 3C 166
Rhicullen. High 1A 158
Rhidorroch. High 4F 163
Rhifail. High 4H 167
Rhigos. Rhon 5C 46
Rhilochan. High 3E 165
Rhiroy. High 5F 163
Rhitongue. High 3G 167
Rhiw. Gwyn 3B 68
Rhiwabon. Wrex 1F 71
Rhiwbina. Card 3E 33
Rhiwbryfdir. Gwyn 1F 69
Rhiwderin. Newp 3F 33
Rhiwlas. Gwyn 2B 70 (nr. Bala)
Rhiwlas. Gwyn 4E 81 (nr. Bangor)
Rhiwlas. Powy 2D 70
Rhodes. G Man 4G 91
Rhodesia. Notts 2C 86
Rhodes Minnis. Kent 1F 29
Rhodiad-y-Brenin. Pemb 2B 42
Rhondda. Rhon 2C 32
Rhonehouse. Dum 4E 111
Rhoose. V Glam 5D 32
Rhos. Carm 2D 45
Rhos. Neat 5H 45
Rhosaman. Carm 4H 45
Rhoscefnhir. IOA 3E 81
Rhoscolyn. IOA 3B 80
Rhos Common. Powy 4E 71
Rhoscrowther. Pemb 4D 42
Rhos-ddu. Gwyn 2B 68
Rhosdylluan. Gwyn 3A 70
Rhosesmor. Flin 4E 82
Rhos-fawr. Gwyn 2C 68
Rhosgadfan. Gwyn 5E 81
Rhosgoch. IOA 2D 80
Rhosgoch. Powy 1E 47
Rhos Haminiog. Cdgn 4E 57
Rhos-hill. Pemb 1B 44
Rhoshirwaun. Gwyn 3A 68
Rhoslan. Gwyn 1D 69
Rhoslefain. Gwyn 5E 69
Rhosllanerchrugog. Wrex 1E 71
Rhos Lligwy. IOA 2D 81
Rhosmaen. Carm 3G 45
Rhosmeirch. IOA 3D 80
Rhosneigr. IOA 3C 80
Rhos-on-Sea. Cnwy 2H 81
Rhossili. Swan 4D 30
Rhosson. Pemb 2B 42
Rhos, The. Pemb 3E 43
Rhostrenwfa. IOA 3D 80
Rhostryfan. Gwyn 5D 81
Rhostyllen. Wrex 1F 71
Rhoswiel. Shrp 2E 71
Rhosybol. IOA 2D 80
Rhos-y-brithdir. Powy 3D 70
Rhos-y-garth. Cdgn 3F 57
Rhos-y-gwaliau. Gwyn 2B 70
Rhos-y-llan. Gwyn 2B 68
Rhos-y-meirch. Powy 4E 59
Rhu. Arg 1D 126
Rhualt. Den 3C 82
Rhubadach. Arg 2B 126
Rhubha Stoer. High 1E 163
Rhuddall Heath. Ches W 4H 83
Rhuddlan. Cdgn 1E 45
Rhuddlan. Den 3C 82
Rhue. High 4E 163
Rhulen. Powy 1E 47
Rhunahaorine. Arg 5F 125
Rhuthun. Den 5D 82
Rhuvoult. High 3C 166
Rhyd. Gwyn 1F 69
Rhydaman. Carm 4G 45
Rhydargaeau. Carm 3E 45
Rhydcymerau. Carm 2F 45
Rhydd. Worc 1D 48
Rhyd-Ddu. Gwyn 5E 81
Rhydding. Neat 3G 31
Rhydfudr. Cdgn 4E 57
Rhydlanfair. Cnwy 5H 81
Rhydlewis. Cdgn 1D 44
Rhydlios. Gwyn 2A 68
Rhydlydan. Cnwy 5A 82
Rhyd-meirionydd. Cdgn 2F 57
Rhydowen. Cdgn 1E 45
Rhyd-Rosser. Cdgn 4E 57
Rhydspence. Powy 1F 47
Rhydtalog. Flin 5E 83
Rhyd-uchaf. Gwyn 2B 70
Rhydwyn. IOA 2C 80
Rhyd-y-clafdy. Gwyn 2C 68
Rhydycroesau. Shrp 2E 71
Rhydyfelin. Cdgn 3E 57
Rhydyfelin. Rhon 3E 32
Rhyd-y-foel. Cnwy 3B 82
Rhyd-y-fro. Neat 5H 45
Rhydymain. Gwyn 3H 69
Rhyd-y-meirch. Mon 5G 47
Rhyd-y-meudwy. Den 5D 82
Rhydymwyn. Flin 4E 82
Rhyd-yr-onen. Gwyn 5F 69
Rhyd-y-sarn. Gwyn 1F 69
Rhyl. Den 2C 82
Rhymney. Cphy 5E 46
Rhymni. Cphy 5E 46
Rhynd. Per 1D 136
Rhynie. Abers 1B 152
Ribbesford. Worc 3B 60
Ribbleton. Lanc 1D 90
Ribby. Lanc 1C 90
Ribchester. Lanc 1E 91
Riber. Derbs 5H 85
Ribigill. High 3F 167
Riby. Linc 4E 95
Riccall. N Yor 1G 93
Riccarton. E Ayr 1D 116
Richards Castle. Here 4G 59
Richborough Port. Kent 4H 41
Richings Park. Buck 3B 38
Richmond. G Lon 3C 38
Richmond. N Yor 4E 105
Rickarton. Abers 5F 153
Rickerby. Cumb 4F 113
Rickerscote. Staf 3D 72
Rickford. N Som 1H 21
Rickham. Devn 5D 8
Rickinghall. Suff 3C 66
Rickleton. Tyne 4F 115
Rickling. Essx 2E 53
Rickling Green. Essx 3F 53
Rickmansworth. Herts 1B 38
Riddings. Derbs 5B 86
Riddlecombe. Devn 1G 11
Riddlesden. W Yor 5C 98
Ridge. Dors 4E 15
Ridge. Herts 5C 52
Ridge. Wilts 3E 23
Ridgebourne. Powy 4C 58
Ridge Lane. Warw 1G 61
Ridgeway. Derbs 5A 86 (nr. Alfreton)
Ridgeway. Derbs 2B 86 (nr. Sheffield)
Ridgeway. Staf 5C 84
Ridgeway Cross. Here 1C 48
Ridgeway Moor. Derbs 2B 86
Ridgewell. Essx 1H 53
Ridgewood. E Sus 3F 27
Ridgmont. C Beds 2H 51
Ridgwardine. Shrp 2A 72
Riding Mill. Nmbd 3D 114
Ridley. Kent 4H 39
Ridley. Nmbd 3A 114
Ridlington. Norf 2F 79
Ridlington. Rut 5F 75
Ridsdale. Nmbd 1C 114
Riemore Lodge. Per 4H 143
Rievaulx. N Yor 1H 99
Rift House. Hart 1B 106
Rigg. Dum 3D 112
Riggend. N Lan 2A 128
Rigsby. Linc 3D 88
Rigside. S Lan 1A 118
Riley Green. Lanc 2E 90
Rileyhill. Staf 4F 73
Rilla Mill. Corn 5C 10
Rillington. N Yor 2C 100
Rimington. Lanc 5H 97
Rimpton. Som 4B 22
Rimsdale. High 4H 167
Rimswell. E Yor 2G 95
Ringasta. Shet 10E 173
Ringford. Dum 4D 111
Ringing Hill. Leics 4B 74
Ringinglow. S Yor 2G 85
Ringland. Norf 4D 78
Ringlestone. Kent 5C 40
Ringmer. E Sus 4F 27
Ringmore. Devn 4C 8 (nr. Kingsbridge)
Ringmore. Devn 5C 12 (nr. Teignmouth)
Ring o' Bells. Lanc 3C 90
Ring's End. Cambs 5C 76
Ringsfield. Suff 2G 67
Ringsfield Corner. Suff 2G 67
Ringshall. Buck 4H 51
Ringshall. Suff 5C 66
Ringshall Stocks. Suff 5C 66
Ringstead. Norf 1G 77
Ringstead. Nptn 3G 63
Ringwood. Hants 2G 15
Ringwould. Kent 1H 29
Rinmore. Abers 2B 152
Rinnigill. Orkn 8C 172
Rinsey. Corn 4C 4
Riof. W Isl 4D 171
Ripe. E Sus 4G 27
Ripley. Derbs 1B 74
Ripley. Hants 3G 15
Ripley. N Yor 3E 99
Ripley. Surr 5B 38
Riplingham. E Yor 1C 94
Riplington. Hants 4E 25
Ripon. N Yor 2F 99
Rippingale. Linc 3H 75
Ripple. Kent 1H 29
Ripple. Worc 2D 48
Ripponden. W Yor 3A 92
Rireavach. High 4E 163
Risabus. Arg 5B 124
Risbury. Here 5H 59
Risby. E Yor 1D 94
Risby. N Lin 3C 94
Risby. Suff 4G 65
Risca. Cphy 2F 33
Rise. E Yor 5F 101
Riseden. E Sus 2H 27
Riseden. Kent 2B 28
Rise End. Derbs 5G 85
Risegate. Linc 2B 76
Riseholme. Linc 3G 87
Riseley. Bed 4H 63
Riseley. Wok 5F 37
Rishangles. Suff 4D 66
Rishton. Lanc 1F 91
Rishworth. W Yor 3A 92
Risley. Derbs 2B 74
Risley. Warr 1A 84
Risplith. N Yor 3E 99
Rispond. High 2E 167
Rivar. Wilts 5B 36
Rivenhall. Essx 4B 54
Rivenhall End. Essx 4B 54
River. Kent 1G 29
River. W Sus 3A 26
River Bank. Cambs 4E 65
Riverhead. Kent 5G 39
Rivington. Lanc 3E 91
Roach Bridge. Lanc 2D 90
Roachill. Devn 4B 20
Roade. Nptn 5E 63
Road Green. Norf 1E 67
Roadhead. Cumb 2G 113
Roadmeetings. S Lan 5B 128
Roadside. High 2D 168
Roadside of Catterline. Abers 1H 145
Roadside of Kinneff. Abers 1H 145
Roadwater. Som 3D 20
Road Weedon. Nptn 5D 62
Roag. High 4B 154
Roa Island. Cumb 3B 96
Roath. Card 4E 33
Roberton. Bord 3G 119
Roberton. S Lan 2B 118
Robertsbridge. E Sus 3B 28
Robertstown. Mor 4G 159
Robertstown. Rhon 5C 46
Roberttown. W Yor 2B 92
Robeston Back. Pemb 3E 43
Robeston Wathen. Pemb 3E 43
Robeston West. Pemb 4C 42
Robin Hood. Lanc 3D 90
Robin Hood. W Yor 2D 92
Robin Hood Airport Doncaster Sheffield. S Yor 1D 86
Robinhood End. Essx 2H 53
Robin Hood's Bay. N Yor 4G 107
Roborough. Devn 1F 11 (nr. Great Torrington)
Roborough. Devn 2B 8 (nr. Plymouth)
Rob Roy's House. Arg 2A 134
Roby Mill. Lanc 4D 90
Rocester. Staf 2F 73
Roch. Pemb 2C 42
Rochdale. G Man 3G 91
Roche. Corn 2D 6
Rochester. Medw 4B 40 & **Medway 204**
Rochester. Nmbd 5C 120
Rochford. Essx 1C 40
Rock. Corn 1D 6
Rock. Nmbd 2G 121
Rock. W Sus 4C 26
Rock. Worc 3B 60
Rockbeare. Devn 3D 12
Rockbourne. Hants 1G 15
Rockcliffe. Cumb 3E 113
Rockcliffe. Dum 4F 111
Rockcliffe Cross. Cumb 3E 113
Rock Ferry. Mers 2F 83
Rockfield. High 5G 165
Rockfield. Mon 4H 47
Rockford. Hants 2G 15
Rockgreen. Shrp 3H 59
Rockhampton. S Glo 2B 34
Rockhead. Corn 4A 10
Rockingham. Nptn 1F 63
Rockland All Saints. Norf 1B 66
Rockland St Mary. Norf 5F 79
Rockland St Peter. Norf 1B 66
Rockley. Wilts 4G 35
Rockwell End. Buck 3F 37
Rockwell Green. Som 1E 13
Rodborough. Glos 5D 48
Rodbourne. Wilts 3E 35
Rodd. Here 4F 59
Roddam. Nmbd 2E 121
Rodden. Dors 4B 14
Roddenloft. E Ayr 2D 117
Roddymoor. Dur 1E 105
Rode. Som 1D 22
Rodeheath. Ches E 4C 84 (nr. Congleton)
Rode Heath. Ches E 5C 84 (nr. Kidsgrove)
Roden. Telf 4H 71
Rodhuish. Som 3D 20
Rodington. Telf 4H 71
Rodington Heath. Telf 4H 71
Rodley. Glos 4C 48
Rodmarton. Glos 2E 35
Rodmell. E Sus 5F 27
Rodmersham. Kent 4D 40
Rodmersham Green. Kent 4D 40
Rodney Stoke. Som 2H 21
Rodsley. Derbs 1G 73
Rodway. Som 2F 21
Rodway. Telf 4A 72
Rodwell. Dors 5B 14
Roecliffe. N Yor 3F 99
Roe Green. Herts 2D 52
Roehampton. G Lon 3D 38
Roesound. Shet 5E 173
Roffey. W Sus 2C 26
Rogart. High 3E 165
Rogate. W Sus 4G 25
Roger Ground. Cumb 5E 103
Rogerstone. Newp 3F 33
Roghadal. W Isl 9C 171
Rogiet. Mon 3H 33
Rogue's Alley. Cambs 5C 76
Roke. Oxon 2E 37
Rokemarsh. Oxon 2E 36
Roker. Tyne 4H 115
Rollesby. Norf 4G 79
Rolleston. Leics 5E 75
Rolleston. Notts 5E 87
Rolleston on Dove. Staf 3G 73
Rolston. E Yor 5G 101
Rolvenden. Kent 2C 28
Rolvenden Layne. Kent 2C 28
Romaldkirk. Dur 2C 104
Roman Bank. Shrp 1H 59
Romanby. N Yor 5A 106
Roman Camp. W Lot 2D 129
Romannobridge. Bord 5E 129
Romansleigh. Devn 4H 19
Romers Common. Worc 4H 59
Romesdal. High 3D 154

Romford. Dors 2F 15
Romford. G Lon 2G 39
Romiley. G Man 1D 84
Romsey. Hants 4B 24
Romsley. Shrp 2B 60
Romsley. Worc 3D 60
Ronague. IOM 4B 108
Ronaldsvoe. Orkn 8D 172
Rookby. Cumb 3B 104
Rookhope. Dur 5C 114
Rooking. Cumb 3F 103
Rookley. IOW 4D 16
Rooks Bridge. Som 1G 21
Rooksey Green. Suff 5B 66
Rook's Nest. Som 3D 20
Rookwood. W Sus 3F 17
Roos. E Yor 1F 95
Roosebeck. Cumb 3B 96
Roosecote. Cumb 3B 96
Rootfield. High 3H 157
Rootham's Green. Bed 5A 64
Rootpark. S Lan 4C 128
Ropley. Hants 3E 25
Ropley Dean. Hants 3E 25
Ropsley. Linc 2G 75
Rora. Abers 3H 161
Rorandle. Abers 2D 152
Rorrington. Shrp 5F 71
Rose. Corn 3B 6
Roseacre. Lanc 1C 90
Rose Ash. Devn 4A 20
Rosebank. S Lan 5B 128
Rosebush. Pemb 2E 43
Rosedale Abbey. N Yor 5E 107
Roseden. Nmbd 2E 121
Rose Green. Essx 3C 54
Rose Green. Suff 1C 54
Rosehall. High 3B 164
Rosehearty. Abers 2G 161
Rose Hill. E Sus 4F 27
Rose Hill. Lanc 1G 91
Rosehill. Shrp 2A 72
(nr. Market Drayton)
Rosehill. Shrp 4G 71
(nr. Shrewsbury)
Roseisle. Mor 2F 159
Rosemarket. Pemb 4D 42
Rosemarkie. High 3B 158
Rosemary Lane. Devn 1E 13
Rosemount. Per 4A 144
Rosenannon. Corn 2D 6
Roser's Cross. E Sus 3G 27
Rosevean. Corn 3E 6
Rosewell. Midl 3F 129
Roseworth. Stoc T 2B 106
Roseworthy. Corn 3D 4
Rosgill. Cumb 3G 103
Roshven. High 1B 140
Roskhill. High 4B 154
Roskorwell. Corn 4E 5
Rosley. Cumb 5E 112
Roslin. Midl 3F 129
Rosliston. Derbs 4G 73
Rosneath. Arg 1D 126
Ross. Dum 5D 110
Ross. Nmbd 1F 121
Ross. Per 1G 135
Ross. Bord 3F 131
Rossendale. Lanc 2F 91
Rossett. Wrex 5F 83
Rossington. S Yor 1D 86
Rosskeen. High 2A 158
Rossland. Ren 2F 127
Ross-on-Wye. Here 3B 48
Roster. High 4E 169
Rostherne. Ches E 2B 84
Rostholme. S Yor 4F 93
Rosthwaite. Cumb 3D 102
Roston. Derbs 1F 73
Rosudgeon. Corn 4C 4
Rosyth. Fife 1E 129
Rothbury. Nmbd 4E 121
Rotherby. Leics 4D 74
Rotherfield. E Sus 3G 27
Rotherfield Greys. Oxon 3F 37
Rotherfield Peppard. Oxon 3F 37
Rotherham. S Yor 1B 86
Rothersthorpe. Nptn 5E 62
Rotherwick. Hants 1F 25
Rothes. Mor 4G 159
Rothesay. Arg 3B 126
Rothienorman. Abers 5E 160
Rothiesholm. Orkn 5F 172
Rothley. Leics 4C 74
Rothley. Nmbd 1D 114
Rothwell. Linc 1A 88
Rothwell. Nptn 2F 63
Rothwell. W Yor 2D 92
Rothwell Haigh. W Yor 2D 92
Rotsea. E Yor 4E 101
Rottal. Ang 2C 144
Rotten End. Suff 4F 67
Rotten Row. Norf 4C 78
Rotten Row. W Ber 4D 36
Rotten Row. W Mid 3F 61
Rottingdean. Brig 5E 27
Rottington. Cumb 3A 102
Roud. IOW 4D 16
Rougham. Norf 3H 77
Rougham. Suff 4B 66
Rough Close. Staf 2D 72
Rough Common. Kent 5F 41
Roughcote. Staf 1D 72
Rough Haugh. High 4H 167
Rough Hay. Staf 3G 73
Roughlee. Lanc 5H 97
Roughley. W Mid 1F 61
Roughsike. Cumb 2G 113
Roughton. Linc 4B 88
Roughton. Norf 2E 78
Roughton. Shrp 1B 60
Roundbush Green. Essx 4F 53
Roundham. Som 2H 13
Roundhay. W Yor 1D 92
Round Hill. Torb 2F 9
Roundhurst. W Sus 2A 26
Round Maple. Suff 1C 54
Round Oak. Shrp 2F 59
Roundstreet Common.
W Sus 3B 26
Roundthwaite. Cumb 4H 103
Roundway. Wilts 5F 35
Roundyhill. Ang 3C 144
Rousdon. Devn 3F 13
Rousham. Oxon 3C 50
Rous Lench. Worc 5E 61
Routh. E Yor 5E 101
Rout's Green. Buck 2F 37
Row. Corn 5A 10
Row. Cumb 1D 96
(nr. Kendal)
Row. Cumb 1H 103
(nr. Penrith)
Rowanburn. Dum 2F 113
Rowanhill. Abers 3H 161
Rowardennan. Stir 4C 134
Rowarth. Derbs 2E 85
Row Ash. Hants 1D 16
Rowberrow. Som 1H 21
Rowde. Wilts 5E 35
Rowden. Devn 3G 11
Rowden Hill. Wilts 4E 35
Rowen. Cnwy 3G 81
Rowfoot. Nmbd 3H 113
Row Green. Essx 3H 53
Row Heath. Essx 4E 55
Rowhedge. Essx 3D 54
Rowhook. W Sus 2C 26
Rowington. Warw 4G 61
Rowland. Derbs 3G 85
Rowland's Castle. Hants 1F 17
Rowlands Gill. Tyne 4E 115
Rowledge. Surr 2G 25
Rowley. Dur 5D 115
Rowley. E Yor 1C 94
Rowley. Shrp 5F 71
Rowley Hill. W Yor 3B 92
Rowley Regis. W Mid 2D 60
Rowlstone. Here 3G 47
Rowly. Surr 1B 26
Rowner. Hants 2D 16
Rowney Green. Worc 3E 61
Rownhams. Hants 1B 16
Rowrah. Cumb 3B 102
Rowsham. Buck 4G 51
Rowsley. Derbs 4G 85
Rowstock. Oxon 3C 36
Rowston. Linc 5H 87
Row, The. Lanc 2D 96
Rowthorne. Derbs 4B 86
Rowton. Ches W 4G 83
Rowton. Shrp 2G 59
(nr. Ludlow)
Rowton. Shrp 4F 71
(nr. Shrewsbury)
Rowton. Telf 4A 72
Row Town. Surr 4B 38
Roxburgh. Bord 1B 120
Roxby. N Lin 3C 94
Roxby. N Yor 3E 107
Roxton. Bed 5A 64
Roxwell. Essx 5G 53
Royal Leamington Spa.
Warw 4H 61
Royal Oak. Darl 2F 105
Royal Oak. Lanc 4C 90
Royal Oak. N Yor 2F 101
Royal's Green. Ches E 1A 72
Royal Tunbridge Wells. Kent 2G 27
Royal Wootton Bassett. Wilts 3F 35
Roybridge. High 5E 149
Roydon. Essx 4E 53
Roydon. Norf 2C 66
(nr. Diss)
Roydon. Norf 3G 77
(nr. King's Lynn)
Roydon Hamlet. Essx 5E 53
Royston. Herts 1D 52
Royston. S Yor 3D 92
Royston Water. Som 1F 13
Royton. G Man 4H 91
Ruabon. Wrex 1F 71
Ruaig. Arg 4B 138
Ruan High Lanes. Corn 5D 6
Ruan Lanihorne. Corn 4C 6
Ruan Major. Corn 5E 5
Ruan Minor. Corn 5E 5
Ruarach. High 1B 148
Ruardean. Glos 4B 48
Ruardean Hill. Glos 4B 48
Ruardean Woodside. Glos 4B 48
Rubery. W Mid 3D 61
Ruchazie. Glas 3H 127
Ruckcroft. Cumb 5G 113
Ruckinge. Kent 2E 29
Ruckland. Linc 3C 88
Rucklers Lane. Herts 5A 52
Ruckley. Shrp 5H 71
Rudbaxton. Pemb 2D 42
Rudby. N Yor 4B 106
Ruddington. Notts 2C 74
Rudford. Glos 3C 48
Rudge. Shrp 1C 60
Rudge. Wilts 1D 22
Rudge Heath. Shrp 1B 60
Rudgeway. S Glo 3B 34
Rudgwick. W Sus 2B 26
Rudhall. Here 3B 48
Rudheath. Ches W 3A 84
Rudley Green. Essx 5B 54
Rudloe. Wilts 4D 34
Rudry. Cphy 3E 33
Rudston. E Yor 3E 101
Rudyard. Staf 5D 84
Rufford. Lanc 3C 90
Rufforth. York 4H 99
Rugby. Warw 3C 62
Rugeley. Staf 4E 73
Ruglen. S Ayr 4B 116
Ruilick. High 4H 157
Ruisaurie. High 4G 157
Ruishton. Som 4F 21
Ruisigearraidh. W Isl 1E 170
Ruislip. G Lon 2B 38
Ruislip Common. G Lon 2B 38
Rumbling Bridge. Per 4C 136
Rumburgh. Suff 2F 67
Rumford. Corn 1C 6
Rumford. Falk 2C 128
Rumney. Card 4F 33
Rumwell. Som 4E 21
Runcorn. Hal 2H 83
Runcton. W Sus 2G 17
Runcton Holme. Norf 5F 77
Rundlestone. Devn 5F 11
Runfold. Surr 2G 25
Runhall. Norf 5C 78
Runham. Norf 4G 79
Runnington. Som 4E 20
Runshaw Moor. Lanc 3D 90
Runswick. N Yor 3F 107
Runtaleave. Ang 2B 144
Runwell. Essx 1B 40
Ruscombe. Wok 4F 37
Rushall. Here 2B 48
Rushall. Norf 2D 66
Rushall. W Mid 5E 73
Rushall. Wilts 1G 23
Rushbrooke. Suff 4A 66
Rushbury. Shrp 1H 59
Rushden. Herts 2D 52
Rushden. Nptn 4G 63
Rushenden. Kent 3D 40
Rushford. Devn 5E 11
Rushford. Suff 2B 66
Rush Green. Herts 3C 52
Rushlake Green. E Sus 4H 27
Rushmere. Suff 2G 67
Rushmere St Andrew. Suff 1E 55
Rushmoor. Surr 2G 25
Rushock. Worc 3C 60
Rusholme. G Man 1C 84
Rushton. Ches W 4H 83
Rushton. Nptn 2F 63
Rushton. Shrp 5A 72
Rushton Spencer. Staf 4D 84
Rushwick. Worc 5C 60
Rushyford. Dur 2F 105
Ruskie. Stir 3F 135
Ruskington. Linc 5H 87
Rusland. Cumb 1C 96
Rusper. W Sus 2D 26
Ruspidge. Glos 4B 48
Russell's Water. Oxon 3F 37
Russel's Green. Suff 3E 67
Russ Hill. Surr 1D 26
Russland. Orkn 6C 172
Rusthall. Kent 2G 27
Rustington. W Sus 5B 26
Ruston. N Yor 1D 100
Ruston Parva. E Yor 3E 101
Ruswarp. N Yor 4F 107
Rutherglen. S Lan 3H 127
Ruthernbridge. Corn 2E 6
Ruthin. Den 5D 82
Ruthin. V Glam 4C 32
Ruthrieston. Aber 3G 153
Ruthven. Abers 4C 160
Ruthven. Ang 4B 144
Ruthven. High 5C 158
(nr. Inverness)
Ruthven. High 4B 150
(nr. Kingussie)
Ruthvoes. Corn 2D 6
Ruthwaite. Cumb 1D 102
Ruthwell. Dum 3C 112
Ruxton Green. Here 4A 48
Ruyton-XI-Towns. Shrp 3F 71
Ryal. Nmbd 2D 114
Ryall. Dors 3H 13
Ryall. Worc 1D 48
Ryarsh. Kent 5A 40
Rychraggan. High 5G 157
Rydal. Cumb 4E 103
Ryde. IOW 3D 16
Rye. E Sus 3D 28
Ryecroft Gate. Staf 4D 84
Ryeford. Here 3B 48
Rye Foreign. E Sus 3D 28
Rye Harbour. E Sus 4D 28
Ryehill. E Yor 2F 95
Rye Street. Worc 2C 48
Ryhall. Rut 4H 75
Ryhill. W Yor 3D 93
Ryhope. Tyne 4H 115
Ryhope Colliery. Tyne 4H 115
Rylands. Notts 2C 74
Rylstone. N Yor 4B 98
Ryme Intrinseca. Dors 1A 14
Ryther. N Yor 1F 93
Ryton. Glos 2C 48
Ryton. N Yor 2B 100
Ryton. Shrp 5B 72
Ryton. Tyne 3E 115
Ryton. Warw 2A 62
Ryton-on-Dunsmore. Warw 3A 62
Ryton Woodside. Tyne 3E 115

S

Saasaig. High 3E 147
Sabden. Lanc 1F 91
Sacombe. Herts 4D 52
Sacriston. Dur 5F 115
Sadberge. Darl 3A 106
Saddell. Arg 2B 122
Saddington. Leics 1D 62
Saddle Bow. Norf 4F 77
Saddlescombe. W Sus 4D 26
Saddleworth. G Man 4H 91
Sadgill. Cumb 4F 103
Saffron Walden. Essx 2F 53
Sageston. Pemb 4E 43
Saham Hills. Norf 5B 78
Saham Toney. Norf 5A 78
Saighdinis. W Isl 2D 170
Saighton. Ches W 4G 83
Sain Dunwyd. V Glam 5C 32
Sain Hilari. V Glam 4D 32
St Abbs. Bord 3F 131
St Agnes. Corn 3B 6
St Albans. Herts 5B 52
St Allen. Corn 3C 6
St Andrews. Fife 2H 137 & 209
St Andrews Major. V Glam 4E 33
St Anne's. Lanc 2B 90
St Ann's. Dum 5C 118
St Ann's Chapel. Corn 5E 11
St Ann's Chapel. Devn 4C 8
St Anthony. Corn 5C 6
St Anthony-in-Meneage. Corn 4E 5
St Arvans. Mon 2A 34
St Asaph. Den 3C 82
Sain Tathan. V Glam 5D 32
St Athan. V Glam 5D 32
St Austell. Corn 3E 6
St Bartholomew's Hill. Wilts 4E 23
St Bees. Cumb 3A 102
St Blazey. Corn 3E 7
St Blazey Gate. Corn 3E 7
St Boswells. Bord 1A 120
St Breock. Corn 1D 6
St Breward. Corn 5A 10
St Briavels. Glos 5A 48
St Brides. Pemb 3B 42
St Bride's Major. V Glam 4B 32
St Bride's Netherwent. Mon 3H 33
St Bride's-super-Ely. V Glam 4D 32
St Brides Wentlooge. Newp 3F 33
St Budeaux. Plym 3A 8
Saintbury. Glos 2G 49
St Buryan. Corn 4B 4
St Catherine. Bath 4C 34
St Catherines. Arg 3A 134
St Clears. Carm 3G 43
St Cleer. Corn 2G 7
St Clement. Corn 4C 6
St Clether. Corn 4C 10
St Colmac. Arg 3B 126
St Columb Major. Corn 2D 6
St Columb Minor. Corn 2C 6
St Columb Road. Corn 3D 6
St Combs. Abers 2H 161
St Cross. Hants 4C 24
St Cross South Elmham. Suff 2E 67
St Cyrus. Abers 2G 145
St David's. Pemb 2B 42
St David's. Per 1B 136
St Day. Corn 4B 6
St Dennis. Corn 3D 6
St Dogmaels. Pemb 1B 44
St Dominick. Corn 2H 7
St Donat's. V Glam 5C 32
St Edith's Marsh. Wilts 5E 35
St Endellion. Corn 1D 6
St Enoder. Corn 3C 6
St Erme. Corn 4C 6
St Erney. Corn 3H 7
St Erth. Corn 3C 4
St Erth Praze. Corn 3C 4
St Ervan. Corn 1C 6
St Eval. Corn 2C 6
St Ewe. Corn 4D 6
St Fagans. Card 4E 32
St Fergus. Abers 3H 161
St Fillans. Per 1F 135
St Florence. Pemb 4E 43
St Gennys. Corn 3B 10
St George. Cnwy 3B 82
St Georges. N Som 5G 33
St Georges. V Glam 4D 32
St George's Hill. Surr 4B 38
St Germans. Corn 3H 7
St Giles in the Wood. Devn 1F 11
St Giles on the Heath. Devn 3D 10
St Giles's Hill. Hants 4C 24
St Gluvias. Corn 5B 6
St Harmon. Powy 3B 58
St Helena. Warw 5G 73
St Helen Auckland. Dur 2E 105
St Helens. Cumb 1B 102
St Helens. E Sus 4C 28
St Helens. IOW 4E 17
St Helens. Mers 1G 83
St Hilary. Corn 3C 4
St Hilary. V Glam 4D 32
Saint Hill. Devn 2D 12
Saint Hill. W Sus 2E 27
St Illtyd. Blae 5F 47
St Ippolyts. Herts 3B 52
St Ishmael. Carm 5D 44
St Ishmael's. Pemb 4C 42
St Issey. Corn 1D 6
St Ive. Corn 2H 7
St Ives. Cambs 3C 64
St Ives. Corn 2C 4
St Ives. Dors 2G 15
St James' End. Nptn 4E 63
St James South Elmham. Suff 2F 67
St Jidgey. Corn 2D 6
St John. Corn 3A 8
St John's. IOM 3B 108
St Johns. Worc 5C 60
St John's Chapel. Devn 4F 19
St John's Chapel. Dur 1B 104
St John's Fen End. Norf 4E 77
St John's Hall. Dur 1D 104
St John's Town of Dalry.
Dum 1D 110
St Judes. IOM 2C 108
St Just. Corn 5C 6
(nr. Falmouth)
St Just. Corn 3A 4
(nr. Penzance)
St Just in Roseland. Corn 5C 6
St Katherines. Abers 5E 161
St Keverne. Corn 4E 5
St Kew. Corn 5A 10
St Kew Highway. Corn 5A 10
St Keyne. Corn 2G 7
St Lawrence. Corn 2E 7
St Lawrence. Essx 5C 54
St Lawrence. IOW 5D 16
St Leonards. Buck 5H 51
St Leonards. Dors 2G 15
St Leonards. E Sus 5B 28
St Levan. Corn 4A 4
St Lythans. V Glam 4E 32
St Mabyn. Corn 5A 10
St Madoes. Per 1D 136
St Margarets. Here 2G 47
St Margaret's. Herts 4A 52
(nr. Hemel Hempstead)
St Margarets. Herts 4D 53
(nr. Hoddesdon)
St Margaret's. Wilts 5G 35
St Margaret's at Cliffe. Kent 1H 29
St Margaret's Hope. Orkn 8D 172
St Margaret South Elmham.
Suff 2F 67
St Mark's. IOM 4B 108
St Martin. Corn 4E 5
(nr. Helston)
St Martin. Corn 3G 7
(nr. Looe)
St Martins. Per 5A 144
St Martin's. Shrp 2F 71
St Mary Bourne. Hants 1C 24
St Marychurch. Torb 2F 9
St Mary Church. V Glam 4D 32
St Mary Cray. G Lon 4F 39
St Mary Hill. V Glam 4C 32
St Mary Hoo. Medw 3C 40
St Mary in the Marsh. Kent 3E 29
St Mary's. Orkn 7D 172
St Mary's Bay. Kent 3E 29
St Maughan's Green. Mon 4H 47
St Mawes. Corn 5C 6
St Mawgan. Corn 2C 6
St Mellion. Corn 2H 7
St Mellons. Card 3F 33
St Merryn. Corn 1C 6
St Mewan. Corn 3D 6
St Michael Caerhays. Corn 4D 6
St Michael Penkevil. Corn 4C 6
St Michaels. Kent 2C 28
St Michaels. Torb 3E 9
St Michaels. Worc 4H 59
St Michael's on Wyre. Lanc 5D 96
St Michael South Elmham.
Suff 2F 67
St Minver. Corn 1D 6
St Monans. Fife 3H 137
St Neot. Corn 2F 7
St Neots. Cambs 4A 64
St Newlyn East. Corn 3C 6
St Nicholas. Pemb 1D 42
St Nicholas. V Glam 4D 32
St Nicholas at Wade. Kent 4G 41

St Nicholas South Elmham. Suff . . . 2F 67
St Ninians. Stir . . . 4H 135
St Olaves. Norf . . . 1G 67
St Osyth. Essx . . . 4E 54
St Osyth Heath. Essx . . . 4E 55
St Owen's Cross. Here . . . 3A 48
St Paul's Cray. G Lon . . . 4F 39
St Paul's Walden. Herts . . . 3B 52
St Peter's. Kent . . . 4H 41
St Peter The Great. Worc . . . 5C 60
St Petrox. Pemb . . . 5D 42
St Pinnock. Corn . . . 2G 7
St Quivox. S Ayr . . . 2C 116
St Ruan. Corn . . . 5E 5
St Stephen. Corn . . . 3D 6
St Stephens. Corn . . . 4D 10 (nr. Launceston)
St Stephens. Corn . . . 3A 8 (nr. Saltash)
St Teath. Corn . . . 4A 10
St Thomas. Devn . . . 3C 12
St Thomas. Swan . . . 3F 31
St Tudy. Corn . . . 5A 10
St Twynnells. Pemb . . . 5D 42
St Veep. Corn . . . 3F 7
St Vigeans. Ang . . . 4F 145
St Wenn. Corn . . . 2D 6
St Weonards. Here . . . 3H 47
St Winnolls. Corn . . . 3H 7
St Winnow. Corn . . . 3F 7
Salcombe. Devn . . . 5D 8
Salcombe Regis. Devn . . . 4E 13
Salcott. Essx . . . 4C 54
Sale. G Man . . . 1B 84
Saleby. Linc . . . 3D 88
Sale Green. Worc . . . 5D 60
Salehurst. E Sus . . . 3B 28
Salem. Carm . . . 3G 45
Salem. Cdgn . . . 2F 57
Salen. Arg . . . 4G 139
Salen. High . . . 2A 140
Salesbury. Lanc . . . 1E 91
Saleway. Worc . . . 5D 60
Salford. C Beds . . . 2H 51
Salford. G Man . . . 1C 84 & **Manchester** 201
Salford. Oxon . . . 3A 50
Salford Priors. Warw . . . 5E 61
Salfords. Surr . . . 1D 27
Salhouse. Norf . . . 4F 79
Saligo. Arg . . . 3A 124
Saline. Fife . . . 4C 136
Salisbury. Wilts . . . 3G 23 & 210
Salkeld Dykes. Cumb . . . 1G 103
Sallachan. High . . . 2D 141
Sallachy. High . . . 3C 164 (nr. Lairg)
Sallachy. High . . . 5B 156 (nr. Stromeferry)
Salle. Norf . . . 3D 78
Salmonby. Linc . . . 3C 88
Salmond's Muir. Ang . . . 5E 145
Salperton. Glos . . . 3F 49
Salph End. Bed . . . 5H 63
Salsburgh. N Lan . . . 3B 128
Salt. Staf . . . 3D 72
Salta. Cumb . . . 5B 112
Saltaire. W Yor . . . 1B 92
Saltash. Corn . . . 3A 8
Saltburn. High . . . 2B 158
Saltburn-by-the-Sea. Red C . . . 2D 106
Saltby. Leics . . . 3F 75
Saltcoats. Cumb . . . 5B 102
Saltcoats. N Ayr . . . 5D 126
Saltdean. Brig . . . 5E 27
Salt End. E Yor . . . 2E 95
Salter. Lanc . . . 3F 97
Salterforth. Lanc . . . 5A 98
Salters Lode. Norf . . . 5E 77
Salterswall. Ches W . . . 4A 84
Salterton. Wilts . . . 3G 23
Saltfleet. Linc . . . 1D 88
Saltfleetby All Saints. Linc . . . 1D 88
Saltfleetby St Clements. Linc . . . 1D 88
Saltfleetby St Peter. Linc . . . 2D 88
Saltford. Bath . . . 5B 34
Salthouse. Norf . . . 1C 78
Saltmarshe. E Yor . . . 2A 94
Saltmead. Card . . . 4E 33
Saltness. Orkn . . . 9B 172
Saltness. Shet . . . 7D 173
Saltney. Flin . . . 4F 83
Salton. N Yor . . . 2B 100
Saltrens. Devn . . . 4E 19
Saltwick. Nmbd . . . 2E 115
Saltwood. Kent . . . 2F 29
Salum. Arg . . . 4B 138
Salwarpe. Worc . . . 4C 60
Salwayash. Dors . . . 3H 13
Samalaman. High . . . 1A 140
Sambourne. Warw . . . 4E 61
Sambourne. Wilts . . . 2D 22
Sambrook. Telf . . . 3B 72
Samhia. W Isl . . . 2C 170
Samlesbury. Lanc . . . 1D 90
Samlesbury Bottoms. Lanc . . . 2E 90
Sampford Arundel. Som . . . 1E 12
Sampford Brett. Som . . . 2D 20
Sampford Courtenay. Devn . . . 2G 11
Sampford Peverell. Devn . . . 1D 12
Sampford Spiney. Devn . . . 5F 11
Samsonlane. Orkn . . . 5F 172
Samuelston. E Lot . . . 2A 130
Sanaigmore. Arg . . . 2A 124
Sancreed. Corn . . . 4B 4
Sancton. E Yor . . . 1C 94
Sand. High . . . 4D 162
Sand. Shet . . . 7E 173
Sand. Som . . . 2H 21
Sandaig. Arg . . . 4A 138
Sandaig. High . . . 3F 147
Sandale. Cumb . . . 5D 112
Sandal Magna. W Yor . . . 3D 92
Sandavore. High . . . 5C 146
Sanday Airport. Orkn . . . 3F 172
Sandbach. Ches E . . . 4B 84
Sandbank. Arg . . . 1C 126
Sandbanks. Pool . . . 4F 15
Sandend. Abers . . . 2C 160
Sanderstead. G Lon . . . 4E 39
Sandfields. Neat . . . 3G 31
Sandford. Cumb . . . 3A 104
Sandford. Devn . . . 2B 12
Sandford. Dors . . . 4E 15
Sandford. Hants . . . 2G 15
Sandford. IOW . . . 4D 16
Sandford. N Som . . . 1H 21
Sandford. Shrp . . . 3F 71 (nr. Oswestry)
Sandford. Shrp . . . 2H 71 (nr. Whitchurch)
Sandford. S Lan . . . 5A 128
Sandfordhill. Abers . . . 4H 161
Sandford-on-Thames. Oxon . . . 5D 50
Sandford Orcas. Dors . . . 4B 22
Sandford St Martin. Oxon . . . 3C 50
Sandgate. Kent . . . 2F 29
Sandgreen. Dum . . . 4C 110
Sandhaven. Abers . . . 2G 161
Sandhead. Dum . . . 4F 109
Sandhill. Cambs . . . 2E 65
Sandhills. Dors . . . 1B 14
Sandhills. Oxon . . . 5D 50
Sandhills. Surr . . . 2A 26
Sandhoe. Nmbd . . . 3C 114
Sand Hole. E Yor . . . 1B 94
Sandholme. E Yor . . . 1B 94
Sandholme. Linc . . . 2C 76
Sandhurst. Brac . . . 5G 37
Sandhurst. Glos . . . 3D 48
Sandhurst. Kent . . . 3B 28
Sandhurst Cross. Kent . . . 3B 28
Sandhutton. N Yor . . . 1F 99 (nr. Thirsk)
Sand Hutton. N Yor . . . 4A 100 (nr. York)
Sandiacre. Derbs . . . 2B 74
Sandilands. Linc . . . 2E 89
Sandiway. Ches W . . . 3A 84
Sandleheath. Hants . . . 1G 15
Sandling. Kent . . . 5B 40
Sandlow Green. Ches E . . . 4B 84
Sandness. Shet . . . 6C 173
Sandon. Essx . . . 5H 53
Sandon. Herts . . . 2D 52
Sandon. Staf . . . 3D 72
Sandonbank. Staf . . . 3D 72
Sandown. IOW . . . 4D 16
Sandplace. Corn . . . 3G 7
Sandridge. Herts . . . 4B 52
Sandridge. Wilts . . . 5E 35
Sandringham. Norf . . . 3F 77
Sandsend. N Yor . . . 3F 107
Sandside. Cumb . . . 2C 96
Sandsound. Shet . . . 7E 173
Sands, The. Surr . . . 2G 25
Sandtoft. N Lin . . . 4H 93
Sandvoe. Shet . . . 2E 173
Sandway. Kent . . . 5C 40
Sandwell Green. Suff . . . 3D 66
Sandwich. Kent . . . 5H 41
Sandwick. Cumb . . . 3F 103
Sandwick. Orkn . . . 6B 172 (on Mainland)
Sandwick. Orkn . . . 9D 172 (on South Ronaldsay)
Sandwick. Shet . . . 9F 173 (on Mainland)
Sandwick. Shet . . . 5G 173 (on Whalsay)
Sandwith. Cumb . . . 3A 102
Sandy. Carm . . . 5E 45
Sandy. C Beds . . . 1B 52
Sandy Bank. Linc . . . 5B 88
Sandycroft. Flin . . . 4F 83
Sandy Cross. Here . . . 5A 60
Sandygate. Devn . . . 5B 12
Sandygate. IOM . . . 2C 108
Sandy Haven. Pemb . . . 4C 42
Sandyhills. Dum . . . 4F 111
Sandylands. Lanc . . . 3D 96
Sandylane. Swan . . . 4E 31
Sandy Lane. Wilts . . . 5E 35
Sandystones. Bord . . . 2H 119
Sandyway. Here . . . 3H 47
Sangobeg. High . . . 2E 167
Sangomore. High . . . 2E 166
Sankyn's Green. Worc . . . 4B 60
Sanna. High . . . 2F 139
Sanndabhaig. W Isl . . . 4G 171 (on Isle of Lewis)
Sanndabhaig. W Isl . . . 4D 170 (on South Uist)
Sannox. N Ayr . . . 5B 126
Sanquhar. Dum . . . 3G 117
Santon. Cumb . . . 4B 102
Santon Bridge. Cumb . . . 4C 102
Santon Downham. Suff . . . 2H 65
Sapcote. Leics . . . 1B 62
Sapey Common. Here . . . 4B 60
Sapiston. Suff . . . 3B 66
Sapley. Cambs . . . 3B 64
Sapperton. Derbs . . . 2F 73
Sapperton. Glos . . . 5E 49
Sapperton. Linc . . . 2H 75
Saracen's Head. Linc . . . 3C 76
Sarclet. High . . . 4F 169
Sardis. Carm . . . 5F 45
Sardis. Pemb . . . 4D 42 (nr. Milford Haven)
Sardis. Pemb . . . 4F 43 (nr. Tenby)
Sarisbury. Hants . . . 2D 16
Sarn. B'end . . . 3C 32
Sarn. Powy . . . 1E 58
Sarnau. Carm . . . 3E 45
Sarnau. Cdgn . . . 5C 56
Sarnau. Gwyn . . . 2B 70
Sarnau. Powy . . . 2D 46 (nr. Brecon)
Sarnau. Powy . . . 4E 71 (nr. Welshpool)
Sarn Bach. Gwyn . . . 3C 68
Sarnesfield. Here . . . 5F 59
Sarn Meyllteyrn. Gwyn . . . 2B 68
Saron. Carm . . . 4G 45 (nr. Ammanford)
Saron. Carm . . . 2D 45 (nr. Newcastle Emlyn)
Saron. Gwyn . . . 4E 81 (nr. Bethel)
Saron. Gwyn . . . 5D 80 (nr. Bontnewydd)
Sarratt. Herts . . . 1B 38
Sarre. Kent . . . 4G 41
Sarsden. Oxon . . . 3A 50
Satley. Dur . . . 5E 115
Satron. N Yor . . . 5C 104
Satterleigh. Devn . . . 4G 19
Satterthwaite. Cumb . . . 5E 103
Satwell. Oxon . . . 3F 37
Sauchen. Abers . . . 2D 152
Saucher. Per . . . 5A 144
Saughall. Ches W . . . 4F 83
Saughtree. Bord . . . 5H 119
Saul. Glos . . . 5C 48
Saundby. Notts . . . 2E 87
Saundersfoot. Pemb . . . 4F 43
Saunderton. Buck . . . 5F 51
Saunderton Lee. Buck . . . 2G 37
Saunton. Devn . . . 3E 19
Sausthorpe. Linc . . . 4C 88
Saval. High . . . 3C 164
Saverley Green. Staf . . . 2D 72
Sawbridge. Warw . . . 4C 62
Sawbridgeworth. Herts . . . 4E 53
Sawdon. N Yor . . . 1D 100
Sawley. Derbs . . . 2B 74
Sawley. Lanc . . . 5G 97
Sawley. N Yor . . . 3E 99
Sawston. Cambs . . . 1E 53
Sawtry. Cambs . . . 2A 64
Saxby. Leics . . . 3F 75
Saxby. Linc . . . 2H 87
Saxby All Saints. N Lin . . . 3C 94
Saxelby. Leics . . . 3D 74
Saxelbye. Leics . . . 3D 74
Saxham Street. Suff . . . 4C 66
Saxilby. Linc . . . 3F 87
Saxlingham. Norf . . . 2C 78
Saxlingham Green. Norf . . . 1E 67
Saxlingham Nethergate. Norf . . . 1E 67
Saxlingham Thorpe. Norf . . . 1E 66
Saxmundham. Suff . . . 4F 67
Saxondale. Notts . . . 1D 74
Saxon Street. Cambs . . . 5F 65
Saxtead. Suff . . . 4E 67
Saxtead Green. Suff . . . 4E 67
Saxthorpe. Norf . . . 2D 78
Saxton. N Yor . . . 1E 93
Sayers Common. W Sus . . . 4D 26
Scackleton. N Yor . . . 2A 100
Scadabhagh. W Isl . . . 8D 171
Scaftworth. Notts . . . 1D 86
Scagglethorpe. N Yor . . . 2C 100
Scaitcliffe. Lanc . . . 2F 91
Scaladal. W Isl . . . 6D 171
Scalasaig. Arg . . . 4A 132
Scalby. E Yor . . . 2B 94
Scalby. N Yor . . . 5H 107
Scalby Mills. N Yor . . . 5H 107
Scaldwell. Nptn . . . 3E 63
Scaleby. Cumb . . . 3F 113
Scaleby Hill. Cumb . . . 3F 113
Scale Houses. Cumb . . . 5G 113
Scales. Cumb . . . 2B 96 (nr. Barrow-in-Furness)
Scales. Cumb . . . 2E 103 (nr. Keswick)
Scalford. Leics . . . 3E 75
Scaling. Red C . . . 3E 107
Scaling Dam. Red C . . . 3E 107
Scalloway. Shet . . . 8E 173
Scalpaigh. W Isl . . . 8E 171
Scalpay House. High . . . 1E 147
Scamblesby. Linc . . . 3B 88
Scamodale. High . . . 1C 140
Scampston. N Yor . . . 2C 100
Scampton. Linc . . . 3G 87
Scaniport. High . . . 5A 158
Scapa. Orkn . . . 7D 172
Scapegoat Hill. W Yor . . . 3A 92
Scar. Orkn . . . 3F 172
Scarasta. W Isl . . . 8C 171
Scarborough. N Yor . . . 1E 101
Scarcliffe. Derbs . . . 4B 86
Scarcroft. W Yor . . . 5F 99
Scardroy. High . . . 3E 156
Scarfskerry. High . . . 1E 169
Scargill. Dur . . . 3D 104
Scarinish. Arg . . . 4B 138
Scarisbrick. Lanc . . . 3B 90
Scarning. Norf . . . 4B 78
Scarrington. Notts . . . 1E 75
Scarth Hill. Lanc . . . 4C 90
Scartho. NE Lin . . . 4F 95
Scarvister. Shet . . . 7E 173
Scatness. Shet . . . 10E 173
Scatwell. High . . . 3F 157
Scaur. Dum . . . 4F 111
Scawby. N Lin . . . 4C 94
Scawby Brook. N Lin . . . 4C 94
Scawsby. S Yor . . . 4F 93
Scawton. N Yor . . . 1H 99
Scayne's Hill. W Sus . . . 3E 27
Scethrog. Powy . . . 3E 46
Scholar Green. Ches E . . . 5C 84
Scholes. G Man . . . 4D 90
Scholes. W Yor . . . 2B 92 (nr. Bradford)
Scholes. W Yor . . . 4B 92 (nr. Holmfirth)
Scholes. W Yor . . . 1D 93 (nr. Leeds)
Scholey Hill. W Yor . . . 2D 93
School Aycliffe. Dur . . . 2F 105
School Green. Ches W . . . 4A 84
School Green. Essx . . . 2H 53
Scissett. W Yor . . . 3C 92
Scleddau. Pemb . . . 1D 42
Scofton. Notts . . . 2D 86
Scole. Norf . . . 3D 66
Scolpaig. W Isl . . . 1C 170
Scolton. Pemb . . . 2D 43
Scone. Per . . . 1D 136
Sconser. High . . . 5E 155
Scoonie. Fife . . . 3F 137
Scopwick. Linc . . . 5H 87
Scoraig. High . . . 4E 163
Scorborough. E Yor . . . 5E 101
Scorrier. Corn . . . 4B 6
Scorriton. Devn . . . 2D 8
Scorton. Lanc . . . 5E 97
Scorton. N Yor . . . 4F 105
Sco Ruston. Norf . . . 3E 79
Scotbheinn. W Isl . . . 3D 170
Scotby. Cumb . . . 4F 113
Scotch Corner. N Yor . . . 4F 105
Scotforth. Lanc . . . 3D 97
Scot Hay. Staf . . . 1C 72
Scothern. Linc . . . 3H 87
Scotland End. Oxon . . . 2B 50
Scotlandwell. Per . . . 3D 136
Scot Lane End. G Man . . . 4E 91
Scotsburn. High . . . 1B 158
Scotsburn. Mor . . . 2G 159
Scotsdike. Cumb . . . 2E 113
Scots Gap. Nmbd . . . 1D 114
Scotstoun. Glas . . . 3G 127
Scotstown. High . . . 2C 140
Scotswood. Tyne . . . 3F 115
Scottas. High . . . 3F 147
Scotter. Linc . . . 4B 94
Scotterthorpe. Linc . . . 4B 94
Scottlethorpe. Linc . . . 3H 75
Scotton. Linc . . . 1F 87
Scotton. N Yor . . . 5E 105 (nr. Catterick Garrison)
Scotton. N Yor . . . 4F 99 (nr. Harrogate)
Scottow. Norf . . . 3E 79
Scoulton. Norf . . . 5B 78
Scounslow Green. Staf . . . 3E 73
Scourie. High . . . 4B 166
Scourie More. High . . . 4B 166
Scousburgh. Shet . . . 10E 173
Scout Green. Cumb . . . 4G 103
Scouthead. G Man . . . 4H 91
Scrabster. High . . . 1C 168
Scrafield. Linc . . . 4C 88
Scrainwood. Nmbd . . . 4D 121
Scrane End. Linc . . . 1C 76
Scraptoft. Leic . . . 5D 74
Scratby. Norf . . . 4H 79
Scrayingham. N Yor . . . 3B 100
Scredington. Linc . . . 1H 75
Scremby. Linc . . . 4D 88
Scremerston. Nmbd . . . 5G 131
Screveton. Notts . . . 1E 75
Scrivelsby. Linc . . . 4B 88
Scriven. N Yor . . . 4F 99
Scronkey. Lanc . . . 5D 96
Scrooby. Notts . . . 1D 86
Scropton. Derbs . . . 2F 73
Scrub Hill. Linc . . . 5B 88
Scruton. N Yor . . . 5F 105
Scuggate. Cumb . . . 2F 113
Sculamus. High . . . 1E 147
Sculcoates. Hull . . . 1D 94
Sculthorpe. Norf . . . 2A 78
Scunthorpe. N Lin . . . 3B 94
Scurlage. Swan . . . 4D 30
Sea. Som . . . 1G 13
Seaborough. Dors . . . 2H 13
Seabridge. Staf . . . 1C 72
Seabrook. Kent . . . 2F 29
Seaburn. Tyne . . . 3H 115
Seacombe. Mers . . . 1F 83
Seacroft. Linc . . . 4E 89
Seacroft. W Yor . . . 1D 92
Seadyke. Linc . . . 2C 76
Seafield. High . . . 5G 165
Seafield. Midl . . . 3F 129
Seafield. S Ayr . . . 2C 116
Seafield. W Lot . . . 3D 128
Seaford. E Sus . . . 5F 27
Seaforth. Mers . . . 1F 83
Seagrave. Leics . . . 4D 74
Seaham. Dur . . . 5H 115
Seahouses. Nmbd . . . 1G 121
Seal. Kent . . . 5G 39
Sealand. Flin . . . 4F 83
Seale. Surr . . . 2G 25
Seamer. N Yor . . . 1E 101 (nr. Scarborough)
Seamer. N Yor . . . 3B 106 (nr. Stokesley)
Seamill. N Ayr . . . 5C 126
Sea Mills. Bris . . . 4A 34
Sea Palling. Norf . . . 3G 79
Searby. Linc . . . 4D 94
Seasalter. Kent . . . 4E 41
Seascale. Cumb . . . 4B 102
Seaside. Per . . . 1E 137
Seater. High . . . 1F 169
Seathorne. Linc . . . 4E 89
Seathwaite. Cumb . . . 3D 102 (nr. Buttermere)
Seathwaite. Cumb . . . 5D 102 (nr. Ulpha)
Seatle. Cumb . . . 1C 96
Seatoller. Cumb . . . 3D 102
Seaton. Corn . . . 3H 7
Seaton. Cumb . . . 1B 102
Seaton. Devn . . . 3F 13
Seaton. Dur . . . 4G 115
Seaton. E Yor . . . 5F 101
Seaton. Nmbd . . . 2G 115
Seaton. Rut . . . 1G 63
Seaton Burn. Tyne . . . 2F 115
Seaton Carew. Hart . . . 2C 106
Seaton Delaval. Nmbd . . . 2G 115
Seaton Junction. Devn . . . 3F 13
Seaton Ross. E Yor . . . 5B 100
Seaton Sluice. Nmbd . . . 2G 115
Seatown. Abers . . . 2C 160
Seatown. Dors . . . 3H 13
Seatown. Mor . . . 2C 160 (nr. Cullen)
Seatown. Mor . . . 1G 159 (nr. Lossiemouth)
Seave Green. N Yor . . . 4C 106
Seaview. IOW . . . 3E 17
Seaville. Cumb . . . 4C 112
Seavington St Mary. Som . . . 1H 13
Seavington St Michael. Som . . . 1H 13
Seawick. Essx . . . 4E 55
Sebastopol. Torf . . . 2F 33
Sebergham. Cumb . . . 5E 113
Seckington. Warw . . . 5G 73
Second Coast. High . . . 4D 162
Sedbergh. Cumb . . . 5H 103
Sedbury. Glos . . . 2A 34
Sedbusk. N Yor . . . 5B 104
Sedgeberrow. Worc . . . 2F 49
Sedgebrook. Linc . . . 2F 75
Sedgefield. Dur . . . 2A 106
Sedgeford. Norf . . . 2G 77
Sedgehill. Wilts . . . 4D 22
Sedgley. W Mid . . . 1D 60
Sedgwick. Cumb . . . 1E 97
Sedlescombe. E Sus . . . 4B 28
Seend. Wilts . . . 5E 35
Seend Cleeve. Wilts . . . 5E 35
Seer Green. Buck . . . 1A 38
Seething. Norf . . . 1F 67
Sefster. Shet . . . 6E 173
Sefton. Mers . . . 4B 90
Sefton Park. Mers . . . 2F 83
Segensworth. Hants . . . 2D 16
Seggat. Abers . . . 4E 161
Seghill. Nmbd . . . 2F 115
Seifton. Shrp . . . 2G 59
Seighford. Staf . . . 3C 72
Seilebost. W Isl . . . 8C 171
Seisdon. Staf . . . 1C 60
Seisiadar. W Isl . . . 4H 171
Selattyn. Shrp . . . 2E 71
Selborne. Hants . . . 3F 25
Selby. N Yor . . . 1G 93
Selham. W Sus . . . 3A 26
Selkirk. Bord . . . 2G 119

Sellack. *Here* 3A 48
Sellafirth. *Shet* 2G 173
Sellick's Green. *Som* 1F 13
Sellindge. *Kent* 2F 29
Selling. *Kent* 5E 41
Sells Green. *Wilts* 5E 35
Selly Oak. *W Mid* 2E 61
Selmeston. *E Sus* 5G 27
Selsdon. *G Lon* 4E 39
Selsey. *W Sus* 3G 17
Selsfield Common. *W Sus* 2E 27
Selside. *Cumb* 5G 103
Selside. *N Yor* 2G 97
Selsley. *Glos* 5D 48
Selsted. *Kent* 1G 29
Selston. *Notts* 5B 86
Selworthy. *Som* 2C 20
Semblister. *Shet* 6E 173
Semer. *Suff* 1D 54
Semington. *Wilts* 5D 35
Semley. *Wilts* 4D 23
Sempringham. *Linc* 2A 76
Send. *Surr* 5B 38
Send Marsh. *Surr* 5B 38
Senghenydd. *Cphy* 2E 32
Sennen. *Corn* 4A 4
Sennen Cove. *Corn* 4A 4
Sennicotts. *W Sus* 2G 17
Sennybridge. *Powy* 3C 46
Serlby. *Notts* 2D 86
Sessay. *N Yor* 2G 99
Setchey. *Norf* 4F 77
Setley. *Hants* 2B 16
Setter. *Shet* 3F 173
Settiscarth. *Orkn* 6C 172
Settle. *N Yor* 3H 97
Settrington. *N Yor* 2C 100
Seven Ash. *Som* 3E 21
Sevenhampton. *Glos* 3F 49
Sevenhampton. *Swin* 2H 35
Sevenoaks. *Kent* 5G 39
Sevenoaks Weald. *Kent* 5G 39
Seven Sisters. *Neat* 5B 46
Seven Springs. *Glos* 4E 49
Severn Beach. *S Glo* 3A 34
Severn Stoke. *Worc* 1D 48
Sevington. *Kent* 1E 29
Sewards End. *Essx* 2F 53
Sewardstone. *Essx* 1E 39
Sewell. *C Beds* 3H 51
Sewerby. *E Yor* 3G 101
Seworgan. *Corn* 5B 6
Sewstern. *Leics* 3F 75
Sgallairidh. *W Isl* 9B 170
Sgarasta Mhor. *W Isl* 8C 171
Sgiogarstaigh. *W Isl* 1H 171
Sgreadan. *Arg* 4A 132
Shabbington. *Buck* 5E 51
Shackerley. *Shrp* 5C 72
Shackerstone. *Leics* 5A 74
Shackleford. *Surr* 1A 26
Shadforth. *Dur* 5G 115
Shadingfield. *Suff* 2G 67
Shadoxhurst. *Kent* 2D 28
Shadsworth. *Bkbn* 2E 91
Shadwell. *Norf* 2B 66
Shadwell. *W Yor* 1D 92
Shaftesbury. *Dors* 4D 22
Shafton. *S Yor* 3D 93
Shafton Two Gates. *S Yor* 3D 93
Shaggs. *Dors* 4D 14
Shakesfield. *Glos* 2B 48
Shalbourne. *Wilts* 5B 36
Shalcombe. *IOW* 4B 16
Shalden. *Hants* 2E 25
Shaldon. *Devn* 5C 12
Shalfleet. *IOW* 4C 16
Shalford. *Essx* 3H 53
Shalford. *Surr* 1B 26
Shalford Green. *Essx* 3H 53
Shallowford. *Devn* 2H 19
Shallowford. *Staf* 3C 72
Shalmsford Street. *Kent* 5E 41
Shalstone. *Buck* 2E 51
Shamley Green. *Surr* 1B 26
Shandon. *Arg* 1D 126
Shandwick. *High* 1C 158
Shangton. *Leics* 1E 62
Shankhouse. *Nmbd* 2F 115
Shanklin. *IOW* 4D 16
Shannochie. *N Ayr* 3D 122
Shap. *Cumb* 3G 103
Shapwick. *Dors* 2E 15
Shapwick. *Som* 3H 21
Sharcott. *Wilts* 1G 23
Shardlow. *Derbs* 2B 74
Shareshill. *Staf* 5D 72
Sharlston. *W Yor* 3D 93
Sharlston Common. *W Yor* 3D 93
Sharnal Street. *Medw* 3B 40
Sharnbrook. *Bed* 5G 63
Sharneyford. *Lanc* 2G 91
Sharnford. *Leics* 1B 62
Sharnhill Green. *Dors* 2C 14
Sharow. *N Yor* 2F 99
Sharpe Green. *Lanc* 1D 90
Sharpenhoe. *C Beds* 2A 52
Sharperton. *Nmbd* 4D 120
Sharpness. *Glos* 5B 48
Sharp Street. *Norf* 3F 79
Sharpthorne. *W Sus* 2E 27
Sharrington. *Norf* 2C 78
Shatterford. *Worc* 2B 60
Shatton. *Derbs* 2G 85
Shaugh Prior. *Devn* 2B 8
Shavington. *Ches E* 5B 84
Shaw. *G Man* 4H 91
Shaw. *W Ber* 5C 36
Shaw. *Wilts* 5D 35
Shawbirch. *Telf* 4A 72
Shawbury. *Shrp* 3H 71
Shawdon Hall. *Nmbd* 3E 121
Shawell. *Leics* 2C 62
Shawford. *Hants* 4C 24
Shawforth. *Lanc* 2G 91
Shaw Green. *Lanc* 3D 90
Shawhead. *Dum* 2F 111
Shaw Mills. *N Yor* 3E 99
Shawwood. *E Ayr* 2E 117
Shearington. *Dum* 3B 112
Shearsby. *Leics* 1D 62
Shearston. *Som* 3F 21
Shebbear. *Devn* 2E 11
Shebdon. *Staf* 3B 72
Shebster. *High* 2C 168
Sheddocksley. *Aber* 3F 153
Shedfield. *Hants* 1D 16
Shedog. *N Ayr* 2D 122
Sheen. *Staf* 4F 85
Sheepbridge. *Derbs* 3A 86
Sheep Hill. *Tyne* 4E 115
Sheepscar. *W Yor* 1D 92
Sheepscombe. *Glos* 4D 49
Sheepstor. *Devn* 2B 8
Sheepwash. *Devn* 2E 11
Sheepwash. *Nmbd* 1F 115
Sheepway. *N Som* 4H 33
Sheepy Magna. *Leics* 5H 73
Sheepy Parva. *Leics* 5H 73
Sheering. *Essx* 4F 53
Sheerness. *Kent* 3D 40
Sheerwater. *Surr* 4B 38
Sheet. *Hants* 4F 25
Sheffield. *S Yor* 2H 85 & 210
Sheffield Bottom. *W Ber* 5E 37
Sheffield Green. *E Sus* 3F 27
Shefford. *C Beds* 2B 52
Shefford Woodlands. *W Ber* 4B 36
Sheigra. *High* 2B 166
Sheinton. *Shrp* 5A 72
Shelderton. *Shrp* 3G 59
Sheldon. *Derbs* 4F 85
Sheldon. *Devn* 2E 12
Sheldon. *W Mid* 2F 61
Sheldwich. *Kent* 5E 40
Sheldwich Lees. *Kent* 5E 40
Shelf. *W Yor* 2B 92
Shelfanger. *Norf* 2D 66
Shelfield. *Warw* 4F 61
Shelfield. *W Mid* 5E 73
Shelford. *Notts* 1D 74
Shelford. *Warw* 2B 62
Shell. *Worc* 5D 60
Shelley. *Suff* 2D 54
Shelley. *W Yor* 3C 92
Shell Green. *Hal* 2H 83
Shellingford. *Oxon* 2B 36
Shellow Bowells. *Essx* 5G 53
Shelsley Beauchamp. *Worc* 4B 60
Shelsley Walsh. *Worc* 4B 60
Shelthorpe. *Leics* 4C 74
Shelton. *Bed* 4H 63
Shelton. *Norf* 1E 67
Shelton. *Notts* 1E 75
Shelton. *Shrp* 4G 71
Shelton Green. *Norf* 1E 67
Shelton Lock. *Derb* 2A 74
Shelve. *Shrp* 1F 59
Shelwick. *Here* 1A 48
Shelwick Green. *Here* 1A 48
Shenfield. *Essx* 1H 39
Shenington. *Oxon* 1B 50
Shenley. *Herts* 5B 52
Shenley Brook End. *Mil* 2G 51
Shenleybury. *Herts* 5B 52
Shenley Church End. *Mil* 2G 51
Shenmore. *Here* 2G 47
Shennanton. *Dum* 3A 110
Shenstone. *Staf* 5F 73
Shenstone. *Worc* 3C 60
Shenstone Woodend. *Staf* 5F 73
Shenton. *Leics* 5A 74
Shenval. *Mor* 1G 151
Shepeau Stow. *Linc* 4C 76
Shephall. *Herts* 3C 52
Shepherd's Bush. *G Lon* 2D 38
Shepherd's Gate. *Norf* 4E 77
Shepherd's Green. *Oxon* 3F 37
Shepherd's Port. *Norf* 2F 77
Shepherdswell. *Kent* 1G 29
Shepley. *W Yor* 4B 92
Sheppardstown. *High* 4D 169
Shepperdine. *S Glo* 2B 34
Shepperton. *Surr* 4B 38
Shepreth. *Cambs* 1D 53
Shepshed. *Leics* 4B 74
Shepton Beauchamp. *Som* 1H 13
Shepton Mallet. *Som* 2B 22
Shepton Montague. *Som* 3B 22
Shepway. *Kent* 5B 40
Sheraton. *Dur* 1B 106
Sherborne. *Bath* 1A 22
Sherborne. *Dors* 1B 14
Sherborne. *Glos* 4G 49
Sherborne Causeway. *Dors* 4D 22
Sherborne St John. *Hants* 1E 24
Sherbourne. *Warw* 4G 61
Sherburn. *Dur* 5G 115
Sherburn. *N Yor* 2D 100
Sherburn Hill. *Dur* 5G 115
Sherburn in Elmet. *N Yor* 1E 93
Shere. *Surr* 1B 26
Shereford. *Norf* 3A 78
Sherfield English. *Hants* 4A 24
Sherfield on Loddon. *Hants* 1E 25
Sherford. *Devn* 4D 9
Sherford. *Dors* 3E 15
Sheriffhales. *Shrp* 4B 72
Sheriff Hutton. *N Yor* 3A 100
Sheriffston. *Mor* 2G 159
Sheringham. *Norf* 1D 78
Sherington. *Mil* 1G 51
Shermanbury. *W Sus* 4D 26
Shernal Green. *Worc* 4D 60
Shernborne. *Norf* 2G 77
Sherrington. *Wilts* 3E 23
Sherston. *Wilts* 3D 34
Sherwood. *Nott* 1C 74
Sherwood Green. *Devn* 4F 19
Shettleston. *Glas* 3H 127
Shevington. *G Man* 4D 90
Shevington Moor. *G Man* 3D 90
Shevington Vale. *G Man* 4D 90
Sheviock. *Corn* 3H 7
Shide. *IOW* 4D 16
Shiel Bridge. *High* 2B 148
Shieldaig. *High* 1H 155 (nr. Charlestown)
Shieldaig. *High* 3H 155 (nr. Torridon)
Shieldhill. *Dum* 1B 112
Shieldhill. *Falk* 2B 128
Shieldhill. *S Lan* 5D 128
Shieldmuir. *N Lan* 4A 128
Shielfoot. *High* 2A 140
Shielhill. *Abers* 3H 161
Shielhill. *Ang* 3D 144
Shifnal. *Shrp* 5B 72
Shilbottle. *Nmbd* 4F 121
Shilbottle Grange. *Nmbd* 4G 121
Shildon. *Dur* 2F 105
Shillford. *E Ren* 4F 127
Shillingford. *Devn* 4C 20
Shillingford. *Oxon* 2D 36
Shillingford St George. *Devn* 4C 12
Shillingstone. *Dors* 1D 14
Shillington. *C Beds* 2B 52
Shillmoor. *Nmbd* 4C 120
Shilton. *Oxon* 5A 50
Shilton. *Warw* 2B 62
Shilvinghampton. *Dors* 4B 14
Shilvington. *Nmbd* 1E 115
Shimpling. *Norf* 2D 66
Shimpling. *Suff* 5A 66
Shimpling Street. *Suff* 5A 66
Shincliffe. *Dur* 5F 115
Shiney Row. *Tyne* 4G 115
Shinfield. *Wok* 5F 37
Shingay. *Cambs* 1D 52
Shingham. *Norf* 5G 77
Shingle Street. *Suff* 1G 55
Shinner's Bridge. *Devn* 2D 9
Shinness. *High* 2C 164
Shipbourne. *Kent* 5G 39
Shipdham. *Norf* 5B 78
Shipham. *Som* 1H 21
Shiphay. *Torb* 2E 9
Shiplake. *Oxon* 4F 37
Shipley. *Derbs* 1B 74
Shipley. *Nmbd* 3F 121
Shipley. *Shrp* 1C 60
Shipley. *W Sus* 3C 26
Shipley. *W Yor* 1B 92
Shipley Bridge. *Surr* 1E 27
Shipmeadow. *Suff* 1F 67
Shippon. *Oxon* 2C 36
Shipston-on-Stour. *Warw* 1A 50
Shipton. *Buck* 3F 51
Shipton. *Glos* 4F 49
Shipton. *N Yor* 4H 99
Shipton. *Shrp* 1H 59
Shipton Bellinger. *Hants* 2H 23
Shipton Gorge. *Dors* 3H 13
Shipton Green. *W Sus* 3G 17
Shipton Moyne. *Glos* 3D 35
Shipton-on-Cherwell. *Oxon* 4C 50
Shiptonthorpe. *E Yor* 5C 100
Shipton-under-Wychwood. *Oxon* 4A 50
Shirburn. *Oxon* 2E 37
Shirdley Hill. *Lanc* 3B 90
Shire. *Cumb* 1H 103
Shirebrook. *Derbs* 4C 86
Shiregreen. *S Yor* 1A 86
Shirehampton. *Bris* 4A 34
Shiremoor. *Tyne* 2G 115
Shirenewton. *Mon* 2H 33
Shireoaks. *Notts* 2C 86
Shires Mill. *Fife* 1C 128
Shirkoak. *Kent* 2D 28
Shirland. *Derbs* 5A 86
Shirley. *Derbs* 1G 73
Shirley. *Sotn* 1C 16
Shirley. *W Mid* 3F 61
Shirleywich. *Staf* 3D 73
Shirl Heath. *Here* 5G 59
Shirrell Heath. *Hants* 1D 16
Shirwell. *Devn* 3F 19
Shiskine. *N Ayr* 3D 122
Shobdon. *Here* 4F 59
Shobnall. *Staf* 3G 73
Shobrooke. *Devn* 2B 12
Shoby. *Leics* 3D 74
Shocklach. *Ches W* 1G 71
Shoeburyness. *S'end* 2D 40
Sholden. *Kent* 5H 41
Sholing. *Sotn* 1C 16
Sholver. *G Man* 4H 91
Shoot Hill. *Shrp* 4G 71
Shop. *Corn* 1C 10 (nr. Bude)
Shop. *Corn* 1C 6 (nr. Padstow)
Shop. *Devn* 1D 11
Shopford. *Cumb* 2G 113
Shoreditch. *G Lon* 2E 39
Shoreditch. *Som* 4F 21
Shoregill. *Cumb* 4A 104
Shoreham. *Kent* 4G 39
Shoreham-by-Sea. *W Sus* 5D 26
Shoresdean. *Nmbd* 5F 131
Shoreswood. *Nmbd* 5F 131
Shore, The. *Fife* 2E 137
Shorncote. *Glos* 2F 35
Shorne. *Kent* 3A 40
Shorne Ridgeway. *Kent* 3A 40
Shortacombe. *Devn* 4F 11
Shortbridge. *E Sus* 3F 27
Shortgate. *E Sus* 4F 27
Short Green. *Norf* 2C 66
Shorthampton. *Oxon* 3B 50
Short Heath. *Leics* 4H 73
Short Heath. *W Mid* 1E 61 (nr. Erdington)
Short Heath. *W Mid* 5D 73 (nr. Wednesfield)
Shortlanesend. *Corn* 4C 6
Shorton. *Torb* 2E 9
Shortstown. *Bed* 1A 52
Shortwood. *S Glo* 4B 34
Shorwell. *IOW* 4C 16
Shoscombe. *Bath* 1C 22
Shotesham. *Norf* 1E 67
Shotgate. *Essx* 1B 40
Shotley. *Suff* 2F 55
Shotley Bridge. *Dur* 4D 115
Shotleyfield. *Nmbd* 4D 114
Shotley Gate. *Suff* 2F 55
Shottenden. *Kent* 5E 41
Shottermill. *Surr* 3G 25
Shottery. *Warw* 5F 61
Shotteswell. *Warw* 1C 50
Shottisham. *Suff* 1G 55
Shottle. *Derbs* 1H 73
Shotton. *Dur* 1B 106 (nr. Peterlee)
Shotton. *Dur* 2A 106 (nr. Sedgefield)
Shotton. *Flin* 4E 83
Shotton. *Nmbd* 2F 115 (nr. Morpeth)
Shotton. *Nmbd* 1C 120 (nr. Town Yetholm)
Shotton Colliery. *Dur* 5G 115
Shotts. *N Lan* 3B 128
Shotwick. *Ches W* 3F 83
Shouldham. *Norf* 5F 77
Shouldham Thorpe. *Norf* 5F 77
Shoulton. *Worc* 5C 60
Shrawardine. *Shrp* 4F 71
Shrawley. *Worc* 4C 60
Shreding Green. *Buck* 2B 38
Shrewley. *Warw* 4G 61
Shrewsbury. *Shrp* 4G 71 & 210
Shrewton. *Wilts* 2F 23
Shripney. *W Sus* 5A 26
Shrivenham. *Oxon* 3H 35
Shropham. *Norf* 1B 66
Shroton. *Dors* 1D 14
Shrub End. *Essx* 3C 54
Shucknall. *Here* 1A 48
Shudy Camps. *Cambs* 1G 53
Shulishadermor. *High* 4D 155
Shulista. *High* 1D 154
Shurdington. *Glos* 4E 49
Shurlock Row. *Wind* 4G 37
Shurrery. *High* 3C 168
Shurton. *Som* 2F 21
Shustoke. *Warw* 1G 61
Shute. *Devn* 3F 13 (nr. Axminster)
Shute. *Devn* 2B 12 (nr. Crediton)
Shutford. *Oxon* 1B 50
Shut Heath. *Staf* 3C 72
Shuthonger. *Glos* 2D 49
Shutlanehead. *Staf* 1C 72
Shutlanger. *Nptn* 1F 51
Shutt Green. *Staf* 5C 72
Shuttington. *Warw* 5G 73
Shuttlewood. *Derbs* 3B 86
Shuttleworth. *G Man* 3G 91
Siabost. *W Isl* 3E 171
Siabost bho Dheas. *W Isl* 3E 171
Siabost bho Thuath. *W Isl* 3E 171
Siadar. *W Isl* 2F 171
Siadar Uarach. *W Isl* 2F 171
Sibbaldbie. *Dum* 1C 112
Sibbertoft. *Nptn* 2D 62
Sibdon Carwood. *Shrp* 2G 59
Sibertswold. *Kent* 1G 29
Sibford Ferris. *Oxon* 2B 50
Sibford Gower. *Oxon* 2B 50
Sible Hedingham. *Essx* 2A 54
Sibsey. *Linc* 5C 88
Sibsey Fen Side. *Linc* 5C 88
Sibson. *Cambs* 1H 63
Sibson. *Leics* 5A 74
Sibster. *High* 3F 169
Sibthorpe. *Notts* 1E 75
Sibton. *Suff* 4F 67
Sicklesmere. *Suff* 4A 66
Sicklinghall. *N Yor* 5F 99
Sid. *Devn* 4E 13
Sidbury. *Devn* 3E 13
Sidbury. *Shrp* 2A 60
Sidcot. *N Som* 1H 21
Sidcup. *G Lon* 3F 39
Siddick. *Cumb* 1B 102
Siddington. *Ches E* 3C 84
Siddington. *Glos* 2F 35
Side of the Moor. *G Man* 3F 91
Sidestrand. *Norf* 2E 79
Sidford. *Devn* 3E 13
Sidlesham. *W Sus* 3G 17
Sidley. *E Sus* 5B 28
Sidlow. *Surr* 1D 26
Sidmouth. *Devn* 4E 13
Sigford. *Devn* 5A 12
Sigglesthorne. *E Yor* 5F 101
Sighthill. *Edin* 2E 129
Sigingstone. *V Glam* 4C 32
Signet. *Oxon* 4H 49
Silchester. *Hants* 5E 37
Sildinis. *W Isl* 6E 171
Sileby. *Leics* 4D 74
Silecroft. *Cumb* 1A 96
Silfield. *Norf* 1D 66
Silian. *Cdgn* 5E 57
Silkstone. *S Yor* 4C 92
Silkstone Common. *S Yor* 4C 92
Silksworth. *Tyne* 4G 115
Silk Willoughby. *Linc* 1H 75
Silloth. *Cumb* 4C 112
Sills. *Nmbd* 4C 120
Sillyearn. *Mor* 3C 160
Silpho. *N Yor* 5G 107
Silsden. *W Yor* 5C 98
Silsoe. *C Beds* 2A 52
Silverbank. *Abers* 4E 152
Silverburn. *Midl* 3F 129
Silverdale. *Lanc* 2D 96
Silverdale. *Staf* 1C 72
Silverdale Green. *Lanc* 2D 96
Silver End. *Essx* 4B 54
Silver End. *W Mid* 2D 60
Silvergate. *Norf* 3D 78
Silver Green. *Norf* 1E 67
Silverhillocks. *Abers* 2E 161
Silverley's Green. *Suff* 3E 67
Silverstone. *Nptn* 1E 51
Silverton. *Devn* 2C 12
Silverton. *W Dun* 2F 127
Silvington. *Shrp* 3A 60
Simm's Cross. *Hal* 2H 83
Simm's Lane End. *Mers* 1H 83
Simonburn. *Nmbd* 2B 114
Simonsbath. *Som* 3A 20
Simonstone. *Lanc* 1F 91
Simprim. *Bord* 5E 131
Simpson. *Pemb* 3C 42
Simpson Cross. *Pemb* 3C 42
Sinclairston. *E Ayr* 3D 116
Sinclairtown. *Fife* 4E 137
Sinderby. *N Yor* 1F 99
Sinderhope. *Nmbd* 4B 114
Sindlesham. *Wok* 5F 37
Sinfin. *Derb* 2A 74
Singleborough. *Buck* 2F 51
Singleton. *Kent* 1D 28
Singleton. *Lanc* 1B 90
Singleton. *W Sus* 1G 17
Singlewell. *Kent* 3A 40
Sinkhurst Green. *Kent* 1C 28
Sinnahard. *Abers* 2B 152
Sinnington. *N Yor* 1B 100
Sinton Green. *Worc* 4C 60
Sipson. *G Lon* 3B 38
Sirhowy. *Blae* 4E 47
Sisland. *Norf* 1F 67
Sissinghurst. *Kent* 2B 28
Siston. *S Glo* 4B 34
Sithney. *Corn* 4D 4
Sittingbourne. *Kent* 4D 40
Six Ashes. *Staf* 2B 60
Six Bells. *Blae* 5F 47
Six Hills. *Leics* 3D 74
Sixhills. *Linc* 2A 88
Six Mile Bottom. *Cambs* 5E 65
Sixpenny Handley. *Dors* 1E 15
Sizewell. *Suff* 4G 67
Skail. *High* 4H 167
Skaill. *Orkn* 6B 172
Skaills. *Orkn* 7E 172
Skares. *E Ayr* 3E 117
Skateraw. *E Lot* 2D 130
Skaw. *Shet* 5G 173
Skeabost. *High* 4D 154

Skeabrae. *Orkn* 5B **172**
Skeeby. *N Yor* 4E **105**
Skeffington. *Leics* 5E **75**
Skeffling. *E Yor* 3G **95**
Skegby. *Notts* 4B **86**
(nr. Mansfield)
Skegby. *Notts* 3E **87**
(nr. Tuxford)
Skegness. *Linc* 4E **89**
Skelberry. *Shet* 10E **173**
(nr. Boddam)
Skelberry. *Shet* 3E **173**
(nr. Housetter)
Skelbo. *High* 4E **165**
Skelbo Street. *High* 4E **165**
Skelbrooke. *S Yor* 3F **93**
Skeldyke. *Linc* 2C **76**
Skelfhill. *Bord* 4G **119**
Skellingthorpe. *Linc* 3G **87**
Skellister. *Shet* 6F **173**
Skellorn Green. *Ches E* 2D **84**
Skellow. *S Yor* 3F **93**
Skelmanthorpe. *W Yor* 3C **92**
Skelmersdale. *Lanc* 4C **90**
Skelmorlie. *N Ayr* 3C **126**
Skelpick. *High* 3H **167**
Skelton. *Cumb* 1F **103**
Skelton. *E Yor* 2A **94**
Skelton. *N Yor* 4D **105**
(nr. Richmond)
Skelton. *N Yor* 3F **99**
(nr. Ripon)
Skelton. *Red C* 3D **106**
Skelton. *York* 4H **99**
Skelton Green. *Red C* 3D **106**
Skelwick. *Orkn* 3D **172**
Skelwith Bridge. *Cumb* 4E **103**
Skendleby. *Linc* 4D **88**
Skendleby Psalter. *Linc* 3D **88**
Skenfrith. *Mon* 3H **47**
Skerne. *E Yor* 4E **101**
Skeroblingarry. *Arg* 3B **122**
Skerray. *High* 2G **167**
Skerricha. *High* 3C **166**
Skerries Airport. *Shet* 4H **173**
Skerton. *Lanc* 3D **97**
Sketchley. *Leics* 1B **62**
Sketty. *Swan* 3F **31**
Skewen. *Neat* 3G **31**
Skewsby. *N Yor* 2A **100**
Skeyton. *Norf* 3E **79**
Skeyton Corner. *Norf* 3E **79**
Skiall. *High* 2C **168**
Skidbrooke. *Linc* 1D **88**
Skidbrooke North End. *Linc* 1D **88**
Skidby. *E Yor* 1D **94**
Skilgate. *Som* 4C **20**
Skillington. *Linc* 3F **75**
Skinburness. *Cumb* 4C **112**
Skinflats. *Falk* 1C **128**
Skinidin. *High* 4B **154**
Skinnet. *High* 2F **167**
Skinningrove. *Red C* 2E **107**
Skipness. *Arg* 4G **125**
Skippool. *Lanc* 5C **96**
Skiprigg. *Cumb* 5E **113**
Skipsea. *E Yor* 4F **101**
Skipsea Brough. *E Yor* 4F **101**
Skipton. *N Yor* 4B **98**
Skipton-on-Swale. *N Yor* 2F **99**
Skipwith. *N Yor* 1G **93**
Skirbeck. *Linc* 1C **76**
Skirbeck Quarter. *Linc* 1C **76**
Skirlaugh. *E Yor* 1E **95**
Skirling. *Bord* 1C **118**
Skirmett. *Buck* 2F **37**
Skirpenbeck. *E Yor* 4B **100**
Skirwith. *Cumb* 1H **103**
Skirwith. *N Yor* 2G **97**
Skirza. *High* 2F **169**
Skitby. *Cumb* 3F **113**
Skitham. *Lanc* 5D **96**
Skittle Green. *Buck* 5F **51**
Skroo. *Shet* 1B **172**
Skulamus. *High* 1E **147**
Skullomie. *High* 2G **167**
Skyborry Green. *Shrp* 3E **59**
Skye Green. *Essx* 3B **54**
Skye of Curr. *High* 1D **151**
Slack. *W Yor* 2H **91**
Slackhall. *Derbs* 2E **85**
Slack Head. *Cumb* 2D **97**
Slackhead. *Mor* 2B **160**
Slackholme End. *Linc* 3E **89**
Slacks of Cairnbanno. *Abers* 4F **161**
Slack, The. *Dur* 2E **105**
Slad. *Glos* 5D **48**
Slade. *Swan* 4D **31**
Slade End. *Oxon* 2D **36**
Slade Field. *Cambs* 2C **64**
Slade Green. *G Lon* 3G **39**
Slade Heath. *Staf* 5D **72**
Slade Hooton. *S Yor* 2C **86**
Sladesbridge. *Corn* 5A **10**
Slade, The. *W Ber* 5D **36**
Slaggyford. *Nmbd* 4H **113**
Slaidburn. *Lanc* 4G **97**
Slaid Hill. *W Yor* 5F **99**
Slaithwaite. *W Yor* 3A **92**
Slaley. *Derbs* 5G **85**
Slaley. *Nmbd* 4C **114**
Slamannan. *Falk* 2B **128**
Slapton. *Buck* 3H **51**
Slapton. *Devn* 4E **9**
Slapton. *Nptn* 1E **51**
Slattock. *G Man* 4G **91**
Slaugham. *W Sus* 3D **26**
Slaughterbridge. *Corn* 4B **10**
Slaughterford. *Wilts* 4D **34**
Slawston. *Leics* 1E **63**
Sleaford. *Hants* 3G **25**
Sleaford. *Linc* 1H **75**
Sleagill. *Cumb* 3G **103**
Sleap. *Shrp* 3G **71**
Sledmere. *E Yor* 3D **100**
Sleightholme. *Dur* 3C **104**
Sleights. *N Yor* 4F **107**
Slepe. *Dors* 3E **15**
Slickly. *High* 2E **169**
Sliddery. *N Ayr* 3D **122**
Sligachan. *High* 1C **146**
Slimbridge. *Glos* 5C **48**
Slindon. *Staf* 2C **72**
Slindon. *W Sus* 5A **26**
Slinfold. *W Sus* 2C **26**
Slingsby. *N Yor* 2A **100**
Slip End. *C Beds* 4A **52**
Slipton. *Nptn* 3G **63**
Slitting Mill. *Staf* 4E **73**
Slochd. *High* 1C **150**
Slockavullin. *Arg* 4F **133**
Sloley. *Norf* 3E **79**
Sloncombe. *Devn* 4H **11**
Sloothby. *Linc* 3D **89**
Slough. *Slo* 2A **38**
Slough Green. *Som* 4F **21**
Slough Green. *W Sus* 3D **27**
Sluggan. *High* 1C **150**
Slyne. *Lanc* 3D **97**
Smailholm. *Bord* 1A **120**
Smallbridge. *G Man* 3H **91**
Smallbrook. *Devn* 3B **12**
Smallburgh. *Norf* 3F **79**
Smallburn. *E Ayr* 2F **117**
Smalldale. *Derbs* 3E **85**
Small Dole. *W Sus* 4D **26**
Smalley. *Derbs* 1B **74**
Smallfield. *Surr* 1E **27**
Small Heath. *W Mid* 2E **61**
Smallholm. *Dum* 2C **112**
Small Hythe. *Kent* 2C **28**
Smallrice. *Staf* 2D **72**
Smallridge. *Devn* 2G **13**
Smallwood Hey. *Lanc* 5C **96**
Smallworth. *Norf* 2C **66**
Smannell. *Hants* 2B **24**
Smardale. *Cumb* 4A **104**
Smarden. *Kent* 1C **28**
Smarden Bell. *Kent* 1C **28**
Smart's Hill. *Kent* 1G **27**
Smeatharpe. *Devn* 1F **13**
Smeeth. *Kent* 2E **29**
Smeeth, The. *Norf* 4E **77**
Smeeton Westerby. *Leics* 1D **62**
Smeircleit. *W Isl* 7C **170**
Smerral. *High* 5D **168**
Smestow. *Staf* 1C **60**
Smethwick. *W Mid* 2E **61**
Smirisary. *High* 1A **140**
Smisby. *Derbs* 4H **73**
Smitham Hill. *Bath* 1A **22**
Smith End Green. *Worc* 5B **60**
Smithfield. *Cumb* 3F **113**
Smith Green. *Lanc* 4D **97**
Smithies, The. *Shrp* 1A **60**
Smithincott. *Devn* 1D **12**
Smith's Green. *Essx* 3F **53**
Smithstown. *High* 1G **155**
Smithton. *High* 4B **158**
Smithwood Green. *Suff* 5B **66**
Smithy Bridge. *G Man* 3H **91**
Smithy Green. *Ches E* 3B **84**
Smithy Lane Ends. *Lanc* 3C **90**
Smockington. *Warw* 2B **62**
Smoogro. *Orkn* 7C **172**
Smyth's Green. *Essx* 4C **54**
Snaigow House. *Per* 4H **143**
Snailbeach. *Shrp* 5F **71**
Snailwell. *Cambs* 4F **65**
Snainton. *N Yor* 1D **100**
Snaith. *E Yor* 2G **93**
Snape. *N Yor* 1E **99**
Snape. *Suff* 5F **67**
Snape Green. *Lanc* 3B **90**
Snapper. *Devn* 3F **19**
Snarestone. *Leics* 5H **73**
Snarford. *Linc* 2H **87**
Snargate. *Kent* 3D **28**
Snave. *Kent* 3E **28**
Sneachill. *Worc* 5D **60**
Snead. *Powy* 1F **59**
Snead Common. *Worc* 4B **60**
Sneaton. *N Yor* 4F **107**
Sneatonthorpe. *N Yor* 4G **107**
Snelland. *Linc* 2H **87**
Snelston. *Derbs* 1F **73**
Snetterton. *Norf* 1B **66**
Snettisham. *Norf* 2F **77**
Snibston. *Leics* 4B **74**
Sniseabhal. *W Isl* 5C **170**
Snitter. *Nmbd* 4E **121**
Snitterby. *Linc* 1G **87**
Snitterfield. *Warw* 5G **61**
Snitton. *Shrp* 3H **59**
Snodhill. *Here* 1G **47**
Snodland. *Kent* 4A **40**
Snods Edge. *Nmbd* 4D **114**
Snowdonia. *Gwyn* 2G **69**
Snowshill. *Glos* 2F **49**
Snow Street. *Norf* 2C **66**
Snydale. *W Yor* 3E **93**
Soake. *Hants* 1E **17**
Soar. *Carm* 3G **45**
Soar. *Gwyn* 2F **69**
Soar. *IOA* 3C **80**
Soar. *Powy* 2C **46**
Soberton. *Hants* 1E **16**
Soberton Heath. *Hants* 1E **16**
Sockbridge. *Cumb* 2F **103**
Sockburn. *Darl* 4A **106**
Sodom. *Den* 3C **82**
Sodom. *Shet* 5G **173**
Soham. *Cambs* 3E **65**
Soham Cotes. *Cambs* 3E **65**
Solas. *W Isl* 1D **170**
Soldon Cross. *Devn* 1D **10**
Soldridge. *Hants* 3E **25**
Solent Breezes. *Hants* 2D **16**
Sole Street. *Kent* 4A **40**
(nr. Meopham)
Sole Street. *Kent* 1E **29**
(nr. Waltham)
Solihull. *W Mid* 3F **61**
Sollers Dilwyn. *Here* 5G **59**
Sollers Hope. *Here* 2B **48**
Sollom. *Lanc* 3C **90**
Solva. *Pemb* 2B **42**
Somerby. *Leics* 4E **75**
Somerby. *Linc* 4D **94**
Somercotes. *Derbs* 5B **86**
Somerford. *Dors* 3G **15**
Somerford. *Staf* 5C **72**
Somerford Keynes. *Glos* 2F **35**
Somerley. *W Sus* 3G **17**
Somerleyton. *Suff* 1G **67**
Somersal Herbert. *Derbs* 2F **73**
Somersby. *Linc* 3C **88**
Somersham. *Cambs* 3C **64**
Somersham. *Suff* 1D **54**
Somerton. *Oxon* 3C **50**
Somerton. *Som* 4H **21**
Somerton. *Suff* 5H **65**
Sompting. *W Sus* 5C **26**
Sonning. *Wok* 4F **37**
Sonning Common. *Oxon* 3F **37**
Sonning Eye. *Oxon* 4F **37**
Sookholme. *Notts* 4C **86**
Sopley. *Hants* 3G **15**
Sopworth. *Wilts* 3D **34**
Sorbie. *Dum* 5B **110**
Sordale. *High* 2D **168**
Sorisdale. *Arg* 2D **138**
Sorn. *E Ayr* 2E **117**
Sornhill. *E Ayr* 1E **117**
Sortat. *High* 2E **169**
Sotby. *Linc* 3B **88**
Sots Hole. *Linc* 4A **88**
Sotterley. *Suff* 2G **67**
Soudley. *Shrp* 1G **59**
(nr. Church Stretton)
Soudley. *Shrp* 3B **72**
(nr. Market Drayton)
Soughton. *Flin* 4E **83**
Soulbury. *Buck* 3G **51**
Soulby. *Cumb* 3A **104**
(nr. Appleby)
Soulby. *Cumb* 2F **103**
(nr. Penrith)
Souldern. *Oxon* 2D **50**
Souldrop. *Bed* 4G **63**
Sound. *Ches E* 1A **72**
Sound. *Shet* 7F **173**
(nr. Lerwick)
Sound. *Shet* 6E **173**
(nr. Tresta)
Soundwell. *Bris* 4B **34**
Sourhope. *Bord* 2C **120**
Sourin. *Orkn* 4D **172**
Sour Nook. *Cumb* 5E **113**
Sourton. *Devn* 3F **11**
Soutergate. *Cumb* 1B **96**
South Acre. *Norf* 4H **77**
Southall. *G Lon* 3C **38**
South Allington. *Devn* 5D **9**
South Alloa. *Falk* 4A **136**
Southam. *Glos* 3E **49**
Southam. *Warw* 4B **62**
South Ambersham. *W Sus* 3A **26**
Southampton. *Sotn* 1C **16** & **211**
Southampton International Airport. *Hants* 1C **16**
Southannan. *N Ayr* 4D **126**
South Anston. *S Yor* 2C **86**
South Ascot. *Wind* 4A **38**
South Baddesley. *Hants* 3B **16**
South Balfern. *Dum* 4B **110**
South Ballachulish. *High* 3E **141**
South Bank. *Red C* 2C **106**
South Barrow. *Som* 4B **22**
South Benfleet. *Essx* 2B **40**
South Bents. *Tyne* 3H **115**
South Bersted. *W Sus* 5A **26**
Southborough. *Kent* 1G **27**
Southbourne. *Bour* 3G **15**
Southbourne. *W Sus* 2F **17**
South Bowood. *Dors* 3H **13**
South Brent. *Devn* 2D **8**
South Brewham. *Som* 3C **22**
South Broomage. *Falk* 1B **128**
South Broomhill. *Nmbd* 4G **121**
Southburgh. *Norf* 5B **78**
South Burlingham. *Norf* 5F **79**
Southburn. *E Yor* 4D **101**
South Cadbury. *Som* 4B **22**
South Carlton. *Linc* 3G **87**
South Cave. *E Yor* 1C **94**
South Cerney. *Glos* 2F **35**
South Chard. *Som* 2G **13**
South Charlton. *Nmbd* 2F **121**
South Cheriton. *Som* 4B **22**
South Church. *Dur* 2F **105**
Southchurch. *S'end* 2D **40**
South Cleatlam. *Dur* 3E **105**
South Cliffe. *E Yor* 1B **94**
South Clifton. *Notts* 3F **87**
South Clunes. *High* 4H **157**
South Cockerington. *Linc* 2C **88**
South Common. *Devn* 2G **13**
South Common. *E Sus* 4E **27**
South Cornelly. *B'end* 3B **32**
Southcott. *Devn* 1E **11**
(nr. Great Torrington)
Southcott. *Devn* 3F **11**
(nr. Okehampton)
Southcott. *Wilts* 1G **23**
Southcourt. *Buck* 4G **51**
South Cove. *Suff* 2G **67**
South Creagan. *Arg* 4D **141**
South Creake. *Norf* 2A **78**
South Crosland. *W Yor* 3B **92**
South Croxton. *Leics* 4D **74**
South Dalton. *E Yor* 5D **100**
South Darenth. *Kent* 4G **39**
Southdean. *Bord* 4A **120**
Southdown. *Bath* 5C **34**
South Downs. *W Sus* 5D **26**
South Duffield. *N Yor* 1G **93**
Southease. *E Sus* 5F **27**
South Elkington. *Linc* 2B **88**
South Elmsall. *W Yor* 3E **93**
Southend. *Arg* 5A **122**
South End. *Cumb* 3B **96**
Southend. *Glos* 2C **34**
South End. *N Lin* 2E **94**
South End. *W Ber* 4D **36**
Southend (London) Airport. *Essx* 2C **40**
Southend-on-Sea. *S'end* 2C **40**
Southerfield. *Cumb* 5C **112**
Southerhouse. *Shet* 8E **173**
Southerly. *Devn* 4F **11**
Southernden. *Kent* 1C **28**
Southerndown. *V Glam* 4B **32**
Southerness. *Dum* 4A **112**
South Erradale. *High* 1G **155**
Southerton. *Devn* 3D **12**
Southery. *Norf* 1F **65**
Southey Green. *Essx* 2A **54**
South Fambridge. *Essx* 1C **40**
South Fawley. *W Ber* 3B **36**
South Feorline. *N Ayr* 3D **122**
South Ferriby. *N Lin* 2C **94**
South Field. *E Yor* 2D **94**
Southfleet. *Kent* 3H **39**
South Garvan. *High* 1D **141**
Southgate. *Cdgn* 2E **57**
Southgate. *G Lon* 1E **39**
Southgate. *Norf* 3D **78**
(nr. Aylsham)
Southgate. *Norf* 2A **78**
(nr. Fakenham)
Southgate. *Swan* 4E **31**
South Gluss. *Shet* 4E **173**
South Godstone. *Surr* 1E **27**
South Gorley. *Hants* 1G **15**
South Green. *Essx* 1A **40**
(nr. Billericay)
South Green. *Essx* 4D **54**
(nr. Colchester)
South Green. *Kent* 4C **40**
South Hanningfield. *Essx* 1B **40**
South Harting. *W Sus* 1F **17**
South Hayling. *Hants* 3F **17**
South Hazelrigg. *Nmbd* 1E **121**
South Heath. *Buck* 5H **51**
South Heath. *Essx* 4E **54**
South Heighton. *E Sus* 5F **27**
South Hetton. *Dur* 5G **115**
South Hiendley. *W Yor* 3D **93**
South Hill. *Corn* 5D **10**
South Hill. *Som* 4H **21**
South Hinksey. *Oxon* 5D **50**
South Hole. *Devn* 4C **18**
South Holme. *N Yor* 2B **100**
South Holmwood. *Surr* 1C **26**
South Hornchurch. *G Lon* 2G **39**
South Huish. *Devn* 4C **8**
South Hykeham. *Linc* 4G **87**
South Hylton. *Tyne* 4G **115**
Southill. *C Beds* 1B **52**
Southington. *Hants* 2D **24**
South Kelsey. *Linc* 1H **87**
South Kessock. *High* 4A **158**
South Killingholme. *N Lin* 3E **95**
South Kilvington. *N Yor* 1G **99**
South Kilworth. *Leics* 2D **62**
South Kirkby. *W Yor* 3E **93**
South Kirton. *Abers* 3E **153**
South Knighton. *Devn* 5B **12**
South Kyme. *Linc* 1A **76**
South Lancing. *W Sus* 5C **26**
South Ledaig. *Arg* 5D **140**
Southleigh. *Devn* 3F **13**
South Leigh. *Oxon* 5B **50**
South Leverton. *Notts* 2E **87**
South Littleton. *Worc* 1F **49**
South Lopham. *Norf* 2C **66**
South Luffenham. *Rut* 5G **75**
South Malling. *E Sus* 4F **27**
South Marston. *Swin* 3G **35**
South Middleton. *Nmbd* 2E **121**
South Milford. *N Yor* 1E **93**
South Milton. *Devn* 4D **8**
South Mimms. *Herts* 5C **52**
Southminster. *Essx* 1D **40**
South Molton. *Devn* 4H **19**
South Moor. *Dur* 4E **115**
Southmoor. *Oxon* 2B **36**
South Moreton. *Oxon* 3D **36**
South Mundham. *W Sus* 2G **17**
South Muskham. *Notts* 5E **87**
South Newbald. *E Yor* 1C **94**
South Newington. *Oxon* 2C **50**
South Newsham. *Nmbd* 2G **115**
South Newton. *N Ayr* 4H **125**
South Newton. *Wilts* 3F **23**
South Normanton. *Derbs* 5B **86**
South Norwood. *G Lon* 4E **39**
South Nutfield. *Surr* 1E **27**
South Ockendon. *Thur* 2G **39**
Southoe. *Cambs* 4A **64**
Southolt. *Suff* 4D **66**
South Ormsby. *Linc* 3C **88**
Southorpe. *Pet* 5H **75**
South Otterington. *N Yor* 1F **99**
South Owersby. *Linc* 1H **87**
Southowram. *W Yor* 2B **92**
South Oxhey. *Herts* 1C **38**
South Perrott. *Dors* 2H **13**
South Petherton. *Som* 1H **13**
South Petherwin. *Corn* 4D **10**
South Pickenham. *Norf* 5A **78**
South Pool. *Devn* 4D **9**
South Poorton. *Dors* 3A **14**
South Port. *Arg* 1H **133**
Southport. *Mers* 3B **90**
Southpunds. *Shet* 10F **173**
South Queensferry. *Edin* 2E **129**
South Radworthy. *Devn* 3A **20**
South Rauceby. *Linc* 1H **75**
South Raynham. *Norf* 3A **78**
Southrepps. *Norf* 2E **79**
South Reston. *Linc* 2D **88**
Southrey. *Linc* 4A **88**
Southrop. *Glos* 5G **49**
Southrope. *Hants* 2E **25**
South Runcton. *Norf* 5F **77**
South Scarle. *Notts* 4F **87**
Southsea. *Port* 3E **17**
South Shields. *Tyne* 3G **115**
South Shore. *Bkpl* 1B **90**
Southside. *Orkn* 5E **172**
South Somercotes. *Linc* 1D **88**
South Stainley. *N Yor* 3F **99**
South Stainmore. *Cumb* 3B **104**
South Stifford. *Thur* 3G **39**
Southstoke. *Bath* 5C **34**
South Stoke. *Oxon* 3D **36**
South Stoke. *W Sus* 4B **26**
South Street. *E Sus* 4E **27**
South Street. *Kent* 5E **41**
(nr. Faversham)
South Street. *Kent* 4F **41**
(nr. Whitstable)
South Tawton. *Devn* 3G **11**
South Thoresby. *Linc* 3D **88**
South Tidworth. *Wilts* 2H **23**
South Town. *Devn* 4C **12**
South Town. *Hants* 3E **25**
Southtown. *Norf* 5H **79**
Southtown. *Orkn* 8D **172**
South View. *Shet* 7E **173**
Southwaite. *Cumb* 5F **113**
South Walsham. *Norf* 4F **79**
South Warnborough. *Hants* 2F **25**
Southwater. *W Sus* 3C **26**
Southwater Street. *W Sus* 3C **26**
Southway. *Som* 2A **22**
South Weald. *Essx* 1G **39**
South Weirs. *Hants* 2A **16**
Southwell. *Dors* 5B **14**
Southwell. *Notts* 5D **86**
South Weston. *Oxon* 2F **37**
South Wheatley. *Corn* 3C **10**
South Wheatley. *Notts* 2E **87**
Southwick. *Hants* 2E **17**
Southwick. *Nptn* 1H **63**
Southwick. *Tyne* 4G **115**
Southwick. *W Sus* 5D **26**
Southwick. *Wilts* 1D **22**
South Widcombe. *Bath* 1A **22**
South Wigston. *Leics* 1C **62**
South Willingham. *Linc* 2A **88**
South Wingfield. *Derbs* 5A **86**
South Witham. *Linc* 4G **75**
Southwold. *Suff* 3H **67**
South Wonston. *Hants* 3C **24**
Southwood. *Norf* 5F **79**
Southwood. *Som* 3A **22**

South Woodham Ferrers. *Essx* 1C 40
South Wootton. *Norf* 3F 77
South Wraxall. *Wilts* 5D 34
South Zeal. *Devn* 3G 11
Soval Lodge. *W Isl* 5F 171
Sowerby. *N Yor* 1G 99
Sowerby. *W Yor* 2A 92
Sowerby Bridge. *W Yor* 2A 92
Sowerby Row. *Cumb* 5E 113
Sower Carr. *Lanc* 5C 96
Sowley Green. *Suff* 5G 65
Sowood. *W Yor* 3A 92
Sowton. *Devn* 3C 12
Soyal. *High* 4C 164
Soyland Town. *W Yor* 2A 92
Spacey Houses. *N Yor* 4F 99
Spa Common. *Norf* 2E 79
Spalding. *Linc* 3B 76
Spaldington. *E Yor* 1A 94
Spaldwick. *Cambs* 3A 64
Spalford. *Notts* 4F 87
Spanby. *Linc* 2H 75
Sparham. *Norf* 4C 78
Sparhamhill. *Norf* 4C 78
Spark Bridge. *Cumb* 1C 96
Sparket. *Cumb* 2F 103
Sparkford. *Som* 4B 22
Sparkwell. *Devn* 3B 8
Sparrow Green. *Norf* 4B 78
Sparrowpit. *Derbs* 2E 85
Sparrow's Green. *E Sus* 2H 27
Sparsholt. *Hants* 3C 24
Sparsholt. *Oxon* 3B 36
Spartylea. *Nmbd* 5B 114
Spath. *Staf* 2E 73
Spaunton. *N Yor* 1B 100
Spaxton. *Som* 3F 21
Spean Bridge. *High* 5E 149
Spear Hill. *W Sus* 4C 26
Speen. *Buck* 2G 37
Speen. *W Ber* 5C 36
Speeton. *N Yor* 2F 101
Speke. *Mers* 2G 83
Speldhurst. *Kent* 1G 27
Spellbrook. *Herts* 4E 53
Spelsbury. *Oxon* 3B 50
Spencers Wood. *Wok* 5F 37
Spennithorne. *N Yor* 1D 98
Spennymoor. *Dur* 1F 105
Spernall. *Warw* 4E 61
Spetchley. *Worc* 5C 60
Spetisbury. *Dors* 2E 15
Spexhall. *Suff* 2F 67
Speybank. *High* 3C 150
Spey Bay. *Mor* 2A 160
Speybridge. *High* 1E 151
Speyview. *Mor* 4G 159
Spilsby. *Linc* 4C 88
Spindlestone. *Nmbd* 1F 121
Spinkhill. *Derbs* 3B 86
Spinney Hills. *Leic* 5D 74
Spinningdale. *High* 5D 164
Spital. *Mers* 2F 83
Spitalhill. *Derbs* 1F 73
Spital in the Street. *Linc* 1G 87
Spithurst. *E Sus* 4F 27
Spittal. *Dum* 4A 110
Spittal. *E Lot* 2A 130
Spittal. *High* 3D 168
Spittal. *Nmbd* 4G 131
Spittal. *Pemb* 2D 43
Spittalfield. *Per* 4A 144
Spittal of Glenmuick. *Abers* 5H 151
Spittal of Glenshee. *Per* 1A 144
Spittal-on-Rule. *Bord* 3H 119
Spixworth. *Norf* 4E 79
Splatt. *Corn* 4C 10
Spofforth. *N Yor* 4F 99
Spondon. *Derb* 2B 74
Spon End. *W Mid* 3H 61
Spooner Row. *Norf* 1C 66
Sporle. *Norf* 4H 77
Spott. *E Lot* 2C 130
Spratton. *Nptn* 3E 62
Spreakley. *Surr* 2G 25
Spreyton. *Devn* 3H 11
Spridlington. *Linc* 2H 87
Springburn. *Glas* 3H 127
Springfield. *Dum* 3E 113
Springfield. *Fife* 2F 137
Springfield. *High* 2A 158
Springfield. *W Mid* 2E 61
Springhill. *Staf* 5D 73
Springholm. *Dum* 2F 111
Springside. *N Ayr* 1C 116
Springthorpe. *Linc* 2F 87
Spring Vale. *IOW* 3E 16
Spring Valley. *IOM* 4C 108
Springwell. *Tyne* 4F 115
Sproatley. *E Yor* 1E 95
Sproston Green. *Ches W* 4B 84
Sprotbrough. *S Yor* 4F 93
Sproughton. *Suff* 1E 55
Sprouston. *Bord* 1B 120
Sprowston. *Norf* 4E 79
Sproxton. *Leics* 3F 75
Sproxton. *N Yor* 1A 100
Sprunston. *Cumb* 5E 113
Spurstow. *Ches E* 5H 83
Squires Gate. *Bkpl* 1B 90
Sraid Ruadh. *Arg* 4A 138
Srannda. *W Isl* 9C 171
Sron an t-Sithein. *High* 2C 140
Sronphadruig Lodge. *Per* 1E 142
Sruth Mor. *W Isl* 2E 170
Stableford. *Shrp* 1B 60
Stackhouse. *N Yor* 3H 97
Stackpole. *Pemb* 5D 43
Stackpole Elidor. *Pemb* 5D 43
Stacksford. *Norf* 1C 66
Stacksteads. *Lanc* 2G 91
Staddiscombe. *Plym* 3B 8
Staddlethorpe. *E Yor* 2B 94
Staddon. *Devn* 2D 10
Staden. *Derbs* 3E 85
Stadhampton. *Oxon* 2E 36
Stadhlaigearraidh. *W Isl* 5C 170
Stafainn. *High* 2D 155
Staffield. *Cumb* 5G 113
Staffin. *High* 2D 155
Stafford. *Staf* 3D 72
Stafford Park. *Telf* 5B 72
Stagden Cross. *Essx* 4G 53
Stagsden. *Bed* 1H 51
Stag's Head. *Devn* 4G 19
Stainburn. *Cumb* 2B 102
Stainburn. *N Yor* 5E 99
Stainby. *Linc* 3G 75
Staincliffe. *W Yor* 2C 92
Staincross. *S Yor* 3D 92
Staindrop. *Dur* 2E 105
Staines-Upon-Thames. *Surr* 3B 38
Stainfield. *Linc* 3H 75 (nr. Bourne)
Stainfield. *Linc* 3A 88 (nr. Lincoln)
Stainforth. *N Yor* 3H 97
Stainforth. *S Yor* 3G 93
Staining. *Lanc* 1B 90
Stainland. *W Yor* 3A 92
Stainsacre. *N Yor* 4G 107
Stainton. *Cumb* 4E 113 (nr. Carlisle)
Stainton. *Cumb* 1E 97 (nr. Kendal)
Stainton. *Cumb* 2F 103 (nr. Penrith)
Stainton. *Dur* 3D 104
Stainton. *Midd* 3B 106
Stainton. *N Yor* 5E 105
Stainton. *S Yor* 1C 86
Stainton by Langworth. *Linc* 3H 87
Staintondale. *N Yor* 5G 107
Stainton le Vale. *Linc* 1A 88
Stainton with Adgarley. *Cumb* 2B 96
Stair. *Cumb* 2D 102
Stair. *E Ayr* 2D 116
Stairhaven. *Dum* 4H 109
Staithes. *N Yor* 3E 107
Stakeford. *Nmbd* 1F 115
Stake Pool. *Lanc* 5D 96
Stakes. *Hants* 2E 17
Stalbridge. *Dors* 1C 14
Stalbridge Weston. *Dors* 1C 14
Stalham. *Norf* 3F 79
Stalham Green. *Norf* 3F 79
Stalisfield Green. *Kent* 5D 40
Stallen. *Dors* 1B 14
Stallingborough. *NE Lin* 3F 95
Stalling Busk. *N Yor* 1B 98
Stallington. *Staf* 2D 72
Stalmine. *Lanc* 5C 96
Stalybridge. *G Man* 1D 84
Stambourne. *Essx* 2H 53
Stamford. *Linc* 5H 75
Stamford. *Nmbd* 3G 121
Stamford Bridge. *Ches W* 4G 83
Stamford Bridge. *E Yor* 4B 100
Stamfordham. *Nmbd* 2D 115
Stamperland. *E Ren* 4G 127
Stanah. *Lanc* 5C 96
Stanborough. *Herts* 4C 52
Stanbridge. *C Beds* 3H 51
Stanbridge. *Dors* 2F 15
Stanbury. *W Yor* 1A 92
Stand. *N Lan* 3A 128
Standburn. *Falk* 2C 128
Standeford. *Staf* 5D 72
Standen. *Kent* 1C 28
Standen Street. *Kent* 2C 28
Standerwick. *Som* 1D 22
Standford. *Hants* 3G 25
Standford Bridge. *Telf* 3B 72
Standingstone. *Cumb* 5D 112
Standish. *Glos* 5D 48
Standish. *G Man* 3D 90
Standish Lower Ground. *G Man* 4D 90
Standlake. *Oxon* 5B 50
Standon. *Hants* 4C 24
Standon. *Herts* 3D 53
Standon. *Staf* 2C 72
Standon Green End. *Herts* 4D 52
Stane. *N Lan* 4B 128
Stanecastle. *N Ayr* 1C 116
Stanfield. *Norf* 3B 78
Stanford. *C Beds* 1B 52
Stanford. *Kent* 2F 29
Stanford Bishop. *Here* 5A 60
Stanford Bridge. *Worc* 4B 60
Stanford Dingley. *W Ber* 4D 36
Stanford in the Vale. *Oxon* 2B 36
Stanford-le-Hope. *Thur* 2A 40
Stanford on Avon. *Nptn* 3C 62
Stanford on Soar. *Notts* 3C 74
Stanford on Teme. *Worc* 4B 60
Stanford Rivers. *Essx* 5F 53
Stanfree. *Derbs* 3B 86
Stanghow. *Red C* 3D 107
Stanground. *Pet* 1B 64
Stanhoe. *Norf* 2H 77
Stanhope. *Dur* 1C 104
Stanhope. *Bord* 1D 118
Stanion. *Nptn* 2G 63
Stanley. *Derbs* 1B 74
Stanley. *Dur* 4E 115
Stanley. *Per* 5A 144
Stanley. *Shrp* 2B 60
Stanley. *Staf* 5D 84
Stanley. *W Yor* 2D 92
Stanley Common. *Derbs* 1B 74
Stanley Crook. *Dur* 1E 105
Stanley Hill. *Here* 1B 48
Stanlow. *Ches W* 3G 83
Stanmer. *Brig* 5E 27
Stanmore. *G Lon* 1C 38
Stanmore. *Hants* 4C 24
Stanmore. *W Ber* 4C 36
Stannersburn. *Nmbd* 1A 114
Stanningfield. *Suff* 5A 66
Stannington. *Nmbd* 2F 115
Stannington. *S Yor* 2H 85
Stansbatch. *Here* 4F 59
Stansfield. *Suff* 5G 65
Stanshope. *Staf* 5F 85
Stanstead. *Suff* 1B 54
Stanstead Abbotts. *Herts* 4D 53
Stansted. *Kent* 4H 39
Stansted (London) Airport. *Essx* 3F 53 & 216
Stansted Mountfitchet. *Essx* 3F 53
Stanthorne. *Ches W* 4A 84
Stanton. *Derbs* 4G 73
Stanton. *Glos* 2F 49
Stanton. *Nmbd* 5F 121
Stanton. *Staf* 1F 73
Stanton. *Suff* 3B 66
Stanton by Bridge. *Derbs* 3A 74
Stanton by Dale. *Derbs* 2B 74
Stanton Chare. *Suff* 3B 66
Stanton Drew. *Bath* 5A 34
Stanton Fitzwarren. *Swin* 2G 35
Stanton Harcourt. *Oxon* 5C 50
Stanton Hill. *Notts* 4B 86
Stanton in Peak. *Derbs* 4G 85
Stanton Lacy. *Shrp* 3G 59
Stanton Long. *Shrp* 1H 59
Stanton-on-the-Wolds. *Notts* 2D 74
Stanton Prior. *Bath* 5B 34
Stanton St Bernard. *Wilts* 5F 35
Stanton St John. *Oxon* 5D 50
Stanton St Quintin. *Wilts* 4E 35
Stanton Street. *Suff* 4B 66
Stanton under Bardon. *Leics* 4B 74
Stanton upon Hine Heath. *Shrp* 3H 71
Stanton Wick. *Bath* 5B 34
Stanwardine in the Fields. *Shrp* 3G 71
Stanwardine in the Wood. *Shrp* 3G 71
Stanway. *Essx* 3C 54
Stanway. *Glos* 2F 49
Stanwell. *Surr* 3B 38
Stanwell Moor. *Surr* 3B 38
Stanwick. *Nptn* 3G 63
Stanydale. *Shet* 6D 173
Staoinebrig. *W Isl* 5C 170
Stape. *N Yor* 5E 107
Stapehill. *Dors* 2F 15
Stapeley. *Ches E* 1A 72
Stapenhill. *Staf* 3G 73
Staple. *Kent* 5G 41
Staple Cross. *Devn* 4D 20
Staplecross. *E Sus* 3B 28
Staplefield. *W Sus* 3D 27
Staple Fitzpaine. *Som* 1F 13
Stapleford. *Cambs* 5D 64
Stapleford. *Herts* 4D 52
Stapleford. *Leics* 4F 75
Stapleford. *Linc* 5F 87
Stapleford. *Notts* 2B 74
Stapleford. *Wilts* 3F 23
Stapleford Abbotts. *Essx* 1G 39
Stapleford Tawney. *Essx* 1G 39
Staplegrove. *Som* 4F 21
Staplehay. *Som* 4F 21
Staple Hill. *S Glo* 4B 34
Staplehurst. *Kent* 1B 28
Staplers. *IOW* 4D 16
Stapleton. *Bris* 4B 34
Stapleton. *Cumb* 2G 113
Stapleton. *Here* 4F 59
Stapleton. *Leics* 1B 62
Stapleton. *N Yor* 3F 105
Stapleton. *Shrp* 5G 71
Stapleton. *Som* 4H 21
Stapley. *Som* 1E 13
Staploe. *Bed* 4A 64
Staplow. *Here* 1B 48
Star. *Fife* 3F 137
Star. *Pemb* 1G 43
Starbeck. *N Yor* 4F 99
Starbotton. *N Yor* 2B 98
Starcross. *Devn* 4C 12
Stareton. *Warw* 3H 61
Starkholmes. *Derbs* 5H 85
Starling. *G Man* 3F 91
Starling's Green. *Essx* 2E 53
Starston. *Norf* 2E 67
Start. *Devn* 4E 9
Startforth. *Dur* 3D 104
Start Hill. *Essx* 3F 53
Startley. *Wilts* 3E 35
Stathe. *Som* 4G 21
Stathern. *Leics* 2E 75
Station Town. *Dur* 1B 106
Staughton Green. *Cambs* 4A 64
Staughton Highway. *Cambs* 4A 64
Staunton. *Glos* 3C 48 (nr. Cheltenham)
Staunton. *Glos* 4A 48 (nr. Monmouth)
Staunton in the Vale. *Notts* 1F 75
Staunton on Arrow. *Here* 4F 59
Staunton on Wye. *Here* 1G 47
Staveley. *Cumb* 5F 103
Staveley. *Derbs* 3B 86
Staveley. *N Yor* 3F 99
Staveley-in-Cartmel. *Cumb* 1C 96
Staverton. *Devn* 2D 9
Staverton. *Glos* 3D 49
Staverton. *Nptn* 4C 62
Staverton. *Wilts* 5D 34
Stawell. *Som* 3G 21
Stawley. *Som* 4D 20
Staxigoe. *High* 3F 169
Staxton. *N Yor* 2E 101
Staylittle. *Powy* 1A 58
Staynall. *Lanc* 5C 96
Staythorpe. *Notts* 5E 87
Stean. *N Yor* 2C 98
Stearsby. *N Yor* 2A 100
Steart. *Som* 2F 21
Stebbing. *Essx* 3G 53
Stebbing Green. *Essx* 3G 53
Stedham. *W Sus* 4G 25
Steel. *Nmbd* 4C 114
Steel Cross. *E Sus* 2G 27
Steelend. *Fife* 4C 136
Steele Road. *Bord* 5H 119
Steel Heath. *Shrp* 2H 71
Steen's Bridge. *Here* 5H 59
Steep. *Hants* 4F 25
Steep Lane. *W Yor* 2A 92
Steeple. *Dors* 4E 15
Steeple. *Essx* 5C 54
Steeple Ashton. *Wilts* 1E 23
Steeple Aston. *Oxon* 3C 50
Steeple Barton. *Oxon* 3C 50
Steeple Bumpstead. *Essx* 1G 53
Steeple Claydon. *Buck* 3E 51
Steeple Gidding. *Cambs* 2A 64
Steeple Langford. *Wilts* 3F 23
Steeple Morden. *Cambs* 1C 52
Steeton. *W Yor* 5C 98
Stein. *High* 3B 154
Steinmanhill. *Abers* 4E 161
Stelling Minnis. *Kent* 1F 29
Stembridge. *Som* 4H 21
Stemster. *High* 2D 169 (nr. Halkirk)
Stemster. *High* 2C 168 (nr. Westfield)
Stenalees. *Corn* 3E 6
Stenhill. *Devn* 1D 12
Stenhouse. *Edin* 2F 129
Stenhousemuir. *Falk* 1B 128
Stenigot. *Linc* 2B 88
Stenscholl. *High* 2D 155
Stenso. *Orkn* 5C 172
Stenson. *Derbs* 3H 73
Stenson Fields. *Derbs* 2H 73
Stenton. *E Lot* 2C 130
Stenwith. *Linc* 2F 75
Steòrnabhagh. *W Isl* 4G 171
Stepaside. *Pemb* 4F 43
Stepford. *Dum* 1F 111
Stepney. *G Lon* 2E 39
Steppingley. *C Beds* 2A 52
Stepps. *N Lan* 3H 127
Sterndale Moor. *Derbs* 4F 85
Sternfield. *Suff* 4F 67
Stert. *Wilts* 1F 23
Stetchworth. *Cambs* 5F 65
Stevenage. *Herts* 3C 52
Stevenston. *N Ayr* 5D 126
Stevenstone. *Devn* 1F 11
Steventon. *Hants* 2D 24
Steventon. *Oxon* 2C 36
Steventon End. *Cambs* 1G 53
Stevington. *Bed* 5G 63
Stewartby. *Bed* 1A 52
Stewarton. *Arg* 4A 122
Stewarton. *E Ayr* 5F 127
Stewkley. *Buck* 3G 51
Stewkley Dean. *Buck* 3G 51
Stewley. *Som* 1G 13
Stewton. *Linc* 2C 88
Steyning. *W Sus* 4C 26
Steynton. *Pemb* 4D 42
Stibb. *Corn* 1C 10
Stibbard. *Norf* 3B 78
Stibb Cross. *Devn* 1E 11
Stibb Green. *Wilts* 5H 35
Stibbington. *Cambs* 1H 63
Stichill. *Bord* 1B 120
Sticker. *Corn* 3D 6
Stickford. *Linc* 4C 88
Sticklepath. *Devn* 3G 11
Sticklinch. *Som* 3A 22
Stickling Green. *Essx* 2E 53
Stickney. *Linc* 5C 88
Stiffkey. *Norf* 1B 78
Stifford's Bridge. *Here* 1C 48
Stileway. *Som* 2H 21
Stillingfleet. *N Yor* 5H 99
Stillington. *N Yor* 3H 99
Stillington. *Stoc T* 2A 106
Stilton. *Cambs* 2A 64
Stinchcombe. *Glos* 2C 34
Stinsford. *Dors* 3C 14
Stiperstones. *Shrp* 5F 71
Stirchley. *Telf* 5B 72
Stirchley. *W Mid* 2E 61
Stirling. *Abers* 4H 161
Stirling. *Stir* 4G 135 & 211
Stirton. *N Yor* 4B 98
Stisted. *Essx* 3A 54
Stitchcombe. *Wilts* 5H 35
Stithians. *Corn* 5B 6
Stittenham. *High* 1A 158
Stivichall. *W Mid* 3H 61
Stixwould. *Linc* 4A 88
Stoak. *Ches W* 3G 83
Stobo. *Bord* 1D 118
Stobo Castle. *Bord* 1D 118
Stoborough. *Dors* 4E 15
Stoborough Green. *Dors* 4E 15
Stobs Castle. *Bord* 4H 119
Stobswood. *Nmbd* 5G 121
Stock. *Essx* 1A 40
Stockbridge. *Hants* 3B 24
Stockbridge. *W Yor* 5C 98
Stockbury. *Kent* 4C 40
Stockcross. *W Ber* 5C 36
Stockdalewath. *Cumb* 5E 113
Stocker's Head. *Kent* 5D 40
Stockerston. *Leics* 1F 63
Stock Green. *Worc* 5D 61
Stocking. *Here* 2B 48
Stockingford. *Warw* 1H 61
Stocking Green. *Essx* 2F 53
Stocking Pelham. *Herts* 3E 53
Stockland. *Devn* 2F 13
Stockland Bristol. *Som* 2F 21
Stockleigh English. *Devn* 2B 12
Stockleigh Pomeroy. *Devn* 2B 12
Stockley. *Wilts* 5F 35
Stocklinch. *Som* 1G 13
Stockport. *G Man* 2D 84
Stocksbridge. *S Yor* 1G 85
Stocksfield. *Nmbd* 3D 114
Stocks, The. *Kent* 4D 28
Stockstreet. *Essx* 3B 54
Stockton. *Here* 4H 59
Stockton. *Norf* 1F 67
Stockton. *Shrp* 1B 60 (nr. Bridgnorth)
Stockton. *Shrp* 5E 71 (nr. Chirbury)
Stockton. *Telf* 4B 72
Stockton. *Warw* 4B 62
Stockton. *Wilts* 3E 23
Stockton Brook. *Staf* 5D 84
Stockton Cross. *Here* 4H 59
Stockton Heath. *Warr* 2A 84
Stockton-on-Tees. *Stoc T* 3B 106
Stockton on Teme. *Worc* 4B 60
Stockton-on-the-Forest. *York* 4A 100
Stockwell Heath. *Staf* 3E 73
Stockwood. *Bris* 5B 34
Stock Wood. *Worc* 5E 61
Stodmarsh. *Kent* 4G 41
Stody. *Norf* 2C 78
Stoer. *High* 1E 163
Stoford. *Som* 1A 14
Stoford. *Wilts* 3F 23
Stogumber. *Som* 3D 20
Stogursey. *Som* 2F 21
Stoke. *Devn* 4C 18
Stoke. *Hants* 1C 24 (nr. Andover)
Stoke. *Hants* 2F 17 (nr. South Hayling)
Stoke. *Medw* 3C 40
Stoke. *W Mid* 3A 62
Stoke Abbott. *Dors* 2H 13
Stoke Albany. *Nptn* 2F 63
Stoke Ash. *Suff* 3D 66
Stoke Bardolph. *Notts* 1D 74
Stoke Bliss. *Worc* 4A 60
Stoke Bruerne. *Nptn* 1F 51
Stoke by Clare. *Suff* 1H 53
Stoke-by-Nayland. *Suff* 2C 54
Stoke Canon. *Devn* 3C 12
Stoke Charity. *Hants* 3C 24
Stoke Climsland. *Corn* 5D 10
Stoke Cross. *Here* 5A 60
Stoke D'Abernon. *Surr* 5C 38
Stoke Doyle. *Nptn* 2H 63
Stoke Dry. *Rut* 1F 63
Stoke Edith. *Here* 1B 48

Stoke Farthing. *Wilts* 4F 23
Stoke Ferry. *Norf* 1G 65
Stoke Fleming. *Devn* 4E 9
Stokeford. *Dors* 4D 14
Stoke Gabriel. *Devn* 3E 9
Stoke Gifford. *S Glo* 4B 34
Stoke Golding. *Leics* 1A 62
Stoke Goldington. *Mil* 1G 51
Stokeham. *Notts* 3E 87
Stoke Hammond. *Buck* 3G 51
Stoke Heath. *Shrp* 3A 72
Stoke Holy Cross. *Norf* 5E 79
Stokeinteignhead. *Devn* 5C 12
Stoke Lacy. *Here* 1B 48
Stoke Lyne. *Oxon* 3D 50
Stoke Mandeville. *Buck* 4G 51
Stokenchurch. *Buck* 2F 37
Stoke Newington. *G Lon* 2E 39
Stokenham. *Devn* 4E 9
Stoke on Tern. *Shrp* 3A 72
Stoke-on-Trent. *Stoke* 1C 72 & 211
Stoke Orchard. *Glos* 3E 49
Stoke Pero. *Som* 2B 20
Stoke Poges. *Buck* 2A 38
Stoke Prior. *Here* 5H 59
Stoke Prior. *Worc* 4D 60
Stoke Rivers. *Devn* 3G 19
Stoke Rochford. *Linc* 3G 75
Stoke Row. *Oxon* 3E 37
Stoke St Gregory. *Som* 4G 21
Stoke St Mary. *Som* 4F 21
Stoke St Michael. *Som* 2B 22
Stoke St Milborough. *Shrp* 2H 59
Stokesay. *Shrp* 2G 59
Stokesby. *Norf* 4G 79
Stokesley. *N Yor* 4C 106
Stoke sub Hamdon. *Som* 1H 13
Stoke Talmage. *Oxon* 2E 37
Stoke Town. *Stoke* 1C 72 & 211
Stoke Trister. *Som* 4C 22
Stoke Wake. *Dors* 2C 14
Stolford. *Som* 2F 21
Stondon Massey. *Essx* 5F 53
Stone. *Buck* 4F 51
Stone. *Glos* 2B 34
Stone. *Kent* 3G 39
Stone. *Som* 3A 22
Stone. *Staf* 2D 72
Stone. *Worc* 3C 60
Stonea. *Cambs* 1D 64
Stoneacton. *Shrp* 1H 59
Stone Allerton. *Som* 1H 21
Ston Easton. *Som* 1B 22
Stonebridge. *N Som* 1G 21
Stonebridge. *Som* 2C 22
Stonebridge. *Surr* 1C 26
Stone Bridge Corner. *Pet* 5B 76
Stonebroom. *Derbs* 5B 86
Stonebyres. *S Lan* 5B 128
Stone Chair. *W Yor* 2B 92
Stone Cross. *E Sus* 5H 27
Stone Cross. *Kent* 2G 27
Stone-edge-Batch. *N Som* 4H 33
Stoneferry. *Hull* 1D 94
Stonefield. *Arg* 5D 140
Stonefield. *S Lan* 4H 127
Stonegate. *E Sus* 3A 28
Stonegate. *N Yor* 4E 107
Stonegrave. *N Yor* 2A 100
Stonehall. *Worc* 1D 49
Stonehaugh. *Nmbd* 2A 114
Stonehaven. *Abers* 5F 153
Stone Heath. *Staf* 2D 72
Stone Hill. *Kent* 2E 29
Stone House. *Cumb* 1G 97
Stonehouse. *Glos* 5D 48
Stonehouse. *Nmbd* 4H 113
Stonehouse. *S Lan* 5A 128
Stone in Oxney. *Kent* 3D 28
Stoneleigh. *Warw* 3H 61
Stoneley Green. *Ches E* 5A 84
Stonely. *Cambs* 4A 64
Stonepits. *Worc* 5E 61
Stoner Hill. *Hants* 4F 25
Stonesby. *Leics* 3F 75
Stonesfield. *Oxon* 4B 50
Stones Green. *Essx* 3E 55
Stone Street. *Kent* 5G 39
Stone Street. *Suff* 2C 54 (nr. Boxford)
Stone Street. *Suff* 2F 67 (nr. Halesworth)
Stonethwaite. *Cumb* 3D 102
Stoneyburn. *W Lot* 3C 128
Stoney Cross. *Hants* 1A 16
Stoneyford. *Devn* 2D 12
Stoneygate. *Leic* 5D 74
Stoneyhills. *Essx* 1D 40
Stoneykirk. *Dum* 4F 109
Stoney Middleton. *Derbs* 3G 85
Stoney Stanton. *Leics* 1B 62
Stoney Stoke. *Som* 3C 22
Stoney Stratton. *Som* 3B 22
Stoney Stretton. *Shrp* 5F 71
Stoneywood. *Aber* 2F 153
Stonham Aspal. *Suff* 5D 66
Stonnall. *Staf* 5E 73
Stonor. *Oxon* 3F 37
Stonton Wyville. *Leics* 1E 63
Stonybreck. *Shet* 1B 172
Stony Cross. *Devn* 4F 19
Stony Cross. *Here* 1C 48 (nr. Great Malvern)
Stony Cross. *Here* 4H 59 (nr. Leominster)
Stony Houghton. *Derbs* 4B 86
Stony Stratford. *Mil* 1F 51
Stoodleigh. *Devn* 3G 19 (nr. Barnstaple)
Stoodleigh. *Devn* 1C 12 (nr. Tiverton)
Stopham. *W Sus* 4B 26
Stopsley. *Lutn* 3B 52
Stoptide. *Corn* 1D 6
Storeton. *Mers* 2F 83
Stormontfield. *Per* 1D 136
Stornoway. *W Isl* 4G 171
Stornoway Airport. *W Isl* 4G 171
Storridge. *Here* 1C 48
Storrington. *W Sus* 4B 26
Storrs. *Cumb* 5E 103
Storth. *Cumb* 1D 97
Storwood. *E Yor* 5B 100
Stotfield. *Mor* 1G 159
Stotfold. *C Beds* 2C 52
Stottesdon. *Shrp* 2A 60
Stoughton. *Leics* 5D 74
Stoughton. *Surr* 5A 38
Stoughton. *W Sus* 1G 17
Stoul. *High* 4F 147
Stoulton. *Worc* 1E 49
Stourbridge. *W Mid* 2C 60
Stourpaine. *Dors* 2D 14
Stourport-on-Severn. *Worc* 3C 60
Stour Provost. *Dors* 4C 22
Stour Row. *Dors* 4D 22
Stourton. *Staf* 2C 60
Stourton. *Warw* 2A 50
Stourton. *W Yor* 1D 92
Stourton. *Wilts* 3C 22
Stourton Caundle. *Dors* 1C 14
Stove. *Orkn* 4F 172
Stove. *Shet* 9F 173
Stoven. *Suff* 2G 67
Stow. *Linc* 2H 75 (nr. Billingborough)
Stow. *Linc* 2F 87 (nr. Gainsborough)
Stow. *Bord* 5A 130
Stow Bardolph. *Norf* 5F 77
Stow Bedon. *Norf* 1B 66
Stowbridge. *Norf* 5F 77
Stow cum Quy. *Cambs* 4E 65
Stowe. *Glos* 5A 48
Stowe. *Shrp* 3F 59
Stowe. *Staf* 4F 73
Stowe-by-Chartley. *Staf* 3E 73
Stowell. *Som* 4B 22
Stowey. *Bath* 1A 22
Stowford. *Devn* 2G 19 (nr. Combe Martin)
Stowford. *Devn* 4D 12 (nr. Exmouth)
Stowford. *Devn* 4E 11 (nr. Tavistock)
Stowlangtoft. *Suff* 4B 66
Stow Longa. *Cambs* 3A 64
Stow Maries. *Essx* 1C 40
Stowmarket. *Suff* 5C 66
Stow-on-the-Wold. *Glos* 3G 49
Stowting. *Kent* 1F 29
Stowupland. *Suff* 5C 66
Straad. *Arg* 3B 126
Strachan. *Abers* 4D 152
Stradbroke. *Suff* 3E 67
Stradbrook. *Wilts* 1E 23
Stradishall. *Suff* 5G 65
Stradsett. *Norf* 5F 77
Stragglethorpe. *Linc* 5G 87
Stragglethorpe. *Notts* 2D 74
Straid. *S Ayr* 5A 116
Straight Soley. *Wilts* 4B 36
Straiton. *Edin* 3F 129
Straiton. *S Ayr* 4C 116
Straloch. *Per* 2H 143
Stramshall. *Staf* 2E 73
Strang. *IOM* 4C 108
Strangford. *Here* 3A 48
Stranraer. *Dum* 3F 109
Strata Florida. *Cdgn* 4G 57
Stratfield Mortimer. *W Ber* 5E 37
Stratfield Saye. *Hants* 5E 37
Stratfield Turgis. *Hants* 1E 25
Stratford. *Glos* 2D 49
Stratford. *G Lon* 2E 39
Stratford St Andrew. *Suff* 4F 67
Stratford St Mary. *Suff* 2D 54
Stratford sub Castle. *Wilts* 3G 23
Stratford Tony. *Wilts* 4F 23
Stratford-upon-Avon. *Warw* 5G 61 & 212
Strath. *High* 1G 155 (nr. Gairloch)
Strath. *High* 3E 169 (nr. Wick)
Strathan. *High* 4B 148 (nr. Fort William)
Strathan. *High* 1E 163 (nr. Lochinver)
Strathan. *High* 2F 167 (nr. Tongue)
Strathan Skerray. *High* 2G 167
Strathaven. *S Lan* 5A 128
Strathblane. *Stir* 2G 127
Strathcanaird. *High* 3F 163
Strathcarron. *High* 4B 156
Strathcoil. *Arg* 5A 140
Strathdon. *Abers* 2A 152
Strathkinness. *Fife* 2G 137
Strathmashie House. *High* 4H 149
Strathmiglo. *Fife* 2E 136
Strathmore Lodge. *High* 4D 168
Strathpeffer. *High* 3G 157
Strathrannoch. *High* 1F 157
Strathtay. *Per* 3G 143
Strathvaich Lodge. *High* 1F 157
Strathwhillan. *N Ayr* 2E 123
Strathy. *High* 1A 158 (nr. Invergordon)
Strathy. *High* 2A 168 (nr. Melvich)
Strathyre. *Stir* 2E 135
Stratton. *Corn* 2C 10
Stratton. *Dors* 3B 14
Stratton. *Glos* 5F 49
Stratton Audley. *Oxon* 3E 50
Stratton-on-the-Fosse. *Som* 1B 22
Stratton St Margaret. *Swin* 3G 35
Stratton St Michael. *Norf* 1E 66
Stratton Strawless. *Norf* 3E 78
Stravithie. *Fife* 2H 137
Stream. *Som* 3D 20
Streat. *E Sus* 4E 27
Streatham. *G Lon* 3D 39
Streatley. *C Beds* 3A 52
Streatley. *W Ber* 3D 36
Street. *Corn* 3C 10
Street. *Lanc* 4E 97
Street. *N Yor* 4E 107
Street. *Som* 2G 13 (nr. Chard)
Street. *Som* 3H 21 (nr. Glastonbury)
Street Ash. *Som* 1F 13
Street Dinas. *Shrp* 2F 71
Street End. *Kent* 5F 41
Street End. *W Sus* 3G 17
Street Gate. *Tyne* 4F 115
Streethay. *Staf* 4F 73
Streethouse. *W Yor* 3D 93
Streetlam. *N Yor* 5A 106
Street Lane. *Derbs* 1A 74
Streetly. *W Mid* 1E 61
Streetly End. *Cambs* 1G 53
Street on the Fosse. *Som* 3B 22
Strefford. *Shrp* 2G 59
Strelley. *Notts* 1C 74
Strensall. *York* 3A 100
Strensall Camp. *York* 4A 100
Stretcholt. *Som* 2F 21
Strete. *Devn* 4E 9
Stretford. *G Man* 1C 84
Stretford. *Here* 5H 59
Strethall. *Essx* 2E 53
Stretham. *Cambs* 3E 65
Stretton. *Ches W* 5G 83
Stretton. *Derbs* 4A 86
Stretton. *Rut* 4G 75
Stretton. *Staf* 4C 72 (nr. Brewood)
Stretton. *Staf* 3G 73 (nr. Burton upon Trent)
Stretton. *Warr* 2A 84
Stretton en le Field. *Leics* 4H 73
Stretton Grandison. *Here* 1B 48
Stretton Heath. *Shrp* 4F 71
Stretton-on-Dunsmore. *Warw* 3B 62
Stretton-on-Fosse. *Warw* 2H 49
Stretton Sugwas. *Here* 1H 47
Stretton under Fosse. *Warw* 2B 62
Stretton Westwood. *Shrp* 1H 59
Strichen. *Abers* 3G 161
Strines. *G Man* 2D 84
Stringston. *Som* 2E 21
Strixton. *Nptn* 4G 63
Stroanfreggan. *Dum* 5F 117
Stroat. *Glos* 2A 34
Stromeferry. *High* 5A 156
Stromemore. *High* 5A 156
Stromness. *Orkn* 7B 172
Stronachie. *Per* 3C 136
Stronachlachar. *Stir* 2D 134
Stronchreggan. *High* 1E 141
Strone. *Arg* 1C 126
Strone. *High* 1H 149 (nr. Drumnadrochit)
Strone. *High* 3B 150 (nr. Kingussie)
Stronenaba. *High* 5E 148
Stronganess. *Shet* 1G 173
Stronmilchan. *Arg* 1A 134
Stronsay Airport. *Orkn* 5F 172
Strontian. *High* 2C 140
Strood. *Kent* 2C 28
Strood. *Medw* 4B 40
Strood Green. *Surr* 1D 26
Strood Green. *W Sus* 3B 26 (nr. Billingshurst)
Strood Green. *W Sus* 2C 26 (nr. Horsham)
Strothers Dale. *Nmbd* 4C 114
Stroud. *Glos* 5D 48
Stroud. *Hants* 4F 25
Stroud Green. *Essx* 1C 40
Stroxton. *Linc* 2G 75
Struan. *High* 5C 154
Struan. *Per* 2F 143
Struanmore. *High* 5C 154
Strubby. *Linc* 2D 88
Strugg's Hill. *Linc* 2B 76
Strumpshaw. *Norf* 5F 79
Strutherhill. *S Lan* 4A 128
Struy. *High* 5F 157
Stryd. *IOA* 2B 80
Stryt-issa. *Wrex* 1E 71
Stuartfield. *Abers* 4G 161
Stubbington. *Hants* 2D 16
Stubbins. *Lanc* 3F 91
Stubble Green. *Cumb* 5B 102
Stubb's Cross. *Kent* 2D 28
Stubbs Green. *Norf* 1F 67
Stubhampton. *Dors* 1E 15
Stubton. *Linc* 1F 75
Stubwood. *Staf* 2E 73
Stuckton. *Hants* 1G 15
Studham. *C Beds* 4A 52
Studland. *Dors* 4F 15
Studley. *Warw* 4E 61
Studley. *Wilts* 4E 35
Studley Roger. *N Yor* 3E 99
Stuntney. *Cambs* 3E 65
Stunts Green. *E Sus* 4H 27
Sturbridge. *Staf* 2C 72
Sturgate. *Linc* 2F 87
Sturmer. *Essx* 1G 53
Sturminster Marshall. *Dors* 2E 15
Sturminster Newton. *Dors* 1C 14
Sturry. *Kent* 4F 41
Sturton. *N Lin* 4C 94
Sturton by Stow. *Linc* 2F 87
Sturton le Steeple. *Notts* 2E 87
Stuston. *Suff* 3D 66
Stutton. *N Yor* 5G 99
Stutton. *Suff* 2E 55
Styal. *Ches E* 2C 84
Stydd. *Lanc* 1E 91
Styrrup. *Notts* 1D 86
Suainebost. *W Isl* 1H 171
Suardail. *W Isl* 4G 171
Succoth. *Abers* 5B 160
Succoth. *Arg* 3B 134
Suckley. *Worc* 5B 60
Suckley Knowl. *Worc* 5B 60
Sudborough. *Nptn* 2G 63
Sudbourne. *Suff* 5G 67
Sudbrook. *Linc* 1G 75
Sudbrook. *Mon* 3A 34
Sudbrooke. *Linc* 3H 87
Sudbury. *Derbs* 2F 73
Sudbury. *Suff* 1B 54
Sudgrove. *Glos* 5E 49
Suffield. *Norf* 2E 79
Suffield. *N Yor* 5G 107
Sugnall. *Staf* 2B 72
Sugwas Pool. *Here* 1H 47
Suisnish. *High* 5E 155
Sulaisiadar. *W Isl* 4H 171
Sùlaisiadar Mòr. *High* 4D 155
Sulby. *IOM* 2C 108
Sulgrave. *Nptn* 1D 50
Sulham. *W Ber* 4E 37
Sulhamstead. *W Ber* 5E 37
Sullington. *W Sus* 4B 26
Sullom. *Shet* 4E 173
Sully. *V Glam* 5E 33
Sumburgh. *Shet* 10F 173
Sumburgh Airport. *Shet* 10E 173
Summer Bridge. *N Yor* 3E 98
Summercourt. *Corn* 3C 6
Summergangs. *Hull* 1E 95
Summerhill. *Aber* 3G 153
Summerhill. *Pemb* 4F 43
Summer Hill. *W Mid* 1D 60
Summerhouse. *Darl* 3F 105
Summersdale. *W Sus* 2G 17
Summerseat. *G Man* 3F 91
Summit. *G Man* 3H 91
Sunbury. *Surr* 4C 38
Sunderland. *Cumb* 1C 102
Sunderland. *Lanc* 4D 96
Sunderland. *Tyne* 4G 115 & 212
Sunderland Bridge. *Dur* 1F 105
Sundon Park. *Lutn* 3A 52
Sundridge. *Kent* 5F 39
Sunk Island. *E Yor* 3F 95
Sunningdale. *Wind* 4A 38
Sunninghill. *Wind* 4A 38
Sunningwell. *Oxon* 5C 50
Sunniside. *Dur* 1E 105
Sunniside. *Tyne* 4F 115
Sunny Bank. *Cumb* 5D 102
Sunny Hill. *Derb* 2H 73
Sunnyhurst. *Bkbn* 2E 91
Sunnylaw. *Stir* 4G 135
Sunnymead. *Oxon* 5D 50
Sunnyside. *S Yor* 1B 86
Sunnyside. *W Sus* 2E 27
Sunton. *Wilts* 1H 23
Surbiton. *G Lon* 4C 38
Surby. *IOM* 4B 108
Surfleet. *Linc* 3B 76
Surfleet Seas End. *Linc* 3B 76
Surlingham. *Norf* 5F 79
Surrex. *Essx* 3B 54
Sustead. *Norf* 2D 78
Susworth. *Linc* 4B 94
Sutcombe. *Devn* 1D 10
Suton. *Norf* 1C 66
Sutors of Cromarty. *High* 2C 158
Sutterby. *Linc* 3C 88
Sutterton. *Linc* 2B 76
Sutterton Dowdyke. *Linc* 2B 76
Sutton. *Buck* 3B 38
Sutton. *Cambs* 3D 64
Sutton. *C Beds* 1C 52
Sutton. *E Sus* 5F 27
Sutton. *G Lon* 4D 38
Sutton. *Kent* 1H 29
Sutton. *Norf* 3F 79
Sutton. *Notts* 2E 75
Sutton. *Oxon* 5C 50
Sutton. *Pemb* 3D 42
Sutton. *Pet* 1H 63
Sutton. *Shrp* 2B 60 (nr. Bridgnorth)
Sutton. *Shrp* 2A 72 (nr. Market Drayton)
Sutton. *Shrp* 3F 71 (nr. Oswestry)
Sutton. *Shrp* 4H 71 (nr. Shrewsbury)
Sutton. *Som* 3B 22
Sutton. *S Yor* 3F 93
Sutton. *Staf* 3B 72
Sutton. *Suff* 1G 55
Sutton. *W Sus* 4A 26
Sutton. *Worc* 4A 60
Sutton Abinger. *Surr* 1C 26
Sutton at Hone. *Kent* 4G 39
Sutton Bassett. *Nptn* 1E 63
Sutton Benger. *Wilts* 4E 35
Sutton Bingham. *Som* 1A 14
Sutton Bonington. *Notts* 3C 74
Sutton Bridge. *Linc* 3D 76
Sutton Cheney. *Leics* 5B 74
Sutton Coldfield. *W Mid* 1F 61
Sutton Corner. *Linc* 3D 76
Sutton Courtenay. *Oxon* 2D 36
Sutton Crosses. *Linc* 3D 76
Sutton cum Lound. *Notts* 2D 86
Sutton Gault. *Cambs* 3D 64
Sutton Grange. *N Yor* 2E 99
Sutton Green. *Surr* 5B 38
Sutton Howgrave. *N Yor* 2F 99
Sutton in Ashfield. *Notts* 5B 86
Sutton-in-Craven. *N Yor* 5C 98
Sutton Ings. *Hull* 1E 94
Sutton in the Elms. *Leics* 1C 62
Sutton Lane Ends. *Ches E* 3D 84
Sutton Leach. *Mers* 1H 83
Sutton Maddock. *Shrp* 5B 72
Sutton Mallet. *Som* 3G 21
Sutton Mandeville. *Wilts* 4E 23
Sutton Montis. *Som* 4B 22
Sutton-on-Hull. *Hull* 1E 94
Sutton on Sea. *Linc* 2E 89
Sutton-on-the-Forest. *N Yor* 3H 99
Sutton on the Hill. *Derbs* 2G 73
Sutton on Trent. *Notts* 4E 87
Sutton Poyntz. *Dors* 4C 14
Sutton St Edmund. *Linc* 4C 76
Sutton St Edmund's Common. *Linc* 5C 76
Sutton St James. *Linc* 4C 76
Sutton St Michael. *Here* 1A 48
Sutton St Nicholas. *Here* 1A 48
Sutton Scarsdale. *Derbs* 4B 86
Sutton Scotney. *Hants* 3C 24
Sutton-under-Brailes. *Warw* 2B 50
Sutton-under-Whitestonecliffe. *N Yor* 1G 99
Sutton upon Derwent. *E Yor* 5B 100
Sutton Valence. *Kent* 1C 28
Sutton Veny. *Wilts* 2E 23
Sutton Waldron. *Dors* 1D 14
Sutton Weaver. *Ches W* 3H 83
Swaby. *Linc* 3C 88
Swadlincote. *Derbs* 4G 73
Swaffham. *Norf* 5H 77
Swaffham Bulbeck. *Cambs* 4E 65
Swaffham Prior. *Cambs* 4E 65
Swafield. *Norf* 2E 79
Swainby. *N Yor* 4B 106
Swainshill. *Here* 1H 47
Swainsthorpe. *Norf* 5E 78
Swainswick. *Bath* 5C 34
Swalcliffe. *Oxon* 2B 50
Swalecliffe. *Kent* 4F 41
Swallow. *Linc* 4E 95
Swallow Beck. *Linc* 4G 87
Swallowcliffe. *Wilts* 4E 23
Swallowfield. *Wok* 5F 37
Swallownest. *S Yor* 2B 86
Swampton. *Hants* 1C 24
Swanage. *Dors* 5F 15
Swanbister. *Orkn* 7C 172
Swanbourne. *Buck* 3G 51
Swanbridge. *V Glam* 5E 33
Swan Green. *Ches W* 3B 84
Swanland. *E Yor* 2C 94
Swanley. *Kent* 4G 39
Swanmore. *Hants* 1D 16
Swannington. *Leics* 4B 74
Swannington. *Norf* 4D 78
Swanpool. *Linc* 3G 87
Swanscombe. *Kent* 3G 39
Swansea. *Swan* 3F 31 & 212

Swansmoor. Staf 3E 73
Swan Street. Essx 3B 54
Swanton Abbott. Norf 3E 79
Swanton Morley. Norf 4C 78
Swanton Novers. Norf 2C 78
Swanton Street. Kent 5C 40
Swanwick. Derbs 5B 86
Swanwick. Hants 2D 16
Swanwick Green. Ches E 1H 71
Swarby. Linc 1H 75
Swardeston. Norf 5E 78
Swarister. Shet 3G 173
Swarkestone. Derbs 3A 74
Swarland. Nmbd 4F 121
Swarraton. Hants 3D 24
Swartha. W Yor 5C 98
Swarthmoor. Cumb 2B 96
Swaton. Linc 2A 76
Swavesey. Cambs 4C 64
Sway. Hants 3A 16
Swayfield. Linc 3G 75
Swaythling. Sotn 1C 16
Sweet Green. Worc 4A 60
Sweetham. Devn 3B 12
Sweetholme. Cumb 3G 103
Sweets. Corn 3B 10
Sweetshouse. Corn 2E 7
Swefling. Suff 4F 67
Swell. Som 4G 21
Swepstone. Leics 4A 74
Swerford. Oxon 2B 50
Swettenham. Ches E 4C 84
Swetton. N Yor 2D 98
Swffyrd. Cphy 2F 33
Swiftsden. E Sus 3B 28
Swilland. Suff 5D 66
Swillington. W Yor 1D 93
Swimbridge. Devn 4G 19
Swimbridge Newland. Devn 3G 19
Swinbrook. Oxon 4A 50
Swincliffe. N Yor 4E 99
Swincliffe. W Yor 2C 92
Swinderby. Linc 4F 87
Swindon. Glos 3E 49
Swindon. Nmbd 5D 121
Swindon. Staf 1C 60
Swindon. Swin 3G 35 & 212
Swine. E Yor 1E 95
Swinefleet. E Yor 2A 94
Swineford. S Glo 5B 34
Swineshead. Bed 4H 63
Swineshead. Linc 1B 76
Swineshead Bridge. Linc 1B 76
Swiney. High 5E 169
Swinford. Leics 3C 62
Swinford. Oxon 5C 50
Swingate. Notts 1C 74
Swingbrow. Cambs 2C 64
Swingfield Minnis. Kent 1G 29
Swingfield Street. Kent 1G 29
Swingleton Green. Suff 1C 54
Swinhill. S Lan 5A 128
Swinhoe. Nmbd 2G 121
Swinhope. Linc 1B 88
Swinister. Shet 3E 173
Swinithwaite. N Yor 1C 98
Swinmore Common. Here 1B 48
Swinscoe. Staf 1F 73
Swinside Hall. Bord 3B 120
Swinstead. Linc 3H 75
Swinton. G Man 4F 91
Swinton. N Yor 2B 100 (nr. Malton)
Swinton. N Yor 2E 98 (nr. Masham)
Swinton. Bord 5E 131
Swinton. S Yor 1B 86
Swithland. Leics 4C 74
Swordale. High 2H 157
Swordly. High 2H 167
Sworton Heath. Ches E 2A 84
Swyddffynnon. Cdgn 4F 57
Swyffrd. Cphy 2F 33
Swynnerton. Staf 2C 72
Swyre. Dors 4A 14
Sycharth. Powy 3E 70
Sychdyn. Flin 4E 83
Sychnant. Powy 3B 58
Sychtyn. Powy 5B 70
Syde. Glos 4E 49
Sydenham. G Lon 3E 39
Sydenham. Oxon 5F 51
Sydenham. Som 3G 21
Sydenham Damerel. Devn 5E 11
Syderstone. Norf 2H 77
Sydling St Nicholas. Dors 3B 14
Sydmonton. Hants 1C 24
Sydney. Ches E 5B 84
Syerston. Notts 1E 75
Syke. G Man 3G 91
Sykehouse. S Yor 3G 93
Sykes. Lanc 4F 97
Syleham. Suff 3E 66
Sylen. Carm 5F 45
Sylfaen. Powy 5D 70
Symbister. Shet 5G 173
Symington. S Ayr 1C 116
Symington. S Lan 1B 118
Symondsbury. Dors 3H 13
Symonds Yat. Here 4A 48
Synod Inn. Cdgn 5D 56
Syre. High 4G 167
Syreford. Glos 3F 49
Syresham. Nptn 1E 51
Syston. Leics 4D 74
Syston. Linc 1G 75
Sytchampton. Worc 4C 60
Sywell. Nptn 4F 63

T

Tabost. W Isl 6F 171 (nr. Cearsiadar)
Tabost. W Isl 1H 171 (nr. Suainebost)
Tachbrook Mallory. Warw 4H 61
Tackley. Oxon 3C 50
Tacleit. W Isl 4D 171
Tacolneston. Norf 1D 66
Tadcaster. N Yor 5G 99
Taddington. Derbs 3F 85
Taddington. Glos 2F 49
Taddiport. Devn 1E 11
Tadley. Hants 5E 36
Tadlow. Cambs 1C 52
Tadmarton. Oxon 2B 50
Tadwick. Bath 4C 34
Tadworth. Surr 5D 38
Tafarnaubach. Blae 4E 46
Tafarn-y-bwlch. Pemb 1E 43
Tafarn-y-Gelyn. Den 4D 82
Taff's Well. Rhon 3E 33
Tafolwern. Powy 5A 70
Taibach. Neat 3A 32
Tai-bach. Powy 3D 70
Taigh a Ghearraidh. W Isl 1C 170
Taigh Bhuirgh. W Isl 8C 171
Tain. High 5E 165 (nr. Invergordon)
Tain. High 2E 169 (nr. Thurso)
Tai-Nant. Wrex 1E 71
Tai'n Lon. Gwyn 5D 80
Tairbeart. W Isl 8D 171
Tairgwaith. Neat 4H 45
Takeley. Essx 3F 53
Takeley Street. Essx 3F 53
Talachddu. Powy 2D 46
Talacre. Flin 2D 82
Talardd. Gwyn 3A 70
Talaton. Devn 3D 12
Talbenny. Pemb 3C 42
Talbot Green. Rhon 3D 32
Taleford. Devn 3D 12
Talerddig. Powy 5B 70
Talgarreg. Cdgn 5D 56
Talgarth. Powy 2E 47
Talisker. High 5C 154
Talke. Staf 5C 84
Talkin. Cumb 4G 113
Talladale. High 1B 156
Talla Linnfoots. Bord 2D 118
Tallaminnock. S Ayr 5D 116
Tallarn Green. Wrex 1G 71
Tallentire. Cumb 1C 102
Talley. Carm 2G 45
Tallington. Linc 5H 75
Talmine. High 2F 167
Talog. Carm 2H 43
Talsarn. Carm 3A 46
Talsarn. Cdgn 5E 57
Talsarnau. Gwyn 2F 69
Talskiddy. Corn 2D 6
Talwrn. IOA 3D 81
Talwrn. Wrex 1E 71
Tal-y-bont. Cdgn 2F 57
Tal-y-Bont. Cnwy 4G 81
Tal-y-bont. Gwyn 3F 81 (nr. Bangor)
Tal-y-bont. Gwyn 3E 69 (nr. Barmouth)
Talybont-on-Usk. Powy 3E 46
Tal-y-cafn. Cnwy 3G 81
Tal-y-coed. Mon 4H 47
Tal-y-llyn. Gwyn 5G 69
Talyllyn. Powy 3E 46
Talysarn. Gwyn 5D 81
Tal-y-waenydd. Gwyn 1F 69
Talywain. Torf 5F 47
Talywern. Powy 5H 69
Tamerton Foliot. Plym 2A 8
Tamworth. Staf 5G 73
Tamworth Green. Linc 1C 76
Tandlehill. Ren 3F 127
Tandridge. Surr 5E 39
Tanerdy. Carm 3E 45
Tanfield. Dur 4E 115
Tanfield Lea. Dur 4E 115
Tangasdale. W Isl 8B 170
Tang Hall. York 4A 100
Tangiers. Pemb 3D 42
Tangley. Hants 1B 24
Tangmere. W Sus 5A 26
Tangwick. Shet 4D 173
Tankerness. Orkn 7E 172
Tankersley. S Yor 1H 85
Tankerton. Kent 4F 41
Tan-lan. Cnwy 4G 81
Tan-lan. Gwyn 1F 69
Tannach. High 4F 169
Tannadice. Ang 3D 145
Tanner's Green. Worc 3E 61
Tannington. Suff 4E 67
Tannochside. N Lan 3A 128
Tan Office Green. Suff 5G 65
Tansley. Derbs 5H 85
Tansley Knoll. Derbs 4H 85
Tansor. Nptn 1H 63
Tantobie. Dur 4E 115
Tanton. N Yor 3C 106
Tanvats. Linc 4A 88
Tanworth-in-Arden. Warw 3F 61
Tan-y-bwlch. Gwyn 1F 69
Tan-y-fron. Cnwy 4B 82
Tanyfron. Wrex 5E 83
Tan-y-goes. Cdgn 1C 44
Tanygrisiau. Gwyn 1F 69
Tan-y-pistyll. Powy 3C 70
Tan-yr-allt. Den 2C 82
Taobh a Chaolais. W Isl 7C 170
Taobh a Deas Loch Aineort. W Isl 6C 170
Taobh a Ghlinne. W Isl 6F 171
Taobh a Tuath Loch Aineort. W Isl 6C 170
Taplow. Buck 2A 38
Tapton. Derbs 3A 86
Tarbert. Arg 1E 125 (on Jura)
Tarbert. Arg 3G 125 (on Kintyre)
Tarbert. W Isl 8D 171
Tarbet. Arg 3C 134
Tarbet. High 4F 147 (nr. Mallaig)
Tarbet. High 4B 166 (nr. Scourie)
Tarbock Green. Mers 2G 83
Tarbolton. S Ayr 2D 116
Tarbrax. S Lan 4D 128
Tardebigge. Worc 4E 61
Tarfside. Ang 1D 145
Tarland. Abers 3B 152
Tarleton. Lanc 2C 90
Tarlogie. High 5E 165
Tarlscough. Lanc 3C 90
Tarlton. Glos 2E 35
Tarnbrook. Lanc 4E 97
Tarnock. Som 1G 21
Tarns. Cumb 5C 112
Tarporley. Ches W 4H 83
Tarpots. Essx 2B 40
Tarr. Som 3E 20
Tarrant Crawford. Dors 2E 15
Tarrant Gunville. Dors 1E 15
Tarrant Hinton. Dors 1E 15
Tarrant Keyneston. Dors 2E 15
Tarrant Launceston. Dors 2E 15
Tarrant Monkton. Dors 2E 15
Tarrant Rawston. Dors 2E 15
Tarrant Rushton. Dors 2E 15
Tarrel. High 5F 165
Tarring Neville. E Sus 5F 27
Tarrington. Here 1B 48
Tarsappie. Per 1D 136
Tarscabhaig. High 3D 147
Tarskavaig. High 3D 147
Tarves. Abers 5F 161
Tarvie. High 3G 157
Tarvin. Ches W 4G 83
Tasburgh. Norf 1E 66
Tasley. Shrp 1A 60
Taston. Oxon 3B 50
Tatenhill. Staf 3G 73
Tathall End. Mil 1G 51
Tatham. Lanc 3F 97
Tathwell. Linc 2C 88
Tatling End. Buck 2B 38
Tatsfield. Surr 5F 39
Tattenhall. Ches W 5G 83
Tatterford. Norf 3A 78
Tattersett. Norf 2H 77
Tattershall. Linc 5B 88
Tattershall Bridge. Linc 5A 88
Tattershall Thorpe. Linc 5B 88
Tattingstone. Suff 2E 55
Tattingstone White Horse. Suff 2E 55
Tattle Bank. Warw 4F 61
Tatworth. Som 2G 13
Taunton. Som 4F 21 & 213
Taverham. Norf 4D 78
Taverners Green. Essx 4F 53
Tavernspite. Pemb 3F 43
Tavistock. Devn 5E 11
Tavool House. Arg 1B 132
Taw Green. Devn 3G 11
Tawstock. Devn 4F 19
Taxal. Derbs 2E 85
Tayinloan. Arg 5E 125
Taynish. Arg 1F 125
Taynton. Glos 3C 48
Taynton. Oxon 4H 49
Taynuilt. Arg 5E 141
Tayport. Fife 1G 137
Tay Road Bridge. Fife 1G 137
Tayvallich. Arg 1F 125
Tealby. Linc 1A 88
Tealing. Ang 5D 144
Teams. Tyne 3F 115
Teangue. High 3E 147
Teanna Machair. W Isl 2C 170
Tebay. Cumb 4H 103
Tebworth. C Beds 3H 51
Tedburn St Mary. Devn 3B 12
Teddington. Glos 2E 49
Teddington. G Lon 3C 38
Tedsmore. Shrp 3F 71
Tedstone Delamere. Here 5A 60
Tedstone Wafer. Here 5A 60
Teesport. Red C 2C 106
Teesside. Stoc T 2C 106
Teeton. Nptn 3D 62
Teffont Evias. Wilts 3E 23
Teffont Magna. Wilts 3E 23
Tegryn. Pemb 1G 43
Teigh. Rut 4F 75
Teigncombe. Devn 4G 11
Teigngrace. Devn 5B 12
Teignmouth. Devn 5C 12
Telford. Telf 4A 72
Telham. E Sus 4B 28
Tellisford. Som 1D 22
Telscombe. E Sus 5F 27
Telscombe Cliffs. E Sus 5E 27
Tempar. Per 3D 142
Templand. Dum 1B 112
Temple. Corn 5B 10
Temple. Glas 3G 127
Temple. Midl 4G 129
Temple Balsall. W Mid 3G 61
Temple Bar. Carm 4F 45
Temple Bar. Cdgn 5E 57
Temple Cloud. Bath 1B 22
Templecombe. Som 4C 22
Temple Ewell. Kent 1G 29
Temple Grafton. Warw 5F 61
Temple Guiting. Glos 3F 49
Templehall. Fife 4E 137
Temple Hirst. N Yor 2G 93
Temple Normanton. Derbs 4B 86
Temple Sowerby. Cumb 2H 103
Templeton. Devn 1B 12
Templeton. Pemb 3F 43
Templeton. W Ber 5B 36
Templetown. Dur 5E 115
Tempsford. C Beds 5A 64
Tenandry. Per 2G 143
Tenbury Wells. Worc 4H 59
Tenby. Pemb 4F 43
Tendring. Essx 3E 55
Tendring Green. Essx 3E 55
Tenga. Arg 4G 139
Ten Mile Bank. Norf 1F 65
Tenterden. Kent 2C 28
Terfyn. Cnwy 3B 82
Terhill. Som 3E 21
Terling. Essx 4A 54
Ternhill. Shrp 2A 72
Terregles. Dum 2G 111
Terrick. Buck 5G 51
Terrington. N Yor 2A 100
Terrington St Clement. Norf 3E 77
Terrington St John. Norf 4E 77
Terry's Green. Warw 3F 61
Teston. Kent 5B 40
Testwood. Hants 1B 16
Tetbury. Glos 2D 35
Tetbury Upton. Glos 2D 35
Tetchill. Shrp 2F 71
Tetcott. Devn 3D 10
Tetford. Linc 3C 88
Tetney. Linc 4G 95
Tetney Lock. Linc 4G 95
Tetsworth. Oxon 5E 51
Tettenhall. W Mid 1C 60
Teversal. Notts 4B 86
Teversham. Cambs 5D 65
Teviothead. Bord 4G 119
Tewel. Abers 5F 153
Tewin. Herts 4C 52
Tewkesbury. Glos 2D 49
Teynham. Kent 4D 40
Teynham Street. Kent 4D 40
Thackthwaite. Cumb 2F 103
Thakeham. W Sus 4C 26
Thame. Oxon 5F 51
Thames Ditton. Surr 4C 38
Thames Haven. Thur 2B 40
Thamesmead. G Lon 2F 39
Thamesport. Medw 3C 40
Thanington Without. Kent 5F 41
Thankerton. S Lan 1B 118
Tharston. Norf 1D 66
Thatcham. W Ber 5D 36
Thatto Heath. Mers 1H 83
Thaxted. Essx 2G 53
Theakston. N Yor 1F 99
Thealby. N Lin 3B 94
Theale. Som 2H 21
Theale. W Ber 4E 37
Thearne. E Yor 1D 94
Theberton. Suff 4G 67
Theddingworth. Leics 2D 62
Theddlethorpe All Saints. Linc 2D 88
Theddlethorpe St Helen. Linc 2D 89
Thelbridge Barton. Devn 1A 12
Thelnetham. Suff 3C 66
Thelveton. Norf 2D 66
Thelwall. Warr 2A 84
Themelthorpe. Norf 3C 78
Thenford. Nptn 1D 50
Therfield. Herts 2D 52
Thetford. Linc 4A 76
Thetford. Norf 2A 66
Thethwaite. Cumb 5E 113
Theydon Bois. Essx 1F 39
Thick Hollins. W Yor 3B 92
Thickwood. Wilts 4D 34
Thimbleby. Linc 3B 88
Thimbleby. N Yor 5B 106
Thingwall. Mers 2E 83
Thirlby. N Yor 1G 99
Thirlestane. Bord 5B 130
Thirn. N Yor 1E 98
Thirsk. N Yor 1G 99
Thirtleby. E Yor 1E 95
Thistleton. Lanc 1C 90
Thistleton. Rut 4G 75
Thistley Green. Suff 3F 65
Thixendale. N Yor 3C 100
Thockrington. Nmbd 2C 114
Tholomas Drove. Cambs 5D 76
Tholthorpe. N Yor 3G 99
Thomas Chapel. Pemb 4F 43
Thomas Close. Cumb 5F 113
Thomastown. Abers 4E 160
Thomastown. Rhon 3D 32
Thompson. Norf 1B 66
Thomshill. Mor 3G 159
Thong. Kent 3A 40
Thongsbridge. W Yor 4B 92
Thoralby. N Yor 1C 98
Thoresby. Notts 3D 86
Thoresway. Linc 1A 88
Thorganby. Linc 1B 88
Thorganby. N Yor 5A 100
Thorgill. N Yor 5E 107
Thorington. Suff 3G 67
Thorington Street. Suff 2D 54
Thorlby. N Yor 4B 98
Thorley. Herts 4E 53
Thorley Street. Herts 4E 53
Thorley Street. IOW 4B 16
Thormanby. N Yor 2G 99
Thorn. Powy 4E 59
Thornaby-on-Tees. Stoc T 3B 106
Thornage. Norf 2C 78
Thornborough. Buck 2F 51
Thornborough. N Yor 2E 99
Thornbury. Devn 2E 11
Thornbury. Here 5A 60
Thornbury. S Glo 3B 34
Thornby. Cumb 4D 112
Thornby. Nptn 3D 62
Thorncliffe. Staf 5E 85
Thorncombe. Dors 2G 13
Thorncombe Street. Surr 1A 26
Thorncote Green. C Beds 1B 52
Thorndon. Suff 4D 66
Thorndon Cross. Devn 3F 11
Thorne. S Yor 3G 93
Thornehillhead. Devn 1E 11
Thorner. W Yor 5F 99
Thorne St Margaret. Som 4D 20
Thorney. Notts 3F 87
Thorney. Pet 5B 76
Thorney. Som 4H 21
Thorney Hill. Hants 3G 15
Thorney Toll. Cambs 5C 76
Thornfalcon. Som 4F 21
Thornford. Dors 1B 14
Thorngrafton. Nmbd 3A 114
Thorngrove. Som 3G 21
Thorngumbald. E Yor 2F 95
Thornham. Norf 1G 77
Thornham Magna. Suff 3D 66
Thornham Parva. Suff 3D 66
Thornhaugh. Pet 5H 75
Thornhill. Cphy 3E 33
Thornhill. Cumb 4B 102
Thornhill. Derbs 2G 85
Thornhill. Dum 5A 118
Thornhill. Sotn 1C 16
Thornhill. Stir 4F 135
Thornhill. W Yor 3C 92
Thornhill Lees. W Yor 3C 92
Thornhills. W Yor 2B 92
Thornholme. E Yor 3F 101
Thornicombe. Dors 2D 14
Thornington. Nmbd 1C 120
Thornley. Dur 1A 106 (nr. Durham)
Thornley. Dur 1E 105 (nr. Tow Law)
Thornley Gate. Nmbd 4B 114
Thornliebank. E Ren 4G 127
Thornroan. Abers 5F 161
Thorns. Suff 5G 65
Thornsett. Derbs 2E 85
Thornthwaite. Cumb 2D 102
Thornthwaite. N Yor 4D 98
Thornton. Ang 4C 144
Thornton. Buck 2F 51
Thornton. E Yor 5B 100
Thornton. Fife 4E 137
Thornton. Lanc 5C 96
Thornton. Leics 5B 74
Thornton. Linc 4B 88
Thornton. Mers 4B 90
Thornton. Midd 3B 106
Thornton. Nmbd 5F 131
Thornton. Pemb 4D 42
Thornton. W Yor 1A 92
Thornton Curtis. N Lin 3D 94
Thorntonhall. S Lan 4G 127
Thornton Heath. G Lon 4E 39

Thornton Hough. *Mers* 2F **83**
Thornton in Craven. *N Yor* 5B **98**
Thornton in Lonsdale. *N Yor* 2F **97**
Thornton-le-Beans. *N Yor* 5A **106**
Thornton-le-Clay. *N Yor* 3A **100**
Thornton-le-Dale. *N Yor* 1C **100**
Thornton le Moor. *Linc* 1H **87**
Thornton-le-Moor. *N Yor* 1F **99**
Thornton-le-Moors. *Ches W* 3G **83**
Thornton-le-Street. *N Yor* 1G **99**
Thorntonloch. *E Lot* 2D **130**
Thornton Rust. *N Yor* 1B **98**
Thornton Steward. *N Yor* 1D **98**
Thornton Watlass. *N Yor* 1E **99**
Thornwood Common. *Essx* 5E **53**
Thornythwaite. *Cumb* 2E **103**
Thoroton. *Notts* 1E **75**
Thorp Arch. *W Yor* 5G **99**
Thorpe. *Derbs* 5F **85**
Thorpe. *E Yor* 5D **101**
Thorpe. *Linc* 2D **89**
Thorpe. *Norf* 1G **67**
Thorpe. *N Yor* 3C **98**
Thorpe. *Notts* 1E **75**
Thorpe. *Surr* 4B **38**
Thorpe Abbotts. *Norf* 3D **66**
Thorpe Acre. *Leics* 3C **74**
Thorpe Arnold. *Leics* 3E **75**
Thorpe Audlin. *W Yor* 3E **93**
Thorpe Bassett. *N Yor* 2C **100**
Thorpe Bay. *S'end* 2D **40**
Thorpe by Water. *Rut* 1F **63**
Thorpe Common. *S Yor* 1A **86**
Thorpe Common. *Suff* 2F **55**
Thorpe Constantine. *Staf* 5G **73**
Thorpe End. *Norf* 4E **79**
Thorpe Fendike. *Linc* 4D **88**
Thorpe Green. *Essx* 3E **55**
Thorpe Green. *Suff* 5B **66**
Thorpe Hall. *N Yor* 2H **99**
Thorpe Hamlet. *Norf* 5E **79**
Thorpe Hesley. *S Yor* 1A **86**
Thorpe in Balne. *S Yor* 3F **93**
Thorpe in the Fallows. *Linc* 2G **87**
Thorpe Langton. *Leics* 1E **63**
Thorpe Larches. *Dur* 2A **106**
Thorpe Latimer. *Linc* 1A **76**
Thorpe-le-Soken. *Essx* 3E **55**
Thorpe le Street. *E Yor* 5C **100**
Thorpe Malsor. *Nptn* 3F **63**
Thorpe Mandeville. *Nptn* 1D **50**
Thorpe Market. *Norf* 2E **79**
Thorpe Marriott. *Norf* 4D **78**
Thorpe Morieux. *Suff* 5B **66**
Thorpeness. *Suff* 4G **67**
Thorpe on the Hill. *Linc* 4G **87**
Thorpe on the Hill. *W Yor* 2D **92**
Thorpe St Andrew. *Norf* 5E **79**
Thorpe St Peter. *Linc* 4D **89**
Thorpe Salvin. *S Yor* 2C **86**
Thorpe Satchville. *Leics* 4E **75**
Thorpe Thewles. *Stoc T* 2B **106**
Thorpe Tilney. *Linc* 5A **88**
Thorpe Underwood. *N Yor* 4G **99**
Thorpe Waterville. *Nptn* 2H **63**
Thorpe Willoughby. *N Yor* 1F **93**
Thorpland. *Norf* 5F **77**
Thorrington. *Essx* 3D **54**
Thorverton. *Devn* 2C **12**
Thrandeston. *Suff* 3D **66**
Thrapston. *Nptn* 3G **63**
Thrashbush. *N Lan* 3A **128**
Threapland. *Cumb* 1C **102**
Threapland. *N Yor* 3B **98**
Threapwood. *Ches W* 1G **71**
Threapwood. *Staf* 1E **73**
Three Ashes. *Here* 3A **48**
Three Bridges. *Linc* 2D **88**
Three Bridges. *W Sus* 2D **27**
Three Burrows. *Corn* 4B **6**
Three Chimneys. *Kent* 2C **28**
Three Cocks. *Powy* 2E **47**
Three Crosses. *Swan* 3E **31**
Three Cups Corner. *E Sus* 3H **27**
Threehammer Common. *Norf* 3F **79**
Three Holes. *Norf* 5E **77**
Threekingham. *Linc* 2H **75**
Three Leg Cross. *E Sus* 2A **28**
Three Legged Cross. *Dors* 2F **15**
Three Mile Cross. *Wok* 5F **37**
Threemilestone. *Corn* 4B **6**
Three Oaks. *E Sus* 4C **28**
Threlkeld. *Cumb* 2E **102**
Threshfield. *N Yor* 3B **98**
Thrigby. *Norf* 4G **79**
Thringarth. *Dur* 2C **104**
Thringstone. *Leics* 4B **74**
Thrintoft. *N Yor* 5A **106**
Thriplow. *Cambs* 1E **53**
Throckenholt. *Linc* 5C **76**
Throcking. *Herts* 2D **52**
Throckley. *Tyne* 3E **115**
Throckmorton. *Worc* 1E **49**
Throop. *Bour* 3G **15**
Throphill. *Nmbd* 1E **115**
Thropton. *Nmbd* 4E **121**
Throsk. *Stir* 4A **136**
Througham. *Glos* 5E **49**
Throughgate. *Dum* 1F **111**
Throwleigh. *Devn* 3G **11**
Throwley. *Kent* 5D **40**
Throwley Forstal. *Kent* 5D **40**
Throxenby. *N Yor* 1E **101**
Thrumpton. *Notts* 2C **74**
Thrumster. *High* 4F **169**
Thrunton. *Nmbd* 3E **121**
Thrupp. *Glos* 5D **48**
Thrupp. *Oxon* 4C **50**
Thrushelton. *Devn* 4E **11**
Thrushgill. *Lanc* 3F **97**
Thrussington. *Leics* 4D **74**
Thruxton. *Hants* 2A **24**
Thruxton. *Here* 2H **47**
Thrybergh. *S Yor* 1B **86**
Thulston. *Derbs* 2B **74**
Thundergay. *N Ayr* 5G **125**
Thundersley. *Essx* 2B **40**
Thundridge. *Herts* 4D **52**
Thurcaston. *Leics* 4C **74**
Thurcroft. *S Yor* 2B **86**
Thurdon. *Corn* 1C **10**
Thurgarton. *Norf* 2D **78**
Thurgarton. *Notts* 1D **74**
Thurgoland. *S Yor* 4C **92**
Thurlaston. *Leics* 1C **62**
Thurlaston. *Warw* 3B **62**
Thurlbear. *Som* 4F **21**
Thurlby. *Linc* 3D **89** (nr. Alford)
Thurlby. *Linc* 4A **76** (nr. Baston)
Thurlby. *Linc* 4G **87** (nr. Lincoln)
Thurleigh. *Bed* 5H **63**
Thurlestone. *Devn* 4C **8**
Thurloxton. *Som* 3F **21**
Thurlstone. *S Yor* 4C **92**
Thurlton. *Norf* 1G **67**
Thurmaston. *Leics* 5D **74**
Thurnby. *Leics* 5D **74**
Thurne. *Norf* 4G **79**
Thurnham. *Kent* 5C **40**
Thurning. *Norf* 3C **78**
Thurning. *Nptn* 2H **63**
Thurnscoe. *S Yor* 4E **93**
Thursby. *Cumb* 4E **113**
Thursford. *Norf* 2B **78**
Thursford Green. *Norf* 2B **78**
Thursley. *Surr* 2A **26**
Thurso. *High* 2D **168**
Thurso East. *High* 2D **168**
Thurstaston. *Mers* 2E **83**
Thurston. *Suff* 4B **66**
Thurston End. *Suff* 5G **65**
Thurstonfield. *Cumb* 4E **112**
Thurstonland. *W Yor* 3B **92**
Thurton. *Norf* 5F **79**
Thurvaston. *Derbs* 2F **73** (nr. Ashbourne)
Thurvaston. *Derbs* 2G **73** (nr. Derby)
Thuxton. *Norf* 5C **78**
Thwaite. *Dur* 3D **104**
Thwaite. *N Yor* 5B **104**
Thwaite. *Suff* 4D **66**
Thwaite Head. *Cumb* 5E **103**
Thwaites. *W Yor* 5C **98**
Thwaite St Mary. *Norf* 1F **67**
Thwing. *E Yor* 2E **101**
Tibbermore. *Per* 1C **136**
Tibberton. *Glos* 3C **48**
Tibberton. *Telf* 3A **72**
Tibberton. *Worc* 5D **60**
Tibenham. *Norf* 2D **66**
Tibshelf. *Derbs* 4B **86**
Tibthorpe. *E Yor* 4D **100**
Ticehurst. *E Sus* 2A **28**
Tichborne. *Hants* 3D **24**
Tickencote. *Rut* 5G **75**
Tickenham. *N Som* 4H **33**
Tickhill. *S Yor* 1C **86**
Ticklerton. *Shrp* 1G **59**
Ticknall. *Derbs* 3H **73**
Tickton. *E Yor* 5E **101**
Tidbury Green. *W Mid* 3F **61**
Tidcombe. *Wilts* 1A **24**
Tiddington. *Oxon* 5E **51**
Tiddington. *Warw* 5G **61**
Tiddleywink. *Wilts* 4D **34**
Tidebrook. *E Sus* 3H **27**
Tideford. *Corn* 3H **7**
Tideford Cross. *Corn* 2H **7**
Tidenham. *Glos* 2A **34**
Tideswell. *Derbs* 3F **85**
Tidmarsh. *W Ber* 4E **37**
Tidmington. *Warw* 2A **50**
Tidpit. *Hants* 1F **15**
Tidworth. *Wilts* 2H **23**
Tidworth Camp. *Wilts* 2H **23**
Tiers Cross. *Pemb* 3D **42**
Tiffield. *Nptn* 5D **62**
Tifty. *Abers* 4E **161**
Tigerton. *Ang* 2E **145**
Tighnabruaich. *Arg* 2A **126**
Tigley. *Devn* 2D **8**
Tilbrook. *Cambs* 4H **63**
Tilbury. *Thur* 3H **39**
Tilbury Green. *Essx* 1H **53**
Tilbury Juxta Clare. *Essx* 1A **54**
Tile Hill. *W Mid* 3G **61**
Tilehurst. *Read* 4E **37**
Tilford. *Surr* 2G **25**
Tilgate Forest Row. *W Sus* 2D **26**
Tillathrowie. *Abers* 5B **160**
Tillers Green. *Glos* 2B **48**
Tillery. *Abers* 1G **153**
Tilley. *Shrp* 3H **71**
Tillicoultry. *Clac* 4B **136**
Tillingham. *Essx* 5C **54**
Tillington. *Here* 1H **47**
Tillington. *W Sus* 3A **26**
Tillington Common. *Here* 1H **47**
Tillybirloch. *Abers* 3D **152**
Tillyfourie. *Abers* 2D **152**
Tilmanstone. *Kent* 5H **41**
Tilney All Saints. *Norf* 4E **77**
Tilney Fen End. *Norf* 4E **77**
Tilney High End. *Norf* 4E **77**
Tilney St Lawrence. *Norf* 4E **77**
Tilshead. *Wilts* 2F **23**
Tilstock. *Shrp* 2H **71**
Tilston. *Ches W* 5G **83**
Tilstone Fearnall. *Ches W* 4H **83**
Tilsworth. *C Beds* 3H **51**
Tilton on the Hill. *Leics* 5E **75**
Tiltups End. *Glos* 2D **34**
Timberland. *Linc* 5A **88**
Timbersbrook. *Ches E* 4C **84**
Timberscombe. *Som* 2C **20**
Timble. *N Yor* 4D **98**
Timperley. *G Man* 2B **84**
Timsbury. *Bath* 1B **22**
Timsbury. *Hants* 4B **24**
Timsgearraidh. *W Isl* 4C **171**
Timworth Green. *Suff* 4A **66**
Tincleton. *Dors* 3C **14**
Tindale. *Cumb* 4H **113**
Tindale Crescent. *Dur* 2F **105**
Tingewick. *Buck* 2E **51**
Tingrith. *C Beds* 2A **52**
Tingwall. *Orkn* 5D **172**
Tinhay. *Devn* 4D **11**
Tinshill. *W Yor* 1C **92**
Tinsley. *S Yor* 1B **86**
Tinsley Green. *W Sus* 2D **27**
Tintagel. *Corn* 4A **10**
Tintern. *Mon* 5A **48**
Tintinhull. *Som* 1A **14**
Tintwistle. *Derbs* 1E **85**
Tinwald. *Dum* 1B **112**
Tinwell. *Rut* 5H **75**
Tippacott. *Devn* 2A **20**
Tipperty. *Abers* 1G **153**
Tipps End. *Cambs* 1E **65**
Tiptoe. *Hants* 3A **16**
Tipton. *W Mid* 1D **60**
Tipton St John. *Devn* 3D **12**
Tiptree. *Essx* 4B **54**
Tiptree Heath. *Essx* 4B **54**
Tirabad. *Powy* 1B **46**
Tircoed. *Swan* 5G **45**
Tiree Airport. *Arg* 4B **138**
Tirinie. *Per* 2F **143**
Tirley. *Glos* 3D **48**
Tirnewydd. *Flin* 3D **82**
Tiroran. *Arg* 1B **132**
Tirphil. *Cphy* 5E **47**
Tirril. *Cumb* 2G **103**
Tirryside. *High* 2C **164**
Tir-y-dail. *Carm* 4G **45**
Tisbury. *Wilts* 4E **23**
Tisman's Common. *W Sus* 2B **26**
Tissington. *Derbs* 5F **85**
Titchberry. *Devn* 4C **18**
Titchfield. *Hants* 2D **16**
Titchmarsh. *Nptn* 3H **63**
Titchwell. *Norf* 1G **77**
Tithby. *Notts* 2D **74**
Titley. *Here* 5F **59**
Titlington. *Nmbd* 3F **121**
Titsey. *Surr* 5F **39**
Titson. *Corn* 2C **10**
Tittensor. *Staf* 2C **72**
Tittleshall. *Norf* 3A **78**
Titton. *Worc* 4C **60**
Tiverton. *Ches W* 4H **83**
Tiverton. *Devn* 1C **12**
Tivetshall St Margaret. *Norf* 2D **66**
Tivetshall St Mary. *Norf* 2D **66**
Tivington. *Som* 2C **20**
Tixall. *Staf* 3D **73**
Tixover. *Rut* 5G **75**
Toab. *Orkn* 7E **172**
Toab. *Shet* 10E **173**
Toadmoor. *Derbs* 5H **85**
Tobermory. *Arg* 3G **139**
Toberonochy. *Arg* 3E **133**
Tobha-Beag. *W Isl* 1E **170** (on North Uist)
Tobha Beag. *W Isl* 5C **170** (on South Uist)
Tobha Mor. *W Isl* 5C **170**
Tobhtarol. *W Isl* 4D **171**
Tobson. *W Isl* 4D **171**
Tocabhaig. *High* 2E **147**
Tocher. *Abers* 5D **160**
Tockenham. *Wilts* 4F **35**
Tockenham Wick. *Wilts* 3F **35**
Tockholes. *Bkbn* 2E **91**
Tockington. *S Glo* 3B **34**
Tockwith. *N Yor* 4G **99**
Todber. *Dors* 4D **22**
Todding. *Here* 3G **59**
Toddington. *C Beds* 3A **52**
Toddington. *Glos* 2F **49**
Todenham. *Glos* 2H **49**
Todhills. *Cumb* 3E **113**
Todmorden. *W Yor* 2H **91**
Todwick. *S Yor* 2B **86**
Toft. *Cambs* 5C **64**
Toft. *Linc* 4H **75**
Toft Hill. *Dur* 2E **105**
Toft Monks. *Norf* 1G **67**
Toft next Newton. *Linc* 2H **87**
Toftrees. *Norf* 3A **78**
Tofts. *High* 2F **169**
Toftwood. *Norf* 4B **78**
Togston. *Nmbd* 4G **121**
Tokavaig. *High* 2E **147**
Tokers Green. *Oxon* 4F **37**
Tolastadh a Chaolais. *W Isl* 4D **171**
Tolladine. *Worc* 5C **60**
Tolland. *Som* 3E **20**
Tollard Farnham. *Dors* 1E **15**
Tollard Royal. *Wilts* 1E **15**
Toll Bar. *S Yor* 4F **93**
Toller Fratrum. *Dors* 3A **14**
Toller Porcorum. *Dors* 3A **14**
Tollerton. *N Yor* 3H **99**
Tollerton. *Notts* 2D **74**
Toller Whelme. *Dors* 2A **14**
Tollesbury. *Essx* 4C **54**
Tolleshunt D'Arcy. *Essx* 4C **54**
Tolleshunt Knights. *Essx* 4C **54**
Tolleshunt Major. *Essx* 4C **54**
Tollie. *High* 3H **157**
Tollie Farm. *High* 1A **156**
Tolm. *W Isl* 4G **171**
Tolpuddle. *Dors* 3C **14**
Tolstadh bho Thuath. *W Isl* 3H **171**
Tolworth. *G Lon* 4C **38**
Tomachlaggan. *Mor* 1F **151**
Tomaknock. *Per* 1A **136**
Tomatin. *High* 1C **150**
Tombuidhe. *Arg* 3H **133**
Tomdoun. *High* 3D **148**
Tomich. *High* 1F **149** (nr. Cannich)
Tomich. *High* 1B **158** (nr. Invergordon)
Tomich. *High* 3D **164** (nr. Lairg)
Tomintoul. *Mor* 2F **151**
Tomnavoulin. *Mor* 1G **151**
Tomsleibhe. *Arg* 5A **140**
Ton. *Mon* 2G **33**
Tonbridge. *Kent* 1G **27**
Tondu. *B'end* 3B **32**
Tonedale. *Som* 4E **21**
Tonfanau. *Gwyn* 5E **69**
Tong. *Shrp* 5B **72**
Tonge. *Leics* 3B **74**
Tong Forge. *Shrp* 5B **72**
Tongham. *Surr* 2G **25**
Tongland. *Dum* 4D **111**
Tong Norton. *Shrp* 5B **72**
Tongue. *High* 3F **167**
Tongue End. *Linc* 4A **76**
Tongwynlais. *Card* 3E **33**
Tonmawr. *Neat* 2B **32**
Tonna. *Neat* 2A **32**
Tonnau. *Neat* 2A **32**
Ton-Pentre. *Rhon* 2C **32**
Ton-Teg. *Rhon* 3D **32**
Tonwell. *Herts* 4D **52**
Tonypandy. *Rhon* 2C **32**
Tonyrefail. *Rhon* 3D **32**
Toot Baldon. *Oxon* 5D **50**
Toot Hill. *Essx* 5F **53**
Toot Hill. *Hants* 1B **16**
Topcliffe. *N Yor* 2G **99**
Topcliffe. *W Yor* 2C **92**
Topcroft. *Norf* 1E **67**
Topcroft Street. *Norf* 1E **67**
Toppesfield. *Essx* 2H **53**
Toppings. *G Man* 3F **91**
Toprow. *Norf* 1D **66**
Topsham. *Devn* 4C **12**
Torbay. *Torb* 2F **9**
Torbeg. *N Ayr* 3C **122**
Torbothie. *N Lan* 3B **128**
Torbryan. *Devn* 2E **9**
Torcross. *Devn* 4E **9**
Tore. *High* 3A **158**
Torgyle. *High* 2F **149**
Torinturk. *Arg* 3G **125**
Torksey. *Linc* 3F **87**
Torlum. *W Isl* 3C **170**
Torlundy. *High* 1F **141**
Tormarton. *S Glo* 4C **34**
Tormitchell. *S Ayr* 5B **116**
Tormore. *High* 3E **147**
Tormore. *N Ayr* 2C **122**
Tornagrain. *High* 4B **158**
Tornaveen. *Abers* 3D **152**
Torness. *High* 1H **149**
Toronto. *Dur* 1E **105**
Torpenhow. *Cumb* 1D **102**
Torphichen. *W Lot* 2C **128**
Torphins. *Abers* 3D **152**
Torpoint. *Corn* 3A **8**
Torquay. *Torb* 2F **9**
Torr. *Devn* 3B **8**
Torra. *Arg* 4B **124**
Torran. *High* 4E **155**
Torrance. *E Dun* 2H **127**
Torrans. *Arg* 1B **132**
Torranyard. *E Ayr* 5E **127**
Torre. *Som* 3D **20**
Torre. *Torb* 2E **9**
Torridon. *High* 3B **156**
Torrin. *High* 1D **147**
Torrisdale. *Arg* 2B **122**
Torrisdale. *High* 2G **167**
Torrish. *High* 2G **165**
Torrisholme. *Lanc* 3D **96**
Torroble. *High* 3C **164**
Torroy. *High* 4C **164**
Torry. *Aber* 3G **153**
Torryburn. *Fife* 1D **128**
Torthorwald. *Dum* 2B **112**
Tortington. *W Sus* 5B **26**
Tortworth. *S Glo* 2C **34**
Torvaig. *High* 4D **155**
Torver. *Cumb* 5D **102**
Torwood. *Falk* 1B **128**
Torworth. *Notts* 2D **86**
Toscaig. *High* 5G **155**
Toseland. *Cambs* 4B **64**
Tosside. *Lanc* 4G **97**
Tostock. *Suff* 4B **66**
Totaig. *High* 3B **154**
Totardor. *High* 5C **154**
Tote. *High* 4D **154**
Totegan. *High* 2A **168**
Tothill. *Linc* 2D **88**
Totland. *IOW* 4B **16**
Totley. *S Yor* 3H **85**
Totnell. *Dors* 2B **14**
Totnes. *Devn* 2E **9**
Toton. *Derbs* 2B **74**
Totronald. *Arg* 3C **138**
Totscore. *High* 2C **154**
Tottenham. *G Lon* 1E **39**
Tottenhill. *Norf* 4F **77**
Tottenhill Row. *Norf* 4F **77**
Totteridge. *G Lon* 1D **38**
Totternhoe. *C Beds* 3H **51**
Tottington. *G Man* 3F **91**
Totton. *Hants* 1B **16**
Touchen-end. *Wind* 4G **37**
Toulvaddie. *High* 5F **165**
Towans, The. *Corn* 3C **4**
Toward. *Arg* 3C **126**
Towcester. *Nptn* 1E **51**
Towednack. *Corn* 3B **4**
Tower End. *Norf* 4F **77**
Tower Hill. *Mers* 4C **90**
Tower Hill. *W Sus* 3C **26**
Towersey. *Oxon* 5F **51**
Towie. *Abers* 2B **152**
Towiemore. *Mor* 4A **160**
Tow Law. *Dur* 1E **105**
Town End. *Cambs* 1D **64**
Town End. *Cumb* 4F **103** (nr. Ambleside)
Town End. *Cumb* 2H **103** (nr. Kirkby Thore)
Town End. *Cumb* 1D **96** (nr. Lindale)
Town End. *Cumb* 1C **96** (nr. Newby Bridge)
Town End. *Mers* 2G **83**
Townend. *W Dun* 2F **127**
Townfield. *Dur* 5C **114**
Towngate. *Cumb* 5G **113**
Towngate. *Linc* 4A **76**
Town Green. *Lanc* 4B **90**
Town Head. *Cumb* 4E **103** (nr. Grasmere)
Town Head. *Cumb* 3H **103** (nr. Great Asby)
Townhead. *Cumb* 1G **103** (nr. Lazonby)
Townhead. *Cumb* 1B **102** (nr. Maryport)
Townhead. *Cumb* 1H **103** (nr. Ousby)
Townhead. *Dum* 5D **111**
Townhead of Greenlaw. *Dum* 3E **111**
Townhill. *Fife* 1E **129**
Townhill. *Swan* 3F **31**
Town Kelloe. *Dur* 1A **106**
Town Littleworth. *E Sus* 4F **27**
Town Row. *E Sus* 2G **27**
Towns End. *Hants* 1D **24**
Townsend. *Herts* 5B **52**
Townshend. *Corn* 3C **4**
Town Street. *Suff* 2G **65**
Town, The. *IOS* 1A **4**
Town Yetholm. *Bord* 2C **120**
Towthorpe. *E Yor* 3C **100**
Towthorpe. *York* 4A **100**
Towton. *N Yor* 1E **93**
Towyn. *Cnwy* 3B **82**
Toxteth. *Mers* 2F **83**
Toynton All Saints. *Linc* 4C **88**
Toynton Fen Side. *Linc* 4C **88**
Toynton St Peter. *Linc* 4D **88**
Toy's Hill. *Kent* 5F **39**
Trabboch. *E Ayr* 2D **116**
Traboe. *Corn* 4E **5**
Tradespark. *High* 3C **158**
Tradespark. *Orkn* 7D **172**
Trafford Park. *G Man* 1B **84**
Trallong. *Powy* 3C **46**
Tranent. *E Lot* 2H **129**
Tranmere. *Mers* 2F **83**
Trantlebeg. *High* 3A **168**
Trantlemore. *High* 3A **168**

Tranwell. *Nmbd* 1E **115**
Trapp. *Carm* 4G **45**
Traquair. *Bord* 1F **119**
Trash Green. *W Ber* 5E **37**
Trawden. *Lanc* 1H **91**
Trawscoed. *Powy* 2D **46**
Trawsfynydd. *Gwyn* 2G **69**
Trawsgoed. *Cdgn* 3F **57**
Treaddow. *Here* 3A **48**
Trealaw. *Rhon* 2D **32**
Treales. *Lanc* 1C **90**
Trearddur. *IOA* 3B **80**
Treaslane. *High* 3C **154**
Treator. *Corn* 1D **6**
Trebanog. *Rhon* 2D **32**
Trebanos. *Neat* 5H **45**
Trebarber. *Corn* 2C **6**
Trebartha. *Corn* 5C **10**
Trebarwith. *Corn* 4A **10**
Trebetherick. *Corn* 1D **6**
Treborough. *Som* 3D **20**
Trebudannon. *Corn* 2C **6**
Trebullett. *Corn* 5D **10**
Treburley. *Corn* 5D **10**
Treburrick. *Corn* 1C **6**
Trebyan. *Corn* 2E **7**
Trecastle. *Powy* 3B **46**
Trecenydd. *Cphy* 3E **33**
Trecott. *Devn* 2G **11**
Trecwn. *Pemb* 1D **42**
Trecynon. *Rhon* 5C **46**
Tredaule. *Corn* 4C **10**
Tredavoe. *Corn* 4B **4**
Tredegar. *Blae* 5E **47**
Trederwen. *Powy* 4E **71**
Tredington. *Glos* 3E **49**
Tredington. *Warw* 1A **50**
Tredinnick. *Corn* 2F **7**
(nr. Bodmin)
Tredinnick. *Corn* 3G **7**
(nr. Looe)
Tredinnick. *Corn* 1D **6**
(nr. Padstow)
Tredogan. *V Glam* 5D **32**
Tredomen. *Powy* 2E **46**
Tredunnock. *Mon* 2G **33**
Tredustan. *Powy* 2E **47**
Treen. *Corn* 4A **4**
(nr. Land's End)
Treen. *Corn* 3B **4**
(nr. St Ives)
Treeton. *S Yor* 2B **86**
Trefaldwyn. *Powy* 1E **58**
Trefasser. *Pemb* 1C **42**
Trefdraeth. *IOA* 3D **80**
Trefdraeth. *Pemb* 1E **43**
Trefecca. *Powy* 2E **47**
Trefechan. *Mer T* 5D **46**
Trefeglwys. *Powy* 1B **58**
Trefeitha. *Powy* 2E **46**
Trefenter. *Cdgn* 4F **57**
Treffgarne. *Pemb* 2D **42**
Treffynnon. *Flin* 3D **82**
Treffynnon. *Pemb* 2C **42**
Trefil. *Blae* 4E **46**
Trefilan. *Cdgn* 5E **57**
Trefin. *Pemb* 1C **42**
Treflach. *Shrp* 3E **71**
Trefnant. *Den* 3C **82**
Trefonen. *Shrp* 3E **71**
Trefor. *Gwyn* 1C **68**
Trefor. *IOA* 2C **80**
Treforest. *Rhon* 3D **32**
Trefrew. *Corn* 4B **10**
Trefriw. *Cnwy* 4G **81**
Tref-y-Clawdd. *Powy* 3E **59**
Trefynwy. *Mon* 4A **48**
Tregada. *Corn* 4D **10**
Tregadillett. *Corn* 4D **10**
Tregare. *Mon* 4H **47**
Tregarne. *Corn* 4E **5**
Tregaron. *Cdgn* 5F **57**
Tregarth. *Gwyn* 4F **81**
Tregear. *Corn* 3C **6**
Tregeare. *Corn* 4C **10**
Tregeiriog. *Wrex* 2D **70**
Tregele. *IOA* 1C **80**
Tregeseal. *Corn* 3A **4**
Tregiskey. *Corn* 4E **6**
Tregole. *Corn* 3B **10**
Tregolwyn. *V Glam* 4C **32**
Tregonetha. *Corn* 2D **6**
Tregonhawke. *Corn* 3A **8**
Tregony. *Corn* 4D **6**
Tregoodwell. *Corn* 4B **10**
Tregorrick. *Corn* 3E **6**
Tregoss. *Corn* 2D **6**
Tregowris. *Corn* 4E **5**
Tregoyd. *Powy* 2E **47**
Tregrehan Mills. *Corn* 3E **7**
Tre-groes. *Cdgn* 1E **45**
Tregullon. *Corn* 2E **7**
Tregurrian. *Corn* 2C **6**
Tregynon. *Powy* 1C **58**
Trehafod. *Rhon* 2D **32**
Trehan. *Corn* 3A **8**
Treharris. *Mer T* 2E **32**
Treherbert. *Rhon* 2C **32**
Trehunist. *Corn* 2H **7**
Trekenner. *Corn* 5D **10**
Trekenning. *Corn* 2D **6**
Treknow. *Corn* 4A **10**
Trelales. *B'end* 3B **32**
Trelan. *Corn* 5E **5**
Trelash. *Corn* 3B **10**
Trelassick. *Corn* 3C **6**
Trelawnyd. *Flin* 3C **82**
Trelech. *Carm* 1G **43**
Treleddyd-fawr. *Pemb* 2B **42**
Trelewis. *Mer T* 2E **32**
Treligga. *Corn* 4A **10**
Trelights. *Corn* 1D **6**
Trelill. *Corn* 5A **10**
Trelissick. *Corn* 5C **6**
Trellech. *Mon* 5A **48**
Trelleck Grange. *Mon* 5H **47**
Trelogan. *Flin* 2D **82**
Trelystan. *Powy* 5E **71**
Tremadog. *Gwyn* 1E **69**
Tremail. *Corn* 4B **10**
Tremain. *Cdgn* 1C **44**
Tremaine. *Corn* 4C **10**
Tremar. *Corn* 2G **7**
Trematon. *Corn* 3H **7**
Tremeirchion. *Den* 3C **82**
Tremore. *Corn* 2E **6**
Tremorfa. *Card* 4F **33**
Trenance. *Corn* 2C **6**
(nr. Newquay)
Trenance. *Corn* 1D **6**
(nr. Padstow)
Trenarren. *Corn* 4E **7**
Trench. *Telf* 4A **72**
Trencreek. *Corn* 2C **6**
Trendeal. *Corn* 3C **6**
Trenear. *Corn* 5A **6**
Treneglos. *Corn* 4C **10**
Trenewan. *Corn* 3F **7**
Trengune. *Corn* 3B **10**
Trent. *Dors* 1A **14**
Trentham. *Stoke* 1C **72**
Trentishoe. *Devn* 2G **19**
Trentlock. *Derbs* 2B **74**
Treoes. *V Glam* 4C **32**
Treorchy. *Rhon* 2C **32**
Treorci. *Rhon* 2C **32**
Tre'r-ddol. *Cdgn* 1F **57**
Tre'r llai. *Powy* 5E **71**
Trerulefoot. *Corn* 3H **7**
Tresaith. *Cdgn* 5B **56**
Trescott. *Staf* 1C **60**
Trescowe. *Corn* 3C **4**
Tresham. *Glos* 2C **34**
Tresigin. *V Glam* 4C **32**
Tresillian. *Corn* 4C **6**
Tresimwn. *V Glam* 4D **32**
Tresinney. *Corn* 4B **10**
Treskillard. *Corn* 5A **6**
Treskinnick Cross. *Corn* 3C **10**
Tresmeer. *Corn* 4C **10**
Tresparrett. *Corn* 3B **10**
Tresparrett Posts. *Corn* 3B **10**
Tressady. *High* 3D **164**
Tressait. *Per* 2F **143**
Tresta. *Shet* 2H **173**
(on Fetlar)
Tresta. *Shet* 6E **173**
(on Mainland)
Treswell. *Notts* 3E **87**
Treswithian. *Corn* 3D **4**
Tre Taliesin. *Cdgn* 1F **57**
Trethomas. *Cphy* 3E **33**
Trethosa. *Corn* 3D **6**
Trethurgy. *Corn* 3E **7**
Tretio. *Pemb* 2B **42**
Tretire. *Here* 3A **48**
Tretower. *Powy* 3E **47**
Treuddyn. *Flin* 5E **83**
Trevadlock. *Corn* 5C **10**
Trevalga. *Corn* 3A **10**
Trevalyn. *Wrex* 5F **83**
Trevance. *Corn* 1D **6**
Trevanger. *Corn* 1D **6**
Trevanson. *Corn* 1D **6**
Trevarrack. *Corn* 3B **4**
Trevarren. *Corn* 2D **6**
Trevarrian. *Corn* 2C **6**
Trevarrick. *Corn* 4D **6**
Tre-vaughan. *Carm* 3E **45**
(nr. Carmarthen)
Trevaughan. *Carm* 3F **43**
(nr. Whitland)
Treveighan. *Corn* 5A **10**
Trevellas. *Corn* 3B **6**
Trevelmond. *Corn* 2G **7**
Treverva. *Corn* 5B **6**
Trevescan. *Corn* 4A **4**
Trevethin. *Torf* 5F **47**
Trevia. *Corn* 4A **10**
Trevigro. *Corn* 2H **7**
Trevilley. *Corn* 4A **4**
Treviscoe. *Corn* 3D **6**
Trevivian. *Corn* 4B **10**
Trevone. *Corn* 1C **6**
Trevor. *Wrex* 1E **71**
Trevor Uchaf. *Den* 1E **71**
Trew. *Corn* 4D **4**
Trewalder. *Corn* 4A **10**
Trewarlett. *Corn* 4D **10**
Trewarmett. *Corn* 4A **10**
Trewassa. *Corn* 4B **10**
Treween. *Corn* 4C **10**
Trewellard. *Corn* 3A **4**
Trewen. *Corn* 4C **10**
Trewennack. *Corn* 4D **5**
Trewern. *Powy* 4E **71**
Trewetha. *Corn* 5A **10**
Trewidland. *Corn* 2G **7**
Trewint. *Corn* 3B **10**
Trewithian. *Corn* 5C **6**
Trewoofe. *Corn* 4B **4**
Trewoon. *Corn* 3D **6**
Treworthal. *Corn* 5C **6**
Trewyddel. *Pemb* 1B **44**
Treyarnon. *Corn* 1C **6**
Treyford. *W Sus* 1G **17**
Triangle. *Staf* 5E **73**
Triangle. *W Yor* 2A **92**
Trickett's Cross. *Dors* 2F **15**
Trimdon. *Dur* 1A **106**
Trimdon Colliery. *Dur* 1A **106**
Trimdon Grange. *Dur* 1A **106**
Trimingham. *Norf* 2E **79**
Trimley Lower Street. *Suff* 2F **55**
Trimley St Martin. *Suff* 2F **55**
Trimley St Mary. *Suff* 2F **55**
Trimpley. *Worc* 3B **60**
Trimsaran. *Carm* 5E **45**
Trimstone. *Devn* 2F **19**
Trinafour. *Per* 2E **142**
Trinant. *Cphy* 2F **33**
Tring. *Herts* 4H **51**
Trinity. *Ang* 2F **145**
Trinity. *Edin* 2F **129**
Trisant. *Cdgn* 3G **57**
Triscombe. *Som* 3E **21**
Trislaig. *High* 1E **141**
Trispen. *Corn* 3C **6**
Tritlington. *Nmbd* 5G **121**
Trochry. *Per* 4G **143**
Troedrhiwdalar. *Powy* 5B **58**
Troedrhiwfuwch. *Cphy* 5E **47**
Troedrhiwgwair. *Blae* 5E **47**
Troedyraur. *Cdgn* 1D **44**
Troedyrhiw. *Mer T* 5D **46**
Trondavoe. *Shet* 4E **173**
Troon. *Corn* 5A **6**
Troon. *S Ayr* 1C **116**
Troqueer. *Dum* 2A **112**
Troston. *Suff* 3A **66**
Trottiscliffe. *Kent* 4H **39**
Trotton. *W Sus* 4G **25**
Troutbeck. *Cumb* 4F **103**
(nr. Ambleside)
Troutbeck. *Cumb* 2E **103**
(nr. Penrith)
Troutbeck Bridge. *Cumb* 4F **103**
Troway. *Derbs* 3A **86**
Trowbridge. *Wilts* 1D **22**
Trowell. *Notts* 2B **74**
Trowle Common. *Wilts* 1D **22**
Trowley Bottom. *Herts* 4A **52**
Trowse Newton. *Norf* 5E **79**
Trudoxhill. *Som* 2C **22**
Trull. *Som* 4F **21**
Trumaisgearraidh. *W Isl* 1D **170**
Trumpan. *High* 2B **154**
Trumpet. *Here* 2B **48**
Trumpington. *Cambs* 5D **64**
Trumps Green. *Surr* 4A **38**
Trunch. *Norf* 2E **79**
Trunnah. *Lanc* 5C **96**
Truro. *Corn* 4C **6**
Trusham. *Devn* 4B **12**
Trusley. *Derbs* 2G **73**
Trusthorpe. *Linc* 2E **89**
Tryfil. *IOA* 2D **80**
Trysull. *Staf* 1C **60**
Tubney. *Oxon* 2C **36**
Tuckenhay. *Devn* 3E **9**
Tuckhill. *Staf* 2B **60**
Tuckingmill. *Corn* 4A **6**
Tuckton. *Bour* 3G **15**
Tuddenham. *Suff* 3G **65**
Tuddenham St Martin. *Suff* 1E **55**
Tudeley. *Kent* 1H **27**
Tudhoe. *Dur* 1F **105**
Tudhoe Grange. *Dur* 1F **105**
Tudorville. *Here* 3A **48**
Tudweiliog. *Gwyn* 2B **68**
Tuesley. *Surr* 1A **26**
Tufton. *Hants* 2C **24**
Tufton. *Pemb* 2E **43**
Tugby. *Leics* 5E **75**
Tugford. *Shrp* 2H **59**
Tughall. *Nmbd* 2G **121**
Tulchan. *Per* 1B **136**
Tullibardine. *Per* 2B **136**
Tullibody. *Clac* 4A **136**
Tullich. *Arg* 2H **133**
Tullich. *High* 4B **156**
(nr. Lochcarron)
Tullich. *High* 1C **158**
(nr. Tain)
Tullich. *Mor* 4H **159**
Tullich Muir. *High* 1B **158**
Tulliemet. *Per* 3G **143**
Tulloch. *Abers* 5F **161**
Tulloch. *High* 4D **164**
(nr. Bonar Bridge)
Tulloch. *High* 5F **149**
(nr. Fort William)
Tulloch. *High* 2D **151**
(nr. Grantown-on-Spey)
Tulloch. *Per* 1C **136**
Tullochgorm. *Arg* 4G **133**
Tullybeagles Lodge. *Per* 5H **143**
Tullymurdoch. *Per* 3A **144**
Tullynessle. *Abers* 2C **152**
Tumble. *Carm* 4F **45**
Tumbler's Green. *Essx* 3B **54**
Tumby. *Linc* 4B **88**
Tumby Woodside. *Linc* 5B **88**
Tummel Bridge. *Per* 3E **143**
Tunbridge Wells, Royal.
Kent 2G **27**
Tunga. *W Isl* 4G **171**
Tungate. *Norf* 3E **79**
Tunley. *Bath* 1B **22**
Tunstall. *E Yor* 1G **95**
Tunstall. *Kent* 4C **40**
Tunstall. *Lanc* 2F **97**
Tunstall. *Norf* 5G **79**
Tunstall. *N Yor* 5F **105**
Tunstall. *Staf* 3B **72**
Tunstall. *Stoke* 5C **84**
Tunstall. *Suff* 5F **67**
Tunstall. *Tyne* 4G **115**
Tunstead. *Derbs* 3F **85**
Tunstead. *Norf* 3E **79**
Tunstead Milton. *Derbs* 2E **85**
Tunworth. *Hants* 2E **25**
Tupsley. *Here* 1A **48**
Tupton. *Derbs* 4A **86**
Turfholm. *S Lan* 1H **117**
Turfmoor. *Devn* 2F **13**
Turgis Green. *Hants* 1E **25**
Turkdean. *Glos* 4G **49**
Turkey Island. *Hants* 1D **16**
Tur Langton. *Leics* 1E **62**
Turleigh. *Wilts* 5D **34**
Turlin Moor. *Pool* 3E **15**
Turnant. *Here* 3G **47**
Turnastone. *Here* 2G **47**
Turnberry. *S Ayr* 4B **116**
Turnchapel. *Plym* 3A **8**
Turnditch. *Derbs* 1G **73**
Turners Hill. *W Sus* 2E **27**
Turners Puddle. *Dors* 3D **14**
Turnford. *Herts* 5D **52**
Turnhouse. *Edin* 2E **129**
Turnworth. *Dors* 2D **14**
Turriff. *Abers* 4E **161**
Tursdale. *Dur* 1A **106**
Turton Bottoms. *Bkbn* 3F **91**
Turtory. *Mor* 4C **160**
Turves Green. *W Mid* 3E **61**
Turvey. *Bed* 5G **63**
Turville. *Buck* 2F **37**
Turville Heath. *Buck* 2F **37**
Turweston. *Buck* 2E **50**
Tushielaw. *Bord* 3F **119**
Tutbury. *Staf* 3G **73**
Tutnall. *Worc* 3D **61**
Tutsbill. *Glos* 2A **34**
Tuttington. *Norf* 3E **79**
Tutts Clump. *W Ber* 4D **36**
Tutwell. *Corn* 5D **11**
Tuxford. *Notts* 3E **87**
Twatt. *Orkn* 5B **172**
Twatt. *Shet* 6E **173**
Twechar. *E Dun* 2A **128**
Tweedale. *Telf* 5B **72**
Tweedmouth. *Nmbd* 4F **131**
Tweedsmuir. *Bord* 2C **118**
Twelveheads. *Corn* 4B **6**
Twemlow Green. *Ches E* 4B **84**
Twenty. *Linc* 3A **76**
Twerton. *Bath* 5C **34**
Twickenham. *G Lon* 3C **38**
Twigworth. *Glos* 3D **48**
Twineham. *W Sus* 3D **26**
Twinhoe. *Bath* 1C **22**
Twinstead. *Essx* 2B **54**
Twinstead Green. *Essx* 2B **54**
Twiss Green. *Warr* 1A **84**
Twiston. *Lanc* 5H **97**
Twitchen. *Devn* 3A **20**
Twitchen. *Shrp* 3F **59**
Two Bridges. *Devn* 5G **11**
Two Bridges. *Glos* 5B **48**
Two Dales. *Derbs* 4G **85**
Two Gates. *Staf* 5G **73**
Two Mile Oak. *Devn* 2E **9**
Twycross. *Leics* 5H **73**
Twyford. *Buck* 3E **51**
Twyford. *Derbs* 3H **73**
Twyford. *Dors* 1D **14**
Twyford. *Hants* 4C **24**
Twyford. *Leics* 4E **75**
Twyford. *Norf* 3C **78**
Twyford. *Wok* 4F **37**
Twyford Common. *Here* 2A **48**
Twyncarno. *Cphy* 5E **46**
Twynholm. *Dum* 4D **110**
Twyning. *Glos* 2D **49**
Twyning Green. *Glos* 2E **49**
Twynllanan. *Carm* 3A **46**
Twyn-y-Sheriff. *Mon* 5H **47**
Twywell. *Nptn* 3G **63**
Tyberton. *Here* 2G **47**
Tyburn. *W Mid* 1F **61**
Tyby. *Norf* 3C **78**
Tycroes. *Carm* 4G **45**
Tycrwyn. *Powy* 4D **70**
Tyddewi. *Pemb* 2B **42**
Tydd Gote. *Linc* 4D **76**
Tydd St Giles. *Cambs* 4D **76**
Tydd St Mary. *Linc* 4D **76**
Tye. *Hants* 2F **17**
Tye Green. *Essx* 3F **53**
(nr. Bishop's Stortford)
Tye Green. *Essx* 3A **54**
(nr. Braintree)
Tye Green. *Essx* 2F **53**
(nr. Saffron Walden)
Tyersal. *W Yor* 1B **92**
Ty Issa. *Powy* 3D **70**
Tyldesley. *G Man* 4E **91**
Tyle. *Carm* 3G **45**
Tyler Hill. *Kent* 4F **41**
Tylers Green. *Buck* 2G **37**
Tyler's Green. *Essx* 5F **53**
Tylorstown. *Rhon* 2D **32**
Tylwch. *Powy* 2B **58**
Ty-nant. *Cnwy* 1B **70**
Tyndrum. *Stir* 5H **141**
Tyneham. *Dors* 4D **15**
Tynehead. *Midl* 4G **129**
Tynemouth. *Tyne* 3G **115**
Tyneside. *Tyne* 3F **115**
Tyne Tunnel. *Tyne* 3G **115**
Tynewydd. *Rhon* 2C **32**
Tyninghame. *E Lot* 2C **130**
Tynron. *Dum* 5H **117**
Ty'n-y-bryn. *Rhon* 3D **32**
Tyn-y-celyn. *Wrex* 2D **70**
Tyn-y-cwm. *Swan* 5G **45**
Tyn-y-ffridd. *Powy* 2D **70**
Tynygongl. *IOA* 2E **81**
Tynygraig. *Cdgn* 4F **57**
Tyn-y-groes. *Cnwy* 3G **81**
Ty'n-yr-eithin. *Cdgn* 4F **57**
Tyn-y-rhyd. *Powy* 4C **70**
Tyn-y-wern. *Powy* 3C **70**
Tyrie. *Abers* 2G **161**
Tyringham. *Mil* 1G **51**
Tythecott. *Devn* 1E **11**
Tythegston. *B'end* 4B **32**
Tytherington. *Ches E* 3D **84**
Tytherington. *Som* 2C **22**
Tytherington. *S Glo* 3B **34**
Tytherington. *Wilts* 2E **23**
Tytherleigh. *Devn* 2G **13**
Tywardreath. *Corn* 3E **7**
Tywardreath Highway. *Corn* 3E **7**
Tywyn. *Cnwy* 3G **81**
Tywyn. *Gwyn* 5E **69**

U

Uachdar. *W Isl* 3D **170**
Uags. *High* 5G **155**
Ubbeston Green. *Suff* 3F **67**
Ubley. *Bath* 1A **22**
Uckerby. *N Yor* 4F **105**
Uckfield. *E Sus* 3F **27**
Uckinghall. *Worc* 2D **48**
Uckington. *Glos* 3E **49**
Uckington. *Shrp* 5H **71**
Uddingston. *S Lan* 3H **127**
Uddington. *S Lan* 1A **118**
Udimore. *E Sus* 4C **28**
Udny Green. *Abers* 1F **153**
Udny Station. *Abers* 1G **153**
Udston. *S Lan* 4A **128**
Udstonhead. *S Lan* 5A **128**
Uffcott. *Wilts* 4G **35**
Uffculme. *Devn* 1D **12**
Uffington. *Linc* 5H **75**
Uffington. *Oxon* 3B **36**
Uffington. *Shrp* 4H **71**
Ufford. *Pet* 5H **75**
Ufford. *Suff* 5E **67**
Ufton. *Warw* 4A **62**
Ufton Nervet. *W Ber* 5E **37**
Ugadale. *Arg* 3B **122**
Ugborough. *Devn* 3C **8**
Ugford. *Wilts* 3F **23**
Uggeshall. *Suff* 2G **67**
Ugglebarnby. *N Yor* 4F **107**
Ugley. *Essx* 3F **53**
Ugley Green. *Essx* 3F **53**
Ugthorpe. *N Yor* 3E **107**
Uidh. *W Isl* 9B **170**
Uig. *Arg* 3C **138**
Uig. *High* 2C **154**
(nr. Balgown)
Uig. *High* 3A **154**
(nr. Dunvegan)
Uigshader. *High* 4D **154**
Uisken. *Arg* 2A **132**
Ulbster. *High* 4F **169**
Ulcat Row. *Cumb* 2F **103**
Ulceby. *Linc* 3D **88**
Ulceby. *N Lin* 3E **94**
Ulceby Skitter. *N Lin* 3E **94**
Ulcombe. *Kent* 1C **28**
Uldale. *Cumb* 1D **102**
Uley. *Glos* 2C **34**
Ulgham. *Nmbd* 5G **121**
Ullapool. *High* 4F **163**
Ullenhall. *Warw* 4F **61**
Ulleskelf. *N Yor* 1F **93**
Ullesthorpe. *Leics* 2C **62**
Ulley. *S Yor* 2B **86**
Ullingswick. *Here* 1A **48**
Ullinish. *High* 5C **154**
Ullock. *Cumb* 2B **102**

Ulpha. *Cumb* 5C 102
Ulrome. *E Yor* 4F 101
Ulsta. *Shet* 3F 173
Ulting. *Essx* 5B 54
Ulva House. *Arg* 5F 139
Ulverston. *Cumb* 2B 96
Ulwell. *Dors* 4F 15
Umberleigh. *Devn* 4G 19
Unapool. *High* 5C 166
Underbarrow. *Cumb* 5F 103
Undercliffe. *W Yor* 1B 92
Underdale. *Shrp* 4H 71
Underhoull. *Shet* 1G 173
Underriver. *Kent* 5G 39
Under Tofts. *S Yor* 2H 85
Underton. *Shrp* 1A 60
Underwood. *Newp* 3G 33
Underwood. *Notts* 5B 86
Underwood. *Plym* 3B 8
Undley. *Suff* 2F 65
Undy. *Mon* 3H 33
Union Mills. *IOM* 4C 108
Union Street. *E Sus* 2B 28
Unstone. *Derbs* 3A 86
Unstone Green. *Derbs* 3A 86
Unthank. *Cumb* 5E 113 (nr. Carlisle)
Unthank. *Cumb* 5H 113 (nr. Gamblesby)
Unthank. *Cumb* 1F 103 (nr. Penrith)
Unthank End. *Cumb* 1F 103
Upavon. *Wilts* 1G 23
Up Cerne. *Dors* 2B 14
Upchurch. *Kent* 4C 40
Upcott. *Devn* 2F 11
Upcott. *Here* 5F 59
Upend. *Cambs* 5G 65
Up Exe. *Devn* 2C 12
Upgate. *Norf* 4D 78
Upgate Street. *Norf* 1C 66
Uphall. *Dors* 2A 14
Uphall. *W Lot* 2D 128
Uphall Station. *W Lot* 2D 128
Upham. *Devn* 2B 12
Upham. *Hants* 4D 24
Uphampton. *Here* 4F 59
Uphampton. *Worc* 4C 60
Up Hatherley. *Glos* 3E 49
Uphill. *N Som* 1G 21
Up Holland. *Lanc* 4D 90
Uplawmoor. *E Ren* 4F 127
Upleadon. *Glos* 3C 48
Upleatham. *Red C* 3D 106
Uplees. *Kent* 4D 40
Uploders. *Dors* 3A 14
Uplowman. *Devn* 1D 12
Uplyme. *Devn* 3G 13
Up Marden. *W Sus* 1F 17
Upminster. *G Lon* 2G 39
Up Nately. *Hants* 1E 25
Upottery. *Devn* 2F 13
Uppat. *High* 3F 165
Upper Affcot. *Shrp* 2G 59
Upper Arley. *Worc* 2B 60
Upper Armley. *W Yor* 1C 92
Upper Arncott. *Oxon* 4E 50
Upper Astrop. *Nptn* 2D 50
Upper Badcall. *High* 4B 166
Upper Bangor. *Gwyn* 3E 81
Upper Basildon. *W Ber* 4D 36
Upper Batley. *W Yor* 2C 92
Upper Beeding. *W Sus* 4C 26
Upper Benefield. *Nptn* 2G 63
Upper Bentley. *Worc* 4D 61
Upper Bighouse. *High* 3A 168
Upper Boddam. *Abers* 5D 160
Upper Boddington. *Nptn* 5B 62
Upper Bogside. *Mor* 3G 159
Upper Booth. *Derbs* 2F 85
Upper Borth. *Cdgn* 2F 57
Upper Boyndlie. *Abers* 2G 161
Upper Brailes. *Warw* 2B 50
Upper Breinton. *Here* 1H 47
Upper Broadheath. *Worc* 5C 60
Upper Broughton. *Notts* 3D 74
Upper Brynamman. *Carm* 4H 45
Upper Bucklebury. *W Ber* 5D 36
Upper Bullington. *Hants* 2C 24
Upper Burgate. *Hants* 1G 15
Upper Caldecote. *C Beds* 1B 52
Upper Canterton. *Hants* 1A 16
Upper Catesby. *Nptn* 5C 62
Upper Chapel. *Powy* 1D 46
Upper Cheddon. *Som* 4F 21
Upper Chicksgrove. *Wilts* 4E 23
Upper Church Village. *Rhon* 3D 32
Upper Chute. *Wilts* 1A 24
Upper Clatford. *Hants* 2B 24
Upper Coberley. *Glos* 4E 49
Upper Coedcae. *Torf* 5F 47
Upper Cokeham. *W Sus* 5C 26
Upper Common. *Hants* 2E 25
Upper Cound. *Shrp* 5H 71
Upper Cudworth. *S Yor* 4D 93
Upper Cumberworth. *W Yor* 4C 92
Upper Cuttlehill. *Abers* 4B 160
Upper Cwmbran. *Torf* 2F 33
Upper Dallachy. *Mor* 2A 160
Upper Dean. *Bed* 4H 63
Upper Dean. *Devn* 2D 8
Upper Denby. *W Yor* 4C 92
Upper Derraid. *High* 5E 159
Upper Diabaig. *High* 2H 155
Upper Dicker. *E Sus* 5G 27
Upper Dinchope. *Shrp* 2G 59
Upper Dochcarty. *High* 2H 157
Upper Dounreay. *High* 2B 168
Upper Dovercourt. *Essx* 2F 55
Upper Dunsforth. *N Yor* 3G 99
Upper Dunsley. *Herts* 4H 51
Upper Eastern Green. *W Mid* 2G 61
Upper Elkstone. *Staf* 5E 85
Upper Ellastone. *Staf* 1F 73
Upper End. *Derbs* 3E 85
Upper Enham. *Hants* 2B 24
Upper Farmcote. *Shrp* 1B 60
Upper Farringdon. *Hants* 3F 25
Upper Framilode. *Glos* 4C 48
Upper Froyle. *Hants* 2F 25
Upper Gills. *High* 1F 169
Upper Glenfintaig. *High* 5E 149
Upper Godney. *Som* 2H 21
Upper Gravenhurst. *C Beds* 2B 52
Upper Green. *Essx* 2E 53
Upper Green. *W Ber* 5B 36
Upper Green. *W Yor* 2C 92
Upper Grove Common. *Here* 3A 48
Upper Hackney. *Derbs* 4G 85
Upper Hale. *Surr* 2G 25
Upper Halliford. *Surr* 4B 38
Upper Halling. *Medw* 4A 40
Upper Hambleton. *Rut* 5G 75
Upper Hardres Court. *Kent* 5F 41
Upper Hardwick. *Here* 5G 59
Upper Hartfield. *E Sus* 2F 27
Upper Haugh. *S Yor* 1B 86
Upper Hayton. *Shrp* 2H 59
Upper Heath. *Shrp* 2H 59
Upper Hellesdon. *Norf* 4E 79
Upper Helmsley. *N Yor* 4A 100
Upper Hengoed. *Shrp* 2E 71
Upper Hergest. *Here* 5E 59
Upper Heyford. *Nptn* 5D 62
Upper Heyford. *Oxon* 3C 50
Upper Hill. *Here* 5G 59
Upper Hindhope. *Bord* 4B 120
Upper Hopton. *W Yor* 3B 92
Upper Howsell. *Worc* 1C 48
Upper Hulme. *Staf* 4E 85
Upper Inglesham. *Swin* 2H 35
Upper Kilcott. *Glos* 3C 34
Upper Killay. *Swan* 3E 31
Upper Kirkton. *Abers* 5E 161
Upper Kirkton. *N Ayr* 4C 126
Upper Knockando. *Mor* 4F 159
Upper Knockchoilum. *High* 2G 149
Upper Lambourn. *W Ber* 3B 36
Upper Langford. *N Som* 1H 21
Upper Langwith. *Derbs* 4C 86
Upper Largo. *Fife* 3G 137
Upper Latheron. *High* 5D 169
Upper Layham. *Suff* 1D 54
Upper Leigh. *Staf* 2E 73
Upper Lenie. *High* 1H 149
Upper Lochton. *Abers* 4E 152
Upper Longdon. *Staf* 4E 73
Upper Longwood. *Shrp* 5A 72
Upper Lybster. *High* 5E 169
Upper Lydbrook. *Glos* 4B 48
Upper Lye. *Here* 4F 59
Upper Maes-coed. *Here* 2G 47
Upper Midway. *Derbs* 3G 73
Uppermill. *G Man* 4H 91
Upper Millichope. *Shrp* 2H 59
Upper Milovaig. *High* 4A 154
Upper Minety. *Wilts* 2F 35
Upper Mitton. *Worc* 3C 60
Upper Nash. *Pemb* 4E 43
Upper Neepaback. *Shet* 3G 173
Upper Netchwood. *Shrp* 1A 60
Upper Nobut. *Staf* 2E 73
Upper North Dean. *Buck* 2G 37
Upper Norwood. *W Sus* 4A 26
Upper Nyland. *Dors* 4C 22
Upper Oddington. *Glos* 3H 49
Upper Ollach. *High* 5E 155
Upper Outwoods. *Staf* 3G 73
Upper Padley. *Derbs* 3G 85
Upper Pennington. *Hants* 3B 16
Upper Poppleton. *York* 4H 99
Upper Quinton. *Warw* 1G 49
Upper Rochford. *Worc* 4A 60
Upper Rusko. *Dum* 3C 110
Upper Sandaig. *High* 2F 147
Upper Sanday. *Orkn* 7E 172
Upper Sapey. *Here* 4A 60
Upper Seagry. *Wilts* 3E 35
Upper Shelton. *C Beds* 1H 51
Upper Sheringham. *Norf* 1D 78
Upper Skelmorlie. *N Ayr* 3C 126
Upper Slaughter. *Glos* 3G 49
Upper Sonachan. *Arg* 1H 133
Upper Soudley. *Glos* 4B 48
Upper Staploe. *Bed* 5A 64
Upper Stoke. *Norf* 5E 79
Upper Stondon. *C Beds* 2B 52
Upper Stowe. *Nptn* 5D 62
Upper Street. *Hants* 1G 15
Upper Street. *Norf* 4F 79 (nr. Horning)
Upper Street. *Norf* 4F 79 (nr. Hoveton)
Upper Street. *Suff* 2E 55
Upper Strensham. *Worc* 2E 49
Upper Studley. *Wilts* 1D 22
Upper Sundon. *C Beds* 3A 52
Upper Swell. *Glos* 3G 49
Upper Tankersley. *S Yor* 1H 85
Upper Tean. *Staf* 2E 73
Upperthong. *W Yor* 4B 92
Upperthorpe. *N Lin* 4A 94
Upper Thurnham. *Lanc* 4D 96
Upper Tillyrie. *Per* 3D 136
Upperton. *W Sus* 3A 26
Upper Tooting. *G Lon* 3D 38
Uppertown. *Derbs* 4H 85 (nr. Ashover)
Upper Town. *Derbs* 5G 85 (nr. Bonsall)
Upper Town. *Derbs* 5G 85 (nr. Hognaston)
Upper Town. *Here* 1A 48
Uppertown. *High* 1F 169
Upper Town. *N Som* 5A 34
Uppertown. *Nmbd* 2B 114
Uppertown. *Orkn* 8D 172
Upper Tysoe. *Warw* 1B 50
Upper Upham. *Wilts* 4H 35
Upper Upnor. *Medw* 3B 40
Upper Urquhart. *Fife* 3D 136
Upper Wardington. *Oxon* 1C 50
Upper Weald. *Mil* 2G 51
Upper Weedon. *Nptn* 5D 62
Upper Wellingham. *E Sus* 4F 27
Upper Whiston. *S Yor* 2B 86
Upper Wield. *Hants* 3E 25
Upper Winchendon. *Buck* 4F 51
Upperwood. *Derbs* 5G 85
Upper Woodford. *Wilts* 3G 23
Upper Wootton. *Hants* 1D 24
Upper Wraxall. *Wilts* 4D 34
Upper Wyche. *Here* 1C 48
Uppincott. *Devn* 2B 12
Uppingham. *Rut* 1F 63
Uppington. *Shrp* 5H 71
Upsall. *N Yor* 1G 99
Upsettlington. *Bord* 5E 131
Upshire. *Essx* 5E 53
Up Somborne. *Hants* 3B 24
Upstreet. *Kent* 4G 41
Up Sydling. *Dors* 2B 14
Upthorpe. *Suff* 3B 66
Upton. *Buck* 4F 51
Upton. *Cambs* 3A 64
Upton. *Ches W* 4G 83
Upton. *Corn* 2C 10 (nr. Bude)
Upton. *Corn* 5C 10 (nr. Liskeard)
Upton. *Cumb* 1E 102
Upton. *Devn* 2D 12 (nr. Honiton)
Upton. *Devn* 4D 8 (nr. Kingsbridge)
Upton. *Dors* 3E 15 (nr. Poole)
Upton. *Dors* 4C 14 (nr. Weymouth)
Upton. *E Yor* 4F 101
Upton. *Hants* 1B 24 (nr. Andover)
Upton. *Hants* 1B 16 (nr. Southampton)
Upton. *IOW* 3D 16
Upton. *Leics* 1A 62
Upton. *Linc* 2F 87
Upton. *Mers* 2E 83
Upton. *Norf* 4F 79
Upton. *Nptn* 4E 62
Upton. *Notts* 3E 87 (nr. Retford)
Upton. *Notts* 5E 87 (nr. Southwell)
Upton. *Oxon* 3D 36
Upton. *Pemb* 4E 43
Upton. *Pet* 5A 76
Upton. *Slo* 3A 38
Upton. *Som* 4H 21 (nr. Somerton)
Upton. *Som* 4C 20 (nr. Wiveliscombe)
Upton. *Warw* 5F 61
Upton. *W Yor* 3E 93
Upton. *Wilts* 3D 22
Upton Bishop. *Here* 3B 48
Upton Cheyney. *S Glo* 5B 34
Upton Cressett. *Shrp* 1A 60
Upton Crews. *Here* 3B 48
Upton Cross. *Corn* 5C 10
Upton End. *C Beds* 2B 52
Upton Grey. *Hants* 2E 25
Upton Heath. *Ches W* 4G 83
Upton Hellions. *Devn* 2B 12
Upton Lovell. *Wilts* 2E 23
Upton Magna. *Shrp* 4H 71
Upton Noble. *Som* 3C 22
Upton Pyne. *Devn* 3C 12
Upton St Leonards. *Glos* 4D 48
Upton Scudamore. *Wilts* 2D 22
Upton Snodsbury. *Worc* 5D 60
Upton upon Severn. *Worc* 1D 48
Upton Warren. *Worc* 4D 60
Upwaltham. *W Sus* 4A 26
Upware. *Cambs* 3E 65
Upwell. *Cambs* 5D 77
Upwey. *Dors* 4B 14
Upwick Green. *Herts* 3E 53
Upwood. *Cambs* 2B 64
Urafirth. *Shet* 4E 173
Uragaig. *Arg* 4A 132
Urchany. *High* 4C 158
Urchfont. *Wilts* 1F 23
Urdimarsh. *Here* 1A 48
Ure. *Shet* 4D 173
Ure Bank. *N Yor* 2F 99
Urgha. *W Isl* 8D 171
Urlay Nook. *Stoc T* 3B 106
Urmston. *G Man* 1B 84
Urquhart. *Mor* 2G 159
Urra. *N Yor* 4C 106
Urray. *High* 3H 157
Usan. *Ang* 3G 145
Ushaw Moor. *Dur* 5F 115
Usk. *Mon* 5G 47
Usselby. *Linc* 1H 87
Usworth. *Tyne* 4G 115
Utkinton. *Ches W* 4H 83
Uton. *Devn* 3B 12
Utterby. *Linc* 1C 88
Uttoxeter. *Staf* 2E 73
Uwchmynydd. *Gwyn* 3A 68
Uxbridge. *G Lon* 2B 38
Uyeasound. *Shet* 1G 173
Uzmaston. *Pemb* 3D 42

V

Valley. *IOA* 3B 80
Valley End. *Surr* 4A 38
Valley Truckle. *Corn* 4B 10
Valsgarth. *Shet* 1H 173
Valtos. *High* 2E 155
Van. *Powy* 2B 58
Vange. *Essx* 2B 40
Varteg. *Torf* 5F 47
Vatsetter. *Shet* 3G 173
Vatten. *High* 4B 154
Vaul. *Arg* 4B 138
Vauld, The. *Here* 1A 48
Vaynol. *Gwyn* 3E 81
Vaynor. *Mer T* 4D 46
Veensgarth. *Shet* 7F 173
Velindre. *Powy* 2E 47
Vellow. *Som* 3D 20
Velly. *Devn* 4C 18
Veness. *Orkn* 5E 172
Venhay. *Devn* 1A 12
Venn. *Devn* 4D 8
Venngreen. *Devn* 1D 11
Vennington. *Shrp* 5F 71
Venn Ottery. *Devn* 3D 12
Venn's Green. *Here* 1A 48
Venny Tedburn. *Devn* 3B 12
Venterdon. *Corn* 5D 10
Ventnor. *IOW* 5D 16
Vernham Dean. *Hants* 1B 24
Vernham Street. *Hants* 1B 24
Vernolds Common. *Shrp* 2G 59
Verwood. *Dors* 2F 15
Veryan. *Corn* 5D 6
Veryan Green. *Corn* 4D 6
Vicarage. *Devn* 4F 13
Vickerstown. *Cumb* 3A 96
Victoria. *Corn* 2D 6
Vidlin. *Shet* 5F 173
Viewpark. *N Lan* 3A 128
Vigo. *W Mid* 5E 73
Vigo Village. *Kent* 4H 39
Village Bay. *High* 3B 154
Vinehall Street. *E Sus* 3B 28
Vine's Cross. *E Sus* 4G 27
Viney Hill. *Glos* 5B 48
Virginia Water. *Surr* 4A 38
Virginstow. *Devn* 3D 11
Vobster. *Som* 2C 22
Voe. *Shet* 5F 173 (nr. Hillside)
Voe. *Shet* 3E 173 (nr. Swinister)
Vole. *Som* 2G 21
Vowchurch. *Here* 2G 47
Voxter. *Shet* 4E 173
Voy. *Orkn* 6B 172
Vulcan Village. *Warr* 1H 83

W

Waberthwaite. *Cumb* 5C 102
Wackerfield. *Dur* 2E 105
Wacton. *Norf* 1D 66
Wadbister. *Shet* 7F 173
Wadborough. *Worc* 1E 49
Wadbrook. *Devn* 2G 13
Waddesdon. *Buck* 4F 51
Waddeton. *Devn* 3E 9
Waddicar. *Mers* 1F 83
Waddingham. *Linc* 1G 87
Waddington. *Lanc* 5G 97
Waddington. *Linc* 4G 87
Waddon. *Devn* 5B 12
Wadebridge. *Corn* 1D 6
Wadeford. *Som* 1G 13
Wadenhoe. *Nptn* 2H 63
Wadesmill. *Herts* 4D 52
Wadhurst. *E Sus* 2H 27
Wadshelf. *Derbs* 3H 85
Wadsley. *S Yor* 1H 85
Wadsley Bridge. *S Yor* 1H 85
Wadswick. *Wilts* 5D 34
Wadwick. *Hants* 1C 24
Wadworth. *S Yor* 1C 86
Waen. *Den* 4C 82 (nr. Bodfari)
Waen. *Den* 4D 82 (nr. Llandyrnog)
Waen. *Den* 4B 82 (nr. Nantglyn)
Waen. *Powy* 1B 58
Waen Fach. *Powy* 4E 70
Waen Goleugoed. *Den* 3C 82
Wag. *High* 1H 165
Wainfleet All Saints. *Linc* 5D 89
Wainfleet Bank. *Linc* 5D 88
Wainfleet St Mary. *Linc* 5D 89
Wainhouse Corner. *Corn* 3B 10
Wainscott. *Medw* 3B 40
Wainstalls. *W Yor* 2A 92
Waitby. *Cumb* 4A 104
Waithe. *Linc* 4F 95
Wakefield. *W Yor* 2D 92
Wakerley. *Nptn* 1G 63
Wakes Colne. *Essx* 3B 54
Walberswick. *Suff* 3G 67
Walberton. *W Sus* 5A 26
Walbottle. *Tyne* 3E 115
Walby. *Cumb* 3F 113
Walcombe. *Som* 2A 22
Walcot. *Linc* 2H 75
Walcot. *N Lin* 2B 94
Walcot. *Swin* 3G 35
Walcot. *Telf* 4H 71
Walcot. *Warw* 5F 61
Walcote. *Leics* 2C 62
Walcot Green. *Norf* 2D 66
Walcott. *Linc* 5A 88
Walcott. *Norf* 2F 79
Walden. *N Yor* 1C 98
Walden Head. *N Yor* 1B 98
Walden Stubbs. *N Yor* 3F 93
Walderslade. *Medw* 4B 40
Walderton. *W Sus* 1F 17
Walditch. *Dors* 3H 13
Waldley. *Derbs* 2F 73
Waldridge. *Dur* 4F 115
Waldringfield. *Suff* 1F 55
Waldron. *E Sus* 4G 27
Wales. *S Yor* 2B 86
Walesby. *Linc* 1A 88
Walesby. *Notts* 3D 86
Walford. *Here* 3F 59 (nr. Leintwardine)
Walford. *Here* 3A 48 (nr. Ross-on-Wye)
Walford. *Shrp* 3G 71
Walford. *Staf* 2C 72
Walford Heath. *Shrp* 4G 71
Walgherton. *Ches E* 1A 72
Walgrave. *Nptn* 3F 63
Walhampton. *Hants* 3B 16
Walkden. *G Man* 4F 91
Walker. *Tyne* 3F 115
Walkerburn. *Bord* 1F 119
Walker Fold. *Lanc* 5F 97
Walkeringham. *Notts* 1E 87
Walkerith. *Linc* 1E 87
Walkern. *Herts* 3C 52
Walker's Green. *Here* 1A 48
Walkerton. *Fife* 3E 137
Walkerville. *N Yor* 5F 105
Walkford. *Dors* 3H 15
Walkhampton. *Devn* 2B 8
Walkington. *E Yor* 1C 94
Walkley. *S Yor* 2H 85
Walk Mill. *Lanc* 1G 91
Wall. *Corn* 3D 4
Wall. *Nmbd* 3C 114
Wall. *Staf* 5F 73
Wallaceton. *Dum* 1F 111
Wallacetown. *Shet* 6E 173
Wallacetown. *S Ayr* 2C 116 (nr. Ayr)
Wallacetown. *S Ayr* 4B 116 (nr. Dailly)
Wallands Park. *E Sus* 4F 27
Wallasey. *Mers* 1F 83
Wallaston Green. *Pemb* 4D 42
Wallbrook. *W Mid* 1D 60
Wallcrouch. *E Sus* 2A 28
Wall End. *Cumb* 1B 96
Wallend. *Medw* 3C 40
Wall Heath. *W Mid* 2C 60
Wallingford. *Oxon* 3E 36
Wallington. *G Lon* 4D 39
Wallington. *Hants* 2D 16
Wallington. *Herts* 2C 52
Wallis. *Pemb* 2E 43

Wallisdown. *Pool* 3F **15**
Walliswood. *Surr* 2C **26**
Wall Nook. *Dur* 5F **115**
Walls. *Shet* 7D **173**
Wallsend. *Tyne* 3G **115**
Wallsworth. *Glos* 3D **48**
Wall under Heywood. *Shrp* 1H **59**
Wallyford. *E Lot* 2G **129**
Walmer. *Kent* 5H **41**
Walmer Bridge. *Lanc* 2C **90**
Walmersley. *G Man* 3G **91**
Walmley. *W Mid* 1F **61**
Walnut Grove. *Per* 1D **136**
Walpole. *Suff* 3F **67**
Walpole Cross Keys. *Norf* 4E **77**
Walpole Gate. *Norf* 4E **77**
Walpole Highway. *Norf* 4E **77**
Walpole Marsh. *Norf* 4D **77**
Walpole St Andrew. *Norf* 4E **77**
Walpole St Peter. *Norf* 4E **77**
Walsall. *W Mid* 1E **61**
Walsall Wood. *W Mid* 5E **73**
Walsden. *W Yor* 2H **91**
Walsgrave on Sowe. *W Mid* 2A **62**
Walsham le Willows. *Suff* 3C **66**
Walshaw. *G Man* 3F **91**
Walshford. *N Yor* 4G **99**
Walsoken. *Cambs* 4D **76**
Walston. *S Lan* 5D **128**
Walsworth. *Herts* 2B **52**
Walter's Ash. *Buck* 2G **37**
Walterston. *V Glam* 4D **32**
Walterstone. *Here* 3G **47**
Waltham. *Kent* 1F **29**
Waltham. *NE Lin* 4F **95**
Waltham Abbey. *Essx* 5D **53**
Waltham Chase. *Hants* 1D **16**
Waltham Cross. *Herts* 5D **52**
Waltham on the Wolds. *Leics* 3F **75**
Waltham St Lawrence. *Wind* 4G **37**
Waltham's Cross. *Essx* 2G **53**
Walthamstow. *G Lon* 2E **39**
Walton. *Cumb* 3G **113**
Walton. *Derbs* 4A **86**
Walton. *Leics* 2C **62**
Walton. *Mers* 1F **83**
Walton. *Mil* 2G **51**
Walton. *Pet* 5A **76**
Walton. *Powy* 5E **59**
Walton. *Som* 3H **21**
Walton. *Staf* 3C **72**
(nr. Eccleshall)
Walton. *Staf* 2C **72**
(nr. Stone)
Walton. *Suff* 2F **55**
Walton. *Telf* 4H **71**
Walton. *Warw* 5G **61**
Walton. *W Yor* 3D **92**
(nr. Wakefield)
Walton. *W Yor* 5G **99**
(nr. Wetherby)
Walton Cardiff. *Glos* 2E **49**
Walton East. *Pemb* 2E **43**
Walton Elm. *Dors* 1C **14**
Walton Highway. *Norf* 4D **77**
Walton-in-Gordano. *N Som* 4H **33**
Walton-le-Dale. *Lanc* 2D **90**
Walton-on-Thames. *Surr* 4C **38**
Walton-on-the-Hill. *Staf* 3D **72**
Walton on the Hill. *Surr* 5D **38**
Walton-on-the-Naze. *Essx* 3F **55**
Walton on the Wolds. *Leics* 4C **74**
Walton-on-Trent. *Derbs* 4G **73**
Walton West. *Pemb* 3C **42**
Walwick. *Nmbd* 2C **114**
Walworth. *Darl* 3F **105**
Walworth Gate. *Darl* 2F **105**
Walwyn's Castle. *Pemb* 3C **42**
Wambrook. *Som* 2F **13**
Wampool. *Cumb* 4D **112**
Wanborough. *Surr* 1A **26**
Wanborough. *Swin* 3H **35**
Wandel. *S Lan* 2B **118**
Wandsworth. *G Lon* 3D **38**
Wangford. *Suff* 2G **65**
(nr. Lakenheath)
Wangford. *Suff* 3G **67**
(nr. Southwold)
Wanlip. *Leics* 4D **74**
Wanlockhead. *Dum* 3A **118**
Wannock. *E Sus* 5G **27**
Wansford. *E Yor* 4E **101**
Wansford. *Pet* 1H **63**
Wanshurst Green. *Kent* 1B **28**
Wanstead. *G Lon* 2F **39**
Wanstrow. *Som* 2C **22**
Wanswell. *Glos* 5B **48**
Wantage. *Oxon* 3C **36**
Wapley. *S Glo* 4C **34**
Wappenbury. *Warw* 4A **62**
Wappenham. *Nptn* 1E **51**
Warbleton. *E Sus* 4H **27**
Warblington. *Hants* 2F **17**
Warborough. *Oxon* 2D **36**
Warboys. *Cambs* 2C **64**
Warbreck. *Bkpl* 1B **90**
Warbstow. *Corn* 3C **10**
Warburton. *G Man* 2A **84**
Warcop. *Cumb* 3A **104**
Warden. *Kent* 3E **40**
Warden. *Nmbd* 3C **114**
Ward End. *W Mid* 2F **61**
Ward Green. *Suff* 4C **66**
Ward Green Cross. *Lanc* 1E **91**
Wardhedges. *C Beds* 2A **52**
Wardhouse. *Abers* 5C **160**
Wardington. *Oxon* 1C **50**
Wardle. *Ches E* 5A **84**
Wardle. *G Man* 3H **91**
Wardley. *Rut* 5F **75**
Wardley. *W Sus* 4G **25**
Wardlow. *Derbs* 3F **85**
Wardsend. *Ches E* 2D **84**
Wardy Hill. *Cambs* 2D **64**
Ware. *Herts* 4D **52**
Ware. *Kent* 4G **41**
Wareham. *Dors* 4E **15**
Warehorne. *Kent* 2D **28**
Warenford. *Nmbd* 2F **121**
Waren Mill. *Nmbd* 1F **121**
Warenton. *Nmbd* 1F **121**
Wareside. *Herts* 4D **53**
Waresley. *Cambs* 5B **64**
Waresley. *Worc* 4C **60**
Warfield. *Brac* 4G **37**
Warfleet. *Devn* 3E **9**
Wargate. *Linc* 2B **76**
Wargrave. *Wok* 4F **37**
Warham. *Norf* 1B **78**
Wark. *Nmbd* 1C **120**
(nr. Coldstream)
Wark. *Nmbd* 2B **114**
(nr. Hexham)
Warkleigh. *Devn* 4G **19**
Warkton. *Nptn* 3F **63**
Warkworth. *Nptn* 1C **50**
Warkworth. *Nmbd* 4G **121**
Warlaby. *N Yor* 5A **106**
Warland. *W Yor* 2H **91**
Warleggan. *Corn* 2F **7**
Warlingham. *Surr* 5E **39**
Warmanbie. *Dum* 3C **112**
Warmfield. *W Yor* 2D **93**
Warmingham. *Ches E* 4B **84**
Warminghurst. *W Sus* 4C **26**
Warmington. *Nptn* 1H **63**
Warmington. *Warw* 1C **50**
Warminster. *Wilts* 2D **23**
Warmley. *S Glo* 4B **34**
Warmsworth. *S Yor* 4F **93**
Warmwell. *Dors* 4C **14**
Warndon. *Worc* 5C **60**
Warners End. *Herts* 5A **52**
Warnford. *Hants* 4E **24**
Warnham. *W Sus* 2C **26**
Warningcamp. *W Sus* 5B **26**
Warninglid. *W Sus* 3D **26**
Warren. *Ches E* 3C **84**
Warren. *Pemb* 5D **42**
Warrenby. *Red C* 2C **106**
Warren Corner. *Hants* 2G **25**
(nr. Aldershot)
Warren Corner. *Hants* 4F **25**
(nr. Petersfield)
Warren Row. *Wind* 3G **37**
Warren Street. *Kent* 5D **40**
Warrington. *Mil* 5F **63**
Warrington. *Warr* 2A **84**
Warsash. *Hants* 2C **16**
Warse. *High* 1F **169**
Warslow. *Staf* 5E **85**
Warsop. *Notts* 4C **86**
Warsop Vale. *Notts* 4C **86**
Warter. *E Yor* 4C **100**
Warthermarske. *N Yor* 2E **98**
Warthill. *N Yor* 4A **100**
Wartling. *E Sus* 5A **28**
Wartnaby. *Leics* 3E **74**
Warton. *Lanc* 2D **97**
(nr. Carnforth)
Warton. *Lanc* 2C **90**
(nr. Freckleton)
Warton. *Nmbd* 4E **121**
Warton. *Warw* 5G **73**
Warwick. *Warw* 4G **61**
Warwick Bridge. *Cumb* 4F **113**
Warwick-on-Eden. *Cumb* 4F **113**
Warwick Wold. *Surr* 5E **39**
Wasbister. *Orkn* 4C **172**
Wasdale Head. *Cumb* 4C **102**
Wash. *Derbs* 2E **85**
Washaway. *Corn* 2E **7**
Washbourne. *Devn* 3E **9**
Washbrook. *Suff* 1E **54**
Wash Common. *W Ber* 5C **36**
Washerwall. *Staf* 1D **72**
Washfield. *Devn* 1C **12**
Washfold. *N Yor* 4D **104**
Washford. *Som* 2D **20**
Washford Pyne. *Devn* 1B **12**
Washingborough. *Linc* 3H **87**
Washington. *Tyne* 4G **115**
Washington. *W Sus* 4C **26**
Washington Village. *Tyne* 4G **115**
Waskerley. *Dur* 5D **114**
Wasperton. *Warw* 5G **61**
Wasp Green. *Surr* 1E **27**
Wasps Nest. *Linc* 4H **87**
Wass. *N Yor* 2H **99**
Watchet. *Som* 2D **20**
Watchfield. *Oxon* 2H **35**
Watchgate. *Cumb* 5G **103**
Watchhill. *Cumb* 5C **112**
Watcombe. *Torb* 2F **9**
Watendlath. *Cumb* 3D **102**
Water. *Devn* 4A **12**
Water. *Lanc* 2G **91**
Waterbeach. *Cambs* 4D **65**
Waterbeach. *W Sus* 2G **17**
Waterbeck. *Dum* 2D **112**
Waterditch. *Hants* 3G **15**
Water End. *C Beds* 2A **52**
Water End. *E Yor* 1A **94**
Water End. *Essx* 1F **53**
Water End. *Herts* 5C **52**
(nr. Hatfield)
Water End. *Herts* 4A **52**
(nr. Hemel Hempstead)
Waterfall. *Staf* 5E **85**
Waterfoot. *E Ren* 4G **127**
Waterfoot. *Lanc* 2G **91**
Waterford. *Herts* 4D **52**
Water Fryston. *W Yor* 2E **93**
Waterhead. *Cumb* 4E **103**
Waterhead. *E Ayr* 3E **117**
Waterhead. *S Ayr* 5C **116**
Waterheads. *Bord* 4F **129**
Waterhouses. *Dur* 5E **115**
Waterhouses. *Staf* 5E **85**
Wateringbury. *Kent* 5A **40**
Waterlane. *Glos* 5E **49**
Waterlip. *Som* 2B **22**
Waterloo. *Cphy* 3E **33**
Waterloo. *Corn* 5B **10**
Waterloo. *Here* 1G **47**
Waterloo. *High* 1E **147**
Waterloo. *Mers* 1F **83**
Waterloo. *Norf* 4E **78**
Waterloo. *N Lan* 4B **128**
Waterloo. *Pemb* 4D **42**
Waterloo. *Per* 5H **143**
Waterloo. *Pool* 3F **15**
Waterloo. *Shrp* 2G **71**
Waterlooville. *Hants* 2E **17**
Watermead. *Buck* 4G **51**
Watermillock. *Cumb* 2F **103**
Water Newton. *Cambs* 1A **64**
Water Orton. *Warw* 1F **61**
Waterperry. *Oxon* 5E **51**
Waterrow. *Som* 4D **20**
Watersfield. *W Sus* 4B **26**
Waterside. *Buck* 5H **51**
Waterside. *Cambs* 3F **65**
Waterside. *Cumb* 5D **112**
Waterside. *E Ayr* 4D **116**
(nr. Ayr)
Waterside. *E Ayr* 5F **127**
(nr. Kilmarnock)
Waterside. *E Dun* 2H **127**
Waterstein. *High* 4A **154**
Waterstock. *Oxon* 5E **51**
Waterston. *Pemb* 4D **42**
Water Stratford. *Buck* 2E **51**
Waters Upton. *Telf* 4A **72**
Water Yeat. *Cumb* 1B **96**
Watford. *Herts* 1B **38**
Watford. *Nptn* 4D **62**
Wath. *Cumb* 4H **103**
Wath. *N Yor* 3D **98**
(nr. Pateley Bridge)
Wath. *N Yor* 2F **99**
(nr. Ripon)
Wath Brow. *Cumb* 3B **102**
Wath upon Dearne. *S Yor* 1B **86**
Watlington. *Norf* 4F **77**
Watlington. *Oxon* 2E **37**
Watten. *High* 3E **169**
Wattisfield. *Suff* 3C **66**
Wattisham. *Suff* 5C **66**
Wattlesborough Heath. *Shrp* 4F **71**
Watton. *Dors* 3H **13**
Watton. *E Yor* 4E **101**
Watton. *Norf* 5B **78**
Watton at Stone. *Herts* 4C **52**
Wattston. *N Lan* 2A **128**
Wattstown. *Rhon* 2D **32**
Wattsville. *Cphy* 2F **33**
Wauldby. *E Yor* 2C **94**
Waulkmill. *Abers* 4D **152**
Waun. *Powy* 4E **71**
Waunarlwydd. *Swan* 3F **31**
Waun Fawr. *Cdgn* 2F **57**
Waunfawr. *Gwyn* 5E **81**
Waungilwen. *Carm* 1H **43**
Waunlwyd. *Blae* 5E **47**
Waun-y-Clyn. *Carm* 5E **45**
Wavendon. *Mil* 2H **51**
Waverbridge. *Cumb* 5D **112**
Waverley. *Surr* 2G **25**
Waverton. *Ches W* 4G **83**
Waverton. *Cumb* 5D **112**
Wavertree. *Mers* 2F **83**
Wawne. *E Yor* 1D **94**
Waxham. *Norf* 3G **79**
Waxholme. *E Yor* 2G **95**
Wayford. *Som* 2H **13**
Way Head. *Cambs* 2D **65**
Waytown. *Dors* 3H **13**
Way Village. *Devn* 1B **12**
Wdig. *Pemb* 1D **42**
Wealdstone. *G Lon* 2C **38**
Weardley. *W Yor* 5E **99**
Weare. *Som* 1H **21**
Weare Giffard. *Devn* 4E **19**
Wearhead. *Dur* 1B **104**
Wearne. *Som* 4H **21**
Weasdale. *Cumb* 4H **103**
Weasenham All Saints. *Norf* 3H **77**
Weasenham St Peter. *Norf* 3A **78**
Weaverham. *Ches W* 3A **84**
Weaverthorpe. *N Yor* 2D **100**
Webheath. *Worc* 4E **61**
Webton. *Here* 2H **47**
Wedderlairs. *Abers* 5F **161**
Weddington. *Warw* 1A **62**
Wedhampton. *Wilts* 1F **23**
Wedmore. *Som* 2H **21**
Wednesbury. *W Mid* 1D **61**
Wednesfield. *W Mid* 5D **72**
Weecar. *Notts* 4F **87**
Weedon. *Buck* 4G **51**
Weedon Bec. *Nptn* 5D **62**
Weedon Lois. *Nptn* 1E **50**
Weeford. *Staf* 5F **73**
Week. *Devn* 4G **19**
(nr. Barnstaple)
Week. *Devn* 2G **11**
(nr. Okehampton)
Week. *Devn* 1H **11**
(nr. South Molton)
Week. *Devn* 2D **9**
(nr. Totnes)
Week. *Som* 3C **20**
Weeke. *Devn* 2A **12**
Weeke. *Hants* 3C **24**
Week Green. *Corn* 3C **10**
Weekley. *Nptn* 2F **63**
Week St Mary. *Corn* 3C **10**
Weel. *E Yor* 1D **94**
Weeley. *Essx* 3E **55**
Weeley Heath. *Essx* 3E **55**
Weem. *Per* 4F **143**
Weeping Cross. *Staf* 3D **72**
Weethly. *Warw* 5E **61**
Weeting. *Norf* 2G **65**
Weeton. *E Yor* 2G **95**
Weeton. *Lanc* 1B **90**
Weeton. *N Yor* 5E **99**
Weetwood Hall. *Nmbd* 2E **121**
Weir. *Lanc* 2G **91**
Welborne. *Norf* 4C **78**
Welbourn. *Linc* 5G **87**
Welburn. *N Yor* 1A **100**
(nr. Kirkbymoorside)
Welburn. *N Yor* 3B **100**
(nr. Malton)
Welbury. *N Yor* 4A **106**
Welby. *Linc* 2G **75**
Welches Dam. *Cambs* 2D **64**
Welcombe. *Devn* 1C **10**
Weld Bank. *Lanc* 3D **90**
Weldon. *Nptn* 2G **63**
Weldon. *Nmbd* 5F **121**
Welford. *Nptn* 2D **62**
Welford. *W Ber* 4C **36**
Welford-on-Avon. *Warw* 5F **61**
Welham. *Leics* 1E **63**
Welham. *Notts* 2E **87**
Welham Green. *Herts* 5C **52**
Well. *Hants* 2F **25**
Well. *Linc* 3D **88**
Well. *N Yor* 1E **99**
Welland. *Worc* 1C **48**
Wellbank. *Ang* 5D **144**
Well Bottom. *Dors* 1E **15**
Welldale. *Dum* 3C **112**
Wellesbourne. *Warw* 5G **61**
Well Hill. *Kent* 4F **39**
Wellhouse. *W Ber* 4D **36**
Welling. *G Lon* 3F **39**
Wellingborough. *Nptn* 4F **63**
Wellingham. *Norf* 3A **78**
Wellingore. *Linc* 5G **87**
Wellington. *Cumb* 4B **102**
Wellington. *Here* 1H **47**
Wellington. *Som* 4E **21**
Wellington. *Telf* 4A **72**
Wellington Heath. *Here* 1C **48**
Wellow. *Bath* 1C **22**
Wellow. *IOW* 4B **16**
Wellow. *Notts* 4D **86**
Wellpond Green. *Herts* 3E **53**
Wells. *Som* 2A **22**
Wellsborough. *Leics* 5A **74**
Wells Green. *Ches E* 5A **84**
Wells-next-the-Sea. *Norf* 1B **78**
Wells of Ythan. *Abers* 5D **160**
Wellswood. *Torb* 2F **9**
Wellwood. *Fife* 1D **129**
Welney. *Norf* 1E **65**
Welsford. *Devn* 4C **18**
Welshampton. *Shrp* 2G **71**
Welsh End. *Shrp* 2H **71**
Welsh Frankton. *Shrp* 2F **71**
Welsh Hook. *Pemb* 2D **42**
Welsh Newton. *Here* 4H **47**
Welsh Newton Common. *Here* 4A **48**
Welshpool. *Powy* 5E **70**
Welsh St Donats. *V Glam* 4D **32**
Welton. *Bath* 1B **22**
Welton. *Cumb* 5E **113**
Welton. *E Yor* 2C **94**
Welton. *Linc* 2H **87**
Welton. *Nptn* 4C **62**
Welton Hill. *Linc* 2H **87**
Welton le Marsh. *Linc* 4D **88**
Welton le Wold. *Linc* 2B **88**
Welwick. *E Yor* 2G **95**
Welwyn. *Herts* 4C **52**
Welwyn Garden City. *Herts* 4C **52**
Wem. *Shrp* 3H **71**
Wembdon. *Som* 3F **21**
Wembley. *G Lon* 2C **38**
Wembury. *Devn* 4B **8**
Wembworthy. *Devn* 2G **11**
Wemyss Bay. *Inv* 2C **126**
Wenallt. *Cdgn* 3F **57**
Wenallt. *Gwyn* 1B **70**
Wendens Ambo. *Essx* 2F **53**
Wendlebury. *Oxon* 4D **50**
Wendling. *Norf* 4B **78**
Wendover. *Buck* 5G **51**
Wendron. *Corn* 5A **6**
Wendy. *Cambs* 1D **52**
Wenfordbridge. *Corn* 5A **10**
Wenhaston. *Suff* 3G **67**
Wennington. *Cambs* 3B **64**
Wennington. *G Lon* 2G **39**
Wennington. *Lanc* 2F **97**
Wensley. *Derbs* 4G **85**
Wensley. *N Yor* 1C **98**
Wentbridge. *W Yor* 3E **93**
Wentnor. *Shrp* 1F **59**
Wentworth. *Cambs* 3D **65**
Wentworth. *S Yor* 1A **86**
Wenvoe. *V Glam* 4E **32**
Weobley. *Here* 5G **59**
Weobley Marsh. *Here* 5G **59**
Wepham. *W Sus* 5B **26**
Wereham. *Norf* 5F **77**
Wergs. *W Mid* 5C **72**
Wern. *Gwyn* 1E **69**
Wern. *Powy* 4E **46**
(nr. Brecon)
Wern. *Powy* 4E **71**
(nr. Guilsfield)
Wern. *Powy* 4B **70**
(nr. Llangadfan)
Wern. *Powy* 3E **71**
(nr. Llanymynech)
Wernffrwd. *Swan* 3E **31**
Wernyrheolydd. *Mon* 4G **47**
Werrington. *Corn* 4D **10**
Werrington. *Pet* 5A **76**
Werrington. *Staf* 1D **72**
Wervin. *Ches W* 3G **83**
Wesham. *Lanc* 1C **90**
Wessington. *Derbs* 5A **86**
West Aberthaw. *V Glam* 5D **32**
West Acre. *Norf* 4G **77**
West Allerdean. *Nmbd* 5F **131**
West Alvington. *Devn* 4D **8**
West Amesbury. *Wilts* 2G **23**
West Anstey. *Devn* 4B **20**
West Appleton. *N Yor* 5F **105**
West Ardsley. *W Yor* 2C **92**
West Arthurlie. *E Ren* 4F **127**
West Ashby. *Linc* 3B **88**
West Ashling. *W Sus* 2G **17**
West Ashton. *Wilts* 1D **23**
West Auckland. *Dur* 2E **105**
West Ayton. *N Yor* 1D **101**
West Bagborough. *Som* 3E **21**
West Bank. *Hal* 2H **83**
West Barkwith. *Linc* 2A **88**
West Barnby. *N Yor* 3F **107**
West Barns. *E Lot* 2C **130**
West Barsham. *Norf* 2B **78**
West Bay. *Dors* 3H **13**
West Beckham. *Norf* 2D **78**
West Bennan. *N Ayr* 3D **123**
Westbere. *Kent* 4F **41**
West Bergholt. *Essx* 3C **54**
West Bexington. *Dors* 4A **14**
West Bilney. *Norf* 4G **77**
West Blackdene. *Dur* 1B **104**
West Blatchington. *Brig* 5D **27**
Westborough. *Linc* 1F **75**
Westbourne. *Bour* 3F **15**
Westbourne. *W Sus* 2F **17**
West Bowling. *W Yor* 1B **92**
West Brabourne. *Kent* 1E **29**
West Bradford. *Lanc* 5G **97**
West Bradley. *Som* 3A **22**
West Bretton. *W Yor* 3C **92**
West Bridgford. *Notts* 2C **74**
West Briggs. *Norf* 4F **77**
West Bromwich. *W Mid* 1D **61**
Westbrook. *Here* 1F **47**
Westbrook. *Kent* 3H **41**
Westbrook. *Wilts* 5E **35**

West Buckland. *Devn* 3G 19
(nr. Barnstaple)
West Buckland. *Devn* 4C 8
(nr. Thurlestone)
West Buckland. *Som* 4E 21
West Burnside. *Abers* 1G 145
West Burrafirth. *Shet* 6D 173
West Burton. *N Yor* 1C 98
West Burton. *W Sus* 4B 26
Westbury. *Buck* 2E 50
Westbury. *Shrp* 5F 71
Westbury. *Wilts* 1D 22
Westbury Leigh. *Wilts* 2D 22
Westbury-on-Severn. *Glos* 4C 48
Westbury on Trym. *Bris* 4A 34
Westbury-sub-Mendip. *Som* 2A 22
West Butsfield. *Dur* 5E 115
West Butterwick. *N Lin* 4B 94
Westby. *Linc* 3G 75
West Byfleet. *Surr* 4B 38
West Caister. *Norf* 4H 79
West Calder. *W Lot* 3D 128
West Camel. *Som* 4A 22
West Carr. *N Lin* 4H 93
West Chaldon. *Dors* 4C 14
West Challow. *Oxon* 3B 36
West Charleton. *Devn* 4D 8
West Chelborough. *Dors* 2A 14
West Chevington. *Nmbd* 5G 121
West Chiltington. *W Sus* 4B 26
West Chiltington Common. *W Sus* 4B 26
West Chinnock. *Som* 1H 13
West Chisenbury. *Wilts* 1G 23
West Clandon. *Surr* 5B 38
West Cliffe. *Kent* 1H 29
Westcliff-on-Sea. *S'end* 2C 40
West Clyne. *High* 3F 165
West Coker. *Som* 1A 14
Westcombe. *Som* 3B 22
(nr. Evercreech)
Westcombe. *Som* 4H 21
(nr. Somerton)
West Compton. *Dors* 3A 14
West Compton. *Som* 2A 22
West Cornforth. *Dur* 1A 106
Westcot. *Oxon* 3B 36
Westcott. *Buck* 4F 51
Westcott. *Devn* 2D 12
Westcott. *Surr* 1C 26
Westcott Barton. *Oxon* 3C 50
West Cowick. *E Yor* 2G 93
West Cranmore. *Som* 2B 22
West Croftmore. *High* 2D 150
West Cross. *Swan* 4F 31
West Cullerlie. *Abers* 3E 153
West Culvennan. *Dum* 3H 109
West Curry. *Corn* 3C 10
West Curthwaite. *Cumb* 5E 113
Westdean. *E Sus* 5G 27
West Dean. *W Sus* 1G 17
West Dean. *Wilts* 4A 24
West Deeping. *Linc* 5A 76
West Derby. *Mers* 1F 83
West Dereham. *Norf* 5F 77
West Down. *Devn* 2F 19
Westdowns. *Corn* 4A 10
West Drayton. *G Lon* 3B 38
West Drayton. *Notts* 3E 86
West Dunnet. *High* 1E 169
West Ella. *E Yor* 2D 94
West End. *Bed* 5G 63
West End. *Cambs* 1D 64
West End. *Dors* 2E 15
West End. *E Yor* 3E 101
(nr. Kilham)
West End. *E Yor* 1E 95
(nr. Preston)
West End. *E Yor* 1C 94
(nr. South Cove)
West End. *E Yor* 4F 101
(nr. Ulrome)
West End. *G Lon* 2D 39
West End. *Hants* 1C 16
West End. *Herts* 5C 52
West End. *Kent* 4F 41
West End. *Lanc* 3D 96
West End. *Linc* 1C 76
West End. *Norf* 4G 79
West End. *N Som* 5H 33
West End. *N Yor* 4D 98
West End. *S Glo* 3C 34
West End. *S Lan* 5C 128
West End. *Surr* 4A 38
West End. *Wilts* 4E 23
West End. *Wind* 4G 37
West End. *Worc* 2F 49
West End Green. *Hants* 5E 37
Westenhanger. *Kent* 2F 29
Wester Aberchalder. *High* 2H 149
Wester Balgedie. *Per* 3D 136
Wester Brae. *High* 2A 158
Wester Culbeuchly. *Abers* 2D 160
Westerdale. *High* 3D 168
Westerdale. *N Yor* 4D 106
Wester Dechmont. *W Lot* 2D 128
Wester Fearn. *High* 5D 164
Westerfield. *Suff* 1E 55
Wester Galcantray. *High* 4C 158
Westergate. *W Sus* 5A 26
Wester Gruinards. *High* 4C 164
Westerham. *Kent* 5F 39
Westerleigh. *S Glo* 4B 34
Westerloch. *High* 3F 169
Wester Mandally. *High* 3E 149
Wester Quarff. *Shet* 8F 173
Wester Rarichie. *High* 1C 158
Wester Shian. *Per* 5F 143
Wester Skeld. *Shet* 7D 173
Westerton. *Ang* 3F 145
Westerton. *Dur* 1F 105
Westerton. *W Sus* 2G 17
Westerwick. *Shet* 7D 173
West Farleigh. *Kent* 5B 40
West Farndon. *Nptn* 5C 62
West Felton. *Shrp* 3F 71
Westfield. *Cumb* 2A 102
Westfield. *E Sus* 4C 28
Westfield. *High* 2C 168
Westfield. *Norf* 5B 78
Westfield. *N Lan* 2A 128
Westfield. *W Lot* 2C 128
Westfields. *Dors* 2C 14
Westfields of Rattray. *Per* 4A 144
West Fleetham. *Nmbd* 2F 121
Westford. *Som* 1E 13
West Garforth. *W Yor* 1D 93
Westgate. *Dur* 1C 104
Westgate. *Norf* 1B 78
Westgate. *N Lin* 4A 94
Westgate on Sea. *Kent* 3H 41
West Ginge. *Oxon* 3C 36
West Grafton. *Wilts* 5H 35
West Green. *Hants* 1F 25
West Grimstead. *Wilts* 4H 23
West Grinstead. *W Sus* 3C 26
West Haddlesey. *N Yor* 2F 93
West Haddon. *Nptn* 3D 62
West Hagbourne. *Oxon* 3D 36
West Hagley. *Worc* 2C 60
West Hall. *Cumb* 3G 113
Westhall. *Suff* 2G 67
West Hallam. *Derbs* 1B 74
Westhall Terrace. *Ang* 5D 144
West Halton. *N Lin* 2C 94
Westham. *Dors* 5B 14
Westham. *E Sus* 5H 27
West Ham. *G Lon* 2E 39
Westham. *Som* 2H 21
Westhampnett. *W Sus* 2G 17
West Handley. *Derbs* 3A 86
West Hanney. *Oxon* 2C 36
West Hanningfield. *Essx* 1B 40
West Hardwick. *W Yor* 3E 93
West Harnham. *Wilts* 4G 23
West Harptree. *Bath* 1A 22
West Harting. *W Sus* 4F 25
West Harton. *Tyne* 3G 115
West Hatch. *Som* 4F 21
Westhay. *Som* 2H 21
Westhead. *Lanc* 4C 90
West Head. *Norf* 5E 77
West Heath. *Hants* 1D 24
(nr. Basingstoke)
West Heath. *Hants* 1G 25
(nr. Farnborough)
West Helmsdale. *High* 2H 165
West Hendred. *Oxon* 3C 36
West Heogaland. *Shet* 4D 173
West Heslerton. *N Yor* 2D 100
West Hewish. *N Som* 5G 33
Westhide. *Here* 1A 48
Westhill. *Abers* 3F 153
West Hill. *Devn* 3D 12
West Hill. *E Yor* 3F 101
Westhill. *High* 4B 158
West Hill. *N Som* 4H 33
West Hill. *W Sus* 2E 27
West Hoathly. *W Sus* 2E 27
West Holme. *Dors* 4D 15
Westhope. *Here* 5G 59
Westhope. *Shrp* 2G 59
West Horndon. *Essx* 2H 39
Westhorp. *Nptn* 5C 62
Westhorpe. *Linc* 2B 76
Westhorpe. *Suff* 4C 66
West Horrington. *Som* 2A 22
West Horsley. *Surr* 5B 38
West Horton. *Nmbd* 1E 121
West Hougham. *Kent* 1G 29
Westhoughton. *G Man* 4E 91
West Houlland. *Shet* 6D 173
Westhouse. *N Yor* 2F 97
Westhouses. *Derbs* 5B 86
West Howe. *Bour* 3F 15
Westhumble. *Surr* 5C 38
West Huntspill. *Som* 2G 21
West Hyde. *Herts* 1B 38
West Hynish. *Arg* 5A 138
West Hythe. *Kent* 2F 29
West Ilsley. *W Ber* 3C 36
Westing. *Shet* 1G 173
West Itchenor. *W Sus* 2G 17
West Keal. *Linc* 4C 88
West Kennett. *Wilts* 5G 35
West Kilbride. *N Ayr* 5D 126
West Kingsdown. *Kent* 4G 39
West Kington. *Wilts* 4D 34
West Kirby. *Mers* 2E 82
West Knapton. *N Yor* 2C 100
West Knighton. *Dors* 4C 14
West Knoyle. *Wilts* 3D 22
West Kyloe. *Nmbd* 5G 131
Westlake. *Devn* 3C 8
West Lambrook. *Som* 1H 13
West Langdon. *Kent* 1H 29
West Langwell. *High* 3D 164
West Lavington. *W Sus* 4G 25
West Lavington. *Wilts* 1F 23
West Layton. *N Yor* 4E 105
West Leake. *Notts* 3C 74
West Learmouth. *Nmbd* 1C 120
Westleigh. *Devn* 4E 19
(nr. Bideford)
Westleigh. *Devn* 1D 12
(nr. Tiverton)
West Leigh. *Devn* 2G 11
(nr. Winkleigh)
Westleigh. *G Man* 4E 91
West Leith. *Buck* 4H 51
Westleton. *Suff* 4G 67
West Lexham. *Norf* 4H 77
Westley. *Shrp* 5F 71
Westley. *Suff* 4H 65
Westley Waterless. *Cambs* 5F 65
West Lilling. *N Yor* 3A 100
West Lingo. *Fife* 3G 137
Westlington. *Buck* 4F 51
Westlinton. *Cumb* 3E 113
West Linton. *Bord* 4E 129
West Littleton. *S Glo* 4C 34
West Looe. *Corn* 3G 7
West Lulworth. *Dors* 4D 14
West Lutton. *N Yor* 3D 100
West Lydford. *Som* 3A 22
West Lyng. *Som* 4G 21
West Lynn. *Norf* 4F 77
West Mains. *Per* 2B 136
West Malling. *Kent* 5A 40
West Malvern. *Worc* 1C 48
Westmancote. *Worc* 2E 49
West Marden. *W Sus* 1F 17
West Markham. *Notts* 3E 86
Westmarsh. *Kent* 4G 41
West Marsh. *NE Lin* 4F 95
West Marton. *N Yor* 4A 98
West Meon. *Hants* 4E 25
West Mersea. *Essx* 4D 54
Westmeston. *E Sus* 4E 27
Westmill. *Herts* 3D 52
(nr. Buntingford)
Westmill. *Herts* 2B 52
(nr. Hitchin)
West Milton. *Dors* 3A 14
Westminster. *G Lon* 3D 39
West Molesey. *Surr* 4C 38
West Monkton. *Som* 4F 21
Westmoor End. *Cumb* 1B 102
West Moors. *Dors* 2F 15
West Morden. *Dors* 3E 15
West Muir. *Ang* 2E 145
(nr. Brechin)
Westmuir. *Ang* 3C 144
(nr. Forfar)
West Murkle. *High* 2D 168
West Ness. *N Yor* 2A 100
Westness. *Orkn* 5C 172
Westnewton. *Cumb* 5C 112
West Newton. *E Yor* 1E 95
West Newton. *Norf* 3F 77
Westnewton. *Nmbd* 1D 120
West Newton. *Som* 4F 21
West Norwood. *G Lon* 3E 39
Westoe. *Tyne* 3G 115
West Ogwell. *Devn* 2E 9
Weston. *Bath* 5C 34
Weston. *Ches E* 5B 84
(nr. Crewe)
Weston. *Ches E* 3D 84
(nr. Macclesfield)
Weston. *Devn* 2E 13
(nr. Honiton)
Weston. *Devn* 4E 13
(nr. Sidmouth)
Weston. *Dors* 5B 14
(nr. Weymouth)
Weston. *Dors* 2A 14
(nr. Yeovil)
Weston. *Hal* 2H 83
Weston. *Hants* 4F 25
Weston. *Here* 5F 59
Weston. *Herts* 2C 52
Weston. *Linc* 3B 76
Weston. *Nptn* 1D 50
Weston. *Notts* 4E 87
Weston. *Shrp* 1H 59
(nr. Bridgnorth)
Weston. *Shrp* 3F 59
(nr. Knighton)
Weston. *Shrp* 3H 71
(nr. Wem)
Weston. *S Lan* 5D 128
Weston. *Staf* 3D 73
Weston. *Suff* 2G 67
Weston. *W Ber* 4B 36
Weston Bampfylde. *Som* 4B 22
Weston Beggard. *Here* 1A 48
Westonbirt. *Glos* 3D 34
Weston by Welland. *Nptn* 1E 63
Weston Colville. *Cambs* 5F 65
Westoncommon. *Shrp* 3G 71
Weston Coyney. *Stoke* 1D 72
Weston Ditch. *Suff* 3F 65
Weston Favell. *Nptn* 4E 63
Weston Green. *Cambs* 5F 65
Weston Green. *Norf* 4D 78
Weston Heath. *Shrp* 4B 72
Weston Hills. *Linc* 4B 76
Weston in Arden. *Warw* 2A 62
Westoning. *C Beds* 2A 52
Weston-in-Gordano. *N Som* 4H 33
Weston Jones. *Staf* 3B 72
Weston Longville. *Norf* 4D 78
Weston Lullingfields. *Shrp* 3G 71
Weston-on-Avon. *Warw* 5F 61
Weston-on-the-Green. *Oxon* 4D 50
Weston-on-Trent. *Derbs* 3B 74
Weston Patrick. *Hants* 2E 25
Weston Rhyn. *Shrp* 2E 71
Weston-sub-Edge. *Glos* 1G 49
Weston-super-Mare. *N Som* 5G 33
Weston Town. *Som* 2C 22
Weston Turville. *Buck* 4G 51
Weston under Lizard. *Staf* 4C 72
Weston under Penyard. *Here* 3B 48
Weston under Wetherley. *Warw* 4A 62
Weston Underwood. *Derbs* 1G 73
Weston Underwood. *Mil* 5F 63
Westonzoyland. *Som* 3G 21
West Orchard. *Dors* 1D 14
West Overton. *Wilts* 5G 35
Westow. *N Yor* 3B 100
Westown. *Per* 1E 137
West Panson. *Devn* 3D 10
West Park. *Hart* 1B 106
West Parley. *Dors* 3F 15
West Peckham. *Kent* 5H 39
West Pelton. *Dur* 4F 115
West Pennard. *Som* 3A 22
West Pentire. *Corn* 2B 6
West Perry. *Cambs* 4A 64
West Pitcorthie. *Fife* 3H 137
West Plean. *Stir* 1B 128
West Poringland. *Norf* 5E 79
West Porlock. *Som* 2B 20
Westport. *Som* 1G 13
West Putford. *Devn* 1D 10
West Quantoxhead. *Som* 2E 20
Westra. *V Glam* 4E 33
West Rainton. *Dur* 5G 115
West Rasen. *Linc* 2H 87
West Ravendale. *NE Lin* 1B 88
Westray Airport. *Orkn* 2D 172
West Raynham. *Norf* 3A 78
Westrigg. *W Lot* 3C 128
West Rounton. *N Yor* 4B 106
West Row. *Suff* 3F 65
West Rudham. *Norf* 3H 77
West Runton. *Norf* 1D 78
Westruther. *Bord* 4C 130
Westry. *Cambs* 1C 64
West Saltoun. *E Lot* 3A 130
West Sandford. *Devn* 2B 12
West Sandwick. *Shet* 3F 173
West Scrafton. *N Yor* 1C 98
Westside. *Orkn* 5C 172
West Sleekburn. *Nmbd* 1F 115
West Somerton. *Norf* 4G 79
West Stafford. *Dors* 4C 14
West Stockwith. *Notts* 1E 87
West Stoke. *W Sus* 2G 17
West Stonesdale. *N Yor* 4B 104
West Stoughton. *Som* 2H 21
West Stour. *Dors* 4C 22
West Stourmouth. *Kent* 4G 41
West Stow. *Suff* 3H 65
West Stowell. *Wilts* 5G 35
West Strathan. *High* 2F 167
West Stratton. *Hants* 2D 24
West Street. *Kent* 5D 40
West Tanfield. *N Yor* 2E 99
West Taphouse. *Corn* 2F 7
West Tarbert. *Arg* 3G 125
West Thirston. *Nmbd* 4F 121
West Thorney. *W Sus* 2F 17
West Thurrock. *Thur* 3G 39
West Tilbury. *Thur* 3A 40
West Tisted. *Hants* 4E 25
West Tofts. *Norf* 1H 65
West Torrington. *Linc* 2A 88
West Town. *Bath* 5A 34
West Town. *Hants* 3F 17
West Town. *N Som* 5H 33
West Tytherley. *Hants* 4A 24
West Tytherton. *Wilts* 4E 35
West View. *Hart* 1C 106
Westville. *Notts* 1C 74
West Walton. *Norf* 4D 76
Westward. *Cumb* 5D 112
Westward Ho!. *Devn* 4E 19
Westwell. *Kent* 1D 28
Westwell. *Oxon* 5H 49
Westwell Leacon. *Kent* 1D 28
West Wellow. *Hants* 1A 16
West Wemyss. *Fife* 4F 137
Westwick. *Cambs* 4D 64
Westwick. *Dur* 3D 104
Westwick. *Norf* 3E 79
West Wick. *N Som* 5G 33
West Wickham. *Cambs* 1G 53
West Wickham. *G Lon* 4E 39
West Williamston. *Pemb* 4E 43
West Willoughby. *Linc* 1G 75
West Winch. *Norf* 4F 77
West Winterslow. *Wilts* 3H 23
West Wittering. *W Sus* 3F 17
West Witton. *N Yor* 1C 98
Westwood. *Devn* 3D 12
Westwood. *Kent* 4H 41
Westwood. *Pet* 1A 64
Westwood. *S Lan* 4H 127
Westwood. *Wilts* 1D 22
West Woodburn. *Nmbd* 1B 114
West Woodhay. *W Ber* 5B 36
West Woodlands. *Som* 2C 22
West Woodside. *Cumb* 5E 112
Westwoodside. *N Lin* 4H 93
West Worldham. *Hants* 3F 25
West Worlington. *Devn* 1A 12
West Worthing. *W Sus* 5C 26
West Wratting. *Cambs* 5F 65
West Wycombe. *Buck* 2G 37
West Wylam. *Nmbd* 3E 115
West Yatton. *Wilts* 4D 34
West Yell. *Shet* 3F 173
West Youlstone. *Corn* 1C 10
Wetheral. *Cumb* 4F 113
Wetherby. *W Yor* 5G 99
Wetherden. *Suff* 4C 66
Wetheringsett. *Suff* 4D 66
Wethersfield. *Essx* 2H 53
Wethersta. *Shet* 5E 173
Wetherup Street. *Suff* 4D 66
Wetley Rocks. *Staf* 1D 72
Wettenhall. *Ches E* 4A 84
Wetton. *Staf* 5F 85
Wetwang. *E Yor* 4D 100
Wetwood. *Staf* 2B 72
Wexcombe. *Wilts* 1A 24
Wexham Street. *Buck* 2A 38
Weybourne. *Norf* 1D 78
Weybourne. *Surr* 2G 25
Weybread. *Suff* 2E 67
Weybridge. *Surr* 4B 38
Weycroft. *Devn* 3G 13
Weydale. *High* 2D 168
Weyhill. *Hants* 2B 24
Weymouth. *Dors* 5B 14 & 215
Weythel. *Powy* 5E 59
Whaddon. *Buck* 2G 51
Whaddon. *Cambs* 1D 52
Whaddon. *Glos* 4D 48
Whaddon. *Wilts* 4G 23
Whale. *Cumb* 2G 103
Whaley. *Derbs* 3C 86
Whaley Bridge. *Derbs* 2E 85
Whaley Thorns. *Derbs* 3C 86
Whalley. *Lanc* 1F 91
Whalton. *Nmbd* 1E 115
Wham. *N Yor* 3G 97
Whaplode. *Linc* 3C 76
Whaplode Drove. *Linc* 4C 76
Whaplode St Catherine. *Linc* 3C 76
Wharfe. *N Yor* 3G 97
Wharles. *Lanc* 1C 90
Wharley End. *C Beds* 1H 51
Wharncliffe Side. *S Yor* 1G 85
Wharram-le-Street. *N Yor* 3C 100
Wharton. *Ches W* 4A 84
Wharton. *Here* 5H 59
Whashton. *N Yor* 4E 105
Whasset. *Cumb* 1E 97
Whatcote. *Warw* 1A 50
Whateley. *Warw* 1G 61
Whatfield. *Suff* 1D 54
Whatley. *Som* 2G 13
(nr. Chard)
Whatley. *Som* 2C 22
(nr. Frome)
Whatlington. *E Sus* 4B 28
Whatmore. *Shrp* 3A 60
Whatstandwell. *Derbs* 5H 85
Whatton. *Notts* 2E 75
Whauphill. *Dum* 5B 110
Whaw. *N Yor* 4C 104
Wheatacre. *Norf* 1G 67
Wheatcroft. *Derbs* 5A 86
Wheathampstead. *Herts* 4B 52
Wheathill. *Shrp* 2A 60
Wheatley. *Devn* 3B 12
Wheatley. *Hants* 2F 25
Wheatley. *Oxon* 5D 50
Wheatley. *S Yor* 4F 93
Wheatley. *W Yor* 2A 92
Wheatley Hill. *Dur* 1A 106
Wheatley Lane. *Lanc* 1G 91
Wheatley Park. *S Yor* 4F 93
Wheaton Aston. *Staf* 4C 72
Wheatstone Park. *Staf* 5C 72
Wheddon Cross. *Som* 3C 20
Wheelerstreet. *Surr* 1A 26
Wheelock. *Ches E* 5B 84
Wheelock Heath. *Ches E* 5B 84
Wheelton. *Lanc* 2E 90

Wheldrake. *York* 5A **100**
Whelford. *Glos* 2G **35**
Whelpley Hill. *Buck* 5H **51**
Whelpo. *Cumb* 1E **102**
Whelston. *Flin* 3E **82**
Whenby. *N Yor* 3A **100**
Whepstead. *Suff* 5H **65**
Wherstead. *Suff* 1E **55**
Wherwell. *Hants* 2B **24**
Wheston. *Derbs* 3F **85**
Whetsted. *Kent* 1A **28**
Whetstone. *G Lon* 1D **38**
Whetstone. *Leics* 1C **62**
Whicham. *Cumb* 1A **96**
Whichford. *Warw* 2B **50**
Whickham. *Tyne* 3F **115**
Whiddon. *Devn* 2E **11**
Whiddon Down. *Devn* 3G **11**
Whigstreet. *Ang* 4D **145**
Whilton. *Nptn* 4D **62**
Whimble. *Devn* 2D **10**
Whimple. *Devn* 3D **12**
Whimpwell Green. *Norf* 3F **79**
Whinburgh. *Norf* 5C **78**
Whin Lane End. *Lanc* 5C **96**
Whinnyfold. *Abers* 5H **161**
Whinny Hill. *Stoc T* 3A **106**
Whippingham. *IOW* 3D **16**
Whipsnade. *C Beds* 4A **52**
Whipton. *Devn* 3C **12**
Whirlow. *S Yor* 2H **85**
Whisby. *Linc* 4G **87**
Whissendine. *Rut* 4F **75**
Whissonsett. *Norf* 3B **78**
Whisterfield. *Ches E* 3C **84**
Whistley Green. *Wok* 4F **37**
Whiston. *Mers* 1G **83**
Whiston. *Nptn* 4F **63**
Whiston. *S Yor* 1B **86**
Whiston. *Staf* 1E **73**
(nr. Cheadle)
Whiston. *Staf* 4C **72**
(nr. Penkridge)
Whiston Cross. *Shrp* 5B **72**
Whiston Eaves. *Staf* 1E **73**
Whitacre Heath. *Warw* 1G **61**
Whitbeck. *Cumb* 1A **96**
Whitbourne. *Here* 5B **60**
Whitburn. *Tyne* 3H **115**
Whitburn. *W Lot* 3C **128**
Whitburn Colliery. *Tyne* 3H **115**
Whitby. *Ches W* 3F **83**
Whitby. *N Yor* 3F **107**
Whitbyheath. *Ches W* 3F **83**
Whitchester. *Bord* 4D **130**
Whitchurch. *Bath* 5B **34**
Whitchurch. *Buck* 3G **51**
Whitchurch. *Card* 4E **33**
Whitchurch. *Devn* 5E **11**
Whitchurch. *Hants* 2C **24**
Whitchurch. *Here* 4A **48**
Whitchurch. *Pemb* 2C **42**
Whitchurch. *Shrp* 1H **71**
Whitchurch Canonicorum. *Dors* 3G **13**
Whitchurch Hill. *Oxon* 4E **37**
Whitchurch-on-Thames. *Oxon* 4E **37**
Whitcombe. *Dors* 4C **14**
Whitcot. *Shrp* 1F **59**
Whitcott Keysett. *Shrp* 2E **59**
Whiteash Green. *Essx* 2A **54**
Whitebog. *High* 2B **158**
Whitebridge. *High* 2G **149**
Whitebrook. *Mon* 5A **48**
Whitecairns. *Abers* 2G **153**
White Chapel. *Lanc* 5E **97**
Whitechurch. *Pemb* 1F **43**
White Colne. *Essx* 3B **54**
White Coppice. *Lanc* 3E **90**
White Corries. *High* 3G **141**
Whitecraig. *E Lot* 2G **129**
Whitecroft. *Glos* 5B **48**
White Cross. *Corn* 4D **5**
(nr. Mullion)
Whitecross. *Corn* 1D **6**
(nr. Wadebridge)
Whitecross. *Falk* 2C **128**
White End. *Worc* 2C **48**
Whiteface. *High* 5E **164**
Whitefarland. *N Ayr* 5G **125**
Whitefaulds. *S Ayr* 4B **116**
Whitefield. *Dors* 3E **15**
Whitefield. *G Man* 4G **91**
Whitefield. *Som* 4D **20**
Whiteford. *Abers* 1E **152**
Whitegate. *Ches W* 4A **84**
Whitehall. *Devn* 1E **13**
Whitehall. *Hants* 1F **25**
Whitehall. *Orkn* 5F **172**
Whitehall. *W Sus* 3C **26**
Whitehaven. *Cumb* 3A **102**
Whitehaven. *Shrp* 3E **71**
Whitehill. *Hants* 3F **25**
Whitehill. *N Ayr* 4D **126**
Whitehills. *Abers* 2D **160**
Whitehills. *Ang* 3D **144**
White Horse Common. *Norf* 3F **79**
Whitehough. *Derbs* 2E **85**
Whitehouse. *Abers* 2D **152**
Whitehouse. *Arg* 3G **125**
Whiteinch. *Glas* 3G **127**
Whitekirk. *E Lot* 1B **130**
White Kirkley. *Dur* 1D **104**
White Lackington. *Dors* 3C **14**
Whitelackington. *Som* 1G **13**
White Ladies Aston. *Worc* 5D **60**
White Lee. *W Yor* 2C **92**
Whiteley. *Hants* 1D **16**
Whiteley Bank. *IOW* 4D **16**
Whiteley Village. *Surr* 4B **38**
Whitemans Green. *W Sus* 3E **27**
White Mill. *Carm* 3E **45**
Whitemire. *Mor* 3D **159**
Whitemoor. *Corn* 3D **6**
Whitenap. *Hants* 4B **24**
Whiteness. *Shet* 7F **173**
White Notley. *Essx* 4A **54**
Whiteoak Green. *Oxon* 4B **50**
Whiteparish. *Wilts* 4H **23**
White Pit. *Linc* 3C **88**
Whiterashes. *Abers* 1F **153**
White Rocks. *Here* 3H **47**
White Roding. *Essx* 4F **53**
Whiterow. *High* 4F **169**
Whiterow. *Mor* 3E **159**
Whiteshill. *Glos* 5D **48**
Whiteside. *Nmbd* 3A **114**
Whiteside. *W Lot* 3C **128**
Whitesmith. *E Sus* 4G **27**
Whitestaunton. *Som* 1F **13**
Whitestone. *Abers* 4D **152**
Whitestone. *Devn* 3B **12**
White Stone. *Here* 1A **48**
Whitestones. *Abers* 3F **161**
Whitestreet Green. *Suff* 2C **54**
Whitewall Corner. *N Yor* 2B **100**
White Waltham. *Wind* 4G **37**
Whiteway. *Glos* 4E **49**
Whitewell. *Lanc* 5F **97**
Whitewell Bottom. *Lanc* 2G **91**
Whiteworks. *Devn* 5G **11**
Whitewreath. *Mor* 3G **159**
Whitfield. *D'dee* 5D **144**
Whitfield. *Kent* 1H **29**
Whitfield. *Nptn* 2E **50**
Whitfield. *Nmbd* 4A **114**
Whitfield. *S Glo* 2B **34**
Whitford. *Devn* 3F **13**
Whitford. *Flin* 3D **82**
Whitgift. *E Yor* 2B **94**
Whitgreave. *Staf* 3C **72**
Whithorn. *Dum* 5B **110**
Whiting Bay. *N Ayr* 3E **123**
Whitington. *Norf* 1G **65**
Whitkirk. *W Yor* 1D **92**
Whitland. *Carm* 3G **43**
Whitleigh. *Plym* 3A **8**
Whitletts. *S Ayr* 2C **116**
Whitley. *N Yor* 2F **93**
Whitley. *Wilts* 5D **35**
Whitley Bay. *Tyne* 2G **115**
Whitley Chapel. *Nmbd* 4C **114**
Whitley Heath. *Staf* 3C **72**
Whitley Lower. *W Yor* 3C **92**
Whitley Thorpe. *N Yor* 2F **93**
Whitlock's End. *W Mid* 3F **61**
Whitminster. *Glos* 5C **48**
Whitmore. *Dors* 2F **15**
Whitmore. *Staf* 1C **72**
Whitnage. *Devn* 1D **12**
Whitnash. *Warw* 4H **61**
Whitney. *Here* 1F **47**
Whitrigg. *Cumb* 4D **112**
(nr. Kirkbride)
Whitrigg. *Cumb* 1D **102**
(nr. Torpenhow)
Whitsbury. *Hants* 1G **15**
Whitsome. *Bord* 4E **131**
Whitson. *Newp* 3G **33**
Whitstable. *Kent* 4F **41**
Whitstone. *Corn* 3C **10**
Whittingham. *Nmbd* 3E **121**
Whittingslow. *Shrp* 2G **59**
Whittington. *Derbs* 3B **86**
Whittington. *Glos* 3F **49**
Whittington. *Lanc* 2F **97**
Whittington. *Shrp* 2F **71**
Whittington. *Staf* 2C **60**
(nr. Kinver)
Whittington. *Staf* 5F **73**
(nr. Lichfield)
Whittington. *Warw* 1G **61**
Whittington. *Worc* 5C **60**
Whittington Barracks. *Staf* 5F **73**
Whittlebury. *Nptn* 1E **51**
Whittleford. *Warw* 1H **61**
Whittle-le-Woods. *Lanc* 2D **90**
Whittlesey. *Cambs* 1B **64**
Whittlesford. *Cambs* 1E **53**
Whittlestone Head. *Bkbn* 3F **91**
Whitton. *N Lin* 2C **94**
Whitton. *Nmbd* 4E **121**
Whitton. *Powy* 4E **59**
Whitton. *Bord* 2B **120**
Whitton. *Shrp* 3H **59**
Whitton. *Stoc T* 2A **106**
Whittonditch. *Wilts* 4A **36**
Whittonstall. *Nmbd* 4D **114**
Whitway. *Hants* 1C **24**
Whitwell. *Derbs* 3C **86**
Whitwell. *Herts* 3B **52**
Whitwell. *IOW* 5D **16**
Whitwell. *N Yor* 5F **105**
Whitwell. *Rut* 5G **75**
Whitwell-on-the-Hill. *N Yor* 3B **100**
Whitwick. *Leics* 4B **74**
Whitwood. *W Yor* 2E **93**
Whitworth. *Lanc* 3G **91**
Whixall. *Shrp* 2H **71**
Whixley. *N Yor* 4G **99**
Whoberley. *W Mid* 3G **61**
Whorlton. *Dur* 3E **105**
Whorlton. *N Yor* 4B **106**
Whygate. *Nmbd* 2A **114**
Whyle. *Here* 4H **59**
Whyteleafe. *Surr* 5E **39**
Wibdon. *Glos* 2A **34**
Wibtoft. *Warw* 2B **62**
Wichenford. *Worc* 4B **60**
Wichling. *Kent* 5D **40**
Wick. *Bour* 3G **15**
Wick. *Devn* 2E **13**
Wick. *High* 3F **169**
Wick. *Shet* 8F **173**
(on Mainland)
Wick. *Shet* 1G **173**
(on Unst)
Wick. *Som* 2F **21**
(nr. Bridgwater)
Wick. *Som* 1G **21**
(nr. Burnham-on-Sea)
Wick. *Som* 4H **21**
(nr. Somerton)
Wick. *S Glo* 4C **34**
Wick. *V Glam* 4C **32**
Wick. *W Sus* 5B **26**
Wick. *Wilts* 4G **23**
Wick. *Worc* 1E **49**
Wick Airport. *High* 3F **169**
Wicken. *Cambs* 3E **65**
Wicken. *Nptn* 2F **51**
Wicken Bonhunt. *Essx* 2E **53**
Wickenby. *Linc* 2H **87**
Wicken Green Village. *Norf* 2H **77**
Wickersley. *S Yor* 1B **86**
Wicker Street Green. *Suff* 1C **54**
Wickford. *Essx* 1B **40**
Wickham. *Hants* 1D **16**
Wickham. *W Ber* 4B **36**
Wickham Bishops. *Essx* 4B **54**
Wickhambreaux. *Kent* 5G **41**
Wickhambrook. *Suff* 5G **65**
Wickhamford. *Worc* 1F **49**
Wickham Green. *Suff* 4C **66**
Wickham Heath. *W Ber* 5C **36**
Wickham Market. *Suff* 5F **67**
Wickhampton. *Norf* 5G **79**
Wickham St Paul. *Essx* 2B **54**
Wickham Skeith. *Suff* 4C **66**
Wickham Street. *Suff* 4C **66**
Wick Hill. *Wok* 5F **37**
Wicklewood. *Norf* 5C **78**
Wickmere. *Norf* 2D **78**
Wick St Lawrence. *N Som* 5G **33**
Wickwar. *S Glo* 3C **34**
Widdington. *Essx* 2F **53**
Widdrington. *Nmbd* 5G **121**
Widdrington Station. *Nmbd* 5G **121**
Widecombe in the Moor. *Devn* 5H **11**
Widegates. *Corn* 3G **7**
Widemouth Bay. *Corn* 2C **10**
Wide Open. *Tyne* 2F **115**
Widewall. *Orkn* 8D **172**
Widford. *Essx* 5G **53**
Widford. *Herts* 4E **53**
Widham. *Wilts* 3F **35**
Widmer End. *Buck* 2G **37**
Widmerpool. *Notts* 3D **74**
Widnes. *Hal* 2H **83**
Widworthy. *Devn* 3F **13**
Wigan. *G Man* 4D **90**
Wigbeth. *Dors* 2F **15**
Wigborough. *Som* 1H **13**
Wiggaton. *Devn* 3E **12**
Wiggenhall St Germans. *Norf* 4E **77**
Wiggenhall St Mary Magdalen. *Norf* 4E **77**
Wiggenhall St Mary the Virgin. *Norf* 4E **77**
Wiggenhall St Peter. *Norf* 4F **77**
Wiggens Green. *Essx* 1G **53**
Wigginton. *Herts* 4H **51**
Wigginton. *Oxon* 2B **50**
Wigginton. *Staf* 5G **73**
Wigginton. *York* 4H **99**
Wigglesworth. *N Yor* 4H **97**
Wiggonby. *Cumb* 4D **112**
Wiggonholt. *W Sus* 4B **26**
Wighill. *N Yor* 5G **99**
Wighton. *Norf* 1B **78**
Wightwick. *Staf* 1C **60**
Wigley. *Hants* 1B **16**
Wigmore. *Here* 4G **59**
Wigmore. *Medw* 4C **40**
Wigsley. *Notts* 3F **87**
Wigsthorpe. *Nptn* 2H **63**
Wigston. *Leics* 1D **62**
Wigtoft. *Linc* 2B **76**
Wigton. *Cumb* 5D **112**
Wigtown. *Dum* 4B **110**
Wigtwizzle. *S Yor* 1G **85**
Wike. *W Yor* 5F **99**
Wilbarston. *Nptn* 2F **63**
Wilberfoss. *E Yor* 4B **100**
Wilburton. *Cambs* 3D **65**
Wilby. *Norf* 2C **66**
Wilby. *Nptn* 4F **63**
Wilby. *Suff* 3E **67**
Wilcot. *Wilts* 5G **35**
Wilcott. *Shrp* 4F **71**
Wilcove. *Corn* 3A **8**
Wildboarclough. *Ches E* 4D **85**
Wilden. *Bed* 5H **63**
Wilden. *Worc* 3C **60**
Wildern. *Hants* 1C **16**
Wilderspool. *Warr* 2A **84**
Wilde Street. *Suff* 3G **65**
Wildhern. *Hants* 1B **24**
Wildmanbridge. *S Lan* 4B **128**
Wildmoor. *Worc* 3D **60**
Wildsworth. *Linc* 1F **87**
Wildwood. *Staf* 3D **72**
Wilford. *Nott* 2C **74**
Wilkesley. *Ches E* 1A **72**
Wilkhaven. *High* 5G **165**
Wilkieston. *W Lot* 3E **129**
Wilksby. *Linc* 4B **88**
Willand. *Devn* 1D **12**
Willaston. *Ches E* 5A **84**
Willaston. *Ches W* 3F **83**
Willaston. *IOM* 4C **108**
Willen. *Mil* 1G **51**
Willenhall. *W Mid* 3A **62**
(nr. Coventry)
Willenhall. *W Mid* 1D **60**
(nr. Wolverhampton)
Willerby. *E Yor* 1D **94**
Willerby. *N Yor* 2E **101**
Willersey. *Glos* 2G **49**
Willersley. *Here* 1G **47**
Willesborough. *Kent* 1E **28**
Willesborough Lees. *Kent* 1E **29**
Willesden. *G Lon* 2D **38**
Willesley. *Wilts* 3D **34**
Willett. *Som* 3E **20**
Willey. *Shrp* 1A **60**
Willey. *Warw* 2B **62**
Willey Green. *Surr* 5A **38**
Williamscot. *Oxon* 1C **50**
Williamsetter. *Shet* 9E **173**
Willian. *Herts* 2C **52**
Willingale. *Essx* 5F **53**
Willingdon. *E Sus* 5G **27**
Willingham. *Cambs* 3D **64**
Willingham by Stow. *Linc* 2F **87**
Willingham Green. *Cambs* 5F **65**
Willington. *Bed* 1B **52**
Willington. *Derbs* 3G **73**
Willington. *Dur* 1E **105**
Willington. *Tyne* 3G **115**
Willington. *Warw* 2A **50**
Willington Corner. *Ches W* 4H **83**
Willisham Tye. *Suff* 5C **66**
Willitoft. *E Yor* 1H **93**
Williton. *Som* 2D **20**
Willoughbridge. *Staf* 1B **72**
Willoughby. *Linc* 3D **88**
Willoughby. *Warw* 4C **62**
Willoughby-on-the-Wolds. *Notts* 3D **74**
Willoughby Waterleys. *Leics* 1C **62**
Willoughton. *Linc* 1G **87**
Willow Green. *Worc* 5B **60**
Willows Green. *Essx* 4H **53**
Willsbridge. *S Glo* 4B **34**
Willslock. *Staf* 2E **73**
Wilmcote. *Warw* 5F **61**
Wilmington. *Bath* 5B **34**
Wilmington. *Devn* 3F **13**
Wilmington. *E Sus* 5G **27**
Wilmington. *Kent* 3G **39**
Wilmslow. *Ches E* 2C **84**
Wilnecote. *Staf* 5G **73**
Wilney Green. *Norf* 2C **66**
Wilpshire. *Lanc* 1E **91**
Wilsden. *W Yor* 1A **92**
Wilsford. *Linc* 1H **75**
Wilsford. *Wilts* 3G **23**
(nr. Amesbury)
Wilsford. *Wilts* 1G **23**
(nr. Devizes)
Wilsill. *N Yor* 3D **98**
Wilsley Green. *Kent* 2B **28**
Wilson. *Here* 3A **48**
Wilson. *Leics* 3B **74**
Wilsontown. *S Lan* 4C **128**
Wilstead. *Bed* 1A **52**
Wilsthorpe. *E Yor* 3F **101**
Wilsthorpe. *Linc* 4H **75**
Wilstone. *Herts* 4H **51**
Wilton. *Cumb* 3B **102**
Wilton. *N Yor* 1C **100**
Wilton. *Red C* 3C **106**
Wilton. *Bord* 3H **119**
Wilton. *Wilts* 5A **36**
(nr. Marlborough)
Wilton. *Wilts* 3F **23**
(nr. Salisbury)
Wimbish. *Essx* 2F **53**
Wimbish Green. *Essx* 2G **53**
Wimblebury. *Staf* 4E **73**
Wimbledon. *G Lon* 3D **38**
Wimblington. *Cambs* 1D **64**
Wimboldsley. *Ches W* 4A **84**
Wimborne Minster. *Dors* 2F **15**
Wimborne St Giles. *Dors* 1F **15**
Wimbotsham. *Norf* 5F **77**
Wimpole. *Cambs* 1D **52**
Wimpstone. *Warw* 1H **49**
Wincanton. *Som* 4C **22**
Winceby. *Linc* 4C **88**
Wincham. *Ches W* 3A **84**
Winchburgh. *W Lot* 2D **129**
Winchcombe. *Glos* 3F **49**
Winchelsea. *E Sus* 4D **28**
Winchelsea Beach. *E Sus* 4D **28**
Winchester. *Hants* 4C **24** & **213**
Winchet Hill. *Kent* 1B **28**
Winchfield. *Hants* 1F **25**
Winchmore Hill. *Buck* 1A **38**
Winchmore Hill. *G Lon* 1E **39**
Wincle. *Ches E* 4D **84**
Windermere. *Cumb* 5F **103**
Winderton. *Warw* 1B **50**
Windhill. *High* 4H **157**
Windle Hill. *Ches W* 3F **83**
Windlesham. *Surr* 4A **38**
Windley. *Derbs* 1H **73**
Windmill. *Derbs* 3F **85**
Windmill Hill. *E Sus* 4H **27**
Windmill Hill. *Som* 1G **13**
Windrush. *Glos* 4G **49**
Windsor. *Wind* 3A **38** & **213**
Windsor Green. *Suff* 5A **66**
Windyedge. *Abers* 4G **153**
Windygates. *Fife* 3F **137**
Windyharbour. *Ches E* 3C **84**
Windyknowe. *W Lot* 3C **128**
Wineham. *W Sus* 3D **26**
Winestead. *E Yor* 2G **95**
Winfarthing. *Norf* 2D **66**
Winford. *IOW* 4D **16**
Winford. *N Som* 5A **34**
Winforton. *Here* 1F **47**
Winfrith Newburgh. *Dors* 4D **14**
Wing. *Buck* 3G **51**
Wing. *Rut* 5F **75**
Wingate. *Dur* 1A **106**
Wingates. *G Man* 4E **91**
Wingates. *Nmbd* 5F **121**
Wingerworth. *Derbs* 4A **86**
Wingfield. *C Beds* 3A **52**
Wingfield. *Suff* 3E **67**
Wingfield. *Wilts* 1D **22**
Wingfield Park. *Derbs* 5A **86**
Wingham. *Kent* 5G **41**
Wingmore. *Kent* 1F **29**
Wingrave. *Buck* 4G **51**
Winkburn. *Notts* 5E **86**
Winkfield. *Brac* 3A **38**
Winkfield Row. *Brac* 4G **37**
Winkhill. *Staf* 5E **85**
Winklebury. *Hants* 1E **24**
Winkleigh. *Devn* 2G **11**
Winksley. *N Yor* 2E **99**
Winkton. *Dors* 3G **15**
Winlaton. *Tyne* 3E **115**
Winlaton Mill. *Tyne* 3E **115**
Winless. *High* 3F **169**
Winmarleigh. *Lanc* 5D **96**
Winnal Common. *Here* 2H **47**
Winnard's Perch. *Corn* 2D **6**
Winnersh. *Wok* 4F **37**
Winnington. *Ches W* 3A **84**
Winnington. *Staf* 2B **72**
Winnothdale. *Staf* 1E **73**
Winscales. *Cumb* 2B **102**
Winscombe. *N Som* 1H **21**
Winsford. *Ches W* 4A **84**
Winsford. *Som* 3C **20**
Winsham. *Devn* 3F **19**
Winsham. *Som* 2G **13**
Winshill. *Staf* 3G **73**
Winsh-wen. *Swan* 3F **31**
Winskill. *Cumb* 1G **103**
Winslade. *Hants* 2E **25**
Winsley. *Wilts* 5C **34**
Winslow. *Buck* 3F **51**
Winson. *Glos* 5F **49**
Winson Green. *W Mid* 2E **61**
Winsor. *Hants* 1B **16**
Winster. *Cumb* 5F **103**
Winster. *Derbs* 4G **85**
Winston. *Dur* 3E **105**
Winston. *Suff* 4D **66**
Winstone. *Glos* 5E **49**
Winswell. *Devn* 1E **11**
Winterborne Clenston. *Dors* 2D **14**
Winterborne Herringston. *Dors* 4B **14**
Winterborne Houghton. *Dors* 2D **14**
Winterborne Kingston. *Dors* 3D **14**

Winterborne Monkton. *Dors* 4B 14
Winterborne St Martin. *Dors* 4B 14
Winterborne Stickland. *Dors* 2D 14
Winterborne Whitechurch. *Dors* 2D 14
Winterborne Zelston. *Dors* 3E 15
Winterbourne. *S Glo* 3B 34
Winterbourne. *W Ber* 4C 36
Winterbourne Abbas. *Dors* 3B 14
Winterbourne Bassett. *Wilts* 4G 35
Winterbourne Dauntsey. *Wilts* 3G 23
Winterbourne Earls. *Wilts* 3G 23
Winterbourne Gunner. *Wilts* 3G 23
Winterbourne Monkton. *Wilts* 4F 35
Winterbourne Steepleton. *Dors* 4B 14
Winterbourne Stoke. *Wilts* 2F 23
Winterbrook. *Oxon* 3E 36
Winterburn. *N Yor* 4B 98
Winter Gardens. *Essx* 2B 40
Winterhay Green. *Som* 1G 13
Winteringham. *N Lin* 2C 94
Winterley. *Ches E* 5B 84
Wintersett. *W Yor* 3D 93
Winterton. *N Lin* 3C 94
Winterton-on-Sea. *Norf* 4G 79
Winthorpe. *Linc* 4E 89
Winthorpe. *Notts* 5F 87
Winton. *Bour* 3F 15
Winton. *Cumb* 3A 104
Winton. *E Sus* 5G 27
Wintringham. *N Yor* 2C 100
Winwick. *Cambs* 2A 64
Winwick. *Nptn* 3D 62
Winwick. *Warr* 1A 84
Wirksworth. *Derbs* 5G 85
Wirswall. *Ches E* 1H 71
Wisbech. *Cambs* 4D 76
Wisbech St Mary. *Cambs* 5D 76
Wisborough Green. *W Sus* 3B 26
Wiseton. *Notts* 2E 86
Wishaw. *N Lan* 4B 128
Wishaw. *Warw* 1F 61
Wisley. *Surr* 5B 38
Wispington. *Linc* 3B 88
Wissenden. *Kent* 1D 28
Wissett. *Suff* 3F 67
Wistanstow. *Shrp* 2G 59
Wistanswick. *Shrp* 3A 72
Wistaston. *Ches E* 5A 84
Wiston. *Pemb* 3E 43
Wiston. *S Lan* 1B 118
Wiston. *W Sus* 4C 26
Wistow. *Cambs* 2B 64
Wistow. *N Yor* 1F 93
Wiswell. *Lanc* 1F 91
Witcham. *Cambs* 2D 64
Witchampton. *Dors* 2E 15
Witchford. *Cambs* 3E 65
Witham. *Essx* 4B 54
Witham Friary. *Som* 2C 22
Witham on the Hill. *Linc* 4H 75
Witham St Hughs. *Linc* 4F 87
Withcall. *Linc* 2B 88
Witherenden Hill. *E Sus* 3H 27
Withergate. *Norf* 3E 79
Witheridge. *Devn* 1B 12
Witheridge Hill. *Oxon* 3E 37
Witherley. *Leics* 1H 61
Withermarsh Green. *Suff* 2D 54
Withern. *Linc* 2D 88
Withernsea. *E Yor* 2G 95
Withernwick. *E Yor* 5F 101
Withersdale Street. *Suff* 2E 67
Withersfield. *Suff* 1G 53
Witherslack. *Cumb* 1D 96
Withiel. *Corn* 2D 6
Withiel Florey. *Som* 3C 20
Withington. *Glos* 4F 49
Withington. *G Man* 1C 84
Withington. *Here* 1A 48
Withington. *Shrp* 4H 71
Withington. *Staf* 2E 73
Withington Green. *Ches E* 3C 84
Withington Marsh. *Here* 1A 48
Withleigh. *Devn* 1C 12
Withnell. *Lanc* 2E 91
Withnell Fold. *Lanc* 2E 90
Withybrook. *Warw* 2B 62
Withycombe. *Som* 2D 20
Withycombe Raleigh. *Devn* 4D 12
Withyham. *E Sus* 2F 27
Withypool. *Som* 3B 20
Witley. *Surr* 1A 26
Witnesham. *Suff* 5D 66
Witney. *Oxon* 4B 50
Wittering. *Pet* 5H 75
Wittersham. *Kent* 3D 28
Witton. *Norf* 5F 79
Witton. *Worc* 4D 60
Witton Bridge. *Norf* 2F 79
Witton Gilbert. *Dur* 5F 115
Witton-le-Wear. *Dur* 1E 105
Witton Park. *Dur* 1E 105
Wiveliscombe. *Som* 4D 20
Wivelrod. *Hants* 3E 25
Wivelsfield. *E Sus* 3E 27
Wivelsfield Green. *E Sus* 4E 27
Wivenhoe. *Essx* 3D 54
Wiveton. *Norf* 1C 78
Wix. *Essx* 3E 55
Wixford. *Warw* 5E 61
Wixhill. *Shrp* 3H 71
Wixoe. *Suff* 1H 53
Woburn. *C Beds* 2H 51
Woburn Sands. *Mil* 2H 51
Woking. *Surr* 5B 38
Wokingham. *Wok* 5G 37
Wolborough. *Devn* 5B 12
Woldingham. *Surr* 5E 39
Wold Newton. *E Yor* 2E 101
Wold Newton. *NE Lin* 1B 88
Wolferlow. *Here* 4A 60
Wolferton. *Norf* 3F 77
Wolfhill. *Per* 5A 144
Wolf's Castle. *Pemb* 2D 42
Wolfsdale. *Pemb* 2D 42
Wolgarston. *Staf* 4D 72
Wollaston. *Nptn* 4G 63
Wollaston. *Shrp* 4F 71
Wollaston. *W Mid* 2C 60
Wollaton. *Nott* 1C 74
Wollerton. *Shrp* 2A 72
Wollescote. *W Mid* 2D 60
Wolseley Bridge. *Staf* 3E 73
Wolsingham. *Dur* 1D 105
Wolstanton. *Staf* 1C 72
Wolston. *Warw* 3B 62
Wolsty. *Cumb* 4C 112
Wolterton. *Norf* 2D 78
Wolvercote. *Oxon* 5C 50
Wolverhampton. *W Mid* 1D 60 & 213
Wolverley. *Shrp* 2G 71
Wolverley. *Worc* 3C 60
Wolverton. *Hants* 1D 24
Wolverton. *Mil* 1G 51
Wolverton. *Warw* 4G 61
Wolverton. *Wilts* 3C 22
Wolverton Common. *Hants* 1D 24
Wolvesnewton. *Mon* 2H 33
Wolvey. *Warw* 2B 62
Wolvey Heath. *Warw* 2B 62
Wolviston. *Stoc T* 2B 106
Womaston. *Powy* 4E 59
Wombleton. *N Yor* 1A 100
Wombourne. *Staf* 1C 60
Wombwell. *S Yor* 4D 93
Womenswold. *Kent* 5G 41
Womersley. *N Yor* 3F 93
Wonersh. *Surr* 1B 26
Wonson. *Devn* 4G 11
Wonston. *Dors* 2C 14
Wonston. *Hants* 3C 24
Wooburn. *Buck* 2A 38
Wooburn Green. *Buck* 2A 38
Wood. *Pemb* 2C 42
Woodacott. *Devn* 2D 11
Woodale. *N Yor* 2C 98
Woodall. *S Yor* 2B 86
Woodbank. *Ches W* 3F 83
Woodbastwick. *Norf* 4F 79
Woodbeck. *Notts* 3E 87
Woodborough. *Notts* 1D 74
Woodborough. *Wilts* 1G 23
Woodbridge. *Devn* 3E 13
Woodbridge. *Dors* 1C 14
Woodbridge. *Suff* 1F 55
Wood Burcote. *Nptn* 1E 51
Woodbury. *Devn* 4D 12
Woodbury Salterton. *Devn* 4D 12
Woodchester. *Glos* 5D 48
Woodchurch. *Kent* 2D 28
Woodchurch. *Mers* 2E 83
Woodcock Heath. *Staf* 3E 73
Woodcombe. *Som* 2C 20
Woodcote. *Oxon* 3E 37
Woodcote Green. *Worc* 3D 60
Woodcott. *Hants* 1C 24
Woodcroft. *Glos* 2A 34
Woodcutts. *Dors* 1E 15
Wood Dalling. *Norf* 3C 78
Woodditton. *Cambs* 5F 65
Woodeaton. *Oxon* 4D 50
Wood Eaton. *Staf* 4C 72
Wood End. *Bed* 4H 63
Woodend. *Cumb* 5C 102
Wood End. *Herts* 3D 52
Woodend. *Nptn* 1E 50
Woodend. *Staf* 3F 73
Wood End. *Warw* 2G 61 (nr. Bedworth)
Wood End. *Warw* 1G 61 (nr. Dordon)
Wood End. *Warw* 3F 61 (nr. Tanworth-in-Arden)
Woodend. *W Sus* 2G 17
Wood Enderby. *Linc* 4B 88
Woodend Green. *Essx* 3F 53
Woodfalls. *Wilts* 4G 23
Woodfield. *Oxon* 3D 50
Woodfields. *Lanc* 1E 91
Woodford. *Corn* 1C 10
Woodford. *Devn* 3D 9
Woodford. *Glos* 2B 34
Woodford. *G Lon* 1E 39
Woodford. *G Man* 2C 84
Woodford. *Nptn* 3G 63
Woodford. *Plym* 3B 8
Woodford Green. *G Lon* 1F 39
Woodford Halse. *Nptn* 5C 62
Woodgate. *Norf* 4C 78
Woodgate. *W Mid* 2D 61
Woodgate. *W Sus* 5A 26
Woodgate. *Worc* 4D 60
Wood Green. *G Lon* 1D 39
Woodgreen. *Hants* 1G 15
Woodgreen. *Oxon* 4B 50
Wood Hall. *E Yor* 1E 95
Woodhall. *Inv* 2E 127
Woodhall. *Linc* 4B 88
Woodhall. *N Yor* 5C 104
Woodhall Spa. *Linc* 4A 88
Woodham. *Surr* 4B 38
Woodham Ferrers. *Essx* 1B 40
Woodham Mortimer. *Essx* 5B 54
Woodham Walter. *Essx* 5B 54
Woodhaven. *Fife* 1G 137
Wood Hayes. *W Mid* 5D 72
Woodhead. *Abers* 2G 161 (nr. Fraserburgh)
Woodhead. *Abers* 5E 161 (nr. Fyvie)
Woodhill. *N Som* 4H 33
Woodhill. *Shrp* 2B 60
Woodhill. *Som* 4G 21
Woodhorn. *Nmbd* 1G 115
Woodhouse. *Leics* 4C 74
Woodhouse. *S Yor* 2B 86
Woodhouse. *W Yor* 1C 92 (nr. Leeds)
Woodhouse. *W Yor* 2D 93 (nr. Normanton)
Woodhouse Eaves. *Leics* 4C 74
Woodhouses. *Ches W* 3H 83
Woodhouses. *G Man* 4H 91 (nr. Failsworth)
Woodhouses. *G Man* 1B 84 (nr. Sale)
Woodhouses. *Staf* 4F 73
Woodhuish. *Devn* 3F 9
Woodhurst. *Cambs* 3C 64
Woodingdean. *Brig* 5E 27
Woodland. *Devn* 2D 9
Woodland. *Dur* 2D 104
Woodland Head. *Devn* 3A 12
Woodlands. *Abers* 4E 153
Woodlands. *Dors* 2F 15
Woodlands. *Hants* 1B 16
Woodlands. *Kent* 4G 39
Woodlands. *N Yor* 4F 99
Woodlands. *S Yor* 4F 93
Woodlands Park. *Wind* 4G 37
Woodlands St Mary. *W Ber* 4B 36
Woodlane. *Shrp* 3A 72
Woodlane. *Staf* 3F 73
Woodleigh. *Devn* 4D 8
Woodlesford. *W Yor* 2D 92
Woodley. *G Man* 1D 84
Woodley. *Wok* 4F 37
Woodmancote. *Glos* 3E 49 (nr. Cheltenham)
Woodmancote. *Glos* 5F 49 (nr. Cirencester)
Woodmancote. *W Sus* 2F 17 (nr. Chichester)
Woodmancote. *W Sus* 4D 26 (nr. Henfield)
Woodmancote. *Worc* 1E 49
Woodmancott. *Hants* 2D 24
Woodmansey. *E Yor* 1D 94
Woodmansgreen. *W Sus* 4G 25
Woodmansterne. *Surr* 5D 39
Woodmanton. *Devn* 4D 12
Woodmill. *Staf* 3F 73
Woodminton. *Wilts* 4F 23
Woodnesborough. *Kent* 5H 41
Woodnewton. *Nptn* 1H 63
Woodnook. *Linc* 2G 75
Wood Norton. *Norf* 3C 78
Woodplumpton. *Lanc* 1D 90
Woodrising. *Norf* 5B 78
Woodrow. *Cumb* 5D 112
Woodrow. *Dors* 1C 14 (nr. Fifehead Neville)
Woodrow. *Dors* 2C 14 (nr. Hazelbury Bryan)
Wood Row. *W Yor* 2D 93
Woods Eaves. *Here* 1F 47
Woodseaves. *Shrp* 2A 72
Woodseaves. *Staf* 3B 72
Woodsend. *Wilts* 4H 35
Woodsetts. *S Yor* 2C 86
Woodsford. *Dors* 3C 14
Wood's Green. *E Sus* 2H 27
Woodshaw. *Wilts* 3F 35
Woodside. *Aber* 3G 153
Woodside. *Brac* 3A 38
Woodside. *Derbs* 1A 74
Woodside. *Dum* 2B 112
Woodside. *Dur* 2E 105
Woodside. *Fife* 3G 137
Woodside. *Herts* 5C 52
Woodside. *Per* 5B 144
Wood Stanway. *Glos* 2F 49
Woodstock. *Oxon* 4C 50
Woodstock Slop. *Pemb* 2E 43
Woodston. *Pet* 1A 64
Wood Street. *Norf* 3F 79
Wood Street Village. *Surr* 5A 38
Woodthorpe. *Derbs* 3B 86
Woodthorpe. *Leics* 4C 74
Woodthorpe. *Linc* 2D 88
Woodthorpe. *York* 5H 99
Woodton. *Norf* 1E 67
Woodtown. *Devn* 4E 19 (nr. Bideford)
Woodtown. *Devn* 4E 19 (nr. Littleham)
Woodvale. *Mers* 3B 90
Woodville. *Derbs* 4H 73
Woodwalton. *Cambs* 2B 64
Woodwick. *Orkn* 5C 172
Woodyates. *Dors* 1F 15
Woody Bay. *Devn* 2G 19
Woofferton. *Shrp* 4H 59
Wookey. *Som* 2A 22
Wookey Hole. *Som* 2A 22
Wool. *Dors* 4D 14
Woolacombe. *Devn* 2E 19
Woolage Green. *Kent* 1G 29
Woolage Village. *Kent* 5G 41
Woolaston. *Glos* 2A 34
Woolavington. *Som* 2G 21
Woolbeding. *W Sus* 4G 25
Woolcotts. *Som* 3C 20
Wooldale. *W Yor* 4B 92
Wooler. *Nmbd* 2D 121
Woolfardisworthy. *Devn* 4D 18 (nr. Bideford)
Woolfardisworthy. *Devn* 2B 12 (nr. Crediton)
Woolfords. *S Lan* 4D 128
Woolgarston. *Dors* 4E 15
Woolhampton. *W Ber* 5D 36
Woolhope. *Here* 2B 48
Woolland. *Dors* 2C 14
Woollard. *Bath* 5B 34
Woolley. *Bath* 5C 34
Woolley. *Cambs* 3A 64
Woolley. *Corn* 1C 10
Woolley. *Derbs* 4A 86
Woolley. *W Yor* 3D 92
Woolley Green. *Wilts* 5D 34
Woolmere Green. *Worc* 4D 60
Woolmer Green. *Herts* 4C 52
Woolminstone. *Som* 2H 13
Woolpit. *Suff* 4B 66
Woolridge. *Glos* 3D 48
Woolscott. *Warw* 4B 62
Woolsery. *Devn* 4D 18
Woolsington. *Tyne* 3E 115
Woolstaston. *Shrp* 1G 59
Woolsthorpe By Belvoir. *Linc* 2F 75
Woolsthorpe-by-Colsterworth. *Linc* 3G 75
Woolston. *Devn* 4D 8
Woolston. *Shrp* 2G 59 (nr. Church Stretton)
Woolston. *Shrp* 3F 71 (nr. Oswestry)
Woolston. *Som* 4B 22
Woolston. *Sotn* 1C 16
Woolston. *Warr* 1A 84
Woolstone. *Glos* 2E 49
Woolstone. *Oxon* 3A 36
Woolston Green. *Devn* 2D 9
Woolton. *Mers* 2G 83
Woolton Hill. *Hants* 5C 36
Woolverstone. *Suff* 2E 55
Woolverton. *Som* 1C 22
Woolwell. *Devn* 2B 8
Woolwich. *G Lon* 3F 39
Woonton. *Here* 5F 59 (nr. Kington)
Woonton. *Here* 4H 59 (nr. Leominster)
Wooperton. *Nmbd* 2E 121
Woore. *Shrp* 1B 72
Wooth. *Dors* 3H 13
Wooton. *Shrp* 2B 60
Wootton. *Bed* 1A 52
Wootton. *Hants* 3H 15
Wootton. *IOW* 3D 16
Wootton. *Kent* 1G 29
Wootton. *Nptn* 5E 63
Wootton. *N Lin* 3D 94
Wootton. *Oxon* 5C 50 (nr. Abingdon)
Wootton. *Oxon* 4C 50 (nr. Woodstock)
Wootton. *Shrp* 3G 59 (nr. Ludlow)
Wootton. *Shrp* 3F 71 (nr. Oswestry)
Wootton. *Staf* 3C 72 (nr. Eccleshall)
Wootton. *Staf* 1F 73 (nr. Ellastone)
Wootton Bridge. *IOW* 3D 16
Wootton Common. *IOW* 3D 16
Wootton Courtenay. *Som* 2C 20
Wootton Fitzpaine. *Dors* 3G 13
Wootton Rivers. *Wilts* 5G 35
Wootton St Lawrence. *Hants* 1D 24
Wootton Wawen. *Warw* 4F 61
Worcester. *Worc* 5C 60 & 214
Worcester Park. *G Lon* 4D 38
Wordsley. *W Mid* 2C 60
Worfield. *Shrp* 1B 60
Work. *Orkn* 6D 172
Workhouse Green. *Suff* 2C 54
Workington. *Cumb* 2A 102
Worksop. *Notts* 3C 86
Worlaby. *N Lin* 3D 94
Worlds End. *Hants* 1E 17
Worldsend. *Shrp* 1G 59
World's End. *W Ber* 4C 36
Worlds End. *W Mid* 2F 61
World's End. *W Sus* 4E 27
Worle. *N Som* 5G 33
Worleston. *Ches E* 5A 84
Worley. *Glos* 2D 34
Worlingham. *Suff* 1G 67
Worlington. *Suff* 3F 65
Worlingworth. *Suff* 4E 67
Wormbridge. *Here* 2H 47
Wormegay. *Norf* 4F 77
Wormelow Tump. *Here* 2H 47
Wormhill. *Derbs* 3F 85
Wormingford. *Essx* 2C 54
Worminghall. *Buck* 5E 51
Wormington. *Glos* 2F 49
Worminster. *Som* 2A 22
Wormit. *Fife* 1F 137
Wormleighton. *Warw* 5B 62
Wormley. *Herts* 5D 52
Wormley. *Surr* 2A 26
Wormshill. *Kent* 5C 40
Wormsley. *Here* 1H 47
Worplesdon. *Surr* 5A 38
Worrall. *S Yor* 1H 85
Worsbrough. *S Yor* 4D 92
Worsley. *G Man* 4F 91
Worstead. *Norf* 3F 79
Worsthorne. *Lanc* 1G 91
Worston. *Lanc* 5G 97
Worth. *Kent* 5H 41
Worth. *W Sus* 2E 27
Wortham. *Suff* 3C 66
Worthen. *Shrp* 5F 71
Worthenbury. *Wrex* 1G 71
Worthing. *Norf* 4B 78
Worthing. *W Sus* 5C 26
Worthington. *Leics* 3B 74
Worth Matravers. *Dors* 5E 15
Worting. *Hants* 1E 24
Wortley. *Glos* 2C 34
Wortley. *S Yor* 1H 85
Wortley. *W Yor* 1C 92
Worton. *N Yor* 5C 104
Worton. *Wilts* 1E 23
Wortwell. *Norf* 2E 67
Wotherton. *Shrp* 5E 71
Wothorpe. *Nptn* 5H 75
Wotter. *Devn* 2B 8
Wotton. *Glos* 4D 48
Wotton. *Surr* 1C 26
Wotton-under-Edge. *Glos* 2C 34
Wotton Underwood. *Buck* 4E 51
Wouldham. *Kent* 4B 40
Wrabness. *Essx* 2E 55
Wrafton. *Devn* 3E 19
Wragby. *Linc* 3A 88
Wragby. *W Yor* 3E 93
Wramplingham. *Norf* 5D 78
Wrangbrook. *W Yor* 3E 93
Wrangle. *Linc* 5D 88
Wrangle Lowgate. *Linc* 5D 88
Wrangway. *Som* 1E 13
Wrantage. *Som* 4G 21
Wrawby. *N Lin* 4D 94
Wraxall. *N Som* 4H 33
Wraxall. *Som* 3B 22
Wray. *Lanc* 3F 97
Wraysbury. *Wind* 3B 38
Wrayton. *Lanc* 2F 97
Wrea Green. *Lanc* 1B 90
Wreay. *Cumb* 5F 113 (nr. Carlisle)
Wreay. *Cumb* 2F 103 (nr. Penrith)
Wrecclesham. *Surr* 2G 25
Wrecsam. *Wrex* 5F 83 & **Wrexham** 214
Wrekenton. *Tyne* 4F 115
Wrelton. *N Yor* 1B 100
Wrenbury. *Ches E* 1H 71
Wreningham. *Norf* 1D 66
Wrentham. *Suff* 2G 67
Wrenthorpe. *W Yor* 2D 92
Wrentnall. *Shrp* 5G 71
Wressle. *E Yor* 1H 93
Wressle. *N Lin* 4C 94
Wrestlingworth. *C Beds* 1C 52
Wretton. *Norf* 1F 65
Wrexham. *Wrex* 5F 83 & 214

Wrexham Industrial Estate.	Wyke Regis. *Dors* 5B **14**	Yarhampton. *Worc* 4B **60**	Yeavering. *Nmbd* 1D **120**	Yockenthwaite. *N Yor* 2B **98**
Wrex 1F **71**	Wyke, The. *Shrp* 5B **72**	Yarkhill. *Here* 1B **48**	Yedingham. *N Yor* 2C **100**	Yockleton. *Shrp* 4G **71**
Wreyland. *Devn* 4A **12**	Wykey. *Shrp* 3F **71**	Yarlet. *Staf* 3D **72**	Yeldersley Hollies.	Yokefleet. *E Yor* 2B **94**
Wrickton. *Shrp* 2A **60**	Wykin. *Leics* 1B **62**	Yarley. *Som* 2A **22**	*Derbs* 1G **73**	Yoker. *Glas* 3G **127**
Wrightlington Bar. *Lanc* 3D **90**	Wylam. *Nmbd* 3E **115**	Yarlington. *Som* 4B **22**	Yelford. *Oxon* 5B **50**	Yonder Bognie. *Abers* 4C **160**
Wright's Green. *Essx* 4F **53**	Wylde Green. *W Mid* 1F **61**	Yarm. *Stoc T* 3B **106**	Yelland. *Devn* 3E **19**	Yonderton. *Abers* 5G **161**
Wrinehill. *Staf* 1B **72**	Wylye. *Wilts* 3F **23**	Yarmouth. *IOW* 4B **16**	Yelling. *Cambs* 4B **64**	**York.** *York* .....4A **100** & **214**
Wrington. *N Som* 5H **33**	Wymering. *Port* 2E **17**	Yarnbrook. *Wilts* 1D **22**	Yelsted. *Kent* 4C **40**	Yorkletts. *Kent* 4E **41**
Writtle. *Essx* 5G **53**	Wymeswold. *Leics* 3D **74**	Yarnfield. *Staf* 2C **72**	Yelvertoft. *Nptn* 3C **62**	Yorkley. *Glos* 5B **48**
Wrockwardine. *Telf* 4A **72**	Wymington. *Bed* 4G **63**	Yarnscombe. *Devn* 4F **19**	Yelverton. *Devn* 2B **8**	Yorkshire Dales. *N Yor* 2H **97**
Wroot. *N Lin* 4H **93**	Wymondham. *Leics* 4F **75**	Yarnton. *Oxon* 4C **50**	Yelverton. *Norf* 5E **79**	Yorton. *Shrp* 3H **71**
Wrotham. *Kent* 5H **39**	**Wymondham.** *Norf* 5D **78**	Yarpole. *Here* 4G **59**	Yenston. *Som* 4C **22**	Yorton Heath. *Shrp* 3H **71**
Wrotham Heath. *Kent* 5H **39**	Wyndham. *B'end* 2C **32**	Yarrow. *Nmbd* 1A **114**	Yeoford. *Devn* 3A **12**	Youlgreave. *Derbs* 4G **85**
Wroughton. *Swin* 3G **35**	Wynford Eagle. *Dors* 3A **14**	Yarrow. *Bord* 2F **119**	Yeolmbridge. *Corn* 4D **10**	Youlthorpe. *E Yor* 4B **100**
Wroxall. *IOW* 4D **16**	Wyng. *Orkn* 8C **172**	Yarrow. *Som* 2G **21**	Yeo Mill. *Devn* 4B **20**	Youlton. *N Yor* 3G **99**
Wroxall. *Warw* 3G **61**	Wynyard Village.	Yarrow Feus. *Bord* 2F **119**	**Yeovil.** *Som* 1A **14**	Young's End. *Essx* 4H **53**
Wroxeter. *Shrp* 5H **71**	*Stoc T* 2B **106**	Yarrow Ford. *Bord* 1G **119**	Yeovil Marsh. *Som* 1A **14**	Young Wood. *Linc* 3A **88**
Wroxham. *Norf* 4F **79**	Wyre Piddle. *Worc* 1E **49**	Yarsop. *Here* 1H **47**	Yeovilton. *Som* 4A **22**	Yoxall. *Staf* 4F **73**
Wroxton. *Oxon* 1C **50**	Wysall. *Notts* 3D **74**	Yarwell. *Nptn* 1H **63**	Yerbeston. *Pemb* 4E **43**	Yoxford. *Suff* 4F **67**
Wyaston. *Derbs* 1F **73**	Wyson. *Here* 4H **59**	Yate. *S Glo* 3C **34**	Yesnaby. *Orkn* 6B **172**	Yr Hob. *Flin* 5F **83**
Wyatt's Green. *Essx* 1G **39**	Wythall. *Worc* 3E **61**	**Yateley.** *Hants* 5G **37**	Yetlington. *Nmbd* 4E **121**	Y Rhws. *V Glam* 5D **32**
Wybers Wood. *NE Lin* 4F **95**	Wytham. *Oxon* 5C **50**	Yatesbury. *Wilts* 4F **35**	Yetminster. *Dors* 1A **14**	Yr Wyddgrug. *Flin* 4E **83**
Wyberton. *Linc* 1C **76**	Wythenshawe. *G Man* 2C **84**	Yattendon. *W Ber* 4D **36**	Yett. *N Lan* 4A **128**	Ysbyty Cynfyn. *Cdgn* 3G **57**
Wyboston. *Bed* 5A **64**	Wythop Mill. *Cumb* 2C **102**	Yatton. *Here* 4G **59**	Yett. *S Ayr* 2D **116**	Ysbyty Ifan. *Cnwy* 1H **69**
Wybunbury. *Ches E* 1A **72**	Wyton. *Cambs* 3B **64**	(nr. Leominster)	Yettington. *Devn* 4D **12**	Ysbyty Ystwyth. *Cdgn* 3G **57**
Wychbold. *Worc* 4D **60**	Wyton. *E Yor* 1E **95**	Yatton. *Here* 2B **48**	Yetts o' Muckhart.	Ysceifiog. *Flin* 3D **82**
Wych Cross. *E Sus* 2F **27**	Wyverstone. *Suff* 4C **66**	(nr. Ross-on-Wye)	*Clac* 3C **136**	Yspitty. *Carm* 3E **31**
Wychnor. *Staf* 4F **73**	Wyverstone Street. *Suff* 4C **66**	Yatton. *N Som* 5H **33**	Y Fali. *IOA* 3B **80**	Ystalyfera. *Neat* 5A **46**
Wychnor Bridges. *Staf* 4F **73**	Wyville. *Linc* 3F **75**	Yatton Keynell. *Wilts* 4D **34**	Y Felinheli. *Gwyn* 4E **81**	Ystrad. *Rhon* 2C **32**
Wyck. *Hants* 3F **25**	Wyvis Lodge. *High* 1G **157**	Yaverland. *IOW* 4E **16**	Y Ferwig. *Cdgn* 1B **44**	Ystrad Aeron. *Cdgn* 5E **57**
Wyck Hill. *Glos* 3G **49**		Yawl. *Devn* 3G **13**	**Y Fflint.** *Flin* 3E **83**	Ystradfellte. *Powy* 4C **46**
Wyck Rissington. *Glos* 3G **49**	**Y**	Yaxham. *Norf* 4C **78**	Y Ffor. *Gwyn* 2C **68**	Ystradffin. *Carm* 1A **46**
Wycliffe. *Dur* 3E **105**	Yaddlethorpe. *N Lin* 4B **94**	Yaxley. *Cambs* 1A **64**	Y Fron. *Gwyn* 5E **81**	Ystradgynlais. *Powy* 4A **46**
Wycombe Marsh. *Buck* 2G **37**	Yafford. *IOW* 4C **16**	Yaxley. *Suff* 3D **66**	Y Gelli Gandryll. *Powy* 1F **47**	Ystradmeurig. *Cdgn* 4G **57**
Wyddial. *Herts* 2D **52**	Yafforth. *N Yor* 5A **106**	Yazor. *Here* 1H **47**	Yielden. *Bed* 4H **63**	Ystrad Mynach. *Cphy* 2E **33**
Wye. *Kent* 1E **29**	Yalding. *Kent* 5A **40**	Y Bala. *Gwyn* 2B **70**	Yieldshields. *S Lan* 4B **128**	Ystradowen. *Carm* 4A **46**
Wyesham. *Mon* 4A **48**	Yanley. *N Som* 5A **34**	Y Bont-Faen. *V Glam* 4C **32**	Yiewsley. *G Lon* 2B **38**	Ystradowen. *V Glam* 4D **32**
Wyfold Grange. *Oxon* 3E **37**	Yanwath. *Cumb* 2G **103**	Y Clun. *Neat* 5B **46**	Yinstay. *Orkn* 6E **172**	Ystumtuen. *Cdgn* 3G **57**
Wyfordby. *Leics* 4E **75**	Yanworth. *Glos* 4F **49**	Y Dref. *Gwyn* 2D **69**	Ynysboeth. *Rhon* 2D **32**	Ythanbank. *Abers* 5G **161**
Wyke. *Devn* 3B **12**	Yapham. *E Yor* 4B **100**	**Y Drenewydd.** *Powy* 1D **58**	Ynysddu. *Cphy* 2E **33**	Ythanwells. *Abers* 5D **160**
Wyke. *Dors* 4C **22**	Yapton. *W Sus* 5A **26**	Yeading. *G Lon* 2C **38**	Ynysforgan. *Swan* 3F **31**	Y Trallwng. *Powy* 5E **70**
Wyke. *Shrp* 5A **72**	Yarburgh. *Linc* 1C **88**	Yeadon. *W Yor* 5E **98**	Ynyshir. *Rhon* 2D **32**	Y Tymbl. *Carm* 4F **45**
Wyke. *Surr* 5A **38**	Yarcombe. *Devn* 2F **13**	Yealand Conyers. *Lanc* 2E **97**	Ynyslas. *Cdgn* 1F **57**	Y Waun. *Wrex* 2E **71**
Wyke. *W Yor* 2B **92**	Yardley. *W Mid* 2F **61**	Yealand Redmayne. *Lanc* 2E **97**	Ynysmaerdy. *Rhon* 3D **32**	
Wyke Champflower. *Som* 3B **22**	Yardley Gobion. *Nptn* 1F **51**	Yealand Storrs. *Lanc* 2D **97**	Ynysmeudwy. *Neat* 5H **45**	**Z**
Wykeham. *Linc* 3B **76**	Yardley Hastings.	Yealmpton. *Devn* 3B **8**	Ynystawe. *Swan* 5G **45**	
Wykeham. *N Yor* 2C **100**	*Nptn* 5F **63**	Yearby. *Red C* 2D **106**	Ynyswen. *Powy* 4B **46**	Zeal Monachorum. *Devn* 2H **11**
(nr. Malton)	Yardley Wood. *W Mid* 2F **61**	Yearngill. *Cumb* 5C **112**	Ynys-wen. *Rhon* 2C **32**	Zeals. *Wilts* 3C **22**
Wykeham. *N Yor* 1D **100**	Yardro. *Powy* 5E **58**	Yearsett. *Here* 5B **60**	Ynys y Barri. *V Glam* 5E **32**	Zelah. *Corn* 3C **6**
(nr. Scarborough)		Yearsley. *N Yor* 2H **99**	Ynysybwl. *Rhon* 2D **32**	Zennor. *Corn* 3B **4**
Wyken. *Shrp* 1B **60**		Yeaton. *Shrp* 4G **71**	Ynysymaerdy. *Neat* 3G **31**	Zouch. *Notts* 3C **74**
Wyken. *W Mid* 2A **62**		Yeaveley. *Derbs* 1F **73**		

Safety Camera Information

More than 4000 fixed and long term road works camera locations are shown, including Gatso, Truvelo, SPECS Monitron and Redspeed camera types. Mobile camera sites and cameras on roads not included in the map specification are not shown. Camera locations are shown as accurately as the scale allows. Symbols do not indicate camera direction. Two or more cameras in close proximity are represented by a multiple camera symbol. Safety camera locations are publicised by the Safer Roads Partnership who operate them in order to encourage drivers to comply with speed limits at these sites. It is the driver's absolute responsibility to be aware of, and adhere to, speed limits at all times. Data accurate at time of printing.
Supplied by PocketGPSWorld.com

Single Camera Locations

This symbol shows single camera locations with their speed limit

Multiple Camera Locations

This symbol is used where multiple cameras are sited in close proximity to each other with the same speed limit

Variable MPH

Single camera    Multiple cameras

These symbols are used where variable speed limits are in force

(1) A strict alphabetical order is used e.g. Benmore Botanic Gdn. follows Ben Macdui but precedes Ben Nevis.

(2) Entries shown without a main map index reference have the name of the appropriate Town Plan and its page number; e.g. Ashmolean Mus. (OX1 2PH) . . . . **Oxford 207**
The Town Plan title is not given when this is included in the name of the Place of Interest.

(3) Entries in italics are not named on the map but are shown with a symbol only.
Entries in italics and enclosed in brackets are not shown on the map.
Where this occurs the nearest town or village may also be given, unless that name is already included in the name of the Place of Interest.

SAT NAV POSTCODES

Postcodes (in brackets) are included as a navigation aid to assist Sat Nav users and are supplied on this basis. It should be noted that postcodes have been selected by their proximity to the Place of Interest and that they may not form part of the actual postal address.
Drivers should follow the Tourist Brown Signs when available.

ABBREVIATIONS USED IN THIS INDEX

Garden : Gdn.
Gardens : Gdns.
Museum : Mus.
National : Nat
Park : Pk.

INDEX

A

Abbeydale Industrial Hamlet (S7 2QW) 2H **85**
Abbey House Mus. (LS5 3EH) 1C **92**
Abbot Hall Art Gallery, Kendal (LA9 5AL) 5G 103
Abbotsbury Sub Tropical Gdns. (DT3 4LA) 4A **14**
Abbotsbury Swannery (DT3 4JG) 4A **14**
Abbotsford (TD6 9BQ) 1H **119**
Aberdeen Maritime Mus. (AB11 5BY) **187**
Aberdour Castle (KY3 0XA) 1E 129
Aberdulais Falls (SA10 8EU) 5A **46**
Aberglasney Gdns. (SA32 8QH) 3F **45**
Abernethy Round Tower (PH2 9RT) 2D **136**
Aberystwyth Castle (SY23 1DZ) **187**
Acorn Bank Gdn. & Watermill (CA10 1SP) . . . 2H **103**
Acton Burnell Castle (SY5 7PF) 5H 71
Acton Scott Historic Working Farm (SY6 6QN) 2G **59**
Adlington Hall (SK10 4LF) 2D **84**
Africa Alive! (NR33 7TF) 2H **67**
Aintree Racecourse (L9 5AS) 1F **83**
Aira Force (CA11 0JX) 2F **103**
A la Ronde (EX8 5BD) 4D **12**
Alderley Edge (SK10 4UB) 3C **84**
Alfriston Clergy House (BN26 5TL) 5G **27**
Alloa Tower (FK10 1PP) 4A **136**
Alnwick Castle (NE66 1NQ) 3F 121
Alnwick Gdn. (NE66 1YU) 3F 121
Althorp (NN7 4HQ) 4D **62**
Alton Towers (ST10 4DB) 1E **73**
Amberley Mus. & Heritage Cen. (BN18 9LT) . . . 4B **26**
American Mus. in Britain (BA2 7BD) 5C **34**
Angel of the North (NE9 6PG) 4F **115**
Anglesey Abbey & Lode Mill (CB25 9EJ) 4E **65**
Angus Folk Mus. (DD8 1RT) 4C **144**
Animalarium at Borth (SY24 5NA) 2F **57**
Anne Hathaway's Cottage (CV37 9HH) 5F **61**
Antonine Wall (FK4 2AA) 2B **128**
Antony (PL11 2QA) 3A **8**
Appuldurcombe House (PO38 3EW) 4D **16**
Arbeia Roman Fort & Mus. (NE33 2BB) 3G **115**
Arbroath Abbey (DD11 1JQ) 4F **145**
Arbury Hall (CV10 7PT) 2H **61**
Arbuthnott House Gdn. (AB30 1PA) 1G **145**
Ardkinglas Woodland Gdns. (PA26 8BG) 2A **134**
Ardnamurchan Point (PH36 4LN) 2F **139**
Arduaine Gdn. (PA34 4XQ) 2E **133**
Ardwell Gdns. (DG9 9LY) 5G **109**
Argyll's Lodging (FK8 1EG) . . . . **Stirling 211**
Arley Hall & Gdns. (CW9 6NA) 2A **84**
Arlington Court (EX31 4LP) 3G **19**
Arlington Row (GL7 5NJ) 5G **49**
Armadale Castle Gdns. (IV45 8RS) 3E **147**
Arniston House (EH23 4RY) 4G **129**
Arundel Castle (BN18 9AB) 5B 26
Arundel Wetland Centre (BN18 9PB) 5B **26**
Ascot Racecourse (SL5 7JX) 4A **38**
Ascott (LU7 0PT) 3G **51**
Ashby-de-la-Zouch Castle (LE65 1BR) 4A 74
Ashdown Forest (TN7 4EU) 2F **27**
Ashdown House (RG17 8RE) 3A **36**
Ashmolean Mus. (OX1 2PH) . . . . **Oxford 207**
Ashridge Estate (HP4 1LT) 4H **51**
Astley Hall Mus. & Art Gallery (PR7 1NP) 3D **90**
Athelhampton House (DT2 7LG) 3C **14**
Attingham Pk. (SY4 4TP) 5H **71**
Auchingarrich Wildlife Centre (PH6 2JE) 2G **135**
Auckland Castle, Bishop Auckland (DL14 7NP) 1F 105
Audley End House & Gdns. (CB11 4JF) 2F **53**
Avebury Stone Circle (SN8 1RE) 4G **35**
Avoncroft Mus. of Historic Buildings (B60 4JR) 4D **60**
Avon Valley Adventure & Wildlife Pk. (BS31 1TP) 5B **34**
Avon Valley Railway (BS30 6HD) 4B **34**
Aydon Castle (NE45 5PJ) 3C 114
Ayr Racecourse (KA8 0JE) **187**
Ayscoughfee Hall Mus. & Gdns. (PE11 2RA) . . . 3B **76**
Aysgarth Falls (DL8 3SR) 1C **98**
Ayton Castle (TD14 5RD) 3F 131

B

Bachelors' Club (KA5 5RB) 2D **116**
Baconsthorpe Castle (NR25 6PS) 2D 78
Baddesley Clinton (B93 0DQ) 3F **61**
Bala Lake Railway (LL23 7DD) 2A **70**
Ballindalloch Castle (AB37 9AX) 5F **159**
Balmacara Estate (IV40 8DN) 1F **147**
Balmoral Castle (AB35 5TB) 4G **151**
Balvaird Castle (PH2 9PY) 2D **136**
Balvenie Castle (AB55 4DH) 4H **159**
Bamburgh Castle (NE69 7DF) 1F 121
Bangor Cathedral (LL57 1DN) 3E **81**
Banham Zoo (NR16 2HE) 2C **66**
Bannockburn Battle Site (FK7 0PL) 4G **135**
Barbara Hepworth Mus. & Sculpture Gdn. (TR26 1AD) 2C **4**
Barnard Castle (DL12 8PR) 3D 104
Barnsdale Gdns. (LE15 8AH) 4G **75**
Barrington Court (TA19 0NQ) 1G **13**
Basildon Pk. (RG8 9NR) 4E **36**
Basing House (RG24 7HB) 1E **25**
Basingwerk Abbey (CH8 7GH) 3D **82**
Bateman's (TN19 7DS) 3A **28**
Bath Abbey (BA1 1LT) **187**
Bath Assembly Rooms & Fashion Mus. (BA1 2QH) **187**
Bath Roman Baths & Pump Room (BA1 1LZ) **187**
Battle Abbey (TN33 0AD) 4B **28**
Battlefield Line Railway (CV13 0BS) 5A **74**
Battle of Britain Memorial Flight Visitors Centre, RAF Coningsby (LN4 4SY) 5B 88
Battle of Hastings Site (TN33 0AD) 4B **28**
Bayham Abbey (TN3 8BE) 2H **27**
Beachy Head (BN20 7YA) 5G **27**
Beamish (DH9 0RG) 4F **115**
Beatles Story, The (L3 4AD) . . . . **Liverpool 200**
Beatrix Potter's House, Hill Top (LA22 0LF) . . . 5E **103**
Beaulieu Abbey (SO42 7ZN) 2B **16**
Beauly Priory (IV4 7BL) 4H **157**
Beaumaris Castle (LL58 8AP) 3F 81
Beck Isle Mus. of Rural Life (YO18 8DU) 1B **100**
Bedgebury Nat. Pinetum (TN17 2SL) 2B **28**
Bedruthan Steps (PL27 7UW) 2C **6**
Beeston Castle & Woodland Pk. (CW6 9TX) . . . 5H 83
Bekonscot Model Village & Railway (HP9 2PL) 1A **38**
Belgrave Hall Mus. & Gdns. (LE4 5PE) 5C **74**
Belmont House & Gdns. (ME13 0HH) 5D **40**
Belsay Hall, Castle & Gdns. (NE20 0DX) 2D **115**
Belton House (NG32 2LS) 2G **75**
Belvoir Castle (NG32 1PD) 2F 75
Beningbrough Hall & Gdns. (YO30 1DD) 4H **99**
Benington Lordship Gdns. (SG2 7BS) 3C **52**
Ben Lawers (PH15 2PA) 4D **142**
Ben Lomond (FK8 3TR) 3C **134**
Ben Macdui (PH22 1RB) 4D **151**
Benmore Botanic Gdn. (PA23 8QU) 1C **126**
Ben Nevis (PH33 6SY) 1F **141**
Benthall Hall (TF12 5RX) 5A **72**
Bentley Wildfowl & Motor Mus. (BN8 5AF) 4F **27**
Berkeley Castle (GL13 9BQ) 2B **34**
Berkhamsted Castle (HP4 1LJ) 5H 51
Berney Arms Windmill (NR31 9HU) 5G **79**
Berrington Hall (HR6 0DW) 4H **59**
Berry Pomeroy Castle (TQ9 6LJ) 2E **9**
Bessie Surtees House (NE1 3JF) . . . . . . **Newcastle 205**
Beverley Minster (HU17 0DP) 1D **94**
Bicton Pk. Botanical Gdns. (EX9 7BJ) 4D **12**
Biddulph Grange Gdn. (ST8 7SD) 5C **84**
Big Ben (SW1A 2PW) . . . . **London 203**
Bignor Roman Villa (RH20 1PH) 4A **26**
Big Pit: Nat. Coal Mus. (NP4 9XP) 5F **47**
Binham Priory (NR21 0DJ) 1B **78**
Birmingham Mus. & Art Gallery (B3 3DH) **188**
Bishop's Waltham Palace (SO32 1DP) 1D **16**
Black Country Living Mus., Dudley (DY1 4SQ) 1D 60
Blackgang Chine (PO38 2HN) 5C **16**
Blackhouse (HS2 9DB) 3F **171**
Blackness Castle (EH49 7NH) 1D **128**
Blackpool Pleasure Beach (FY4 1EZ) 1B **90**
Blackpool Zoo (FY3 8PP) 1B 90
Blackwell, The Arts & Crafts House (LA23 3JR) 5F **103**
Blaenavon Ironworks (NP4 9RJ) 5F **47**
Blaenavon World Heritage Cen. (NP4 9AS) . . . 5F 47
Blair Castle (PH18 5TL) 2F **143**
Blair Drummond Safari & Adventure Pk. (FK9 4UR) 4G **135**
Blairquhan Castle (KA19 7LZ) 4C **116**
Blakeney Point (NR25 7SA) 1C **78**
Blakesley Hall (B25 8RN) 2F **61**
Blenheim Palace (OX20 1PX) 4C **50**
Bletchley Pk. (MK3 6EB) 2G **51**
Blickling Estate (NR11 6NF) 3D **78**
Blists Hill Victorian Town, Telford (TF7 5DS) . . 5A 72
Bluebell Railway (TN22 3QL) 3E **27**
Blue John Cavern (S33 8WP) 2F **85**
Blue Reef Aquarium, Bristol (BS1 5TT) **189**
Blue Reef Aquarium, Hastings (TN34 3DW) . . . 5C **28**
Blue Reef Aquarium, Newquay (TR7 1DU) 2C **6**
[Blue Reef Aquarium, Portsmouth, Southsea (PO5 3PB)] 3E 17
Blue Reef Aquarium, Tynemouth (NE30 4JF) 2G **115**
Boath Doocot (IV12 5TD) 3D **158**
Bocketts Farm Pk. (KT22 9BS) 5C **38**
Bodelwyddan Castle (LL18 5YA) 3B **82**
Bodiam Castle (TN32 5UA) 3B 28
Bodmin & Wenford Railway (PL31 1AQ) 2E **7**
Bodmin Moor (PL15 7TN) 5B **10**
Bodnant Gdn. (LL28 5RE) 3H **81**
Bodrhyddan Hall (LL18 5SB) 3C **82**
Bolingbroke Castle (PE23 4HH) 4C **88**
Bolsover Castle (S44 6PR) 3B 86
Bolton Castle (DL8 4ET) 5D **104**
Bolton Priory (BD23 6AL) 4C **98**
Bonawe Historic Iron Furnace (PA35 1JQ) 5E **141**
Bo'ness & Kinneil Railway (EH51 9AQ) 1C **128**
Booth Mus. of Natural History (BN1 5AA) . . . . **Brighton & Hove 189**
Borde Hill Gdn. (RH16 1XP) 3E **27**
Boscobel House (ST19 9AR) 5C **72**
Boston Stump (PE21 6NQ) 1C **76**
Bosworth Field Battle Site (CV13 0AB) 5A **74**
Bothwell Castle (G71 8BL) 4H **127**
Boughton (NN14 1BJ) 2G **63**
Boughton House & Gdns. (NN14 1BJ) 4E **63**
Bowes Castle (DL12 9LE) 3C 104
Bowes Mus., The (DL12 8NP) 3D **104**
Bowhill House & Country Estate (TD7 5ET) . . . 2G **119**
Bowood House & Gdns. (SN11 0LZ) 5E **35**
Box Hill (KT20 7LF) 5C **38**
Braemar Castle (AB35 5XR) 4F **151**
Bramall Hall, Bramhall (SK7 3NX) 2C 84
Bramber Castle (BN44 3FJ) 4C **26**
Bramham Pk. (LS23 6ND) 5G **99**
Brands Hatch Motor Circuit (DA3 8NG) 4G **39**
Brantwood (LA21 8AD) 5E **102**
Breamore House (SP6 2DF) 1G **15**
Brean Down (TA8 2RS) 1F **21**
Brecon Beacons Nat. Pk. (CF44 9JG) 4B **46**
Brecon Mountain Railway (CF48 2UP) 4D **46**
Bressingham Steam & Gdns. (IP22 2AB) 2C **66**
Brimham Rocks (HG3 4DW) 3E **98**
Brindley Mill & Mus. (ST13 8FA) 5D **85**
Brinkburn Priory (NE65 8AR) 5F **121**
Bristol Cathedral (BS1 5TJ) **189**
Bristol Zoo Gdns. (BS8 3HA) **189**
Britannia Bridge (LL61 5BZ) 3E **81**
British Golf Mus. (KY16 9AB) . . . . **St Andrews 209**
British Library (NW1 2DB) . . . . **London 203**
British Mus. (WC1B 3DG) . . . . **London 203**
Broadlands (SO51 9ZD) 4B **24**
Broads, The (NR3 1BQ) 5G **79**
Broadway Tower (WR12 7LB) 2G **49**
Brobury House Gdns. (HR3 6BS) 1G **47**
Brockhampton Estate (WR6 5TB) 5A **60**
Brockhole, Lake District Visitor Centre (LA23 1LJ) 4E **103**
Brodick Castle & Gdn. (KA27 8HY) 2E **123**
Brodie Castle (IV36 2TE) 3D **159**
Brodsworth Hall & Gdns. (DN5 7XJ) 4F **93**
Brogdale (ME13 8XU) 5E **40**
Bronllys Castle (LD3 0HL) 2E **47**
Brontë Parsonage Mus. (BD22 8DR) 1A **92**
Broseley Pipe Works (TF12 5LX) 5A 72
Brougham Castle (CA10 2AA) 2G 103
Brough Castle (CA17 4EJ) 3A **104**
Broughton Castle (OX15 5EB) 2C **50**
Broughton House & Gdn. (DG6 4JX) 4D **111**
Brownsea Island (BH13 7EE) 4F 15
Bruce's Stone (DG7 3SQ) 2C **110**
Brunel's SS Great Britain (BS1 6TY) . . . . . . **Bristol 189**
Buckfast Abbey (TQ11 0EE) 2D **8**
Buckingham Palace (SW1A 1AA) . . . . **London 202**
Buckland Abbey (PL20 6EY) 2A **8**
Buckler's Hard Martime Mus. (SO42 7XB) 3C **16**
Buildwas Abbey (TF8 7BW) 5A **72**
Bungay Castle (NR35 1DD) 2F 67
Bure Valley Railway (NR11 6BW) 3E **79**
Burford House Gdns. (WR15 8HQ) 4H **59**
Burghley (PE9 3JY) 5H **75**
Burleigh Castle (KY13 9TD) 3D **136**
Burnby Hall Gdns. & Mus. (YO42 2QF) 5C **100**
Burns Cottage, Alloway (KA7 4PY) 3C 116
Burns House Mus. (KA5 5BZ) 2D **117**
[Burrell Collection, Pollokshaws (G43 1AT)] . . . 3G 127
Burton Agnes Hall (YO25 4ND) 3F **101**
Burton Constable Hall (HU11 4LN) 1E **95**
Bury St Edmunds Abbey (IP33 1RS) 4A **66**
Buscot Pk. (SN7 8BU) 2H **35**
Butser Ancient Farm (PO8 0QF) 1F **17**
Butterfly & Wildlife Pk. (PE12 9LF) 3D **76**
Buttertubs, The (DL11 6DR) 5B **104**
Buxton Pavilion Gdns. (SK17 6XN) 3E **85**
Byland Abbey (YO61 4BD) 2H 99

C

Cadair Idris (LL40 1TN) 4F **69**
Cadbury World (B30 1JR) 2E **61**
Caerlaverock Castle (DG1 4RU) 3B **112**
Caerleon Roman Fortress (NP18 1AY) 2G **33**
Caernarfon Castle (LL55 2AY) **190**
Caerphilly Castle (CF83 1JD) 3E 33
Cairngorms Nat. Pk. (PH26 3HG) 3E **151**
Cairnpapple Hill (EH48 4NW) 2C **128**
Caister Castle & Motor Mus. (NR30 5SN) 4H **79**
Calanais (Callanish) Standing Stones (HS2 9DY) 4E **171**
Caldey Island (SA70 7UH) 5F **43**
Caldicot Castle (NP26 5JB) 3H 33
Caledonian Railway (DD9 7AF) 3F **145**
Calke Abbey (DE73 7LE) 3A **74**
Calshot Castle (SO45 1BR) 2C 16
Camber Castle (TN31 7TB) 4D **28**
Cambo Gdns. (KY16 8QD) 2H **137**
Cambridge University Botanic Gdn. (CB2 1JF) . . . **191**
Camelot Theme Pk. (PR7 5LP) 3D **90**
Camperdown Wildlife Centre (DD2 4TF) 5C **144**
Canal Mus. (NN12 7SE) 5E **63**
Cannock Chase (WS12 4PW) 4D **73**
Cannon Hall Mus. (S75 4AT) 4C **92**
Canons Ashby House (NN11 3SD) 5C **62**
Canterbury Cathedral (CT1 2EH) **190**
Capesthorne Hall (SK11 9JY) 3C **84**
Cape Wrath (IV27 4QQ) 1C **166**
Captain Cook Schoolroom Mus. (TS9 6NB) 3C **106**
Cardiff Castle (CF10 3RB) **191**
Cardoness Castle (DG7 2EH) 4C **110**
Carew Castle & Tidal Mill (SA70 8SL) 4E 43
Carisbrooke Castle (PO30 1XY) 4C **16**
Carlisle Castle (CA3 8UR) **192**
Carlisle Cathedral (CA3 8TZ) **192**
Carlyle's Birthplace (DG11 3DG) 2C **112**
Carnassarie Castle (PA31 8RQ) 3F **133**
Carn Euny Ancient Village (TR20 8RB) 4B **4**
Carreg Cennen Castle & Farm (SA19 6UA) 4G **45**
Carsluith Castle (DG8 7DY) 4B **110**
Cartmel Priory Church (LA11 6QQ) 2C 96
Castell Coch, Tongwynlais (CF15 7JS) 3E 33
Castell Dinas Bran (LL20 8DY) 1E **70**
Castell y Bere (LL36 9TP) 5F **69**
Castle Acre Castle (PE32 2XB) 4H 77
Castle Acre Priory (PE32 2XD) 4H **77**
Castle & Gdns. of Mey (KW14 8XH) 1E **169**
Castle Campbell & Gdn. (FK14 7PP) 4B **136**
Castle Drogo (EX6 6PB) 3H **11**
Castle Fraser (AB51 7LD) 2E **152**
Castle Howard (YO60 7DA) 2B **100**
Castle Kennedy Gdns. (DG9 8SJ) 3G **109**
Castle Leod (IV14 9AA) 3G **157**
Castle Menzies (PH15 2JD) 4F **143**
Castlerigg Stone Circle (CA12 4RN) 2D **102**
Castle Rising Castle (PE31 6AH) 3F 77
Catalyst Science Discovery Centre (WA8 0DF) 2H **83**
Cawdor Castle (IV12 5RD) 4C 158
Cecil Higgins Art Gallery (MK40 3RP) . . . . **Bedford 188**
Ceramica (ST6 3DS) 1C **72**
Cerne Giant (DT2 7TS) 2B **14**
Chanonry Point (IV10 8SD) 3B **158**
Charlecote Pk. (CV35 9ER) 5G **61**
Charleston (BN8 6LL) 5F **27**
Chartwell (TN16 1PS) 5F **39**
Chastleton House (GL56 0SU) 3H **49**
Chatsworth (DE45 1PP) 3G **85**
Chavenage House (GL8 8XP) 2D **34**
Cheddar Gorge (BS40 7XT) 1H **21**
Chedworth Roman Villa (GL54 3LJ) 4F **49**
Cheltenham Racecourse (GL50 4SH) 3E 49
Chenies Manor House & Gdns. (WD3 6ER) 1B **38**
Chepstow Castle (NP16 5EZ) 2A 34
Chepstow Racecourse (NP16 6EG) 2A **34**
Chesil Beach (DT3 4ED) 4B **14**
Chessington World of Adventures (KT9 2NE) . . . 4C **38**
Chester Cathedral (CH1 2HU) **192**
Chester Roman Amphitheatre (CH1 1RF) **192**
Chesters Roman Fort & Mus. (NE46 4ET) 2C **114**
Chester Zoo (CH2 1LH) 3G **83**
Chettle House (DT11 8DB) 1E **15**
Chichester Cathedral (PO19 1PX) 2G **17**
Chiddingstone Castle (TN8 7AD) 1F **27**
Chillingham Castle (NE66 5NJ) 2E 121
Chillingham Wild Cattle (NE66 5NJ) 2E **121**
Chillington Hall (WV8 1RE) 5C **72**
Chiltern Hills (RG9 6DR) 3E **37**
Chiltern Open Air Mus. (HP8 4AB) 1B **38**
China Clay Country Pk. (Wheal Martyn) (PL26 8XG) 3E **6**
Chirk Castle (LL14 5AF) 2E **71**
Cholmondeley Castle Gdns. (SY14 8AH) 5H **83**
Christchurch Castle & Norman House (BH23 1BW) 3G **15**
Christchurch Mansion (IP4 2BE) . . . . **Ipswich 198**
Churchill War Rooms (SW1A 2AQ) . . . . . . **London 203**
Churnet Valley Railway (ST13 7EE) 5D **85**
Chysauster Ancient Village (TR20 8XA) 3B **4**
Cilgerran Castle (SA43 2SF) 1B 44
Cissbury Ring (BN14 0SQ) 5C **26**
Clandon Pk. (GU4 7RQ) 5B **38**
Claremont Landscape Gdn. (KT10 9JG) 4C **38**
Claydon (MK18 2EY) 3F **51**
Clearwell Caves (GL16 8JR) 5A **48**
Cleeve Abbey (TA23 0PS) 2D **20**
Clevedon Court (BS21 6QU) 4H **33**
Clifford's Tower (YO1 9SA) . . . . **York 214**
Clifton Suspension Bridge (BS8 3PA) . . . . . **Bristol 189**
Cliveden (SL6 0JA) 2A **38**
Clouds Hill (BH20 7NQ) 3D **14**
Clumber Pk. (S80 3BX) 3D **86**
Clun Castle (SY7 8JR) 2E 59
Clyde Muirshiel Regional Pk. (PA10 2PZ) 3D **126**
Coalbrookdale Mus. of Iron (TF8 7DQ) 5A **72**
Coalport China Mus. (TF8 7HT) 5A **72**
Coed y Brenin Visitor Centre (LL40 2HZ) 3G **69**
Coggeshall Grange Barn (CO6 1RE) 3B **54**
Coity Castle (CF35 6AU) 3C 32
Colby Woodland Gdn. (SA67 8PP) 4F **43**
Colchester Castle Mus. (CO1 1TJ) 3D **54**
Colchester Zoo (CO3 0SL) 3C **54**
Coleridge Cottage (TA5 1NQ) 3E **21**
Coleton Fishacre (TQ6 0EQ) 3F **9**
Colour Experience (BD1 2JB) . . . . **Bradford 190**
Colzium Walled Gdn. (G65 0PY) 2A **128**
Combe Martin Wildlife & Dinosaur Pk. (EX34 0NG) 2F **19**
Compton Acres (BH13 7ES) 4F **15**
Compton Castle (TQ3 1TA) 2E 9
Compton Verney (CV35 9HZ) 5H **61**
Conisbrough Castle (DN12 3BU) 1C 86
Conishead Priory (LA12 9QQ) 2C **96**
Conkers (DE12 6GA) 4H **73**
Constable Burton Hall Gdns. (DL8 5LJ) 5E **105**
Conwy Castle (LL32 8LD) 3G 81
Corbridge Roman Town (NE45 5NT) 3C **114**
Corfe Castle (BH20 5EZ) 4E 15
Corgarff Castle (AB36 8YP) 3G **151**
Corinium Mus. (GL7 2BX) 5F **49**
Cornish Mines & Engines (TR15 3NP) 4A **6**
Corrieshalloch Gorge (IV23 2PJ) 1E **156**
Corsham Court (SN13 0BZ) 4D **35**
Cotehele (PL12 6TA) 2A **8**
Coton Manor Gdn. (NN6 8RQ) 3D **62**
Cotswold Farm Pk. (GL54 5UG) 3G **49**
Cotswold Hills (GL8 8NU) 5E **49**
Cotswold Water Pk. (GL7 5TL) 2F **35**
Cottesbrooke Hall & Gdns. (NN6 8PF) 3E **62**
Cotton Mechanical Music Mus. (IP14 4QN) 4C **66**
Coughton Court (B49 5JA) 4E **61**
Courts Gdn., The (BA14 6RR) 5D **34**
Coventry Cathedral (CV1 5AB) **192**
Coventry Transport Mus. (CV1 1JD) **192**
Cowdray House (GU29 9AL) 4G **25**
Cragside (NE65 7PX) 4E **121**
Craig Castle (AB54 4LP) 1B **152**
Craigievar Castle (AB33 8JF) 3C **152**
Craigmillar Castle (EH16 4SY) 2F 129
Craignethan Castle (ML11 9PL) 5B **128**
Craigston Castle (AB53 5PX) 3E **161**
Cranborne Manor Gdn. (BH21 5PS) 1F **15**
Cranwell Aviation Heritage Centre (NG34 8QR) 1H **75**
Crarae Gdn. (PA32 8YA) 4G **133**
Crathes Castle & Gdn. (AB31 5QJ) 4E **153**
Creswell Crags (S80 3LH) 3C **86**
Crewe Heritage Centre (CW1 2DD) 5B **84**
Criccieth Castle (LL52 0DP) 2D 69
Crichton Castle (EH37 5XA) 3G **129**

Crich Tramway Village (DE4 5DP) 5H 85
Croft Castle (HR6 9PW) 4G 59
Croft Motor Circuit (DL2 2PL) 4F 105
Cromford Mill (DE4 3RQ) 5G 85
Cromwell Mus. (PE29 3LF) 3B 64
Crookston Castle (G53 5RR) 3G 127
Croome (WR8 9JS) 1D 49
Crossraguel Abbey (KA19 8HQ) 4B 116
Croxden Abbey (ST14 5JG) 2E 73
Croxteth Hall (L12 0HB) 1G 83
Cruachan Power Station (PA33 1AN) 1H 133
Culloden Battlefield Visitor Centre (IV2 5EU) 4B 158
Culloden Battle Site (IV2 5EU) 4B 158
Culross Palace (KY12 8JH) 1C 128
Culzean Castle (KA19 8LE) 3B 116
Curraghs Wildlife Pk. (IM7 5EA) 2C 108
Cusworth Hall (DN5 7TU) 4F 93
Cymer Abbey (LL40 2HE) 4G 69

D

Dalemain (CA11 0HB) 2F 103
Dales Countryside Mus. (DL8 3NT) 5B 104
Dallas Dhu Historic Distillery (IV36 2RR) 3E 159
Dalmeny House (EH30 9TQ) 2E 129
Darby Houses (TF8 7DQ) 5A 72
Dartington Crystal (EX38 7AN) 1E 11
Dartington Hall Gdns. (TQ9 6EL) 2E 9
Dartmoor Nat. Pk. (TQ13 9JQ) 4F 11
Dartmoor Zoo (PL7 5DG) 3B 8
Dartmouth Castle (TQ6 0JN) 3E 9
Dartmouth Steam Railway (TQ4 6AF) 3E 9
Dawyck Botanic Gdn. (EH45 9JU) 1D 118
Deal Castle (CT14 7BA) 5H 41
Dean Castle (KA3 1XB) 1D 116
Dean Forest Railway (GL15 4ET) 5B 48
Deene Pk. (NN17 3EW) 1G 63
Deep Sea World (KY11 1JR) 1E 129
Deep, The (HU1 4DP) **Hull 199**
Delamere Forest (CW8 2JD) 3H 83
Delgatie Castle (AB53 5TD) 3E 161
Denbigh Castle (LL16 3NB) 4C 82
Devil's Dyke (BN45 7DE) 4D 26
Devil's Punch Bowl (GU26 6AB) 3G 25
Dewa Roman Experience (CH1 1NL) **Chester 192**
DH Lawrence Birthplace Mus. (NG16 3AW) 1B 74
Dickens House Mus. (CT10 1QS) 4H 41
[Dickens World, Chatham (ME4 4LL)] 3B 40
Didcot Railway Centre (OX11 7NJ) 2D 36
Dinefwr Castle (SA19 6PF) 3G 45
Dinefwr Pk. (SA19 6RT) 3G 45
Dinorwig Power Station (Electric Mountain) (LL55 4UR) 5E 81
Dinosaur Adventure (NR9 5JW) 4D 78
Dinosaur Mus. (DT1 1EW) 3B 14
Dirleton Castle & Gdn. (EH39 5ER) 1B 130
Discovery Mus. (NE1 4JA) **Newcastle 205**
Discovery Point & RRS Discovery (DD1 4XA) **Dundee 194**
Dock Mus. (LA14 2PW) 3A 96
Doddington Hall & Gdns. (LN6 4RU) 4F 87
Doddington Place Gdns. (ME9 0BB) 5D 40
Dolaucothi Gold Mines (SA19 8RR) 2G 45
Dolbadarn Castle (LL55 4SU) 5E 81
Dolforwyn Castle (SY15 6JH) 1D 58
Dolwyddelan Castle (LL25 0JD) 5G 81
Domestic Fowl Trust and Honeybourne Rare Breeds (WR11 7QZ) 1G 49
Doncaster Racecourse (DN2 6BB) 4G 93
Donington Grand Prix Collection, Castle Donington (DE74 2RP) 3B 74
Donington Pk. Motor Circuit (DE74 2RP) 3B 74
Donnington Castle (RG14 2LE) 5C 36
Dorfold Hall (CW5 8LD) 5A 84
Dorothy Clive Gdn. (TF9 4EU) 2B 72
Doune Castle (FK16 6EA) 3G 135
Dove Cottage (Wordsworth Mus.) (LA22 9SH) 4E 103
Dove Dale (DE6 1NL) 5F 85
Dover Castle (CT16 1HU) 193
Down House (BR6 7JT) 4F 39
Dozmary Pool (PL15 7TP) 5B 10
Drayton Manor Theme Pk. (B78 3TW) 5F 73
Drum Castle & Gdn. (AB31 5EY) 3E 153
Drumlanrig Castle (DG3 4AQ) 5A 118
Drummond Gdns. (PH5 2AA) 2H 135
Drusillas (BN26 5QS) 5G 27
Dryburgh Abbey (TD6 0RQ) 1H 119
Dryslwyn Castle (SA32 8JQ) 3F 45
Duart Castle (PA64 6AP) 5B 140
[Dudley Zoological Gdns. & Castle (DY1 4AS)] 1D 60
Dudmaston Estate (WV15 6QN) 2B 60
Duff House Country Gallery (AB45 3SX) 2D 160
Duffus Castle (IV30 5RH) 2F 159
Dukeries, The (S80 3BT) 3D 86
Dumbarton Castle (G82 1JJ) 2F 127
Dunblane Cathedral (FK15 0AQ) 3G 135
Dun Carloway (HS2 9AZ) 3D 171
Duncombe Pk. (YO62 5EB) 1A 100
Dundonald Castle (KA2 9HD) 1C 116
Dundrennan Abbey (DG6 4QH) 5E 111
Dunfermline Abbey & Palace (KY12 7PE) 1D 129
Dungeon Ghyll Force (LA22 9JY) 4D 102
Dunge Valley Rhododendron Gdns. (SK23 7RF) 3D 85
Dunham Massey (WA14 4SJ) 2B 84
Dunkeld Cathedral (PH8 0AW) 4H 143
Dunkery Beacon (TA24 7AT) 2B 20
Dunnet Head (KW14 8XS) 1D 169
Dunninald (DD10 9TD) 3G 145
Dunnottar Castle (AB39 2TL) 5F 153
Dunrobin Castle (KW10 6SF) 3F 165
Dunstaffnage Castle (PA37 1PZ) 5C 140
Dunstanburgh Castle (NE66 3TG) 2G 121
Dunster Castle (TA24 6SL) 2C 20
Dunvegan Castle (IV55 8WF) 4B 154
Durdle Door (BH20 5PU) 4D 14
Durham Cathedral (DH1 3EH) 194
Dyffryn Gdns. (CF5 6SU) 4D 32
Dylan Thomas Boathouse (SA33 4SD) 3H 43
Dyrham Pk. (SN14 8ER) 4C 34

E

Eagle Heights Wildlife Pk. (DA4 0JB) 4G 39
Easby Abbey (DL10 7JU) 4E 105
East Anglian Railway Mus. (CO6 2DS) 3B 54
East Bergholt Place Gdn. (CO7 6UP) 2D 54
East Kent Railway (CT15 7PD) 1G 29
East Lambrook Manor Gdns. (TA13 5HH) 1H 13
East Lancashire Railway (BL9 0EY) 2G 91
East Riddlesden Hall (BD20 5EL) 5C 98
East Somerset Railway (BA4 4QP) 2B 22
Eastnor Castle (HR8 1RD) 2C 48
Eden Project (PL24 2SG) 3E 7
Edinburgh Castle (EH1 2NG) 194
Edinburgh Zoo (EH12 6TS) 2F 129
Edzell Castle & Gdn. (DD9 7UE) 2E 145
Egglestone Abbey (DL12 9TN) 3D 104
Eilean Donan Castle (IV40 8DX) 1A 148
Elcho Castle (PH2 8QQ) 1D 136
Electric Mountain (Dinorwig Power Station) (LL55 4UR) 4E 81
Elgar Birthplace Mus. (WR2 6RH) 5C 60
Elgin Cathedral (IV30 1EL) 2G 159
Eltham Palace & Gdns. (SE9 5QE) 3F 39
Elton Hall & Gdns. (PE8 6SH) 1H 63
Ely Cathedral (CB7 4DL) 2E 65
Embsay & Bolton Abbey Steam Railway (BD23 6AF) 4C 98
Emmetts Gdn. (TN14 6BA) 5F 39
Enginuity (TF8 7DQ) 5A 72
Epsom Downs Racecourse (KT18 5LQ) 5D 38
Erddig (LL13 0YT) 1F 71
Escot (EX11 1LU) 3D 12
Etal Castle (TD12 4TN) 1D 120
Eureka! The Nat. Children's Mus., Halifax (HX1 2NE) 2A 92
Euston Hall (IP24 2QW) 3A 66
Ewloe Castle (CH5 3BZ) 4E 83
Exbury Gdns. (SO45 1AZ) 2C 16
Exeter Cathedral (EX1 1HS) 195
Exmoor Nat. Pk. (TA22 9HL) 2A 20
Eyam Hall (S32 5QW) 3G 85
Eye Castle (IP23 7AP) 3D 66
Eynsford Castle (DA4 0AA) 4G 39

F

Fairbourne Steam Railway (LL38 2PZ) 4F 69
Fairhaven Woodland & Water Gdn. (NR13 6DZ) 4F 79
Falkirk Wheel (FK1 4RS) 1B 128
Falkland Palace (KY15 7BU) 3E 137
Falls of Glomach (IV40 8DS) 1C 148
Falstaff Experience - Tudor World (CV37 6EE) **Stratford 212**
Farleigh Hungerford Castle (BA2 7RS) 1D 22
Farmland Mus. & Denny Abbey (CB25 9PQ) 4D 65
Farnborough Hall (OX17 1DU) 1C 50
Farne Islands (NE68 7SY) 1G 121
Farnham Castle Keep (GU9 0AE) 2G 25
Felbrigg Hall (NR11 8PR) 2D 78
Fell Foot Pk. (LA12 8NN) 1C 96
Ferniehirst Castle (TD8 6NX) 3A 120
Ffestiniog Railway (LL49 9NF) 1F 69
Fiddleford Manor (DT10 2BU) 1D 14
Finchale Priory (DH1 5SH) 5F 115
Finchcocks (TN17 1HH) 2A 28
Finch Foundry (EX20 2NW) 3G 11
Fingal's Cave (PA73 6NA) 5E 138
Finlaystone Country Estate (PA14 6TJ) 2E 127
Firle Place (BN8 6LP) 5F 27
Fishbourne Roman Palace & Gdns. (PO19 3QR) 2G 17
Fitzwilliam Mus. (CB2 1RB) **Cambridge 191**
Five Sisters of Kintail (IV40 8HQ) 2B 148
Flambards Experience (TR13 0QA) 4D 4
Flamingo Land (YO17 6UX) 2B 100
Fleet Air Arm Mus. (BA22 8HT) 4A 22
Flint Castle (CH6 5PE) 3E 83
Floors Castle & Gdns. (TD5 7SF) 1B 120
Fonmon Castle (CF62 3ZN) 5D 32
Forde Abbey & Gdns. (TA20 4LU) 2G 13
Ford Green Hall (ST6 1NG) 5C 84
Forest of Dean (GL15 4SL) 5B 48
Fort George (IV2 7TD) 3B 158
Forth Bridge (EH30 9TB) 2E 129
Fort Nelson (Royal Armouries) (PO17 6AN) 2E 16
Fountains Abbey & Studley Royal (HG4 3DY) 3E 99
Foxfield Steam Railway (ST11 9BG) 1D 72
Foxton Locks (LE16 7RA) 2D 62
Framlingham Castle (IP13 9BP) 4E 67
Froghall Wharf (ST10 2HH) 1E 73
Furness Abbey (LA13 0PG) 2B 96
Furzey Gdns. (SO43 7GL) 1A 16
Fyne Court (TA5 2EQ) 3F 21
Fyvie Castle (AB53 8JS) 5E 161

G

Gainsborough Old Hall (DN21 2NB) 1F 87
Gainsborough's House (CO10 2EU) 1B 54
Gallery of Modern Art (G1 3AH) **Glasgow 196**
Galloway Forest Pk. (DG8 6TA) 1B 110
Galloway House Gdns. (DG8 8HF) 5B 110
Galloway Wildlife Conservation Pk. (DG6 4XX) 4E 111
Garden House, The (PL20 7LQ) 2A 8
Gdns. of the Rose (AL2 3NR) 5B 52
Gawsworth Hall (SK11 9RN) 4C 84
Gawthorpe Hall (BB12 8UA) 1G 91
Geevor Tin Mine Mus. (TR19 7EW) 3A 4
George Stephenson's Birthplace (NE41 8BP) 3E 115
Georgian House (EH2 4DR) **Edinburgh 194**
Gibside (NE16 6BG) 4E 115
Gilbert White's House & Gdn. (GU34 3JH) 3F 25
Gisborough Priory (TS14 6BU) 3D 106
Gladstone Pottery Mus. (ST3 1PQ) 1D 72
Gladstone's Land (EH1 2NT) **Edinburgh 194**
Glamis Castle (DD8 1QJ) 4C 144
Glastonbury Abbey (BA6 9EL) 3A 22
Glastonbury Tor (BA6 8BG) 3A 22
Glenarn (G84 8LL) 1D 126
Glenbuchat Castle (AB36 8TN) 2A 152
Glencoe Gorge (PH50 4SG) 3F 141
Glendurgan Gdn. (TR11 5JZ) 4E 5
Glenfinnan Monument (PH37 4LT) 5B 148
Glenluce Abbey (DG8 0LW) 4G 109
Glenmore Forest Pk. Visitor Centre (PH22 1QY) 3D 150
Glenwhan Gdns. (DG9 8PH) 4G 109
Gloucester Cathedral (GL1 2LR) 196
Gloucestershire Warwickshire Railway (GL54 5DT) 2F 49
Gloucester Waterways Mus. (GL1 2EH) 196
Glynde Place (BN8 6SX) 5F 27
Godinton House & Gdns. (TN23 3BP) 1D 28
Godolphin (TR13 9RE) 3D 4
Goodnestone Pk. Gdns. (CT3 1PL) 5G 41
Goodrich Castle (HR9 6HY) 3A 48
Goodwood House (PO18 0PX) 2G 17
Goodwood Racecourse (PO18 0PS) 1G 17
Gordale Scar (BD23 4DL) 3B 98
Grampian Transport Mus. (AB33 8AE) 2C 152
Grange at Northington, The (SO24 9TG) 3D 24
Graves Gallery (S1 1XZ) **Sheffield 210**
Graythwaite Hall Gdns. (LA12 8BA) 5E 103
Great Central Railway (LE11 1RW) 4C 74
Great Central Railway (Nottingham) (NG11 6NX) 2C 74
Great Chalfield Manor & Gdn. (SN12 8NH) 5D 34
Great Comp Gdn. (TN15 8QS) 5H 39
Great Dixter (TN31 6PH) 3C 28
Great North Mus. : Hancock (NE2 4PT) **Newcastle 205**
Greenbank House & Gdn. (G76 8RB) 4G 127
Greenknowe Tower (TD3 6JL) 5C 130
Greenway (TQ5 0ES) 3E 9
Gretna Green Old Blacksmith's Shop (DG16 5EA) 3E 112
Grey Mare's Tail Waterfall (DG10 9LH) 3D 118
Greys Court (RG9 4PG) 3F 37
Grimes Graves (IP26 5DE) 1H 65
Grimsby Fishing Heritage Centre (DN31 1UZ) 4F 95
Grimspound (PL20 6TB) 4H 11
Grimsthorpe Castle (PE10 0LZ) 3H 75
Grizedale Forest (LA22 0QJ) 5E 103
Groombridge Place Gdns. (TN3 9QG) 2G 27
Grove Mus. (IM8 3UA) 2D 108
Gulliver's Dinosaur & Farm Pk. (MK15 0DT) 2G 51
Gulliver's Matlock Bath (DE4 3PG) 5G 85
Gulliver's Milton Keynes (MK15 0DT) 204
Gulliver's Warrington (WA5 9YZ) 1H 83
Gunby Hall (PE23 5SS) 4D 88
Gwydir Castle (LL26 0PN) 4G 81

H

Haddo House (AB41 7EQ) 5F 161
Haddon Hall (DE45 1LA) 4G 85
Hadleigh Castle (SS7 2AR) 2C 40
Hadrian's Wall (NE47 6NN) 3A 114
Hailes Abbey (GL54 5PB) 2F 49
Hailes Castle (EH41 3SB) 2B 130
Hall i' th' Wood Mus. (BL1 8UA) 3F 91
Hall Place & Gdns. (DA5 1PQ) 3G 39
Hamerton Zoo Pk. (PE28 5RE) 2A 64
Ham House & Gdn. (TW10 7RS) 3C 38
Hammerwood Pk. (RH19 3QE) 2F 27
Hampden Pk. (G42 9AY) 3G 127
Hampton Court Castle & Gdns. (HR6 0PN) 5H 59
Hampton Court Palace (KT8 9AU) 4C 38
Hanbury Hall (WR9 7EA) 4D 60
Handel House Mus. (W1K 4HB) **London 202**
Hardknott Roman Fort (LA20 6EQ) 4D 102
Hardwick Hall (S44 5QJ) 4B 86
Hardy Monument (DT2 9HY) 4B 14
Hardy's Cottage (DT2 8QJ) 3C 14
Hare Hill (SK10 4QA) 3C 84
Harewood House (LS17 9LG) 5F 99
Harlech Castle (LL46 2YH) 2E 69
Harley Gallery (S80 3LW) 3C 86
Hartland Abbey & Gdns. (EX39 6DT) 4C 18
Harvington Hall (DY10 4LR) 3C 60
Harwich Redoubt (CO12 3NL) 2F 55
Hatchlands Pk. (GU4 7RT) 5B 38
Hatfield House (AL9 5NQ) 5C 52
Haughmond Abbey (SY4 4RW) 4H 71
Haverfordwest Castle (SA61 2BW) 3D 42
Haverfordwest Priory (SA61 1RN) 3D 42
Hawk Conservancy Trust (SP11 8DY) 2B 24
Haydock Pk. Racecourse (WA12 0HQ) 1H 83
Head of Steam - Darlington Railway Mus. (DL3 6ST) 3F 105
Heale Gdns. (SP4 6NT) 3G 23
Heaton Hall (M25 2SW) 4G 91
Hedingham Castle (CO9 3DJ) 2A 54
Heights of Abraham (DE4 3PB) 5G 85
Hellens (HR8 2LY) 2B 48
Helmingham Hall Gdns. (IP14 6EF) 5D 66
Helmshore Mills Textile Mus. (BB4 4NP) 2F 91
Helmsley Castle (YO62 5AB) 1A 100
Helvellyn (CA12 4TP) 3E 103
[Henry Moore Institute, Leeds (LS1 3AH)] **Leeds 199**
Heptonstall Mus. (HX7 7PL) 2H 91
Hereford Cathedral (HR1 2NG) 197
Hereford Cider Mus. (HR4 0LW) 2A 48
Hergest Croft Gdns. (HR5 3EG) 5E 59
Heritage Motor Centre (CV35 0BJ) 5A 62
Hermitage Castle (TD9 0LU) 5H 119
Herstmonceux Castle & Gdn. (BN27 1RN) 4H 27
Hestercombe Gdns. (TA2 8LG) 4F 21
Hever Castle & Gdns. (TN8 7NG) 1F 27
Hexham Abbey (NE46 3NB) 3C 114
Hidcote (GL55 6LR) 1G 49
High Beeches Gdns. (RH17 6HQ) 2D 27
Highclere Castle (RG20 9RN) 1C 24
Highland Folk Mus. (PH20 1AY) 4B 150
Highland Wildlife Pk. (PH21 1NL) 3C 150
Hill House (G84 9AJ) 1D 126
Hill of Tarvit Mansionhouse & Gdns. (KY15 5PB) 2F 137
Hill Top (LA22 0LF) 5E 103
Hinton Ampner (SO24 0LA) 4D 24
Hirsel (TD12 4LP) 5E 131
Historic Dockyard Chatham (ME4 4TZ) **Medway 204**
HMS Victory (PO1 3LJ) **Portsmouth 209**
HMS Warrior 1860 (PO1 3QX) **Portsmouth 209**
Hodnet Hall Gdns. (TF9 3NN) 3A 72
Hoghton Tower (PR5 0SH) 2E 90
Hog's Back (GU3 1AQ) 1A 26
Holburne Mus. of Art (BA2 4DB) **Bath 187**
Holdenby House Gdns. & Falconry Centre (NN6 8DJ) 4D 62
Holehird Gdns. (LA23 1NP) 4F 103
Holker Hall & Gdns. (LA11 7PL) 2C 96
Holkham (NR23 1AB) 1A 78
Hollycombe (GU30 7LP) 4G 25
Holst Birthplace Mus. (GL52 2AY) **Cheltenham 192**
Holy Jesus Hospital (NE1 2AS) **Newcastle 205**
Holyrood Abbey (EH8 8DX) **Edinburgh 194**
Hopetoun (EH30 9SL) 2D 129
Hop Farm Family Pk. (TN12 6PY) 1A 28
Houghton Hall (PE31 6TZ) 3G 77
Houghton House (MK45 2EZ) 2A 52
Houghton Lodge Gdns. (SO20 6LQ) 3B 24
House of Dun (DD10 9LQ) 3F 145
House of Manannan Mus., Peel (IM5 1TA) 3B 108
House of the Binns (EH49 7NA) 1D 128
Houses of Parliament (SW1A 0RS) **London 203**
Housesteads Roman Fort & Mus. (NE47 6NN) 3A 114
Hoveton Hall Gdns. (NR12 8RJ) 3F 79
Hovingham Hall (YO62 4LU) 2A 100
Howick Hall Gdns. (NE66 3LB) 3G 121
Howletts Wild Animal Pk. (CT4 5EL) 5F 41
Hughenden Manor (HP14 4LA) 2G 37
Hugh Miller Mus. & Birthplace Cottage (IV11 8XA) 2B 158
Hunstanton Sea Life Sanctuary (PE36 5BH) 1F 77
Hunterian Mus. (G12 8QQ) 3G 127
Huntingtower Castle (PH1 3JL) 1C 136
Huntly Castle (AB54 4SH) 4C 160
Hurst Castle (SO41 0TP) 4B 16
Hutton-in-the-Forest (CA11 9TH) 1F 103
Hylands House & Gdns. (CM2 8WQ) 5G 53

I

Iceni Village & Mus. (PE37 8AG) 5G 77
Ickworth (IP29 5QE) 4H 65
Iford Manor (Peto Gdn.) (BA15 2BA) 1D 22
Ightham Mote (TN15 0NT) 5G 39
Ilam Pk. (DE6 2AZ) 5F 85
Ilfracombe Aquarium (EX34 9EQ) 2F 19
Imperial War Mus. Duxford (CB22 4QR) 1E 53
Imperial War Mus. London (SE1 6HZ) 203
Imperial War Mus. North, Trafford Park (M17 1TZ) 1C 84
Inchcolm Abbey (KY3 0XR) 1E 129
Inchmahome Priory (FK8 3RD) 3E 135
Ingatestone Hall (CM4 9NS) 1A 40
International Centre for Birds of Prey (GL18 1JJ) 3C 48
Inveraray Castle (PA32 8XE) 3H 133
Inveresk Lodge Gdn. (EH21 7TE) 2G 129
Inverewe Gdn. (IV22 2LG) 5C 162
Inverlochy Castle (PH33 6TQ) 1F 141
Inverness Mus. & Art Gallery (IV2 3EB) 198
Iona (PA76 6SP) 2A 132
Iron Bridge (TF8 7JP) 5A 72
Isel Hall (CA13 0QG) 1C 102
Isle of Man Steam Railway (IM1 4LL) 4C 108
Isle of Wight Steam Railway (PO33 4DS) 4D 16
Ivinghoe Beacon (LU6 2EG) 4H 51
Izaak Walton's Cottage (ST15 0PA) 3C 72

J

Jackfield Tile Mus. (TF8 7ND) 5A 72
Jane Austen Centre (BA1 2NT) **Bath 187**
Jane Austen's House Mus. (GU34 1SD) 3F 25
Jarlshof Prehistoric & Norse Settlement (ZE3 9JN) 10E 173
Jedburgh Abbey (TD8 6JQ) 3A 120
Jervaulx Abbey (HG4 4PH) 1D 98
JM Barrie's Birthplace (DD8 4BX) 3C 144
Jodrell Bank Discovery Centre (SK11 9DL) 3B 84
Jorvik Viking Centre (YO1 9WT) **York 214**

K

Kedleston Hall (DE22 5JH) 1H 73
Keighley & Worth Valley Railway (BD22 8NJ) 1A 92
Kelburn Castle & Country Centre (KA29 0BE) 4D 126
Keld Chapel (CA10 3QF) 3G 103
Kelham Island Mus. (S3 8RY) **Sheffield 210**
Kellie Castle & Gdn. (KY10 2RF) 3H 137
Kelmarsh Hall & Gdns. (NN6 9LY) 3E 63
Kelmscott Manor (GL7 3HJ) 2A 36
Kelso Abbey (TD5 7BB) 1B 120
Kelvingrove Art Gallery & Mus., Glasgow (G3 8AG) 3G 127
Kempton Pk. Racecourse (TW16 5AE) 3C 38
Kenilworth Castle (CV8 1NE) 3G 61
Kent & East Sussex Railway (TN30 6HE) 3C 28
Kentwell (CO10 9BA) 1B 54
Kenwood House (NW3 7JR) 2D 38
Keswick Mus. & Gallery (CA12 4NF) 2D 102
Kettle's Yard (CB3 0AQ) **Cambridge 191**
Kew Gdns. (TW9 3AB) 3C 38
Kidwelly Castle (SA17 5BQ) 5E 45
Kielder Water & Forest Pk. (NE48 1QZ) 1H 113
Kiftsgate Court Gdns. (GL55 6LN) 1G 49
Kilchurn Castle (PA33 1AF) 1A 134
Kildrummy Castle (AB33 8RA) 2B 152
Killerton (EX5 3LE) 2C 12
Kilmartin Glen Prehistoric Sites (PA31 8RQ) 4F 133
Kilmartin House Mus. (PA31 8RQ) 4F 133
Kinder Scout (S33 7ZJ) 2E 85
King's College Chapel (CB2 1TN) **Cambridge 191**
Kingston Bagpuize House & Gdn. (OX13 5AX) 2C 36
Kingston Lacy (BH21 4EA) 2E 15
Kingston Maurward Animal Pk. & Gdns. (DT2 8PY) 3C 14
Kinnersley Castle (HR3 6QF) 1G 47
Kinver Edge (DY7 5NP) 2C 60
Kiplin Hall (DL10 6AT) 5F 105
Kirby Hall (NN17 3EN) 1G 63
Kirby Muxloe Castle (LE9 2DH) 5C 74
Kirkham Priory (YO60 7JS) 3B 100
Kirklees Light Railway (HD8 9XJ) 3C 92
Kirkstall Abbey (LS5 3EH) 1C 92
Kirkwall Cathedral (KW15 1JF) 6D 172
Knaresborough Castle (HG5 8BB) 4F 99
Knebworth House (SG3 6PY) 3C 52
Knightshayes Court (EX16 7RQ) 1C 12
Knockhill Motor Circuit (KY12 9TF) 4C 136
Knole (TN15 0RP) 5G 39

Knoll Gdns. (BH21 7ND) . . . 2F 15
Knowsley Safari Pk. (L34 4AN) . . . 1G 83

L

Lacock Abbey (SN15 2LG) . . . 5E 35
Lady Lever Art Gallery (CH62 5EQ) . . . 2F 83
Laing Art Gallery (NE1 8AG) . . . Newcastle 205
Lake District Nat. Pk. (LA9 7RL) . . . 3E 103
Lakeside & Haverthwaite Railway (LA12 8AL) . . . 1C 96
Lamb House (TN31 7ES) . . . 3D 28
Lamphey Bishop's Palace (SA71 5NT) . . . 4E 43
Lamport Hall & Gdns. (NN6 9HD) . . . 3E 63
Lancaster Castle (LA1 1YJ) . . . 3D 96
Landmark Forest Adventure Pk. (PH23 3AJ) . . . 1D 150
Land's End (TR19 7AA) . . . 4A 4
Lanercost Priory (CA8 2HQ) . . . 3G 113
Langdale Pikes (LA22 9JY) . . . 4D 102
Langley Chapel (SY5 7HU) . . . 1H 59
Lanhydrock (PL30 5AD) . . . 2E 7
Lappa Valley Steam Railway (TR8 5LX) . . . 3C 6
Larmer Tree Gdns. (SP5 5PZ) . . . 1E 15
Laugharne Castle (SA33 4SA) . . . 3H 43
Launceston Castle (PL15 7DR) . . . 4D 10
Launceston Steam Railway (PL15 8DA) . . . 4D 10
Lauriston Castle (EH4 5QD) . . . 2F 129
Lavenham Guildhall (CO10 9QZ) . . . 1C 54
Laxey Wheel (IM4 7NL) . . . 3D 108
Layer Marney Tower (CO5 9US) . . . 4C 54
Leeds Castle (Kent) (ME17 1PL) . . . 5C 40
Leeds City Mus. (LS1 3AA) . . . 199
Legoland (SL4 4AY) . . . 3A 38
Leighton Buzzard Railway (LU7 4TN) . . . 3H 51
Leighton Hall (LA5 9ST) . . . 2E 97
Leiston Abbey (IP16 4TD) . . . 4G 67
Leith Hall (AB54 4NQ) . . . 1C 152
Leith Hill (RH5 6LX) . . . 1C 26
Lennoxlove House (EH41 4NZ) . . . 2B 130
Levant Mine & Beam Engine (TR19 7SX) . . . 3A 4
Levens Hall & Gdns. (LA8 0PD) . . . 1D 97
Lewes Castle (BN7 1YE) . . . 4F 27
Lichfield Cathedral (WS13 7LD) . . . 4F 73
Life (NE1 4EP) . . . Newcastle 205
Lightwater Valley (HG4 3HT) . . . 2E 99
Lilleshall Abbey (TF10 9HW) . . . 4B 72
Lincoln Castle (LN1 3AA) . . . 198
Lincoln Cathedral (LN2 1PZ) . . . 198
Lincoln Medieval Bishops' Palace (LN2 1PU) . . . 198
Lincolnshire Road Transport Mus. (LN6 3QT) . . . 4G 87
Lindisfarne (TD15 2SF) . . . 5H 131
Lindisfarne Castle (TD15 2SH) . . . 5H 131
Lindisfarne Priory (TD15 2RX) . . . 5H 131
Linlithgow Palace (EH49 7AL) . . . 2D 128
Linton Zoo (CB21 4XN) . . . 1F 53
Little Clarendon (SP3 5DZ) . . . 3F 23
Little Malvern Court (WR14 4JN) . . . 1C 48
Little Moreton Hall (CW12 4SD) . . . 5C 84
Liverpool Cathedral (L1 7AZ) . . . 2F 83
Liverpool Metropolitan RC Cathedral (L3 5TQ) . . . 200
Lizard Point (TR12 7NU) . . . 5E 5
Llanberis Lake Railway (LL55 3HB) . . . 4E 81
Llanerchaeron (SA48 8DG) . . . 5D 57
Llangollen Railway (LL20 7AJ) . . . 1D 70
Llansteffan Castle (SA33 5JX) . . . 4D 44
Llawhaden Castle (SA67 8HL) . . . 3E 43
Llechwedd Slate Caverns (LL41 3NB) . . . 1G 69
Llywernog Silver-Lead Mine (SY23 3AB) . . . 2G 57
Lochalsh Woodland Gdn. (IV40 8DN) . . . 1F 147
Loch Doon Castle (KA6 7QE) . . . 5D 117
Lochleven Castle (KY13 8ET) . . . 3D 136
Loch Lomond (G83 8PA) . . . 4C 134
Loch Lomond & The Trossachs Nat. Pk. (FK8 3UA) . . . 2D 134
Lochmaben Castle (DG11 1JE) . . . 1B 112
Loch Ness Exhibition Centre (IV63 6TU) . . . 5H 157
"Locomotion" Nat. Railway Mus. Shildon (DL4 1PQ) . . . 2F 105
Lodge Pk. (GL54 3PP) . . . 4G 49
Lodge RSPB Nature Reserve, The (SG19 2DL) . . . 1B 52
Logan Botanic Gdn. (DG9 9ND) . . . 5F 109
Logan Fish Pond & Marine Life Centre (DG9 9NF) . . . 5F 109
London 2012 Olympic Pk. (E20 2ST) . . . 2E 39
London Dungeon (SE1 2SZ) . . . 203
London Eye (SE1 7PB) . . . 203
London Film Mus. (SE1 3PB) . . . 203
London Zoo (NW1 4RY) . . . 202
Long Cross Victorian Gdns. (PL29 3TF) . . . 1D 6
Longleat Safari & Adventure Pk. (BA12 7NW) . . . 2D 22
Long Mynd (SY7 8BH) . . . 1G 59
Longthorpe Tower (PE3 6SU) . . . 1A 64
Longtown Castle (HR2 0LE) . . . 3G 47
Lord Leycester Hospital & The Master's Gdn., Warwick (CV34 4BH) . . . 4G 61
Loseley Pk. (GU3 1HS) . . . 1A 26
Lost Gdns. of Heligan (PL26 6EN) . . . 4D 6
Lotherton Hall (LS25 3EB) . . . 1E 93
Loughwood Meeting House (EX13 7DU) . . . 3F 13
[Lowry, The, Salford (M50 3AZ)] . . . 1C 84
Ludgershall Castle (SP11 9QS) . . . 1A 24
Ludlow Castle (SY8 1AY) . . . 3H 59
Lullingstone Castle & World Gdn. (DA4 0JA) . . . 4G 39
Lullingstone Roman Villa (DA4 0JA) . . . 4G 39
Lulworth Castle (BH20 5QS) . . . 4D 14
Lundy Island (EX39 2LY) . . . 2B 18
Lyddington Bede House (LE15 9LZ) . . . 1F 63
Lydford Castle & Saxon Town (EX20 4BH) . . . 4F 11
Lydford Gorge (EX20 4BH) . . . 4F 11
Lydiard House & Pk. (SN5 3PA) . . . 3G 35
Lydney Pk. Gdns. (GL15 6BU) . . . 5B 48
Lyme Pk. (SK12 2NX) . . . 2D 84
Lytes Cary Manor (TA11 7HU) . . . 4A 22
Lyveden New Bield (PE8 5AT) . . . 2G 63

M

Macclesfield Silk Museums (SK11 6PD) . . . 3D 84
Macduff Marine Aquarium (AB44 1SL) . . . 2E 160
MacLellan's Castle (DG6 4JD) . . . 4D 111
Madame Tussaud's (NW1 5LR) . . . London 202
Maeshowe Chambered Cairn (KW16 3HQ) . . . 6C 172
MAGNA Science Adventure Centre (S60 1DX) . . . 1B 86
Maiden Castle (DT2 9PP) . . . 4B 14
Major Oak (NG21 9HN) . . . 4D 86
Malham Cove (BD23 4DJ) . . . 3A 98
Malham Tarn (BD24 9PU) . . . 3A 98
Malleny Gdn. (EH14 7AF) . . . 3E 129
Malton Mus. (YO17 7LP) . . . 2B 100
Malvern Hills (HR8 1EN) . . . 2C 48
Manchester Art Gallery (M2 3JL) . . . 201
M & D's (Scotland's Theme Pk.), Motherwell (ML1 3RT) . . . 4A 128
Manderston (TD11 3PP) . . . 4E 130
Mannington Gdns. (NR11 7BB) . . . 2D 78
Manorbier Castle (SA70 7SY) . . . 5E 43
Manx Electric Railway (IM2 4NR) . . . 3D 108
Manx Mus. (IM1 3LY) . . . 4C 108
Mapledurham House (RG4 7TR) . . . 4E 37
Marble Hill House (TW1 2NL) . . . 3C 38
Markenfield Hall (HG4 3AD) . . . 3E 99
Mar Lodge Estate (AB35 5YJ) . . . 5E 151
Martin Mere Wetland Centre (L40 0TA) . . . 3C 90
Marwell Wildlife (SO21 1JH) . . . 4D 24
Marwood Hill Gdns. (EX31 4EB) . . . 3F 19
Mary Arden's Farm (CV37 9UN) . . . 5F 61
Mary, Queen of Scots' House (TD8 6EN) . . . 2A 120
Mary Rose Ship & Mus. (PO1 3LX) . . . Portsmouth 209
Max Gate (DT1 2AB) . . . 3C 14
Megginch Castle Gdns. (PH2 7SW) . . . 1E 137
Melbourne Hall (DE73 8EN) . . . 3A 74
Melford Hall (CO10 9AA) . . . 1B 54
Mellerstain House (TD3 6LG) . . . 1A 120
Melrose Abbey (TD6 9LG) . . . 1H 119
Menai Suspension Bridge (LL59 5HH) . . . 3E 81
Mendip Hills (BS40 7XS) . . . 1H 21
Merriments Gdns. (TN19 7RA) . . . 3B 28
Merseyside Maritime Mus. (L3 4AQ) . . . Liverpool 200
Mertoun Gdns. (TD6 0EA) . . . 1A 120
Michelham Priory (BN27 3QS) . . . 5G 27
Middleham Castle (DL8 4QR) . . . 1D 98
Midland Railway Centre (DE5 3QZ) . . . 5B 86
Mid-Norfolk Railway (NR19 1DF) . . . 5C 78
Millennium Coastal Pk. (SA15 2LG) . . . 3D 31
Millennium Stadium (CF10 1NS) . . . Cardiff 191
Milton Manor House (OX14 4EN) . . . 2C 36
Milton's Cottage (HP8 4JH) . . . 1A 38
Minack Theatre (TR19 6JU) . . . 4A 4
Minsmere (IP17 3BY) . . . 4G 67
Minterne Gdns. (DT2 7AU) . . . 2B 14
Mirehouse (CA12 4QE) . . . 2D 102
Misarden Pk. Gdns. (GL6 7JA) . . . 5E 49
Mistley Towers (CO11 1ET) . . . 2E 54
Mompesson House (SP1 2EL) . . . Salisbury 210
Monk Bretton Priory (S71 5QE) . . . 4D 93
Monkey Forest at Trentham (ST4 8AY) . . . 2C 72
Monkey Sanctuary (PL13 1NZ) . . . 3G 7
Monkey World (BH20 6HH) . . . 4D 14
Monk's House (BN7 3HF) . . . 5F 27
Montacute House (TA15 6XP) . . . 1H 13
Monteviot House (TD8 6UH) . . . 2A 120
Montgomery Castle (SY15 6HN) . . . 1E 58
Moreton Corbet Castle, Shawbury (SY4 4DW) . . . 3H 71
Morwellham Quay (PL19 8JL) . . . 2A 8
Moseley Old Hall, Wolverhampton (WV10 7HY) . . . 5D 72
Mother Shipton's Cave & the Petrifying Well (HG5 8DD) . . . 4F 99
Mottisfont (SO51 0LP) . . . 4B 24
Mount Edgcumbe House (PL10 1HZ) . . . 3A 8
Mount Ephraim Gdns. (ME13 9TX) . . . 4E 41
Mountfitchet Castle (CM24 8SP) . . . 3F 53
Mount Grace Priory (DL6 3JG) . . . 5B 106
Mount Stuart (PA20 9LR) . . . 4C 126
Mr Straw's House (S81 0JG) . . . 2C 86
Muchelney Abbey (TA10 0DQ) . . . 4H 21
Muchelney Priest's House (TA10 0DQ) . . . 4H 21
Mull of Kintyre (PA28 6RU) . . . 5A 122
Muncaster Castle & Gdns. (CA18 1RQ) . . . 5C 102
Mus. of Army Flying (SO20 8DY) . . . 3B 24
Mus. of East Anglian Life (IP14 1DL) . . . 5C 66
Mus. of Lakeland Life & Industry, Kendal (LA9 5AL) . . . 5G 103
Mus. of Lincolnshire Life (LN1 3LY) . . . Lincoln 198
Mus. of London (EC2Y 5HN) . . . 203
Mus. of Science & Industry (M3 4FP) . . . Manchester 201
Mus. of Scottish Lighthouses (AB43 9DU) . . . 2G 161
Mus. of the Gorge (TF8 7NH) . . . 5A 72
Mus. of the Isles (IV45 8RS) . . . 3E 147
Mus. of the Jewellery Quarter (B18 6HA) . . . Birmingham 188

N

Nat. Botanic Gdn. of Wales (SA32 8HG) . . . 4F 45
Nat. Coal Mining Mus. for England (WF4 4RH) . . . 3C 92
Nat. Coracle Centre (SA38 9JL) . . . 1C 44
Nat. Exhibition Centre (NEC) (B40 1NT) . . . 2F 61
Nat. Football Mus. (M4 3BG) . . . Manchester 201
Nat. Forest, The (DE12 6HZ) . . . 4H 73
Nat. Gallery (WC2N 5DN) . . . London 203
Nat. Gallery of Scotland (EH2 2EL) . . . Edinburgh 194
Nat. Glass Centre (SR6 0GL) . . . 4H 115
Nat. Horseracing Mus. (CB8 8JL) . . . 4F 65
Nat. Marine Aquarium (PL4 0LF) . . . Plymouth 208
Nat. Maritime Mus., Greenwich (SE10 9NF) . . . 3E 39
Nat. Maritime Mus. Cornwall, Falmouth (TR11 3QY) . . . 5C 6
Nat. Media Mus. (BD1 1NQ) . . . Bradford 190
Nat. Memorial Arboretum (DE13 7AR) . . . 4F 73
National Mining Mus. Scotland (EH22 4QN) . . . 3G 129
Nat. Motorcycle Mus. (B92 0EJ) . . . 2G 61
Nat. Motor Mus., (Beaulieu) (SO42 7ZN) . . . 2B 16
Nat. Mus. Cardiff (CF10 3NP) . . . 191
Nat. Mus. of Costume (DG2 8HQ) . . . 3A 112
Nat. Mus. of Flight (EH39 5LF) . . . 2B 130
Nat. Mus. of Rural Life Scotland (G76 9HR) . . . 4H 127
Nat. Mus. of Scotland (EH1 1JF) . . . Edinburgh 194
Nat. Portrait Gallery (WC2H 0HE) . . . London 203
Nat. Railway Mus. (YO26 4XJ) . . . York 214
Nat. Roman Legion Mus., Caerleon, Caerleon (NP18 1AE) . . . 2G 33
Nat. Sea Life Centre (B1 2HL) . . . Birmingham 188
Nat. Seal Sanctuary (TR12 6UG) . . . 4E 5
Nat. Showcaves Centre for Wales (SA9 1GJ) . . . 4B 46
Nat. Slate Mus. (LL55 4TY) . . . 4E 81
Nat. Space Centre (LE4 5NS) . . . 5C 74
Nat. Waterfront Mus. (SA1 3RD) . . . Swansea 212
Nat. Waterways Mus. (CH65 4FW) . . . 3G 83
Nat. Wool Mus. (SA44 5UP) . . . 2D 44
Natural History Mus. (SW7 5BD) . . . London 202
Natural History Mus. at Tring (HP23 6AP) . . . 4H 51
Neath Abbey (SA10 7DW) . . . 3G 31
Needles, The (PO39 0JH) . . . 4A 16
Nene Valley Railway (PE8 6LR) . . . 1A 64
Ness Botanic Gdns. (CH64 4AY) . . . 3F 83
Nessieland Castle Monster Centre (IV63 6TU) . . . 5H 157
Nether Winchendon House (HP18 0DY) . . . 4F 51
Netley Abbey (SO31 5HB) . . . 2C 16
New Abbey Corn Mill (DG2 8DX) . . . 3A 112
Newark Air Mus. (NG24 2NY) . . . 5F 87
Newark Castle (Newark-on-Trent) (NG24 1BN) . . . 5E 87
Newark Castle (Port Glasgow) (PA14 5NG) . . . 2E 127
Newark Pk. (GL12 7PZ) . . . 2C 34
New Art Gallery Walsall (WS2 8LG) . . . 1E 61
Newburgh Priory (YO61 4AS) . . . 2H 99
Newbury Racecourse (RG14 7NZ) . . . 5C 36
Newby Hall & Gdns. (HG4 5AE) . . . 3F 99
Newcastle Castle (Bridgend) (CF31 4JW) . . . 3B 32
Newcastle Upon Tyne Castle Keep (NE1 1RQ) . . . 205
New Forest Nat. Pk. (SO43 7BD) . . . 2H 15
New Lanark World Heritage Site Visitor Centre (ML11 9DB) . . . 5B 128
Newmarket Racecourse (CB8 0TG) . . . 4F 65
Newquay Zoo (TR7 2LZ) . . . 2C 6
Newstead Abbey (NG15 8NA) . . . 5C 86
Nine Ladies Stone Circle (DE4 2LF) . . . 4G 85
Norfolk Lavender (PE31 7JE) . . . 2F 77
Norham Castle (TD15 2LL) . . . 5F 131
Normanby Hall Mus. (DN15 9HU) . . . 3B 94
North Downs (GU10 5QE) . . . 5C 38
North Norfolk Railway (NR26 8RA) . . . 1D 78
Northumberland Nat. Pk. (NE46 1BS) . . . 1A 114
North York Moors Nat. Pk. (YO18 8RN) . . . 5E 107
North Yorkshire Moors Railway (YO18 7AJ) . . . 1C 100
Norton Conyers (HG4 5EQ) . . . 2F 99
Norton Priory Mus. & Gdns. (WA7 1SX) . . . 2H 83
Norwich Castle Mus. & Art Gallery (NR1 3JU) . . . 205
Norwich Cathedral (NR1 4DH) . . . 205
Nostell Priory (WF4 1QE) . . . 3E 93
Nunney Castle (BA11 4LN) . . . 2C 22
Nunnington Hall (YO62 5UY) . . . 2A 100
Nymans (RH17 6EB) . . . 3D 26

O

Oakham Castle (LE15 6DR) . . . 5F 75
Oakwell Hall, Birstall (WF17 9LG) . . . 2C 92
Oakwood Theme Pk. (SA67 8DE) . . . 3E 43
Observatory Science Centre (BN27 1RN) . . . 4A 28
Oceanarium (BH2 5AA) . . . Bournemouth 190
Offa's Dyke (NP16 7NQ) . . . 5A 48
Okehampton Castle (EX20 1JA) . . . 3F 11
Old Beaupre Castle (CF71 7LT) . . . 4D 32
Old Gorhambury House (AL3 6AH) . . . 5B 52
Old Oswestry Hill Fort (SY10 7AA) . . . 2E 71
Old Sarum (SP1 3SD) . . . 3G 23
Old Wardour Castle (SP3 6RR) . . . 4E 23
Old Winchester Hill Hill Fort (GU32 1HN) . . . 4E 25
Olympic Pk. (London 2012) (E20 2ST) . . . 2E 39
Orford Castle (IP12 2NF) . . . 1H 55
Orford Ness (IP12 2NU) . . . 1H 55
Ormesby Hall (TS7 9AS) . . . 3C 106
Osborne House (PO32 6JX) . . . 3D 16
Osterley Pk. & House (TW7 4RB) . . . 3C 38
Oulton Pk. Motor Circuit (CW6 9BW) . . . 4H 83
Our Dynamic Earth (EH8 8AS) . . . Edinburgh 194
Overbeck's (TQ8 8LW) . . . 5D 8
Owletts (DA12 3AP) . . . 4A 40
Oxburgh Hall (PE33 9PS) . . . 5G 77
Oxford Christ Church Cathedral (OX1 4JF) . . . 207
Oxwich Castle (SA3 1LU) . . . 4D 31
Oystermouth Castle (SA3 5TA) . . . 4F 31

P

Packwood House (B94 6AT) . . . 3F 61
Paignton Zoo (TQ4 7EU) . . . 3E 9
Painshill Pk. (KT11 1JE) . . . 5B 38
Painswick Rococo Gdn. (GL6 6TH) . . . 4D 48
Palace of Holyroodhouse (EH8 8DX) . . . Edinburgh 194
Papplewick Pumping Station (NG15 9AJ) . . . 5C 86
Paradise Pk. (Hayle) (TR27 4HB) . . . 3C 4
Paradise Wildlife Pk. (EN10 7QZ) . . . 5D 52
Parcevall Hall Gdns. (BD23 6DE) . . . 3C 98
Parham (RH20 4HS) . . . 4B 26
Pashley Manor Gdns. (TN5 7HE) . . . 3B 28
Paul Corin's Magnificent Music Machines (PL14 4SH) . . . 2G 7
Paultons Pk. (SO51 6AL) . . . 1B 16
Paxton House (TD15 1SZ) . . . 4F 131
Paycocke's (CO6 1NS) . . . 3B 54
Peak Cavern (S33 8WS) . . . 2F 85
Peak District Nat. Pk. (DE45 1AE) . . . 3F 85
Peak Rail (DE4 3NA) . . . 4G 85
Peckover House & Gdn. (PE13 1JR) . . . 5D 76
Peel Castle (IM5 1AB) . . . 3B 108
Pembroke Castle (SA71 4LA) . . . 4D 43
Pembrokeshire Coast Nat. Pk. (SA41 3XD) . . . 3C 42
Pencarrow (PL30 3AG) . . . 5A 10
Pendennis Castle (TR11 4LP) . . . 5C 6
Penhow Castle (NP26 3AD) . . . 2H 33
Penrhyn Castle (LL57 4HN) . . . 3F 81
Penrith Castle (CA11 7JB) . . . 2G 103
Penshurst Place & Gdns. (TN11 8DG) . . . 1G 27
Peover Hall (WA16 9HW) . . . 3B 84
Perth Mus. & Art Gallery (PH1 5LB) . . . 207
Peterborough Cathedral (PE1 1XZ) . . . 208
Petworth House & Pk. (GU28 0AE) . . . 3A 26
Pevensey Castle (BN24 5LE) . . . 5H 27
Peveril Castle (S33 8WQ) . . . 2F 85
Philipps House (SP3 5HH) . . . 3F 23
Pickering Castle (YO18 7AX) . . . 1C 100
Picton Castle (SA62 4AS) . . . 3E 43
Piel Castle (LA13 0QN) . . . 3B 96
Pistyll Rhaeadr (SY10 0BZ) . . . 3C 70
Pitmedden Gdn. (AB41 7PD) . . . 1F 153
Pitt Rivers Mus. (OX1 3PP) . . . Oxford 207
Plantasia (SA1 2AL) . . . Swansea 212
Plas Brondanw Gdn. (LL48 6SW) . . . 1F 69
Plas Newydd (Llanfairpwllgwyngyll) (LL61 6DQ) . . . 4E 81
Plas Newydd (Llangollen) (LL20 8AW) . . . 1E 70
Plas yn Rhiw (LL53 8AB) . . . 3B 68
Pleasurewood Hills (NR32 5DZ) . . . 1H 67
Poldark Mine (TR13 0ES) . . . 5A 6
Polesden Lacey (RH5 6BD) . . . 5C 38
Pollok House, Glasgow (G43 1AT) . . . 3G 127
Pontcysyllte Aqueduct (LL20 7YS) . . . 1E 71
Portchester Castle (PO16 9QW) . . . 2E 17
Portland Castle (DT5 1AZ) . . . 5B 14
Port Lympne Wild Animal Pk. (CT21 4PD) . . . 2F 29
Portsmouth Historic Dockyard (PO1 3LJ) . . . 209
Potteries Mus. & Art Gallery (ST1 3DW) . . . Stoke 211
Powderham Castle (EX6 8JQ) . . . 4C 12
Powis Castle & Gdn. (SY21 8RF) . . . 5E 70
Prebendal Manor House (PE8 6QG) . . . 1H 63
Prestongrange Mus. (EH32 9RX) . . . 2G 129
Preston Manor (BN1 6SD) . . . 5E 27
Preston Mill & Phantassie Doocot (EH40 3DS) . . . 2B 130
Preston Tower (Northumberland) (NE67 5DH) . . . 2F 121
Preston Tower, Prestonpans (EH32 9NN) . . . 2G 129
Prideaux Place (PL28 8RP) . . . 1D 6
Prior Pk. Landscape Gdn. (BA2 5AH) . . . 5C 34
Provan Hall (G34 9NJ) . . . 3H 127
Prudoe Castle (NE42 6NA) . . . 3D 115

Q

Quantock Hills (TA4 4AP) . . . 3E 21
Quarry Bank Mill (DL8 3SG) . . . 2C 84
Quebec House (TN16 1TD) . . . 5F 39
Queen Elizabeth Country Pk. (PO8 0QE) . . . 1F 17
Queen Elizabeth Forest Pk. (FK8 3UZ) . . . 4D 134
Quex House & Gdns. (CT7 0BH) . . . 4H 41
Quilt Mus. & Gallery (YO1 7PW) . . . York 214

R

Raby Castle (DL2 3AH) . . . 2E 105
RAF Holmpton (HU19 2RG) . . . 2G 95
RAF Mus. Cosford (TF11 8UP) . . . 5B 72
RAF Mus. London (NW9 5LL) . . . 1D 38
Raglan Castle (NP15 2BT) . . . 5H 47
Ragley (B49 5NJ) . . . 5E 61
Ramsey Island (SA62 6SA) . . . 2B 42
Ravenglass & Eskdale Railway (CA18 1SW) . . . 4C 102
Raveningham Gdns. (NR14 6NS) . . . 1F 67
Ravenscraig Castle (KY1 2AZ) . . . 4E 137
Reculver Towers (CT6 6SX) . . . 4G 41
Renishaw Hall & Gdns. (S21 3WB) . . . 3B 86
Restoration House (ME1 1RF) . . . Medway 204
Restormel Castle (PL22 0HN) . . . 2F 7
Revolution House (S41 9LA) . . . 3A 86
Rheged Centre (CA11 0DQ) . . . 2G 103
Rheidol Power Station & Vis. Cen. (SY23 3NF) . . . 3G 57
Rhossili Bay (SA3 1PR) . . . 4D 30
RHS Gdn. Harlow Carr (HG3 1QB) . . . 4E 99
RHS Gdn. Hyde Hall (CM3 8ET) . . . 1B 40
RHS Gdn. Rosemoor (EX38 8PH) . . . 1F 11
RHS Gdn. Wisley (GU23 6QB) . . . 5B 38
Rhuddlan Castle (LL18 5AD) . . . 3C 82
Ribchester Roman Mus. (PR3 3XS) . . . 1E 91
Richmond Castle (DL10 4QW) . . . 4E 105
Rievaulx Abbey (YO62 5LB) . . . 1H 99
Rievaulx Terrace (YO62 5LJ) . . . 1H 99
Ripley Castle (HG3 3AY) . . . 3E 99
Ripon Cathedral (HG4 1QT) . . . 2F 99
River & Rowing Mus. (RG9 1BF) . . . 3F 37
Riverside Mus., Glasgow (G3 8RS) . . . 3G 127
Robert Burns Birthplace Mus. (KA7 4PQ) . . . 3C 116
Robert Burns House (DG1 2PS) . . . Dumfries 193
Roche Abbey (S66 8NW) . . . 2C 86
Rochester Castle (ME1 1SW) . . . Medway 204
Rochester Cathedral (ME1 1SX) . . . Medway 204
Rockbourne Roman Villa (SP6 3PG) . . . 1G 15
Rockingham Castle (LE16 8TH) . . . 1F 63
Rockingham Motor Speedway (NN17 5AF) . . . 1G 63
Rode Hall (ST7 3QP) . . . 5C 84
Rodmarton Manor (GL7 6PF) . . . 2E 35
Rokeby Pk. (DL12 9RZ) . . . 3D 105
Rollright Stones (OX7 5QB) . . . 2A 50
Roman Army Mus. (CA8 7JB) . . . 3H 113
Roman Painted House (CT17 9AJ) . . . Dover 193
Roman Vindolanda (NE47 7JN) . . . 3A 114
Romney, Hythe & Dymchurch Railway (TN28 8PL) . . . 3E 29
Roseberry Topping (TS9 6QX) . . . 3C 106
Rothesay Castle (PA20 0DA) . . . 3B 126
Rothiemurchus Centre (PH22 1QH) . . . 2D 150
Rousham House Gdns. (OX25 4QX) . . . 3C 50
Royal Academy of Arts (W1J 0BD) . . . London 202
Royal Albert Bridge (PL12 4GT) . . . 3A 8
Royal Armouries Mus. (LS10 1LT) . . . Leeds 199
Royal Botanic Gdn. Edinburgh (EH3 5LR) . . . 2F 129
Royal Botanic Gdns., Kew (TW9 3AB) . . . 3C 38
Royal Cornwall Mus. (TR1 2SJ) . . . 4C 6
Royal Crown Derby Mus. (DE23 8JZ) . . . 193
Royal Navy Submarine Mus. (PO12 2AS) . . . 3E 16
Royal Pavilion (BN1 1EE) . . . Brighton & Hove 189
Royal Pump Room Mus. (HG1 2RY) . . . Harrogate 197
Royal Yacht Britannia (EH6 6JJ) . . . 2F 129
Ruddington Framework Knitters' Mus. (NG11 6HE) . . . 2C 74
Rufford Abbey (NG22 9DF) . . . 4D 86
Rufford Old Hall (L40 1SG) . . . 3C 90
Rufus Stone (SO43 7HN) . . . 1A 16
Runnymede (RG18 9NA) . . . 3A 38
Rushton Triangular Lodge (NN14 1RP) . . . 2F 63
Russell-Cotes Art Gallery & Mus. (BH1 3AA) . . . Bournemouth 190
Rutland County Mus. (LE15 6HW) . . . 5F 75
Rutland Railway Mus. (LE15 7BX) . . . 4F 75
Rutland Water (LE15 8BL) . . . 5G 75
Rydal Mount & Gdns. (LA22 9LU) . . . 4E 103
Ryedale Folk Mus. (YO62 6UA) . . . 5E 107
Ryton Gdns. (CV8 3LG) . . . 3B 62

S

Saatchi Gallery (SW3 4RY) . . . London 202
Sainsbury Centre for Visual Arts (NR4 7TJ) . . . 5D 78
St Abb's Head (TD14 5QF) . . . 3F 131
St Albans Cathedral (AL1 1BY) . . . 5B 52
St Andrews Aquarium (KY16 9AS) . . . 209
St Andrews Cathedral (KY16 9QL) . . . 209
St Augustine's Abbey (CT1 1PF) . . . Canterbury 190
St David's Cathedral & Bishop's Palace (SA62 6RD) . . . 2B 42
St Dogmaels Abbey (SA43 3JH) . . . 1B 44

St Fagans: Nat. History Mus. (CF5 6XB) 4E 32
St Giles' Cathedral (EH1 1RE) **Edinburgh 194**
St John's Jerusalem (DA4 9HQ) 3G 39
St Mary's Cathedral, Glasgow (G4 9JB) 3G 127
St Mary's House & Gdns. (BN44 3WE) 4C 26
St Mawes Castle (TR2 5DE) 5C 6
St Michael's Mount (TR17 0HS) 4C 4
St Paul's Cathedral (EC4M 8AE) **London 203**
Salford Mus. & Art Gallery (M5 4WU) **Manchester 201**
Salisbury Cathedral (SP1 2EG) **210**
Saltaire World Heritage Village (BD18 4PL) 1B 92
Saltram (PL7 1UH) 3B 8
Samlesbury Hall (PR5 0UP) 1E 90
Sandford Orcas Manor House (DT9 4SB) 4B 22
Sandham Memorial Chapel (RG20 9JT) 5C 36
Sandown Pk. Racecourse (KT10 9AJ) 4C 38
Sandringham (PE35 6EP) 3F 77
Sarehole Mill (B13 0BD) 2E 61
Savill Gdn., The (SL4 2HT) 3A 38
Sawley Abbey (BB7 4LE) 5G 97
Saxtead Green Post Mill (IP13 9QQ) 4E 67
Scafell Pike (CA20 1EX) 4D 102
Scampston Hall (YO17 8NG) 2C 100
Scarborough Castle (YO11 1HY) 1E 101
Science Mus. (SW7 2DD) **London 202**
Scone Palace (PH2 6BD) 1D 136
Scotch Whisky Experience (EH1 2NE) **Edinburgh 194**
Scotney Castle (TN3 8JN) 2A 28
Scotstarvit Tower (KY15 5PA) 2F 137
Scottish Deer Centre (KY15 4NQ) 2F 137
[Scottish Exhibition & Conference Centre (SECC), Glasgow (G3 8YW)] 3G 127
Scottish Fisheries Mus. (KY10 3AB) 3H 137
Scottish Industrial Railway Centre (KA6 7JF) 4D 116
Scottish Maritime Mus. (KA12 8QE) 1C 116
Scottish Nat. Gallery of Modern Art, Edinburgh (EH4 3DR) 2F 129
Scottish Nat. Portrait Gallery (EH2 1JD) **Edinburgh 194**
Scottish Parliament (EH99 1SP) **Edinburgh 194**
Scottish Sea Life Sanctuary (PA37 1SE) 4D 140
Sea Life Adventure, Southend-on-Sea (SS1 2ER) 2C 40
Sea Life Blackpool (FY1 5AA) **188**
Sea Life Brighton (BN2 1TB) **Brighton & Hove 189**
Sea Life Great Yarmouth (NR30 3AH) **196**
Sea Life Loch Lomond (G83 8QL) 1E 127
Sea Life London Aquarium (SE1 7PB) **203**
Sea Life Scarborough (YO12 6RP) 5H 107
Sea Life Weymouth (DT4 7SX) 4B 14
SeaQuarium, Rhyl (LL18 3AF) 2C 82
SeaQuarium, Weston-super-Mare (BS23 1BE) 5G 33
Seaton Delaval Hall (NE26 4QR) 2G 115
Seaton Tramway (EX12 2NQ) 3F 13
Seaview Wildlife Encounter (PO34 5AP) 3E 16
Selby Abbey (YO8 4PF) 1G 93
Selly Manor (B30 2AD) 2E 61
Severn Valley Railway (DY12 1BG) 2B 60
Sewerby Hall & Gdns. (YO15 1EA) 3G 101
Sezincote (GL56 9AW) 2G 49
Shaftesbury Abbey Mus. & Gdns. (SP7 8JR) 4D 22
Shakespeare's Birthplace (CV37 6QW) **Stratford 212**
Shandy Hall (YO61 4AD) 2H 99
Shap Abbey (CA10 3NB) 3G 103
Shaw's Corner (AL6 9BX) 4B 52
Sheffield Pk. & Gdn. (TN22 3QX) 3F 27
Sheffield Winter Gdn. (S1 2PP) **210**
Shepreth Wildlife Pk. (SG8 6PZ) 1D 53
Sherborne Castle (DT9 3PY) 1B 14
Sherborne Old Castle (DT9 3SA) 1B 14
Sherwood Forest (NG21 9HN) 4D 86
Shibden Hall (HX3 6XG) 2B 92
Shipton Hall (TF13 6JZ) 1H 59
Shoe Mus. (BA16 0EQ) 3H 21
Shrewsbury Castle (SY1 2AT) **210**
Shugborough (ST17 0XB) 3D 73
Shute Barton (EX13 7PT) 3F 13
Shuttleworth Collection (SG18 9EP) 1B 52
Silbury Hill (SN8 1QH) 5G 35
Silverstone Motor Circuit (NN12 8TN) 1E 51
Sir Harold Hillier Gdns. (SO51 0QA) 4B 24
Sir Walter Scott's Courtroom (TD7 4BT) 2G 119
Sissinghurst Castle Gdn. (TN17 2AB) 2C 28
Sizergh Castle & Gdn. (LA8 8AE) 1D 97
Skara Brae Prehistoric Village (KW16 3LR) 6B 172
Skenfrith Castle (NP7 8UH) 3H 47
Skiddaw (CA12 4QE) 2D 102
Skipness Castle (PA29 6XU) 4H 125
Skipton Castle (BD23 1AW) 4B 98
Skokholm Island (SA62 3BL) 4B 42
Skomer Island (SA62 3BL) 4B 42
Sledmere House (YO25 3XG) 3D 100
Slimbridge Wetland Centre (GL2 7BT) 5C 48
Smailholm Tower (TD5 7PG) 1A 120
Smallhythe Place (TN30 7NG) 3D 28
Snaefell Mountain Railway (IM4 7NL) 3D 108
Snibston (LE67 3LN) 4B 74
Snowdon (LL55 4UL) 5F 81
Snowdonia Nat. Pk. (LL48 6LF) 2G 69
Snowdon Mountain Railway (LL55 4TY) 5F 81
Snowshill Manor & Gdn. (WR12 7JU) 2F 49
Somerleyton (NR32 5QQ) 1G 67
Sorn Castle (KA5 6HR) 2E 117
Souter Lighthouse (SR6 7NH) 3H 115
South Devon Railway (TQ11 0DZ) 2D 8
South Downs Nat. Pk. (GU29 9SB) 4F 27
South Lakes Wild Animal Pk. (LA15 8JR) 2B 96
South Tynedale Railway (CA9 3JB) 5A 114
Southwell Minster (NG25 0HD) 5E 86
Spa Valley Railway (TN2 5QY) 2G 27
Speedwell Cavern (S33 8WA) 2F 85
Speke Hall (L24 1XD) 2G 83
Spetchley Pk. Gdns. (WR5 1RR) 5C 60
Spinners Gdn. (SO41 5QE) 3B 16
Spofforth Castle (HG3 1DA) 4F 99
Sprivers Gdn. (TN12 8DR) 1A 28
Spurn Head (HU12 0UG) 3H 95
Spynie Palace (IV30 5QG) 2G 159
Squerryes (TN16 1SJ) 5F 39
Stafford Castle (ST16 1DJ) 3D 72
Stagshaw Gdn. (LA22 0HE) 4E 103
Stanage Edge (S33 0AD) 2G 85
Standen (RH19 4NE) 2E 27
Stanford Hall (LE17 6DH) 3C 62
Stansted Pk. (PO9 6DX) 2F 17
Stanway House & Fountain (GL54 5PQ) 2F 49
Staunton Harold Church (LE65 1RT) 3A 74
Steam - Mus. of the Great Western Railway (SN2 2EY) 3G 35
Stirling Castle (FK8 1EJ) **211**
Stoke Pk. Pavilions (NN12 7RZ) 1F 51
Stokesay Castle (SY7 9AH) 2G 59
Stoke-sub-Hamdon Priory (TA14 6QP) 1H 13
Stoneacre (ME15 8RS) 5C 40
Stonehenge (SP4 7DE) 2G 23
Stoneleigh Abbey (CV8 2LF) 3H 61
Stonor (RG9 6HF) 3F 37
Storybook Glen (AB12 5FT) 4F 153
Stott Pk. Bobbin Mill (LA12 8AX) 1C 96
Stourhead (BA12 6QD) 3C 22
Stourton House Flower Gdn. (BA12 6QF) 3C 22
Stowe House (MK18 5EH) 2E 51
Stowe Landscape Gdns. (MK18 5EH) 2E 51
Strata Florida Abbey (SY25 6BJ) 4G 57
Stratfield Saye House (RG7 2BZ) 5F 37
Strathaven Castle (ML10 6QS) 5A 128
Strathspey Railway (PH22 1PY) 2D 150
Strawberry Hill, Twickenham (TW1 4ST) 3C 38
Strome Castle (IV54 8YJ) 5A 156
Sudbury Hall (DE6 5HT) 2F 73
Sudeley Castle (GL54 5JD) 3F 49
Sufton Court (HR1 4LU) 2A 48
Sulgrave Manor (OX17 2SD) 1D 50
Summerlee - Mus. of Scottish Industrial Life (ML5 1QD) 3A 128
Sundown Adventureland (DN22 0HX) 3E 87
Sutton Hoo (IP12 3DJ) 1F 55
Sutton Pk. (YO61 1DP) 3H 99
Sutton Scarsdale Hall (S44 5UT) 4B 86
Sutton Valence Castle (ME17 3DA) 1C 28
Swaledale Mus. (DL11 6QT) 5D 104
Swallow Falls (LL24 0DH) 5G 81
Swansea RC Cathedral (SA1 2BX) **212**
Sweetheart Abbey (DG2 8BU) 3A 112
Swindon & Cricklade Railway (SN25 2DA) 2G 35
Swiss Gdn. (SG18 9ER) 1B 52
Syon Pk. (TW8 8JF) 3C 38

T

Tabley House (WA16 0HB) 3B 84
Talley Abbey (SA19 7AX) 2G 45
Talyllyn Railway (LL36 9EY) 5F 69
Tamworth Castle (B79 7NA) 5G 73
Tank Mus. (BH20 6JG) 4D 14
Tantallon Castle (EH39 5PN) 1B 130
Tarn Hows (LA22 0PR) 5E 103
Tar Tunnel (TF8 7HS) 5A 72
Tate Britain (SW1P 4RG) **London 203**
Tate Liverpool (L3 4BB) **200**
Tate Modern (SE1 9TG) **London 203**
Tate St Ives (TR26 1TG) 2C 4
Tattershall Castle (LN4 4NR) 5B 88
Tatton Pk. (WA16 6QN) 2B 84
Tay Forest Pk. (PH17 2QG) 3C 142
Teifi Valley Railway (SA44 5TD) 1D 44
Temple Newsam (LS15 0AE) 1D 92
Tenby Castle (SA70 7BP) 4F 43
Thames Barrier (SE18 5NJ) 3F 39
Thetford Forest Pk. (IP26 5DB) 1A 66
Thetford Priory (IP24 1AZ) 2A 66
Thirlestane Castle (TD2 6RU) 5B 130
Thoresby Gallery (NG22 9EP) 3D 86
Thornham Walled Gdn. (IP23 8HH) 3D 66
Thornton Abbey & Gatehouse (DN39 6TU) 3E 94
Thorpe Pk. (KT16 8PN) 4B 38
Thorp Perrow Arboretum (DL8 2PR) 1E 99
Threave Castle (DG7 2AB) 3E 111
Threave Gdn. (DG7 1RX) 3E 111
Thrigby Hall Wildlife Gdns. (NR29 3DR) 4G 79
Thruxton Motor Circuit (SP11 8PW) 2A 24
Thursford Collection (NR21 0AS) 2B 78
Tilbury Fort (RM18 7NR) 3H 39
Tintagel Castle (PL34 0HE) 4A 10
Tintagel Visitor Information Centre (PL34 0AJ) 4A 10
Tintern Abbey (NP16 6SH) 5A 48
Tintinhull Gdn. (BA22 8QL) 4A 22
Titchfield Abbey (PO15 5RA) 2D 16
Tiverton Castle (EX16 6RP) 1C 12
Tolpuddle Martyrs Mus. (DT2 7EH) 3C 14
Tolquhon Castle (AB41 7LP) 1F 153
Torridon Countryside Centre (IV22 2EW) 3B 156
Totnes Castle (TQ9 5NU) 2E 9
Tower Bridge (SE1 2UP) **London 203**
Tower of London, The (EC3N 4AB) **203**
Towneley Hall Art Gallery & Mus. (BB11 3RQ) 1G 91
Townend (LA23 1LB) 4F 103
Traquair House (EH44 6PW) 1F 119
Treasurer's House, Martock (TA12 6JL) 1H 13
Treasurer's House, York (YO1 7JL) **214**
Trebah Gdn. (TR11 5JZ) 4E 5
Tredegar House (NP10 8YW) 3F 33
Tregrehan Gdn. (PL24 2SJ) 3E 7
Trelissick Gdn. (TR3 6QL) 5C 6
Trengwainton Gdn. (TR20 8RZ) 3B 4
Trentham Gdns. (ST4 8NF) 1C 72
Trerice (TR8 4PG) 3C 6
Tresco Abbey Gdns. (TR24 0QQ) 1A 4
Tretower Castle & Court (NP8 1RF) 3E 47
Trewithen (TR2 4DD) 4D 6
Tropical Birdland (LE9 9GN) 5B 74
Trossachs, The (FK17 8HZ) 3E 135
Tudor Merchant's House (SA70 7BX) 4F 43
Turner Contemporary (CT9 1HG) 3H 41
Turton Tower (BL7 0HG) 3F 91
Tutbury Castle (DE13 9JF) 3G 73
Twycross Zoo (CV9 3PX) 5H 73
Ty Mawr Wybrnant (LL25 0HJ) 5G 81
Tynemouth Castle (NE30 4BZ) 3G 115
Tyntesfield (BS48 1NT) 4A 34

U

[U-Boat Story, Birkenhead (CH41 6DU)] 2F 83
Uffington White Horse (SN7 7QJ) 3B 36
Ugbrooke (TQ13 0AD) 5B 12
Upnor Castle (ME2 4XG) 3B 40
Uppark (GU31 5QR) 1F 17
Upton Castle Gdns. (SA72 4SE) 4E 43
Upton House & Gdns. (OX15 6HT) 1B 50
Urquhart Castle (IV63 6XJ) 1H 149
Usher Gallery (LN2 1NN) **Lincoln 198**
Usk Castle (NP15 1SD) 5G 47

V

Vale of Rheidol Railway (SY23 1PG) 3F 57
Valle Crucis Abbey (LL20 8DT) 1E 70
Valley Gdns. (SL4 2HT) 4A 38
Veddw House Gdn. (NP16 6PH) 2H 33
Verulamium Mus., St Albans (AL3 4SW) 5B 52
Victoria & Albert Mus. (SW7 2RL) **London 202**
Vyne, The (RG24 9HL) 1E 25

W

Waddesdon Manor (HP18 0JH) 4F 51
Wakehurst Place (RH17 6TN) 2E 27
Walker Art Gallery (L3 8EL) **Liverpool 200**
Wallington (NE61 4AR) 1D 114
Walmer Castle & Gdns. (CT14 7LJ) 1H 29
Walsingham Abbey (NR22 6BL) 2B 78
Warkworth Castle & Hermitage (NE65 0UJ) 4G 121
Warwick Castle (CV34 4QX) 4G 61
Washington Old Hall (NE38 7LE) 4G 115
Watercress Line (SO24 9JG) 3E 25
Watermouth Castle (EX34 9SL) 2F 19
Waterperry Gdns. (OX33 1JZ) 5E 51
Watersmeet (EX35 6NT) 2H 19
Weald & Downland Open Air Mus. (PO18 0EU) 1G 17
Weaver Hall Mus. & Workhouse (CW9 8AB) 3A 84
Weaver's Cottage (PA10 2JG) 3E 127
Wedgwood Visitor Centre (ST12 9ER) 2C 72
Weir, The (HR4 7QF) 1H 47
Wells & Walsingham Light Railway (NR23 1QB) 1B 78
Wells Cathedral (BA5 2UE) 2A 22
Welney Wetland Centre (PE14 9TN) 1E 65
Welsh Highland Heritage Railway (LL49 9DY) 2E 69
Welsh Highland Railway (LL54 5UP) **Caernarfon 190**
Welsh Mountain Zoo, Colwyn Bay (LL28 5UY) 3H 81
Welshpool & Llanfair Light Railway (SY21 0SF) 5D 70
Wembley Stadium (HA9 0WS) 2C 38
Wenlock Edge (SY7 9JH) 2G 59
Wenlock Priory (TF13 6HS) 5A 72
Wentworth Castle Gdns. (S75 3ET) 4D 92
Weobley Castle (SA3 1HB) 3D 31
Weoley Castle (B29 5RX) 2E 61
Wesley Cottage (PL15 7TG) 4C 10
Westbury Court Gdn. (GL14 1PD) 4C 48
West Green House Gdn. (RG27 8JB) 1F 25
West Highland Mus. (PH33 6AJ) 1F 141
West Midland Safari & Leisure Pk. (DY12 1LF) 3C 60
Westminster Abbey (SW1P 3PA) **London 203**
Westminster RC Cathedral (SW1P 1QH) **London 202**
Westonbirt Nat. Arboretum (GL8 8QS) 3D 34
Weston Pk. (TF11 8LE) 4C 72
West Somerset Railway (TA24 5BG) 4E 21
Westwood Manor (BA15 2AF) 1D 22
West Wycombe Pk. (HP14 3AJ) 2G 37
Wetlands Animal Pk. (DN22 8SB) 2D 86
Whalley Abbey (BB7 9TN) 1F 91
Whipsnade Tree Cathedral (LU6 2LL) 4A 52
Whipsnade Zoo (LU6 2LF) 4A 52
Whitby Abbey (YO22 4JT) 3G 107
White Castle (NP7 8UD) 4G 47
Whitehorse Hill (SN7 7QJ) 3B 36
White Scar Cave (LA6 3AW) 2G 97
Whithorn Priory & Mus. (DG8 8PY) 5B 110
Whitmore Hall (ST5 5HW) 1C 72
Whitworth Art Gallery, Hulme (M15 6ER) 1C 84
Wicken Fen Nat. Nature Reserve (CB7 5YG) 3E 65
Wicksteed Pk. (NN15 6NJ) 3F 63
Wightwick Manor & Gdns. (WV6 8EE) 1C 60
Wigmore Castle (HR6 9UJ) 4G 59
Wilberforce House Mus. (HU1 1NE) **Hull 199**
Wilderhope Manor (TF13 6EG) 1H 59
Wilton House (SP2 0BJ) 3F 23
Wimbledon Lawn Tennis Mus. (SW19 5HP) 3D 38
Wimpole Hall & Gdns. (SG8 0BW) 5C 64
Winchester Cathedral (SO23 9LS) **213**
Windmill Hill (SN4 9NW) 4F 35
Windsor Castle (SL4 1NJ) **213**
Wingfield Manor (DE55 7NH) 5A 86
Winkworth Arboretum (GU8 4AD) 1A 26
Witley Court & Gdns. (WR6 6JT) 4B 60
Woburn Abbey (MK17 9WA) 2H 51
Woburn Safari Pk. (MK17 9QN) 2H 51
Wolds, The (Lincolnshire) (LN8 6BL) 1B 88
Wolds, The (Yorkshire) (YO25 9EN) 4D 100
Wolfeton House (DT2 9QN) 3B 14
Wollaton Hall (NG8 2AE) 2C 74
Wolseley Cen. (ST17 0WT) 3E 73
Wolterton Pk. (NR11 7BB) 2D 78
Wolvesey Castle (SO23 9NB) **Winchester 213**
Woodchester Mansion (GL10 3TS) 5D 48
Woodhenge (SP4 7AR) 2G 23
Wookey Hole (BA5 1BB) 2A 22
Woolsthorpe Manor (NG33 5PD) 3G 75
Worcester Cathedral (WR1 2LH) **214**
Worcester Porcelain Mus. (WR1 2NE) **214**
Worcestershire County Mus. (DY11 7XZ) 3C 60
Wordsworth House (CA13 9RX) 1C 102
Wordsworth Mus. (Dove Cottage) (LA22 9SH) 4E 103
Wotton House Landscape Gdns. (HP18 0SB) 4E 51
Wrest Pk. (MK45 4HR) 2A 52
Wrexham RC Cathedral (LL11 1RB) **214**
Wroxeter Roman City (SY5 6PH) 5H 71
Wroxton Abbey Gdns. (OX15 6PX) 1C 50
Wylfa Visitor Centre (LL67 0DH) 1C 80
Wyre Forest (DY14 9UH) 3B 60
Wythenshawe Hall (M23 0AB) 2C 84

Y

Yarmouth Castle (PO41 0PB) 4B 16
York Art Gallery (YO1 7EW) **214**
York Castle Mus. (YO1 9RY) **214**
York Minster (YO1 7JN) **214**
York Racecourse (YO23 1EX) 5H 99
Yorkshire Dales Nat. Pk. (BD23 5LB) 1A 98
Yorkshire Mus. (YO30 7DR) **York 214**
Yorkshire Mus. of Farming (YO19 5GH) 4A 100
Yorkshire Sculpture Pk. (WF4 4LG) 3C 92

FSC
www.fsc.org
MIX
Paper from responsible sources
FSC® C005461

Limited Interchange Motorway Junctions are shown on the maps by RED junction indicators

M1

Junction 2
Northbound: No exit, access from A1 only
Southbound: No access, exit to A1 only

Junction 4
Northbound: No exit, access from A41 only
Southbound: No access, exit to A41 only

Junction 6a
Northbound: No exit, access from M25 only
Southbound: No access, exit to M25 only

Junction 17
Northbound: No access, exit to M45 only
Southbound: No exit, access from M45 only

Junction 19
Northbound: Exit to M6 only, access from A14 only
Southbound: Access from M6 only, exit to A14 only

Junction 21a
Northbound: No access, exit to A46 only
Southbound: No exit, access from A46 only

Junction 24a
Northbound: Access from A50 only
Southbound: Exit to A50 only

Junction 35a
Northbound: No access, exit to A616 only
Southbound: No exit, access from A616 only

Junction 43
Northbound: Exit to M621 only
Southbound: Access from M621 only

Junction 48
Eastbound: Exit to A1(M) Northbound only
Westbound: Access from A1(M) Southbound only

M2

Junction 1
Eastbound: Access from A2 Eastbound only
Westbound: Exit to A2 Westbound only

M3

Junction 8
Westbound: No access, exit to A303 only
Eastbound: No exit, access from A303 only

Junction 10
Northbound: No access from A31
Southbound: No exit to A31

Junction 13
Southbound: No access from A335 to M3 leading to M27 Eastbound

M4

Junction 1
Westbound: Access from A4 Westbound only
Eastbound: Exit to A4 Eastbound only

Junction 21
Westbound: No access from M48
Eastbound: No exit to M48

Junction 23
Westbound: No exit to M48
Eastbound: No access from M48

Junction 25
Westbound: No access
Eastbound: No exit

Junction 25a
Westbound: No access
Eastbound: No exit

Junction 29
Westbound: No access, exit to A48(M) only
Eastbound: No exit, access from A48(M) only

Junction 38
Westbound: No access, exit to A48 only

Junction 39
Westbound: No exit, access from A48 only
Eastbound: No access or exit

Junction 42
Westbound: No exit to A48
Eastbound: No access from A48

M5

Junction 10
Southbound: No access, exit to A4019 only
Northbound: No exit, access from A4019 only

Junction 11a
Southbound: No exit to A417 Westbound

Junction 18a
Southbound: No exit to M49
Northbound: No access from M49

M6

Junction 3a
Eastbound: No exit to M6 TOLL
Westbound: No access from M6 TOLL

Junction 4
Northbound: No exit to M42 Northbound
No access from M42 Southbound
Southbound: No exit to M42
No access from M42 Southbound

Junction 4a
Northbound: No exit, access from M42 Southbound only
Southbound: No access, exit to M42 only

Junction 5
Northbound: No access, exit to A452 only
Southbound: No exit, access from A452 only

Junction 10a
Northbound: No access, exit to M54 only
Southbound: No exit, access from M54 only

Junction 11a
Northbound: No exit to M6 TOLL
Southbound: No access from M6 TOLL

Junction 20
Northbound: No exit to M56 Eastbound
Southbound: No access from M56 Westbound

Junction 24
Northbound: No exit, access from A58 only
Southbound: No access, exit to A58 only

Junction 25
Northbound: No access, exit to A49 only
Southbound: No exit, access from A49 only

Junction 30
Northbound: No exit, access from M61 Northbound only
Southbound: No access, exit to M61 Southbound only

Junction 31a
Northbound: No access, exit to B6242 only
Southbound: No exit, access from B6242 only

Junction 45
Northbound: No access onto A74(M)
Southbound: No exit from A74(M)

M6 TOLL

Junction T1
Northbound: No exit
Southbound: No access

Junction T2
Northbound: No access or exit
Southbound: No access

Junction T5
Northbound: No exit
Southbound: No access

Junction T7
Northbound: No access from A5
Southbound: No exit

Junction T8
Northbound: No exit to A460 Northbound
Southbound: No exit

M8

Junction 8
Westbound: No access from M73 Southbound
Eastbound: No exit to M73 Northbound

Junction 9
Westbound: No exit, access only
Eastbound: No access, exit only

Junction 13
Westbound: No exit to M80 Northbound
Eastbound: No access from M80 Southbound

Junction 14
Westbound: No exit, access only
Eastbound: No access, exit only

Junction 16
Westbound: No access, exit only
Eastbound: No exit, access only

Junction 17
Westbound: No access, exit to A82 only
Eastbound: No exit, access from A82 only

Junction 18
Westbound: No exit, access only

Junction 19
Westbound: No access from A814 Westbound
Eastbound: No exit to A814 Eastbound

Junction 20
Westbound: No access, exit only
Eastbound: No exit, access only

Junction 21
Westbound: No exit, access only
Eastbound: No access, exit only

Junction 22
Westbound: No access, exit to M77 only
Eastbound: No exit, access from M77 only

Junction 23
Westbound: No access, exit to B768 only
Eastbound: No exit, access from B768 only

Junction 25
Westbound and Eastbound:
Exit to A739 Northbound only
Access from A739 Southbound only

Junction 25a
Eastbound: Access only
Westbound: Exit only

Junction 28
Westbound: no access, exit to airport only
Eastbound: no exit, access from airport only

M9

Junction 1a
Northbound: No access, exit to M9 spur only
Southbound: No exit, access from M9 spur only

Junction 2
Northbound: No exit, access from B8046 only
Southbound: No access, exit to B8046 only

Junction 3
Northbound: No access, exit to A803 only
Southbound: No exit, access from A803 only

Junction 6
Northbound: No exit, access only
Southbound: No access, exit to A905 only

Junction 8
Northbound: No access, exit to M876 only
Southbound: No exit, access from M876 only

Junction with A90
Northbound: Exit onto A90 westbound only
Southbound: Access from A90 eastbound only

M11

Junction 4
Northbound: No exit, access from A406 Eastbound only
Southbound: No access, exit to A406 Westbound only

Junction 5
Northbound: No access, exit to A1168 only
Southbound: No exit, access from A1168 only

Junction 8a
Northbound: No access, exit only
Southbound: No exit, access only

Junction 9
Northbound: No access, exit only
Southbound: No exit, access only

Junction 13
Northbound: No access, exit only
Southbound: No exit, access only

Junction 14
Northbound: No access from A428 Eastbound
No exit to A428 Westbound
Southbound: No exit, access from A428 Eastbound only

M20

Junction 2
Eastbound: No access, exit to A20 only (access via M26 Junction 2a)
Westbound: No exit, access only (exit via M26 Junction 2a)

Junction 3
Eastbound: No exit, access from M26 Eastbound only
Westbound: No access, exit to M26 Westbound only

Junction 11a
Westbound: No exit to Channel Tunnel
Eastbound: No access from Channel Tunnel

M23

Junction 7
Southbound: No access from A23 Northbound
Northbound: No exit to A23 Southbound

Junction 10a
Northbound: No exit, access only
Southbound: No access, exit only

M25

Junction 5
Clockwise: No exit to M26 Eastbound
Anti-clockwise: No access from M26 Westbound

Spur to A21
Southbound: No access from M26 Westbound
Northbound: No exit to M26 Eastbound

Junction 19
Clockwise: No access exit only
Anti-clockwise: No exit access only

Junction 21
Clockwise and Anti-clockwise:
No exit to M1 Southbound
No access from M1 Northbound

Junction 31
Southbound: No exit access only (exit via Junction 30)
Northbound: No access exit only (access via Junction 30)

M26

Junction with M25 (M25 Junc. 5)
Westbound: No exit to M25 anti-clockwise or spur to A21 Southbound
Eastbound: No access from M25 clockwise or spur from A21 Northbound

Junction with M20 (M20 Junc. 3)
Eastbound: No exit to M20 Westbound
Westbound: No access from M20 Eastbound

M27

Junction 4
Eastbound and Westbound: No exit to A33 Southbound (Southampton)
No access from A33 Northbound

Junction 10
Eastbound: No exit, access from A32 only
Westbound: No access, exit to A32 only

M40

Junction 3
North-Westbound: No access, exit to A40 only
South-Eastbound: No exit, access from A40 only

Junction 7
South-Eastbound: No exit, access only
North-Westbound: No access, exit only

Junction 13
South-Eastbound: No exit, access only
North-Westbound: No access, exit only

Junction 14
South-Eastbound: No access, exit only
North-Westbound: No exit, access only

Junction 16
South-Eastbound: No access, exit only
North-Westbound: No exit, access only

M42

Junction 1
Eastbound: No exit
Westbound: No access

Junction 7
Northbound: No access, exit to M6 only
Southbound: No exit, access from M6 Northbound only

Junction 8
Northbound: No exit, access from M6 Southbound only
Southbound: Exit to M6 Northbound only
Access from M6 Southbound only

M45

Junction with M1 (M1 Junc. 17)
Eastbound: No exit to M1 Northbound
Westbound: No access from M1 Southbound

Junction with A45 east of Dunchurch
Eastbound: No access, exit to A45 only
Westbound: No exit, access from A45 Northbound only

M48

Junction with M4 (M4 Junc. 21)
Westbound: No access from M4 Eastbound
Eastbound: No exit to M4 Westbound

Junction with M4 (M4 Junc. 23)
Westbound: No exit to M4 Eastbound
Eastbound: No access from M4 Westbound

M53

Junction 11
Southbound and Northbound: No access from M56 Eastbound, no exit to M56 Westbound

M56

Junction 1
Westbound: No access from M60
South-Eastbound:
No access from A34 Northbound
Eastbound: No exit to M60 North-Westbound
No exit to A34 Southbound

Junction 2
Westbound: No access, exit to A560 only
Eastbound: No exit, access from A560 only

Junction 3
Westbound: No exit, access only
Eastbound: No access, exit only

Junction 4
Westbound: No access, exit only
Eastbound: No exit, access only

Junction 7
Westbound: No exit, access only

Junction 8
Westbound: No exit, access from A556 only
Eastbound: No access or exit

Junction 9
Westbound: No exit to M6 Southbound
Eastbound: No access from M6 Northbound

Junction 15
Westbound: No access from M53
Eastbound: No exit to M53

M57

Junction 3
Northbound: No exit, access only
Southbound: No access, exit only

Junction 5
Northbound: No exit, access from A580
Westbound only
Southbound: No access, exit to A580
Eastbound only

M58

Junction 1
Eastbound: No exit, access from A506 only
Westbound: No access, exit to A506 only

M60

Junction 2
Nth.-Eastbound: No access, exit to A560 only
Sth.-Westbound: No exit,
access from A560 only

Junction 3
Westbound: No exit to A34 Northbound
Eastbound: No access from A34 Southbound

Junction 4
Westbound: No access from A34 Southbound
No access from M56 Eastbound
Eastbound: No exit to M56 South-Westbound
No exit to A34 Northbound

Junction 5
South-Eastbound: No access from or exit to A5103 Northbound
North-Westbound: No access from or exit to A5103 Southbound

Junction 14
Eastbound: No exit to A580
No access from A580 Westbound
Westbound: No exit to A580 Eastbound
No access from A580

Junction 16
Eastbound: No exit, access from A666 only
Westbound: No access, exit to A666 only

Junction 20
Eastbound: No access from A664
Westbound: No exit to A664

Junction 22
Westbound: No access from A62

Junction 25
South-Westbound:
No access from A560/A6017

Junction 26
North-Eastbound: No access or exit

Junction 27
North-Eastbound: No access, exit only
South-Westbound: No exit, access only

M61

Junctions 2 and 3
North-Westbound:
No access from A580 Eastbound
Sth.-Eastbound: No exit to A580 Westbound

Junction with M6 (M6 Junc. 30)
North-Westbound:
No exit to M6 Southbound
South-Eastbound:
No access from M6 Northbound

M62

Junction 23
Eastbound: No access, exit to A640 only
Westbound: No exit, access from A640 only

M65

Junction 9
Nth.-Eastbound: No access, exit to A679 only
Sth.-Westbound:
No exit, access from A679 only

Junction 11
North-Eastbound: No exit, access only
South-Westbound: No access, exit only

M66

Junction 1
Southbound: No exit, access from A56 only
Northbound: No access, exit to A56 only

M67

Junction 1
Eastbound: Access from A57 Eastbound only
Westbound: Exit to A57 Westbound only

Junction 1a
Eastbound: No access, exit to A6017 only
Westbound: No exit, access from A6017 only

Junction 2
Eastbound: No exit, access from A57 only
Westbound: No access, exit to A57 only

M69

Junction 2
North-Eastbound:
No exit, access from B4669 only
South-Westbound:
No access, exit to B4669 only

M73

Junction 1
Southbound: No exit to A74 Eastbound

Junction 2
Northbound: No access from M8 Eastbound
No exit to A89 Eastbound
Southbound: No exit to M8 Westbound
No access from A89 Westbound

Junction 3
Northbound: No exit to A80 South-Westbound
Southbound:
No access from A80 North-Eastbound

M74

Junction 1
Eastbound: No access from M8 Westbound
Westbound: No exit to M8 Westbound

Junction 3
Eastbound: No exit
Westbound: No access

Junction 3a
Eastbound: No access
Westbound: No exit

Junction 7
Southbound: No access, exit to A72 only
Northbound: No exit, access from A72 only

Junction 9
Southbound: No access, exit to B7078 only
Northbound: No access or exit

Junction 10
Southbound: No exit, access from B7078 only

Junction 11
Southbound: No access, exit to B7078 only
Northbound: No exit, access from B7078 only

Junction 12
Southbound: No exit, access from A70 only
Northbound: No access, exit to A70 only

M77

Junction with M8 (M8 Junc. 22)
Southbound: No access from M8 Eastbound
Northbound: No exit to M8 Westbound

Junction 4
Southbound: No access
Northbound: No exit

Junction 6
Southbound: No access from A77
Northbound: No exit to A77

Junction 7
Northbound: No access from A77
No exit to A77

M80

Junction 1
Northbound: No access from M8 Westbound
Southbound: No exit to M8 Eastbound

Junction 4a
Northbound: No access
Southbound: No exit

Junction 6a
Northbound: No exit
Southbound: No access

Junction 8
Northbound: No access from M876
Southbound: No exit to M876

M90

Junction 2a
Northbound: No access, exit to A92 only
Southbound: No exit, access from A92 only

Junction 7
Northbound: No exit, access from A91 only
Southbound: No access, exit to A91 only

Junction 8
Northbound: No access, exit to A91 only
Southbound: No exit, access from A91 only

Junction 10
Northbound: No access from A912
Exit to A912 Northbound only
Southbound: No exit to A912
Access from A912 Southbound only

M180

Junction 1
Eastbound: No access, exit only
Westbound: No exit, access from A18 only

M606

Junction 2
Northbound: No access, exit only

M621

Junction 2a
Eastbound: No exit, access only
Westbound: No access, exit only

Junction 4
Southbound: No exit

Junction 5
Northbound: No access, exit to A61 only
Southbound: No exit, access from A61 only

Junction 6
Northbound: No access, exit only
Southbound: No exit, access only

Junction 7
Westbound: No exit, access only
Eastbound: No access, exit only

Junction 8
Northbound: No access, exit only
Southbound: No exit, access only

M876

Junction with M80 (M80 Junc. 5)
North-Eastbound:
No access from M80 Southbound
South-Westbound: No exit to M80 Northbound
Junction with M9 (M9 Junc. 8)
North-Eastbound: No exit to M9 Northbound
South-Westbound:
No access from M9 Southbound

A1(M) (Hertfordshire Section)

Junction 2
Southbound: No exit, access from A1001 only
Northbound: No access, exit only

Junction 3
Southbound: No access, exit only

Junction 5
Northbound: No exit, access only
Southbound: No access or exit

A1(M) (Cambridgeshire Section)

Junction 13a
Northbound: No exit to B1043
Southbound: No access from B1043

Junction 14
Northbound: No exit, access only
Southbound: No access, exit only

A1(M) (Leeds Section)

Junction 40
Southbound: Exit to A1 Southbound only

Junction 43
Northbound: Access from M1 Eastbound only
Southbound: Exit to M1 Westbound only

A1(M) (Durham Section)

Junction 57
Northbound: No access,
exit to A66(M) only
Southbound: No exit, access from A66(M)

Junction 65
Northbound: Exit to A1 North-Westbound,
and to A194(M) only
Southbound: Access from A1 South-Eastbound,
and from A194(M) only

A3(M)

Junction 4
Northbound: No access, exit only
Southbound: No exit, access only

A38(M) Aston Expressway

Junction with Victoria Road, Aston
Northbound: No exit, access only
Southbound: No access, exit only

A48(M)

Junction with M4 (M4 Junc. 29)
South-Westbound: access from M4 Westbound
North-Eastbound: exit to M4 Eastbound only

Junction 29a
South-Westbound: Exit to A48 Westbound only
North-Eastbound:
Access from A48 Eastbound only

A57(M) Mancunian Way

Junction with A34 Brook Street, Manchester
Eastbound: No access, exit to A34 Brook Street
Southbound only
Westbound: No exit, access only

A58(M) Leeds Inner Ring Road

Junction with Park Lane/ Westgate
Southbound: No access, exit only

A64(M) Leeds Inner Ring Road
(Continuation of A58(M))

Junction with A58 Clay Pit Lane
Eastbound: No Access
Westbound: No exit

A66(M)

Junction with A1(M) (A1(M) Junc. 57)
South-Westbound:
Exit to A1(M) Southbound only
North-Eastbound:
Access from A1(M) Northbound only

A74(M)

Junction 18
Northbound: No access
Southbound: No exit

A167(M) Newcastle Central Motorway

Junction with Camden Street
Northbound: No exit, access only
Southbound: No access or exit

A194(M)

Junction with A1(M) (A1(M) Junc. 65) and A1 Gateshead Western By-Pass
Southbound: Exit to A1(M) only
Northbound: Access from A1(M) only

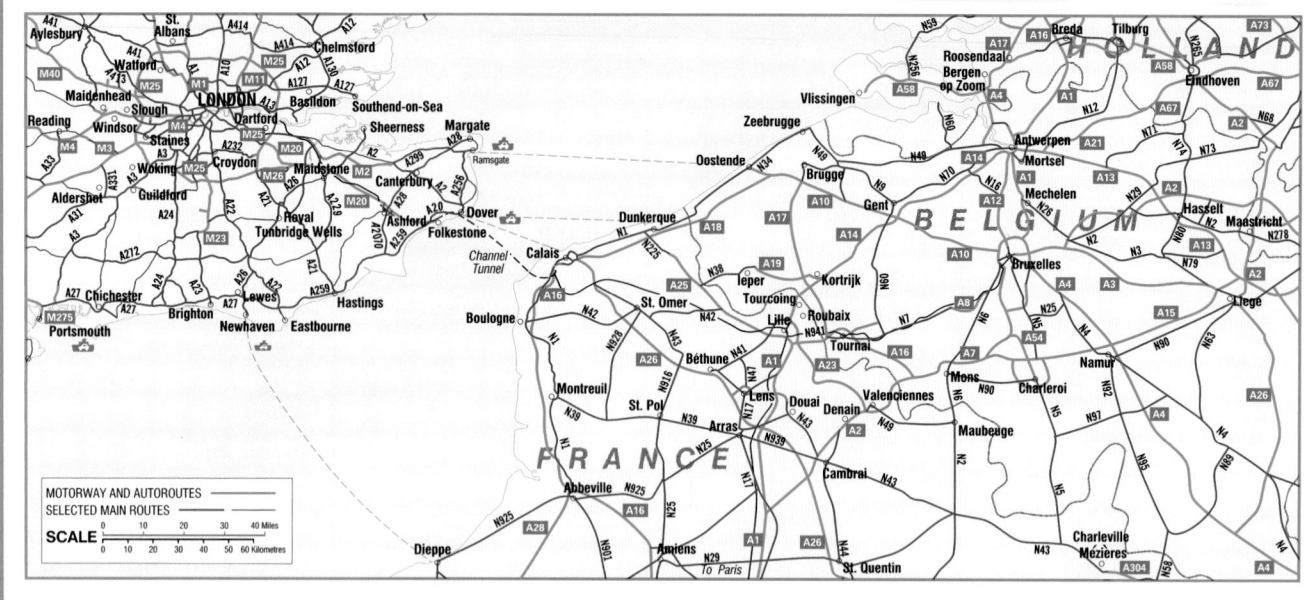

MOTORWAY AND AUTOROUTES
SELECTED MAIN ROUTES
SCALE
0 10 20 30 40 Miles
0 10 20 30 40 50 60 Kilometres

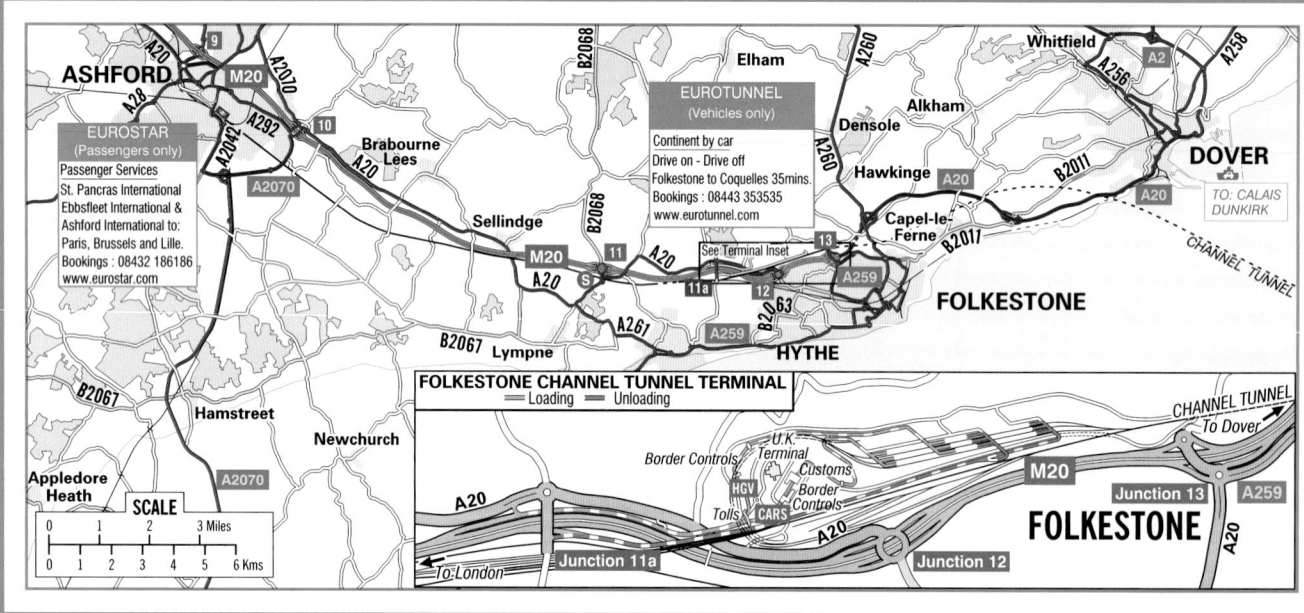

EUROSTAR
(Passengers only)
Passenger Services
St. Pancras International
Ebbsfleet International &
Ashford International to:
Paris, Brussels and Lille.
Bookings : 08432 186186
www.eurostar.com

EUROTUNNEL
(Vehicles only)
Continent by car
Drive on - Drive off
Folkestone to Coquelles 35mins.
Bookings : 08443 353535
www.eurotunnel.com

FOLKESTONE CHANNEL TUNNEL TERMINAL
Loading   Unloading

SCALE
0 1 2 3 Miles
0 1 2 3 4 5 6 Kms

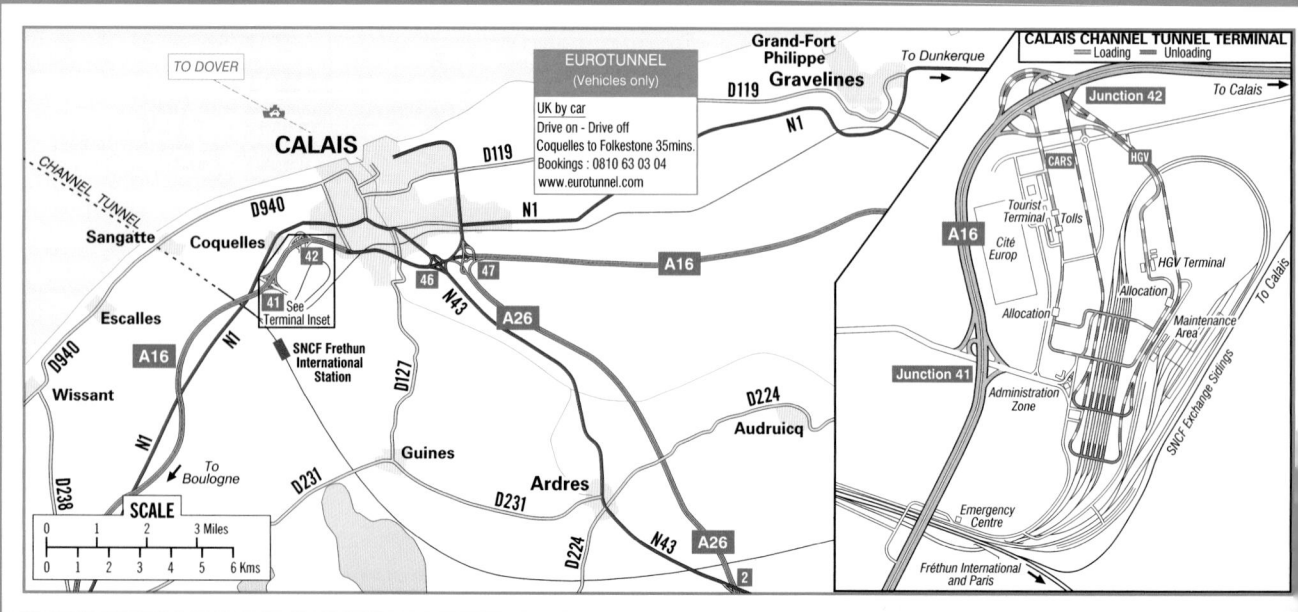

EUROTUNNEL
(Vehicles only)
UK by car
Drive on - Drive off
Coquelles to Folkestone 35mins.
Bookings : 0810 63 03 04
www.eurotunnel.com

CALAIS CHANNEL TUNNEL TERMINAL
Loading   Unloading

SCALE
0 1 2 3 Miles
0 1 2 3 4 5 6 Kms

Which map to choose?

> NATIONAL - THE COUNTRY MAP

> **NATIONAL maps give an overall picture of your route.**

> REGIONAL - WITH PRACTICAL INFORMATION

> **REGIONAL maps show primary & secondary networks.**

> LOCAL - DETAILED & COMPREHENSIVE

> **LOCAL maps provide detailed coverage of France and Italy. They are perfect for fully exploring these countries and ideal for cyclists.**

> ZOOM - THE TOURIST MAP

> Zoom maps cover major towns and tourist areas, with a high level of detail in an easy to use format.